# POLITICAL AND CIVIL RIGHTS
## IN THE
# UNITED STATES

---

A Collection of Legal and Related Materials

by

**THOMAS I. EMERSON**

*Professor of Law, Yale University*

and

**DAVID HABER**

*Associate Professor of Law, Yale University*

Foreword by

ROBERT M. HUTCHINS

*Associate Director, The Ford Foundation*

CASE BOOK
UNITED STATES
SERIES

**DENNIS & CO., INC.**

Law Book Publishers

Buffalo, New York

1952

# FOREWORD

This is the only comprehensive collection of cases and materials on the most important subject in the world today.

The editors have taken soundings in all the areas in which the freedom of individuals and of private groups is in controversy. They have not limited themselves to the decisions of courts. The reader will find here questions raised and answers given by philosophers and journalists, politicians and businessmen. The collection amounts to a complete bibliography. It portrays the state of the discussion as it is today; it includes such recent material as the *Dennis* case, the *Miracle* case, and the opinions of the United States Supreme Court on the Feinberg law.

Perhaps the best thing that can be said about the law in this field is that it is unsettled. Even the question whether the first eight Amendments are made to apply to the States by the Fourteenth has not yet received a unanimous answer from the Supreme Court. The law is being made now; the *Gitlow* case, which is cited in almost every discussion of the subject, was decided only a little more than twenty-five years ago. Just yesterday motion pictures were brought under the First Amendment.

The number and vigor of opinions concurring in the result, to say nothing of the number and vigor of dissents, suggest that anything may happen when a case involving civil liberties gets before the Supreme Court. Five-to-four decisions, with the majority splitting on the reasons, are the order of the day; and some of the most important cases have been "decided", when one justice was absent or disqualified, by a court that was equally divided and that could only affirm the holding of the court below.

If there ever was a branch of the law that was "developing", this is it. This collection should assist development by showing citizens, scholars, judges and future judges, lawyers and future lawyers in one comprehensive view what the issues are. If they understand what the issues are, we may have some hope that even the Cold War will not indefinitely postpone a rational settlement.

Everybody knows by now that this subject affects the position of the United States in the world just as much as it does that of the American citizen at home. The fact that civil liberties do not exist in Soviet Russia has not prevented the propagandists of that country from exploiting the failure of America to make good the promise of the Bill of Rights and of the Thirteenth,

iii

Fourteenth and Fifteenth Amendments. A country that calls to others in the name of liberty must make sure that its practice conforms to its professed ideals. Even in those sections of the field in which great progress has been made, such as the rights of the Negro, we have a long way to go. In others, such as the freedom to differ and to espouse unpopular causes, we seem to be losing ground.

These cases and materials will force the reader to re-think the most fundamental questions: the purpose of human life and of organized society; the relation of man to the state; the conflict between freedom and security; and even, as in the opinion of Chief Justice Vinson in *U.S. v. Dennis*, the nature of truth itself. This collection may make its most important contribution by driving the reader back to examine his preconceptions; for it is doubtful if we can make our political behavior rational unless we attempt to clarify our basic ideas.

ROBERT M. HUTCHINS

# INTRODUCTION

## I

The American people today are in broad agreement concerning the basic values and fundamental principles of a democratic society. But in the attempt to realize the common values and to apply the accepted principles sharp differences of opinion have arisen. This book undertakes to collect some of the materials relevant to one aspect of these problems of democracy in action. It deals with the operation of the vital mechanisms of the democratic process. Its aim is to throw light upon those institutions, rules and procedures of our society which keep the system functioning on a democratic level, which permit our people to solve their problems through the exercise of democratic choice, which, in short, form the ground rules for the practice of democracy.

The problems here treated flow immediately from practical application of the accepted principles. In a society based upon human dignity and the development of the individual personality, clearly all members are entitled to security of the person—protection from bodily harm, involuntary servitude, and the fear of physical restraint. Yet in some areas of the nation, and for some groups in our society, this basic right is consistently or intermittently infringed. How is this problem to be met? What should the role of the Federal Government be? Is additional legislation necessary? How can our police and court systems be adjusted to guarantee effective protection?

Our tradition calls for the extension of various procedural safeguards to individuals who come into conflict with the law. We accept an accusatorial rather than an inquisitorial system of justice. Our theory is that the individual, pitted against the overwhelming power, prestige and resources of the government, is entitled to certain equalizing rights, even though some of the guilty escape as a result. These protections constitute a major portion of the Bill of Rights embodied in our Constitution. But how far should the police go in seeking to extract a confession from a suspected prisoner? What is the extent of the right to counsel and how can it be assured in fact? What are the rights of the police to search for and seize evidence? Should their investigatory powers extend to tapping telephone wires or the use of similar devices for obtaining evidence? Where is the line to be drawn between protection of the individual and the right of society to solve its crime problem? And how can the courts and other institutions most effectively afford in practice the rights conceded in theory?

In a democratic state it is acknowledged that all citizens should have the right to participate in government through exercise of the franchise. But some are not accorded this right at all, and others are seriously hampered in exercising it. To what extent should the courts, and particularly the Federal courts, strike down legislative or executive action denying or abridging this right, or afford protection against private infringement? What institutional devices are available to assure its full protection?

It is a fundamental principle of democracy that all individuals should have the right to influence the political process through full freedom of political organization and political expression. In the First Amendment to our Constitution this right is guaranteed in unconditional and unequivocal terms. Should there be any limits to.the right? Does the acknowledged power of the state to preserve order and to protect itself against external threat outweigh the individual's right of political opposition and, if so, under what circumstances? What is the effect of the growth of the Communist Party abroad and in the United States? Are there any limits to the power of legislative committees to inquire into political activities, associations or beliefs? Are sedition laws, registration laws, loyalty oaths or tests, an appropriate response to the development of anti-democratic ideologies and organizations? And what should be the respective function of the courts, the legislature and the executive in dealing with these problems?

The theory of freedom of expression extends beyond the political sphere and embraces all forms of expression. It is designed to keep open the channels of communication in every guise. But when may communication be restricted because it is claimed to be obscene, or libellous of an individual? What if it is alleged to defame a whole group and to stir up racial or religious hatred, fear and discord? What limits may be imposed upon the use of public parks or streets for communication, or upon various techniques of persuasion, such as picketing or sound trucks? What problems arise from the growth of the organs of mass communication—the modern newspaper, radio, television and movies—and particularly from the trend toward concentration of ownership and uniformity of content? Should the government attempt to maintain diversity of ownership, and how can this be done? Should government attempt to control content?

An important bastion of a free society is, or can be, its academic institutions. Through the principle of academic freedom

It is imperative that we seek to understand and appraise the new elements in the picture. The basic principles of the democratic process remain unaltered and as valid today as when they were formulated. But the economic, social and political matrix in which they operate, and the specific issues which arise in their application, have undergone important changes. At the same time the tools at hand for fashioning a solution to the problems in their new form are significantly improved over any past period. What is true of our civilization generally is true of the field of political and civil rights. We are living in a period of great stress, of great difficulty, and of great promise.

In broad outline the new factors on the scene are not difficult to sketch. They arise from both internal and external sources. The vast industrial development of the United States, with the accompanying growth in population, in technology, in the size and concentration of economic units, in the interdependence of economic relations, have profoundly changed the economic basis of our society. The principles of democratic freedom must now be applied not in a context of laissez-faire, a free market, and the largely unregulated competition of numerous small and independent business units, but in the context of regulated monopoly or semi-monopoly. This means that the economic forces which originally sponsored and fought for the principles of individual liberty against absolutist executive authority may find their interests today more on the side of maintaining the status quo and hence leaning toward a closed society than on the side of encouraging opportunities for change and hence fostering an open society.

Similarly the role of the government is now quite different. The era when government was confined primarily to the preservation of domestic order and protection of our foreign interests no longer exists. Far-reaching state controls, accompanied by the inevitable government bureaucracy, have become essential to the maintenance of economic order and prosperity. Hence the problem is no longer the relatively simple one of curbing unfair or oppressive actions of a state machine with narrowly circumscribed functions, but rather of accepting and using a powerful and effective government apparatus while at the same time holding it within bounds.

And, again, the control of a complex industrial society, dependent for smooth operation upon the rapid use of an intricate set of regulatory devices, does not allow the same tolerance for discussion, delay, individual variation or experimentation.

The situation of today is likewise profoundly affected by important social changes. Many elements in modern society—the denser population, our systems of mass production, the development of transportation and communication, the concentration of control over the organs of mass communication, and others—drive us steadily toward standardization and conformity. Greater social values become attached to orthodoxy and greater social deprivations assigned to deviation. Thus the majority becomes more coalesced, more demanding of unity, and the individual or the minority finds less toleration for non-conformities. Hence the maintenance of political and civil rights comes to require not only a battle against government power but a struggle against oppressive, non-governmental, majorities. In this contest the individual or minority group may actually look to the government for aid. In any event the issue arises whether the government should take a positive responsibility for creating conditions and promulgating controls by which individual and minority freedoms may be encouraged and preserved.

Other social changes have important effects. Thus the trend toward urbanization has an impact on the problem of crime and hence has repercussions on fair trial procedures.

Changes have also taken place in the techniques of organization and of political appeal. The development of private associations of great power in nearly every phase of national life presents new issues both of government restriction and of governmentally enforced internal democracy. The growth of highly integrated and closely disciplined political parties poses questions substantially different from those involved in looser groupings of persons with kindred political interests. Even more important the totalitarian parties of the world have developed to a high pitch the techniques of mass emotional appeal. And these methods are by no means confined to totalitarian countries or parties. Hence the underlying assumption of the framers of the doctrines of free speech—that open discussion of issues would produce well-considered and rational results—may require significant qualification. These possibilities of political manipulation through an emotional appeal to latent insecurities, frustrations and prejudice raise issues of which our ancestors were only dimly aware.

Other difficulties that arise to perplex us grow out of unsettled and turbulent world conditions. The growth of the Communist movement, the stirrings of nationalism in many parts of the world, the hurried strivings for industrialization in less advanced areas, the growing division of the world into two hostile camps—all create problems that impinge upon political and civil rights. We are concerned with national security, we are engaged in large scale military activities and preparations, we feel the need to protect ourselves from espionage and fifth column activities, we seek to present a united front to the rest of the world. The danger that American democratic institutions will be engulfed in a rising tide of totalitarianism is a real one, to which we cannot remain oblivious. Measures to meet the challenge must be taken. But the wisest and most effective course of action is by no means clear. And grave danger exists that we will be misled by confusion, insecurity and panic into steps that undermine the very principles we seek to protect and dissipate the very strength upon which our position is built.

The present status of the United States in the world today introduces a new factor into all our decisions on issues of political and civil rights. Our claim to moral leadership in world affairs is based in large part upon our principles and practices of individual freedom and equality. This is perhaps our major contribution and our principal appeal to the world. Hence the eyes of all peoples are upon us in all we do or fail to do to advance freedom among our own people. No decision we make, particularly in the area of racial equality, can ignore this direct impact upon our world position.

All of these, as well as many other factors, make more difficult the present task of translating our democratic principles into democratic practice. But we have certain advantages too. First of all we know far more than we did about the human mind and personality. We are better able to understand and take into account the drives and motivations of human conduct. Moreover, we know more about the relationship of the individual to the group and of the varying groups to each other. The causes of prejudice and antagonisms, the possibilities of compromise and adjustment, can be explored. We can decide important questions, such as the psychological and social effects of segregation, with some degree of scientific insight. We know more, too, about the possibilities of education and methods of training individuals in democratic attitudes and practices. We have added to our knowledge of such matters as the techniques of government administration and devices for securing both effective government action and the protection of individual rights. Thus, as the problems have become more complex, the tools at our disposal have become more refined.

The mechanisms of democracy, up to now, have on the whole operated well in the United States. We have applied them with confidence and growing skill. And the results, taken as a whole, have been as good as Milton foresaw they could be. Our people, with significant exceptions, have been more free to live and work and play than probably any other people in history. The nation as a whole has prospered. We have remained an alert and vigorous people, reasonably tolerant, ready to experiment, improvise and adjust. The crucial question before us now is whether, under the new conditions of the modern world which press upon us, we can continue to maintain the practices of democratic freedom or whether we shall abandon them for a stagnant and servile existence.

## III

We have approached these problems in this book principally from a legal point of view. The legal aspects are of special significance for a number of reasons.

In the first place, underlying the entire mechanism of democracy is the cardinal principle that individuals should be restricted by government action only in accordance with general principles of law. Within the limits of human frailty, no person is to be subject to the compulsion of the state through the accident or caprice of an ad hoc decision, but only through the application of general rules that treat like situations alike. From this it follows that the techniques, training and discipline of the legal method must play an important part in the successful operation of democratic procedures.

Secondly, two related legal institutions have always been important factors in the maintenance of political and civil rights. One is the written constitution. It has been traditional in the United States to embody in constitutional form those guarantees of individual and minority rights, and those restrictions on the exercise of government power, which form the basic structure of the democratic process. These constitutional provisions, notably in the Federal Constitution, not only are exceptionally difficult to change but have come to possess a unique prestige and public support. Hence many, or most, of the crucial issues of political and civil rights are ultimately framed as constitutional questions.

The related legal institution of importance here is that of judicial review,—the power of the courts, functioning under broad constitutional provisions, to act as final arbitrator between the rights of individual and government, of minority and the current majority. By reason of their appointment for life or for long terms, judges may be more independent of day-to-day pressures and passing moods. Selected from a group trained to make decisions in terms of principle, and frequently men of broad interests and outlook, they can and often do bring a calmer and more judicious approach to problems than the active participants in partisan conflict. And, along with the written constitution, the judiciary has come to have a symbolic prestige as defender of democratic rights. There is great difference of opinion over the role that the judiciary does or should play in a democratic society, but it can hardly be disputed that in our society the doctrines of judicial review have been a major influence.

Finally it has also been a tradition in the United States for lawyers to participate actively in both the legislative and executive branches of government. The effect has been to stamp all of our political institutions and practices with legal ways of action and modes of thought.

For these reasons, as well as others, most of the important issues relating to the workings of our democratic system ultimately come before the courts and are decided in terms of legal doctrine.

This book grew out of a law school course in these legal problems. It was undertaken in the first instance as a collection of materials for law students, and it was hoped that making the materials readily available would stimulate other courses on these vital questions or facilitate their consideration in advanced constitutional law courses.

As the project developed the authors were motivated by another consideration, that of making the book useful to the growing number of lawyers who deal with matters involving political and civil rights, or who have an interest in that field. With this in mind we have attempted to supplement the basic materials with somewhat elaborate notes collecting the major legal and related references. Although much has been written on various aspects of political and civil rights there is no comprehensive legal treatise on this branch of the law in existence today. Our purpose has been to fill, in part and temporarily, this unfortunate gap in legal scholarship.

It has also been our hope that the book would have a wider appeal. The law of political and civil rights is too important a matter to be left to the lawyers. Solution of the problems involved will require the combined assistance of all intellectual disciplines. Above all it will require the fullest attention and understanding of all citizens. We therefore dare to encourage students and workers in the social sciences, and also the general reader, to make use of these materials. We have not stinted on the legal technicalities or attempted to simplify the legal issues. Some of the extracts may prove difficult going for the non-lawyer. He may find this particularly true of the Supreme Court decisions in the first chapter, where the Court has exercised a full measure of legal ingenuity in interpreting the Fourteenth Amendment and the Federal Civil Rights Acts. But actually the law, at least in the field of political and civil rights, is not as mysterious as laymen may suppose. And even legal writing can have literary merit. In any event the particular problems with which the materials deal are human, vital and all-important ones.

THOMAS I. EMERSON
DAVID HABER

New Haven, Conn.
August 1952.

# PREFACE

The materials have been organized in terms of problems rather than of legal doctrine. Thus issues of freedom of speech under the First Amendment, or "state action" under the Fourteenth, run through a number of chapters. We have used this organization in order to emphasize the concrete issues at stake and to bring to bear on those issues all relevant considerations, whether from legal or other sources. In order to facilitate use of the book along doctrinal lines, however, we have striven to make the index as complete as possible.

The necessities of space have forced us to limit or omit materials on a number of important problems. We particularly regret the lack of space to deal adequately with issues relating to aliens, political and civil rights in periods of emergency, problems of military law, and human rights in the world community. Nor have we dealt adequately with the right of private association or the operation of the democratic process within private organizations.

Although many of the footnotes attached to extracts reprinted have been retained, many others have been omitted. Except where we have wished to call the omitted footnote to the reader's attention, we have not indicated the omission. Nor have we attempted to renumber the footnotes.

The authors confess to a strong bias in favor of political and civil rights. We have accepted throughout the assumptions inherent in a system of democratic values. Within this framework, however, we have attempted to present the materials in an objective manner. Our purpose has been to bring to the reader, so far as possible, the relevant facts and the significant points of view, leaving it up to each individual to make his own judgment.

It is a healthy sign of a vigorous interest in political and civil rights that so many persons have given so generously of their time and effort to assist in the preparation of this volume. We can acknowledge here only a few. We are particularly indebted to our colleague, Professor Theodore M. Greene, who prepared a special contribution for the chapter on Academic Freedom; to Sheila Spaulding, who was responsible for a substantial share of that chapter; and to Ruth Calvin Goldman, who did research on a number of chapters. We wish also to record the valuable assistance rendered by David Helfeld, Richard Schifter, Lisa Sandler, Yolanda Chambers, William and Georgia Delano,

xv

Charles Fielding, Shirley Fingerhood, Joseph Finley, Arthur Galub, Marvin and Rhoda Karpatkin, Peter Marcuse, Herbert Morris, John Silverstone and Henry Winestine. Grateful appreciation is extended to Mollie McCall and her patient and tireless stenographic staff. Dean Wesley A. Sturges and our colleagues on the law faculty have given us ready and valuable aid whenever called upon. And finally we express our warmest gratitude to Bertha Emerson who performed her wifely duties of critic, exhorter and proofreader with unfailing skill and devotion.

# TABLE OF CONTENTS

xvii

†

# CHAPTER I

# THE RIGHT TO SECURITY OF THE PERSON

## A. IDEAL AND REALITY

### TO SECURE THESE RIGHTS—THE REPORT OF THE PRESIDENT'S COMMITTEE ON CIVIL RIGHTS [1]

Washington: U. S. Government Printing Office, 1947, pp. 6, 20–30

Freedom can exist only where the citizen is assured that his person is secure against bondage, lawless violence, and arbitrary arrest and punishment. Freedom from slavery in all its forms is clearly necessary if all men are to have equal opportunity to use their talents and to lead worthwhile lives. Moreover, to be free, men must be subject to discipline by society only for commission of offenses clearly defined by law and only after trial by due process of law. Where the administration of justice is discriminatory, no man can be sure of security. Where the threat of violence by private persons or mobs exists, a cruel inhibition of the sense of freedom of activity and security of the person inevitably results. Where a society permits private and arbitrary violence to be done to its members, its own integrity is inevitably corrupted. It cannot permit human beings to be imprisoned or killed in the absence of due process of law without degrading its entire fabric. . . .

Most Americans enjoy this right, but it is not yet secure for all. Too many of our people still live under the harrowing fear of violence or death at the hands of a mob or of brutal treatment by police officers. Many fear entanglement with the law because of the knowledge that the justice rendered in some courts is not equal for all persons. In a few areas the freedom to move about and choose one's job is endangered by

---

[1] The President's Committee on Civil Rights was appointed by President Truman on December 5, 1946 to study and make recommendations for strengthening and improving "the civil rights of the people." The Committee was composed of 15 distinguished citizens, headed by Mr. Charles E. Wilson, President of the General Electric Company. After a comprehensive survey, extending over a year, the Committee issued its findings and recommendations in a report. The following extract from the report embodies the Committee's findings with respect to the status of the right to security of the person at the end of 1947. The Committee's appraisal may be taken as an authoritative, if perhaps moderate, statement of the problem.

attempts to hold workers in peonage or other forms of involuntary servitude.

THE CRIME OF LYNCHING

In 1946 at least six persons in the United States were lynched by mobs. Three of them had not been charged, either by the police or anyone else, with an offense. Of the three that had been charged, one had been accused of stealing a saddle. (The real thieves were discovered after the lynching.) Another was said to have broken into a house. A third was charged with stabbing a man. All were Negroes. During the same year, mobs were prevented from lynching 22 persons, of whom 21 were Negroes, 1 white.

On July 20, 1946, a white farmer, Loy Harrison, posted bond for the release of Roger Malcolm from the jail at Monroe, Georgia. Malcolm, a young Negro, had been involved in a fight with his white employer during the course of which the latter had been stabbed. It is reported that there was talk of lynching Malcolm at the time of the incident and while he was in jail. Upon Malcolm's release, Harrison started to drive Malcolm, Malcolm's wife, and a Negro overseas veteran, George Dorsey, and his wife, out of Monroe. At a bridge along the way a large group of unmasked white men, armed with pistols and shotguns, was waiting. They stopped Harrison's car and removed Malcolm and Dorsey. As they were leading the two men away, Harrison later stated, one of the women called out the name of a member of the mob. Thereupon the lynchers returned and removed the two women from the car. Three volleys of shots were fired as if by a squad of professional executioners. The coroner's report said that at least 60 bullets were found in the scarcely recognizable bodies. Harrison consistently denied that he could identify any of the unmasked murderers. State and federal grand juries reviewed the evidence in the case, but no person has yet been indicted for the crime.

Later that summer, in Minden, Louisiana, a young Negro named John Jones was arrested on suspicion of housebreaking. Another Negro youth, Albert Harris, was arrested at about the same time, and beaten in an effort to implicate Jones. He was then released, only to be rearrested after a few days. On August 6th, early in the evening, and before there had been any trial of the charges against them, Jones and Harris were released by a deputy sheriff. Waiting in the jail yard was a group of white men. There was evidence that, with the aid of the deputy sheriff, the young men were put into a car. They were then driven into the country. Jones was beaten to death. Harris, left for dead, revived and escaped. Five persons, including two

**2**                                                         [Emerson]

deputy sheriffs, were indicted and brought to trial in a federal court for this crime. All were acquitted.

These are two of the less brutal lynchings of the past years. The victims in these cases were not mutilated or burned. . . .

While available statistics show that, decade by decade, lynchings have decreased, this Committee has found that in the year 1947 lynching remains one of the most serious threats to the civil rights of Americans. It is still possible for a mob to abduct and murder a person in some sections of the country with almost certain assurance of escaping punishment for the crime. The decade from 1936 through 1946 saw at least 43 lynchings. No person received the death penalty, and the majority of the guilty persons were not even prosecuted.

The communities in which lynchings occur tend to condone the crime. Punishment of lynchers is not accepted as the responsibility of state or local governments in these communities. Frequently, state officials participate in the crime, actively or passively. Federal efforts to punish the crime are resisted. Condonation of lynching is indicated by the failure of some local law enforcement officials to make adequate efforts to break up a mob. It is further shown by failure in most cases to make any real effort to apprehend or try those guilty. If the federal government enters a case, local officials sometimes actively resist the federal investigation. Local citizens often combine to impede the effort to apprehend the criminals by convenient "loss of memory"; grand juries refuse to indict; trial juries acquit in the face of overwhelming proof of guilt.

The large number of attempted lynchings highlights, even more than those which have succeeded, the widespread readiness of many communities to resort to mob violence. Thus, for seven of the years from 1937 to 1946 for which statistics are reported, the conservative estimates of the Tuskegee Institute show that 226 persons were rescued from threatened lynching. Over 200 of these were Negroes. . . .

The devastating consequences of lynchings go far beyond what is shown by counting the victims. When a person is lynched and the lynchers go unpunished, thousands wonder where the evil will appear again and what mischance may produce another victim. And every time lynchers go unpunished, Negroes have learned to expect other forms of violence at the hands of private citizens or public officials. In describing the thwarted efforts of the Department of Justice to identify those responsible for one lynching, J. Edgar Hoover stated to the Committee: "The arrogance of most of the white population of that county was unbelievable, and the fear of the Negroes was almost unbelievable."

**3**

The almost complete immunity from punishment enjoyed by lynchers is merely a striking form of the broad and general immunity from punishment enjoyed by whites in many communities for less extreme offenses against Negroes. Moreover, lynching is the ultimate threat by which his inferior status is driven home to the Negro. As a terrorist device, it reinforces all the other disabilities placed upon him. The threat of lynching always hangs over the head of the southern Negro; the knowledge that a misinterpreted word or action can lead to his death is a dreadful burden.

POLICE BRUTALITY

We have reported the failure of some public officials to fulfill their most elementary duty—the protection of persons against mob violence. We must also report more widespread and varied forms of official misconduct. These include violent physical attacks by police officers on members of minority groups, the use of third degree methods to extort confessions, and brutality against prisoners. Civil rights violations of this kind are by no means universal and many law enforcement agencies have gone far in recent years toward stamping out these evils.

In various localities, scattered throughout the country, unprofessional or undisciplined police, while avoiding brutality, fail to recognize and to safeguard the civil rights of the citizenry. Insensitive to the necessary limits of police authority, untrained officers frequently overstep the bounds of their proper duties. At times this appears in unwarranted arrests, unduly prolonged detention before arraignment, and abuse of the search and seizure power. Cases involving these breaches of civil rights constantly come before the courts. The frequency with which such cases arise is proof that improper police conduct is still widespread, for it must be assumed that there are many instances of the abuse of police power which do not reach the courts. Most of the victims of such abuses are ignorant, friendless persons, unaware of their rights, and without the means of challenging those who have violated those rights.

Where lawless police forces exist, their activities may impair the civil rights of any citizen. In one place the brunt of illegal police activity may fall on suspected vagrants, in another on union organizers, and in another on unpopular racial or religious minorities, such as Negroes, Mexicans, or Jehovah's Witnesses. But wherever unfettered police lawlessness exists, civil rights may be vulnerable to the prejudices of the region or of dominant local groups, and to the caprice of individual policemen. Unpopular, weak, or defenseless groups are most apt to suffer. . . .

4

Much of the illegal official action which has been brought to the attention of the Committee is centered in the South. There is evidence of lawless police action against whites and Negroes alike, but the dominant pattern is that of race prejudice. J. Edgar Hoover referred, in his testimony before the Committee, to a particular jail where "it was seldom that a Negro man or woman was incarcerated who was not given a severe beating, which started off with a pistol whipping and ended with a rubber hose. . . ."

The total picture—adding the connivance of some police officials in lynchings to their record of brutality against Negroes in other situations—is, in the opinion of this Committee, a serious reflection on American justice. We know that Americans everywhere deplore this violence. We recognize further that there are many law enforcement officers in the South and the North who do not commit violent acts against Negroes or other friendless culprits. We are convinced, however, that the incidence of police brutality against Negroes is disturbingly high. . . .

INVOLUNTARY SERVITUDE

Slavery was abolished in this country nearly a century ago, and in its traditional form has disappeared. But the temptation to force poor and defenseless persons, by one device or another, into a condition of virtual slavery still exists. As recently as 1944, in the case of *Pollock* v. *Williams,* the Supreme Court struck down as a violation of the Thirteenth Amendment to the Constitution an Alabama statute which enabled employers to force employees, in debt on account of advanced wage payments, to continue to work for them under threat of criminal punishment. This is one of the more subtle devices for securing forced labor. More direct is the practice whereby sheriffs in some areas free prisoners into the custody of local entrepreneurs who pay fines or post bonds. The prisoners then work for their "benefactors" under threat of returning to jail. Sometimes the original charge against the prisoners is trumped up for the purpose of securing labor by this means. In still other instances persons have been held in peonage by sheer force or by threats of prosecution for debt.

Since the Civil Rights Section [of the Department of Justice] was established in 1939, a widespread decline in peonage and involuntary servitude has occurred. However, the threat has not entirely disappeared. In 1945, the Department of Justice prosecuted a case in which a Negro woman and her ten year old son had been held in captivity by a Mississippi farmer. Forced to work on a farm by day, they were locked in a crude, windowless, chimneyless cabin by night. The mother had made three

**5**

unsuccessful efforts to escape before federal authorities were informed of the situation. And as recently as 1947, an involuntary servitude case was successfully prosecuted by the federal government in California.

Where large numbers of people are frightened, uneducated, and underprivileged, the dangers of involuntary servitude remain. If economic conditions deteriorate, a more general recurrence of peonage may be anticipated.

## Note

Outbreaks of violence, involving serious infringement upon the right to security of the person, have occurred on various occasions since the issuance of the Committee's report. On August 27, 1949, an open air meeting near Peekskill, N. Y., at which Paul Robeson was scheduled to sing, was broken up by a mob; and a week later, after the concert was held, a mob attacked those leaving the meeting, injuring several hundred persons. See N. Y. Times, Aug. 28, Sept. 5–7, 1949; American Civil Liberties Union, *Violence in Peekskill*. In July, 1951, a mob rioted for several days in Cicero, Illinois, and prevented a Negro family from moving into the city, an all-white community, See Jack, *Cicero's Nightmare*, The Nation, July 28, 1951, p. 64; Miller, *Cicero's Covenants*, The New Republic, Aug. 6, 1951, p. 11. On Christmas night the same year a bomb placed under the home of Harry T. Moore, a leader in the National Association for the Advancement of Colored People in Mims, Florida, killed Moore and his wife. N. Y. Times, Dec. 27–30, 1951. Other bombings and intimidation in Florida, Cairo, Illinois, and elsewhere are described in Schroeter, *Dixie—A Pattern of Violence*, The New Republic, Feb. 11, 1952; Schroeter, *Force and Violence in Illinois*, The Nation, Feb. 9, 1952; N. Y. Times, Feb. 17, 1952.

Among the voluminous materials describing other infringements upon security of the person, see Whipple, *The Story of Civil Liberty in the United States* (1927); Hays, *Let Freedom Ring* (1928); Wecter, *When Johnny Comes Marching Home* (1944); Carr, *Federal Protection of Civil Rights* 14–20 (1947); the annual reports of the American Civil Liberties Union; *Civil Rights in the United States*, annual reports prepared by the American Jewish Congress and the National Association for the Advancement of Colored People.

With respect to the Negro's problem, see Cutler, *Lynch–law* (1905); White, *Rope and Faggot* (1929); Raper, *The Tragedy of Lynching* (1933); Chadbourn, *Lynching and the Law* (1933); Shay, *Judge Lynch* (1938); Myrdal, *An American Dilemma*, Part VI, esp. ch. 27 (1944); Cox, *Caste, Class and Race*, pp. 548–64 (1948); Davie, *Negroes in American Society*, ch. 16, with bibliography (1949); Murray, *The Negro Handbook*, 1942, 1944, 1947, and 1949.

For accounts of violence directed against other groups, see Report of the Senate Committee on Education and Labor pursuant to S. Res. 266, 74th Cong., 1st Sess., *Violations of Free Speech and the Rights of Labor* (LaFollette Report) ; Rotnem and Folsom, *Recent Restrictions Upon Religious Liberty,* 36 Am. Pol. Sci. Rev. 1053 (1942).

The results of the investigation by the Wickersham Commission into police brutality may be found in National Commission on Law Observance and Enforcement, *Report on Lawlessness in Law Enforcement* (1931). See also Hopkins, *Our Lawless Police* (1931).

A recent survey of involuntary servitude in the United States and elsewhere may be found in Herling, *Slavery Throughout the World,* The Survey, Sept. 1951, p. 377.

## B. THE ROLE OF THE FEDERAL GOVERNMENT

Infringements upon security of the person through violence, threats of violence, involuntary servitude and similar forms of coercion constitute, of course, violations of the ordinary criminal law of the states and localities. Moreover, a number of states, including some in the South, have specific laws directed at lynching, mob violence, the wearing of masks or hoods, the burning of crosses, and other forms of intimidation. See Mangum, *The Legal Status of the Negro,* pp. 290–307 (1940) ; Note, *Constitutionality of Proposed Federal Anti-Lynching Legislation,* 34 Va. L. Rev. 944, 945 (1948). There is, therefore, no lack of legal power to assure protection for the basic right of physical security. The problem arises out of the failure of the states and localities to enforce their laws and thus maintain the theoretical right in actual practice.

The issue thus becomes the extent to which the Federal government should undertake to afford protection through Federal legislation and the Federal machinery of justice. Generally speaking, of course, the Federal government, under our constitutional framework, has no authority or responsibility in the area of the ordinary crimes against the person. But should it assume jurisdiction where the state and local authorities have proven themselves unwilling or unable to protect the basic right involved?

The argument in favor of Federal intervention was carefully formulated by the President's Committee on Civil Rights. The argument against Federal intervention rests upon the well-known principles of state responsibility and states rights. Samples of the debate are given in the following extracts.

## TO SECURE THESE RIGHTS—THE REPORT OF THE PRESIDENT'S COMMITTEE ON CIVIL RIGHTS

Washington: U. S. Government Printing Office, 1947, pp. 99–104

The National Government of the United States must take the lead in safeguarding the civil rights of all Americans. We believe that this is one of the most important observations that can be made about the civil rights problem in our country today. We agree with words used by the President, in an address at the Lincoln Memorial in Washington in June, 1947:

> We must make the Federal Government a friendly, vigilant defender of the rights and equalities of all Americans. . . . Our National Government must show the way.

. . . There are several reasons why we believe the federal government must play a leading role in our efforts as a nation to improve our civil rights record.

First, many of the most serious wrongs against individual rights are committed by private persons or by local public officers. In the most flagrant of all such wrongs—lynching—private individuals, aided upon occasion by state or local officials, are the ones who take the law into their own hands and deprive the victim of his life. The very fact that these outrages continue to occur, coupled with the fact that the states have been unable to eliminate them, points clearly to a strong need for federal safeguards.

Second, it is a sound policy to use the idealism and prestige of our whole people to check the wayward tendencies of a part of them. It is true that the conscience of a nation is colored by the moral sense of its local communities. Still, the American people have traditionally shown high national regard for civil rights, even though the record in many a community has been far from good. We should not fail to make use of this in combating civil rights violations. . . .

Third, our civil rights record has growing international implications. These cannot safely be disregarded by the government at the national level which is responsible for our relations with the world, and left entirely to government at the local level for proper recognition and action. Many of man's problems, we have been learning, are capable of ultimate solution only through international cooperation and action. The subject of human rights, itself, has been made a major concern of the United Nations. It would indeed be ironical if in our own country the argument should prevail that safeguarding the rights of the individual is the exclusive or even the primary concern of local government.

8

A lynching in a rural American community is not a challenge to that community's conscience alone. The repercussions of such a crime are heard not only in the locality, or indeed only in our own nation. They echo from one end of the globe to the other, and the world looks to the American national government for both an explanation of how such a shocking event can occur in a civilized country and remedial action to prevent its recurrence. . . .

Fourth, the steadily growing tendency of the American people to look to the national government for the protection of their civil rights is highly significant. This popular demand does not by itself prove the case for national government action. But the persistent and deep-felt desire of the American citizen for federal action safeguarding his civil rights is neither a request for spoils by a selfish pressure group, nor is it a shortsighted and opportunistic attempt by a temporary majority to urge the government into a dubious or unwise course of action. It is a demand rooted in the folkways of the people, sound in instinct and reason, and impossible to ignore. The American people are loyal to the institutions of local self-government, and distrust highly centralized power. But we have never hesitated to entrust power and responsibility to the national government when need for such a course of action has been demonstrated and the people themselves are convinced of that need.

Finally, the national government should assume leadership in our American civil rights program because there is much in the field of civil rights that it is squarely responsible for in its own direct dealings with millions of persons. It is the largest single employer of labor in the country. More than two million persons are on its payroll. The freedom of opinion and expression enjoyed by these people is in many ways dependent upon the attitudes and practices of the government. By not restricting this freedom beyond a point necessary to insure the efficiency and loyalty of its workers, the government, itself, can make a very large contribution to the effort to achieve true freedom of thought in America. By scrupulously following fair employment practices, it not only sets a model for other employers to follow, but also directly protects the rights of more than two million workers to fair employment. The same is true of the armed forces. Their policies are completely determined by the federal government. That government has the power, the opportunity and the duty to see that discrimination and prejudice are completely eliminated from the armed services, and that the American soldier or sailor enjoys as full a measure of civil liberty as is commensurate with military service. . . .

Leadership by the federal government in safeguarding civil rights does not mean exclusive action by that government. There is much that the states and local communities can do in this field, and much that they alone can do. The Committee believes that Justice Holmes' view of the states as 48 laboratories for social and economic experimentation is still valid. The very complexity of the civil rights problem calls for much experimental, remedial action which may be better undertaken by the states than by the national government. Parallel state and local action supporting the national program is highly desirable. It is obvious that even though the federal government should take steps to stamp out the crime of lynching, the states cannot escape the responsibility to employ all of the powers and resources available to them for the same end. Or again, the enactment of a federal fair employment practice act will not render similar state legislation unnecessary.

In certain areas the states must do far more than parallel federal action. Either for constitutional or administrative reasons, they must remain the primary protectors of civil rights.

. . .

## COLLINS—THE CONSTITUTIONAL ASPECTS OF THE TRUMAN CIVIL RIGHTS PROGRAM

44 Ill. L. Rev. 1, at pp. 1, 11–12 (1949)

When on February 2, 1948,[1] President Truman asserted Federal jurisdiction over the civil rights of individual persons throughout the United States he precipitated a conflict which involves the fundamental question of the nature and form of our system of Government. It involves considerations of origin and destiny. . . .

Our American ancestors sought and won freedom. They built on virgin soil a new form of government to make men free. In the short space of our national life—only 159 years—our republican form of government has shown how freedom can be achieved under the Rule of Law. Nevertheless the student of the Constitution must now face the fact that a considerable body of public opinion now supports radical changes in our theory of government with the emphasis on personal security rather than freedom.

The last ten or fifteen years have brought to bear upon the minds of the American people cataclysmic concepts of human relations and we have learned a new vocabulary. We became acquainted with national stateism in Russia, Italy and Germany.

---

[1] 94 Cong. Rec., Feb. 2, 1948, at 960.

And in the war with the first as an ally, and with the other two as enemies, we also, under the centralizing forces of national defense and war, followed their example by going far into national stateism ourselves. And the influence of this centralization and national planning of everything for everybody has been carried over into the post-war period. Thus many are now coming to look to the Federal Government for the satisfaction of all of their needs and desires. They look to the centralized state for succor and protection from the cradle to the grave. "Rugged individualism"—the symbol of freedom and adventure—has become to them a term of reproach.

Within this new school of thought which is trying to bend the Constitution to its will without seeking formal amendments, religious values are also playing a part and they are frankly stated in the report of the President's Committee on Civil Rights. They are supported as legitimate Federal aims by a number of influential religious organizations. The Federal Government is urged to make effective the "brotherhood of man" because all men are the "children of God". The "democratic way of life" becomes of national concern. This also is a religious or moral concept because it denotes a rule of conduct of the individual. It is different from the concept of democracy as a form of government.

Under this civil rights plan the federal legislation recommended would carry heavy civil and criminal penalties for violations by individual persons and by state officials. The strong arm of the Federal Government with its enlarged and specially trained secret police would go out to detect and punish those who failed to observe these new laws.

Although to an old line student of the Constitution this situation may present a constitutional nightmare, he cannot afford to ignore it. We have already come a long way in this movement to change the fundamental nature of our form of government by evasion, subterfuge, indirection and emotionalism. In the near future it bids fair to become one of the chief political issues before the country. New party alignments may arise because of it. It has already been the occasion for the States Rights Democratic revolt in the South. But it is not a local or regional question. It is a question of the survival of the Constitution.

## Note

Further in support of Federal intervention, see Lusky, *Minority Rights and the Public Interest*, 52 Yale L. J. 1 (1942); Konvitz, *The Constitution and Civil Rights*, ch. 3 and 4 (1947); Carr, *Progress in Civil Rights*, in Wilcox (ed.) *Civil Liberties Under Attack*, pp. 31–7 (1951).

For the contrary argument see Sloan, *Federal Civil Rights Legislation and the Constitution,* 1 So. Car. L. Q. 245 (1949); Note, *Constitutionality of Proposed Federal Anti-Lynching Legislation,* 34 Va. L. Rev. 944 (1948); opinion of Mr. Justice Roberts in *Screws v. U. S.,* printed *infra.*

See also Hearings before Subcommittee of Committee on the Judiciary on S. 42, S. 1352, S. 1465, 80th Cong., 2d Sess. (1948), and Hearings before Subcommittee No. 4 of the Committee on the Judiciary, House of Representatives, on H. R. 41 et al., 80th Cong., 2d Sess. (1948) (hearings on anti-lynching bills).

For a similar controversy over proposals for an International Bill of Human Rights, see Holman, *An "International Bill of Rights": Proposals Have Dangerous Implications for U. S.,* 34 A. B. A. J. 984 (1948) and McDougal and Leighton, *The Rights of Man in the World Community: Constitutional Illusions Versus Rational Action,* 14 Law and Contemp. Prob. 490 (1949), 59 Yale L. J. 60 (1949).

## C. CONSTITUTIONAL AND STATUTORY BASIS FOR FEDERAL ACTION

### 1. Historical Development of Federal Power

Prior to the Civil War there had been little or no effort to invoke the authority of the Federal government in protection of the right to security of the person. Indeed the Constitution seemed to afford no legal basis for such intervention. It might have been possible to predicate Federal power upon the Bill of Rights, embodied in the first eight amendments, but the Supreme Court squarely held in 1833 that the Bill of Rights imposed restrictions only upon the Federal government, not upon state or local governments or their officials, or upon private individuals. *Barron v. Baltimore,* 7 Peters 243, 8 L. Ed. 672 (1833). This ruling has never been seriously challenged.

Another source of Federal power might have been the privileges and immunities clause in Article IV, Section 2 of the Constitution. This provides that "the citizens of each state shall be entitled to all privileges and immunities of citizens in the several states." See *Corfield v. Coryell,* 6 Fed. Cas. 546, No. 3230 (E.D. Pa. 1823). But this provision has now been interpreted to require only that no state may deprive a citizen of another state of the "privileges and immunities", whatever they may be, enjoyed by its own citizens. Thus even if the phrase "privileges and immunities" were interpreted broadly, which it has not been, the provision would afford protection only for discrimination by states against citizens of other states. *Slaughter-House Cases,* 16 Wall. 36, 21 L. Ed. 394 (1873); Rottschaefer, *Handbook of American Constitutional Law,* pp. 123–34 (1939); Hale,

*Some Basic Constitutional Rights of Economic Significance*, 51 Col. L. Rev. 271, 288–304 (1951).

In the aftermath of the Civil War, however, the country turned sharply in the direction of invoking Federal power for the protection of rights to security of the person. In the Thirteenth, Fourteenth and Fifteenth Amendments, and in the Civil Rights Acts, there was created the basis for a vast expansion of Federal authority.

## THIRTEENTH AMENDMENT (1865)

SECTION 1. Neither slavery nor involuntary servitude, except as a punishment for crime whereof the party shall have been duly convicted, shall exist within the United States, or any place subject to their jurisdiction.

SECTION 2. Congress shall have power to enforce this article by appropriate legislation.

## FOURTEENTH AMENDMENT (1868)

SECTION 1. All persons born or naturalized in the United States, and subject to the jurisdiction thereof, are citizens of the United States and of the State wherein they reside. No State shall make or enforce any law which shall abridge the privileges or immunities of citizens of the United States; nor shall any State deprive any person of life, liberty, or property, without due process of law; nor deny to any person within its jurisdiction the equal protection of the laws.

SECTION 2. Representatives shall be apportioned among the several States according to their respective numbers, counting the whole number of persons in each State, excluding Indians not taxed. But when the right to vote at any election for the choice of electors for President and Vice President of the United States, Representatives in Congress, the Executive and Judicial officers of a State, or the members of the Legislature thereof, is denied to any of the male inhabitants of such State, being twenty-one years of age, and citizens of the United States, or in any way abridged, except for participation in rebellion, or other crime, the basis of representation therein shall be reduced in the proportion which the number of such male citizens shall bear to the whole number of male citizens twenty-one years of age in such State.

. . . . . . . . . .

SECTION 5. The Congress shall have power to enforce, by appropriate legislation, the provisions of this article.

## FIFTEENTH AMENDMENT (1870)

SECTION 1. The right of citizens of the United States to vote shall not be denied or abridged by the United States or by any State on account of race, color, or previous condition of servitude.

SECTION 2. The Congress shall have power to enforce this article by appropriate legislation.

## CARR—FEDERAL PROTECTION OF CIVIL RIGHTS

### pp. 36–39 (1947)

The meaning and purpose of these Civil War Amendments has been the subject of much controversy. But one can build a strong case contending that their congressional framers meant them to serve as a basis for a positive, comprehensive federal program—a program defining fundamental civil rights protected by federal machinery against both state and private encroachment.[5] Perhaps the best evidence supporting this contention is that during and just after the period when the Amendments were framed, Congress passed seven statutes establishing just such a federal program. There were members of Congress who argued against the constitutionality of this program and voted against the bills, just as there were members of Congress who opposed the three Amendments. But the Amendments and statutes received the necessary majorities in both houses of Congress. The significance of the nearly simultaneous action of Congress in passing the three Amendments and seven statutes implementing them cannot be overlooked. . . .

Five of the statutes by which Congress tried to implement the Civil War Amendments were general civil rights acts. The first of these was the Act of April 9, 1866, which was passed at a time when only the Thirteenth Amendment had gone into effect. Known as the Civil Rights or Enforcement Act, it was entitled "An Act to protect all Persons in the United States in their Civil Rights, and furnish the Means of their Vindication." The Act was aimed at outlawing the "Black Codes," enacted by the southern states immediately after the close of the war, which restricted the movement and occupation of Negroes. It provided

---

[5] See Carl B. Swisher, *American Constitutional Development*, chap. 15, and H. E. Flack, *The Adoption of the Fourteenth Amendment* (Baltimore: The Johns Hopkins Press, 1908). While Flack's study is concerned only with the Fourteenth Amendment, he concludes that "according to the purpose and intention of the Amendment as disclosed in the debates in Congress and in the several state Legislatures and in other ways, Congress had the constitutional power to enact direct legislation to secure the rights of citizens against violation by individuals as well as by States" (p. 277).

that all persons born in the United States were citizens thereof, and it endeavored to place members of all races on an equal basis as to their rights "to make and enforce contracts, to sue, be parties, and give evidence, to inherit, purchase, lease, sell, hold and convey real and personal property, and to full and equal benefit of all laws and proceedings for the security of persons and property." The federal courts were given exclusive jurisdiction of cases arising under the Act, severe penalties were prescribed for its violation, and the President was empowered to use the land and naval forces to secure its enforcement.[6]

The second Civil Rights, or Enforcement Act, was passed by Congress on May 31, 1870, and was entitled, "An Act to enforce the Right of Citizens of the United States to vote in the several States of this Union, and for other purposes." This second statute was amended by an Act of February 28, 1871. The general purpose of these two acts was to make the Fourteenth and Fifteenth Amendments effective. More specifically, they were designed to protect the right to vote by providing federal machinery to supervise elections in the states. Severe penalties for any interference, based on race or color, with the exercise of the right of suffrage at federal or state elections were provided. In addition, it was made a felony for two or more persons to conspire to interfere with the free exercise by a citizen of any right granted to him by the laws or Constitution of the United States.[7]

The Act of April 20, 1871, often known as the Ku Klux Klan Act, or the Antilynching Act, was entitled "An Act to enforce the Provisions of the Fourteenth Amendment to the Constitution of the United States." This Act penalized action, under color of law, which deprived persons of their rights under the laws or Constitution of the United States. The Act also provided penalties for conspiring to overthrow the government of the United States, or to prevent the execution of its laws. The President was authorized to use the military force to suppress unlawful action, when the states were unable or unwilling to prevent interferences with citizens' rights or the obstruction of the federal government processes.[8]

Finally, there was the Civil Rights Act of March 1, 1875, entitled "An Act to protect all Citizens in their civil and legal rights." This Act was designed to guarantee to Negroes equal accommodations with white citizens in all inns, public conveyances, theaters, and other places of amusement. Refusal by pri-

---

[6] 14 Stat. 27. . . .
[7] 16 Stat. 140, and 16 Stat. 433.
[8] 17 Stat. 13.

vate persons to provide such accommodations was declared to be a misdemeanor, and injured parties were given the right to sue for damages.[9]

Two of the seven statutes were more limited in purpose. These were the Slave Kidnaping Act of May 21, 1866, and the Peonage Abolition Act of March 2, 1867, which were designed to implement the Thirteenth Amendment. The former was entitled "An Act to prevent and punish Kidnapping," and made it a federal crime to kidnap or carry away a person with the intention of placing him in slavery or involuntary servitude. The latter statute was entitled "An Act to abolish and forever prohibit the System of Peonage in the Territory of New Mexico and other parts of the United States." While aimed primarily at practices prevailing in New Mexico, it also was designed to define "involuntary servitude" and to provide specific criminal penalties for violations of the Thirteenth Amendment.[10]

It is clear that in these seven acts, Congress intended to make extensive use of the "sword" technique in providing federal protection of the rights of individuals against interferences either by public officers or by private individuals. These acts admittedly were motivated by a general concern on the part of Congress for the newly freed Negro, and by a specific desire to safeguard his rights. But, without exception, no mention is made of the Negro as such. Instead the wording is sufficiently broad to cover the rights of *all citizens,* if not all inhabitants or persons. . . . .

## Note

The literature on adoption of the Civil War Amendments is extensive. In addition to Flack and Swisher, cited in the extract from Carr, see Guthrie, *The Fourteenth Article of Amendment to the Constitution of the United States* (1898) ; Collins, *The Fourteenth Amendment and the States* (1912) ; Graham, *The "Conspiracy Theory" of the Fourteenth Amendment,* 47 Yale L. J. 371 (1938) ; Boudin, *Truth and Fiction About the Fourteenth Amendment,* 16 N. Y. U. L. Q. Rev. 19 (1938) ; *Adamson v. Cal.* 332 U. S. 46, 91 L. Ed. 1903, 67 S. Ct. 1672 (1947) ; Fairman, *Does the Fourteenth Amendment Incorporate the Bill of Rights?,* 2 Stanford L. Rev. 5 (1949) ; Frank and Munro, *The Original Understanding of "Equal Protection of the Laws,"* 50 Col. L. Rev. 131 (1950).

With reference to the Civil Rights Acts see Biddle, *Civil Rights and the Federal Law* in Wilcox (ed.), *Safeguarding Civil Liberty Today* (1945) ; Fraenkel, *The Federal Civil Rights Laws,* 31 Minn. L. Rev. 301 (1947) ; Berger, *Equality by Statute,* pp. 8–13 (1952). The

---

[9] 18 Stat. 335.

[10] 14 Stat. 50 and 546.

text of the legislation may be found in Carr, *Federal Protection of Civil Rights*, Appen. 1, pp. 211–251 (1947).

For the economic, political and social background see McLaughlin, *A Constitutional History of the United States*, ch. XLIV–XLIX (1935); Randall, *The Civil War and Reconstruction* (1937); Kelly and Harbison, *The American Constitution*, ch. 17 and 18, and material cited on pp. 876–7 (1948); Graham, *The Early Antislavery Backgrounds of the Fourteenth Amendment*, 1950 Wis. L. Rev. 479; TenBroek, *The Antislavery Origins of the Fourteenth Amendment* (1951).

The Civil War Amendments and the Civil Rights Acts came before the Supreme Court in a series of cases in the following decades. The most significant, with respect to the problems of this chapter, are the *Slaughter-House Cases*, the *Civil Rights Cases* and the *Cruikshank Case.*

## SLAUGHTER-HOUSE CASES

Supreme Court of the United States, 1873
16 Wall. 36, 21 L. Ed. 394

[A Louisiana statute, passed in 1869, chartered a private corporation and granted to it exclusive rights for 25 years to conduct all slaughtering operations in 3 parishes, including the city of New Orleans. All persons were forbidden to slaughter cattle except in the facilities operated by the new corporation. Maximum prices for the services rendered by the corporation were fixed by the statute. Proponents of the legislation justified it as a health measure. A group of butchers in New Orleans challenged the constitutionality of the statute on the grounds, among others, that it violated the Thirteenth and Fourteenth Amendments. The argument under the Thirteenth Amendment was that the restriction upon free use of property imposed by the statute constituted a "servitude." This position was rejected by the Court. After discussing the background of the Civil War Amendments the majority opinion of Justice Miller considers the argument under the Fourteenth Amendment.]

MR. JUSTICE MILLER . . .

We repeat, then, in the light of this recapitulation of events, almost too recent to be called history, but which are familiar to us all; and on the most casual examination of the language of these amendments, no one can fail to be impressed with the one pervading purpose found in them all, lying at the foundation of each, and without which none of them would have been even suggested; we mean the freedom of the slave race, the security and firm establishment of that freedom, and the protection of the newly-made freeman and citizen from the oppressions of those who had formerly exercised unlimited dominion over him. It is true that only the fifteenth amendment, in terms, mentions the negro by speaking of his color and his slavery. But it is just as true that each of the other articles was addressed to the grievances of that race, and designed to remedy them as the fifteenth. . . .

"All persons born or naturalized in the United States, and subject to the jurisdiction thereof, are citizens of the United States and of the State wherein they reside."

The first observation we have to make on this clause is, that it puts at rest both the questions which we stated to have been the subject of differences of opinion. It declares that persons may be citizens of the United States without regard to their citizenship of a particular State, and it overturns the Dred Scott decision by making *all persons* born within the United States and subject to its jurisdiction citizens of the United States. That its main purpose was to establish the citizenship of the negro can admit of no doubt. The phrase, "subject to its jurisdiction" was intended to exclude from its operation children of ministers, consuls, and citizens or subjects of foreign States born within the United States.

The next observation is more important in view of the arguments of counsel in the present case. It is, that the distinction between citizenship of the United States and citizenship of a State is clearly recognized and established. Not only may a man be a citizen of the United States without being a citizen of a State, but an important element is necessary to convert the former into the latter. He must reside within the State to make him a citizen of it, but it is only necessary that he should be born or naturalized in the United States to be a citizen of the Union.

It is quite clear, then, that there is a citizenship of the United States, and a citizenship of a State, which are distinct from each other, and which depend upon different characteristics or circumstances in the individual.

We think this distinction and its explicit recognition in this amendment of great weight in this argument, because the next paragraph of this same section, which is the one mainly relied on by the plaintiffs in error, speaks only of privileges and immunities of citizens of the United States, and does not speak of those of citizens of the several States. . . .

The language is, "No State shall make or enforce any law which shall abridge the privileges or immunities of citizens of *the United States.*" It is a little remarkable, if this clause was intended as a protection to the citizen of a State against the legislative power of his own State, that the word citizen of the State

18                                                                    [Emerson]

should be left out when it is so carefully used, and used in contradistinction to citizens of the United States, in the very sentence which precedes it. It is too clear for argument that the change in phraseology was adopted understandingly and with a purpose. . . .

[The Court then discusses Article IV, Section 2 of the Constitution: "The citizens of each State shall be entitled to all privileges and immunities of citizens of the several States."]

Fortunately we are not without judicial construction of this clause of the Constitution. The first and the leading case on the subject is that of *Corfield v. Coryell,* decided by Mr. Justice Washington in the Circuit Court for the District of Pennsylvania in 1823.*

"The inquiry," he says, "is, what are the privileges and immunities of citizens of the several States? We feel no hesitation in confining these expressions to those privileges and immunities which are *fundamental;* which belong of right to the citizens of all free governments, and which have at all times been enjoyed by citizens of the several States which compose this Union, from the time of their becoming free, independent, and sovereign. What these fundamental principles are, it would be more tedious than difficult to enumerate. They may all, however, be comprehended under the following general heads: protection by the government, with the right to acquire and possess property of every kind, and to pursue and obtain happiness and safety, subject, nevertheless, to such restraints as the government may prescribe for the general good of the whole." . . .

The constitutional provision there alluded to did not create those rights, which it called privileges and immunities of citizens of the States. It threw around them in that clause no security for the citizen of the State in which they were claimed or exercised. Nor did it profess to control the power of the State governments over the rights of its own citizens.

Its sole purpose was to declare to the several States, that whatever those rights, as you grant or establish them to your own citizens, or as you limit or qualify, or impose restrictions on their exercise, the same, neither more nor less, shall be the measure of the rights of citizens of other States within your jurisdiction.

It would be the vainest show of learning to attempt to prove by citations of authority, that up to the adoption of the recent amendments, no claim or pretence was set up that those rights depended on the Federal government for their existence or protection, beyond the very few express limitations which the Fed-

---

* 4 Washington's Circuit Court, 371.

eral Constitution imposed upon the States—such, for instance, as the prohibition against ex post facto laws, bills of attainder, and laws impairing the obligation of contracts. But with the exception of these and a few other restrictions, the entire domain of the privileges and immunities of citizens of the States, as above defined, lay within the constitutional and legislative power of the States, and without that of the Federal government. Was it the purpose of the fourteenth amendment, by the simple declaration that no State should make or enforce any law which shall abridge the privileges and immunities of *citizens of the United States,* to transfer the security and protection of all the civil rights which we have mentioned, from the States to the Federal government? And where it is declared that Congress shall have the power to enforce that article, was it intended to bring within the power of Congress the entire domain of civil rights heretofore belonging exclusively to the States?

All this and more must follow, if the proposition of the plaintiffs in error be sound. For not only are these rights subject to the control of Congress whenever in its discretion any of them are supposed to be abridged by State legislation, but that body may also pass laws in advance, limiting and restricting the exercise of legislative power by the States, in their most ordinary and usual functions, as in its judgment it may think proper on all such subjects. And still further, such a construction followed by the reversal of the judgments of the Supreme Court of Louisiana in these cases, would constitute this court a perpetual censor upon all legislation of the States, on the civil rights of their own citizens, with authority to nullify such as it did not approve as consistent with those rights, as they existed at the time of the adoption of this amendment. The argument we admit is not always the most conclusive which is drawn from the consequences urged against the adoption of a particular construction of an instrument. But when, as in the case before us, these consequences are so serious, so far-reaching and pervading, so great a departure from the structure and spirit of our institutions; when the effect is to fetter and degrade the State governments by subjecting them to the control of Congress, in the exercise of powers heretofore universally conceded to them of the most ordinary and fundamental character; when in fact it radically changes the whole theory of the relations of the State and Federal governments to each other and of both these governments to the people; the argument has a force that is irresistible, in the absence of language which expresses such a purpose too clearly to admit of doubt.

We are convinced that no such results were intended by the

**20**

Congress which proposed these amendments, nor by the legislatures of the States which ratified them.

Having shown that the privileges and immunities relied on in the argument are those which belong to citizens of the States as such, and that they are left to the State governments for security and protection, and not by this article placed under the special care of the Federal government, we may hold ourselves excused from defining the privileges and immunities of citizens of the United States which no State can abridge, until some case involving those privileges may make it necessary to do so.

But lest it should be said that no such privileges and immunities are to be found if those we have been considering are excluded, we venture to suggest some which owe their existence to the Federal government, its National character, its Constitution, or its laws.

One of these is well described in the case of *Crandall v. Nevada*.* It is said to be the right of the citizen of this great country, protected by implied guarantees of its Constitution, "to come to the seat of government to assert any claim he may have upon that government, to transact any business he may have with it, to seek its protection, to share its offices, to engage in administering its functions. He has the right of free access to its seaports, through which all operations of foreign commerce are conducted, to the subtreasuries, land offices, and courts of justice in the several States." . . .

Another privilege of a citizen of the United States is to demand the care and protection of the Federal government over his life, liberty, and property when on the high seas or within the jurisdiction of a foreign government. Of this there can be no doubt, nor that the right depends upon his character as a citizen of the United States. The right to peaceably assemble and petition for redress of grievances, the privilege of the writ of *habeas corpus,* are rights of the citizen guaranteed by the Federal Constitution. The right to use the navigable waters of the United States, however they may penetrate the territory of the several States, all rights secured to our citizens by treaties with foreign nations, are dependent upon citizenship of the United States, and not citizenship of a State. One of these privileges is conferred by the very article under consideration. It is that a citizen of the United States can, of his own volition, become a citizen of any State of the Union by a *bona fide* residence therein, with the same rights as other citizens of that State. To these may be added the rights secured by the thirteenth and fifteenth articles of amendment, and by the other clause of the fourteenth, next to be considered.

---

* 6 Wallace, 36.

But it is useless to pursue this branch of the inquiry, since we are of opinion that the rights claimed by these plaintiffs in error, if they have any existence, are not privileges and immunities of citizens of the United States within the meaning of the clause of the fourteenth amendment under consideration. . . .

[The Court then went on to hold that neither the due process nor equal protection clauses of the Fourteenth Amendment constituted grounds for invalidating the Louisiana statute.]

MR. JUSTICE FIELD, dissenting. . . .

The first clause of the fourteenth amendment changes this whole subject [the issue of who is a citizen of the United States], and removes it from the region of discussion and doubt. It recognizes in express terms, if it does not create, citizens of the United States, and it makes their citizenship dependent upon the place of their birth, or the fact of their adoption, and not upon the constitution or laws of any State or the condition of their ancestry. A citizen of a State is now only a citizen of the United States residing in that State. The fundamental rights, privileges, and immunities which belong to him as a free man and a free citizen, now belong to him as a citizen of the United States, and are not dependent upon his citizenship of any State. The exercise of these rights and privileges, and the degree of enjoyment received from such exercise, are always more or less affected by the condition and the local institutions of the State, or city, or town where he resides. They are thus affected in a State by the wisdom of its laws, the ability of its officers, the efficiency of its magistrates, the education and morals of its people, and by many other considerations. This is a result which follows from the constitution of society, and can never be avoided, but in no other way can they be affected by the action of the State, or by the residence of the citizen therein. They do not derive their existence from its legislation, and cannot be destroyed by its power.

The amendment does not attempt to confer any new privileges or immunities upon citizens, or to enumerate or define those already existing. It assumes that there are such privileges and immunities which belong of right to citizens as such, and ordains that they shall not be abridged by State legislation. If this inhibition has no reference to privileges and immunities of this character, but only refers, as held by the majority of the court in their opinion, to such privileges and immunities as were before its adoption specially designated in the Constitution or necessarily implied as belonging to citizens of the United States, it was a vain and idle enactment, which accomplished nothing, and most unnecessarily excited Congress and the people on its passage. With privileges and immunities thus designated or implied no State could ever have interfered by its laws, and no new constitutional provision was required to inhibit such interference. The supremacy of the Constitution and the laws of the United States always controlled any State legislation of that character. But if the amendment refers to the natural and inalienable rights which belong to all citizens, the inhibition has a profound significance and consequence.

What, then, are the privileges and immunities which are secured against abridgment by State legislation? . . .

The terms, privileges and immunities, are not new in the amendment; they were in the Constitution before the amendment was adopted. They are found in the second section of the fourth article. . . .

[The opinion then discusses the interpretation of Article IV, Section 2, in *Corfield v. Coryell*.]

It will not be pretended that under the fourth article of the Constitution any State could create a monopoly in any known trade or manufacture in favor of her own citizens, or any portion of them, which would exclude an equal participation in the trade or manufacture monopolized by citizens of other States. . . .

Now, what the clause in question does for the protection of citizens of one State against the creation of monopolies in favor of citizens of other States, the fourteenth amendment does for the protection of every citizen of the United States against the creation of any monopoly whatever. The privileges and immunities of citizens of the United States, of every one of them, is secured against abridgment in any form by any State. The fourteenth amendment places them under the guardianship of the National authority. All monopolies in any known trade or manufacture are an invasion of these privileges, for they encroach upon the liberty of citizens to acquire property and pursue happiness, and were held void at common law in the great *Case of Monopolies*, decided during the reign of Queen Elizabeth. . . .

I am authorized by THE CHIEF JUSTICE, MR. JUSTICE SWAYNE, and MR. JUSTICE BRADLEY, to state that they concur with me in the dissenting opinion.

[Justices Bradley and Swayne also delivered separate opinions].[1]

---

[1] For discussion of the *Slaughter-House* cases see Franklin, *The Foundations and Meaning of the Slaughterhouse Cases*, 18 Tulane L. Rev. 1, 218 (1943); Konvitz, *The Constitution and Civil Rights*, pp. 31–6 (1947); and materials cited *infra*.

## CIVIL RIGHTS CASES

Supreme Court of the United States, 1883
109 U. S. 3, 27 L. Ed. 835, 3 Sup. Ct. 18

[The cases arose under the Civil Rights Act of March 1, 1875, which provided in part:

"That all persons within the jurisdiction of the United States shall be entitled to the full and equal enjoyment of the accommodations, advantages, facilities, and privileges of inns, public conveyances on land or water, theatres, and other places of public amusement; subject only to the conditions and limitations established by law, and applicable alike to citizens of every race and color, regardless of any previous condition of servitude."

The proceedings involved several indictments charging refusal to grant accommodations to Negroes in a hotel and in theaters in San Francisco and New York, and a civil action alleging refusal to permit a Negro woman to ride in the ladies' car of a railroad in Tennessee.]

Mr. Justice Bradley . . .

The essence of the law is, not to declare broadly that all persons shall be entitled to the full and equal enjoyment of the accommodations, advantages, facilities, and privileges of inns, public conveyances, and theatres; but that such enjoyment shall not be subject to any conditions applicable only to citizens of a particular race or color, or who had been in a previous condition of servitude.

. . .

Has Congress constitutional power to make such a law? Of course, no one will contend that the power to pass it was contained in the Constitution before the adoption of the last three amendments. . . .

[The Court then refers to Section 1 of the Fourteenth Amendment.]

It is State action of a particular character that is prohibited. Individual invasion of individual rights is not the subject-matter of the amendment. It has a deeper and broader scope. It nullifies and makes void all State legislation, and State action of every kind, which impairs the privileges and immunities of citizens of the United States, or which injures them in life, liberty or property without due process of law, or which denies to any of them the equal protection of the laws. It not only does this, but, in order that the national will, thus declared, may not be a mere *brutum fulmen,* the last section of the amendment invests Congress with power to enforce it by appropriate legislation. To

**24**

enforce what? To enforce the prohibition. To adopt appropriate legislation for correcting the effects of such prohibited State laws and State acts, and thus to render them effectually null, void, and innocuous. This is the legislative power conferred upon Congress, and this is the whole of it. It does not invest Congress with power to legislate upon subjects which are within the domain of State legislation; but to provide modes of relief against State legislation, or State action, of the kind referred to. It does not authorize Congress to create a code of municipal law for the regulation of private rights; but to provide modes of redress against the operation of State laws, and the action of State officers executive or judicial, when these are subversive of the fundamental rights specified in the amendment. Positive rights and privileges are undoubtedly secured by the Fourteenth Amendment; but they are secured by way of prohibition against State laws and State proceedings affecting those rights and privileges, and by power given to Congress to legislate for the purpose of carrying such prohibition into effect: and such legislation must necessarily be predicated upon such supposed State laws or State proceedings, and be directed to the correction of their operation and effect. A quite full discussion of this aspect of the amendment may be found in *United States* v. *Cruikshank*, 92 U. S. 542; *Virginia* v. *Rives*, 100 U. S. 313; and *Ex parte Virginia*, 100 U. S. 339.

An apt illustration of this distinction may be found in some of the provisions of the original Constitution. Take the subject of contracts, for example. The Constitution prohibited the States from passing any law impairing the obligation of contracts. This did not give to Congress power to provide laws for the general enforcement of contracts; nor power to invest the courts of the United States with jurisdiction over contracts, so as to enable parties to sue upon them in those courts. It did, however, give the power to provide remedies by which the impairment of contracts by State legislation might be counteracted and corrected: and this power was exercised. The remedy which Congress actually provided was that contained in the 25th section of the Judiciary Act of 1789, 1 Stat. 85, giving to the Supreme Court of the United States jurisdiction by writ of error to review the final decisions of State courts whenever they should sustain the validity of a State statute or authority alleged to be repugnant to the Constitution or laws of the United States. . . .

If this legislation is appropriate for enforcing the prohibitions of the amendment, it is difficult to see where it is to stop. Why may not Congress with equal show of authority enact a code of laws for the enforcement and vindication of all rights of life, liberty, and property? If it is supposable that the States may deprive persons of life, liberty, and property without due process of law (and the amendment itself does suppose this), why should not Congress proceed at once to prescribe due process of law for the protection of every one of these fundamental rights, in every possible case, as well as to prescribe equal privileges in inns, public conveyances, and theatres? . . .

In this connection it is proper to state that civil rights, such as are guaranteed by the Constitution against State aggression, cannot be impaired by the wrongful acts of individuals, unsupported by State authority in the shape of laws, customs, or judicial or executive proceedings. The wrongful act of an individual, unsupported by any such authority, is simply a private wrong, or a crime of that individual; an invasion of the rights of the injured party, it is true, whether they affect his person, his property, or his reputation; but if not sanctioned in some way by the State, or not done under State authority, his rights remain in full force, and may presumably be vindicated by resort to the laws of the State for redress. An individual cannot deprive a man of his right to vote, to hold property, to buy and sell, to sue in the courts, or to be a witness or a juror; he may, by force or fraud, interfere with the enjoyment of the right in a particular case; he may commit an assault against the person, or commit murder, or use ruffian violence at the polls, or slander the good name of a fellow citizen; but, unless protected in these wrongful acts by some shield of State law or State authority, he cannot destroy or injure the right; he will only render himself amenable to satisfaction or punishment; and amenable therefor to the laws of the State where the wrongful acts are committed. . . .

Of course, these remarks do not apply to those cases in which Congress is clothed with direct and plenary powers of legislation over the whole subject, accompanied with an express or implied denial of such power to the States, as in the regulation of commerce with foreign nations, among the several States, and with the Indian tribes, the coining of money, the establishment of post offices and post roads, the declaring of war, etc. In these cases Congress has power to pass laws for regulating the subjects specified in every detail, and the conduct and transactions of individuals in respect thereof. But where a subject is not submitted to the general legislative power of Congress, but is only submitted thereto for the purpose of rendering effective some prohibition against particular State legislation or State action in reference to that subject, the power given is limited by its object, and any legislation by Congress in the matter must necessarily be corrective in its character, adapted to counteract and redress

26

the operation of such prohibited State laws or proceedings of State officers. . . .

We have discussed the question presented by the law on the assumption that a right to enjoy equal accommodation and privileges in all inns, public conveyances, and places of public amusement, is one of the essential rights of the citizen which no State can abridge or interfere with. Whether it is such a right, or not, is a different question which, in the view we have taken of the validity of the law on the ground already stated, it is not necessary to examine.

We have also discussed the validity of the law in reference to cases arising in the States only; and not in reference to cases arising in the Territories or the District of Columbia, which are subject to the plenary legislation of Congress in every branch of municipal regulation. Whether the law would be a valid one as applied to the Territories and the District is not a question for consideration in the cases before us: they all being cases arising within the limits of States. And whether Congress, in the exercise of its power to regulate commerce amongst the several States, might or might not pass a law regulating rights in public conveyances passing from one State to another, is also a question which is not now before us, as the sections in question are not conceived in any such view.

But the power of Congress to adopt direct and primary, as distinguished from corrective legislation, on the subject in hand, is sought, in the second place, from the Thirteenth Amendment, which abolishes slavery. . . .

This amendment, as well as the Fourteenth, is undoubtedly self-executing without any ancillary legislation, so far as its terms are applicable to any existing state of circumstances. By its own unaided force and effect it abolished slavery, and established universal freedom. Still, legislation may be necessary and proper to meet all the various cases and circumstances to be affected by it, and to prescribe proper modes of redress for its violation in letter or spirit. And such legislation may be primary and direct in its character; for the amendment is not a mere prohibition of State laws establishing or upholding slavery, but an absolute declaration that slavery or involuntary servitude shall not exist in any part of the United States.

It is true, that slavery cannot exist without law, any more than property in lands and goods can exist without law: and, therefore, the Thirteenth Amendment may be regarded as nullifying all State laws which establish or uphold slavery. But it has a reflex character also, establishing and decreeing universal civil and political freedom throughout the United States; and it is

**27**

assumed, that the power vested in Congress to enforce the article by appropriate legislation, clothes Congress with power to pass all laws necessary and proper for abolishing all badges and incidents of slavery in the United States: and upon this assumption it is claimed, that this is sufficient authority for declaring by law that all persons shall have equal accommodations and privileges in all inns, public conveyances, and places of amusement; the argument being, that the denial of such equal accommodations and privileges is, in itself, a subjection to a species of servitude within the meaning of the amendment. Conceding the major proposition to be true, that Congress has a right to enact all necessary and proper laws for the obliteration and prevention of slavery with all its badges and incidents, is the minor proposition also true, that the denial to any person of admission to the accommodations and privileges of an inn, a public conveyance, or a theatre, does subject that person to any form of servitude, or tend to fasten upon him any badge of slavery? If it does not, then power to pass the law is not found in the Thirteenth Amendment. . . .

The long existence of African slavery in this country gave us very distinct notions of what it was, and what were its necessary incidents. Compulsory service of the slave for the benefit of the master, restraint of his movements except by the master's will, disability to hold property, to make contracts, to have a standing in court, to be a witness against a white person, and such like burdens and incapacities, were the inseparable incidents of the institution. Severer punishments for crimes were imposed on the slave than on free persons guilty of the same offences. Congress, as we have seen, by the Civil Rights Bill of 1866, passed in view of the Thirteenth Amendment, before the Fourteenth was adopted, undertook to wipe out these burdens and disabilities, the necessary incidents of slavery, constituting its substance and visible form; and to secure to all citizens of every race and color, and without regard to previous servitude, those fundamental rights which are the essence of civil freedom, namely, the same right to make and enforce contracts, to sue, be parties, give evidence, and to inherit, purchase, lease, sell and convey property, as is enjoyed by white citizens. Whether this legislation was fully authorized by the Thirteenth Amendment alone, without the support which it afterward received from the Fourteenth Amendment, after the adoption of which it was re-enacted with some additions, it is not necessary to inquire. It is referred to for the purpose of showing that at that time (in 1866) Congress did not assume, under the authority given by the Thirteenth Amendment, to adjust what may be called the social rights of men and races in the community; but only to declare and vindicate those fundamental rights which appertain to the essence of citizenship, and the enjoyment or deprivation of which constitutes the essential distinction between freedom and slavery. . . .

After giving to these questions all the consideration which their importance demands, we are forced to the conclusion that such an act of refusal has nothing to do with slavery or involuntary servitude, and that if it is violative of any right of the party, his redress is to be sought under the laws of the State; or if those laws are adverse to his rights and do not protect him, his remedy will be found in the corrective legislation which Congress has adopted, or may adopt, for counteracting the effect of State laws, or State action, prohibited by the Fourteenth Amendment. It would be running the slavery argument into the ground to make it apply to every act of discrimination which a person may see fit to make as to the guests he will entertain, or as to the people he will take into his coach or cab or car, or admit to his concert or theatre, or deal with in other matters of intercourse or business. Innkeepers and public carriers, by the laws of all the States, so far as we are aware, are bound, to the extent of their facilities, to furnish proper accommodation to all unobjectionable persons who in good faith apply for them. If the laws themselves make any unjust discrimination, amenable to the prohibitions of the Fourteenth Amendment, Congress has full power to afford a remedy under that amendment and in accordance with it.

When a man has emerged from slavery, and by the aid of beneficient legislation has shaken off the inseparable concomitants of that state, there must be some stage in the progress of his elevation when he takes the rank of a mere citizen, and ceases to be the special favorite of the laws, and when his rights as a citizen, or a man, are to be protected in the ordinary modes by which other men's rights are protected. There were thousands of free colored people in this country before the abolition of slavery, enjoying all the essential rights of life, liberty and property the same as white citizens; yet no one, at that time, thought that it was any invasion of his personal status as a freeman because he was not admitted to all the privileges enjoyed by white citizens, or because he was subjected to discriminations in the enjoyment of accommodations in inns, public conveyances and places of amusement. Mere discriminations on account of race or color were not regarded as badges of slavery. If, since that time, the enjoyment of equal rights in all these respects has become established by constitutional enactment, it is not by force of the Thirteenth Amendment (which merely abolishes

**29**

slavery), but by force of the Fourteenth and Fifteenth Amendments. . . .

MR. JUSTICE HARLAN dissenting.

The opinion in these cases proceeds, it seems to me, upon grounds entirely too narrow and artificial. I cannot resist the conclusion that the substance and spirit of the recent amendments of the Constitution have been sacrificed by a subtle and ingenious verbal criticism. "It is not the words of the law but the internal sense of it that makes the law: the letter of the law is the body; the sense and reason of the law is the soul." Constitutional provisions, adopted in the interest of liberty, and for the purpose of securing, through national legislation, if need be, rights inhering in a state of freedom, and belonging to American citizenship, have been so construed as to defeat the ends the people desired to accomplish, which they attempted to accomplish, and which they supposed they had accomplished by changes in their fundamental law. By this I do not mean that the determination of these cases should have been materially controlled by considerations of mere expediency or policy. I mean only, in this form, to express an earnest conviction that the court has departed from the familiar rule requiring, in the interpretation of constitutional provisions, that full effect be given to the intent with which they were adopted. . . .

The Thirteenth Amendment, it is conceded, did something more than to prohibit slavery as an *institution*, resting upon distinctions of race, and upheld by positive law. My brethren admit that it established and decreed universal *civil freedom* throughout the United States. But did the freedom thus established involve nothing more than exemption from actual slavery? Was nothing more intended than to forbid one man from owning another as property? Was it the purpose of the nation simply to destroy the institution, and then remit the race, theretofore held in bondage, to the several States for such protection, in their civil rights, necessarily growing out of freedom, as those States, in their discretion, might choose to provide? Were the States against whose protest the institution was destroyed, to be left free, so far as national interference was concerned, to make or allow discriminations against that race, as such, in the enjoyment of those fundamental rights which by universal concession, inhere in a state of freedom? . . .

That there are burdens and disabilities which constitute badges of slavery and servitude, and that the power to enforce by appropriate legislation the Thirteenth Amendment may be exerted by legislation of a direct and primary character, for the eradication, not simply of the institution, but of its badges and incidents,

are propositions which ought to be deemed indisputable. . . .
I do not contend that the Thirteenth Amendment invests Congress with authority, by legislation, to define and regulate the entire body of the civil rights which citizens enjoy, or may enjoy, in the several States. But I hold that since slavery, as the court has repeatedly declared, *Slaughter-house Cases,* 16 Wall. 36; *Strauder* v. *West Virginia,* 100 U. S. 303, was the moving or principal cause of the adoption of that amendment, and since that institution rested wholly upon the inferiority, as a race, of those held in bondage, their freedom necessarily involved immunity from, and protection against, all discrimination against them, because of their race, in respect of such civil rights as belong to freemen of other races. Congress, therefore, under its express power to enforce that amendment, by appropriate legislation, may enact laws to protect that people against the deprivation, *because of their race,* of any civil rights granted to other freemen in the same State; and such legislation may be of a direct and primary character, operating upon States, their officers and agents, and, also, upon, at least, such individuals and corporations as exercise public functions and wield power and authority under the State. . . .

[Justice Harlan then turns to a consideration of the Fourteenth Amendment.]

The assumption that this amendment consists wholly of prohibitions upon State laws and State proceedings in hostility to its provisions, is unauthorized by its language. The first clause of the first section—"All persons born or naturalized in the United States, and subject to the jurisdiction thereof, are citizens of the United States, and of the State wherein they reside"—is of a distinctly affirmative character. In its application to the colored race, previously liberated, it created and granted, as well citizenship of the United States, as citizenship of the State in which they respectively resided. It introduced all of that race, whose ancestors had been imported and sold as slaves, at once, into the political community known as the "People of the United States." They became, instantly, citizens of the United States, *and* of their respective States. Further, they were brought, by this supreme act of the nation, within the direct operation of that provision of the Constitution which declares that "the citizens of each State shall be entitled to all privileges and immunities of citizens in the several States." Art. 4, § 2.

The citizenship thus acquired, by that race, in virtue of an affirmative grant from the nation, may be protected, not alone by the judicial branch of the government, but by congressional legislation of a primary direct character; this, because the power

**31**

of Congress is not restricted to the enforcement of prohibitions upon State laws or State action. It is, in terms distinct and positive, to enforce "the *provisions* of *this article*" of amendment; not simply those of a prohibitive character, but the provisions—*all* of the provisions—affirmative and prohibitive, of the amendment. It is, therefore, a grave misconception to suppose that the fifth section of the amendment has reference exclusively to express prohibitions upon State laws or State action. If any right was created by that amendment, the grant of power, through appropriate legislation, to enforce its provisions, authorizes Congress by means of legislation, operating throughout the entire Union, to guard, secure, and protect that right. . . .

But what was secured to colored citizens of the United States—as between them and their respective States—by the national grant to them of State citizenship? With what rights, privileges, or immunities did this grant invest them? There is one, if there be no other—exemption from race discrimination in respect of any civil right belonging to citizens of the white race in the same State. That, surely, is their constitutional privilege when within the jurisdiction of other States. And such must be their constitutional right, in their own State, unless the recent amendments be splendid baubles, thrown out to delude those who deserved fair and generous treatment at the hands of the nation. Citizenship in this country necessarily imports at least equality of civil rights among citizens of every race in the same State. It is fundamental in American citizenship that, in respect of such rights, there shall be no discrimination by the State, or its officers, or by individuals or corporations exercising public functions or authority, against any citizen because of his race or previous condition of servitude. . . .

It is said that any interpretation of the Fourteenth Amendment different from that adopted by the majority of the court, would imply that Congress had authority to enact a municipal code for all the States, covering every matter affecting the life, liberty, and property of the citizens of the several States. Not so. Prior to the adoption of that amendment the constitutions of the several States, without perhaps an exception, secured all *persons* against deprivation of life, liberty, or property, otherwise than by due process of law, and, in some form, recognized the right of all *persons* to the equal protection of the laws. Those rights, therefore, existed before that amendment was proposed or adopted, and were not created by it. If, by reason of that fact, it be assumed that protection in these rights of persons still rests primarily with the States, and that Congress may not interfere except to enforce, by means of corrective legislation, the prohibitions upon State laws or State proceedings inconsistent with those rights, it does not at all follow, that privileges which have been *granted by the nation,* may not be protected by primary legislation upon the part of Congress. The personal rights and immunities recognized in the prohibitive clauses of the amendment were, prior to its adoption, under the protection, primarily, of the States, while rights, created by or derived from the United States, have always been, and in the nature of things, should always be, primarily, under the protection of the general government. Exemption from race discrimination in respect of the civil rights which are fundamental in *citizenship* in a republican government, is, as we have seen, a new right, created by the nation, with express power in Congress, by legislation, to enforce the constitutional provision from which it is derived. If, in some sense, such race discrimination is, within the letter of the last clause of the first section, a denial of that equal protection of the laws which is secured against State denial of all persons, whether citizens or not, it cannot be possible that a mere prohibition upon said State denial, or a prohibition upon State laws abridging the privileges and immunities of citizens of the United States, takes from the nation the power which it has uniformly exercised of protecting, by direct primary legislation, those privileges and immunities which existed under the Constitution before the adoption of the Fourteenth Amendment, or have been created by that amendment in behalf of those thereby made *citizens* of their respective States. . . .

But if it were conceded that the power of Congress could not be brought into activity until the rights specified in the act of 1875 had been abridged or denied by some State law or State action, I maintain that the decision of the court is erroneous. There has been adverse State action within the Fourteenth Amendment as heretofore interpreted by this court. . . .

[Mr. Justice Harlan here discusses *Ex parte Virginia,* 100 U. S. 334, 25 L. Ed. 676, summarized *infra.*]

In every material sense applicable to the practical enforcement of the Fourteenth Amendment, railroad corporations, keepers of inns, and managers of places of public amusement are agents or instrumentalities of the State, because they are charged with duties to the public, and are amenable, in respect of their duties and functions, to governmental regulation. It seems to me that, within the principle settled in *Ex parte Virginia,* a denial, by these instrumentalities of the State, to the citizen, because of his race, of that equality of civil rights secured to him by law, is a denial by the State, within the meaning of the Fourteenth Amendment. If it be not, then that race is left, in respect of the civil rights in question, practically at the mercy of corporations and individuals wielding power under the States.

But the court says that Congress did not, in the act of 1866, assume, under the authority given by the Thirteenth Amendment, to adjust what may be called the social rights of men and races in the community. I agree that government has nothing to do with social, as distinguished from technically legal, rights of individuals. No government ever has brought, or ever can bring, its people into social intercourse against their wishes. Whether one person will permit or maintain social relations with another is a matter with which government has no concern. I agree that if one citizen chooses not to hold social intercourse with another, he is not and cannot be made amenable to the law for his conduct in that regard; for even upon grounds of race, no legal right of a citizen is violated by the refusal of others to maintain merely social relations with him. What I affirm is that no State, nor the officers of any State, nor any corporation or individual wielding power under State authority for the public benefit or the public convenience, can, consistently either with the freedom established by the fundamental law, or with that equality of civil rights which now belongs to every citizen, discriminate against freemen or citizens, in those rights, because of their race, or because they once labored under the disabilities of slavery imposed upon them as a race. The rights which Congress, by the act of 1875, endeavored to secure and protect are legal, not social rights. The right, for instance, of a colored citizen to use the accommodations of a public highway, upon the same terms as are permitted to white citizens, is no more a social right than his right, under the law, to use the public streets of a city or a town, or a turnpike road, or a public market, or a post office, or his right to sit in a public building with others, of whatever race, for the purpose of hearing the political questions of the day discussed. . . .

My brethren say, that when a man has emerged from slavery, and by the aid of beneficent legislation has shaken off the inseparable concomitants of that state, there must be some stage in the progress of his elevation when he takes the rank of a mere citizen, and ceases to be the special favorite of the laws, and when his rights as a citizen, or a man, are to be protected in the ordinary modes by which other men's rights are protected. It is, I submit, scarcely just to say that the colored race has been the special favorite of the laws. The statute of 1875, now adjudged to be unconstitutional, is for the benefit of citizens of every race and color. What the nation, through Congress, has sought to accomplish in reference to that race, is—what had already been

[Emerson]

done in every State of the Union for the white race—to secure and protect rights belonging to them as freemen and citizens; nothing more. It was not deemed enough "to help the feeble up, but to support him after." The one underlying purpose of congressional legislation has been to enable the black race to take the rank of mere citizens. The difficulty has been to compel a recognition of the legal right of the black race to take the rank of citizens, and to secure the enjoyment of privileges belonging, under the law, to them as a component part of the people for whose welfare and happiness government is ordained. At every step, in this direction, the nation has been confronted with class tyranny, which a contemporary English historian says is, of all tyrannies, the most intolerable, "for it is ubiquitous in its operation, and weighs, perhaps, most heavily on those whose obscurity or distance would withdraw them from the notice of a single despot." To-day, it is the colored race which is denied, by corporations and individuals wielding public authority, rights fundamental in their freedom and citizenship. At some future time, it may be that some other race will fall under the ban of race discrimination. If the constitutional amendments be enforced, according to the intent with which, as I conceive, they were adopted, there cannot be, in this republic, any class of human beings in practical subjection to another class, with power in the latter to dole out to the former just such privileges as they may choose to grant. The supreme law of the land has decreed that no authority shall be exercised in this country upon the basis of discrimination, in respect of civil rights, against freemen and citizens because of their race, color, or previous condition of servitude. To that decree—for the due enforcement of which, by appropriate legislation, Congress has been invested with express power—every one must bow, whatever may have been, or whatever now are, his individual views as to the wisdom or policy, either of the recent changes in the fundamental law, or of the legislation which has been enacted to give them effect.

For the reasons stated I feel constrained to withhold my assent to the opinion of the court.[1]

---

[1] For discussion of the case see Konvitz, *The Constitution and Civil Rights*, ch. 2 (1947).

## UNITED STATES v. CRUIKSHANK

Supreme Court of the United States, 1875
92 U. S. 542, 23 L. Ed. 588

[Defendants were among more than 100 persons jointly indicted in the Federal Court in Louisiana, charged with offenses in violation of the Enforcement Act of May 31, 1870. Section 6 of that statute provided in part:

> "That if two or more persons shall band or conspire together, or go in disguise upon the public highway, or upon the premises of another, with intent to violate any provision of this act, or to injure, oppress, threaten, or intimidate any citizen, with intent to prevent or hinder his free exercise and enjoyment of any right or privilege granted or secured to him by the constitution or laws of the United States, or because of his having exercised the same, such persons shall be held guilty of felony . . ."

The first eight counts charged defendants with "banding" and the second eight with "conspiring" together to hinder and prevent Negroes from the exercise of certain rights and privileges granted to them under the constitution or laws of the United States. The issue arose on a motion in arrest of judgment after a verdict of guilty.]

MR. CHIEF JUSTICE WAITE . . .
We have in our political system a government of the United States and a government of each of the several States. Each one of these governments is distinct from the others, and each has citizens of its own who owe it allegiance, and whose rights, within its jurisdiction, it must protect. The same person may be at the same time a citizen of the United States and a citizen of a State, but his rights of citizenship under one of these governments will be different from those he has under the other. *Slaughter-House Cases,* 16 Wall. 74. . . .
We now proceed to an examination of the indictment, to ascertain whether the several rights, which it is alleged the defendants intended to interfere with, are such as had been in law and in fact granted or secured by the constitution or laws of the United States.

The first and ninth counts state the intent of the defendants to have been to hinder and prevent the citizens named in the free exercise and enjoyment of their "lawful right and privilege to peaceably assemble together with each other and with other citizens of the United States for a peaceful and lawful purpose." The right of the people peaceably to assemble for lawful purposes existed long before the adoption of the Constitution of the United States. In fact, it is, and always has been, one of the attributes of citizenship under a free government. It "derives its source," to use the language of Chief Justice Marshall, in *Gibbons* v. *Ogden,* 9 Wheat. 211, "from those laws whose authority is acknowledged by civilized man throughout the world." It is found wherever civilization exists. It was not, therefore, a right granted to the people by the Constitution. The government of the United States when established found it in existence, with the obligation on the part of the States to afford it protection. As no direct power over it was granted to Congress, it remains, according to the ruling in *Gibbons* v. *Ogden,* id. 203, subject to State jurisdiction. Only such existing rights were committed by the people to the protection of Congress as came within the general scope of the authority granted to the national government.

The first amendment to the Constitution prohibits Congress from abridging "the right of the people to assemble and to petition the government for a redress of grievances." This, like the other amendments proposed and adopted at the same time, was not intended to limit the powers of the State governments in respect to their own citizens, but to operate upon the National government alone. . . .

The particular amendment now under consideration assumes the existence of the right of the people to assemble for lawful purposes, and protects it against encroachment by Congress. The right was not created by the amendment; neither was its continuance guaranteed, except as against congressional interference. For their protection in its enjoyment, therefore, the people must look to the States. The power for that purpose was originally placed there, and it has never been surrendered to the United States.

The right of the people peaceably to assemble for the purpose of petitioning Congress for a redress of grievances, or for any thing else connected with the powers or the duties of the national government, is an attribute of national citizenship, and, as such, under the protection of, and guaranteed by, the United States. The very idea of a government, republican in form, implies a right on the part of its citizens to meet peaceably for consultation in respect to public affairs and to petition for a redress of grievances. If it had been alleged in these counts that the object of the defendants was to prevent a meeting for such a purpose, the case would have been within the statute, and within the scope of the sovereignty of the United States. Such, however, is not the case. The offence, as stated in the indictment, will be made out, if it be shown that the object of the conspiracy was to prevent a meeting for any lawful purpose whatever.

**37**

The second and tenth counts are equally defective. The right there specified is that of "bearing arms for a lawful purpose." This is not a right granted by the Constitution. Neither is it in any manner dependent upon that instrument for its existence. The second amendment declares that it shall not be infringed; but this, as has been seen, means no more than that it shall not be infringed by Congress. This is one of the amendments that has no other effect than to restrict the powers of the national government, leaving the people to look for their protection against any violation by their fellow-citizens of the rights it recognizes, to what is called, in *The City of New York* v. *Miln,* 11 Pet. 139, the "powers which relate to merely municipal legislation, or what was, perhaps, more properly called internal police," "not surrendered or restrained" by the Constitution of the United States.

The third and eleventh counts are even more objectionable. They charge the intent to have been to deprive the citizens named, they being in Louisiana, "of their respective several lives and liberty of person without due process of law." This is nothing else than alleging a conspiracy to falsely imprison or murder citizens of the United States, being within the territorial jurisdiction of the State of Louisiana. The rights of life and personal liberty are natural rights of man. "To secure these rights," says the Declaration of Independence, "governments are instituted among men, deriving their just powers from the consent of the governed." The very highest duty of the States, when they entered into the Union under the Constitution, was to protect all persons within their boundaries in the enjoyment of these "unalienable rights with which they were endowed by their Creator." Sovereignty, for this purpose, rests alone with the States. It is no more the duty or within the power of the United States to punish for a conspiracy to falsely imprison or murder within a State, than it would be to punish for false imprisonment or murder itself.

The fourteenth amendment prohibits a State from depriving any person of life, liberty, or property, without due process of law; but this adds nothing to the rights of one citizen as against another. It simply furnishes an additional guaranty against any encroachment by the States upon the fundamental rights which belong to every citizen as a member of society. As was said by Mr. Justice Johnson, in *Bank of Columbia* v. *Okely,* 4 Wheat. 244, it secures "the individual from the arbitrary exercise of the powers of government, unrestrained by the established principles of private rights and distributive justice." These counts in the indictment do not call for the exercise of any of the powers conferred by this provision in the amendment.

The fourth and twelfth counts charge the intent to have been to prevent and hinder the citizens named, who were of African descent and persons of color, in "the free exercise and enjoyment of their several right and privilege to the full and equal benefit of all laws and proceedings, then and there, before that time, enacted or ordained by the said State of Louisiana and by the United States; and then and there, at that time, being in force in the said State and District of Louisiana aforesaid, for the security of their respective persons and property, then and there, at that time enjoyed at and within said State and District of Louisiana by white persons, being citizens of said State of Louisiana and the United States, for the protection of the persons and property of said white citizens." There is no allegation that this was done because of the race or color of the persons conspired against. When stripped of its verbiage, the case as presented amounts to nothing more than that the defendants conspired to prevent certain citizens of the United States, being within the State of Louisiana, from enjoying the equal protection of the laws of the State and of the United States.

The fourteenth amendment prohibits a State from denying to any person within its jurisdiction the equal protection of the laws; but this provision does not, any more than the one which precedes it, and which we have just considered, add any thing to the rights which one citizen has under the Constitution against another. The equality of the rights of citizens is a principle of republicanism. Every republican government is in duty bound to protect all its citizens in the enjoyment of this principle, if within its power. That duty was originally assumed by the States; and it still remains there. The only obligation resting upon the United States is to see that the States do not deny the right. This the amendment guarantees, but no more. The power of the national government is limited to the enforcement of this guaranty.

No question arises under the Civil Rights Act of April 9, 1866 (14 Stat. 27), which is intended for the protection of citizens of the United States in the enjoyment of certain rights, without discrimination on account of race, color, or previous condition of servitude, because, as has already been stated, it is nowhere alleged in these counts that the wrong contemplated against the rights of these citizens was on account of their race or color.
. . .

[The sixth, seventh, fourteenth and fifteenth counts, charging interference with the right to vote in a Louisiana election were held insufficient in the absence of allegations that the interference was on account of race, color, or previous condition of servitude.

See Chapter III, *infra*. The fifth, eighth, thirteenth and sixteenth counts, charging generally interference with rights granted and secured to citizens of the United States, were found insufficient as being too vague and general.

Mr. Justice Clifford concurred in the result, on the grounds that the pleadings were defective, without passing on the constitutionality of the Enforcement Act.]

## Note

1. In a number of other cases, decided in the decades after adoption of the Civil War Amendments, the Supreme Court invalidated various provisions of the Civil Rights Acts:

In *U. S. v. Reese*, 92 U. S. 214, 23 L. Ed. 563 (1876), two election inspectors in a Kentucky Municipal election were indicted, for refusing to receive and count the vote of a Negro, under provisions of the Civil Rights Acts which prohibited interference with the right to vote. The Court, considering only the Fifteenth Amendment issue, held these provisions unconstitutional as going beyond the Fifteenth Amendment in that the statute was not limited to interference on account of race, color or previous condition of servitude. Mr. Justice Hunt dissented.

In *U. S. v. Harris*, 106 U. S. 629, 27 L. Ed. 290, 1 S. Ct. 601 (1883), twenty members of a Tennessee lynch mob seized four prisoners held by a state deputy sheriff and beat them severely, killing one. They were indicted under a provision of the Civil Rights Acts prohibiting a conspiracy by two or more persons to deprive another of equal protection of the laws or equal privileges or immunities under the laws, or from hindering State authorities from giving such protection. The Court followed the *Cruikshank* case, holding that the Fourteenth Amendment applied only to State, not private, action, and that no other part of the Constitution afforded authority for the statutory provision. Mr. Justice Harlan dissented, but expressed no opinion on the merits.

In *Baldwin v. Franks,* 120 U. S. 678, 32 L. Ed. 766, 7 S. Ct. 656 (1887), petitioner was arrested for assaulting Chinese citizens and driving them out of a California town. In habeas corpus proceedings the Supreme Court directed his release, again holding invalid the provision involved in the *Harris* case. The fact that the Chinese citizens were protected under a treaty might have afforded basis for Federal power, the Court held, but the provision was too broadly worded. Mr. Justice Harlan dissented.

In *James v. Bowman*, 190 U. S. 127, 47 L. Ed. 979, 23 S. Ct. 678 (1903), two persons were indicted, for bribing and preventing a Negro from voting in a Kentucky Congressional election, under a provision prohibiting any person from hindering or intimidating another from voting by various enumerated means. The Court held this provision invalid under the Fifteenth Amendment on the ground that the Fifteenth, like the Fourteenth, was directed only at State action, not private action. The Court also refused to uphold the provision under the general Federal power over elections conferred by Article I, Section

4 on the ground that the statute applied to all elections, state as well as Federal, and hence was too broad.   Justices Harlan and Brown dissented.

In *Hodges v. U. S.*, 203 U. S. 1, 51 L. Ed. 65, 27 S. Ct. 6 (1906), the defendants were indicted for intimidating a group of Negroes employed under contracts in a lumber mill and driving them out of work. The Civil Rights Acts provided that all persons had the same right to make contracts as white persons, and, under the provision considered in the *Cruikshank* case, prohibited conspiracies to injure or oppress persons in the free exercise of rights secured by the constitution or laws.   The Court applied the rule of previous cases that the statute could not be upheld under the Fourteenth Amendment since it applied to private, not State, action.   It also held the provisions not within the protection of the Thirteenth Amendment.   Justices Harlan and Day dissented.

See also *U. S. v. Powell*, 212 U. S. 564, 53 L. Ed. 653, 29 S. Ct. 690 (1909), aff'g 151 F. 648 (C. C. N. D. Ala., 1907).

2. On the other hand certain other provisions of the Civil Rights Acts were upheld:

In *Ex parte Virginia*, 100 U. S. 339, 25 L. Ed. 676 (1880), the Supreme Court upheld the indictment of a Virginia judge charged with excluding Negroes from state juries in violation of a specific prohibition of the Civil Rights Acts.   The Court ruled that the action of the judge constituted State action under the Fourteenth Amendment.   To the same effect were *Strauder v. West Virginia*, 100 U. S. 303, 25 L. Ed. 664 (1880), and *Virginia v. Rives*, 100 U. S. 313, 25 L. Ed. 667 (1880). Justices Field and Crawford dissented in all three cases.

In *Ex parte Siebold*, 100 U. S. 371, 25 L. Ed. 717 (1880), Maryland election officials were indicted for stuffing ballot boxes in a Congressional election.   The provisions of the Civil Rights Acts making this a criminal offense were sustained under the Federal power to control elections conferred by Article I, Section 4.   Justices Field and Crawford again dissented.   In *Ex parte Yarbrough*, 110 U. S. 651, 28 L. Ed. 274, 4 S. Ct. 152 (1884), the conviction of private indivduals who had used violence against a Negro voting in a Congressional election in Georgia was sustained on the same ground.   Two provisions of the Civil Rights Acts were invoked, one of which was the same as that involved in the *Cruikshank* case.   See Chapter III, *infra*.

In *U. S. v. Waddell*, 112 U. S. 76, 28 L. Ed. 673, 5 S. Ct. 35 (1884), defendants were charged with using violence to drive a homesteader off his land which he had settled pursuant to the Federal Homestead Act. The statutory provision involved was the same, with minor revisions, as that at issue in the *Cruikshank* and *Yarbrough* cases.   The Court held that the defendants' actions deprived the homesteader of rights secured to him by the laws of the United States and affirmed the validity of the provision in its application to the case before it.

In *Logan v. U. S.*, 144 U. S. 263, 36 L. Ed. 429, 12 S. Ct. 617 (1892), the Court upheld the same provision as the basis for conviction of three men charged with mob violence against prisoners in the custody of a United States marshal.   The Court held that the prisoners, who were

**41**

awaiting trial for an offense against the United States, had a federal right to be protected in their persons while in United States custody. While the Constitution grants no specific Congressional power to provide for the punishment of crimes, the Court said, "no one doubts the power of Congress to provide for the punishment of all crimes and offenses against the United States . . . and persons arrested and held pursuant to such laws are in the exclusive custody of the United States and are not subject to the judicial process or executive warrant of any state. . . . The United States, having the absolute right to hold such prisoners, have an equal duty to protect them, while so held, against assault or injury from any quarter. The existence of that duty on the part of the government necessarily implies a corresponding right of the prisoners to be so protected; and this right of the prisoners is a right secured to them by the Constitution and laws of the United States." 144 U. S. at 283–4.

In *Motes v. U. S.*, 178 U. S. 458, 44 L. Ed. 1150, 20 S. Ct. 993 (1900), the Court held the same way in the case of defendants who had murdered a person who had informed Federal revenue agents of the illegal operation of a distillery in Alabama. Accord is *In re Quarles and Butler*, 158 U. S. 532, 39 L. Ed. 1080, 15 S. Ct. 959 (1895).

The above cases are summarized in the opinion of Mr. Justice Frankfurter in *U. S. v. Williams*, 341 U. S. 70, 77–81, 95 L. Ed. 758, 71 S. Ct. 581 (1951). See *infra*.

The Peonage Abolition Act was upheld in *Clyatt v. U. S.*, 197 U. S. 207, 49 L. Ed. 726, 25 S. Ct. 429 (1905). The validity of the Slave Kidnapping Act has never been seriously questioned.

For a review of the cases during this period in the lower Federal courts, see Carr, *Federal Protection of Civil Rights*, pp. 57–77 (1947).

3. In 1877, 1894 and 1909 many of the provisions of the Civil Rights Acts were repealed. See Carr, *supra*, pp. 45–6.

4. For discussion of the treatment of the Civil Rights Acts by the Supreme Court see Warren, *The Supreme Court in United States History*, ch. XXXII–XXXIV (1932 ed.) ; Carr, *supra*, pp. 9–14, 35–84; 2 Boudin, *Government by Judiciary*, ch. XXII–XXIV (1932) ; Waite, *The Negro in the Supreme Court*, 30 Minn. L. Rev. 219, 224–65 (1946) ; Frantz, *Enforcement of the Fourteenth Amendment*, 9 Law. Guild Rev. 122 (1949) ; Watt and Orlikoff, *The Coming Vindication of Mr. Justice Harlan*, 44 Ill. L. Rev. 13 (1949) ; Berger, *Equality by Statute*, pp. 37–60 (1952).

Material on the economic, social and political forces of the period may be found in McLaughlin, *A Constitutional History of the United States*, ch. XLV–XLIX (1935) ; Swisher, *American Constitutional Development*, ch. 15 (1943) ; Kelly and Harbison, *The American Constitution*, ch. 17 and 18 (1948) ; Dunning, *Essays on the Civil War and Reconstruction* (1904) ; Dunning, *Reconstruction, Political and Economic, 1865–1877* (1907) ; Randall, *The Civil War and Reconstruction*, ch. XXX–XXXVII (1937) ; Hesseltine, *The South in American History*, ch. XXIV–XXVIII (1943) ; Hesseltine, *Economic Factors in Abandonment of Reconstruction*, 22 Miss. Valley Historical Rev. 191 (1935) ; Williams, *The Louisiana Unification Movement of 1873*, 11 Jo. Southern

History 349 (1945). Particularly on the "Deal of 1877" see Haworth, *The Hayes-Tilden Disputed Presidential Election of 1876* (1906); Woodward, *Reunion and Reaction* (1951).

## 2. Current Status of Federal Constitutional and Statutory Power

### a. *Criminal Provisions of Federal Civil Rights Acts*

As a result of the revisions of 1909 the major surviving criminal provisions of the Civil Rights Acts (in addition to the anti-peonage provisions) became Sections 19 and 20 of the Criminal Code, which became Sections 51 and 52 of Title 18 U. S. C. (1926 codification), which in turn became Sections 241 and 242 of Title 18 U. S. C. (1948 codification). In their present form Sections 241 and 242 read:

"§ 241. Conspiracy against rights of citizens.

"If two or more persons conspire to injure, oppress, threaten, or intimidate any citizen in the free exercise or enjoyment of any right or privilege secured to him by the Constitution or laws of the United States, or because of his having so exercised the same; or

"If two or more persons go in disguise on the highway, or on the premises of another, with intent to prevent or hinder his free exercise or enjoyment of any right or privilege so secured—

"They shall be fined not more than $5,000 or imprisoned not more than ten years, or both."

"§ 242. Deprivation of rights under color of law.

"Whoever, under color of any law, statute, ordinance, regulation, or custom, willfully subjects any inhabitant of any State, Territory, or District to the deprivation of any rights, privileges, or immunities secured or protected by the Constitution or laws of the United States, or to different punishments, pains, or penalties, on account of such inhabitant being an alien, or by reason of his color, or race, than are prescribed for the punishment of citizens, shall be fined not more than $1,000 or imprisoned not more than one year, or both."

The surviving provisions of the Civil Rights Acts are printed in Appendix 2 to Carr, *Federal Protection of Civil Rights* (1947). The history of Sections 241 and 242 is traced in the Appendix to Mr. Justice Frankfurter's opinion in *U. S. v. Williams*, 341 U.S. 70, 83, 95 L. Ed. 758, 71 S. Ct. 581 (1951).

In the 30 years from 1909 to 1939 the provisions of the Civil

Rights Acts remained largely dormant. In *U. S. v. Mosley*, 238 U.S. 383, 59 L. Ed. 1355, 35 S. Ct. 904 (1915), the predecessor of Section 241 was upheld in the prosecution of members of a state election board for failing to count ballots in a Federal election. But in *U. S. v. Gradwell*, 243 U.S. 476, 61 L. Ed. 857, 37 S. Ct. 407 (1917), and *U. S. v. Bathgate*, 246 U. S. 220, 62 L. Ed. 676, 38 S. Ct. 269 (1918), the provision was narrowly construed as not covering the procuring of illegal voters or bribing voters. See Chapter III, *infra*.

The other major decision under the predecessor of Section 241 was also adverse to the statute. In *U. S. v. Wheeler*, 254 U. S. 281, 65 L. Ed. 270, 41 S. Ct. 133 (1920), 25 men were indicted for seizing and forcibly deporting a group of several hundred persons, who were not residents of Arizona, from that state into New Mexico. The Court dismissed the indictment, holding that the privileges and immunities clause of Article IV, Section 2 was applicable only to state action and that the right of ingress or egress from and into a state, except where there was a direct interference with Federal matters, did not constitute a violation of the statute.

During this period no cases under the predecessor of Section 242 reached the Supreme Court.[1]

In 1939 Attorney General Frank Murphy created a Civil Rights Section in the Department of Justice. The function of this section was "to pursue a program of vigilant action in the prosecution of infringement" of civil liberties. As a result of setting up the Civil Rights Section, and as part of a general reawakening of interest, a new era in the life of the Civil Rights Acts began. Many more cases were brought, both criminal and civil, and the law began to develop rapidly.

The first cases to reach the Supreme Court involved election frauds. In *U. S. v. Classic*, 313 U. S. 299, 85 L. Ed. 1368, 61 S. Ct. 1031 (1941), the Court upheld an indictment under Sections 241 and 242 of election officials who had made a fraudulent count of the ballots in a Federal primary election. In *U. S. v. Saylor*, 322 U.S. 385, 88 L. Ed. 1341, 64 S. Ct. 1101 (1944), the Court held that Section 241 could be invoked against election officials who stuffed ballot boxes in a Federal election. See Chapter III, *infra*. In 1945 came the *Screws* case. This case, and the two *Williams* cases in 1951, set forth the present position of the Court on the protection afforded by the Civil Rights Acts to security of the person.

---

[1] For scattered cases in which the predecessors of Sections 241 and 242 were invoked and considered in the lower Federal courts, see Carr, *supra*, pp. 57–77.

## SCREWS v. UNITED STATES

Supreme Court of the United States, 1945
325 U. S. 91, 89 L. Ed. 1495, 65 S. Ct. 1031

MR. JUSTICE DOUGLAS announced the judgment of the Court and delivered the following opinion, in which the CHIEF JUSTICE, MR. JUSTICE BLACK and MR. JUSTICE REED concur.

This case involves a shocking and revolting episode in law enforcement. Petitioner Screws was sheriff of Baker County, Georgia. He enlisted the assistance of petitioner Jones, a policeman, and petitioner Kelley, a special deputy, in arresting Robert Hall, a citizen of the United States and of Georgia. The arrest was made late at night at Hall's home on a warrant charging Hall with theft of a tire. Hall, a young negro about thirty years of age, was handcuffed and taken by car to the court house. As Hall alighted from the car at the court-house square, the three petitioners began beating him with their fists and with a solid-bar blackjack about eight inches long and weighing two pounds. They claimed Hall had reached for a gun and had used insulting language as he alighted from the car. But after Hall, still handcuffed, had been knocked to the ground they continued to beat him from fifteen to thirty minutes until he was unconscious. Hall was then dragged feet first through the court-house yard into the jail and thrown upon the floor dying. An ambulance was called and Hall was removed to a hospital where he died within the hour and without regaining consciousness. There was evidence that Screws held a grudge against Hall and had threatened to "get" him.

An indictment was returned against petitioners—one count charging a violation of § 20 of the Criminal Code, 18 U.S.C. § 52 and another charging a conspiracy to violate § 20 contrary to § 37 of the Criminal Code, 18 U.S.C. § 88. . . . The indictment charged that petitioners, acting under color of the laws of Georgia, "willfully" caused Hall to be deprived of "rights, privileges, or immunities secured or protected" to him by the Fourteenth Amendment—the right not to be deprived of life without due process of law; the right to be tried, upon the charge on which he was arrested, by due process of law and if found guilty to be punished in accordance with the laws of Georgia; that is to say that petitioners "unlawfully and wrongfully did assault, strike and beat the said Robert Hall about the head with human fists and a blackjack causing injuries" to Hall "which were the proximate and immediate cause of his death." A like charge was made in the conspiracy count.

The case was tried to a jury. The court charged the jury that due process of law gave one charged with a crime the right

**45**

to be tried by a jury and sentenced by a court. On the question of intent it charged that

". . . if these defendants, without its being necessary to make the arrest effectual or necessary to their own personal protection, beat this man, assaulted him or killed him while he was under arrest, then they would be acting illegally under color of law, as stated by this statute, and would be depriving the prisoner of certain constitutional rights guaranteed to him by the Constitution of the United States and consented to by the State of Georgia."

The jury returned a verdict of guilty and a fine and imprisonment on each count was imposed. The Circuit Court of Appeals affirmed the judgment of conviction, one judge dissenting. 140 F.2d 662. The case is here on a petition for a writ of certiorari which we granted because of the importance in the administration of the criminal laws of the questions presented.

I

We are met at the outset with the claim that § 20 is unconstitutional, insofar as it makes criminal acts in violation of the due process clause of the Fourteenth Amendment. The argument runs as follows: It is true that this Act as construed in *United States v. Classic,* 313 U.S. 299, 328, was upheld in its application to certain ballot box frauds committed by state officials. But in that case the constitutional rights protected were the rights to vote specifically guaranteed by Art. I, § 2 and § 4 of the Constitution. Here there is no ascertainable standard of guilt. There have been conflicting views in the Court as to the proper construction of the due process clause. The majority have quite consistently construed it in broad general terms. Thus it was stated in *Twining v. New Jersey,* 211 U.S. 78, 101, that due process requires that "no change in ancient procedure can be made which disregards those fundamental principles, to be ascertained from time to time by judicial action, which have relation to process of law and protect the citizen in his private right, and guard him against the arbitrary action of government." In *Snyder v. Massachusetts,* 291 U.S. 97, 105, it was said that due process prevents state action which "offends some principle of justice so rooted in the traditions and conscience of our people as to be ranked as fundamental." The same standard was expressed in *Palko v. Connecticut,* 302 U.S. 319, 325, in terms of a "scheme of ordered liberty." And the same idea was recently phrased as follows: "The phrase formulates a concept less rigid and more fluid than those envisaged in other specific and particular provisions of the Bill of Rights. Its application is less a matter of rule.

Asserted denial is to be tested by an appraisal of the totality of facts in a given case. That which may, in one setting, constitute a denial of fundamental fairness, shocking to the universal sense of justice, may, in other circumstances, and in the light of other considerations, fall short of such denial." *Betts* v. *Brady,* 316 U.S. 455, 462.

It is said that the Act must be read as if it contained those broad and fluid definitions of due process and that if it is so read it provides no ascertainable standard of guilt. It is pointed out that in *United States* v. *Cohen Grocery Co.,* 255 U. S. 81, 89, an Act of Congress was struck down, the enforcement of which would have been "the exact equivalent of an effort to carry out a statute which in terms merely penalized and punished all acts detrimental to the public interest when unjust and unreasonable in the estimation of the court and jury." In that case the act declared criminal was the making of "any unjust or unreasonable rate or charge in handling or dealing in or with any necessaries." 255 U.S. p. 86. The Act contained no definition of an "unjust or unreasonable rate" nor did it refer to any source where the measure of "unjust or unreasonable" could be ascertained. In the instant case the decisions of the courts are, to be sure, a source of reference for ascertaining the specific content of the concept of due process. But even so the Act would incorporate by reference a large body of changing and uncertain law. That law is not always reducible to specific rules, is expressible only in general terms, and turns many times on the facts of a particular case. Accordingly, it is argued that such a body of legal principles lacks the basic specificity necessary for criminal statutes under our system of government. Congress did not define what it desired to punish but referred the citizen to a comprehensive law library in order to ascertain what acts were prohibited. To enforce such a statute would be like sanctioning the practice of Caligula who "published the law, but it was written in a very small hand, and posted up in a corner so that no one could make a copy of it." Suetonius, Lives of the Twelve Caesars, p. 278.

The serious character of that challenge to the constitutionality of the Act is emphasized if the customary standard of guilt for statutory crimes is taken. As we shall see, specific intent is at times required. Holmes, The Common Law, pp. 66 *et seq.* But the general rule was stated in *Ellis* v. *United States,* 206 U.S. 246, 257, as follows: "If a man intentionally adopts certain conduct in certain circumstances known to him, and that conduct is forbidden by the law under those circumstances, he intentionally breaks the law in the only sense in which the law ever considers

**47**

intent." And see *Horning* v. *District of Columbia,* 254 U.S. 135, 137; *Nash* v. *United States,* 229 U. S. 373, 377. Under that test a local law enforcement officer violates § 20 and commits a federal offense for which he can be sent to the penitentiary if he does an act which some court later holds deprives a person of due process of law. And he is a criminal though his motive was pure and though his purpose was unrelated to the disregard of any constitutional guarantee. The treacherous ground on which state officials—police, prosecutors, legislators, and judges—would walk is indicated by the character and closeness of decisions of this Court interpreting the due process clause of the Fourteenth Amendment. A confession obtained by too long questioning (*Ashcraft* v. *Tennessee,* 322 U.S. 143); the enforcement of an ordinance requiring a license for the distribution of religious literature (*Murdock* v. *Pennsylvania,* 319 U.S. 105); the denial of the assistance of counsel in certain types of cases (Cf. *Powell* v. *Alabama,* 287 U.S. 45 with *Betts* v. *Brady, supra*); the enforcement of certain types of anti-picketing statutes (*Thornhill* v. *Alabama,* 310 U.S. 88); the enforcement of state price control laws (*Olsen* v. *Nebraska,* 313 U.S. 236); the requirement that public school children salute the flag (*Board of Education* v. *Barnette,* 319 U.S. 624)—these are illustrative of the kind of state action which might or might not be caught in the broad reaches of § 20 dependent on the prevailing view of the Court as constituted when the case arose. Those who enforced local law today might not know for many months (and meanwhile could not find out) whether what they did deprived some one of due process of law. The enforcement of a criminal statute so construed would indeed cast law enforcement agencies loose at their own risk on a vast uncharted sea.

If such a construction is not necessary, it should be avoided. This Court has consistently favored that interpretation of legislation which supports its constitutionality. . . .

We hesitate to say that when Congress sought to enforce the Fourteenth Amendment in this fashion it did a vain thing. We hesitate to conclude that for 80 years this effort of Congress, renewed several times, to protect the important rights of the individual guaranteed by the Fourteenth Amendment has been an idle gesture. Yet if the Act falls by reason of vagueness so far as due process of law is concerned, there would seem to be a similar lack of specificity when the privileges and immunities clause (*Madden* v. *Kentucky,* 309 U.S. 83) and the equal protection clause (*Smith* v. *Texas,* 311 U.S. 128; *Hill* v. *Texas,* 316 U.S. 400) of the Fourteenth Amendment are involved. Only if no construction can save the Act from this claim of unconstitutionality are we willing to reach that result. We do not reach it, for we are of the view that if § 20 is confined more narrowly than the lower courts confined it, it can be preserved as one of the sanctions to the great rights which the Fourteenth Amendment was designed to secure.

## II

. . . An analysis of the cases in which "willfully" has been held to connote more than an act which is voluntary or intentional would not prove helpful as each turns on its own peculiar facts. Those cases, however, make clear that if we construe "willfully" in § 20 as connoting a purpose to deprive a person of a specific constitutional right, we would introduce no innovation. The Court, indeed, has recognized that the requirement of a specific intent to do a prohibited act may avoid those consequences to the accused which may otherwise render a vague or indefinite statute invalid. The constitutional vice in such a statute is the essential injustice to the accused of placing him on trial for an offense, the nature of which the statute does not define and hence of which it gives no warning. See *United States* v. *Cohen Grocery Co.*, *supra*. But where the punishment imposed is only for an act knowingly done with the purpose of doing that which the statute prohibits, the accused cannot be said to suffer from lack of warning or knowledge that the act which he does is a violation of law. The requirement that the act must be willful or purposeful may not render certain, for all purposes, a statutory definition of the crime which is in some respects uncertain. But it does relieve the statute of the objection that it punishes without warning an offense of which the accused was unaware. . . .

It is said, however, that this construction of the Act will not save it from the infirmity of vagueness since neither a law enforcement official nor a trial judge can know with sufficient definiteness the range of rights that are constitutional. But that criticism is wide of the mark. For the specific intent required by the Act is an intent to deprive a person of a right which has been made specific either by the express terms of the Constitution or laws of the United States or by decisions interpreting them. Take the case of a local officer who persists in enforcing a type of ordinance which the Court has held invalid as violative of the guarantees of free speech or freedom of worship. Or a local official continues to select juries in a manner which flies in the teeth of decisions of the Court. If those acts are done willfully, how can the officer possibly claim that he had no fair warning that his acts were prohibited by the statute? He violates the statute not merely because he has a bad purpose but because he acts in defiance of announced rules of law. He who defies a decision interpreting the Constitution knows precisely what he is doing. If sane, he hardly may be heard to say that he knew not what he did. Of course, willful conduct cannot make definite that which is undefined. But willful violators of constitutional requirements, which have been defined, certainly are in no position to say that they had no adequate advance notice that they would be visited with punishment. When they act willfully in the sense in which we use the word, they act in open defiance or in reckless disregard of a constitutional requirement which has been made specific and definite. When they are convicted for so acting, they are not punished for violating an unknowable something. . . .

The difficulty here is that this question of intent was not submitted to the jury with the proper instructions. The court charged that petitioners acted illegally if they applied more force than was necessary to make the arrest effectual or to protect themselves from the prisoner's alleged assault. But in view of our construction of the word "willfully" the jury should have been further instructed that it was not sufficient that petitioners had a generally bad purpose. To convict it was necessary for them to find that petitioners had the purpose to deprive the prisoner of a constitutional right, e.g. the right to be tried by a court rather than by ordeal. And in determining whether that requisite bad purpose was present the jury would be entitled to consider all the attendant circumstances—the malice of petitioners, the weapons used in the assault, its character and duration, the provocation, if any, and the like. . . .

## III

It is said, however, that petitioners did not act "under color of any law" within the meaning of § 20 of the Criminal Code. We disagree. We are of the view that petitioners acted under "color" of law in making the arrest of Robert Hall and in assaulting him. They were officers of the law who made the arrest. By their own admissions they assaulted Hall in order to protect themselves and to keep their prisoner from escaping. It was their duty under Georgia law to make the arrest effective. Hence, their conduct comes within the statute.

Some of the arguments which have been advanced in support of the contrary conclusion suggest that the question under § 20 is whether Congress has made it a federal offense for a state officer to violate the law of his State. But there is no warrant for treating the question in state law terms. The problem is not whether state law has been violated but whether an inhabitant of a State has been deprived of a federal right by one who acts

[Emerson]

under "color of any law." He who acts under "color" of law may be a federal officer or a state officer. He may act under "color" of federal law or of state law. The statute does not come into play merely because the federal law or the state law under which the officer purports to act is violated. It is applicable when and only when someone is deprived of a federal right by that action. The fact that it is also a violation of state law does not make it any the less a federal offense punishable as such. Nor does its punishment by federal authority encroach on state authority or relieve the state from its responsibility for punishing state offenses.

We agree that when this statute is applied to the action of state officials, it should be construed so as to respect the proper balance between the States and the federal government in law enforcement. Violation of local law does not necessarily mean that federal rights have been invaded. The fact that a prisoner is assaulted, injured, or even murdered by state officials does not necessarily mean that he is deprived of any right protected or secured by the Constitution or laws of the United States. Cf. *Logan* v. *United States*, 144 U.S. 263, dealing with assaults by federal officials. The Fourteenth Amendment did not alter the basic relations between the States and the national government. *United States* v. *Harris*, 106 U.S. 629; *In re Kemmler*, 136 U.S. 436, 448. Our national government is one of delegated powers alone. Under our federal system the administration of criminal justice rests with the States except as Congress, acting within the scope of those delegated powers, has created offenses against the United States. *Jerome* v. *United States*, 318 U.S. 101, 105. As stated in *United States* v. *Cruikshank*, 92 U.S. 542, 553–554, "It is no more the duty or within the power of the United States to punish for a conspiracy to falsely imprison or murder within a State, than it would be to punish for false imprisonment or murder itself." And see *United States* v. *Fox*, 95 U.S. 670, 672. It is only state action of a "particular character" that is prohibited by the Fourteenth Amendment and against which the Amendment authorizes Congress to afford relief. *Civil Rights Cases*, 109 U.S. 3, 11, 13. Thus Congress in § 20 of the Criminal Code did not undertake to make all torts of state officials federal crimes. It brought within § 20 only specified acts done "under color" of law and then only those acts which deprived a person of some right secured by the Constitution or laws of the United States. . . .

Since there must be a new trial, the judgment below is

*Reversed.*

MR. JUSTICE RUTLEDGE, concurring in the result. . . .

In effect, [defendants urge] it is murder they have done, not deprivation of constitutional right. Strange as the argument is the reason. It comes to this, that abuse of state power creates immunity to federal power. Because what they did violated the state's laws, the nation cannot reach their conduct. It may deprive the citizen of his liberty and his life. But whatever state officers may do in abuse of their official capacity can give this Government and its courts no concern. This, though the prime object of the Fourteenth Amendment and § 20 was to secure these fundamental rights against wrongful denial by exercise of the power of the states. . . .

. . . the generality of the section's terms simply has not worked out to be a hazard of unconstitutional, or even serious, proportions. It has not proved a source of practical difficulty. In no other way can be explained the paucity of the objection's appearance in the wealth of others made. If experience is the life of the law, as has been said, this has been true preeminently in the application of §§ 19 and 20.

Moreover, statutory specificity has two purposes, to give due notice that an act has been made criminal before it is done and to inform one accused of the nature of the offense charged, so that he may adequately prepare and make his defense. More than this certainly the Constitution does not require. Cf. Amend. VI. All difficulty on the latter score vanishes, under § 20, with the indictment's particularization of the rights infringed and the acts infringing them. . . .

In the other aspect of specificity, two answers, apart from experience, suffice. One is that § 20, and § 19, are no more general and vague, Fourteenth Amendment rights included, than other criminal statutes commonly enforced against this objection. The Sherman Act is the most obvious illustration.

Furthermore, the argument of vagueness, to warn men of their conduct, ignores the nature of the criminal act itself and the notice necessarily given from this. Section 20 strikes only at abuse of official functions by state officers. It does not reach out for crimes done by men in general. Not murder per se, but murder by state officers in the course of official conduct and done with the aid of state power, is outlawed. These facts, inherent in the crime, give all the warning constitutionally required. For one, so situated, who goes so far in misconduct can have no excuse of innocence or ignorance.

Generally state officials know something of the individual's basic legal rights. If they do not, they should, for they assume that duty when they assume their office. Ignorance of the law is no excuse for men in general. It is less an excuse for men whose special duty is to apply it, and therefore to know and observe it. If their knowledge is not comprehensive, state officials know or should know when they pass the limits of their authority, so far at any rate that their action exceeds honest error of judgment and amounts to abuse of their office and its function. When they enter such a domain in dealing with the citizen's rights, they should do so at their peril, whether that be created by state or federal law. . . .

What has been said supplies all the case requires to be decided on the question of criminal intent. If the criminal act is limited, as I think it must be and the statute intends, to infraction of constitutional rights, including rights secured by the Fourteenth Amendment, by conduct which amounts to abuse of one's official place or reckless disregard of duty, no undue hazard or burden can be placed on state officials honestly seeking to perform the rightful functions of their office. Others are not entitled to greater protection.

[Mr. Justice Rutledge then goes on to discuss "the fear grounded in concern for possible maladjustment of federal-state relations."]

. . . Enough has been said to show that the fear is not well grounded. The same fear was expressed, by some in exaggerated and highly emotional terms, when § 2 of the Civil Rights Act, the antecedent of § 20, was under debate in Congress. The history of the legislation's enforcement gives it no support. The fear was not realized in later experience. Eighty years should be enough to remove any remaining vestige. The volume of prosecutions and convictions has been small, in view of the importance of the subject matter and the length of time the statutes have been in force. There are reasons for this, apart from self-restraint of federal prosecuting officials.

One lies in the character of the criminal act and the intent which must be proved. A strong case must be made to show abuse of official function, and therefore to secure indictment or conviction. Trial must be "by an impartial jury of the State and the district wherein the crime shall have been committed." Const., Amend. VI; cf. Art. III, § 2. For all practical purposes this means within the state of which the accused is an officer. Citizens of the state have not been, and will not be, ready to indict or convict their local officers on groundless charges or in doubtful cases. The sections can be applied effectively only when twelve of them concur in a verdict which accords with the prosecuting official's belief that the accused has violated another's fundamental rights. A federal official therefore faces both a delicate and a difficult task when he undertakes to charge and try a state officer under the terms of §§ 19 and 20. The restraint which has been shown is as much enforced by these limitations as it has been voluntary.

These are the reasons why prosecution has not been frequent, has been brought only in cases of gross abuse, and therefore has produced no grave or substantial problem of interference by federal authority in state affairs. But if the problem in this phase of the case were more serious than it has been or is likely to be, the result legally could not be to give state officials immunity from the obligations and liabilities the Amendment and its supporting legislation have imposed. For the verdict of the struggle which brought about adoption of the Amendment was to the contrary. . . .

[Mr. Justice Rutledge then states that he would vote to affirm the judgment except for the fact that such a vote would leave the Court without a majority for any disposition of the case. Accordingly, to avoid this result, he concurs in the disposition required by the opinion of Mr. Justice Douglas.]

MR. JUSTICE MURPHY, dissenting.

I dissent. Robert Hall, a Negro citizen, has been deprived not only of the right to be tried by a court rather than by ordeal. He has been deprived of the right to life itself. That right belonged to him not because he was a Negro or a member of any particular race or creed. That right was his because he was an American citizen, because he was a human being. As such, he was entitled to all the respect and fair treatment that befits the dignity of man, a dignity that is recognized and guaranteed by the Constitution. Yet not even the semblance of due process has been accorded him. He has been cruelly and unjustifiably beaten to death by local police officers acting under color of authority derived from the state. It is difficult to believe that such an obvious and necessary right is indefinitely guaranteed by the Constitution or is foreign to the knowledge of local police officers so as to cast any reasonable doubt on the conviction under § 20 of the Criminal Code of the perpetrators of this "shocking and revolting episode in law enforcement." . . .

It is an illusion to say that the real issue in this case is the alleged failure of § 20 fully to warn the state officials that their actions were illegal. The Constitution, § 20 and their own consciences told them that. They knew that they lacked any mandate or authority to take human life unnecessarily or without due process of law in the course of their duties. They knew that their excessive and abusive use of authority would only subvert the ends of justice. The significant question, rather, is whether law enforcement officers and those entrusted with authority shall be allowed to violate with impunity the clear constitutional rights of the inarticulate and the friendless. Too often unpopular minorities, such as Negroes, are unable to find effective refuge from the cruelties of bigoted and ruthless authority. States are undoubtedly capable of punishing their officers who commit such outrages. But where, as here, the states are unwilling for some reason to prosecute such crimes the federal government must step in unless constitutional guarantees are to become atrophied. . . .

Mr. Justice Roberts, Mr. Justice Frankfurter and Mr. Justice Jackson, dissenting. . . .

Of course the petitioners are punishable. The only issue is whether Georgia alone has the power and duty to punish, or whether this patently local crime can be made the basis of a federal prosecution. The practical question is whether the States should be relieved from responsibility to bring their law officers to book for homicide, by allowing prosecutions in the federal courts for a relatively minor offense carrying a short sentence. The legal question is whether, for the purpose of accomplishing this relaxation of State responsibility, hitherto settled principles for the protection of civil liberties shall be bent and tortured.

## I

. . . Accordingly, Congress passed various measures for its [the Fourteenth Amendment's] enforcement. It is familiar history that much of this legislation was born of that vengeful spirit which to no small degree envenomed the Reconstruction era. Legislative respect for constitutional limitations was not at its height and Congress passed laws clearly unconstitutional. See *Civil Rights Cases*, 109 U. S. 3. One of the laws of this period was the Act of May 31, 1870, 16 Stat. 140. In its present form, as § 20, it is now here for the first time on full consideration as to its meaning and its constitutionality, unembarrassed by preoccupation both on the part of counsel and Court with the more compelling issue of the power of Congress to control State procedure for the election of federal officers. . . .

The Fourteenth Amendment prohibited a State from so acting as to deprive persons of new federal rights defined by it. Section 5 of the Amendment specifically authorized enabling legislation to enforce that prohibition. Since a State can act only through its officers, Congress provided for the prosecution of any officer who deprives others of their guaranteed rights and denied such an officer the right to defend by claiming the authority of the State for his action. In short, Congress said that no State

**55**

can empower an officer to commit acts which the Constitution forbade the State from authorizing, whether such unauthorized command be given for the State by its legislative or judicial voice, or by a custom contradicting the written law. See *Nashville, C. & St. L. R. Co.* v. *Browning*, 310 U. S. 362, 369. The present prosecution is not based on an officer's claim that that for which the United States seeks his punishment was commanded or authorized by the law of his State. On the contrary, the present prosecution is based on the theory that Congress made it a federal offense for a State officer to violate the explicit law of his State. We are asked to construe legislation which was intended to effectuate prohibitions against States for defiance of the Constitution, to be equally applicable where a State duly obeys the Constitution, but an officer flouts State law and is unquestionably subject to punishment by the State for his disobedience. . . .

Such a distortion of federal power devised against recalcitrant State authority never entered the minds of the proponents of the legislation.

[The opinion here discusses the legislative history of Section 20.]

Were it otherwise it would indeed be surprising. It was natural to give the shelter of the Constitution to those basic human rights for the vindication of which the successful conduct of the Civil War was the end of a long process. And the extension of federal authority so as to guard against evasion by any State of these newly created federal rights was an obvious corollary. But to attribute to Congress the making overnight of a revolutionary change in the balance of the political relations between the National Government and the States without reason, is a very different thing. And to have provided for the National Government to take over the administration of criminal justice from the States to the extent of making every lawless act of the policeman on the beat or in the station house, whether by way of third degree or the illegal ransacking for evidence in a man's house (see *Gouled* v. *United States*, 255 U. S. 298; *Byars* v. *United States*, 273 U. S. 28; *Brown* v. *Mississippi*, 297 U. S. 278; *Chambers* v. *Florida*, 309 U. S. 227), a federal offense, would have constituted a revolutionary break with the past overnight. The desire for such a dislocation in our federal system plainly was not contemplated by the Lyman Trumbulls and the John Shermans, and not even by the Thaddeus Stevenses. . . .

Nor is there a body of judicial opinion which bids us find in the unbridled excess of a State officer, constituting a crime under his State law, action taken "under color of law" which federal law forbids. . . .

56

It may well be that Congress could, within the bounds of the Fourteenth Amendment, treat action taken by a State official even though in defiance of State law and not condoned by ultimate State authority as the action of "a State." It has never been satisfactorily explained how a State can be said to deprive a person of liberty or property without due process of law when the foundation of the claim is that a minor official has disobeyed the authentic command of his State. See *Raymond* v. *Chicago Traction Co.*, 207 U. S. 20, 40, 41. Although action taken under such circumstances has been deemed to be deprivation by a "State" of rights guaranteed by the Fourteenth Amendment for purposes of federal jurisdiction, the doctrine has had a fluctuating and dubious history. Compare *Barney* v. *City of New York*, 193 U. S. 430, with *Raymond* v. *Chicago Traction Co.*, *supra; Memphis* v. *Cumberland Telephone Co.*, 218 U. S. 624, with *Home Tel. & Tel. Co.* v. *Los Angeles*, 227 U. S. 278. *Barney* v. *City of New York*, *supra*, which ruled otherwise, although questioned, has never been overruled. See, for instance, *Iowa-Des Moines Bank* v. *Bennett*, 284 U. S. 239, 246–247, and *Snowden* v. *Hughes*, 321 U. S. 1, 13.

But assuming unreservedly that conduct such as that now before us, perpetrated by State officers in flagrant defiance of State law, may be attributed to the State under the Fourteenth Amendment, this does not make it action under "color of any law." Section 20 is much narrower than the power of Congress. Even though Congress might have swept within the federal criminal law any action that could be deemed within the vast reach of the Fourteenth Amendment, Congress did not do so. The presuppositions of our federal system, the pronouncements of the statesmen who shaped this legislation, and the normal meaning of language powerfully counsel against attributing to Congress intrusion into the sphere of criminal law traditionally and naturally reserved for the States alone. . . .

## II

. . . All but two members of the Court apparently agree that insofar as § 20 purports to subject men to punishment for crime it fails to define what conduct is made criminal. As misuse of the criminal machinery is one of the most potent and familiar instruments of arbitrary government, proper regard for the rational requirement of definiteness in criminal statutes is basic to civil liberties. As such it is included in the constitutional guaranty of due process of law. But four members of the Court are of the opinion that this plain constitutional principle of definiteness in criminal statutes may be replaced by an elaborate scheme of constitutional exegesis whereby that which Con-

**57**

gress has not defined the courts can define from time to time, with varying and conflicting definiteness in the decisions, and that, in any event, an undefined range of conduct may become sufficiently definite if only such undefined conduct is committed "willfully."

In subjecting to punishment "deprivation of any rights, privileges, or immunities secured or protected by the Constitution and laws of the United States," § 20 on its face makes criminal deprivation of the whole range of undefined appeals to the Constitution. Such is the true scope of the forbidden conduct. Its domain is unbounded and therefore too indefinite. Criminal statutes must have more or less specific contours. This has none.

To suggest that the "right" deprivation of which is made criminal by § 20 "has been made specific either by the express terms of the Constitution or by decisions interpreting it" hardly adds definiteness beyond that of the statute's own terms. What provision is to be deemed "specific" "by the express terms of the Constitution" and what not "specific"? If the First Amendment safeguarding free speech be a "specific" provision, what about the Fourth? "All unreasonable searches and seizures are absolutely forbidden by the Fourth Amendment." *Nathanson* v. *United States,* 290 U. S. 41, 46. Surely each is among the "rights, privileges, or immunities secured or protected by the Constitution," deprivation of which is a crime under § 20. In any event, what are the criteria by which to determine what express provisions of the Constitution are "specific" and what provisions are not "specific"? And if the terms of § 20 in and of themselves are lacking in sufficient definiteness for a criminal statute, restriction within the framework of "decisions interpreting" the Constitution cannot show the necessary definiteness. The illustrations given in the Court's opinion underline the inescapable vagueness due to the doubts and fluctuating character of decisions interpreting the Constitution.

This intrinsic vagueness of the terms of § 20 surely cannot be removed by making the statute applicable only where the defendant has the "requisite bad purpose." Does that not amount to saying that the black heart of the defendant enables him to know what are the constitutional rights deprivation of which the statute forbids, although we as judges are not able to define their classes or their limits, or, at least, are not prepared to state what they are unless it be to say that § 20 protects whatever rights the Constitution protects? . . .

## III

. . . The Government recognizes that "this is the first case brought before this Court in which § 20 has been applied to deprivations of rights secured by the Fourteenth Amendment." It is not denied that the Government's contention would make a potential offender against this act of any State official who as a judge admitted a confession of crime, or who as judge of a State court of last resort sustained admission of a confession, which we should later hold constitutionally inadmissible, or who as a public service commissioner issued a regulatory order which we should later hold denied due process or who as a municipal officer stopped any conduct we later should hold to be constitutionally protected. The Due Process Clause of the Fourteenth Amendment has a content the scope of which this Court determines only as cases come here from time to time and then not without close division and reversals of position. Such a dubious construction of a criminal statute should not be made unless language compels.

That such a pliable instrument of prosecution is to be feared appears to be recognized by the Government. It urges three safeguards against abuse of the broad powers of prosecution for which it contends. (1) Congress, it says, will supervise the Department's policies and curb excesses by withdrawal of funds. It surely is casting an impossible burden upon Congress to expect it to police the propriety of prosecutions by the Department of Justice. Nor would such detailed oversight by Congress make for the effective administration of the criminal law. (2) The Government further urges that, since prosecutions must be brought in the district where the crime was committed, the judge and jurors of that locality can be depended upon to protect against federal interference with State law enforcement. Such a suggestion would, for practical purposes, transfer the functions of this Court, which adjudicates questions concerning the proper relationship between the federal and State governments, to jurors whose function is to resolve factual questions. Moreover, if federal and State prosecutions are subject to the same influences, it is difficult to see what need there is for taking the prosecution out of the hands of the State. After all, Georgia citizens sitting as a federal grand jury indicted and other Georgia citizens sitting as a federal trial jury convicted Screws and his associates; and it was a Georgia judge who charged more strongly against them than this Court thinks he should have.

Finally, the Department of Justice gives us this assurance of its moderation:

"(3) The Department of Justice has established a policy of strict self-limitation with regard to prosecutions under the civil rights acts. When violations of such statutes are reported, the Department requires that efforts be made to encourage state officials to take appropriate action under state law. To assure consistent observance of this policy in the enforcement of the civil rights statutes, all United States Attorneys have been instructed to submit cases to the Department for approval before prosecutions or investigations are instituted. The number of prosecutions which have been brought under the civil rights statutes is small. No statistics are available with respect to the number of prosecutions prior to 1939, when a special Civil Rights Section was established in the Department of Justice. Only two cases during this period have been reported: *United States* v. *Buntin*, 10 Fed. 730 (C.C.S.D. Ohio), and *United States* v. *Stone*, 188 Fed. 836 (D.Md.). Since 1939, the number of complaints received annually by the Civil Rights Section has ranged from 8,000 to 14,000, but in no year have prosecutions under both Sections 20 and 19, its companion statute, exceeded 76. In the fiscal year 1943, for example, 31 full investigations of alleged violations of Section 20 were conducted, and three cases were brought to trial. In the following fiscal year there were 55 such investigations, and prosecutions were instituted in 12 cases.

"Complaints of violations are often submitted to the Department by local law enforcement officials who for one reason or another may feel themselves powerless to take action under state law. It is primarily in this area, namely, where the official position of the wrongdoers has apparently rendered the State unable or unwilling to institute proceedings, that the statute has come into operation. . . ."

But such a "policy of strict self-limitation" is not accompanied by assurance of permanent tenure and immortality of those who make it the policy. Evil men are rarely given power; they take it over from better men to whom it had been entrusted. There can be no doubt that this shapeless and all-embracing statute can serve as a dangerous instrument of political intimidation and coercion in the hands of those so inclined.

We are told local authorities cannot be relied upon for courageous and prompt action, that often they have personal or political reasons for refusing to prosecute. If it be significantly true that crimes against local law cannot be locally prosecuted, it is an ominous sign indeed. In any event, the cure is a reinvigoration of State responsibility. It is not an undue incursion of remote federal authority into local duties with consequent debilitation of local responsibility. . . .[1]

---

1. On retrial of the case, following the remand, defendants were acquitted by the jury. See Carr, *Federal Protection of Civil Rights*, p. 114 (1947).

For comment on the *Screws* case, see also Cohen, *The Screws Case: Federal Protection of Negro Rights*, 46 Col. L. Rev. 94 (1946) ; Carr, *Screws v. U. S.: The Georgia Police Brutality Case*, 31 Corn. L. Q. 48 (1945) ; Notes

## WILLIAMS v. UNITED STATES

Supreme Court of the United States, 1951
341 U. S. 97, 95 L. Ed. 774, 71 S. Ct. 576

MR. JUSTICE DOUGLAS delivered the opinion of the Court.

The question in this case is whether a special police officer who in his official capacity subjects a person suspected of crime to force and violence in order to obtain a confession may be prosecuted under § 20 of the Criminal Code, 18 U. S. C. (1946 ed.) § 52, now 18 U. S. C. § 242. . . .

The facts are these: The Lindsley Lumber Co. suffered numerous thefts and hired petitioner, who operated a detective agency, to ascertain the identity of the thieves. Petitioner held a special police officer's card issued by the City of Miami, Florida and had taken an oath and qualified as a special police officer. Petitioner and others over a period of three days took four men to a paint shack on the company's premises and used brutal methods to obtain a confession from each of them. A rubber hose, a pistol, a blunt instrument, a sash cord and other implements were used in the project. One man was forced to look at a bright light for fifteen minutes; when he was blinded he was repeatedly hit with a rubber hose and a sash cord and finally knocked to the floor. Another was knocked from a chair and hit in the stomach again and again. He was put back in the chair and the procedure was repeated. One was backed against the wall and jammed in the chest with a club. Each was beaten, threatened, and unmercifully punished for several hours until he confessed. One Ford, a policeman, was sent by his superior to lend authority to the proceedings. And petitioner, who committed the assaults, went about flashing his badge.

The indictment charged among other things that petitioner acting under color of law used force to make each victim confess to his guilt and implicate others, and that the victims were denied the right to be tried by due process of law and if found guilty to be sentenced and punished in accordance with the laws of the state. Petitioner was found guilty by a jury under instructions which conformed with the rulings of the Court in *Screws v. United States*, 325 U. S. 91. The Court of Appeals affirmed. 179 F. 2d 656. The case, which is a companion to No. 26, *United States v. Williams* [341 U. S. 70], and No. 134, *United States v. Williams* [341 U. S. 58], decided this day, is here on certiorari.

We think it clear that petitioner was acting "under color" of law within the meaning of § 20, or at least that the jury could

in 55 Yale L. J. 576 (1946), 8 Ga. Bar. J. 320 (1946), 40 Ill. L. Rev. 263 (1945), 44 Mich. L. Rev. 814 (1946).

properly so find. We interpreted this phrase of § 20 in *United States v. Classic*, 313 U. S. 299, 326, "Misuse of power, possessed by virtue of state law and made possible only because the wrongdoer is clothed with the authority of state law, is action taken 'under color of' state law." And see *Screws v. United States, supra*, 107–111. It is common practice, as we noted in *Labor Board v. Jones & Laughlin Co.*, 331 U. S. 416, 429, for private guards or detectives to be vested with policemen's powers. We know from the record that that is the policy of Miami, Florida. Moreover, this was an investigation conducted under the aegis of the State, as evidenced by the fact that a regular police officer was detailed to attend it. We need go no further to conclude that the lower court to whom we give deference on local law matters, see *Gardner v. New Jersey*, 329 U. S. 565, 583, was correct in holding that petitioner was no mere interloper but had a semblance of policeman's power from Florida. There was, therefore, evidence that he acted under authority of Florida law; and the manner of his conduct of the interrogations makes clear that he was asserting the authority granted him and not acting in the role of a private person. In any event, the charge to the jury drew the line between official and unofficial conduct which we explored in *Screws v. United States, supra*, 111, and gave petitioner all of the protection which "color of" law as used in § 20 offers.

The main contention is that the application of section 20 so as to sustain a conviction for obtaining a confession by use of force and violence is unconstitutional. The argument is the one that a clear majority of the Court rejected in *Screws v. United States*.

. . .

Many criminal statutes might be extended to circumstances so extreme as to make their application unconstitutional. Conversely, as we held in *Screws v. United States*, a close construction will often save an act from vagueness that is fatal. The present case is as good an illustration as any. It is as plain as a pikestaff that the present confessions would not be allowed in evidence whatever the school of thought concerning the scope and meaning of the Due Process Clause. This is the classic use of force to make a man testify against himself. The result is as plain as if the rack, the wheel, and the thumb screw—the ancient methods of securing evidence by torture (*Brown v. Mississippi*, 297 U. S. 278, 285–286; *Chambers v. Florida*, 309 U.S. 227, 237)—were used to compel the confession. Some day the application of § 20 to less obvious methods of coercion may be presented and doubts as to the adequacy of the standard of guilt may be presented. There may be a similar doubt when an officer is tried under § 20 for beating a man to death. That was a doubt stirred in the *Screws* case; and it was the reason we held that the purpose must be plain, the deprivation of the constitutional right willful. But where police take matters in their own hands, seize victims, beat and pound them until they confess, there cannot be the slightest doubt that the police have deprived the victim of a right under the Constitution. It is the right of the accused to be tried by a legally constituted court, not by a kangaroo court. Hence when officers wring confessions from the accused by force and violence, they violate some of the most fundamental, basic, and well established constitutional rights which every citizen enjoys. Petitioner and his associates acted willfully and purposely; their aim was precisely to deny the protection that the Constitution affords.* It was an arrogant and brutal deprivation of rights which the Constitution specifically guarantees. Section 20 would be denied the high service for which it was designed if rights so palpably plain were denied its protection. Only casuistry could make vague and nebulous what our constitutional scheme makes so clear and specific. . . .

*Affirmed.*

MR. JUSTICE BLACK dissents.

MR. JUSTICE FRANKFURTER, MR. JUSTICE JACKSON and MR. JUSTICE MINTON, dissenting.

Experience in the effort to apply the doctrine of *Screws v. United States*, 325 U. S. 91, leads MR. JUSTICE FRANKFURTER, MR. JUSTICE JACKSON and MR. JUSTICE MINTON to dissent for the reasons set forth in dissent in that case.

---

* The trial judge charged in part on this phase of the case: "The law denies to anyone acting under color of law, statute, ordinance, regulation, or custom the right to try a person by ordeal; that is, for the officer himself to inflict such punishment upon the person as he thinks the person should receive. Now in determining whether this requisite of willful intent was present in this case as to these counts you gentlemen are entitled to consider all the attendant circumstances; the malice, if any, of the defendants toward these men; the weapon used in the assault, if any; and the character and duration of the investigation, if any, of the assault, if any, and the time and manner in which it was carried out. All these facts and circumstances may be taken into consideration from the evidence that has been submitted for the purpose of determining whether the acts of the defendants were willful and for the deliberate and willful purpose of depriving these men of their Constitutional rights to be tried by a jury just like everyone else."

## UNITED STATES v. WILLIAMS

Supreme Court of the United States, 1951

341 U. S. 70, 95 L. Ed. 758, 71 S. Ct. 581

[This is a companion case to *Williams v. U. S., supra.* In addition to the prosecution under § 242, Williams and three others were indicted for violation of § 241. The indictment alleged that "acting under the laws of the State of Florida" the defendants "conspired to injure . . . a citizen of the United States and of the State of Florida, in the free exercise and enjoyment of the rights and privileges secured to him and protected by the Fourteenth Amendment . . . ." All the defendants were convicted; but on appeal the Court of Appeals for the Fifth Circuit reversed. 179 F. 2d 644.]

MR. JUSTICE FRANKFURTER announced the judgment of the Court and an opinion in which THE CHIEF JUSTICE, MR. JUSTICE JACKSON and MR. JUSTICE MINTON joined.

. . . we agree that § 241 (to use the current designation for what was § 19 of the Criminal Code) does not reach the conduct laid as an offense in the prosecution here. This is not because we deny the power of Congress to enforce by appropriate criminal sanction every right guaranteed by the Due Process Clause of the Fourteenth Amendment; nor is it because we fully accept the course of reasoning of the court below. We base our decision on the history of § 241, its text and context, the statutory framework in which it stands, its practical and judicial application—controlling elements in construing a federal criminal provision that affects the wise adjustment between State responsibility and national control of essentially local affairs. The elements all converge in one direction. They lead us to hold that § 241 only covers conduct which interferes with rights arising from the substantive powers of the Federal Government.

What is now known as § 241 originated as § 6 of the Act of May 31, 1870, 16 Stat. 140. . . . [Section 17 of the same Act is the predecessor of § 242.]

The dominant conditions of the Reconstruction Period were not conducive to the enactment of carefully considered and coherent legislation. Strong post-war feeling caused inadequate deliberation and led to loose and careless phrasing of laws relating to the new political issues. The sections before us are no exception. Although enacted together, they were proposed by different sponsors and hastily adopted. They received little attention in debate. While the discussion of the bill as a whole fills about 100 pages of the Congressional Globe, only two or three related to

§ 6, and these are in good part a record of complaint that the section was inadequately considered or understood.

Nevertheless some conclusions are warranted. The first is that interference with civil rights by State officers was dealt with fully by § 17 of the Act. Three years before its enactment Congress had passed the first general conspiracy statute. Act of March 2, 1867, § 30, 14 Stat. 484; R. S. § 5440, now 18 U. S. C. § 371. This provision, in conjunction with § 17, reached conspiracies under color of State law to deprive persons of rights guaranteed by the Fourteenth Amendment. No other provision of the Act of 1870 was necessary for that purpose.

The second conclusion is that if language is to carry any meaning at all it must be clear that the principal purpose of § 6, unlike § 17, was to reach private action rather than officers of a State acting under its authority. Men who "go in disguise upon the public highway, or upon the premises of another" are not likely to be acting in official capacities. The history of the times—the lawless activities of private bands, of which the Klan was the most conspicuous—explains why Congress dealt with both State disregard of the new constitutional prohibitions and private lawlessness. The sponsor of § 6 in the Senate made explicit that the purpose of his amendment was to control private conduct.

These two conclusions strongly suggest a third: that the rights which § 6 protects are those which Congress can beyond doubt constitutionally secure against interference by private individuals. Decisions of this Court have established that this category includes rights which arise from the relationship of the individual and the Federal Government. The right of citizens to vote in congressional elections, for instance, may obviously be protected by Congress from individual as well as from State interference. *Ex parte Yarbrough*, 110 U. S. 651. On the other hand, we have consistently held that the category of rights which Congress may constitutionally protect from interference by private persons excludes those rights which the Constitution merely guarantees from interference by a State. Thus we held that an individual's interest in receiving a fair trial in State courts cannot be constitutionally vindicated by federal prosecution of private persons. *United States v. Powell*, 212 U. S. 564; accord, *Hodges v. United States*, 203 U. S. 1; *United States v. Wheeler*, 254 U. S. 281. The distinction which these decisions draw between rights that flow from the substantive powers of the Federal Government and may clearly be protected from private interference, and interests which the Constitution only guarantees from interference by States, is a familiar one in American law. See, *e. g., Strauder v. West Virginia*, 100 U. S. 303, 310.

To construe § 6 so as to protect interests not arising from the relationship of the individual with the Federal Government, but only guaranteed by the Constitution from interference by the States, would make its scope duplicate the coverage of § 17 and the general conspiracy clause. That this is not in fact what Congress desired is confirmed by further examination of the text of the statute. Full allowance for hasty draftsmanship cannot obscure the clear indications from the text that the category of interests protected by § 6 does not include the rights against State action secured by § 17.

Thus, when Congress wished to protect from State action interests guaranteed by the Fourteenth Amendment, it described them in § 17 as rights "secured or protected" by the Constitution. But in § 6 the narrower phrase "granted or secured" is used to define the interests protected from interference by individuals. When Congress wanted to reach action by State officers, the explicit reference in § 17 to "color" of State law demonstrates that Congress knew how to make this purpose known. Similarly, reference in §§ 2 and 3 to "persons or officers" indicates that Congress was able explicitly to draft a section applicable to persons acting in private and official capacities alike. In contrast, § 6 was made applicable simply to "persons." Nothing in its terms indicates that color of State law was to be relevant to prosecution under it.

[The opinion then reviews prior decisions under § 241. For digests of most of these cases see Note, *supra*.]

In none of these decisions was the precise issue before us decided, for in none was it alleged that the defendants acted under color of State law. But the validity of a conviction under § 241 depends on the scope of that section, which cannot be expanded by the draftsmen of an indictment. The uses to which a statute has been put are strong evidence of the ends it was intended to serve. In this instance the decisions buttress what common sense and a spontaneous reading of the statute independently make clear, and give added significance to repeated reenactment without substantial change. All the evidence points to the same conclusion: that § 241 applies only to interference with rights which arise from the relation of the victim and the Federal Government, and not to interference by state officers with rights which the Federal Government merely guarantees from abridgment by the States.

To reject this evidence and hold the indictment valid under § 241 not only involves a new, distorting construction of an old statute. It also makes for redundancy and confusion and raises some needless constitutional problems. For if we assume that a

[Emerson]

conspiracy such as that described here is under color of State law, it can be reached under § 242 and the general conspiracy statute. . . . Unlike § 242, the section now before us is not qualified by the requirement that the defendants have acted "wilfully," and the very specialized content attributed to that word was found essential to sustaining § 242 in *Screws v. United States,* 325 U. S. 91. Nor does the defined crime have as an ingredient that the conspiracy be under color of State law. Criminal statutes should be given the meaning their language most obviously invites. Their scope should not be extended to conduct not clearly within their terms.

We therefore hold that including an allegation that the defendants acted under color of State law in an indictment under § 241 does not extend the protection of the section to rights which the Federal Constitution merely guarantees against abridgment by the States. Since under this interpretation of the statute the indictment must fall, the judgment of the court below is

*Affirmed.*

[Appendix omitted.]

[Mr. Justice Black concurred on grounds of *res adjudicata,* thus finding it unnecessary to determine whether § 241, as applied, "is too vague and uncertain in scope to be consistent with the Fifth Amendment."]

Mr. Justice Douglas, with whom Mr. Justice Reed, Mr. Justice Burton, and Mr. Justice Clark concur, dissenting.

Sections 19 and 20 of the Criminal Code, now 18 U.S.C. §§ 241 and 242, are companion sections designed for the protection of great rights won after the Nation's most critical internal conflict. . . .

Mr. Justice Rutledge in *Screws v. United States,* 325 U. S. 91, 119, wrote that in spite of the difference in wording of §§ 19 and 20 there are "no differences in the basic rights guarded. Each protects in a different way the rights and privileges secured to individuals by the Constitution." One would indeed have to strain hard at words to find any difference of substance between "any right or privilege secured" by the Constitution or laws of the United States (§ 19) and "any rights, privileges, or immunities secured or protected by the Constitution and laws of the United States" (§ 20). If § 20 embraces a broader range of rights than § 19, it must be because it includes "immunities" as well as "rights" and "privileges" and "protects" them as well as "secures" them. When no major difference between §§ 19 and 20 is apparent from the words themselves, it is strange to hear it said that though § 20 extends to rights guaranteed against

**67**

state action by the Fourteenth Amendment, § 19 is limited to rights which the Federal Government can secure against invasion by private persons. The division of powers between the State and Nation is so inherent in our republican form of government and so well established throughout our history that if Congress had desired to draw a distinction along that line, it is hard to imagine that it would not have made its purpose clear in the language used. . . .

The distinction now urged has not been noticed by students of the period. Thus Flack, in Adoption of the Fourteenth Amendment (1908), p. 223, wrote, "The bill as passed by the Houses was signed by the President May 31, 1870, and so became a law, and was, therefore, the first law for the enforcement of the Fourteenth and Fifteenth Amendments." And see Mr. Justice Roberts in *Hague v. C. I. O.*, 307 U. S. 496, 510. If the drastic restriction now proposed for § 19 had been part of the architectural scheme for the Act of May 31, 1870, it is difficult to imagine that some trace of the purpose would not have been left in the legislative history. What we find points indeed the other way. Senator Pool of North Carolina, who introduced the section from which § 19 evolved, indicated that it was his purpose to extend the protection of the new provision to the Fourteenth as well as to the Fifteenth Amendment. It has, indeed, long been assumed that § 19 had a coverage broad enough to include all constitutional rights. Thus in *United States v. Mosley*, 238 U. S. 383, 387, Mr. Justice Holmes observed that § 19 "dealt with Federal rights, and with all Federal rights."

There is no decision, prior to that of the Court of Appeals in this case, which is opposed to that view. Fourteenth Amendment rights have sometimes been asserted under § 19 and denied by the Court. That was true in *United States v. Cruikshank*, 92 U. S. 542. But the denial had nothing to do with the issues in the present case. The Fourteenth Amendment protects the individual against *state action*, not against wrongs done by *individuals*. See *Civil Rights Cases*, 109 U. S. 3; *Shelley v. Kraemer*, 334 U. S. 1. The *Cruikshank* case, like others, involved wrongful action by *individuals* who did not act for a state nor under color of state authority. . . .

. . . Those attempts which failed did so not because § 19 was construed to have too narrow a scope, but because the action complained of was *individual* action, not *state* action. See, *e. g.*, *United States v. Powell*, 151 F 648, aff'd 212 U. S. 564; *Powe v. United States*, 109 F.2d 147.

. . . It certainly cannot be doubted that state officers, or those acting under color of state law, who conspire to wring confessions from an accused by force and violence, are included in "two or more persons" within the meaning of § 19. As we hold in No. 365, *Williams v. United States* [341 U. S. 97], decided this day, such an act deprives the accused of the kind of trial which the Fourteenth guarantees. He is therefore denied the enjoyment of that right, within the meaning of § 19.

In *Screws v. United States, supra,* we relieved § 20 of the risk of unconstitutionality by reason of vagueness. We held that "a requirement of a specific intent to deprive a person of a federal right made definite by decision or other rule of law saves the Act from any charge of unconstitutionality on the grounds of vagueness." 325 U. S. at p. 103. The same analysis does like service here, as evidenced both by the construction of § 19 and the charge to the jury in this case.

A conspiracy by definition is a criminal agreement for a specific venture. It is "a partnership in crime." *United States v. Socony-Vacuum Oil Co.,* 310 U. S. 150, 253. As stated by Mr. Justice Holmes in *Frohwerk v. United States,* 249 U. S. 204, 209, an "intent to accomplish an object cannot be alleged more clearly than by stating that parties conspired to accomplish it." The trial court in its charge to the jury followed the ruling in the *Screws* case and gave precise application to this concept in avoidance of any claim of unconstitutionality of § 19 on the grounds of vagueness. The court, after explaining to the jury what rights, enumerated in the indictment, were guaranteed under the Fourteenth Amendment, gave numerous charges on the element of intent. The following is typical:

> "In order to convict under this indictment, it is necessary for the jury to find that the defendants had in mind the specific purpose of depriving the complaining witnesses of those rights guaranteed them under the Fourteenth Amendment to the Constitution of the United States, which are enumerated in the indictment, while acting under color of the laws of the State of Florida.
>
> "The proof, if any, of a general intent to do the complaining witnesses a wrong is not sufficient, but a specific intent to deprive them of a Constitutional right, as the object of the conspiracy, if any, is a burden the law casts upon the Government. In considering whether the defendants had such specific intent, you may take into consideration all the circumstances of the case in the light of the evidence as it has been developed."

In view of the nature of the conspiracy and charge to the jury in the instant case, it would be incongruous to strike § 19 down

**69**

on the grounds of vagueness and yet sustain § 20 as we did in the *Screws* case. • • •

## Note

1. Section 241 has occasionally been invoked against violence by private persons which interfered with the rights of individuals secured by Federal statute. See *U. S. v. Waddell*, 112 U. S. 76, 28 L. Ed. 673, 5 S. Ct. 35 (1884), *supra*, followed in *Nixon v. U. S.*, 289 F. 177 (C. A. 9, 1923), cert. den. 263 U. S. 703 (1923). In *U. S. v. Mary Helen Coal Co.* (E. D. Ky., 1938, unreported) more than 50 defendants, including 16 coal companies, 18 coal company operators, the Harlan County Coal Operators' Union, and 22 hired deputy sheriffs were indicted under Section 241, for using force and other methods to prevent labor organizers and miners from engaging in labor union activity, thereby depriving them of the right to organize and bargain collectively established by the National Labor Relations Act. The Federal District Judge overruled a demurrer to the indictment, but the case ended in a jury disagreement. A similar attempt in *U. S. v. Fitzgerald Cotton Mills* (S. D. Ga., 1940, unreported) also was upheld against attack by demurrer but resulted in an acquittal. See Schweinhaut, *The Civil Liberties Section of the Department of Justice*, 1 Bill of Rights Rev. 206 (1941); Konvitz, *The Constitution and Civil Rights*, pp. 44–5 (1947). But see *U. S. v. Berke Cake Co.*, 50 F. Supp. 311 (E. D. N. Y. 1943), appeal dis., 320 U. S. 807 (1943) (sustaining demurrer to an indictment alleging conspiracy by employers and labor union officials to use threats of discharge and other economic coercion to prevent employees from filing suits for damages under the Fair Labor Standards Act).

2. The constitutional rights which are protected by Section 241 against interference by private individuals remain somewhat obscure. Clearly Section 241 would apply to interference by violence with the exercise of the Federal franchise. See *Ex parte Yarbrough*, 110 U. S. 651, 28 L. Ed. 274, 4 S. Ct. 152 (1884), *supra; U. S. v. Classic*, 313 U. S. 299, 85 L. Ed. 1368, 61 S. Ct. 1031 (1941); and other cases cited in Chapter III, *infra*. Other constitutional rights protected are those recognized in *Logan v. U. S.*, 144 U. S. 263, 36 L. Ed. 429, 12 S. Ct. 617 (1892), and *Motes v. U. S.*, 178 U. S. 458, 44 L. Ed. 1150, 20 S. Ct. 993 (1900) *supra*. Labor cases in accord are *Foss v. U. S.*, 266 Fed. 881 (C. A. 9, 1920) and *Nicholson v. U. S.*, 79 F.2d 387 (C. A. 8, 1935).

With respect to interference by violence with the right to freedom of speech, press and assembly the dictum in the *Cruikshank* case, *supra*, would indicate that the right of assembly for purposes "connected with the powers or the duties of the national government" would be protected under Section 241. In *Powe v. U. S.*, 109 F.2d 147 (C. A. 5, 1940), cert. den. 309 U. S. 679 (1940), five defendants were indicted for attempting by blackmail to prevent the editor of a local newspaper from publishing attacks upon local officials for their failure to suppress gambling. The court sustained a demurrer to the indictment but quoted the *Cruikshank* dictum and added:

> "Because the federal government is a republican one in which the will of the people ought to prevail, and because that will ought

to be expressive of an informed public opinion, the freedom of speaking and printing on subjects relating to that government, its elections, its laws, its operations and its officers is vital to it. Assuming that for this reason Congress, if it finds it necessary, can legislate to maintain such freedom in that field, it does not follow that Congress can legislate generally to preserve such freedom in discussing religious affairs, or social or artistic matters, or matters of purely State concern. Again, by Art. 4, Sect. 4, of the Constitution the United States shall guarantee to every State a republican form of government. Should a tyranny be set up in a State accompanied by a suppression of free speech and press, conceivably the Congress might be called on, temporarily in the execution of this guaranty, to pass a law securing against individual violence free speech in such State; but the section before us is not such a law." [1]

See *Collins v. Hardyman, infra,* and other cases arising under the civil provisions of the Federal Civil Rights Acts. See also *Hague v. C. I. O.,* 307 U. S. 496, 83 L. Ed. 1423, 59 S. Ct. 954 (1939) ; *Edwards v. California,* 314 U. S. 160, 86 L. Ed. 119, 62 S. Ct. 164 (1941) (concurring opinions).

3. Following the *Screws* case convictions were obtained under Section 242, as construed in the *Screws* decision, in *Crews v. U. S.,* 160 F.2d 746 (C. A. 5, 1947) (constable whipped Negro and forced him to jump in a river, thereby causing him to drown) ; *Apodaca v. U. S.,* 188 F.2d 932 (C. A. 10, 1951) (police officials used torture in an attempt to extract confession) ; *Lynch v. U. S.,* 189 F.2d 476 (C. A. 5, 1951), cert. den. 342 U. S. 831 (1951) (police officials surrendered Negro prisoners to Ku Klux Klan mob which administered beating) ; *Koehler v. U. S.* 189 F.2d 711 (C.A. 5, 1951), cert. den, 342 U. S. 852 (1951) (police officials took individual into custody and beat and tortured him) ; *Clark v. U. S.,* 193 F.2d 294 (C.A. 5, 1951). In the *Apodaca* case the charge to the jury included a statement that "intent is merely the purpose or willingness to commit the act charged" and "does not require knowledge that such act is a violation of law" (188 F.2d at 937). For a case in which a charge to the jury in accordance with the *Screws* doctrine resulted in an acquittal, see Carr, *Federal Protection of Civil Rights,* pp. 161–2 (1947). See also *Pullen v. U. S.,* 164 F.2d 756 (C. A. 5, 1947) (demurrer sustained where indictment failed to allege requisite intent and charge was held insufficient). For a detailed account of the cases up to 1947 see Carr at pp. 151–176. See also Note, 40 Geo. L. J. 566 (1952).

4. In the *Apodaca, Lynch* and *Koehler* cases, *supra,* the prosecution was based upon a denial of equal protection as well as due process of law under the Fourteenth Amendment. This was also true in *Catlette v. U. S.,* 132 F. 2d 902 (C. A. 4, 1943), decided before the *Screws* case. In *U. S. v. Classic,* 313 U. S. 299, 85 L. Ed. 1368, 61 S. Ct. 1031 (1941), the equal protection point was raised but not passed upon by the Supreme Court. Presumably all rights guaranteed against state

---

[1] The *Powe* case is discussed in 40 Col. L. Rev. 902 (1940).

infringement by the Fourteenth Amendment, including rights to freedom of speech, press and assembly, are protected under Section 242 against violent interference by persons acting under color of law. See *Hague v. C. I. O., supra.* Similarly other constitutional rights, implicit or explicit, and rights based upon Federal statute are protected under Section 242. See *U. S. v. Classic, supra;* and see also cases arising under the civil provisions of the Federal Civil Rights Acts, *infra.*

On the privileges and immunities clause of the Fourteenth Amendment, see *U. S. v. Wheeler,* 254 U. S. 281, 65 L. Ed. 270, 41 S. Ct. 133 (1920); *Hague v. C. I. O., supra;* Meyers, *Federal Privileges and Immunities: Application to Ingress and Egress,* 29 Corn. L. Q. 489 (1944); Note, *The Adamson Case: A Study in Constitutional Technique,* 58 Yale L. J. 268 (1949); Hale, *Some Basic Constitutional Rights of Economic Significance,* 51 Col. L. Rev. 271, 288–304 (1951).

5. With respect to the issue of when an individual will be deemed to be acting under "color of law", see especially the *Crews, Lynch* and *Koehler* cases, *supra.* In the *Lynch* case the failure of police officials to afford adequate protection was held to fall within the terms of Section 242. See also *Catlette v. U. S., supra;* Cohen, *The Screws Case: Federal Protection of Negro Rights,* 46 Col. L. Rev. 94, 104–6 (1946); cases involving the civil provisions of the Federal Civil Rights Acts, *infra.* For more generalized discussion of what constitutes "state action", see Hale, *Rights Under the Fourteenth and Fifteenth Amendments Against Injuries Inflicted by Private Individuals,* 6 Law. Guild Rev. 627 (1946); Hale, *Some Basic Constitutional Rights of Economic Significance,* 51 Col. L. Rev. 271, 317–26 (1951); Barnett, *What Is "State" Action Under the Fourteenth, Fifteenth and Nineteenth Amendments of the Constitution?* 24 Ore. L. Rev. 227 (1945); Notes in 48 Col. L. Rev. 1241 (1948); 96 U. Pa. L. Rev. 402 (1948); 44 Ill. L. Rev. 199 (1949). See also Chapter IX, *infra.*

6. By combining Section 242 and the general conspiracy statute (18 U. S. C. § 371) it has been possible to apply the heavier penalties of the conspiracy statute to violations of Section 242. *Apodaca v. U. S.,* 188 F.2d 932 (C. A. 10, 1951). Through the same combination the conviction of private persons who conspired with state officials has been upheld. *Culp v. U. S.,* 131 F.2d 93 (C. A. 8, 1942); *U. S. v. Trierweiler,* 52 F. Supp. 4 (E. D. Ill., 1943); *Koehler v. U. S., supra.*

7. With respect to rights under the Thirteenth Amendment and the peonage and slavery statutes (18 U. S. C. §§ 1581–8), see *Peonage Cases,* 123 F. 671 (M. D. Ala. 1903); *Clyatt v. U. S.,* 197 U. S. 207, 49 L. Ed. 726, 25 S. Ct. 429 (1905); *Bailey v. Alabama,* 219 U. S. 219, 55 L. Ed. 191, 31 S. Ct. 145 (1911); *U. S. v. Broughton,* 235 U. S. 133, 59 L. Ed. 162, 35 S. Ct. 86 (1914); *Taylor v. Georgia,* 315 U. S. 25, 86 L. Ed. 615, 62 S. Ct. 415 (1942); *U. S. v. Gaskin,* 320 U. S. 527, 88 L. Ed. 287, 64 S. Ct. 318 (1944); *Pollock v. Williams,* 322 U. S. 4, 88 L. Ed. 1095, 64 S. Ct. 792 (1944); *Pierce v. U. S.,* 146 F.2d 84 (C. A. 5, 1944), cert. den. 324 U. S. 873 (1945); *U. S. v. Ingalls,* 73 F. Supp. 76 (S. D. Cal. 1947). See also Carr, *Federal Protection of Civil Rights,* pp. 77–84, 116–20 (1947); Hale, *Some Basic Constitutional Rights of Economic Significance,* 51 Col. L. Rev. 271, 271–8 (1951); Folsom, *A Slave Trade*

*Law in a Contemporary Setting*, 29 Corn. L. Q. 203 (1943); Brodie, *The Federally-Secured Right to be Free From Bondage*, 40 Geo. L. J. 367 (1952).

8. General discussion of the criminal provisions of the Federal Civil Rights Acts may be found in Carr, *supra*, and in Note, *Federal Power to Prosecute Violence Against Minority Groups*, 57 Yale L. J. 855 (1948); Hale, *Unconstitutional Acts as Federal Crimes*, 60 Harv. L. Rev. 65 (1946); Fraenkel, *The Federal Civil Rights Laws*, 31 Minn. L. Rev. 301 (1947); Konvitz, *The Constitution and Civil Rights*, ch. 3 and 4 (1947). See also Rotnem, *The Federal Civil Right "Not To Be Lynched"*, 28 Wash. U. L. Q. 57 (1943); Coleman, *Freedom from Fear on the Home Front*, 29 Iowa L. Rev. 415 (1944); Newman, *A Forgotten Right of United States Citizenship*, 39 Ill. L. Rev. 367 (1945); Clark, *A Federal Prosecutor Looks at the Civil Rights Statutes*, 47 Col. L. Rev. 175 (1947); Note, 25 So. Cal. L. Rev. 125 (1951) (note on *Williams* cases); Note, 162 A.L.R. 1373 (1946).

### b. Civil Provisions of Federal Civil Rights Acts

The Civil Rights Acts contained, in addition to the criminal provisions, a series of provisions giving injured persons the right to sue for civil damages or to obtain injunctive or other civil relief. Of those remaining on the statute books, the two most important are Sections 43 and 47(3) of Title 8 of the United States Code, which read as follows:

"§ 43. **Civil action for deprivation of rights.**

"Every person who, under color of any statute, ordinance, regulation, custom, or usage, of any State or Territory, subjects or causes to be subjected, any citizen of the United States or other person within the jurisdiction thereof to the deprivation of any rights, privileges, or immunities secured by the Constitution and laws, shall be liable to the party injured in an action at law, suit in equity, or other proper proceeding for redress."

"§ 47(3). **Conspiracies: to deprive citizens of rights or privileges.**

"If two or more persons in any State or Territory conspire or go in disguise on the highway or on the premises of another, for the purpose of depriving, either directly or indirectly, any person or class of persons of the equal protection of the laws, or of equal privileges and immunities under the laws; or for the purpose of preventing or hindering the constituted authorities of any State or Territory from giving or securing to all persons within such State or Territory the equal protection of the laws; or if two or more persons conspire to prevent by force, intimidation, or threat, any citizen who is lawfully entitled to vote, from giving his support or advocacy in a legal manner, toward or in favor of the election of any lawfully qualified person as an elector for President or Vice President, or as a Member of Congress of the United States; or to injure any citizen in person or property on account of such support or advocacy; in any case of conspiracy set forth in this section, if one or more persons engaged therein do, or cause to be done, any act in furtherance of the object of such conspiracy, whereby another is injured in his person or property, or deprived of having and exercising any right or privilege of a citizen of the United States, the party so injured or deprived may have an action for the recovery of damages occasioned by such injury or deprivation, against any one or more of the conspirators."

Other provisions establish the right of all citizens to vote without distinction of race, color, or previous condition of servitude (8 U. S. C. § 31); the right of all persons to make and enforce contracts, to sue, be parties, give evidence, and to the full and equal benefit of all laws and proceedings for the security of persons and property, to the same extent as white citizens (8 U. S. C. § 41); the right of all citizens to inherit, purchase, lease, sell, hold, and convey real or personal property to the same extent as white citizens (8 U. S. C. § 42); afford civil relief against conspiracies to prevent by force, intimidation, or threat, any person from holding office or discharging the duties of office under the United States (8 U. S. C. § 47(1)); afford civil relief against like conspiracies to interfere with parties or witnesses in United States courts, or to impede, hinder, obstruct or defeat justice with intent to deny any citizen the equal protection of the laws (8 U. S. C. § 47(2)); and provide an action for damages against any person who, having knowledge of wrongs about to be committed contrary to Section 47, and power to prevent them, neglects or refuses to do so (8 U. S. C. § 48). The text of these and additional provisions are set forth in Carr, *Federal Protection of Civil Rights,* Appendix 2 (1947).

## Note

1. Section 43, like Section 242 of Title 18, is applicable only to persons acting under "color of statute".[1] But, unlike Section 242, it is limited to acts done under color of law "of any State or Territory" and hence does not apply to acts done under color of Federal law. *Gregoire v. Biddle,* 177 F.2d 579 (C. A. 2, 1949), cert. den. 339 U. S. 949 (1950). Where the requisite "color of law" is present, however, Section 43

[1] The phrase "color of statute" in Section 43 has been interpreted to mean the same as "color of law" in Section 242. *Picking v. Pennsylvania R. Co.,* 151 F. 2d 240 (C. A. 3, 1945), cert. den. 332 U. S. 776 (1947).

affords civil relief against deprivation of (1) rights secured by the Federal Constitution against state action; (2) rights secured by the Federal Constitution against individual action; and (3) rights secured by Federal Statute. The courts were originally reluctant to sanction the use of Section 43. See *Carter v. Greenhow*, 114 U. S. 317, 29 L. Ed. 202, 5 S. Ct. 928 (1885); *Holt v. Indiana Manufacturing Co.*, 176 U. S. 68, 44 L. Ed. 374, 20 S. Ct. 272 (1900); *Giles v. Harris*, 189 U. S. 475, 47 L. Ed. 909, 23 S. Ct. 639 (1903). But more recently the section has been successfully invoked to protect a wide variety of constitutional and statutory rights. In a number of these cases the right involved has been protected against the use of violence or physical intimidation; presumably any of the rights covered by Section 43 would be safeguarded against such infringement. Among the significant situations in which Section 43 has been held applicable are the following:

*Unjustified violence in the administration of law: Picking v. Pennsylvania R. Co.*, 151 F. 2d 240 (C. A. 3, 1945) (complaint alleging false arrest and assault while in custody of police upheld as denial of due process under Fourteenth Amendment); *Refoule v. Ellis*, 74 F. Supp. 336 (N. D. Ga., 1947) (complaint alleging arrest without warrant, illegal detention and use of third degree upheld as denial of due process); *State v. Central Sur. & Ins. Corp*, 102 F. Supp. 444 (W. D. Ark, 1952); *Gordon v. Garrson*, 77 F. Supp. 477 (E. D. Ill., 1948) (complaint charging prison superintendent with violent treatment of prisoner upheld); but cf. *Siegel v. Ragen*, 180 F.2d 785 (C. A. 7, 1950), cert. den. 339 U. S. 990 (1950) (prisoner has no right to practice law or interfere with internal prison discipline). Presumably the actions of the defendants in the *Screws* and *Williams* cases would also fall within Section 43.

*Other abuse of the judicial process: Picking v. Pennsylvania R. Co.*, *supra* (false arrest); *McShane v. Moldovan*, 172 F. 2d 1016 (C. A. 6, 1949) (complaint charging false arrest and fraudulent trial upheld as denial of due process); *Burt v. City of New York*, 156 F. 2d 791 (C. A. 2, 1946) (allegation of "purposeful discrimination" in administration of building regulations upheld as denial of equal protection); *Cooper v. Hutchinson*, 184 F. 2d 119 (C. A. 3, 1950) (allegation that judge arbitrarily denied accused right to choose own counsel in capital case upheld). But in the absence of clear-cut fraud or bad faith the courts have been reluctant to approve the use of Section 43 in cases charging abuse of the judicial process, frequently relying upon doctrines of immunity for judicial, administrative and prosecuting officials. *Viles v. Symes*, 129 F. 2d 828 (C. A. 10, 1942), cert. den. 317 U. S. 633 (1942); *Bottone v. Lindsley*, 170 F. 2d 705 (C. A. 10, 1948), cert. den. 336 U. S. 944 (1949); *Campo v. Niemeyer*, 182 F. 2d 115 (C. A. 7, 1950); *Papagianakis v. S. S. Samos*, 186 F. 2d 257 (C. A. 4, 1950); *Moffett v. Commerce Trust Co.*, 187 F. 2d 242 (C. A. 8, 1951), cert. den. 342 U. S. 818 (1951); see *Gregoire v. Biddle*, *supra*. See also Note, *Liability of Public Officers to Suit Under the Civil Rights Acts*, 46 Col. L. Rev. 614 (1946). Moreover, the courts have tended to exercise discretion to refuse equitable relief where the grant-

**75**

ing of such relief would interrupt the course of judicial proceedings actually in progress. See, *e. g., Cooper v. Hutchinson, supra,* noted in 60 Yale L. J. 720 (1951), where the Court declined to grant equitable relief "at least until it has become apparent that state procedure cannot avert irreparable harm to these appellants." 184 F. 2d at 124. And see *Stefanelli v. Minard,* discussed *infra* in Note following *Collins v. Hardyman.* Apart from this problem the courts would presumably be more favorably disposed to grant an injunction or declaratory judgment than to sustain a suit seeking damages. And note, further, that all the above cases sustaining rights under Section 43 arose on the pleadings; whether sufficient proof could be adduced is another matter.

*Right of franchise: Smith v. Allwright,* 321 U. S. 649, 88 L. Ed. 987, 64 S. Ct. 757 (1944) (refusal to permit Negroes to participate in Federal primary elections held denial of rights under Fifteenth Amendment) ; see also other cases in Chapter III, *infra.*

*Right of free speech and assembly: Hague v. C.I.O.,* 307 U. S. 496, 83 L. Ed. 1423, 59 S. Ct. 954 (1939) (interference by Jersey City officials with efforts of union organizers to hold meetings and conduct other organizational activity enjoined, the Court disagreeing upon whether the right involved was protected by the privileges and immunities or the due process clause of the Fourteenth Amendment); *Oney v. Oklahoma City,* 120 F. 2d 861 (C. A. 10, 1941) ; *Sellers v. Johnson,* 163 F. 2d 877 (C. A. 8, 1947), cert. den. 332 U. S. 851 (1948). But in *Douglas v. City of Jeannette,* 319 U. S. 157, 87 L. Ed. 1324, 63 S. Ct. 877 (1943), the Court, while holding that a suit alleging the invalidity of a city ordinance as infringing freedom of speech was within the jurisdiction of the Federal courts, refused as a matter of equitable discretion to grant an injunction against criminal prosecutions brought under the ordinance. Accord is *Ackerman v. International Longshoremen's & Warehousemen's Union,* 187 F. 2d 860 (C. A. 9, 1951), cert. den. 342 U. S. 859 (1951). See also *Tenney v. Brandhove,* 341 U. S. 367, 95 L. Ed. 1019, 71 S. Ct. 783 (1951) (suit against members of state legislative committee dismissed on grounds of legislative immunity). In *Robeson v. Fanelli* a complaint alleging failure to afford police protection to public meetings in Peekskill, called in part to raise funds for and discuss national issues, was first sustained, 94 F. Supp. 62 (S. D. N. Y., 1950), and then, after the decision in *Collins v. Hardyman, infra,* dismissed (unreported; see N. Y. Times, Jan. 24, 1952).

*Discrimination on account of race or color: Kerr v. Enoch Pratt Free Library,* 149 F. 2d 212 (C. A. 4, 1945), cert. den. 326 U. S. 721 (1945) (exclusion of Negro from library training class at library owned and supported by city but operated by private persons) ; *Morris v. Williams,* 149 F. 2d 703 (C. A. 8, 1945) (discrimination in salaries against Negro teachers) ; *Valle v. Stengel,* 176 F. 2d 697 (C. A. 3, 1949) (refusal of managers of amusement park, aided by police, to admit Negroes to swimming pool held denial of privileges and immunities secured by Article IV and Fourteenth Amendment as well as denial of equal protection); but *cf. Watkins v. Oaklawn Jockey*

*Club,* 183 F. 2d 440 (C. A. 8, 1950). The civil provisions of the Civil Rights Acts have perhaps been most frequently used in this type of situation. See cases in Chapter IX, *infra.*

*Other rights: Bomar v. Keyes,* 162 F. 2d 136 (C. A. 2, 1947), cert. den. 332 U. S. 825 (1947) (complaint against city officials for discharge of teacher who served on jury sustained).

2. The question of what constitutes state action, or action under "color of law," raises the same issues as under Section 242. See the *Kerr, Picking, Valle, Robeson* and *Watkins* cases, *supra.* The issue of vagueness has arisen under Section 43, but has not prevented the courts from finding a valid cause of action stated in the cases set forth above. See especially the *Picking* and *Burt* cases, *supra.* Private persons, who would not be operating under color of law if acting alone, have been brought under Section 43 when cooperating with state officials on the theory that they were conspiring with or aiding and abetting such officials. See the *Picking, Valle, Robeson* and *Watkins* cases, *supra.*

3. Section 47(3), like Section 241 applicable to private individuals engaged in a conspiracy, has been much less frequently invoked than Section 43. In *Love v. Chandler,* 124 F. 2d 785 (C. A. 8, 1942), a suit for damages was brought against Federal and state officials and private persons for conspiracy to prevent plaintiff from obtaining and holding employment under the Works Progress Administration, the complaint alleging that defendants in pursuance of this objective had subjected plaintiff to threats, assaults, insanity proceedings and temporary wrongful deprivation of liberty. The court dismissed the action on the ground that the right to employment under W. P. A. was not a federally guaranteed right. See also *Ferrer v. Fronton Exhibition Co.,* 188 F. 2d 954 (C. A. 5, 1951) (court dismissed suit charging conspiracy to import alien contract labor, contrary to Federal statute, thereby depriving plaintiff of employment); *Schatte v. I. A. T. S. E.,* 182 F. 2d 158 (C. A. 9, 1950), cert. den. 340 U. S. 827 (1950). In *Mitchell v. Greenough,* 100 F. 2d 184 (C. A. 9, 1938), cert. den. 306 U. S. 659 (1939), a suit alleging conspiracy by various officials and private individuals to convict plaintiff of a crime through false testimony, thereby resulting in his disbarment from the practice of law, was dismissed on the ground that the right to practice law in a state was not a Federal right and that no purpose to deprive plaintiff of equal protection was shown. Similar holdings that no denial of equal protection was shown were made in *Allen v. Corsano,* 56 F. Supp. 169 (D. Del., 1944) and *Campo v. Niemeyer, supra.* But *cf. Burt v. City of New York, supra.* See also *Viles v. Symes, supra.* In *Hardyman v. Collins,* 183 F. 2d 308 (C. A. 9, 1950), and *Robeson v. Fanelli, supra,* complaints alleging violent interference with the right of freedom of speech and assembly were originally upheld.

## COLLINS v. HARDYMAN

Supreme Court of the United States, 1951

341 U. S. 651, 95 L. Ed. 1253, 71 S. Ct. 937.

MR. JUSTICE JACKSON delivered the opinion of the Court.

This controversy arises under 8 U. S. C. § 47 (3), which provides civil remedies for certain conspiracies. A motion to dismiss the amended complaint raises the issue of its sufficiency and, of course, requires us to accept its well-pleaded facts as the hypothesis for decision.

Its essential allegations are that plaintiffs are citizens of the United States, residents of California, and members or officers of a voluntary association or political club organized for the purpose of participating in the election of officers of the United States, petitioning the national government for redress of grievances, and engaging in public meetings for the discussion of national public issues. It planned a public meeting for November 14, 1947, on the subject, "The Cominform and the Marshall Plan," at which it was intended to adopt a resolution opposing said Marshall Plan, to be forwarded, by way of a petition for the redress of grievances, to appropriate federal officials.

The conspiracy charged as being within the Act is that defendants, with knowledge of the meeting and its purposes, entered into an agreement to deprive the plaintiffs, "as citizens of the United States, of privileges and immunities as citizens of the United States, of the rights peaceably to assemble for the purpose of discussing and communicating upon national public issues. . . ." And further, "to deprive the plaintiffs as well as the members of the said club as citizens of the United States, of equal privileges and immunities under the laws of the United States. . . ." This is amplified by allegations that defendants knew of many public meetings in the locality, at which resolutions were adopted by groups with whose opinions defendants agreed, and with which defendants did not interfere or conspire to interfere. "With respect to the meeting aforesaid on November 14, 1947, however, the defendants conspired to interfere with said meeting for the reason that the defendants opposed the views of the plaintiffs. . . ."

In the effort to bring the case within the statute, the pleader also alleged that defendants conspired "to go in disguise upon the highways" and that they did in fact go in disguise "consisting of the unlawful and unauthorized wearing of caps of the American Legion." The District Court disposed of this part of the complaint by holding that wearing such headgear did not constitute the disguise or concealment of identity contemplated by the Act. Plaintiffs thereupon abandoned that part of the complaint and do not here rely upon it to support their claims.

The complaint then separately sets out the overt acts of injury and damage relied upon to meet the requirements of the Act. To carry out the conspiracy, it is alleged that defendants proceeded to the meeting place and, by force and threats of force, did assault and intimidate plaintiffs and those present at the meeting and thereby broke up the meeting, thus interfering with the right of the plaintiffs to petition the Government for redress of grievances. Both compensatory and punitive damages are demanded.

It is averred that the cause of action arises under the statute cited and under the Constitution of the United States. But apparently the draftsman was scrupulously cautious not to allege that it arose under the Fourteenth Amendment, or that defendants had conspired to deprive plaintiffs of rights secured by that Amendment, thus seeking to avoid the effect of earlier decisions of this Court in Fourteenth Amendment cases.

The complaint makes no claim that the conspiracy or the overt acts involved any action by state officials, or that defendants even pretended to act under color of state law. It is not shown that defendants had or claimed any protection or immunity from the law of the State, or that they in fact enjoyed such because of any act or omission by state authorities. Indeed, the trial court found that the acts alleged are punishable under the laws of California relating to disturbance of the peace, assault, and trespass, and are also civilly actionable. . . .

This statutory provision [§ 47(3)] has long been dormant. It was introduced into the federal statutes by the Act of April 20, 1871, entitled, "An Act to enforce the Provisions of the Fourteenth Amendment to the Constitution of the United States, and for other Purposes." The Act was among the last of the reconstruction legislation to be based on the "conquered province" theory which prevailed in Congress for a period following the Civil War. This statute, without separability provisions, established the civil liability with which we are here concerned as well as other civil liabilities, together with parallel criminal liabilities.
. . .

The Act, popularly known as the Ku Klux Act, was passed by a partisan vote in a highly inflamed atmosphere. It was preceded by spirited debate which pointed out its grave character and susceptibility to abuse, and its defects were soon realized when its execution brought about a severe reaction.[8]

---

[8] The background of this Act, the nature of the debates which preceded its passage, and the reaction it produced are set forth in Bowers, The Tragic Era, 340–348.

The provision establishing criminal conspiracies in language indistinguishable from that used to describe civil conspiracies came to judgment in *United States v. Harris,* 106 U. S. 629. It was held unconstitutional. This decision was in harmony with that of other important decisions during that period by a Court, every member of which had been appointed by Presidents Lincoln, Grant, Hayes, Garfield or Arthur—all indoctrinated in the cause which produced the Fourteenth Amendment, but convinced that it was not to be used to centralize power so as to upset the federal system.

While we have not been in agreement as to the interpretation and application of some of the post-Civil War legislation, the Court recently unanimously declared, through the Chief Justice:

> "Since the decision of this Court in the *Civil Rights Cases,* 109 U. S. 3 (1883), the principle has become firmly embedded in our constitutional law that the action inhibited by the first section of the Fourteenth Amendment is only such action as may fairly be said to be that of the States. That Amendment erects no shield against merely private conduct, however discriminatory or wrongful. . . ."[12]

It is apparent that, if this complaint meets the requirements of this Act, it raises constitutional problems of the first magnitude that, in the light of history, are not without difficulty. These would include issues as to congressional power under and apart from the Fourteenth Amendment, the reserved power of the States, the content of rights derived from national as distinguished from state citizenship, and the question of separability of the Act in its application to those two classes of rights. The latter question was long ago decided adversely to the plaintiffs. *Baldwin v. Franks,* 120 U. S. 678. Before we embark upon such a constitutional inquiry, it is necessary to satisfy ourselves that the attempt to allege a cause of action within the purview of the statute has been successful.

The section under which this action is brought falls into two divisions. The forepart defines conspiracies that may become the basis of liability, and the latter portion defines overt acts necessary to consummate the conspiracy as an actionable wrong. While a mere unlawful agreement or conspiracy may be made a federal crime, as it was at common law, this statute does not make the mere agreement or understanding for concerted action which constitutes the forbidden conspiracy an actionable wrong unless it matures into some action that inflicts injury. That, we

---

[12] *Shelley v. Kraemer,* 334 U. S. 1, 13.

think, is the significance of the second division of the section.
. . .

In the light of the dictum in *United States v. Cruikshank*, 92
U. S. 542, 552, we assume, without deciding, that the facts pleaded
show that defendants did deprive plaintiffs "of having and exercising" a federal right which, provided the defendants were engaged in a "conspiracy set forth in this section," would bring the
case within the Act.

The "conspiracy" required is differently stated from the required overt act and we think the difference is not accidental but
significant. Its essentials, with emphasis supplied, are that two
or more persons must conspire (1) for the purpose of *depriving*
any person or class of persons of the *equal protection of the laws*,
or of *equal privileges and immunities under the law;* or (2) for
the purpose of preventing or hindering the constituted authorities from giving or securing to all persons the equal protection of
the laws; or (3) to prevent by force, intimidation, or threat, any
citizen entitled to vote from giving his support or advocacy in a
legal manner toward election of an elector for President or a
member of Congress; or (4) to injure any citizen in person or
property on account of such support or advocacy. There is no
claim that any allegation brings this case within the provisions
that we have numbered (2), (3), and (4), so we may eliminate
any consideration of those categories. The complaint is within
the statute only if it alleges a conspiracy of the first described
class. It is apparent that this part of the Act defines conspiracies
of a very limited character. They must, we repeat, be "for the
purpose of *depriving* . . . of the *equal protection of the laws*,
or of *equal privileges and immunities under the laws*". (Italics
supplied.)

Passing the argument, fully developed in the *Civil Rights Cases*,
that an individual or group of individuals not in office cannot
*deprive* anybody of constitutional rights, though they may invade
or violate those rights, it is clear that this statute does not
attempt to reach a conspiracy to deprive one of rights, unless
it is a deprivation of equality, of "equal protection of the law,"
or of "equal privileges and immunities under the laws." That
accords with the purpose of the Act to put the lately freed Negro
on an equal footing before the law with his former master. The
Act apparently deemed that adequate and went no further.

What we have here is not a conspiracy to affect in any way
these plaintiffs' equality of protection by the law, or their equality
of privileges and immunities under the law. There is not the
slightest allegation that defendants were conscious of or trying to
influence the law, or were endeavoring to obstruct or interfere

with it. The only inequality suggested is that the defendants broke up plaintiffs' meeting and did not break up meetings of others with whose sentiments they agreed. To be sure, this is not equal injury, but it is no more a deprivation of "equal protection" or of "equal privileges and immunities" than it would be for one to assault one neighbor without assaulting them all, or to libel some persons without mention of others. Such private discrimination is not inequality before the law unless there is some manipulation of the law or its agencies to give sanction or sanctuary for doing so. Plaintiffs' rights were certainly invaded, disregarded and lawlessly violated, but neither their rights nor their equality of rights under the law have been, or were intended to be, denied or impaired. Their rights *under the laws* and to *protection of the laws* remain untouched and equal to the rights of every other Californian, and may be vindicated in the same way and with the same effect as those of any other citizen who suffers violence at the hands of a mob.

We do not say that no conspiracy by private individuals could be of such magnitude and effect as to work a deprivation of equal protection of the laws, or of equal privileges and immunities under laws. Indeed, the post-Civil War Ku Klux Klan, against which this Act was fashioned, may have, or may reasonably have been thought to have, done so. It is estimated to have had a membership of around 550,000, and thus to have included "nearly the entire adult male white population of the South."[15] It may well be that a conspiracy, so far-flung and embracing such numbers, with a purpose to dominate and set at naught the "carpet-bag" and "scalawag" governments of the day, was able effectively to deprive Negroes of their legal rights and to close all avenues of redress or vindication, in view of the then disparity of position, education and opportunity between them and those who made up the Ku Klux Klan. We do not know. But here nothing of that sort appears. We have a case of a lawless political brawl, precipitated by a handful of white citizens against other white citizens. California courts are open to plaintiffs and its laws offer redress for their injury and vindication for their rights.

We say nothing of the power of Congress to authorize such civil actions as respondents have commenced or otherwise to redress such grievances as they assert. We think that Congress has not, in the narrow class of conspiracies defined by this statute, included the conspiracy charged here. We therefore reach no constitutional questions. The facts alleged fall short of a conspiracy to alter, impair or deny equality of rights under the law, though they do show a lawless invasion of rights for which there are remedies

---

[15] 8 Encyc. Soc. Sci., 606, 607.

[Emerson]

in the law of California. It is not for this Court to compete with Congress or attempt to replace it as the Nation's law-making body.

The judgment of the Court of Appeals is

*Reversed.*

MR. JUSTICE BURTON, with whom MR. JUSTICE BLACK and MR. JUSTICE DOUGLAS concur, dissenting.

I cannot agree that the respondents in their complaint have failed to state a cause of action under R. S. § 1980 (3), 8 U. S. C. § 47 (3).

The right alleged to have been violated is the right to petition the Federal Government for a redress of grievances. The right is equally recognized by the First Amendment and this Court has said that "The very idea of a government, republican in form, implies a right on the part of its citizens to meet peaceably for consultation in respect to public affairs and to petition for a redress of grievances." *United States v. Cruikshank,* 92 U. S. 542, 552, and see *In re Quarles and Butler,* 158 U. S. 532, 535. The source of the right in this case is not the Fourteenth Amendment. The complaint alleges that petitioners "knowingly" did not interfere with the "many public meetings" whose objectives they agreed with, but that they did conspire to break up respondents' meeting because petitioners were opposed to respondents' views, which were expected to be there expressed. Such conduct does not differ materially from the specific conspiracies which the Court recognizes that the statute was intended to reach.

The language of the statute refutes the suggestion that action under color of state law is a necessary ingredient of the cause of action which it recognizes. R. S. § 1980 (3) speaks of "two or more persons in any State or Territory" conspiring. That clause is not limited to state officials. Still more obviously, where the section speaks of persons going "in disguise on the highway . . . for the purpose of depriving . . . any person or class of persons of the equal protection of the laws," it certainly does not limit its reference to actions of that kind by state officials. When Congress, at this period, did intend to limit comparable civil rights legislation to action under color of state law, it said so in unmistakable terms. In fact, R. S. § 1980 (3) originally was § 2 of the Act of April 20, 1871, and § 1 of that same Act said "That any person who, *under color of any law,* statute, ordinance, regulation, custom, or usage of any State, shall subject . . . any person within the jurisdiction of the United States to the deprivation of any rights, privileges, or immunities secured by the Constitution of the United States, shall . . . be liable to the party injured . . . ." (Emphasis added.) 17 Stat. 13.

**83**

Congress certainly has the power to create a federal cause of action in favor of persons injured by private individuals through the abridgment of federally created constitutional rights. It seems to me that Congress has done just this in R. S. § 1980(3). This is not inconsistent with the principle underlying the Fourteenth Amendment. That amendment prohibits the respective states from making laws abridging the privileges or immunities of citizens of the United States or denying to any person within the jurisdiction of a state the equal protection of the laws. Cases holding that those clauses are directed only at state action are not authority for the contention that Congress may not pass laws supporting rights which exist apart from the Fourteenth Amendment.

Accordingly, I would affirm the judgment of the Court of Appeals.

## Note

1. In *Stefanelli v. Minard*, 342 U. S. 117, 96 L. Ed. —, 72 S. Ct. 118 (1951), suit was brought under Section 43 to enjoin the use of certain evidence in a New Jersey criminal prosecution. The evidence was obtained under circumstances that, if Federal officials had been involved, would have been in violation of the provision against unreasonable searches and seizures in the Fourth Amendment. The Court had previously held that the use of such evidence in state prosecutions did not constitute a violation of the Fourteenth Amendment. *Wolf v. Colorado*, 338 U. S. 25, 93 L. Ed. 1782, 69 S. Ct. 1359 (1949), set forth in Chapter II, *infra*. Hence it would appear that no deprivation of a right secured by the Federal Constitution or laws was alleged. The Court did not consider, however, whether the complaint stated a cause of action under Section 43, but held that in any event the Federal courts should exercise discretion to refuse equitable relief to interfere with criminal prosecutions, particularly in state courts. The Court pointed out that a contrary holding would open the Federal courts to interlocutory proceedings involving challenges to numerous aspects of state criminal prosecutions alleged to violate the Fourteenth Amendment. See Chapter II, *infra*. Mr. Justice Frankfurter, writing for the majority, characterized the Federal Civil Rights Acts as "the remaining fragments of a comprehensive enactment, dismembered by partial repeal and invalidity, loosely and blindly drafted in the first instance, and drawing on the whole Constitution itself for its scope and meaning." 342 U. S. at 121. Justices Black and Clark concurred in the result. Mr. Justice Minton did not participate. Mr. Justice Douglas dissented.

2. The civil provisions of the Civil Rights Acts are discussed in Konvitz, *The Constitution and Civil Rights*, ch. 5 (1947); Note, *Federal Power to Prosecute Violence Against Minority Groups*, 57 Yale L. J. 855 (1948); Note, *Freedom to Contract—A New Civil Right*, 59 Yale L. J. 1167 (1950); Note, 3 Stan. L. Rev. 142 (1950).

The Supreme Court's decision in the *Hardyman* case is reviewed in Frantz, *The New Supreme Court Decisions on the Federal Civil Rights Statutes,* 11 Law. Guild Rev. 142 (1951), and in Note, 100 U. Pa. L. Rev. 121 (1951).

With respect to the question of the jurisdiction of Federal courts over civil actions see Notes in 39 Mich. L. Rev. 284 (1940) ; 62 Harv. L. Rev. 659 (1949).

### c. Other Sources of Federal Power

In addition to the constitutional powers considered in the foregoing cases, certain other sources of Federal power to protect the security of the person have been suggested. These include the power of the Federal Government to guarantee to every state a republican form of government (Art. IV, § 4), the treaty power (Art. II, § 2), and the Federal power over the District of Columbia and the territories. See *To Secure These Rights—The Report of the President's Committee on Civil Rights,* pp. 107–112 (1947) ; Carr, *Federal Protection of Civil Rights,* pp. 203–8 (1947) ; Hale, *Unconstitutional Acts as Federal Crimes,* 60 Harv. L. Rev. 65 (1946) ; Note, 40 Col. L. Rev. 902 (1940).

Certain other statutory provisions are also available, including the Hatch Act (18 U. S. C. § 594), prohibiting intimidation against voters in final Federal elections, and Sections 1503 and 1505 of Title 18, U. S. C., prohibiting intimidation of witnesses in Federal judicial or administrative proceedings. See Note, *Federal Power to Prosecute Violence Against Minority Groups,* 57 Yale L. J. 855, 863–4 (1948). See also Marcus, *Civil Rights and the Anti-Trust Laws,* 18 U. Chic. L. Rev. 171 (1951).

In *Bell v. Hood* plaintiffs sued a number of FBI agents for damages alleged to have been suffered as a result of the illegal seizure of plaintiffs' documents and illegal arrest. The suit was not predicated upon any statute providing for damages under such circumstances (Section 43 applying only to persons acting under color of state law) but was based directly upon the claimed violation of the Fourth and Fifth Amendments. After dismissal below for lack of jurisdiction the Supreme Court, holding that the Federal courts had jurisdiction, reversed and remanded. 327 U. S. 678, 90 L. Ed. 939, 66 S. Ct. 773 (1946). In further proceedings in the District Court the complaint was dismissed for failure to state a claim upon which relief could be granted. 71 F. Supp. 813 (S. D. Cal., 1947). See also *Georgia v. Wenger,* 187 F. 2d 285 (C. A. 7, 1951), cert. den. 342 U. S. 822 (1951).

## D. ADMINISTRATION AND ENFORCEMENT

### TO SECURE THESE RIGHTS—THE REPORT OF THE PRESIDENT'S COMMITTEE ON CIVIL RIGHTS

U. S. Government Printing Office, 1947, at pp. 114, 119–25, 129–33.

From the days of the civil rights legislation of the 1860's and 1870's, there remained on the federal statute books scattered provisions of civil rights law. Responsibility for the enforcement of these laws rested with the Department of Justice. From time to time, it took prosecutive action under them but no coordinated program was developed. However, in 1939, to encourage more vigorous use of these laws and to centralize responsibility for their enforcement, Attorney General Frank Murphy established a Civil Rights Section in the Criminal Division of the Department.

This agency has now had eight years of experience. The President's Committee on Civil Rights has regarded an examination of the Sections' organization and achievements as one of its most important assignments. We wish to point out at once that we believe that the Section's record is a remarkable one. In many instances during these eight years, the Section, the FBI and the United States Attorneys in the field have done invaluable work. They deserve the highest praise for the imagination and courage they have often shown. Indeed, we have found that the total achievement of the Department of Justice in the civil rights field during the period of the Section's existence goes well beyond anything that had previously been accomplished. Yet the record is by no means a perfect one, and it seems clear that the time has come to evaluate the experiment, to note criticisms of the program, and to suggest ways of improving it.

As our recommendations will show, one of the most important objectives of this Committee is to strengthen the federal civil rights enforcement machinery. We believe that the achievements of these agencies offer great promise for the future. But only by remedying some of the imperfections in the machinery can this progress be assured. Some of these imperfections will now be discussed. . . .

2. *Insufficient personnel.*—At the present time the Civil Rights Section has a complement of seven lawyers, all stationed in Washington. It depends on the FBI for all investigative work, and on the regional United States Attorneys for prosecution of specific cases. Enforcement of the civil rights statutes is not its only task. It also administers the criminal provisions of the Fair Labor Standards Act, the Safety Appliance Act, the Hatch Act, and certain other statutes. It is responsible for processing most

of the mail received by the federal government which in any way bears on civil rights. Although other resources of the Department of Justice are available to supplement the Civil Rights Section staff, the Section is the only agency in the Department with specialized experience in civil rights work. This small staff is inadequate either for maximum enforcement of existing civil rights statutes, or for enforcement of additional legislation such as that recommended by this Committee.

The Committee has found that relatively few cases have been prosecuted by the Section, and that in part this is the result of its insufficient personnel. The Section simply does not have an adequate staff for the careful, continuing study of civil rights violations, often highly elusive and technically difficult, which occur in many areas of human relations.

On the other hand, there is much misunderstanding about the discrepancy between the very large volume of mail received by the Section and the small number of cases it takes to court. An analysis has shown that approximately 22 percent of the agency's incoming mail contains complaints of civil rights violations and that these complaints number from 1,500 to 2,500 each year. The Civil Rights Section has prosecuted about 178 cases in eight years.[1]

There are a number of possible explanations of the small number of cases prosecuted. In the beginning of its existence, the Civil Rights Section was required to move slowly in order to find cases which would be most useful in delineating the scope of the civil rights statutes. Although the period of legal experimentation is substantially over, the case law developed in this period in certain respects hampers forceful prosecution. In addition, it must be realized that investigation of many "complaints" shows that they do not present a basis for prosecution. With due regard to these points, however, it is our judgment that the number of cases prosecuted merits some criticism.

3. *Adequacy of cooperation by United States Attorneys.*— Whenever a complaint of a civil rights violation appears to merit prosecutive action it must, under the organization of the Department of Justice, be processed through the office of the United

---

[1] [Ed. note]. Tom C. Clark, writing in 1947 when he was Attorney General, gave the following figures on the work of the Civil Rights Section: "Since its establishment in 1939 the Section has received nearly 70,000 complaints, of which about 13,000 may be considered as concerned with invasion of federally secured rights. The vast majority, of course, show no federal jurisdiction on their face. Nearly 850 complaints were investigated; prosecution was instituted in 178 cases; and more than 130 defendants were convicted." Clark, *A Federal Prosecutor Looks At the Civil Rights Statutes*, 47 Col. L. Rev. 175, 181 (1947). See also Carr, *Federal Protection of Civil Rights*, pp. 125, 133 (1947).

States Attorney in the district where the prosecution is to be brought.

The Civil Rights Section frequently seeks the advice of those Attorneys before deciding whether a complaint should be investigated. The opinion of these men will often determine whether the case will be prosecuted. Intelligent and sympathetic cooperation of the United States Attorneys is, therefore, crucial to effective federal enforcement of the civil rights laws. Many United States Attorneys extend such cooperation. However, a staff survey of a random selection of the Section's case files disclosed serious shortcomings in the work of some United States Attorneys.

It should be remembered that these men are local lawyers appointed by the President, subject to confirmation by the Senate, for a term of four years. To them is entrusted the task of initiating proceedings where there has been a civil rights violation, and of prosecuting the actual cases. This often places the United States Attorney in the unenviable position of having to take a public stand in court against the ingrained prejudices and mores of his own community. There have been outstanding examples of United States Attorneys, whatever their personal beliefs, courageously and vigorously assuming this position; there are indications that others have been less willing to set themselves up against local public opinion.

In one case involving interference with the rights of Negroes to vote, the United States Attorney insisted that the evidence developed by the investigation did not make out a case under federal law and recommended that the file be closed. Noting the "clear admissions" of the public officers against whom the charge of interference had been filed, the Civil Rights Section promptly overruled the United States Attorney, who then wrote the Section:

> "Assuming that you will direct prosecution, I wish to suggest that inasmuch as you have a unit set up within the Department for the prosecution of these cases that you assign an attorney for the trial of this case and for drawing the bill of indictment; in other words, take charge of the case with all the assistance our office can give. . . . The reason I am requesting this is because I have a deep conviction that I cannot win it. We have had several of these cases and have not yet had a true bill."

Similarly, in a case in which a local constable had brutally killed a Negro, the local United States Attorney was asked for his views, after an FBI investigation had been made. He expressed grave doubts as to the advisability of proceeding under Section 52.

In the same letter, he expressed his personal belief that Section 52 was unconstitutional, quoting liberally from the arguments of the dissenting justices in the *Screws* case. The Civil Rights Section prosecuted anyway, and obtained a conviction.

In another case involving the killing of a Negro by a deputy sheriff, the Civil Rights Section sought the advice of the United States Attorney on July 30, and referred him to the FBI report of its investigation in the case. On September 13, the Section again asked for the advice of the United States Attorney. On October 10, it repeated its request for the third time. On October 14, the United States Attorney wrote that he had not received the FBI report, but would express his views to the Section as soon as he obained it. On October 17, he advised that he had received the report and he thought the matter should be closed. He gave no reason for his opinion. The Civil Rights Section closed the case, apparently because the Civil Rights Section attorney in charge reported, according to a note in the file, that "X will not go on anything."

These delays are very serious, for they may have a fatal effect upon the prosecution of cases. Public interest in the case dies and it becomes increasingly difficult to persuade a grand jury to indict. Witnesses scatter, evidence grows cold, and a conviction, always difficult to obtain in a civil rights case, may become impossible.

All too frequently, United States Attorneys are allowed to become the final arbiters in the disposition of civil rights cases. The Department of Justice should make more vigorous use of its authority to stimulate, educate, prod, and even overrule United States Attorneys in the handling of cases in this area.

4. *The Civil Rights Section's dependence upon the FBI for its investigative work.*—The FBI handles virtually all of the investigative work in federal civil rights cases. It is unnecessary to comment on the remarkably successful record of the FBI in the general field of law enforcement. In the civil rights field there are many cases where high caliber investigative work has been done by the Bureau. However, there are also indications that upon occasion investigations in this very difficult and highly specialized area have not measured up to the Bureau's high standard in the handling of other types of cases.

There is evidence in the civil rights case files in the Department of Justice that the Bureau has sometimes felt that it was burdensome and difficult to undertake as many specific civil rights investigations as are requested. Moreover, investigations have not always been as full as the needs of the situation would warrant.

**89**

Such shortcomings should be remedied by streamlining the somewhat cumbersome administrative relationships among the Civil Rights Section, the Criminal Division of the Department of Justice, the Office of the Attorney General and the Federal Bureau of Investigation.

The tendency of FBI agents to work in close cooperation with local police officers has sometimes been detrimental to the handling of civil rights investigations. At times, these local officers are themselves under suspicion. Even where this is not so, the victims or witnesses in civil rights cases are apt to be weak and frightened people who are not encouraged to tell their stories freely to federal agents where the latter are working closely with local police officers. In ordinary crime detection work, it is highly desirable for the FBI to cooperate closely with the local police. Having in general established such a wholly sound relationship, it is sometimes difficult for the FBI agent to break this relationship and to work without, or even against, the local police when a civil rights case comes along.

A second difficulty which explains investigative shortcomings in some civil rights cases is the fact that the FBI agent must be trained broadly in law enforcement work and must be active on a wide front in enforcing the great variety of federal criminal statutes which now exist. Accordingly, the agent is not always prepared to cope with the elusive and difficult aspects of a civil rights case. More highly specialized training of agents in this field would overcome some of the occasional shortcomings which are now present in the Bureau's work in cases of this type.

5. *Hostility of local officers and local communities.*—The prejudices of communities where civil rights violations occur often defeat federal law enforcement. Evidence of this is found in the behavior of juries. A recent example was the 1946, Minden, Louisiana, lynching when two Negroes were released from the local jail into the hands of a mob and so unmercifully beaten that one, a veteran, died. Mr. Hoover called it "the best case we have ever made out; we had clear-cut, uncontroverted evidence of the conspiracy." Five of the mob members were indicted by the federal government and promptly acquitted by the jury.

The Minden case was at least partially successful. It survived the grand jury stage and went to trial. In other cases federal grand juries simply refuse to return indictments.

Similar local prejudice thwarts the efforts of the FBI to obtain information from local citizens—even including local law-enforcement officers. Speaking of the problems encountered by the FBI in civil rights cases, Mr. Hoover stated: "We are faced,

90

usually, in these investigations, with what I would call an iron curtain, in practically every one of these cases in the communities in which the investigations have to be conducted. Now we are absolutely powerless, as investigators, unless the citizens of a community come forward with information. In other words, our function is to go out and get the evidence. We have to have sources of information, we have got to be able to go to citizens and have them talk freely and frankly to us, so that we may prepare the case for the prosecuting attorney."

A case in point is the 1946, Monroe, Georgia, lynching. Four Negroes had been killed. Twenty agents were assigned to the case; 2,790 individuals interviewed; and 106 witnesses presented to the grand jury—which failed to return an indictment. . . .

Local prejudice also interferes with the efforts of federal law enforcement officers because of the fear it instills and the silence it inspires in government witnesses. In 1945, an alleged police brutality case was reported to the Civil Rights Section. The affidavit of the complainant, a Negro minister, suggested a clear-cut case. The minister, who was an eye-witness to the incident, had fled from his southern home to Chicago because of threats by both the local police and citizenry. When interviewed by the FBI, he confirmed his allegations, but positively stated that he would not be willing to testify in the community where the offense occurred. The FBI, in the same investigation, met similar evidences of intimidation of Negro witnesses. Some of them flatly refused to sign statements, or, if called as witnesses, to testify in court.

6. *The position of the Civil Rights Section in the Department of Justice.*—The Civil Rights Section's name suggests to many citizens that it is a powerful arm of the government devoting its time and energy to the protection of all our valued civil liberties. This is, of course, incorrect. The Section is only one unit in the Criminal Division of the Department of Justice. As such, it lacks the prestige and authority which may be necessary to deal effectively with other parts of the Department and to secure the kind of cooperation necessary to a thorough-going enforcement of civil rights law. There have been instances where the Section has not asserted itself when United States Attorneys are uncooperative or investigative reports are inadequate. As the organization of the Department now stands, the Section is in a poor position to take a strong stand in such contingencies.

It may easily be a direct result of the Civil Rights Section's subordinate position that the total picture of work derived from the staff survey is that of a sincere, hardworking, but perhaps overcautious agency. Its relative lack of prestige in the Depart-

**91**

ment of Justice, the legal and constitutional difficulties which confront it, the problems caused by its administrative relation to the FBI, the hostility of some United States Attorneys, the force of local prejudice, and the size of its staff all combine to make the Section less effective and less self-assured than the challenge of its assignment demands. . . . .

[The Report then goes on to say that "even where the federal government has failed to win convictions, the mere attempt to invoke criminal penalties in civil rights cases where flagrant wrongs have been committed has often had a sobering influence upon local attitudes and practices."]

The use of civil sanctions to supplement criminal penalties in securing the enforcement of civil rights legislation is desirable. The writ of injunction and the suit for damages have often been used in civil rights cases. But their use has depended upon the initiative of the individual victim, since he has the burden of invoking them. . . . .

The potential use of civil sanctions in civil rights cases is very great. In general, they are of little value in combating intermittent civil rights violations. They obviously could not prevent a lynching. But many violations of rights are of a persistent type; they take the form of long-standing denials of the right to vote, or refusal to give certain persons access to government services or to places of public accommodation. In these cases civil penalties can frequently be effectively invoked. In many instances a civil action will accomplish results when criminal prosecution will not, because a jury which might be reluctant to convict a defendant in a criminal prosecution for a violation of civil rights might not hesitate to afford relief in the form of a civil penalty. However, there is a need to give the government itself greater power to use civil sanctions. . . . .

The Committee does believe that we must show both courage and imagination in devising and using new tools for the enforcement of civil rights policy. It believes that the national government has at its command varied powers and administrative machinery which are capable of being used with great profit in safeguarding civil rights. Experimentation in the use of these powers and this machinery for such a worthwhile purpose is eminently desirable and should be undertaken immediately. . . . .

## Note

1. The President's Committee on Civil Rights made the following recommendations for strengthening enforcement machinery (Report, pp. 151–5):

"1. The reorganization of the Civil Rights Section of the Department of Justice to provide for:

The establishment of regional offices;

A substantial increase in its appropriation and staff to enable it to engage in more extensive research and to act more effectively to prevent civil rights violations;

An increase in investigative action in the absence of complaints;

The greater use of civil sanctions;

Its elevation to the status of a full division in the Department of Justice.

"2. The establishment within the FBI of a special unit of investigators trained in civil rights work.

"3. The establishment by the state governments of law enforcement agencies comparable to the federal Civil Rights Section.

"4. The establishment of a permanent Commission on Civil Rights in the Executive Office of the President, preferably by Act of Congress;

"And the simultaneous creation of a Joint Standing Committee on Civil Rights in Congress.

"5. The establishment by the states of permanent commissions on civil rights to parallel the work of the federal Commission at the state level.

"6. The increased professionalization of state and local police forces."

2. At the end of 1950 the work of the Civil Rights Section was being carried on at the same pace as at the time of the President's Committee report. Henry Putzel, Jr., an attorney in the Civil Rights Section, reports that there were seven attorneys in the Section and the number of cases prosecuted averaged about 20 a year. "Acquittals and convictions seem to be almost equally divided." Putzel, *Federal Civil Rights Enforcement: A Current Appraisal*, 99 U. Pa. L. Rev. 439, 449 (1951).

A fuller discussion of the problems in enforcement of the Civil Rights Acts may be found in Carr, *Federal Protection of Civil Rights*, pp. 121–210 (1947). See also, in addition to the Putzel article, *supra*, Maslow and Robison, *Civil Rights—A Program for the President's Committee*, 7 Law. Guild Rev. 112 (1947); Schwartz, *Federal Criminal Jurisdiction and Prosecutors' Discretion*, 13 Law and Contemp. Prob. 64 (1948); Davie, *Negroes in American Society*, pp. 352–8 (1949); Rebecca West, *Lynching Trials in America*, 17 Medico-Legal Journal 90 (1949).

3. With respect to problems of enforcement in the Reconstruction Period, see Davis, *The Federal Enforcement Acts*, in *Studies in Southern History and Politics*, pp. 205–28 (1914); Cummings and McFarland, *Federal Justice*, pp. 230–49 (1937).

4. On the work of civil liberties organizations prepared to assist in the enforcement process, see *Private Attorneys-General: Group Action in the Fight For Civil Liberties*, 58 Yale L. J. 574 (1949); Robison, *Organizations Promoting Civil Rights and Liberties*, 275 Annals of the Am. Acad. of Pol. and Soc. Sci. 18 (1951).

## E. PROPOSED REVISION OF FEDERAL STATUTES

For a number of years prior to the Report of the President's Committee on Civil Rights efforts had been made to amend and expand Federal legislation in order to afford more adequate Federal protection to security of the person. These attempts were uniformly unsuccessful. See Walter, *Proposals for a Federal Anti-Lynching Law*, 28 Am. Pol. Sci. Rev. 436 (1934); *The Federal Anti-Lynching Bill*, 38 Col. L. Rev. 199 (1938); Konvitz, *The Constitution and Civil Rights*, ch. 4 (1947).

In 1947 the Report of the President's Committee set forth detailed recommendations for further legislation, Report, pp. 156–9. On February 2, 1948 President Truman sent a special message to the Congress urging legislation to carry out these recommendations. 94 Cong. Rec. 927–9. A pledge to enact civil rights legislation was incorporated in the Democratic Party Platform in 1948 and, following the election, Senator McGrath introduced bills embodying the Committee's and the President's proposals.[1] The main elements of this legislative program pertaining to security of the person were incorporated in two bills, of which the significant provisions follow.

### S. 1725

81st Congress
1st Session

### IN THE SENATE OF THE UNITED STATES
April 28 (legislative day, April 11), 1949
Mr. McGrath introduced the following bill; which was read twice and referred to the Committee on the Judiciary

### A BILL

To provide means of securing and protecting the civil rights of persons within the jurisdiction of the United States.

*Be it enacted by the Senate and House of Representatives of the*

---

[1] Meanwhile hearings had been held before Senate and House Committees on various anti-lynching bills in 1948. Hearings before Senate Subcommittee of the Committee on the Judiciary, 80th Cong., 2d Sess., on S. 42, S. 1352 and S. 1465 (1948); Hearings before subcommittee 4 of the House Committee on the Judiciary, 80th Cong., 2d Sess. (1948). The Senate Judiciary Committee reported out a modified anti-lynching bill in June 1948. Sen. Rep't. 1625, 94 Cong. Rec. 8075–6. But no legislation resulted.

*United States of America in Congress assembled,* That this Act, divided into titles and parts according to the following table of contents, may be cited as the "Civil Rights Act of 1949". . . .

SEC. 2. (a) The Congress hereby finds that, despite the continuing progress of our Nation with respect to protection of the rights of individuals, the civil rights of some persons within the jurisdiction of the United States are being denied, abridged, or threatened, and that such infringements upon the American principle of freedom and equality endanger our form of government and are destructive of the basic doctrine of the integrity and dignity of the individual upon which this Nation was founded and which distinguishes it from the totalitarian nations. The Congress recognizes that it is essential to the national security and the general welfare that this gap between principle and practice be closed; and that more adequate protection of the civil rights of individuals must be provided to preserve our American heritage, halt the undermining of our constitutional guaranties, and prevent serious damage to our moral, social, economic, and political life, and to our international relations.

(b) The Congress therefore declares that it is its purpose to strengthen and secure the civil rights of the people of the United States under the Constitution, and that it is the national policy to protect the right of the individual to be free from discrimination based upon race, color, religion, or national origin.

(c) The Congress further declares that the succeeding provisions of this Act are necessary for the following purposes:

(i) To insure the more complete and full enjoyment by all persons of the rights, privileges, and immunities secured and protected by the Constitution of the United States, and to enforce the provisions of the Constitution.

(ii) To safeguard to the several States and Territories of the United States a republican form of government from the lawless conduct of persons threatening to destroy the several systems of public criminal justice and frustrate the functioning thereof through duly constituted officials.

(iii) To promote universal respect for, and observance of, human rights and fundamental freedoms for all, without distinction as to race or religion, in accordance with the undertaking of the United States under the United Nations Charter, and to further the national policy in that regard by securing to all persons under the jurisdiction of the United States effective recognition of certain of the rights and freedoms proclaimed by the General Assembly of the United Nations in the Universal Declaration of Human Rights.

(d) To the end that these policies may be effectively carried out by a positive program of Federal action the provisions of this Act are enacted. . . .

[Title I establishes a Commission on Civil Rights, composed of five members appointed by the President with the consent of the Senate, to gather information concerning civil rights; to appraise the policies, practices, and enforcement program of the Federal Government with respect to civil rights; to appraise the activities of Federal, state and local governments and of private individuals and groups pertaining to civil rights; and to make findings and recommendations with respect to civil rights matters. It also provides for the organization of a Civil Rights Division, under a separate Assistant Attorney General in the Department of Justice, and for an increase in the personnel of the FBI, for the purpose of strengthening enforcement of civil rights legislation. And it creates a Joint Congressional Committee on Civil Rights, with power of subpoena, to maintain a continuing study of matters relating to civil rights.]

## TITLE II—PROVISIONS TO STRENGTHEN PROTECTION OF THE INDIVIDUAL'S RIGHTS TO LIBERTY, SECURITY, CITIZENSHIP AND ITS PRIVILEGES

### PART 1—AMENDMENTS AND SUPPLEMENTS TO EXISTING CIVIL RIGHTS STATUTES

SEC. 201. Title 18, United States Code, section 241, is amended to read as follows:

"SEC. 241. (a) If two or more persons conspire to injure, oppress, threaten, or intimidate any inhabitant of any State, Territory, or District in the free exercise or enjoyment of any right or privilege secured to him by the Constitution or laws of the United States, or because of his having so exercised the same; or if two or more persons go in disguise on the highway, or on the premises of another, with intent to prevent or hinder his free exercise or enjoyment of any right or privilege so secured they shall be fined not more than $5,000 or imprisoned not more than ten years, or both.

"(b) If any person injures, oppresses, threatens, or intimidates any inhabitant of any State, Territory or District in the free exercise or enjoyment of any right or privilege secured to him by the Constitution or laws of the United States, or because of his having so exercised the same; or if any person goes in disguise on the highway, or on the premises of another, with intent to prevent or hinder his free exercise or enjoyment of any right or privilege so secured such person shall be fined not more than $1,000 or imprisoned not more than one year, or both; or shall be fined not more than $10,000 or imprisoned not more than twenty years, or both, if the injury or other wrongful conduct herein shall cause the death or maiming of the person so injured or wronged.

"(c) Any person or persons violating the provisions of subsections (a) and (b) of this section shall be subject to suit by the party injured, or by his estate, in an action at law, suit in equity, or other proper proceeding for damages or preventive or declaratory or other relief. The district courts, concurrently with State and territorial courts, shall have jurisdiction of all proceedings under this subsection without regard to the sum or value of the matter in controversy. . . ."

SEC. 202. Title 18, United States Code, section 242, is amended to read as follows:

"SEC. 242. Whoever, under color of any law, statute, ordinance, regulation, or custom, willfully subjects, or causes to be subjected, any inhabitant of any State, Territory, or District to the deprivation of any rights, privileges, or immunities secured or protected by the Constitution and laws of the United States, or to different punishments, pains, or penalties, on account of such inhabitant being an alien, or by reason of his color, or race, than are prescribed for the punishment of citizens, shall be fined not more than $1,000 or imprisoned not more than one year, or both; or shall be fined not more than $10,000 or imprisoned not more than twenty years, or both, if the deprivation, different punishment or other wrongful conduct herein shall cause the death or maiming of the person so injured or wronged."

SEC. 203. Title 18, United States Code, is amended by adding after section 242 thereof the following new section:

"SEC. 242A. The rights, privileges, and immunities referred to in title 18, United States Code, section 242, shall be deemed to include, but shall not be limited to, the following:

"(1) The right to be immune from exactions of fines, or deprivations of property, without due process of law.

"(2) The right to be immune from punishment for crime or alleged criminal offenses except after a fair trial and upon conviction and sentence pursuant to due process of law.

"(3) The right to be immune from physical violence applied to exact testimony or to compel confession of crime or alleged offenses.

"(4) The right to be free of illegal restraint of the person.

[Emerson]—7

"(5) The right to protection of person and property without discrimination by reason of race, color, religion, or national origin.

"(6) The right to vote as protected by Federal law."

. . .

## S. 1726

[S. 1726, to be known as the "Federal Anti-Lynching Act," sets forth the same purposes as are recited in Section 2(c) of S. 1725 and then continues:]

SEC. 3.   It is hereby declared that the right to be free from lynching is a right of all persons within the jurisdiction of the United States.   Such right is in addition to any similar rights they may have as citizens of any of the several States or as persons within their jurisdiction.

SEC. 4.   Any assemblage of two or more persons which shall, without authority of law (a) commit or attempt to commit violence upon any person or persons or on his or their property because of his or their race, color, religion, or national origin, or (b) exercise or attempt to exercise, by physical violence against person or property, any power of correction or punishment over any person or persons in the custody of any peace officer or suspected of, charged with, or convicted of the commission of any criminal offense, with the purpose or consequence of preventing the apprehension or trial or punishment by law of such person or persons, or of imposing a punishment not authorized by law, shall constitute a lynch mob within the meaning of this Act. Any such violence or attempt by a lynch mob shall constitute lynching within the meaning of this Act.

SEC. 5.   Any person whether or not a member of a lynch mob who willfully instigates, incites, organizes, aids, abets, or commits a lynching by any means whatsoever, and any member of a lynch mob, shall, upon conviction, be fined not more than $1,000, or imprisoned not more than one year, or both; or shall be fined not more than $10,000, or imprisoned not more than twenty years, or both, if the wrongful conduct herein results in death or maiming, or damage to property as amounts to an infamous crime under applicable State or Territorial law.   An infamous crime, for the purposes of this section, shall be deemed one which under applicable State or Territorial law is punishable by imprisonment for more than one year.

SEC. 6.   (a) Whenever a lynching shall occur, any peace officer of a State or any governmental subdivision thereof, who shall have been charged with the duty or shall have possessed the authority as such officer to prevent the acts constituting the lynching, but shall have neglected, refused, or willfully failed

[Emerson]

to make all diligent efforts to prevent the lynching, and any such officer who shall have had custody of the person or persons lynched and shall have neglected, refused, or willfully failed to make all diligent efforts to protect such person or persons from lynching, and any such officer who, in violation of his duty as such officer, shall neglect, refuse, or willfully fail to make all diligent efforts to apprehend or keep in custody the members or any member of the lynching mob, shall be guilty of a felony and, upon conviction, shall be punished by a fine not exceeding $5,000, or by imprisonment not exceeding five years, or both.

(b) Whenever a lynching shall occur in any Territory, possession, District of Columbia, or in any other area in which the United States shall exercise exclusive criminal jurisdiction, any peace officer of the United States or of such Territory, possession, District, or area, who shall have been charged with the duty or shall have possessed the authority as such officer to prevent the acts constituting the lynching, but shall have neglected, refused, or willfully failed to make all diligent efforts to prevent the lynching, and any such officer who shall have had custody of the person or persons lynched and shall have neglected, refused, or willfully failed to make diligent efforts to protect such person or persons from lynching, and any such officer who, in violation of his duty as such officer, shall neglect, refuse, or willfully fail to make all diligent efforts to apprehend or keep in custody the members or any member of the lynching mob, shall be guilty of a felony and, upon conviction, shall be punished by a fine not exceeding $5,000 or by imprisonment not exceeding five years, or both.

SEC. 7.   For the purposes of this Act the term "peace officer" shall include those officers, their deputies and assistants, who perform the functions of police personnel, sheriffs, constables, marshals, jailers, or jail wardens, by whatever nomenclature they are designated.

SEC. 8.   The crime defined in and punishable under the Act of June 22, 1932, as amended (18 U. S. C. 1201, 1202, 10) shall include knowingly transporting, or causing to be transported, in interstate or foreign commerce, any person unlawfully abducted and held because of his race, color, religion or national origin, or for purposes of punishment, correction, or intimidation. . . .

## Note

Similar bills were introduced in the House by Congressman Celler. H. R. 4682 and 4683, 81st Cong., 1st Sess. Hearings were held in June 1949 and January 1950. Hearings before Subcommittee No. 3 of the House Committee on the Judiciary on H. R. 115 et al., 81st

Cong., 1st and 2d Sess. (1950). The Senate Committee on the Judiciary again reported out an anti-lynching bill but no legislation was passed. Comparable bills have been introduced at later sessions. See, *e.g.,* H. R. 28 and 29, 82d Cong., 1st Sess. (1951), S. 1733, 1735, 1737 and 1739, 82d Cong., 1st Sess. (1951).

The constitutional issues raised by this legislation are discussed at length in the hearings. See also *Constitutional Basis for Federal Anti-Lynching Legislation,* 6 Law. Guild Rev. 643 (1946); Ford, *Constitutionality of Proposed Federal Anti-Lynching Legislation,* 34 Va. L. Rev. 944 (1948); and the material cited in Note, 57 Yale L. J. 855, at 870–1 (1948).

## F. BEYOND LEGISLATION

### TO SECURE THESE RIGHTS—THE REPORT OF THE PRESIDENT'S COMMITTEE ON CIVIL RIGHTS

U. S. Government Printing Office, 1947, pp. 133–5

The adoption of specific legislation, the implementation of laws or the development of new administrative policies and procedures cannot alone bring us all the way to full civil rights. The strong arm of government can cope with individual acts of discrimination, injustice and violence. But in one sense, the actual infringements of civil rights by public or private persons are only symptoms. They reflect the imperfections of our social order, and the ignorance and moral weaknesses of some of our people.

There are social and psychological conditions which foster civil rights; there are others which imperil them. In a world forever tottering on the brink of war, civil rights will be precarious at best. In a nation wracked by depression and widespread economic insecurity, the inclination to consider civil rights a luxury will be more easily accepted. We need peace and prosperity for their own sake; we need them to secure our civil rights as well. We must make constructive efforts to create an appropriate national outlook—a climate of public opinion which will outlaw individual abridgements of personal freedom, a climate of opinion as free from prejudice as we can make it.

We do not have sufficient information to know all about the many variations of prejudice. We do know that most prejudice is learned. We know that it may result from actual experience, or propaganda, or both. It may derive from foolish generalizations about groups, from personal frustration, from economic or social competition, or from local environments that are built on discrimination. It ranges from the mild, secret feeling of the social snob to the violent, murderous impulses of the insanely prejudiced. It seems probable that no one can become a bigoted fanatic unless he has need for prejudice towards others to begin with. This may be a need for a feeling of superiority, for a feeling of being strong enough to exclude others from equality. The fear or insecurity which makes someone need prejudice is probably not enough to make a fanatic. There must also be ignorance to sustain the prejudice. Most prejudice cannot survive real understanding of the great variations among people in any one group; or of the scientific findings which establish the equality of groups, and disprove racist nonsense; or of the fact that in a democratic commonwealth, prejudice is an immoral outlaw attitude.

The achievement of full civil rights in law may do as much to end prejudice as the end of prejudice may do to achieve full civil rights. The fewer the opportunities there are to use inequality in the law as a reinforcement of prejudice, the sooner prejudice will vanish. In addition, people must be taught about the evil effects of prejudice. They must be helped to understand why they have developed prejudices. It means trying to show them that it is unfair and stupid to condemn whole groups, that in every group they will find about the same proportion of people whom they will like or dislike; that each man must be judged by himself, on his own merits and faults.

We know from research studies that this can be done. We also know that we are not yet sufficiently skilled to have complete confidence in our educational methods. Since many bigots need their prejudices for reasons of their own, they do not like to give them up. Accordingly, they are very successful at avoiding written or spoken presentations which may disturb their prejudices.

One thing, however, which we can do, is to make certain that all Americans are familiar with the fundamental rights to which they are entitled and which they owe to one another. This is not the case at present. In October, 1946, the National Opinion Research Center at the University of Denver, asked a cross-section of our adult population a series of questions about the Bill of Rights. Only one out of five Americans had a reasonably accurate knowledge of what is in the first 10 Amendments to the Constitution. Completely confused and inaccurate descriptions were offered by 12 per cent. More than a third had heard of the Bill of Rights but could not identify it in any way. Another third had not even heard of it. The NORC also reported that "Even among the best informed people, however—the more privileged, educationally, economically, and occupationally—less than a majority can satisfactorily identify the Bill of Rights." There is no excuse for this kind of ignorance. It represents a dismal failure of our schools, our homes and our media of communication. Where efforts to overcome prejudice directly may boomerang, informing the people of the legally guaranteed rights to which all are entitled, almost certainly cannot. It is at least possible that this kind of information will ease the task of overcoming deep-rooted prejudice.

We are thus extremely sensitive to the general existence of lingering prejudices which must be overcome. It will take time. How much time will depend in a large measure on how quickly and aggressively we inaugurate a program of action under the leadership of the federal government. All of our governments, federal, state, and local, must be uncompromising enemies of discrimination, which is prejudice come to life. In turn, they must be reinforced by education—education through carefully planned experience, to break down the fears of groups; education through information to dispel ignorance about our heritage and our civil rights. There is no need to choose between these approaches. Neither one is adequate for the complete securing of our rights; both are indispensable to it.

## Note

For material from the social sciences which bears upon the basic problem of security of the person, see Dollard, *Frustration and Aggression* (1939); Cantril, *The Psychology of Social Movements* (1941); Fromm, *Escape From Freedom* (1941); Myrdal, *An American Dilemma* (1944); Mayo, *The Social Problems of An Industrial Civilization* (1945); West, *Conscience and Society* (1945); Lewin, *Resolving Social Conflicts* (1948); Bettelheim and Janowitz, *Dynamics of Prejudice* (1950); Lowenthal and Guterman, *Prophets of Deceit* (1949); Arendt, *The Origins of Totalitarianism* (1951).

# CHAPTER II

## FAIRNESS IN GOVERNMENTAL PROCEDURES

The problem considered in this chapter is that of fairness in the procedures by which governmental power is applied against the individual citizen. Mr. Justice Frankfurter has remarked that "the history of American freedom is, in no small measure, the history of procedure."[1] And that procedure, throughout the development of Anglo-American jurisprudence, has been marked by a deliberate effort to establish and maintain a series of safeguards designed to curb the power of the government in its dealings with the individual. The strong feeling that individual freedom demands such protection has its historical roots in the struggle against the arbitrary and excessive power of the English kings and their representatives. It retains its current justification in the fact that an individual citizen increasingly finds himself at a serious disadvantage when confronted by the overwhelming power, prestige and resources of the state. Further, the procedural rights characteristic of Anglo-American law are based upon the principle not only that innocent and guilty alike are necessarily entitled to share the protections but that fairness to the innocent will inevitably result in some of the guilty escaping punishment. On the other side of the scale must, of course, be placed the fundamental interest of the community in being able to protect itself effectively against anti-social conduct.

In its broader aspects the problem encompasses not only fairness in judicial proceedings—criminal and civil—but fairness in executive or administrative proceedings and also in legislative proceedings. The materials in the present chapter, however, will be confined to certain aspects of criminal procedure.

The right to security of the person against abuse of governmental process in the Federal system of criminal law rests upon certain provisions of the United States Constitution. The chief of these are the guarantee of the right to habeas corpus and certain of the provisions of the Bill of Rights:

### ARTICLE I, SECTION 9, CLAUSE 2

The Privilege of the Writ of Habeas Corpus shall not be sus-

---

[1] *Malinski v. N. Y.*, 324 U. S. 401, 414, 89 L. Ed. 1029, 65 S. Ct. 781 (1945).

pended, unless when in Cases of Rebellion or Invasion the Public Safety may require it.

## FOURTH AMENDMENT

The right of the people to be secure in their persons, houses, papers, and effects, against unreasonable searches and seizures, shall not be violated, and no Warrants shall issue, but upon probable cause, supported by Oath or affirmation, and particularly describing the place to be searched, and the persons or things to be seized.

## FIFTH AMENDMENT

No person shall be held to answer for a capital, or otherwise infamous crime, unless on a presentment or indictment of a Grand Jury, except in cases arising in the land or naval forces, or in the Militia, when in actual service in time of War or public danger; nor shall any person be subject for the same offence to be twice put in jeopardy of life or limb, nor shall be compelled in any criminal case to be a witness against himself, nor be deprived of life, liberty, or property, without due process of law; nor shall private property be taken for public use, without just compensation.

## SIXTH AMENDMENT

In all criminal prosecutions, the accused shall enjoy the right to a speedy and public trial, by an impartial jury of the State and district wherein the crime shall have been committed, which district shall have been previously ascertained by law, and to be informed of the nature and cause of the accusation; to be confronted with the witnesses against him; to have compulsory process for obtaining Witnesses in his favor, and to have the Assistance of Counsel for his defence.

## EIGHTH AMENDMENT

Excessive bail shall not be required, nor excessive fines imposed, nor cruel and unusual punishments inflicted.

Identical or similar provisions are incorporated in the constitutions of the States and furnish the basis for protection of individual rights in state and local administration of the criminal law.

In addition to these fundamental constitutional guarantees the safeguards against abuse of the criminal process rest upon numerous statutes and court decisions and, equally important, the actual practices in criminal law administration. These, of course, vary from state to state.

A further issue of major current significance, as in the case of the right to personal security against the acts of private individuals or groups, is the extent to which the Federal Constitution and courts afford protection against unfairness in the procedure of state and local authorities. In the case of *Barron v. Baltimore*, 7 Pet. 243 (1833), as pointed out in the previous chapter, the Bill of Rights in the United States Constitution was held not to operate as a limitation upon the states. Hence the major restrictions embodied in the Federal constitution were those in the provisions forbidding states to enact bills of attainder or ex post facto laws (Art. I, Sec. 10). The adoption of the post Civil War Amendments, particularly the Fourteenth Amendment, opened the door to vastly increased Federal control over state and local procedures. The development began, for practical purposes, with the decision in *Powell v. Alabama* and came to a focus in *Adamson v. California*.

It is not possible within the confines of this book to consider all aspects of fairness in criminal procedures. Emphasis has therefore been placed upon the Federal system and upon the control by the Federal constitution and courts over state and local procedures. Three major issues, which are of particular importance in the field of civil liberties and which illustrate the nature of the problems, have been chosen for development. These are the question of police brutality, the right to counsel, and the law of searches and seizures. Other rights are dealt with only in summary form.

### Note

In general, see Lusky, *Minority Rights and the Public Interest*, 52 Yale L. J. 1 (1942); Fraenkel, *Our Civil Liberties*, pp. 120–84, 235–49, 254–7 (1944); Green, *The Bill of Rights, the Fourteenth Amendment and the Supreme Court*, 46 Mich. L. Rev. 869 (1948); Fraenkel, *The Supreme Court and Civil Liberties* (3d revision, 1949); Fraenkel, *The Supreme Court as Protector of Civil Rights: Criminal Justice*, 275 Annals of the Amer. Acad. of Pol. and Soc. Sci. 86 (1951); Reppy, *Civil Rights in the United States*, ch. VIII (1951); Wood, *Due Process of Law*, ch. III (1951); Sanders, *Criminal Law Administration Prior to Trial: Recent Constitutional Developments*, 4 Vand. L. Rev. 766 (1951); Whalen, *Punishment for Crime: The Supreme Court and the Constitution*, 35 Minn. L. Rev. 109 (1951).

For comprehensive treatments of criminal law and administration, see Dession, *Criminal Law, Administration and Public Order*, ch. V and VI and Part IV (1948); Michael and Wechsler, *Criminal Law and its Administration*, ch. XIV (1940).

## A. POLICE VIOLENCE AND COERCED CONFESSIONS

### 1. The Problem

## NATIONAL COMMISSION ON LAW OBSERVANCE AND ENFORCEMENT—REPORT ON LAWLESSNESS IN LAW ENFORCEMENT

U. S. Government Printing Office, 1931, pp. 152–155.

CONCLUSIONS AS TO THE EXISTENCE OF THE THIRD DEGREE

There are difficulties in forming conclusions as to the prevalence of the third degree. Since the practice is illegal, there are bound to be professional denials of its existence from the police. On the other hand, the assertions of prisoners and their counsel are likely to be biased and exaggerated. The problem is one of police administration and therefore local. Conditions may differ in near-by localities, even in cities in the same State subject to the same laws. Conditions in a given locality may change with a change of administration. (The only thorough-going investigation in any community would be one by persons clothed, as we were not, with the power by subpoena to compel the attendance of witnesses.)

But after making all deductions for the inherent uncertainties of the subject matter, we regard the following propositions as established:

#### I. EXISTENCE

The third degree—the inflicting of pain, physical or mental, to extract confessions or statements—is widespread throughout the country.

#### II. PHYSICAL BRUTALITY

Physical brutality is extensively practiced. The methods are various. They range from beating to harsher forms of torture. The commoner forms are beating with the fists or with some implement, especially the rubber hose, that inflicts pain but is not likely to leave permanent visible scars.

#### III. PROTRACTED QUESTIONING

The method most commonly employed is protracted questioning. By this we mean questioning—at times by relays of questioners—so protracted that the prisoner's energies are spent and his powers of resistance overcome. At times such questioning is the only method used. At times the questioning is accompanied by blows or by throwing continuous straining light upon the face of the suspect. At times the suspect is kept standing for hours,

106

or deprived of food or sleep, or his sleep is periodically interrupted to resume questioning.

### IV. THREATS

Methods of intimidation adjusted to the age or mentality of the victim are frequently used alone or in combination with other practices. The threats are usually of bodily injury. They have gone to the extreme of procuring a confession at the point of a pistol or through fear of a mob.

### V. ILLEGAL DETENTION

Prolonged illegal detention is a common practice. The law requires prompt production of a prisoner before a magistrate. In a large majority of the cities we have investigated this rule is constantly violated.

Through illegal detention, time is obtained for police investigation. Various devices are employed to extend this time, such as taking the prisoner to an outlying station, sometimes to another city, sometimes even to a neighboring State, misleading friends or counsel as to the place of detention and, in the meantime, shifting the prisoner to another place. In one large city the practice of shifting the prisoner from station to station has been so highly developed as to have, in local speech, a name of its own. But the practice is not confined to this city nor to the State in which it lies.

Though illegal detention is frequently a mere expedient to gain time for investigation, it may also be effective in "softening" the prisoner and making him more ready to confess. Especially is this so where, as in more than one city, many prisoners are jammed into the same cell, with the result that the air is vile, the sanitary facilities inadequate, the surroundings filthy and verminous, and sleep or rest next to impossible. Illegal detention is at times definitely used for purposes of compulsion—prisoners are told they will be detained until they confess.

The practice of holding persons *incommunicado*—unable to get in touch with their families, friends or counsel—is frequently encountered, so much so in certain places that there are cells called *"incommunicado* cells."

### VI. BRUTALITY IN MAKING ARRESTS

We have not included as third-degree practices, cases of brutality at the time of making the arrest. A policeman who makes an arrest may have to use force, and force, if necessary to overcome resistance, is justifiable. But the use of force to obtain evidence cannot be justified under existing institutions.

Despite the distinction, there is often a connection—sometimes an intentional connection—between brutality in arrests and the third degree. A man who is beaten when arrested is likely, out of fear of further violence, to be more amenable to police questioning.

### VII. Where the Practice Has Been Found to Exist

In considerably over half of the States, instances of the third degree practice have occurred in the last 10 years. . . .

Fifteen representative cities were visited during the last 12 months by our field investigators. In 10 of them there was no doubt as to the existence of third-degree practices at that time.

The practice is by no means confined to cities. Over one-third of the cases judicially reported since 1920 arose in places of less than 10,000 inhabitants. Other data in our possession confirm the occurrence of this practice in rural communities.

Outside of the reports of a rather mild and sporadic use of the third degree in the enforcement of the narcotic laws, we find little evidence of third-degree practice by Federal officials. (The field of prohibition enforcement, including issues of brutality in connection therewith, lies outside the scope of this section.)

We are without information that would enable us to state whether the practice, taking the country as a whole, is increasing or decreasing. In certain cities, notably Philadelphia and Cincinnati, there has been a marked decrease in recent years. We know of no city in which there has been a definite increase.

When all allowances are made, it remains beyond doubt that the practice is shocking in its character and extent, violative of American traditions and institutions, and not to be tolerated.[1]

## TO SECURE THESE RIGHTS—THE REPORT OF THE PRESIDENT'S COMMITTEE ON CIVIL RIGHTS

U. S. Government Printing Office, 1947, pp. 25–6.

We have reported the failure of some public officials to fulfill their most elementary duty—the protection of persons against mob violence. We must also report more widespread and varied forms of official misconduct. These include violent physical attacks by police officers on members of minority groups, the use of third degree methods to extort confessions, and brutality against prisoners. Civil rights violations of this kind are by no means universal and many law enforcement agencies have gone far in recent years toward stamping out these evils.

In various localities, scattered throughout the country, un-

---

[1] Further details are given on pp. 38–152 of the Report.

professional or undisciplined police, while avoiding brutality, fail to recognize and to safeguard the civil rights of the citizenry. Insensitive to the necessary limits of police authority, untrained officers frequently overstep the bounds of their proper duties. At times this appears in unwarranted arrests, unduly prolonged detention before arraignment, and abuse of the search and seizure power. Cases involving these breaches of civil rights constantly come before the courts. The frequency with which such cases arise is proof that improper police conduct is still widespread, for it must be assumed that there are many instances of the abuse of police power which do not reach the courts. Most of the victims of such abuses are ignorant, friendless persons, unaware of their rights, and without the means of challenging those who have violated those rights.

Where lawless police forces exist, their activities may impair the civil rights of any citizen. In one place the brunt of illegal police activity may fall on suspected vagrants, in another on union organizers, and in another on unpopular racial or religious minorities, such as Negroes, Mexicans, or Jehovah's Witnesses. But wherever unfettered police lawlessness exists, civil rights may be vulnerable to the prejudices of the region or of dominant local groups, and to the caprice of individual policemen. Unpopular, weak, or defenseless groups are most apt to suffer.

Considerable evidence in the files of the Department of Justice supports this assertion.

## Note

In addition to the conclusions of the two official commissions set forth in the above extracts there is substantial evidence from other sources that the use of third degree methods continues to be widespread and serious. News reports frequently recount instances of the practice, as in the following item from NAIRO Reporter for October 1951 (published by the National Association of Intergroup Relations Officials) p. 4:

"Three Negro suspects confessed to a murder in the Sunflower County, Miss., jail late one night last July. The next morning, the man whose 'murder' they had confessed was found to be alive. Sheriff George Marshall said 'some heat probably had been applied' to the suspects to elicit their confession. 'I imagine they probably used a leather strap.' Released, the three 'confessed murderers' showed signs of severe beating; one required medical attention. The sheriff said he planned no action against the officers who had interrogated the suspects."

Further evidence of the practice may be found in the annual reports of the American Civil Liberties Union. See also Note, *The Third Degree*, 43 Harv. L. Rev. 617 (1930); Lavine, *The Third Degree* (1930); Hopkins, *Our Lawless Police* (1931); Myrdal, *An American*

*Dilemma,* pp. 540–3 (1944) ; McCormick, *Some Problems and Developments in the Admissibility of Confessions,* 24 Tex. L. Rev. 239 (1946) ; Barnes and Teeters, *New Horizons in Criminology,* pp. 274–82 (1945). For criticism of the report of the National Commission, see Waite, *Report on Lawlessness in Law Enforcement: Comment,* 30 Mich. L. Rev. 54 (1931).

For a statement concerning the practice from the police point of view see Bruce Smith, *Police Systems in the United States,* p. 11 (rev. ed. 1949) : "While the practice of police forces varies widely, even some of the most scrupulous administrators hold that under special circumstances the use of force, or the threat of force, in securing a confession is justified by the practical exigencies of police work. This in general represents the official attitude of the better police organizations. Untrained and inefficient police bodies employ the third degree with greater frequency, and there are those which rely upon it as an easy short cut to the successful investigation of cases involving familiar criminal characters."

## 2. The Inadmissibility of Involuntary Confessions

The use of third degree methods by police officials would normally constitute a violation of state criminal law. Some states have special statutes directed specifically at third degree practices. See *Report on Lawlessness in Law Enforcement, supra,* at pp. 29–31 and Appendix III. Police officials are, of course, subject to discipline for infringement of law or regulations. And civil remedies in the form of an action for damages are available in all states to individuals who have been the object of unwarranted attacks. In addition, the Federal Civil Rights Acts afford both criminal and civil remedies under certain circumstances in the Federal courts. See Chapter I, *supra.* But it is generally recognized that these methods of combating unlawful police violence are inadequate. Prosecutions are rare, the difficulties of bringing suit and proving a case are enormous, and the whole machinery of law enforcement imposes obstacles to such modes of relief. See Hall, *The Law of Arrest in Relation to Contemporary Social Problems,* 3 U. of Chi. L. Rev. 345, 346–53 (1936) ; Plumb, *Illegal Enforcement of the Law,* 24 Corn. L. Q. 337, 385–9 (1939) ; Note, *Legal Consequences of the Third Degree,* 9 Ohio St. L. J. 514, 519–24 (1948) ; Note, *Judicial Control of Illegal Search and Seizure,* 58 Yale L. J. 144, 146–7 (1948) ; Orfield, *Criminal Procedure from Arrest to Appeal,* pp. 28–31 (1947).

See also *Wolf v. Colorado, infra.* In any event, regardless of possible criminal or civil remedies, police violence has a direct bearing upon the fairness of any subsequent prosecution.

The primary issue to which attention is here directed, therefore, is the effect of third degree methods upon the trial of the accused. The underlying principles of law were stated in the Report on Lawlessness in Law Enforcement.

## NATIONAL COMMISSION ON LAW OBSERVANCE AND ENFORCEMENT—REPORT ON LAWLESSNESS IN LAW ENFORCEMENT

U. S. Government Printing Office, 1931, pp. 24–9.

Apart from its violation of fundamental traditions of personal security until after conviction, the third degree conflicts with two definite legal principles recognized everywhere in the United States—the rule that a man shall not be compelled to furnish evidence against himself, and the rule that confessions obtained by duress are not admissible in evidence.

The first rule, against self-incrimination, is part of the English common law which has been embodied in the United States Constitution and in the constitutions of all the States, except two—Iowa and New Jersey, where it is established by judicial decisions. Many States also recognize this privilege in their statutes.[8]

The history of this rule that a man shall not be compelled to furnish evidence against himself is narrated by Mr. Wigmore.[9] It did not exist under the Tudors and early Stuarts. The Star Chamber statute of 1487 sanctioned the examination of the accused under oath at his trial because "little or nothing may be found by inquiry" of the ordinary sort,[10]—a reason which resembles contemporary apologies for the third degree. The practice of putting the suspect under oath without any formal charge against him was a favorite method in heresy trials in the later Middle Ages and was taken over after the Reformation by the English ecclesiastical courts. In their pursuit of heretics and schismatics, this compulsory questioning tended to degenerate into the process of poking about in the hope of finding something chargeable. For a time the opposition to this compulsory examination centered on points of procedure, such as the necessity of a formal charge against the person interrogated and the limitation of the questions to the scope of this charge. Eventually, the whole process of compulsion came to share the odium which attached to the courts extensively employing it—the Star Chamber and the High Commission. After the abolition of these courts under the Long Parliament it became settled that there was no obligation upon defendants in ecclesiastical courts to

---

[8] 4 Wigmore [2d ed., 1923], sec. 2252, note 3.

[9] Id. sec. 2250. Additional historical material discovered by Mrs. John M. Maguire (Mary Hume) is mentioned in 37 Harv. L. Rev. 520.

[10] Stat. 3 Henry VII, c. 1.

**111**

answer questions on any criminal matters. In the ordinary courts of common law there was at first no similar opposition to the compulsory examination of accused persons, but the hostility arising from the struggle in the ecclesiastical courts soon extended to criminal trials generally, and the assertion was frequently made that no man is bound to incriminate himself on any charge in any court. By the end of the reign of Charles II this claim was usually conceded by the English judges although there were occasional instances of compulsory questioning until after 1700 and the privilege of refusal to answer was not mentioned in the Bill of Rights of 1689. The early colonial settlers brought over the practice of compulsory questioning, at least to Massachusetts. The circumstances of its subsequent disappearance in this country during the 18th century and the adoption here of the contemporary English common law have not been investigated, but many of the thirteen original States insisted on prohibiting self-incrimination in the Federal Bill of Rights of 1791 and in their own revolutionary constitutions.[11]

Thus, this privilege originated in the opposition to compulsory examination in courts, especially courts which were themselves unpopular. In time, the advantage of the privilege of silence was extended from the defendants in criminal cases to witnesses (even in civil suits); and the privilege can now be claimed, not only in ordinary trials in court but also in any other proceedings in which testimony is to be taken, for example, investigations by a grand jury or a legislative committee.

Since the privilege exists during the trial in open court of a person who has been formally charged with crime, it seems even more applicable to the preliminary inquisition of a suspect by police or prosecutors before any judicial proceeding or formal charge. It is true that there is some difference of opinion whether the third degree violates the privilege against self-incrimination; a few courts say that it does not because the questioning does not involve any kind of judicial process for the taking of testimony. This seems a narrow limitation of a constitutional right, and many courts declare that the third degree is forbidden by constitutions as well as by the common-law confession rule.

The consequences of the privilege are numerous. Information obtained in violation of it before trial is not properly admissible in evidence. The judicial authority may not lawfully be exerted to compel a man to testify so as to incriminate himself, and his

---

[11] Moody, J., Twining v. New Jersey, 211 United States 78, 91 (1908), lists the constitutions of North Carolina, Pennsylvania, Virginia (all 1776), Massachusetts (1780), New Hampshire (1784), also Maryland (1776), which was less strict, and says that in the rest of the original States there seems to be no doubt that the privilege was recognized by the courts.

refusal to do so is not punishable as contempt of court. A violation of the privilege may lead to a reversal of a conviction.

The rule excluding involuntary confessions is directed specifically against improper methods of obtaining evidence of guilt from a suspect before trial. It developed quite independently of the privilege against self-incrimination.[16] The use of torture to extract confessions was common in England until the middle of the sixteen hundreds, and the resulting confessions were employed at trials without scruple. The last instance of torture in England was apparently in 1640, but as late as 1664 a defendant said that he was threatened with the rack. In Scotland it survived until 1690 at least; the torture scene in Scott's Old Mortality describes in part an actual case. Even after the cessation of torture there is no indication of any general doctrine limiting the admissibility of confessions which had been procured by milder forms of compulsion until well on in the eighteenth century. By the end of our Revolution the modern rule had been definitely established by the English judges that a confession would be excluded if it was made under the pressure of fear (or of hope of some promised benefit, like a pardon or light sentence, which lies outside this investigation). In 1792 the same doctrine was judicially recognized in this country.[18] It is accepted by all American courts and is embodied in the statutes of several States.[19] . . .

The main reason, at least, given by the courts for excluding a confession made under improper pressure, is the risk that the confession may not have been true—that the accused said what was desired of him, whether true or false, in order to end the suffering or danger which he might otherwise continue to undergo.

Among the forms of compulsion that are everywhere recognized as excluding a confession are force and threats of force. There is more difference of judicial opinion about other forms of pressure—protracted questioning, inflicting severe fatigue, loss of sleep, or other serious discomfort. A few cases cited by Wigmore and supported by him admit confessions so obtained. On the other hand, although interrogations by the police and prosecutors after arrest do not *per se* fall within our definition of the third degree, they are brought within it if accompanied by mental suffering of the types mentioned; and numerous cases exclude confessions thus procured. Thus, in Wan *v.* United

---

[16] For the history see 2 Wigmore, op. cit., supra, sec. 818 ff.; also A. L. Lowell, Judicial Use of Torture, 11 Harv. L. Rev. 220, 290 (1897).

[18] Commonwealth *v.* Dillon, 4 Dall. 116 (Pa. 1792).

[19] These are collected in 2 Wigmore, op. cit., supra, sec. 831, note 2 . . .

States, a case of protracted questioning, Mr. Justice Brandeis said:[23]

> In the Federal courts the requisite of voluntariness is not satisfied by establishing merely that the confession was not induced by a promise or a threat. A confession is voluntary in law if, and only if, it was, in fact, voluntarily made. A confession may have been given voluntarily, although it was made to police officers, while in custody, and in answer to an examination conducted by them. But a confession obtained by compulsion must be excluded, whatever may have been the character of the compulsion and whether the compulsion was applied in a judicial proceeding or otherwise.

On several other aspects of the confession rule the decisions in the various States differ considerably, such as the respective functions of judge and jury in determining the presence or absence of compulsion, the necessity of corroboration, the admissibility of confessions when verified by the discovery of objective facts. But discussion of these points is not necessary here.

The self-incrimination rule and the confession rule do not operate in precisely the same ways and are not coextensive.[24] However, they both forbid testimony obtained by compulsion, and they frequently overlap in their application to the third degree.

### Note

1. For detailed discussion of the state law see Wigmore, *Evidence*, § 851 (3d ed. 1940); McCormick, *Some Problems and Developments in the Admissibility of Confessions*, 24 Tex. L. Rev. 239 (1946). See also Machen, *The Law of Arrest* (1950); Orfield, *Criminal Procedure from Arrest to Appeal* (1947); Note, *Some Proposals for Modernizing the Law of Arrest*, 39 Calif. L. Rev. 96 (1951).

2. Further material on the history of the privilege against self-incrimination may be found in Pittman, *The Colonial and Constitutional History of the Privilege Against Self-Incrimination in America*, 21 Va. L. Rev. 763 (1935); Morgan, *The Privilege Against Self-Incrimination*, 34 Minn. L. Rev. 1 (1949).

See also, on self-incrimination, Section D, *infra*, and Chapter IV, *infra*.

---

[23] 266 U. S. 1, 14 (1924).

[24] Thus the confession rule excludes confessions obtained by promises of a pardon and other benefits, but these would not violate the privilege. Other differences are suggested by 4 Wigmore, op. cit., supra, sec. 2266; 2 Wigmore, op. cit., supra, sec. 823.

[Emerson]

## BROWN v. MISSISSIPPI

Supreme Court of the United States, 1936
297 U. S. 278, 80 L. Ed. 682, 56 S. Ct. 461

MR. CHIEF JUSTICE HUGHES delivered the opinion of the Court.

The question in this case is whether convictions, which rest solely upon confessions shown to have been extorted by officers of the State by brutality and violence, are consistent with the due process of law required by the Fourteenth Amendment of the Constitution of the United States.

Petitioners were indicted for the murder of one Raymond Stewart, whose death occurred on March 30, 1934. They were indicted on April 4, 1934, and were then arraigned and pleaded not guilty. Counsel were appointed by the court to defend them. Trial was begun the next morning and was concluded on the following day, when they were found guilty and sentenced to death.

Aside from the confessions, there was no evidence sufficient to warrant the submission of the case to the jury. After a preliminary inquiry, testimony as to the confessions was received over the objection of defendants' counsel. Defendants then testified that the confessions were false and had been procured by physical torture. The case went to the jury with instructions, upon the request of defendants' counsel, that if the jury had reasonable doubt as to the confessions having resulted from coercion, and that they were not true, they were not to be considered as evidence. On their appeal to the Supreme Court of the State, defendants assigned as error the inadmissibility of the confessions. The judgment was affirmed. 158 So. 339. . . .

[On motion for a new trial the Supreme Court of Mississippi again affirmed. 161 So. 465.]

The opinion of the state court did not set forth the evidence as to the circumstances in which the confessions were procured. That the evidence established that they were procured by coercion was not questioned. The state court said: "After the state closed its case on the merits, the appellants, for the first time, introduced evidence from which it appears that the confessions were not made voluntarily but were coerced." *Id.*, p. 466. There is no dispute as to the facts upon this point and as they are clearly and adequately stated in the dissenting opinion of Judge Griffith (with whom Judge Anderson concurred)—showing both the extreme brutality of the measures to extort the confessions and the participation of the state authorities—we quote this part of his opinion in full, as follows (*Id.*, pp. 470, 471):

"The crime with which these defendants, all ignorant negroes,

**115**

are charged, was discovered about one o'clock p.m. on Friday, March 30, 1934. On that night one Dial, a deputy sheriff, accompanied by others, came to the home of Ellington, one of the defendants, and requested him to accompany them to the house of the deceased, and there a number of white men were gathered, who began to accuse the defendant of the crime. Upon his denial they seized him, and with the participation of the deputy they hanged him by a rope to the limb of a tree, and having let him down, they hung him again, and when he was let down the second time, and he still protested his innocence, he was tied to a tree and whipped, and still declining to accede to the demands that he confess, he was finally released and he returned with some difficulty to his home, suffering intense pain and agony. The record of the testimony shows that the signs of the rope on his neck were plainly visible during the so-called trial. A day or two thereafter the said deputy, accompanied by another, returned to the home of the said defendant and arrested him, and departed with the prisoner towards the jail in an adjoining county, but went by a route which led into the State of Alabama; and while on the way, in that State, the deputy stopped and again severely whipped the defendant, declaring that he would continue the whipping until he confessed, and the defendant then agreed to confess to such a statement as the deputy would dictate, and he did so, after which he was delivered to jail.

"The other two defendants, Ed Brown and Henry Shields, were also arrested and taken to the same jail. On Sunday night, April 1, 1934, the same deputy, accompanied by a number of white men, one of whom was also an officer, and by the jailer, came to the jail, and the two last named defendants were made to strip and they were laid over chairs and their backs were cut to pieces with a leather strap with buckles on it, and they were likewise made by the said deputy definitely to understand that the whipping would be continued unless and until they confessed, and not only confessed, but confessed in every matter of detail as demanded by those present; and in this manner the defendants confessed the crime, and as the whippings progressed and were repeated, they changed or adjusted their confession in all particulars of detail so as to conform to the demands of their torturers. When the confessions had been obtained in the exact form and contents as desired by the mob, they left with the parting admonition and warning that, if the defendants changed their story at any time in any respect from that last stated, the perpetrators of the outrage would administer the same or equally effective treatment.

"Further details of the brutal treatment to which these helpless prisoners were subjected need not be pursued. It is sufficient to say that in pertinent respects the transcript reads more like pages torn from some medieval account, than a record made within the confines of a modern civilization which aspires to an enlightened constitutional government. . . ."

[The confessions actually used in the trial were obtained the following day from the defendants in jail.]

1. The State stresses the statement in *Twining* v. *New Jersey*, 211 U. S. 78, 114, that "exemption from compulsory self-incrimination in the courts of the States is not secured by any part of the Federal Constitution," and the statement in *Snyder* v. *Massachusetts*, 291 U. S. 97, 105, that "the privilege against self-incrimination may be withdrawn and the accused put upon the stand as a witness for the State." But the question of the right of the State to withdraw the privilege against self-incrimination is not here involved. The compulsion to which the quoted statements refer is that of the processes of justice by which the accused may be called as a witness and required to testify. Compulsion by torture to extort a confession is a different matter.

The State is free to regulate the procedure of its courts in accordance with its own conceptions of policy, unless in so doing it "offends some principle of justice so rooted in the traditions and conscience of our people as to be ranked as fundamental." *Snyder* v. *Massachusetts, supra; Rogers* v. *Peck*, 199 U. S. 425, 434. The State may abolish trial by jury. It may dispense with indictment by a grand jury and substitute complaint or information. *Walker* v. *Sauvinet*, 92 U. S. 90; *Hurtado* v. *California*, 110 U. S. 516; *Snyder* v. *Massachusetts, supra.* But the freedom of the State in establishing its policy is the freedom of constitutional government and is limited by the requirement of due process of law. Because a State may dispense with a jury trial, it does not follow that it may substitute trial by ordeal. The rack and torture chamber may not be substituted for the witness stand. The State may not permit an accused to be hurried to conviction under mob domination—where the whole proceeding is but a mask—without supplying corrective process. *Moore* v. *Dempsey*, 261 U. S. 86, 91. The State may not deny to the accused the aid of counsel. *Powell* v. *Alabama*, 287 U. S. 45. Nor may a State, through the action of its officers, contrive a conviction through the pretense of a trial which in truth is "but used as a means of depriving a defendant of liberty through a deliberate deception of court and jury by the presentation of testimony known to be perjured." *Mooney* v. *Holohan*, 294 U. S. 103, 112. And the trial equally is a mere pretense where the state authorities have contrived a conviction resting solely upon confessions obtained by violence. The due process clause requires "that state action, whether through one agency or another, shall be consistent with the fundamental principles of liberty and justice which lie at the base of all our civil and political institutions." *Hebert* v. *Louisiana,* 272 U. S. 312, 316. It would be difficult to conceive of methods more revolting to the sense of justice than those taken to procure the confessions of these petitioners, and the use of the confessions thus obtained as the basis for conviction and sentence was a clear denial of due process.

2. It is in this view that the further contention of the State must be considered. That contention rests upon the failure of counsel for the accused, who had objected to the admissibility of the confessions, to move for their exclusion after they had been introduced and the fact of coercion had been proved. It is a contention which proceeds upon a misconception of the nature of petitioners' complaint. That complaint is not of the commission of mere error, but of a wrong so fundamental that it made the whole proceeding a mere pretense of a trial and rendered the conviction and sentence wholly void. *Moore* v. *Dempsey, supra.* We are not concerned with a mere question of state practice, or whether counsel assigned to petitioners were competent or mistakenly assumed that their first objections were sufficient. In an earlier case the Supreme Court of the State had recognized the duty of the court to supply corrective process where due process of law had been denied. . . .

In the instant case, the trial court was fully advised by the undisputed evidence of the way in which the confessions had been procured. The trial court knew that there was no other evidence upon which conviction and sentence could be based. Yet it proceeded to permit conviction and to pronounce sentence. The conviction and sentence were void for want of the essential elements of due process, and the proceeding thus vitiated could be challenged in any appropriate manner. *Mooney* v. *Holohan, supra.* It was challenged before the Supreme Court of the State by the express invocation of the Fourteenth Amendment. That court entertained the challenge, considered the federal question thus presented, but declined to enforce petitioners' constitutional right. The court thus denied a federal right fully established and specially set up and claimed and the judgment must be

*Reversed.*

## Note

1. In *Chambers v. Florida,* 309 U. S. 227, 84 L. Ed. 716, 60 S. Ct. 472 (1940), the defendants were questioned for a period of five days, concluding with an all night examination under circumstances such "as to fill petitioners [defendants] with terror and frightful misgivings." Reversing convictions for murder Mr. Justice Black concluded:

"We are not impressed by the argument that law enforcement

methods such as those under review are necessary to uphold our laws. The Constitution proscribes such lawless means irrespective of the end. And this argument flouts the basic principle that all people must stand on an equality before the bar of justice in every American court. Today, as in ages past, we are not without tragic proof that the exalted power of some governments to punish manufactured crime dictatorially is the handmaid of tyranny. Under our constitutional system, courts stand against any winds that blow as havens of refuge for those who might otherwise suffer because they are helpless, weak, outnumbered, or because they are non-conforming victims of prejudice and public excitement. Due process of law, preserved for all by our Constitution, commands that no such practice as that disclosed by this record shall send any accused to his death. No higher duty, no more solemn responsibility, rests upon this Court, than that of translating into living law and maintaining this constitutional shield deliberately planned and inscribed for the benefit of every human being subject to our Constitution—of whatever race, creed, or persuasion." 309 U. S. at 240–1.

2. In *Rochin v. California*, 342 U. S. 165, 96 L. Ed. —, 72 S. Ct. 205 (1952), the police entered Rochin's house without a warrant, forced open the door to his bedroom and arrested him. In the process Rochin swallowed two capsules which were lying on the night stand beside the bed. The police thereupon handcuffed Rochin, took him to a hospital and through the use of a stomach pump, forced him to vomit. The capsules thus recovered were found to contain morphine. They were admitted as evidence in Rochin's trial. The Supreme Court reversed the conviction, holding that the methods employed by the police violated the due process clause of the Fourteenth Amendment. Mr. Justice Douglas, concurring, pointed out that most states admit evidence derived from blood tests or other personal examination. Such cases also raise issues of unreasonable search and seizure.

## WATTS v. INDIANA

Supreme Court of the United States, 1949
338 U. S. 49, 93 L. Ed. 1801, 69 S. Ct. 1347

MR. JUSTICE FRANKFURTER announced the judgment of the Court and an opinion in which MR. JUSTICE MURPHY and MR. JUSTICE RUTLEDGE join.

Although the Constitution puts protection against crime predominantly in the keeping of the States, the Fourteenth Amendment severely restricted the States in their administration of criminal justice. Thus, while the State courts have the responsibility for securing the rudimentary requirements of a civilized order, in discharging that responsibility there hangs over them the reviewing power of this Court.[1] Power of such delicacy and

---

[1] Of course this Court does not have the corrective power over State courts that it has over the lower federal courts. See, e. g., *McNabb v. United*

import must, of course, be exercised with the greatest forbearance. When, however, appeal is made to it, there is no escape. And so this Court once again must meet the uncongenial duty of testing the validity of a conviction by a State court for a State crime by what is to be found in the Due Process Clause of the Fourteenth Amendment. This case is here because the Supreme Court of Indiana rejected petitioner's claim that confessions elicited from him were procured under circumstances rendering their admission as evidence against him a denial of due process of law.[2] 226 Ind. 655, 82 N.E.2d 846. The grounds on which our review was sought seemed sufficiently weighty to grant the petition for certiorari. 336 U. S. 917.

On review here of State convictions, all those matters which are usually termed issues of fact are for conclusive determination by the State courts and are not open for reconsideration by this Court. Observance of this restriction in our review of State courts calls for the utmost scruple. But "issue of fact" is a coat of many colors. It does not cover a conclusion drawn from uncontroverted happenings, when that conclusion incorporates standards of conduct or criteria for judgment which in themselves are decisive of constitutional rights. Such standards and criteria, measured against the requirements drawn from constitutional provisions, and their proper applications, are issues for this Court's adjudication. *Hooven & Allison Co.* v. *Evatt,* 324 U. S. 652, 659, and cases cited. Especially in cases arising under the Due Process Clause is it important to distinguish between issues of fact that are here foreclosed and issues which, though cast in the form of determinations of fact, are the very issues to review which this Court sits. See *Norris* v. *Alabama,* 294 U. S. 587, 589–90; *Marsh* v. *Alabama,* 326 U. S. 501, 510.

In the application of so embracing a constitutional concept as "due process," it would be idle to expect at all times unanimity of views. Nevertheless, in all the cases that have come here during the last decade from the courts of the various States in which it was claimed that the admission of coerced confessions vitiated

---

*States,* 318 U. S. 332. In the main, the proper administration of the criminal law of the States rests with the State courts. The nature of the Due Process Clause, however, potentially gives wide range to the reviewing power of this Court over State-court convictions.

[2] In the petitioner's statements there was acknowledgment of the possession of an incriminating gun, the existence of which the police independently established. But a coerced confession is inadmissible under the Due Process Clause even though statements in it may be independently established as true. See *Lisenba* v. *People of State of California,* 314 U. S. 219, 236–237.

convictions for murder,[3] there has been complete agreement that any conflict in testimony as to what actually led to a contested confession is not this Court's concern. Such conflict comes here authoritatively resolved by the State's adjudication. Therefore only those elements of the events and circumstances in which a confession was involved that are unquestioned in the State's version of what happened are relevant to the constitutional issue here. But if force has been applied, this Court does not leave to local determination whether or not the confession was voluntary. There is torture of mind as well as body; the will is as much affected by fear as by force. And there comes a point where this Court should not be ignorant as judges of what we know as men. See Taft, C. J., in the *Child Labor Tax Case*, 259 U. S. 20, 37.

This brings us to the undisputed circumstances which must determine the issue of due process in this case. Thanks to the forthrightness of counsel for Indiana, these circumstances may be briefly stated.

On November 12, 1947, a Wednesday, petitioner was arrested and held as the suspected perpetrator of an alleged criminal assault earlier in the day. Later the same day, in the vicinity of this occurrence, a woman was found dead under conditions suggesting murder in the course of an attempted criminal assault. Suspicion of murder quickly turned towards petitioner and the police began to question him. They took him from the county jail to State Police Headquarters, where he was questioned by officers in relays from about 11:30 that night until sometime between 2:30 and 3 o'clock the following morning. The same procedure of persistent interrogation from about 5:30 in the afternoon until about 3 o'clock the following morning, by a relay of six to eight officers, was pursued on Thursday the 13th, Friday the 14th, Saturday the 15th, Monday the 17th. Sunday was a day of rest from interrogation. About 3 o'clock on Tuesday morning, November 18, the petitioner made an incriminating statement after continuous questioning since 6 o'clock of the

[3] The validity of a conviction because an allegedly coerced confession was used has been called into question in the following cases:

(A) Confession was found to be procured under circumstances violative of the Due Process Clause in *Haley v. Ohio*, 332 U. S. 596; *Malinski v. New York*, 324 U. S. 401; *Ashcraft v. Tennessee*, 322 U. S. 143; *Ward v. Texas*, 316 U. S. 547; *Lomax v. Texas*, 313 U. S. 544; *Vernon v. Alabama*, 313 U. S. 547; *White v. Texas*, 310 U. S. 530; *Canty v. Alabama*, 309 U. S. 629; *White v. Texas*, 309 U. S. 631; *Chambers v. Florida*, 309 U. S. 227; *Brown v. Mississippi*, 297 U. S. 278; and see *Ashcraft v. Tennessee*, 327 U. S. 274.

(B) Confession was found to have been procured under circumstances not violative of the Due Process Clause in *Lyons v. Oklahoma*, 322 U. S. 596, and *Lisenba v. California*, 314 U. S. 219.

preceding evening. The statement did not satisfy the prosecutor who had been called in and he then took petitioner in hand. Petitioner, questioned by an interrogator of twenty years' experience as lawyer, judge and prosecutor, yielded a more incriminating document.

Until his inculpatory statements were secured, the petitioner was a prisoner in the exclusive control of the prosecuting authorities. He was kept for the first two days in solitary confinement in a cell aptly enough called "the hole" in view of its physical conditions as described by the State's witnesses. Apart from the five night sessions, the police intermittently interrogated Watts during the day and on three days drove him around town, hours at a time, with a view to eliciting identifications and other disclosures. Although the law of Indiana required that petitioner be given a prompt preliminary hearing before a magistrate, with all the protection a hearing was intended to give him, the petitioner was not only given no hearing during the entire period of interrogation but was without friendly or professional aid and without advice as to his constitutional rights. Disregard of rudimentary needs of life—opportunities for sleep and a decent allowance of food—are also relevant, not as aggravating elements of petitioner's treatment, but as part of the total situation out of which his confessions came and which stamped their character.

A confession by which life becomes forfeit must be the expression of free choice. A statement to be voluntary of course need not be volunteered. But if it is the product of sustained pressure by the police it does not issue from a free choice. When a suspect speaks because he is overborne, it is immaterial whether he has been subjected to a physical or a mental ordeal. Eventual yielding to questioning under such circumstances is plainly the product of the suction process of interrogation and therefore the reverse of voluntary. We would have to shut our minds to the plain significance of what here transpired to deny that this was a calculated endeavor to secure a confession through the pressure of unrelenting interrogation. The very relentlessness of such interrogation implies that it is better for the prisoner to answer than to persist in the refusal of disclosure which is his constitutional right. To turn the detention of an accused into a process of wrenching from him evidence which could not be extorted in open court with all its safeguards, is so grave an abuse of the power of arrest as to offend the procedural standards of due process.

This is so because it violates the underlying principle in our enforcement of the criminal law. Ours is the accusatorial as opposed to the inquisitorial system. Such has been the characteristic of Anglo-American criminal justice since it freed itself from practices borrowed by the Star Chamber from the Continent whereby an accused was interrogated in secret for hours on end. See Ploscowe, *The Development of Present-Day Criminal Procedures in Europe and America*, 48 Harv. L. Rev. 433, 457–58, 467–473 (1935). Under our system society carries the burden of proving its charge against the accused not out of his own mouth. It must establish its case, not by interrogation of the accused even under judicial safeguards, but by evidence independently secured through skillful investigation. "The law will not suffer a prisoner to be made the deluded instrument of his own conviction." 2 Hawkins, Pleas of the Crown, c. 46, § 34 (8th ed., 1824). The requirement of specific charges, their proof beyond a reasonable doubt, the protection of the accused from confessions extorted through whatever form of police pressures, the right to a prompt hearing before a magistrate, the right to assistance of counsel, to be supplied by government when circumstances make it necessary, the duty to advise an accused of his constitutional rights—these are all characteristics of the accusatorial system and manifestations of its demands. Protracted, systematic and uncontrolled subjection of an accused to interrogation by the police for the purpose of eliciting disclosures or confessions is subversive of the accusatorial system. It is the inquisitorial system without its safeguards. For while under that system the accused is subjected to judicial interrogation, he is protected by the disinterestedness of the judge in the presence of counsel. See Keedy, *The Preliminary Investigation of Crime in France*, 88 U. of Pa. L. Rev., 692, 708–712 (1940).

In holding that the Due Process Clause bars police procedure which violates the basic notions of our accusatorial mode of prosecuting crime and vitiates a conviction based on the fruits of such procedure, we apply the Due Process Clause to its historic function of assuring appropriate procedure before liberty is curtailed or life is taken. We are deeply mindful of the anguishing problems which the incidence of crime presents to the States. But the history of the criminal law proves overwhelmingly that brutal methods of law enforcement are essentially self-defeating, whatever may be their effect in a particular case. See, e. g., Radzinowicz, A History of English Criminal Law and its Administration from 1750, *passim* (1948). Law triumphs when the natural impulses aroused by a shocking crime yield to the safeguards which our civilization has evolved for an administration of criminal justice at once rational and effective.

We have examined petitioner's other contentions and do not sustain them.

*Reversed.*

MR. JUSTICE BLACK concurs in the judgment of the Court on the authority of *Chambers v. Florida,* 309 U. S. 277; *Ashcraft v. Tennessee,* 322 U. S. 143.

On the record before us and in view of the consideration given to the evidence by the state courts and the conclusion reached, THE CHIEF JUSTICE, MR. JUSTICE REED and MR. JUSTICE BURTON believe that the judgment should be affirmed.

MR. JUSTICE DOUGLAS, concurring. . . .

It would be naive to think that this protective custody was less than the inquisition. The man was held until he broke. Then and only then was he arraigned and given the protection which the law provides all accused. Detention without arraignment is a time-honored method for keeping an accused under the exclusive control of the police. They can then operate at their leisure. The accused is wholly at their mercy. He is without the aid of counsel or friends; and he is denied the protection of the magistrate. We should unequivocally condemn the procedure and stand ready to outlaw, as we did in *Malinski v. New York,* 324 U. S. 401, and *Haley v. Ohio,* 332 U. S. 596, any confessions obtained during the period of the unlawful detention. The procedure breeds coerced confessions. It is the root of the evil. It is the procedure without which the inquisition could not flourish in the country.

[In two similar cases, decided the same day, the same justices reached similar conclusions. *Turner* v. *Pennsylvania,* 338 U. S. 62, 93 L. Ed. 1810, 69 Sup. Ct. 1352; *Harris* v. *South Carolina,* 338 U. S. 68, 93 L. Ed. 1815, 69 Sup. Ct. 1354. Mr. Justice Jackson concurred in the *Watts* case but dissented in the *Turner* and *Harris* cases in the following opinion:]

MR. JUSTICE JACKSON concurring in the result in No. 610 and dissenting in Nos. 76 and 107.

These three cases, from widely separated states, present essentially the same problem. Its recurrence suggests that it has roots in some condition fundamental and general to our criminal system.

In each case police were confronted with one or more brutal murders which the authorities were under the highest duty to solve. Each of these murders was unwitnessed, and the only positive knowledge on which a solution could be based was possessed by the killer. In each there was reasonable ground to *suspect* an individual but not enough legal evidence to *charge* him with guilt. In each the police attempted to meet the situation by taking the suspect into custody and interrogating him. This extended over varying periods. In each, confessions were made and received in evidence at the trial. Checked with external evidence, they are inherently believable, and were not shaken as to truth by anything that occurred at the trial. Each confessor was convicted by a jury and state courts affirmed. This Court sets all three convictions aside.

The seriousness of the Court's judgment is that no one suggests that any course held promise of solution of these murders other than to take the suspect into custody for questioning. The alternative was to close the books on the crime and forget it, with the suspect at large. This is a grave choice for a society in which two-thirds of the murders already are closed out as insoluble.

. . .

Amid much that is irrelevant or trivial one serious situation seems to me to stand out in these cases. The suspect neither had nor was advised of his right to get counsel. This presents a real dilemma in a free society. To subject one without counsel to questioning which may and is intended to convict him, is a real peril to individual freedom. To bring in a lawyer means a real peril to solution of the crime because under our adversary system, he deems that his sole duty is to protect his client—guilty or innocent—and that in such a capacity he owes no duty whatever to help society solve its crime problem. Under this conception of criminal procedure, any lawyer worth his salt will tell the suspect in no uncertain terms to make no statement to police under any circumstances.

If the State may arrest on suspicion and interrogate without counsel, there is no denying the fact that it largely negates the benefits of the constitutional guaranty of the right to assistance of counsel. Any lawyer who has ever been called into a case after his client has "told all" and turned any evidence he has over to the Government, knows how helpless he is to protect his client against the facts thus disclosed.

I suppose the view one takes will turn on what one thinks should be the right of an accused person against the State. Is it his right to have the judgment on the facts? Or is it his right to have a judgment based on only such evidence as he cannot conceal from the authorities, who cannot compel him to testify in court and also cannot question him before? Our system comes close to the latter by any interpretation, for the defendant is shielded by such safeguards as no system of law except the Anglo-American concedes to him.

Of course, no confession that has been obtained by any form of physical violence to the person is reliable and hence no conviction should rest upon one obtained in that manner. Such treatment not only breaks the will to conceal or lie, but may even break the will to stand by the truth. Nor is it questioned that the same result can sometimes be achieved by threats, promises, or inducements, which torture the mind but put no scar on the body. If the opinion of MR. JUSTICE FRANKFURTER in the *Watts* case were based solely on the State's admissions as to the treatment of Watts, I should not disagree. But if ultimate quest in a criminal trial is the truth and if the circumstances indicate no violence or threats of it, should society be deprived of the suspect's help in solving a crime merely because he was confined and questioned when uncounseled?

We must not overlook that in these, as in some previous cases, once a confession is obtained it supplies ways of verifying its trustworthiness. In these cases before us the verification is sufficient to leave me in no doubt that the admissions of guilt were genuine and truthful. Such corroboration consists in one case of finding a weapon where the accused has said he hid it, and in others that conditions which could only have been known to one who was implicated correspond with his story. It is possible, but it is rare, that a confession, if repudiated on the trial, standing alone will convict unless there is external proof of its verity.

In all such cases, along with other conditions criticized, the continuity and duration of the questioning is invoked and it is called an "inquiry," "inquest" or "inquisition," depending mainly on the emotional state of the writer. But as in some of the cases here, if interrogation is permissible at all, there are sound reasons for prolonging it—which the opinions here ignore. The suspect at first perhaps makes an effort to exculpate himself by alibis or other statements. These are verified, found false, and he is then confronted with his falsehood. Sometimes (though such cases do not reach us) verification proves them true or credible and the suspect is released. Sometimes, as here, more than one crime is involved. The duration of an interrogation may well depend on the temperament, shrewdness and cunning of the accused and the competence of the examiner. But assuming a right to examine at all, the right must include what is made reasonably necessary by the facts of the particular case.

If the right of interrogation be admitted, then it seems to me that we must leave it to trial judges and juries and state appellate courts to decide individual cases, unless they show some want of proper standards of decision. I find nothing to indicate that any of the courts below in these cases did not have a correct understanding of the Fourteenth Amendment, unless this Court thinks it means absolute prohibition of interrogation while in custody before arraignment.

I suppose no one would doubt that our Constitution and Bill

**126**

of Rights, grounded in revolt against the arbitrary measures of George III and in the philosophy of the French Revolution, represent the maximum restrictions upon the power of organized society over the individual that are compatible with the maintenance of organized society itself. They were so intended and should be so interpreted. It cannot be denied that, even if construed as these provisions traditionally have been, they contain an aggregate of restrictions which seriously limit the power of society to solve such crimes as confront us in these cases. Those restrictions we should not for that reason cast aside, but that is good reason for indulging in no unnecessary expansion of them.

I doubt very much if they require us to hold that the State may not take into custody and question one suspected reasonably of an unwitnessed murder. If it does, the people of this country must discipline themselves to seeing their police stand by helplessly while those suspected of murder prowl about unmolested. Is it a necessary price to pay for the fairness which we know as "due process of law"? And if not a necessary one, should it be demanded by this Court? I do not know the ultimate answer to these questions; but, for the present, I should not increase the handicap on society.

## Note

1. Following the Supreme Court's decision in the *Watts, Turner* and *Harris* cases the Supreme Court of Pennsylvania held admissible the confession of one Johnson, a co-defendant of Turner. Both Turner and Johnson had been arrested at approximately the same time and were interrogated and allegedly beaten while being held incommunicado for at least five days. The Pennsylvania court distinguished the *Turner* case on the facts, primarily on the ground that Johnson had been questioned for fewer hours than Turner. *Pennsylvania v. Johnson,* 365 Pa. 303, 74 Atl. 2d 144 (1950). The Supreme Court, however, reversed per curiam, Justices Reed and Jackson objecting to the summary disposition of the case. *Johnson v. Pennsylvania,* 340 U. S. 881, 95 L. Ed. 640, 71 S. Ct. 191 (1950).

2. In *Gallegos v. Nebraska,* 342 U. S. 55, 96 L. Ed. —, 72 S. Ct. 141 (1951), Gallegos, a Mexican farm hand who could neither speak nor write English, was arrested on September 19, 1949, by Texas police at the request of the Federal immigration service. Gallegos was booked on a charge of vagrancy, although he was working at the time. He was held in the Texas jail for a period of eight days, during which he was questioned intermittently by the Texas police. Part of the time he was kept in an 8' x 8' cell, known as the "dark room", and food was scarce, perhaps not more than a meal a day. According to the police Gallegos was not treated or threatened with violence and the questioning never lasted more than an hour or two on any one day. According to Gallegos he was threatened but not hit. It was not

denied that he was told he might be turned over to Mexican authorities for more severe interrogation. At no time was a formal charge filed against him, nor was he brought before a magistrate.

During this confinement Gallegos was questioned concerning his activities in Nebraska the previous year. At first he concealed his identity but on the third day after arrest he admitted he had been in Nebraska. The following day Gallegos confessed to having murdered his paramour in Nebraska and buried her body. This was the first knowledge by Texas or Nebraska authorities that such a crime had been committed. A statement regarding the crime was prepared in English, read to Gallegos in Spanish, and signed by him.

The Nebraska police were notified and, after checking and finding the body, sent a sheriff to Texas who removed Gallegos to a jail in Nebraska. On October 1 Gallegos signed a second confession prepared in English. There was no claim of mistreatment by the Nebraska authorities. Gallegos was brought before a court for the first time on October 13 where, at a preliminary hearing, he pleaded guilty. After counsel had been assigned by the court Gallegos withdrew his plea. At the trial both confessions and the plea were admitted in evidence. Gallegos was convicted of manslaughter and sentenced to 10 years in prison.

The Supreme Court held that the admission of the confessions and plea did not violate the Fourteenth Amendment. Mr. Justice Reed, joined by Chief Justice Vinson and Justices Burton and Clark, said in the prevailing opinion:

"So far as due process affects admissions before trial of the defendant, the accepted test is their voluntariness. This requires appraisal of the facts of each particular case open to consideration by this Court. In recent cases, where undisputed facts existed far more likely to produce involuntary confessions than those in this case, there was disagreement as to whether due process was violated. The facts here to support a claim of denial of due process are not so convincing. . . .

"We have carefully weighed the circumstances of the petitioner's lack of education and familiarity with our law, his experience and condition in life, his need for advice of counsel as to the law of homicide and the probable effect on such a man of interrogation during confinement. We have also taken into consideration Gallegos' uncontradicted testimony about his accommodations, his limited amounts of food and certain threats made by a Texas assistant sheriff not present at the trial. The uncertain character of this uncontradicted testimony, its lack of definiteness, and the action of the trial judge and jury lead us to place little weight upon it. Our position is confirmed by Gallegos' reiteration of his confession while in custody in Nebraska, when he charges no coercion except detention. See *Lyons v. Oklahoma,* 322 U. S. 596, 603.

"We cannot say that Nebraska has here violated standards of decency or justice in this conviction."

Mr. Justice Minton did not participate in the decision. Justices Jackson and Frankfurter concurred in the decision, saying:

"For three days, Gallegos refused to tell his name. But when he finally revealed his identity, he went on and told all. He may have been of the impression that the authorities who were holding him knew more than they did. Only the fact that he was in custody, the fear that his deeds were known, and the weight of the crime on his conscience can be said to have coerced this confession."

Mr. Justice Black, joined by Mr. Justice Douglas, dissented:

"As is usual in this type of case the deputies say that the confession was wholly 'voluntary'; petitioner says that it was due to fear engendered by his incarceration and the actions of the deputies. Even if the officers' story should happen to be correct, I believe the Constitution forbids the use of confessions obtained by the kind of secret inquisition these deputies conducted.

"There are countries where arbitrary arrests like this, followed by secret imprisonment and systematic questioning until confessions are obtained, are still recognized and permissible legal procedures. See 'The Trap Closes' by Robert A. Vogeler with Leigh White, The Saturday Evening Post, November 3, 1951, p. 36 *et seq.* My own belief is that only by departure from the Constitution as properly interpreted can America tolerate such practices."

3. The usual procedure for deciding whether an allegedly coerced confession should be admitted is for the trial judge to conduct a preliminary examination in the absence of the jury. If the judge finds the confession involuntary he excludes it; if not, all facts are presented again to the jury and the final decision left to it. See Wigmore, *Evidence,* § 861 (3d ed. 1940). With regard to other procedural issues in raising the defense, see *Townsend v. Burke,* 334 U. S. 736, 92 L. Ed. 1690, 68 S. Ct. 1252 (1948); *Taylor v. Alabama,* 335 U. S. 252, 92 L. Ed. 1935, 68 S. Ct. 1415 (1948); Note, 56 Yale L. J. 1076 (1947); 1 A. L. R. 2d 1012.

4. In *Lee v. Mississippi,* 332 U. S. 742, 92 L. Ed. 330, 68 S. Ct. 300 (1948), the Court held that the denial by a defendant that he had made any confession did not preclude him from raising the defense that the confession was coerced. For the effect of a second confession, given after a coerced confession, see *Malinski v. New York,* 324 U. S. 401, 89 L. Ed. 1029, 65 S. Ct. 781 (1945).

5. Of the 1400 to 1500 cases presented to the Supreme Court each term, a substantial number raise the issue of alleged coerced confessions. The Court, however, disposes of all but a few—not more than two or three a term—without passing on the merits. See, *e. g., Agoston v. Pennsylvania,* 364 Pa. 464, 72 Atl.2d 575 (1950) cert. den. 340 U. S. 844, 95 L. Ed. 619, 71 S. Ct. 9 (1950), Justices Black and Douglas dissenting, in which Mr. Justice Frankfurter took occasion to "reiterate our settled rule" that the denial of certiorari "carries no support of the decision in that case, nor of any of the views in the opinion supporting it." See Harper and Rosenthal, *What the Supreme Court Did Not Do in the 1949 Term—An Appraisal of Certiorari,* 99 U. Pa. L. Rev. 293 (1950); Harper and Etherington, *What the Supreme Court Did Not Do During the 1950 Term,* 100 U. Pa. L. Rev. 354, esp. 374–8

(1951); Frank, *The United States Supreme Court: 1950–51*, 19 U. Chi. L. Rev. 165, 201 (1952).

6. With respect to the question whether the Supreme Court decisions in these cases have resulted in a decrease in the use of third degree methods by state and local police, note the statement of one commentator: "Far from stamping out the 'third degree' and its kindred refinements, judicial denunciation has merely tended to drive it underground where it has challenged the ingenuity of those who practice it to continue to do so free of the danger of detection. Instruments which leave tell-tale marks have fallen into disfavor. The rubber hose has taken the place of the whip.

"A defendant from whom a confession has skillfully been extorted is generally without practical remedy. The only witnesses to the coercive practices are those who participated in and encouraged them. The issue, if raised on the trial, is one of credibility between the defendant, an interested witness, whose only salvation lies in nullifying the confession, and officers sworn to uphold the law. The issue is almost universally resolved against the defendant." Bader, *Coerced Confessions and the Due Process Clause*, 15 Brooklyn L. Rev. 51, 70 (1948).

7. Further discussion of the problem of the admissibility of coerced confessions may be found in McCormick, *Some Problems and Developments in the Admissibility of Confessions*, 24 Tex. L. Rev. 239 (1946); Boskey and Pickering, *Federal Restrictions on State Criminal Procedure*, 13 U. Chi. L. Rev. 266, 282–95 (1946); Wood, *Due Process of Law*, pp. 218–37 (1951).

## 3. Confessions Obtained During Illegal Detention

### McNABB v. UNITED STATES

Supreme Court of the United States, 1943
318 U. S. 332, 87 L. Ed. 819, 63 S. Ct. 608

MR. JUSTICE FRANKFURTER delivered the opinion of the Court.
The petitioners are under sentence of imprisonment for forty-five years for the murder of an officer of the Alcohol Tax Unit of the Bureau of Internal Revenue engaged in the performance of his official duties. (18 U. S. C. § 253.) They were convicted of second-degree murder in the District Court for the Eastern District of Tennessee, and on appeal to the Circuit Court of Appeals for the Sixth Circuit the convictions were sustained. 123 F. 2d 848. We brought the case here because the petition for certiorari presented serious questions in the administration of federal criminal justice. 316 U. S. 658. Determination of these questions turns upon the circumstances relating to the admission in evidence of incriminating statements made by the petitioners.

On the afternoon of Wednesday, July 31, 1940, information was received at the Chattanooga office of the Alcoholic Tax Unit that several members of the McNabb family were planning to

[Emerson]

sell that night whiskey on which federal taxes had not been paid. The McNabbs were a clan of Tennessee mountaineers living about twelve miles from Chattanooga in a section known as the McNabb Settlement. Plans were made to apprehend the McNabbs while actually engaged in their illicit enterprise. That evening four revenue agents, accompanied by the Government's informers, drove to the McNabb Settlement. When they approached the rendezvous arranged between the McNabbs and the informers, the officers got out of the car. The informers drove on and met five of the McNabbs, of whom three—the twin brothers Freeman and Raymond, and their cousin Benjamin—are the petitioners here. (The two others, Emuil and Barney McNabb, were acquitted at the direction of the trial court.) The group proceeded to a spot near the family cemetery where the liquor was hidden. While cans containing whiskey were being loaded into the car, one of the informers flashed a prearranged signal to the officers, who thereupon came running. One of these called out, "All right, boys, federal officers!", and the McNabbs took flight.

Instead of pursuing the McNabbs, the officers began to empty the cans. They heard noises coming from the direction of the cemetery, and after a short while a large rock landed at their feet. An officer named Leeper ran into the cemetery. He looked about with his flashlight but discovered no one. Noticing a couple of whiskey cans there, he began to pour out their contents. Shortly afterwards the other officers heard a shot; running into the cemetery they found Leeper on the ground, fatally wounded. A few minutes later—at about ten o'clock—he died without having identified his assailant. A second shot slightly wounded another officer. A search of the cemetery proved futile, and the officers left.

About three or four hours later—between one and two o'clock Thursday morning—federal officers went to the home of Freeman, Raymond, and Emuil McNabb and there placed them under arrest. Freeman and Raymond were twenty-five years old. Both had lived in the Settlement all their lives; neither had gone beyond the fourth grade in school; neither had ever been farther from his home than Jasper, twenty-one miles away. Emuil was twenty-two years old. He, too, had lived in the Settlement all his life, and had not gone beyond the second grade.

Immediately upon arrest, Freeman, Raymond, and Emuil were taken directly to the Federal Building at Chattanooga. They were not brought before a United States commissioner or a judge. Instead, they were placed in a detention room (where there was nothing they could sit or lie down on, except the floor), and kept there for about fourteen hours, from three o'clock Thursday

**131**

morning until five o'clock that afternoon. They were given some sandwiches. They were not permitted to see relatives and friends who attempted to visit them. They had no lawyer. There is no evidence that they requested the assistance of counsel, or that they were told that they were entitled to such assistance.

Barney McNabb, who had been arrested early Thursday morning by the local police, was handed over to the federal authorities about nine or ten o'clock that morning. He was twenty-eight years old; like the other McNabbs he had spent his entire life in the Settlement, had never gone beyond Jasper, and his schooling stopped at the third grade. Barney was placed in a separate room in the Federal Building where he was questioned for a short period. The officers then took him to the scene of the killing, brought him back to the Federal Building, questioned him further for about an hour, and finally removed him to the county jail three blocks away.

In the meantime, direction of the investigation had been assumed by H. B. Taylor, district supervisor of the Alcohol Tax Unit, with headquarters at Louisville, Kentucky. Taylor was the Government's chief witness on the central issue of the admissibility of the statements made by the McNabbs. Arriving in Chattanooga early Thursday morning, he spent the day in study of the case before beginning his interrogation of the prisoners. Freeman, Raymond, and Emuil, who had been taken to the county jail about five o'clock Thursday afternoon, were brought back to the Federal Building early that evening. According to Taylor, his questioning of them began at nine o'clock. Other officers set the hour earlier.

Throughout the questioning, most of which was done by Taylor, at least six officers were present. At no time during its course was a lawyer or any relative or friend of the defendants present. Taylor began by telling "each of them before they were questioned that we were Government officers, what we were investigating, and advised them that they did not have to make a statement, that they need not fear force, and that any statement made by them would be used against them, and that they need not answer any questions asked unless they desired to do so."

The men were questioned singly and together. As described by one of the officers, "They would be brought in, be questioned possibly at various times, some of them half an hour, or maybe an hour, or maybe two hours." Taylor testified that the questioning continued until one o'clock in the morning when the defendants were taken back to the county jail.

The questioning was resumed Friday morning, probably sometime between nine and ten o'clock. "They were brought down from the jail several times, how many I don't know. They were questioned one at a time, as we would finish one he would be sent back and we would try to reconcile the facts they told, connect up the statements they made, and then we would get two of them together. I think at one time we probably had all five together trying to reconcile their statements. . . . When I knew the truth I told the defendants what I knew. I never called them damned liars, but I did say they were lying to me. . . . It would be impossible to tell all the motions I made with my hands during the two days of questioning, however, I didn't threaten anyone. None of the officers were prejudiced towards these defendants nor bitter toward them. We were only trying to find out who killed our fellow officer."

Benjamin McNabb, the third of the petitioners, came to the office of the Alcohol Tax Unit about eight or nine o'clock Friday morning and voluntarily surrendered. Benjamin was twenty years old, had never been arrested before, had lived in the McNabb Settlement all his life, and had not got beyond the fourth grade in school. He told the officers that he had heard that they were looking for him but that he was entirely innocent of any connection with the crime. The officers made him take his clothes off for a few minutes because, so he testified, "they wanted to look at me. This scared me pretty much." He was not taken before a United States Commissioner or a judge. Instead, the officers questioned him for about five or six hours. When finally in the afternoon he was confronted with the statement that the others accused him of having fired both shots, Benjamin said, "If they are going to accuse me of that, I will tell the whole truth; you may get your pencil and paper and write it down." He then confessed that he had fired the first shot, but denied that he had also fired the second.

Because there were "certain discrepancies in their stories, and we were anxious to straighten them out," the defendants were brought to the Federal Building from the jail between nine and ten o'clock Friday night. They were again questioned, sometimes separately, sometimes together. Taylor testified that "We had Freeman McNabb on the night of the second [Friday] for about three and one-half hours. I don't remember the time but I remember him particularly because he certainly was hard to get anything out of. He would admit he lied before, and then tell it all over again. I knew some of the things about the whole truth and it took about three and one-half hours before he would say it was the truth, and I finally got him to tell a story which he said was true and which certainly fit better with the physical facts and circumstances than any other story he had told. It took me three and one-half hours to get a story that was satis-

**133**

factory or that I believed was nearer the truth than when we started."

The questioning of the defendants continued until about two o'clock Saturday morning, when the officers finally "got all the discrepancies straightened out." Benjamin did not change his story that he had fired only the first shot. Freeman and Raymond admitted that they were present when the shooting occurred, but denied Benjamin's charge that they had urged him to shoot. Barney and Emuil, who were acquitted at the direction of the trial court, made no incriminating admissions.

Concededly, the admissions made by Freeman, Raymond and Benjamin constituted the crux of the Government's case against them, and the convictions cannot stand if such evidence be excluded. Accordingly, the question for our decision is whether these incriminating statements, made under the circumstances we have summarized,[5] were properly admitted. Relying upon the guarantees of the Fifth Amendment that no person "shall be compelled in any criminal case to be a witness against himself, nor be deprived of life, liberty, or property, without due process of law," the petitioners contend that the Constitution itself forbade the use of this evidence against them. The Government counters by urging that the Constitution proscribes only "involuntary" confessions, and that judged by appropriate criteria of "voluntariness" the petitioners' admissions were voluntary and hence admissible. . . .

In the view we take of the case, however, it becomes unnecessary to reach the Constitutional issue pressed upon us. For, while the power of this Court to undo convictions in state courts is limited to the enforcement of those "fundamental principles of liberty and justice," *Hebert* v. *Louisiana*, 272 U. S. 312, 316, which are secured by the Fourteenth Amendment, the scope of our reviewing power over convictions brought here from the federal courts is not confined to ascertainment of Constitutional validity. Judicial supervision of the administration of criminal justice in the federal courts implies the duty of establishing and maintaining civilized standards of procedure and evidence. Such standards are not satisfied merely by observance of those minimal historic safeguards for securing trial by reason which are summarized as "due process of law" and below which we reach what is really trial by force. Moreover, review by this Court of state action expressing its notion of what will best further its own security in the administration of criminal justice demands ap-

---

5. . . . we have treated as facts only the testimony offered on behalf of the Government and so much of the petitioners' evidence as is neither contradicted by nor inconsistent with that of the Government.

propriate respect for the deliberative judgment of a state in so basic an exercise of its jurisdiction. Considerations of large policy in making the necessary accommodations in our federal system are wholly irrelevant to the formulation and application of proper standards for the enforcement of the federal criminal law in the federal courts.

The principles governing the admissibility of evidence in federal criminal trials have not been restricted, therefore, to those derived solely from the Constitution. In the exercise of its supervisory authority over the administration of criminal justice in the federal courts, see *Nardone* v. *United States*, 308 U. S. 338, 341–42, this Court has, from the very beginning of its history, formulated rules of evidence to be applied in federal criminal prosecutions. . . . And in formulating such rules of evidence for federal criminal trials the Court has been guided by considerations of justice not limited to the strict canons of evidentiary relevance.

Quite apart from the Constitution, therefore, we are constrained to hold that the evidence elicited from the petitioners in the circumstances disclosed here must be excluded. For in their treatment of the petitioners the arresting officers assumed functions which Congress has explicitly denied them. They subjected the accused to the pressures of a procedure which is wholly incompatible with the vital but very restricted duties of the investigating and arresting officers of the Government and which tends to undermine the integrity of the criminal proceeding. Congress has explicitly commanded that "It shall be the duty of the marshal, his deputy, or other officer, who may arrest a person charged with any crime or offense, to take the defendant before the nearest United States commissioner or the nearest judicial officer having jurisdiction under existing laws for a hearing, commitment, or taking bail for trial . . ." 18 U. S. C. § 595. Similarly, the Act of June 18, 1934, c. 595, 48 Stat. 1008, 5 U. S. C. § 300a, authorizing officers of the Federal Bureau of Investigation to make arrests, requires that "the person arrested shall be immediately taken before a committing officer." Compare also the Act of March 1, 1879, c. 125, 20 Stat. 327, 341, 18 U. S. C. § 593, which provides that when arrests are made of persons in the act of operating an illicit distillery, the arrested persons shall be taken forthwith before some judicial officer residing in the county where the arrests were made, or if none, in the county nearest to the place of arrest. Similar legislation, requiring that arrested persons be promptly taken before a committing authority, appears on the statute books of nearly all the states.

The purpose of this impressively pervasive requirement of

criminal procedure is plain. A democratic society, in which respect for the dignity of all men is central, naturally guards against the misuse of the law enforcement process. Zeal in tracking down crime is not in itself an assurance of soberness of judgment. Disinterestedness in law enforcement does not alone prevent disregard of cherished liberties. Experience has therefore counseled that safeguards must be provided against the dangers of the overzealous as well as the despotic. The awful instruments of the criminal law cannot be entrusted to a single functionary. The complicated process of criminal justice is therefore divided into different parts, responsibility for which is separately vested in the various participants upon whom the criminal law relies for its vindication. Legislation such as this, requiring that the police must with reasonable promptness show legal cause for detaining arrested persons, constitutes an important safeguard— not only in assuring protection for the innocent but also in securing conviction of the guilty by methods that commend themselves to a progressive and self-confident society. For this procedural requirement checks resort to those reprehensible practices known as the "third degree" which, though universally rejected as indefensible, still find their way into use. It aims to avoid all the evil implications of secret interrogation of persons accused of crime. It reflects not a sentimental but a sturdy view of law enforcement. It outlaws easy but self-defeating ways in which brutality is substituted for brains as an instrument of crime detection.[8] A statute carrying such purposes is expressive of a general legislative policy to which courts should not be heedless when appropriate situations call for its application.

The circumstances in which the statements admitted in evidence against the petitioners were secured reveal a plain disregard of the duty enjoined by Congress upon federal law officers. Freeman and Raymond McNabb were arrested in the middle of the night at their home. Instead of being brought before a United States commissioner or a judicial officer, as the law requires, in order to determine the sufficiency of the justification for their detention, they were put in a barren cell and kept there for fourteen hours. For two days they were subjected to unremitting

---

[8] "During the discussions which took place on the Indian Code of Criminal Procedure in 1872 some observations were made on the reasons which occasionally lead native police officers to apply torture to prisoners. An experienced civil officer observed, 'There is a great deal of laziness in it. It is far pleasanter to sit comfortably in the shade rubbing red pepper into a poor devil's eyes than to go about in the sun hunting up evidence.' This was a new view to me, but I have no doubt of its truth." Sir James Fitzjames Stephen, A History of the Criminal Law of England (1883), vol. 1, p. 442 note. Compare §§ 25 and 26 of the Indian Evidence Act (1872),

questioning by numerous officers. Benjamin's confession was secured by detaining him unlawfully and questioning him continuously for five or six hours. The McNabbs had to submit to all this without the aid of friends or the benefit of counsel. The record leaves no room for doubt that the questioning of the petitioners took place while they were in the custody of the arresting officers and before any order of commitment was made. Plainly, a conviction resting on evidence secured through such a flagrant disregard of the procedure which Congress has commanded cannot be allowed to stand without making the courts themselves accomplices in willful disobedience of law. Congress has not explicitly forbidden the use of evidence so procured. But to permit such evidence to be made the basis of a conviction in the federal courts would stultify the policy which Congress has enacted into law.

Unlike England, where the Judges of the King's Bench have prescribed rules for the interrogation of prisoners while in the custody of police officers, we have no specific provisions of law governing federal law enforcement officers in procuring evidence from persons held in custody. But the absence of specific restraints going beyond the legislation to which we have referred does not imply that the circumstances under which evidence was secured are irrelevant in ascertaining its admissibility. The mere fact that a confession was made while in the custody of the police does not render it inadmissible. Compare *Hopt* v. *Utah*, 110 U. S. 574; *Sparf* v. *United States*, 156 U. S. 51, 55; *United States ex rel. Bilokumsky* v. *Tod*, 263 U. S. 149, 157; *Wan* v. *United States*, 266 U. S. 1, 14. But where in the course of a criminal trial in the federal courts it appears that evidence has been obtained in such violation of legal rights as this case discloses, it is the duty of the trial court to entertain a motion for the exclusion of such evidence and to hold a hearing, as was done here, to determine whether such motion should be granted or denied. Cf. *Gouled* v. *United States*, 255 U. S. 298, 312–13; *Amos* v. *United States*, 255 U. S. 313; *Nardone* v. *United States*, 308 U. S. 338, 341–42. The interruption of the trial for this purpose should be no longer than is required for a competent determination of the substantiality of the motion. . . .

In holding that the petitioners' admissions were improperly received in evidence against them, and that having been based on this evidence their convictions cannot stand, we confine ourselves to our limited function as the court of ultimate review of the standards formulated and applied by federal courts in the trial of criminal cases. We are not concerned with law enforcement practices except in so far as courts themselves become instruments of law enforcement. We hold only that a decent regard for the duty of courts as agencies of justice and custodians of liberty forbids that men should be convicted upon evidence secured under the circumstances revealed here. In so doing, we respect the policy which underlies Congressional legislation. The history of liberty has largely been the history of observance of procedural safeguards. And the effective administration of criminal justice hardly requires disregard of fair procedures imposed by law.

*Reversed.*

MR. JUSTICE RUTLEDGE took no part in the consideration or decision of this case.

MR. JUSTICE REED, dissenting:

I find myself unable to agree with the opinion of the Court in this case. An officer of the United States was killed while in the performance of his duties. From the circumstances detailed in the Court's opinion, there was obvious reason to suspect that the petitioners here were implicated in firing the fatal shot from the dark. The arrests followed. As the guilty parties were known only to the McNabbs who took part in the assault at the burying ground, it was natural and proper that the officers would question them as to their actions.

. . . statements made while under interrogation may be used at a trial if it may fairly be said that the information was given voluntarily. A frank and free confession of crime by the culprit affords testimony of the highest credibility and of a character which may be verified easily. Equally frank responses to officers by innocent people arrested under misapprehension give the best basis for prompt discharge from custody. The realization of the convincing quality of a confession tempts officials to press suspects unduly for such statements. To guard accused persons against the danger of being forced to confess, the law admits confessions of guilt only when they are voluntarily made. While the connotation of voluntary is indefinite, it affords an understandable label under which can be readily classified the various acts of terrorism, promises, trickery and threats which have led this and other courts to refuse admission as evidence to confessions. The cases cited in the Court's opinion show the broad coverage of this rule of law. Through it those coerced into confession have found a ready defense from injustice.

Were the Court today saying merely that in its judgment the confessions of the McNabbs were not voluntary, there would be no occasion for this single protest. A notation of dissent would suffice. The opinion, however, does more. Involuntary confessions are not constitutionally admissible because violative of the provision of self-incrimination in the Bill of Rights. Now the Court leaves undecided whether the present confessions are voluntary or involuntary and declares that the confessions must be excluded because in addition to questioning the petitioners, the arresting officers failed promptly to take them before a committing magistrate. The Court finds a basis for the declaration of this new rule of evidence in its supervisory authority over the administration of criminal justice. I question whether this offers to the trial courts and the peace officers a rule of admissibility as clear as the test of the voluntary character of the confession. I am opposed to broadening the possibilities of defendants escaping punishment by these more rigorous technical requirements in the administration of justice. If these confessions are otherwise voluntary, civilized standards, in my opinion, are not advanced by setting aside these judgments because of acts of omission which are not shown to have tended toward coercing the admissions.

Our police officers occasionally overstep legal bounds. This record does not show when the petitioners were taken before a committing magistrate. No point was made of the failure to commit by defendant or counsel. No opportunity was given to the officers to explain. Objection to the introduction of the confessions was made only on the ground that they were obtained through coercion. This was determined against the accused both by the court, when it appraised the fact as to the voluntary character of the confessions preliminarily to determining the legal question of their admissibility, and by the jury. The court saw and heard witnesses for the prosecution and the defense. The defendants did not take the stand before the jury. The uncontradicted evidence does not require a different conclusion. The officers of the Alcohol Tax Unit should not be disciplined by overturning this conviction.[1]

## Note

1. In a similar case, decided the same day, the Court also held the confessions inadmissible. *Anderson v. United States*, 318 U. S. 350, 87 L. Ed. 829, 63 S. Ct. 599 (1943). The cases were widely noted in the law reviews. See, *e.g.*, 56 Harv. L. Rev. 1008 (1943); 42 Mich. L. Rev. 679, 909 (1944); 28 Minn. L. Rev. 73 (1943); 22 Tex. L. Rev. 473 (1944); 1945 Wis. L. Rev. 105; 53 Yale L. J. 758 (1944).

---

[1] On retrial the McNabbs were convicted of voluntary manslaughter. The court found that they had been arraigned on a different charge and held there was "no substantial evidence that the confessions were elicited by means of illegal procedure." 142 F. 2d 904, 907 (C. A. 6, 1944), cert. den. 323 U. S. 771 (1944).

2. The *McNabb* decision met with considerable opposition from police and prosecuting officials, from some commentators, and even from the lower Federal courts. See *Upshaw v. United States, infra.* A bill was introduced in the House of Representatives to nullify the decision and, in a somewhat modified form, passed the House. The Senate, however, took no action. For an account of the reception accorded the *McNabb* decision see Dession, *The New Federal Rules of Criminal Procedure,* 55 Yale L. J. 694, 706–14 (1946).

3. In *United States v. Mitchell,* 322 U. S. 65, 88 L. Ed. 1140, 64 S. Ct. 896 (1944), the defendant was arrested on a charge of housebreaking at 7 o'clock in the evening, taken to the police station and, within a few minutes, admitted his guilt. Thereafter he was held by the police for 8 days without arraignment, during which time he assisted the police in clearing up thirty housebreakings in which he had participated. The Court, in an opinion by Mr. Justice Frankfurter, distinguished the *McNabb* case and upheld the conviction:

"Here there was no disclosure induced by illegal detention, no evidence was obtained in violation of any legal rights, but instead the consent to a search of his home, the prompt acknowledgment by an accused of his guilt, and the subsequent rueing apparently of such spontaneous cooperation and concession of guilt." 322 U. S. at 70.

Justices Douglas and Rutledge concurred without opinion; Mr. Justice Reed concurred in a separate opinion; and Mr. Justice Black dissented without opinion.

4. The Federal Rules of Criminal Procedure, which became effective March 21, 1946, do not deal specifically with the admissibility issue but provide with respect to detention:

"5(a) Appearance before the Commissioner. An officer making an arrest under a warrant issued upon a complaint or any person making an arrest without a warrant shall take the arrested person without unnecessary delay before the nearest available commissioner or before any other nearby officer empowered to commit persons charged with offenses against the laws of the United States. When a person arrested without a warrant is brought before a commissioner or other officer, a complaint shall be filed forthwith." 18 U. S. C.

Subdivision (b) of Rule 5 provides that the commissioner shall inform the accused of the complaint against him, of his right to counsel, and of his right to have a preliminary examination. The accused is also to be advised that he is not required to make a statement and that any statement made by him may be used in evidence. The commissioner may also set bail.

## UPSHAW v. UNITED STATES

Supreme Court of the United States, 1948
335 U. S. 410, 93 L. Ed. 100, 69 S. Ct. 170

MR. JUSTICE BLACK delivered the opinion of the Court.

The petitioner was convicted of grand larceny in the United States District Court for the District of Columbia and sentenced to serve sixteen months to four years in prison. Pre-trial confessions of guilt without which petitioner could not have been convicted were admitted in evidence against his objection that they had been illegally obtained. The confessions had been made during a 30-hour period while petitioner was held a prisoner after the police had arrested him on suspicion and without a warrant.

Petitioner's objection to the admissibility of the confessions rested on Rule 5(a) of the Federal Rules of Criminal Procedure and our holding in *McNabb v. United States,* 318 U. S. 332. . . . Petitioner contended that the officers had violated this rule in detaining him as they did without taking him before a committing magistrate. In the *McNabb* case we held that confessions had been improperly admitted where they were the plain result of holding and interrogating persons without carrying them "forthwith" before a committing magistrate as the law commands. . . .

We hold that this case falls squarely within the *McNabb* ruling and is not taken out of it by what was decided in the *Mitchell* case. In the *McNabb* case we held that the plain purpose of the requirement that prisoners should promptly be taken before committing magistrates was to check resort by officers to "secret interrogation of persons accused of crime." We then pointed out the circumstances under which petitioners were interrogated and confessed. This was done to show that the record left no doubt that the McNabbs were not promptly taken before a judicial officer as the law required, but instead were held for secret questioning, and "that the questioning of petitioners took place while they were in the custody of the arresting officers and before any order of commitment was made." The McNabb confessions were thus held inadmissible because the McNabbs were questioned while held in "plain disregard of the duty enjoined by Congress upon Federal officers" promptly to take them before a judicial officer. In the *McNabb* case there were confessions "induced by illegal detention," *United States v. Mitchell, supra,* at 70, a fact which this Court found did not exist in the *Mitchell* case.

In the *Mitchell* case although the defendant was illegally held eight days, the court accepted the record as showing that Mitchell promptly and spontaneously admitted his guilt within a few

**141**

minutes after his arrival at the police station. Mitchell's confessions therefore were found to have been made before any illegal detention had occurred. . . . The *Mitchell* case at page 68, however, reaffirms the *McNabb* rule that a confession is inadmissible if made during illegal detention due to failure promptly to carry a prisoner before a committing magistrate, whether or not the "confession is the result of torture, physical or psychological . . . ."

In this case we are left in no doubt as to why this petitioner was not brought promptly before a committing magistrate. The arresting officer himself stated that petitioner was not carried before a magistrate on Friday or Saturday morning after his arrest on Friday at 2 a. m., because the officer thought there was not "a sufficient case" for the court to hold him, adding that even "if the police court did hold him we would lose custody of him and I no longer would be able to question him." Thus the arresting officer in effect conceded that the confessions here were "the fruits of wrongdoing" by the police officers. He conceded more: He admitted that petitioner was illegally detained for at least thirty hours for the very purpose of securing these challenged confessions. He thereby refutes any possibility of an argument that after arrest he was carried before a magistrate "without unnecessary delay."

The argument was made to the trial court that this method of arresting, holding, and questioning people on mere suspicion, was in accordance with the "usual police procedure of questioning a suspect . . . ." However usual this practice, it is in violation of law, and confessions thus obtained are inadmissible under the *McNabb* rule. We adhere to that rule.

*Reversed.*

MR. JUSTICE REED, with whom THE CHIEF JUSTICE, MR. JUSTICE JACKSON and MR. JUSTICE BURTON join, dissenting. . . .

My objection to this Court's action of today in what seems to me an extension of the scope of nonadmissibility of confessions in the federal courts is not to its power so to act but to the advisibility of such an additional step. . . .

The judicial approach to the problem, of course, must be in a spirit of cooperation with the police officials in the administration of justice. They are directly charged with the responsibility for the maintenance of law and order and are under the same obligation as the judicial arm to discharge their duties in a manner consistent with the Constitution and statutes. The prevention and punishment of crime is a difficult and dangerous task, for the most part performed by security and prosecuting personnel in a spirit of public service to the community. Only by the maintenance of order may the rights of the criminal and the law abiding elements of the population be protected. . . .

During detention in violation of the federal commitment statute is the likelihood that police officials will use coercion for the extraction of an involuntary confession so strong as to justify the exclusion by this Court of all confessions to the police obtained after their failure to conform to the requirement of prompt production of the accused before a magistrate? I think not. It must be admitted that a prompt hearing gives an accused an opportunity to obtain a lawyer; to secure from him advice as to maintaining an absolute silence to all questions, no matter how apparently innocuous; to gain complete freedom from police interrogation in all bailable offenses; and that these privileges are more valuable to the illiterate and inexperienced than to the educated and well-briefed accused. Proper protection of the ignorant is of course desirable, but the rule now announced forces exclusion of all confessions given during illegal restraint. It will shift the inquiry to the legality of the arrest and restraint, rather than to whether the confession was voluntary. Such exclusion becomes automatic on proof of detention in violation of the commitment statute, followed by a confession to police officials before commitment. It is now made analogous to the exclusion of evidence obtained in violation of the Bill of Rights through unreasonable search and seizure or through compulsion or by denial of due process. I do not think this is the doctrine of the *McNabb* case or that it should now be made an explicit rule of federal law. . . .

This brings me to a statement of the true rule of the *McNabb* case, as I understand it. This rule is that purposeful, unlawful detention illegally to extract evidence and the successful extraction of confessions under psychological pressure, other than mere detention for limited periods, makes confessions so obtained inadmissible. . . . It means that pressure short of coercion but beyond mere detention makes confessions inadmissible. Obviously there is a wide range of discretion as to how much psychological pressure is necessary. If any material amount is sufficient, the rule differs little from one denying admissibility if obtained during illegal restraint. If almost coercion is required, the rule will differ little from that excluding an involuntary confession. Under this interpretation of *McNabb*, I suppose, as in coerced confessions, it should be left to a jury to decide whether there was enough evidence of pressure where the admitted facts do not show improper pressure as a matter of law. . . . I think there was less psychological pressure upon

Upshaw than there was upon the McNabbs. That precedent, therefore, if the true *McNabb* rule is properly stated . . . above, does not require me to declare Upshaw's confession inadmissible. In the McNabbs' case, the facts of their illegal detention that caused this Court's action appear from the opinion. . . . As for Upshaw the facts are detailed in the footnote.[25] The time between confession and commitment is not significant. *United States v. Mitchell, supra.* The indications of pressure on the McNabbs that lead me to conclude that the Court should hold Upshaw's confession admissible under my understanding of the *McNabb* rule before this present holding are the lack of experience of the McNabbs, the "breaking" of Benjamin by confrontation of charges of his guilt by his relatives and confederates, the greater number of officers questioning them, and the longer time the McNabb group was interrogated. . . .

I do not agree that we should now extend the *McNabb* rule by saying that every confession obtained by police after unnecessary delay in arraignment for commitment and before magisterial commitment must be barred from the trial. Those most concerned with a proper administration of the criminal law are against any extension.

(1) The departure of the *McNabb* and *Anderson* cases from well-established methods for protection against coercion has been condemned by the House of Representatives and not acted upon by the Senate.[27]

(2) Officers charged with enforcement of the criminal law have objected for the reason that fear of the application of its

---

[25] Upshaw, a Negro man able to read and write who had completed one year of high school, was arrested at his room by Detectives Furr and Culpepper on a charge of larceny of a wrist watch at about 2 a. m., Friday, June 6. He was taken to No. 10 precinct and questioned for about 30 minutes. Furr testified that petitioner was under the influence of alcohol at the time. Upshaw denied this. He was coughing sporadically at the time of his arrest and subsequently until his commitment. At approximately 10 a. m., June 6, he was questioned again by Furr, at which time he denied guilt. Culpepper questioned him through the bars in the cell block at 11 a. m. and again at 5:30 p. m. on June 6. Furr questioned him again for approximately 30 minutes at 7:30 p. m. on the same day. At 9 a. m. June 7, Upshaw confessed, and at 9:30 a. m. he signed a statement which he identified as his statement at 2 p. m., June 7. Thus some 31 hours intervened between the arrest and the confession. At 9 p. m. that night Upshaw was taken to the home of the complaining witness where he repeated his confession to her.

The petitioner was taken before a magistrate for commitment on Monday, June 9. The officers testified that they had not had him committed sooner because they did not have a sufficient case against him to cause the Police Court to hold him and because they wanted to continue their investigation.

[27] 93 Cong. Rec. 1392; H. R. Rep. No. 29, 80th Cong., 1st Sess.

drastic penalties deterred officers from questioning during reasonable delays in commitment.[28]

(3) State courts under similar laws and conditions have refused to follow the *McNabb* example.[29]

(4) Law Review comment generally condemns the rule.[30] . . .

Such condemnation of even the restricted *McNabb* rule by those immediately responsible for the enactment and administration of our criminal laws should make this Court, so far removed from the actualities of crime prevention, hesitate long before pushing farther by judicial legislation its conception of the proprieties in criminal investigation. It takes this step in the belief that thereby it strengthens criminal administration by protecting a prisoner. A prisoner should have protection but it is well to remember that law and order is an essential prerequisite to the protection of the security of all. Today's decision puts another weapon in the hand of the criminal world. Apparently the Court intends to make the rule of commitment "without unnecessary delay" an iron rule without flexibility to meet the emergencies of conspiracies, search for confederates, or examining into the ramifications of criminality. The Court does this by failing to distinguish between necessary and unnecessary delay in commitment. It uses words like "forthwith" and "promptly" and thus destroys the leeway given by the Rule to police investigations. All, I think, without any need for such action since every coerced confession has been inadmissible for generations. The position stated in this dissent does not envisage a surrender to evils in the handling of criminals. If there is a prevalent abuse of the right to question prisoners, the sounder remedy lies in police discipline, in statutory punishment of offending officials, in vigorous judicial protection against unconstitutional pressures for confessions, and in legislative enactments for inquiries into circumstances surrounding crimes by methods that protect both the public and suspects—for example, an inquiry before a magistrate with sealed evidence.

I would affirm this conviction in reliance upon the verdict of the properly instructed jury that this was a voluntary confession.

---

[28] International Association of Chiefs of Police, Hearings, *supra*, 43; National Sheriffs Association Hearings, *supra*, 26; Attorney General of the United States, H. R. Rep. No. 29, *supra*.

[29] [Citing state cases.]

[30] Inbau, The Confession Dilemma in the United States Supreme Court, 43 Ill. L. Rev. 442; 42 Mich. L. Rev. 679; 56 Harv. L. Rev. 1008; 47 Col. L. Rev. 1214. See Statement of Special Committee on the Bill of Rights of the American Bar Association, p. VI, which advocates maintenance of *McNabb* rule until a better system for dealing with confessions to police can be devised.

## Note

1. In *United States v. Carignan*, 342 U. S. 36, 96 L. Ed. —, 72 S. Ct. 97 (1951), the defendant was detained by the police on a charge of assault with intent to rape. The same day he confessed to the assault, was arrested, and was committed to jail. During his original detention, and on two days after his commitment and while in jail, the defendant was questioned, under circumstances indicating some psychological pressure, about a murder which had occurred six weeks before in connection with an attempted rape. The defendant then confessed to the murder, was convicted on the murder charge, and sentenced to death. Mr. Justice Reed, writing for the majority, held that since the confession was not given during an illegal detention the case did not fall within the *McNabb* rule. The Court added that the *McNabb* rule should not be extended to cover such a situation, saying:

"Another extension of the *McNabb* rule would accentuate the shift of the inquiry as to admissibility from the voluntariness of the confession to the legality of the arrest and restraint. Complete protection is afforded the civil rights of an accused who makes an involuntary confession or statement when such confession must be excluded by the judge or disregarded by the jury upon proof that it is not voluntary. Such a just and merciful rule preserves the rights of accused and society alike. It does not sacrifice justice to sentimentality. An extension of a mechanical rule based on the time of a confession would not be a helpful addition to the rules of criminal evidence. We decline to extend the *McNabb* fixed rule of exclusion to statements to police or wardens concerning other crimes while prisoners are legally in detention on criminal charges."

Mr. Justice Minton did not participate in the case. Mr. Justice Douglas, joined by Justices Black and Frankfurter, disagreed:

"There are time-honored police methods for obtaining confessions from an accused. One is detention without arraignment, the problem we dealt with in *McNabb v. United States*, 318 U. S. 332. Then the accused is under the exclusive control of the police, subject to their mercy, and beyond the reach of counsel or of friends. What happens behind doors that are opened and closed at the sole discretion of the police is a black chapter in every country—the free as well as the despotic, the modern as well as the ancient. In the *McNabb* case we tried to rid the federal system of those breeding grounds for coerced confessions.

"Another time-honored police method for obtaining confessions is to arrest a man on one charge (often a minor one) and use his detention for investigating a wholly different crime. This is an easy short cut for the police. How convenient it is to make detention the vehicle of investigation! Then the police can have access to the prisoner day and night. Arraignment for one crime gives some protection. But when it is a pretense or used as the device for breaking the will of the prisoner on long, relentless, or repeated questionings, it is abhorrent.

[Emerson]

We should free the federal system of that disreputable practice which has honeycombed the municipal police system in this country. We should make illegal such a perversion of a 'legal' detention."

2. Evidence that it is a frequent practice for Federal police officers to question a prisoner regarding crimes other than the one for which he was arraigned appears in Note, *Post-Arraignment Safeguards for Jailhouse Interrogation*, 60 Yale L. J. 1228, 1230-1 (1951). With respect to the practice of holding a suspect as a material witness, see *People v. Perez*, 300 N. Y. 208, 647, 90 N. E. 2d 40, 499 (1949), cert. den. 338 U. S. 952 (1950), discussed in Note, *Material Witnesses and "Involuntary" Confessions*, 17 U. Chi. L. Rev. 706 (1950). As to what constitutes "unnecessary delay" and the effect of night, holiday and weekend arrests, see the cases and references cited in Note, *supra*, 60 Yale L. J. at 1230; see also Note, 100 U. Pa. L. Rev. 136 (1951). See also Note, *Use of Vagrancy-Type Laws for Arrest and Detention of Suspicious Persons*, 59 Yale L. J. 1351 (1950).

3. Legislation requiring prompt arraignment exists in all states, although under some state laws the requirement is not applicable to all arrests. See Note, 53 Yale L. J. 758, 758-9 (1944). But most of the state courts which have considered the issue have refused to follow the *McNabb* rule. See McCormick, *Some Problems and Developments in the Admissibility of Confessions*, 24 Tex. L. Rev. 239, 275-6 (1946); cases cited in Mr. Justice Reed's opinion in the *Upshaw* case, 335 U. S. at 434-5. In *Gallegos v. Nebraska*, *supra*, the Supreme Court reiterated that the *McNabb* rule will not be applied to state proceedings by the Federal Courts.

4. Under English law and practice statements made in response to police interrogation after arrest are inadmissible in evidence at the trial. But the police are permitted to question suspects to determine whether there are reasonable grounds for arrest, and statements so obtained are admissible. See Note, *Illegal Detention and the Admissibility of Confessions*, 53 Yale L. J. 758, 767-8 (1944); McCormick, *supra*, 24 Tex. L. Rev. at 254-8; Johnston, *The Legal Limitations of the Interrogation of Suspects and Prisoners in England and Wales*, 39 J. of Am. Inst. of Cr. L. and Criminology 89 (1948).

5. For general discussion of the problem of illegal detention and the third degree, see Note, *supra*, 53 Yale L. J. 758 (1944); Waite, *Police Regulation by Rules of Evidence*, 42 Mich. L. Rev. 679 (1944); Committee on the Bill of Rights of the American Bar Association, *Memorandum on Detention of Arrested Persons* (1944); McCormick, *supra*, 24 Tex. L. Rev. 239 (1946); Note, *The McNabb Rule Transformed*, 47 Col. L. Rev. 1214 (1947); Inbau, *The Confession Dilemma in the United States Supreme Court*, 43 Ill. L. Rev. 442 (1948); Bruce Smith, *Police Systems in the United States*, pp. 10–14, 342–6 (rev. ed. 1949); Note, *supra*, 60 Yale L. J. 1228 (1951); 19 A. L. R. 2d 1331. Discussion of other proposals for eliminating the third degree may be found in Chafee, *Remedies for the Third Degree*, 148 Atlantic Monthly 621 (1931); Kauper, *Judicial Examination of the Accused—A Remedy for the Third Degree*, 30 Mich. L. Rev. 1224 (1932); O'Connor,

*The "Third Degree,"* 9 St. John's L. Rev. 180 (1934) ; Warner, *How Can the Third Degree Be Eliminated?*, 1 Bill of Rights Rev. 24 (1940) ; McCormick, *supra*, 24 Tex. L. Rev. at 276-8 (1946) ; Barnes and Teeters, *New Horizons in Criminology*, pp. 280-2 (1945). For the suggestion that the courts be "supplied with an independent prosecuting arm" to aid them in eliminating police lawlessness, see Note, *Judicial Control of Illegal Search and Seizure*, 58 Yale L. J. 144, 163-4 (1948). See also Moscovitz, *Civil Liberties and Injunctive Protection*, 39 Ill. L. Rev. 144 (1944).

## B. THE RIGHT TO COUNSEL

The Sixth Amendment to the United States Constitution declares that in all criminal prosecutions the accused shall enjoy the right "to have the assistance of counsel for his defense." State constitutions contain similar provisions.[1] The application of these provisions, however, raise many problems, both with regard to the meaning of the constitutional guarantee and with regard to its effectiveness in actual operation. A good introduction to the subject is the famous *Scottsboro* case,—*Powell v. Alabama.*

### POWELL v. ALABAMA

Supreme Court of the United States, 1932
287 U. S. 45, 77 L. Ed. 158, 53 S. Ct. 55

MR. JUSTICE SUTHERLAND delivered the opinion of the Court.
[The defendants, seven young Negroes, were charged with raping two white girls on March 25, 1931. Defendants were indicted on March 31 and were tried a few days later in three groups, each trial being completed within a single day. The juries found defendants guilty and imposed the death penalty upon all. The Alabama Supreme Court affirmed the convictions, Chief Justice Anderson dissenting. 224 Ala. 524, 531, 540; 141 So. 215, 195, 201. The judgments were assailed in the United States Supreme Court as constituting a denial of due process and equal protection under the Fourteenth Amendment in that defendants (1) were not given a fair, impartial and deliberate trial; (2) were denied the right to counsel; and (3) were tried before juries from which Negroes were systematically excluded. The Supreme Court considered only the second issue.]
The record shows that on the day when the offense is said to have been committed, these defendants, together with a number

---

[1] In Virginia the constitution contains no specific provision but the courts have held that the right to counsel is included in the due process clause. *Barnes v. Commonwealth*, 92 Va. 794, 23 S. E. 784 (1895).

of other negroes, were upon a freight train on its way through Alabama. On the same train were seven white boys and the two white girls. A fight took place between the negroes and the white boys, in the course of which the white boys, with the exception of one named Gilley, were thrown off the train. A message was sent ahead, reporting the fight and asking that every negro be gotten off the train. The participants in the fight, and the two girls, were in an open gondola car. The two girls testified that each of them was assaulted by six different negroes in turn, and they identified the seven defendants as having been among the number. None of the white boys was called to testify, with the exception of Gilley, who was called in rebuttal.

Before the train reached Scottsboro, Alabama, a sheriff's posse seized the defendants and two other negroes. Both girls and the negroes then were taken to Scottsboro, the county seat. Word of their coming and of the alleged assault had preceded them, and they were met at Scottsboro by a large crowd. It does not sufficiently appear that the defendants were seriously threatened with, or that they were actually in danger of, mob violence; but it does appear that the attitude of the community was one of great hostility. The sheriff thought it necessary to call for the militia to assist in safeguarding the prisoners. Chief Justice Anderson pointed out in his opinion that every step taken from the arrest and arraignment to the sentence was accompanied by the military. Soldiers took the defendants to Gadsden for safekeeping, brought them back to Scottsboro for arraignment, returned them to Gadsden for safekeeping while awaiting trial, escorted them to Scottsboro for trial a few days later, and guarded the court house and grounds at every stage of the proceedings. It is perfectly apparent that the proceedings, from beginning to end, took place in an atmosphere of tense, hostile and excited public sentiment. During the entire time, the defendants were closely confined or were under military guard. The record does not disclose their ages, except that one of them was nineteen; but the record clearly indicates that most, if not all, of them were youthful, and they are constantly referred to as "the boys." They were ignorant and illiterate. All of them were residents of other states, where alone members of their families or friends resided.

However guilty defendants, upon due inquiry, might prove to have been, they were, until convicted, presumed to be innocent. It was the duty of the court having their cases in charge to see that they were denied no necessary incident of a fair trial. With any error of the state court involving alleged contravention of the state statutes or constitution we, of course, have nothing to do.

**149**

The sole inquiry which we are permitted to make is whether the federal Constitution was contravened (*Rogers* v. *Peck,* 199 U.S. 425, 434; *Hebert* v. *Louisiana,* 272 U.S. 312, 316) ; and as to that, we confine ourselves, as already suggested, to the inquiry whether the defendants were in substance denied the right of counsel, and if so, whether such denial infringes the due process clause of the Fourteenth Amendment.

*First.* The record shows that immediately upon the return of the indictment defendants were arraigned and pleaded not guilty. Apparently they were not asked whether they had, or were able to employ, counsel, or wished to have counsel appointed; or whether they had friends or relatives who might assist in that regard if communicated with. That it would not have been an idle ceremony to have given the defendants reasonable opportunity to communicate with their families and endeavor to obtain counsel is demonstrated by the fact that, very soon after conviction, able counsel appeared in their behalf. . . .

It is hardly necessary to say that, the right to counsel being conceded, a defendant should be afforded a fair opportunity to secure counsel of his own choice. Not only was that not done here, but such designation of counsel as was attempted was either so indefinite or so close upon the trial as to amount to a denial of effective and substantial aid in that regard. This will be amply demonstrated by a brief review of the record. . . .

It thus will be seen that until the very morning of the trial no lawyer had been named or definitely designated to represent the defendants. Prior to that time, the trial judge had "appointed all the members of the bar" for the limited "purpose of arraigning the defendants." Whether they would represent the defendants thereafter if no counsel appeared in their behalf, was a matter of speculation only, or, as the judge indicated, of mere anticipation on the part of the court. Such a designation, even if made for all purposes, would, in our opinion, have fallen far short of meeting, in any proper sense, a requirement for the appointment of counsel. How many lawyers were members of the bar does not appear; but, in the very nature of things, whether many or few, they would not, thus collectively named, have been given that clear appreciation of responsibility or impressed with that individual sense of duty which should and naturally would accompany the appointment of a selected member of the bar, specifically named and assigned.

That this action of the trial judge in respect of appointment of counsel was little more than an expansive gesture, imposing no substantial or definite obligation upon any one, is borne out by the fact that prior to the calling of the case for trial on April

6, a leading member of the local bar accepted employment on the side of the prosecution and actively participated in the trial. It is true that he said that before doing so he had understood Mr. Roddy would be employed as counsel for the defendants. This the lawyer in question, of his own accord, frankly stated to the court; and no doubt he acted with the utmost good faith. Probably other members of the bar had a like understanding. In any event, the circumstance lends emphasis to the conclusion that during perhaps the most critical period of the proceedings against these defendants, that is to say, from the time of their arraignment until the beginning of their trial, when consultation, thoroughgoing investigation and preparation were vitally important, the defendants did not have the aid of counsel in any real sense, although they were as much entitled to such aid during that period as at the trial itself. *People ex rel. Burgess* v. *Risley*, 66 How. Pr. (N.Y.) 67; *Batchelor* v. *State*, 189 Ind. 69, 76; 125 N.E. 773.

Nor do we think the situation was helped by what occurred on the morning of the trial. At that time . . . Mr. Roddy stated to the court that he did not appear as counsel, but that he would like to appear along with counsel that the court might appoint; that he had not been given an opportunity to prepare the case; that he was not familiar with the procedure in Alabama, but merely came down as a friend of the people who were interested; that he thought the boys would be better off if he should step entirely out of the case. Mr. Moody, a member of the local bar, expressed a willingness to help Mr. Roddy in anything he could do under the circumstances. To this the court responded, "All right, all the lawyers that will; of course I would not require a lawyer to appear if —." And Mr. Moody continued, "I am willing to do that for him as a member of the bar; I will go ahead and help do any thing I can do." With this dubious understanding, the trials immediately proceeded. The defendants, young, ignorant, illiterate, surrounded by hostile sentiment, haled back and forth under guard of soldiers, charged with an atrocious crime regarded with especial horror in the community where they were to be tried, were thus put in peril of their lives within a few moments after counsel for the first time charged with any degree of responsibility began to represent them.

It is not enough to assume that counsel thus precipitated into the case thought there was no defense, and exercised their best judgment in proceeding to trial without preparation. Neither they nor the court could say what a prompt and thoroughgoing investigation might disclose as to the facts. No attempt was made to investigate. No opportunity to do so was given. Defendants were immediately hurried to trial. Chief Justice Anderson, after disclaiming any intention to criticize harshly counsel who attempted to represent defendants at the trials, said: ". . . the record indicates that the appearance was rather *pro forma* than zealous and active . . ." Under the circumstances disclosed, we hold that defendants were not accorded the right of counsel in any substantial sense. To decide otherwise, would simply be to ignore actualities. . . . [citing state cases].

*Second.* The Constitution of Alabama provides that in all criminal prosecutions the accused shall enjoy the right to have the assistance of counsel; and a state statute requires the court in a capital case, where the defendant is unable to employ counsel, to appoint counsel for him. The state supreme court held that these provisions had not been infringed, and with that holding we are powerless to interfere. The question, however, which it is our duty, and within our power, to decide, is whether the denial of the assistance of counsel contravenes the due process clause of the Fourteenth Amendment to the federal Constitution.

If recognition of the right of a defendant charged with a felony to have the aid of counsel depended upon the existence of a similar right at common law as it existed in England when our Constitution was adopted, there would be great difficulty in maintaining it as necessary to due process. Originally, in England, a person charged with treason or felony was denied the aid of counsel, except in respect of legal questions which the accused himself might suggest. At the same time parties in civil cases and persons accused of misdemeanors were entitled to the full assistance of counsel. After the revolution of 1688, the rule was abolished as to treason, but was otherwise steadily adhered to until 1836, when by act of Parliament the full right was granted in respect of felonies generally. 1 Cooley's Const. Lim., 8th ed., 698, *et seq.,* and notes.

An affirmation of the right to the aid of counsel in petty offenses, and its denial in the case of crimes of the gravest character, where such aid is most needed, is so outrageous and so obviously a perversion of all sense of proportion that the rule was constantly, vigorously and sometimes passionately assailed by English statesmen and lawyers. As early as 1758, Blackstone, although recognizing that the rule was settled at common law, denounced it as not in keeping with the rest of the humane treatment of prisoners by the English law. "For upon what face of reason," he says, "can that assistance be denied to save the life of a man, which yet is allowed him in prosecutions for every petty trespass?" 4 Blackstone 355. One of the grounds upon which Lord Coke defended the rule was that in felonies the court itself was counsel for the prisoner. 1 Cooley's Const. Lim., *supra*. But how can a judge, whose functions are purely judicial, effectively discharge the obligations of counsel for the accused? He can and should see to it that in the proceedings before the court the accused shall be dealt with justly and fairly. He cannot investigate the facts, advise and direct the defense, or participate in those necessary conferences between counsel and accused which sometimes partake of the inviolable character of the confessional.

The rule was rejected by the colonies. . . . [The Court then reviews various provisions of the constitutions of the colonies.]

It thus appears that in at least twelve of the thirteen colonies the rule of the English common law, in the respect now under consideration, had been definitely rejected and the right to counsel fully recognized in all criminal prosecutions, save that in one or two instances the right was limited to capital offenses or to the more serious crimes. . . .

One test which has been applied to determine whether due process of law has been accorded in given instances is to ascertain what were the settled usages and modes of proceeding under the common and statute law of England before the Declaration of Independence, subject, however, to the qualification that they be shown not to have been unsuited to the civil and political conditions of our ancestors by having been followed in this country after it became a nation. *Lowe* v. *Kansas*, 163 U.S. 81, 85. Compare *Murray's Lessee* v. *Hoboken Land & Improvement Co.*, 18 How. 272, 276–277; *Twining* v. *New Jersey*, 211 U.S. 78, 100–101. Plainly, as appears from the foregoing, this test, as thus qualified, has not been met in the present case.

We do not overlook the case of *Hurtado* v. *California*, 110 U. S. 516, where this court determined that due process of law does not require an indictment by a grand jury as a prerequisite to prosecution by a state for murder. In support of that conclusion the court (pp. 534–535) referred to the fact that the Fifth Amendment, in addition to containing the due process of law clause, provides in explicit terms that "No person shall be held to answer for a capital, or otherwise infamous crime, unless on a presentment or indictment of a grand jury, . . .", and said that since no part of this important amendment could be regarded as superfluous, the obvious inference is that in the sense of the Constitution due process of law was not intended to include, *ex vi termini*, the institution and procedure of a grand jury in any case; and that the same phrase, employed in the Fourteenth Amendment to restrain the action of the states, was to be interpreted as having been used in the same sense and with

**153**

no greater extent; and that if it had been the purpose of that Amendment to perpetuate the institution of the grand jury in the states, it would have embodied, as did the Fifth Amendment, an express declaration to that effect.

The Sixth Amendment, in terms, provides that in all criminal prosecutions the accused shall enjoy the right "to have the assistance of counsel for his defense." In the face of the reasoning of the *Hurtado* case, if it stood alone, it would be difficult to justify the conclusion that the right to counsel, being thus specifically granted by the Sixth Amendment, was also within the intendment of the due process of law clause. But the *Hurtado* case does not stand alone. In the later case of *Chicago, Burlington & Quincy R. Co. v. Chicago,* 166 U. S. 226, 241, this court held that a judgment of a state court, even though authorized by statute, by which private property was taken for public use without just compensation, was in violation of the due process of law required by the Fourteenth Amendment, notwithstanding that the Fifth Amendment explicitly declares that private property shall not be taken for public use without just compensation. This holding was followed in *Norwood v. Baker,* 172 U. S. 269, 277; *Smyth* v. *Ames,* 169 U. S. 466, 524; and *San Diego Land Co.* v. *National City,* 174 U. S. 739, 754.

Likewise, this court has considered that freedom of speech and of the press are rights protected by the due process clause of the Fourteenth Amendment, although in the First Amendment, Congress is prohibited in specific terms from abridging the right. *Gitlow* v. *New York,* 268 U. S. 652, 666; *Stromberg* v. *California,* 283 U. S. 359, 368; *Near* v. *Minnesota,* 283 U. S. 697, 707.

These later cases establish that notwithstanding the sweeping character of the language in the *Hurtado* case, the rule laid down is not without exceptions. The rule is an aid to construction, and in some instances may be conclusive; but it must yield to more compelling considerations whenever such considerations exist. The fact that the right involved is of such a character that it cannot be denied without violating those "fundamental principles of liberty and justice which lie at the base of all our civil and political institutions" (*Hebert* v. *Louisiana,* 272 U. S. 312, 316), is obviously one of those compelling considerations which must prevail in determining whether it is embraced within the due process clause of the Fourteenth Amendment, although it be specifically dealt with in another part of the federal Constitution. Evidently this court, in the later cases enumerated, regarded the rights there under consideration as of this fundamental character. . . . While the question has never been categorical-

ly determined by this court, a consideration of the nature of the
right and a review of the expressions of this and other courts,
makes it clear that the right to the aid of counsel is of this
fundamental character.

It has never been doubted by this court, or any other so far
as we know, that notice and hearing are preliminary steps essential to the passing of an enforceable judgment, and that they,
together with a legally competent tribunal having jurisdiction
of the case, constitute basic elements of the constitutional requirement of due process of law. The words of Webster, so often
quoted, that by "the law of the land" is intended "a law which
hears before it condemns," have been repeated in varying forms
of expression in a multitude of decisions. . . .

What, then, does a hearing include? Historically and in practice, in our own country at least, it has always included the right
to the aid of counsel when desired and provided by the party
asserting the right. The right to be heard would be, in many
cases, of little avail if it did not comprehend the right to be
heard by counsel. Even the intelligent and educated layman has
small and sometimes no skill in the science of law. If charged
with crime, he is incapable, generally, of determining for himself whether the indictment is good or bad. He is unfamiliar
with the rules of evidence. Left without the aid of counsel he
may be put on trial without a proper charge, and convicted
upon incompetent evidence, or evidence irrelevant to the issue or
otherwise inadmissible. He lacks both the skill and knowledge
adequately to prepare his defense, even though he have a perfect
one. He requires the guiding hand of counsel at every step
in the proceedings against him. Without it, though he be not
guilty, he faces the danger of conviction because he does not know
how to establish his innocence. If that be true of men of intelligence, how much more true is it of the ignorant and illiterate,
or those of feeble intellect. If in any case, civil or criminal, a
state or federal court were arbitrarily to refuse to hear a party by
counsel, employed by and appearing for him, it reasonably may
not be doubted that such a refusal would be a denial of a hearing, and, therefore, of due process in the constitutional sense.
. . .

In the light of the facts outlined in the forepart of this opinion
—the ignorance and illiteracy of the defendants, their youth, the
circumstances of public hostility, the imprisonment and the close
surveillance of the defendants by the military forces, the fact
that their friends and families were all in other states and communication with them necessarily difficult, and above all that they
stood in deadly peril of their lives—we think the failure of the

trial court to give them reasonable time and opportunity to secure counsel was a clear denial of due process.

But passing that, and assuming their inability, even if opportunity had been given, to employ counsel, as the trial court evidently did assume, we are of opinion that, under the circumstances just stated, the necessity of counsel was so vital and imperative that the failure of the trial court to make an effective appointment of counsel was likewise a denial of due process within the meaning of the Fourteenth Amendment. Whether this would be so in other criminal prosecutions, or under other circumstances, we need not determine. All that it is necessary now to decide, as we do decide, is that in a capital case, where the defendant is unable to employ counsel, and is incapable adequately of making his own defense because of ignorance, feeble mindedness, illiteracy, or the like, it is the duty of the court, whether requested or not, to assign counsel for him as a necessary requisite of due process of law; and that duty is not discharged by an assignment at such a time or under such circumstances as to preclude the giving of effective aid in the preparation and trial of the case. To hold otherwise would be to ignore the fundamental postulate, already adverted to, "that there are certain immutable principles of justice which inhere in the very idea of free government which no member of the Union may disregard." *Holden* v. *Hardy* [169 U. S. 366]. In a case such as this, whatever may be the rule in other cases, the right to have counsel appointed, when necessary, is a logical corollary from the constitutional right to be heard by counsel. . . .

Let us suppose the extreme case of a prisoner charged with a capital offense, who is deaf and dumb, illiterate and feeble minded, unable to employ counsel, with the whole power of the state arrayed against him, prosecuted by counsel for the state without assignment of counsel for his defense, tried, convicted and sentenced to death. Such a result, which, if carried into execution, would be little short of judicial murder, it cannot be doubted would be a gross violation of the guarantee of due process of law; and we venture to think that no appellate court, state or federal, would hesitate so to decide. . . . The duty of the trial court to appoint counsel under such circumstances is clear, as it is clear under circumstances such as are disclosed by the record here; and its power to do so, even in the absence of a statute, can not be questioned. Attorneys are officers of the court, and are bound to render service when required by such an appointment. See Cooley, Const. Lim., *supra,* 700 and note.

The United States by statute and every state in the Union by express provision of law, or by the determination of its courts, make it the duty of the trial judge, where the accused is unable to employ counsel, to appoint counsel for him. In most states the rule applies broadly to all criminal prosecutions, in others it is limited to the more serious crimes, and in a very limited number, to capital cases. A rule adopted with such unanimous accord reflects, if it does not establish, the inherent right to have counsel appointed, at least in cases like the present, and lends convincing support to the conclusion we have reached as to the fundamental nature of that right.

The judgments must be reversed and the causes remanded for further proceedings not inconsistent with this opinion.

*Judgments reversed.*

MR. JUSTICE BUTLER, dissenting.

The Court, putting aside—they are utterly without merit—all other claims that the constitutional rights of petitioners were infringed, grounds its opinion and judgment upon a single assertion of fact. It is that petitioners "were denied the right of counsel, with the accustomed incidents of consultation and opportunity of preparation for trial." If that is true, they were denied due process of law and are entitled to have the judgments against them reversed.

But no such denial is shown by the record. . . .

The informality disclosed by the colloquy between court and counsel, which is quoted in the opinion of this Court and so heavily leaned on, is not entitled to any weight. It must be inferred from the record that Mr. Roddy at all times was in touch with the defendants and the people who procured him to act for them. Mr. Moody and others of the local bar also acted for defendants at the time of the first arraignment and, as appears from the part of the record that is quoted in the opinion, thereafter proceeded in the discharge of their duty, including conferences with the defendants. There is not the slightest ground to suppose that Roddy or Moody were by fear or in any manner restrained from full performance of their duties. Indeed, it clearly appears that the State, by proper and adequate show of its purpose and power to preserve order, furnished adequate protection to them and the defendants.

When the first case was called for trial, defendants' attorneys had already prepared, and then submitted, a motion for change of venue together with supporting papers. They were ready to and did at once introduce testimony of witnesses to sustain that demand. They had procured and were ready to offer evidence to show that the defendants Roy Wright and Eugene Williams were under age. The record shows that the State's evidence was ample to warrant a conviction. And three defendants each,

**157**

while asserting his own innocence, testified that he saw others accused commit the crime charged. When regard is had to these and other disclosures that may have been and probably were made by petitioners to Roddy and Moody before the trial, it would be difficult to think of anything that counsel erroneously did or omitted for their defense. . . .

If correct, the ruling that the failure of the trial court to give petitioners time and opportunity to secure counsel was denial of due process is enough, and with this the opinion should end. But the Court goes on to declare that "the failure of the trial court to make an effective appointment of counsel was likewise a denial of due process within the meaning of the Fourteenth Amendment." This is an extension of federal authority into a field hitherto occupied exclusively by the several States. Nothing before the Court calls for a consideration of the point. It was not suggested below, and petitioners do not ask for its decision here. The Court, without being called upon to consider it, adjudges without a hearing an important constitutional question concerning criminal procedure in state courts.

It is a wise rule, firmly established by a long course of decisions here, that constitutional questions—even when properly raised and argued—are to be decided only when necessary for a determination of the rights of the parties in controversy before it. . . .

The record wholly fails to reveal that petitioners have been deprived of any right guaranteed by the Federal Constitution, and I am of opinion that the judgment should be affirmed.

MR. JUSTICE MCREYNOLDS concurs in this opinion.*

---

* The case is discussed in 13 Boston U. L. Rev. 92 (1933); 31 Mich. L. Rev. 245 (1932); 17 Minn. L. Rev. 415 (1933); and 11 Tex. L. Rev. 546 (1933).

After reversal by the Supreme Court one of the defendants, Patterson, was tried again and convicted, but the conviction was set aside by the trial judge. Thereafter Patterson was tried a third time, along with Norris; both were convicted and sentenced to death. This conviction was reversed by the United States Supreme Court on the ground that Negroes had been systematically excluded from the jury in violation of the equal protection clause of the Fourteenth Amendment. *Norris v. Alabama*, 294 U. S. 587, 79 L. Ed. 1074, 55 S. Ct. 579 (1935). In 1936 Patterson was tried for the fourth time, convicted, and sentenced to 75 years imprisonment. This conviction was affirmed by the Alabama Supreme Court, 234 Ala. 342, 175 So. 371 (1937). In 1937 Norris and two other defendants were tried again, convicted, and sentenced,—Norris to death, the others to 99 and 75 years in prison. Norris' sentence was later commuted. Charges against the others were dropped. Norris and the two convicted with him were paroled in 1944. In 1948 Patterson escaped from prison. In 1950 Patterson was arrested by the FBI in Detroit but the Governor of Michigan refused to grant extradition. See Patterson and Conrad, *Scottsboro Boy* (1950);

## Note

Further material on the historical background of the right to counsel may be found in 1 Stephen, *A History of the Criminal Law of England*, pp. 424-5 (1883); Plucknett, *Concise History of the Common Law*, p. 410 (4th ed. 1948); Holtzoff, *The Right of Counsel Under the Sixth Amendment*, 20 N. Y. U. L. Q. Rev. 1 (1944); Fellman, *The Constitutional Right to Counsel in Federal Courts*, 30 Neb. L. Rev. 559 (1951).

After the *Powell* case the law with respect to the right of counsel developed rapidly. The following materials consider first the present status of the right in the Federal courts under the Sixth Amendment.

## JOHNSON v. ZERBST

Supreme Court of the United States, 1938
304 U. S. 458, 82 L. Ed. 1461, 58 S. Ct. 1019

[Two enlisted men in the Marines were arrested while on leave in Charleston, S. C., and charged with passing and possessing counterfeit bills. Both men were from other states and, lacking bail, were confined to jail awaiting action by the Grand Jury. Two months later they were indicted. Two days afterwards they were brought to the Federal District Court, arraigned, tried, convicted, and sentenced to four and one-half years in the penitentiary, all on the same day. Although they were represented by counsel at the time of arrest they were unable to obtain counsel for the trial. They made no request to the trial judge for counsel. One of them contended that he had asked the District Attorney for assistance of counsel and that the District Attorney had stated that the court would appoint counsel only in capital cases. The District Attorney denied this. At the arraignment the defendants said they had no counsel but, in response to an inquiry from the court, stated they were ready for trial. One of them attempted to act as his own counsel at the trial. After conviction both defendants were taken back to jail, where their requests for counsel were denied, and they were then taken to the Federal penitentiary. No appeal was filed until the time for appeal had expired.

Johnson, one of the defendants, subsequently brought a habeas corpus proceeding in the Federal District Court. Upon denial of relief the case reached the Supreme Court.]

MR. JUSTICE BLACK delivered the opinion of the Court. . . .
*One.* The Sixth Amendment guarantees that "In all criminal

Reynolds, *Courtroom* pp. 248–314 (1950); Chalmers, *They Shall Be Free* (1951).

prosecutions, the accused shall enjoy the right . . . to have the Assistance of Counsel for his defence." This is one of the safeguards of the Sixth Amendment deemed necessary to insure fundamental human rights of life and liberty. Omitted from the Constitution as originally adopted, provisions of this and other Amendments were submitted by the first Congress convened under that Constitution as essential barriers against arbitrary or unjust deprivation of human rights. The Sixth Amendment stands as a constant admonition that if the constitutional safeguards it provides be lost, justice will not "still be done." It embodies a realistic recognition of the obvious truth that the average defendant does not have the professional legal skill to protect himself when brought before a tribunal with power to take his life or liberty, wherein the prosecution is presented by experienced and learned counsel. That which is simple, orderly and necessary to the lawyer, to the untrained layman may appear intricate, complex and mysterious. Consistently with the wise policy of the Sixth Amendment and other parts of our fundamental charter, this Court has pointed to ". . . the humane policy of the modern criminal law . . ." which now provides that a defendant ". . . if he be poor, . . . may have counsel furnished him by the state . . . not infrequently . . . more able than the attorney for the state."[9] . . .

The Sixth Amendment withholds from federal courts,[11] in all criminal proceedings, the power and authority to deprive an accused of his life or liberty unless he has or waives the assistance of counsel.

*Two.* There is insistence here that petitioner waived this constitutional right. The District Court did not so find. It has been pointed out that "courts indulge every reasonable presumption against waiver" of fundamental constitutional rights[12] and that we "do not presume acquiescence in the loss of fundamental rights."[13] A waiver is ordinarily an intentional relinquishment or abandonment of a known right or privilege. The determination of whether there has been an intelligent waiver of the right to counsel must depend, in each case, upon the particular facts and circumstances surrounding that case, including the background, experience, and conduct of the accused. . . .

The constitutional right of an accused to be represented by counsel invokes, of itself, the protection of a trial court, in which

[9] *Patton v. United States*, 281 U. S. 276, 308.

[11] Cf., *Barron v. The Mayor*, 7 Pet. 243, 247; *Edwards v. Elliott*, 21 Wall. 532, 557.

[12] *Aetna Ins. Co. v. Kennedy*, 301 U. S. 389, 393; *Hodges v. Easton*, 106 U. S. 408, 412.

[13] *Ohio Bell Telephone Co. v. Public Utilities Comm'n*, 301 U. S. 292, 307.

the accused—whose life or liberty is at stake—is without counsel. This protecting duty imposes the serious and weighty responsibility upon the trial judge of determining whether there is an intelligent and competent waiver by the accused. While an accused may waive the right to counsel, whether there is a proper waiver should be clearly determined by the trial court, and it would be fitting and appropriate for that determination to appear upon the record.

*Three.* The District Court, holding petitioner could not obtain relief by *habeas corpus,* said:

"It is unfortunate, if petitioners lost their right to a new trial through ignorance or negligence, but such misfortune cannot give this Court jurisdiction in a habeas corpus case to review and correct the errors complained of."

The purpose of the constitutional guaranty of a right to counsel is to protect an accused from conviction resulting from his own ignorance of his legal and constitutional rights, and the guaranty would be nullified by a determination that an accused's ignorant failure to claim his rights removes the protection of the Constitution. True, *habeas corpus* cannot be used as a means of reviewing errors of law and irregularities—not involving the question of jurisdiction—occurring during the course of trial;[15] and the "writ of *habeas corpus* cannot be used as a writ of error."[16] These principles, however, must be construed and applied so as to preserve—not destroy—constitutional safeguards of human life and liberty. The scope of inquiry in *habeas corpus* proceedings has been broadened—not narrowed—since the adoption of the Sixth Amendment. In such a proceeding, "it would be clearly erroneous to confine the inquiry to the proceedings and judgment of the trial court"[17] and the petitioned court has "power to inquire with regard to the jurisdiction of the inferior court, either in respect to the subject matter or to the person, even if such inquiry . . . [involves] an examination of facts outside of, but not inconsistent with, the record."[18] . . .

Since the Sixth Amendment constitutionally entitles one charged with crime to the assistance of counsel, compliance with this constitutional mandate is an essential jurisdictional prerequisite to a federal court's authority to deprive an accused of his life or liberty. When this right is properly waived, the assistance of counsel is no longer a necessary element of the court's jurisdiction to proceed to conviction and sentence. If

---

[15] Cf., *Ex parte Watkins,* 3 Pet. 193; *Knewal v. Egan,* 268 U. S. 442; *Harlan v. McGourin,* 218 U. S. 442.

[16] *Woolsey v. Best,* 299 U. S. 1, 2.

[17] *Frank v. Mangum,* 237 U. S. 309, 327.

[18] *In re Mayfield,* 141 U. S. 107, 116; *Cuddy, Petitioner,* 131 U. S. 280.

the accused, however, is not represented by counsel and has not competently and intelligently waived his constitutional right, the Sixth Amendment stands as a jurisdictional bar to a valid conviction and sentence depriving him of his life or his liberty.
. . .

It must be remembered, however, that a judgment can not be lightly set aside by collateral attack, even on *habeas corpus*. When collaterally attacked, the judgment of a court carries with it a presumption of regularity. Where a defendant, without counsel, acquiesces in a trial resulting in his conviction and later seeks release by the extraordinary remedy of *habeas corpus*, the burden of proof rests upon him to establish that he did not competently and intelligently waive his constitutional right to assistance of counsel. If in a *habeas corpus* hearing, he does meet this burden and convinces the court by a preponderance of evidence that he neither had counsel nor properly waived his constitutional right to counsel, it is the duty of the court to grant the writ. . . .

The cause is reversed and remanded to the District Court for action in harmony with this opinion.

*Reversed.*

[Mr. Justice Reed concurred in the reversal. Justices McReynolds and Butler dissented. Mr. Justice Cardozo did not participate.]

## Note

1. Following *Johnson v. Zerbst* a large number of petitions for habeas corpus, based upon an alleged denial of counsel, were filed by Federal prisoners. In the District which included Alcatraz Penitentiary, for example, 75 such petitions were filed in the ensuing three years. See Fellman, *The Constitutional Right to Counsel in Federal Courts*, 30 Neb. L. Rev. 559, 571 (1951).

The Supreme Court, however, continued to give a liberal interpretation to the Sixth Amendment. In *Walker v. Johnston*, 312 U. S. 275, 85 L. Ed. 830, 61 S. Ct. 574 (1941), the Court held that if a defendant was not advised of his right to counsel and did not knowingly waive it, or was deceived or coerced by the prosecutor into pleading guilty, he was deprived of his rights under the Sixth Amendment. The entering of a guilty plea was considered not in itself to indicate a waiver. Accord is *Von Moltke v. Gillies*, 332 U. S. 708, 92 L. Ed. 309, 68 S. Ct. 316 (1948) (a "mere routine inquiry" by the judge may not be sufficient basis for the necessary "informed decision" as to waiver); but on remand the District Court and the Court of Appeals, Judge McAllister dissenting, found that the defendant had made an intelligent waiver. *Von Moltke v. U. S.*, 189 F. 2d 56 (C. A. 6, 1951), aff'd by an equally divided Court, 343 U. S. 922 (1952). *Cf.* also *Adams v. U. S.*,

[Emerson]

317 U. S. 269, 87 L. Ed. 268, 63 S. Ct. 236 (1942). In *Glasser v. U. S.*, 315 U. S. 60, 86 L. Ed. 680, 62 S. Ct. 457 (1942), the Court ruled that the appointment of an attorney who also represented a co-defendant with conflicting interests did not afford "the effective assistance of counsel guaranteed by the Sixth Amendment." The right to competent counsel at all stages of the court proceedings was also declared in the first *Von Moltke* case, *supra*.

2. The Federal rule on the right to appointment of counsel in all criminal cases was incorporated in Rule 44 of the Federal Rules of Criminal Procedure, effective March 21, 1946:

> "If the defendant appears in court without counsel, the court shall advise him of his right to counsel and assign counsel to represent him at every stage of the proceeding unless he elects to proceed without counsel or is able to obtain counsel." 18 U. S. C.

Rule 5 (b) provides that when an arrested person is brought before a commissioner the latter shall inform him of his right to retain counsel and "shall allow the defendant reasonable time and opportunity to consult counsel."

Since 1944 Federal legislation has provided for a court reporter to transcribe all criminal proceedings in open court, thus eliminating much of the prior uncertainty with respect to whether the defendant had actually waived his right. See Fellman, *supra*, 30 Neb. L. Rev. at 566, 571-6.

3. In *Coplon v. U. S.*, 191 F. 2d 749 (C. A. D. C., 1951), cert. den. 342 U. S. 926 (1952), the Court held that wiretapping by the F.B.I. of telephone conversations between defendant and her attorney would deprive defendant of the right to private consultation with her attorney and hence would deny her the effective aid of counsel in violation of the Sixth Amendment.

4. The right to assignment of counsel in the Federal courts does not appear to extend to proceedings at the stage of police interrogation or proceedings preliminary to the indictment. See *Gilmore v. U. S.*, 129 F. 2d 199 (C. A. 10, 1942), cert. den. 317 U. S. 631 (1942); *Burall v. Johnston*, 146 F. 2d 230 (C. A. 9, 1944), cert. den. 325 U. S. 887 (1945); *Setser v. Welch*, 159 F. 2d 703 (C. A. 4, 1947), cert. den. 331 U. S. 840 (1947). *Cf. Wood v. U. S.*, 128 F. 2d 265 (C. A. D. C., 1942).

5. Full discussion of the Federal rules on right to counsel may be found in Fellman, *supra*, 30 Neb. L. Rev. 559 (1951); Heller, *The Sixth Amendment*, ch. VI (1951); Holtzoff, *The Right of Counsel Under the Sixth Amendment*, 20 N. Y. U. L. Q. Rev. 1 (1944). See also 42 Col. L. Rev. 271 (1942); 23 Tex. L. Rev. 66 (1944); 17 U. Chi. L. Rev. 718 (1950); 84 L. Ed. 383 (1940); 146 A. L. R. 369 (1943); 3 A. L. R. 2d 1003 (1949). For discussion of the operation of the Federal rules in actual practice see the note following *Gibbs v. Burke, infra*.

6. State law and practice with respect to the right of counsel, and the extent of Federal control over state law and practice, are considered in the series of cases that followed the *Powell* case, beginning with *Betts v. Brady*.

## BETTS v. BRADY

Supreme Court of the United States, 1942
316 U. S. 455, 86 L. Ed. 1595, 62 S. Ct. 1252

MR. JUSTICE ROBERTS delivered the opinion of the Court.

The petitioner was indicted for robbery in the Circuit Court of Carroll County, Maryland. Due to lack of funds, he was unable to employ counsel, and so informed the judge at his arraignment. He requested that counsel be appointed for him. The judge advised him that this would not be done, as it was not the practice in Carroll County to appoint counsel for indigent defendants, save in prosecutions for murder and rape.

Without waiving his asserted right to counsel, the petitioner pleaded not guilty and elected to be tried without a jury. At his request witnesses were summoned in his behalf. He cross-examined the State's witnesses and examined his own. The latter gave testimony tending to establish an alibi. Although afforded the opportunity, he did not take the witness stand. The judge found him guilty and imposed a sentence of eight years.

[Some months later, Betts filed a petition for a writ of habeas corpus before the Chief Judge of the Court of Appeals of Maryland, but relief was denied. He then applied to the United States Supreme Court for a writ of certiorari, which was granted. The first part of the Court's opinion holds that Betts had exhausted his remedies in the Maryland courts and that the Supreme Court had jurisdiction.]

Was the petitioner's conviction and sentence a deprivation of his liberty without due process of law, in violation of the Fourteenth Amendment, because of the court's refusal to appoint counsel at his request?

The Sixth Amendment of the national Constitution applies only to trials in federal courts. The due process clause of the Fourteenth Amendment does not incorporate, as such, the specific guarantees found in the Sixth Amendment,[10] although a denial by a State of rights or privileges specifically embodied in that and others of the first eight amendments may, in certain circumstances, or in connection with other elements, operate, in a given case, to deprive a litigant of due process of law in violation of the Fourteenth.[11] Due process of law is secured against invasion

[10] *Hurtado v. California*, 110 U. S. 516; *Maxwell v. Dow*, 176 U. S. 581; *West v. Louisiana*, 194 U. S. 258; *Twining v. New Jersey*, 211 U. S. 78; *Frank v. Mangum*, 237 U. S. 309; *Snyder v. Massachusetts*, 291 U. S. 97; *Palko v. Connecticut*, 302 U. S. 319.

[11] Compare *Twining v. New Jersey*, 211 U. S. 78, 98; *Powell v. Alabama*, 287 U. S. 45; *Palko v. Connecticut*, 302 U. S. 319, 323 ff.

by the federal Government by the Fifth Amendment, and is safeguarded against state action in identical words by the Fourteenth. The phrase formulates a concept less rigid and more fluid than those envisaged in other specific and particular provisions of the Bill of Rights. Its application is less a matter of rule. Asserted denial is to be tested by an appraisal of the totality of facts in a given case. That which may, in one setting, constitute a denial of fundamental fairness, shocking to the universal sense of justice, may, in other circumstances, and in the light of other considerations, fall short of such denial.[12] In the application of such a concept, there is always the danger of falling into the habit of formulating the guarantee into a set of hard and fast rules, the application of which in a given case may be to ignore the qualifying factors therein disclosed.

The petitioner, in this instance, asks us, in effect, to apply a rule in the enforcement of the due process clause. He says the rule to be deduced from our former decisions is that, in every case, whatever the circumstances, one charged with crime, who is unable to obtain counsel, must be furnished counsel by the State. Expressions in the opinions of this court lend color to the argument,[13] but, as the petitioner admits, none of our decisions squarely adjudicates the question now presented.

In *Powell* v. *Alabama*, 287 U. S. 45, ignorant and friendless negro youths, strangers in the community, without friends or means to obtain counsel, were hurried to trial for a capital offense without effective appointment of counsel on whom the burden of preparation and trial would rest, and without adequate opportunity to consult even the counsel casually appointed to represent them. This occurred in a State whose statute law required the appointment of counsel for indigent defendants prosecuted for the offense charged. Thus the trial was conducted in disregard of every principle of fairness and in disregard of that which was declared by the law of the State a requisite of a fair trial. This court held the resulting convictions were without due process of law. . . .

[The Court then discusses *Avery* v. *Alabama*, 308 U. S. 444.]

In *Smith* v. *O'Grady*, 312 U. S. 329, the petition for *habeas corpus* alleged a failure to appoint counsel but averred other facts which, if established, would prove that the trial was a mere sham and pretense, offensive to the concept of due process. There also,

---

[12] Compare *Lisenba* v. *California*, 314 U. S. 219, 236–237.

[13] *Powell* v. *Alabama*, 287 U. S. 45, 73; *Grosjean* v. *American Press Co.*, 297 U. S. 233, 243, 244; *Johnson* v. *Zerbst*, 304 U. S. 458, 462; *Avery* v. *Alabama*, 308 U. S. 444, 447.

state law required the appointment of counsel for one on trial for the offense involved.

Those cases, which are the petitioner's chief reliance, do not rule this. The question we are now to decide is whether due process of law demands that in every criminal case, whatever the circumstances, a State must furnish counsel to an indigent defendant. Is the furnishing of counsel in all cases whatever dictated by natural, inherent, and fundamental principles of fairness? The answer to the question may be found in the common understanding of those who have lived under the Anglo-American system of law. By the Sixth Amendment the people ordained that, in all criminal prosecutions, the accused should "enjoy the right . . . to have the assistance of counsel for his defence." We have construed the provision to require appointment of counsel in all cases where a defendant is unable to procure the services of an attorney, and where the right has not been intentionally and competently waived.[14] Though, as we have noted, the Amendment lays down no rule for the conduct of the States, the question recurs whether the constraint laid by the Amendment upon the national courts expresses a rule so fundamental and essential to a fair trial, and so, to due process of law, that it is made obligatory upon the States by the Fourteenth Amendment. Relevant data on the subject are afforded by constitutional and statutory provisions subsisting in the colonies and the States prior to the inclusion of the Bill of Rights in the national Constitution, and in the constitutional, legislative, and judicial history of the States to the present date. These constitute the most authoritative sources for ascertaining the considered judgment of the citizens of the States upon the question.

The Constitutions of the thirteen original States, as they were at the time of federal union, exhibit great diversity in respect of the right to have counsel in criminal cases. Rhode Island had no constitutional provision on the subject until 1843, North Carolina and South Carolina had none until 1868. Virginia has never had any. Maryland, in 1776, and New York, in 1777, adopted provisions to the effect that a defendant accused of crime should be "allowed" counsel. A constitutional mandate that the accused should have a right to be heard by himself and by his counsel was adopted by Pennsylvania in 1776, New Hampshire in 1774, by Delaware in 1782, and by Connecticut in 1818. In 1780 Massachusetts ordained that the defendant should have the right to be heard by himself or his counsel at his election. In 1798 Georgia provided that the accused might be heard by himself or counsel, or both. In 1776 New Jersey guaranteed the accused the same

---

[14] *Johnson v. Zerbst*, 304 U. S. 458.

privileges of witnesses and counsel as their prosecutors "are or shall be entitled to."

[The Court then reviews the history of the law in England. See *Powell v. Alabama, supra.*]

In the light of this common law practice, it is evident that the constitutional provisions to the effect that a defendant should be "allowed" counsel or should have a right "to be heard by himself and his counsel," or that he might be heard by "either or both," at his election, were intended to do away with the rules which denied representation, in whole or in part, by counsel in criminal prosecutions, but were not aimed to compel the State to provide counsel for a defendant. At the least, such a construction by State courts and legislators can not be said to lack reasonable basis.

The statutes in force in the thirteen original States at the time of the adoption of the Bill of Rights are also illuminating. It is of interest that the matter of appointment of counsel for defendants, if dealt with at all, was dealt with by statute rather than by constitutional provision. The contemporary legislation exhibits great diversity of policy.[20]

The constitutions of all of the States, presently in force, save that of Virginia, contain provisions with respect to the assistance of counsel in criminal trials. Those of nine States may be said to embody a guarantee textually the same as that of the Sixth Amendment, or of like import. In the fundamental law of most States, however, the language used indicates only that a defendant is not to be denied the privilege of representation by counsel of his choice.

In three States, the guarantee, whether or not in the exact phraseology of the Sixth Amendment, has been held to require appointment in all cases where the defendant is unable to procure counsel. In six, the provisions (one of which is like the Sixth Amendment) have been held not to require the appointment of counsel for indigent defendants. In eight, provisions, one of which is the same as that of the Sixth Amendment, have evidently not been viewed as requiring such appointment, since the courts have enforced statutes making appointment discretionary, or obligatory only in prosecutions for capital offenses or felonies.

In twelve States, it seems to be understood that the constitutional provision does not require appointment of counsel, since statutes of greater or less antiquity, call for such appointment only in capital cases or cases of felony or other grave crime, or refer the matter to the discretion of the court. In eighteen

---

[20] [Ed. note: This footnote, and subsequent footnotes citing state constitutions and decisions, are omitted.]

States the statutes now require the court to appoint in all cases where defendants are unable to procure counsel.[28] But this has not always been the statutory requirement in some of those States. And it seems to have been assumed by many legislatures that the matter was one for regulation from time to time as deemed necessary, since laws requiring appointment in all cases have been modified to require it only in the case of certain offenses.

This material demonstrates that, in the great majority of the States, it has been the considered judgment of the people, their representatives and their courts that appointment of counsel is not a fundamenal right, essential to a fair trial. On the contrary, the matter has generally been deemed one of legislative policy. In the light of this evidence, we are unable to say that the concept of due process incorporated in the Fourteenth Amendment obligates the States, whatever may be their own views, to furnish counsel in every such case. Every court has power, if it deems proper, to appoint counsel where that course seems to be required in the interest of fairness. . . .

In this case there was no question of the commission of a robbery. The State's case consisted of evidence identifying the petitioner as the perpetrator. The defense was an alibi. Petitioner called and examined witnesses to prove that he was at another place at the time of the commission of the offense. The simple issue was the veracity of the testimony for the State and that for the defendant. As Judge Bond says, the accused was not helpless, but was a man forty-three years old, of ordinary intelligence, and ability to take care of his own interests on the trial of that narrow issue. He had once before been in a criminal court, pleaded guilty to larceny and served a sentence and was not wholly unfamiliar with criminal procedure. It is quite clear that in Maryland, if the situation had been otherwise and it had appeared that the petitioner was, for any reason, at a serious disadvantage by reason of the lack of counsel, a refusal to appoint would have resulted in the reversal of a judgment of conviction. Only recently the Court of Appeals has reversed a conviction because it was convinced on the whole record that an accused, tried

---

[28] . . . At least as early as 1903 (3 Edw. 7, c. 38) England adopted a Poor Prisoners' Defence Act, under which a rule was adopted whereby an accused might defend by counsel assigned by the court. Bowen-Rowlands, Criminal Proceedings, London (1904) pp. 46–47. The existing statute is the Poor Prisoners' Defence Act (1930) 20 & 21 Geo. 5, c. 32. See Archbold's Criminal Pleading, Evidence and Practice, 30th Ed. (1938) p. 167. Under this act a poor defendant is entitled as of right to counsel on a charge of murder, but assignment of counsel is discretionary in other cases.

without counsel, had been handicapped by the lack of representation.

To deduce from the due process clause a rule binding upon the States in this matter would be to impose upon them, as Judge Bond points out, a requirement without distinction between criminal charges of different magnitude or in respect of courts of varying jurisdiction. As he says: "Charges of small crimes tried before justices of the peace and capital charges tried in the higher courts would equally require the appointment of counsel. Presumably it would be argued that trials in the Traffic Court would require it." And, indeed, it was said by petitioner's counsel both below and in this court, that as the Fourteenth Amendment extends the protection of due process to property as well as to life and liberty, if we hold with the petitioner, logic would require the furnishing of counsel in civil cases involving property.

As we have said, the Fourteenth Amendment prohibits the conviction and incarceration of one whose trial is offensive to the common and fundamental ideas of fairness and right, and while want of counsel in a particular case may result in a conviction lacking in such fundamental fairness, we cannot say that the Amendment embodies an inexorable command that no trial for any offense, or in any court, can be fairly conducted and justice accorded a defendant who is not represented by counsel.

The judgment is

*Affirmed.*

MR. JUSTICE BLACK, dissenting, with whom MR. JUSTICE DOUGLAS and MR. JUSTICE MURPHY concur.

To hold that the petitioner had a constitutional right to counsel in this case does not require us to say that "no trial for any offense, or in any court, can be fairly conducted and justice accorded a defendant who is not represented by counsel." This case can be determined by a resolution of a narrower question: whether in view of the nature of the offense and the circumstances of his trial and conviction, this petitioner was denied the procedural protection which is his right under the Federal Constitution. I think he was.

The petitioner, a farm hand, out of a job and on relief, was indicted in a Maryland state court on a charge of robbery. He was too poor to hire a lawyer. He so informed the court and requested that counsel be appointed to defend him. His request was denied. Put to trial without a lawyer, he conducted his own defense, was found guilty, and was sentenced to eight years' imprisonment. The court below found that the petitioner had "at least an ordinary amount of intelligence." It is clear from his examination of witnesses that he was a man of little education.

If this case had come to us from a federal court, it is clear we should have to reverse it, because the Sixth Amendment makes the right to counsel in criminal cases inviolable by the Federal Government. I believe that the Fourteenth Amendment made the Sixth applicable to the states. But this view, although often urged in dissents, has never been accepted by a majority of this Court and is not accepted today. A statement of the grounds supporting it is, therefore, unnecessary at this time. I believe, however, that, under the prevailing view of due process, as reflected in the opinion just announced, a view which gives this Court such vast supervisory powers that I am not prepared to accept it without grave doubts, the judgment below should be reversed.

This Court has just declared that due process of law is denied if a trial is conducted in such manner that it is "shocking to the universal sense of justice" or "offensive to the common and fundamental ideas of fairness and right." On another occasion, this Court has recognized that whatever is "implicit in the concept of ordered liberty" and "essential to the substance of a hearing" is within the procedural protection afforded by the constitutional guaranty of due process. *Palko* v. *Connecticut*, 302 U. S. 319, 325, 327.

The right to counsel in a criminal proceeding is "fundamental." *Powell* v. *Alabama*, 287 U. S. 45, 70; *Grosjean* v. *American Press Co.*, 297 U. S. 233, 243–244. It is guarded from invasion by the Sixth Amendment, adopted to raise an effective barrier against arbitrary or unjust deprivation of liberty by the Federal Government. *Johnson* v. *Zerbst*, 304 U. S. 458, 462. . . .

[The dissent then quotes from the *Powell* case the statement that a hearing includes the right to aid of counsel.]

A practice cannot be reconciled with "common and fundamental ideas of fairness and right," which subjects innocent men to increased dangers of conviction merely because of their poverty. Whether a man is innocent cannot be determined from a trial in which, as here, denial of counsel has made it impossible to conclude, with any satisfactory degree of certainty, that the defendant's case was adequately presented. No one questions that due process requires a hearing before conviction and sentence for the serious crime of robbery. As the Supreme Court of Wisconsin said, in 1859, ". . . would it not be a little like mockery to secure to a pauper these solemn constitutional guaranties for a fair and full trial of the matters with which he was charged, and yet say to him when on trial, that he must

**170**

employ his own counsel, who could alone render these guaranties of any real permanent value to him. . . . Why this great solicitude to secure him a fair trial if he cannot have the benefit of counsel?" *Carpenter* v. *Dane County,* 9 Wis. 274, 276–277.

Denial to the poor of the request for counsel in proceedings based on charges of serious crime has long been regarded as shocking to the "universal sense of justice" throughout this country. In 1854, for example, the Supreme Court of Indiana said: "It is not to be thought of, in a civilized community, for a moment, that any citizen put in jeopardy of life or liberty, should be debarred of counsel because he was too poor to employ such aid. No Court could be respected, or respect itself, to sit and hear such a trial. The defence of the poor, in such cases, is a duty resting somewhere, which will be at once conceded as essential to the accused, to the Court, and to the public." *Webb* v. *Baird,* 6 Ind. 13, 18. And most of the other States have shown their agreement by constitutional provisions, statutes, or established practice judicially approved, which assure that no man shall be deprived of counsel merely because of his poverty.[2] Any other practice seems to me to defeat the promise of our democratic society to provide equal justice under the law.

[The appendix to the dissenting opinion, summarizing the law in individual states, is omitted.]

## Note

The issues raised in *Betts v. Brady* were again discussed at length in *Bute v. Illinois,* 333 U. S. 640, 92 L. Ed. 986, 68 S. Ct. 763 (1948). The majority in the *Bute* case formulated a distinction between cases involving charges of crime carrying the death penalty and cases involving lesser sentences. In the capital cases the right to counsel in state courts guaranteed by the Fourteenth Amendment appears to be equivalent to that required in Federal courts by the Sixth Amendment. Hence in a capital case the state courts are required to assign counsel whether or not the defendant requests it. *Williams v. Kaiser,* 323 U. S. 471, 89 L. Ed. 398, 65 S. Ct. 363 (1945); *Tomkins v. Missouri,* 323 U. S. 485, 89 L. Ed. 407, 65 S. Ct. 370 (1945); *Marino v. Ragen,* 332

---

2 In thirty-five states, there is some clear legal requirement or an established practice that indigent defendants in serious non-capital as well as capital criminal cases (*e. g.,* where the crime charged is a felony, a "penitentiary offense," an offense punishable by imprisonment for several years) be provided with counsel on request. In nine states, there are no clearly controlling statutory or constitutional provisions and no decisive reported cases on the subject. In two states, there are dicta in judicial decisions indicating a probability that the holding of the court below in this case would be followed under similar circumstances. In only two states (including the one in which this case arose) has the practice here upheld by this Court been affirmatively sustained. Appended to this opinion is a list of the several states divided into these four categories.

U. S. 561, 92 L. Ed. 170, 68 S. Ct. 240 (1947). And counsel must have sufficient time in which to prepare the case. *Hawk v. Olson*, 326 U. S. 271, 90 L. Ed. 61, 66 S. Ct. 116 (1945). But the defendant may, by plea of guilty or otherwise, waive his right. *Carter v. Illinois*, 329 U. S. 173, 91 L. Ed. 172, 67 S. Ct. 216 (1946).

In non-capital cases, if the defendant is refused the right to have counsel of his own selection the Court will find a violation of the Fourteenth Amendment. *House v. Mayo*, 324 U. S. 42, 89 L. Ed. 739, 65 S. Ct. 517 (1945). Otherwise the Fourteenth Amendment guarantees an accused the assistance of counsel only where "there are special circumstances showing that, otherwise, the defendant would not enjoy that fair notice and adequate hearing which constitute the foundation of due process of law in the trial of any criminal charge." *Bute v. Illinois*, 333 U. S. at 677. Or, as the majority put it in *Uveges v. Pennsylvania*, "when a crime subject to capital punishment is not involved, each case depends upon its own facts." 335 U. S. 437, 441, 93 L. Ed. 127, 69 S. Ct. 184 (1948). The application of this principle is illustrated by *Gibbs v. Burke*, set forth below.

## GIBBS v. BURKE

Supreme Court of the United States, 1949
337 U. S. 773, 93 L. Ed. 1686, 69 S. Ct. 1247

MR. JUSTICE REED delivered the opinion of the Court.

This case raises the question whether under the circumstances of petitioner's trial for larceny in a state court without counsel, Pennsylvania deprived him of a federal constitutional right, protected by the due process clause of the Fourteenth Amendment.

Petitioner, a man in his thirties, was arrested in Pennsylvania in 1947 for the larceny of certain clothing and other personal effects allegedly belonging to one James Blades. Upon the return of an indictment he pleaded not guilty, was tried before a jury which found him guilty, and was sentenced to a term of two and one-half to five years in the penitentiary. The record shows neither a request for counsel by the petitioner nor an offer of counsel by the court. Petitioner conducted his own defense.

. . .

[Subsequently Gibbs filed a petition for writ of habeas corpus in the Supreme Court of Pennsylvania, which was denied. The United States Supreme Court then granted his petition for certiorari.]

James Blades, the prosecuting witness, Mrs. Lafield, his mother, Constable Fleming, the arresting officer, and James Silverstein, a second-hand dealer, testified for the state. Briefly summarized, their testimony tended to prove that petitioner came to Blades' home on the morning of the alleged theft, looked in Blades' room, where the stolen articles were in plain view, and, finding Blades absent, departed. When Blades returned home that day he noticed that the articles were missing from his room and, upon learning from his mother that Gibbs had been there, he notified the police. He and Constable Fleming found some of the missing articles in a pawnshop and found the petitioner in a taproom wearing Blades' hat and watch. Later Blades' wallet was found in the jail cell in which petitioner was incarcerated. Silverstein, the secondhand dealer in the pawnshop, testified that Gibbs had brought the missing clothing in and had sold them to him.

Petitioner, by means of cross-examination, sought to establish that the articles had been taken, and some of them sold, pursuant to an understanding between him and Blades.

Several events occurring at the trial are pertinent to petitioner's claim that failure to appoint counsel violated the federal Constitution. (1) Considerable inadmissible hearsay and otherwise incompetent evidence was allowed to go in without objection by Gibbs.[1] (2) When petitioner recalled the prosecuting witness Blades for further cross-examination the trial judge accepted the prosecutor's suggestion and made Blades the petitioner's witness for the purpose of the unfavorable testimony then elicited.[2] Thus he made this testimony binding on the petitioner although the Pennsylvania rule would seem to be that an adverse witness can be so examined and yet remain the witness of the

---

[1] Blades: "Then she [witness's mother] tells me about him [petitioner] being there."

Constable Fleming: "I got a telephone call from the Chief of Police, Mr. Miller, to go up to Mrs. Lafield's to investigate a robbery that occurred there. . . . I asked Jim, where was the suitcase. He said, the suitcase was by the bed. . . ."

"I went to three pawnshops and they gave me a description of Edward Gibbs. . . ."

The District Attorney's unsworn offer of proof concerning the missing articles was as follows:

"Mr. Johnson: I want to offer into evidence the wallet, the watch, which were identified and found—The watch was found in the possession of the defendant. This wallet, containing the papers of Mr. Blade, which was found in the jail cell that had been occupied by the defendant.

"The Court: What about the radio?

"Mr. Johnson: It has been recovered and returned to the owner."

[2] "The Defendant: May I call the prosecutor [Blades] back on the stand?

"Mr. Johnson: He desires to call the prosecutor as his witness."

In his charge to the jury the judge said with reference to this episode:

"As he has presented no evidence of his own except having called Mr. Blades and certain questions were asked Mr. Blades and certain answers were made; that is the only evidence he presented."

opposing party.[3] (3) Although, as we have already noted, petitioner attempted to defend himself on the ground that he took and sold the articles pursuant to an agreement with the prosecuting witness, he was prevented from proving a fact clearly relevant to that defense,[4] i.e., that Blades had previously made a baseless criminal charge against him under similar circumstances.[5] (4) The trial judge also advised petitioner in the presence of the jury, so far as the record shows, as to his opportunity to avail himself of the privilege against self-incrimination which was his under Pennsylvania law. In doing so he made reference to possible past convictions.[6] So to require him to claim his constitutional safeguard in the presence of the jury was, petitioner claims, a violation of Pennsylvania law. Cf. *Philadelphia v. Cline,* 158 Pa. Super. 179, 185, 44 A. 2d 610; *Commonwealth v. Valeroso,* 273 Pa. 213, 116 A. 828. Respondent does not claim otherwise. The information given by the judge as to past convictions could have been given by a lawyer to the petitioner beyond the jury's hearing. (5) Finally, when sentencing petitioner the judge used language which, it is claimed, evinced a hostile and thoroughly injudicial attitude.[7] . . .

---

[3] *Commonwealth v. Reeves,* 267 Pa. 631, 362–363, 110 A. 158; *Commonwealth v. Eisenhower,* 181 Pa. 470, 476, 37 A. 521, 59 Am. St. Rep. 670.

[4] *Commonwealth v. Farrell,* 187 Pa. 408, 423–424, 41 A. 382; see 3 Wigmore, Evidence (3d ed., 1940) § 950.

[5] "Q. Last fall, last year, didn't you wreck your own automobile and enter a complaint that I stole your car and wrecked it?

"Mr. Johnson: Objected to.

"The Court: Objection sustained. It has nothing to do with this case.

"The Defendant: All right."

[6] "The Court: Now then, Gibbs, you may, if you want to, take the stand and say anything you want to say, but I warn you if you do, if you have any record of any prior conviction, any felonies or any misdemeanors in the nature of what we call crimen falsi, the commonwealth may offer the record of any convictions you may have had. I am warning you in advance. You may, however, take the stand and testify or you may refuse to take the stand and if you do refuse to take the stand, the commonwealth and the court may not comment unfavorably about your failure to take the stand and testify. I want to warn you fully before you do take the stand.

"Do you want to take the stand?

"The Defendant: No, I don't have anything to say in court."

[7] "By the Court:

"Q. Gibbs, do you have anything to say before we impose sentence?

"A. No, I guess not.

"Q. How long have you been in jail?

"A. Two months and a half.

"Q. What is the matter with you; why can't you keep out of trouble?

"A. I don't know, sir.

"Q. You don't know why you can't do it? What do you do, get drunk or something, or are you just ornery?

Since it is clear that a failure to request counsel does not constitute a waiver when the defendant does not know of his right to counsel, *Uveges v. Pennsylvania,* 335 U. S. 437, we proceed to the merits. We consider this case on the theory upheld in *Betts v. Brady,* 316 U. S. 455, that the Constitution does not guarantee to every person charged with a serious crime in a state court the right to the assistance of counsel regardless of the circumstances. *Betts v. Brady* rejected the contention that the Fourteenth Amendment automatically afforded such protection. In so doing, however, it did not, of course, hold or intimate that counsel was never required in noncapital cases in state courts in order to satisfy the necessity for basic fairness which is formulated in that Amendment.

There have been made to this Court without avail arguments based on the long practice as to counsel in state courts to convince us that under the Fourteenth Amendment a state may refuse to furnish counsel even when needed by the accused in serious felonies other than capital. Our decisions have been that where the ignorance, youth, or other incapacity of the defendant made

---

"Mr. Johnson: Don't you think this man would be better if he were sent to the Eastern Penitentiary?

"By the Court:

"Q. Do you realize you can be put away for the rest of your life?

"A. (No answer).

"The Court: It is a wonder the district attorney doesn't indict you for it. You can be indicted.

"Mr. Johnson: If he comes back again, I will take it as my personal job to indict him.

"The Court: In 1928 you were found guilty of burglary, larceny, receiving stolen goods, before Judge Fronefield—one to two years, county jail. In 1931, plead guilty to larceny—$100 fine and costs, one to two years, Judge McDade. 1932 found guilty of larceny and receiving stolen goods, $50 fine and costs, six months to three years in county jail, Judge Morrow. That is three. 1934 larceny, found guilty, $100 fine and costs, six months to three years in county jail; sentenced to one year in county jail for violation of parole; Judge Fronefield. That is four. 1937, receiving stolen goods, $10 fine and costs, one to three years county jail, sentence suspended by Judge McDade. That is five. 1938, larceny; found guilty, one and half to three years county jail, Judge Crichton. I don't believe there is anyone you missed up to now. You were before me a year ago. No, just last March. You beat that, not guilty. Now, here you are the seventh time.

"All I can do is give him two and a half to five years, if you don't want to indict these fourth offenders.

"Sentence.

"On No. 417 September Sessions 1947, the sentence of the court is that you undergo imprisonment in the Eastern State Penitentiary at solitary confinement and hard labor for two and a half to five years and stand committed until this sentence be complied with. If I could give you life, I would do it.

"Take him away."

a trial without counsel unfair, the defendant is deprived of his liberty contrary to the Fourteenth Amendment. Counsel necessary for his adequate defense would be lacking.

Respondent argues that to hold to such precedents leaves the state prosecuting authorities uncertain as to whether to offer counsel to all accused who are without adequate funds and under serious charges in state courts. We cannot offer a panacea for the difficulty. Such an interpretation of the Fourteenth Amendment would be an unwarranted federal intrusion into state control of its criminal procedure. The due process clause is not susceptible to reduction to a mathematical formula.

Furthermore, the fair conduct of a trial depends largely on the wisdom and understanding of the trial judge. He knows the essentials of a fair trial. The primary duty falls on him to determine the accused's need of counsel at arraignment and during trial. He may guide a defendant without a lawyer past the errors that make trials unfair. Cf. *Uveges v. Pennsylvania, supra.* Failure to protect properly the rights of one accused of serious offenses is unusual. Obviously a fair trial test necessitates an appraisal before and during the trial of the facts of each case to determine whether the need for counsel is so great that the deprivation of the right to counsel works a fundamental unfairness. The recent discussion of the problem in *Uveges v. Pennsylvania, supra,* makes further elaboration unnecessary. We think that the facts of this case, particularly the events occurring at the trial, reveal, in the light of that opinion and the precedents there cited, that petitioner was handicapped by lack of counsel to such an extent that his constitutional right to a fair trial was denied. This case is of the type referred to in *Betts v. Brady, supra,* at 473, as lacking fundamental fairness because neither counsel nor adequate judicial guidance or protection was furnished at the trial.

A defendant who pleads not guilty and elects to go to trial is usually more in need of the assistance of a lawyer than is one who pleads guilty. The record in this case evidences petitioner's helplessness, without counsel and without more assistance from the judge, in defending himself against this charge of larceny. We take no note of the tone of the comments at the time of the sentence. The trial was over. The questionable issues allowed to pass unnoticed as to procedure, evidence, privilege, and instructions detailed in the first part of this opinion demonstrate to us that petitioner did not have a trial that measures up to the test of fairness prescribed by the Fourteenth Amendment.

Reversed and remanded for proceedings not inconsistent with this opinion.

*Reversed and remanded.*

MR. JUSTICE BLACK and MR. JUSTICE DOUGLAS concur in the judgment of the Court. They think that *Betts v. Brady* should be overruled. If that case is to be followed, however, they agree with the Court's opinion insofar as it holds that petitioner is entitled to relief under the *Betts v. Brady* doctrine.

MR. JUSTICE MURPHY and MR. JUSTICE RUTLEDGE concur in the result.

## Note

1. Failure to provide counsel in non-capital cases in the state courts was held a denial of due process in *De Meerleer v. Michigan*, 329 U. S. 663, 91 L. Ed. 584, 67 S. Ct. 596 (1947); *Wade v. Mayo*, 334 U. S. 672, 92 L. Ed. 1647, 68 S. Ct. 1270 (1948); *Townsend v. Burke*, 334 U. S. 736, 92 L. Ed. 1690, 68 S. Ct. 1252 (1948) (defendant pleaded guilty but was prejudiced by lack of counsel at sentencing); *Uveges v. Pennsylvania*, 335 U. S. 437, 93 L. Ed. 127, 69 S. Ct. 184 (1948); *cf. Rice v. Olson*, 324 U. S. 786, 89 L. Ed. 1367, 65 S. Ct. 989 (1945); *Palmer v. Ashe*, 342 U. S. 134, 96 L. Ed. —, 72 S. Ct. 191 (1951). The contrary result was reached in *Canizio v. New York*, 327 U. S. 82, 90 L. Ed. 545, 66 S. Ct. 452 (1946) (defendant had counsel at sentencing, who could have withdrawn plea of guilty at that time); *Foster v. Illinois*, 332 U. S. 134, 91 L. Ed. 1955, 67 S. Ct. 1716 (1947); *Gayes v. New York*, 332 U. S. 145, 91 L. Ed. 1962, 67 S. Ct. 1711 (1947); *Bute v. Illinois*, 333 U. S. 640, 92 L. Ed. 986, 68 S. Ct. 763 (1948); *Gryger v. Burke*, 334 U. S. 728, 92 L. Ed. 1683, 68 S. Ct. 1256 (1948); *Quicksall v. Michigan*, 339 U. S. 660, 94 L. Ed. 1188, 70 S. Ct. 910 (1950).

As in the case of alleged coerced confessions, the Supreme Court grants petitions for certiorari in only a small fraction of the cases presented to it.

2. Under the doctrine of the foregoing cases, unless prejudice appears from all the circumstances, there is no requirement that the state show that the defendant was advised of his right to representation by counsel. See the *Bute*, *Foster* and *Quicksall* cases, *supra*. But the doctrine does take into consideration, as part of the relevant circumstances, whether the defendant was afforded adequate time to consult with his counsel, whether counsel had sufficient opportunity for preparation of the case, and, to a lesser extent, whether counsel was competent. See *House v. Mayo*, 324 U. S. 42, 89 L. Ed. 739, 65 S. Ct. 517 (1945); *White v. Ragen*, 324 U. S. 760, 89 L. Ed. 1348, 65 S. Ct. 978 (1945); Fellman, *The Federal Right to Counsel in State Courts*, 31 Neb. L. Rev. 15, 51–3 (1951); Note, 47 Col. L. Rev. 115 (1947).

3. The procedure for raising the issue of denial of counsel often confronts the defendant with complex technical problems. When the question can be presented to the Supreme Court on direct appeal from the state court conviction, as in *Powell v. Alabama*, no difficulties arise. But usually the issue is raised by collateral attack in the state courts through habeas corpus or similar proceedings. Here the defendant meets the rule, consistently and strictly applied, that he must

fully exhaust his state remedies before his case will be considered by the Supreme Court. See *Ex parte Hawk,* 321 U. S. 114, 88 L. Ed. 572, 64 S. Ct. 448 (1944); for an extreme application of the rule see *Gayes v. New York, supra.* Where there is uncertainty or complexity in the state procedures the application of the rule can result in false starts and long delays. See *Marino v. Ragen,* 332 U. S. 561, 92 L. Ed. 170, 68 S. Ct. 240 (1947); *Young v. Ragen,* 337 U. S. 235, 93 L. Ed. 1333, 69 S. Ct. 1073 (1949); *Jennings v. Illinois,* 342 U. S. 104, 96 L. Ed. —, 72 S. Ct. 123 (1951). The defendant must also exhaust his remedies in the state courts before he may apply to a Federal District Court for a writ of habeas corpus. See 28 U. S. C. §§ 2241-55 (Supp. 1950). This rule has been extended to require the defendant to apply to the United States Supreme Court for a writ of certiorari from the state court decision on habeas corpus, before a Federal court may entertain a petition. *Darr v. Burford,* 339 U. S. 200, 94 L. Ed. 761, 70 S. Ct. 587 (1950), overruling *Wade v. Mayo, supra.* For a discussion of the procedural problems see Fellman, *supra,* 31 Neb. L. Rev. at 31–48.

4. Where factual issues are in dispute the Supreme Court, as in the case of alleged coerced confessions, is limited by the record and findings of the state court proceedings. Where the defendant raises substantial issues of fact in a habeas corpus proceeding, either in a state or Federal court, he is entitled to a hearing in which he may submit his evidence. See, *e. g., Hawk v. Olson,* 326 U. S. 271, 90 L. Ed. 61, 66 S. Ct. 116 (1945); *Wade v. Mayo, supra; Palmer v. Ashe, supra.* There is greater leeway for Federal factfinding, however, when the issue is presented by petition for habeas corpus in the Federal court. See *Wade v. Mayo, supra.*

5. With respect to the right to be represented in a state court by counsel from outside the state, see *Cooper v. Hutchinson,* 184 F. 2d 119 (C. A. 3, 1950); Note, 51 Col. L. Rev. 127 (1951).

6. For discussion of Federal control over state court practices on the right to counsel, see Fellman, *supra,* 31 Neb. L. Rev. 15 (1951); Heller, *The Sixth Amendment,* ch. VI (1951); Wood, *Due Process of Law,* pp. 192–218 (1951); Note, *The Substance of the Right to Counsel,* 17 U. of Chi. L. Rev. 718 (1950); Note, *The Right of Counsel Today,* 43 Ill. L. Rev. 664 (1948); Boskey and Pickering, *Federal Restrictions on State Criminal Procedure,* 13 U. of Chi. L. Rev. 266, 267–79 (1946). See also Notes, 48 Col. L. Rev. 1076 (1948); 1948 Wis. L. Rev. 235; 33 Va. L. Rev. 731 (1947); 23 Tex. L. Rev. 66 (1944); 42 Col. L. Rev. 271 (1942); 3 A. L. R. 2d 1003.

7. Within the standards imposed by the due process clause of the Fourteenth Amendment the law in the various states differs with respect to when counsel must be assigned, when and how the defendant must be informed of his rights, what constitutes adequate opportunity for consultation and preparation, and similar matters. In general see Orfield, *Criminal Procedure from Arrest to Appeal,* pp. 417–28 (1947); Mangum, *The Legal Status of the Negro,* ch. XIV (1940); Notes, 28 Tex. L. Rev. 236 (1949); 47 Col. L. Rev. 115 (1947); 3 A. L. R. 2d 1003.

[Emerson]

## POLLOCK—THE VOLUNTARY DEFENDER AS COUNSEL FOR THE DEFENSE

32 J. of Am. Jud. Soc. 174, at pp. 174–7 (1949)

Recent pronouncements of the Supreme Court of the United States broadening the interpretation of the constitutional right of an accused to the assistance of counsel have caused concern among law makers, judges and lawyers. How, they ask, should the growing demand for legal assistance to impoverished defendants in criminal cases be met? Donald Freeman thinks the answer is the public defender.[1] William Scott Stewart stands squarely opposed to that view and, by implication at least, favors the old, traditional system of assignment of private counsel in individual cases.[2] In my opinion, some practical objections to these two methods are overcome by a third—the representation of indigent defendants by the voluntary defender.

The old concept of supplying legal representation to indigent defendants on the basis of charity has gradually given away to the concept of representation as a matter of right. The haphazard system of assigning private lawyers in individual cases has not kept pace in urban areas with the need for assistance created by this change in attitude so clearly reflected in the recent decisions of the Supreme Court of the United States.

Under the assignment system a person charged with the commission of a crime often goes to trial without legal representation, unless the court sees fit to assign counsel to him. Not infreqeuntly assigned counsel has little or no criminal trial experience. Pressed into service without notice he has no means of adequately preparing his defense. Since there is no provision for compensation, or even for reimbursement of expenses in many states, counsel cannot be expected, and he is in some instances financially unable, to spend the time or money required to find witnesses and procure their appearance in court. While counsel may graciously accept an assignment and do all that can reasonably be expected under the circumstances, he lacks the means at hand of properly representing the man. This is particularly so in large metropolitan districts where the pressure of court business is such that large numbers of uncounselled defendants may be brought to trial on little or no notice. Where such conditions exist it is imperative that counsel be supplied as soon after arrest as is feasible so that the man's case may be prepared within the

---

[1] "The Public Defender System," 32 J. Am. Jud. Soc. 74 (Oct., 1948).

[2] "The Public Defender System is Unsound in Principle," 32 J. Am. Jud. Soc. 115 (Dec., 1948).

brief time that elapses before trial. This cannot be done under the unregulated assignment system.

### ORGANIZATION IS NECESSARY

It is generally agreed that today legal assistance to the accused poor can be effectively rendered only on an organized basis—be it private or public. Some communities, recognizing the weaknesses of the appointive system, have sought to satisfy the needs of indigent defendants for legal aid by setting up private voluntary associations, while others sought solution in the statutory creation of the office of public defender. While the purposes of these two bodies are essentially the same, their organizational structure may frequently determine the quality of the services they perform.

Mr. Stewart's spirited attack on the public defender system rose out of his conviction that a public official, whether he be appointed by the court or elected by the people cannot take the place of the lawyer for the defense; that he cannot, because of his position, satisfy the essentials of due process. Mr. Stewart maintains that the public defender's master is the court rather than the client; that he tries his case to please the judge and dare not be too critical of the prosecutor. From all this he concludes that the public defender system is unsound in principle.

I cannot agree with the assertion that the public defender system is unsound in principle. . . . Mr. Stewart's charge that the public defender merely goes through the motions of pretending to be a lawyer for the defense, persuades his client to waive jury trial, or causes him to plead guilty to save time is to indict not only the lawyer but the court, and in the end the entire bar which supinely permits such a state of affairs to exist. Doubtless the setting in which a public defender works affects the manner in which he discharges his duty to his client. If his office is hemmed in by statutory limitations and political pressures, or if his relationship to the court is such that his efforts to fulfill his duties may easily be curbed by lazy or tyrannical judges to whom he owes his appointment, his effectiveness as the poor man's advocate will be diminished. This does not mean that the public defender doctrine is unsound. It merely means that its implementation is sometimes beset with serious obstacles.

### HOW IT IS DONE IN PHILADELPHIA

Many informed persons believe that the rights of indigent defendants require independent protection against the excesses or abuses of official authority. They are convinced that the rep-

**180**

resentation of impoverished defendants by public officials is neither traditional nor desirable from a practical standpoint. It is this belief which has been responsible in a number of cities for the establishment of voluntary defender organizations. Such an organization, supported by the Community Chest, exists in Philadelphia. It is designedly housed in a private office building rather than in the county court house. This is done in order to make it plain that the Voluntary Defender is not a public official. Structurally the Association is organized as a non-profit corporation governed by a Board of Directors principally composed of leaders of the Philadelphia Bar. The Board of Directors selects the Defender and places on him the full responsibility of carrying out the purpose and policies of the Association. The judges in no way control this selection, and the Defender stands before the court in the same position as private counsel.

On the Defender staff are three lawyers, five investigators and three clerical workers. All are engaged on a full time basis, and the lawyers are precluded from taking any private work. The legal staff is augmented by volunteer attorneys assigned for specific periods of time by the larger law offices. These volunteers work on a full time basis and assist in the preparation and trial of cases. . . .

I do not pretend that the voluntary defender method of supplying counsel approaches perfection, but I do say that it can afford to an indigent defendant the same kind and quality of independent representation traditionally enjoyed by those financially able to engage private counsel.

## Note

1. In the Federal courts there is no provision for payment of compensation to attorneys assigned to represent indigent defendants. See Holtzoff, *The Right of Counsel Under the Sixth Amendment*, 20 N. Y. U. L. Q. Rev. 1, 17–9 (1944); Fellman, *The Constitutional Right to Counsel in Federal Courts*, 30 Neb. L. Rev. 559, 596–9 (1951) (both articles criticize the lack of compensation and discuss proposed legislation). In over half the states some provision for payment of fees is made. See Baird, *Compensation for Court Appointed Counsel*, 31 J. Am. Inst. of Cr. L. and Crim. 731, 734–5 (1941). Nevertheless criticism of the operation of the assignment system in practice is almost universal among commentators. See e. g., Pollock and Baird, *supra;* Elson, *The Rushcliffe Report*, 13 U. of Chi. L. Rev. 131 (1946); Bennett, *To Secure the Right to Counsel*, 32 J. of Am. Jud. Soc. 177 (1949); Potts, *Right to Counsel in Criminal Cases: Legal Aid or Public Defender*, 28 Tex. L. Rev. 491 (1950). But *cf.* Holtzoff, *supra.*

Public defender systems exist in 5 states and about a dozen cities. The quality of service rendered has been vigorously attacked (see the

Stewart article cited in the extract from Pollock, *supra*) and equally strongly defended (see Bennett, *supra;* Potts, *supra;* Freeman, *The Public Defender System,* 32 J. of Am. Jud. Soc. 74 (1948)). In addition voluntary public defender systems, supported by the Community Chest, are functioning in Philadelphia and Boston; and in New York, Pittsburgh, New Orleans and Cincinnati the Legal Aid Societies render public defender service. See Brownell, *Legal Aid and Democracy,* 34 Corn. L. Q. 580, 583 (1949). Altogether the assistance of a public defender is thus available to only a small portion of the total population.

2. In general, on the whole question of the availability and effectiveness of legal services for low and middle income groups see, in addition to the material above cited, Smith, *Justice and the Poor* (3d ed. 1924); Smith and Bradway, *The Growth of Legal Aid Work in the United States,* Dept. of Labor Bull. No. 607 (1936); Mangum, *The Legal Status of the Negro,* ch. XIV (1940); *The Availability of Legal Services,* 10 Law. Guild Rev. 8 (1950) (collecting much of the available material); Brownell, *Legal Aid in the United States* (1951). On legal aid systems in other countries see Schweinburg, *Legal Assistance Abroad,* 17 U. Chi. L. Rev. 270 (1950); Note, *The British Legal Aid and Advice Bill,* 59 Yale L. J. 320 (1950); Smith, *The English Legal Assistance Plan,* 35 A. B. A. J. 453 (1949).

3. A further problem in connection wth the effective right to counsel concerns the zeal or aggressiveness with which an attorney may advocate his client's cause. The lawyer's conduct in the courtroom must, generally speaking, be kept within the bounds sanctioned by the presiding judge. By Federal statute and decision strict limitations have been imposed upon the power of a judge to punish by summary citation for contempt of court. See *Ex parte Terry,* 128 U. S. 289, 32 L. Ed. 405, 9 S. Ct. 77 (1888); *Cooke v. U. S.,* 267 U. S. 517, 69 L. Ed. 767, 45 S. Ct. 390 (1925); *In re Oliver,* 333 U. S. 257, 92 L. Ed. 682, 68 S. Ct. 499 (1948); Nelles, *Summary Power to Punish for Contempt,* 31 Col. L. Rev. 956 (1931). And see Rule 42 of the Federal Rules of Criminal Procedure, 18 U. S. C. (1951). But the power still remaining, plus the fact that an attorney may normally expect to appear before the same judge on later occasions, renders the control exercised by the judge in practice a pervasive and decisive one. See, *e. g., Fisher v. Pace,* 336 U. S. 155, 93 L. Ed. 569, 69 S. Ct. 425 (1949); *cf.* the material on the right to comment on judicial proceedings, Chapter IV, *infra.*

Issues of this nature are likely to arise in cases where the attorney is representing an unpopular cause. This problem is not new. Clashes between judge and attorney occurred in the English seditious libel cases. See, *e. g.,* Oswald, *Contempt of Court,* pp. 51-2 (3d ed. 1911). And similar conflicts took place in trials under the Alien and Sedition Acts. See Raby, *Fifty Famous Trials,* pp. 66–72 (1937); *The Impeachment Trial of Justice Samuel Chase (Report of the Trial)* pp. 18–55, Appendix pp. 3–6 (1805); Miller, *Crisis in Freedom,* p. 217 (1951); see also *The Trial of John Peter Zenger,* 17 How. St. Tr.

675 (1735). More recent trials involving unpopular political minorities that have resulted in contempt proceedings against attorneys for the defense include the first Communist trial and the trial of Harry Bridges for perjury. See *Sacher v. U. S.*, 182 F. 2d 416 (C. A. 2, 1950), 343 U. S. 1, 96 L. Ed. —, 72 S. Ct. 451 (1952) (Communist trial); *Hallinan v. U. S.*, 182 F. 2d 880 (C. A. 9, 1950), cert. den. 341 U. S. 952 (1951), rehearing den. 342 U. S. 956 (1952) (Bridges trial); *MacInnis v. U. S.*, 191 F. 2d 157 (C. A. 9, 1951), cert. den. 342 U. S. 953 (1952) (Bridges trial); Harper and Haber, *Lawyer Troubles in Political Trials*, 60 Yale L. J. 1 (1951). For the disbarment proceedings against Sacher and Isserman, see N. Y. Times, January 5, 1952, March 25, 1952; Weissman, *Sacher and Isserman in the Courts*, 12 Law. Guild Rev. 39 (1952). See also *Cooper v. Hutchinson*, 184 F. 2d 119 (C. A. 3d, 1950).

4. With reference to the obligation of the legal profession to furnish legal assistance to members of unpopular political groups charged with crime, note the statement of President Truman to the American Bar Association: "A second contribution which I think the Bar may make relates to fair administrative and legislative hearings for persons under investigation and fair trials for persons accused of crime involving security. The Bar has a notable tradition of willingness to protect the rights of the accused. It seems to me that if this tradition is to be meaningful today it must extend to all defendants, including persons accused of such abhorrent crimes as conspiracy to overthrow the Government by force, espionage, and sabotage. Undoubtedly, some uninformed persons will always identify the lawyer with the client. But I believe that most Americans recognize how important it is to our tradition of fair trial that there be adequate representation by competent counsel.

"Lawyers in the past have risked the obloquy of the uninformed to protect the rights of the most degraded. Unless they continue to do so in the future, an important part of our rights will be gone." N. Y. Times, Sept. 19, 1951.

See also Joughlin, *The Legal Defense of Hated Men*, The Nation, Jan. 13, 1951, p. 10.

## C. SEARCHES AND SEIZURES

The Fourth Amendment provides that "the right of the people to be secure in their persons, houses, papers and effects, against unreasonable searches and seizures, shall not be violated, and no Warrants shall issue, but upon probable cause, supported by Oath or affirmation, and particularly describing the place to be searched, and the persons or things to be seized." All state constitutions contain similar provisions. See Cornelius, *The Law of Search and Seizure*, pp. 8–11 (2d ed. 1930); dissenting opinion of Mr. Justice Frankfurter in *Harris v. U. S.*, 331 U. S. 145, 91 L. Ed. 1399, 67 S. Ct. 1098 (1947).

The first important Supreme Court decision interpreting the Fourth Amendment was *Boyd v. United States,* set forth below.

## BOYD v. UNITED STATES

Supreme Court of the United States, 1886
116 U. S. 616, 29 L. Ed. 746, 6 S. Ct. 524

[The government had seized 35 cases of plate glass alleged to have been fraudulently imported by Boyd & Sons in violation of the customs law. Boyd claimed the goods were not subject to forfeiture. At the trial the government found it important to establish the quantity and value of the glass contained in 29 cases previously imported by Boyd. Acting under a statute authorizing the procedure, the government moved for an order of the court directing Boyd to produce the invoice covering the earlier 29 cases, which order was granted. The statute provided that if the papers were not produced pursuant to such motion and order the facts alleged in the motion would be taken as admitted. Boyd asserted that the procedure and the statute violated the Fourth Amendment and the self-incrimination provisions of the Fifth Amendment.]

MR. JUSTICE BRADLEY delivered the opinion of the court. . . .
But, in regard to the Fourth Amendment, it is contended that, whatever might have been alleged against the constitutionality of the acts of 1863 and 1867, that of 1874, under which the order in the present case was made, is free from constitutional objection, because it does not authorize the search and seizure of books and papers, but only requires the defendant or claimant to produce them. That is so; but it declares that if he does not produce them, the allegations which it is affirmed they will prove shall be taken as confessed. This is tantamount to compelling their production; for the prosecuting attorney will always be sure to state the evidence expected to be derived from them as strongly as the case will admit of. It is true that certain aggravating incidents of actual search and seizure, such as forcible entry into a man's house and searching amongst his papers, are wanting, and to this extent the proceeding under the act of 1874 is a mitigation of that which was authorized by the former acts; but it accomplishes the substantial object of those acts in forcing from a party evidence against himself. It is our opinion, therefore, that a compulsory production of a man's private papers to establish a criminal charge against him, or to forfeit his property, is within the scope of the Fourth Amendment to the Constitution, in all cases in which a search and seizure would be; because it is

a material ingredient, and effects the sole object and purpose of search and seizure.

The principal question, however, remains to be considered. Is a search and seizure, or, what is equivalent thereto, a compulsory production of a man's private papers, to be used in evidence against him in a proceeding to forfeit his property for alleged fraud against the revenue laws—is such a proceeding for such a purpose an *"unreasonable* search and seizure" within the meaning of the Fourth Amendment of the Constitution? or, is it a legitimate proceeding? It is contended by the counsel for the government, that it is a legitimate proceeding, sanctioned by long usage, and the authority of judicial decision. . . . Even the act under which the obnoxious writs of assistance were issued did not go as far as this, but only authorized the examination of ships and vessels, and persons found therein, for the purpose of finding goods prohibited to be imported or exported, or on which the duties were not paid, and to enter into and search any suspected vaults, cellars, or warehouses for such goods. The search for and seizure of stolen or forfeited goods, or goods liable to duties and concealed to avoid the payment thereof, are totally different things from a search for and seizure of a man's private books and papers for the purpose of obtaining information therein contained, or of using them as evidence against him. The two things differ *toto coelo*. In the one case, the government is entitled to the *possession* of the property; in the other it is not. The seizure of stolen goods is authorized by the common law; and the seizure of goods forfeited for a breach of the revenue laws, or concealed to avoid the duties payable on them, has been authorized by English statutes for at least two centuries past; and the like seizures have been authorized by our own revenue acts from the commencement of the government. The first statute passed by Congress to regulate the collection of duties, the act of July 31, 1789, 1 Stat. 29, 43, contains provisions to this effect. As this act was passed by the same Congress which proposed for adoption the original amendments to the Constitution, it is clear that the members of that body did not regard searches and seizures of this kind as "unreasonable," and they are not embraced within the prohibition of the amendment. So, also, the supervision authorized to be exercised by officers of the revenue over the manufacture or custody of excisable articles, and the entries thereof in books required by law to be kept for their inspection, are necessarily excepted out of the category of unreasonable searches and seizures. So, also, the laws which provide for the search and seizure of articles and things which it is unlawful for a person to have in his possession

**185**

for the purpose of issue or disposition, such as counterfeit coin, lottery tickets, implements of gambling, &c., are not within this category. *Commonwealth v. Dana*, 2 Met. (Mass.) 329. Many other things of this character might be enumerated. The entry upon premises, made by a sheriff or other officer of the law, for the purpose of seizing goods and chattels by virtue of a judicial writ, such as an attachment, a sequestration, or an execution, is not within the prohibition of the Fourth or Fifth Amendment, or any other clause of the Constitution; nor is the examination of a defendant under oath after an ineffectual execution, for the purpose of discovering secreted property or credits, to be applied to the payment of a judgment against him, obnoxious to those amendments.

But, when examined with care, it is manifest that there is a total unlikeness of these official acts and proceedings to that which is now under consideration. In the case of stolen goods, the owner from whom they were stolen is entitled to their possession; and in the case of excisable or dutiable articles, the government has an interest in them for the payment of the duties thereon, and until such duties are paid has a right to keep them under observation, or to pursue and drag them from concealment; and in the case of goods seized on attachment or execution, the creditor is entitled to their seizure in satisfaction of his debt; and the examination of a defendant under oath to obtain a discovery of concealed property or credits is a proceeding merely civil to effect the ends of justice, and is no more than what the court of chancery would direct on a bill for discovery. Whereas, by the proceeding now under consideration, the court attempts to extort from the party his private books and papers to make him liable for a penalty or to forfeit his property.

In order to ascertain the nature of the proceedings intended by the Fourth Amendment to the Constitution under the terms "unreasonable searches and seizures," it is only necessary to recall the contemporary or then recent history of the controversies on the subject, both in this country and in England. The practice had obtained in the colonies of issuing writs of assistance to the revenue officers, empowering them, in their discretion, to search suspected places for smuggled goods, which James Otis pronounced "the worst instrument of arbitrary power, the most destructive of English liberty, and the fundamental principles of law, that ever was found in an English law book;" since they placed "the liberty of every man in the hands of every petty officer." * This was in February, 1761, in Boston, and the famous

---

* *Note by the Court.*—Cooley's Constitutional Limitations, 301–303, (5th ed. 368, 369). A very full and interesting account of this discussion will

debate in which it occurred was perhaps the most prominent event which inaugurated the resistance of the colonies to the oppressions of the mother country. "Then and there," said John Adams, "then and there was the first scene of the first act of opposition to the arbitrary claims of Great Britain. Then and there the child Independence was born."

These things, and the events which took place in England immediately following the argument about writs of assistance in Boston, were fresh in the memories of those who achieved our independence and established our form of government. In the period from 1762, when the North Briton was started by John Wilkes, to April, 1766, when the House of Commons passed resolutions condemnatory of general warrants, whether for the seizure of persons or papers, occurred the bitter controversy between the English government and Wilkes, in which the latter appeared as the champion of popular rights, and was, indeed, the pioneer in the contest which resulted in the abolition of some grievous abuses which had gradually crept into the administration of public affairs. Prominent and principal among these was the practice of issuing general warrants by the Secretary of State, for searching private houses for the discovery and seizure of books and papers that might be used to convict their owner of the charge of libel. Certain numbers of the North Briton, particularly No. 45, had been very bold in denunciation of the government, and were esteemed heinously libellous. By authority of the secretary's warrant Wilkes's house was searched, and his papers were indiscriminately seized. For this outrage he sued the perpetrators and obtained a verdict of £1000 against Wood, one of the party who made the search, and £4000 against Lord Halifax, the Secretary of State who issued the warrant. The case, however, which will always be celebrated as being the occasion of Lord Camden's memorable discussion of the subject, was that of *Entick v. Carrington and Three Other King's Messengers*, reported at length in 19 Howell's State Trials, 1029. The action was trespass for entering the plaintiff's dwelling-house in November, 1762, and breaking open his desks, boxes, &c., and searching and examining his papers. The jury rendered a special verdict, and the case was twice solemnly argued at the bar. Lord Camden pronounced the judgment of the court in Michaelmas Term, 1765, and the law as expounded by him has been regarded

---

be found in the works of John Adams, vol. 2, Appendix A, pp. 523–525; vol. 10, pp. 183, 233, 244, 256, &c., and in Quincy's Reports, pp. 469–482; and see *Paxton's Case*, do. 51–57, which was argued in November of the same year (1761). An elaborate history of the writs of assistance is given in the Appendix to Quincy's Reports, above referred to, written by Horace Gray, Jr., Esq., now a member of this court.

as settled from that time to this, and his great judgment on that occasion is considered as one of the landmarks of English liberty. It was welcomed and applauded by the lovers of liberty in the colonies as well as in the mother country. It is regarded as one of the permanent monuments of the British Constitution, and is quoted as such by the English authorities on that subject down to the present time.*

As every American statesmen, during our revolutionary and formative period as a nation, was undoubtedly familiar with this monument of English freedom, and considered it as the true and ultimate expression of constitutional law, it may be confidently asserted that its propositions were in the minds of those who framed the Fourth Amendment to the Constitution, and were considered as sufficiently explanatory of what was meant by unreasonable searches and seizures. . . .

The principles laid down in this opinion affect the very essence of constitutional liberty and security. They reach farther than the concrete form of the case then before the court, with its adventitious circumstances; they apply to all invasions on the part of the government and its employés of the sanctity of a man's home and the privacies of life. It is not the breaking of his doors, and the rummaging of his drawers, that constitutes the essence of the offence; but it is the invasion of his indefeasible right of personal security, personal liberty and private property, where that right has never been forfeited by his conviction of some public offence,—it is the invasion of this sacred right which underlies and constitutes the essence of Lord Camden's judgment. Breaking into a house and opening boxes and drawers are circumstances of aggravation; but any forcible and compulsory extortion of a man's own testimony or of his private papers to be used as evidence to convict him of crime or to forfeit his goods, is within the condemnation of that judgment. In this regard the Fourth and Fifth Amendments run almost into each other. . . .

We think that the notice to produce the invoice in this case, the order by virtue of which it was issued, and the law which authorized the order, were unconstitutional and void, and that the inspection by the district attorney of said invoice, when produced in obedience to said notice, and its admission in evidence by the court, were erroneous and unconstitutional proceedings. We are of opinion, therefore, that

---

*Note by the Court.*—See May's Constitutional History of England, vol. 3, (American ed., vol. 2) chap. 11; Broom's Constitutional Law, 558; Cox's Institutions of the English Government, 437.

*The judgment of the Circuit Court should be reversed, and the cause remanded, with directions to award a new trial.*

[Chief Justice Waite and Mr. Justice Miller concurred in the result, agreeing with the majority on the Fifth Amendment. As to the Fourth Amendment, they felt that no "search and seizure" was involved.]

## Note

1. Further discussion of the historical background of the Fourth Amendment may be found in Reynard, *Freedom from Unreasonable Search and Seizure—A Second Class Constitutional Right?*, 25 Ind. L. J. 259, 259–77 (1950); Mr. Justice Frankfurter's dissenting opinions in *Davis v. U. S.*, 328 U. S. 582, 90 L. Ed. 1453, 66 S. Ct. 1256 (1946) and *Harris v. U. S.*, 331 U. S. 145, 91 L. Ed. 1399, 67 S. Ct. 1098 (1947).

2. Warrants for search and seizure may be issued only under specific authorization of a statute. The Federal statutes embodying such authorization, all of which are applicable only in cases charging a felony, are listed in Mr. Justice Frankfurter's dissenting opinion in the *Davis* case, *supra*. The procedure for issuance, execution and return of the warrant is set forth in Rule 41(c) and (d) of the Federal Rules of Criminal Procedure, 18 U. S. C. (1951). See also Machen, *The Law of Search and Seizure*, ch. I (1950); Note, 46 Harv. L. Rev. 1307 (1933); 14 A. L. R. 2d 605. Other forms of compulsory process issued by executive officials, such as supoenas, must likewise be specifically authorized by statute. See *Cudahy Packing Co. v. Holland*, 315 U. S. 357, 86 L. Ed. 895, 62 S. Ct. 651 (1942); *Fleming v. Mohawk Wrecking & Lumber Co.*, 331 U. S. 111, 91 L. Ed. 1375, 67 S. Ct. 1129 (1947).

3. The doctrine of the *Boyd* case, that a valid search can be conducted only for limited categories of articles, such as contraband and stolen goods, was reiterated and clarified in *Gouled v. U. S.*, 255 U. S. 298, 65 L. Ed. 647, 41 S. Ct. 261 (1921). Gouled was indicted for defrauding the United States on Army contracts. Under a search warrant the government seized certain other contracts, bills for legal fees, and similar papers in defendant's office, which were admitted in evidence. The Court, reversing the conviction, held that search warrants "may not be used as a means of gaining access to a man's house or office and papers solely for the purpose of making search to secure evidence to be used against him in a criminal or penal proceeding, but . . . they may be resorted to only when a primary right to such search and seizure may be found in the interest which the public or the complainant may have in the property to be seized, or in the right to the possession of it, or when a valid exercise of the police power renders possession of the property by the accused unlawful and provides that it may be taken" 255 U. S. at 309. The rule is usually stated that only contraband, stolen goods or articles used in connection with the crime may be seized. See Fraenkel, *Recent Developments in the Federal Law of Searches and Seizures*, 33 Iowa L. Rev. 472, 487–8 (1948). And these

restrictions are embodied in Rule 41(b) of the Federal Rules of Criminal Procedure. 18 U. S. C.

As time has gone on, however, the category of articles used in connection with the crime has broadened. See the *Marron* case, discussed in the *Rabinowitz* case, *infra*. And the Court has permitted the use of subpoenas or other compulsory process to require extensive production of business records showing Federal jurisdiction over the enterprise and violation of Federal economic regulation. *Oklahoma Press Publishing Co. v. Walling*, 327 U. S. 186, 90 L. Ed. 614, 66 S. Ct. 494 (1946); *U. S. v. Morton Salt Co.*, 338 U. S. 632, 94 L. Ed. 401, 70 S. Ct. 357 (1950). See also *Shapiro v. U. S.*, 335 U. S. 1, 92 L. Ed. 1787, 68 S. Ct. 1375 (1948) (records required by law to be kept); *Zap v. U. S.*, 328 U. S. 624, 90 L. Ed. 1477, 66 S. Ct. 1277 (1946) (contractor with government agreed to permit inspection of books), vacated on other grounds, 330 U. S. 800, 91 L. Ed. 1259, 67 S. Ct. 857 (1947).

4. The articles seized under a search warrant must be only those "particularly described" in the warrant. See the *Marron* case, and compare the *Harris* case, both discussed in the *Rabinowitz* case, *infra*. And a warrant cannot be general. See the *Agnello* case, discussed in the *Rabinowitz* case, *infra*. The Fourth Amendment protects against seizure by trickery as well as by force. *Gouled v. U. S.*, *supra;* but *cf. On Lee v. U. S.*, 343 U. S. —, 96 L. Ed. —, 72 S. Ct. 967 (1952) (no violation of Fourth Amendment where evidence obtained by radio transmitter concealed in pocket of government informer who engaged defendant in conversation at his place of business; four justices dissented). The Fourth Amendment does not apply where consent is given to the seizure. See *Amos v. U. S.*, 255 U. S. 313, 65 L. Ed. 654, 41 S. Ct. 266 (1921); *Zap v. U. S.*, *supra*. And where the article concerned is government property consent will be more readily implied. *Davis v. U. S.*, *supra*. With regard to the right of inspection by health officers, see *District of Columbia v. Little*, 339 U. S. 1, 94 L. Ed. 599, 70 S. Ct. 468 (1950); Note, 17 U. of Chi. L. Rev. 733 (1950).

5. The enactment of prohibition and the great development of Federal economic regulation produced a series of new problems under the Fourth Amendment. One of the major ones has been the extent to which a search and seizure may be undertaken without a warrant at all. The shifting position of the Supreme Court on this important problem is revealed in the opinions of the justices in *U. S. v. Rabinowitz*.

## UNITED STATES v. RABINOWITZ

Supreme Court of the United States, 1950

339 U. S. 56, 94 L. Ed. 653, 70 S. Ct. 430

MR. JUSTICE MINTON delivered the opinion of the Court.

Respondent was convicted of selling and of possessing and concealing forged and altered obligations of the United States with intent to defraud. The question presented here is the reasonableness of a search without a search warrant of a place of business consisting of a one-room office, incident to a valid arrest.

On February 1, 1943, a printer who possessed plates for forging "overprints" on canceled stamps was taken into custody. He disclosed that respondent, a dealer in stamps, was one of the customers to whom he had delivered large numbers of stamps bearing forged overprints.[1]  On Saturday, February 6, 1943, with this information concerning respondent and his activities in the hands of Government officers, a postal employee was sent to respondent's place of business to buy stamps bearing overprints. He bought four stamps.  On Monday, February 8, the stamps were sent to an expert to determine whether the overprints were genuine.  On February 9 the report was received showing the overprints to be forgeries, having been placed upon the stamps after cancellation, and not before as was the Government's practice.  On February 11 a further statement was obtained from the printer who had made the overprints.  On February 16, 1943, a warrant for the arrest of respondent was obtained. . . .

Armed with this valid warrant for arrest, the Government officers, accompanied by two stamp experts, went to respondent's place of business, a one-room office open to the public.  The officers thereupon arrested the respondent, and over his objection searched the desk, safe, and file cabinets in the office for about an hour and a half.  They found and seized 573 stamps, on which it was later determined that overprints had been forged, along with some other stamps which were subsequently returned to respondent. . . .

Respondent made timely motions for suppression and to strike the evidence pertaining to the 573 stamps, all of which were eventually denied.  Respondent was convicted on both counts after trial before a jury in which he offered no evidence.  Relying on *Trupiano v. United States,* 334 U.S. 699, the Court of Appeals, one judge dissenting, reversed on the ground that since the officers had had time in which to procure a search warrant and had failed to do so the search was illegal, and the evidence therefore should have been excluded.  176 F.2d 732.  We granted certiorari to determine the validity of the search because of the question's importance in the administration of the law of search and seizure.  338 U.S. 884.

Were the 573 stamps, the fruits of this search, admissible in evidence?  If legally obtained, these stamps were competent evidence to show intent under the first count of the indictment, and

---

[1] The stamps involved were genuine postage stamps.  At certain times the Government has printed the name of a particular state or possession on stamps prior to post office sale.  Canceled stamps bearing these overprints have an unusual value for stamp collectors.

they were the very things the possession of which was the crime charged in the second count. . . .

It is unreasonable searches that are prohibited by the Fourth Amendment. *Carroll v. United States,* 267 U.S. 132, 147. It was recognized by the framers of the Constitution that there were reasonable searches for which no warrant was required. The right of the "people to be secure in their persons" was certainly of as much concern to the framers of the Constitution as the property of the person. Yet no one questions the right, without a search warrant, to search the person after a valid arrest. The right to search the person incident to arrest always has been recognized in this country and in England. *Weeks v. United States,* 232 U.S. 383, 392. Where one had been placed in the custody of the law by valid action of officers, it was not unreasonable to search him.

Of course, a search without warrant incident to an arrest is dependent initially on a valid arrest. Here the officers had a warrant for respondent's arrest which was, as far as can be ascertained, broad enough to cover the crime of possession charged in the second count, and consequently respondent was properly arrested. Even if the warrant of arrest were not sufficient to authorize the arrest for possession of the stamps, the arrest therefor was valid because the officers had probable cause to believe that a felony was being committed in their very presence. *Carroll v. United States,* 267 U.S. 132, 156–57.

The arrest was therefore valid in any event, and respondent's person could be lawfully searched. Could the officers search his desk, safe and file cabinets, all within plain sight of the parties, and all located under respondent's immediate control in his one-room office open to the public?

Decisions of this Court have often recognized that there is a permissible area of search beyond the person proper. Thus in *Agnello v. United States,* 269 U.S. 20, 30, this Court stated:

"The right without a search warrant contemporaneously to search persons lawfully arrested while committing crime and to search the place where the arrest is made in order to find and seize things connected with the crime as its fruits or as the means by which it was committed, as well as weapons and other things to effect an escape from custody is not to be doubted."

The right "to search the place where the arrest is made in order to find and seize things connected with the crime as its fruits or as the means by which it was committed" seems to have stemmed not only from the acknowledged authority to search the person, but also from the long-standing practice of searching for other proofs of guilt within the control of the

192

accused found upon arrest. *Weeks v. United States,* 232 U.S. 383, 392. It became accepted that the premises where the arrest was made, which premises were under the control of the person arrested and where the crime was being committed, were subject to search without a search warrant. Such a search was not "unreasonable." *Agnello v. United States,* 269 U.S. 20, 30; *Carroll v. United States,* 267 U.S. 132, 158; *Boyd v. United States,* 116 U.S. 616, 623–24.

In *Marron v. United States,* 275 U.S. 192, the officers had a warrant to search for liquor, but the warrant did not describe a certain ledger and invoices pertaining to the operation of the business. The latter were seized during the search of the place of business but were not returned on the search warrant as they were not described therein. The offense of maintaining a nuisance under the National Prohibition Act was being committed in the room by the arrested bartender in the officers' presence. The search warrant was held not to cover the articles seized, but the arrest for the offense being committed in the presence of the officers was held to authorize the search for and seizure of the ledger and invoices, this Court saying:

"The officers were authorized to arrest for crime being committed in their presence, and they lawfully arrested Birdsall. They had a right without a warrant contemporaneously to search the place in order to find and seize the things used to carry on the criminal enterprise. . . . The closet in which liquor and the ledger were found was used as a part of the saloon. And, if the ledger was not as essential to the maintenance of the establishment as were bottles, liquors and glasses, it was none the less a part of the outfit or equipment actually used to commit the offense. And, while it was not on Birdsall's person at the time of his arrest, it was in his immediate possession and control. The authority of officers to search and seize the things by which the nuisance was being maintained extended to all parts of the premises used for the unlawful purpose." *Marron v. United States,* 275 U.S. 192, 198–199.

We do not understand the *Marron* case to have been drained of contemporary vitality by *Go-Bart Co. v. United States,* 282 U.S. 344, and *United States v. Lefkowitz,* 285 U.S. 452. Those cases condemned general exploratory searches, which cannot be undertaken by officers with or without a warrant. In the instant case the search was not general or exploratory for whatever might be turned up. Specificity was the mark of the search and seizure here. There was probable cause to believe that respondent was conducting his business illegally. The search was for stamps overprinted illegally, which were thought upon the most

[Emerson]—13

**193**

reliable information to be in the possession of and concealed by respondent in the very room where he was arrested, over which room he had immediate control and in which he had been selling such stamps unlawfully. *Harris v. United States,* 331 U.S. 145, which has not been overruled, is ample authority for the more limited search here considered. In all the years of our Nation's existence, with special attention to the Prohibition Era, it seems never to have been questioned seriously that a limited search such as here conducted as incident to a lawful arrest was a reasonable search and therefore valid.[5] It has been considered in the same pattern as search of the person after lawful arrest.

What is a reasonable search is not to be determined by any fixed formula. The Constitution does not define what are "unreasonable" searches and, regrettably, in our discipline we have no ready litmus-paper test. The recurring questions of the reasonableness of searches must find resolution in the facts and circumstances of each case. *Go-Bart Co. v. United States,* 282 U.S. 344, 357. Reasonableness is in the first instance for the District Court to determine. We think the District Court's conclusion that here the search and seizure were reasonable should be sustained because: (1) the search and seizure were incident to a valid arrest; (2) the place of the search was a business room to which the public, including the officers, was invited; (3) the room was small and under the immediate and complete control of respondent; (4) the search did not extend beyond the room used for unlawful purposes; (5) the possession of the forged and altered stamps was a crime, just as it is a crime to possess burglars' tools, lottery tickets or counterfeit money.[6]

Assuming that the officers had time to procure a search warrant, were they bound to do so? We think not, because the search was otherwise reasonable, as previously concluded. In a recent opinion, *Trupiano v. United States,* 334 U.S. 699, this Court first enunciated the requirement that search warrants must be procured when "practicable" in a case of search incident to arrest. On the occasion of the previous suggestion of such a test, *Taylor v. United States,* 286 U.S. 1, the Court had been scrupulous to restrict the opinion to the familiar situation there presented. Prohibition agents, having received complaints for

---

[5] [Ed. note. The Court here cites various state cases.]

[6] There is no dispute that the objects searched for and seized here, having been utilized in perpetrating a crime for which arrest was made, were properly subject to seizure. Such objects are to be distinguished from merely evidentiary materials which may not be taken into custody. *United States v. Lefkowitz, supra,* at 464–66; *Gouled v. United States,* 255 U. S. 298, 309–11. This is a distinction of importance, for "limitations upon the fruit to be gathered tend to limit the quest itself. . . ." *United States v. Poller,* 43 F. 2d 911, 914.

**194**                                               [Emerson]

about a year, went at 2:30 a. m. to a garage adjacent to a house, flashed a light through a small opening, and then broke in and seized liquor. The Court emphasized that "No one was within the place, and there was no reason to think otherwise." *Id.* at 5. . . .

A rule of thumb requiring that a search warrant always be procured whenever practicable may be appealing from the vantage point of easy administration. But we cannot agree that this requirement should be crystallized into a *sine qua non* to the reasonableness of a search. It is fallacious to judge events retrospectively and thus to determine, considering the time element alone, that there was time to procure a search warrant. Whether there was time may well be dependent upon considerations other than the ticking off of minutes or hours. The judgment of the officers as to when to close the trap on a criminal committing a crime in their presence or who they have reasonable cause to believe is committing a felony is not determined solely upon whether there was time to procure a search warrant. Some flexibility will be accorded law officers engaged in daily battle with criminals for whose restraint criminal laws are essential.

It is appropriate to note that the Constitution does not say that the right of the people to be secure in their persons should not be violated without a search warrant if it is practicable for the officers to procure one. The mandate of the Fourth Amendment is that the people shall be secure against *unreasonable* searches. It is not disputed that there may be reasonable searches, incident to an arrest, without a search warrant. Upon acceptance of this established rule that some authority to search follows from lawfully taking the person into custody, it becomes apparent that such searches turn upon the reasonableness under all the circumstances and not upon the practicability of procuring a search warrant for the warrant is not required. To the extent that *Trupiano v. United States,* 334 U. S. 699, requires a search warrant solely upon the basis of the practicability of procuring it rather than upon the reasonableness of the search after a lawful arrest, that case is overruled. The relevant test is not whether it is reasonable to procure a search warrant, but whether the search was reasonable. That criterion in turn depends upon the facts and circumstances—the total atmosphere of the case. It is a sufficient precaution that law officers must justify their conduct before courts which have always been, and must be, jealous of the individual's right of privacy within the broad sweep of the Fourth Amendment. . . .

*Reversed.*

MR. JUSTICE DOUGLAS took no part in the consideration or decision of this case.

[Mr. Justice Black dissented on the ground that the *Trupiano* case should be followed. He had previously dissented in the *Trupiano* case.]

MR. JUSTICE FRANKFURTER, whom MR. JUSTICE JACKSON joins, dissenting.

The clear-cut issue before us is this: in making a lawful arrest, may arresting officers search without a search warrant not merely the person under arrest or things under his immediate physical control, but the premises where the arrest is made, although there was ample time to secure such a warrant and no danger that the "papers and effects" for which a search warrant could be issued would be despoiled or destroyed?

The old saw that hard cases make bad law has its basis in experience. But petty cases are even more calculated to make bad law. The impact of a sordid little case is apt to obscure the implications of the generalization to which the case gives rise. Only thus can I account for a disregard of the history embedded in the Fourth Amendment and the great place which belongs to that Amendment in the body of our liberties as recognized and applied by unanimous decisions over a long stretch of the Court's history.

It is a fair summary of history to say that the safeguards of liberty have frequently been forged in controversies involving not very nice people. And so, while we are concerned here with a shabby defrauder, we must deal with his case in the context of what are really the great themes expressed by the Fourth Amendment. A disregard of the historic materials underlying the Amendment does not answer them.

1. It is true also of journeys in the law that the place you reach depends on the direction you are taking. And so, where one comes out on a case depends on where one goes in. It makes all the difference in the world whether one approaches the Fourth Amendment as the Court approached it in *Boyd v. United States*, 116 U.S. 616, in *Weeks v. United States*, 232 U.S. 383, in *Silverthorne Lumber Co. v. United States*, 251 U.S. 385, in *Gouled v. United States*, 255 U.S. 298, or one approaches it as a provision dealing with a formality. It makes all the difference in the world whether one recognizes the central fact about the Fourth Amendment, namely, that it was a safeguard against recurrence of abuses so deeply felt by the Colonies as to be one of the potent causes of the Revolution, or one thinks of it as merely a requirement for a piece of paper.

2. . . . These words [of the Fourth Amendment] are not just a literary composition. They are not to be read as they might be read by a man who knows English but has no knowledge of the history that gave rise to the words. The clue to the meaning and scope of the Fourth Amendment is John Adams' characterization of Otis' argument against search by the police that "American independence was then and there born." 10 Adams, *Works* 247. One cannot wrench "unreasonable searches" from the text and context and historic content of the Fourth Amendment. It was the answer of the Revolutionary statesmen to the evils of searches without warrants and searches with warrants unrestricted in scope. Both were deemed "unreasonable." Words must be read with the gloss of the experience of those who framed them. Because the experience of the framers of the Bill of Rights was so vivid, they assumed that it would be carried down the stream of history and that their words would receive the significance of the experience to which they were addressed—a significance not to be found in the dictionary. When the Fourth Amendment outlawed "unreasonable searches" and then went on to define the very restricted authority that even a search warrant issued by a magistrate could give, the framers said with all the clarity of the gloss of history that a search is "unreasonable" unless a warrant authorizes it, barring only exceptions justified by absolute necessity. Even a warrant cannot authorize it except when it is issued "upon probable cause . . . and particularly describing the place to be searched, and the persons or things to be seized." With all respect I suggest that it makes a mockery of the Fourth Amendment to sanction search without a search warrant merely because of the legality of an arrest. . . .

3. This brings me to a consideration of the right of search and seizure "incident to arrest." Undue haste in coming to that issue too readily leads to getting off the track of the Fourth Amendment. The Government argued as though the Constitution said search of premises may be at large whenever an arrest is made in them. The utterly free hand, for all practical purposes, this gives the arresting officers to rummage all over the house is, I think, inevitable unless the basis of any right to search as an incident to arrest is put in proper focus. Photographs can be so taken as to make a midget look like a giant, and vice versa. The same kind of distortion results if a legal doctrine embedded in a larger matrix of principle is taken out of the matrix and elevated to an independent position. In plain English, the right to search incident to arrest is merely one of those very narrow exceptions to the "guaranties and immunities which we had in-

**197**

herited from our English ancestors, and which had from time immemorial been subject to certain well-recognized exceptions arising from the necessities of the case." *Robertson v. Baldwin,* 165 U.S. 275, 281.

4. What, then, is the exception to the prohibition by the Fourth Amendment of search without a warrant in case of a legal arrest, whether the arrest is on a warrant or based on the historic right of arrest without a warrant if a crime is committed in the presence of the arrester? The exception may in part be a surviving incident of the historic role of "hue and cry" in early Anglo-Saxon law. See Judge Cardozo in *People v. Chiagles,* 237 N.Y. 193, 196, 142 N.E. 583, 584. Its basic roots, however, lie in necessity. What is the necessity? Why is search of the arrested person permitted? For two reasons: first, in order to protect the arresting officer and to deprive the prisoner of potential means of escape, *Closson v. Morrison,* 47 N.H. 482, and, secondly, to avoid destruction of evidence by the arrested person. See *Reifsnyder v. Lee,* 44 Iowa 101, 103; *Holker v. Hennessey,* 141 Mo. 527, 540, 42 S.W. 1090, 1093. From this it follows that officers may search and seize not only the things physically on the person arrested, but those within his immediate physical control. What a farce it makes of the whole Fourth Amendment to say that because for many legal purposes everything in a man's house is under his control therefore his house—his rooms— may be searched. Of course in this field of law, as in others, opinions sometimes use language not with fastidious precision. Apart from such instances of loose use of language, the doctrine of search incidental to arrest has, until very recently, been strictly confined to the necessities of the situation, *i. e.,* the search of the person and those immediate physical surroundings which may fairly be deemed to be an extension of his person.

5. Another exception to the constitutional prohibition of unreasonable searches is likewise rooted in necessity. The search without a warrant of moving objects—vehicles and vessels—was sanctioned in *Carroll v. United States,* 267 U.S. 132, on the ground that "it is not practicable to secure a warrant, because the vehicle can be quickly moved out of the locality or jurisdiction in which the warrant must be sought." 267 U.S. at 153. Furthermore, the limits of the exception were carefully defined in terms of necessity, for the Court added:

"In cases where the securing of a warrant is reasonably practicable, it must be used and when properly supported by affidavit and issued after judicial approval protects the seizing officer against a suit for damages. In cases where seizure is impossible except without warrant, the seizing officer acts unlawfully and at his peril unless he can show the court probable cause." 267 U.S. at 156. Even as to moving vehicles, this Court did not lay down an absolute rule dispensing with a search warrant. It limited dispensation to the demands of necessity, where want of time precluded the obtaining of a warrant. The necessity founded on the time factor which guided the Court in the *Carroll* case cannot justify the search here made of the respondent's premises, for there was ample time to obtain a warrant before the arrest and even on the occasion of the arrest.

6. It is in this connection that the body of congressional enactments becomes significant, particularly legislation contemporaneous with the adoption of the Bill of Rights. If explicit legislation was deemed necessary to inspect without warrant even vessels and vehicles, and if Congress has been very niggardly in giving authority to search even with a warrant—niggardly both as to the officers who may obtain such warrants and as to strictly defined circumstances under which search is allowed—the attitude disclosed by this impressive legislation bears powerfully on the historic purposes of the Fourth Amendment and the functions that it fulfills in our democracy. It deserves to be recalled that Congress, despite repeated requests by Attorneys General, long refused to make search by warrant generally available as an aid to criminal prosecution. It did not do so until the First World War and even then it did not do so except under conditions most carefully circumscribed.[2]

7. With only rare deviations, such as today's decision, this Court has construed the Fourth Amendment "liberally to safeguard the right of privacy." *United States v. Lefkowitz*, 285 U.S. 452, 464. . . .

8. The opinion of the Court insists, however, that its major premise—that an arrest creates a right to search the place of arrest—finds support in decisions beginning with *Weeks v. United States*, 232 U.S. 383. These decisions do not justify today's decision. They merely prove how a hint becomes a suggestion, is loosely turned into dictum and finally elevated to a decision. . . .

[The opinion then discusses dicta in the *Weeks*, *Carroll* and *Agnello* cases.]

In *Marron v. United States*, 275 U.S. 192, these carelessly phrased dicta were for the first time reflected in the result. The statement in the opinion that officers "had a right without a warrant contemporaneously to search the place in order to find and seize the things used to carry on the criminal enterprise,"

---

[2] See Title XI of the Act of June 15, 1917, 40 Stat. 217, 228, now Rule 41 of the Federal Rules of Criminal Procedure. . . .

275 U.S. at 199, was drastically qualified by *Go-Bart Co. v. United States,* 282 U.S. 344, and *United States v. Lefkowitz,* 285 U.S. 452. The teaching of those cases is that the warrant of arrest carries with it authority to seize all that is on the person, or in such immediate physical relation to the one arrested as to be in a fair sense a projection of his person. The *Lefkowitz* decision emphasized that the things seized in *Marron* "being in plain view were picked up by the officers as an incident of the arrest. No search for them was made." 285 U. S. at 465. Thus explained, *Marron* stands merely for the historically justified right to seize visible instruments of crime at the scene of the arrest.

In reliance on the prior dicta and on the Marron decision, it was asserted in *Harris v. United States,* 331 U. S. 145, 150, that "Search and seizure incident to lawful arrest is a practice of ancient origin." Literally, this is true: the right to search the person arrested and to seize visible instruments of crime has a good legal title. But judicial history cannot be avouched if this statement is meant to cover the right to search the place of arrest. Such a claim can only be made by sliding from a search of the person to a search for things in his "possession" or "in his immediate control," without regard to the treacherous ambiguity of these terms, and then using these phrases, taken out of their original context, so as to include the entire premises.

The short of it is that the right to search the place of arrest is an innovation based on confusion, without historic foundation, and made in the teeth of a historic protection against it.

9. If the exception of search without a warrant incidental to a legal arrest is extended beyond the person and his physical extension, search throughout the house necessarily follows. I am aware that most differences in the law depend on differences of degree. But differences though of degree must not be capricious; the differences must permit rational classification. If upon arrest you may search beyond the immediate person and the very restricted area that may fairly be deemed part of the person, what rational line can be drawn short of searching as many rooms as arresting officers may deem appropriate for finding "the fruits of the crime"? Is search to be restricted to the room in which the person is arrested but not to another open room into which it leads? Or take a house or an apartment consisting largely of one big room serving as dining room, living room and bedroom. May search be made in a small room but not in such a large room? If you may search the bedroom part of a large room, why not a bedroom separated from the dining room by a partition? These are not silly hard cases. They put the principle to a test. The right to search an arrested person and to take

the stuff on top of the desk at which he sits has a justification of necessity which does not eat away the great principle of the Fourth Amendment. But to assume that this exception of a search incidental to arrest permits a freehanded search without warrant is to subvert the purpose of the Fourth Amendment by making the exception displace the principle. History and the policy which it represents alike admonish against it.

10. To tear "unreasonable" from the context and history and purpose of the Fourth Amendment in applying the narrow exception of search as an incident to an arrest is to disregard *the* reason to which reference must be made when a question arises under the Fourth Amendment. It is to make the arrest an incident to an unwarranted search instead of a warrantless search an incident to an arrest. The test by which searches and seizures must be judged is whether conduct is consonant with the main aim of the Fourth Amendment. The main aim of the Fourth Amendment is against invasion of the right of privacy as to one's effects and papers without regard to the result of such invasion. The purpose of the Fourth Amendment was to assure that the existence of probable cause as the legal basis for making a search was to be determined by a judicial officer before arrest and not after, subject only to what is necessarily to be excepted from such requirement. The exceptions cannot be enthroned into the rule. The justification for intrusion into a man's privacy was to be determined by a magistrate uninfluenced by what may turn out to be a successful search for papers, the desire to search for which might be the very reason for the Fourth Amendment's prohibition. . . .

11. By the Bill of Rights the founders of this country subordinated police action to legal restraints not in order to convenience the guilty but to protect the innocent. Nor did they provide that only the innocent may appeal to these safeguards. They knew too well that the successful prosecution of the guilty does not require jeopardy to the innocent. The knock at the door under the guise of a warrant of arrest for a venial or spurious offense was not unknown to them. Compare the statement in *Weeks* v. *United States,* 232 U. S. 383, 390, that searches and seizures had been made under general warrants in England "in support of charges, real or imaginary." We have had grim reminders in our day of their experience. Arrest under a warrant for a minor or a trumped-up charge has been familiar practice in the past, is a commonplace in the police state of today, and too well-known in this country. See *Lanzetta* v. *New Jersey,* 306 U. S. 451. The progress is too easy from police action unscrutinized by judicial authorization to the police state. The

founders wrote into the Constitution their conviction that law enforcement does not require the easy but dangerous way of letting the police determine when search is called for without prior authorization by a magistrate. They have been vindicated in that conviction. It may safely be asserted that crime is most effectively brought to book when the principles underlying the constitutional restraints upon police action are most scrupulously observed. . . .

13. Even if the test of reasonableness is to be taken out of the context of the history and purpose of the Fourth Amendment, the test should not be limited to examination of arresting officers' conduct in making the arrest. Their conduct prior to arrest is no less relevant. In any event, therefore, the presence or absence of an ample opportunity for getting a search warrant becomes very important. It is not a rule of thumb. It is a rule of the Fourth Amendment and of the reasons for its adoption. It is not a rule invented in *Trupiano v. United States*, 334 U. S. 699. It is not a rule of those who came on this Court in recent years. The decision in *Taylor v. United States*, 286 U. S. 1, turned on it. . . .

14. It is not as though we are asked to extend a mischievous doctrine that has been shown to hamper law enforcers. We are asked to overrule decisions based on a long course of prior unanimous decisions, drawn from history and legislative experience. In overruling *Trupiano* we overrule the underlying principle of a whole series of recent cases: *United States v. Di Re*, 332 U. S. 581; *Johnson v. United States*, 333 U. S. 10; *McDonald v. United States*, 335 U. S. 451, based on the earlier cases. For these cases ought not to be allowed to remain as derelicts on the stream of the law, if we overrule *Trupiano*. These are not outmoded decisions eroded by time. Even under normal circumstances, the Court ought not to overrule such a series of decisions where no mischief flowing from them has been made manifest. Respect for continuity in law, where reasons for change are wanting, alone requires adherence to *Trupiano* and the other decisions. Especially ought the Court not reenforce needlessly the instabilities of our day by giving fair ground for the belief that Law is the expression of chance—for instance, of unexpected changes in the Court's composition and the contingencies in the choice of successors.

## Note

1. In *Harris v. U. S.*, 331 U. S. 145, 91 L. Ed. 1399, 67 S. Ct. 1098 (1947), the defendant was charged with two Federal offenses involved in forging and cashing a check. Five agents of the FBI, acting under valid warrants of arrest, went to the defendant's four-room apart-

ment and arrested him. After the arrest, which took place in the living room, the agents searched the entire apartment for approximately five hours. They were looking for two stolen cancelled checks which might have been employed in accomplishing the forgery, as well as for burglar tools, pens or other articles that might have been used. Nothing connected with the forgery was found. But toward the end of the search, in a bureau drawer in the bedroom, the FBI agents found and seized an envelope containing Classification Cards and Registration Certificates used in the Selective Service System. The defendant was prosecuted and convicted for illegal possession of these draft cards. A majority of the Supreme Court held that the search was lawful as an incident to a valid arrest, observing that "the same meticulous investigation which would be appropriate in a search for two small cancelled checks could not be considered reasonable where agents are seeking a stolen automobile or an illegal still." 331 U. S. at 152. The majority also found no violation of the Fourth Amendment in the seizure of the draft cards, although they were related to a different crime, on the ground that they were government property illegally held. Justices Frankfurter, Murphy, Jackson and Rutledge vigorously dissented. The separate opinions of Justices Frankfurter, Murphy and Jackson include discussion of the problem of law enforcement and the implications of the decision in the prosecution of political minorities.

2. The decision in the *Carroll* case on the search of moving vehicles was followed in *Brinegar v. U. S.*, 338 U. S. 160, 93 L. Ed. 1879, 69 S. Ct. 1302 (1949). See also *Casey v. U. S.*, 343 U. S. —, 96 L. Ed. —, 72 S. Ct. 999 (1952).

3. A chart analysis of the Supreme Court decisions involving searches and seizures, from the *Weeks* case to the *Davis* case, may be found in the appendix to Mr. Justice Frankfurter's dissenting opinion in the *Harris* case. Some of the leading state cases are listed in the footnotes in the *Harris* and *Rabinowitz* cases, *supra*, and the *Wolf* case, *infra*. See also 82 A. L. R. 782; 169 A. L. R. 1419.

4. Ever since the *Weeks* case the Federal courts have consistently ruled that evidence obtained through an illegal search and seizure will, upon timely motion, be returned or suppressed and hence may not be used in evidence. A majority of the state courts do not follow this practice. Some of the issues involved are considered in *Wolf v. Colorado*, set forth below, where the Supreme Court for the first time considered the question whether the admission by a state court of evidence illegally secured violated the due process clause of the Fourteenth Amendment.

## WOLF v. COLORADO

Supreme Court of the United States, 1949
338 U. S. 25, 93 L. Ed. 1782, 69 S. Ct. 1359

MR. JUSTICE FRANKFURTER delivered the opinion of the Court. The precise question for consideration is this: Does a conviction by a State court for a State offense deny the "due process of law" required by the Fourteenth Amendment, solely because evidence that was admitted at the trial was obtained under circumstances which would have rendered it inadmissible in a prosecution for violation of a federal law in a court of the United States because there deemed to be an infraction of the Fourth Amendment as applied in *Weeks v. United States,* 232 U. S. 383? The Supreme Court of Colorado has sustained convictions in which such evidence was admitted, 117 Col. 279, 187 P. 2d 926; 117 Col. 321, 187 P. 2d 928, and we brought the cases here. 333 U. S. 879.

Unlike the specific requirements and restrictions placed by the Bill of Rights (Amendments I to VIII) upon the administration of criminal justice by federal authority, the Fourteenth Amendment did not subject criminal justice in the States to specific limitations. The notion that the "due process of law" guaranteed by the Fourteenth Amendment is shorthand for the first eight amendments of the Constitution and thereby incorporates them has been rejected by this Court again and again, after impressive consideration. See, e. g., *Hurtado v. California,* 110 U. S. 516; *Twining v. New Jersey,* 211 U. S. 78; *Brown v. Mississippi,* 297 U. S. 278; *Palko v. Connecticut,* 302 U. S. 319. Only the other day the Court reaffirmed this rejection after thorough reexamination of the scope and function of the Due Process Clause of the Fourteenth Amendment. *Adamson v. California,* 332 U. S. 46. The issue is closed. . . .

The security of one's privacy against arbitrary intrusion by the police—which is at the core of the Fourth Amendment—is basic to a free society. It is therefore implicit in "the concept of ordered liberty" and as such enforceable against the States through the Due Process Clause. The knock at the door, whether by day or by night, as a prelude to a search, without authority of law but solely on the authority of the police, did not need the commentary of recent history to be condemned as inconsistent with the conception of human rights enshrined in the history and the basic constitutional documents of English-speaking peoples.

Accordingly, we have no hesitation in saying that were a State affirmatively to sanction such police incursion into privacy it would run counter to the guaranty of the Fourteenth Amendment. But the ways of enforcing such a basic right raise questions of a different order. How such arbitrary conduct should be checked, what remedies against it should be afforded, the means by which the right should be made effective, are all questions that are not to be so dogmatically answered as to preclude the varying solutions which spring from an allowable range of judgment on issues not susceptible of quantitative solution.

In *Weeks v. United States, supra,* this Court held that in a federal prosecution the Fourth Amendment barred the use of evidence secured through an illegal search and seizure. This ruling was made for the first time in 1914. It was not derived from the explicit requirements of the Fourth Amendment; it was not based on legislation expressing Congressional policy in the enforcement of the Constitution. The decision was a matter of judicial implication. Since then it has been frequently applied and we stoutly adhere to it. But the immediate question is whether the basic right to protection against arbitrary intrusion by the police demands the exclusion of logically relevant evidence obtained by an unreasonable search and seizure because, in a federal prosecution for a federal crime, it would be excluded. As a matter of inherent reason, one would suppose this to be an issue as to which men with complete devotion to the protection of the right of privacy might give different answers. When we find that in fact most of the English-speaking world does not regard as vital to such protection the exclusion of evidence thus obtained, we must hesitate to treat this remedy as an essential ingredient of the right. The contrariety of views of the States is particularly impressive in view of the careful reconsideration which they have given the problem in the light of the *Weeks* decision.

I. Before the *Weeks* decision 27 States had passed on the admissibility of evidence obtained by unlawful search and seizure.

    (a) Of these, 26 States opposed the *Weeks* doctrine. (See Appendix, Table A.)

    (b) Of these, 1 State anticipated the *Weeks* doctrine. (Table B.)

II. Since the *Weeks* decision 47 States all told have passed on the *Weeks* doctrine. (Table C.)

    (a) Of these, 20 passed on it for the first time.

        (1) Of the foregoing States, 6 followed the *Weeks* doctrine. (Table D.)

        (2) Of the foregoing States, 14 rejected the *Weeks* doctrine. (Table E.)

    (b) Of these, 26 States reviewed prior decisions contrary to the *Weeks* doctrine.

        (1) Of these, 10 States have followed *Weeks*, overruling or distinguishing their prior decisions. (Table F.)

(2) Of these, 16 States adhered to their prior decisions against *Weeks*. (Table G.)

(c) Of these, 1 State repudiated its prior formulation of the *Weeks* doctrine. (Table H.)

III. As of today 31 States reject the *Weeks* doctrine, 16 States are in agreement with it. (Table I.)

IV. Of 10 jurisdictions within the United Kingdom and the British Commonwealth of Nations which have passed on the question, none has held evidence obtained by illegal search and seizure inadmissible. (Table J.) *

The jurisdictions which have rejected the *Weeks* doctrine have not left the right to privacy without other means of protection.[1] Indeed, the exclusion of evidence is a remedy which directly serves only to protect those upon whose person or premises something incriminating has been found. We cannot, therefore, regard it as a departure from basic standards to remand such persons, together with those who emerge scatheless from a search, to the remedies of private action and such protection as the internal discipline of the police, under the eyes of an alert public opinion, may afford. Granting that in practice the exclusion of evidence may be an effective way of deterring unreasonable searches, it is not for this Court to condemn as falling below the minimal standards assured by the Due Process Clause a State's reliance upon other methods which, if consistently enforced, would be equally effective. Weighty testimony against such an insistence on our own view is furnished by the opinion of Mr. Justice (then Judge) Cardozo in *People v. Defore*, 242 N. Y. 13, 150 N. E. 585. We cannot brush aside the experience of States which deem the incidence of such conduct by the police

---

* [Ed. note: The Appendix, listing cases in each category, is omitted.]

[1] The common law provides actions for damages against the searching officer . . . ; against one who procures the issuance of a warrant maliciously and without probable cause . . . ; against a magistrate who has acted without jurisdiction in issuing a warrant . . . ; and against persons assisting in the execution of an illegal search. . . . One may also without liability use force to resist an unlawful search. . . .

Statutory sanctions in the main provide for the punishment of one maliciously procuring a search warrant or willfully exceeding his authority in exercising it. . . . Some statutes more broadly penalize unlawful searches. . . . Virginia also makes punishable one who issues a general search warrant or a warrant unsupported by affidavit. . . . A few States have provided statutory civil remedies. . . . And in one State, misuse of a search warrant may be an abuse of process punishable as contempt of court. . . .

[Ed. note: The decisions and statutes cited by the Court to illustrate the foregoing statements have been omitted.]

too slight to call for a deterrent remedy not by way of disciplinary measures but by overriding the relevant rules of evidence. There are, moreover, reasons for excluding evidence unreasonably obtained by the federal police which are less compelling in the case of police under State or local authority. The public opinion of a community can far more effectively be exerted against oppressive conduct on the part of police directly responsible to the community itself than can local opinion, sporadically aroused, be brought to bear upon remote authority pervasively exerted throughout the country.

We hold, therefore, that in a prosecution in a State court for a State crime the Fourteenth Amendment does not forbid the admission of evidence obtained by an unreasonable search and seizure. And though we have interpreted the Fourth Amendment to forbid the admission of such evidence, a different question would be presented if Congress under its legislative powers were to pass a statute purporting to negate the *Weeks* doctrine. We would then be faced with the problem of the respect to be accorded the legislative judgment on an issue as to which, in default of that judgment, we have been forced to depend upon our own. Problems of a converse character, also not before us, would be presented should Congress under § 5 of the Fourteenth Amendment undertake to enforce the rights there guaranteed by attempting to make the *Weeks* doctrine binding upon the States.

*Affirmed.*

MR. JUSTICE BLACK, concurring. . . .

For reasons stated in my dissenting opinion in *Adamson v. California,* 332 U. S. 46, 68, I agree with the conclusion of the Court that the Fourth Amendment's prohibition of "unreasonable searches and seizures" is enforceable against the states. Consequently, I should be for reversal of this case if I thought the Fourth Amendment not only prohibited "unreasonable searches and seizures," but also, of itself, barred the use of evidence so unlawfully obtained. But I agree with what appears to be a plain implication of the Court's opinion that the federal exclusionary rule is not a command of the Fourth Amendment but is a judicially created rule of evidence which Congress might negate. See *McNabb v. United States,* 318 U. S. 332. This leads me to concur in the Court's judgment of affirmance.

It is not amiss to repeat my belief that the Fourteenth Amendment was intended to make the Fourth Amendment in its entirety applicable to the states. The Fourth Amendment was designed to protect people against unrestrained searches and seizures by sheriffs, policemen and other law enforcement officers. Such protection is an essential in a free society. And I am unable to agree that the protection of people from over-zealous or ruthless state officers is any less essential in a country of "ordered liberty" than is the protection of people from over-zealous or ruthless federal officers. Certainly there are far more state than federal enforcement officers and their activities, up to now, have more frequently and closely touched the intimate daily lives of people than have the activities of federal officers. A state officer's "knock at the door . . . as a prelude to a search, without authority of law," may be, as our experience shows, just as ominous to "ordered liberty" as though the knock were made by a federal officer.

MR. JUSTICE DOUGLAS, dissenting.

I believe for the reasons stated by MR. JUSTICE BLACK in his dissent in *Adamson v. California*, 332 U. S. 46, 68, that the Fourth Amendment is applicable to the States. I agree with MR. JUSTICE MURPHY that the evidence obtained in violation of it *must* be excluded in state prosecutions as well as in federal prosecutions, since in absence of that rule of evidence the Amendment would have no effective sanction. I also agree with him that under that test this evidence was improperly admitted and that the judgments of conviction must be reversed.

MR. JUSTICE MURPHY, with whom MR. JUSTICE RUTLEDGE joins, dissenting.

It is disheartening to find so much that is right in an opinion which seems to me so fundamentally wrong. Of course I agree with the Court that the Fourteenth Amendment prohibits activities which are proscribed by the search and seizure clause of the Fourth Amendment. See my dissenting views, and those of MR. JUSTICE BLACK, in *Adamson v. California*, 332 U. S. 46, 68, 123. Quite apart from the blanket application of the Bill of Rights to the States, a devotee of democracy would ill suit his name were he to suggest that his home's protection against unlicensed governmental invasion was not "of the very essence of a scheme of ordered liberty." *Palko v. Connecticut*, 302 U. S. 319, 325. It is difficult for me to understand how the Court can go this far and yet be unwilling to make the step which can give some meaning to the pronouncements it utters.

Imagination and zeal may invent a dozen methods to give content to the commands of the Fourth Amendment. But this Court is limited to the remedies currently available. It cannot legislate the ideal system. If we would attempt the enforcement of the search and seizure clause in the ordinary case today, we are limited to three devices: judicial exclusion of the illegally obtained evidence; criminal prosecution of violators; and civil action against violators in the action of trespass.

Alternatives are deceptive. Their very statement conveys the impression that one possibility is as effective as the next. In this case their statement is blinding. For there is but one alternative to the rule of exclusion. That is no sanction at all.

This has been perfectly clear since 1914, when a unanimous Court decided *Weeks v. United States*, 232 U. S. 383, 393. "If letters and private documents can thus be seized and held and used in evidence against a citizen accused of an offense," we said, "the protection of the Fourth Amendment, declaring his right to be secure against such searches and seizures, is of no value, and, so far as those thus placed are concerned, might as well be stricken from the Constitution." "It reduces the Fourth Amendment to a form of words." Holmes, J., for the Court, in *Silverthorne Lumber Co. v. United States*, 251 U. S. 385, 392.

Today the Court wipes those statements from the books with its bland citation of "other remedies." Little need be said concerning the possibilities of criminal prosecution. Self-scrutiny is a lofty ideal, but its exaltation reaches new heights if we expect a District Attorney to prosecute himself or his associates for well-meaning violations of the search and seizure clause during a raid the District Attorney or his associates have ordered.[1] But there is an appealing ring in another alternative. A trespass action for damages is a venerable means of securing reparation for unauthorized invasion of the home. Why not put the old writ to a new use? When the Court cites cases permitting the action, the remedy seems complete.

But what an illusory remedy this is, if by "remedy" we mean a positive deterrent to police and prosecutors tempted to violate the Fourth Amendment. The appealing ring softens when we recall that in a trespass action the measure of damages is simply the extent of the injury to physical property. If the officer searches with care, he can avoid all but nominal damages—a penny, or a dollar. Are punitive damages possible? Perhaps. But a few states permit none, whatever the circumstances.[2] In those that do, the plaintiff must show the real ill will or malice

---

[1] See Pound, Criminal Justice in America (New York, 1930): "Under our legal system the way of the prosecutor is hard, and the need of 'getting results' puts pressure upon prosecutors to . . . indulge in that lawless enforcement of law which produces a vicious circle of disrespect for law." P. 186.

And note the statement of the Wickersham Commission, with reference to arrests: ". . . in case of persons of no influence or little or no means the legal restrictions are not likely to give an officer serious trouble." II National Commission on Law Observance and Enforcement, Report on Criminal Procedure (1931), p. 19.

[2] [Ed. note: Citations in the footnotes to this paragraph have been omitted.]

[Emerson]—14

of the defendant, and surely it is not unreasonable to assume that one in honest pursuit of crime bears no malice toward the search victim. If that burden is carried, recovery may yet be defeated by the rule that there must be physical damages before punitive damages may be awarded. In addition, some states limit punitive damages to the actual expenses of litigation. See 61 Harv. L. Rev. 113, 119–120. Others demand some arbitrary ratio between actual and punitive damages before a verdict may stand. See Morris, *Punitive Damages in Tort Cases*, 44 Harv. L. Rev. 1173, 1180–1181. Even assuming the ill will of the officer, his reasonable grounds for belief that the home he searched harbored evidence of crime is admissible in mitigation of punitive damages. *Gamble v. Keyes*, 35 S. D. 644, 153 N. W. 888; *Simpson v. McCaffrey*, 13 Ohio 508. The bad reputation of the plaintiff is likewise admissible. *Banfill v. Byrd*, 122 Miss. 288, 84 So. 227. If the evidence seized was actually used at a trial, that fact has been held a complete justification of the search, and a defense against the trespass action. *Elias v. Pasmore* [1934] 2 K. B. 164. And even if the plaintiff hurdles all these obstacles, and gains a substantial verdict, the individual officer's finances may well make the judgment useless—for the municipality, of course, is not liable without its consent. Is it surprising that there is so little in the books concerning trespass actions for violation of the search and seizure clause?

The conclusion is inescapable that but one remedy exists to deter violations of the search and seizure clause. That is the rule which excludes illegally obtained evidence. Only by exclusion can we impress upon the zealous prosecutor that violation of the Constitution will do him no good. And only when that point is driven home can the prosecutor be expected to emphasize the importance of observing constitutional demands in his instructions to the police.

If proof of the efficacy of the federal rule were needed, there is testimony in abundance in the recruit training programs and in-service courses provided the police in states which follow the federal rule.[5] St. Louis, for example, demands extensive training in the rules of search and seizure, with emphasis upon the

---

[5] The material which follows is gleaned from letters and other material from Commissioners of Police and Chiefs of Police in twenty-six cities. Thirty-eight large cities in the United States were selected at random, and inquiries directed concerning the instructions provided police on the rules of search and seizure. Twenty-six replies have been received to date. Those of any significance are mentioned in the text of this opinion. The sample is believed to be representative, but it cannot, of course, substitute for a thoroughgoing comparison of present-day police procedures by a completely objective observer. A study of this kind would be of inestimable value.

[Emerson]

ease with which a case may collapse if it depends upon evidence obtained unlawfully. Current court decisions are digested and read at roll calls. The same general pattern prevails in Washington, D. C. In Dallas, officers are thoroughly briefed and instructed that "the courts will follow the rules very closely and will detect any frauds." In Milwaukee, a stout volume on the law of arrest and search and seizure is made the basis of extended instruction. Officer preparation in the applicable rules in Jackson, Mississippi, has included the lectures of an Associate Justice of the Mississippi Supreme Court. The instructions on evidence and search and seizure given to trainees in San Antonio carefully note the rule of exclusion in Texas, and close with this statement: "Every police officer should know the laws and rules of evidence. Upon knowledge of these facts determines whether the . . . defendant will be convicted or acquitted. . . . When you investigate a case . . . remember throughout your investigation that only admissible evidence can be used."

But in New York City, we are informed simply that "copies of the State Penal Law and Code of Criminal Procedure" are given to officers, and that they are "kept advised" that illegally obtained evidence may be admitted in New York courts. In Baltimore, a "Digest of Laws" is distributed, and it is made clear that the statutory section excluding evidence "is limited in its application to the trial of misdemeanors. . . . It would appear . . . that . . . evidence illegally obtained may still be admissible in the trial of felonies." In Cleveland, recruits and other officers are told of the rules of search and seizure, but "instructed that it is admissible in the courts of Ohio. The Ohio Supreme Court has indicated very definitely and clearly that Ohio belongs to the 'admissionist' group of states when evidence obtained by an illegal search is presented to the court." A similar pattern emerges in Birmingham, Alabama.

The contrast between states with the federal rule and those without it is thus a positive demonstration of its efficacy. There are apparent exceptions to the contrast—Denver, for example, appears to provide as comprehensive a series of instructions as that in Chicago, although Colorado permits introduction of the evidence and Illinois does not. And, so far as we can determine from letters, a fairly uniform standard of officer instruction appears in other cities, irrespective of the local rule of evidence. But the examples cited above serve to ground an assumption that has motivated this Court since the *Weeks* case: that this is an area in which judicial action has positive effect upon the breach of law; and that without judicial action, there are simply no effective sanctions presently available.

I cannot believe that we should decide due process questions by simply taking a poll of the rules in various jurisdictions, even if we follow the *Palko* "test." Today's decision will do inestimable harm to the cause of fair police methods in our cities and states. Even more important, perhaps, it must have tragic effect upon public respect for our judiciary. For the Court now allows what is indeed shabby business: lawlessness by officers of the law.

Since the evidence admitted was secured in violation of the Fourth Amendment, the judgment should be reversed.

[The separate dissenting opinion of Mr. Justice Rutledge is omitted.]

## Note

1. No comprehensive material is available to indicate the extent to which police officials engage in illegal search and seizure. The large number of cases reaching the appellate courts as well as other evidence, however, suggests that the practice is fairly widespread. See, e.g., *Report of the President's Committee on Civil Rights*, pp. 25–29 (1947); statement of Senator Dunnigan in 1 *New York State Constitutional Convention, Revised Record* 365 (1938); N. Y. Times, Feb. 28, 1949. There is also considerable material supporting Mr. Justice Murphy's position that criminal or civil proceedings against police officials, and internal police discipline, have been ineffective in remedying or curbing the practice. See material cited *supra* in connection with the problem of police brutality; see also Rudd, *Present Significance of Constitutional Guaranties Against Unreasonable Searches and Seizures,* 18 U. of Cin. L. Rev. 387, 389–90 (1949). For further discussion of the justification for the Federal rule of exclusion, see Plumb, *Illegal Enforcement of the Law,* 24 Corn. L. Q. 337 (1939); Note, *Judicial Control of Illegal Search and Seizure,* 58 Yale L. J. 144 (1948) (collecting prior material at p. 151).

2. The Federal rule of exclusion is now incorporated in Rule 41(e) of the Federal Rules of Criminal Procedure, 18 U. S. C. (1951). This Rule also prescribes the procedure for raising the issue through a motion to return or suppress the evidence.

3. The doctrine of exclusion, as applied in the Federal courts and in the state courts that follow the Federal principle, is subject to two important exceptions. One is that only a person whose rights have actually been infringed by the illegal search and seizure may claim protection of the exclusionary rule. See *Goldstein v. U. S.,* 316 U. S. 114, 86 L. Ed. 1312, 62 S. Ct. 1000 (1942), and lower Federal court cases collected in Note, *supra,* 58 Yale L. J. at 154–6; but note the dissents in the *Goldstein* case. And see *U. S. v. Jeffers,* 342 U. S. 48, 96 L. Ed. —, 72 S. Ct. 93 (1951) (evidence secured by illegal search of premises occupied by third parties, but made available to defendant, could not be used against defendant); *McDonald v. U. S.,* 335 U. S. 451, 93 L. Ed. 153, 69 S. Ct. 191 (1948) (guest, who was co-defendant with occupant of premises, protected). The other exception is that the rule of exclusion does not apply to evidence illegally seized by persons other

than officials of the prosecuting government. *Weeks v. U. S.*, 232 U. S. 383, 58 L. Ed. 652, 34 S. Ct. 341 (1914) (evidence illegally seized by state officers held admissible); *Burdeau v. McDowell*, 256 U. S. 465, 65 L. Ed. 1048, 41 S. Ct. 574 (1921) (evidence illegally seized by private persons held admissible); but note the contrary views of some of the justices in *Lustig v. U. S.*, 338 U. S. 74, 93 L. Ed. 1819, 69 S. Ct. 1372 (1949). While the courts will not sanction collusion between the officers of the prosecuting government and other officers or individuals, the line is often hard to draw. See the *Lustig* case, *supra*. The two exceptions, particularly the latter, open substantial possibilities for evasion of the exclusionary rule. See Note, *supra*, 58 Yale at 154–60.

4. Following the *Wolf* case, the defendant in a New Jersey prosecution filed suit in the Federal District Court for an injunction under the Federal Civil Rights Acts (8 U. S. C. § 43) to prevent use in the New Jersey prosecution of illegally seized evidence. The Supreme Court, Justices Douglas, Murphy and Rutledge dissenting, held that the Federal courts should exercise discretion to refuse equitable relief. *Stefanelli v. Minard*, 342 U. S. 117, 96 L. Ed. —, 72 S. Ct. 118 (1951).

5. The Federal and state cases dealing with the admissibility of evidence illegally obtained are collected in Wigmore, *Evidence*, §§ 2183–4 (3d ed. 1940); 150 A. L. R. 566. Among the voluminous materials discussing the main problems of searches and seizures the most useful is Reynard, *Freedom from Unreasonable Search and Seizure*, 25 Ind. L. J. 259 (1950); Allen, *The Wolf Case: Search and Seizure, Federalism, and the Civil Liberties*, 45 Ill. L. Rev. 1 (1950); Note, *supra*, 58 Yale L. J. 144 (1948) (collecting the earlier material in footnote 32, p. 151); Fraenkel, *Recent Developments in the Federal Law of Searches and Seizures*, 33 Iowa L. Rev. 472 (1948); Machen, *The Law of Search and Seizure* (1950). See also the articles and notes in 14 So. Cal. L. Rev. 359 (1941); 15 So. Cal. L. Rev. 60 (1941); 42 Mich. L. Rev. 147 (1943); 47 Mich. L. Rev. 1137 (1949); 18 U. of Cin. L. Rev. 387 (1949); 50 Col. L. Rev. 364 (1950); 36 Corn. L. Q. 125 (1950); 35 Minn. L. Rev. 457 (1951); 25 So. Cal. L. Rev. 1 (1951). For discussion of the law in England and other countries in Europe, see Ploscowe, *Measures of Constraint in European and Anglo-American Criminal Procedure*, 23 Geo. L. J. 762 (1935).

## Wiretapping

Few issues have been more hotly debated in the field of criminal procedure than the practice by the police of intercepting private communications through the use of wiretaps or other technical devices. The question first reached the Supreme Court in a case growing out of the attempt to aid the enforcement of the prohibition laws by resort to wiretapping. *Olmstead v. U. S.*, 277 U. S. 438, 72 L. Ed. 944, 48 S. Ct. 564 (1928).

In this case 75 individuals had been indicted on charges of conspiracy to import, transport and sell liquor in violation of the National Prohibition Act. A substantial part of the government's evidence was obtained by tapping the office and house telephones of the members of the group over a period of months. Several of the defendants who had been convicted appealed to the Supreme Court on the ground that the evidence obtained from wiretapping should have been excluded as in violation of the Fourth Amendment and the self-incrimination provisions of the Fifth Amendment. In a 5 to 4 decision the Court upheld the convictions. Chief Justice Taft, writing for the majority, dismissed the argument based on the Fifth Amendment with the statement: "There was no evidence of compulsion to induce the defendants to talk over their many telephones. They were continually and voluntarily transacting business without knowledge of the interception." 277 U. S. at 462. He then held there was no violation of the Fourth Amendment:

"There was no searching. There was no seizure. The evidence was secured by the use of the sense of hearing and that only. There was no entry of the houses or offices of the defendants. . . .

"Nor can we, without the sanction of congressional enactment, subscribe to the suggestion that the courts have a discretion to exclude evidence, the admission of which is not unconstitutional, because unethically secured. This would be at variance with the common law doctrine generally supported by authority. . . .

"A standard which would forbid the reception of evidence if obtained by other than nice ethical conduct by government officials would make society suffer and give criminals greater immunity than has been known heretofore. . . ." 277 U. S. at 464, 468.

Justices Holmes, Brandeis, Butler and Stone vigorously dissented. In an opinion in which he referred to wiretapping as "dirty business" Mr. Justice Holmes said:

"It is desirable that criminals should be detected, and to that end that all available evidence should be used. It also is desirable that the Government should not itself foster and pay for other crimes, when they are the means by which the evidence is to be obtained. If it pays its officers for having got evidence by crime, I do not see why it may not as well pay them for getting it in the same way, and I can attach no importance to protestations of disapproval if it knowingly accepts and pays and announces that in future it will pay for the fruits. We have to choose, and for my part I think it a less evil that some criminals should escape than that the Government should play an ignoble part." 277 U. S. at 470.

Justice Brandeis, in a long opinion, declared:

"The progress of science in furnishing the Government with means of espionage is not likely to stop with wire-tapping. Ways may some day be developed by which the Government, without removing papers from secret drawers, can reproduce them in court, and by which it will be enabled to expose to a jury the most intimate occurrences of the home. Advances in the psychic and related sciences may bring means of exploring unexpressed beliefs, thoughts and emotions. 'That places the liberty of every man in the hands of every petty officer' was said by James Otis of much lesser intrusions than these. To Lord Camden, a far slighter intrusion seemed 'subversive of all the comforts of society.' Can it be that the Constitution affords no protection against such invasions of individual security? . . ."

"Whenever a telephone line is tapped, the privacy of the persons at both ends of the line is invaded and all conversations between them upon any subject, and although proper, confidential and privileged, may be overheard. Moreover, the tapping of one man's telephone line involves the tapping of the telephone of every other person whom he may call or who may call him. As a means of espionage, writs of assistance and general warrants are but puny instruments of tyranny and oppression when compared with wire-tapping. . . ."

"The makers of our Constitution undertook to secure conditions favorable to the pursuit of happiness. They recognized the significance of man's spiritual nature, of his feelings and of his intellect. They knew that only a part of the pain, pleasure and satisfactions of life are to be found in material things. They sought to protect Americans in their beliefs, their thoughts, their emotions and their sensations. They conferred, as against the Government, the right to be let alone—the most comprehensive of rights and the right most valued by civilized men. To protect that right, every unjustifiable intrusion by the Government upon the privacy of the individual, whatever the means employed, must be deemed a violation of the Fourth Amendment. And the use, as evidence in a criminal proceeding, of facts ascertained by such intrusion must be deemed a violation of the Fifth. . . ." 277 U. S. at 474–9.

Pointing out that wiretapping was a violation of the laws of the state, of many other states, and of the Federal Radio Act, Mr. Justice Brandeis added:

"Decency, security and liberty alike demand that government officials shall be subjected to the same rules of conduct that are commands to the citizen. In a government of laws, existence of the government will be imperilled if it fails to observe the law scrupulously. Our Government is the potent, the omnipresent teacher. For good or for ill, it teaches the whole people by its example. Crime is contagious. If the Government becomes a lawbreaker, it breeds contempt for law; it invites every man to become a law unto himself; it invites anarchy. To declare that in the administration of the criminal law the end justifies the means—to declare that the Government may commit crimes in order to secure the conviction of a private criminal—would bring terrible retribution. Against that pernicious doctrine this Court should resolutely set its face." 277 U. S. at 485.

The *Olmstead* case settled the constitutional question. But nine years later the issue came before the Court again in statutory form. Section 605 of the Federal Communications Act of 1934— in a provision similar to that in the prior Federal Radio Act— states:

". . . no person not being authorized by the sender shall intercept any communication and divulge or publish the existence, contents, substance, purport, effect, or meaning of such intercepted communication to any person; . . . and no person having received such intercepted communication . . . shall . . . use the same or any information therein contained for his own benefit or the benefit of another not entitled thereto . . ." 47 U. S. C. § 605 (1948).

In *Nardone v. U. S.*, 302 U. S. 379, 82 L. Ed. 314, 58 S. Ct. 275 (1937), the defendants were convicted of smuggling alcohol, a substantial part of the evidence used against them being obtained from tapping of their telephone conversations. Mr. Justice Roberts, speaking for the majority, ruled that the evidence was obtained in violation of Section 605 and was inadmissible:

"Taken at face value the phrase 'no person' comprehends federal agents, and the ban on communication to 'any person' bars testimony to the content of an intercepted message." 302 U. S. at 381.

To the argument that it was not the intention of Congress to prohibit wiretapping by Federal officials Mr. Justice Roberts answered:

"We nevertheless face the fact that the plain words of § 605 forbid anyone, unless authorized by the sender, to intercept a telephone message, and direct in equally clear language that '*no person*' shall divulge or publish the message or its substance to '*any person*.' To recite the contents of the message in testimony before a court is to divulge the message. The conclusion that the act forbids such testimony seems to us unshaken by the government's arguments. . . ."

216

"It is urged that a construction be given the section which would exclude federal agents since it is improbable Congress intended to hamper and impede the activities of the government in the detection and punishment of crime. The answer is that the question is one of policy. Congress may have thought it less important that some offenders should go unwhipped of justice than that officers should resort to methods deemed inconsistent with ethical standards and destructive of personal liberty. The same considerations may well have moved the Congress to adopt § 605 as evoked the guaranty against practices and procedures violative of privacy, embodied in the Fourth and Fifth Amendments of the Constitution. . . ."

"For years controversy has raged with respect to the morality of the practice of wire-tapping by officers to obtain evidence. It has been the view of many that the practice involves a grave wrong. In the light of these circumstances we think another well recognized principle leads to the application of the statute as it is written so as to include within its sweep federal officers as well as others. That principle is that the sovereign is embraced by general words of a statute intended to prevent injury and wrong. . . ." 302 U. S. at 382–4.

Justices Sutherland and McReynolds dissented on the ground that the word "person" as used in the statute "does not include an officer of the federal government, actually engaged in the detection of crime and the enforcement of the criminal statutes of the United States. . . . The decision just made will necessarily have the effect of enabling the most depraved criminals to further their criminal plans over the telephone, in the secure knowledge that even if these plans involve kidnapping and murder, their telephone conversations can never be intercepted by officers of the law and revealed in court." 302 U. S. at 385.

Subsequently Nardone and his associates were tried again and again convicted. This time the wiretap evidence was not used directly but, the defendants contended, much of the evidence was obtained through leads developed by the wiretapping. The Court again reversed, holding that "knowledge gained by the Government's own wrong cannot be used by it" and that the defendants should have been given the opportunity to establish the use to which the information obtained from wiretapping had been put. Foreseeing some of the complications likely to ensue from this ruling Mr. Justice Frankfurter went on to say:

"In practice this generalized statement may conceal concrete complexities. Sophisticated argument may prove a causal connection between information obtained through illicit wire-tapping and the Government's proof. As a matter of good sense, however, such connection may have become so attenuated as to dissipate the taint. A sensible way of dealing with such a situation—fair to the intendment of § 605, but fair also to the purposes of the criminal law—ought to be within the reach of experienced trial judges. The burden is, of course, on the accused in the first instance to prove to the trial court's satisfaction that wire-tapping was unlawfully employed. Once that is established —as was plainly done here—the trial judge must give opportunity, however closely confined, to the accused to prove that a substantial portion of the case against him was a fruit of the poisonous tree. This leaves ample opportunity to the Government to convince the trial court that its proof had an independent origin." *Nardone v. U. S.*, 308 U. S. 338, 341, 84 L. Ed. 307, 60 S. Ct. 266 (1939).

Mr. Justice McReynolds again dissented.

In a case decided the same day as the second *Nardone* case the Court laid down two further propositions: (1) Section 605 of the Communications Act is applicable to intrastate as well as interstate and foreign communications, at least where the wires used in the intrastate conversation are part of an interstate network; and (2) an authorization to disclose the intercepted communication, given by one of the parties to the conversation who has turned state's evidence, does not constitute a consent to the divulgence within the meaning of the statute. *Weiss v. U. S.*, 308 U. S. 321, 84 L. Ed. 298, 60 S. Ct. 269 (1939).[1]

Three years later, however, the Court in two decisions refused to extend the judicial ban on wiretapping further. In *Goldstein v. U. S.*, 316 U. S. 114, 86 L. Ed. 1312, 62 S. Ct. 1000 (1942), a number of individuals were indicted under the mail fraud and conspiracy statutes. By revealing wiretap recordings of conversations the police induced two of those indicted to confess and turn state's evidence. Their testimony played an important part in convicting Goldstein and other defendants tried with him. None of the convicted defendants were parties to the intercepted conversations. The Court upheld the conviction, pointing out that "the federal courts in numerous cases, and with unanimity, have denied standing to one not the victim of an unconstitutional search and seizure to object to the introduction in evidence of that which was seized. *A fortiori* the same rule should apply to the introduction of evidence induced by the use or disclosure thereof to a witness other than the victim of the seizure. We think no broader sanction should be imposed upon the Govern-

---

[1] In accord on the second proposition is *U. S. v. Polakoff*, 112 F. 2d 888 (C. A. 2d, 1940), holding that under Section 605 the consent of both parties to the conversation is necessary. Judge Clark dissented.

ment in respect of violations of the Communications Act." 316 U. S. at 121. Chief Justice Stone and Justices Frankfurter and Murphy dissented on the ground that using wiretaps to obtain confessions was in violation of the "use for benefit" prohibition of Section 605, and that the logic and policy of the *Nardone* cases would forbid use of the tainted evidence in this manner.

*Goldman v. U. S.*, 316 U. S. 129, 86 L. Ed. 1322, 62 S. Ct. 993 (1942), involved a situation where federal agents placed a detectaphone on the wall of an adjoining room and thus picked up conversations in the defendant's office. The Court ruled, following *Olmstead*, that the use of the listening device did not infringe the Fourth Amendment. It also held that the overhearing of defendant's end of his telephone conversations did not constitute a violation of Section 605. Mr. Justice Murphy wrote a strong dissenting opinion, and Chief Justice Stone and Mr. Justice Frankfurter also indicated their agreement with the dissenters in *Olmstead*.[2]

The law of the Supreme Court stands as set forth in the foregoing decisions.[3] But the law in action is a somewhat different matter. Two important problems require further exploration. The first is the extent to which Federal and state officers continue to engage in wiretapping in spite of the Supreme Court decisions; the second relates to practical problems in the application of the *Nardone* rule.

The prevalence of wiretapping in Federal and state police work is not easy to determine. A certain amount of wiretapping is publicly acknowledged. There is evidence of extensive wiretapping not openly admitted.

The policy of the Department of Justice on the issue of wiretapping has fluctuated. Prior to 1924 wiretapping was apparently freely practiced.[4] In that year Attorney General Stone banned

---

[2] In *On Lee v. U. S.*, 343 U. S. ——, 96 L. Ed. ——, 72 S. Ct. 967 (1952), noted *supra*, a conversation was admitted in evidence obtained by a Federal agent on a radio receiver tuned to a concealed transmitter in the pocket of an informer who had entered the defendant's place of business and engaged him in conversation. The Court held that no violation of the Fourth Amendment or of Section 605 was involved. Nor would the Court exclude the testimony in the exercise of its supervisory power over Federal criminal administration. Justices Black, Frankfurter, Douglas and Burton dissented.

[3] Numerous proposals have been introduced in Congress to change Section 605 of the Federal Communications Act, but no legislation has resulted. For a full analysis see Helfeld, *A Study of the Justice Department Policies on Wire Tapping*, 9 Law. Guild Rev. 57 (1949); Note, *Congressional Wiretapping Policy Overdue*, 2 Stan. L. Rev. 744 (1950).

[4] The statements in this and the succeeding paragraph are based upon material documented in Helfeld, *supra*, pp. 59–66, and 2 Stan. L. Rev., *supra*, pp. 748–50.

the use of wiretapping by the Federal Bureau of Investigation as "unethical tactics." This policy prevailed until 1931 when Attorney General Mitchell relaxed the regulations. After the *Nardone* decision in 1937 the Department made unsuccessful efforts for several years to get the court rule reversed. In 1940, however, Attorney General Jackson prohibited wiretapping by Department agents, saying it could not be done "under the existing state of the law and decisions."[5] At about the same time Mr. J. Edgar Hoover, Director of the FBI, termed it an "archaic and inefficient" practice which "has proved a definite handicap or barrier in the development of ethical, scientific, and sound investigative technique."[6]

A year later, however, the Department changed its position. In August 1941 agents of the FBI tapped the wires of Harry Bridges in connection with a deportation proceeding.[7] In February 1949 Mr. Hoover, in the first official statement on the matter for some years, announced the policy as follows:

"It is no secret that the FBI does tap telephones in a very limited type of cases with the express approval in each instance of the Attorney General of the United States, but only in cases involving espionage, sabotage, grave risks to internal security, or when human lives are in jeopardy."[8]

The present Department practice is justified on the legal theory that Section 605 does not prohibit interception alone but only interception *and* divulging, and that communication of the results of wiretapping by one Federal agent to another does not constitute "divulging" within the meaning of the statute.[9] The extent of wiretapping by the FBI under this policy has never been fully revealed, but plainly it sanctions broad use of the device in many situations.[10]

---

[5] N. Y. Times, Mar. 18, 1940; reprinted in 86 Cong. Rec. App. 1471–2 (1940).

[6] Quoted in Note, 53 Harv. L. Rev. 863, 870 (1940).

[7] See the decision of Sears, *In the Matter of Harry Bridges*, pp. 183–4 (1941).

[8] Hoover, *A Comment on the Article "Loyalty Among Government Employees,"* 58 Yale L. J. 401, 405 (1949). This policy was affirmed by Attorney General Clark and Attorney General McGrath. Dep't of Justice Press Releases, Mar. 31, 1949 and Jan. 8, 1950.

[9] See, *e. g.*, the statement of Attorney General Biddle, N. Y. Times, Oct. 9, 1941; Dep't of Justice Press Releases, *supra* note 8. This interpretation has been severely criticized. See, *e. g.*, statement of James L. Fly, former Chairman of the Federal Communications Commission, Washington Post, Jan. 7, 1950. In the New York *Coplon* case both the trial judge and the Court of Appeals stated that wiretapping by Federal officials violated Section 605. *U. S. v. Coplon*, 88 F. Supp. 921, 925 (S. D. N. Y., 1950), 185 F. 2d 629, 636, 640 (C. A. 2d, 1950).

[10] On January 15, 1950 Mr. Hoover stated that the FBI had 170 taps

On the other hand the Treasury Department takes the position that Section 605 prohibits wiretapping and that it is not used in Treasury investigations.[11] The policy of other Federal agencies is not clear.[12]

The constitution and statutes of New York authorize law enforcement officials to tap wires in criminal cases upon securing an ex parte court order. N. Y. Const. Art. I, § 12 (1938); N. Y. Code of Crim. Proc. § 813-a (1942). And the Court of Appeals of New York has approved the use in evidence of wiretap information thus procured. *People v. Stemmer*, 298 N. Y. 728, 83 N. E. 2d 141 (1948). Efforts to test the constitutionality of the New York law have hitherto failed to achieve a decision on the merits. *Stemmer v. N. Y.*, 336 U. S. 963, 93 L. Ed. 1115, 69 S. Ct. 936 (1949) (affirmance of *People v. Stemmer* by an equally divided court); *Hoffman v. O'Brien*, 88 F. Supp. 490 (S. D. N. Y., 1949), appeal dismissed 339 U. S. 955 (1950) (suit for a declaratory judgment and injunction by the N. Y. County Criminal Courts Bar Association and the President of the Association as an individual, dismissed as not presenting a justiciable issue). Again, full data on the extent of wiretapping under the New York law are not available. In 1949, however, it was reported by the New York Times that wiretapping was used in New York City in about 350 cases a year. N. Y. Times, Feb. 25, 1949.

The incidence of unacknowledged wire tapping by police and others cannot readily be estimated. But available evidence indicates the volume is substantial.[13] In any event there is widespread suspicion on the part of government officials and others that telephones are frequently tapped.[14]

---

in existence on that day, confined to internal security cases. Dep't of Justice Press Release, Jan. 15, 1950. The number for other periods and the question whether the taps were multiple taps were not disclosed. For an example of FBI wiretapping in an espionage case see the New York *Coplon* case, *supra* note 9, and the Washington *Coplon* case, *U. S. v. Coplon*, 91 F. Supp. 867 (D. C. D. C., 1950), 191 F. 2d 749 (C. A. D. C., 1951). Certiorari was denied in both cases. 342 U. S. 920, 926 (1952).

[11] See Note, *supra*, 2 Stan. L. Rev. at 744, referring to a letter from the Under Secretary of the Treasury.

[12] *Ibid.*

[13] See, *e. g., Investigation of Alleged Wire Tapping*, Hearings before Subcommittee of the Committee on Interstate Commerce pursuant to Sen. Res. 224, 76th Cong., 3d Sess. (1940); Richards, *Is Your Telephone Tapped?*, N. Y. Star, Sept. 27 to Oct. 1, 1948; N. Y. Times, Feb. 25, 1949; Mellin, *I was a Wire Tapper*, Sat. Eve. Post, Sept. 10, 1949, p. 59; Fly, *The Wire-Tapping Outrage*, The New Republic, Feb. 6, 1950, p. 14; N. Y. Times, Dec. 28, 1950; *Report on Certain Alleged Practices of the FBI*, 10 Law. Guild Rev. 185, 190–2 (1950); Westin, *Wire-Tapping: Supreme Court v. FBI*, The Nation, Feb. 23, 1952, p. 172.

[14] See, *e. g.*, N. Y. Times, Mar. 14, 1949: ". . . tapping, illegal or

Despite the frequency of wiretapping there is only one reported case of a prosecution for violation of Section 605 of the Federal Communications Act.[15] No prosecutions have been brought against Federal or state officials under Section 605. Prosecutions for violation of state laws are reported occasionally.[16]

The Federal courts continue to follow the rule of the *Nardone* cases that evidence obtained directly or indirectly from wiretapping must be excluded. But serious problems have arisen in the concrete application of this basic principle.

Under the *Nardone* rule evidence secured by wiretapping does not thereby become "sacred and inaccessible" to the government forever; if knowledge of the same facts is obtained by the government from independent sources they may be proved like any other facts. See 308 U. S. at 341. This necessary qualification of the *Nardone* rule in practice allows the government considerable leeway to establish the same information obtained by wiretaps from other untainted sources. The tracing of such information to the wiretapping alone presents the defendant with an almost insurmountable problem.[17]

Comparable difficulties arise in deciding how closely connected the evidence must be with the wiretapping to constitute "the fruit of the poisonous tree."[18]

Even more of a problem for the defendant, however, is the establishment of the right to a hearing on the wiretapping issue at all. Under the second *Nardone* case the defendant must first "prove to the trial court's satisfaction" that wiretapping has

---

with the required [N. Y.] Supreme Court order, admittedly has reached such proportions that astute city officials have abandoned use of the telephone for any conversation that even borders on the confidential side." See also Kilpatrick, *Washington Worry-Go-Round*, '48 Magazine, March 1948, pp. 126–32.

[15] *U. S. v. Gruber*, 123 F. 2d 307 (C. A. 2d, 1941), conviction of an attorney for tapping the wires of Federal officials.

[16] See materials cited in Note following this section.

[17] Thus in the *Coplon* case the FBI obtained information that the defendant intended to make a trip to New York (in the course of which she was arrested) through its wiretaps. But the government was able to show that it also secured the same information from the defendant's supervisor. In both the Washington and the New York trials the judge held it sufficiently demonstrated that the information had come from legitimate sources. *U. S. v. Coplon*, 88 F. Supp. 921 (S. D. N. Y. 1950); 91 F. Supp. 867 (D. C. D. C. 1950). The ruling was affirmed by the Court of Appeals for the District of Columbia, 191 F. 2d 749, 756–7, but not passed on by the Court of Appeals for the Second Circuit, 185 F. 2d 629.

[18] See decision of Judge Ryan in the *Coplon* case, 88 F. Supp. 921, 928–30 (S. D. N. Y., 1950); but *cf.* the discussion by the Court of Appeals, 185 F. 2d 629, 639–40. See also the ruling of the Court of Appeals for the District of Columbia, 191 F. 2d 749, 756–7.

occurred; only then is the judge required to hold a hearing in which the full facts may be uncovered.[19] In practice the defendant may find it difficult or impossible to obtain the necessary facts. The admission of wiretapping was obtained in the *Coplon* case only by the most strenuous efforts, after initial concealment of the facts from the judge.[20] In the trial of the second group of Communists in New York the defendants' motion for a hearing was supported by affidavits alleging that (1) it was the admitted practice of the FBI to tap telephones in "security cases"; (2) an examination by a technician of the telephones at Communist Party headquarters revealed that the telephones were tapped, but that the source of the tap was not found; and (3) the wife of one of the defendants on picking up her home telephone heard a conversation referring to wiretapping equipment. The government in an answering affidavit did not deny wiretapping but stated that no evidence secured from wiretapping would be used in the trial. The District Judge ruled that the defendants' allegations of wiretapping "depend on the merest innuendo" and denied a hearing.[21] Actually there are only four reported instances in which the preliminary hearing on wiretapping has been allowed by the courts in the 15 years since the *Nardone* case.[22]

It may thus be fairly concluded that the policy expressed by the Supreme Court in the *Nardone* cases has been only partially realized in practice.

## Note

Most of the states have legislation prohibiting wiretapping, but prosecutions under these statutes have been rare. See Rosenzweig, *The Law of Wire Tapping*, 33 Corn. L. Q. 73, 73–90 (1947). Those states which have passed on the question have agreed with the *Olmstead*

---

[19] The Court of Appeals for the Second Circuit has held that in such a hearing the burden shifts to the government to prove that the evidence it proposes to introduce was not obtained from tainted sources. *U. S. v. Goldstein*, 120 F. 2d 485, 488 (C. A. 2d, 1941); *U. S. v. Coplon*, 185 F. 2d 629, 639 (C. A. 2d 1950). Thus once the right to a hearing is established the defendant is in a strong position to discover all the facts relating to the wiretapping. In the *Coplon* case the Court further held that the government must produce all its wiretap material regardless of the claim that to do so would reveal information injurious to national security.

[20] See Lowenthal, *The Federal Bureau of Investigation*, pp. 434–7 (1950).

[21] *U. S. v. Flynn*, decision of Judge Conger (S. D. N. Y., Dec. 21, 1952), unreported. The same result was reached in the prosecution of Communist Party members in Baltimore, *U. S. v. Frankfeld*, 100 F. Supp. 934 (D. Md., 1951); and in *U. S. v. Pillon*, 36 F. Supp. 567 (E. D. N. Y., 1941).

[22] The *Goldman*, *Weiss* and *Coplon* cases, *supra*, and *U. S. v. Lewis*, 87 F. Supp. 970 (D. C. D. C. 1950), rev'd on other grounds *sub. nom. Billeci v. U. S.*, 184 F. 2d 394 (C. A. D. C., 1950). In all four cases the showing that wiretapping was utilized came about through unusual circumstances.

decision that wiretapping does not constitute a violation of constitutional provisions prohibiting unreasonable searches and seizures. *Ibid.* Nor have the states excluded evidence obtained from wiretapping on the ground that it was illegally obtained in violation of state law or Section 605 of the Federal Communications Act. *Ibid.;* see also Note, *Wire Tapping,* 3 Miami L. Q. 604, 608–12 (1949). Of course, strict enforcement of Section 605 would effectively prevent the use of wiretapping evidence in the state courts.

The state statutes and decisions on wiretapping are collected and discussed in Rosenzweig, *supra;* Wigmore, *Evidence,* § 2184(b) (3d ed. 1940).

For general discussion of the law of wiretapping, including the arguments advanced for and against wiretapping (or restricted forms of wiretapping) see in addition to the above material, Rosenzweig, *The Law of Wire Tapping,* 32 Corn. L. Q. 514 (1947); Helfeld, *supra,* 9 Law. Guild Rev. 57 (1949); Note, *supra,* 2 Stan. L. Rev. 744 (1950); Note, 40 J. of Am. Inst. of Cr. L. and Crim. 476 (1949); Woodring, *Wire Tapping* (Editorial Research Reports, 1949); Bernstein, *The Fruit of the Poisonous Tree,* 37 Ill. L. Rev. 99 (1942); *Wiretapping, Congress and the Department of Justice,* 9 Internat'l Jur. Ass'n Bull. 97 (1941); Note, 53 Harv. L. Rev. 863 (1940).

With respect to the procedures for raising the wiretapping issue in a criminal prosecution, see Note, *The Coplon Case: Wiretapping, State Secrets, and National Security,* 60 Yale L. J. 736 (1951); Bernstein, *supra,* 37 Ill. L. Rev. at 100–8; Note, 55 Harv. L. Rev. 141 (1941).

For a description of some of the scientific and political potentialities of unrestricted wiretapping read George Orwell's novel, *Nineteen Eighty-Four* (1949).

A full discussion of wiretapping, unfortunately not available when this section was prepared, may be found in Westin, *The Wire-Tapping Problem: An Analysis and a Legislative Proposal,* 52 Col. L. Rev. 165 (1952).

## D. OTHER AREAS OF PROTECTION

Federal and state constitutions, statutes and decisions provide many other forms of protection to the individual against arbitrary or unjust action by the government in criminal prosecutions. Of these safeguards, the most significant of the constitutional rights secured by the Federal Constitution are noted briefly below. Virtually all state constitutions contain similar guarantees, but substantial variation is frequently found in the interpretation and in the practical application of these provisions. The extent to which the Fourteenth Amendment compels state proceedings to conform with the constitutional standards required in Federal proceedings is a question that constantly recurs throughout the cases. The conflicting views of the Supreme Court justices on this matter, already noted in the previous sections of this chapter, came to a sharp focus in the *Adamson* case, set forth below.

## Free, Fair and Unbiased Trial

The due process clause of the Fifth and Fourteenth Amendments guarantees the accused a trial free from mob domination or pressure. *Moore v. Dempsey*, 261 U. S. 86, 67 L. Ed. 543, 43 S. Ct. 265 (1923). *Cf. Spies v. Illinois*, 123 U. S. 131, 31 L. Ed. 80, 8 S. Ct. 21 (1887) (Haymarket trial) ; *Frank v. Mangum*, 237 U. S. 309, 59 L. Ed. 969, 35 S. Ct. 582 (1915). See also *Shepherd v. Florida*, 341 U. S. 50, 95 L. Ed. 740, 71 S. Ct. 549 (1951). Rule 21(a) of the Federal Rules of Criminal Procedure authorizes a change of venue on grounds of prejudice in the district where a trial is to be held. Likewise a conviction obtained by prosecuting officials through the use of fraud or trickery, the knowing use of perjured testimony, or the suppression of evidence is also a violation of the due process clause. *Mooney v. Holohan*, 294 U. S. 103, 79 L. Ed. 791, 55 S. Ct. 340 (1935) (the famous Tom Mooney case) ; *Smith v. O'Grady*, 312 U. S. 329, 85 L. Ed. 859, 61 S. Ct. 572 (1941) ; *Pyle v. Kansas*, 317 U. S. 213, 87 L. Ed. 214, 63 S. Ct. 177 (1942). *Cf. Cochran v. Kansas*, 316 U. S. 255, 86 L. Ed. 1453, 62 S. Ct. 1068 (1942) (refusal of prison authorities to allow defendant to file appeal held denial of equal protection). But *cf. Buchalter v. N. Y.*, 319 U. S. 427, 87 L. Ed. 1492, 63 S. Ct. 1129 (1943).

Where the trial takes place in a state court, however, the rule requiring the exhaustion of state remedies and the Supreme Court's reliance upon the factual determinations of the state courts impose substantial obstacles to vindication of the foregoing rights in the Federal courts. Thus in the end Mooney failed to obtain judicial relief. See *In re Mooney*, 10 Cal. 2d 1, 73 Pac. 2d 554 (1937), cert. den. 305 U. S. 598. Mooney was ultimately pardoned by the Governor Olsen of California, who said he was convinced of Mooney's innocence. N. Y. Times, Jan. 8, 1939. See also *Hysler v. Florida*, 315 U. S. 411, 86 L. Ed. 932, 62 S. Ct. 688 (1942) ; *Ex parte Hawk*, 321 U. S. 114, 88 L. Ed. 572, 64 S. Ct. 448 (1944) ; *White v. Ragen*, 324 U. S. 760, 89 L. Ed. 1348, 65 S. Ct. 978 (1945).

For discussion of the *Frank* and *Moore* cases see Schofield, *Federal Courts and Mob Domination of State Courts: Leo Frank's Case*, 10 Ill. L. Rev. 479 (1916) ; Note, *Mob Domination of a Trial as a Violation of the Fourteenth Amendment*, 37 Harv. L. Rev. 247 (1923) ; Waterman and Overton, *The Aftermath of Moore v. Dempsey*, 18 St. Louis L. Rev. 117 (1933). See, generally, Boskey and Pickering, *Federal Restrictions on State Criminal Procedure*, 13 U. Chi. L. Rev. 266, 295–7 (1946) ; Hays, *Trial by Prejudice* (1933) ; Mangum, *The Legal Status of the Negro*, ch. XI (1940). With reference to control over the press and radio in connection with criminal prosecutions, see Chapter IV, *infra*.

The accused likewise has a constitutional right under the due process clause to trial before an unbiased judge. *Tumey v. Ohio*, 273 U. S. 510, 71 L. Ed. 749, 47 S. Ct. 437 (1927) (judge's fees derived from fines imposed) ; *cf. Berger v. U. S.*, 255 U. S. 22, 65 L. Ed. 481, 41 S. Ct. 230 (1921). But *cf. Dugan v. Ohio*, 277 U. S. 61, 72 L. Ed. 784, 48 S. Ct. 439 (1928). For discussion of this issue in the Sacco-Vanzetti case, see Fraenkel, *The Sacco-Vanzetti Case*, pp. 178–82 (1931). See also Notes, 1 U. Cin. L. Rev. 338 (1927) ; 36 Yale L. J. 1171 (1927) ; Frank, *Disqualification of Judges*, 56 Yale L. J. 605 (1947).

Other safeguards under the due process clause include the rule against vagueness and the rule against unreasonable presumptions. See Fraenkel, *The Supreme Court as Protector of Civil Rights: Criminal Justice*, 275 Annals of the Am. Acad. of Pol. and Soc. Sci. 86, 94–5 (1951).

## Indictment by Grand Jury

The guarantee of indictment by grand jury in the Fifth Amendment applies only to a "capital, or otherwise infamous crime." The term "infamous crime" has been interpreted to mean an offense punishable by imprisonment in a penitentiary or involving hard labor. *U. S. v. Moreland*, 258 U. S. 433, 66 L. Ed. 700, 42 S. Ct. 368 (1922). Rule 7(a) of the Federal Rules of Criminal Procedure now provides for an indictment in all capital cases and, unless waived, in cases involving an offense subject to imprisonment for a term exceeding one year or at hard labor; otherwise a prosecution may be initiated by information. The requirement of an indictment is not incorporated into the Fourteenth Amendment and hence is not applicable to the states. *Hurtado v. California*, 110 U. S. 516, 28 L. Ed. 232, 4 S. Ct. 111 (1884). See Orfield, *Criminal Procedure from Arrest to Appeal*, ch. V (1947) ; Dession, *From Indictment to Information: Implications of the Shift*, 42 Yale L. J. 163 (1932).

## Double Jeopardy

The double jeopardy provision of the Fifth Amendment affords protection primarily against a second trial for the same offense

**226**

after acquittal, and against an increase in the punishment originally imposed. It does not prevent a second trial when the defendant has obtained a reversal on appeal; nor does it prevent a prosecution under state law based on the same facts as a Federal prosecution. See Fraenkel, *Our Civil Liberties*, ch. XII (1944); Parker, *Some Aspects of Double Jeopardy*, 25 St. John's L. Rev. 188 (1951); see also *Sealfron v. U. S.*, 332 U. S. 575, 92 L. Ed. 180, 68 S. Ct. 237 (1948). The double jeopardy provision of the Fifth Amendment is not, as such, incorporated in the Fourteenth. *Palko v. Connecticut*, 302 U. S. 319, 82 L. Ed. 288, 58 S. Ct. 149 (1937).

## Self-Incrimination

The historical background and certain features of the privilege against self-incrimination have already been discussed in connection with coerced confessions and searches and seizures. The application of the privilege in cases involving political activity—perhaps the most significant aspect of the privilege today—is treated in Chapter IV, *infra*.

In general, the privilege may be claimed in any kind of government proceeding as a ground for refusing to answer questions that might tend to subject the person questioned to criminal penalties or forfeitures. *McCarthy v. Arndstein*, 266 U. S. 34, 69 L. Ed. 158, 45 S. Ct. 16 (1924); *Counselman v. Hitchcock*, 142 U. S. 547, 35 L. Ed. 1110, 12 S. Ct. 195 (1892); *Smith v. U. S.*, 337 U. S. 137, 93 L. Ed. 1264, 69 S. Ct. 1000 (1949). But the privilege is for the personal protection of the claimant and may not be invoked on behalf of anyone else. *Hale v. Henkel*, 201 U. S. 43, 50 L. Ed. 652, 26 S. Ct. 370 (1906); *U. S. v. Field*, 193 F. 2d 92 (C. A. 2d, 1951), cert. den. 342 U. S. 894 (1951). And it has been held not available to protect corporations or associations from the production of their books or records. *Wilson v. U. S.*, 221 U. S. 361, 55 L. Ed. 771, 31 S. Ct. 538 (1911); *U. S. v. White*, 322 U. S. 694, 88 L. Ed. 1542, 64 S. Ct. 1248 (1944); see also *Shapiro v. U. S.*, 335 U. S. 1, 92 L. Ed. 1787, 68 S. Ct. 1375 (1948). Moreover, it has been held that the Federal privilege may be invoked only where the claimant fears incrimination under Federal laws, and does not apply where incrimination is feared under the laws of a state or another sovereignty. *U. S. v. Murdock*, 284 U. S. 141, 76 L. Ed. 210, 52 S. Ct. 63 (1931). But cf. *U. S. v. Di Carlo*, 102 F. Supp. 597 (N. D. Ohio, 1952). Under an immunity statute, exempting the witness from prosecution arising out of his testimony, he may be compelled to testify. *Brown v. Walker*, 161 U. S. 591, 40 L. Ed. 819, 16 S. Ct. 644 (1896); *U. S. v. Monia*, 317 U. S. 424, 87 L. Ed. 376, 63 S. Ct.

409 (1943) ; cf. *Feldman v. U. S.*, 322 U. S. 487, 88 L. Ed. 1408, 64 S. Ct. 1082 (1944) (testimony compelled under state immunity statute admissible in Federal prosecution).

The determination of when the privilege against self-incrimination may be invoked rests with the court. *Hoffman v. U. S.*, 341 U. S. 479, 95 L. Ed. 1118, 71 S. Ct. 814 (1951). But once it appears that the claimant is in danger he is allowed wide latitude in judging whether a particular question will tend to incriminate him. *Hoffman v. U.S., supra; Mason v. U. S.*, 244 U. S. 362, 61 L. Ed. 1198, 37 S. Ct. 621 (1917).

With respect to the right to comment to the jury on the defendant's failure to testify and the question of whether the privilege is incorporated in the Fourteenth Amendment, see *Adamson v. California, infra.*

In general see Corwin, *The Supreme Court's Construction of the Self-Incrimination Clause*, 29 Mich. L. Rev. 1, 191 (1930) ; 8 Wigmore, *Evidence*, §§ 2250–84 (3d ed. 1940) ; Morgan, *The Privilege Against Self-Incrimination*, 34 Minn. L. Rev. 1 (1949) ; Inbau, *Self-Incrimination* (1950) ; Grant, *Immunity from Compulsory Self-Incrimination in a Federal System of Government*, 9 Temple L. Q. 57, 194 (1934–5) ; Gold, *Privilege Against Self-Incrimination in Federal Grand Jury Proceedings*, 24 Temple L. Q. 395 (1951) ; Note, 61 Yale L. J. 105 (1952).

## Public Trial, Notice, Confrontation

The Sixth Amendment guarantees, "in all criminal prosecutions," the right of the accused to a "speedy and public trial," "to be informed of the nature and cause of the accusation," and "to be confronted with the witnesses against him." The nature of these rights was set forth by the Supreme Court in *In re Oliver*, 333 U. S. 257, 92 L. Ed. 682, 68 S. Ct. 499 (1948). In that case a Michigan judge, sitting as a one man grand jury, found that one of the witnesses before him had testified falsely and sentenced him to jail for contempt. The public was excluded from the proceeding and much of the evidence upon which the judge based his decision was considered confidential and not revealed to the defendant. The Supreme Court reversed the conviction, holding that the due process clause of the Fourteenth Amendment was violated by the exclusion of the public and the failure to afford the defendant a reasonable opportunity to defend himself. The Court noted that the right to a public trial did not forbid the court to exclude certain members of the public from the courtroom under special circumstances, but said that "no court in this country has ever before held, so far as we can find, that an accused can be tried, convicted, and sent to jail, when everyone else is denied entrance to the court, except the judge and his attaches." 333 U. S. at 271. With respect to the second question the Court said: "A person's right to reasonable notice of a charge against him, and an opportunity to be heard in his defense—a right to his day in court—are basic in our system of jurisprudence; and these rights include, as a minimum, a right to examine the witnesses against him, to offer testimony, and to be represented by counsel." 333 U. S. at 273.

Further, with respect to the right of public trial, see *U. S. v. Kobli*, 172 F. 2d 919 (C. A. 3, 1949); Radin, *The Right to a Public Trial*, 6 Temple L. Q. 381 (1932); Notes, 49 Col. L. Rev. 110 (1949), 97 U. Pa. L. Rev. 276 (1948). Concerning the problem of publicity in connection with judicial proceedings, see Chapter IV, *infra*. The right to prosecution only on a charge that is actually made was affirmed in *DeJonge v. Oregon*, 299 U. S. 353, 81 L. Ed. 278, 57 S. Ct. 255 (1937); *Cole v. Arkansas*, 333 U. S. 196, 92 L. Ed. 644, 68 S. Ct. 514 (1948). With respect to the right to a speedy trial, see *U. S. v. McWilliams*, 163 F. 2d 695 (C. A. D. C., 1947) (dismissing the indictment in the trial of alleged pro-Nazis under the Smith Act). On confrontation, see Note, 3 Okla. L. Rev. 321 (1950).

The rights here involved have been limited by a strict interpretation of "criminal prosecution." Thus they do not apply to the judge's determination, on the basis of a probation report not made available to the defendant, what the sentence should be, *Williams v. N. Y.*, 337 U. S. 241, 93 L. Ed. 1337, 69 S. Ct. 1079 (1949); nor to the decision of the governor of a state as to whether a defendant sentenced to death had become insane after conviction, *Solesbee v. Balkcom*, 339 U. S. 9, 94 L. Ed. 604, 70 S. Ct. 457 (1950). See also Note, 60 Yale L. J. 736, 738–9 (1951). But *cf. U. S. v. Coplon*, 185 F. 2d 629 (C. A. 2, 1950). The rights are also not infringed in those situations where the judge may punish summarily for contempt of court. See *In re Oliver, supra*.

In recent years these rights to public trial, notice and confrontation have been challenged particularly in matters alleged to involve national security. This phase of the problem is considered in Chapter IV, *infra*.

As indicated in the right to counsel cases, not all the rights guaranteed by the Sixth Amendment have been held to be secured against state action under the Fourteenth.

In general, see Heller, *The Sixth Amendment* (1951).

## Bail

The present Federal law with respect to bail before conviction is stated in Rule 46(a)(1) of the Federal Rules of Criminal Procedure:

"A person arrested for an offense not punishable by death shall be admitted to bail. A person arrested for an offense punishable by death may be admitted to bail by any court or judge authorized by law to do so in the exercise of discretion, giving due weight to the evidence and to the nature and circumstances of the offense." 18 U. S. C. (1951).

The guarantee in the Sixth Amendment protects only the right to bail at common law and hence applies only to bail before conviction. The right to bail after the conviction is provided for in Rule 46(a)(2) which states that bail "may be allowed pending appeal or certiorari only if it appears that the case involves a substantial question which should be determined by the appellate court."

The important question of the amount of bail is a matter in the first instance for the commissioner or trial judge, but is subject to review by appeal.

For material on the historical background of the bail system, see Petersdorff, *A Practical Treatise on the Law of Bail* (1835); 2 Pollock and Maitland, *The History of English Law*, p. 584 (2d ed. 1905); DeHaas, *Antiquities of Bail* (1940); Longsdorf, *Is Bail a Rich Man's Privilege?* 7 Fed. Rules Dec. 309 (1947). Generally on problems of bail see Yankwich, *Release on Bond by Trial and Appellate Courts*, 7 Fed. Rules Dec. 271 (1947); Notes, 25 Mich. L. Rev. 646 (1927); 41 Yale L. J. 293 (1931); 35 Va. L. Rev. 496 (1949). For material on the actual operation of bail systems, see Beeley, *The Bail System* in *Chicago* (1927); Cleveland Crime Commission Report, *A Study of Criminal Court Bail Bonds in Cleveland* (1936); Barnes and Teeters, *New Horizons in Criminology*, pp. 294–6 (1945).

## Cruel and Unusual Punishment

The only case in which the Supreme Court has set aside a punishment as cruel and unusual is one which arose under the Philippine Bill of Rights. *Weems v. U. S.*, 217 U. S. 349, 54 L. Ed. 793, 30 S. Ct. 544 (1910). In this case the punishment involved a prison term at hard labor, the prisoner to wear a chain hung from wrist to ankle. A more recent decision discussing the constitutional issue is *Louisiana ex rel. Francis v. Resweber*, 329 U. S. 459, 91 L. Ed. 422, 67 S. Ct. 374 (1947). Here the Court, by a 5 to 4 vote, held that a second attempt at electrocution, the first having failed, would not constitute cruel and unusual punishment. See also *Johnson v. Dye,* 175 F. 2d 250 (C. A. 3, 1949), rev'd on other grounds, 338 U. S. 864 (1949); *Johnson v. Matthews,* 182 F. 2d 677 (C. A. D. C., 1950), cert. den. 340 U. S. 828 (1950).

See, generally, Sutherland, *Due Process and Cruel Punishment,* 64 Harv. L. Rev. 271 (1950); Notes, 34 Minn. L. Rev. 134 (1950); 4 Vand. L. Rev. 680 (1951).

## Jury Trial

In addition to the requirements of the Sixth Amendment the Federal Constitution provides in Article III, Section 2, that "the trial of all crimes, except in cases of impeachment, shall be by jury." The historical background of the jury system is traced in 1 Holdsworth, *A History of English Law,* pp. 312–50 (5th ed. 1931); 1 Stephen, *A History of the Criminal Law of England,* pp. 250–72 (1883); 1 Pollock and Maitland, *The History of English Law,* pp. 136–53, (2d ed., 1905); Lesser, *The Historical Development of the Jury System* (1894); Stephens, *The Growth of Trial by Jury in England,* 10 Harv. L. Rev. 150 (1896); Coleman, *Origin and Development of Trial by Jury,* 6 Va. L. Rev. 77 (1919); Henry, *The Story of the Criminal Jury,* in Legal Essays in Tribute to Orrin Kip McMurray pp. 135–63 (Max Radin ed., 1935); Heller, *The Sixth Amendment,* ch. I and II (1951).

The right to trial by jury may be waived. *Patton v. U. S.,* 281 U. S. 276, 74 L. Ed 854, 50 S. Ct. 253 (1930); *Adams v. U. S. ex rel. McCann,* 317 U. S. 269, 87 L. Ed. 268, 63 S. Ct. 236 (1942). And Congress has power to provide for the trial of minor offenses without a jury. *District of Columbia v. Clawans,* 300 U. S. 617, 81 L. Ed. 843, 57 S. Ct. 660 (1937); *cf. Callan v. Wilson,* 127 U. S. 540, 32 L. Ed. 223, 8 S. Ct. 1301 (1888). Furthermore the Federal constitutional provisions do not require a jury trial in the state courts. See *Jordan v. Mass.,* 225 U. S. 167, 56 L. Ed. 1038, 32 S. Ct. 651 (1912).

The Sixth Amendment's guarantee of an "impartial jury" requires that the jury represent "a cross-section of the community." *Glasser v. U. S.,* 315 U. S. 60, 86 L. Ed. 680, 62 S. Ct. 457 (1942). Hence exclusion from the jury panel of persons on account of race, economic status or, at least where women are qualified to serve, sex, would not conform to constitutional requirements. See *Glasser v. U. S., supra; Thiel v. Southern Pacific Co.,* 328 U. S. 217, 90 L. Ed. 1181, 66 S. Ct. 984 (1946); *Ballard v. U. S.,* 329 U. S. 187, 91 L. Ed. 181, 67 S. Ct. 261 (1946). But the courts will not reject a system of jury selection because of the absence of members of an economic class without a strong showing of discrimination. *U. S. v. Dennis*, 183 F. 2d 201 (C. A. 2, 1950). And the presence of government employees upon a jury has been held not to infringe constitutional protections. *Frazier v. U. S.*, 335 U. S. 497, 93 L. Ed. 187, 69 S. Ct. 201 (1948) ; *Dennis v. U. S.*, 339 U. S. 162, 94 L. Ed. 734, 70 S. Ct. 519 (1950) ; but see *Morford v. U. S.*, 339 U. S. 258, 94 L. Ed. 815, 70 S. Ct. 586 (1950).

The equal protection clause of the Fourteenth Amendment imposes upon the states a similar requirement that the jury be selected without discrimination. The Supreme Court has consistently reversed convictions in state courts upon a showing of systematic exclusion of Negroes from jury service. *Strauder v. W. Va.*, 100 U. S. 303, 25 L. Ed. 664 (1880) ; *Norris v. Alabama*, 294 U. S. 587, 79 L. Ed. 1074, 55 S. Ct. 579 (1935) (the second Scottsboro case) ; *Cassell v. Texas*, 339 U. S. 282, 94 L. Ed. 839, 70 S. Ct. 629 (1950) ; but *cf. Akins v. Texas*, 325 U. S. 398, 89 L. Ed. 1692, 65 S. Ct. 1276 (1945). See Mangum, *The Legal Status of the Negro*, ch. XII (1940). But the Court has refused to hold illegal the New York system of "blue ribbon" juries on the ground that no sufficient showing of discrimination has been made. *Fay v. N. Y.*, 332 U. S. 261, 91 L. Ed. 2043, 67 S. Ct. 1613 (1947) ; *Moore v. N. Y.*, 333 U. S. 565, 92 L. Ed. 881, 68 S Ct. 705 (1948). See also 1 A.L.R. 2d 1291 ; 9 A.L.R. 2d 661.

In general, on jury questions, see Orfield, *Criminal Procedure from Arrest to Appeal*, ch. IV and VII (1947) ; Heller, *The Sixth Amendment*, ch. IV (1951) ; Frankfurter and Corcoran, *Petty Federal Offenses and the Constitutional Guaranty of Trial by Jury*, 39 Harv. L. Rev. 917 (1926) ; Scott, *The Supreme Court's Control over State and Federal Criminal Juries*, 34 Iowa L. Rev. 577 (1949) ; Note, *Disqualification of Federal Employees From Jury Service in Cases Involving "Subversives,"* 49 Col. L. Rev. 1131 (1949) ; Note, *Justice, Jury Trials, and Government Service*, 35 Corn. L. Q. 814 (1950).

## Miscellaneous

On bill of attainder and ex post facto laws see Chapter IV, *infra*.

With reference to the question of discriminatory enforcement of non-discriminatory laws, see *Yick Wo v. Hopkins*, 118 U. S. 356, 30 L. Ed. 220, 6 S. Ct. 1064 (1886) ; *Snowden v. Hughes*, 321 U. S. 1, 88 L. Ed. 497, 64 S. Ct. 397 (1944) ; Note, *Discriminatory Law Enforcement and Equal Protection From the Law*, 59 Yale L. J. 354 (1950). On the question of discrimination in sentencing see Mangum, *supra*, ch. XVII ; *Hampton v. Commonwealth*, 190 Va. 531, 554–7, 58 S. E. 2d 288, 298–9 (1950), cert. den. 339 U. S. 989 (1950), 340 U. S. 914 (1951).

## ADAMSON v. CALIFORNIA

Supreme Court of the United States, 1947
332 U. S. 46, 91 L. Ed. 1903, 67 S. Ct. 1672

MR. JUSTICE REED delivered the opinion of the Court.

The appellant, Adamson, a citizen of the United States, was convicted, without recommendation for mercy, by a jury in a Superior Court of the State of California of murder in the first degree. . . . The provisions of California law which were challenged in the state proceedings as invalid under the Fourteenth Amendment to the Federal Constitution are those of the state constitution and penal code in the margin. They permit the failure of a defendant to explain or to deny evidence against him to be commented upon by court and by counsel and to be considered by court and jury.[3] The defendant did not testify. As the trial court gave its instructions and the District Attorney argued the case in accordance with the constitutional and statutory provisions just referred to, we have for decision the question of their constitutionality in these circumstances under the limitations of § 1 of the Fourteenth Amendment.

The appellant was charged in the information with former convictions for burglary, larceny and robbery and pursuant to § 1025, California Penal Code, answered that he had suffered the previous convictions. This answer barred allusion to these charges of convictions on the trial. Under California's interpretation of § 1025 of the Penal Code and § 2051 of the Code of Civil Procedure, however, if the defendant, after answering affirmatively charges alleging prior convictions, takes the witness stand to deny or explain away other evidence that has been introduced "the commission of these crimes could have been revealed to the jury on cross-examination to impeach his testimony." *People* v. *Adamson,* 27 Cal. 2d 478, 494, 165 P. 2d 3, 11; *People* v. *Braun,* 14 Cal. 2d 1, 6, 92 P. 2d 402, 405. This forces

---

[3] Constitution of California, Art. I, § 13:

". . . No person shall be twice put in jeopardy for the same offense; nor be compelled, in any criminal case, to be a witness against himself; nor be deprived of life, liberty, or property without due process of law; but in any criminal case, whether the defendant testifies or not, his failure to explain or to deny by his testimony any evidence or facts in the case against him may be commented upon by the court and by counsel, and may be considered by the court or the jury. . . ."

Penal Code of California, § 1323: "A defendant in a criminal action or proceeding cannot be compelled to be a witness against himself; but if he offers himself as a witness, he may be cross-examined by the counsel for the people as to all matters about which he was examined in chief. The failure of the defendant to explain or to deny by his testimony any evidence or facts in the case against him may be commented upon by counsel."

an accused who is a repeated offender to choose between the risk of having his prior offenses disclosed to the jury or of having it draw harmful inferences from uncontradicted evidence that can only be denied or explained by the defendant. . . .

We shall assume, but without any intention thereby of ruling upon the issue,[6] that permission by law to the court, counsel and jury to comment upon and consider the failure of defendant "to explain or to deny by his testimony any evidence or facts in the case against him" would infringe defendant's privilege against self-incrimination under the Fifth Amendment if this were a trial in a court of the United States under a similar law. Such an assumption does not determine appellant's rights under the Fourteenth Amendment. It is settled law that the clause of the Fifth Amendment, protecting a person against being compelled to be a witness against himself, is not made effective by the Fourteenth Amendment as a protection against state action on the ground that freedom from testimonial compulsion is a right of national citizenship, or because it is a personal privilege or immunity secured by the Federal Constitution as one of the rights of man that are listed in the Bill of Rights. . . .

[The Court here discusses *Barron v. Baltimore*, the *Slaughter-House Cases*, *Twining v. N. J.*, and other cases.]

Appellant secondly contends that if the privilege against self-incrimination is not a right protected by the privileges and immunities clause of the Fourteenth Amendment against state action, this privilege, to its full scope under the Fifth Amendment, inheres in the right to a fair trial. A right to a fair trial is a right admittedly protected by the due process clause of the Fourteenth Amendment. Therefore, appellant argues, the due process clause of the Fourteenth Amendment protects his privilege against self-incrimination. The due process clause of the Fourteenth Amendment, however, does not draw all the rights of the federal Bill of Rights under its protection. That contention was made and rejected in *Palko* v. *Connecticut*, 302 U. S. 319, 323. It was rejected with citation of the cases excluding several of the rights, protected by the Bill of Rights, against infringement by the National Government. Nothing has been

---

6 . . . The Fifth Amendment forbids compulsion on a defendant to testify. *Boyd v. United States*, 116 U. S. 616, 631, 632; cf. *Davis v. United States*, 328 U. S. 582, 587, 593. A federal statute that grew out of the extension of permissible witnesses to include those charged with offenses negatives a presumption against an accused for failure to avail himself of the right to testify in his own defense. 28 U. S. C. § 632; *Bruno v. United States*, 308 U. S. 287. It was this statute which is interpreted to protect the defendant against comment for his claim of privilege. *Wilson v. United States*, 149 U. S. 60, 66; *Johnson v. United States*, 318 U. S. 189, 199.

called to our attention that either the framers of the Fourteenth Amendment or the states that adopted intended its due process clause to draw within its scope the earlier amendments to the Constitution. *Palko* held that such provisions of the Bill of Rights as were "implicit in the concept of ordered liberty," p. 325, became secure from state interference by the clause. But it held nothing more.

Specifically, the due process clause does not protect, by virtue of its mere existence, the accused's freedom from giving testimony by compulsion in state trials that is secured to him against federal interference by the Fifth Amendment. *Twining* v. *New Jersey,* 211 U. S. 78, 99–114; *Palko* v. *Connecticut, supra,* p. 323. For a state to require testimony from an accused is not necessarily a breach of a state's obligation to give a fair trial. Therefore, we must examine the effect of the California law applied in this trial to see whether the comment on failure to testify violates the protection against state action that the due process clause does grant to an accused. . . .

Generally, comment on the failure of an accused to testify is forbidden in American jurisdictions.[15] This arises from state constitutional or statutory provisions similar in character to the federal provisions. Fifth Amendment and 28 U. S. C. § 632. California, however, is one of a few states that permit limited comment upon a defendant's failure to testify.[16] That permission is narrow. The California law is set out in note 3 and authorizes comment by court and counsel upon the "failure of the defendant to explain or to deny by his testimony any evidence or facts in the case against him." This does not involve any presumption, rebuttable or irrebuttable, either of guilt or of the truth of any fact, that is offered in evidence. Compare *Tot* v. *United States,* 319 U. S. 463, 470. It allows inferences to be drawn from proven facts. . . . There is here no lack of power in the trial court to adjudge and no denial of a hearing. California has prescribed a method for advising the jury in the search for truth. However sound may be the legislative conclusion that an accused should not be compelled in any criminal case to be a witness against himself, we see no reason why comment should not be made upon his silence. It seems quite natural that

---

[15] [8 Wigmore, *Evidence,* p. 412 (3d ed. 1940).]

[16] The cases and statutory references are collected in VIII Wigmore, *supra,* at pp. 413 *et seq.* New Jersey, Ohio and Vermont permit comment. The question of permitting comment upon the failure of an accused to testify has been a matter for consideration in recent years. See Reports of American Bar Association (1931) 137; Proceedings, American Law Institute, 1930–31, 202; Reeder, *Comment Upon Failure of Accused to Testify,* 31 Mich. L. Rev. 40; Bruce, *The Right to Comment on the Failure of the Defendant to Testify, Id.,* 226.

when a defendant has opportunity to deny or explain facts and determines not to do so, the prosecution should bring out the strength of the evidence by commenting upon defendant's failure to explain or deny it. The prosecution evidence may be of facts that may be beyond the knowledge of the accused. If so, his failure to testify would have little if any weight. But the facts may be such as are necessarily in the knowledge of the accused. In that case a failure to explain would point to an inability to explain.

Appellant sets out the circumstances of this case, however, to show coercion and unfairness in permitting comment. The guilty person was not seen at the place and time of the crime. There was evidence, however, that entrance to the place or room where the crime was committed might have been obtained through a small door. It was freshly broken. Evidence showed that six fingerprints on the door were petitioner's. Certain diamond rings were missing from the deceased's possession. There was evidence that appellant, sometime after the crime, asked an unidentified person whether the latter would be interested in purchasing a diamond ring. As has been stated, the information charged other crimes to appellant and he admitted them. His argument here is that he could not take the stand to deny the evidence against him because he would be subjected to a cross-examination as to former crimes to impeach his veracity and the evidence so produced might well bring about his conviction. . . .

It is true that if comment were forbidden, an accused in this situation could remain silent and avoid evidence of former crimes and comment upon his failure to testify. We are of the view, however, that a state may control such a situation in accordance with its own ideas of the most efficient administration of criminal justice. The purpose of due process is not to protect an accused against a proper conviction but against an unfair conviction. When evidence is before a jury that threatens conviction, it does not seem unfair to require him to choose between leaving the adverse evidence unexplained and subjecting himself to impeachment through disclosure of former crimes. Indeed, this is a dilemma with which any defendant may be faced. If facts, adverse to the defendant, are proven by the prosecution, there may be no way to explain them favorably to the accused except by a witness who may be vulnerable to impeachment on cross-examination. The defendant must then decide whether or not to use such a witness. The fact that the witness may also be the defendant makes the choice more difficult but a denial of due process does not emerge from the circumstances.

There is no basis in the California law for appellant's objection on due process or other grounds that the statutory authorization to comment on the failure to explain or deny adverse testimony shifts the burden of proof or the duty to go forward with the evidence. Failure of the accused to testify is not an admission of the truth of the adverse evidence. Instructions told the jury that the burden of proof remained upon the state and the presumption of innocence with the accused. . . . The Supreme Court of California called attention to the fact that the prosecutor's argument approached the borderline in a statement that might have been construed as asserting "that the jury should infer guilt solely from defendant's silence." That court felt that it was improbable the jury was misled into such an understanding of their power. We shall not interfere with such a conclusion. *People* v. *Adamson,* 27 Cal. 2d 478, 494–95, 165 P. 2d 3, 12. . . .

We find no other error that gives ground for our intervention in California's administration of criminal justice.

*Affirmed.*

MR. JUSTICE FRANKFURTER, concurring. . . .
This does not create an issue different from that settled in the *Twining* case. Only a technical rule of law would exclude from consideration that which is relevant, as a matter of fair reasoning, to the solution of a problem. Sensible and just-minded men, in important affairs of life, deem it significant that a man remains silent when confronted with serious and responsible evidence against himself which it is within his power to contradict. The notion that to allow jurors to do that which sensible and right-minded men do every day violates the "immutable principles of justice" as conceived by a civilized society is to trivialize the importance of "due process." Nor does it make any difference in drawing significance from silence under such circumstances that an accused may deem it more advantageous to remain silent than to speak, on the nice calculation that by taking the witness stand he may expose himself to having his credibility impugned by reason of his criminal record. Silence under such circumstances is still significant. A person in that situation may express to the jury, through appropriate requests to charge, why he prefers to keep silent. A man who has done one wrong may prove his innocence on a totally different charge. To deny that the jury can be trusted to make such discrimination is to show little confidence in the jury system. The prosecution is frequently compelled to rely on the testimony of shady characters whose credibility is bound to be the chief target of the defense. It is a common practice in criminal trials to draw out of a vulnerable witness'

**237**

mouth his vulnerability, and then convince the jury that nevertheless he is telling the truth in this particular case. This is also a common experience for defendants.

For historical reasons a limited immunity from the common duty to testify was written into the Federal Bill of Rights, and I am prepared to agree that, as part of that immunity, comment on the failure of an accused to take the witness stand is forbidden in federal prosecutions. It is so, of course, by explicit act of Congress. 20 Stat. 30; see *Bruno* v. *United States,* 308 U. S. 287. But to suggest that such a limitation can be drawn out of "due process" in its protection of ultimate decency in a civilized society is to suggest that the Due Process Clause fastened fetters of unreason upon the States. . . .

Between the incorporation of the Fourteenth Amendment into the Constitution and the beginning of the present membership of the Court—a period of seventy years—the scope of that Amendment was passed upon by forty-three judges. Of all these judges, only one, who may respectfully be called an eccentric exception, ever indicated the belief that the Fourteenth Amendment was a shorthand summary of the first eight Amendments theretofore limiting only the Federal Government, and that due process incorporated those eight Amendments as restrictions upon the powers of the States. Among these judges were not only those who would have to be included among the greatest in the history of the Court, but—it is especially relevant to note—they included those whose services in the cause of human rights and the spirit of freedom are the most conspicuous in our history. It is not invidious to single out Miller, Davis, Bradley, Waite, Matthews, Gray, Fuller, Holmes, Brandeis, Stone and Cardozo (to speak only of the dead) as judges who were alert in safeguarding and promoting the interests of liberty and human dignity through law. But they were also judges mindful of the relation of our federal system to a progressively democratic society and therefore duly regardful of the scope of authority that was left to the States even after the Civil War. And so they did not find that the Fourteenth Amendment, concerned as it was with matters fundamental to the pursuit of justice, fastened upon the States procedural arrangements which, in the language of Mr. Justice Cardozo, only those who are "narrow or provincial" would deem essential to "a fair and enlightened system of justice." *Palko* v. *Connecticut,* 302 U. S. 319, 325. To suggest that it is inconsistent with a truly free society to begin prosecutions without an indictment, to try petty civil cases without the paraphernalia of a common law jury, to take into consideration that one who has full opportunity to make a defense remains silent is, in de Tocqueville's phrase, to confound the familiar with the necessary.

The short answer to the suggestion that the provision of the Fourteenth Amendment, which ordains "nor shall any State deprive any person of life, liberty, or property, without due process of law," was a way of saying that every State must thereafter initiate prosecutions through indictment by a grand jury, must have a trial by a jury of twelve in criminal cases, and must have trial by such a jury in common law suits where the amount in controversy exceeds twenty dollars, is that it is a strange way of saying it. It would be extraordinarily strange for a Constitution to convey such specific commands in such a roundabout and inexplicit way. . . . Arguments that may now be adduced to prove that the first eight Amendments were concealed within the historic phrasing of the Fourteenth Amendment were not unknown at the time of its adoption. A surer estimate of their bearing was possible for judges at the time than distorting distance is likely to vouchsafe. Any evidence of design or purpose not contemporaneously known could hardly have influenced those who ratified the Amendment. Remarks of a particular proponent of the Amendment, no matter how influential, are not to be deemed part of the Amendment. What was submitted for ratification was his proposal, not his speech. Thus, at the time of the ratification of the Fourteenth Amendment the constitutions of nearly half of the ratifying States did not have the rigorous requirements of the Fifth Amendment for instituting criminal proceedings through a grand jury. It could hardly have occurred to these States that by ratifying the Amendment they uprooted their established methods for prosecuting crime and fastened upon themselves a new prosecutorial system.

Indeed, the suggestion that the Fourteenth Amendment incorporates the first eight Amendments as such is not unambiguously urged. Even the boldest innovator would shrink from suggesting to more than half the States that they may no longer initiate prosecutions without indictment by grand jury, or that thereafter all the States of the Union must furnish a jury of twelve for every case involving a claim above twenty dollars. There is suggested merely a selective incorporation of the first eight Amendments into the Fourteenth Amendment. Some are in and some are out, but we are left in the dark as to which are in and which are out. Nor are we given the calculus for determining which go in and which stay out. If the basis of selection is merely that those provisions of the first eight Amendments are incorporated which commend themselves to individual justices as indispensable to the dignity and happiness of a free man, we are thrown back to a merely subjective test. The protection against unreasonable search and seizure might have primacy for one judge, while trial by a jury of twelve for every claim above twenty dollars might appear to another as an ultimate need in a free society. In the history of thought "natural law" has a much longer and much better founded meaning and justification than such subjective selection of the first eight Amendments for incorporation into the Fourteenth. . . .

A construction which gives to due process no independent function but turns it into a summary of the specific provisions of the Bill of Rights would, as has been noted, tear up by the roots much of the fabric of law in the several States, and would deprive the States of opportunity for reforms in legal process designed for extending the area of freedom. It would assume that no other abuses would reveal themselves in the course of time than those which had become manifest in 1791. Such a view not only disregards the historic meaning of "due process." It leads inevitably to a warped construction of specific provisions of the Bill of Rights to bring within their scope conduct clearly condemned by due process but not easily fitting into the pigeonholes of the specific provisions. It seems pretty late in the day to suggest that a phrase so laden with historic meaning should be given an improvised content consisting of some but not all of the provisions of the first eight Amendments, selected on an undefined basis, with improvisation of content for the provisions so selected. . . .

The judicial judgment in applying the Due Process Clause must move within the limits of accepted notions of justice and is not to be based upon the idiosyncrasies of a merely personal judgment. The fact that judges among themselves may differ whether in a particular case a trial offends accepted notions of justice is not disproof that general rather than idiosyncratic standards are applied. An important safeguard against such merely individual judgment is an alert deference to the judgment of the State court under review.

MR. JUSTICE BLACK, dissenting. . . .

This decision reasserts a constitutional theory spelled out in *Twining* v. *New Jersey*, 211 U. S. 78, that this Court is endowed by the Constitution with boundless power under "natural law" periodically to expand and contract constitutional standards to conform to the Court's conception of what at a particular time constitutes "civilized decency" and "fundamental liberty and justice." Invoking this *Twining* rule, the Court concludes that although comment upon testimony in a federal court would violate the Fifth Amendment, identical comment in a state court does not violate today's fashion in civilized decency and fundamentals and is therefore not prohibited by the Federal Constitution as amended.

The *Twining* case was the first, as it is the only, decision of this Court which has squarely held that states were free, notwithstanding the Fifth and Fourteenth Amendments, to extort evidence from one accused of crime.[2] I agree that if *Twining* be reaffirmed, the result reached might appropriately follow. But I would not reaffirm the *Twining* decision. I think that decision and the "natural law" theory of the Constitution upon which it relies degrade the constitutional safeguards of the Bill of Rights and simultaneously appropriate for this Court a broad power which we are not authorized by the Constitution to exercise. Furthermore, the *Twining* decision rested on previous cases and broad hypotheses which have been undercut by intervening decisions of this Court. See Corwin, The Supreme Court's Construction of the Self-Incrimination Clause, 29 Mich. L. Rev. 1, 191, 202. My reasons for believing that the *Twining* decision should not be revitalized can best be understood by reference to the constitutional, judicial, and general history that preceded and followed the case. That reference must be abbreviated far more than is justified but for the necessary limitations of opinion-writing.

The first ten amendments were proposed and adopted largely because of fear that Government might unduly interfere with prized individual liberties. . . .

But these limitations were not expressly imposed upon state court action. In 1833, *Barron* v. *Baltimore, supra,* was decided by this Court. It specifically held inapplicable to the states that provision of the Fifth Amendment which declares: "nor shall private property be taken for public use, without just compensation." In deciding the particular point raised, the Court there said that it could not hold that the first eight amendments applied to the states. This was the controlling constitutional rule when the Fourteenth Amendment was proposed in 1866.

My study of the historical events that culminated in the Fourteenth Amendment, and the expressions of those who sponsored and favored, as well as those who opposed its submission and passage, persuades me that one of the chief objects that the pro-

---

[2] "The question in the case at bar has been twice before us, and been left undecided, as the cases were disposed of on other grounds." *Twining v. New Jersey, supra,* 92. In *Palko v. Connecticut,* 302 U. S. 319, relied on by the Court, the issue was double jeopardy and not enforced self-incrimination.

visions of the Amendment's first section, separately, and as a whole, were intended to accomplish was to make the Bill of Rights, applicable to the states.[5] With full knowledge of the import of the *Barron* decision, the framers and backers of the Fourteenth Amendment proclaimed its purpose to be to overturn the constitutional rule that case had announced. This historical purpose has never received full consideration or exposition in any opinion of this Court interpreting the Amendment.

. . .

For this reason, I am attaching to this dissent an appendix which contains a résumé, by no means complete, of the Amendment's history. In my judgment that history conclusively demonstrates that the language of the first section of the Fourteenth Amendment, taken as a whole, was thought by those responsible for its submission to the people, and by those who opposed its submission, sufficiently explicit to guarantee that thereafter no state could deprive its citizens of the privileges and protections of the Bill of Rights. Whether this Court ever will, or whether it now should, in the light of past decisions, give full effect to what the Amendment was intended to accomplish is not necessarily essential to a decision here. However that may be, our prior decisions, including *Twining,* do not prevent our carrying out that purpose, at least to the extent of making applicable to the states, not a mere part, as the Court has, but the full protection of the Fifth Amendment's provision against compelling evidence from an accused to convict him of crime. And I further contend that the "natural law" formula which the Court uses to reach its conclusion in this case should be abandoned as an incongruous excrescence on our Constitution. I believe that formula to be itself a violation of our Constitution, in that it subtly conveys to courts, at the expense of legislatures, ultimate power over public policies in fields where no specific provision of the Constitution limits legislative power. And my belief seems to be in accord with the views expressed by this Court, at least

---

[5] Another prime purpose was to make colored people citizens entitled to full equal rights as citizens despite what this Court decided in the Dred Scott case. *Scott v. Sandford,* 19 How. 393.

A comprehensive analysis of the historical origins of the Fourteenth Amendment, Flack, The Adoption of the Fourteenth Amendment (1908) 94, concludes that "Congress, the House and the Senate, had the following objects and motives in view for submitting the first section of the Fourteenth Amendment to the States for ratification:

"1. To make the Bill of Rights (the first eight Amendments) binding upon, or applicable to, the States.

"2. To give validity to the Civil Rights Bill.

"3. To declare who were citizens of the United States."

[Emerson]

for the first two decades after the Fourteenth Amendment was adopted. . . .

[Mr. Justice Black then analyzes the Fourteenth Amendment cases from *Slaughter-House* to *Twining* to show that the Court, through "natural law concepts," had withdrawn the protection of the Fourteenth Amendment from state infringement of the personal liberties guaranteed in the Bill of Rights, while at the same time extending the due process clause of the Fourteenth Amendment to protect business activities against state regulation.]

The *Twining* decision, rejecting the compelled testimony clause of the Fifth Amendment, and indeed rejecting all the Bill of Rights, is the end product of one phase of this philosophy. . . . For the *Twining* decision, giving separate consideration to "due process" and "privileges or immunities," went all the way to say that the "privileges or immunities" clause of the Fourteenth Amendment "did not forbid the States to abridge the personal rights enumerated in the first eight Amendments . . ." *Twining* v. *New Jersey, supra,* 99. And in order to be certain, so far as possible, to leave this Court wholly free to reject all the Bill of Rights as specific restraints upon state action, the decision declared that even if this Court should decide that the due process clause forbids the states to infringe personal liberties guaranteed by the Bill of Rights, it would do so, not "because those rights are enumerated in the first eight Amendments, but because they are of such a nature that they are included in the conception of due process of law." *Ibid.*

At the same time that the *Twining* decision held that the states need not conform to the specific provisions of the Bill of Rights, it consolidated the power that the Court had assumed under the due process clause by laying even broader foundations for the Court to invalidate state and even federal regulatory legislation. For under the *Twining* formula, which includes non-regard for the first eight amendments, what are "fundamental rights" and in accord with "canons of decency," as the Court said in *Twining,* and today reaffirms, is to be independently "ascertained from time to time by judicial action . . ." *Id.* at 101; "what is due process of law depends on circumstances." *Moyer* v. *Peabody,* 212 U. S. 78, 84. . . .

Later decisions of this Court have completely undermined that phase of the *Twining* doctrine which broadly precluded reliance on the Bill of Rights to determine what is and what is not a "fundamental" right. Later cases have also made the *Hurtado* case an inadequate support for this phase of the *Twining* formula. For despite *Hurtado* and *Twining,* this Court has now held that the Fourteenth Amendment protects from state invasion the following "fundamental" rights safeguarded by the Bill of Rights: right to counsel in criminal cases, *Powell* v. *Alabama,* 287 U. S. 45, 67, limiting the *Hurtado* case; see also *Betts* v. *Brady,* 316 U. S. 455, and *De Meerleer* v. *Michigan,* 329 U. S. 663; freedom of assembly, *De Jonge* v. *Oregon,* 299 U. S. 353, 364; at the very least, certain types of cruel and unusual punishment and former jeopardy, *State of Louisiana ex rel. Francis* v. *Resweber,* 329 U. S. 459; the right of an accused in a criminal case to be informed of the charge against him, see *Snyder* v. *Massachusetts,* 291 U. S. 97, 105; the right to receive just compensation on account of taking private property for public use, *Chicago, B. & Q. R. Co.* v. *Chicago,* 166 U. S. 226. And the Court has now through the Fourteenth Amendment literally and emphatically applied the First Amendment to the States in its very terms. *Everson* v. *Board of Education,* 330 U. S. 1; *Board of Education* v. *Barnette,* 319 U. S. 624, 639; *Bridges* v. *California,* 314 U. S. 252, 268.

In *Palko* v. *Connecticut, supra,* a case which involved former jeopardy only, this Court re-examined the path it had traveled in interpreting the Fourteenth Amendment since the *Twining* opinion was written. In *Twining* the Court had declared that none of the rights enumerated in the first eight amendments were protected against state invasion because they were incorporated in the Bill of Rights. But the Court in *Palko, supra,* at 323, answered a contention that all eight applied with the more guarded statement, similar to that the Court had used in *Maxwell* v. *Dow, supra* at 597, that "there is no such general rule." Implicit in this statement, and in the cases decided in the interim between *Twining* and *Palko* and since, is the understanding that some of the eight amendments do apply by their very terms. . . .

It seems rather plain to me why the Court today does not attempt to justify all of the broad *Twining* discussion. That opinion carries its own refutation on what may be called the factual issue the Court resolved. The opinion itself shows, without resort to the powerful argument in the dissent of Mr. Justice Harlan, that outside of Star Chamber practices and influences, the "English-speaking" peoples have for centuries abhorred and feared the practice of compelling people to convict themselves of crime. I shall not attempt to narrate the reasons. They are well known and those interested can read them in both the majority and dissenting opinions in the *Twining* case, in *Boyd* v. *United States,* 116 U. S. 616, and in the cases cited in notes 8, 9, 10, and 11 of *Ashcraft* v. *Tennessee* [322 U. S. 143]. Nor does the history of the practice of compelling testimony in this country, relied on in the *Twining* opinion, support the degraded rank which that opinion gave the Fifth Amendment's privilege against compulsory self-incrimination. I think the history there recited by the Court belies its conclusion. . . .

I cannot consider the Bill of Rights to be an outworn 18th Century "strait jacket" as the *Twining* opinion did. Its provisions may be thought outdated abstractions by some. And it is true that they were designed to meet ancient evils. But they are the same kind of human evils that have emerged from century to century wherever excessive power is sought by the few at the expense of the many. In my judgment the people of no nation can lose their liberty so long as a Bill of Rights like ours survives and its basic purposes are conscientiously interpreted, enforced and respected so as to afford continuous protection against old, as well as new, devices and practices which might thwart those purposes. I fear to see the consequences of the Court's practice of substituting its own concepts of decency and fundamental justice for the language of the Bill of Rights as its point of departure in interpreting and enforcing that Bill of Rights. If the choice must be between the selective process of the *Palko* decision applying some of the Bill of Rights to the States, or the *Twining* rule applying none of them, I would choose the *Palko* selective process. But rather than accept either of these choices, I would follow what I believe was the original purpose of the Fourteenth Amendment—to extend to all the people of the nation the complete protection of the Bill of Rights. To hold that this Court can determine what, if any, provisions of the Bill of Rights will be enforced, and if so to what degree, is to frustrate the great design of a written Constitution. . . .

It is an illusory apprehension that literal application of some or all of the provisions of the Bill of Rights to the States would unwisely increase the sum total of the powers of this Court to invalidate state legislation. The Federal Government has not been harmfully burdened by the requirement that enforcement of federal laws affecting civil liberty conform literally to the Bill of Rights. Who would advocate its repeal? It must be conceded, of course, that the natural-law-due-process formula, which the Court today reaffirms, has been interpreted to limit substantially this Court's power to prevent state violations of the individual civil liberties guaranteed by the Bill of Rights.[16] But this formula also has been used in the past, and can be used in the future, to license this Court, in considering regulatory legislation, to roam at large in the broad expanses of policy and morals

[16] See, *e. g.*, *Betts v. Brady*, 316 U. S. 455; *Feldman v. United States*, 322 U. S. 487.

and to trespass, all too freely, on the legislative domain of the States as well as the Federal Government. . . .

[The appendix attached to Mr. Justice Black's opinion is omitted.]

MR. JUSTICE DOUGLAS joins in this opinion.

MR. JUSTICE MURPHY, with whom MR. JUSTICE RUTLEDGE concurs, dissenting.

While in substantial agreement with the views of MR. JUSTICE BLACK, I have one reservation and one addition to make.

I agree that the specific guarantees of the Bill of Rights should be carried over intact into the first section of the Fourteenth Amendment. But I am not prepared to say that the latter is entirely and necessarily limited by the Bill of Rights. Occasions may arise where a proceeding falls so far short of conforming to fundamental standards of procedure as to warrant constitutional condemnation in terms of a lack of due process despite the absence of a specific provision in the Bill of Rights.

That point, however, need not be pursued here inasmuch as the Fifth Amendment is explicit in its provision that no person shall be compelled in any criminal case to be a witness against himself. That provision, as MR. JUSTICE BLACK demonstrates, is a constituent part of the Fourteenth Amendment.

Moreover, it is my belief that this guarantee against self-incrimination has been violated in this case. Under California law, the judge or prosecutor may comment on the failure of the defendant in a criminal trial to explain or deny any evidence or facts introduced against him. As interpreted and applied in this case, such a provision compels a defendant to be a witness against himself in one of two ways:

1. If he does not take the stand, his silence is used as the basis for drawing unfavorable inferences against him as to matters which he might reasonably be expected to explain. Thus he is compelled, through his silence, to testify against himself. And silence can be as effective in this situation as oral statements.

2. If he does take the stand, thereby opening himself to cross-examination, so as to overcome the effects of the provision in question, he is necessarily compelled to testify against himself. In that case, his testimony on cross-examination is the result of the coercive pressure of the provision rather than his own volition.

Much can be said pro and con as to the desirability of allowing comment on the failure of the accused to testify. But policy arguments are to no avail in the face of a clear constitutional command. This guarantee of freedom from self-incrimination is grounded on a deep respect for those who might prefer to remain silent before their accusers. To borrow language from *Wilson* v. *United States*, 149 U. S. 60, 66: "It is not every one who can safely venture on the witness stand though entirely innocent of the charge against him. Excessive timidity, nervousness when facing others and attempting to explain transactions of a suspicious character, and offences charged against him, will often confuse and embarrass him to such a degree as to increase rather than remove prejudices against him. It is not every one, however honest, who would, therefore, willingly be placed on the witness stand."

We are obliged to give effect to the principle of freedom from self-incrimination. That principle is as applicable where the compelled testimony is in the form of silence as where it is composed of oral statements. Accordingly, I would reverse the judgment below.

## Note

1. The argument has been renewed from time to time in subsequent cases. See, *e.g., Wolf v. Colorado, supra*, and especially *Rochin v. California*, 342 U. S. 165, 96 L. Ed. —, 72 S. Ct. 205 (1952).

2. Comment on the issues raised in the *Adamson* case may be found in *Note, The Adamson Case: A Study in Constitutional Technique*, 58 Yale L. J. 268 (1949); Morrison, *Does the Fourteenth Amendment Incorporate the Bill of Rights? The Judicial Interpretation*, 2 Stan. L. Rev. 140 (1949); Green, *The Supreme Court, The Bill of Rights and the States*, 97 U. of Pa. L. Rev. 608 (1949); Notes, 36 Geo. L. J. 398 (1948); 33 Iowa L. Rev. 666 (1948); 46 Mich. L. Rev. 372 (1948). Mr. Justice Black's interpretation of the history of the Fourteenth Amendment has been challenged in Fairman, *Does the Fourteenth Amendment Incorporate the Bill of Rights? The Original Understanding*, 2 Stan. L. Rev. 5 (1949). But see ten Broek, *The Antislavery Origins of the Fourteenth Amendment* (1951). And see materials cited in Chapter I, *supra*.

# CHAPTER III

# THE RIGHT OF FRANCHISE

The materials in this chapter and the next deal with the rights of individuals to participate directly in the process of government. Chapter III considers the basic right of franchise and closely related matters. Chapter IV takes up other aspects of the right of political organization and political expression.

In the two prior chapters the problems related primarily to the rights of persons in their individual capacities. In this chapter and the following ones the issues are somewhat broader. They involve at many points the rights of individuals to form groups or associations, the control by government over such organizations, and the relationship of the individual to the group. This right of association is basic to a democratic society. It embraces not only the right to form political associations but also the right to organize business, labor, agricultural, cultural, recreational and numerous other groups that represent the manifold activities and interests of a democratic people. In many of these areas an individual can function effectively in a modern industrial community only through the medium of such organizations. Chapters III and IV, however, direct attention primarily to political associations.

The United States Constitution nowhere explicitly recognizes a right to form political organizations. Indeed many of the founding fathers looked upon political parties with some suspicion, referring to them as "factions." Yet it is generally accepted that the rights in the First Amendment to freedom of speech, press and assembly, and to petition the government for redress of grievances, taken in combination, establish a broader guarantee to the right of political association. The legal issues have revolved around the extent to which the state can regulate or restrict such organizations and the position of individuals who wish to participate in their activities.[1]

---

[1] See Wyzanski, *The Open Window and the Open Door*, 35 Calif. L. Rev. 336 (1947); Fraenkel, *Our Civil Liberties*, pp. 114–6 (1944); *Bryant v. Zimmerman*, 278 U. S. 63, 72–3, 73 L. Ed. 184, 49 S. Ct. 61 (1928); *De Jonge v. Oregon*, 299 U. S. 353, 364–6, 81 L. Ed. 278, 57 S. Ct. 255 (1937); *Bowe v. Secretary of the Commonwealth*, 320 Mass. 230, 251–3, 69 N. E. 2d 115, 130–1 (1946).

## A. BACKGROUND

The right of all qualified citizens to participate in the power process through exercise of the franchise is, of course, fundamental to any democratic society. In the United States today the general right to vote is legally recognized and popularly accepted. Yet the concept of universal suffrage developed only slowly in America. And in practice the right of franchise has never been fully secured to all citizens nor, even when assured, fully exercised.

In colonial times not only were women, slaves and indentured servants wholly denied the right of franchise but property qualifications were universal, religious and character restrictions were frequently imposed, and racial and other limitations were common. At the time of ratification of the Constitution probably not more than a quarter of the adult males were entitled to vote.[1]

At the Constitutional Convention the delegates differed sharply with respect to the right of franchise. Some delegates favored a broad franchise; others urged property qualifications based on land ownership; still others wanted no popular election in the Federal government at all.[2] As finally approved the Constitution contained no provisions expressly securing the right of franchise. Senators were to be chosen by the state legislatures (Art. I, Sec. 3); members of the House were to be elected by those persons in each state having the qualifications requisite for electors of the most numerous branch of the state legislature (Art. I, Sec. 2); and the President was to be selected by electors appointed in such manner as the state legislatures should direct (Art. II, Sec. 1). The only significant control over the franchise to be exercised by the Federal government appeared in Article I, Section 4:

> "The Times, Places and Manner of holding Elections for Senators and Representatives, shall be prescribed in each State by the Legislature thereof; but the Congress may at any time by Law make or alter such Regulations, except as to the Places of chusing Senators."[3]

The American and French revolutions gave impetus to the

---

[1] See Beard, *An Economic Interpretation of the Constitution of the United States*, pp. 324–5 (1944 ed.); McKinley, *The Suffrage Franchise in the Thirteen English Colonies in America*, p. 488 (1905).

[2] See Holcombe, *The Middle Classes in American Politics*, pp. 137–42 (1940).

[3] Article II, Section 1, also provided that "the Congress may determine the Time of chusing the Electors [for President and Vice-President], and the Day on which they shall give their Votes; which Day shall be the same throughout the United States."

growing movement against restrictions on the right to vote. Religious qualifications soon disappeared. But property qualifications persisted, in diminishing form and extent, until the middle of the century.[4]

Racial restrictions, at least against the Negro, existed in most states until the Civil War.

Popular election of Presidential electors was authorized by some state legislatures at an early period and became established in all states by 1868. The Seventeenth Amendment, adopted in 1913, provided for the election of Senators in the same manner as members of the House, that is by the people of each state having qualifications to vote for the most numerous branch of the state legislature. And the Nineteenth Amendment, adopted in 1920, extended the franchise to women and completed the legal framework of universal suffrage.

The most dramatic, and probably the most significant, restrictions upon actual exercise of the franchise have been those which exist in the southern states, particularly with respect to the Negro. Prior to the Civil War only five states (Maine, New Hampshire, Vermont, Massachusetts and Rhode Island) made no distinction in exercise of the franchise because of race. In addition Negroes were permitted to vote in Wisconsin as a result of a popular referendum in 1849 and, subject to special property qualifications, in New York. Twenty-three states restricted suffrage to free white males. With the adoption of the Thirteenth, Fourteenth and particularly the Fifteenth Amendments, all states were forced to abandon overt legal discriminations.

In the southern states the effort to enfranchise the Negro met with vigorous resistance. The Civil War Amendments were implemented by the Federal Civil Rights Acts, of which the two measures passed in 1870 and 1871 were specifically directed at protection of the right to vote. See Chapter I, *supra*. Under these amendments and enforcing statutes, but more importantly by reason of the military occupation, Negroes during the Reconstruction Period exercised the franchise on a substantial scale. Southern resistance took the form of violence and intimidation, spearheaded by the Ku Klux Klan and similar organizations. With the withdrawal of military forces and the end of Reconstruction the Negroes were unable to maintain their position. By 1877 or shortly thereafter the Negro in the South was for all practical purposes disenfranchised.

---

[4] Even at the present time in some states the possession of property, or the payment of taxes, operates to qualify a person as a voter who would otherwise be disqualified for residence, literacy or other reasons.

Although this result was accomplished primarily through force and threats of force, the southern states sought, particularly in the two decades beginning about 1890, to establish the disenfranchisement of the Negro on a legal basis. For this purpose various devices were adopted, designed to circumvent the Fifteenth Amendment. These included various literacy, property, residence and character qualifications, the grandfather clause, the poll tax, and, with the ultimate establishment of the one-party system, the white primary. In some states these legal devices were pushed through by the conservative forces, who probably also had in mind the disenfranchisement of poor white as well as Negro voters. But in Georgia and South Carolina the initiative for their adoption came from the Populist groups, apparently fearful of the domination of the Negro vote by their conservative opponents.[5]

These attempts at legal disenfranchisement were supplemented by discriminatory administration of the election laws. And the use or threat of force continued to remain as a basic factor in the political scene.

As time went on the various obstacles to Negro voting in the South came under legal attack. These court battles have been fought with increasing intensity during the past three decades. This chapter is, in large part, concerned with the history and present status of this legal struggle.

Restrictions upon free exercise of the franchise, however, are by no means confined to the Negro or to the South. Other forms of infringement include the lack of fair apportionment among voting districts, corrupt practices of various kinds, and excessive obstacles placed in the path of new or minority parties. The curtailment of political activity by government employees likewise restricts the right of franchise of a rapidly growing portion of our population. The cumulative effect of these various limitations on exercise of the franchise would appear to present a problem of serious proportions for modern democracy.

Closely connected with these positive restrictions upon voting is the failure of many voters to cast a ballot even though qualified to do so. The legal questions discussed in this chapter must be considered in the context of this broader problem of political apathy.

### Note

For the history of suffrage during the colonial period, see Bishop, *History of Elections in the American Colonies* (1893); McKinley, *The Suffrage Franchise in the Thirteen English Colonies in America,*

---

[5] See Key, *Southern Politics*, pp. 539–50 (1949).

pp. 478–81 (1905). With respect to later periods see Porter, *A History of Suffrage in the United States* (1918); Beard and Beard, *Rise of American Civilization*, pp. 543–5 (1930); Gosnell, *Democracy, The Threshold of Freedom* (1948); McGovney, *The American Suffrage Medley*, ch. I–III (1949).

Generally with respect to Negro suffrage see Key, *Southern Politics, Part Five* (1949); Davie, *Negroes in American Society*, ch. 14 (1949) (containing bibliography); Moon, *Balance of Power: The Negro Vote* (1948); Myrdal, *An American Dilemma*, Part V (1944); Hesseltine, *The South in American History*, ch. XXV–XXVI (1943); Mangum, *The Legal Status of the Negro*, ch. XVIII (1940); Lewinson, *Race, Class and Party: A History of Negro Suffrage and White Politics in the South* (1932); Note, *Negro Disenfranchisement—A Challenge to the Constitution*, 47 Col. L. Rev. 76 (1947).

As to the impact of Negro voting on the South in the Reconstruction Period historians are in conflict. For the traditional view that the Negro electorate was widely and easily corrupted, and that Negro officeholders were largely venal, incompetent and destructive, see Dunning, *Reconstruction, Political and Economic* (1907); Donald, *The Negro Freedman* (1952). For the contrary view see Woodson, *The Negro in our History* (1947); Franklin, *From Slavery to Freedom* (1947); DuBois, *Black Reconstruction* (1935); Lewinson, *supra*. See also Aptheker, *A Documentary History of the Negro People in the United States*, pp. 559–65 (1951).

On women's suffrage see Stanton, Anthony, Gage and Harper, *History of Woman Suffrage* (1889–1922); Catt and Shuler, *Woman Suffrage and Politics* (1923); Squire, *The Woman Movement in America* (1911).

The present voting laws of the various states may be found in *Book of the States*, pp. 96–102 (1950).

# B. VIOLENCE, FRAUD AND CORRUPTION

## TO SECURE THESE RIGHTS—THE REPORT OF THE PRESIDENT'S COMMITTEE ON CIVIL RIGHTS

U. S. Government Printing Office, 1947, at pp. 35–6, 40

The denial of the suffrage on account of race is the most serious present interference with the right to vote. Until very recently, American Negro citizens in most southern states found it difficult to vote. Some Negroes have voted in parts of the upper South for the last twenty years. In recent years the situation in the deep South has changed to the point where it can be said that Negroes are beginning to exercise the political rights of free Americans. In the light of history, this represents progress, limited and precarious, but nevertheless progress.

This report cannot adequately describe the history of Negro disfranchisement. At different times, different methods have

been employed. As legal devices for disfranchising the Negro
have been held unconstitutional, new methods have been improvised to take their places. Intimidation and the threat of
intimidation have always loomed behind these legal devices to
make sure that the desired result is achieved. . . .

[The Report then discusses the white primary, educational
requirements, the poll tax, and similar restrictions.]

In addition to formal, legal methods of disfranchisement, there
are the long-standing techniques of terror and intimidation, in
the face of which great courage is required of the Negro who
tries to vote. In the regions most characterized by generalized
violence against Negroes, little more than "advice" is often necessary to frighten them away from the polls. They have learned,
through the years, to discover threats in mood and atmosphere.
In one case in a deep southern state, a middle-class Negro who
had courageously attempted to vote and to complain to the Department of Justice when he was refused access to the polls,
subsequently became so afraid of reprisal that he indicated
uncertainty whether he would be willing to testify in court. He
asked, if he should decide to testify, to be given ample notice of
the date so that he could first move his family out of the region.

### Note

Additional evidence showing the use of violence or threats of violence in recent years to prevent Negroes from voting may be found
in Minority Report of the Special Committee to Investigate Campaign
Expenditures, 80th Cong., 1st Sess. (1946) (dealing with the primary
campaign of Senator Bilbo of Mississippi); Davie, *Negroes in American Society*, p. 266 (1949); Myrdal, *An American Dilemma*, pp. 485–6
1944).

---

State legislation in all states is technically adequate to safeguard the right of franchise against all forms of violence, fraud
and corruption. The problem arises when state legislation is not
in practice enforced. As in the case of security for the person
against intimidation generally, the major issues have revolved
around the constitutional and statutory power of the Federal
Government to afford protection, and the enforcement of such
Federal power as exists.

The main course of Supreme Court decision in the post Civil
War decades has already been summarized in Chapter I. The
Fifteenth Amendment, the Court had held, authorized Federal
protection of the franchise against violence, fraud or corruption
only where abridgment of the right was "on account of race,
color or previous condition of servitude." Hence those pro-

**253**

visions of the Act of 1870 which prohibited interference with the right to vote in general terms were ruled unconstitutional as going beyond the authority of the Fifteenth Amendment. *U. S. v. Reese,* 92 U. S. 214, 23 L. Ed. 563 (1876).[1] And the Fourteenth Amendment had been held applicable only to abridgment through state action. *U. S. v. Harris,* 106 U. S. 629, 27 L. Ed. 290, 1 S. Ct. 601 (1883); *Civil Rights Cases,* 109 U. S. 3, 27 L. Ed. 835, 3 S. Ct. 18 (1883). A further aspect of Federal constitutional and statutory power was presented in the *Yarbrough* case, set forth below.

## EX PARTE YARBROUGH

Supreme Court of the United States, 1884
110 U. S. 651, 28 L. Ed. 274, 4 S. Ct. 152

[Yarbrough and seven others were convicted of violating Revised Statutes Section 5508, the predecessor of 18 U. S. C. § 241 (see Chapter I, *supra*) and Revised Statutes Section 5520. The latter made it a criminal offense for two or more persons to conspire "to prevent by force, intimidation, or threat, any citizen who is lawfully entitled to vote, from giving his support or advocacy, in a legal manner, toward or in favor of the election of any lawfully qualified person as an elector for President or Vice President, or as a member of the Congress of the United States; or to injure any citizen in person or property on account of such support or advocacy."]

MR. JUSTICE MILLER delivered the opinion of the Court . . .

Stripped of its technical verbiage, the offence charged in this indictment is that the defendants conspired to intimidate Berry Saunders, a citizen of African descent, in the exercise of his right to vote for a member of the Congress of the United States, and in the execution of that conspiracy they beat, bruised, wounded and otherwise maltreated him; and in the second count that they did this on account of his race, color, and previous condition of servitude, by going in disguise and assaulting him on the public highway and on his own premises.

If the question were not concluded in this court, as we have already seen that it is by the decision of the Circuit Court, we entertain no doubt that the conspiracy here described is one which is embraced within the provisions of the Revised Statutes which we have cited.

---

[1] The statute had previously been held valid by the Federal Circuit Court in Ohio, *U. S. v. Canter,* Fed. Cas. No. 14,719 (C. C. S. D. Ohio, 1870), and in South Carolina, *U. S. v. Crosby,* Fed. Cas. No. 14,893 (C. C. S. C., 1871).

That a government whose essential character is republican, whose executive head and legislative body are both elective, whose most numerous and powerful branch of the legislature is elected by the people directly, has no power by appropriate laws to secure this election from the influence of violence, of corruption, and of fraud, is a proposition so startling as to arrest attention and demand the gravest consideration.

If this government is anything more than a mere aggregation of delegated agents of other States and governments, each of which is superior to the general government, it must have the power to protect the elections on which its existence depends from violence and corruption.

If it has not this power it is left helpless before the two great natural and historical enemies of all republics, open violence and insidious corruption.

The proposition that it has no such power is supported by the old argument often heard, often repeated, and in this court never assented to, that when a question of the power of Congress arises the advocate of the power must be able to place his finger on words which expressly grant it. The brief of counsel before us, though directed to the authority of that body to pass criminal laws, uses the same language. Because there is no *express* power to provide for preventing violence exercised on the voter as a means of controlling his vote, no such law can be enacted. It destroys at one blow, in construing the Constitution of the United States, the doctrine universally applied to all instruments of writing, that what is implied is as much a part of the instrument as what is expressed. This principle, in its application to the Constitution of the United States, more than to almost any other writing, is a necessity, by reason of the inherent inability to put into words all derivative powers—a difficulty which the instrument itself recognizes by conferring on Congress the authority to pass all laws necessary and proper to carry into execution the powers expressly granted and all other powers vested in the government or any branch of it by the Constitution. Article I, sec. 8, clause 18.

We know of no express authority to pass laws to punish theft or burglary of the treasury of the United States. Is there therefore no power in the Congress to protect the treasury by punishing such theft and burglary?

Are the mails of the United States and the money carried in them to be left to the mercy of robbers and of thieves who may handle the mail because the Constitution contains no express words of power in Congress to enact laws for the punishment of those offences? The principle, if sound, would abolish the entire criminal jurisdiction of the courts of the United States and the laws which confer that jurisdiction.

It is said that the States can pass the necessary law on this subject, and no necessity exists for such action by Congress. But the existence of State laws punishing the counterfeiting of the coin of the United States has never been held to supersede the acts of Congress passed for that purpose, or to justify the United States in failing to enforce its own laws to protect the circulation of the coin which it issues. . . .

It was not until 1842 that Congress took any action under [Article I, Section 4], when, conceiving that the system of electing all the members of the House of Representatives from a State by general ticket, as it was called, that is, every elector voting for as many names as the State was entitled to representatives in that house, worked injustice to other States which did not adopt that system, and gave an undue preponderance of power to the political party which had a majority of votes in the State, however small, enacted that each member should be elected by a separate district, composed of contiguous territory. 5 Stat. 491.

And to remedy more than one evil arising from the election of members of Congress occurring at different times in the different States, Congress, by the act of February 2, 1872, thirty years later, required all the elections for such members to be held on the Tuesday after the first Monday in November in 1876, and on the same day of every second year thereafter.

The frequent failures of the legislatures of the States to elect senators at the proper time, by one branch of the legislature voting for one person and the other branch for another person, and refusing in any manner to reconcile their differences, led Congress to pass an act which compelled the two bodies to meet in joint convention, and fixing the day when this should be done, and requiring them so to meet on every day thereafter and vote for a senator until one was elected.

In like manner Congress has fixed a day, which is to be the same in all the States, when the electors for President and Vice-President shall be appointed. . . .

Will it be denied that it is in the power of that body to provide laws for the proper conduct of those elections? To provide, if necessary, the officers who shall conduct them and make return of the result? And especially to provide, in an election held under its own authority, for security of life and limb to the voter while in the exercise of this function? Can it be doubted that Congress can by law protect the act of voting, the place where it is done, and the man who votes, from personal violence or intimidation and the election itself from corruption and fraud?

256

If this be so, and it is not doubted, are such powers annulled because an election for State officers is held at the same time and place? Is it any less important that the election of members of Congress should be the free choice of all the electors because State officers are to be elected at the same time? *Ex parte Siebold,* 100 U. S. 371.

These questions answer themselves; and it is only because the Congress of the United States, through long habit and long years of forbearance, has, in deference and respect to the States, refrained from the exercise of these powers, that they are now doubted.

But when, in the pursuance of a new demand for action, that body, as it did in the cases just enumerated, finds it necessary to make additional laws for the free, the pure, and the safe exercise of this right of voting, they stand upon the same ground and are to be upheld for the same reasons.

It is said that the parties assaulted in these cases are not officers of the United States, and their protection in exercising the right to vote by Congress does not stand on the same ground.

But the distinction is not well taken. The power in either case arises out of the circumstance that the function in which the party is engaged or the right which he is about to exercise is dependent on the laws of the United States.

In both cases it is the duty of that government to see that he may exercise this right freely, and to protect him from violence while so doing, or on account of so doing. This duty does not arise solely from the interest of the party concerned, but from the necessity of the government itself, that its service shall be free from the adverse influence of force and fraud practised on its agents, and that the votes by which its members of Congress and its President are elected shall be the *free* votes of the electors, and the officers thus chosen the free and uncorrupted choice of those who have the right to take part in that choice.

This proposition answers also another objection to the constitutionality of the laws under consideration, namely, that the right to vote for a member of Congress is not dependent upon the Constitution or laws of the United States, but is governed by the law of each State respectively.

If this were conceded, the importance to the general government of having the actual election—the voting for those members —free from force and fraud is not diminished by the circumstance that the qualification of the voter is determined by the law of the State where he votes. It equally affects the government, it is as indispensable to the proper discharge of the great function of legislating for that government, that those who are to control

[Emerson]—17

this legislation shall not owe their election to bribery or violence, whether the class of persons who shall vote is determined by the law of the State, or by law of the United States, or by their united result.

But it is not correct to say that the right to vote for a member of Congress does not depend on the Constitution of the United States.

The office, if it be properly called an office, is created by that Constitution and by that alone. It also declares how it shall be filled, namely, by election. . . .

The States in prescibing the qualifications of voters for the most numerous branch of their own legislatures, do not do this with reference to the election for members of Congress. Nor can they prescribe the qualification for voters for those *eo nomine*. They define who are to vote for the popular branch of their own legislature, and the Constitution of the United States says the same persons shall vote for members of Congress in that State. It adopts the qualification thus furnished as the qualification of its own electors for members of Congress.

It is not true, therefore, that electors for members of Congress owe their right to vote to the State law in any sense which makes the exercise of the right to depend exclusively on the law of the State. . . .

In the case of *United States* v. *Reese* [92 U. S. 214], so much relied on by counsel, this court said in regard to the Fifteenth Amendment, that "it has invested the citizens of the United States with a new constitutional right which is within the protecting power of Congress. That right is an exemption from discrimination in the exercise of the elective franchise on account of race, color, or previous condition of servitude." This new constitutional right was mainly designed for citizens of African descent. The principle, however, that the protection of the exercise of this right is within the power of Congress, is as necessary to the right of other citizens to vote as to the colored citizen, and to the right to vote in general as to the right to be protected against discrimination.

The exercise of the right in both instances is guaranteed by the Constitution, and should be kept free and pure by congressional enactments whenever that is necessary.

The reference to cases in this court in which the power of Congress under the first section of the Fourteenth Amendment has been held to relate alone to acts done under State authority, can afford petitioners no aid in the present case. For, while it may be true that acts which are mere invasions of private rights, which acts have no sanction in the statutes of a State, or which

[Emerson]

are not committed by any one exercising its authority, are not within the scope of that amendment, it is quite a different matter when Congress undertakes to protect the citizen in the exercise of rights conferred by the Constitution of the United States essential to the healthy organization of the government itself. . . .

*The rule is discharged, and the writ of habeas corpus is denied.*

## Note

1. Several years before, in *Ex parte Siebold,* 100 U. S. 371, 25 L. Ed. 717 (1880), the Court had upheld the conviction, under other provisions of the Civil Rights Acts, of state election officials who had stuffed the ballot boxes in an election involving Congressional candidates. The power of Congress to control election procedures in Federal elections under Article I, Section 4 was scarcely questioned, the case turning upon issues of Federal and state concurrent powers in the field. Justices Field and Clifford dissented.

2. In 1894 the specific provisions of the Act of 1870 dealing with elections, including R. S. 5520 involved in the *Yarbrough* case, were repealed. This left in effect the general provisions of R. S. 5508 (later Section 241 of Title 18), the other statutory basis for *Yarbrough.* In *U. S. v. Mosley,* 238 U. S. 383, 59 L. Ed. 1355, 35 S. Ct. 904 (1915), the Court held that, despite the repeal of the specific election provisions, the general provisions of R. S. 5508 (making it unlawful to conspire to "injure, oppress, threaten or intimidate any citizen in the free exercise or enjoyment" of rights secured by the Constitution or laws) would prohibit interference with the right to vote for a member of Congress. The *Mosley* case did not involve violence, but false counting of the ballots, which the Court found to come within the statute. Mr. Justice Lamar dissented.

3. Two decisions restricting the application of R. S. 5508 followed the *Mosley* case. In *U. S. v. Gradwell,* 243 U. S. 476, 61 L. Ed. 857, 37 S. Ct. 407 (1917), the indictment charged defendants with conspiracy to injure and oppress three candidates for nomination as Senator by procuring a thousand persons, who were not qualified, to vote for an opposing candidate. The Court held that the rights of candidates in a state primary election were not constitutionally protected against defendants' action. In *U. S. v. Bathgate,* 246 U. S. 220, 62 L. Ed. 676, 38 S. Ct. 269 (1918), the defendants bribed voters in a general election at which Federal offices were to be filled. The Court, pointing out that the specific provisions of the Act of 1870 relating to bribery had been repealed, held that the general provision remaining in effect did not cover bribery. The statute protected only personal rights, in the Court's view, and "not the political, non-judicable one common to all that the public shall be protected against harmful acts." 246 U. S. at 226.

4. The power of Congress to protect the right of franchise under the Fifteenth Amendment arose again in *James v. Bowman,* 190 U. S.

127, 47 L. Ed. 979, 23 S. Ct. 678 (1903). That case involved an indictment under R. S. 5507, which prohibited interference with the right to vote of persons whose right is guaranteed by the Fifteenth Amendment. The Court held the statute invalid on the ground that it purported to prohibit individual action whereas the Fifteenth Amendment prohibited action only "by the United States or by any State." The Court further held that the statute could not be sustained under other powers to regulate Federal elections because the statute was not so confined but applied to all elections.

5. The question of whether the authority of Congress under Article I, Section 4, extends to primary elections and the nomination of candidates was raised in *Newberry v. U. S.*, 256 U. S. 232, 65 L. Ed. 913, 41 S Ct 469 (1921). Newberry and others were indicted for spending more money in his primary campaign for Senator in Michigan than was permitted under the Federal Corrupt Practices Act. The conviction was reversed by the Supreme Court, but without a majority being agreed upon the constitutional issues. See discussion of the case in *U. S. v. Classic, infra.*

## UNITED STATES v. CLASSIC

Supreme Court of the United States, 1941
313 U. S. 299, 85 L. Ed. 1368, 61 S. Ct. 1031

MR. JUSTICE STONE delivered the opinion of the Court.

Two counts of an indictment found in a federal district court charged that appellees, Commissioners of Elections, conducting a primary election under Louisiana law, to nominate a candidate of the Democratic Party for representative in Congress, willfully altered and falsely counted and certified the ballots of voters cast in the primary election. The questions for decision are whether the right of qualified voters to vote in the Louisiana primary and to have their ballots counted is a right "secured by the Constitution" within the meaning of §§ 19 and 20 of the Criminal Code [now 18 U. S. C. §§ 241 and 242], and whether the acts of appellees charged in the indictment violate those sections.

. . .

[The District Court sustained a demurrer to both counts, relying upon the *Gradwell* and *Newberry* cases.]

Section 19 of the Criminal Code condemns as a criminal offense any conspiracy to injure a citizen in the exercise "of any right or privilege secured to him by the Constitution or laws of the United States." Section 20 makes it a penal offense for anyone who, acting "under color of any law," "willfully subjects, or causes to be subjected, any inhabitant of any State . . . to the deprivation of any rights, privileges, and immunities secured and protected by the Constitution and laws of the United States."

The Government argues that the right of a qualified voter in a Louisiana congressional primary election to have his vote counted as cast is a right secured by Article I, §§ 2 and 4 of the Constitution, and that a conspiracy to deprive the citizen of that right is a violation of § 19, and also that the willful action of appellees as state officials, in falsely counting the ballots at the primary election and in falsely certifying the count, deprived qualified voters of that right and of the equal protection of the laws guaranteed by the Fourteenth Amendment, all in violation of § 20 of the Criminal Code. . . .

Pursuant to the authority given by § 2 of Article I of the Constitution, and subject to the legislative power of Congress under § 4 of Article I, and other pertinent provisions of the Constitution, the states are given, and in fact exercise, a wide discretion in the formulation of a system for the choice by the people of representatives in Congress. In common with many other states, Louisiana has exercised that discretion by setting up machinery for the effective choice of party candidates for representative in Congress by primary elections, and by its laws it eliminates or seriously restricts the candidacy at the general election of all those who are defeated at the primary. All political parties, which are defined as those that have cast at least 5 per cent of the total vote at specified preceding elections, are required to nominate their candidates for representative by direct primary elections. Louisiana Act No. 46, Regular Session, 1940, §§ 1 and 3.

The primary is conducted by the state at public expense. Act No. 46, *supra*, § 35. The primary, as is the general election, is subject to numerous statutory regulations as to the time, place and manner of conducting the election, including provisions to insure that the ballots cast at the primary are correctly counted, and the results of the count correctly recorded and certified to the Secretary of State, whose duty it is to place the names of the successful candidates of each party on the official ballot.[1] The Secretary of State is prohibited from placing on the official

---

[1] The ballots are printed at public expense, § 35 of Act No. 46, Regular Session, 1940, are furnished by the Secretary of State, § 36 in a form prescribed by statute, § 37. Close supervision of the delivery of the ballots to the election commissioners is prescribed, §§ 43–46. The polling places are required to be equipped to secure secrecy, §§ 48–50; §§ 54–57. The selection of election commissioners is prescribed, § 61 and their duties detailed. The commissioners must swear to conduct the election impartially, § 64 and are subject to punishment for deliberately falsifying the returns or destroying the lists and ballots, §§ 98, 99. They must identify by certificate the ballot boxes used, § 67, keep a triplicate list of voters, § 68, publicly canvass the return, § 74 and certify the same to the Secretary of State, § 75.

**261**

ballot the name of any person as a candidate for any political party not nominated in accordance with the provisions of the Act. Act 46, § 1. . . .

The right to vote for a representative in Congress at the general election is, as a matter of law, thus restricted to the successful party candidate at the primary, to those not candidates at the primary who file nomination papers, and those whose names may be lawfully written into the ballot by the electors. Even if, as appellees argue, contrary to the decision in *Serpas* v. *Trebucq* [1 So. 2d 346, 705] voters may lawfully write into their ballots, cast at the general election, the name of a candidate rejected at the primary and have their ballots counted, the practical operation of the primary law in otherwise excluding from the ballot on the general election the names of candidates rejected at the primary is such as to impose serious restrictions upon the choice of candidates by the voters save by voting at the primary election. In fact, as alleged in the indictment, the practical operation of the primary in Louisiana is, and has been since the primary election was established in 1900, to secure the election of the Democratic primary nominee for the Second Congressional District of Louisiana.

Interference with the right to vote in the Congressional primary in the Second Congressional District for the choice of Democratic candidate for Congress is thus, as a matter of law and in fact, an interference with the effective choice of the voters at the only stage of the election procedure when their choice is of significance, since it is at the only stage when such interference could have any practical effect on the ultimate result, the choice of the Congressman to represent the district. The primary in Louisiana is an integral part of the procedure for the popular choice of Congressman. The right of qualified voters to vote at the Congressional primary in Louisiana and to have their ballots counted is thus the right to participate in that choice.

We come then to the question whether that right is one secured by the Constitution. Section 2 of Article I commands that Congressmen shall be chosen by the people of the several states by electors, the qualifications of which it prescribes. The right of the people to choose, whatever its appropriate constitutional limitations, where in other respects it is defined, and the mode of its exercise is prescribed by state action in conformity to the Constitution, is a right established and guaranteed by the Constitution, and hence is one secured by it to those citizens and inhabitants of the state entitled to exercise the right. *Ex parte Yarbrough*, 110 U. S. 651; *United States* v. *Mosley*, 238 U. S. 383. And see *Hague* v. *C. I. O.*, 307 U. S. 496, 508, 513, 526, 527,

**262**

529, giving the same interpretation to the like phrase "rights" "secured by the Constitution" appearing in § 1 of the Civil Rights Act of 1871, 17 Stat. 13. While, in a loose sense, the right to vote for representatives in Congress is sometimes spoken of as a right derived from the states, see *Minor* v. *Happersett,* 21 Wall. 162, 170; *United States* v. *Reese,* 92 U. S. 214, 217–218; *McPherson* v. *Blacker,* 146 U. S. 1, 38–39; *Breedlove* v. *Suttles,* 302 U. S. 277, 283, this statement is true only in the sense that the states are authorized by the Constitution, to legislate on the subject as provided by § 2 of Art. I, to the extent that Congress has not restricted state action by the exercise of its powers to regulate elections under § 4 and its more general power under Article I, § 8, clause 18 of the Constitution "to make all laws which shall be necessary and proper for carrying into execution the foregoing powers." See *Ex parte Siebold,* 100 U. S. 371; *Ex parte Yarbrough, supra,* 663, 664; *Swafford* v. *Templeton,* 185 U. S. 487; *Wiley* v. *Sinkler,* 179 U. S. 58, 64.

Obviously included within the right to choose, secured by the Constitution, is the right of qualified voters within a state to cast their ballots and have them counted at Congressional elections. This Court has consistently held that this is a right secured by the Constitution. *Ex parte Yarbrough, supra; Wiley* v. *Sinkler, supra; Swafford* v. *Templeton, supra; United States* v. *Mosley, supra;* see *Ex parte Siebold, supra; In re Coy,* 127 U. S. 731; *Logan* v. *United States,* 144 U. S. 263. And since the constitutional command is without restriction or limitation, the right, unlike those guaranteed by the Fourteenth and Fifteenth Amendments, is secured against the action of individuals as well as of states. *Ex parte Yarbrough, supra; Logan* v. *United States, supra.*

But we are now concerned with the question whether the right to choose at a primary election, a candidate for election as representative, is embraced in the right to choose representatives secured by Article I, § 2. We may assume that the framers of the Constitution in adopting that section, did not have specifically in mind the selection and elimination of candidates for Congress by the direct primary any more than they contemplated the application of the commerce clause to interstate telephone, telegraph and wireless communication, which are concededly within it. But in determining whether a provision of the Constitution applies to a new subject matter, it is of little significance that it is one with which the framers were not familiar. For in setting up an enduring framework of government they undertook to carry out for the indefinite future and in all the vicissitudes of the changing affairs of men, those fundamental purposes which the instrument itself discloses. Hence we read its words, not as we read legislative codes which are subject to continuous revision with the changing course of events, but as the revelation of the great purposes which were intended to be achieved by the Constitution as a continuing instrument of government. Cf. *Davidson* v. *New Orleans*, 96 U. S. 97; *Brown* v. *Walker*, 161 U. S. 591, 595; *Robertson* v. *Baldwin*, 165 U. S. 275, 281, 282. If we remember that "it is a Constitution we are expounding," we cannot rightly prefer, of the possible meanings of its words, that which will defeat rather than effectuate the constitutional purpose.

That the free choice by the people of representatives in Congress, subject only to the restrictions to be found in §§ 2 and 4 of Article I and elsewhere in the Constitution, was one of the great purposes of our constitutional scheme of government cannot be doubted. We cannot regard it as any the less the constitutional purpose, or its words as any the less guarantying the integrity of that choice, when a state, exercising its privilege in the absence of Congressional action, changes the mode of choice from a single step, a general election, to two, of which the first is the choice at a primary of those candidates from whom, as a second step, the representative in Congress is to be chosen at the election.

Nor can we say that that choice which the Constitution protects is restricted to the second step because § 4 of Article I, as a means of securing a free choice of representatives by the people, has authorized Congress to regulate the manner of elections, without making any mention of primary elections. For we think that the authority of Congress, given by § 4, includes the authority to regulate primary elections when, as in this case, they are a step in the exercise by the people of their choice of representatives in Congress. The point whether the power conferred by § 4 includes in any circumstances the power to regulate primary elections was reserved in *United States* v. *Gradwell, supra,* 487. In *Newberry* v. *United States, supra,* four Justices of this Court were of opinion that the term "elections" in § 4 of Article I did not embrace a primary election, since that procedure was unknown to the framers. A fifth Justice, who with them pronounced the judgment of the Court, was of opinion that a primary, held under a law enacted before the adoption of the Seventeenth Amendment, for the nomination of candidates for Senator, was not an election within the meaning of § 4 of Article I of the Constitution, presumably because the choice of the primary imposed no legal restrictions on the election of Senators by the state legislatures to which their election had been committed by Article

I, § 3.  The remaining four Justices were of the opinion that a primary election for the choice of candidates for Senator or Representative were elections subject to regulation by Congress within the meaning of § 4 of Article I.  The question then has not been prejudged by any decision of this Court. . . .

There is no historical warrant for supposing that the framers were under the illusion that the method of effecting the choice of the electors would never change or that, if it did, the change was for that reason to be permitted to defeat the right of the people to choose representatives for Congress which the Constitution had guaranteed.  The right to participate in the choice of representatives for Congress includes, as we have said, the right to cast a ballot and to have it counted at the general election, whether for the successful candidate or not.  Where the state law has made the primary an integral part of the procedure of choice, or where in fact the primary effectively controls the choice, the right of the elector to have his ballot counted at the primary is likewise included in the right protected by Article I, § 2.  And this right of participation is protected just as is the right to vote at the election, where the primary is by law made an integral part of the election machinery, whether the voter exercises his right in a party primary which invariably, sometimes or never determines the ultimate choice of the representative.  Here, even apart from the circumstance that the Louisiana primary is made by law an integral part of the procedure of choice, the right to choose a representative is in fact controlled by the primary because, as is alleged in the indictment, the choice of candidates at the Democratic primary determines the choice of the elected representative.  Moreover, we cannot close our eyes to the fact, already mentioned, that the practical influence of the choice of candidates at the primary may be so great as to affect profoundly the choice at the general election, even though there is no effective legal prohibition upon the rejection at the election of the choice made at the primary, and may thus operate to deprive the voter of his constitutional right of choice.  This was noted and extensively commented upon by the concurring Justices in *Newberry* v. *United States, supra*, 263–269, 285, 287.

Unless the constitutional protection of the integrity of "elections" extends to primary elections, Congress is left powerless to effect the constitutional purpose, and the popular choice of representatives is stripped of its constitutional protection save only as Congress, by taking over the control of state elections, may exclude from them the influence of the state primaries.  Such an expedient would end that state autonomy with respect to elections which the Constitution contemplated that Congress

**265**

should be free to leave undisturbed, subject only to such minimum regulation as it should find necessary to insure the freedom and integrity of the choice. Words, especially those of a constitution, are not to be read with such stultifying narrowness. The words of §§ 2 and 4 of Article I, read in the sense which is plainly permissible and in the light of the constitutional purpose, require us to hold that a primary election which involves a necessary step in the choice of candidates for election as representatives in Congress, and which in the circumstances of this case controls that choice, is an election within the meaning of the constitutional provision and is subject to congressional regulation as to the manner of holding it. . . .

There remains the question whether §§ 19 and 20 are an exercise of the congressional authority applicable to the acts with which appellees are charged in the indictment. Section 19 makes it a crime to conspire to "injure" or "oppress" any citizen "in the free exercise or enjoyment of any right or privilege secured to him by the Constitution." In *Ex parte Yarbrough, supra,* and in *United States v. Mosley, supra,* as we have seen, it was held that the right to vote in a congressional election is a right secured by the Constitution, and that a conspiracy to prevent the citizen from voting, or to prevent the official count of his ballot when cast, is a conspiracy to injure and oppress the citizen in the free exercise of a right secured by the Constitution within the meaning of § 19. In reaching this conclusion the Court found no uncertainty or ambiguity in the statutory language, obviously devised to protect the citizen "in the free exercise or enjoyment of any right or privilege secured to him by the Constitution" and concerned itself with the question whether the right to participate in choosing a representative is so secured. Such is our function here. Conspiracy to prevent the official count of a citizen's ballot, held in *United States* v. *Mosley, supra,* to be a violation of § 19 in the case of a congressional election, is equally a conspiracy to injure and oppress the citizen when the ballots are cast in a primary election prerequisite to the choice of party candidates for a congressional election. In both cases the right infringed is one secured by the Constitution. The injury suffered by the citizen in the exercise of the right is an injury which the statute describes and to which it applies in the one case as in the other.

The suggestion that § 19, concededly applicable to conspiracies to deprive electors of their votes at congressional elections, is not sufficiently specific to be deemed applicable to primary elections, will hardly bear examination. Section 19 speaks neither of elections nor of primaries. In unambiguous language it protects "any right or privilege secured by the Constitution," a phrase which, as we have seen, extends to the right of the voter to have his vote counted in both the general election and in the primary election, where the latter is a part of the election machinery, as well as to numerous other constitutional rights which are wholly unrelated to the choice of a representative in Congress. *United States* v. *Waddell,* 112 U. S. 76; *Logan* v. *United States,* 144 U. S. 263; *In re Quarles,* 158 U. S. 532; *Motes* v. *United States,* 178 U. S. 458; *Guinn* v. *United States,* 238 U. S. 347. . . .

To withdraw from the scope of the statute an effective interference with the constitutional right of choice, because other wholly different situations not now before us may not be found to involve such an interference, cf. *United States* v. *Bathgate,* 246 U. S. 220; *United States* v. *Gradwell,* 243 U. S. 476, is to say that acts plainly within the statute should be deemed to be without it because other hypothetical cases may later be found not to infringe the constitutional right with which alone the statute is concerned. . . .

The right of the voters at the primary to have their votes counted is, as we have stated, a right or privilege secured by the Constitution, and to this § 20 also gives protection. The alleged acts of appellees were committed in the course of their performance of duties under the Louisiana statute requiring them to count the ballots, to record the result of the count, and to certify the result of the election. Misuse of power, possessed by virtue of state law and made possible only because the wrongdoer is clothed with the authority of state law, is action taken "under color of" state law. *Ex parte Virginia,* 100 U. S. 339, 346; *Home Telephone & Telegraph Co.* v. *Los Angeles,* 227 U. S. 278, 287, et seq.; *Hague* v. *CIO,* 307 U. S. 496, 507, 519; *cf.* 101 F. 2d 774, 790. Here the acts of appellees infringed the constitutional right and deprived the voters of the benefit of it within the meaning of § 20, unless by its terms its application is restricted to deprivations "on account of such inhabitant being an alien or by reason of his color, or race."

The last clause of § 20 protects inhabitants of a state from being subjected to different punishments, pains or penalties, by reason of alienage, color or race, than are prescribed for the punishment of citizens. That the qualification with respect to alienage, color and race, refers only to differences in punishment and not to deprivations of any rights or privileges secured by the Constitution, is evidenced by the structure of the section and the necessities of the practical application of its provisions. The qualification as to alienage, color and race, is a parenthetical phrase in the clause penalizing different punishments "than are prescribed

**267**

for citizens," and in the common use of language could refer only to the subject-matter of the clause and not to that of the earlier one relating to the deprivation of rights to which it makes no reference in terms. . . .

We think that § 20 authorizes the punishment of two different offenses. The one is willfully subjecting any inhabitant to the deprivation of rights secured by the Constitution; the other is willfully subjecting any inhabitant to different punishments on account of his alienage, color or race, than are prescribed for the punishment of citizens. The meager legislative history of the section supports this conclusion.

So interpreted, § 20 applies to deprivation of the constitutional rights of qualified voters to choose representatives in Congress. The generality of the section, made applicable as it is to deprivations of any constitutional right, does not obscure its meaning or impair its force within the scope of its application, which is restricted by its terms to deprivations which are willfully inflicted by those acting under color of any law, statute and the like.

We do not discuss the application of § 20 to deprivations of the right to equal protection of the laws guaranteed by the Fourteenth Amendment, a point apparently raised and discussed for the first time in the Government's brief in this Court. The point was not specially considered or decided by the court below, and has not been assigned as error by the Government. Since the indictment on its face does not purport to charge a deprivation of equal protection to voters or candidates, we are not called upon the construe the indictment in order to raise a question of statutory validity or construction which we are alone authorized to review upon this appeal.

*Reversed.*

THE CHIEF JUSTICE took no part in the consideration or decision of this case.

[Justices Douglas, Black and Murphy, in an opinion by the first, agreed with the majority that constitutional power existed in Congress to regulate all phases of the Federal election process, including primaries, but dissented on the ground that Section 19 should not be construed to apply to primaries. Relying upon the *Bathgate* and *Gradwell* decisions these justices would read Section 19 "so as to exclude all acts which do not have the direct effect of depriving voters of their right to vote at general elections."]

## Note

1. The *Classic* case is discussed in Notes, 41 Col. L. Rev. 1101 (1941); 10 Geo. Wash. L. Rev. 625 (1942); 36 Ill. L. Rev. 475 (1941); 40 Mich. L. Rev. 460 (1942); 20 N. C. L. Rev. 93 (1941).

2. In *U. S. v. Saylor*, 322 U. S. 385, 88 L. Ed. 1341, 64 S. Ct. 1101 (1944), the Court upheld a conviction under Section 241 for stuffing the ballot box in an election of a Senator in Kentucky. The Court distinguished the *Bathgate* case and followed the *Mosley* case. Justices Douglas, Black and Reed dissented, construing Section 241 as restricted "to those cases where a voter is deprived of his right to cast a ballot or have his ballot counted."

Section 241 has been used frequently in recent years to prosecute election frauds. See, e. g., *Walker v. U. S.*, 93 F. 2d 383 (C. A. 8, 1937), cert. den. 303 U. S. 644 (1938); *Ledford v. U. S.*, 155 F. 2d 574 (C. A. 6, 1946), cert. den. 329 U. S. 733 (1946); *Klein v. U. S.*, 176 F. 2d 184 (C. A. 8, 1949), cert. den. 338 U. S. 870 (1949); *Prichard v. U. S.*, 181 F. 2d 326 (C. A. 6, 1950), aff'd 339 U. S. 974 (1950). But it has been invoked only rarely to prosecute interference with the right of franchise by violence or intimidation. In *U. S. v. Ellis*, 43 F. Supp. 321 (W. D. S. C., 1942), the members of an Election Registration Board in South Carolina were indicted under Section 241 for conspiracy to prevent by threats and intimidation certain citizens from registering to vote. The District Judge overruled a demurrer to the indictment, but on trial defendants were acquitted by the jury. See Carr, *Federal Protection of Civil Rights*, pp. 138–9, 176–80 (1947).

## SNOWDEN v. HUGHES

Supreme Court of the United States, 1944
321 U. S. 1, 88 L. Ed. 497, 64 S. Ct. 397.

MR. CHIEF JUSTICE STONE delivered the opinion of the Court.

Petitioner, a citizen of Illinois, brought this suit at law in the District Court for Northern Illinois against respondents, citizens of Illinois, to recover damages for infringement of his civil rights in violation of the Fourteenth Amendment and 8 U. S. C. §§ 41, 43 and 47 (3). . . .

The complaint makes the following allegations. Petitioner was one of several candidates at the April 9, 1940, Republican primary election held in the Third Senatorial District of Illinois pursuant to Ill. Rev. Stat. (State Bar Assn. Ed.), Ch. 46, Art. 8 for nominees for the office of representative in the Illinois General Assembly. By reason of appropriate action taken respectively by the Republican and Democratic Senatorial Committees of the Third Senatorial District in conformity to the scheme of proportional representation authorized by Ill. Rev. Stat., Ch. 46, §§ 8–13, two candidates for representative in the General Assembly were to be nominated on the Republican ticket and one on the Democratic ticket. Since three representatives were to be elected, Ill. Const., Art. IV, §§ 7 and 8, and only three were to be nominated by the primary election, election at the primary as one of the two Republican nominees was, so the complaint alleges, tantamount to election to the office of representative.

The votes cast at the primary election were duly canvassed by the Canvassing Board of Cook County, which, as required by Ill. Rev. Stat., Ch. 46, § 8–15, certified and forwarded to the Secretary of State a tabulation showing the results of the primary election in the Third Senatorial District. By this tabulation the Board certified that petitioner and another had received respectively the second highest and highest number of votes for the Republican nominations. Ill. Rev. Stat., Ch. 46, § 8–13 requires that the candidates receiving the highest votes shall be declared nominated.

Respondents Hughes and Lewis, and Henry Horner whose executors were joined as defendants and are respondents here, constituted the State Primary Canvassing Board for the election year 1940. By Ill. Rev. Stat., Ch. 46, § 8–15 it was made their duty to receive the certified tabulated statements of votes cast, including that prepared by the Canvassing Board of Cook County, to canvass the returns, to proclaim the results and to issue certificates of nomination to the successful candidates. Such a certificate is a prerequisite to the inclusion of a candidate's name on the ballot. Ill. Rev. Stat., Ch. 46, § 10–14. Acting in their official capacity as State Primary Canvassing Board they issued, on April 29, 1940, their official proclamation which designated only one nominee for the office of representative in the General Assembly from the Third Senatorial District on the Republican ticket and excluded from the nomination petitioner, who had received the second highest number of votes for the Republican nomination.

After setting out these facts the complaint alleges that Horner and respondents Hughes and Lewis, "willfully, maliciously and arbitrarily" failed and refused to file with the Secretary of State a correct certificate showing that petitioner was one of the Republican nominees, that they conspired and confederated together for that purpose, and that their action constituted "an unequal, unjust and oppressive administration" of the laws of Illinois. It alleges that Horner, Hughes and Lewis, acting as state officials under color of the laws of Illinois, thereby deprived petitioner of the Republican nomination for representative in the General Assembly and of election to that office, to his damage in the amount of $50,000, and by so doing deprived petitioner, in contravention of 8 U. S. C. §§ 41, 43 and 47(3), of rights, privileges and immunities secured to him as a citizen of the United States, and of the equal protection of the laws, both guaranteed to him by the Fourteenth Amendment.

The District Court granted motions by respondents to strike the complaint and dismiss the suit. . . .

Section 43 provides that "Every person who, under color of any statute, ordinance, regulation, custom, or usage, of any State . . . , subjects, or causes to be subjected, any citizen of the United States or other person . . . to the deprivation of any rights, privileges, or immunities secured by the Constitution and laws, shall be liable to the party injured in an action at law . . . for redress." Section 47(3), so far as now relevant, gives an action for damages to any person "injured in his person or property, or deprived of having and exercising any right or privilege of a citizen of the United States," by reason of a conspiracy of two or more persons entered into "for the purpose of depriving . . . any person . . . of the equal protection of the laws, . . . or of equal privileges and immunities under the laws." . . .

Three distinct provisions of the Fourteenth Amendment guarantee rights of persons and property. It declares that "No State shall make or enforce any law which shall abridge the privileges or immunities of citizens of the United States; nor shall any State deprive any person of life, liberty, or property, without due process of law; nor deny to any person within its jurisdiction the equal protection of the laws."

The protection extended to citizens of the United States by the privileges and immunities clause includes those rights and privileges which, under the laws and Constitution of the United States, are incident to citizenship of the United States, but does not include rights pertaining to state citizenship and derived solely from the relationship of the citizen and his state established by state law. *Slaughter-House Cases*, 16 Wall. 36, 74, 79; *Maxwell* v. *Bugbee*, 250 U. S. 525, 538; *Prudential Insurance Co.* v. *Cheek*, 259 U. S. 530, 539; *Madden* v. *Kentucky*, 309 U. S. 83, 90–93. The right to become a candidate for state office, like the right to vote for the election of state officers, *Minor* v. *Happersett*, 21 Wall. 162, 170–78; *Pope* v. *Williams*, 193 U. S. 621, 632; *Breedlove* v. *Suttles*, 302 U. S. 277, 283, is a right or privilege of state citizenship, not of national citizenship which alone is protected by the privileges and immunities clause.

More than forty years ago this Court determined that an unlawful denial by state action of a right to state political office is not a denial of a right of property or of liberty secured by the due process clause. *Taylor & Marshall* v. *Beckham*, 178 U. S. 548. Only once since has this Court had occasion to consider the question and it then reaffirmed that conclusion, *Cave* v. *Newell*, 246 U. S. 650, as we reaffirm it now.

Nor can we conclude that the action of the State Primary Canvassing Board, even though it be regarded as state action within the prohibitions of the Fourteenth Amendment, was a denial of the equal protection of the laws. The denial alleged is of the right of petitioner to be a candidate for and to be elected to public office upon receiving a sufficient number of votes. The right is one secured to him by state statute and the deprivation of right is alleged to result solely from the Board's failure to obey state law. There is no contention that the statutes of the state are in any respect inconsistent with the guarantees of the Fourteenth Amendment. There is no allegation of any facts tending to show that in refusing to certify petitioner as a nominee, the Board was making any intentional or purposeful discrimination between persons or classes. On the argument before us petitioner disclaimed any contention that class or racial discrimination is involved. The insistence is rather that the Board, merely by failing to certify petitioner as a duly elected nominee, has denied to him a right conferred by state law and has thereby denied to him the equal protection of the laws secured by the Fourteenth Amendment.

But not every denial of a right conferred by state law involves a denial of the equal protection of the laws, even though the denial of the right to one person may operate to confer it on another. Where, as here, a statute requires official action discriminating between a successful and an unsuccessful candidate, the required action is not a denial of equal protection since the distinction between the successful and the unsuccessful candidate is based on a permissible classification. And where the official action purports to be in conformity to the statutory classification, an erroneous or mistaken performance of the statutory duty, although a violation of the statute, is not without more a denial of the equal protection of the laws.

The unlawful administration by state officers of a state statute fair on its face, resulting in its unequal application to those who are entitled to be treated alike, is not a denial of equal protection unless there is shown to be present in it an element of intentional or purposeful discrimination. This may appear on the face of the action taken with respect to a particular class or person, cf. *McFarland* v. *American Sugar Co.*, 241 U. S. 79, 86–7, or it may only be shown by extrinsic evidence showing a discriminatory design to favor one individual or class over another not to be inferred from the action itself, *Yick Wo v. Hopkins*, 118 U. S. 356, 373–4. But a discriminatory purpose is not presumed, *Tarrance v. Florida*, 188 U. S. 519, 520; there must be a showing of "clear and intentional discrimination," *Gundling v. Chicago*, 177 U. S. 183, 186; see *Ah Sin v. Wittman*, 198 U. S. 500, 507–8; *Bailey v. Alabama*, 219 U. S. 219, 231. Thus the denial of equal protection by the exclusion of negroes from a jury may be shown by extrinsic evidence of a purposeful discriminatory administration of a statute fair on its face. *Neal v. Delaware*, 103 U. S. 370, 394, 397; *Norris v. Alabama*, 294 U. S. 587, 589; *Pierre v. Louisiana*, 306 U. S. 354, 357; *Smith v. Texas*, 311 U. S. 128, 130–31; *Hill v. Texas*, 316 U. S. 400, 404. But a mere showing that negroes were not included in a particular jury is not enough; there must be a showing of actual discrimination because of race. *Virginia v. Rives*, 100 U. S. 313, 322–3; *Martin v. Texas*, 200 U. S. 316, 320–21; *Thomas v. Texas*, 212 U. S. 278, 282; cf. *Williams v. Mississippi*, 170 U. S. 213, 225.

Another familiar example is the failure of state taxing officials to assess property for taxation on a uniform standard of valuation as required by the assessment laws. It is not enough to establish a denial of equal protection that some are assessed at a higher valuation than others. The difference must be due to a purposeful discrimination, which may be evidenced, for example, by a systematic under-valuation of the property of some taxpayers and a systematic over-valuation of the property of others, so that the practical effect of the official breach of law is the same as though the discrimination were incorporated in and proclaimed by the statute. . . .

Where discrimination is sufficiently shown, the right to relief under the equal protection clause is not diminished by the fact that the discrimination relates to political rights. *McPherson v. Blacker*, 146 U. S. 1, 23–4; *Nixon v. Herndon*, 273 U. S. 536, 538; *Nixon v. Condon*, 286 U. S. 73; see *Pope v. Williams, supra*, 634. But the necessity of a showing of purposeful discrimination is no less in a case involving political rights than in any other. It was not intended by the Fourteenth Amendment and the Civil Rights Acts that all matters formerly within the exclusive cognizance of the states should become matters of national concern.

A construction of the equal protection clause which would find a violation of federal right in every departure by state officers from state law is not to be favored. And it is not without significance that we are not cited to and have been unable to find a single instance in which this Court has entertained the notion that an unlawful denial by state authority of the right to state office is without more a denial of any right secured by the Fourteenth Amendment. See *Taylor & Marshall v. Beckhan, supra,* and authorities cited; *Cave v. Newell, supra.* . . .

As we conclude that the right asserted by petitioner is not one secured by the Fourteenth Amendment and affords no basis for a suit brought under the sections of the Civil Rights Acts relied upon, we find it unnecessary to consider whether the action by the State Board of which petitioner complains is state action within the meaning of the Fourteenth Amendment. The authority of *Barney v. City of New York* [193 U. S. 430], on which the court below relied, has been so restricted by our later decisions, see *Raymond v. Chicago Traction Co.,* 207 U. S. 20, 37; *Home Tel. & Tel. Co. v. Los Angeles,* 227 U. S. 278, 294; *Iowa-Des Moines Bank v. Bennett* [284 U. S. 239, 246]; cf. *United States v. Classic,* 313 U. S. 299, 326, that our determination may be more properly and more certainly rested on petitioner's failure to assert a right of a nature such as the Fourteenth Amendment protects against state action.

The judgment is accordingly affirmed for failure of the complaint to state a cause of action within the jurisdiction of the District Court.

*Affirmed.*

MR. JUSTICE RUTLEDGE concurs in the result.

MR. JUSTICE FRANKFURTER, concurring. . . .

The Constitution does not assure uniformity of decisions or immunity from merely erroneous action, whether by the courts or the executive agencies of a state. See *McGovern v. New York,* 229 U. S. 363, 370–1. However, in forbidding a state to "deny to any person within its jurisdiction the equal protection of the laws," the Fourteenth Amendment does not permit a state to deny the equal protection of its laws because such denial is not wholesale. The talk in some of the cases about systematic discrimination is only a way of indicating that in order to give rise to a constitutional grievance a departure from a norm must be rooted in design and not derive merely from error or fallible judgment. Speaking of a situation in which conscious discrimination by a state touches "the plaintiff alone," this Court tersely expressed the governing principle by observing that "we suppose that no one would contend that the plaintiff was given the equal protection of the laws." *McFarland v. American Sugar Co.,* 241 U. S. 79, 86, 87. And if the highest court of a state should candidly deny to one litigant a rule of law which it concededly would apply to all other litigants in similar situations, could it escape condemnation as an unjust discrimination and therefore a denial of the equal protection of the laws? See *Backus v. Fort Street Union Depot Co.,* 169 U. S. 557, 571.

[Emerson]

But to constitute such unjust discrimination the action must be that of the state. Since the state, for present purposes, can only act through functionaries, the question naturally arises what functionaries, acting under what circumstances, are to be deemed the state for purposes of bringing suit in the federal courts on the basis of illegal state action. The problem is beset with inherent difficulties and not unnaturally has had a fluctuating history in the decisions of the Court. Compare *Barney v. City of New York*, 193 U. S. 430, with *Raymond v. Chicago Traction Co.*, 207 U. S. 20, *Memphis v. Cumberland Telephone Co.*, 218 U. S. 624, with *Home Tel. & Tel. Co. v. Los Angeles*, 227 U. S. 278. It is not to be resolved by abstract considerations such as the fact that every official who purports to wield power conferred by a state is *pro tanto* the state. Otherwise every illegal discrimination by a policeman on the beat would be state action for purpose of suit in a federal court.

Our question is not whether a remedy is available for such an illegality, but whether it is available in the first instance in a federal court. Such a problem of federal judicial control must be placed in the historic context of the relationship of the federal courts to the states, with due regard for the natural sensitiveness of the states and for the appropriate responsibility of state courts to correct the action of lower state courts and state officials. . . .

I am clear, therefore, that the action of the Canvassing Board taken, as the plaintiff himself acknowledges, in defiance of the duty of that Board under Illinois law, cannot be deemed the action of the State, certainly not until the highest court of the State confirms such action and thereby makes it the law of the State. I agree, in a word, with the court below that *Barney v. City of New York*, 193 U.S. 430, is controlling. See Isseks, *Jurisdiction of the Lower Federal Courts to Enjoin Unauthorized Action of State Officials*, 40 Harv. L. Rev. 969. Neither the wisdom of its reasoning nor its holding has been impaired by subsequent decisions. A different problem is presented when a case comes here on review from a decision of a state court as the ultimate voice of state law. See for instance *Iowa-Des Moines Bank v. Bennett*, 284 U. S. 239. And the case is wholly unlike *Lane v. Wilson*, 307 U. S. 268, in which the election officials acted not in defiance of a statute of a state but under its authority.

MR. JUSTICE DOUGLAS, with whom MR. JUSTICE MURPHY concurs, dissenting:

My disagreement with the majority of the Court is on a narrow ground. I agree that the equal protection clause of the Fourteenth Amendment should not be distorted to make the federal courts the supervisor of the state elections. That would place the federal judiciary in a position "to supervise and review the political administration of a state government by its own officials and through its own courts" (*Wilson v. North Carolina*, 169 U. S. 586, 596)—matters on which each State has the final say. I also agree that a candidate for public office is not denied the equal protection of the law in the constitutional sense merely because he is the victim of unlawful administration of a state election law. I believe, as the opinion of the Court indicates, that a denial of equal protection of the laws requires an invidious, purposeful discrimination. But I depart from the majority when it denies Snowden the opportunity of showing that he was in fact the victim of such discriminatory action. His complaint seems to me to be adequate to raise the issue. He charges a conspiracy to wilfully, maliciously and arbitrarily refuse to designate him as one of the nominees of the Republican party, that such action was an "unequal" administration of the Illinois law and a denial to him of the equal protection of the laws, and that the conspiracy had that purpose. While the complaint could have drawn the issue more sharply, I think it defines it sufficiently to survive the motion to dismiss.

No doubt unconstitutional discriminations against a class, such as those which we have recently condemned in *Lane v. Wilson*, 307 U. S. 268, and *Skinner v. Oklahoma*, 316 U. S. 535, may be more readily established than a discrimination against an individual *per se*. But though the proof is exacting, the latter may be shown as in *Cochran v. Kansas*, 316 U. S. 255, where a prisoner was prevented from perfecting an appeal. The criteria are the same whether one has been denied the opportunity to be a candidate for public office, to enter private business, or to have the protection of the courts. If the law is "applied and administered by public authority with an evil eye and an unequal hand, so as practically to make unjust and illegal discriminations between persons in similar circumstances" (*Yick Wo v. Hopkins*, 118 U. S. 356, 373–374), it is the same as if the invidious discrimination were incorporated in the law itself. If the action of the Illinois Board in effect were the same as an Illinois law that Snowden could not run for office, it would run afoul of the equal protection clause whether that discrimination were based on the fact that Snowden was a Negro, Catholic, Presbyterian, Free Mason, or had some other characteristic or belief which the authorities did not like. Snowden should be allowed the opportunity to make that showing no matter how thin his chances of success may seem.

### Note

The civil provisions of the Federal Civil Rights Acts have not been of practical importance in situations involving interference with the right of franchise through violence, fraud or corruption. For their more successful application to other kinds of infringement see Sections D and E of this Chapter, *infra*. See also Chapter I, *supra*. In *Johnson v. Stevenson*, 170 F. 2d 108 (C. A. 5, 1948), cert. den. 336 U. S. 904 (1949), the Court held that the Federal courts had no jurisdiction to enjoin the results of a primary Senatorial election, where the defeated candidate claimed illegal votes were cast, but that such an election contest must be brought in the state courts. On state remedies for fraud in elections see Note, *Correction of Election Frauds*, 48 Yale L. J. 1434 (1939).

## TO SECURE THESE RIGHTS—THE REPORT OF THE PRESIDENT'S COMMITTEE ON CIVIL RIGHTS

U. S. Government Printing Office, 1947, at pp. 160–1

*To strengthen the right to citizenship and its privileges, the President's Committee recommends:* . . .

2. **The enactment by Congress of a statute protecting the right of qualified persons to participate in federal primaries and elections against interference by public officers and private persons.**

This statute would apply only to federal elections. There is no doubt that such a law can be applied to primaries which are an integral part of the federal electoral process or which affect or determine the result of a federal election. It can also protect participation in federal election campaigns and discussions of matters relating to national political issues. This statute should authorize the Department of Justice to use both civil and criminal sanctions. Civil remedies should be used wherever possible to test the legality of threatened interferences with the suffrage before voting rights have been lost.

3. **The enactment by Congress of a statute protecting the right to qualify for, or participate in, federal or state primaries or elections against discriminatory action by state officers based on race or color, or depending on any other unreasonable classification of persons for voting purposes.**

This statute would apply to both federal and state elections, but it would be limited to the protection of the right to vote against discriminatory interferences based on race, color, or other unreasonable classification. Its constitutionality is clearly indicated by the Fourteenth and Fifteenth Amendments. Like the legislation suggested under (2) it should authorize the use of civil and criminal sanctions by the Department of Justice.

## Note

1. The recommendations of the President's Committee have been embodied in a bill introduced by Senator Humphrey and six other Senators. S. 1738, 82d Cong., 1st Sess. (1951).

2. The Hatch Political Activity Act makes it a misdemeanor to intimidate, threaten, or coerce, or to attempt to intimidate, threaten, or coerce any voter at a Federal election. 18 U. S. C. § 594 (1950). This statute has been held not to apply to primaries, an express provision extending coverage to primaries having been eliminated from the original bill. *U. S. v. Malphurs,* 41 F. Supp. 817 (S. D. Fla., 1941), rev'd on other grounds, 316 U. S. 1 (1942). The Hatch Act seems to have been invoked only rarely in this connection.

3. It may be noted that, while Federal power over state elections is substantially more limited than over Federal elections, most elections involve voting for both Federal and state officials. Furthermore, attempts to abridge the right of franchise through intimidation rarely distinguish between Federal and state elections. Hence the Federal power potentially permeates most of the election process.

4. The problems with respect to enforcement of Federal statutes safeguarding the right of franchise against interference by violence, fraud or corruption are similar to those arising with respect to enforcement of other provisions protecting security of the person. See Chapter I, *supra.*

5. For further discussion of the cases treated in this section, see Carr, *Federal Protection of Civil Rights,* pp. 52–3, 64–7, 85–9, 97–9, 176–80 (1947), and other references cited in Chapter I, *supra.*

## C. THE POLL TAX

The poll tax was one of the most common electoral devices adopted by the Southern states in the period following Reconstruction. At one time 11 states imposed such a tax: Florida (1889), Mississippi (1890), Tennessee (1890), Arkansas (1893), South Carolina (1895), Louisiana (1898), North Carolina (1900), Alabama (1901), Virginia (1902), Texas (1902), and Georgia (adopted in 1804). The tax has now been repealed in 6 of these states: North Carolina (1920), Louisiana (1934), Florida (1937), Georgia (1945), South Carolina (1951), and Tennessee (1951).[1]

---

[1] In Tennessee the tax is still technically in force (a repeal law having been declared unconstitutional) but is limited to the payment of taxes assessed in 1871 and is thus without effect. Tenn. Code tit. 6, § 2027 (Supp. 1951).

The details of the tax and its administration vary considerably from state to state. In general the tax is a capitation tax, due annually, and its payment is a prerequisite of voting. In amount the tax ranges from $1 to $2 in the different states; in some states counties or cities are authorized to levy a further amount, but in no case more than $1 additional. Some statutes provide for exemptions for women, older persons and the like; apart from the provisions relating to women, the exemptions may cover up to 15 per cent of the otherwise eligible voters. As a revenue raising device the tax is without significance.

The extent to which a poll tax diminishes voting in any state depends upon a number of factors. Frequently the tax is cumulative; that is, back taxes must be paid before voting is permitted. Of the existing poll tax systems, Mississippi, Alabama and Virginia contain some cumulative provisions. In all states the tax must be paid some months, ranging from 3 to 18, before the primaries. The evidence required to show proof of payment in order to register or vote again varies between the states, in most instances the presentation of a certificate of payment being required at the time of voting. Normally little effort is made by state officials to collect the tax, and in some cases payment may require a visit to the courthouse or a comparable affirmative effort by the taxpayer. In some states there is no legal penalty for failure to pay the tax, and in no state is there any significant program of enforcement through legal process.

At the present time there are increasing efforts on the part of political machines, civic organizations, labor organizations and other private groups to secure payment of the tax by potential voters. In most states it is possible for the political machines to obtain books of blank receipts and "block payments" are common. These practices have undoubtedly afforded facility for manipulation and corruption. And the administration of a poll tax in other respects affords the opportunity for various discriminatory tactics.

The actual effect of the poll tax in disenfranchising Negroes and others is a matter of some dispute. There is evidence that the volume of poll tax payments varies with economic conditions, indicating that the tax does constitute an important burden. But the evidence here is inconclusive. In those states which have repealed the poll tax there has been a substantial increase in voting, but other factors (which may have produced the repeal itself) must be reckoned with. Comparisons of similar poll tax and non-poll tax states, such as Kentucky and Tennessee, reveal a substantially higher percentage of voting in non-poll tax states; but other factors, such as the one party system (of which the poll tax system is itself a part), again make it difficult to isolate the effect of the poll tax.

Despite differences of opinion, however, there is general agreement upon the following propositions: (1) The poll tax does have a substantial effect in diminishing voting, whether that effect be measured in terms of hundreds of thousands or of millions of voters. (2) Insofar as the poll tax has operated to curtail voting it has affected white voters as well as Negroes, Mexican-Americans and others; probably the effect has been greater on white voters. (3) The effect of the poll tax on the Negro vote has thus far been of less significance than the effect of other devices for disenfranchisement, such as white primaries, literacy tests, and other restrictions.

Professor V. O. Key, who has made a careful and moderate analysis of the poll tax in his book *Southern Politics,* concludes that "elimination of the poll tax alone would increase voting in most southern states by no more than 5 to 10 per cent of the potential number of white voters;" that this is "by no means negligible," however, since "in some states the addition of 5 or 10 per cent of the potential white electorate to the voting population brings a substantial increase—a third or a fourth—in the number of voting citizens;" that "the poll tax has had little or no bearing on Negro disenfranchisement," which "has been accomplished by extralegal restraints and by the white primary;" and that "probably the tax would constitute a far more serious deterrent to voting than it now does if some of the allied obstacles to high electoral interest were removed." Key, *Southern Politics,* pp. 617–8 (1949).

## Note

1. The impact of the poll tax on the southern political scene is put in stronger terms by Prof. Maurice R. Davie in *Negroes in American Society,* pp. 267–8 (1949):

"The poll tax does not produce much revenue, nor does it act as a qualitative guarantee for electors. It is openly admitted in every state that a large number, in some cases a majority, of the poll-tax receipts are paid for by politicians who hold them and vote them wholesale. The poll tax is only partially a racial question; fundamentally, it is a weapon against progressive politics, a device to maintain the *status quo,* an instrument for perpetuating control by a minority composed of the local middle class, Northern commercial and industrial interests, and local political machines. In the 1932 presidential election only 22.2 per cent of the adult citizens in the poll-tax states voted as compared with 70.7 per cent in the other states. In the 1936 election the percentages were 22 as against 72; in the 1940 elections 21.1 as against 70.6; in the 1944 election 19 as against 57. Thus in the poll-tax states hardly one out of four qualified voters cast a ballot as compared with almost three out of four in the other states of the union. While the rest of the country casts approximately 100,000 votes in electing each of its Congressmen, the poll-tax states elect theirs with about 30,000 votes each. Because of this situation the tenure of Congressmen from these states is unduly lengthened, and through seniority they come to hold a disproportionate number of committee chairmanships in both House and Senate. As of 1944 no less than eighteen Congressmen from poll-tax states had been perpetuated in office for more than twenty years, and by virtue of seniority they held chairmanships of 17 of the 47 standing House committees and second-ranking positions on 11 others. In the Senate, poll-tax Senators presided over 10 of the 33 standing committees and had twice their share on other Senate committees. Wielding a large influence on national affairs, these Congressional committee chairmen obstruct social and labor legislation and favor discriminatory laws which injure not only the South but the citizens of all states.

"Along with the one-party system and the white primary, the poll tax has reduced democracy to a mere travesty in the South and perpetuated a form of economic feudalism. . . ."

For an extreme statement see the speech of Congressman Bender of Ohio in support of the anti-poll tax bill in the House of Representatives on July 21, 1947, in which he declared that the poll tax "disenfranchises 10,000,000 of our citizens—Negro and white alike." 93 Cong. Rec., p. 9528.

2. Further discussion of the poll tax problem may be found in U. S. Library of Congress Bulletin No. 15, *Poll Tax as a Prerequisite to Voting* (1942); McGovney, *The American Suffrage Medley,* ch. VII (1949); *To Secure These Rights,* Report of the President's Committee on Civil Rights, pp. 38–9 (1947); Strong, *The Poll Tax: The Case of Texas,* 38 Amer. Pol. Sci. Rev. 693 (1944); Stoney, *Suffrage in the South,* 29 Survey Graphic 4 (1940); Note, *Disenfranchisement by Means of the Poll Tax,* 53 Harv. L. Rev. 645 (1940); hearings and reports on proposed Federal legislation, *infra.*

## BREEDLOVE v. SUTTLES

Supreme Court of the United States, 1937
302 U. S. 277, 82 L. Ed. 252, 58 S. Ct. 205

APPEAL from a judgment which affirmed the dismissal of appellant's petition for a writ of mandamus requiring the appellee to allow the appellant to register for voting for federal and state officers at primary and general elections, without payment of poll taxes.

MR. JUSTICE BUTLER delivered the opinion of the Court.

A Georgia statute provides that there shall be levied and collected each year from every inhabitant of the State between the ages of 21 and 60 a poll tax of one dollar, but that the tax shall not be demanded from the blind or from females who do not register for voting. Georgia Code, 1933, § 92–108. The state constitution declares that to entitle a person to register and vote at any election he shall have paid all poll taxes that he may have had opportunity to pay agreeably to law. Art. II, § I, par. III; Code, § 2–603. The form of oath prescribed to qualify an elector contains a clause declaring compliance with that requirement. § 34–103. Tax collectors may not allow any person to register for voting unless satisfied that his poll taxes have been paid. § 34–114. Appellant brought this suit in the superior court of Fulton county to have the clause of the constitution and the statutory provisions above mentioned declared repugnant to various provisions of the Federal Constitution and to compel appellee to allow him to register for voting without payment of poll taxes. The court dismissed his petition. The state supreme court affirmed. 183 Ga. 189; 188 S. E. 140.

The pertinent facts alleged in the petition are these. March 16, 1936, appellant, a white male citizen 28 years old, applied to appellee to register him for voting for federal and state officers at primary and general elections. He informed appellee he had neither made poll tax returns nor paid any poll taxes and had not registered to vote because a receipt for poll taxes and an oath that he had paid them are prerequisites to registration. He demanded that appellee administer the oath, omitting the part declaring payment of poll taxes, and allow him to register. Appellee refused.

Appellant maintains that the provisions in question are repugnant to the equal protection clause and the privileges and immunities clause of the Fourteenth Amendment and to the Nineteenth Amendment.

1. He asserts that the law offends the rule of equality in that it extends only to persons between the ages of 21 and 60 and to women only if they register for voting and in that it makes payment a prerequisite to registration. He does not suggest that exemption of the blind is unreasonable.

Levy by the poll has long been a familiar form of taxation, much used in some countries and to a considerable extent here, at first in the Colonies and later in the States. To prevent burdens deemed grievous and oppressive, the constitutions of some States prohibit or limit poll taxes. That of Georgia prevents more than a dollar a year. Art VII, § II, par. III; Code § 2–5004. Poll taxes are laid upon persons without regard to their occupations or property to raise money for the support of government or some more specific end.[1] The equal protection clause does not require

---

[1] Dowell, History of Taxation and Taxes in England, Vol. III, c. 1.

absolute equality. While possible by statutory declaration to levy a poll tax upon every inhabitant of whatsoever sex, age or condition, collection from all would be impossible for always there are many too poor to pay. Attempt equally to enforce such a measure would justify condemnation of the tax as harsh and unjust. See *Faribault* v. *Misener,* 20 Minn. 396, 398; *Thurston County* v. *Tenino Stone Quarries,* 44 Wash. 351, 355; 87 Pac. 634; *Salt Lake City* v. *Wilson,* 46 Utah 60, 66, *et seq.;* 148 Pac. 1104. Collection from minors would be to put the burden upon their fathers or others upon whom they depend for support. It is not unreasonable to exclude them from the class taxed.

Men who have attained the age of 60 are often, if not always, excused from road work, jury duty and service in the militia. They have served or have been liable to be called on to serve the public to the extent that the State chooses to require. So far as concerns equality under the equal protection clause, there is no substantial difference between these exemptions and exemption from poll taxes. The burden laid upon appellant is precisely that put upon other men. The rate is a dollar a year, commencing at 21 and ending at 60 years of age.

The tax being upon persons, women may be exempted on the basis of special considerations to which they are naturally entitled. In view of burdens necessarily borne by them for the preservation of the race, the State reasonably may exempt them from poll taxes. Cf. *Muller* v. *Oregon,* 208 U. S. 412, 421, *et seq.* *Quong Wing* v. *Kirkendall,* 223 U. S. 59, 63. *Riley* v. *Massachusetts,* 232 U. S. 671. *Miller* v. *Wilson,* 236 U. S. 373. *Bosley* v. *McLaughlin,* 236 U. S. 385. The laws of Georgia declare the husband to be the head of the family and the wife to be subject to him. § 53–501. To subject her to the levy would be to add to his burden. Moreover, Georgia poll taxes are laid to raise money for educational purposes, and it is the father's duty to provide for education of the children. § 74–105. Discrimination in favor of all women being permissible, appellant may not complain because the tax is laid only upon some or object to registration of women without payment of taxes for previous years. *Aetna Insurance Co.* v. *Hyde,* 275 U. S. 440, 447. *Rosenthal* v. *New York,* 226 U. S. 260, 270.

Payment as a prerequisite is not required for the purpose of denying or abridging the privilege of voting. It does not limit the tax to electors; aliens are not there permitted to vote, but

Bryce, the American Commonwealth, c. XLIII. Cooley, The Law of Taxation (4th ed.) §§ 40, 1773. *Hylton* v. *United States,* 3 Dall. 171, 175, 182. *Short* v. *Maryland,* 80 Md. 392, 397, *et seq.;* 31 Atl. 322. *Faribault* v. *Misener,* 20 Minn. 396.

the tax is laid upon them, if within the defined class. It is not laid upon persons of 60 or more years old, whether electors or not. Exaction of payment before registration undoubtedly serves to aid collection from electors desiring to vote, but that use of the State's power is not prevented by the Federal Constitution. Cf. *Magnano Co.* v. *Hamilton,* 292 U. S. 40, 44.

2. To make payment of poll taxes a prerequisite of voting is not to deny any privilege or immunity protected by the Fourteenth Amendment. Privilege of voting is not derived from the United States, but is conferred by the State and, save as restrained by the Fifteenth and Nineteenth Amendments and other provisions of the Federal Constitution, the State may condition suffrage as it seems appropriate. *Minor* v. *Happersett,* 21 Wall. 162, 170 *et seq. Ex parte Yarbrough,* 110 U. S. 651, 664–775. *McPherson* v. *Blacker,* 146 U. S. 1, 37–38. *Guinn* v. *United States,* 238 U. S. 347, 362. The privileges and immunities protected are only those that arise from the Constitution and laws of the United States and not those that spring from other sources. *Hamilton* v. *Regents,* 293 U. S. 245, 261.

3. The Nineteenth Amendment, adopted in 1920, declares: "The right of citizens of the United States to vote shall not be denied or abridged by the United States or by any State on account of sex." It applies to men and women alike and by its own force supersedes inconsistent measures, whether federal or state. *Leser* v. *Garnett,* 258 U. S. 130, 135. Its purpose is not to regulate the levy or collection of taxes. The construction for which appellant contends would make the amendment a limitation upon the power to tax. Cf. *Minor* v. *Happersett, supra,* 173; *Bowers* v. *Kerbaugh-Empire Co.,* 271 U. S. 170, 173–174. The payment of poll taxes as a prerequisite to voting is a familiar and reasonable regulation long enforced in many States and for more than a century in Georgia. That measure reasonably may be deemed essential to that form of levy. Imposition without enforcement would be futile. Power to levy and power to collect are equally necessary. And, by the exaction of payment before registration, the right to vote is neither denied nor abridged on account of sex. It is fanciful to suggest that the Georgia law is a mere disguise under which to deny or abridge the right of men to vote on account of their sex. The challenged enactment is not repugnant to the Nineteenth Amendment.

*Affirmed.*

## Note

1. Subsequent efforts to outlaw the poll tax through judicial decision have likewise failed. In *Pirtle* v. *Brown,* 118 F. 2d 218 (C. A. 6, 1941), cert. den. 314 U. S. 621 (1941), the Tennessee poll tax was at-

tacked as unconstitutional in its application to a person, otherwise qualified, seeking to vote in a special Congressional election. The court held the *Breedlove* case controlling.

A collateral attack on the Virginia poll tax was made in *Saunders v. Wilkins*, 152 F. 2d 235 (C. A. 4, 1945), cert. den. 328 U. S. 870 (1946) (Mr. Justice Douglas dissenting). Here action was brought against the Secretary of State of Virginia to recover damages under 8 U. S. C. § 43 for failure to certify the plaintiff as a candidate for election as Representative-at-Large to Congress. The theory of the action was that Virginia, through its poll tax legislation, had deprived 60 per cent of its voters of the right of franchise; that consequently, under Section 2 of the Fourteenth Amendment, the representation of Virginia in the House of Representatives should be reduced from nine to four; that the allocation of nine representatives by Congress and the apportionment by Virginia of these nine representatives to districts were unconstitutional; and hence that Virginia's four representatives must be elected at large. The court dismissed the suit, holding that the issue was "political in its nature [and] must be determined by the legislative branch of the government." 152 F. 2d at 237.

In *Butler v. Thompson*, 97 F. Supp. 17 (E. D. Va., 1951), aff'd 341 U. S. 937 (1951) (Mr. Justice Douglas dissenting), the Virginia poll tax was again challenged in a suit brought to compel an election registrar to register plaintiff, a Negro who had not paid her poll tax, and for damages. It was alleged that the Virginia poll tax law had been passed to disenfranchise Negro voters and was being administered in a manner that discriminated against Negroes. A three-judge court found the evidence did not support the allegations of discrimination and dismissed the suit.

See also *Caven v. Clark*, 78 F. Supp. 295 (W. D. Ark., 1948), in which a suit under 8 U. S. C. § 43 for mandatory injunction or declaratory judgment to purge the poll tax list of the names of 2502 persons alleged to be holders of illegal poll tax receipts was dismissed for lack of equity jurisdiction.

Cases in the state courts upholding the poll tax are summarized in *Saunders v. Wilkins, supra,* and in Note, 139 A. L. R. 557.

2. For discussion of the foregoing cases see Note, *Negro Disenfranchisement—A Challenge to the Constitution,* 47 Col. L. Rev. 76, 92–4 (1947); Boudin, *State Poll Taxes and the Federal Constitution,* 28 Va. L. Rev. 1 (1941); and materials on the constitutionality of Federal anti-poll tax legislation, cited *infra.*

82d CONGRESS
1st Session

## S. 1734

### IN THE SENATE OF THE UNITED STATES

June 25 (legislative day, June 21), 1951

MR. HUMPHREY (for himself, MR. BENTON, MR. DOUGLAS, MR. LEHMAN, MR. MAGNUSON, MR. MORSE, MR. MURRAY, MR. NEELY, and MR. PASTORE) introduced the following bill; which was read twice and referred to the Committee on Rules and Administration.

### A BILL

Outlawing the poll tax as a condition of voting in any primary or other election for national officers.

*Be it enacted by the Senate and House of Representatives of the United States of America in Congress assembled,* That this Act may be cited as the "Federal Anti-Poll-Tax Act".

SEC. 2. When used in this Act—

(a) The term "poll tax" shall be construed to include specifically, but not by way of limitation, any tax, however designated, which is, or at any time was, imposed, increased, accelerated, or otherwise unfavorably modified, as a direct or indirect prerequisite to or consequence of voting in a national election.

(b) The term "voting in a national election" shall mean voting or registering to vote in any primary or other election for President, Vice President, or elector or electors for President or Vice President, or for United States Senator or for Member of the House of Representatives.

SEC. 3. It shall be unlawful for any person, whether or not acting on behalf of any State or any governmental subdivision thereof or therein, to levy, collect, or require the payment of any poll tax, or otherwise interfere with any person's voting in any national election by reason of such person's failure or refusal to pay or assume the obligation of payment of any poll tax. Any such action by any such person shall be deemed an interference with the manner of holding such elections, an abridgment of the right and privilege of citizens of the United States to vote for such officers, and an obstruction of the operations of the Federal Government.

SEC. 4. (a) In the event of a violation or threatened violation of this Act, either the United States, or any person aggrieved or likely to be aggrieved by such violation or threatened violation, may apply to the appropriate district court of the United States for an order enjoining such violation or threatened violation, or for an order compelling compliance with this Act. Upon proof of such violation or threatened violation, the court shall issue, without bond, such restraining order, temporary or permanent injunction, writ of mandamus, or other order or orders as may be appropriate to insure prompt and effective compliance with this Act. . . .

(c) In any action brought under subsection (a) of this section 4, any appeal to the appropriate court of appeals and any review thereof by the Supreme Court shall be heard expeditiously and shall, where practicable, be determined before the next national election in connection with which the violation or threatened violation of this Act is alleged. . . .

## Note

1. Proposals for eliminating the poll tax by Federal legislation have been advanced for many years. The first anti-poll tax bill was introduced in Congress in 1939. In 1947 the President's Committee on Civil Rights recommended such legislation. *To Secure These Rights*, p. 160 (1947). And pledges to enact anti-poll tax legislation were incorporated in both the Republican and Democratic platforms of 1948 and in the Republican platform of 1952. The House of Representatives has passed anti-poll tax bills on five occasions: in 1942 (H. R. 1024, 77th Cong., 2d Sess.), 1943 (H. R. 7, 78th Cong., 1st Sess.), 1945 (H. R. 7, 79th Cong., 1st Sess.), 1947 (H. R. 29, 80th Cong., 1st Sess.), and 1949 (H. R. 3199, 81st Cong., 1st Sess). In each case Senate action was blocked by filibuster. No attempt to pass the bill in the Senate was made in 1950, 1951 or 1952.

Hearings were held on the legislation before the House Committee on the Judiciary in 1940 (not printed); before the House Committee on Administration, Subcommittee on Elections in 1947 and 1949 (not printed); before the Senate Committee on the Judiciary in 1942 and 1943; before the Senate Committee on Rules and Administration in 1948.

For accounts of the legislative history see Kallenbach, *Constitutional Aspects of Federal Anti-Poll Tax Legislation*, 45 Mich. L. Rev. 717, 717–22 (1947); Christensen, *The Constitutionality of National Anti-Poll Tax Bills*, 33 Minn. L. Rev. 217, 218–21 (1949).

2. During World War II Congress passed legislation abolishing the requirement of the payment of a poll tax by servicemen desiring to vote in Federal elections. 56 Stat. 753 (1942), amended by 58 Stat. 136 (1944); 50 U. S. C. § 301 (1951). Some of the states passed similar legislation. See Kallenbach, *supra*, at p. 719.

3. The constitutionality of Federal anti-poll tax legislation has been much debated. Proponents argue that (1) the right to vote in Federal elections is a right derived from the Constitution and may not be taxed or infringed by the states; (2) adequate power exists under Article I, Section 4, authorizing Congress to make regulations

concerning the "times, places and manner of holding elections"; (3) the poll tax is a source of fraud and corruption and hence its elimination is necessary to protect the integrity of Federal elections, an argument similar to that supporting the Hatch Act's regulation of elections; (4) the purpose and effect of the poll tax is to disenfranchise Negro and poor white voters, and therefore Congress may implement the equal protection clause of the Fourteenth Amendment and the Fifteenth Amendment; (5) power may be derived from Article IV, Section 4, providing that the United States "shall guarantee to every State . . . a republican form of government"; and (6) the requirement of payment of a poll tax is not a "qualification" for voting, in that it has no relevance to a voter's competence, and hence is not within the exclusive power of the states.

On the other hand opponents of the legislation contend that (1) under Article I, Section 2, Article II, Section 1, and the Seventeenth Amendment, power to determine the qualification of voters is a function of the states, not the Federal government; and (2) *Williams v. Mississippi, infra,* and *Breedlove v. Suttles, supra,* establish that the requirement of a poll tax is reasonable and appropriate.

For full discussion of the constitutional issues see the Christensen and Kallenbach articles, *supra,* reaching the conclusion that the legislation is constitutional, and McGovney, *The American Suffrage Medley,* ch. VIII (1949), coming to the opposite conclusion. See also, on behalf of constitutionality, Boudin, *State Poll Taxes and the Federal Constitution,* 28 Va. L. Rev. 1 (1941); Crockett, *The Constitutionality of Federal Anti-Poll Tax Legislation,* 2 Nat. Bar J. 46 (1944); articles and notes in 2 Law. Guild Rev., No. 2, p. 11 (1942); 3 Law. Guild Rev. No. 5, p. 9 (1943); 28 Corn. L. Q. 104 (1942); 21 N. Y. U. L. Q. Rev. 113 (1946). On behalf of unconstitutionality, see Looney, *Constitutionality of Anti-Poll Tax Measures,* 7 Tex. Bar. J. 70 (1944); Morse, *A Study on the Unconstitutionality of the Proposed Federal Abolition of the Poll Tax,* 10 Ga. B. J. 37 (1947); Note, 53 Harv. L. Rev. 645 (1940). In addition, the constitutional issues are discussed in the hearings and reports of the Congressional committees considering the legislation.

## D. THE WHITE PRIMARY

The white primary system in the southern states involves the exclusion of Negroes from voting in Democratic Party primary elections and, indeed, from taking any part in the organization or functioning of the Democratic Party. The exclusion of Negroes from Democratic Party activities was a natural development of the Reconstruction Period. The practice continued through the establishment of that party as the single dominant party in the South and, with the exception of isolated areas, prevailed throughout the entire South. It thus came to constitute the major legal, or pseudo-legal, device upon which the system of Negro disenfranchisement rested.[1]

Legal attack upon the white primary system first reached the Supreme Court in the case of *Nixon* v. *Herndon* in 1927. The course of the legal controversy is traced in *Smith* v. *Allwright*.

### Note

For background on the white primary system see Key, *Southern Politics,* pp. 619–24 (1949); McGovney, *The American Suffrage Medley,* pp. 99–104 (1949); Mangum, *The Legal Status of the Negro,* pp. 405–24 (1940).

## SMITH v. ALLWRIGHT

Supreme Court of the United States, 1944
321 U. S. 649, 88 L. Ed. 987, 64 S. Ct. 757

MR. JUSTICE REED delivered the opinion of the Court.

This writ of certiorari brings here for review a claim for damages in the sum of $5,000 on the part of petitioner, a Negro citizen of the 48th precinct of Harris County, Texas, for the refusal of respondents, election and associate election judges respectively of that precinct, to give petitioner a ballot or to permit him to cast a ballot in the primary election of July 27, 1940, for the nomination of Democratic candidates for the United States Senate and House of Representatives, and Governor and other state officers. The refusal is alleged to have been solely because of the race and color of the proposed voter.

The actions of respondents are said to violate §§ 31 and 43 to Title 8[1] of the United States Code in that petitioner was deprived of rights secured by §§ 2 and 4 of Article I and the Fourteenth, Fifteenth and Seventeenth Amendments to the United States

---

[1] In most southern states the Republican Party does not hold primaries. See Davie, *Negroes in American Society,* pp. 272–3 (1949).

[1] 8 U. S. C. § 31:

"All citizens of the United States who are otherwise qualified by law to vote at any election by the people in any State, Territory, district, county, city, parish, township, school district, municipality, or other territorial subdivision, shall be entitled and allowed to vote at all such elections, without distinction of race, color, or previous condition of servitude; any constitution, law, custom, usage, or regulation of any State or Territory, or by or under its authority, to the contrary notwithstanding."

§ 43: "Every person who, under color of any statute, ordinance, regulation, custom, or usage, of any State or Territory, subjects, or causes to be subjected, any citizen of the United States or other person within the jurisdiction thereof to the deprivation of any rights, privileges, or immunities secured by the Constitution and laws, shall be liable to the party injured in an action at law, suit in equity, or other proper proceeding for redress."

Constitution. The suit was filed in the District Court of the United States for the Southern District of Texas, which had jurisdiction under Judicial Code § 24, subsection 14.

The District Court denied the relief sought and the Circuit Court of Appeals quite properly affirmed its action on the authority of *Grovey* v. *Townsend*, 295 U. S. 45. We granted the petition for certiorari to resolve a claimed inconsistency between the decision in the *Grovey* case and that of *United States* v. *Classic*, 313 U. S. 299. 319 U. S. 738.

The State of Texas by its Constitution and statutes provides that every person, if certain other requirements are met which are not here in issue, qualified by residence in the district or county "shall be deemed a qualified elector." Constitution of Texas, Article VI, § 2; Vernon's Civil Statutes (1939 ed.), Article 2955. Primary elections for United States Senators, Congressmen and state officers are provided for by Chapters Twelve and Thirteen of the statutes. Under these chapters, the Democratic party was required to hold the primary which was the occasion of the alleged wrong to petitioner. A summary of the state statutes regulating primaries appears in the footnote.[6] These nominations are to be made by the qualified voters of the party. Art. 3101.

The Democratic party of Texas is held by the Supreme Court of that State to be a "voluntary association," *Bell* v. *Hill*, 123 Tex. 531, 534, protected by § 27 of the Bill of Rights, Art. I, Constitution of Texas, from interference by the State except that:

"In the interest of fair methods and a fair expression by their members of their preferences in the selection of their nominees, the State may regulate such elections by proper laws." p. 545. That court stated further:

"Since the right to organize and maintain a political party is one guaranteed by the Bill of Rights of this State, it necessarily follows that every privilege essential or reasonably appropriate to the exercise of that right is likewise guaranteed,—including, of course, the privilege of determining the policies of the party and its membership. Without the privilege of determining the policy of a political association and its membership, the right to organize such an association would be a mere mockery. We think these rights,—that is, the right to determine the membership of a political party and to determine its policies, of necessity are to be exercised by the state convention of such party, and cannot, under any circumstances, be conferred upon a state or governmental agency." p. 546. Cf. *Waples* v. *Marrast*, 108 Tex. 5, 184 S. W. 180.

---

[6] [Footnote omitted.]

The Democratic party on May 24, 1932, in a state convention adopted the following resolution, which has not since been "amended, abrogated, annulled or avoided":

"Be it resolved that all white citizens of the State of Texas who are qualified to vote under the Constitution and laws of the State shall be eligible to membership in the Democratic party and, as such, entitled to participate in its deliberations."

It was by virtue of this resolution that the respondents refused to permit the petitioner to vote.

Texas is free to conduct her elections and limit her electorate as she may deem wise, save only as her action may be affected by the prohibitions of the United States Constitution or in conflict with powers delegated to and exercised by the National Government. The Fourteenth Amendment forbids a State from making or enforcing any law which abridges the privileges or immunities of citizens of the United States and the Fifteenth Amendment specifically interdicts any denial or abridgment by a State of the right of citizens to vote on account of color. Respondents appeared in the District Court and the Circuit Court of Appeals and defended on the ground that the Democratic party of Texas is a voluntary organization with members banded together for the purpose of selecting individuals of the group representing the common political beliefs as candidates in the general election. As such a voluntary organization, it was claimed, the Democratic party is free to select its own membership and limit to whites participation in the party primary. Such action, the answer asserted, does not violate the Fourteenth, Fifteenth or Seventeenth Amendment as officers of government cannot be chosen at primaries and the Amendments are applicable only to general elections where governmental officers are actually elected. Primaries, it is said, are political party affairs, handled by party, not governmental, officers. No appearance for respondents is made in this Court. Arguments presented here by the Attorney General of Texas and the Chairman of the State Democratic Executive Committee of Texas, as amici curiae, urged substantially the same grounds as those advanced by the respondents.

The right of a Negro to vote in the Texas primary has been considered heretofore by this Court. The first case was *Nixon* v. *Herndon*, 273 U. S. 536. At that time, 1924, the Texas statute, Art. 3093a, afterwards numbered Art. 3107 (Rev. Stat. 1925) declared "in no event shall a Negro be eligible to participate in a Democratic Party primary election in the State of Texas." Nixon was refused the right to vote in a Democratic primary and brought a suit for damages against the election officers under R. S. §§ 1979 and 2004, the present §§ 43 and 31 of Title 8,

U. S. C., respectively. It was urged to this Court that the denial of the franchise to Nixon violated his Constitutional rights under the Fourteenth and Fifteenth Amendments. Without consideration of the Fifteenth, this Court held that the action of Texas in denying the ballot to Negroes by statute was in violation of the equal protection clause of the Fourteenth Amendment and reversed the dismissal of the suit.

The legislature of Texas reenacted the article but gave the State Executive Committee of a party the power to prescribe the qualifications of its members for voting or other participation. This article remains in the statutes. The State Executive Committee of the Democratic party adopted a resolution that white Democrats and none other might participate in the primaries of that party. Nixon was refused again the privilege of voting in a primary and again brought suit for damages by virtue of § 31, Title 8, U. S. C. This Court again reversed the dismissal of the suit for the reason that the Committee action was deemed to be state action and invalid as discriminatory under the Fourteenth Amendment. The test was said to be whether the Committee operated as representative of the State in the discharge of the State's authority. *Nixon* v. *Condon*, 286 U. S. 73. The question of the inherent power of a political party in Texas "without restraint by any law to determine its own membership" was left open. *Id.*, 84–85.

In *Grovey* v. *Townsend*, 295 U. S. 45, this Court had before it another suit for damages for the refusal in a primary of a county clerk, a Texas officer with only public functions to perform, to furnish petitioner, a Negro, an absentee ballot. The refusal was solely on the ground of race. This case differed from *Nixon* v. *Condon, supra,* in that a state convention of the Democratic party had passed the resolution of May 24, 1932, hereinbefore quoted. It was decided that the determination by the state convention of the membership of the Democratic party made a significant change from a determination by the Executive Committee. The former was party action, voluntary in character. The latter, as had been held in the *Condon* case, was action by authority of the State. The managers of the primary election were therefore declared not to be state officials in such sense that their action was state action. A state convention of a party was said not to be an organ of the State. This Court went on to announce that to deny a vote in a primary was a mere refusal of party membership with which "the State need have no concern," *loc. cit.* at 55, while for a State to deny a vote in a general election on the ground of race or color violated the Constitution. Consequently, there was found no ground for holding that the county clerk's refusal of a ballot because of racial ineligibility for party membership denied the petitioner any right under the Fourteenth or Fifteenth Amendment.

Since *Grovey* v. *Townsend* and prior to the present suit, no case from Texas involving primary elections has been before this Court. We did decide, however, *United States* v. *Classic*, 313 U. S. 299. We there held that § 4 of Article I of the Constitution authorized Congress to regulate primary as well as general elections, 313 U. S. at 316, 317, "where the primary is by law made an integral part of the election machinery." 313 U. S. at 318. Consequently, in the *Classic* case, we upheld the applicability to frauds in a Louisiana primary of §§ 19 and 20 of the Criminal Code. Thereby corrupt acts of election officers were subjected to Congressional sanctions because that body had power to protect rights of federal suffrage secured by the Constitution in primary as in general elections. 313 U. S. at 323. This decision depended, too, on the determination that under the Louisiana statutes the primary was a part of the procedure for choice of federal officials. By this decision the doubt as to whether or not such primaries were a part of "elections" subject to federal control, which had remained unanswered since *Newberry* v. *United States*, 256 U. S. 232, was erased. The *Nixon Cases* were decided under the equal protection clause of the Fourteenth Amendment without a determination of the status of the primary as a part of the electoral process. The exclusion of Negroes from the primaries by action of the State was held invalid under that Amendment. The fusing by the *Classic* case of the primary and general elections into a single instrumentality for choice of officers has a definite bearing on the permissibility under the Constitution of excluding Negroes from primaries. This is not to say that the *Classic* case cuts directly into the rationale of *Grovey* v. *Townsend*. This latter case was not mentioned in the opinion. *Classic* bears upon *Grovey* v. *Townsend* not because exclusion of Negroes from primaries is any more or less state action by reason of the unitary character of the electoral process but because the recognition of the place of the primary in the electoral scheme makes clear that state delegation to a party of the power to fix the qualifications of primary elections is delegation of a state function that may make the party's action the action of the State. When *Grovey* v. *Townsend* was written, the Court looked upon the denial of a vote in a primary as a mere refusal by a party of party membership. 295 U. S. at 55. As the Louisiana statutes for holding primaries are similar to those of Texas, our ruling in *Classic* as to the unitary character of the electoral process calls for a re-

**293**

examination as to whether or not the exclusion of Negroes from a Texas party primary was state action.

The statutes of Texas relating to primaries and the resolution of the Democratic party of Texas extending the privileges of membership to white citizens only are the same in substance and effect today as they were when *Grovey* v. *Townsend* was decided by a unanimous Court. The question as to whether the exclusionary action of the party was the action of the State persists as the determinative factor. In again entering upon consideration of the inference to be drawn as to state action from a substantially similar factual situation, it should be noted that *Grovey* v. *Townsend* upheld exclusion of Negroes from primaries through the denial of party membership by a party convention. A few years before, this Court refused approval of exclusion by the State Executive Committee of the party. A different result was reached on the theory that the Committee action was state authorized and the Convention action was unfettered by statutory control. Such a variation in the result from so slight a change in form influences us to consider anew the legal validity of the distinction which has resulted in barring Negroes from participating in the nominations of candidates of the Democratic party in Texas. Other precedents of this Court forbid the abridgement of the right to vote. *United States* v. *Reese*, 92 U. S. 214, 217; *Neal* v. *Delaware*, 103 U. S. 370, 388; *Guinn* v. *United States*, 238 U. S. 347, 361; *Myers* v. *Anderson*, 238 U. S. 368, 379; *Lane* v. *Wilson*, 307 U. S. 268.

It may now be taken as a postulate that the right to vote in such a primary for the nomination of candidates without discrimination by the State, like the right to vote in a general election, is a right secured by the Constitution. *United States* v. *Classic*, 313 U. S. at 314; *Myers* v. *Anderson*, 238 U. S. 368; *Ex parte Yarbrough*, 110 U. S. 651, 663 *et seq.* By the terms of the Fifteenth Amendment that right may not be abridged by any State on account of race. Under our Constitution the great privilege of the ballot may not be denied a man by the State because of his color.

We are thus brought to an examination of the qualifications for Democratic primary electors in Texas, to determine whether state action or private action has excluded Negroes from participation. Despite Texas' decision that the exclusion is produced by private or party action, *Bell* v. *Hill, supra,* federal courts must for themselves appraise the facts leading to that conclusion. It is only by the performance of this obligation that a final and uniform interpretation can be given to the Constitution, the "supreme Law of the Land." *Nixon* v. *Condon,* 286 U. S. 73, 88;

*Standard Oil Co.* v. *Johnson,* 316 U. S. 481, 483; *Bridges* v. *California,* 314 U. S. 252; *Lisenba* v. *California,* 314 U. S. 219, 238; *Union Pacific R. Co.* v. *United States,* 313 U. S. 450, 467; *Drivers Union* v. *Meadowmoor Co.,* 312 U. S. 287, 294; *Chambers* v. *Florida,* 309 U. S. 227, 228. Texas requires electors in a primary to pay a poll tax. Every person who does so pay and who has the qualifications of age and residence is an acceptable voter for the primary. Art. 2955. As appears above in the summary of the statutory provisions set out in note 6, Texas requires by the law the election of the county officers of a party. These compose the county executive committee. The county chairmen so selected are members of the district executive committee and choose the chairman for the district. Precinct primary election officers are named by the county executive committee. Statutes provide for the election by the voters of precinct delegates to the county convention of a party and the selection of delegates to the district and state conventions by the county convention. The state convention selects the state executive committee. No convention may place in platform or resolution any demand for specific legislation without endorsement of such legislation by the voters in a primary. Texas thus directs the selection of all party officers.

Primary elections are conducted by the party under state statutory authority. The county executive committee selects precinct election officials and the county, district or state executive committees, respectively, canvass the returns. These party committees or the state convention certify the party's candidates to the appropriate officers for inclusion on the official ballot for the general election. No name which has not been so certified may appear upon the ballot for the general election as a candidate of a political party. No other name may be printed on the ballot which has not been placed in nomination by qualified voters who must take oath that they did not participate in a primary for the selection of a candidate for the office for which the nomination is made.

The state courts are given exclusive original jurisdiction of contested elections and of mandamus proceedings to compel party officers to perform their statutory duties.

We think that this statutory system for the selection of party nominees for inclusion on the general election ballot makes the party which is required to follow these legislative directions an agency of the State in so far as it determines the participants in a primary election. The party takes its character as a state agency from the duties imposed upon it by state statutes; the duties do not become matters of private law because they are performed by a political party. The plan of the Texas primary

**295**

follows substantially that of Louisiana, with the exception that in Louisiana the State pays the cost of the primary while Texas assesses the cost against candidates. In numerous instances, the Texas statutes fix or limit the fees to be charged. Whether paid directly by the State or through state requirements, it is state action which compels. When primaries become a part of the machinery for choosing officials, state and national, as they have here, the same tests to determine the character of discrimination or abridgement should be applied to the primary as are applied to the general election. If the State requires a certain electoral procedure, prescribes a general election ballot made up of party nominees so chosen and limits the choice of the electorate in general elections for state offices, practically speaking, to those whose names appear on such a ballot, it endorses, adopts and enforces the discrimination against Negroes, practiced by a party entrusted by Texas law with the determination of the qualifications of participants in the primary. This is state action within the meaning of the Fifteenth Amendment. *Guinn* v. *United States,* 238 U. S. 347, 362.

The United States is a constitutional democracy. Its organic law grants to all citizens a right to participate in the choice of elected officials without restriction by any State because of race. This grant to the people of the opportunity for choice is not to be nullified by a State through casting its electoral process in a form which permits a private organization to practice racial discrimination in the election. Constitutional rights would be of little value if they could be thus indirectly denied. *Lane* v. *Wilson,* 307 U. S. 268, 275.

The privilege of membership in a party may be, as this Court said in *Grovey* v. *Townsend,* 295 U. S. 45, 55, no concern of a State. But when, as here, that privilege is also the essential qualification for voting in a primary to select nominees for a general election, the State makes the action of the party the action of the State. In reaching this conclusion we are not unmindful of the desirability of continuity of decision in constitutional questions. However, when convinced of former error, this Court has never felt constrained to follow precedent. In constitutional questions, where correction depends upon amendment and not upon legislative action this Court throughout its history has freely exercised its power to reexamine the basis of its constitutional decisions. This has long been accepted practice,[9] and this practice has continued to this day.[10] This is particularly true when the decision believed erroneous is the application of

[9 and 10 These footnotes collect cases in which the Supreme Court has overruled prior constitutional decisions.]

a constitutional principle rather than an interpretation of the Constitution to extract the principle itself. Here we are applying, contrary to the recent decision in *Grovey* v. *Townsend,* the well-established principle of the Fifteenth Amendment, forbidding the abridgement by a State of a citizen's right to vote. *Grovey* v. *Townsend* is overruled.

*Judgment reversed.*

MR. JUSTICE FRANKFURTER concurs in the result.

MR. JUSTICE ROBERTS:

In *Mahnich* v. *Southern Steamship Co.,* 321 U. S. 96, 105, I have expressed my views with respect to the present policy of the court freely to disregard and to overrule considered decisions and the rules of law announced in them. This tendency, it seems to me, indicates an intolerance for what those who have composed this court in the past have conscientiously and deliberately concluded, and involves an assumption that knowledge and wisdom reside in us which was denied to our predecessors. I shall not repeat what I there said for I consider it fully applicable to the instant decision, which but points the moral anew. . . .

[Mr. Justice Roberts then reviews the *Nixon* cases and *Grovey* v. *Townsend.*]

I believe it will not be gainsaid the case [*Grovey* v. *Townsend*] received the attention and consideration which the questions involved demanded and the opinion represented the views of all the justices. It appears that those views do not now commend themselves to the court. I shall not restate them. They are exposed in the opinion and must stand or fall on their merits. Their soundness, however, is not a matter which presently concerns me.

The reason for my concern is that the instant decision, overruling that announced about nine years ago, tends to bring adjudications of this tribunal into the same class as a restricted railroad ticket, good for this day and train only. I have no assurance, in view of current decisions, that the opinion announced today may not shortly be repudiated and overruled by justices who deem they have new light on the subject. . . .

I do not stop to call attention to the material differences between the primary election laws of Louisiana under consideration in the *Classic* case and those of Texas which are here drawn in question. These differences were spelled out in detail in the Government's brief in the *Classic* case and emphasized in its oral argument. It is enough to say that the Louisiana statutes required the primary to be conducted by state officials and made it a state election, whereas, under the Texas statute, the primary is a party election conducted at the expense of members of the party and by officials chosen by the party. If this court's opinion in the *Classic* case discloses its method of overruling earlier decisions, I can only protest that, in fairness, it should rather have adopted the open and frank way of saying what it was doing than, after the event, characterize its past action as overruling *Grovey* v. *Townsend* though those less sapient never realized the fact.

It is regrettable that in an era marked by doubt and confusion, an era whose greatest need is steadfastness of thought and purpose, this court, which has been looked to as exhibiting consistency in adjudication, and a steadiness which would hold the balance even in the face of temporary ebbs and flows of opinion, should now itself become the breeder of fresh doubt and confusion in the public mind as to the stability of our institutions.

## Note

1. *Smith v. Allwright* is discussed in Cushman, *The Texas "White Primary" Case—Smith v. Allwright*, 30 Corn. L. Q. 66 (1944); Hastie, *Appraisal of Smith v. Allwright*, 5 Law. Guild Rev. 65 (1945); Notes, 23 Ore. L. Rev. 264 (1944); 22 Tex. L. Rev. 498 (1944). For analysis of the cases leading up to *Smith v. Allwright* see Evans, *Primary Elections and the Constitution*, 32 Mich. L. Rev. 451 (1934); Mangum, *The Legal Status of the Negro*, pp. 410–24 (1940); Notes and articles, 41 Yale L. J. 1212 (1932); 43 Col. L. Rev. 1026 (1943); 20 Temple L. Q. 488 (1947).

2. The Supreme Court's decision in *Smith v. Allwright* had an important effect upon Negro suffrage in the South. Texas made no further effort to maintain the white primary. The same result followed in Tennessee and North Carolina, where the system had already tended to disappear, and in Virginia where it had been outlawed by a lower Federal court decision some years before. After further litigation the system was abandoned in Alabama, Florida, Georgia and Louisiana. See Note, *Negro Disenfranchisement—A Challenge to the Constitution*, 47 Col. L. Rev. 76, 78–80 (1947) (collecting the cases); Weeks, *The White Primary: 1944–1948*, 42 Am. Pol. Sci. Rev. 500 (1948); Key, *Southern Politics*, pp. 625–43 (1949). However, Arkansas, Mississippi and, notably, South Carolina sought further legal devices to perpetuate the white primary. The South Carolina story appears in *Rice v. Elmore* and *Brown v. Baskin*.

## RICE v. ELMORE

United States Court of Appeals for the Fourth Circuit, 1947
165 F. 2d 387, cert. den. 333 U. S. 875

Before PARKER, SOPER and DOBIE, Circuit Judges.

PARKER, Circuit Judge.

This is an appeal from a decree adjudging that Negroes are entitled to vote in Democratic primary elections in South Carolina and enjoining defendants, who conduct such elections, from denying to Negro electors the right to vote therein. Plaintiff, who has brought this as a class suit in behalf of all Negro electors similarly situated, is a Negro duly qualified to vote under the Constitution and laws of the State of South Carolina. He has been denied the right to vote in the Democratic primary of that state by rules promulgated by the Democratic Party limiting the right to vote in the primary to white persons. The defendants are officials of the Democratic Party of South Carolina, who have charge of the primary in the county and precinct where plaintiff resides. . . .

For half a century or more the Democratic Party has absolutely controlled the choice of elective officers in the State of South Carolina. The real elections within that state have been contests within the Democratic Party, the general elections serving only to ratify and give legal validity to the party choice. So well has this been recognized that only a comparatively few persons participate in the general elections. In the election of 1946, for instance, 290,223 votes were cast for Governor in the Democratic primary, only 26,326 in the general election.

In South Carolina, as in most other states of the Union, the primary had become an integral part of the election machinery recognized and regulated by law. Article II, sec. 10, of the State Constitution of 1895 directed that the Legislature provide by law for the regulation of party primary elections, and pursuant thereto a complete set of primary laws had been adopted and were in effect when the Supreme Court of the United States decided the case of Smith v. Allwright, 321 U. S. 649, 64 S. Ct. 757, 88 L. Ed. 987, 151 A. L. R. 1110, holding that the right to vote in a primary election held under state law might not be denied on the ground of race or color. Immediately following this decision, the then Governor of South Carolina convened the state legislature and recommended that it repeal all laws with relation to primaries with the avowed purpose of preventing voting by Negroes in the Democratic primaries of the state. Pursuant to this recommendation, the primary laws of the state were repealed and the Democratic primary was conducted thereafter under rules prescribed by the Democratic Party. That the primary when conducted by the party fulfilled the same function in the election machinery of the state and was managed in practically the same way as when conducted under state law, does not admit of doubt. With respect to this, the District Judge, after describing the procedure when the statutes regulating the primary were in effect, went on to say [72 F. Supp. 525]:

"In 1944 substantially the same process was gone through, although at that time and before the State Convention assembled, the statutes had been repealed by action of the General Assembly, heretofore set out. The State Convention that year adopted a complete new set of rules and regulations, these however embodying practically all of the provisions of the repealed statutes. Some minor changes were made but these amounted to very little more than the usual change of procedure in detail from year to year. . . .

"In 1946 substantially the same procedure was used in the organization of the Democratic Party and another set of rules adopted which were substantially the same as the 1944 rules, excepting that the voting age was lowered to 18 and party officials were allowed the option of using voting machines, and the rules relative to absentee voting were simplified . . ."

The question presented for our decision is whether, by permitting a party to take over a part of its election machinery, a state can avoid the provisions of the Constitution forbidding racial discrimination in elections and can deny to a part of the electorate, because of race and color, any effective voice in the government of the state. It seems perfectly clear that this question must be answered in the negative.

The fundamental error in defendant's position consists in the premise that a political party is a mere private aggregation of individuals, like a country club, and that the primary is a mere piece of party machinery. The party may, indeed, have been a mere private aggregation of individuals in the early days of the Republic, but with the passage of the years, political parties have become in effect state institutions, governmental agencies through which sovereign power is exercised by the people. Party primaries are of more recent growth. Originating in the closing years of the last century as a means of making parties more responsive to the popular will in the nomination of candidates for office, they had been adopted by 1917 in all except four of the states of the Union as a vital and integral part of the state election machinery. Encylopedia of the Social Sciences, vol. 6, p. 396.

. . .

As primaries have become imbedded in the election machinery of the country, there has come gradually a recognition by the courts of the function they perform and the application to them of the laws relating to elections. In the Newberry case [256 U. S. 232], decided in 1921, the Supreme Court, by a bare majority, had held the Federal Corrupt Practices Act, 2 U. S. C. A. § 241 et seq., not applicable to a primary election held for United States Senator under a law adopted prior to the 17th Amendment. In United States v. Classic, 313 U. S. 299, 61 S. Ct. 1031, 85 L. Ed. 1368, decided in 1941, however, it was expressly held that a primary was an election within the meaning of art. 1 sec. 4 of the Constitution and the court pointed out that the Newberry case could not be considered authority to the contrary. . . .

[Here the Court discusses the *Herndon, Condon, Townsend* and *Allwright* cases.]

It is true, as defendants point out, that the primary involved in Smith v. Allwright was conducted under the provisions of state law and not merely under party rules, as is the case here, but we do not think this a controlling distinction. State law relating to the general election gives effect to what is done in the primary and makes it just as much a part of the election machinery of the state by which the people choose their officers as if it were regulated by law, as formerly. Elections in South Carolina remain a two step process, whether the party primary be accounted a preliminary of the general election, or the general election be regarded as giving effect to what is done in the primary; and those who control the Democratic Party as well as the state government cannot by placing the first of the steps under officials of the party rather than of the state, absolve such officials from the limitations which the federal Constitution imposes. When these officials participate in what is a part of the state's election machinery, they are election officers of the state de facto if not de jure, and as such must observe the limitations of the Constitution. Having undertaken to perform an important function relating to the exercise of sovereignty by the people, they may not violate the fundamental principles laid down by the Constitution for its exercise. Cf. Steele v. Louisville & N. R. Co., 323 U. S. 192, 65 S. Ct. 226, 89 L. Ed. 173; Kerr v. Enoch Pratt Free Library, 4 Cir., 149 F. 2d 212, 218. As said in the case last cited, "We know of no reason why the state cannot create separate agencies to carry on its work in this manner, and when it does so, they become subject to the constitutional restraints imposed upon the state itself." . . .

[Here the Court discusses the *Classic* case.]

An essential feature of our form of government is the right of the citizen to participate in the governmental process. The political philosophy of the Declaration of Independence is that governments derive their just powers from the consent of the governed; and the right to a voice in the selection of officers of government on the part of all citizens is important, not only as a means of insuring that government shall have the strength of popular support, but also as a means of securing to the individual citizen proper consideration of his rights by those in power. The disfranchised can never speak with the same force as those who are able to vote. The Fourteenth and Fifteenth Amendments were written into the Constitution to insure to the Negro, who had recently been liberated from slavery, the equal protection of the laws and the right to full participation in the process of government. These amendments have had the effect of creating a federal basis of citizenship and of protecting the rights of individuals and minorities from many abuses of governmental power which were not contemplated at the time. Their primary purpose must not be lost sight of, however; and no election machinery can be upheld if its purpose or effect is to deny to the Negro, on account of his race or color, any effective voice in the government of his country or the state or community wherein he lives. . . .

Affirmed.

## Note

The case is discussed in Note, *Negro Disenfranchisement—A Challenge to the Constitution*, 47 Col. L. Rev. 76, 80–90 (1947); and Notes, 46 Mich. L. Rev. 793 (1948); 33 Iowa L. Rev. 412 (1948); 19 Miss. L. Rev. 244 (1948); 15 U. of Chi. L. Rev. 756 (1948); 1 Vand. L. Rev. 645 (1948).

## BROWN v. BASKIN

United States District Court for the Eastern District of
South Carolina, 1948
78 F. Supp. 933

[Following the denial of certiorari by the Supreme Court in *Rice v. Elmore*, the Democratic Party of South Carolina met in convention and adopted certain changes in the rules governing party organization and the conduct of primary elections. The Party was organized into clubs, open only to white Democrats. All duly enrolled club members were entitled to vote in the primaries. All qualified Negro electors were also entitled to vote in the primaries "if they present their general election

**302**

certificates." No person, white or Negro, could vote in the primary unless he took an oath which included the following:

"I further solemnly swear that I believe in and will support the principles of the Democratic Party of South Carolina, and that I believe in and will support the social and educational separation of races.

"I further solemnly swear that I believe in the principles of States' Rights, and that I am opposed to the proposed Federal so-called F. E. P. C. law."

Brown, a Negro qualified elector, brought suit on behalf of himself and others similarly situated against the Democratic Party officials of South Carolina under 8 U. S. C. §§ 31 and 43. Brown sought declaratory and injunctive relief to compel defendants to enroll him and other Negroes as Democratic Party members, to cease discrimination by requiring of Negroes a general election certificate in order to vote, and to permit Negroes to vote without taking the oath.

The matter came before Judge Waring on a motion for preliminary injunction, which would allow plaintiff and others to participate in the forthcoming primaries.]

WARING, District Judge . . .

The action of the Democratic State Convention in May 1948 was therefore [in light of the previous decision in *Rice v. Elmore, supra*] somewhat of a surprie to all who had any knowledge of the matter. The convention frankly set up two standards of qualifications for voting: one applicable to the members of the white race, and the other to Negroes. This of course was in direct contradiction of all law and custom, which must or should have been well known to any students or even casual inquirers in regard to such matters. Such a flagrant disregard of basic rights must have sprung from either gross ignorance or a conscious determination to evade the issue and to refuse to obey the law of the land. It is hardly credible that a convention composed of a large number of persons, many of whom have had long years of experience and were experts in political matters and a number of whom had actually taken part in the presentation and hearings of the Elmore case as attorneys or witnesses, should have been so crassly ignorant. It would therefore seem that the action of the convention was a deliberate attempt to evade the apparent consequence of the Elmore case. This belief is further supported by the fact that no apparent attention was paid to the opinion that was filed in the Elmore case and only the bald language of the order was followed. The order in that case was based entirely upon the prayer of the complaint but the

**303**

opinion discussed the whole matter of voting in primaries in this State, together with all of its implications, and this court said (72 F. Supp. at page 528):

"The plaintiff and others similarly situated are entitled to *be enrolled* and to vote in the primaries conducted by the Democratic Party of South Carolina." (Emphasis added)

Of course it is true that that case applied only to the officials of Richland County, South Carolina, but the law was clearly and succinctly stated, and anyone who can read the English language must have known what it meant. So it is apparent that the rules above quoted (Rules 6 and 7), which provide for a double standard for the enrollment and voting of whites and Negroes, is a clear and flagrant evasion of the law as enunciated not only by this court but approved by the Circuit Court of Appeals for the Fourth Circuit and by the Supreme Court of the United States.

And the oath which was adopted by the convention (Rule 36) is another attempt to evade the American principle of allowing all persons to freely exercise the suffrage. To require, as a prerequisite to voting, that qualified electors take an oath subscribing to the views of the State Convention and/or its Executive Committee, is a flagrant disregard of the rights of American citizens to exercise their own views and opinions in the choice of representatives in their national government.

Neither in South Carolina nor in any other State in this union have American citizens as yet come to a pass where a group of party officials, in violation of basic American rights, can prescribe oaths, methods and a code of thought for voters. To carry this to its logical conclusion, it is wondered why the State Convention did not require an oath that all parties enrolling or voting should elect them in perpetuity and with satisfactory emoluments. The one party system has reached its apex in this State where the right is claimed not only to segregate according to race, to prescribe different methods of gaining the right to vote, to forbid participation in the organization for government of the party, but to prescribe mental tests and set up a code of thought which, far from being a bill of rights, might rather be called a bill of persecutions. . . .

It is important that once and for all, the members of this Party be made to understand—and that is the purpose of this opinion—that they will be required to obey and carry out the orders of this court, not only in the technical respects but in the true spirit and meaning of the same. This court is convinced that they are fully aware of what is the law, and it will not excuse further evasions, subterfuges or attempts to get around the same. It is time that either the present officials of the Party, or such as may be in the future chosen, realize that the people of the United States expect them to follow the American way of elections. It is believed that the great body of people in this State as well as in this Nation, truly believe in the American ideals and methods, and it is hoped that the actions of the Party officials do not represent the true view of the people of South Carolina. But irrespective of whether that be true or not, it becomes the duty of this court to say to the Party officials that they will have to obey the true intent of the law, which is so clear and apparent that even they must know what it is, and that no excuse or evasion in the future will be tolerated.

An Order providing for a Temporary Injunction will be issued.

. . .

[After further proceedings Judge Waring issued a permanent injunction. 80 F. Supp. 1017 (1948). The case was affirmed by the Court of Appeals in *Baskin v. Brown*, 174 F. 2d 391 (C. A. 4, 1949).]

## Note

1. Arkansas and Mississippi likewise sought to impose oaths unacceptable to Negro voters as a condition of voting in primaries. See Key, *Southern Politics*, pp. 637–43 (1949). These requirements are presumably invalid under *Brown v. Baskin*.

2. In *Perry v. Cyphers*, 186 F. 2d 608 (C. A. 5, 1951), suit was brought to prevent the Citizens Party of Harrison County, Texas, from refusing to permit Negroes to vote in primaries involving county and precinct officers. The Citizens Party was the dominant party in the county. The court followed the *Allwright* case and ordered an injunction granted.

In *Adams v. Terry*, 193 F. 2d 600 (C. A. 5, 1952), however, the same Court reached a different result. Here there had existed for some time in Fort Bend County, Texas, an organization known as the Jaybird Democratic Association of Fort Bend County. This organization, which excluded Negroes, held its own primaries for county and precinct officers each year several months before the regular Democratic primaries. The winner of the Jaybird primary could then enter the regular Democratic primary on his own. The Jaybird primaries were not conducted under Texas election statutes, and the winner was not certified to election officials nor given any status under the election laws. In practice, with a few exceptions, the person receiving the Jaybird endorsement was unopposed in the Democratic primary. In a suit for declaratory judgment under 8 U. S. C. §§ 31 and 43 the District Judge held that the prior cases controlled and that Negroes should be permitted to vote in the Jaybird primaries. The Court of Appeals reversed, saying that "the Jaybird Democratic Association does not in any way or manner operate as a part or parcel of, or in liason with, state political or elective machinery," and hence no state action was involved. Petition for certiorari was filed in the Supreme Court. 21 U. S. Law Week 3002.

3. For more general discussion of what constitutes "state action" under the Fourteenth and Fifteenth Amendments, see Hale, *Rights Under the Fourteenth and Fifteenth Amendments Against Injuries Inflicted by Private Individuals*, 6 Law. Guild Rev. 627 (1946) ; Note, *Negro Disenfranchisement—A Challenge to the Constitution*, 47 Col. L. Rev. 76, 85–90 (1947) ; Note, *The Disintegration of a Concept—State Action Under the 14th and 15th Amendments*, 96 U. Pa. L. Rev. 402 (1948); Note, 61 Harv. L. Rev. 344 (1948). See also Chapter IX, *infra*.

4. Following the white primary decisions several of the southern states changed their election laws, particularly with respect to educational, residence and similar requirements. This development is considered in the next section of this Chapter.

## E. EDUCATIONAL AND OTHER QUALIFICATIONS

Literacy, other educational, character and similar qualifications for voting have been established parts of the franchise system of a number of states for many years. On their face these requirements may be entirely reasonable, although the need for educational tests in a period of universal compulsory education has been questioned. Serious problems arise, however, from two circumstances. One is that qualifications of this kind can be manipulated to prescribe standards which will permit certain groups to vote but exclude others, the differentiation actually resting on grounds of race, religion or similar factors. The other is that these requirements are readily subject to discriminatory administration. Residence requirements may be manipulated in the same manner.

In the post-Civil War South educational, character and residence requirements were among the earliest of the quasi-legal devices employed to disenfranchise the Negro. Under the revised constitution of 1890, and subsequent legislation, Mississippi adopted a series of qualifications for voting which included, in addition to a cumulative poll tax, the requirements that an elector must (1) have a residence of two years in the state and one year in the election district; (2) register four months before an election; (3) not have been convicted of the crimes of bribery, burglary, theft, arson, obtaining money or goods under false pretenses, perjury, forgery, embezzlement or bigamy; (4) "be able to read any section of the Constitution of this State; or he shall be able to understand the same when read to him, or give a reasonable interpretation thereof"; and (5) swear that he will answer truthfully all questions put to him concerning his right to vote (false answers constituting perjury). The purpose of these requirements was frankly to prevent most Negroes from qualifying as voters.

In the next several years similar qualifications were adopted by South Carolina, Louisiana, North Carolina, Alabama, Virginia and Georgia. Most of them imposed the requirement that a voter be able to read and write a provision of the state constitution, and were also more restrictive in other ways.

The constitutionality of the Mississippi provisions was attacked in *Williams* v. *Mississippi*, 170 U. S. 213, 42 L. Ed. 1012, 18 S. Ct. 583 (1898). The issue arose collaterally in a murder case. The defendant, a Negro, moved to quash the indictment on the grounds that the grand jury was by law composed of electors and the constitutional and statutory provisions governing the qualification of electors were unconstitutional under the Fourteenth Amendment. Specifically it was argued that the provisions were intended to and did discriminate against Negro voters, that they conferred unfettered discretion upon election officials to register or not register voters, and that the provisions were being administered in a discriminatory manner. The Supreme Court rejected these contentions. It found the claim of discriminatory administration inadequately pleaded and concluded as to the other issues:

"If weakness were to be taken advantage of, it was to be done 'within the field of permissible action under the limitations imposed by the Federal Constitution,' and the means of it were the alleged characteristics of the negro race, not the administration of the law by officers of the State. Besides, the operation of the constitution and laws is not limited by their language or effects to one race. They reach weak and vicious white men as well as weak and vicious black men, and whatever is sinister in their intention, if anything, can be prevented by both races by the exertion of that duty which voluntarily pays taxes and refrains from crime.

"It cannot be said, therefore, that the denial of the equal protection of the laws arises primarily from the constitution and laws of Mississippi . . ." 170 U. S. at 222.

In *Pope* v. *Williams*, 193 U. S. 621, 48 L. Ed. 817, 24 S. Ct. 573 (1904), the Court upheld a Maryland residence requirement which provided that persons coming to live in the state from outside must file a declaration of intent to become residents and citizens, and were not eligible to vote until a year after making such a declaration.

One feature of the educational and character requirements did, somewhat later, fall before the Supreme Court. Many of the states, in order to avoid disenfranchising white voters, provided that the educational qualifications need not be met by certain classes of persons, so defined as to exclude Negroes. This device was known as the "grandfather clause". At one time it existed in seven states. The grandfather clause adopted by an amendment to the Oklahoma Constitution in 1910 provided that the literacy test (ability to read and write any section of the Oklahoma Constitution) should not be applicable to any person "who was, on January 1, 1866, or at any time prior thereto, entitled to vote under any form of government, or who at that time resided in some foreign nation, and [any] lineal descendant of such person." The Supreme Court, in 1915, held that this provision violated the Fifteenth Amendment. *Guinn* v. *U. S.,* 238 U. S. 347, 59 L. Ed. 1340, 35 S. Ct. 926 (1915). See also *Myers* v. *Anderson,* 238 U. S. 363, 59 L. Ed. 1349, 35 S. Ct. 932 (1915).

In 1916, soon after the *Guinn* decision, the legislature of Oklahoma passed a new registration law providing that those who had voted in the 1914 election (when the grandfather clause was in force) automatically remained qualified voters; that others must apply for registration between April 30 and May 11, 1916, if then qualified; and that those who did not then apply lost permanently the right to register. In 1939 the Supreme Court struck down this scheme under the Fifteenth Amendment, saying "The Amendment nullifies sophisticated as well as simple-minded modes of discrimination." *Lane* v. *Wilson,* 307 U. S. 268, 275, 83 L. Ed. 1281, 59 S. Ct. 872 (1939).

With the exception of the grandfather clauses, the educational, character, residence and similar requirements remained in operation in the southern states which originally adopted them. The most restrictive were the Georgia and Louisiana provisions that a prospective voter must "understand the duties and obligations of citizenship under a republican form of government," and the Louisiana and Mississippi provisions that he must give a "reasonable interpretation" of the Constitution of the United States.

More important than the abstract requirements, however, has been the factor of administration. Professor V. O. Key has said:

"A solemn recapitulation of the formal literacy and understanding requirements verges on the ridiculous. In practice literacy and understanding have little to do with the acquisition of the right to vote. Whether a person can register to vote depends on what the man down at the courthouse says, and he usually has the final say. It is how the tests are administered that matters."[1]

---

[1] Key, *Southern Politics,* p. 560 (1949).

Speaking of the administration of the qualifications in the southern states Professor Key concludes:

"No matter from what direction one looks at it, the southern literacy test is a fraud and nothing more. The simple fact seems to be that the constitutionally prescribed test of ability to read and write a section of the constitution is rarely administered to whites. It is applied chiefly to Negroes and not always to them. When Negroes are tested on their ability to read and write, only in exceptional instances is the test administered fairly. Insofar as is known, no southern registration official has utilized an objective test of literacy. In some states, of course, the constitution prescribes the method for testing, but in other states it would be legally possible to employ a simple objective test similar to that used by some northern states that prescribe literacy as a voting prerequisite.

"A literacy test fairly administered would even now exclude large numbers of Negroes from the suffrage and relatively few whites. It would also enable literate Negroes now excluded from the electorate to qualify to vote. . . ."[2]

Following the white primary decisions Alabama, Georgia and South Carolina revised their franchise systems to tighten up the educational and other registration provisions. The Alabama and Georgia laws were tested in *Davis* v. *Schnell* and *Franklin* v. *Harper,* set forth below.

### Note

For an account of the development of educational, character and residence qualifications in the South during the post-Civil War period, see Porter, *A History of Suffrage in the United States,* 208–27 (1918); Mangum, *The Legal Status of the Negro,* pp. 390–405 (1940). For discussion of the current provisions and their operation, see Key, *Southern Politics,* ch. 26 (1949); Davie, *Negroes in American Society,* pp. 264–5 (1949); McGovney, *The American Suffrage Medley,* ch. V (1949); Myrdal, *An American Dilemma,* pp. 479–484 (1944); Notes, 47 Col. L. Rev. 76, 90–2, 94–7 (1947); 49 Col. L. Rev. 1144 (1949). A discussion of the Oklahoma grandfather clause may be found in Monnet, *The Latest Phase of Negro Disfranchisement,* 26 Harv. L. Rev. 42 (1912).

---

[2] *Ibid.* p. 576.

## DAVIS v. SCHNELL

United States District Court for the Southern District
of Alabama, 1949

81 F. Supp. 872, aff'd 336 U. S. 933, 93 L. Ed. 1093, 69 S. Ct. 749 (1949)

Before McCORD, Circuit Judge, MULLINS and McDUFFIE, District Judges.

MULLINS, District Judge.

This case was tried before a duly constituted three-judge District Court.

Under the amended complaint, this suit is brought by ten Negro citizens of Mobile County, Alabama, against the Board of Registrars of said County and the individual members thereof, to declare and secure their rights to register as electors. The plaintiffs bring the action on their own behalf, and on behalf of all Alabama citizens similarly situated.

The plaintiffs allege that registration is a prerequisite of the right of a citizen of Alabama to vote in any election, Federal, State or local.

The plaintiffs allege that at a general election held on November 7, 1946, there was submitted to and adopted by the people of Alabama an amendment to Section 181 of the Constitution of Alabama (popularly called and referred to herein as the Boswell Amendment), changing the requirements for registration of electors so that only those persons who can "understand and explain" any article of the Federal Constitution can be registered as electors.[2] They allege that this amendment was purposely sponsored, its adoption obtained, and its provisions are being

---

[2] Section 181 of the Constitution of Alabama, as amended:
"After the first day of January, nineteen hundred and three, the following persons, and no others, who, if their place of residence shall remain unchanged, will have, at the date of the next general election, the qualifications as to residence, prescribed in section 178 of this article, shall be qualified to register as electors provided they shall not be disqualified under section 182 of this constitution: those who can read and write, understand and explain any article of the constitution of the United States in the English language and who are physically unable to work and those who can read and write, understand and explain any article of the constitution of the United States in the English language and who have worked or been regularly engaged in some lawful employment, business, or occupation, trade, or calling for the greater part of the twelve months next preceding the time they offer to register, including those who are unable to read and write if such inability is due solely to physical disability; provided, however, no persons shall be entitled to register as electors except those who are of good character and who understand the duties and obligations of good citizenship under a republican form of government." [Amend. No. 55].

**310**

administered so as to prevent the plaintiffs and others, because of their race, from exercising their right to vote.

The plaintiffs aver that they appeared before the defendants, members of the Board of Registrars for Mobile County, Alabama, and, acting under color of law, the defendants required the plaintiffs, all members of the Negro race, to explain an article of the Federal Constitution, which they did, and the defendants informed them that the defendants were not satisfied with the explanations given, and refused to register them.

It is further averred that said Section 181, as amended, requiring applicants for registration to "understand and explain" any article of the United States Constitution, together with the provisions of Title 17, Section 33, Code of Alabama 1940,[3] vests in the Board of Registrars unlimited discretion to grant or deny the plaintiffs and others similarly situated the right to register as electors; that said Amendment provides no definite, reasonable or recognizable standard or test to be applied in determining the qualifications of electors; that defendants refused to register plaintiffs and other qualified Negro applicants, while at the same time defendants were registering white applicants with less qualifications; that plaintiffs, solely because of their race and color, were required to make lengthy explanations of articles of the Constitution of the United States, while white applicants were being registered without being required to make any such explanations. . . .

Plaintiffs seek a declaratory judgment declaring the Boswell Amendment unconstitutional and ask for injunctive relief against the further enforcement of the provisions of the same. Plaintiffs waived their prayer for damages.

The defendant board and two of the individual members thereof answered the complaint. They deny that the Boswell Amendment is unconstitutional and deny that they administer the registration laws differently as to white and Negro applicants, and aver that they administer the laws fairly to all applicants for registration, without regard to race or color. . . .

Only two of the plaintiffs, Hunter Davis and Julius B. Cook, testified on the trial. From the evidence we find that these two plaintiffs presented themselves to the defendant board seeking to register as electors and that they presented satisfactory evidence of their qualifications to register as electors, but their applications were denied. The evidence shows they had the residen-

---

3 Title 17, Section 33, Code of Alabama 1940:

"Any person making application to the board of registrars for registration who fails to establish by evidence to the reasonable satisfaction of the board of registrars that he or she is qualified to register, may be refused registration."

tial qualifications prescribed by Section 178 of the Constitution of Alabama, having continuously resided in the State of Alabama, in the County of Mobile, and in the precinct or ward where they lived for more than two years immediately preceding the time when they applied for registration; that they were over the age of twenty-one years, and had been regularly engaged in lawful employment, business or occupation for the greater part of the twelve months next preceding the time at which they offered to register; that they are citizens of Alabama and of the United States, of good character, and possess all other qualifications of electors, unless it be said that they can be required to "understand and explain" any article of the United States Constitution to the reasonable satisfaction of the members of the defendant board. These two plaintiffs have none of the disqualifications set out in Section 182 of the Alabama Constitution.

We further find from the evidence that prior to the filing of this suit said Board of Registrars required Negro applicants for registration as electors in Mobile County to attempt to explain at least some article of the United States Constitution, while no such requirement was exacted of white applicants. We also find that the plaintiffs Davis and Cook were refused registration as electors because of their race or color.

Prior to this suit defendant board did not keep records of rejected applicants, whether white or Negro. The members of said board went into office on October, 1947. Registration records of said board, which were not disputed, were introduced showing that during their tenure, prior to March 1, 1948 (the filing date of this suit), 39 colored applicants were registered; that subsequent to March 1, 1948, 65 colored applicants were registered and 57 were rejected, the records of these 57 rejected applicants showing, in substance, that they were rejected because they could not "understand and explain" an article of the Federal Constitution. These records show that three white persons who were registered after this action was filed were asked to explain a provision of the Federal Constitution. The records of 11 rejected white applicants show that they were denied registration on grounds other than the requirements of the Boswell Amendment. The defendants offered nine colored witnesses, all of whom with one exception were public school teachers of good education, who testified that they were registered by the defendant board, some of them being asked if they could explain provisions of the Federal Constitution. The members of the defendant board generally required Negro applicants to explain or interpret provisions of the Federal Constitution, and did not generally require white applicants to do so.

The evidence shows that during the incumbency of the defendant board that more than 2800 white persons have been registered and approximately 104 Negroes. The estimated population of Mobile County is 230,000 of which approximately 64 per cent is white and 36 per cent is colored.

The States, not the Federal Government, prescribe the qualifications for the exercise of the franchise, and Federal Courts are not interested in these qualifications unless they contravene the Fifteenth Amendment or other provisions of the United States Constitution. The States have a right to prescribe a literacy test for electors. Guinn v. United States, 238 U. S. 347, 35 S. Ct. 926, 59 L. Ed. 1340, L. R. A. 1916A, 1124. However, state action which denies due process or equal protection of the laws in the exercise of the right of suffrage is prohibited by the Fourteenth Amendment. Nixon v. Herndon, 273 U. S. 536, 47 S. Ct. 446, 71 L. Ed. 759; Nixon v. Condon, 286 U. S. 73, 52 S. Ct. 484, 76 L. Ed. 984, 88 A. L. R. 458. The Fifteenth Amendment guarantees the free exercise of the right of franchise as against state discrimination based upon race or color. Guinn v. United States, supra; Lane v. Wilson, 307 U. S. 268, 59 S. Ct. 872, 83 L. Ed. 1281.

The subject matter of the Boswell Amendment is within state power, and its validity depends upon whether it squares with the Fourteenth and Fifteenth Amendments. We think it does not.

The original Section 181 of the Constitution of Alabama has stood for nearly 50 years and has provided definite standards for passing upon the qualifications of prospective electors. The original section provided for two qualifications, the possession of either of which was sufficient to permit registration. An applicant was required to be able to "read and write any article of the constitution of the United States in the English language," or in the alternative, he could qualify if he owned, assessed and paid taxes on real or personal property of an assessed value of $300. The Boswell Amendment dropped the property qualification, and adopted a qualification requiring not only that an applicant be able to "read and write" but also that he be able to "understand and explain any article of the constitution of the United States in the English language."

Do the words "understand and explain" as used in the Boswell Amendment furnish a reasonable standard whereby boards of registrars may pass on qualifications of prospective electors, or are these words so ambiguous, uncertain, and indefinite in meaning that they confer upon said boards arbitrary power to register or to refuse to register whomever they please.

**313**

"Understand" is a word of many meanings and "a verb of very extensive signification." Understanding may be based upon learning or knowledge or upon rumor or hearsay. It may mean to apprehend, or to comprehend, partially or fully. It may deal with meaning, import, intention or motive. It may mean to appreciate the force or value of a thing or proposition. It may mean that a person is informed or that he had merely received notice or heard of something. To understand may mean to imply, infer or assume, or it may contemplate knowing the meaning or the supposed meaning. It may mean to interpret.

"Explain" is also a word of indefinite meaning; it may mean to make plain, manifest or intelligible; to clear of obscurity; to expound, to illustrate by discourse or by notes.

The Boswell Amendment requires a prospective elector to "understand and explain any article of the constitution of the United States in the English language." There is no requirement that the understanding or explanation be in writing. The language does not call for a simple, fair or reasonable understanding or explanation. It does not say that the understanding and explanation must be partial, full, complete, definite, proper, fair, reasonable, plain, precise, correct, accurate, or give any rule, guide or test as to the nature of the understanding or explanation that is required. The Amendment does not say to whose satisfaction the applicant must "understand and explain," but under the statutes, it must be to the reasonable satisfaction of a majority of the members of one of the 67 boards of registrars that are provided for the 67 counties of Alabama.

The members of these boards are not required to be lawyers or learned in the law, and it is fair to assume that many members of these boards do not have a good or correct understanding of the various articles of the Constitution, and that they might not be able to give any explanation of many of them. Many members of the boards of registrars might justly and properly say to an applicant for registration, "My legs do better understand me, sir, than I understand what you mean."

No uniform, objective or standardized test or examination is provided whereby an impartial board could determine whether the applicant has a reasonable understanding and can give a reasonable explanation of the articles of the Constitution (if, indeed, the test were to be a *reasonable* understanding and a *reasonable* explanation). If such a test or examination were provided to be administered to all prospective electors alike, then the boards of registrars would have definite guides to control their judgment in determining whether or not an applicant could "understand and explain" the provisions of the Constitution.

Under such a test with proper questions or guides a record could be made which would give a rejected applicant a definite basis upon which he could seek and obtain a proper judicial review of the board's action, and the reviewing court would have something definite to act upon in ascertaining whether an applicant had been rightfully or arbitrarily and unjustly denied the right of suffrage.

As pointed out, "understand" may mean to interpret. This meaning requires an exceedingly high, if not impossible, standard. The distinguished Justices of the Supreme Court of the United States have frequently disagreed in their interpretations of various articles of the Constitution. We learn from history that many of the makers of the Constitution did not understand its provisions; many of them understood and believed that its provisions gave the Supreme Court no power to declare an act of Congress unconstitutional. An understanding or explanation given by the Supreme Court a few years ago as to the meaning of the commerce clause does not apply today. Among our most learned judges there are at least four different understandings and explanations of the Fourteenth Amendment to the Constitution as to whether it made the first eight Amendments applicable to state action.[7] Such a rigorous standard—to interpret—is clearly within the legitimate range of the meanings of the phrase "understand and explain," and illustrates the completeness with which any individual or group of prospective electors, whether white or Negro, may be deprived of the right of franchise by boards of registrars inclined to apply this one of the innumerable meanings of such an indefinite phrase.

The words "understand and explain" do not provide a reasonable standard. A simple test may be given one applicant; a long, tedious, complex one to another; one applicant may be examined on one article of the Constitution; another may be called upon to "understand and explain" every article and provision of the entire instrument.

To state it plainly, the sole test is: Has the applicant by oral examination or otherwise understood and explained the Constitution to the satisfaction of the particular board? To state it more plainly, the board has a right to reject one applicant and accept another, depending solely upon whether it likes or dislikes the understanding and explanation offered. To state it even more plainly, the board, by the use of the words "understand and explain," is given the arbitrary power to accept or reject any prospective elector that may apply, or, to use the language of

---

[7] Cf. *Adamson v. California*, 1947, 332 U. S. 46, 67 S. Ct. 1672, 91 L. Ed. 1903, 171 A. L. R. 1223.

Yick Wo v. Hopkins, 118 U. S. 356, 366, 6 S. Ct. 1064, 1069, 30 L. Ed. 220, these words "actually do confer not a discretion to be exercised upon a consideration of the circumstances of each case, but a naked and arbitrary power to give or withhold consent . . . ." The board has the power to establish two classes, those to whom they consent and those to whom they do not—those who may vote and those who may not. Such arbitrary power amounts to a denial of equal protection of the law within the meaning of the Fourteenth Amendment to the Constitution, and is condemned by the Yick.Wo and many other decisions of the Supreme Court.

When a word or phrase in a statute or constitution is ambiguous, it is the duty of the court, in construing the meaning of that word or phrase, to attempt to determine whether an exact meaning was intended and if so, to ascertain that meaning. If an exact meaning of the phrase "understand and explain" were to be discovered by a process of construction in this case, it might be that a suitable and definite standard could be found, which would not give to the board of registrars arbitrary power. However, a careful consideration of the legislative and other history of the adoption of this Amendment to the Constitution of Alabama discloses that the ambiguity inherent in the phrase "understand and explain" cannot be resolved, but, on the contrary, was purposeful and used with a view of meeting the decision of the Supreme Court of the United States in Smith v. Allwright, 321 U. S. 649, 64 S. Ct. 757, 88 L. Ed. 987, 151 A. L. R. 1110. The history of the period immediately preceding the adoption of the Boswell Amendment, of which we take judicial notice, and the evidence in this case prove this.

The State Democratic Executive Committee is an official arm of the State and its action constitutes state action. Smith v. Allwright, supra. The activities of this committee in sponsoring and leading the fight for the adoption of the Boswell Amendment are admissible and material in determining whether the Boswell Amendment is a contrivance by the State to thwart equality in the enjoyment of the right to vote by citizens of the United States on account of race or color.

The State Democratic Executive Committee spent its funds and led the fight to secure the adoption of the Boswell Amendment in its endeavor "to make the Democratic Party in Alabama the 'White Man's Party.' "[9] The chairman of this committee was

[9] In a letter dated August 27, 1946, addressed to the members of the State Democratic Executive Committee, the chairman of that committee, among other things, said . . .

"I might add that while a few members of our State Committee have expressed the thought that the funds of the State Committee should not be

instrumental in originating the Amendment and in making recommendations to the legislative committee as to changes he
deemed advisable in Alabama's election laws to meet the "Texas
case," under which Democratic primaries could no longer be
limited to white voters. An overwhelming majority of the
membership of this committee "took the position that we should
be Militant Democrats and continue to fight for white supremacy
in our State." . . .

In the Alabama Lawyer, the official organ of the State Bar of
Alabama, in the July 1946 issue, a distinguished Alabama lawyer,
writing in opposition to the adoption of the Boswell Amendment,
which was at that time awaiting action at the hands of the people
of Alabama, said:

"Let us be frank and honest with ourselves. You and I know
that the people of our State are expected to adopt this Amendment in order to give the Registrars arbitrary power to exclude
Negroes from voting."

In the October 1946 issue of the same official publication, an
equally distinguished Alabama lawyer, who favored the adoption
of the Boswell Amendment, declared with reference to that
Amendment:

". . . I earnestly favor a law that will make it impossible for
a Negro to qualify, if that is possible. If it is impossible, then
I favor a law, more especially a constitutional provision, that
will come as near as possible, making possible, the impossible."

All of the foregoing but illustrates the intention and general
understanding of the Legislature and electorate of Alabama at
the time this Amendment was proposed and adopted by a small
majority of a light vote. Such a history further demonstrates
that this restrictive Amendment, coming on the heels of the decision of the Supreme Court of the United States in the Smith
v. Allwright case, was intended as a grant of arbitrary power in
an attempt to obviate the consequences of that decision. . . .

The Alabama Democrat, a campaign document in the form
of a newspaper published in support of the adoption of the Boswell
Amendment consisted in its entirety of arguments urging the
voters to adopt the Amendment for the purpose of restricting

expended in a campaign either for or against the adoption of the proposed
'Boswell Amendment,' yet the great majority of the members of our Committee have taken the position that since the emblem of our Party is a
crowing rooster with the words 'White Supremacy' above the rooster, and
the words 'For the Right' below the rooster, that it is entirely proper that
the State Democratic Executive Committee should lead the fight to maintain the traditions of our Party in this State by adopting the proposed
amendment to our Constitution and endeavoring, as far as it can legally
be done, to make the Democratic Party in Alabama the 'White Man's Party.'" (From Plaintiffs' Exhibit 5)

**317**

voting by Negroes. This document carried the headline: "WARNING IS SOUNDED: BLACKS WILL TAKE OVER IF AMENDMENT LOSES" and the footline: "VOTE WHITE— VOTE RIGHT—VOTE FOR AMENDMENT NO. 4." . . .

Furthermore, the administration of the Boswell Amendment by the defendant board demonstrates that the ambiguous standard prescribed has, in fact, been arbitrarily used for the purpose of excluding Negro applicants for the franchise, while white applicants with comparable qualifications were being accepted. The evidence is without dispute that this Amendment has been used to disqualify many Negro applicants for registration while it does not definitely disclose that it has been used to disqualify a single white applicant. It is further shown that as a rule the Boswell test of "understand and explain" is required of Negroes while no such exaction is made of white applicants.

It, thus, clearly appears that this Amendment was intended to be, and is being used for the purpose of discriminating against applicants for the franchise on the basis of race or color. Therefore, we are necessarily brought to the conclusion that this Amendment to the Constitution of Alabama, both in its object and the manner of its administration, is unconstitutional, because it violates the Fifteenth Amendment. While it is true that there is no mention of race or color in the Boswell Amendment, this does not save it. The Fifteenth Amendment "nullifies sophisticated as well as simple-minded modes of discrimination," and "It hits onerous procedural requirements which effectively handicap exercise of the franchise by the colored race although the abstract right to vote may remain unrestricted as to race." Lane v. Wilson, 307 U. S. 268, 275, 59 S. Ct. 872, 876, 83 L. Ed. 1281. Cf. Smith v. Allwright, supra; Guinn v. United States, supra.

We cannot ignore the impact of the Boswell Amendment upon Negro citizens because it avoids mention of race or color; "To do this would be to shut our eyes to what all others than we can see and understand."[13]

The Amendment being unconstitutional, the plaintiffs are entitled to injunctive relief.

McCORD, Circuit Judge, and McDUFFIE, District Judge concurring.

### Note

1. The Supreme Court affirmed per curiam, citing *Lane v. Wilson* and *Yick Wo v. Hopkins, supra,* and noting for comparison *Williams*

---

[13] United States v. Butler, 297 U. S. 1, 61, 56 S. Ct. 312, 317, 80 L. Ed 477, 102 A. L. R. 914.

*v. Mississippi, supra.* The case is discussed in Notes, 1 Ala. L. Rev. 262 (1949); 49 Col. L. Rev. 1144 (1949); 12 Ga. B. J. 94 (1949); 2 Vand. L. Rev. 696 (1949). Cf. *Trudeau v. Barnes,* 65 F. 2d 563 (C. A. 5, 1933). For debate on passage of the Boswell Amendment see articles in 7 Ala. Lawyer 291 and 375 (1946).

2. Subsequent to the Supreme Court decision in *Smith v. Allwright,* outlawing the white primary, the registration of Negro voters in Georgia increased substantially. In 1946 it was estimated that 150,000 Negroes were registered to vote. See Section F, *infra.* In 1949, under the sponsorship of Governor Talmadge, the Georgia legislature passed the Voters' Registration Act requiring all prospective voters to register anew under revised procedures. Opponents of the bill charged that "the sole purpose of the bill is to purge as many Negro voters as possible." N. Y. Times, Feb. 11, 1949. The validity of the new law came before the courts in *Franklin v. Harper.* In 1951 Alabama adopted similar requirements, by constitutional amendment, to replace the Boswell Amendment. Acts of Ala. 1950–1, pp. 760–1, amending Const. of 1901, Art. 8, § 181.

## FRANKLIN v. HARPER

Supreme Court of Georgia, 1949

205 Ga. 779, 55 S. E. 2d 221, appeal dismissed 339 U. S. 946 (1950)

[The Georgia Constitution as amended in 1945 established as eligible to register and vote those who, in addition to other requirements, met the following qualifications:

"1. All persons who are of good character and understand the duties and obligations of citizenship under a republican form of government; or

"2. All persons who can correctly read in the English language any paragraph of the Constitution of the United States or of this State and correctly write the same in the English language when read to them by any one of the registrars, and all persons who solely because of physical disability are unable to comply with the above requirements but who can understand and give a reasonable interpretation of any paragraph of the Constitution of the United States or of this State that may be read to them by any one of the registrars."

This provision was implemented by the Voters' Registration Act of 1949. Plaintiffs, who were County Registrars appointed under the Act, brought suit for mandamus against a county official who refused to pay their salaries on the ground that the Act was unconstitutional. The issue was framed by demurrer and the lower court granted the petition for mandamus.]

ALMAND, Justice. . . .

2. By general demurrers the defendant makes a general attack on the Voters' Registration Act of 1949 as a whole, and does not attack any specific portion thereof; charging that the act is violative of certain specified provisions of the Federal and State Constitutions. We therefore turn to the act itself as a whole, to ascertain if it is subject to the attacks made.

Section 55 declares that the intent of the General Assembly is to provide by this act "for a new and exclusive method of qualifying voters, such revision being necessary in order to make the laws of this State conform to the requirements of the Constitution of Georgia adopted in the year 1945." Section 1 provides that from and after the effective date of the act no person shall be permitted to vote in any election in this State for presidential electors, members of Congress, United States Senators, Governor, Lieutenant-Governor, State House officers, members of the General Assembly, county officers, justices of the peace, or members of county boards of education, unless such person has been registered and qualified as provided in this act. Section 3 provides that the first registration list shall be prepared in 1950, and that the process of registration shall start immediately. It is provided in section 4 that the registration shall be permanent, but electors are required to maintain their status as qualified voters by the exercise of their franchise once every two years. Section 6 provides that the judge of the superior court of each county shall quadrennially appoint three upright and intelligent citizens of the county as a Board of Registrars from a list of six names recommended by the grand jury; the judge having the right to remove a member of the board on recommendation of the grand jury or upon proof of failure to discharge his duties, or because of unfitness of any member of the board. The act provides that the registrars shall take an oath; and under section 9 the tax commissioner or tax collector of the county shall be a deputy to the Board of Registrars. Section 11 provides a form of registration card whereby the applicant under oath is required to state that he is a citizen of the United States; state his age; that he has resided for six months in the county; that he possesses the qualifications of an elector required by the Constitution; and that he is not disfranchised by reason of any offense committed against the State. On this card the deputy or registrar certifies: (1) that the applicant could or could not intelligibly read a specified paragraph of the Constitution of Georgia or the United States; (2) that the applicant wrote or could not write a specified paragraph of the Constitution legibly; (3) that the applicant stated that due solely to physical infirmity he could not read, and a specified paragraph of the Constitution was read to him, and he explained it intelligibly, or could not explain it intelligibly; (4) that the applicant was served with notice to appear before the Board of Registrars on a stated date.

Sections 15, 16, and 17 provide how the applicant shall apply for registration, and the manner of filling out the cards and entry of the answers by the deputy or registrar. If the applicant states that he cannot read, and his inability to do so "is not due to physical infirmity but that he desires to qualify as a voter by reason of his good character and his understanding of the duties and obligations of citizenship under a republican form of government, the fact that he cannot read and write should be noted on the card." The registration cards are then turned over to the registrars for their consideration. Section 18 provides that a failure on the part of the applicant to disclose information sought by direct questions in connection with his application, or the giving of false information, shall be cause for the rejection of the application by the registrars on their own motion. Section 19 provides that all decisions of the registrars are appealable to the superior court.

Section 20 provides that, as the cards are turned over to the registrars, they shall proceed to a consideration of the application in the following manner: (1) Where the application is on the basis of literacy, and it appears that the applicant read the selected portion of the Constitution intelligibly, and wrote it legibly, or that by reason of physical disability he could not read it, but was able to interpret it reasonably when read to him, and the card shows no reason for disqualifying him for noncompliance with the law, the registrars shall pass an order declaring the applicant prima facie qualified. "The interpretation in this case shall be in the applicant's own words, giving words the significance ordinarily attached to them by laymen of average intellect and attainments." (2) In those cases where the applicant applies for qualification solely on the basis of his good character and his understanding of the duties of citizenship under a republican form of government, he shall be notified in writing to appear before the full Board of Registrars, and shall at that time be subjected to an examination as to his or her qualifications, to be conducted in accordance with the procedure hereinafter prescribed (in section 21). . . .

. . . We are here concerned only with the validity of the voters' registration statute as a whole. In this case, an omnibus attack on the act will fail unless the statute is invalid in every part for some reason asserted. . . .

[The Court then holds that the legislature had power to compel a new registration of voters and that the Voters' Registration Act of 1949 does not violate the Georgia Constitution.]

5. It is asserted that the act as a whole violates the Fourteenth Amendment to the Federal Constitution, because it abridges the privileges and immunities of citizens, and deprives them of liberty without due process of law, since the right to vote is the very foundation of a democratic form of government, and said act sets up a board "which has power to discriminate and censor the right of citizens to vote." In substance, the defendant says that the act denies, (a) persons liberty without due process of law, (b) a citizen of the equal protection of the law, because it sets up a board with power to censor the right of a citizen to vote; but it is not pointed out how or in what manner the act denies to him without due process of law a right or liberty which is guaranteed by the Fourteenth Amendment. He asserts that the act denies to citizens the liberty of voting. As we have shown, the Fourteenth Amendment does not confer upon a citizen of this State the right to vote. United States v. Cruikshank, 92 U. S. 542 . . . . Nor is such right a privilege of a citizen of the United States. Pope v. Williams, 193 U. S. 621 . . . . It is a political right, not a civil or property right. Morris v. Colorado Midland Ry. Co., 48 Colo. 147 (109 Pac. 430) ; Walls v. Brundidge, 109 Ark. 250 (160 S. W. 230) ; Minor v. Happersett, 88 U. S. 162 (22 L. ed. 627). We have further shown that the Fourteenth Amendment does not prevent a State from enacting laws requiring qualified voters to register. Unless such laws nullify or unreasonably abridge the right to vote, they are not subject to the charge that they violate the Fourteenth Amendment.

As to the charge that the act as a whole sets up a board of censors "which has power to discriminate and censor the right of citizens to vote," we take it that the plaintiff attempts to assert that the act violates the equal-protection clause of the Fourteenth Amendment. However, he does not show how or in what manner the act operates to his hurt or to the hurt of others. There is no assertion that he or anyone else who is qualified under the Constitution to vote has sought to register and been unlawfully denied the right to register. Nor does he point out how or in what manner the act empowers the Board of Registrars to discriminate against his right or that of any other citizen. . . .

So we are of the opinion that the ground of demurrer which attacks the Voters' Registration Act as violative of the Fourteenth Amendment to the Federal Constitution was properly overruled.

6. It is next asserted that the Voters' Registration Act violates the Fifteenth Amendment to the Federal Constitution,

[Emerson]

because it abridges the right of citizens to vote because of race or color, and leaves to three men unlimited and arbitrary power to declare them ineligible to vote. This amendment only denies to the States the authority to discriminate on account of race, color, or previous condition of servitude. United States v. Reese, 92 U. S. 214 (23 L. ed. 563) ; Guinn v. United States, 238 U. S. 347 . . . . We find nothing in the act to indicate that the law has the effect of denying to any qualified voter the right to register on account of race, color, or previous condition of servitude, so as to form the basis for the defendant to challenge the statute as violating the Fifteenth Amendment.

In support of his contention that the act violates this amendment, counsel for the plaintiff cite the cases of Davis v. Schnell, 81 Fed. Supp. 872, and Smith v. Allwright, 321 U. S. 649 (64 Sup. Ct. 757, 88 L. ed. 987, 151 A.L.R. 1110). In each of these cases, the person challenging the statute in question was a member of a class that the court held the statute proposed to discriminate against. No contention is made here that the act as a whole discriminates against the class of which the defendant is a member. Neither of the cases cited is controlling upon the question that the defendant makes in this case.

The mere possibility that the Board of Registrars may under this statute act arbitrarily or recklessly in administering the law and thereby violate constitutional rights is not a ground for declaring the act as a whole unconstitutional. Monongahela Bridge Co. v. United States, 216 U. S. 177 (30 Sup. Ct. 356, 54 L. ed. 435).

We are therefore of the opinion that the ground of demurrer that the Voters' Registration Act in its entirety violates the Fifteenth Amendment to the Federal Constitution was properly overruled. . . .

## Note

1. After *Rice v. Elmore* and *Brown v. Baskin, supra* Section D, South Carolina also revised its franchise system to require prospective voters in both primary and final elections to read and write a section of the 1895 State Constitution, the requirement not to apply to those who paid taxes on property in the state assessed at $300 or more. Persons convicted of certain enumerated crimes were also disqualified. Acts of S. C. (1950) No. 858, § 3–B (p. 2060). The New York Times reported that "well-informed quarters estimated that the new state law would reduce Negro participation by at least 50 per cent." N. Y. Times, April 14, 1950.

2. Persons denied the right to register or vote have frequently obtained judicial relief through suits for damages under the Federal Civil Rights Acts (8 U. S. C. §§ 31 and 43). See, *e. g.*, the *Nixon* cases,

*Smith v. Allwright, Lane v. Wilson, supra.* But *cf. Trudeau v. Barnes,*
65 F. 2d 563 (C. A. 5, 1933), cert. den. 290 U. S. 659 (1933) (requiring
an exhaustion of administrative remedies), presumably superseded
by *Lane v. Wilson.* A suit for damages may raise the basic constitutionality of the statute involved, and in such circumstances would appear to afford adequate relief. But where a suit for damages is predicated upon discriminatory administration of an otherwise valid statute its effects would be more limited.

Where equitable relief has been sought to vindicate the right of
franchise, certain obstacles have at times been presented. One of the
earliest unsuccessful efforts to obtain equitable relief was in *Giles
v. Harris,* 189 U. S. 475, 47 L. Ed. 909, 23 S. Ct. 639 (1903). Here
a Negro sued on behalf of himself and more than 5000 other Negroes
in the same county similarly situated, seeking to compel the board
of registrars to register him and other qualified persons as voters
and to declare certain parts of the Alabama franchise laws unconstitutional. The complaint alleged that the plaintiff and a large number
of other Negroes had been refused registration because of their race.
The Supreme Court, in an opinion by Mr. Justice Holmes, denied equitable relief. The Court took the view that the plaintiff was inconsistent in asking to be registered under an allegedly unconstitutional
system of laws, and further that a court could not grant effective
relief in a situation so political in nature. Justices Brewer, Brown
and Harlan dissented.

The *Giles* case has been influential in limiting equitable relief in
some later franchise cases. See *Giles v. Teasley,* 193 U. S. 146, 48
L. Ed. 655, 24 S. Ct. 359 (1904) ; *Caven v. Clark,* 78 F. Supp. 295 (W. D.
Ark, 1948) (refusal to enjoin registration of voters allegedly holding
illegal poll tax receipts). *Cf. Colegrove v. Green,* Section G, *infra.*
But it did not prevent the granting of equitable relief, for the plaintiff and those similarly situated, in *Rice v. Elmore, Brown v. Baskin*
and *Davis v. Schnell, supra.* Similar relief was obtained in *Mitchell
v. Wright, infra; Hall v. Nagel,* 154 F. 2d 931 (C. A. 5, 1946);
*Dean v. Thomas,* 93 F. Supp. 129 (E. D. La., 1950). See Note, *Injunctive Protection of Political Rights in the Federal Courts,* 62 Harv.
L. Rev. 659 (1949) ; Note, 33 Iowa L. Rev. 412, 416–9 (1948).

The doctrine of exhausting administrative remedies has also been
urged as a defense. This has been unsuccessful where the state
remedy was judicial in nature, *Mitchell v. Wright,* 154 F. 2d 924 (C.
A. 5, 1946), cert. den. 329 U. S. 733 (1946), but successful where state
law provided an administrative appeal, *Peay v. Cox,* 190 F. 2d 123
(C. A. 5, 1951), cert. den. 342 U. S. 896 (1951).

Efforts to enjoin an election or to upset the results of an election
through suit in the Federal courts have also been unsuccessful. See
*Johnson v. Stevenson,* 170 F. 2d 108 (C. A. 5, 1948), cert. den. 336
U. S. 904 (1949) ; *cf. South v. Peters,* 339 U. S. 276, 94 L. Ed. 834, 70
S. Ct. 641 (1950), discussed in Section G, *infra.*

3. Where judicial relief is available substantial litigation difficulties
remain. These include the willingness of prospective voters to bring
court action, the finances necessary to carry on court proceedings, the

obtaining of counsel, and the like. Establishing the facts of either individual or systematic discrimination also presents serious problems. Compare the comparable issue of proving systematic exclusion of Negroes from juries, as evidenced in *Akins v. Texas,* 325 U. S. 398, 410, 89 L. Ed. 1692, 65 S. Ct. 1276 (1945).

4. Educational qualifications for voting are to be found in a number of states outside the South, including Arizona, California, Connecticut, Delaware, Maine, Massachusetts, New Hampshire, New York, Oregon, Washington and Wyoming. Most of these require an ability to read or write a provision of the Constitution. See McGovney, *The American Suffrage Medley,* ch. V (1949); Notes, 47 Col. L. Rev. 76, 91 (1947); 49 Col. L. Rev. 1144, 1145–6 (1949).

5. Section 2 of the Fourteenth Amendment provides that when the right to vote for Federal or state officials is denied to the inhabitants of any state the basis of such state's representation in the House of Representative shall be proportionately reduced. No legislation to enforce this provision has ever been enacted. The attempt to enforce it through judicial decision has been unsuccessful. *Saunders v. Wilkins,* 152 F. 2d 235 (C. A. 4, 1945), cert. den. 328 U. S. 870 (1946).

## F. TRENDS OF NEGRO VOTING IN THE SOUTH

After reviewing the course of legal development relating to the right of franchise in the South, one may well ask: What has been the actual trend of Negro voting in the southern states? And what part, if any, have judicial decisions played in such trend? On the first question there is some material, albeit far from adequate. On the second there is very little data.

All observers are agreed on the general trend. There has been a substantial increase in Negro registration and voting over the past decade. But the amount of the increase is difficult to ascertain. Only Florida and Louisiana keep official figures on the number of Negroes registered. In other states an estimate can be made only by collecting data from local official or unofficial sources or by sheer guess work. The table below represents the best available estimate of Negro registration, probably on the conservative side. But the figures, except for Florida and Louisiana, can be taken only as indicating the general trend.

## NEGRO REGISTRATION IN THE SOUTH

| | 1940[1] | 1946[2] | 1947[3] | 1950[4] |
|---|---|---|---|---|
| ALABAMA | 2,000 | 10,000 | 6,000 | 50,000 |
| ARKANSAS | 4,000 | 16,000 | 47,000 | 65,000 |
| FLORIDA | 18,000 | 50,000 | 49,000 | 116,145 |
| GEORGIA | 20,000 | 150,000 | 125,000 | 133,000 |
| LOUISIANA | 908 | 7,561 | 10,000 | 51,675 |
| MISSISSIPPI | 2,000 | 5,000 | 5,000 | 8,000 |
| NORTH CAROLINA | 35,000 | 75,000 | 75,000 | 70,000 |
| SOUTH CAROLINA | 3,000 | 5,000 | 50,000 | 73,000 |
| TENNESSEE | 20,000 | 55,000 | 80,000 | 85,000 |
| TEXAS | 30,000 | 200,000 | 100,000 | 110,000 |
| VIRGINIA | 15,000 | 50,000 | 48,000 | 66,000 |
| Total | 149,908 | 623,561 | 595,000 | 827,820 |

As to the effect of the court rulings upon the increase in Negro registration the available data is extremely meager. It seems clear that the Supreme Court's decision in *Smith v. Allwright* and the subsequent white primary cases have been an important influence in eliminating a major obstacle and in stimulating Negro voting generally. See, *e.g.*, Key, *Southern Politics*, ch. 29 (1949); Jackson, *Race and Suffrage in the South Since 1940*, 3 New South Nos. 5 and 6, p. 13 (June–July 1948). It is also clear that other forces have been at work. A fuller estimate of the effect of judicial decision, however, would depend upon studies of a nature not now being made and perhaps not possible to make.

## Note

For discussion of the course of Negro voting in the South, including consideration of many factors in addition to strictly legal developments, see Key and Jackson, *supra;* Moon, *Balance of Power: The Negro Vote* (1948); Heard, *A Two-Party South?* (1952); Strong, *The Rise of Negro Voting in Texas*, 42 Am. Pol. Sci. Rev. 510 (1948).

---

[1] Except for the Louisiana figure, which is official, all estimates for 1940 are those of the late Luther P. Jackson, Professor of History at Virginia State College, as published in 3 New South, Nos. 5 and 6, p. 4 (June–July 1948).

[2] All 1946 figures are those reported by the National Association for the Advancement of Colored People, except Louisiana (official). Key, *Southern Politics*, p. 523 (1949).

[3] All 1947 figures are taken from Jackson, *supra* note 1.

[4] All 1950 figures were supplied by the Southern Regional Council, Atlanta, Ga., except Florida and Louisiana (both official). In July 1951 the New York Times reported that there were 20,000 Negroes registered in Mississippi. N. Y. Times, July 29, 1951. In February 1952 Negroes registered in Louisiana totaled 86,000.

# G. OTHER ASPECTS OF THE RIGHT OF FRANCHISE
## 1. Apportionment

One of the major factors in the full and fair exercise of the right of franchise is the apportionment of population among voting districts. In some situations the lack of equal population in voting districts was deliberately designed to achieve a justifiable, or arguably justifiable, aim. The outstanding example of this is the election of two Senators from each state, regardless of population. Many state constitutions contain similar provisions with respect to one house of the legislature. But in other situations disproportion has arisen through shifts in population, antiquated constitutional or statutory provisions, gerrymandering or the like, where in theory the districts were intended to be of roughly equal population. In such case the vote of an elector in the larger district carries proportionately less weight than the vote of an elector in the smaller district.

This problem, so far as it concerns Congressional voting districts, was considered by the Supreme Court in *Colegrove v. Green.*

## COLEGROVE v. GREEN
Supreme Court of the United States, 1946
328 U. S. 549, 90 L. Ed. 1432, 66 S. Ct. 1198

MR. JUSTICE FRANKFURTER announced the judgment of the Court and an opinion in which MR. JUSTICE REED and MR. JUSTICE BURTON concur.

This case is appropriately here, under § 266 of the Judicial Code, 28 U. S. C. § 380, on direct review of a judgment of the District Court of the Northern District of Illinois, composed of three judges, dismissing the complaint of the appellants. These are three qualified voters in Illinois districts which have much larger populations than other Illinois Congressional districts. They brought this suit against the Governor, the Secretary of State, and the Auditor of the State of Illinois, as members *ex officio* of the Illinois Primary Certifying Board, to restrain them, in effect, from taking proceedings for an election in November 1946, under the provisions of Illinois law governing Congressional districts. Illinois Laws of 1901, p. 3. Formally, the appellants asked for a decree, with its incidental relief, § 274 (d) Judicial Code, 28 U. S. C. § 400, declaring these provisions to be invalid because they violated various provisions of the United States Constitution and § 3 of the Reapportionment Act of August 8, 1911,

37 Stat. 13, as amended, 2 U. S. C. § 2a, in that by reason of subsequent changes in population the Congressional districts for the election of Representatives in the Congress created by the Illinois Laws of 1901 (Ill. Rev. Stat. Ch. 46 (1945) §§ 154–56) lacked compactness of territory and approximate equality of population. The District Court feeling bound by this Court's opinion in *Wood* v. *Broom,* 287 U. S. 1, dismissed the complaint. 64 F. Supp. 632.

The District Court was clearly right in deeming itself bound by *Wood* v. *Broom, supra,* and we could also dispose of this case on the authority of *Wood* v. *Broom.* The legal merits of this controversy were settled in that case, inasmuch as it held that the Reapportionment Act of June 18, 1929, 46 Stat. 21, as amended, 2 U. S. C. § 2 (a), has no requirements "as to the compactness, contiguity and equality in population of districts." 287 U. S. at 8. The Act of 1929 still governs the districting for the election of Representatives. It must be remembered that not only was the legislative history of the matter fully considered in *Wood* v. *Broom,* but the question had been elaborately before the Court in *Smiley* v. *Holm,* 285 U. S. 355, *Koenig* v. *Flynn,* 285 U. S. 375, and *Carroll* v. *Becker,* 285 U. S. 375, argued a few months before *Wood* v. *Broom* was decided. Nothing has now been adduced to lead us to overrule what this Court found to be the requirements under the Act of 1929, the more so since seven Congressional elections have been held under the Act of 1929 as construed by this Court. No manifestation has been shown by Congress even to question the correctness of that which seemed compelling to this Court in enforcing the will of Congress in *Wood* v. *Broom.*

But we also agree with the four Justices (Brandeis, Stone, Roberts, and Cardozo, JJ.) who were of opinion that the bill in *Wood* v. *Broom, supra,* should be "dismissed for want of equity." To be sure, the present complaint, unlike the bill in *Wood* v. *Broom,* was brought under the Federal Declaratory Judgment Act which, not having been enacted until 1934, was not available at the time of *Wood* v. *Broom.* But that Act merely gave the federal courts competence to make a declaration of rights even though no decree of enforcement be immediately asked. It merely permitted a freer movement of the federal courts within the recognized confines of the scope of equity. The Declaratory Judgment Act "only provided a new form of procedure for the adjudication of rights in conformity" with "established equitable principles." *Great Lakes Co.* v. *Huffman,* 319 U. S. 293, 300. And so, the test for determining whether a federal court has authority to make a declaration such as is here asked, is whether the controversy "would be justiciable in this Court if presented in a suit for injunction . . ." *Nashville, C. & St. L. R. Co.* v. *Wallace,* 288 U. S. 249, 262.

We are of opinion that the appellants ask of this Court what is beyond its competence to grant. This is one of those demands on judicial power which cannot be met by verbal fencing about "jurisdiction." It must be resolved by considerations on the basis of which this Court, from time to time, has refused to intervene in controversies. It has refused to do so because due regard for the effective working of our Government revealed this issue to be of a peculiarly political nature and therefore not meet for judicial determination.

This is not an action to recover for damage because of the discriminatory exclusion of a plaintiff from rights enjoyed by other citizens. The basis for the suit is not a private wrong, but a wrong suffered by Illinois as a polity. Compare *Nixon* v. *Herndon,* 273 U. S. 536 and *Lane* v. *Wilson,* 307 U. S. 268, with *Giles* v. *Harris,* 189 U. S. 475. In effect this is an appeal to the federal courts to reconstruct the electoral process of Illinois in order that it may be adequately represented in the councils of the Nation. Because the Illinois legislature has failed to revise its Congressional Representative districts in order to reflect great changes, during more than a generation, in the distribution of its population, we are asked to do this, as it were, for Illinois.

Of course no court can affirmatively re-map the Illinois districts so as to bring them more in conformity with the standards of fairness for a representative system. At best we could only declare the existing electoral system invalid. The result would be to leave Illinois undistricted and to bring into operation, if the Illinois legislature chose not to act, the choice of members for the House of Representatives on a state-wide ticket. The last stage may be worse than the first. The upshot of judicial action may defeat the vital political principle which led Congress, more than a hundred years ago, to require districting. This requirement, in the language of Chancellor Kent, "was recommended by the wisdom and justice of giving, as far as possible, to the local subdivisions of the people of each state, a due influence in the choice of representatives, so as not to leave the aggregate minority of the people in a state, though approaching perhaps to a majority, to be wholly overpowered by the combined action of the numerical majority, without any voice whatever in the national councils." 1 Kent, *Commentaries* (12th ed., 1873) 230–31, n. (c). Assuming acquiescence on the part of the authorities of Illinois in the selection of its Representatives by a mode that defies the direction of Congress for selection by districts, the House of Representatives may not acquiesce. In the exercise of its power to judge the qualifications of its own members, the House may reject a delegation of Representatives-at-large. Article I, § 5, Cl. 1. For the detailed system by which Congress supervises the election of its members, see *e.g.*, 2 U. S. C. §§ 201–226; Bartlett, *Contested Elections in the House of Representatives* (2 vols.) ; Alexander, *History and Procedure of the House of Representatives* (1916) c. XVI. Nothing is clearer than that this controversy concerns matters that bring courts into immediate and active relations with party contests. From the determination of such issues this Court has traditionally held aloof. It is hostile to a democratic system to involve the judiciary in the politics of the people. And it is not less pernicious if such judicial intervention in an essentially political contest be dressed up in the abstract phrases of the law. . . .

The short of it is that the Constitution has conferred upon Congress exclusive authority to secure fair representation by the States in the popular House and left to that House determination whether States have fulfilled their responsibility. If Congress failed in exercising its powers, whereby standards of fairness are offended, the remedy ultimately lies with the people. Whether Congress faithfully discharges its duty or not, the subject has been committed to the exclusive control of Congress. An aspect of government from which the judiciary, in view of what is involved, has been excluded by the clear intention of the Constitution cannot be entered by the federal courts because Congress may have been in default in exacting from States obedience to its mandate.

The one stark fact that emerges from a study of the history of Congressional apportionment is its embroilment in politics, in the sense of party contests and party interests. The Constitution enjoins upon Congress the duty of apportioning Representatives "among the several States . . . according to their respective Numbers, . . ." Article I, § 2. Yet, Congress has at times been heedless of this command and not apportioned according to the requirements of the Census. It never occurred to anyone that this Court could issue mandamus to compel Congress to perform its mandatory duty to apportion. "What might not be done directly by mandamus, could not be attained indirectly by injunction." Chafee, *Congressional Reapportionment* (1929) 42 Harv. L. Rev. 1015, 1019. Until 1842 there was the greatest diversity among the States in the manner of choosing Representatives because Congress had made no requirement for districting. 5 Stat. 491. Congress then provided for the election of Representatives by districts. Strangely enough, the power to do so was seriously questioned; it was still doubted by a Committee of

Congress as late as 1901. See *e.g.,* Speech of Mr. (afterwards Mr. Justice) Clifford, Cong. Globe, April 28, 1842, 27th Cong., 2d Sess., App., p. 347; 1 Bartlett, *Contested Elections in the House of Representatives* (1865) 47, 276; H. R. Rep. No. 3000, 56th Cong., 2d Sess. (1901); H. R. Doc. No. 2052, 64th Cong., 2d Sess. (1917) 43; *United States* v. *Gradwell,* 243 U. S. 476, 482, 483. In 1850 Congress dropped the requirement. 9 Stat. 428, 432–33. The Reapportionment Act of 1862 required that the districts be of contiguous territory. 12 Stat. 572. In 1872 Congress added the requirement of substantial equality of inhabitants. 17 Stat. 28. This was reinforced in 1911. 37 Stat. 13, 14. But the 1929 Act, as we have seen, dropped these requirements. 46 Stat. 21. Throughout our history, whatever may have been the controlling Apportionment Act, the most glaring disparities have prevailed as to the contours and the population of districts. Appendix I summarizes recent disparities in the various Congressional Representative districts throughout the country and Appendix II gives fair samples of prevailing gerrymanders. For other illustrations of glaring inequalities, see 71 Cong. Rec. 2278–79, 2480 *et seq.;* 86 Cong. Rec. 4369, 4370–71, 76th Cong., 2d Sess. (1940); H. R. Rep. No. 1695, 61st Cong., 2d Sess. (1910); (1920) 24 Law Notes 124; (October 30, 1902) 75 The Nation 343; and see, generally, Schmeckebier, *Congressional Apportionment* (1941); and on gerrymandering, see Griffith, *The Rise and Development of the Gerrymander* (1907).

To sustain this action would cut very deep into the very being of Congress. Courts ought not to enter this political thicket. The remedy for unfairness in districting is to secure State legislatures that will apportion properly, or to invoke the ample powers of Congress. The Constitution has many commands that are not enforceable by courts because they clearly fall outside the conditions and purposes that circumscribe judicial action. Thus, "on Demand of the executive Authority," Art. IV, § 2, of a State it is the duty of a sister State to deliver up a fugitive from justice. But the fulfilment of this duty cannot be judicially enforced. *Kentucky* v. *Dennison,* 24 How. 66. The duty to see to it that the laws are faithfully executed cannot be brought under legal compulsion, *Mississippi* v. *Johnson,* 4 Wall. 475. Violation of the great guaranty of a republican form of government in States cannot be challenged in the courts. *Pacific Telephone Co.* v. *Oregon,* 223 U. S. 118. The Constitution has left the performance of many duties in our governmental scheme to depend on the fidelity of the executive and legislative action and, ultimately, on the vigilance of the people in exercising their political rights.

Dismissal of the complaint is affirmed.

331

MR. JUSTICE JACKSON took no part in the consideration or decision of this case.

[The appendices to Mr. Justice Frankfurter's opinion are omitted.

Mr. Justice Rutledge concurred in the result, holding that under *Smiley v. Holm* a justiciable issue was presented but that the Court should decline to exercise its jurisdiction to grant equitable relief. He reached this conclusion because the relief sought "pitches this Court into delicate relation to the functions of state officials and Congress"; the shortness of the time remaining "makes it doubtful whether action could, or would, be taken in time to secure for petitioners the effective relief they seek;" and to force an election at large would deprive Illinois citizens of "representation by districts which the prevailing policy of Congress demands." 328 U. S. at 565–6.]

MR. JUSTICE BLACK, dissenting.

The complaint alleges the following facts essential to the position I take: Appellants, citizens and voters of Illinois, live in congressional election districts, the respective populations of which range from 612,000 to 914,000. Twenty other congressional election districts have populations that range from 112,116 to 385,207. In seven of these districts the population is below 200,000. The Illinois Legislature established these districts in 1901 on the basis of the Census of 1900. The Federal Census of 1910, of 1920, of 1930, and of 1940, each showed a growth of population in Illinois and a substantial shift in the distribution of population among the districts established in 1901. But up to date, attempts to have the State Legislature reapportion congressional election districts so as more nearly to equalize their population have been unsuccessful. A contributing cause of this situation, according to appellants, is the fact that the State Legislature is chosen on the basis of state election districts inequitably apportioned in a way similar to that of the 1901 congressional election districts. The implication is that the issues of state and congressional apportionment are thus so interdependent that it is to the best interest of state legislators to perpetuate the inequitable apportionment of both state and congressional election districts. Prior to this proceeding a series of suits had been brought in the state courts challenging the State's local and federal apportionment system. In all these cases the Supreme Court of the State had denied effective relief.[1]

---

[1] *People v. Thompson*, 155 Ill. 451, 40 N. E. 307; *Fergus v. Marks*, 321 Ill. 510, 152 N. E. 557; *Fergus v. Kinney*, 333 Ill. 437, 164 N. E. 665; *People v. Clardy*, 334 Ill. 160, 165 N. E. 638; *People v. Blackwell*, 342 Ill. 223, 173

In the present suit the complaint attacked the 1901 State Apportionment Act on the ground that it among other things violates Article I and the Fourteenth Amendment of the Constitution. Appellants claim that since they live in the heavily populated districts their vote is much less effective than the vote of those living in a district which under the 1901 Act is also allowed to choose one Congressman, though its population is sometimes only one-ninth that of the heavily populated districts. Appellants contend that this reduction of the effectiveness of their vote is the result of a wilful legislative discrimination against them and thus amounts to a denial of the equal protection of the laws guaranteed by the Fourteenth Amendment. They further assert that this reduction of the effectiveness of their vote also violates the privileges and immunities clause of the Fourteenth Amendment in abridging their privilege as citizens of the United States to vote for Congressmen, a privilege guaranteed by Article I of the Constitution. They further contend that the State Apportionment Act directly violates Article I which guarantees that each citizen eligible to vote has a right to vote for Congressmen and to have his vote counted. The assertion here is that the right to have their vote counted is abridged unless that vote is given approximately equal weight to that of other citizens. It is my judgment that the District Court had jurisdiction;[2] that the complaint presented a justiciable case and controversy;[3] and that appellants had standing to sue, since the facts alleged show that they have been injured as individuals.[4] Unless previous decisions of this Court are to be overruled, the suit is not one against the State but against state officials as individuals.[5] The complaint attacked the 1901 Apportionment Act as unconstitutional and alleged facts indicating that the Act denied appellants the full right to vote and the equal protection of the laws. These allegations have not been denied. Under these circumstances, and since there is no adequate legal remedy for depriving a citizen of his right to vote, equity can and should grant relief.

It is difficult for me to see why the 1901 State Apportionment Act does not deny appellants equal protection of the laws. The

N. E. 750; *Daly v. Madison County,* 378 Ill. 357, 38 N. E. 2d 160. Cf. *Moran v. Bowley,* 347 Ill. 148, 179 N. E. 526.

[2] 28 U. S. C. 41 (14); *Bell v. Hood,* 327 U. S. 678.

[3] *Smiley v. Holm,* 285 U. S. 355; *Koenig v. Flynn,* 285 U. S. 375; *Carroll v. Becker,* 285 U. S. 380; *Wood v. Broom,* 287 U. S. 1; *Nixon v. Herndon,* 273 U. S. 536, 540; *McPherson v. Blacker,* 146 U. S. 1, 23–24; see also cases collected in 2 A. L. R. note, 1337 *et seq.*

[4] *Coleman v. Miller,* 307 U. S. 433, 438, 467.

[5] *Ex parte Young,* 209 U. S. 123; *Sterling v. Constantin,* 287 U. S. 378, 393.

failure of the Legislature to reapportion the congressional election districts for forty years, despite census figures indicating great changes in the distribution of the population, has resulted in election districts the populations of which range from 112,000 to 900,000. One of the appellants lives in a district of more than 900,000 people. His vote is consequently much less effective than that of each of the citizens living in the district of 112,000. And such a gross inequality in the voting power of citizens irrefutably demonstrates a complete lack of effort to make an equitable apportionment. The 1901 State Apportionment Act if applied to the next election would thus result in a wholly indefensible discrimination against appellants and all other voters in heavily populated districts. The equal protection clause of the Fourteenth Amendment forbids such discrimination. . . .

The 1901 State Apportionment Act in reducing the effectiveness of appellants' votes abridges their privilege as citizens to vote for Congressmen and violates Article I of the Constitution. Article I provides that Congressmen "shall be . . . chosen . . . by the People of the several States . . ." It thus gives those qualified a right to vote and a right to have their vote counted. *Ex parte Yarbrough*, 110 U. S. 651; *United States* v. *Mosley*, 238 U. S. 383. This Court in order to prevent "an interference with the effective choice of the voters" has held that this right extends to primaries. *United States* v. *Classic*, 313 U. S. 299, 314. While the Constitution contains no express provision requiring that congressional election districts established by the States must contain approximately equal populations, the constitutionally guaranteed right to vote and the right to have one's vote counted clearly imply the policy that state election systems, no matter what their form, should be designed to give approximately equal weight to each vote cast. To some extent this implication of Article I is expressly stated by § 2 of the Fourteenth Amendment which provides that "Representatives shall be apportioned among the several States according to their respective numbers . . ." The purpose of this requirement is obvious: It is to make the votes of the citizens of the several States equally effective in the selection of members of Congress. It was intended to make illegal a nation-wide "rotten borough" system as between the States. The policy behind it is broader than that. It prohibits as well congressional "rotten boroughs" within the States, such as the ones here involved. The policy is that which is laid down by all the constitutional provisions regulating the election of members of the House of Representatives, including Article I which guarantees the right to vote and to have that vote effectively counted: All groups, classes, and individuals shall to the extent that it is practically feasible be given equal representation in the House of Representatives, which, in conjunction with the Senate, writes the laws affecting the life, liberty, and property of all the people. . . .

Had Illinois passed an Act requiring that all of its twenty-six Congressmen be elected by the citizens of one county, it would clearly have amounted to a denial to the citizens of the other counties of their constitutionally guaranteed right to vote. And I cannot imagine that an Act that would have apportioned twenty-five Congressmen to the State's smallest county and one Congressman to all the others, would have been sustained by any court. Such an Act would clearly have violated the constitutional policy of equal representation. The 1901 Apportionment Act here involved violates that policy in the same way. The policy with respect to federal elections laid down by the Constitution, while it does not mean that the courts can or should prescribe the precise methods to be followed by state legislatures and the invalidation of all Acts that do not embody those precise methods, does mean that state legislatures must make real efforts to bring about approximately equal representation of citizens in Congress. Here the Legislature of Illinois has not done so. Whether that was due to negligence or was a wilful effort to deprive some citizens of an effective vote, the admitted result is that the constitutional policy of equality of representation has been defeated. Under these circumstances it is the Court's duty to invalidate the state law.

It is contended, however, that a court of equity does not have the power, or even if it has the power, that it should not exercise it in this case. To do so, it is argued, would mean that the Court is entering the area of "political questions." I cannot agree with that argument. There have been cases, such as *Coleman v. Miller, supra,* pp. 454, 457, where this Court declined to decide a question because it was political. In the *Miller* case, however, the question involved was ratification of a constitutional amendment, a matter over which the Court believed Congress had been given final authority. To have decided that question would have amounted to a trespass upon the constitutional power of Congress. Here we have before us a state law which abridges the constitutional rights of citizens to cast votes in such way as to obtain the kind of congressional representation the Constitution guarantees to them.

It is true that voting is a part of elections and that elections are "political." But as this Court said in *Nixon v. Herndon* [273 U. S. 536], it is a mere "play upon words" to refer to a controversy such as this as "political" in the sense that courts have nothing

**335**

to do with protecting and vindicating the right of a voter to cast an effective ballot. The *Classic* case, among myriads of others, refutes the contention that courts are impotent in connection with evasions of all "political" rights. *Wood* v. *Broom*, 287 U. S. 1, does not preclude the granting of equitable relief in this case. There this Court simply held that the State Apportionment Act did not violate the Congressional Reapportionment Act of 1929, 46 Stat. 21, 26, 27, since that Act did not require election districts of equal population. The Court expressly reserved the question of "the right of the complainant to relief in equity." *Giles* v. *Harris*, 189 U. S. 475, also did not hold that a court of equity could not, or should not, exercise its power in a case like this. As we said with reference to that decision in *Lane* v. *Wilson*, 307 U. S. 268, 272–273, it stands for the principle that courts will not attempt to "supervise" elections. Furthermore, the author of the *Giles* v. *Harris* opinion also wrote the opinion in *Nixon* v. *Herndon,* in which a voter's right to cast a ballot was held to give rise to a justiciable controversy. . . .

Nor is there any more difficulty in enforcing a decree in this case than there was in the *Smiley* case. It is true that declaration of invalidity of the State Act and the enjoining of state officials would result in prohibiting the State from electing Congressmen under the system of the old congressional districts. But it would leave the State free to elect them from the State at large, which, as we held in the *Smiley* case, is a manner authorized by the Constitution. It is said that it would be inconvenient for the State to conduct the election in this manner. But it has an element of virtue that the more convenient method does not have—namely, it does not discriminate against some groups to favor others, it gives all the people an equally effective voice in electing their representatives as is essential under a free government, and it is constitutional.

MR. JUSTICE DOUGLAS and MR. JUSTICE MURPHY join in this dissent.

### Note

1. Motions for rehearing and for reargument before the full bench were denied, the Chief Justice (Vinson, just appointed) and Mr. Justice Jackson not participating. 329 U. S. 825, 828 (1946).

In a subsequent series of cases the Supreme Court was faced with somewhat similar problems in connection with the Georgia County Unit System. Under Georgia statutes, in primary elections for Federal and the leading state offices, the candidate receiving the highest popular vote in each county receives the electoral vote for that county. This electoral vote varies with the population, the eight most populous counties casting six votes, others four, and most of the counties two.

According to the 1940 census, Fulton County (the largest) had a population of 392,866, and Echols County (the smallest) a population of 2964. In 1946 qualified voters brought suit for a declaratory judgment and an injunction to restrain Georgia election officials from certifying a candidate as winner of a Congressional primary who had received a majority of the county unit vote but not the popular vote. The District Court denied relief on the authority of *Colegrove v. Green*. *Cook v. Fortson*, 68 F. Supp. 624 (N. D. Ga., 1946). A similar suit challenging the gubernatorial primary was also dismissed. *Turman v. Duckworth*, 68 F. Supp. 744 (N. D. Ga., 1946). The Supreme Court, on October 28, 1946, dismissed both appeals per curiam, citing only a case of dismissal for mootness. Justices Black and Douglas were of the opinion that probable jurisdiction should be noted. Mr. Justice Rutledge thought the question of jurisdiction should be postponed until a hearing on the merits. 329 U. S. 675, 91 L. Ed. 596, 67 S. Ct. 21.

In 1950 a suit was instituted prior to the primaries, again challenging the Georgia County Unit System. Voters in Fulton County contended that a vote in the smallest county was worth 120 times a vote in Fulton County, and that in 45 counties a vote would be worth twenty times the weight of a vote in Fulton County. The District Court again dismissed the suit. *South v. Peters*, 89 F. Supp. 672 (N. D. Ga., 1950), Judge Andrews dissenting. The Supreme Court affirmed per curiam, saying "Federal courts consistently refuse to exercise their equity powers in cases posing political issues arising from a state's geographical distribution of electoral strength among its political subdivisions." Justices Douglas and Black dissented, pointing out, among other things, that "there is a heavy Negro population in the large cities" and that "the County Unit System heavily disenfranchises that urban Negro population." *South v. Peters*, 339 U. S. 276, 94 L. Ed. 834, 70 S. Ct. 641 (1950).

A third attempt was made in *Cox v. Peters*, 208 Ga. 498, 67 S. E. 2d 579 (1951). Here suit was brought for damages under 8 U. S. C. § 43 against Georgia election officials, alleging that a voter in the 1950 gubernatorial primaries had been denied full enjoyment of his right to vote by reason of the County Unit System. The Georgia Supreme Court affirmed a dismissal of the suit, saying that the right to vote in a gubernatorial primary was not derived from the United States Constitution and that the Georgia constitutional and statutory provisions did not apply to primaries. The United States Supreme Court dismissed for want of a substantial federal question, Justices Black and Douglas dissenting. *Cox v. Peters*, 342 U. S. 936 (1952).

2. In 1947 the Illinois legislature passed legislation remapping the Congressional districts in that state. Ill. Rev. Stat. (1947) ch. 46, § 156. The validity of this reapportionment was upheld in *People ex rel. Barrett v. Anderson*, 398 Ill. 480, 76 N. E. 2d 773 (1947). A new bill was passed in 1951. Act of Aug. 2, 1951, Ill. Rev. Stat. (1951) ch. 46, § 156d.

3. For discussion of the Congressional apportionment problem see, in addition to the material cited in the *Colegrove* opinions, Bowman, *Congressional Redistricting and the Constitution*, 31 Mich. L. Rev.

149 (1932); Note, *Constitutional Right to Congressional Districts of Equal Population*, 56 Yale L. J. 127 (1946); Note, *Methods for Guaranteeing Equality in Congressional Districts*, 43 Ill. L. Rev. 180 (1948); Note, 3 Stan. L. Rev. 129 (1950). Comment on the *Colegrove* case may be found in Note, *supra*, 56 Yale L. J. 127 (1946); Notes, 35 Calif. L. Rev. 296 (1947); 41 Ill. L. Rev. 578 (1946); 45 Mich. L. Rev. 368 (1947); 25 Tex. L. Rev. 419 (1947). With respect to the Georgia County Unit System cases, see Note, *Georgia County Unit Vote*, 47 Col. L. Rev. 284 (1947); Note, 4 Vand. L. Rev. 691 (1951). On the issue of equitable relief see Note, *Injunctive Protection of Political Rights in the Federal Courts*, 62 Harv. L. Rev. 659 (1949); Note, 56 Yale 139 (1946).

Concerning Congressional apportionment of seats in the House of Representatives among the states, see Note, *Apportionment of the House of Representatives*, 58 Yale L. J. 1360 (1949); Note, 35 Corn. L. Q. 367 (1950); Chafee, *Reapportionment of the House of Representatives Under the 1950 Census*, 36 Corn. L. Q. 643 (1951).

4. Lack of equal apportionment of state legislative districts is a perennial problem in most of the states. Efforts to obtain judicial relief in the state courts encounter many of the obstacles revealed in *Colegrove v. Green* and the Georgia County Unit System cases. But where the basis for unequal apportionment rests on a statutory, rather than a constitutional, basis, some state courts have afforded relief. See, generally, Walter, *Reapportionment and Urban Representation*, 195 Annals of the Am. Acad. of Pol. and Soc. Sci. 11 (1938); Walter, *Reapportionment of State Legislative Districts*, 37 Ill. L. Rev. 20 (1942); Shull, *Legislative Apportionment and the Law*, 18 Temple L. Q. 388 (1944); Durfee, *Apportionment of Representation in the Legislature: A Study of State Constitutions*, 43 Mich. L. Rev. 1091 (1945); MacNeil, *Urban Representation in State Legislatures*, 18 State Government 59 (1945); Note, *supra*, 56 Yale L. J. 127 (collecting materials in footnote 15, p. 131) (1946); Note, 1949 Wis. L. Rev. 761.

The Federal courts, following *Colegrove v. Green*, have refused to pass on the validity of state districting laws. *Colegrove v. Barrett*, decided by the District Court for the Eastern District of Illinois, Jan. 28, 1947 (unreported), app. dis. 330 U. S. 804 (1947). See *Turman v. Duckworth, supra*.

5. The effect of unequal apportionment in most cases is to favor rural over urban voters. For discussion of the impact of this on the political structure of the country see, in addition to the material cited above, Hurst, *The Growth of American Law*, pp. 41–3 (1950); Neuberger, *Our Rotten-Borough Legislatures*, The Survey, Feb. 1950, p. 53; Neuberger, *Farmers in the Saddle*, New Republic, Oct. 2, 1950, p. 13.

## 2. Rights of Minority Parties

### MacDOUGALL v. GREEN

Supreme Court of the United States, 1948
335 U. S. 281, 93 L. Ed. 3, 69 S. Ct. 1

PER CURIAM.

This action was brought before a three-judge court convened in the Northern District of Illinois under 28 U. S. C. § 2281 and § 2284. The object of the action is an injunction against the enforcement of a provision which, in 1935, was added to a statute of Illinois and which requires that a petition to form and to nominate candidates for a new political party be signed by at least 25,000 qualified voters, "Provided, that included in the aggregate total of twenty-five thousand (25,000) signatures are the signatures of two hundred (200) qualified voters from each of at least fifty (50) counties within the State." Ill. Rev. Stat. c. 46, § 10–2 (1947). Appellants are the "Progressive Party," its nominees for United States Senator, Presidential Electors, and State offices, and several Illinois voters. Appellees are the Governor, the Auditor of Public Accounts, and the Secretary of State of Illinois, members of the Boards of Election Commissioners of various cities, and the County Clerks of various counties. The District Court found want of jurisdiction and denied the injunction. 80 F. Supp. 725. Appellants invoke the jurisdiction of this Court under 28 U. S. C. § 1253.

The action arises from the finding of the State Officers Electoral Board that appellants had not obtained the requisite number of signatures from the requisite number of counties and its consequent ruling that their nominating petition was "not sufficient in law to entitle the said candidates' names to appear on the ballot." The appellants' claim to equitable relief against this ruling is based upon the peculiar distribution of population among Illinois' 102 counties. They allege that 52% of the State's registered voters are residents of Cook County alone, 87% are residents of the 49 most populous counties, and only 13% reside in the 53 least populous counties. Under these circumstances, they say, the Illinois statute is so discriminatory in its application as to amount to a denial of the due-process, equal-protection, and privileges-and-immunities clauses of the Fourteenth Amendment, as well as Article I, §§ 2 and 4, Article II, § 1, and the Seventeenth Amendment of the Constitution of the United States.

It is clear that the requirement of 200 signatures from at least 50 counties gives to the voters of the less populous counties of Illinois the power completely to block the nomination of candidates whose support is confined to geographically limited areas.

**339**

But the State is entitled to deem this power not disproportionate: of 25,000 signatures required, only 9,800, or 39%, need be distributed; the remaining 61% may be obtained from a single county. And Cook County, the largest, contains not more than 52% of the State's voters. It is allowable State policy to require that candidates for state-wide office should have support not limited to a concentrated locality. This is not a unique policy. See New York Laws 1896, c. 909, § 57, now N. Y. Elec. Law § 137(4); 113 Laws of Ohio 349, Gen. Code, § 4785-91 (1929), now Ohio Code Ann. (Cum. Supp. 1947) § 4785-91; Mass. Acts 1943, c. 334, § 2, now Mass. Ann. Laws c. 53, § 6 (1945). To assume that political power is a function exclusively of numbers is to disregard the practicalities of government. Thus, the Constitution protects the interests of the smaller against the greater by giving in the Senate entirely unequal representation to populations. It would be strange indeed, and doctrinaire, for this Court, applying such broad constitutional concepts as due process and equal protection of the laws, to deny a State the power to assure a proper diffusion of political initiative as between its thinly populated counties and those having concentrated masses, in view of the fact that the latter have practical opportunities for exerting their political weight at the polls not available to the former. The Constitution—a practical instrument of government—makes no such demands on the States. *Colegrove* v. *Green*, 328 U. S. 549, and *Colegrove* v. *Barrett*, 330 U. S. 804.

On the record before us, we need not pass upon purely local questions, also urged by appellants, having no federal constitutional aspect.

*Judgment affirmed.*

[Mr. Justice Rutledge concurred in the result on the ground that the Court should decline to exercise its equity jurisdiction for the reason that, with only 12 days remaining before the election, the ballots already printed and absentee ballots already distributed, judicial action might prove ineffective and disrupt the entire Illinois electoral process.]

MR. JUSTICE DOUGLAS, with whom MR. JUSTICE BLACK and MR. JUSTICE MURPHY concur, dissenting.

I think that the 1935 amendment of the Illinois Election Code, Ill. Rev. Stat. c. 46, § 10-2 (1947), as construed and applied in this case, violates the Equal Protection Clause of the Fourteenth Amendment.

That statute requires the nominating petition of a new political party, which places candidates on the ballot for the general election, to contain 200 signatures from each of at least 50 of the 102 counties in the state. The statute does not attempt to make the required signatures proportionate to the population of each county. One effect of this requirement is that the electorate in 49 of the counties which contain 87% of the registered voters could not form a new political party and place its candidates on the ballot. Twenty-five thousand of the remaining 13% of registered voters, however, properly distributed among the 53 remaining counties could form a new party to elect candidates to office. That regulation thus discriminates against the residents of the populous counties of the state in favor of rural sections. It therefore lacks the equality to which the exercise of political rights is entitled under the Fourteenth Amendment. . . .

None would deny that a state law giving some citizens twice the vote of other citizens in either the primary or general election would lack that equality which the Fourteenth Amendment guarantees. See *Nixon* v. *Herndon*, 273 U. S. 536. The dilution of political rights may be as complete and effective if the same discrimination appears in the procedure prescribed for nominating petitions. See *State* v. *Junkin*, 85 Neb. 1, 122 N. W. 473. It would, of course, be palpably discriminatory in violation of the Equal Protection Clause if this law were aimed at the Progressive Party in the manner that the state law in *Nixon* v. *Herndon, supra,* was aimed at negroes. But the effect of a state law may bring it under the condemnation of the Equal Protection Clause however innocent its purpose. It is invalid if discrimination is apparent in its operation. The test is whether it has some foundation in experience, practicality, or necessity. See *Skinner* v. *Oklahoma,* 316 U. S. 535, 541–542.

It is not enough to say that this law can stand that test because it is designed to require statewide support for the launching of a new political party rather than support from a few localities. There is no attempt here, as I have said, to make the required signatures even approximately proportionate to the distribution of voters among the various counties of the state. No such proportionate allocation could of course be mathematically exact. Nor would it be required. But when, as here, the law applies a rigid, arbitrary formula to sparsely settled counties and populous counties alike, it offers no basis whatever to justify giving greater weight to the individual votes of one group of citizens than to those of another group. This legislation therefore has the same inherent infirmity as that which some of us saw in *Colegrove* v. *Green,* 328 U. S. 549, 569. The fact that the Constitution itself sanctions inequalities in some phases of our political system does not justify us in allowing a state to create additional ones. The theme of the Constitution is equality among citizens in the exercise of their political rights. The notion that

**341**

one group can be granted greater voting strength than another is hostile to our standards for popular representative government.

Federal courts should be most hesitant to use the injunction in state elections. See *Wilson* v. *North Carolina*, 169 U. S. 586, 596. If federal courts undertook the role of superintendence, disruption of the whole electoral process might result, and the elective system that is vital to our government might be paralyzed. Cf. *Johnson* v. *Stevenson*, 170 F. 2d 108. The equity court, moreover, must always be alert in the exercise of its discretion to make sure that its decree will not be a futile and ineffective thing. But the case, as made before us, does not indicate that either of those considerations should deter us in striking down this unconstitutional statute and in freeing the impending Illinois election of its impediments. The state officials who are responsible for the election and who at this bar confessed error in the decision of the District Court make no such intimation or suggestion. We are therefore not authorized to assume that our decree would interfere with the orderly process of the election.

### Note

For full discussion see Note, *Legal Obstacles to Minority Party Success*, 57 Yale L. J. 1276 (1948); Note, *Denial of Equal Voting Facilities to Minor Parties*, 50 Col. L. Rev. 712 (1950); Note, *The Right to Form a Political Party*, 43 Ill. L. Rev. 832 (1949); Note, *Legal Barriers Confronting Third Parties*, 16 U. of Chi. L. Rev. 499 (1949); Note, 34 Corn. L. Q. 620 (1949); American Civil Liberties Union, *Minority Parties on the Ballot* (rev. 1943).

With respect to the rights of political groups alleged to be subversive, see Chapter IV, *infra*.

### 3. Restraints on Electioneering

Extensive Federal and state legislation regulates the conduct of elections and election campaigns. The great bulk of this legislation raises no question of undue restraint upon exercise of the franchise and has been subject to criticism only for its inadequacy and ineffectiveness. But serious issues have arisen with respect to two more recent developments in this field. One concerns the restraints imposed upon political expenditures by labor organizations; the other relates to political activities by government employees.

THE RIGHT OF FRANCHISE

## SECTION 304 OF THE TAFT-HARTLEY ACT

### 18 U. S. C. § 610 (1951)

It is unlawful for any national bank, or any corporation organized by authority of any law of Congress, to make a contribution or expenditure in connection with any election to any political office, or in connection with any primary election or political convention or caucus held to select candidates for any political office, or for any corporation whatever, or any labor organization to make a contribution or expenditure in connection with any election at which Presidential and Vice Presidential electors or a Senator or Representative in, or a Delegate or Resident Commissioner to Congress are to be voted for, or in connection with any primary election or political convention or caucus held to select candidates for any of the foregoing offices, or for any candidate, political committee, or other person to accept or receive any contribution prohibited by this section.

Every corporation or labor organization which makes any contribution or expenditure in violation of this section shall be fined not more than $5,000; and every officer or director of any corporation, or officer of any labor organization, who consents to any contribution or expenditure by the corporation or labor organization, as the case may be, and any person who accepts or receives any contribution, in violation of this section shall be fined not more than $1,000 or imprisoned not more than one year, or both; and if the violation was willful, shall be fined not more than $10,000 or imprisoned not more than two years, or both.

### Note

1. The Congress of Industrial Organizations sought to test the constitutionality of Section 304 in *United States v. Congress of Industrial Organizations*, 335 U. S. 106, 92 L. Ed. 1849, 68 S. Ct. 1349 (1948). The indictment charged that the CIO and its president published with union funds a regular periodical containing an editorial favoring one candidate in a Maryland Congressional election, and expended union funds to print and distribute extra copies in the election district. The defendants contended that Section 304 violated, among other constitutional provisions, the right to freedom of speech, press and assembly and to petition the Government for redress of grievances, as guaranteed by the First Amendment. But the Supreme Court sidestepped the constitutional issues, holding that the indictment failed to state an offense under the statute: "We are unwilling to say that Congress by its prohibition against corporations or labor organizations making an 'expenditure in connection with any election' of candidates

for federal office intended to outlaw such a publication. We do not think [§ 304] reaches such a use of corporate or labor organization funds." 335 U. S. at 123–4. Mr. Justice Rutledge concurred in the result, with Justices Black, Douglas and Murphy joining him, arguing that the case came squarely within the prohibition of Section 304, but that the statute constituted a prior restraint on freedom of expression and assembly and violated the First Amendment.

Other efforts to challenge Section 304 likewise resulted in dismissal of the indictments on grounds that the conduct of the defendants was not prohibited by the statute. *U. S. v. Painters Local Union No. 481,* 172 F. 2d 854 (C. A. 2, 1949) (indictment charged union with making expenditures to purchase political advertisements in a newspaper and on the radio); *U. S. v. Construction and General Laborers Local Union No. 264,* 101 F. Supp. 869 (W. D. Mo., 1951) (three employees of the union devoted a considerable portion of their time to political campaign).

For discussion of Section 304 and the above cases, see Note, *Section 304, Taft-Hartley Act: Validity of Restrictions on Union Political Activity,* 57 Yale L. J. 806 (1948); Kallenbach, *The Taft-Hartley Act and Union Political Contributions and Expenditures,* 33 Minn. L. Rev. 1 (1948); Notes, 34 Va. L. Rev. 461 (1948); 27 Tex. L. Rev. 565 (1949); 7 Wash. and Lee L. Rev. 87 (1950). For comparable state legislation see Kallenbach, *supra,* at pp. 9–11; *Bowe v. Secretary of the Commonwealth,* 320 Mass. 230, 69 N. E. 2d 115 (1946); Note, 2 Wyo. L. J. 124 (1948).

2. With respect to the general problem of corrupt practices legislation, see Key, *Politics, Parties and Pressure Groups,* ch. 15 (2d ed. 1948); Overacker, *Presidential Campaign Funds,* 39 Am. Pol. Sci. Rev. 899 (1945); Lederle, *Political Committee Expenditures and the Hatch Act,* 44 Mich. L. Rev. 294 (1945); Clark, *Federal Regulation of Election Campaign Activities,* 6 Fed. B. J. 5 (1944); H. R. Rept. No. 2093, 78th Cong., 2d Sess. (1944); Sen. Rept. No. 101, 79th Cong., 1st Sess. (1945). For the Federal legislation, see 18 U. S. C. §§ 591–612 (1950); 2 U. S. C. §§ 241–56 (1951). The basic constitutionality of such legislation was upheld in *Burroughs v. U. S.,* 290 U. S. 534, 78 L. Ed. 484, 54 S. Ct. 287 (1934).

# SECTION 9 OF THE HATCH ACT

## 5 U. S. C. 118i (1950)

(a) It shall be unlawful for any person employed in the executive branch of the Federal Government, or any agency or department thereof, to use his official authority or influence for the purpose of interfering with an election or affecting the result thereof. No officer or employee in the executive branch of the Federal Government, or any agency or department thereof, shall take any active part in political management or in political campaigns. All such persons shall retain the right to vote as they may choose and to express their opinions on all political subjects and candidates. For the purposes of this section the term "officer" or "employee" shall not be construed to include (1) the President and Vice President of the United States; (2) persons whose compensation is paid from the appropriation for the office of the President; (3) heads and assistant heads of executive departments; (4) officers who are appointed by the President, by and with the advice and consent of the Senate, and who determine policies to be pursued by the United States in its relations with foreign powers or in the Nation-wide administration of Federal laws. . . .

(b) Any person violating the provisions of this section shall be removed immediately from the position or office held by him, and thereafter no part of the funds appropriated by any Act of Congress for such position or office shall be used to pay the compensation of such person. . . .

## Note

1. The constitutionality of Section 9 of the Hatch Act was sustained in *United Public Workers v. Mitchell*, 330 U. S. 75, 91 L. Ed. 754, 67 S. Ct. 556 (1947). In a suit for injunction and declaratory judgment the Court considered the application of the Act to a Federal employee, a roller in the Philadelphia mint, who had served as a "ward executive committeeman" and "on election day as a worker at the polls and a paymaster for the services of other party workers." 330 U. S. at 92. The Court found no violation of the First, Fifth, Ninth or Tenth Amendments, holding that the activity prohibited could be "reasonably deemed by Congress to interfere with the efficiency of the public service." 330 U. S. at 101. Justices Black and Rutledge dissented. Mr. Justice Douglas also dissented on the more limited ground that the Act could not be validly applied to an industrial worker as distinct from an administrative employee. Justices Murphy and Jackson did not participate.

Another provision of the Hatch Act applies the same restrictions to state employees "whose principal employment is in connection with any activity which is financed in whole or in part by loans or grants made by the United States or by any Federal agency." 5 U. S. C. § 118k (1950). This provision was upheld in *Oklahoma v. United States Civil Service Commission*, 330 U. S. 127, 91 L. Ed. 794, 67 S. Ct. 544 (1947). Justices Black and Rutledge dissented and Justices Murphy and Jackson did not participate.

For discussion of the Hatch Act and the *Mitchell* and *Oklahoma* decisions, see Kirchheimer, *The Historical and Comparative Background of the Hatch Law*, II Public Policy 341 (1941); Starr, *The Hatch Act—An Interpretation*, 30 National Municipal Rev. 418 (1941); Note, *Political Sterilization of Government Employees*, 47 Col. L. Rev. 295 (1947); Mosher, *Government Employees Under the Hatch Act*, 22 N. Y. U. L. Q. Rev. 233 (1947); Notes, 33 Corn. L. Q. 133 (1947); 15

Geo. Wash. L. Rev. 443 (1947); 32 Minn. L. Rev. 176, 301 (1948); Esman, *The Hatch Act—A Reappraisal,* 60 Yale L. J. 986 (1951).

Of a more general nature, see Mosher and Kingsley, *Public Personnel Administration* (1936); Morstein Marx, *Elements of Public Administration* (1946); Spero, *Government as Employer* (1948).

With respect to the treatment of the problem in other countries, see White et al., *Civil Service Abroad* (1935); Kingsley, *Representative Bureaucracy* (1944); Morstein Marx, *Comparative Administrative Law: Political Activity of Civil Servants,* 29 Va. L. Rev. 52 (1942); Emerson and Helfeld, *Loyalty Among Government Employees,* 58 Yale L. J. 1, 120–133 (1948).

2. In *Ray v. Blair,* 343 U. S. 214, 96 L. Ed. —, 72 S. Ct. 654 (1952), the Supreme Court ruled that candidates for Presidential electors could be required by the Alabama State Democratic Committee, as a condition of running in the Democratic primary, to pledge that they would "aid and support the nominees of the National Convention of the Democratic Party for President and Vice President," even though such nominees had not yet been selected. Justices Jackson and Douglas dissented. Justices Black and Frankfurter did not participate. For other material on the efforts of state parties to avoid supporting the national candidate of the party, see Note, 34 Va. L. Rev. 619 (1948). See also Note, 34 Corn. L. Q. 430 (1949).

On proposals to revise the system of electing the President and Vice-President, see Wechsler, *Presidential Elections and the Constitution: A Comment on Proposed Amendment,* 35 A. B. A. J. 181 (1949); Silva, *The Lodge-Gossett Resolution: A Critical Analysis,* 44 Am. Pol. Sci. Rev. 86 (1950).

3. With respect to the right to a secret ballot see Nutting, *Freedom of Silence: Constitutional Protection Against Governmental Intrusions in Political Affairs,* 47 Mich. L. Rev. 181, 181–200 (1948); *Smith v. Blackwell,* 115 F. 2d 186 (C. A. 4, 1940).

4. The denial of the franchise to residents of the District of Columbia is discussed in the Report of the President's Committee on Civil Rights, *To Secure These Rights,* pp. 35, 161 (1947); *Bar Association Members Urge Vote for District of Columbia,* 13 J. of the Bar Assn of the D. C. 30 (1946); Bendiner, *Colonial Washington,* The Nation, Apr. 1, 1950, p. 292.

5. On the right of Indians to vote see *Harrison v. Laveen,* 67 Ariz. 337, 196 Pac. 2d 456 (1948).

# CHAPTER IV

# FREEDOM OF SPEECH: RIGHT OF POLITICAL ORGANIZATION AND POLITICAL EXPRESSION

## A. THE TRADITION

### MILTON—AREOPAGITICA

A Speech for the Liberty of Unlicensed Printing, To the Parliament
of England (1644)
Everyman's Library, pp. 23–38 (1927)

[Milton's speech was directed against an order of Parliament of June 14, 1643, which among other things provided that no book "shall from henceforth be printed or put to sale, unless the same be first approved of and licensed by such person or persons as both or either of the said Houses (of Parliament) shall appoint for the licensing of the same." After discussing the history of licensing, the values of reading, the ineffectiveness of the order to suppress scandalous, seditious or libellous books, and the inhibitions it places upon scholars and writers, Milton goes on to consider the effect of the licensing system upon the growth and development of the country as a whole.]

And as it is a particular disesteem of every knowing person alive, and most injurious to the written labours and monuments of the dead, so to me it seems an undervaluing and vilifying of the whole Nation. I cannot set so light by all the invention, the art, the wit, the grave and solid judgment which is in England, as that it can be comprehended in any twenty capacities how good soever, much less that it should not pass except their superintendence be over it, except it be sifted and strained with their strainers, that it should be uncurrent without their manual stamp. Truth and understanding are not such wares as to be monopolised and traded in by tickets and statutes and standards. We must not think to make a staple commodity of all the knowledge in the land, to mark and licence it like our broadcloth and our woolpacks. What is it but a servitude like that imposed by the Philistines, not to be allowed the sharpening of our own axes and coulters, but we must repair from all quarters to twenty licensing forges? Had anyone written and divulged erroneous things and scandalous to honest life, misusing and forfeiting the esteem had of his reason among men, if after conviction this only censure were adjudged him that he should never henceforth

**347**

write but what were first examined by an appointed officer, whose hand should be annexed to pass his credit for him that now he might be safely read; it could not be apprehended less than a disgraceful punishment. Whence to include the whole Nation, and those that never yet thus offended, under such a diffident and suspectful prohibition, may plainly be understood what a disparagement it is. So much the more, whenas debtors and delinquents may walk abroad without a keeper, but unoffensive books must not stir forth without a visible jailer in their title.

Nor is it to the common people less than a reproach; for if we be so jealous over them, as that we dare not trust them with an English pamphlet, what do we but censure them for a giddy, vicious, and ungrounded people; in such a sick and weak state of faith and discretion, as to be able to take nothing down but through the pipe of a licenser? That this is care or love of them, we cannot pretend, whenas, in those popish places where the laity are most hated and despised, the same strictness is used over them. Wisdom we cannot call it, because it stops but one breach of licence, nor that neither: whenas those corruptions, which it seeks to prevent, break in faster at other doors which cannot be shut. . . .

Well knows he who uses to consider, that our faith and knowledge thrives by exercise, as well as our limbs and complexion. Truth is compared in Scripture to a streaming fountain; if her waters flow not in a perpetual progression, they sicken into a muddy pool of conformity and tradition. A man may be a heretic in the truth; and if he believe things only because his Pastor says so, or the Assembly so determines, without knowing other reason, though his belief be true, yet the very truth he holds becomes his heresy. . . .

There be who perpetually complain of schisms and sects, and make it such a calamity that any man dissents from their maxims. 'Tis their own pride and ignorance which causes the disturbing, who neither will hear with meekness, nor can convince; yet all must be suppressed which is not found in their Syntagma. They are the troublers, they are the dividers of unity, who neglect and permit not others to unite those dissevered pieces which are yet wanting to the body of Truth. To be still searching what we know not by what we know, still closing up truth to truth as we find it (for all her body is homogeneal and proportional), this is the golden rule in theology as well as in arithmetic, and makes up the best harmony in a Church; not the forced and outward union of cold and neutral, and inwardly divided minds.

Lords and Commons of England, consider what Nation it is whereof ye are, and whereof ye are the governors: a Nation not slow and dull, but of a quick, ingenious and piercing spirit, acute to invent, subtle and sinewy to discourse, not beneath the reach of any point, the highest that human capacity can soar to. . . .

Behold now this vast City: a city of refuge, the mansion house of liberty, encompassed and surrounded with His protection; the shop of war hath not there more anvils and hammers waking, to fashion out the plates and instruments of armed Justice in defence of beleaguered Truth, than there be pens and heads there, sitting by their studious lamps, musing, searching, revolving new notions and ideas wherewith to present, as with their homage and their fealty, the approaching Reformation: others as fast reading, trying all things, assenting to the force of reason and convincement. What could a man require more from a Nation so pliant and so prone to seek after knowledge? What wants there to such a towardly and pregnant soil, but wise and faithful labourers, to make a knowing people, a Nation of Prophets, of Sages, and of Worthies? We reckon more than five months yet to harvest; there need not be five weeks; had we but eyes to lift up, the fields are white already.

Where there is much desire to learn, there of necessity will be much arguing, much writing, many opinions; for opinion in good men is but knowledge in the making. Under these fantastic terrors of sect and schism, we wrong the earnest and zealous thirst after knowledge and understanding which God hath stirred up in this city. What some lament of, we rather should rejoice at, should rather praise this pious forwardness among men, to reassume the ill-reputed care of their Religion into their own hands again. A little generous prudence, a little forbearance of one another, and some grain of charity might win all these diligences to join, and unite in one general and brotherly search after Truth. . . .

Yet these are the men cried out against for schismatics and sectaries; as if, while the temple of the Lord was building, some cutting, some squaring the marble, others hewing the cedars, there should be a sort of irrational men who could not consider there must be many schisms and many dissections made in the quarry and in the timber, ere the house of God can be built. And when every stone is laid artfully together, it cannot be united into a continuity, it can but be contiguous in this world; neither can every piece of the building be of one form; nay rather the perfection consists in this, that, out of many moderate varieties and brotherly dissimilitudes that are not vastly disproportional, arises the goodly and the graceful symmetry that commends the whole pile and structure. . . .

The adversary again applauds, and waits the hour: When they have branched themselves out, saith he, small enough into

349

parties and partitions, then will be our time. Fool! he sees not the firm root, out of which we all grow, though into branches: nor will be ware until he see our small divided maniples cutting through at every angle of his ill-united and unwieldy brigade. And that we are to hope better of all these supposed sects and schisms, and that we shall not need that solicitude, honest perhaps though over-timorous of them that vex in his behalf, but shall laugh in the end at those malicious applauders of our differences, I have these reasons to persuade me.

First, when a City shall be as it were besieged and blocked about, her navigable river infested, inroads and incursions round, defiance and battle oft rumoured to be marching up even to her walls and suburb trenches, that then the people, or the greater part, more than at other times, wholly taken up with the study of highest and most important matters to be reformed, should be disputing, reasoning, reading, inventing, discoursing, even to a rarity and admiration, things not before discoursed or written of, argues first a singular goodwill, contentedness and confidence in your prudent foresight and safe government, Lords and Commons; and from thence derives itself to a gallant bravery and well-grounded contempt of their enemies, as if there were no small number of as great spirits among us, as his was, who when Rome was nigh besieged by Hannibal, being in the city, bought that piece of ground at no cheap rate, whereon Hannibal himself encamped his own regiment.

Next, it is a lively and cheerful presage of our happy success and victory. For as in a body, when the blood is fresh, the spirits pure and vigorous, not only to vital but to rational faculties, and those in the acutest and the pertest operations of wit and subtlety, it argues in what good plight and constitution the body is so when the cheerfulness of the people is so sprightly up, as that it has not only wherewith to guard well its own freedom and safety, but to spare, and to bestow upon the solidest and sublimest points of controversy and new invention, it betokens us not degenerated, nor drooping to a fatal decay, but casting off the old and wrinkled skin of corruption to outlive these pangs and wax young again, entering the glorious ways of truth and prosperous virtue, destined to become great and honourable in these latter ages. Methinks I see in my mind a noble and puissant nation rousing herself like a strong man after sleep, and shaking her invincible locks. Methinks I see her as an eagle mewing her mighty youth, and kindling her undazzled eyes at the full midday beam; purging and unscaling her long-abused sight at the fountain itself of heavenly radiance; while the whole noise of timorous and flocking birds, with those also that love the twilight, flutter about, amazed at what she means, and in their envious gabble would prognosticate a year of sects and schisms.

What would ye do then? should ye suppress all this flowery crop of knowledge and new light sprung up and yet springing daily in this city? should ye set an oligarthy of twenty engrossers over it, to bring a famine upon our minds again, when we shall know nothing but what is measured to us by their bushel? . . .

And now the time in special is, by privilege to write and speak what may help to the further discussing of matters in agitation. The temple of Janus with his two controversial faces might now not unsignificantly be set open. And though all the winds of doctrine were let loose to play upon the earth, so Truth be in the field, we do injuriously, by licensing and prohibiting, to misdoubt her strength. Let her and Falsehood grapple; who ever knew Truth put to the worse, in a free and open encounter? Her confuting is the best and surest suppressing. . . .

I fear yet this iron yoke of outward conformity hath left a slavish print upon our necks; the ghost of a linen decency yet haunts us. We stumble and are impatient at the least dividing of one visible congregation from another, though it be not in fundamentals; and through our forwardness to suppress, and our backwardness to recover any enthralled piece of truth out of the gripe of custom, we care not to keep truth separated from truth, which is the fiercest rent and disunion of all. We do not see that, while we still affect by all means a rigid external formality, we may as soon fall again into a gross conforming stupidity, a stark and dead congealment of wood and hay and stubble, forced and frozen together, which is more to the sudden degenerating of a Church than many subdichotomies of petty schisms.

Not that I can think well of every light separation, or that all in a Church is to be expected gold and silver and precious stones: it is not possible for man to sever the wheat from the tares, the good fish from the other fry; that must be the Angels' Ministry at the end of mortal things. Yet if all cannot be of one mind— as who looks they should be?—this doubtless is more wholesome, more prudent, and more Christian that many be tolerated, rather than all compelled. I mean not tolerated popery, and open superstition, which, as it extirpates all religions and civil supremacies, so itself should be extirpate, provided first that all charitable and compassionate means be used to win and regain the weak and the misled: that also which is impious or evil absolutely either against faith or manners no law can possibly permit, that intends not to unlaw itself: but those neighbouring differences, or rather indifferences, are what I speak of, whether in some point of doctrine or of discipline, which, though they may be many, yet need not interrupt the unity of Spirit, if we could but find among us the bond of peace.

In the meantime if any one would write, and bring his helpful hand to the slow-moving Reformation which we labour under, if Truth have spoken to him before others, or but seemed at least to speak, who hath so bejesuited us that we should trouble that man with asking licence to do so worthy a deed? and not consider this, that if it come to prohibiting, there is not aught more likely to be prohibited than truth itself; whose first appearance to our eyes, bleared and dimmed with prejudice and custom, is more unsightly and unplausible than many errors, even as the person is of many a great man slight and contemptible to see to. And what do they tell us vainly of new opinions, when this very opinion of theirs, that none must be heard, but whom they like, is the worst and newest opinion of all others; and is the chief cause why sects and schisms do so much abound, and true knowledge is kept at distance from us. . . .

## DECLARATION OF INDEPENDENCE
### July 4, 1776

When in the Course of human events, it becomes necessary for one people to dissolve the political bands, which have connected them with another, and to assume, among the powers of the earth, the separate and equal station, to which the Laws of Nature and of Nature's God entitle them, a decent respect to the Opinions of mankind requires that they should declare the causes which impel them to the separation.—We hold these truths to be self-evident, that all men are created equal, that they are endowed by their Creator with certain unalienable Rights, that among these are Life, Liberty and the pursuit of Happiness.— That to secure these rights, Governments are instituted among Men, deriving their just powers from the consent of the governed, —That whenever any Form of Government becomes destructive of these ends, it is the Right of the People to alter or to abolish it, and to institute new Government, laying its foundation on such principles and organizing its powers in such form, as to them shall seem most likely to effect their Safety and Happiness. Prudence, indeed, will dictate that Governments long established should not be changed for light and transient causes; and accordingly all experience hath shewn, that mankind are more disposed to suffer, while evils are sufferable, than to right themselves by abolishing the forms to which they are accustomed. But when a long train of abuses and usurpations, pursuing invariably the same Object evinces a design to reduce them under absolute Despotism, it is their right, it is their duty to throw off such Government, and to provide new Guards for their future security. —Such has been the patient sufferance of these Colonies; and such is now the necessity which constrains them to alter their former Systems of Government.

## JEFFERSON—FIRST INAUGURAL ADDRESS

### March 4, 1801

Padover, The Complete Jefferson, pp. 384–5 (1943)

During the contest of opinion through which we have passed, the animation of discussion and of exertions has sometimes worn an aspect which might impose on strangers unused to think freely and to speak and to write what they think; but this being now decided by the voice of the nation, announced according to the rules of the constitution, all will, of course, arrange themselves under the will of the law, and unite in common efforts for the common good. All, too, will bear in mind this sacred principle, that though the will of the majority is in all cases to prevail, that will, to be rightful, must be reasonable; that the minority possess their equal rights, which equal laws must protect, and to violate which would be oppression. Let us, then, fellow-citizens, unite with one heart and one mind. Let us restore to social intercourse that harmony and affection without which liberty and even life itself are but dreary things. And let us reflect that having banished from our land that religious intolerance under which mankind so long bled and suffered, we have yet gained little if we countenance a political intolerance as despotic, as wicked, and capable of as bitter and bloody persecutions. During the throes and convulsions of the ancient world, during the agonizing spasms of infuriated man, seeking through blood and slaughter his long-lost liberty, it was not wonderful that the agitation of the billows should reach even this distant and peaceful shore; that this should be more felt and feared by some and less by others; that this should divide opinions as to measures of safety. But every difference of opinion is not a difference of principle. We have called by different names brethren of the same principle. We are all republicans—we are federalists. If there be any among us who would wish to dissolve this Union or to change its republican form, let them stand undisturbed as monuments of the safety with which error of opinion may be tolerated where reason is left free to combat it. I know, indeed, that some honest men fear that a republican government cannot be strong; that this government is not strong enough. But would the honest patriot, in the full tide of successful experiment, abandon a government which has so far kept us free and firm, on the theoretic and visionary fear that this government, the world's best hope, may by possibility want energy to preserve itself? I trust not. I believe this, on the contrary, the strongest government on earth. I believe it is the only one where every man, at the call of the laws, would fly to the standard of the law, and would meet invasions of the public order as his own personal concern. Sometimes it is said that man cannot be trusted with the government of himself. Can he, then, be trusted with the government of others? Or have we found angels in the forms of kings to govern him? Let history answer this question.

## JOHN STUART MILL—ON LIBERTY
### 1859

McCallum ed., pp. 15, 24–5, 30–1, 40–1, 47–8 (1946)

First: The opinion which it is attempted to suppress by authority may possibly be true. Those who desire to suppress it, of course deny its truth; but they are not infallible. They have no authority to decide the question for all mankind, and exclude every other person from the means of judging. To refuse a hearing to an opinion, because they are sure that it is false, is to assume that *their* certainty is the same thing as *absolute* certainty. All silencing of discussion is an assumption of infallibility. Its condemnation may be allowed to rest on this common argument, not the worse for being common. . . .

But, indeed, the dictum that truth always triumphs over persecution is one of those pleasant falsehoods which men repeat after one another till they pass into commonplaces, but which all experience refutes. History teems with instances of truth put down by persecution. If not suppressed for ever, it may be thrown back for centuries. To speak only of religious opinions: the Reformation broke out at least twenty times before Luther, and was put down. Arnold of Brescia was put down. Fra Dolcino was put down. Savonarola was put down. The Albigeois were put down. The Vaudois were put down. The Lollards were put down. The Hussites were put down. Even after the era of Luther, wherever persecution was persisted in, it was successful. In Spain, Italy, Flanders, the Austrian Empire, Protestantism was rooted out; and, most likely, would have been so in England, had Queen Mary lived, or Queen Elizabeth died. Persecution has always succeeded, save where the heretics were too strong

[Emerson]

a party to be effectually persecuted. No reasonable person can doubt that Christianity might have been extirpated in the Roman Empire. It spread, and became predominant, because the persecutions were only occasional, lasting but a short time, and separated by long intervals of almost undisturbed propagandism. It is a piece of idle sentimentality that truth, merely as truth, has any inherent power denied to error of prevailing against the dungeon and the stake. Men are not more zealous for truth than they often are for error, and a sufficient application of legal or even of social penalties will generally succeed in stopping the propagation of either. The real advantage which truth has consists in this, that when an opinion is true, it may be extinguished once, twice, or many times, but in the course of ages there will generally be found persons to rediscover it, until some one of its reappearances falls on a time when from favourable circumstances it escapes persecution until it has made such head as to withstand all subsequent attempts to suppress it. . . .

Let us now pass to the second division of the argument, and dismissing the supposition that any of the received opinions may be false, let us assume them to be true, and examine into the worth of the manner in which they are likely to be held, when their truth is not freely and openly canvassed. However unwillingly a person who has a strong opinion may admit the possibility that his opinion may be false he ought to be moved by the consideration that, however true it may be, if it is not fully, frequently, and fearlessly discussed, it will be held as a dead dogma, not a living truth.

There is a class of persons (happily not quite so numerous as formerly) who think it enough if a person assents undoubtingly to what they think true, though he has not knowledge whatever of the grounds of the opinion, and could not make a tenable defence of it against the most superficial objections. Such persons, if they can once get their creed taught from authority, naturally think that no good, and some harm, comes of its being allowed to be questioned. Where their influence prevails, they make it nearly impossible for the received opinion to be rejected wisely and considerately, though it may still be rejected rashly and ignorantly; for to shut out discussion entirely is seldom possible, and when it once gets in, beliefs not grounded on conviction are apt to give way before the slightest semblance of an argument. Waiving, however, this possibility—assuming that the true opinion abides in the mind, but abides as a prejudice, a belief independent of, and proof against, argument—this is not the way in which truth ought to be held by a rational being. This is not knowing the truth. Truth, thus held, is but one supersti-

**355**

tion the more, accidentally clinging to the words which enunciate a truth. . . .

It still remains to speak of one of the principal causes which make diversity of opinion advantageous, and will continue to do so until mankind shall have entered a stage of intellectual advancement which at present seems at an incalculable distance. We have hitherto considered only two possibilities: that the received opinion may be false, and some other opinion, consequently, true; or that, the received opinion being true, a conflict with the opposite error is essential to a clear apprehension and deep feeling of its truth. But there is a commoner case than either of these; when the conflicting doctrines, instead of being one true and the other false, share the truth between them; and the nonconforming opinion is needed to supply the remainder of the truth, of which the received doctrine embodies only a part. Popular opinions, on subjects not palpable to sense, are often true, but seldom or never the whole truth. They are a part of the truth; sometimes a greater, sometimes a smaller part, but exaggerated, distorted, and disjointed from the truths by which they ought to be accompanied and limited. Heretical opinions, on the other hand, are generally some of these suppressed and neglected truths, bursting the bonds which kept them down, and either seeking reconciliation with the truth contained in the common opinion, or fronting it as enemies, and setting themselves up, with similar exclusiveness, as the whole truth. The latter case is hitherto the most frequent, as, in the human mind, one-sidedness has always been the rule, and many-sidedness the exception. Hence, even in revolutions of opinion, one part of the truth usually sets while another rises. Even progress, which ought to superadd, for the most part only substitutes, one partial and incomplete truth for another; improvement consisting chiefly in this, that the new fragment of truth is more wanted, more adapted to the needs of the time, than that which it displaces. Such being the partial character of prevailing opinions, even when resting on a true foundation, every opinion which embodies somewhat of the portion of truth which the common opinion omits, ought to be considered precious, with whatever amount of error and confusion that truth may be blended. No sober judge of human affairs will feel bound to be indignant because those who force on our notice truths which we should otherwise have overlooked, overlook some of those which we see. Rather, he will think that so long as popular truth is one-sided, it is more desirable than otherwise that unpopular truth should have one-sided assertors too; such being usually the most energetic, and the most likely to compel reluctant attention to the fragment of wisdom which they proclaim as if it were the whole. . . .

356

Before quitting the subject of freedom of opinion, it is fit to take some notice of those who say, that the free expression of all opinions should be permitted, on condition that the manner be temperate, and do not pass the bounds of fair discussion. Much might be said on the impossibility of fixing where these supposed bounds are to be placed; for if the test be offence to those whose opinions are attacked, I think experience testifies that this offence is given whenever the attack is telling and powerful, and that every opponent who pushes them hard, and whom they find it difficult to answer, appears to them, if he shows any strong feeling on the subject, an intemperate opponent. But this, though an important consideration in a practical point of view, merges in a more fundamental objection. Undoubtedly the manner of asserting an opinion, even though it be a true one, may be very objectionable, and may justly incur severe censure. But the principal offences of the kind are such as it is mostly impossible, unless by accidental self-betrayal, to bring home to conviction. The gravest of them is, to argue sophistically, to suppress facts or arguments, to misstate the elements of the case, or misrepresent the opposite opinion. But all this, even to the most aggravated degree, is so continually done in perfect good faith, by persons who are not considered, and in many other respects may not deserve to be considered, ignorant or incompetent, that it is rarely possible, on adequate grounds, conscientiously to stamp the misrepresentation as morally culpable; and still less could law presume to interfere with this kind of controversial misconduct. With regard to what is commonly meant by intemperate discussion, namely invective, sarcasm, personality, and the like, the denunciation of these weapons would deserve more sympathy if it were ever proposed to interdict them equally to both sides; but it is only desired to restrain the employment of them against the prevailing opinion: against the unprevailing they may not only be used without general disapproval, but will be likely to obtain for him who uses them the praise of honest zeal and righteous indignation. Yet whatever mischief arises from their use, is greatest when they are employed against the comparatively defenceless; and whatever unfair advantage can be derived by any opinion from this mode of asserting it, accrues almost exclusively to received opinions. The worst offence of this kind which can be committed by a polemic, is to stigmatise those who hold the contrary opinion as bad and immoral men. To calumny of this sort, those who hold any unpopular opinion are peculiarly exposed, because they are in general few and uninfluential, and nobody but themselves feels much interested in seeing justice done them; but this weapon is, from the nature of the case, denied to those who attack a prevailing opinion: they can neither use

**357**

it with safety to themselves, nor, if they could, would it do anything but recoil on their own cause. In general, opinions contrary to those commonly received can only obtain a hearing by studied moderation of language, and the most cautious avoidance of unnecessary offence, from which they hardly ever deviate even in a slight degree without losing ground: while unmeasured vituperation employed on the side of the prevailing opinion really does deter people from professing contrary opinions, and from listening to those who profess them. For the interest, therefore, of truth and justice, it is far more important to restrain this employment of vituperative language than the other; and, for example, if it were necessary to choose, there would be much more need to discourage offensive attacks on infidelity than on religion. It is, however, obvious that law and authority have no business with restraining either, while opinion ought, in every instance, to determine its verdict by the circumstances of the individual case; condemning every one, on whichever side of the argument he places himself, in whose mode of advocacy either want of candour, or malignity, bigotry, or intolerance of feeling manifest themselves; but not inferring these vices from the side which a person takes, though it be the contrary side of the question to our own: and giving merited honour to every one, whatever opinion he may hold, who has calmness to see and honesty to state what his opponents and their opinions really are, exaggerating nothing to their discredit, keeping nothing back which tells, or can be supposed to tell, in their favour. This is the real morality of public discussion: and if often violated, I am happy to think that there are many controversialists who to a great extent observe it, and a still greater number who conscientiously strive towards it.

## MR. JUSTICE HOLMES—DISSENTING OPINION IN ABRAMS v. UNITED STATES

250 U. S. 616, pp. 630–1, 63 L. Ed. 1173, p. 1180, 40 S. Ct. 17, p. 22 (1919)

Persecution for the expression of opinions seems to me perfectly logical. If you have no doubt of your premises or your power and want a certain result with all your heart you naturally express your wishes in law and sweep away all opposition. To allow opposition by speech seems to indicate that you think the speech impotent, as when a man says that he has squared the circle, or that you do not care wholeheartedly for the result, or that you doubt either your power or your premises. But when men have realized that time has upset many fighting faiths, they may come to believe even more than they believe the very foundations of their own conduct that the ultimate good desired is better reached by free trade in ideas—that the best test of truth is the power of the thought to get itself accepted in the competition of the market, and that truth is the only ground upon which their wishes safely can be carried out. That at any rate is the theory of our Constitution. It is an experiment, as all life is an experiment. Every year if not every day we have to wager our salvation upon some prophecy based upon imperfect knowledge. While that experiment is part of our system I think that we should be eternally vigilant against attempts to check the expression of opinions that we loathe and believe to be fraught with death, unless they so imminently threaten immediate interference with the lawful and pressing purposes of the law that an immediate check is required to save the country. . . . Only the emergency that makes it immediately dangerous to leave the correction of evil counsels to time warrants making any exception to the sweeping command, "Congress shall make no law . . . abridging the freedom of speech."

## MR. JUSTICE BRANDEIS—CONCURRING OPINION IN WHITNEY v. CALIFORNIA

274 U. S. 357, pp. 375–6, 71 L. Ed. 1095, pp. 1105–6, 47 S. Ct. 641, p. 648 (1927)

Those who won our independence believed that the final end of the State was to make men free to develop their faculties; and that in its government the deliberative forces should prevail over the arbitrary. They valued liberty both as an end and as a means. They believed liberty to be the secret of happiness and courage to be the secret of liberty. They believed that freedom to think as you will and to speak as you think are means indispensable to the discovery and spread of political truth; that without free speech and assembly discussion would be futile; that with them, discussion affords ordinarily adequate protection against the dissemination of noxious doctrine; that the greatest menace to freedom is an inert people; that public discussion is a political duty; and that this should be a fundamental principle of the American government. They recognized the risks to which all human institutions are subject. But they knew that order cannot be secured merely through fear of punishment for its infraction; that it is hazardous to discourage thought, hope and imagination; that fear breeds repression; that repression breeds hate; that hate menaces stable government; that the path of safety lies in the opportunity to discuss freely supposed grievances and proposed remedies; and that the fitting remedy for evil counsels is good ones. Believing in the power of reason as applied through public discussion, they eschewed silence coerced by law—the argument of force in its worst form. Recognizing the occasional tyrannies of governing majorities, they amended the Constitution so that free speech and assembly should be guaranteed.

## MEIKLEJOHN—FREE SPEECH AND ITS RELATION TO SELF-GOVERNMENT

Copyright, 1948, by Harper & Brothers, pp. 15–6, 25–7

Our preliminary remarks about the Constitution of the United States may, then, be briefly summarized. That Constitution is based upon a twofold political agreement. It is ordained that all authority to exercise control, to determine common action, belongs to "We, the People." We, and we alone, are the rulers. But it is ordained also that We, the People, are, all alike, subject to control. Every one of us may be told what he is allowed to do, what he is not allowed to do, what he is required to do. But this agreed-upon requirement of obedience does not transform a ruler into a slave. Citizens do not become puppets of the state when, having created it by common consent, they pledge allegiance to it and keep their pledge. Control by a self-governing nation is utterly different in kind from control by an irresponsible despotism. And to confuse these two is to lose all understanding of what political freedom is. Under actual conditions, there is no freedom for men except by the authority of government. Free men are not non-governed. They are governed—by themselves. . . .

The First Amendment, then, is not the guardian of unregulated talkativeness. It does not require that, on every occasion, every citizen shall take part in public debate. Nor can it even give assurance that everyone shall have opportunity to do so. . . . What is essential is not that everyone shall speak, but that everything worth saying shall be said. To this end, for example, it may be arranged that each of the known conflicting points of view shall have, and shall be limited to, an assigned share of the time available. But however it be arranged, the vital point, as stated negatively, is that no suggestion of policy shall be denied a hearing because it is on one side of the issue rather than another. And this means that though citizens may, on other grounds, be barred from speaking, they may not be barred because their views are thought to be false or dangeruos. No plan of action shall be outlawed because someone in control thinks it unwise, unfair, un-American. No speaker may be declared "out of order" because we disagree with what he intends to say. And the reason for this equality of status in the field of ideas lies deep in the very foundations of the self-governing process. When men govern themselves, it is they—and no one else—who must pass judgment upon unwisdom and unfairness and danger. And that means that unwise ideas must have a hearing as well as wise ones, unfair as well as fair, dangerous as well as safe, un-American as well as American. Just so far as, at any point, the citizens who are to decide an issue are denied acquaintance with information or opinion or doubt or disbelief or criticism which is relevant to that issue, just so far the result must be ill-considered, ill-balanced planning for the general good. *It is that mutilation of the thinking process of the community against which the First Amendment to the Constitution is directed.* The principle of the freedom of speech springs from the necessities of the program of self-government. It is not a Law of Nature or of Reason in the abstract. It is a deduction from the basic American agreement that public issues shall be decided by universal suffrage.

If, then, on any occasion in the United States it is allowable to say that the Constitution is a good document it is equally allowable, in that situation, to say that the Constitution is a bad document. If a public building may be used in which to say, in time of war, that the war is justified, then the same building may be used in which to say that it is not justified. If it be publicly argued that conscription for armed service is moral and necessary, it may likewise be publicly argued that it is immoral and unnecessary. If it may be said that American political institutions are superior to those of England or Russia or Germany, it may, with equal freedom, be said that those of England or Russia or Germany are superior to ours. These conflicting views may be expressed, must be expressed, not because they are valid, but because they are relevant. If they are responsibly entertained by anyone, we, the voters, need to hear them. When a question of policy is "before the house," free men choose to meet it not with their eyes shut, but with their eyes open. To be afraid of ideas, any idea, is to be unfit for self-government. Any such suppression of ideas about the common good, the First Amendment condemns with its absolute disapproval. The freedom of ideas shall not be abridged.

### Note

For other contributions to the tradition of freedom of political expression, see Locke, *The Second Treatise of Civil Government* (1690); Paine, *The Rights of Man* (1791); Condorcet, *Outlines of an Historical*

*View of the Progress of the Human Mind* (1796) ; Jefferson, *The Kentucky Resolutions* (1798) in Padover, *The Complete Jefferson*, pp. 128–34 (1943) ; Bagehot, *Physics and Politics* (1873) ; Bagehot, *The Metaphysical Basis of Toleration* (1874).

Modern protagonists of freedom of political expression include: Dewey, *Freedom and Culture* (1939) ; Chafee, *Free Speech in the United States* (2d ed., 1941) ; Commager, *The Pragmatic Necessity for Freedom* in Wilcox (ed.), *Civil Liberties Under Attack* (1951) ; Lasswell, *Political Writings of Harold D. Lasswell* (1951) ; Mumford, *The Conduct of Life* (1951) ; Anshen (ed.), *Freedom: Its Meaning* (1940) ; Maritain, *Freedom in the Modern World* (1936) ; Laski, *Liberty in the Modern State* (1930).

Collections of basic materials may be found in Chafee, *Documents on Fundamental Human Rights* (prelim. ed., 1951) ; Coker, *Democracy, Liberty and Property* (1942) ; MacIver, *Great Expressions of Human Rights* (1950) ; H. M. Jones, *Primer of Intellectual Freedom* (1949) ; B. Smith, *The Democratic Spirit* (1941). See also Hacker, *The Shaping of the American Tradition* (1947).

For the historical development of freedom of expression see Bury, *A History of Freedom of Thought* (1913) ; Lecky, *A History of the Rise and Influence of the Spirit of Rationalism in Europe* (1866) ; Acton, *Essays on Freedom and Power*, esp. ch. II–IV (Himmelfarb ed., 1948) ; Laski, *The Rise of European Liberalism* (1936) ; Sabine, *A History of Political Theory* (rev. ed., 1950) ; Curti, *The Roots of American Loyalty* (1946).

For discussions of the problem in its modern setting, see Riesman, *Civil Liberties in a Period of Transition*, in III Public Policy (1942) ; Fromm, *Escape from Freedom* (1941) ; Fromm, *Man for Himself* (1947) ; West, *Conscience and Society* (1942) ; Flügel, *Man, Morals and Society* (1945) ; De Grazia, *The Political Community: A Study of Anomie* (1948) ; Kluckhohn, *Mirror for Man* (1949) ; Emerson, *An Essay on Freedom of Political Expression Today*, 11 Law. Guild Rev. 1 (1951).

For discussion of the function of a written constitution and institutions such as judicial review in achieving democratic liberties see McIlwain, *Constitutionalism: Ancient and Modern* (rev. ed., 1947) ; Patterson, *The Evolution of Constitutionalism*, 32 Minn. L. Rev. 427 (1948) ; Dowling, *Cases on Constitutional Law*, pp. 1–70 (bibliography at pp. 69–70) (4th. ed., 1950) ; Lieber, *On Civil Liberty and Self-Government* (1853).

With respect to the impact on freedom of modern government and its accompanying economic controls, see Hayek, *The Road to Serfdom* (1944) ; Wootton, *Freedom under Planning* (1945) ; Mannheim, *Freedom, Power, and Democratic Planning* (1950) ; Russell, *Authority and the Individual* (1949) ; Schumpeter, *Capitalism, Socialism and Democracy*, (1950).

For studies of anti-democratic thought processes, see Spitz, *Patterns of Anti-Democratic Thought* (1949) ; Alexander, *The Emotional Structure of Totalitarianism*, in *Our Age of Unreason* (1942) ; Arendt, *The Origins of Totalitarianism* (1951).

For philosophic critiques of democratic thought, see Hobbes, *Leviathan* (1651); Nietzsche, *Beyond Good and Evil* and *The Will to Power* (*The Complete Works of Friedrich Nietzsche*, 1924); Pareto, *The Mind and Society* (1935); Plato, *The Republic*. See also Chapters VII and VIII, *infra*.

## B. FREEDOM OF POLITICAL EXPRESSION IN UNITED STATES HISTORY

### 1. Background of the First Amendment

The United States Constitution, as originally adopted, contained no provision dealing expressly with the right to freedom of political expression. The delegates to the Constitutional Convention seemed to have assumed that the Federal Government, possessing only the enumerated powers, would not be authorized to legislate in the field of political expression and that no express limitation upon its power in that area was necessary. But popular pressure forced the adoption of the Bill of Rights in 1791, the first of which expressly guaranteed:

"Congress shall make no law respecting the establishment of religion, or prohibiting the free exercise thereof; or abridging the freedom of speech, or of the press; or the right of the people peaceably to assemble, and to petition the Government for a redress of grievances."

The meaning and significance of the First Amendment to the people of the new nation is to be found in the existing law of England and the colonies dealing with restrictions upon freedom of speech, press and assembly. Apart from the law of civil libel and slander, the law dealing with blasphemy, and the law concerning obscenity, there were two significant legal doctrines with which the First Amendment was concerned. One was the law of censorship; the other was the law of seditious libel.

The history of English censorship has been summarized by Story:

"The art of printing soon after its introduction, we are told, was looked upon, as well in England as in other countries, as merely a matter of state, and subject to the coercion of the crown. It was, therefore, regulated in England by the king's proclamations, prohibitions, charters of privilege, and licenses, and finally by the decrees of the Court of Star-Chamber, which limited the number of printers and of presses which each should employ, and prohibited new publications, unless previously approved by proper licensers. On the demolition of this odious jurisdiction, in 1641, the Long Parliament of Charles the First, after their

**363**

rupture with that prince, assumed the same powers which the Star-Chamber exercised with respect to licensing books; and during the Commonwealth (such is human frailty and the love of power even in republics!) they issued their ordinances for that purpose, founded principally upon a Star-Chamber decree in 1637. After the restoration of Charles the Second, a statute on the same subject was passed, copied, with some few alterations, from the parliamentary ordinances. The act expired in 1679, and was revived and continued for a few years after the revolution of 1688. Many attempts were made by the government to keep it in force; but it was so strongly resisted by Parliament that it expired in 1694, and has never since been revived."[1]

The law of seditious libel, however, was effectively and vigorously enforced in the pre-Revolutionary period. In England some 70 prosecutions for seditious libel took place in the three decades before adoption of the First Amendment, resulting in 50 convictions. These included such well known cases as the prosecution of John Wilkes and the publishers of Junius' *Letter to the King*. Prosecutions for seditious libel had also occurred in the colonies, of which the most famous was that of Peter Zenger, New York printer, in 1734.

Prof. Chafee, in the following extract, discusses the significance of the First Amendment in the light of this background.

## CHAFEE—FREE SPEECH IN THE UNITED STATES
### pp. 18–21 (1941)

If we apply Coke's test of statutory construction, and consider what mischief in the existing law the framers of the First Amendment wished to remedy by a new safeguard, we can be sure that it was not the censorship. This had expired in England in 1695, and in the colonies by 1725.[34] They knew from books that it destroyed liberty of the press; and if they ever thought of its revival as within the range of practical possibilities, they must have regarded it as clearly prohibited by the First Amendment. But there was no need to go to all the trouble of pushing through a constitutional amendment just to settle an issue that had been dead for decades. What the framers did have plenty of reason to fear was an entirely different danger to political writers and speakers.

For years the government here and in England had substituted

---

[1] Story, 2 *Commentaries on the Constitution of the United States*, § 1882 (5th ed., 1891).

[34] Macaulay, *History of England*, chap. xxi; C. A. Duniway, *Freedom of Speech in Massachusetts*, p. 89 n. ....

for the censorship rigorous and repeated prosecutions for seditious libel, which were directed against political discussion, and for years these prosecutions were opposed by liberal opinion and popular agitation. Primarily the controversy raged around two legal contentions of the great advocates for the defense, such as Erskine and Andrew Hamilton. They argued, first, that the jury and not the judge ought to decide whether the writing was seditious, and secondly, that the truth of the charge ought to prevent conviction. The real issue, however, lay much deeper. Two different views of the relation of rulers and people were in conflict. According to one view, the rulers were the superiors of the people, and therefore must not be subjected to any censure that would tend to diminish their authority. The people could not make adverse criticism in newspapers or pamphlets, but only through their lawful representatives in the legislature, who might be petitioned in an orderly manner. According to the other view, the rulers were agents and servants of the people, who might therefore find fault with their servants and discuss questions of their punishment or dismissal, and of governmental policy.

Under the first view, which was officially accepted until the close of the eighteenth century, developed the law of seditious libel. This was defined as "the intentional publication, without lawful excuse or justification, of written blame of any public man, or of the law, or of any institution established by law." There was no need to prove any intention on the part of the defendant to produce disaffection or excite an insurrection. It was enough if he intended to publish the blame, because it was unlawful in him merely to find fault with his masters and betters. Such, in the opinion of the best authorities, was the common law of sedition.[36]

It is obvious that under this law liberty of the press was nothing more than absence of the censorship, as Blackstone said. All through the eighteenth century, however, there existed beside this definite legal meaning of liberty of the press, a definite popular meaning: the right of unrestricted discussion of public affairs. There can be no doubt that this was in a general way what freedom of speech meant to the framers of the Constitution. Thus Madison, who drafted the First Amendment, bases his explanation of it in 1799 on "the essential difference between the British Government and the American constitutions." In the United States the people and not the government possess the

---

[36] Madison, Report on the Virginia Resolutions, 1799, *Elliot's Debates* (2d ed.), IV, 596 ff.; Stephen, *History of the Criminal Law*, II, 299, 353, and chap. xxiv, *passim*; Schofield [*Freedom of Speech in the United States*, in II *Essays on Constitutional Law of Equity* (1914)], 511 ff., gives an excellent summary with especial reference to American conditions. • • •

absolute sovereignty, and the legislature as well as the executive is under limitations of power. Hence, Congress is not free to punish anything which was criminal at English common law. A government which is "elective, limited and responsible" in all its branches may well be supposed to require "a greater freedom of animadversion"[37] than might be tolerated by one that is composed of an irresponsible hereditary king and upper house, and an omnipotent legislature. . . .

There are a few early judicial decisions to the contrary, but they ought not to weigh against the statements of Madison and the general temper of the time. . . . I must therefore strongly dissent, with Justice Holmes,[40] from the position sometimes taken in arguments on the Espionage Act, that the founders of our government left the common law as to seditious libel in force and merely intended by the First Amendment "to limit the new government's statutory powers to penalize utterances as seditious, to those which were seditious under the then accepted common-law rule."[41] The founders had seen seventy English prosecutions for libel since 1760, and fifty convictions under that common-law rule, which made conviction easy.[42] That rule had been detested in this country ever since it was repudiated by jury and populace in the famous trial of Peter Zenger, the New York printer, the account of which went through fourteen editions before 1791.[43] The close relation between the Zenger trial and the prosecutions under George III in England and America is shown by the quotations on reprints of the trial and the dedication of the 1784 London edition to Erskine, as well as by reference to Zenger in the discussions preceding the First Amendment. Nor was this the only colonial sedition prosecution under the common law, and many more were threatened. All the American cases before 1791 prove that our common law of sedition was exactly like that of England, and it would be extraordinary if the First Amendment enacted the English sedition law of that time, which was repudiated by

[37] Madison's Report on the Virginia Resolutions, *Elliot's Debates* (2d ed.), IV, 596–598. As draftsman of the Amendment, Madison's views about its interpretation carry great weight, although they were written down eight years after its adoption and may have been somewhat modified during the interval by his opposition to the Sedition Act of 1798. The same distinction was made by Erastus Root, *Report of the New York Constitutional Convention of 1821*, p. 489. See also *Speeches of Charles Pinckney* (1800), pp. 116 ff.

[40] Abrams v. U. S., 250 U. S. 616 (1919).

[41] W. R. Vance, in "Freedom of Speech and the Press," 2 *Minnesota Law Review*, 239, 259.

[42] May, *Constitutional History of England* (2d ed.), II, 9 n.

[43] 17 How. St. Tr. 675 (1735); Rutherford, *John Peter Zenger* (New York, 1904). See also the life of Zenger's counsel, Andrew Hamilton, by William Henry Loyd, in *Great American Lawyers*, I, 1.

every American and every liberal Englishman,[44] and altered through Fox's Libel Act by Parliament itself in the very next year, 1792. . . . The First Amendment was written by men to whom Wilkes and Junius were household words, who intended to wipe out the common law of sedition, and make further prosecutions for criticism of the government, without any incitement to law-breaking, forever impossible in the United States of America.

## Note

In addition to the material cited in the above extract from Prof. Chafee, see on the English and colonial background, Holdsworth, *Press Control and Copyright in the 16th and 17th Centuries*, 29 Yale L. J. 841 (1920); Glenn, *Censorship at Common Law and Under Modern Dispensation*, 82 U. of Pa. L. Rev. 114 (1933); Whipple, *Our Ancient Liberties*, ch. VII (1927); Corwin, *Freedom of Speech and Press Under the First Amendment: A Résumé*, 30 Yale L. J. 48 (1920); Walsh, *Is the New Judicial and Legislative Interpretation of Freedom of Speech, and of the Freedom of the Press, Sound Constitutional Development?*, 21 Geo. L. J. 35, 161 (1932–3); Shientag, *From Seditious Libel to Freedom of the Press*, 11 Brook. L. Rev. 125 (1942); *Patterson v. Colorado*, 205 U. S. 454, 51 L. Ed. 879, 27 S. Ct. 556 (1907); *Near v. Minnesota*, 283 U. S. 697, 75 L. Ed. 1357, 51 S. Ct. 625 (1931).

With regard to the adoption of the Bill of Rights, see U. S. Constitution Sesquicentennial Commission, *History of the Formation of the Union Under the Constitution*, pp. 62–3, 280–328 (1941); Warren, *Congress, the Constitution, and the Supreme Court*, ch. 3 (1935); Whipple, *supra*, ch. IV (1927).

Generally, with respect to the history of freedom of political expression in the United States, see Chafee, *Free Speech in the United States* (2d ed., 1941); Whipple, *The Story of Civil Liberty in the United States* (1927); Biddle, *The Fear of Freedom* (1951); Schroeder, *Free Speech Bibliography* (1922); U. S. Library of Congress, *The Bill of Rights, A List of References* (1940).

## 2. The Alien and Sedition Acts

The first serious challenge to freedom of political expression came with the Alien and Sedition Acts, passed in 1798. The United States at the time was on the verge of war with France. The impact of ideas generated by the French Revolution aroused fear and hostility in some segments of the American population. Rumors of French plots and charges of French espionage were sweeping the country. Antagonism to French and Irish immigrants ran high in some quarters. A bitter controversy raged

---

[44] May, *Constitutional History of England*, vol. II, chap. ix; Stephen, *History of the Criminal Law*, vol. II, chap. xxiv.

between the Federalists, then in power, and the Republicans. Spearheading the Republican attack was an aggressive press, many of the editors of which were non-citizens. The polemics hurled by both sides were violent in tone, frequently scurrilous.

Under these circumstances the more extreme among the Federalists proposed a series of measures to curb the power of aliens and of the Republican party and press. Although not supported by such Federalists as Hamilton and Marshall the laws were passed by Congress. The Naturalization Act extended the period of residence required for naturalization from five to fourteen years. 1 Stat. 566. The Enemy Alien Act provided that in the event of war, "or any invasion or predatory incursion . . . perpetuated, attempted, or threatened," all subjects of the hostile nation within the United States who were not naturalized "shall be liable to be apprehended, restrained, secured and removed, as alien enemies." 1 Stat. 577. The important parts of the Alien Act and the Sedition Act are set forth below.

## AN ACT CONCERNING ALIENS
1 Stat. 570, June 25, 1798

Section 1. *Be it enacted by the Senate and House of Representatives of the United States of America in Congress assembled,* That it shall be lawful for the President of the United States at any time during the continuance of this act, to *order* all such *aliens* as he shall judge dangerous to the peace and safety of the United States, or shall have reasonable grounds to suspect are concerned in any treasonable or secret machinations against the government thereof, to depart out of the territory of the United States, within such time as shall be expressed in such order. . . . And in case any alien, so ordered to depart, shall be found at large within the United States after the time limited in such order for his departure, and not having obtained a *license* from the President to reside therein, or having obtained such *license* shall not have conformed thereto, every such alien shall, on conviction thereof, be imprisoned for a term not exceeding three years, and shall never after be admitted to become a citizen of the United States. . . .

AN ACT IN ADDITION TO THE ACT, ENTITLED
"AN ACT FOR THE PUNISHMENT OF CERTAIN
CRIMES AGAINST THE UNITED STATES"

1 Stat. 596, July 14, 1798

Sec. 2. *And be it further enacted,* That if any person shall
write, print, utter or publish, or shall cause to procure to be
written, printed, uttered or published, or shall knowingly and
willingly assist or aid in writing, printing, uttering or publishing
any false, scandalous and malicious writing or writings against
the government of the United States, or either house of the
Congress of the United States, or the President of the United
States, with intent to defame the said government, or either
house of the said Congress, or the said President, or to bring
them, or either of them, into contempt or disrepute; or to excite
against them, or either or any of them, the hatred of the good
people of the United States, or to stir up sedition within the
United States, or to excite any unlawful combinations therein, for
opposing or resisting any law of the United States, or any act
of the President of the United States, done in pursuance of any
such law, or of the powers in him vested by the constitution of
the United States, or to resist, oppose, or defeat any such law or
act, or to aid, encourage or abet any hostile designs of any foreign
nation against the United States, their people or government,
then such person, being thereof convicted before any court of
the United States having jurisdiction thereof, shall be punished
by a fine not exceeding two thousand dollars, and by imprisonment not exceeding two years.

Sec. 3. *And be it further enacted and declared,* That if any
person shall be prosecuted under this act, for the writing or publishing any libel aforesaid, it shall be lawful for the defendant,
upon the trial of the cause, to give in evidence in his defence,
the truth of the matter contained in the publication charged as a
libel. And the jury who shall try the cause, shall have a right
to determine the law and the fact, under the direction of the
court, as in other cases.

---

The Alien Act and the Enemy Alien Act were never formally
invoked but their very existence forced a number of aliens to
leave the country or go into hiding. By their terms these acts
expired in two years.

The Sedition Act was vigorously enforced, the victims in all
cases being members of the Republican Party. Republican
newspapers were scanned for seditious material and prosecutions were brought against the four leading Republican papers

as well as against some of those less influential. Cases were also instituted against at least three of the more outspoken Republican office holders. The number of arrests made is not entirely certain but there were at least 25, with at least 15 indictments. Prosecutions were brought in every state except New Hampshire and Rhode Island, where Republican strength was low, and the states of the far South and West. The cases, often tried before openly hostile Federalist judges, resulted in 10 convictions.

The nature of these prosecutions is revealed by the first one brought, against Congressman Mathew Lyon, Republican of Vermont. Lyon, who was one of the Republican politicians most hated by the Federalists, was indicted for (1) publishing an article in which he vigorously attacked the Adams administration, asserting that under President Adams "every consideration of the public welfare was swallowed up in a continual grasp for power, in an unbounded thirst for ridiculous pomp, foolish adulation, and selfish avarice"; (2) publishing a letter from Joel Barlow, then in France, in which Barlow stated that Congress should commit President Adams to the mad house but, instead, treated him "with more servility than ever George III experienced from either House of Parliament." Lyon was convicted and sentenced to a fine of $1000 and four months in prison. He was immediately hurried off to jail and thrown into a filthy cell. While in jail Lyon was reelected to Congress.

Another prosecution, of less significant figures, arose out of an incident in Dedham, Massachusetts. Here some of the inhabitants erected a liberty pole on which they placed the inscription: "No Stamp Act, no Sedition, no Alien bills, no Land Tax; downfall to the Tyrants of America, peace and retirement to the President." Federalist officials obtained the indictment of two of those responsible. One of these recanted and received a fine of $5 and 6 hours in prison,—the only lenient sentence imposed under the Sedition Act. The other participant remained obdurate, refused to disclose the names of his associates and was sentenced to a fine of $400 and 18 months in jail. Unable to pay his fine at the end of his term, he remained in prison altogether for two years.

The constitutional issues raised by the Alien and Sedition Acts never reached the Supreme Court. The validity of the Sedition Act, however, was sustained by the lower Federal courts and by three Supreme Court Justices sitting on circuit. It was argued in support that the Act merely restated, with some liberalizing modifications, the common law of seditious libel, that the First Amendment prohibited only prior censorship, and that

[Emerson]

the exercise of Federal power was derived from the necessary and proper clause. The Act was attacked on the ground that it lay outside the sphere of Federal power and violated the First Amendment. Jefferson and Madison led the campaign against the Alien and Sedition Acts, the most famous expressions of their views being embodied in the Kentucky and Virginia Resolutions.

It is generally agreed that the Alien and Sedition laws profoundly shocked the country and were a major factor in the defeat of the Federalists in the election of 1800. The Sedition Act expired on March 3, 1801. Jefferson pardoned all those who had been convicted under it and eventually Congress repaid most of the fines.

## Note

The most comprehensive account of the Alien and Sedition Acts is Miller, *Crisis in Freedom* (1951), which contains a bibliography. For a vivid description of the Mathew Lyon's case and the general background, see Bowers, *Jefferson and Hamilton*, pp. 374–80 (1933).

The Federalist argument for constitutionality was incorporated in *Report of a Select Committee to Consider Petitions for Repeal of the Alien and Sedition Laws*, 5 Annals (5th Cong.) 2985. The oposition argument was set forth in the Kentucky and Virginia Resolutions, reprinted in Commager, *Documents of American History*, pp. 178–83 (1948); and in a report prepared by Madison known as *The Virginia Report of 1799*, 4 Elliot's Debates (2d ed.) 546, reprinted as Sen. Doc. No. 873, 62d Cong., 2d Sess. (1921).

The four trials that are fully reported are *U. S. v. Lyon*, Wharton's St. Tr. 333 (1798); *U. S. v. Haswell*, Wharton's St. Tr. 684 (1800); *U. S. v. Cooper*, Wharton's St. Tr. 659 (1800); *U. S. v. Callender*, Wharton's St. Tr. 688 (1800).

For further discussion of the enforcement and legal issues, see Anderson, *The Enforcement of the Alien and Sedition Laws*, Annual Report of the American Historical Association, p. 115 (1912); Carroll, *Freedom of Speech and of the Press in the Federalist Period: The Sedition Act*, 18 Mich. L. Rev. 615 (1920); Corwin, *Freedom of Speech and Press Under the First Amendment: A Résumé*, 30 Yale L. J. 48 (1920); Walsh, *supra*, 21 Geo. L. J. 35, 161.

For the impact of the French Revolution on prosecutions for seditious libel in England, see Brown, *The French Revolution in English History* (1918); Sutherland, *British Trials for Disloyal Association During the French Revolution*, 34 Corn. L. Q. 303 (1949); Biddle, *The Fear of Freedom*, pp. 42–53 (1951).

## 3. The Civil War Period

Following the Alien and Sedition Acts the question of whether

**371**

the Federal Government should impose restrictions upon political expression did not arise as a prominent issue until the crisis precipitated by the Civil War. However, full freedom of political expression was subject to significant limitations, frequently from non-governmental sources, at various times and in various areas. The two most significant problems arose out of the nativist movements in the 1830's and the controversy over abolition which mounted in intensity up to the Civil War.

Leon Whipple, in *The Story of Civil Liberty in the United States* (1927), summarizes the first situation in the following terms:

"From 1828 to 1855, and especially from 1833 to 1843, came a veritable mob era. The masses, charmed by this idea of the rule of the people, were convinced that it made small difference whether you downed the minority by ballots or by brick-bats, which they understood better. This form of tyranny by majority had not been anticipated by the statesmen who expected the colder process of voting down the minority to prevail over the warmer sport of killing them.

"Social conditions helped establish these notions. Urban centralization had begun. Immigration, encouraged to bring in cheap labor, first the Irish and later the Chinese, aroused economic, racial and religious prejudices. There was an ardent 'nativism,' by citizens who had themselves but yesterday come from foreign shores. There was an almost inexplicable dread of secret political or religious organizations, expressed in crusades against the Masons, Catholics, and Mormons. Beneath all, the growing machine industry was producing a proletariat. Wage-labor was slowly reaching economic self-consciousness, later to align itself against the wageless institution of Negro slavery. In a few places, direct action by the people approximated a rough sort of government, as in the Vigilantes and other extemporized 'law and order' bodies of the frontier. They did some necessary natural policing before courts or State arrived. . . ." (p. 51)[1]

The abolitionist movement was strongly resisted, especially in the South. In part this took the form of state legislation. Thus a statute passed in Georgia in 1829 prohibited, subject to the death penalty, "aiding or assisting in the circulation or bringing into this state . . . any . . . pamphlet, paper, or circular, for

[1] See, for details, Whipple, *supra*, pp. 49–83; Curti, *The Roots of American Loyalty*, ch. III (1946); G. Myers, *History of Bigotry in the United States*, ch. XIII–XIX (1943); Billington, *The Protestant Crusade 1800–1860* (1938), bibliography contained on pp. 498–504; M. Williams, *The Shadow of the Pope*, pp. 51–94 (1932).

the purposes of exciting to insurrection, conspiracy or resistance among the slaves, negroes, or free persons of colour . . . " Geo. Acts, 1829, pp. 170–1. A similar statute in Louisiana provided that anyone who wrote, printed, published or distributed "any thing having a tendency to produce discontent among the free coloured population of the state, or insubordination among the slaves therein, shall on conviction thereof . . . be sentenced to imprisonment at hard labour for life, or suffer death, at the discretion of the court." La. Acts, 1830, p. 96. The southern states, with some assistance from the Federal Government, also attempted to ban abolitionist literature from coming into the state through the mails. See, e.g., Va. Acts, 1836, p. 44.

Throughout this period suppression of abolitionist views was undertaken by extra-legal sanctions enforced by private individuals and groups. Mob action in both North and South became common. Thus in Boston William Lloyd Garrison was mobbed and dragged through the streets. And a series of violent outbreaks occurred in St. Louis and Alton, Illinois, where the offices and printing presses of Rev. E. P. Lovejoy, publisher of a religious journal, were destroyed and Lovejoy himself killed. During these years lynch law, hitherto known only in frontier areas, spread through many parts of the country. As the Civil War neared, the abolitionists gradually received a better reception in the North, but in the South expressions of opinion favoring abolition were in effect totally suppressed.[2]

With the outbreak of the Civil War President Lincoln, acting under executive power, took a series of measures to meet the crisis. One of these was the suspension of the privilege of the writ of habeas corpus, an action later ratified by Congress. Act of March 3, 1863, 12 Stat. 755 (1863). The story of the period is suggested in the following extracts.


## HALL—FREE SPEECH IN WARTIME

### 21 Col. L. Rev. 526, 527 (1921)

During the Civil War it was deemed politically inexpedient to legislate against disloyal utterances in general. In the earlier

---

[2] For the history of these events see 6 von Holst, *The Constitutional and Political History of the United States*, ch. VI (1889); 1 and 2, H. Wilson, *History of the Rise and Fall of the Slave Power in America* (1872 and 1874); O. Johnson, *William Lloyd Garrison and His Times* (1880); W. L. Garrison, *The New "Reign of Terror" in the Slaveholding States, for 1859–60* (1860); J. E. Cutler, *Lynch-Law*, ch. IV (1905); Whipple, *supra*, ch. III; C. Eaton, *Freedom of Thought in the Old South* (1940); C. Eaton, *Censorship of the Southern Mails*, 48 Am. Hist. Rev. 266 (1943).

stages of the contest Lincoln earnestly sought to hold the border slaves states in the Union. He was represented as praying: "Oh, Lord, we earnestly hope that Thou will favor our cause, but we must have Kentucky." Men not irreconcilably of Southern sympathies were to be won over, if possible, by the methods of persuasion. Many utterances that in Massachusetts would have been treated as clearly indicative of disloyalty, in Kentucky were the natural expressions of men sorely perplexed and reluctant to make a decision that either way was fraught with sorrow. Legislation applying to all alike would have been unjust and alienating to the border state doubters, and would have been widely criticized as an illustration of the despotism so often charged against Lincoln by his opponents. But, without the sanction of the legislation, the federal government arrested by the thousand men whom it knew or suspected to be dangerous or disaffected, and confined them without charges and without trial in military prisons as long as it saw fit—and public opinion generally acquiesced in this as a fairly necessary measure of war-time precaution. The number of such executive arrests has been variously estimated up to as high as 38,000. The War Department records, confessedly very incomplete, show over 13,000.

## LINCOLN'S DEFENSE OF HIS SUSPENSION OF HABEAS CORPUS

Message to Congress in Special Session, July 4, 1861—Nicolay and Hay, *Lincoln, Complete Works*, vol. II, p. 55 (1894)

Of course some consideration was given to the questions of power and propriety before this matter was acted upon. The whole of the laws which were required to be faithfully executed were being resisted and failing of execution in nearly one third of the States. Must they be allowed to finally fail of execution, even had it been perfectly clear that by the use of the means necessary to their execution some single law, made in such extreme tenderness of the citizen's liberty that, practically, it relieves more of the guilty than of the innocent should to a very limited extent be violated? To state the question more directly, are all the laws but one to go unexecuted, and the government itself go to pieces lest that one be violated? Even in such a case, would not the official oath be broken if the government should be overthrown, when it was believed that disregarding the single law would tend to preserve it? But it was not believed that this question was presented. It was not believed that any law was violated. The provision of the Constitution that "the privilege of the writ of habeas corpus shall not be suspended, unless when, in cases of rebellion or invasion, the public safety may require it," is equivalent to a provision—is a provision—that such privilege may be suspended when, in case of rebellion or invasion, the public safety does require it. It was decided that we have a case of rebellion, and that the public safety does require the qualified suspension of the privilege of the writ which was authorized to be made. Now it is insisted that Congress and not the executive, is vested with this power. But the Constitution itself is silent as to which or who is to exercise the power; and as the provision was plainly made for a dangerous emergency, it cannot be believed the framers of the instrument intended that in every case the danger should run its course until Congress could be called together, the very assembling of which might be prevented, as was intended in this case, by the rebellion.[1]

## Note

1. The issue of the authority of a military commission to arrest and try a citizen on criminal or other charges came before the Supreme Court after the War was over in *Ex parte Milligan,* 71 U. S. 2, 18 L. Ed. 281 (1866). A majority held that a military commission could have no such jurisdiction, and the writ of habeas corpus could not be suspended, so long as the courts were open and functioning. "Martial law cannot arise from a *threatened* invasion. The necessity must be actual and present; the invasion real, such as effectually closes the courts and deposes the civil administration." 71 U. S. at 127. Four justices concurred in the result, holding that a military commission had not been authorized by Congress but that Congress had power to set up such a Commission if it chose to do so.

An earlier case raising similar issues was *Ex parte Merryman,* Fed. Cas. No. 9,487 (C. C. D. Md., 1861). See also *Ex parte Vallandigham,* 68 U. S. 243, 17 L. Ed. 589 (1864).

The *Milligan* case has long been famous as an outstanding statement of the right to constitutional protections in a period of emergency. For material on the case see Klaus, *The Milligan Case* (1929) (a complete text of the record and arguments, with bibliography); 2 Warren, *The Supreme Court in United States History, 1836–1918,* ch. XXIX (1932); Fairman, *Mr. Justice Miller and the Supreme Court,* pp. 90–7 (1939); Frank, *Ex parte Milligan v. The Five Companies: Martial Law in Hawaii,* 44 Col. L. Rev. 639 (1944).

2. For additional material concerning the impact of the Civil War on civil liberties, including restrictions on the press, see Whipple, *The Story of Civil Liberty in the United States,* ch. IV (1927); Randall,

---

[1] It should be noted that, although the Civil War commenced with the firing on Fort Sumter April 12, 1861, Lincoln did not call a special session of Congress until July 4, 1861. J. G. Randall, *Constitutional Problems Under Lincoln,* p. 52 (rev. ed., 1951).

*Constitutional Problems Under Lincoln* (rev. ed., 1951) (bibliography on pp. 531–63); W. A. Dunning, *Essays on the Civil War and Reconstruction*, ch. 1 (1898); Schlesinger, *Political and Social History of the United States, 1829–1925*, pp. 215–16 (1932); 3 Rhodes, *History of the United States*, pp. 554–58 (1902); N. W. Stephenson, *Abraham Lincoln and the Union*, pp. 160–67 (1918); 2 Beard, *The Rise of American Civilization*, pp. 78–81 (1928).

## 4. The First World War

In the period following the Civil War freedom of political expression began to encounter the problems growing out of the rapid industrialization of the nation. The struggles of a rising labor movement, often accompanied with violence, created bitterness and aroused fears. The militant activities of small groups of political extremists, such as the anarchists and later the Industrial Workers of the World, received widespread attention and added to the tensions of a turbulent period. Signs were accumulating that the basic principles of Milton, Jefferson, Mill and the others were to be subjected to a severe test under new and trying conditions.

The Haymarket bomb and the subsequent prosecutions presaged some of the problems. In 1886 the country was in a state of agitation over the growth of the Knights of Labor, the demand for an eight hour day, the activities of the anarchists, and similar matters. A meeting of labor sympathizers was being held in Haymarket Square, Chicago, when a detachment of police approached to disperse the crowd. At this moment someone threw a bomb at the police, the explosion killing eight policemen and wounding a number of other persons. It was never discovered who had thrown the bomb. But eight anarchists were tried for murder and convicted on the ground that their speeches and publications had been responsible for the killing. One of the convicted men committed suicide and four were hanged. The others, who were in prison, were pardoned three years later by Governor Altgeld.[1]

In 1902, shortly after the assassination of President McKinley,

---

[1] *Spies v. People*, 122 Ill. 1 (1887); *Spies v. Illinois*, 123 U. S. 131, 31 L. Ed. 80, 8 S. Ct. 21 (1887). For accounts of the Haymarket prosecutions see *The Chicago Martyrs: The Famous Speeches of the Eight Anarchists in Judge Gary's Court and Altgeld's Reasons for Pardoning Fielden, Neebe and Schwab*, No. 1, Free Society Library (1899); Altgeld, *Reasons for Pardoning Fielden, Neebe and Schwab* (1893); Zeisler, *Reminiscences of the Anarchist Case*, 21 Ill. L. Rev. 224 (1926); Whipple, *The Story of Civil Liberty in the United States*, pp. 255–8 (1927); Browne, *Altgeld of Illinois*, pp. 74–115 (1924); Barnard, *Eagle Forgotten*, pp. 165–267 (1938).

New York passed the first state anti-sedition law. This statute made it a criminal offense to advocate "criminal anarchy," defined as "the doctrine that organized government should be overthrown by force or violence," or to join any organization which taught or advocated the doctrine.[2]

Both the Haymarket prosecutions and the New York criminal anarchy law raised important issues as to the limits which the state was entitled to impose upon political expression. But the problem did not emerge in full scale until the first World War. Then there was added to the accumulating pressures of the previous period, the public excitement and hysteria of war, and later the fears, insecurities and conflicts produced by the Bolshevik Revolution. The result was a period in which suppression of political expression assumed widespread proportions.

The main restrictions upon freedom of expression during the war arose from the administration of the Federal Espionage Act and similar state legislation.

## CHAFEE—WAR-TIME PROSECUTIONS

Free Speech in the United States, pp. 37–41, 51–2, 100–1 (1941)

[T]he government had at its disposal several criminal statutes enacted during the Civil War. These it could and did use to punish conspiracies by Emma Goldman and others aiming to resist recruiting and conscription by riots and other forcible means, or seeking by speeches and publications to induce men to evade the draft.[3] In some respects, however, these statutes were felt by the Department of Justice to be incomplete. (1) It was not a crime to persuade a man not to enlist voluntarily. (2) Inasmuch as one man cannot make a conspiracy all by himself, a deliberate attempt by an isolated individual to obstruct the draft, if unsuccessful, was beyond the reach of the law, except when his conduct was sufficiently serious to amount to treason. The treason statute, the only law on the books affecting the conduct of the individual, was of little service,[4] since there

---

[2] N. Y. Laws of 1902, ch. 371. This was the statute involved in *Gitlow v. N. Y.*, set forth in Section C, *infra*.

[3] These statutes are now 18 U. S. C. A. (1926), §§ 4, 6, 88, 550. . . . World War conspiracy cases thereunder include Emma Goldman *v.* United States, 245 U. S. 474 (1918); Wells *v.* U. S., 257 Fed. 605 (C. C. A., 1919); U. S. *v.* Phillips, Bull. Dept. Just., No. 14 (1917); Bryant *v.* U. S., 257 Fed. 378 (C. C. A., 1919); Orear *v.* U. S., 261 Fed. 267 (C. C. A., 1919); U. S. *v.* Reeder, Bull. Dept. Just., No. 161 (1918).

[4] O'Brian, [*Civil Liberty in War Time*, 42 Rep. N. Y. Bar Assn. 275, 277 (1919)]. The treason statute is now 18 U. S. C. A. (1926) §§ 1, 2; see Warren, "What is Giving Aid and Comfort to the Enemy?" 27 *Yale Law*

**377**

was considerable doubt whether it applied to utterances. Therefore, although it is probable that under the circumstances the existing conspiracy statutes would have taken care of any serious danger to the prosecution of the war, new legislation was demanded.

If the government had been content to limit itself to meeting the tangible needs just mentioned, the effect on discussion of the war would probably have been very slight, for treason, conspiracies, and actual attempts constitute a direct and dangerous interference with the war, outside the protection of freedom of speech as defined in the preceding chapter. Two additional factors, however, influenced the terms of the new statutes, and even more the spirit in which they were enforced. First came the recollection of the opposition during the Civil War, which was handled under martial law in so far as it was suppressed at all. Some persons, full of old tales of Copperheads, were eager to treat all opponents of this war as spies and traitors. A bill was actually introduced into the Senate which made the whole United States "a part of the zone of operations conducted by the enemy," and declared that any person who published anything endangering the successful operation of our forces could be tried as a spy by a military tribunal and put to death. President Wilson wished to head off such legislation as unwise and unconstitutional.[5] A turmoil would arise if army officers could thus dispose of the liberties and lives of civilians. Any control of the government over civilians outside actual war areas ought to be exercised through judges and juries. And yet the legal advisers of the administration felt that the conspiracy statutes were not enough to enable the ordinary courts to handle on a large scale dangerous activities short of treason. So it would be easier to resist pressure to take matters away from judges and juries, if a new criminal statute gave judges and juries wider and stiffer powers. The second factor was the fear of German propaganda, and the knowledge of legislation and administrative regulations guarding against it in Great Britain and Canada.[6] Although we did not adopt the British administrative control,

---

*Journal* 331 (1918). . . . World War treason cases include U. S. *v.* Werner, 247 Fed. 708 (1918); U. S. *v.* Robinson, 259 Fed. 685 (1919); U. S. *v.* Fricke, 259 Fed. 673 (1919).

[5] On this Chamberlain bill and similar proposals, see Thomas F. Carroll, "Freedom of Speech and of the Press in War Time: The Espionage Act," 17 *Michigan Law Review* 621, 663 note (1919); cited hereafter as Carroll. The bill seems clearly unconstitutional under *Ex parte* Milligan, 4 Wallace 2 (1866). . . .

[6] As to England, see 31 *Harvard Law Review* 296 (by Laski); Laski, *Authority in the Modern State*, p. 101. As to Canada, see Carroll, at 621 note.

**378**

which combined flexibility with possibilities of despotism, it was easy to forget our own policy of non-interference with minorities and put the United States also in a position to deal severely with written and spoken opposition to the war. . . .

The result of these various influences was the third section of Title I of the Espionage Act. As originally enacted on June 15, 1917 (and still in force in 1940), this section established three new offenses:

> (1) Whoever, when the United States is at war, shall willfully make or convey false reports or false statements with intent to interfere with the operation or success of the military or naval forces of the United States or to promote the success of its enemies (2) and whoever, when the United States is at war, shall willfully cause or attempt to cause insubordination, disloyalty, mutiny, or refusal of duty, in the military or naval forces of the United States, (3) or shall willfully obstruct the recruiting or enlistment service of the United States, to the injury of the service or of the United States, shall be punished by a fine of not more than $10,000 or imprisonment for not more than twenty years, or both.[7]

Although most of the Espionage Act deals with entirely different subjects, like actual espionage, the protection of military secrets and the enforcement of neutrality in future conflicts between other nations, the section just quoted is buttressed by several provisions. Section 4 of the same Title (50 U.S.C.A. § 34) punishes persons conspiring to violate section 3, if any one of them does any act to effect the object of the conspiracy. Title XI (18 U.S.C.A. §§ 611–633) authorizes the issue of search warrants for the seizure of property used as the means of committing a felony, which would include violations of the section just quoted. It was under this provision that the moving-picture film was confiscated in the *Spirit of '76* case, and raids were made on the offices of anti-war organizations. Finally, Title XII (18 U.S.C.A. §§ 343, 344) makes non-mailable any matter violating the Act, or advocating treason, insurrection, or forcible resistance to any law of the United States, directs that it shall not be conveyed or delivered, and imposes heavy penalties for attempting to use the mails for its transmission.

Eleven months later the Espionage Act was greatly expanded by a second statute. Attorney General Gregory thought the

---

[7] Act of June 15, 1917, c. 30, Title I, § 3, now 50 U. S. C. A. (1926), § 33. The numerals are inserted by me. As to the provisions of this statute against real spying, see Gorin *v.* United States, 61 Sup. Ct. 429 (1941).

original 1917 Act did not go far enough in some respects. He stated that although it had proved an effective instrumentality against deliberate or organized disloyal propaganda, it did not reach the individual casual or impulsive disloyal utterances. Also some District Courts gave what he considered a narrow construction of the word "obstruct" in clause 3, so that, as he described it, "most of the teeth which we tried to put in were taken out."[9] . . .

The history of subsequent events shows what is likely to happen in times of panic, when sedate lawyers ask for "just a wee drappie mair of suppression, and where's the harm in that." The Attorney General requested only a brief amendment of the Espionage Act by the addition of attempts to obstruct the recruiting service, and the punishment of efforts intentionally made to discredit and interfere with the flotation of war loans. The Senate Committee on the Judiciary, being thus stirred up, took the bit in its teeth, and decided to stamp on all utterances of a disloyal character. It went for a model of legislation affecting freedom of discussion to a recent sweeping sedition statute of the state of Montana, and inserted most of its clauses into the new federal law.

This amendment of May 16, 1918 (repealed in 1921),[11] which is sometimes called the Sedition Act, inserted "attempts to obstruct" in the third of the original offenses, and added nine more offenses, as follows: (4) saying or doing anything with intent to obstruct the sale of United States bonds, except by way of bona fide and not disloyal advice; (5) uttering, printing, writing, or publishing any disloyal, profane, scurrilous, or abusive language, or language intended to cause contempt, scorn, contumely or disrepute as regards the form of government of the United States; (6) or the Constitution; (7) or the flag; (8) or the uniform of the Army or Navy; (9) or any language intended to incite resistance to the United States or promote the cause of its enemies; (10) urging any curtailment of production of any things necessary to the prosecution of the war with intent to hinder its prosecution; (11) advocating, teaching, defending, or suggesting the doing of any of these acts; and (12) words or acts supporting or favoring the cause of any country at war with us, or opposing the cause of the United States therein. Whoever committed any one of these offenses during the war was liable to the maximum penalty of the original Act, $10,000 fine or twenty years' imprisonment, or both. . . .

---

[9] 4 *American Bar Association Journal*, 306.

[11] 40 Stat. 553 (1918). As to the repeal in 1921, see 41 Stat. 1359–1360; 60 *Congressional Record*, 293–4, 4207–8.

It is unnecessary to review the two thousand Espionage Act prosecutions in detail, but a few general results may be presented here. The courts treated opinions as statements of fact and then condemned them as false because they differed from the President's speech or the resolution of Congress declaring war. . . . Under the second and third clauses against causing insubordination or obstructing recruiting, only a few persons were convicted for actually urging men to evade the draft or not to enlist. Almost all the convictions were for expressions of opinion about the merits and conduct of the war.

It became criminal to advocate heavier taxation instead of bond issues, to state that conscription was unconstitutional though the Supreme Court had not yet held it valid, to say that the sinking of merchant vessels was legal, to urge that a referendum should have preceded our declaration of war, to say that war was contrary to the teachings of Christ. Men have been punished for criticising the Red Cross and the Y.M.C.A., while under the Minnesota Espionage Act it has been held a crime to discourage women from knitting by the remark, "No soldier ever sees these socks."[30] It was in no way necessary that these expressions of opinion should be addressed to soldiers or men on the point of enlisting or being drafted. Most judges held it enough if the words might conceivably reach such men. They have made it impossible for an opponent of the war to write an article or even a letter in a newspaper of general circulation because it will be read in some training camp where it might cause insubordination or interfere with military success. He cannot address a large audience because it is liable to include a few men in uniform; and some judges have held him punishable

---

[30] State v. Freerks, 140 Minn. 349 (1918). Among the many cases illustrating the statements of this paragraph, I cite the following convictions: Sandberg (revd. in 257 Fed. 643); Miller (Bull. 104); Nagler (Bull. 127, 252 Fed. 217); Goldsmith (Bull. 133); Kaufman (Bull. 134); Weist (Bull. 169); Kirchner (Bulls. 69, 174, 255 Fed. 301); Shaffer (Bull. 125, 190, 255 Fed. 886); Albers (Bull. 191, 263 Fed. 27); Krafft (Bull. 6, 84, 249 Fed. 919, 247 U. S. 520); Boutin (251 Fed. 313); Granzow (revd. in 261 Fed. 172); Hitchcock (Bull. 122); Weinsberg (Bull. 123); Denson (Bull. 142); Von Bank (Bull. 164, revd. in 258 Fed. 641); White (263 Fed. 17). A few of these convictions have been reversed as noted above and most of the other sentences were considerably reduced by the President after the armistice, but that does not excuse the conduct of the trial courts. . . .

A great many of the Espionage Act cases have never been reported in detail in print. The total number of persons convicted was stated by the Attorney General in his annual Reports as 877, out of 1,956 cases commenced. His Reports also show pardons and commutations of sentences.

A main source for these prosecutions is Bulletins of the Department of Justice on the Interpretation of War Statutes, cited herein as Bull. For other sources, see 32 *Harvard Law Review* 417.

if it contains men between eighteen and forty-five, since they may be called into the army eventually; some have emphasized the possible presence of shipbuilders and munition-makers. All genuine discussion among civilians of the justice and wisdom of continuing a war thus becomes perilous. . . .

One would have supposed that the federal Espionage Act was a sufficient safeguard against opposition to the war, but many states were not satisfied with either its terms or its enforcement, and enacted similar but more drastic laws of their own.[107]  These were particularly common in western states, where feeling ran high against the Non-Partisan League or the I.W.W.  The most important of these statutes, that of Minnesota, made it unlawful to say "that men should not enlist in the military or naval forces of the United States or the State of Minnesota," or that residents of that state should not aid the United States in carrying on war with the public enemies.[108]  There were a very large number of prosecutions and many convictions under this statute, chiefly of members of the Non-Partisan League, culminating in the condemnation of its president, A. C. Townley. . . .

## Note

1. For a full discussion of the Federal and state statutes and their administration in the war and post war period, see Chafee, *supra*, Parts I and II (1941).  The Supreme Court and other court decisions dealing with these laws are considered in Section C of this Chapter, *infra*.

2. In the post war period suppression of political expression continued to increase.  The highlights of the period are:

(a) *Passage of additional state criminal anarchy, criminal syndicalism and similar anti-sedition laws.*  These laws were similar to the New York law of 1902 and the California statute discussed in *Whitney v. California*, Section C, *infra*.  Two thirds of the states passed such laws from 1917 to 1921.  Prosecutions under them were frequent.  See Chafee, *supra*, ch. 4, 7, 8 and 10, App. III; Dowell, *A History of Criminal*

---

[107] These statutes are listed in Appendix III.  On the constitutionality of the Minnesota war statute and similar laws, see Chapter VII, section I.

. . . .

Other state cases arising out of war utterances involved breaches of the peace; municipal ordinances regulating newspaers (see Pound, *Cases on Equitable Relief against Defamation*, 2d ed., p. 44n.) ; conspiracy to compel newsdealer to handle distasteful newspaper; libel in war controversy; expulsion of college student for pacifism (*id.* 108) ; ordinance prohibiting German opera (*infra*, Chapter IV, note 29) ; ordinance making opponent of war a vagrant (*Ex parte* Taft v. Shaw, 284 Mo. 531; 27 *Illinois Law Review* 67).

[108] Minn. Laws, 1917, c. 463.  This was superseded in 1919 by a still more drastic act, to take care of future wars—Laws, 1919, c. 93; Mason's Minn. Stat. (1927), § 9972.

*Syndicalism Legislation in the United States* (1939); Smith, *Subversive Propaganda, The Past and the Present,* 29 Geo. L. J. 809 (1941). In addition a number of states passed red flag laws. See Section C, *infra.*

(b) *The Palmer raids.* In January 1920 Attorney General Palmer conducted a nation-wide raid on aliens who were members of the Communist Party or the Communist Labor Party. Some 4000 aliens were rounded up; many were arrested and held without warrants; papers, documents and other evidence were seized, also frequently without warrant; many of the raids were conducted at night and the persons arrested immediately hustled off to jail. Subsequent hearings before immigration officials violated some of the basic elements of due process and in many instances were reversed by the courts. In the end only a relatively few of the aliens were deported, but the effect upon political expression was obviously substantial. See *Report upon the Illegal Practices of the United States Department of Justice,* prepared under the auspices of the National Popular Government League by 12 eminent lawyers (including Profs. Chafee, Felix Frankfurter, Ernst Freund, Dean Roscoe Pound and Frank P. Walsh) (1920); Post, *The Deportations Delirium of Nineteen-Twenty* (1923); Brown, *The Disloyalty of Socialism,* 53 Am. L. Rev. 681 (1919); Dunn (ed.), *The Palmer Raids* (1948); Chafee, *supra,* ch. 5; *Colyer v. Skeffington,* 265 Fed. 17 (D. Mass., 1920); Cummings and McFarland, *Federal Justice,* pp. 429–30 (1937); Lowenthal, *The Federal Bureau of Investigation,* ch. 14 (1950).

(c) *Expulsion of Socialists from the legislature.* Victor L. Berger, a leader of the Socialist Party, was indicted for conspiracy under the Espionage Act. In November 1918, before the trial, he was elected to Congress as a Representative from Wisconsin. At the opening of Congress in the spring of 1919 the House of Representatives refused to seat him. A special election was held in November 1919 and Berger was again the victor. He was again refused his seat in Congress. Berger was convicted at his trial in December 1918 and sentenced to 20 years' imprisonment. On appeal the Supreme Court reversed on the ground that the judge should have disqualified himself for prejudice. *Berger v. U. S.,* 255 U. S. 22, 65 L. Ed. 481, 41 S. Ct. 230 (1921). See Chafee, *supra,* pp. 247–69.

In January 1920 five members of the Socialist Party, who had been sworn in as members of the New York Assembly, were ousted from their seats pending investigation of their eligibility. In spite of strong protest, led by Charles Evans Hughes, the Judiciary Committee recommended expulsion and the Assembly voted overwhelmingly to expel. See State of New York, *Legislative Document No. 30,* Jan. 26, 1920; Chafee, *supra,* pp. 269–82; Chamberlain, *Loyalty and Legislative Action,* pp. 48–51 (1951).

(d) *The Lusk Committee.* The Lusk Committee was one of the first of the legislative committees set up in modern times to investigate the loyalty of private citizens. Prof. Chafee describes its operations: "On March 26, 1919, the [New York] legislature set up a joint committee of six under the chairmanship of Senator Lusk to investigate seditious activities and report to the legislature. Although in no sense a body for the prosecution of crime, it proceeded to conduct a series of spectacular illegal raids on the offices of the Rand School and other radical organizations, instigate prosecutions of radical leaders like Gitlow, and fill the press with a flow of terrorizing descriptions of the Red menace. And now it was the moving spirit in ousting the Socialist Assemblymen." Chafee, *supra*, p. 271. For an account of the operation of the Lusk Committee see Chamberlain, *supra*, pp. 9–52. Gov. Alfred E. Smith's famous statements on vetoing the Lusk bill in 1920 and signing the bill repealing the Lusk Laws in 1923 may be found in *Public Papers of Governor Smith,* pp. 227 et seq. (1920) and *Public Papers of Alfred E. Smith, Governor, 1923,* pp. 292 et seq. (1924).

(e) *Teacher's loyalty oaths.* Many states passed legislation requiring loyalty oaths of teachers and restraining teachers in their political views and activities. See Chapter VII, *infra.*

3. For further description of the World War I period see F. L. Allen, *Only Yesterday,* pp. 45–77 (1931); Slosson, *The Great Crusade and After, 1914–1928,* ch. I–III (1931); O'Brian, *Loyalty Tests and Guilt by Association,* 61 Harv. L. Rev. 592, 593–6 (1948); Biddle, *The Fear of Freedom,* pp. 54–69 (1951).

4. In World War II there was no repetition of the excesses of the World War I period. The major issues of political freedom involved (1) the exclusion of the Japanese from the West Coast and their detention; (2) the prosecution of the Minneapolis Troskyites; and (3) the prosecution of a group of alleged pro-Nazis. On these issues, see Section D, *infra.* The post World War II period is discussed at length *infra.*

## C. DEVELOPMENT OF THE LEGAL PRINCIPLES

Enforcement of the Federal Espionage Act and comparable state legislation during World War I brought about major developments in the constitutional principles underlying the traditional doctrine of freedom in political expression. Actually none of the World War I prosecutions reached the Supreme Court until the war was over. Beginning in 1919, however, the Court considered a series of fundamental issues, first relating to wartime legislation and later to legislation applicable in times of peace. Throughout the 1920's the trend of Supreme Court decision tended to uphold the government's authority to restrict political expression. Commencing with *Near v. Minnesota* in 1931 and extending into the middle 1940's, however, the Court built up a body of principles and precedent that severely limited government power in this area.

The first Supreme Court decision came in *Schenck v. United States,* 249 U. S. 47, 63 L. Ed. 470, 39 S. Ct. 247 (1919). Schenck was indicted under the original provisions of the Espionage

Act for causing insubordination in the armed forces of the United States and for obstructing recruiting and enlistment during the war. Schenck, the general secretary of the Socialist Party, had participated in printing and mailing 15,000 leaflets, many of which went to men who had been called for duty by their draft boards. The leaflet asserted that the draft was unconstitutional and that it constituted "a monstrous wrong against humanity in the interests of Wall Street's chosen few"; it contained other arguments and urged recipients to "assert your opposition to the draft." Mr. Justice Holmes, writing for a unanimous court, disposed of the First Amendment issue in the following language:

". . . We admit that in many places and in ordinary times the defendants in saying all that was said in the circular would have been within their constitutional rights. But the character of every act depends upon the circumstances in which it is done. *Aikens* v. *Wisconsin,* 195 U. S. 194, 205, 206. The most stringent protection of free speech would not protect a man in falsely shouting fire in a theatre and causing a panic. It does not even protect a man from an injunction against uttering words that may have all the effect of force. *Gompers* v. *Bucks Stove & Range Co.,* 221 U. S. 418, 439. The question in every case is whether the words used are used in such circumstances and are of such a nature as to create a clear and present danger that they will bring about the substantive evils that Congress has a right to prevent. It is a question of proximity and degree. When a nation is at war many things that might be said in time of peace are such a hindrance to its effort that their utterance will not be endured so long as men fight and that no Court could regard them as protected by any constitutional right. It seems to be admitted that if an actual obstruction of the recruiting service were proved, liability for words that produced that effect might be enforced. The statute of 1917 in § 4 punishes conspiracies to obstruct as well as actual obstruction. If the act, (speaking, or circulating a paper,) its tendency and the intent with which it is done are the same, we perceive no ground for saying that success alone warrants making the act a crime. *Goldman* v. *United States,* 245 U. S. 474, 477. Indeed that case might be said to dispose of the present contention if the precedent covers all *media concludendi*. But as the right to free speech was not referred to specially, we have thought fit to add a few words." 249 U. S. at 52.

This was the first enunciation of the famous clear and present danger test.

Similar results were reached in three other cases decided at the same time or shortly afterwards, all involving prosecutions for creating insubordination in the armed forces. The best known of these was the prosecution of Eugene V. Debs. Debs had made a speech on the general theme of socialism and opposition to the war, in the course of which he had praised certain individuals who had been convicted for resisting the draft or causing insubordination in the armed forces. His most extreme statement was, "you need to know that you are fit for something better than slavery and cannon fodder." The jury had held Debs guilty, thus finding that the intent of the speech was to encourage his hearers to obstruct the recruiting service. Holding the First Amendment issue decided by the *Schenck* case the Court unanimously affirmed the conviction. The sentence was 10 years' imprisonment. *Debs v. United States*, 249 U. S. 211, 63 L. Ed. 566, 39 S. Ct. 252 (1919).[1]

The only case to come before the Court that involved the 1918 amendments to the Espionage Act was *Abrams v. United States*, 250 U. S. 616, 63 L. Ed. 1173, 40 S. Ct. 17 (1919). Here the defendants were indicted for publishing abusive language about the form of government, for publishing language intended to bring the form of government into contempt, for encouraging resistance to the United States in the war, and for inciting curtailment of production of war materials. The charges were based upon two leaflets which the defendants had printed and distributed by throwing them out the window of a building. The first leaflet denounced President Wilson as a coward and hypocrite for sending troops to Russia, and ended:

> "The Russian Revolution cries: Workers of the World! Awake! Rise! Put down your enemy and mine!
> "Yes! friends, there is only one enemy of the workers of the world and that is CAPITALISM.
> "Awake! Awake, you Workers of the World."
> "Revolutionists."

The second leaflet, addressed primarily to workers in the factories, declared, " . . . you are producing bullets, bayonets, cannon, to murder not only the Germans, but also your dearest, best, who are in Russia and are fighting for freedom"; "our reply to the barbaric intervention has to be a general

---

[1] Debs began his sentence on April 13, 1919 at the age of 63. In 1920, while in prison, he was the Socialist candidate for President, receiving 919,799 votes. President Harding released him on Christmas Day, 1921, without restoration of citizenship. 5 Dictionary of American Biography 183.

The other two cases mentioned in the text are *Sugarman v. U. S.*, 249 U. S. 182, 63 L. Ed. 550, 39 S. Ct. 191 (1919), and *Frohwerk v. U. S.*, 249 U. S. 204, 63 L. Ed. 561, 39 S. Ct. 249 (1919).

**386**                                            [Emerson]

strike!"; "workers, up to fight"; "woe unto those who will be in the way of progress. Let solidarity live!" It was signed, "The Rebels."

The majority of the Court held that "the plain purpose of their propaganda was to excite, at the supreme crisis of the war, disaffection, sedition, riots, and, as they hoped, revolution, in this country for the purpose of embarrassing and if possible defeating the military plans of the Government in Europe." 250 U. S. at 623. It thus found evidence to sustain the conviction on the third and fourth charges.

For the first time Justices Holmes and Brandeis dissented. The opinion of Mr. Justice Holmes goes on the ground that the intent required by the statute, to hinder the prosecution of the war, was not shown. Mr. Justice Holmes elaborated his remarks in the *Schenck* case in the following language:

"I never have seen any reason to doubt that the questions of law that alone were before this Court in the cases of *Schenck*, *Frohwerk* and *Debs*, 249 U. S. 47, 204, 211, were rightly decided. I do not doubt for a moment that by the same reasoning that would justify punishing persuasion to murder, the United States constitutionally may punish speech that produces or is intended to produce a clear and imminent danger that it will bring about forthwith certain substantive evils that the United States constitutionally may seek to prevent. The power undoubtedly is greater in time of war than in time of peace because war opens dangers that do not exist at other times.

"But as against dangers peculiar to war, as against others, the principle of the right to free speech is always the same. It is only the present danger of immediate evil or an intent to bring it about that warrants Congress in setting a limit to the expression of opinion where private rights are not concerned. Congress certainly cannot forbid all effort to change the mind of the country. Now nobody can suppose that the surreptitious publishing of a silly leaflet by an unknown man, without more, would present any immediate danger that its opinions would hinder the success of the government arms or have any appreciable tendency to do so. Publishing those opinions for the very purpose of obstructing however, might indicate a greater danger and at any rate would have the quality of an attempt. So I assume that the second leaflet if published for the purposes alleged in the fourth count might be punishable. But it seems pretty clear to me that nothing less than that would bring these papers within the scope of this law." 250 U. S. at 627-8.

## Note

1. Other important cases arising under the Espionage Act were:

*Schaefer v. U. S.*, 251 U. S. 466, 64 L. Ed. 360, 40 S. Ct. 259 (1920), in which convictions were upheld of the officers of a German-language newspaper charged with printing false and distorted accounts of the war. Justices Holmes and Brandeis dissented on free speech grounds; Mr. Justice Clark dissented on grounds of error in the conduct of the trial.

*Pierce v. U. S.*, 252 U. S. 239, 64 L. Ed. 542, 40 S. Ct. 205 (1920), in which convictions were upheld of three Socialists who had distributed a pamphlet denouncing the war. Justices Holmes and Brandeis again dissented.

*United States ex rel Milwaukee Social Democrat Publishing Co. v. Burleson*, 255 U. S. 407, 65 L. Ed. 704, 41 S. Ct. 352 (1921), in which the Court upheld the Postmaster General's revocation of the second class mailing privileges of Victor Berger's *Milwaukee Leader*. The action was taken under Title XII of the Espionage Act which made non-mailable any matter violating the Act. The Court sanctioned not only denial of the second class mailing privilege to issues of the newspaper found to violate the law but denial of the privilege to all future issues. Justices Holmes and Brandeis once more dissented.

The remaining cases, of less significance, were *Stilson v. U. S.*, 250 U. S. 583, 63 L. Ed. 1154, 40 S. Ct. 28 (1919); *O'Connell v. U. S.*, 253 U. S. 142, 64 L. Ed. 827, 40 S. Ct. 444 (1920).

2. One of the earliest, and most interesting, cases under the Espionage Act was *Masses Publishing Co. v. Patten*, 244 Fed. 535 (S. D. N. Y., 1917), in which Judge Learned Hand enjoined the New York Postmaster from excluding from the mails the August 1917 issue of *The Masses*, a left wing publication. Holding that the Espionage Act, in its original form, could not be construed to prohibit the statements involved, Judge Hand attempted to draw the line between protected and unprotected speech:

"One may not counsel or advise others to violate the law as it stands. Words are not only the keys of persuasion, but the triggers of action, and those which have no purport but to counsel the violation of law cannot by any latitude of interpretation be a part of that public opinion which is the final source of government in a democratic state. . . . Political agitation, by the passions it arouses or the convictions it engenders, may in fact stimulate men to the violation of law. Detestation of existing policies is easily transformed into forcible resistance of the authority which puts them in execution, and it would be folly to disregard the causal relation between the two. Yet to assimilate agitation, legitimate as such, with direct incitement to violent resistance, is to disregard the tolerance of all methods of political agitation which in normal times is a safeguard of free government. The distinction is not a scholastic subterfuge, but a hard-bought acquisition in the fight for freedom, and the purpose to disregard it must be evident when the power exists. If one stops short of urging upon others that it is their duty or their interest to resist the law, it seems to me one should not be held to have attempted to cause its violation. If that be not the test, I can see no escape from the conclusion that under this section every political agitation which can be shown to be apt to create a seditious temper is illegal. I am confident that by such language Congress had no such revolutionary purpose in view." 244 Fed. at 540.

On appeal Judge Hand's decision was reversed. 246 Fed. 24 (C. A. 2, 1917).

For discussion of the *Masses* and other cases in the lower Federal courts, see Chafee, *Free Speech in the United States*, pp. 42–79 (1941). The cases up to July 1918, including many not elsewhere reported, are collected in Nelles, *Espionage Act Cases*, published by the National Civil Liberties Bureau (1918).

3. In *Gilbert v. Minnesota*, 254 U. S. 325, 65 L. Ed. 287, 41 S. Ct. 125 (1920), the Supreme Court upheld the Minnesota statute, comparable to the Federal Espionage Act, which prohibited teaching or advocating that men should not enlist or aid in prosecution of the war. The Court ruled that (1) the subject matter of the statute was within the power of the states and not exclusively within Federal power; and (2) assuming the right of free speech to be guaranteed against state action, the legislation did not violate any such right. Mr. Justice Brandeis dissented, arguing that "the right to speak freely concerning functions of the Federal Government is a privilege or immunity of every citizen of the United States which, even before the adoption of the Fourteenth Amendment, a State was powerless to curtail." 254 U. S. at 337.

4. The broader issues raised by anti-sedition legislation not directed exclusively against interference with the operation of war came before the Supreme Court in *Gitlow v. New York.*

## GITLOW v. NEW YORK

Supreme Court of the United States, 1925
268 U. S. 652, 69 L. Ed. 1138, 45 S. Ct. 625

MR. JUSTICE SANFORD delivered the opinion of the Court.

Benjamin Gitlow was indicted in the Supreme Court of New York, with three others for the statutory crime of criminal anarchy. New York Penal Laws, §§ 160, 161.[1] He was separately tried, convicted, and sentenced to imprisonment. The judgment was affirmed by the Appellate Division and by the Court of Appeals. 195 App. Div. 773; 234 N. Y. 132 and 539. The case is here on writ of error to the Supreme Court, to which the record was remitted. 260 U. S. 703.

The contention here is that the statute, by its terms and as applied in this case, is repugnant to the due process clause of the Fourteenth Amendment. Its material provisions are:

---

[1] Laws of 1909, ch. 88; Consol. Laws, 1909, ch. 40. This statute was originally enacted in 1902. Laws of 1902, ch. 371.

"§ 160. *Criminal anarchy defined.* Criminal anarchy is the doctrine that organized government should be overthrown by force or violence, or by assassination of the executive head or of any of the executive officials of government, or by any unlawful means. The advocacy of such doctrine either by word of mouth or writing is a felony.

"§ 161. *Advocacy of criminal anarchy.* Any person who:

"1. By word of mouth or writing advocates, advises or teaches the duty, necessity or propriety of overthrowing or overturning organized government by force or violence, or by assassination of the executive head or of any of the executive officials of government, or by any unlawful means; or,

"2. Prints, publishes, edits, issues or knowingly circulates, sells, distributes or publicly displays any book, paper, document, or written or printed matter in any form, containing or advocating, advising or teaching the doctrine that organized government should be overthrown by force, violence or any unlawful means . . . ,

"Is guilty of a felony and punishable" by imprisonment or fine, or both.

The indictment was in two counts. The first charged that the defendant had advocated, advised and taught the duty, necessity and propriety of overthrowing and overturning organized government by force, violence and unlawful means, by certain writings therein set forth entitled "The Left Wing Manifesto"; the second that he had printed, published and knowingly circulated and distributed a certain paper called "The Revolutionary Age," containing the writings set forth in the first count advocating, advising and teaching the doctrine that organized government should be overthrown by force, violence and unlawful means.

The following facts were established on the trial by undisputed evidence and admissions: The defendant is a member of the Left Wing Section of the Socialist Party, a dissenting branch or faction of that party formed in opposition to its dominant policy of "moderate Socialism." Membership in both is open to aliens as well as citizens. The Left Wing Section was organized nationally at a conference in New York City in June, 1919, attended by ninety delegates from twenty different States. The conference elected a National Council, of which the defendant was a member, and left to it the adoption of a "Manifesto." This was published in The Revolutionary Age, the official organ of the Left Wing. The defendant was on the board of managers of the paper and was its business manager. He arranged for the printing of the paper and took to the printer the manuscript

**390**

of the first issue which contained the Left Wing Manifesto, and also a Communist Program and a Program of the Left Wing that had been adopted by the conference. Sixteen thousand copies were printed, which were delivered at the premises in New York City used as the office of the Revolutionary Age and the headquarters of the Left Wing, and occupied by the defendant and other officials. These copies were paid for by the defendant, as business manager of the paper. Employees at this office wrapped and mailed out copies of the paper under the defendant's direction; and copies were sold from this office. It was admitted that the defendant signed a card subscribing to the Manifesto and Program of the Left Wing, which all applicants were required to sign before being admitted to membership; that he went to different parts of the State to speak to branches of the Socialist Party about the principles of the Left Wing and advocated their adoption; and that he was responsible for the Manifesto as it appeared, that "he knew of the publication, in a general way and he knew of its publication afterwards, and is responsible for its circulation."

There was no evidence of any effect resulting from the publication and circulation of the Manifesto.

No witnesses were offered in behalf of the defendant.

Extracts from the Manifesto are set forth in the margin.[2] Coupled with a review of the rise of Socialism, it condemned the dominant "moderate Socialism" for its recognition of the necessity of the democratic parliamentary state; repudiated its policy of introducing Socialism by legislative measures; and advocated, in plain and unequivocal language, the necessity of accomplishing the "Communist Revolution" by a militant and "revolutionary Socialism", based on "the class struggle" and mobilizing the "power of the proletariat in action," through mass industrial revolts developing into mass political strikes and "revolutionary mass action", for the purpose of conquering and destroying the parliamentary state and establishing in its place, through a "revolutionary dictatorship of the proletariat", the system of Communist Socialism. The then recent strikes in Seattle and Winnipeg were cited as instances of a development already verging on revolutionary action and suggestive of proletarian dictatorship, in which the strike-workers were "trying to usurp the functions of municipal government"; and revolutionary Socialism, it was urged, must use these mass industrial revolts to broaden the strike, make it general and militant, and develop it into mass political strikes and revolutionary mass action for the annihilation of the parliamentary state. . . .

---

[2] [The footnote, quoting the Manifesto, is omitted.]

The sole contention here is, essentially, that as there was no evidence of any concrete result flowing from the publication of the Manifesto or of circumstances showing the likelihood of such result, the statute as construed and applied by the trial court penalizes the mere utterance, as such, of "doctrine" having no quality of incitement, without regard either to the circumstances of its utterance or to the likelihood of unlawful sequences; and that, as the exercise of the right of free expression with relation to government is only punishable "in circumstances involving likelihood of substantive evil," the statute contravenes the due process clause of the Fourteenth Amendment. The argument in support of this contention rests primarily upon the following propositions: 1st, That the "liberty" protected by the Fourteenth Amendment includes the liberty of speech and of the press; and 2nd, That while liberty of expression "is not absolute," it may be restrained "only in circumstances where its exercise bears a causal relation with some substantive evil, consummated, attempted or likely," and as the statute "takes no account of circumstances," it unduly restrains this liberty and is therefore unconstitutional.

The precise question presented, and the only question which we can consider under this writ of error, then is, whether the statute, as construed and applied in this case by the state courts, deprived the defendant of his liberty of expression in violation of the due process clause of the Fourteenth Amendment.

The statute does not penalize the utterance or publication of abstract "doctrine" or academic discussion having no quality of incitement to any concrete action. It is not aimed against mere historical or philosophical essays. It does not restrain the advocacy of changes in the form of government by constitutional and lawful means. What it prohibits is language advocating, advising or teaching the overthrow of organized government by unlawful means. These words imply urging to action. Advocacy is defined in the Century Dictionary as: "1. The act of pleading for, supporting, or recommending; active espousal." It is not the abstract "doctrine" of overthrowing organized government by unlawful means which is denounced by the statute, but the advocacy of action for the accomplishment of that purpose.

. . .

The Manifesto, plainly, is neither the statement of abstract doctrine nor, as suggested by counsel, mere prediction that industrial disturbances and revolutionary mass strikes will result spontaneously in an inevitable process of evolution in the economic system. It advocates and urges in fervent language mass action which shall progressively foment industrial disturbances

**392**

and through political mass strikes and revolutionary mass action overthrow and destroy organized parliamentary government. It concludes with a call to action in these words: "The proletariat revolution and the Communist reconstruction of society— *the struggle for these*—is now indispensable. . . . The Communist International calls the proletariat of the world to the final struggle!" This is not the expression of philosophical abstraction, the mere prediction of future events; it is the language of direct incitement.

The means advocated for bringing about the destruction of organized parliamentary government, namely, mass industrial revolts usurping the functions of municipal government, political mass strikes directed against the parliamentary state, and revolutionary mass action for its final destruction, necessarily imply the use of force and violence, and in their essential nature are inherently unlawful in a constitutional government of law and order. That the jury were warranted in finding that the Manifesto advocated not merely the abstract doctrine of overthrowing organized government by force, violence and unlawful means, but action to that end, is clear.

For present purposes we may and do assume that freedom of speech and of the press—which are protected by the First Amendment from abridgment by Congress—are among the fundamental personal rights and "liberties" protected by the due process clause of the Fourteenth Amendment from impairment by the States. We do not regard the incidental statement in *Prudential Ins. Co.* v. *Cheek,* 259 U. S. 530, 543, that the Fourteenth Amendment imposes no restrictions on the States concerning freedom of speech, as determinative of this question.

It is a fundamental principle, long established, that the freedom of speech and of the press which is secured by the Constitution, does not confer an absolute right to speak or publish, without responsibility, whatever one may choose, or an unrestricted and unbridled license that gives immunity for every possible use of language and prevents the punishment of those who abuse this freedom. 2 Story on the Constitution, 5th ed., § 1580, p. 634; *Robertson* v. *Baldwin,* 165 U. S. 275, 281; *Patterson* v. *Colorado,* 205 U. S. 454, 462; *Fox* v. *Washington,* 236 U. S. 273, 276; *Schenck* v. *United States,* 249 U. S. 47, 52 . . .

That a State in the exercise of its police power may punish those who abuse this freedom by utterances inimical to the public welfare, tending to corrupt public morals, incite to crime, or disturb the public peace, is not open to question. *Robertson* v. *Baldwin, supra,* p. 281; *Patterson* v. *Colorado, supra,* p. 462; *Fox* v. *Washington, supra,* p. 277; *Gilbert* v. *Minnesota* [254 U. S. 325,

339] ; *People* v. *Most,* 171 N. Y. 423, 431 ; *State* v. *Holm,* 139 Minn. 267, 275 ; *State* v. *Hennessy,* 114 Wash. 351, 359 ; *State* v. *Boyd,* 86 N. J. L. 75, 79 ; *State* v. *McKee,* 73 Conn. 18, 27. Thus it was held by this Court in the *Fox Case,* that a State may punish publications advocating and encouraging a breach of its criminal laws ; and, in the *Gilbert Case,* that a State may punish utterances teaching or advocating that its citizens should not assist the United States in prosecuting or carrying on war with its public enemies.

And, for yet more imperative reasons, a State may punish utterances endangering the foundations of organized government and threatening its overthrow by unlawful means. These imperil its own existence as a constitutional State. Freedom of speech and press, said Story (*supra*) does not protect disturbances to the public peace or the attempt to subvert the government. It does not protect publications or teachings which tend to subvert or imperil the government or to impede or hinder it in the performance of its governmental duties. *State* v. *Holm, supra,* p. 275. It does not protect publications prompting the overthrow of government by force ; the punishment of those who publish articles which tend to destroy organized society being essential to the security of freedom and the stability of the State. *People* v. *Most, supra,* pp. 431, 432. And a State may penalize utterances which openly advocate the overthrow of the representative and constitutional form of government of the United States and the several States, by violence or other unlawful means. *People* v. *Lloyd,* 304 Ill. 23, 34. See also, *State* v. *Tachin,* 92 N. J. L. 269, 274 ; and *People* v. *Steelik,* 187 Cal. 361, 375. In short this freedom does not deprive a State of the primary and essential right of self preservation ; which, so long as human governments endure, they cannot be denied. *Turner* v. *Williams,* 194 U. S. 279, 294. . . .

By enacting the present statute the State has determined, through its legislative body, that utterances advocating the overthrow of organized government by force, violence and unlawful means, are so inimical to the general welfare and involve such danger of substantive evil that they may be penalized in the exercise of its police power. That determination must be given great weight. Every presumption is to be indulged in favor of the validity of the statute. *Mugler* v. *Kansas,* 123 U. S. 623, 661. And the case is to be considered "in the light of the principle that the State is primarily the judge of regulations required in the interest of public safety and welfare;" and that its police "statutes may only be declared unconstitutional where they are arbitrary or unreasonable attempts to exercise authority vested in the State in the public interest." *Great Northern Ry.* v. *Clara City,* 246 U. S. 434, 439. That utterances inciting to the over-throw of organized government by unlawful means, present a sufficient danger of substantive evil to bring their punishment within the range of legislative discretion, is clear. Such utter-ances, by their very nature, involve danger to the public peace and to the security of the State. They threaten breaches of the peace and ultimate revolution. And the immediate danger is none the less real and substantial, because the effect of a given utterance cannot be accurately foreseen. The State cannot rea-sonably be required to measure the danger from every such utter-ance in the nice balance of a jeweler's scale. A single revolution-ary spark may kindle a fire that, smouldering for a time, may burst into a sweeping and destructive conflagration. It cannot be said that the State is acting arbitrarily or unreasonably when in the exercise of its judgment as to the measures necessary to pro-tect the public peace and safety, it seeks to extinguish the spark without waiting until it has enkindled the flame or blazed into the conflagration. It cannot reasonably be required to defer the adoption of measures for its own peace and safety until the revolutionary utterances lead to actual disturbances of the public peace or imminent and immediate danger of its own destruction; but it may, in the exercise of its judgment, suppress the threat-ened danger in its incipiency. . . .

We cannot hold that the present statute is an arbitrary or unreasonable exercise of the police power of the State unwarrant-ably infringing the freedom of speech or press; and we must and do sustain its constitutionality.

This being so it may be applied to every utterance—not too trivial to be beneath the notice of the law—which is of such a character and used with such intent and purpose as to bring it within the prohibition of the statute. . . . In other words, when the legislative body has determined generally, in the con-stitutional exercise of its discretion, that utterances of a certain kind involve such danger of substantive evil that they may be punished, the question whether any specific utterance coming within the prohibited class is likely, in and of itself, to bring about the substantive evil, is not open to consideration. It is sufficient that the statute itself be constitutional and that the use of the language comes within its prohibition.

It is clear that the question in such cases is entirely different from that involved in those cases where the statute merely pro-hibits certain acts involving the danger of substantive evil, with-out any reference to language itself, and it is sought to apply its provisions to language used by the defendant for the purpose of bringing about the prohibited results. There, if it be contended that the statute cannot be applied to the language used by the defendant because of its protection by the freedom of speech or press, it must necessarily be found, as an original question, without any previous determination by the legislative body, whether the specific language used involved such likelihood of bringing about the substantive evil as to deprive it of the constitutional protection. In such cases it has been held that the general provisions of the statute may be constitutionally applied to the specific utterance of the defendant if its natural tendency and probable effect was to bring about the substantive evil which the legislative body might prevent. *Schenck* v. *United States, supra,* p. 51; *Debs* v. *United States* [249 U. S. at 215, 216]. And the general statement in the *Schenck Case* (p. 52) that the "question in every case is whether the words are used in such circumstances and are of such a nature as to create a clear and present danger that they will bring about the substantive evils,"—upon which great reliance is placed in the defendant's argument—was manifestly intended, as shown by the context, to apply only in cases of this class, and has no application to those like the present, where the legislative body itself has previously determined the danger of substantive evil arising from utterances of a specified character. . . .

It was not necessary, within the meaning of the statute, that the defendant should have advocated "some definite or immediate act or acts" of force, violence or unlawfulness. It was sufficient if such acts were advocated in general terms; and it was not essential that their immediate execution should have been advocated. Nor was it necessary that the language should have been "reasonably and ordinarily calculated to incite certain persons" to acts of force, violence or unlawfulness. The advocacy need not be addressed to specific persons. Thus, the publication and circulation of a newspaper article may be an encouragement or endeavor to persuade to murder, although not addressed to any person in particular. *Queen* v. *Most*, L. R., 7 Q. B. D. 244.

We need not enter upon a consideration of the English common law rule of seditious libel or the Federal Sedition Act of 1798, to which reference is made in the defendant's brief. These are so unlike the present statute, that we think the decisions under them cast no helpful light upon the questions here.

And finding, for the reasons stated, that the statute is not in itself unconstitutional, and that it has not been applied in the present case in derogation of any constitutional right, the judgment of the Court of Appeals is

*Affirmed.*

396

MR. JUSTICE HOLMES, dissenting.

MR. JUSTICE BRANDEIS and I are of opinion that this judgment should be reversed. The general principle of free speech, it seems to me, must be taken to be included in the Fourteenth Amendment, in view of the scope that has been given to the word 'liberty' as there used, although perhaps it may be accepted with a somewhat larger latitude of interpretation than is allowed to Congress by the sweeping language that governs or ought to govern the laws of the United States. If I am right, then I think that the criterion sanctioned by the full Court in *Schenck* v. *United States*, 249 U. S. 47, 52, applies. "The question in every case is whether the words used are used in such circumstances and are of such a nature as to create a clear and present danger that they will bring about the substantive evils that [the State] has a right to prevent." It is true that in my opinion this criterion was departed from in *Abrams* v. *United States*, 250 U. S. 616, but the convictions that I expressed in that case are too deep for it to be possible for me as yet to believe that it and *Schaefer* v. *United States*, 251 U. S. 466, have settled the law. If what I think the correct test is applied, it is manifest that there was no present danger of an attempt to overthrow the government by force on the part of the admittedly small minority who shared the defendant's views. It is said that this manifesto was more than a theory, that it was an incitement. Every idea is an incitement. It offers itself for belief and if believed it is acted on unless some other belief outweighs it or some failure of energy stifles the movement at its birth. The only difference between the expression of an opinion and an incitement in the narrower sense is the speaker's enthusiasm for the result. Eloquence may set fire to reason. But whatever may be thought of the redundant discourse before us it had no chance of starting a present conflagration. If in the long run the beliefs expressed in proletarian dictatorship are destined to be accepted by the dominant forces of the community, the only meaning of free speech is that they should be given their chance and have their way.

If the publication of this document had been laid as an attempt to induce an uprising against government at once and not at some indefinite time in the future it would have presented a different question. The object would have been one with which the law might deal, subject to the doubt whether there was any danger that the publication could produce any result, or in other words, whether it was not futile and too remote from possible consequences. But the indictment alleges the publication and nothing more.

## WHITNEY v. CALIFORNIA

Supreme Court of the United States, 1927
274 U. S. 357, 71 L. Ed. 1095, 47 S. Ct. 641

MR. JUSTICE SANFORD delivered the opinion of the Court.

By a criminal information filed in the Superior Court of Alameda County, California, the plaintiff in error was charged, in five counts, with violations of the Criminal Syndicalism Act of that State. Statutes, 1919, c. 188, p. 281. She was tried, convicted on the first count, and sentenced to imprisonment. . . .

The pertinent provisions of the Criminal Syndicalism Act are:

"Section 1. The term 'criminal syndicalism' as used in this act is hereby defined as any doctrine or precept advocating, teaching or aiding and abetting the commission of crime, sabotage (which word is hereby defined as meaning wilful and malicious physical damage or injury to physical property), or unlawful acts of force and violence or unlawful methods of terrorism as a means of accomplishing a change in industrial ownership or control, or effecting any political change.

"Sec. 2. Any person who: . . . 4. Organizes or assists in organizing, or is or knowingly becomes a member of, any organization, society, group or assemblage of persons organized or assembled to advocate, teach or aid and abet criminal syndicalism

. . .

"Is guilty of a felony and punishable by imprisonment."

The first count of the information, on which the conviction was had, charged that on or about November 28, 1919, in Alameda County, the defendant, in violation of the Criminal Syndicalism Act, "did then and there unlawfully, wilfully, wrongfully, deliberately and feloniously organize and assist in organizing, and was, is, and knowingly became a member of an organization, society, group and assemblage of persons organized and assembled to advocate, teach, aid and abet criminal syndicalism." . . .

The following facts, among many others, were established on the trial by undisputed evidence: The defendant, a resident of Oakland, in Alameda County, California, had been a member of the Local Oakland branch of the Socialist Party. This Local sent delegates to the national convention of the Socialist Party held in Chicago in 1919, which resulted in a split between the "radical" group and the old-wing Socialists. The "radicals"—to whom the Oakland delegates adhered—being ejected, went to another hall, and formed the Communist Labor Party of America. Its Constitution provided for the membership of persons subscribing to the principles of the Party and pledging themselves to be guided by its Platform, and for the formation of state

**398**

organizations conforming to its Platform as the supreme declaration of the Party. In its "Platform and Program" the Party declared that it was in full harmony with "the revolutionary working class parties of all countries" and adhered to the principles of Communism laid down in the Manifesto of the Third International at Moscow, and that its purpose was "to create a unified revolutionary working class movement in America," organizing the workers as a class, in a revolutionary class struggle to conquer the capitalist state, for the overthrow of capitalist rule, the conquest of political power and the establishment of a working class government, the Dictatorship of the Proletariat, in place of the state machinery of the capitalists, which should make and enforce the laws, reorganize society on the basis of Communism and bring about the Communist Commonwealth—advocated, as the most important means of capturing state power, the action of the masses, proceeding from the shops and factories, the use of the political machinery of the capitalist state being only secondary; the organization of the workers into "revolutionary industrial unions"; propaganda pointing out their revolutionary nature and possibilities; and great industrial battles showing the value of the strike as a political weapon—commended the propaganda and example of the Industrial Workers of the World and their struggles and sacrifices in the class war—pledged support and cooperation to "the revolutionary industrial proletariat of America" in their struggles against the capitalist class—cited the Seattle and Winnipeg strikes and the numerous strikes all over the country "proceeding without the authority of the old reactionary Trade Union officials," as manifestations of the new tendency —and recommended that strikes of national importance be supported and given a political character, and that propagandists and organizers be mobilized "who can not only teach, but actually help to put in practice the principles of revolutionary industrial unionism and Communism."

Shortly thereafter the Local Oakland withdrew from the Socialist Party, and sent accredited delegates, including the defendant, to a convention held in Oakland in November, 1919, for the purpose of organizing a California branch of the Communist Labor Party. The defendant, after taking out a temporary membership in the Communist Labor Party, attended this convention as a delegate and took an active part in its proceedings. She was elected a member of the Credentials Committee, and, as its chairman, made a report to the convention upon which the delegates were seated. She was also appointed a member of the Resolutions Committee, and as such signed the following resolution in reference to political action, among others proposed by the

Committee: "The C. L. P. of California fully recognizes the value of political action as a means of spreading communist propaganda; it insists that in proportion to the development of the economic strength of the working class, it, the working class, must also develop its political power. The C. L. P. of California proclaims and insists that the capture of political power, locally or nationally by the revolutionary working class can be of tremendous assistance to the workers in their struggle of emancipation. Therefore, we again urge the workers who are possessed of the right of franchise to cast their votes for the party which represents their immediate and final interest—the C. L. P.—at all elections, being fully convinced of the utter futility of obtaining any real measure of justice or freedom under officials elected by parties owned and controlled by the capitalist class." The minutes show that this resolution, with the others proposed by the committee, was read by its chairman to the convention before the Committee on the Constitution had submitted its report. According to the recollection of the defendant, however, she herself read this resolution. Thereafter, before the report of the Committee on the Constitution had been acted upon, the defendant was elected an alternate member of the State Executive Committee. The Constitution, as finally read, was then adopted. This provided that the organization should be named the Communist Labor Party of California; that it should be "affiliated with" the Communist Labor Party of America, and subscribe to its Program, Platform and Constitution, and "through this affiliation" be "joined with the Communist International of Moscow;" and that the qualifications for membership should be those prescribed in the National Constitution. The proposed resolutions were later taken up and all adopted, except that on political action, which caused a lengthy debate, resulting in its defeat and the acceptance of the National Program in its place. After this action, the defendant, without, so far as appears, making any protest, remained in the convention until it adjourned. She later attended as an alternate member one or two meetings of the State Executive Committee in San Jose and San Francisco, and stated, on the trial, that she was then a member of the Communist Labor Party. She also testified that it was not her intention that the Communist Labor Party of California should be an instrument of terrorism or violence, and that it was not her purpose or that of the Convention to violate any known law.

In the light of this preliminary statement, we now take up, in so far as they require specific consideration, the various grounds upon which it is here contended that the Syndicalism Act and its application in this case is repugnant to the due process and equal protection clauses of the Fourteenth Amendment.

1. While it is not denied that the evidence warranted the jury in finding that the defendant became a member of and assisted in organizing the Communist Labor Party of California, and that this was organized to advocate, teach, aid or abet criminal syndicalism as defined by the Act, it is urged that the Act, as here construed and applied, deprived the defendant of her liberty without due process of law in that it has made her action in attending the Oakland convention unlawful by reason of "a subsequent event brought about against her will, by the agency of others," with no showing of specific intent on her part to join in the forbidden purpose of the association, and merely because, by reason of a lack of "prophetic" understanding she failed to forsee the quality that others would give to the convention. The argument is, in effect, that the character of the state organization could not be forecast when she attended the convention; that she had no purpose of helping to create an instrument of terrorism and violence; that she "took part in formulating and presenting to the convention a resolution which, if adopted, would have committed the new organization to a legitimate policy of political reform by the use of the ballot"; that it was not until after the majority of the convention turned out to be "contrary-minded, and other less temperate policies prevailed" that the convention could have taken on the character of criminal syndicalism; and that as this was done over her protest, her mere presence in the convention, however violent the opinions expressed therein, could not thereby become a crime. This contention, while advanced in the form of a constitutional objection to the Act, is in effect nothing more than an effort to review the weight of the evidence for the purpose of showing that the defendant did not join and assist in organizing the Communist Labor Party of California with a knowledge of its unlawful character and purpose. This question, which is foreclosed by the verdict of the jury—sustained by the Court of Appeal over the specific objection that it was not supported by the evidence—is one of fact merely which is not open to review in this Court, involving as it does no constitutional question whatever. And we may add that the argument entirely disregards the facts: that the defendant had previously taken out a membership card in the National Party, that the resolution which she supported did not advocate the use of the ballot to the exclusion of violent and unlawful means of bringing about the desired changes in industrial and political conditions; and that, after the constitution of the California Party had been adopted, and this resolution had been voted down and the Na-

tional Program accepted, she not only remained in the convention, without protest, until its close, but subsequently manifested her acquiescence by attending as an alternate member of the State Executive Committee and continuing as a member of the Communist Labor Party.

2. It is clear that the Syndicalism Act is not repugnant to the due process clause by reason of vagueness and uncertainty of definition. It has no substantial resemblance to the statutes held void for uncertainty under the Fourteenth and Fifth Amendments in *International Harvester Co.* v. *Kentucky*, 234 U. S. 216, 221; and *United States* v. *Cohen Grocery*, 255 U. S. 81, 89, because not fixing an ascertainable standard of guilt. The language of § 2, subd. 4, of the Act, under which the plaintiff in error was convicted, is clear; the definition of "criminal syndicalism" specific.

The Act, plainly, meets the essential requirement of due process that a penal statute be "sufficiently explicit to inform those who are subject to it, what conduct on their part will render them liable to its penalties," and be couched in terms that are not "so vague that men of common intelligence must necessarily guess at its meaning and differ as to its application." *Connally* v. *General Construction Co.*, 269 U. S. 385, 391. And see *United States* v. *Brewer*, 139 U. S. 278, 288; *Chicago, etc., Railway* v. *Dey*, (C. C.) 35 Fed. 866, 876; *Tozer* v. *United States*, (C. C.) 52 Fed. 917, 919. . . .

And similar Criminal Syndicalism statutes of other States, some less specific in their definitions, have been held by the State courts not to be void for indefiniteness. *State* v. *Hennessy*, 114 Wash. 351, 364; *State* v. *Laundy*, 103 Ore. 443, 460; *People* v. *Ruthenberg*, 229 Mich. 315, 325. And see *Fox* v. *Washington*, 236 U. S. 273, 277; *People* v. *Steelik*, 187 Cal. 361, 372; *People* v. *Lloyd*, 304 Ill. 23, 34.

3. Neither is the Syndicalism Act repugnant to the equal protection clause, on the ground that, as its penalties are confined to those who advocate a resort to violent and unlawful methods as a means of changing industrial and political conditions, it arbitrarily discriminates between such persons and those who may advocate a resort to these methods as a means of maintaining such conditions.

It is settled by repeated decisions of this Court that the equal protection clause does not take from a State the power to classify in the adoption of police laws, but admits of the exercise of a wide scope of discretion, and avoids what is done only when it is without any reasonable basis and therefore is purely arbitrary; and that one who asasils the classification must carry the burden of showing that it does not rest upon any reasonable basis, but is

[Emerson]

essentially arbitrary. *Lindsley* v. *National Carbonic Gas Co.,* 220 U. S. 61, 78, and cases cited. . . .

The Syndicalism Act is not class legislation; it affects all alike, no matter what their business associations or callings, who come within its terms and do the things prohibited. See *State* v. *Hennessy, supra,* 361; *State* v. *Laundy, supra,* 460. And there is no substantial basis for the contention that the legislature has arbitrarily or unreasonably limited its application to those advocating the use of violent and unlawful methods to effect changes in industrial and political conditions; there being nothing indicating any ground to apprehend that those desiring to maintain existing industrial and political conditions did or would advocate such methods. That there is a wide-spread conviction of the necessity for legislation of this character is indicated by the adoption of similar statutes in several other States.

4. Nor is the Syndicalism Act as applied in this case repugnant to the due process clause as a restraint of the rights of free speech, assembly, and association.

That the freedom of speech which is secured by the Constitution does not confer an absolute right to speak, without responsibility, whatever one may choose, or an unrestricted and unbridled license giving immunity for every possible use of language and preventing the punishment of those who abuse this freedom; and that a State in the exercise of its police power may punish those who abuse this freedom by utterances inimical to the public welfare, tending to incite to crime, disturb the public peace, or endanger the foundations of organized government and threaten its overthrow by unlawful means, is not open to question. *Gitlow* v. *New York,* 268 U. S. 652, 666–668, and cases cited.

By enacting the provisions of the Syndicalism Act the State has declared, through its legislative body, that to knowingly be or become a member of or assist in organizing an association to advocate, teach or aid and abet the commission of crimes or unlawful acts of force, violence or terrorism as a means of accomplishing industrial or political changes, involves such danger to the public peace and the security of the State, that these acts should be penalized in the exercise of its police power. That determination must be given great weight. . . .

The essence of the offense denounced by the Act is the combining with others in an association for the accomplishment of the desired ends through the advocacy and use of criminal and unlawful methods. It partakes of the nature of a criminal conspiracy. See *People* v. *Steelik, supra,* 376. That such united and joint action involves even greater danger to the public peace and

**403**

security than the isolated utterances and acts of individuals, is clear. We cannot hold that, as here applied, the Act is an unreasonable or arbitrary exercise of the police power of the State, unwarrantably infringing any right of free speech, assembly or association, or that those persons are protected from punishment by the due process clause who abuse such rights by joining and furthering an organization thus menacing the peace and welfare of the State. . . .

The order dismissing the writ of error will be vacated and set aside, and the judgment of the Court of Appeal

*Affirmed.*

MR. JUSTICE BRANDEIS, concurring.

Miss Whitney was convicted of the felony of assisting in organizing, in the year 1919, the Communist Labor Party of California, of being a member of it, and of assembling with it. These acts are held to constitute a crime, because the party was formed to teach criminal syndicalism. The statute which made these acts a crime restricted the right of free speech and of assembly theretofore existing. The claim is that the statute, as applied, denied to Miss Whitney the liberty guaranteed by the Fourteenth Amendment.

The felony which the statute created is a crime very unlike the old felony of conspiracy or the old misdemeanor of unlawful assembly. The mere act of assisting in forming a society for teaching syndicalism, of becoming a member of it, or of assembling with others for that purpose is given the dynamic quality of crime. There is guilt although the society may not contemplate immediate promulgation of the doctrine. Thus the accused is to be punished, not for contempt, incitement or conspiracy, but for a step in preparation, which, if it threatens the public order at all, does so only remotely. The novelty in the prohibition introduced is that the statute aims, not at the practice of criminal syndicalism, nor even directly at the preaching of it, but at association with those who propose to preach it.

The right of free speech, the right to teach and the right of assembly are, of course, fundamental rights. . . . These may not be denied or abridged. But, although the rights of free speech and assembly are fundamental, they are not in their nature absolute. Their exercise is subject to restriction, if the particular restriction proposed is required in order to protect the State from destruction or from serious injury, political, economic or moral. That the necessity which is essential to a valid restriction does not exist unless speech would produce, or is intended to produce, a clear and imminent danger of some substantive evil which the State constitutionally may seek to prevent has been settled. See *Schenck* v. *United States*, 249 U. S. 47, 52.

It is said to be the function of the legislature to determine whether at a particular time and under the particular circumstances the formation of, or assembly with, a society organized to advocate criminal syndicalism constitutes a clear and present danger of substantive evil; and that by enacting the law here in question the legislature of California determined that question in the affirmative. Compare *Gitlow* v. *New York*, 268 U. S. 652, 668–671. The legislature must obviously decide, in the first instance, whether a danger exists which calls for a particular protective measure. But where a statute is valid only in case certain conditions exist, the enactment of the statute cannot alone establish the facts which are essential to its validity. Prohibitory legislation has repeatedly been held invalid, because unnecessary, where the denial of liberty involved was that of engaging in a particular business. The power of the courts to strike down an offending law is no less when the interests involved are not property rights, but the fundamental personal rights of free speech and assembly.

This Court has not yet fixed the standard by which to determine when a danger shall be deemed clear; how remote the danger may be and yet be deemed present; and what degree of evil shall be deemed sufficiently substantial to justify resort to abridgement of free speech and assembly as the means of protection. To reach sound conclusions on these matters, we must bear in mind why a State is, ordinarily, denied the power to prohibit dissemination of social, economic and political doctrine which a vast majority of its citizens believes to be false and fraught with evil consequence.

[Here follows the passage quoted in Section A, *supra*.]

Fear of serious injury cannot alone justify suppression of free speech and assembly. Men feared witches and burnt women. It is the function of speech to free men from the bondage of irrational fears. To justify suppression of free speech there must be reasonable ground to fear that serious evil will result if free speech is practiced. There must be reasonable ground to believe that the danger apprehended is imminent. There must be reasonable ground to believe that the evil to be prevented is a serious one. Every denunciation of existing law tends in some measure to increase the probability that there will be violation of it. Condonation of a breach enhances the probability. Expressions of approval add to the probability. Propagation of the criminal state of mind by teaching syndicalism increases it. Advocacy of law-breaking heightens it still further. But even advocacy of violation, however reprehensible morally, is not a justification for denying free speech where the advocacy falls short of incitement and there is nothing to indicate that the advocacy would be immediately acted on. The wide difference between advocacy and incitement, between preparation and attempt, between assembling and conspiracy, must be borne in mind. In order to support a finding of clear and present danger it must be shown either that immediate serious violence was to be expected or was advocated, or that the past conduct furnished reason to believe that such advocacy was then contemplated.

Those who won our independence by revolution were not cowards. They did not fear political change. They did not exalt order at the cost of liberty. To courageous, self-reliant men, with confidence in the power of free and fearless reasoning applied through the processes of popular government, no danger flowing from speech can be deemed clear and present, unless the incidence of the evil apprehended is so imminent that it may befall before there is opportunity for full discussion. If there be time to expose through discussion the falsehoods and fallacies, to avert the evil by the processes of education, the remedy to be applied is more speech, not enforced silence. Only an emergency can justify repression. Such must be the rule if authority is to be reconciled with freedom. Such, in my opinion, is the command of the Constitution. It is therefore always open to Americans to challenge a law abridging free speech and assembly by showing that there was no emergency justifying it.

Moreover, even imminent danger cannot justify resort to prohibition of these functions essential to effective democracy, unless the evil apprehended is relatively serious. Prohibition of free speech and assembly is a measure so stringent that it would be inappropriate as the means for averting a relatively trivial harm to society. A police measure may be unconstitutional merely because the remedy, although effective as means of protection, is unduly harsh or oppressive. Thus, a State might, in the exercise of its police power, make any trespass upon the land of another a crime, regardless of the results or of the intent or purpose of the trespasser. It might, also, punish an attempt, a conspiracy, or an incitement to commit the trespass. But it is hardly conceivable that this Court would hold constitutional a statute which punished as a felony the mere voluntary assembly with a society formed to teach that pedestrians had the moral right to cross unenclosed, unposted, waste lands and to advocate their doing so, even if there was imminent danger that advocacy would lead to a trespass. The fact that speech is likely to result in some violence

**406**

or in destruction of property is not enough to justify its suppression. There must be the probability of serious injury to the State. Among free men, the deterrents ordinarily to be applied to prevent crime are education and punishment for violations of the law, not abridgment of the rights of free speech and assembly.

The California Syndicalism Act recites in § 4:

"Inasmuch as this act concerns and is necessary to the immediate preservation of the public peace and safety, for the reason that at the present time large numbers of persons are going from place to place in this state advocating, teaching and practicing criminal syndicalism, this act shall take effect upon approval by the Governor."

This legislative declaration satisfies the requirement of the constitution of the State concerning emergency legislation. *In re McDermott*, 180 Cal. 783. But it does not preclude enquiry into the question whether, at the time and under the circumstances, the conditions existed which are essential to validity under the Federal Constitution. As a statute, even if not void on its face, may be challenged because invalid as applied, *Dahnke-Walker Milling Co.* v. *Bondurant*, 257 U. S. 282, the result of such an enquiry may depend upon the specific facts of the particular case. Whenever the fundamental rights of free speech and assembly are alleged to have been invaded, it must remain open to a defendant to present the issue whether there actually did exist at the time a clear danger; whether the danger, if any, was imminent; and whether the evil apprehended was one so substantial as to justify the stringent restriction interposed by the legislature. The legislative declaration, like the fact that the statute was passed and was sustained by the highest court of the State, creates merely a rebuttable presumption that these conditions have been satisfied.

Whether in 1919, when Miss Whitney did the things complained of, there was in California such clear and present danger of serious evil, might have been made the important issue in the case. She might have required that the issue be determined either by the court or the jury. She claimed below that the statute as applied to her violated the Federal Constitution; but she did not claim that it was void because there was no clear and present danger of serious evil, nor did she request that the existence of these conditions of a valid measure thus restricting the rights of free speech and assembly be passed upon by the court or a jury. On the other hand, there was evidence on which the court or jury might have found that such danger existed. I am unable to assent to the suggestion in the opinion of the

Court that assembling with a political party, formed to advocate the desirability of a proletarian revolution by mass action at some date necessarily far in the future, is not a right within the protection of the Fourteenth Amendment. In the present case, however, there was other testimony which tended to establish the existence of a conspiracy, on the part of members of the International Workers of the World, to commit present serious crimes; and likewise to show that such a conspiracy would be furthered by the activity of the society of which Miss Whitney was a member. Under these circumstances the judgment of the state court cannot be disturbed. . . . .

MR. JUSTICE HOLMES joins in this opinion.

### Note

1. Accord is *Burns v. U. S.*, 274 U. S. 328, 71 L. Ed. 1077, 47 S. Ct. 650 (1927).

2. On the same day the Supreme Court also decided *Fiske v. Kansas*, 274 U. S. 380, 71 L. Ed. 1108, 47 S. Ct. 655 (1927), involving the Kansas Criminal Syndicalism Act. In that case an organizer for the I. W. W. had been convicted under the Kansas statute on charges of advocating criminal syndicalism and procuring members for a local union of the I. W. W. The only evidence introduced against him consisted of the preamble to the I. W. W. Constitution, which included such statements as, "Between these two classes a struggle must go on until the workers of the World organize as a class, take possession of the earth, and the machinery of production and abolish the wage system." A unanimous Court held that the proof did not constitute evidence of advocacy of the use of unlawful methods and that the Kansas statute, as thus applied, violated the due process clause of the Fourteenth Amendment. Fiske was the first defendant to be successful in the Supreme Court.

3. The *Gitlow* and *Fiske* cases were the first in which the Court expressly included the free speech guarantees of the First Amendment within the scope of the Fourteenth Amendment and hence applicable to the states. For comment on this aspect of the cases, see Chafee, *Free Speech in the United States*, pp. 320–5 (1941); Warren, *The New "Liberty" Under the Fourteenth Amendment*, 39 Harv. L. Rev. 431 (1926); Green, *Liberty Under the Fourteenth Amendment*, 27 Wash. U. L. Q., 497 (1942); Note, 14 Va. L. Rev. 49 (1927).

4. The state red flag laws did not come before the Supreme Court until later. See *Stromberg v. California*, noted *infra*. Nor did the New York Lusk Laws, or similar legislation in other states aimed at sedition in the schools, reach the Supreme Court at this time. For an account of the application of the Lusk Laws to the Rand School, see Chafee, *supra*, ch. 8. See also Chapter VII, Academic Freedom, *infra*.

5. The most complete treatment of the Supreme Court decisions on the Espionage Act and state anti-sedition laws is in Chafee, *supra*,

Parts I and II. See also Wigmore, *Abrams v. U. S.: Freedom of Speech and Freedom of Thuggery in War-Time and Peace-Time*, 14 Ill. L. Rev. 539 (1920); Black, *Debs v. The United States—A Judicial Milepost on the Road to Absolutism*, 81 U. of Pa. L. Rev. 160 (1932); Walsh, *Is the New Judicial and Legislative Interpretation of Freedom of Speech, and of the Freedom of the Press, Sound Constitutional Development?*, 21 Geo. L. J. 161, 168–91 (1933); Million, *Political Crimes*, 5 Mo. L. Rev. 164 (1940); Notes, 33 Harv. L. Rev. 442 (1920); 35 Col. L. Rev. 917 (1935); 84 U. of Pa. L. Rev. 390 (1936); 51 Yale L. J. 798, 802–10 (1942). The state anti-sedition laws of the period and state decisions are collected in Chafee, *supra*, ch. 4, 7 and 10, App. II; Lipsig, *Sedition, Criminal Syndicalism, Criminal Anarchy Laws* (mimeographed publication of American Civil Liberties Union, 1937); Dowell, *A History of Criminal Syndicalism Legislation in the United States*, pp. 14–5, App. I (1939). See also Million, *supra*, 5 Mo. L. Rev. 293 (1940); Note, 36 Ill. L. Rev. 357 (1941). These laws were uniformly upheld by the state courts, and in applying the laws the state courts did not normally follow the clear and present danger test. See Antieau, *The Rule of Clear and Present Danger: Scope of Its Applicability*, 48 Mich. L. Rev. 811, 813, 817 (1950).

6. Prosecutions under state anti-sedition laws dwindled off during the 1920's. They were revived to some extent in the depression years of the 1930's, see Note, 35 Col. L. Rev. 917 (1935), and more vigorously after World War II. See *infra*.

## NEAR v. MINNESOTA

Supreme Court of the United States, 1931
283 U. S. 697, 75 L. Ed. 1357, 51 S. Ct. 625

[Chapter 285 of the Session Laws of Minnesota for the year 1925 provided in Section 1:

"Any person who, as an individual, or as a member or employee of a firm, or association or organization, or as an officer, director, member or employee of a corporation, shall be engaged in the business of regularly or customarily producing, publishing or circulating, having in possession, selling or giving away

(a) an obscene, lewd and lascivious newspaper, magazine, or other periodical, or

(b) a malicious, scandalous and defamatory newspaper, magazine or other periodical,

is guilty of a nuisance, and all persons guilty of such nuisance may be enjoined, as hereinafter provided."

Under clause (b) of the above statute the County Attorney of Hennepin County brought suit to enjoin the defendants from publishing a newspaper known as *The Saturday Press*. The lower court, after trial, granted a permanent injunction and this was upheld by the Supreme Court of Minnesota. The defendants then appealed to the United States Supreme Court.]

MR. CHIEF JUSTICE HUGHES delivered the opinion of the Court. . . .

Without attempting to summarize the contents of the voluminous exhibits attached to the complaint, we deem it sufficient to say that the articles charged in substance that a Jewish gangster was in control of gambling, bootlegging and racketeering in Minneapolis, and that law enforcing officers and agencies were not energetically performing their duties. Most of the charges were directed against the Chief of Police; he was charged with gross neglect of duty, illicit relations with gangsters, and with participation in graft. The County Attorney was charged with knowing the existing conditions and with failure to take adequate measures to remedy them. The Mayor was accused of inefficiency and dereliction. One member of the grand jury was stated to be in sympathy with the gangsters. A special grand jury and a special prosecutor were demanded to deal with the situation in general, and, in particular, to investigate an attempt to assassinate one Guilford, one of the original defendants, who, it appears from the articles, was shot by gangsters after the first issue of the periodical had been published. There is no question but that the articles made serious accusations against the public officers named and others in connection with the prevalence of crimes and the failure to expose and punish them . . . .

This statute, for the suppression as a public nuisance of a newspaper or periodical, is unusual, if not unique, and raises questions of grave importance transcending the local interests involved in the particular action. It is no longer open to doubt that the liberty of the press, and of speech, is within the liberty safeguarded by the due process clause of the Fourteenth Amendment from invasion by state action. . . .

If we cut through mere details of procedure, the operation and effect of the statute in substance is that public authorities may bring the owner or publisher of a newspaper or periodical before a judge upon a charge of conducting a business of publishing scandalous and defamatory matter—in particular that the matter consists of charges against public officers of official dereliction—and, unless the owner or publisher is able and disposed to bring competent evidence to satisfy the judge that the charges are true and are published with good motives and for justifiable ends, his newspaper or periodical is suppressed and further publication is made punishable as a contempt. This is of the essence of censorship.

The question is whether a statute authorizing such proceedings in restraint of publication is consistent with the conception of the liberty of the press as historically conceived and guaranteed. In determining the extent of the constitutional protection, it has been generally, if not universally, considered that it is the chief purpose of the guaranty to prevent previous restraints upon publication. The struggle in England, directed against the legislative power of the licenser, resulted in renunciation of the censorship of the press. . . .

[It] is recognized that punishment for the abuse of the liberty accorded to the press is essential to the protection of the public, and that the common law rules that subject the libeler to responsibility for the public offense, as well as for the private injury, are not abolished by the protection extended in our constitution. *id.* pp. 883, 884. The law of criminal libel rests upon that secure foundation. There is also the conceded authority of courts to punish for contempt when publications directly tend to prevent the proper discharge of judicial functions. *Patterson v. Colorado* [205 U. S. 454]; *Toledo Newspaper Co.* v. *United States*, 247 U. S. 402, 419. In the present case, we have no occasion to inquire as to the permissible scope of subsequent punishment. For whatever wrong the appellant has committed or may commit, by his publications, the State appropriately affords both public and private redress by its libel laws. As has been noted, the statute in question does not deal with punishments; it provides for no punishment, except in case of contempt for violation of the court's order, but for suppression and injunction, that is, for restraint upon publication.

The objection has also been made that the principle as to immunity from previous restraint is stated too broadly, if every such restraint is deemed to be prohibited. That is undoubtedly true; the protection even as to previous restraint is not absolutely unlimited. But the limitation has been recognized only in exceptional cases: "When a nation is at war many things that might be said in time of peace are such a hindrance to its effort that their utterance will not be endured so long as men fight and that no Court could regard them as protected by any constitutional right." *Schenck* v. *United States*, 249 U. S. 47, 52. No one would question but that a government might prevent actual obstruction to its recruiting service or the publication of the sailing dates of transports or the number and location of troops. On similar grounds, the primary requirements of decency may be enforced against obscene publications. The security of the community life may be protected against incitements to acts of violence and the overthrow by force of orderly government. The

**411**

constitutional guaranty of free speech does not "protect a man from an injunction against uttering words that may have all the effect of force. *Gompers* v. *Buck Stove & Range Co.*, 221 U. S. 418, 439." *Schenck* v. *United States, supra.* These limitations are not applicable here. Nor are we now concerned with questions as to the extent of authority to prevent publications in order to protect private rights according to the principles governing the exercise of the jurisdiction of courts of equity.

The exceptional nature of its limitations places in a strong light the general conception that liberty of the press, historically considered and taken up by the Federal Constitution, has meant, principally although not exclusively, immunity from previous restraints or censorship. The conception of the liberty of the press in this country had broadened with the exigencies of the colonial period and with the efforts to secure freedom from oppressive administration. That liberty was especially cherished for the immunity it afforded from previous restraint of the publication of censure of public officers and charges of official misconduct. . . .

The fact that for approximately one hundred and fifty years there has been almost an entire absence of attempts to impose previous restraints upon publications relating to the malfeasance of public officers is significant of the deep-seated conviction that such restraints would violate constitutional right. Public officers, whose character and conduct remain open to debate and free discussion in the press, find their remedies for false accusations in actions under libel laws providing for redress and punishment, and not in proceedings to restrain the publication of newspapers and periodicals. The general principle that the constitutional guaranty of the liberty of the press gives immunity from previous restraints has been approved in many decisions under the provisions of state constitutions.[11]

The importance of this immunity has not lessened. While reckless assaults upon public men, and efforts to bring obloquy upon those who are endeavoring faithfully to discharge official duties, exert a baleful influence and deserve the severest condemnation in public opinion, it cannot be said that this abuse is greater, and it is believed to be less, than that which characterized the period in which our institutions took shape. Meanwhile, the administration of government has become more complex, the opportunities for malfeasance and corruption have multiplied, crime has grown to most serious proportions, and the danger of its protection by unfaithful officials and of the impairment of the fundamental security of life and property by criminal alliances and official neglect, emphasizes the primary need of a vigilant and

---

[11] [The footnote, collecting numerous state cases, is omitted.]

courageous press, especially in great cities. The fact that the liberty of the press may be abused by miscreant purveyors of scandal does not make any the less necessary the immunity of the press from previous restraint in dealing with official misconduct. Subsequent punishment for such abuses as may exist is the appropriate remedy, consistent with constitutional privilege. . . .

Nor can it be said that the constitutional freedom from previous restraint is lost because charges are made of derelictions which constitute crimes. With the multiplying provisions of penal codes, and of municipal charters and ordinances carrying penal sanctions, the conduct of public officers is very largely within the purview of criminal statutes. The freedom of the press from previous restraint has never been regarded as limited to such animadversions as lay outside the range of penal enactments. Historically, there is no such limitation; it is inconsistent with the reason which underlies the privilege, as the privilege so limited would be of slight value for the purposes for which it came to be established.

The statute in question cannot be justified by reason of the fact that the publisher is permitted to show, before injunction issues, that the matter published is true and is published with good motives and for justifiable ends. If such a statute, authorizing suppression and injunction on such a basis, is constitutionally valid, it would be equally permissible for the legislature to provide that at any time the publisher of any newspaper could be brought before a court, or even an administrative officer (as the constitutional protection may not be regarded as resting on mere procedural details) and required to produce proof of the truth of his publication, or of what he intended to publish, and of his motives, or stand enjoined. If this can be done, the legislature may provide machinery for determining in the complete exercise of its discretion what are justifiable ends and restrain publication accordingly. And it would be but a step to a complete system of censorship. The recognition of authority to impose previous restraint upon publication in order to protect the community against the circulation of charges of misconduct, and especially of official misconduct, necessarily would carry with it the admission of the authority of the censor against which the constitutional barrier was erected. The preliminary freedom, by virtue of the very reason for its existence, does not depend, as this Court has said, on proof of truth. *Patterson* v. *Colorado, supra.*

Equally unavailing is the insistence that the statute is designed to prevent the circulation of scandal which tends to disturb the public peace and to provoke assaults and the commission of crime. Charges of reprehensible conduct, and in particular of official malfeasance, unquestionably create a public scandal, but the theory of the constitutional guaranty is that even a more serious public evil would be caused by authority to prevent publication. "To prohibit the intent to excite those unfavorable sentiments against those who administer the Government, is equivalent to a prohibition of the actual excitement of them; and to prohibit the actual excitement of them is equivalent to a prohibition of discussions having that tendency and effect; which, again, is equivalent to a protection of those who administer the Government, if they should at any time deserve the contempt or hatred of the people, against being exposed to it by free animadversions on their characters and conduct."[12] . . . The danger of violent reactions becomes greater with effective organization of defiant groups resenting exposure, and, if this consideration warranted legislative interference with the initial freedom of publication, the constitutional protection would be reduced to a mere form of words.

For these reasons we hold the statute, so far as it authorized the proceedings in this action under clause (b) of section one, to be an infringement of the liberty of the press guaranteed by the Fourteenth Amendment. . . .

Judgment reversed.

MR. JUSTICE BUTLER, dissenting.

The decision of the Court in this case declares Minnesota and every other State powerless to restrain by injunction the business of publishing and circulating among the people malicious, scandalous and defamatory periodicals that in due course of judicial procedure has been adjudged to be a public nuisance. It gives to freedom of the press a meaning and a scope not heretofore recognized and construes "liberty" in the due process clause of the Fourteenth Amendment to put upon the States a federal restriction that is without precedent. . . .

The Minnesota statute does not operate as a *previous* restraint on publication within the proper meaning of that phrase. It does not authorize administrative control in advance such as was formerly exercised by the licensers and censors, but prescribes a remedy to be enforced by a suit in equity. In this case there was previous publication made in the course of the business of regularly producing malicious, scandalous, and defamatory periodicals. The business and publications unquestionably constitute an

---

[12] [Madison, Report on the Virginia Resolutions, Madison's Works, vol. iv, 549.]

abuse of the right of free press. The statute denounces the things done as a nuisance on the ground, as stated by the state supreme court, that they threaten morals, peace, and good order. There is no question of the power of the State to denounce such transgressions. The restraint authorized is only in respect of continuing to do what has been duly adjudged to constitute a nuisance. . . . There is nothing in the statute purporting to prohibit publications that have not been adjudged to constitute a nuisance. It is fanciful to suggest similarity between the granting or enforcement of the decree authorized by this statute to prevent *further* publication of malicious, scandalous, and defamatory articles and the *previous restraint* upon the press by licensers as referred to by Blackstone and described in the history of the times to which he alludes.

The opinion seems to concede that under clause (a) of the Minnesota law the business of regularly publishing and circulating an obscene periodical may be enjoined as a nuisance. It is difficult to perceive any distinction, having any relation to constitutionality, between clause (a) and clause (b) under which this action was brought. Both nuisances are offensive to morals, order, and good government. As that resulting from lewd publications constitutionally may be enjoined, it is hard to understand why the one resulting from a regular business of malicious defamation may not.

It is well known, as found by the state supreme court, that existing libel laws are inadequate effectively to suppress evils resulting from the kind of business and publications that are shown in this case. The doctrine that measures such as the one before us are invalid because they operate as previous restraints to infringe freedom of press exposes the peace and good order of every community and the business and private affairs of every individual to the constant and protracted false and malicious assaults of any insolvent publisher who may have purpose and sufficient capacity to contrive and put into effect a scheme or program for oppression, blackmail or extortion.

The judgment should be affirmed.

MR. JUSTICE VAN DEVANTER, MR. JUSTICE MCREYNOLDS, and MR. JUSTICE SUTHERLAND concur in this opinion.[1]

---

[1] The case is discussed in Notes, 31 Col. L. Rev. 1148 (1931); 9 N. Y. U. L. Q. Rev. 64 (1931); 41 Yale L. J. 262 (1931). On political expression in the press see also *Grosjean v. American Press Co.*, 297 U. S. 233, 80 L. Ed. 660, 56 S. Ct. 444 (1936).

## DE JONGE v. OREGON

Supreme Court of the United States, 1937
299 U. S. 353, 81 L. Ed. 278, 57 S. Ct. 255

MR. CHIEF JUSTICE HUGHES delivered the opinion of the Court.

Appellant, Dirk De Jonge, was indicted in Multonomah County, Oregon, for violation of the Criminal Syndicalism Law of that State. The act . . . defines "criminal syndicalism" as "the doctrine which advocates crime, physical violence, sabotage or any unlawful acts or methods as a means of accomplishing or effecting industrial or political change or revolution." With this preliminary definition the Act proceeds to describe a number of offenses, embracing the teaching of criminal syndicalism, the printing or distribution of books, pamphlets, etc., advocating that doctrine, the organization of a society or assemblage which advocates it, and presiding at or assisting in conducting a meeting of such an organization, society or group. The prohibited acts are made felonies, punishable by imprisonment for not less than one year nor more than ten years, or by a fine of not more than $1,000, or by both.

We are concerned with but one of the described offenses and with the validity of the statute in this particular application. The charge is that appellant assisted in the conduct of a meeting which was called under the auspices of the Communist Party, an organization advocating criminal syndicalism. The defense was that the meeting was public and orderly and was held for a lawful purpose; that while it was held under the auspices of the Communist Party, neither criminal syndicalism nor any unlawful conduct was taught or advocated at the meeting either by appellant or by others. Appellant moved for a direction of acquittal, contending that the statute as applied to him, for merely assisting at a meeting called by the Communist Party at which nothing unlawful was done or advocated, violated the due process clause of the Fourteenth Amendment of the Constitution of the United States.

This contention was overruled. Appellant was found guilty as charged and was sentenced to imprisonment for seven years.

• • •

The record does not present the evidence adduced at the trial. The parties have substituted a stipulation of facts . . .

The stipulation, after setting forth the charging part of the indictment, recites in substance the following: That on July 27, 1934, there was held in Portland, a meeting which had been advertised by handbills issued by the Portland section of the Communist Party; that the number of persons in attendance was

**416**

variously estimated at from 150 to 300; that some of those present, who were members of the Communist Party, estimated that not to exceed ten to fifteen per cent. of those in attendance were such members; that the meeting was open to the public without charge and no questions were asked of those entering, with respect to their relation to the Communist Party; that the notice of the meeting advertised it as a protest against illegal raids on workers' halls and homes and against the shooting of striking longshoremen by Portland police; that the chairman stated that it was a meeting held by the Communist Party; that the first speaker dwelt on the activities of the Young Communist League; that the defendant De Jonge, the second speaker, was a member of the Communist Party and went to the meeting to speak in its name; that in his talk he protested against conditions in the county jail, the action of city police in relation to the maritime strike then in progress in Portland and numerous other matters; that he discussed the reason for the raids on the Communist headquarters and workers' halls and offices; that he told the workers that these attacks were due to efforts on the part of the steamship companies and stevedoring companies to break the maritime longshoremen's and seamen's strike; that they hoped to break the strike by pitting the longshoremen and seamen against the Communist movement; that there was also testimony to the effect that defendant asked those present to do more work in obtaining members for the Communist Party and requested all to be at the meeting of the party to be held in Portland on the following evening and to bring their friends to show their defiance to local police authority and to assist them in their revolutionary tactics; that there was also testimony that defendant urged the purchase of certain communist literature which was sold at the meeting; that while the meeting was still in progress it was raided by the police; that the meeting was conducted in an orderly manner; that defendant and several others who were actively conducting the meeting were arrested by the police and that on searching the hall the police found a quantity of communist literature.

The stipulation then set forth various extracts from the literature of the Communist Party to show its advocacy of criminal syndicalism. The stipulation does not disclose any activity by the defendant as a basis for his prosecution other than his participation in the meeting in question. Nor does the stipulation show that the communist literature distributed at the meeting contained any advocacy of criminal syndicalism or of any unlawful conduct. It was admitted by the Attorney General of the State in his argument at the bar of this Court that

[Emerson]—27                                                              **417** the literature distributed in the meeting was not of that sort and that the extracts contained in the stipulation were taken from communist literature found elsewhere. Its introduction in evidence was for the purpose of showing that the Communist Party as such did advocate the doctrine of criminal syndicalism, a fact which is not disputed on this appeal. . . .

It thus appears that, while defendant was a member of the Communist Party, he was not indicted for participating in its organization, or for joining it, or for soliciting members or for distributing its literature. He was not charged with teaching or advocating criminal syndicalism or sabotage or any unlawful acts, either at the meeting or elsewhere. He was accordingly deprived of the benefit of evidence as to the orderly and lawful conduct of the meeting and that it was not called or used for the advocacy of criminal syndicalism or sabotage or any unlawful action. His sole offense as charged, and for which he was convicted and sentenced to imprisonment for seven years, was that he had assisted in the conduct of a public meeting, albeit otherwise lawful, which was held under the auspices of the Communist Party.

The broad reach of the statute as thus applied is plain. While defendant was a member of the Communist Party, that membership was not necessary to conviction on such a charge. A like fate might have attended any speaker, although not a member, who "assisted in the conduct" of the meeting. However innocuous the object of the meeting, however lawful the subjects and tenor of the addresses, however reasonable and timely the discussion, all those assisting in the conduct of the meeting would be subject to imprisonment as felons if the meeting were held by the Communist Party. This manifest result was brought out sharply at this bar by the concessions which the Attorney General made, and could not avoid, in the light of the decision of the state court. Thus if the Communist Party had called a public meeting in Portland to discuss the tariff, or the foreign policy of the Government, or taxation, or relief, or candidacies for the offices of President, members of Congress, Governor, or state legislators, every speaker who assisted in the conduct of the meeting would be equally guilty with the defendant in this case, upon the charge as here defined and sustained. The list of illustrations might be indefinitely extended to every variety of meetings under the auspices of the Communist Party although held for the discussion of political issues or to adopt protests and pass resolutions of an entirely innocent and proper character.

While the States are entitled to protect themselves from the abuse of the privileges of our institutions through an attempted

**418**                                                    [Emerson]

substitution of force and violence in the place of peaceful political action in order to effect revolutionary changes in government, none of our decisions go to the length of sustaining such a curtailment of the right of free speech and assembly as the Oregon statute demands in its present application. In *Gitlow* v. *New York*, 268 U. S. 652, under the New York statute defining criminal anarchy, the defendant was found to be responsible for a "manifesto" advocating the overthrow of the government by violence and unlawful means. *Id.*, pp. 656, 662, 663. In *Whitney* v. *California*, 274 U. S. 357, under the California statute relating to criminal syndicalism, the defendant was found guilty of wilfully and deliberately assisting in the forming of an organization for the purpose of carrying on a revolutionary class struggle by criminal methods. The defendant was convicted of participation in what amounted to a conspiracy to commit serious crimes. *Id.*, pp. 363, 364, 367, 379. The case of *Burns* v. *United States*, 274 U. S. 328, involved a similar ruling under the California statute as extended to the Yosemite National Park. *Id.*, pp. 330, 331. On the other hand, in *Fiske* v. *Kansas*, 274 U. S. 380, the criminal syndicalism act of that State was held to have been applied unconstitutionally and the judgment of conviction was reversed, where it was not shown that unlawful methods had been advocated. *Id.*, p. 387. See, also *Stromberg* v. *California*, 283 U. S. 359.

Freedom of speech and of the press are fundamental rights which are safeguarded by the due process clause of the Fourteenth Amendment of the Federal Constitution. *Gitlow* v. *New York, supra*, p. 666; *Stromberg* v. *California, supra*, p. 368; *Near* v. *Minnesota*, 283 U. S. 697, 707; *Grosjean* v. *American Press Co.*, 297 U. S. 233, 243, 244. The right of peaceable assembly is a right cognate to those of free speech and free press and is equally fundamental. As this Court said in *United States* v. *Cruikshank*, 92 U. S. 542, 552: "The very idea of a government, republican in form, implies a right on the part of its citizens to meet peaceably for consultation in respect to public affairs and to petition for a redress of grievances." The First Amendment of the Federal Constitution expressly guarantees that right against abridgment by Congress. But explicit mention there does not argue exclusion elsewhere. For the right is one that cannot be denied without violating those fundamental principles of liberty and justice which lie at the base of all civil and political institutions,—principles which the Fourteenth Amendment embodies in the general terms of its due process clause. *Hebert* v. *Louisiana*, 272 U. S. 312, 316; *Powell* v. *Alabama*, 287 U. S. 45, 67; *Grosjean* v. *American Press Co., supra*.

These rights may be abused by using speech or press or assembly in order to incite to violence and crime. The people through their legislatures may protect themselves against that abuse. But the legislative intervention can find constitutional justification only by dealing with the abuse. The rights themselves must not be curtailed. The greater the importance of safeguarding the community from incitements to the overthrow of our institutions by force and violence, the more imperative is the need to preserve inviolate the constitutional rights of free speech, free press and free assembly in order to maintain the opportunity for free political discussion, to the end that government may be responsive to the will of the people and that changes, if desired, may be obtained by peaceful means. Therein lies the security of the Republic, the very foundation of constitutional government.

It follows from these considerations that, consistently with the Federal Constitution, peaceable assembly for lawful discussion cannot be made a crime. The holding of meetings for peaceable political action cannot be proscribed. Those who assist in the conduct of such meetings cannot be branded as criminals on that score. The question, if the rights of free speech and peaceable assembly are to be preserved, is not as to the auspices under which the meeting is held but as to its purpose; not as to the relations of the speakers, but whether their utterances transcend the bounds of the freedom of speech which the Constitution protects. If the persons assembling have committed crimes elsewhere, if they have formed or are engaged in a conspiracy against the public peace and order, they may be prosecuted for their conspiracy or other violation of valid laws. But it is a different matter when the State, instead of prosecuting them for such offenses, seizes upon mere participation in a peaceable assembly and a lawful public discussion as the basis for a criminal charge.

We are not called upon to review the findings of the state court as to the objectives of the Communist Party. Notwithstanding those objectives, the defendant still enjoyed his personal right of free speech and to take part in a peaceable assembly having a lawful purpose, although called by that Party. The defendant was none the less entitled to discuss the public issues of the day and thus in a lawful manner, without incitement to violence or crime to seek redress of alleged grievances. That was of the essence of his guaranteed personal liberty.

We hold that the Oregon statute as applied to the particular charge as defined by the state court is repugnant to the due process clause of the Fourteenth Amendment. The judgment

**420**

of conviction is reversed and the cause is remanded for further proceedings not inconsistent with this opinion.

*Reversed.*

MR. JUSTICE STONE took no part in the consideration or decision of this case.[1]

---

Several additional cases decided by the Supreme Court in the period from 1931 to 1945 made further contributions to the law relating to freedom of political expression.

In *Stromberg v. California*, 283 U. S. 359, 75 L. Ed. 1117, 51 S. Ct. 532 (1931), the defendant was convicted under the California Red Flag law, providing that "any person who displays a red flag, banner or badge . . . as a sign, symbol or emblem of opposition to organized government or as an invitation or stimulus to anarchistic action or as an aid to propaganda that is of a seditious character is guilty of a felony." The defendant, who conducted a children's camp, had daily raised "a camp-made reproduction of the flag of Soviet Russia, which was also the flag of the Communist Party in the United States." The California Court defined the statutory terms "anarchistic action" and "seditious character" to mean unlawful and violent action. But it interpreted the term "opposition to organized government" broadly to include "peaceful and orderly opposition to government by legal means." Under the judge's charge the defendant could have been found guilty if she had displayed the flag for any of the three purposes set forth in the statute.

The Supreme Court, speaking through Chief Justice Hughes, said, "We have no reason to doubt the validity of the second and third clauses of the statute as construed by the state court to relate to such incitements to violence." But it held the first clause invalid and, since the defendant might have been found guilty under that clause, reversed the conviction:

"The maintenance of the opportunity for free political discussion to the end that government may be responsive to the will of the people and that changes may be obtained by lawful means, an opportunity essential to the security of the Republic, is a fundamental principle of our constitutional system. A statute which upon its face, and as authoritatively construed, is so vague and indefinite as to permit the punishment of the fair use of this opportunity is repugnant to the guaranty of liberty contained in the Fourteenth Amendment." 283 U. S. at 369.

---

[1] The *De Jonge* case is discussed in Notes, 46 Yale L. J. 862 (1937); 4 U. of Chi. L. Rev. 489 (1937); 37 Col. L. Rev. 857 (1937); 25 Calif. L. Rev. 496 (1937). For further material on the right of assembly see Chapter VI, *infra.*

In *Herndon v. Lowry*, 301 U. S. 242, 81 L. Ed. 1066, 57 S. Ct. 732 (1937), the defendant was convicted under a Georgia insurrection statute which prohibited "any attempt, by persuasion or otherwise, to induce others to join in any combined resistance to the lawful authority of the State." The evidence showed that the defendant, a Communist Party organizer, had procured members for the Communist Party in Atlanta and that he had in his possession Communist literature which stated the Communist Party was based "upon the revolutionary theory of Marxism", referred to the need for "overthrow of . . . class rule in the Black Belt" as necessary for the "self-determination" of the Negroes, and contained similar references to the "revolutionary struggle for power." The Georgia Supreme Court interpreted the statute to require an intent to resort to force but that it did not require "that the alleged offender should have intended that an insurrection should follow instantly or at any given time, but as to this element it would be sufficient if he intended that it should happen at any time within which he might reasonably expect his influence to continue to be directly operative in causing such action by those whom he sought to induce . . ." 301 U. S. at 254–5.

The Supreme Court reversed, saying that the *Gitlow* case did not hold that under a general law "the standard of guilt may be made the 'dangerous tendency' of his words." Mr. Justice Roberts, writing for the Court, went on:

"The power of a state to abridge freedom of speech and of assembly is the exception rather than the rule and the penalizing even of utterances of a defined character must find its justification in a reasonable apprehension of danger to organized government. The judgment of the legislature is not unfettered. The limitation upon individual liberty must have appropriate relation to the safety of the state. Legislation which goes beyond this need violates the principle of the Constitution. . . .

"We are of opinion that the requisite proof is lacking . . . His membership in the Communist Party and his solicitation of a few members wholly fails to establish an attempt to incite others to insurrection. Indeed, so far as appears, he had but a single copy of the booklet the State claims to be objectionable; that copy he retained. The same may be said with respect to the other books and pamphlets, some of them of more innocent purport. In these circumstances, to make membership in the party and solicitation of members for that party a criminal offense, punishable by death, in the discretion of a jury, is an unwarranted invasion of the right of freedom of speech." 301 U. S. at 258–61.

The Court further held:

"The statute, as construed and applied in the appellant's trial, does not furnish a sufficiently ascertainable standard of guilt. The Act does not prohibit incitement to violent interference with any given activity or operation of the state. By force of it, as construed, the judge and jury trying an alleged offender cannot appraise the circumstances and character of the defendant's utterances or activities as begetting a clear and present danger of forcible obstruction of a particular state function. Nor is any specified conduct or utterance of the accused made an offense. . . .

"If the jury conclude that the defendant should have contemplated that any act or utterance of his in opposition to the established order or advocating a change in that order, might, in the distant future, eventuate in a combination to offer forcible resistance to the State, or as the State says, if the jury believe he should have known that his words would have 'a dangerous tendency' then he may be convicted. To be guilty under the law, as construed, a defendant need not advocate resort to force. He need not teach any particular doctrine to come within its purview. Indeed, he need not be active in the formation of a combination or group if he agitate for a change in the frame of government, however peaceful his own intent. If, by the exercise of prophesy, he can forecast that, as a result of a chain of causation, following his proposed action a group may arise at some future date which will resort to force, he is bound to make the prophesy and abstain, under pain of punishment, possibly of execution. Every person who attacks existing conditions, who agitates for a change in the form of government, must take the risk that if a jury should be of opinion he ought to have foreseen that his utterances might contribute in any measure to some future forcible resistance to the existing government he may be convicted of the offense of inciting insurrection. . . .

"The statute, as construed and applied, amounts merely to a dragnet which may enmesh anyone who agitates for a change of government if a jury can be persuaded that he ought to have foreseen his words would have some effect in the future conduct of others. No reasonably ascertainable standard of guilt is prescribed. So vague and indeterminate are the boundaries thus set to the freedom of speech and assembly that the law necessarily violates the guarantees of liberty embodied in the Fourteenth Amendment." 301 U. S. at 261-4.

Justices Van Devanter, McReynolds, Sutherland and Butler dissented.[1]

---

[1] For an earlier stage of the case see *Herndon v. Georgia*, 295 U. S. 441, 79 L. Ed. 1530, 55 S. Ct. 794 (1935).

*Taylor v. Mississippi*, 319 U. S. 583, 87 L. Ed. 1600, 63 S. Ct. 1200 (1943), involved the conviction of three Jehovah's Witnesses during World War II for violation of a Mississippi statute which, among other things, prohibited teaching or disseminating literature "designed and calculated to encourage violence, sabotage, or disloyalty to the government of the United States, or the state of Mississippi," or which "reasonably tends to create an attitude of stubborn refusal to salute, honor or respect the flag or government." The conviction of all three defendants for advocating and teaching refusal to salute the flag was set aside on the basis of *West Virginia State Board of Education v. Barnette*, 319 U. S. 624, 87 L. Ed. 1628, 63 S. Ct. 1178 (1943), decided the same day. See Chapter VIII, *infra*. Two of the defendants were also convicted for stating that "it was wrong for the President to send our boys across in uniform to fight our enemies," that "these boys were being shot down for no purpose at all", and other remarks to the same effect. Their convictions for encouraging disloyalty by these statements were also set aside:

"The statute as construed in these cases makes it a criminal offense to communicate to others views and opinions respecting government policies, and prophecies concerning the future of our own and other nations. As applied to the appellants, it punishes them although what they communicated is not claimed or shown to have been done with an evil or sinister purpose, to have advocated or incited subversive action against the nation or state, or to have threatened any clear and present danger to our institutions or our Government. What these appellants communicated were their beliefs and opinions concerning domestic measures and trends in national and world affairs.

"Under our decisions criminal sanctions cannot be imposed for such communication." 319 U. S. at 589–90.

*Schneiderman v. United States*, 320 U. S. 118, 87 L. Ed. 1796, 63 S. Ct. 1333 (1943), involved a denaturalization proceeding. The Government sued, in 1939, to cancel the certificate of citizenship issued to Schneiderman in 1927, on the ground that at the time of obtaining citizenship Schneiderman was not "attached to the principles of the Constitution of the United States" as required by the naturalization statute. It was admitted that Schneiderman was a member of the Communist Party in 1927 and later became secretary of the Party in California. The Government produced evidence from two former Communist Party members that the Party advocated abolition of the present form of government "through the dictatorship of the proletariat," which would be brought about through a "revolutionary

**424**

process." The Government also introduced the basic writings of Marx, Engels, Lenin and Stalin which contained similar language. Schneiderman testified that neither he nor the party advocated overthrow of the government by violence, and that "he believed and hoped the Marxist program could be achieved by democratic processes but history showed that the ruling minority had always used force against the majority before surrendering power." There was no evidence that Schneiderman himself "believed in and advocated the employment of force and violence, instead of peaceful persuasion, as a means of attaining political ends." 320 U. S. at 146.

The Supreme Court held that in a denaturalization proceeding the Government must establish that citizenship had been illegally procured by "clear, unequivocal, and convincing" evidence and that this standard of proof had not been met. Mr. Justice Murphy, writing the prevailing opinion, rejected the contention that "one who advocates radical changes is necessarily not attached to the Constitution." As to the evidence that the Communist Party advocated overthrow of the government by force and violence, he found it unnecessary to decide "what interpretation of the Party's attitude toward force and violence is the most probable on the basis of the present record." "We hold only that where two interpretations of an organization's program are possible, the one reprehensible and a bar to naturalization and the other permissible, a court in a denaturalization proceeding . . . is not justified in canceling a certificate of citizenship by imputing the reprehensible interpretation to a member of the organization in the absence of overt acts indicating that such was his interpretation." 320 U. S. at 158–9. Mr. Justice Murphy emphasized the latter point in the following language:

". . . under our traditions beliefs are personal and not a matter of mere association, and . . . men in adhering to a political party or other organization notoriously do not subscribe unqualifiedly to all its platforms or asserted principles." 320 U. S. at 136.

Mr. Justice Douglas joined in the prevailing opinion but added that in his view "the judgment of naturalization is final and conclusive except for fraud." 320 U. S. at 165. Mr. Justice Rutledge, without expressly passing on the question, indicated similar views. Chief Justice Stone and Justices Roberts and Frankfurter dissented.[1]

---

[1] For citation of materials discussing the *Schneiderman* case, see Weiner, *"Freedom for the Thought That We Hate: Is It a Principle of the Constitution?"* 37 A. B. A. J. 177 (1951).

## Note

1. In *Bridges v. Wixon*, 326 U. S. 135, 89 L. Ed. 2103, 65 S. Ct. 1443 (1945), the Supreme Court reversed an order for the deportation of Harry Bridges, West Coast labor leader. The government's case rested upon allegations that Bridges was deportable because of membership in or affiliation with the Communist Party, an organization advocating overthrow of the government by force and violence. The Court found that the evidence, while establishing cooperation with the Communist Party, did not show membership or affiliation within the meaning of the statute. It also held that the administrative proceeding had been unfair in that certain evidence was improperly received. Mr. Justice Jackson took no part in the case; Mr. Justice Murphy concurred in a separate opinion; Chief Justice Stone and Justices Roberts and Frankfurter dissented. For further discussion of the political rights of aliens see Section D, *infra*.

Other decisions during the 1931–1945 period which have an important bearing on freedom of political expression are *Thornhill v. Alabama*, 310 U. S. 88, 84 L. Ed. 1093, 60 S. Ct. 736 (1940) (picketing); *Thomas v. Collins*, 323 U. S. 516, 89 L. Ed. 430, 65 S. Ct. 315 (1945) (license required to solicit union members); *Lovell v. Griffin*, 303 U. S. 444, 82 L. Ed. 949, 58 S. Ct. 666 (1938) (right to distribute literature); and others discussed in Chapter VI, *infra*. Also *Hague v. C. I. O.*, 307 U. S. 496, 83 L. Ed. 1423, 59 S. Ct. 954 (1939), noted in Chapter I, *supra; Bridges v. California*, 314 U. S. 252, 86 L. Ed. 192, 62 S. Ct. 190 (1941), noted in Section E, *infra; West Virginia Board of Education v. Barnette*, 319 U. S. 624, 87 L. Ed. 1628, 63 S. Ct. 1178 (1943), discussed in Chapter VIII, *infra*. All the significant cases are collected and discussed in Mr. Justice Frankfurter's opinion in *Dennis v. U. S.*, 341 U. S. 494, 529–39, 95 L. Ed. 1137, 71 S. Ct. 857 (1951).

2. For general discussion of the 1931–1945 decisions and the legal doctrines enunciated therein, see Chafee, *Free Speech in the United States*, ch. 11 (1941); Fraenkel, *One Hundred and Fifty Years of the Bill of Rights*, 23 Minn. L. Rev. 719 (1939); Wechsler in *Symposium on Civil Liberties*, 9 Am. L. S. Rev. 881 (1941); Lusky, *Minority Rights and the Public Interest*, 52 Yale L. J. 1 (1942); *The Constitutional Right to Advocate Political, Social and Economic Change*, 7 Law. Guild Rev. 57 (1947); Green, *The Supreme Court, the Bill of Rights and the States*, 97 U. of Pa. L. Rev. 608 (1949); Antieau, *Judicial Delimitation of the First Amendment Freedoms*, 34 Marq. L. Rev. 57 (1950).

3. For discussion of the various specific doctrines developed during the period see:

*Presumption in Favor of Rights Guaranteed by the First Amendment: U. S. v. Carolene Products Co.*, 304 U. S. 144, 152–3 n. 4, 82 L. Ed. 1234, 58 S. Ct 778 (1938); *Schneider v State*, 308 U. S. 147, 161, 84 L. Ed. 155, 60 S. Ct. 146 (1939); *Thomas v. Collins, supra*, at 550; see also compilation of cases in concurrence of Mr. Justice Frankfurter in *Kovacs v. Cooper*, 336 U. S. 77, 90–94 (and comment of Mr. Justice Rutledge at 106), 93 L. Ed. 513, 69 S. Ct. 448 (1949); Note, *Presumption of Constitutionality not Applicable to Statutes dealing with*

*Civil Liberties,* 40 Col. L. R. 531 (1940); Notes, 33 Minn. L. R. 390, 392 fn. 17–20 (1949); 47 Col. L. R. 595, 603–4, 607 fn. 93 (1947); 61 Harv. L. R. 1208, 1209–10 (1948); Richardson, *Freedom of Expression and the Function of Courts,* 65 Harv. L. R. 1, 2 fn. 3, 47–51 (1951); Kauper, *The First Ten Amendments,* 37 A. B. A. J. 717 (1951); Hyman, *Judicial Standards for the Protection of Basic Freedoms,* 1 Buffalo L. Rev. 221 (1952).

*Clear and Present Danger Test: Thornhill v. Alabama, supra,* at 105; *Thomas v. Collins, supra,* at 527 fn. 12, 530; Green, *Liberty Under the Fourteenth Amendment,* 27 Wash. U. L. Q. 497, 539–560 (1942); Meiklejohn, *Free Speech and its Relation to Self-Government,* ch. II (1948); Chafee, Book Review (of Meiklejohn) 62 Harv. L. Rev. 891 (1949); Notes, 28 Calif. L. R. 733 (1940); 47 Col. L. R. 595, 605–6 (1947); 57 Yale L. J. 806, 818 (1948); Antieau, *The Rule of Clear and Present Danger—Its Origin and Application,* 13 U. of Detroit L. J. 198 (1950); Antieau, *The Rule of Clear and Present Danger: Scope of its Applicability,* 48 Mich. L. Rev. 811 (1950); Antieau, *"Clear and Present Danger"—Its Meaning and Significance,* 25 Notre Dame Lawyer 603 (1950); Mendelson, *Clear and Present Danger—From Schenck to Dennis,* 52 Col. L. Rev. 313 (1952).

*Rule Against Vagueness: Lanzetta v. N. J.,* 306 U. S. 451, 83 L. Ed. 888, 59 S. Ct. 618 (1939); *Musser v. Utah,* 333 U. S. 95, 97, 92 L. Ed. 562, 68 S. Ct. 397 (1948); see also concurrence of Mr. Justice Rutledge, *U. S. v. C. I. O.,* 335 U. S. 106, 150–5, 92 L. Ed. 1849, 68 S. Ct. 1349 (1948); and *Winters v. N. Y.,* 333 U. S. 507, 92 L. Ed. 840, 68 S. Ct. 665 (1948); Note, *Due Process Requirements of Definiteness in Statutes,* 62 Harv. L. R. 77, 82–4 (1948); Freund, *The Supreme Court and Civil Liberties,* 4 Vand. L. R. 533, 540–1 (1951).

*Statute Must be Narrowly Drawn: Lovell v. Griffin,* 303 U. S. 444, 451, 82 L. Ed. 949, 58 S. Ct. 666 (1938); *Schneider v. State, supra,* at 162–4; *Hague v. C. I. O., supra* at 516; *Thornhill v. Alabama, supra,* at 97–8; *Carlson v. California,* 310 U. S. 106, 112, 84 L. Ed. 1104, 60 S. Ct. 746 (1940); *Cantwell v. Connecticut,* 310 U. S. 296, 307–8, 84 L. Ed. 1213, 60 S. Ct. 900, 128 A. L. R. 1352 (1940); see also, *U. S. v. C. I. O., supra,* at 153; and *Saia v. N. Y.,* 334 U. S. 558, 92 L. Ed. 1574, 68 S. Ct. 1148 (1948); Notes, 47 Col. L. R. 595, 606–7 (1947); 61 Harv. L. R. 1208 (1948); 57 Yale L. J. 806, 821 fn. 54 (1948); Freund, *supra,* at 540–1 (1951).

*Guilt by Association: Bridges v. Wixon, supra,* concurrence of Mr. Justice Murphy at 163; but see *Kessler v. Strecker,* 307 U. S. 22, 29–31, 83 L. Ed. 1082, 59 S. Ct. 694 (1939); O'Brian, *Loyalty Tests and Guilt by Association,* 61 Harv. L. Rev. 592 (1948); Emerson and Helfeld, *Loyalty Among Government Employees,* 58 Yale L. J. 1, 91–94 (1948); Notes, 32 Geo. L. J. 405 (1944); 17 U. of Chi. L. Rev. 148 (1949).

*Role of the Supreme Court in Protecting Political Rights:* Frank, *The United States Supreme Court: 1949–50,* 18 U. of Chi. L. Rev. 1, 3, 7–9, 29–33 (1950); Bernard, *Avoidance of Constitutional Issues in the United States Supreme Court: Liberties of the First Amendment,* 50 Mich. L. R. 261 (1951); Freund, *The Supreme Court and Civil Liber-*

*ties, supra;* Freund, *On Understanding the Supreme Court,* pp. 9–14, 22–28, 30–31, 61–62, 69 (1949); Note, *The Supreme Court, 1950 Term,* 65 Harv. L. R. 107, 129–38 (1951); Richardson, *supra;* Frank, *The United States Supreme Court: 1950–51,* 19 U. of Chi. L. Rev. 165, 166, 185–201, 231–2 (1952); Hyman, *supra.*

## D. THE RIGHT OF POLITICAL EXPRESSION IN THE PERIOD FOLLOWING WORLD WAR II

It is generally agreed that freedom of political expression has been subjected to broader legal restrictions and more intensive private pressures in the period following the Second World War than perhaps at any other time in the history of the United States. Opinions differ markedly as to the reasons for this development and as to whether the curtailment of political expression is justified, in whole, in part, or not at all. Many of these differing points of view appear, expressly or by implication, in the material set forth in this Section. Space does not permit an elaboration of them at this point. But it is necessary to keep in mind that one's attitude toward the specific measures discussed below depends in large part upon one's conclusions or assumptions concerning the need for American society to adjust to changing technological, economic, social and political conditions in this country and throughout the world; the soundest methods of achieving that adjustment, if any is necessary, within the framework of democratic institutions; the nature and the sources of strength and weakness of the Communist movement in this country and abroad; the same with respect to fascist movements; the effectiveness of restrictive measures; the impact of restrictive measures upon liberal thought and action; the advantages and risks of a relatively open society as against one that is relatively confined; and many other considerations of a similar character.

In the material below the major measures which operate to limit political expression have been grouped into five categories: (1) the activity of legislative committees; (2) the enforcement of the Smith Act and similar anti-sedition legislation; (3) the denial of privileges or positions of influence to alleged subversives; (4) loyalty qualifications for employment; and (5) the Internal Security Act of 1950 (the McCarran Act) and similar recent legislation.

### Note

Among the vast and growing literature dealing with recent developments in this field, the following is representative of some of the major points of view:

In support of severe restrictive measures see the reports of the House Committee on Un-American Activities, especially *Report on the Communist Party of the United States as an Advocate of Overthrow of Government by Force and Violence*, H. Rept. No. 1920, 80th Cong., 2d Sess. (1948); and *The Communist Party of the United States as an Agent of a Foreign Power*, H. Rept. 209, 80th Cong., 1st Sess. (1947); House Committee on Foreign Affairs, *The Strategy and Tactics of World Communism*, H. Doc. 619, 80th Cong., 2d Sess. (1948); reports of the committees recommending passage of the Internal Security Act of 1950 (see *infra*); Hoover, *Menace of Communism*, reprinted as Sen. Doc. No. 26, 80th Cong., 1st Sess. (1947); Ober, *Communism vs. the Constitution*, 34 A. B. A. J. 645 (1948); Oneal and Werner, *American Communism* (1947); Crotty, *A Few Observations: The Communist Manifesto in America*, 37 A. B. A. J. 413 (1951). See also the opinion of Mr. Justice Jackson in *American Communications Assn. v. Douds*, 339 U. S. 382, 424–33, 94 L. Ed. 925, 70 S. Ct. 674 (1950); Sutherland, *Freedom and Internal Security*, 64 Harv. L. Rev. 383 (1951); Wyzanski, *The Communist Party and the Law*, The Atlantic Monthly, May 1951, p. 27.

Expressions of concern over the restrictions on political freedom and suggestions of a more positive approach may be found in Barth, *The Loyalty of Free Men* (1951); Biddle, *The Fear of Freedom* (1951); Wilcox (ed.), *Civil Liberties Under Attack* (1951); Gellhorn, *Security, Loyalty, and Science* (1950); McWilliams, *Witch Hunt* (1950); Douglas, *The Black Silence of Fear*, N. Y. Times Magazine, Jan. 13, 1952, p. 7; Cushman, *American Civil Liberties in Mid-Twentieth Century*, 275 Annals of the Am. Acad. of Pol. and Soc. Sci. 1 (1951); Joyce, *Liberty or Fear—The Final Choice*, The Survey, Jan. 1951, p. 7; Chafee, *The Free and the Brave*, a letter to the House Committee on Un-American Activities on the Mundt-Nixon Bill, published by the American Civil Liberties Union (1950); Commager, *The Real Danger—Fear of Ideas*, N. Y. Times Magazine, June 26, 1949, p. 7 (reprinted by the American Civil Liberties Union); Fosdick, *We Must Not be Afraid of Change*, N. Y. Times Magazine, Apr. 3, 1949, p 7; Commager, *Who is Loyal to America*, Harper's Magazine, Sept. 1947, p. 193. For a statement of the argument that political restrictions ostensibly directed against extreme radicals may in reality be aimed at any social change, see Lerner, *Freedom: Image and Reality* in *Safeguarding Civil Liberty Today* (Cornell U. Press, 1945).

See also Lasswell, *National Security and Individual Freedom* (1950); MacIver, *The Ramparts We Guard* (1950); Kennan, *Where Do You Stand on Communism*, N. Y. Times Magazine, May 27, 1951, p. 7; Marx, *Effects of International Tension on Liberty Under Law*, 48 Col. L. Rev. 555 (1948); Ebon, *World Communism Today* (1948); Palmer, *The Communist Problem in America* (1951); J. E. Johnson, *Should the Communist Party be Outlawed*, The Reference Shelf, vol. 20, no. 7 (1949).

For general discussions of the restrictions from the legal point of view see Cohen and Fuchs, *Communism's Challenge and the Consti-*

POLITICAL AND CIVIL RIGHTS

*tution,* 34 Corn. L. Q. 182, 352 (1948 and 1949); Note, *Restraints On American Communist Activities,* 96 U. of Pa. L. Rev. 381 (1948); Note, *Conduct Proscribed as Promoting Violent Overthrow of the Government,* 61 Harv. L. Rev. 1215 (1948); Note, *Impact of the First Amendment on Federal Legislation Affecting "Subversive" Movements,* 49 Col. L. Rev. 363 (1949); Note, *Control of Communist Activities,* 1 Stan. L. Rev. 85 (1948); Note, 34 Va. L. Rev. 439 (1948). For a recent survey of state restrictions see Gellhorn, *The States and Subversion* (1952).

## 1. Legislative Investigating Committees

The need for disclosing and curtailing alleged subversive activities in the United States was initially raised, and has been most consistently and dramatically pressed, by legislative investigating committees. The operation of these committees, both Federal and state, has probably been the most significant single factor in shaping public attitudes and influencing governmental and private action toward radical and unorthodox thought and activity during the past decade and a half.

The most significant, and the most controversial, of the legislative investigating committees has been the House Committee on Un-American Activities. This Committee was established by House Resolution on May 26, 1938 as a select committee to investigate "(1) the extent, character, and objects of un-American propaganda activities in the United States; (2) the diffusion within the United States of subversive and un-American propaganda that is instigated from foreign countries or of a domestic origin and attacks the principle of the form of government as guaranteed by our Constitution; and (3) all other questions in relation thereto that would aid Congress in any necessary remedial legislation."[1] Under the chairmanship of Congressman Martin Dies and his successors the life of the Committee was renewed by each Congress until 1946, when the Committee was given permanent status under the Legislative Reorganization Act. Its present powers are substantially the same as those conferred by the original resolution.[2]

In the course of its existence the Committee has conducted investigations and issued reports on alleged subversive activities in the Federal Government, labor organizations, the motion picture industry, peace organizations and many other areas; on Communist espionage, particularly in connection with atomic energy; and on many organizations and individuals claimed to be subversive. Its most famous investigation was that dealing

[1] H. R. 282, 75th Cong., 2d Sess. (1938).
[2] 60 Stat. 812, 828 (1946).

**430**

with the Chambers-Hiss testimony, which led to the conviction of Alger Hiss for perjury. The Committee has also published lists of organizations and individuals which it has found to be subversive and maintains files containing data on alleged subversive activities of individuals and organizations.

The Committee has described its function in the following terms:

"It has been the established policy of the House Committee on Un-American Activities since its inception that in a great, virile, free republic like the United States, one of the most effective weapons against un-American activities is their continuous exposure to the spotlight of publicity. It has also been our consistent position that the people of the United States —to whom this Government rightfully belongs—are entitled to a clear picture of the extent of disloyal and inimical influences working secretly to destroy our free institutions whether they operate from within or without the Government. . . .

"As contrasted with the FBI and the grand jury, the House Committee on Un-American Activities has a separate and a very special responsibility. It functions to permit the greatest court in the world—the court of American public opinion—to have an undirected, uncensored, and unprejudiced opportunity to render a continuing verdict on all of its public officials and to evaluate the merit of many in private life who either openly associate and assist disloyal groups or covertly operate as members or fellow travelers of such organizations. It is as necessary to the success of this committee that it reveal its findings to the public as it is to the success of the FBI that it conceal its operations from the public view." [3]

Prof. Robert K. Carr has summarized the Committee's activities in more critical language:

"Congressional investigating committees have traditionally been regarded as having three proper functions: they may seek information that will enable Congress to legislate wisely; they may undertake to check administrative agencies, with particular respect to the enforcement of law or the expenditure of public funds; and they may attempt to influence public opinion. The Un-American Activities Committee has certainly shown an interest in all of these functions—an increasing interest in the order in which the functions are named. But always its interest in public opinion has been paramount. The Committee has been concerned lest the American people fail to share its understanding of the nature of subversive activity and the many forms it may

---

[3] Interim Report on Hearings Regarding Communist Espionage in the United States Government, 80th Cong., 2d Sess., p. 1–2 (1948).

take, or appreciate the seriousness of the threat offered by this activity to the 'American way of life' as seen by itself.

"In addition to these three functions the Committee has tried to exercise two others. First, it has tried in a non-statutory way to define subversive or 'un-American' activity and thereby to set the standards of American thought and conduct with respect to orthodoxy and heresy in politics. Second, it has tried in varying ways to take over the function of administrative or judicial agencies in the enforcement of public policy with respect to subversive activity."[4]

For the first ten years of its existence the Committee did not recommend any significant legislation.[5] In 1948 it drafted and reported out the Mundt-Nixon bill. In somewhat altered form this legislation was passed as the Internal Security Act of 1950.

In addition to the Committee on Un-American Activities a number of other Congressional Committees have made investigations in fields relating to political expression. The most active of these have been the Internal Security Subcommittee of the Senate Committee on the Judiciary (the McCarran Committee) and the House Committee on Education and Labor.[6] Similar investigating committees have been established in a number of states, of which the best known are the Rapp-Coudert Committee in New York, the Tenney Committee in California, the Canwell Committee in Washington and the Broyles Commission in Illinois.

The constitutional authority of legislative investigating committees was challenged in a series of cases in the years following the war. The *Barsky* case, set forth below, illustrates the issues involved.

## Note

1. For the history of the Congressional investigations, see Eberling, *Congressional Investigations* (1928); Dimock, *Congressional Investigating Committees* (1929); McGeary, *The Developments of Congressional Investigative Power* (1940). The most comprehensive treatment of the present use of the investigative power may be found

---

[4] Carr, *The Un-American Activities Committee*, 18 U. of Chi. L. Rev. 598, 599–600 (1951).

[5] The only legislation passed in this period for which the Committee was responsible was the rider to an appropriation bill which cut off the salaries of Robert Morse Lovett, Goodwin B. Watson and William E. Dodd, Jr. The rider was declared unconstitutional as a bill of attainder in *U. S. v. Lovett*, 328 U. S. 303, 90 L. Ed. 1252, 66 S. Ct. 1073 (1946).

[6] The most recent Congressional investigation was launched when the House passed a resolution sponsored by Congressman Eugene Cox to investigate charitable foundations and universities. H. R. 561, 82d Cong., 2d Sess., passed April 4, 1952. See 98 Cong. Rec. 3550.

in *Congressional Investigations,* a symposium in 18 U. of Chi. L. Rev. 421–685 (the Spring 1951 issue). See also White, *An Inquiry Into Congressional Inquiries,* N. Y. Times Magazine, Mar. 23, 1952, p. 11; and material cited in the *Barsky* case and the following Note, *infra.*

The extent to which the investigatory power is currently being exercised by Congress appears from the fact that the Eighty-Second Congress, from January 3, 1951 to May 22, 1952 had instituted 225 distinct inquiries in addition to routine legislative and appropriations work. N. Y. Times, Mar. 23, 1952.

2. The work of the Committee on Un-American Activities is revealed by its numerous reports, some of which have been cited above. The earlier years of the Committee's work are appraised in Ogden, *The Dies Committee* (1945); see also Gellermann, *Martin Dies* (1944). The more recent operations are discussed in Carr, *The Un-American Activities Committee,* 18 U. of Chi. L. Rev. 598 (1951). The Committee has been severely criticized on grounds that it equates loyalty with orthodoxy, that it has substituted emotion and hysteria for rational discussion of the issues, that it has seriously damaged the reputations of citizens not guilty of any legal offense, that its procedures have been unfair, and the like. See Gellhorn, *Report on a Report of the House Committee on Un-American Activities,* 60 Harv. L. Rev. 1193 (1947), criticizing the Committee's *Report on the Southern Conference for Human Welfare,* H. R. Rept. No. 592, 80th Cong. 1st Sess. (1947); Emerson and Helfeld, *Loyalty Among Government Employees,* 58 Yale L. J. 1, 8–14 (1948); Emerson, *The National Lawyers Guild: Legal Bulwark of Democracy,* 10 Law. Guild Rev. 93 (1950), a reply to the Committee's Report, *The National Lawyers Guild: Legal Bulwark of the Communist Party,* Sept. 17, 1950; Barth, *The Loyalty of Free Men,* ch. III and IV (1951); Biddle, *The Fear of Freedom,* pp. 110–32 (1951) (Biddle also discusses the predecessors of the Committee, pp. 112–4). A volume on the work of the Committee by Prof. Carr is to be published as part of the Cornell Studies in Civil Liberties (see *infra*).

Prof. Owen Latimore's account of his investigation by a Subcommittee of the Senate Foreign Relations Committee has been published under the title *Ordeal by Slander* (1950). See also Welborn, *The Ordeal of Dr. Condon,* Harper's Magazine, Jan. 1950, p. 46.

3. For material on state legislative committees, see their reports. Discussion of their work, mostly critical, may be found in the following books published as part of the Cornell Studies in Civil Liberties, Prof. Robert E. Cushman, Editor; Gellhorn, *The States and Subversion* (1952); Barrett, *The Tenney Committee: Legislative Investigation of Subversive Activities in California* (1951); Chamberlain, *Loyalty and Legislative Action: A Survey of Activity by the New York State Legislature, 1919–1949* (1951); Countryman, *Un-American Activities in the State of Washington* (1951). See also Biddle, *supra,* pp. 133–54.

## BARSKY ET. AL v. UNITED STATES

United States Court of Appeals, District
of Columbia, 1948
167 F. 2d 241

Before EDGERTON, CLARK and PRETTYMAN, Associate Justices.

PRETTYMAN, Associate Justice. . . .

These appellants were indicted, tried before a jury, convicted, and sentenced for willful failure to produce records before a committee of the Congress pursuant to subpoenas, in violation of Section 192 of Title 2 of the United States Code Annotated. The indictment alleged that appellants were members of the governing body of an unincorporated association known as the Joint Anti-Fascist Refugee Committee and that, having been subpoenaed by the Congressional Committee known as the Committee on Un-American Activities of the House of Representatives, to produce the records of their association relating to the receipt and disbursement of certain money and certain correspondence with persons in foreign countries, they willfully failed to produce those documents.

Upon the trial it was shown that the Congressional Committee existed by virtue of House Resolution No. 5 of the 79th Congress, and that the Joint Anti-Fascist Refugee Committee was a private voluntary association engaged in the collection of funds from the public in this country upon representations that such funds were to be used for relief purposes abroad, and in the disbursement of those funds in foreign countries. It was further shown that the Congressional Committee had received "a large number" of complaints that the funds collected by appellants' organization were being used for political propaganda and not for relief. It made inquiry of the President's War Relief Control Board and, consistently with suggestions there obtained, requested that one of its investigators be permitted to examine the records of the collection and disbursement of the funds. This request was denied. Testimony, including that of an official of the State Department and a person who said that she had observed the operation of appellants' association abroad, was taken. In effect, this testimony sustained the burden of the complaints. Thereupon the Committee issued the subpoenaes above described. Appellants appeared before the Committee but declined to produce, or to cause the production of, the described books and documents. They were thereupon indicted, as above described, and appeal from the judgments upon conviction.

Appellants' first point is that the Resolution creating the Congressional Committee was unconstitutional because it au-

[Emerson]

thorized inquiry into political opinion and expression, in violation of the First Amendment.

The Resolution which created this Congressional Committee authorized it by one of three subclauses to investigate "the diffusion within the United States of subversive and un-American propaganda that is instigated from foreign countries or of a domestic origin and attacks the principle of the form of government as guaranteed by our Constitution."

These appellants were not asked to state their political opinions. They were asked to account for funds. We are unable to visualize the particular in which civil rights are violated by a requirement that persons who collect funds from the public in this country for relief purposes abroad account for the collection and distribution of such funds. Moreover, the fact of the existence of such official bodies as UNRRA and the President's War Relief Control Board, and the then-pending proposals for loans to foreign governments, clearly justified Congressional inquiry into the disbursement abroad of private funds collected in this country avowedly for relief but reasonably represented as being spent for political purposes in Europe.

Appellants' point is not premised upon the specific question asked them but upon the scope of possible inquiry under the Resolution. So we examine the contention in the light of the possibility, indicated by the preliminary data before the Committee, that answers to the inquiry might reveal that the appellants were believers in Communism or members of the Communist Party.

The problem thus presented is difficult and delicate. In it we have not only the frequent "real problem of balancing the public interest against private security," but in this instance we must do so in the midst of swirling currents of public emotion in both directions. We are presented with extreme declarations in respect to Communists and equally extreme declarations in respect to the Congressional Committee. The duty of the courts is no less than to render judgment with utter detachment.

Congressional powers of investigation have been explored and debated by scholars for many years in the United States and other countries.[5] We shall not venture upon a treatise on the

[5] Some outstanding examples, which include many other references, are: Ehrmann, The Duty of Disclosure in Parliamentary Investigation, 11 Chi. L. Rev. 1, 117 (1943); Gose, The Limits of Congressional Investigating Power, 10 Wash. L. Rev. 61 (1935); Hamilton, The Inquisitorial Power of Congress, 23 A. B. A. J. 511 (1937); Comment, 19 Ill. L. Rev. 452 (1925); Loring, Powers of Congressional Investigation Committees, 8 Minn. L. Rev. 595 (1924); Coudert, Congressional Inquisition vs. Individual Liberty, 15 Va. L. Rev. 537 (1929); Stebbins, Limitations of the Powers of

subject but confine ourselves to the specific question before us. Nor shall we elaborate by discussion the principles we deem controlling. We state them and leave support of them to the authorities cited.

We think that even if the inquiry here had been such as to elicit the answer that the witness was a believer in Communism or a member of the Communist Party, Congress had power to make the inquiry.

The first phase of the question thus posed concerns the power of the Congress to inquire into the subject described in the above quotation from the Resolution.

Preliminary inquiry has from the earliest times been considered an essential of the legislative process. By it are to be determined both the advisability for and the content of legislation. So that even as to ordinary subjects, the power of inquiry by the legislature is coextensive with the power of legislation and is not limited to the scope or the content of contemplated legislation. Constitutional legislation might ensue from information derived by an inquiry upon the subject described in the quotation from H. R. Res. No. 5. That potentiality is the measure of the power of inquiry.[7] The fact is that at least eight legislative proposals have been submitted to the Congress by this Committee as the result of its investigations.[8] Obviously, the possibility that invalid as well as valid legislation might ensue from an inquiry does not limit the power of inquiry; invalid legislation might ensue from any inquiry.

The permissible breadth of governmental investigation was indicated many years ago when the Supreme Court held that "the requiring of information concerning a business is not regulation of that business,"[9] and refused to confine investigation to activities which might be regulated. And that breadth has increased considerably in recent years.[10] The Supreme Court has recently held[11] that the First Amendment does not preclude a subpoena by an administrative official requiring a newspaper to

---

Congressional Investigating Committees, 16 A. B. A. J. 425 (1930); Herwitz and Mulligan, The Legislative Investigating Committee, 33 Col. L. Rev. 4 (1933); Landis, Constitutional Limitations on the Congressional Power of Investigation, 40 Harv. L. Rev. 153 (1926).

[7] McGrain v. Daugherty, 1927, 273 U. S. 135, 177–179, 47 S. Ct. 319, 71 L. Ed. 580, 50 A. L. R. 1.

[8] H. R. Rep. No. 2742, 79th Cong., 2d Sess. (1947).

[9] Interstate Commerce Commission v. Goodrich Transit Co., 1912, 224 U. S. 194, 211, 32 S. Ct. 436, 440, 56 L. Ed. 729, 736.

[10] See the exhaustive study of the cases in Davis's "The Administrative Power of Investigation" in the Yale Law Journal, Vol. 56, p. 1111 (1947).

[11] Oklahoma Press Pub. Co. v. Walling, 1946, 327 U. S. 186, 66 S. Ct. 494, 509, 90 L. Ed. 614, 166 A. L. R. 531. . . .

disclose the interstate distribution of its paper, dissemination of its news, or the source and receipt of its advertisements; that it is not necessary that a charge of violation of law be pending, or that the inquiry be limited by "forecasts of the probable results of the investigation." The official might, the Court held, make "preliminary investigation of possibly existing violations", so long as the investigation be for a lawfully authorized purpose within the power of Congress to command. The power of Congress to investigate by means of a Committee of its own can be no less restricted than the power which it may validly confer upon an administrative official. In the case at bar we do not approach the wide boundaries indicated by the Supreme Court in that case.

Moreover, the power to inquire into the subject described in this Resolution rests upon a foundation deeper than a mere auxiliary to the ordinary legislative or administrative process. . . .

[The] existing machinery of government has power to inquire into potential threats to itself, not alone for the selfish reason of self-protection, but for the basic reason that having been established by the people as an instrumentality for the protection of the rights of people, it has an obligation to its creators to preserve itself. Moreover, the process whereby a change in the form of government can be accomplished has been prescribed by the people in the same document which records the establishment of the presently existing machinery, and that process requires the Congress to initiate proposed amendments. We think that inquiry into threats to the existing form of government by extra-constitutional processes of change is a power of Congress under its prime obligation to protect for the people that machinery of which it is a part, and inquiry into the desirability vel non of other forms of government is a power of Congress under its mandate to initiate amendments if such become advisable.

Moreover, Congress is charged with part of the responsibility imposed upon the federal government by that clause of the Constitution which provides that "The United States shall guarantee to every State in this Union a Republican Form of Government * * * ." Art. 4, § 4. This clause alone would supply the authority for Congressional inquiry into potential threats to the republican forms of the governments of the States.

If Congress has power to inquire into the subjects of Communism and the Communist Party, it has power to identify the individuals who believe in Communism and those who belong to the party. The nature and scope of the program and activities depend in large measure upon the character and number

**437**

of their adherents. Personnel is part of the subject. Moreover, the accuracy of the information obtained depends in large part upon the knowledge and the attitude of the witness, whether present before the Committee or represented by the testimony of another. We note at this point that the arguments directed to the invalidity of this inquiry under the First Amendment would apply to an inquiry directed to another person as well as to one directed to the individual himself. The right to refuse self-incrimination is not involved. The problem relates to the power of inquiry into a matter which is not a violation of law.

The Congressional power of inquiry is not unrestricted.[15] One obvious limitation upon this particular sort of inquiry is that some reasonable cause for concern must appear. We are referred to the "clear and present danger" rule expressed by Mr. Justice Holmes in *Schenck* v. *United States*[16] and extending through the line of cases cited and discussed in *Bridges* v. *State of California*.[17] But all those cases dealt with statutes which actually imposed a restriction upon speech or publication. In our view, it would be sheer folly as a matter of governmental policy for an existing government to refrain from inquiry into potential threats to its existence or security until danger was clear and present. And for the judicial branch of government to hold the legislative branch to be without power to make such inquiry until the danger is clear and present, would be absurd. How, except upon inquiry, would the Congress know whether the danger is clear and present? There is a vast difference between the necessities for inquiry and the necessities for action. The latter may be only when danger is clear and present, but the former is when danger is reasonably represented as potential.

There was justification here, within the bounds of the foregoing restriction, for the exercise of the power of inquiry. The President, pursuant to the constitutional requirement that "He shall from time to time give to the Congress Information of the State of the Union" (Art. II, Sec. 3), has announced to the Congress the conclusion that agressive tendencies of totalitarian regimes imposed on free peoples threaten the security of the United States, and he mentioned the activities of Communists in that connection. That proposition underlies much of the current

---

[15] *Kilbourn* v. *Thompson*, 1881, 103 U. S. 168, 26 L. Ed. 377, lays down one rule of restriction, which, however, is applicable to an inquiry into subjects far distant from that here involved. See also *McGrain* v. *Daugherty*, *supra* note 7.

[16] 1919, 249 U. S. 47, 52, 39 S. Ct. 247, 249, 63 L. Ed. 470, 473.

[17] 1941, 314 U. S. 252, 62 S. Ct. 190, 86 L. Ed. 192, 159 A. L. R. 1346; see also *Thomas* v. *Collins*, 1945, 323 U. S. 516, 530, 65 S. Ct. 315, 89 L. Ed. 430.

foreign policy of the Government. It is also the premise upon which much important legislation is now pending. These culminations of responsible governmental consideration sufficiently demonstrate the necessity for Congressional knowledge of the subject and so justify its course in inquiring into it.

Moreover, that the governmental ideology described as Communism and held by the Communist Party is antithetical to the principles which underlie the form of government incorporated in the Federal Constitution and guaranteed by it to the States, is explicit in the basic documents of the two systems; and the view that the former is a potential menace to the latter is held by sufficiently respectable authorities, both judicial and lay, to justify Congressional inquiry into the subject. In fact, the recitations in the opinion of the Supreme Court in *Schneiderman* v. *United States*, 1943, 320 U. S. 118, 63 S. Ct. 1333, 87 L. Ed. 1796, are sufficient to justify inquiry. To remain uninformed upon a subject thus represented would be a failure in Congressional responsibility.

The next phase of the problem is whether the power of inquiry was validly delegated by the Congress to the Committee.

It is said that the Resolution is too vague to be valid. Perhaps the one phrase "un-American propaganda activities," taken alone as it appears in subclause (i) of the Resolution, would be subject to that condemnation. But the clause, above-quoted, "subversive and un-American propaganda that * * * attacks the principle of the form of government as guaranteed by our Constitution," which is subclause (ii), is definite enough. It conveys a clear meaning, and that is all that is required. The principles which underlie the form of the existing government in this country are well-enough defined in basic documents preceding the Constitution, are obvious in the undebated unanimity which prevailed on many basic propositions in the Convention of 1787, were stated during the consideration of the adoption of the Constitution, are stated in countless scholarly works upon principles of government, and, indeed, are taught even to high school students in our schools. Aliens seeking naturalization are required to swear that they are "attached to the principles of the Constitution of the United States." 8 U. S. C. A. § 732 (a) (17). If the part of the Resolution involved in the instant case be clear and certain, it is of no importance that another part, not here involved, is vague or uncertain. . . .

Appellants argue that since an answer that the witness is a Communist would subject him to embarrassment and damage, the asking of the question is an unconstitutional burden upon free speech. It is no doubt true that public revelation at the

**439**

present time of Communist belief and activity on the part of an individual would result in embarrassment and damage. This result would not occur because of the Congressional act itself; that is, the Congress is not imposing a liability, or attaching by direct enactment a stigma. The result would flow from the current unpopularity of the revealed belief and activity. Contra, it is suggested that since the pressure of unpopularity affects only sensitive or timid people, there need be less concern, on the theory that democratic processes must necessarily contemplate rugged courage on the part of those who hold convictions, or even beliefs, on government. But it is true, realistically, that even one fully equipped to formulate a personal preference for a system of government at odds in basic respects with that presently existing, may be deterred from his conclusion by fear of, or distaste for, the unpopularity attached to it. We proceed upon the theory that even the most timid and sensitive cannot be unconstitutionally restrained in the freedom of his thought. But this consideration does not solve the problem, because the problem is the relative necessity of the public interest as against the private rights. Even assuming private rights of the timid to be of the fullest weight, the problem remains whether they outweigh the public necessities in this matter.[28] That the protection of private rights upon occasion involves an invasion of those rights is in theory a paradox but, in the world as it happens to be, is a realistic problem requiring a practical answer. That invasion should never occur except upon necessity, but unless democratic government (by which we mean government premised upon individual human rights) can protect itself by means commensurate with danger, it is doomed. That it cannot do so is the hope of its opponents, the query of its skeptics, the fear of its supporters. While we will not give less consideration to the private rights involved because they may be those of the more sensitive or less courageous, on the other hand we cannot say that merely because those affected are of less courage or greater

---

[28] Other requirements having similar restrictive effects upon the less hardy have been sustained in the public interest. For example, newspapers are required to publish their ownership, and to reveal the sources of their income to governmental inspection. An interesting light upon these contentions is cast by the history of our method of elections. The right of a qualified citizen to vote as he pleases is certainly a fundamental right and is a basic concept in our system of government. Public voting subjected even the most hardy to pressure and also to violence. But it was never thought, or suggested, that public voting violated constitutional rights. The secret ballot does not seem to have appeared in this country until February, 1888, when the newly-devised Australian system was adopted for municipal elections in Louisville, Kentucky. On this subject see Wigmore's Australian Ballot System.

sensitivity than the average, therefore the public interest must be waived or given less consideration. . . .

Appellants press upon us representations as to the conduct of the Congressional Committee, critical of its behavior in various respects. Eminent persons have stated similar views.[33] But such matters are not for the courts. We so held in *Townsend* v. *United States* [92 F. 2d 352], citing *Hearst* v. *Black* [87 F. 2d 68]. The remedy for unseemly conduct, if any, by Committees of Congress is for Congress, or for the people; it is political and not judicial. "It must be remembered that legislatures are ultimate guardians of the liberties and welfare of the people in quite as great a degree as the courts."[36] The courts have no authority to speak or act upon the conduct by the legislative branch of its own business, so long as the bounds of power and pertinency are not exceeded,[37] and the mere possibility that the power of inquiry may be abused "affords no ground for denying the power."[38] The question presented by these contentions must be viewed in the light of the established rule of absolute immunity of governmental officials, Congressional and administrative, from liability for damage done by their acts or speech, even though knowingly false or wrong.[39] The basis of so drastic and rigid a rule is the overbalancing of the individual hurt by the public necessity for untrammeled freedom of legislative and adminstrative activity, within the respective powers of the legislature and the executive.

We hold that in view of the representations to the Congress as to the nature, purposes and program of Communism and the Communist Party, and in view of the legislation proposed, pending and possible in respect to or premised upon that subject, and in view of the involvement of that subject in the foreign policy of the Government, Congress has power to make an inquiry of an individual which may elicit the answer that the witness is a be-

---

[33] E. g., Gellhorn, Report on a Report of the House Committee on Un-American Activities, 60 Harv. L. Rev. 1193 (1947); Letter to the President by Members of Yale Faculty of Law, 34 A. B. A. J. 15, 16 (1948).

[36] Mr. Justice Frankfurter, concurring in *United States* v. *Lovett*, 1946, 328 U. S. 303, 319, 66 S. Ct. 1073, 1080, 90 L. Ed. 1252, quoting Mr. Justice Holmes in *Missouri, K. & T. Ry. of Texas* v. *May*, 1904, 194 U. S. 267, 270, 24 S. Ct. 638, 48 L. Ed. 971, 973.

[37] *McGrain* v. *Daugherty*, *supra* note 7, 273 U. S. at pages 175, 176, 47 S. Ct. at page 329, 71 L. Ed. 580, 50 A. L. R. 1.

[38] *Id.*, 273 U. S. at page 175, 47 S. Ct. at page 329.

[39] U. S. Const. Art. I, § 6; *Kilbourn* v. *Thompson*, *supra* note 15; *Cochran* v. *Couzens*, 1930, 59 App. D. C. 374, 42 F. 2d 783, certiorari denied, 1930, 282 U. S. 874, 51 S. Ct. 79, 75 L. Ed. 772; *Spalding* v. *Vilas*, 1896, 161 U. S. 483, 16 S. Ct. 631, 40 L. Ed. 780; *Glass* v. *Ickes*, 1940, 73 App. D. C. 3, 117 F. 2d 273, 132 A. L. R. 1328; *Jones* v. *Kennedy*, 1941, 73 App. D. C. 292, 121 F. 2d 40.

liever in Communism or a member of the Communist Party. And we further hold that the provision we have quoted from House Resolution No. 5 is sufficiently clear, definite and authoritative to permit this particular Committee to make that particular inquiry. We hold no more than that. . . .

It follows that the judgments of the District Court must be, and they are

Affirmed.

EDGERTON, Associate Justice (dissenting).

In my opinion the House Committee's investigation abridges freedom of speech and inflicts punishment without trial; and the statute the appellants are convicted of violating provides no ascertainable standard of guilt. It follows that the convictions should be reversed on constitutional grounds.

The First Amendment forbids Congress to make any law "abridging the freedom of speech, or of the press." If this "is to mean anything, it must restrict powers which are * * * granted by the Constitution to Congress."[1] Legislation abridging the freedoms guaranteed by the First Amendment is not made valid by the fact that it would be valid if it did not abridge them.

The *Murdock, Opelika,* and *Busey* cases make this plain. Clear and necessary as the taxing power is, it does not extend to sales of propaganda not made for profit; a license tax, although imposed for the legitimate purpose of raising revenue, is unconstitutional in its application to such sales.[2] . . .

It was not the weakness of the taxing power but the strength of the First Amendment that made the *Murdock* and *Opelika* taxes unconstitutional. Yet this court now holds that the First Amendment, which restricts the express power of taxation, does not restrict the implied power of investigation. Investigation in general, and this investigation in particular, is not more necessary than taxation. There is no basis in authority, policy, or logic for holding that it is entitled to a preferred constitutional position. "Freedoms of speech, press, and religion are entitled to a preferred constitutional position."[7] The power of investigation, like the power of taxation, stops short of restricting the freedoms protected by the First Amendment.

Quite as clearly as the taxes in the *Murdock, Opelika,* and *Busey* cases, the House Committee's investigation is on its "face * * *

---

[1] Chafee, Free Speech in the United States, 30–31.

[2] *Jones* v. *City of Opelika,* 319 U. S. 103, 63 S. Ct. 890, 87 L. Ed. 1290; *Murdock* v. *Commonwealth of Pennsylvania,* 319 U. S. 105, 63 S. Ct. 870, 875, 87 L. Ed. 1292, 146 A. L. R. 81; *Busey* v. *District of Columbia* [319 U. S. 579.]

[7] *Busey* v. *District of Columbia,* 78 U. S. App. D. C. 189, 192, 138 F. 2d 592, 595. . . .

442

a restriction of the free exercise of those freedoms." It actually restricts them and puts a substantial clog upon them. It is therefore more clearly unconstitutional than the taxes.

The investigation restricts the freedom of speech by uncovering and stigmatizing expressions of unpopular views. The Committee gives wide publicity to its proceedings. This exposes the men and women whose views are advertised to risks of insult, ostracism, and lasting loss of employment.[8] Persons disposed to express unpopular views privately or to a selected group are often not disposed to risk the consequences to themselves and their families that publication may entail. The Committee's practice of advertising and stigmatizing unpopular views is therefore a strong deterrent to any expression, however private, of such views.

The investigation also restricts freedom of speech by forcing people to express views. Freedom of speech is freedom in respect to speech and includes freedom not to speak. "To force an American citizen publicly to profess any statement of belief" is to violate the First Amendment. "If there is any fixed star in our constitutional constellation, it is that no official, high or petty, can prescribe what shall be orthodox in politics, nationalism, religion, or other matters of opinion or force citizens to confess by word or act their faith therein." That is the rule of the *Barnette* case,[11] which involved pressure on school children to profess approved beliefs. Witnesses before the House Committee are under pressure to profess approved beliefs. They cannot express others without exposing themselves to disastrous consequences. Yet if they have previously expressed others they cannot creditably or credibly profess those that are approved. If they decline "publicly to profess any statement of belief" they invite punishment for contempt. The privilege of choosing between speech that means ostracism and speech that means perjury is not freedom of speech.

"Under our traditions beliefs are personal and not a matter of mere association."[12] Yet the House Committee attributes unpopular and "communistic" beliefs to persons and groups on the basis of mere association with other persons and groups.[13] By

---

[8] "Hollywood Fires 10 Cited in Contempt. Film Heads Rule They Must Swear They're Not Reds To Be Rehired". Head and subhead in Washington Post, Nov. 26, 1947, p. 1, col. 4.

[11] *West Virginia State Board of Education* v. *Barnette*, 319 U. S. 624, 634, 642 . . .

[12] *Schneiderman* v. *United States*, 320 U. S. 118, 136, 63 S. Ct. 1333, 1342, 87 L. Ed. 1796.

[13] Robert E. Cushman, Goldwin Smith Professor of Government in Cornell University, has said: "Under the guise of attacking Communism [Mr. Dies]

this device it greatly extends the restraining effect of its investigation. Its treatment of the Southern Conference for Human Welfare[14] illustrates its practice.[15] It further extends the restraining effect of its investigation by stigmatizing a remarkably wide range of beliefs as un-American.[16]

That the Committee's investigation does in fact restrict speech [17] is too clear for dispute. The prosecution does not deny it and the court concedes it. The effect is not limited to the people whom the committee stigmatizes or calls before it, but extends to others who hold similar views and to still others who might be disposed to adopt them. It is not prudent to hold views or to join groups that the Committee has condemned. People have grown wary of expressing any unorthodox opinions. No one can measure the inroad the Committee has made in the American sense of freedom to speak. There has been some suggestion that it restrains only timid people. I think it nearer the truth to say that, among the more articulate, it affects in one degree or another all but the very courageous, the very orthodox, and the

---

was able to attack all so-called liberal ideas in the field of politics and economics. This was done by pinning the label of Communism on all persons who belonged to any society or organization in which there ever had been any Communist member, or any idea, theory, or action of which any Communist had ever approved." Civil Liberty and Public Opinion; in Safeguarding Civil Liberty Today, Bernays lectures of 1944 at Cornell University, 81, 100.

[14] One suspicious circumstance, in the Committee's view, was that an entertainer at one meeting of the Conference was employed by a New York night club whose owner's brother was a Communist. H. Rep. No. 592, 80th Cong., 1st Sess., 10 (1947). Professor Gellhorn of Columbia University has made a thorough study of this Report. Gellhorn, Report on a Report of the House Committee on Un-American Activities, 60 Harv. L. Rev. 1193.

[15] Cf. a subcommittee's action on Dr. Condon, Director of the National Bureau of Standards; reported in Washington Post, (Washington) Evening Star, March 5, 1948.

[16] *Infra* at note 26. Professor Cushman says: "The opprobrious epithet 'un-American' was applied to all those who indulged in any open criticism of our existing institutions, our so-called American way of life, or of Mr. Dies. * * * Good loyal American citizens who ought to know better were persuaded to give their support to the suppression of free speech and free press on the grotesque theory that they were thereby showing their loyalty to the basic principles of American democracy. Bigotry was made not merely respectable but noble. By the skillful use of labels, or slogans, American public opinion was inoculated with the dangerous idea that true Americanism consists in the stalwart defense of the *status quo* and the suppression of those dangerous and disloyal people who are unpatriotic enough to want to criticize it or suggest any change in it." *Op. cit. supra* note 13, at 100.

[17] Its effect on people in the moving picture industry has been described in the newspapers and in a report in the New Yorker of Feb. 21, 1948, p. 32.

**444**

very secure.[18] But nothing turns on this question of fact. The views of timid people are not necessarily worthless to society. No one needs self-expression more. The Constitution protects them as it protects others. If it be true that the Committee's investigation would not restrain a determined man, this matters no more than the fact that the taxes in the *Murdock* and *Opelika* cases would not restrain a rich man. Some people speak freely whatever it costs, but this does not mean that speech is free whatever it costs. . . .

[In] the present case neither the inclusion nor the burdening of propaganda is incidental. The House Committee's enabling Act concerns, specifically and exclusively, "propaganda activities," and the Committee's principal purpose is to restrain them. Its purpose is shown clearly by its acts and conclusively by its statements. The Committee and its members have repeatedly said in terms or in effect that its main purpose is to do by exposure and publicity what it believes may not validly be done by legislation.[19] This is as much as to say that its purpose is to punish or burden propaganda. The Committee has "embarked upon a systematic campaign to suppress freedom of political and economic opinion."[21]

What Congress may not restrain, Congress may not restrain by exposure and obloquy. If it be thought that the Committee's purpose does not include "punishment, in the ordinary sense," this is immaterial to the present point.[22] The First

---

[18] Even in 1943, after less than five years of existence, the Committee had accumulated a file of over 1,000,000 cards containing information on individuals and organizations. H. Rep. No. 2748, 77th Cong., 2d Sess., 2 (1943).

[19] When the House of Representatives first authorized the Committee as a special committee Mr. Dies, its first chairman, said "I am not in a position to say whether we can legislate effectively in reference to this matter, but I do know that exposure in a democracy of subversive activities is the most effective weapon we have in our possession." 83 Cong. Rec. 7570 (1938). . . .

The Committee's Reports declare its purpose. "While Congress does not have the power to deny to citizens the right to believe in, teach, or advocate communism, fascism, and nazism, it does have the right to focus the spotlight of publicity upon their activities." H. Rep. No. 2, 76th Cong., 1st Sess., 13 (1939). . . . The Committee is "empowered to explore and expose activities by un-American individuals and organizations which, while sometimes being legal, are nonetheless inimical to our American concepts and our American future." H. Rep. No. 2742, 79th Cong., 2d Sess., 16 (1947). . . .

[21] Cushman, *op. cit. supra* note 13, at 100.

[22] *Near* v. *State of Minnesota*, 283 U. S. 697, 711, 51 S. Ct. 625, 629, 75 L. Ed. 1357.

**445**

Amendment forbids Congress purposely to burden forms of expression that it may not punish.[23]

It is said that Congress may punish propaganda that advocates overthrow of the government by force or violence; that it may therefore investigate to determine whether such legislation is necessary; and that it may do this even if the investigation burdens such propaganda and is intended to do so. In short, it is said that the House Committee's investigation is a necessary means to a constitutional end and is therefore constitutional. To this there are at least three answers.

(1) Investigation of possible need for legislation making it unlawful to advocate overthrow of the government by force or violence has not been necessary and has not been among the purposes of Congress or of the House Committee at any time since 1940. On the contrary, the broadest possible legislation of that sort was passed in that year and is still on the books.[24]

(2) The Committee's enabling Act says nothing about force or violence or overthrow of the government. It is broad enough to include investigation of propaganda advocating such things, but it is not by any means limited to such propaganda, and neither is the Committee's actual investigation. Though the Committee has concerned itself largely with communism, and formerly with fascism, it has also concerned itself with propaganda unrelated to any possible overthrow of the government by force and plainly beyond any power of Congress to burden or restrain. "In the course of its inquiries such diverse groups have come under its scrutiny as the American Civil Liberties Union, the C. I. O., the National Catholic Welfare Conference, * * * the Farmer-Labor party, sit-down strikes, the Federal Theatre Project, consumers' organizations, * * * the magazine Time." Among various "other criteria which the Committee or its agents have from time to time suggested as indicative of activity within the scope of its inquiries are: opposition to 'the American system of checks and balances,' opposition to the protection of property rights, belief in dictatorship, opposition to the Franco government of Spain, opposition to General MacArthur, advocacy of a world state, advocacy of the dissolution of the British Empire, criticism of members of Congress, and criticism of the Committee on Un-American Activities."[26] Obviously there could

---

[23] A purpose to reduce the circulation of newspapers makes a tax law unconstitutional. *Grosjean* v. *American Press Co.*, 297 U. S. 233, 250, 56 S. Ct. 444, 80 L. Ed. 660.

[24] [Quoting Section 2(a) of the Alien Registration Act of 1940, 18 U. S. C. A. § 2385 (1951).]

[26] [47 Col. L. Rev.], at 418, 422–423. The quoted statements are supported by specific references.

be no necessity for many of the Committee's activities, and no excuse for the restraints they impose, even if the Act of 1940 were not on the books.

Legislative action that restrains constitutionally protected speech along with other speech cannot be enforced against either. Legislation is unconstitutional as a whole if it "does not aim specifically at evils within the allowable area of state control but * * * sweeps within its ambit other activities that in ordinary circumstances constitute an exercise of freedom of speech or of the press. The existence of such a statute * * * results in a continuous and pervasive restraint on all freedom of discussion that might reasonably be regarded as within its purview. * * * An accused, after arrest and conviction under such a statute, does not have to sustain the burden of demonstrating that the State could not constitutionally have written a different and specific statute covering his activities as disclosed by the charge and the evidence introduced against him. * * * Where regulations of the liberty of free discussion are concerned, there are special reasons for observing the rule that it is the statute, and not the accusation or the evidence under it, which prescribes the limits of permissible conduct and warns against transgression."[27] . . .

(3) The problem is not, as the court suggests, that of balancing public or social interests against private interests. "The principle on which speech is classified as lawful or unlawful involves the balancing against each other of two very important social interests, in public safety and in the search for truth. * * * Imprisonment of 'half-baked' agitators for 'foolish talk' may often discourage wise men from publishing valuable criticism of governmental policies. * * * The great interest in free speech should be sacrificed only when the interest in

The Committee has also scrutinized, e. g., radio commentators who have changed their names or who "can hardly speak English," and Army orientation material which "sought to teach that any person who claimed to be any one or all of the following was a Fascist, or was likely to become a Fascist very shortly: '100 percent American, anti-Jew, anti-Negro, anti-labor, anti-foreign-born, anti-Catholic.'" H. Rep. No. 2233, 79th Cong., 2d Sess., 9–13, 14 (1946).

The Committee said in its first Report: "* * * (5) Any organization or individual who believes in or advocates a system of political, economic, or social regimentation based upon a planned economy is un-American. (6) Any organization or individual who believes in or advocates the destruction of the American system of checks and balances with its three independent coordinate branches of government is un-American." H. Rep. No. 2, 76th Cong., 1st Sess., 12 (1939).

[27] *Thornhill* v. *State of Alabama*, 310 U. S. 88, 97–98, 60 S. Ct. 736, 742, 84 L. Ed. 1093. Cf. *Yu Cong Eng* v. *Trinidad*, 271 U. S. 500, 523, 46 S. Ct. 619, 70 L. Ed. 1059.

public safety is really imperiled. * * * The American policy is to meet force by force, and talk by talk."[29]

This policy is embodied in American constitutional law. "The penalizing even of utterances of a defined character must find its justification in a reasonable apprehension of danger to organized government."[30] "The question in every case is whether the words used are used in such circumstances and are of such a nature as to create a clear and present danger that they will bring about the substantive evils that Congress has a right to prevent";[31] "danger of action of a kind the State is empowered to prevent and punish."[32]

There is no evidence in the record that propaganda has created danger, clear and present or obscure and remote, that the government of the United States or any government in the United States will be overthrown by force or violence. "When legislation appears on its face to affect the use of speech, press, or religion, and when its validity depends upon the existence of facts which are not proved, their existence should not be presumed * * * ."[33] "The usual presumption supporting legislation is balanced by the preferred place given in our scheme to the great, the indispensable democratic freedoms secured by the First Amendment."[34]

The court asks "How, except upon inquiry, would the Congress know whether the danger is clear and present?" . . . But a congressional inquiry, however superfluous, to discover whether there is clear and present danger, could be authorized and could be conducted without violating the First Amendment. The premise that the government must have power to protect itself by discovering whether it is in clear and present danger of overthrow by violence is sound. But it does not support the conclusion that Congress may compel men to disclose their personal opinions, to a committee and also to the world, on topics ranging

---

[29] Chafee, *op. cit. supra* note 1, at 35 ix, 180.

[30] *Herndon* v. *Lowry*, . . . 310 U. S. at page 258, 57 S. Ct. at page 739.

[31] *Schenck* v. *United States*, 249 U. S. 47, 52, 39 S. Ct. 247, 249, 63 L. Ed. 470.

[32] *West Virginia State Board of Education* v. *Barnette*, . . . 319 U. S. at page 633, 63 S. Ct. at page 1183, 87 L. Ed. 1628, 147 A. L. R. 674. "What finally emerges from the 'clear and present danger' cases is a working principle that the substantive evil must be extremely serious and the degree of imminence extremely high before utterances can be punished." *Bridges* v. *State of California*, 314 U. S. 252, 263, 62 S. Ct. 190, 194, 86 L. Ed. 192, 159 A. L. R. 1346.

[33] *Busey* v. *District of Columbia, supra note* 7, 78 U. S. App. D. C. at page 192, 138 F. 2d 595.

[34] *Thomas* v. *Collins*, 323 U. S. 516, 529–530, 65 S. Ct. 315, 322, 89 L. Ed. 430. . . .

from communism, however remotely and peaceably achieved, to the "American system of checks and balances," the British Empire, and the Franco government of Spain. Since the premise does not support this conclusion it has nothing to do with this case. It justifies no punitive exposure. It justifies a very different investigation from the one the House Committee conducts. . . .

[Judge Edgerton's opinion goes on to hold that the "Committee inflicts punishment for unorthodox opinions or associations" without any of the safeguards of a judicial trial, and that the enabling resolution is too vague and indefinite to provide any reasonably clear meaning.]

Appellants appeared and testified before the Committee but did not produce the demanded records. The court says "These appellants were not asked to state their political opinions. They were asked to account for funds." This distinction merely makes any possible pertinence to the Committee's investigation the more remote. The appellants were asked to account for funds in order to reveal their political opinions. Accordingly the court says: "We are considering a specific question only, which is whether this Congressional Committee may inquire whether an individual is or is not a believer in Communism or a member of the Communist Party." That specific question is before us, if at all, as an aspect of the larger question whether courts may punish individuals for not responding to an inquiry by this Committee into their political opinions. My answer to both questions is no. The Committee's specific inquiry abridged appellants' freedom of speech and attempted to inflict punishment without trial. The Committee's entire investigation was unconstitutional both as abridging freedom of speech and as attempting to punish without trial; and there is no duty to respond to inquiries in an unconstitutional proceeding. The statute the appellants are convicted of violating provides no ascertainable standard of guilt. . . .

## Note

1. The Supreme Court denied certiorari in the *Barsky* case. 334 U. S. 843 (1948), petition for rehearing denied, 339 U. S. 971 (1950), Justices Black and Douglas dissenting.

A short time before the *Barsky* decision the Court of Appeals for the Second Circuit reached the same conclusion in the case of Leon Josephson, convicted for refusing to be sworn or give testimony. Judge Clark dissented. *U. S. v. Josephson*, 165 F. 2d 82 (1947). The Supreme Court also denied certiorari in this case. 333 U. S. 838 (1948), Justices Douglas, Murphy and Rutledge dissenting; rehearing denied, 335 U. S. 899 (1948).

The Committee's investigation of the motion picture industry in

1947 led to the citation of 10 witnesses for contempt in refusing to answer, among others, the question, "Are you now or have you ever been a member of the Communist Party?" In two test cases convictions were upheld by the Court of Appeals for the District of Columbia. *Lawson v. U. S.*, and *Trumbo v. U. S.*, 176 F. 2d 49 (1949), and again the Supreme Court denied certiorari. 339 U. S. 934, 972 (1950), Justices Black and Douglas dissenting. All the "Hollywood Ten" served prison sentences.

The refusal of George Marshall to produce the books and records of the National Federation for Constitutional Liberties led to his conviction for contempt, again sustained by the Court of Appeals, *Marshall v. U. S.*, 176 F. 2d 473 (C. A. D. C., 1949), and certiorari denied, 339 U. S. 933 (1950), Justice Black dissenting.

Although the Supreme Court has, by its denials of certiorari, consistently refused to pass on the basic issues of the Committee's power, it has ruled on certain collateral issues. In *Dennis v. U. S.*, 339 U. S. 162, 94 L. Ed. 734, 70 S. Ct. 519 (1950), it held that the presence of Federal government employees on the jury in the trial of Eugene Dennis for contempt of the Committee did not constitute the denial of an "impartial trial," under the Sixth Amendment. But in *Morford v. U. S.*, 339 U. S. 258, 94 L. Ed. 815, 70 S. Ct. 586 (1950), it reversed per curiam a contempt conviction because the defendant had not been permitted to question prospective jurors, who were government employees, concerning the possible effect upon them of the Loyalty Order. On retrial Morford was convicted again and the Supreme Court denied certiorari. 184 F. 2d 864 (1950), cert. den. 340 U. S. 878 (1950). In another case Gerhart Eisler was convicted of contempt of the Committee for refusing to be sworn until he had read a statement. The Court of Appeals upheld the conviction. *Eisler v. U. S.*, 170 F. 2d 273 (C. A. D. C., 1948). The Supreme Court granted certiorari, 335 U. S. 857 (1948), but later dismissed the case as moot after Eisler had fled the country. 338 U. S. 189 (1949). And in *U. S. v. Fleischman*, 339 U. S. 349, 94 L. Ed. 906, 70 S. Ct. 739 (1950), the Court, reversing the Court of Appeals of the District of Columbia, held that the defendant, a member of the executive board of the Joint Anti-Fascist Committee, had not made such efforts to produce the organization's records as would absolve her of contempt for failure of the board to produce them. On retrial Fleischman was convicted. 183 F. 2d 996, cert. den. 340 U. S. 866 (1950). See also *Bryan v. U. S.*, noted *infra*.

See also *U. S. v. Browder* (D. C. D. C., Mar. 14, 1951, unreported), discussed in 40 Geo. L. J. 137 (1951).

Moving toward the other end of the political spectrum, Joseph P. Kamp, executive vice chairman of the Constitutional Educational League, was convicted of contempt of the House Special Committee to Investigate Campaign Expenditures for refusing to produce the books and records of the League. *Kamp v. U. S.*, 176 F. 2d 618 (C. A. D. C., 1948), cert. den. 339 U. S. 957 (1950). Kamp was convicted again in 1951 for refusing to produce financial records before the House Select Committee on Lobbying Activities. N. Y. Times, June 29, 1951.

**450**                                                          [Emerson]

At about the same time Edward A. Rumely, executive secretary of the Committee for Constitutional Government, was found guilty of contempt of the same House Committee for refusing to reveal the names of purchasers of *The Road Ahead* and other books distributed by Rumely's organization. This conviction was reversed by the Court of Appeals for the District of Columbia on the ground that the authority given the Committee by the enabling resolution to investigate "all activities intended to influence, encourage, promote, or retard legislation" or activities designed "to influence legislation indirectly by influencing public opinion" was beyond any power conferred on Congress by the Constitution and violated the First Amendment. *Rumely v. U. S.,* — F. 2d — (C. A. D. C., 1952). Judge Bazelon dissented. Judge Prettyman, writing for the majority, distinguished the *Barsky* case:

"In that case the tenets of Communism and the apparent nature of the Communist party created a public necessity for congressional inquiry. In the case at bar no such dangerous factors are represented to us. There is no suggestion that the publication or distribution of these books and documents constitutes any public danger, clear or otherwise, present or otherwise." — F. 2d at —.

For an account of earlier trials of Kamp and Rumely, which resulted in acquittals, see Note, 35 Geo. L. J. 527 (1947).

2. For general discussion of the legal powers of legislative investigating committees, and the earlier court decisions, see in addition to the material cited in the *Barsky* opinion, Morgan, *Congressional Investigations and Judicial Review,* 37 Calif. L. Rev. 556 (1949); McGeary, *Historical Development,* in the symposium in 18 U. of Chi. L. Rev. 421, 425 (1951); Carr, *The Un-American Activities Committee and the Courts,* 11 La. L. Rev. 282, 283–99 (1951); Notes 45 Ill. L. Rev. 633 (1950); 26 Tulane L. Rev. 381 (1952). For discussion of the issues raised by the *Barsky* case see, Note, *Constitutional Limitations on the Un-American Activities Committee,* 47 Col. L. Rev. 416 (1947); Note, *Congressional Contempt Power in Investigations into the Area of Civil Liberties,* 14 U. of Chi. L. Rev. 256 (1947); Nutting, *Freedom of Silence: Constitutional Protection Against Government Intrusions in Political Affairs,* 47 Mich. L. Rev. 181, 200–222 (1948); Boudin, *Congressional and Agency Investigations,* 35 Va. L. Rev. 143 (1949); Carr *supra,* 11 La. L. Rev. at 299–315; Notes, 33 Corn. L. Q. 565 (1948); 43 Ill. L. Rev. 253 (1948); 46 Mich. L. Rev. 521 (1948).

For discussion of state decisions on the powers of legislative investigating committees see Herwitz and Mulligan, *The Legislative Investigating Committee—A Survey and Critique,* 33 Col. L. Rev. 4 (1933); Cousens, *The Purposes and Scope of Investigations Under Legislative Authority,* 26 Geo. L. J. 905 (1938). State cases similar to the *Barsky* case and reaching the same result are *State v. James,* 36 Wash. 2d 882, 221 Pac. 2d 482 (1950), cert. den. 341 U. S. 911 (1951); *Ex parte Coon,* 44 Cal. App. 2d 531, 112 Pac. 2d 767 (1941). See also *Tenney v. Brandhove,* 341 U. S. 367, 95 L. Ed. 1019, 71 S. Ct. 783 (1951), noted in Chapter I, *supra.*

**451**

# BLAU v. UNITED STATES

Supreme Court of the United States, 1950
340 U. S. 159, 95 L. Ed. 170, 71 S. Ct. 223

MR. JUSTICE BLACK delivered the opinion of the Court.

In response to a subpoena, petitioner appeared as a witness before the United States District Court Grand Jury at Denver, Colorado. There she was asked several questions concerning the Communist Party of Colorado and her employment by it.[1] Petitioner refused to answer these questions on the ground that the answers might tend to incriminate her. She was then taken before the district judge where the questions were again propounded and where she again claimed her constitutional privilege against self-incrimination and refused to testify. The district judge found petitioner guilty of contempt of court and sentenced her to imprisonment for one year. The Court of Appeals for the Tenth Circuit affirmed. 180 F. 2d 103. We granted certiorari because the decision appeared to deny rights guaranteed by the Fifth Amendment.[2] The holding below also was in conflict with recent decisions of the Fifth and Ninth Circuits. *Estes* v. *Potter*, 183 F. 2d 865; *Alexander* v. *United States*, 181 F. 2d 480.

At the time petitioner was called before the grand jury, the Smith Act was on the statute books making it a crime among other things to advocate knowingly the desirability of overthrow of the Government by force or violence; to organize or help to organize any society or group which teaches, advocates or encourages such overthrow of the Government; to be or become a member of such a group with knowledge of its purposes.[3] These provisions made future prosecution of petitioner far more than "a mere imaginary possibility. . . ." *Mason* v. *United States*,

---

[1] The grand jury's questions which petitioner refused to answer were as follows: "Mrs. Blau, do you know the names of the State officers of the Communist Party of Colorado?" "Do you know what the organization of the Communist Party of Colorado is, the table of organization of the Communist Party of Colorado?" "Were you ever employed by the Communist Party of Colorado?" "Mrs. Blau, did you ever have in your possession or custody any of the books and records of the Communist Party of Colorado?" "Did you turn the books and records of the Communist Party of Colorado over to any particular person?" "Do you know the names of any persons who might now have the books and records of the Communist Party of Colorado?" "Could you describe to the grand jury any books and records of the Communist Party of Colorado?"

[2] The Fifth Amendment provides: "No person . . . shall be compelled in any criminal case to be a witness against himself . . . ." U. S. Const., Amend. V.

[3] 62 Stat. 808, 18 U. S. C. § 2385.

**452**

244 U. S. 362, 366; she reasonably could fear that criminal charges might be brought against her if she admitted employment by the Communist Party or intimate knowledge of its workings. Whether such admissions by themselves would support a conviction under a criminal statute is immaterial. Answers to the questions asked by the grand jury would have furnished a link in the chain of evidence needed in a prosecution of petitioner for violation of (or conspiracy to violate) the Smith Act. Prior decisions of this Court have clearly established that under such circumstances, the Constitution gives a witness the privilege of remaining silent. The attempt by the courts below to compel petitioner to testify runs counter to the Fifth Amendment as it has been interpreted from the beginning. *United States* v. *Burr*, 25 Fed. Cas., Case No. 14,692e, decided by Chief Justice Marshall in the Circuit Court of the United States for the District of Virginia; *Counselman* v. *Hitchcock*, 142 U. S. 547; *Ballmann* v. *Fagin*, 200 U. S. 186; *Arndstein* v. *McCarthy*, 254 U. S. 71; *Boyd* v. *United States*, 116 U. S. 616; cf. *United States* v. *White*, 322 U. S. 694, 698, 699.

*Reversed.*

MR. JUSTICE CLARK took no part in the consideration or decision of this case.

## Note

1. In *Blau* v. *U. S.*, 340 U. S. 332, 95 L. Ed. 306, 71 S. Ct. 301 (1951), the Supreme Court upheld the right of Irving Blau, the husband of the defendant in the first *Blau* case, to decline to answer questions concerning his wife's whereabouts, the information being considered a privileged communication between husband and wife.

2. *Rogers* v. *U. S.*, 340 U. S. 367, 95 L. Ed. 344, 71 S. Ct. 438 (1951), involved the same Grand Jury investigation as the two *Blau* cases. Here the defendant testified that she was Treasurer of the Communist Party of Denver and that she had been in possession of the membership lists and dues records of the Party, but had turned them over to another person. Upon demand of the Grand Jury to identify the person who had received the books the defendant refused, giving as her reason, "I don't feel that I should subject a person or persons to the same thing that I'm going through." The Court upheld her conviction for contempt. It ruled that, having voluntarily testified to her status as an officer of the Communist Party, "response to the specific question in issue here would not further incriminate her" and hence she could no longer invoke the privilege: "To uphold a claim of privilege in this case would open the way to distortion of facts by permitting a witness to select any stopping place in the testimony." 340 U. S. at 369, 373, 371. The Court further held that the defendant could not claim the privilege as grounds for refusing to produce organizational records she held in her capacity as officer of an association.

Justices Black, Frankfurter and Douglas, dissenting in an opinion by the first, said:

"Apparently, the Court's holding is that at some uncertain point in petitioner's testimony, regardless of her intention, admission of associations with the Communist Party automatically effected a 'waiver' of her constitutional protection as to all related questions. To adopt such a rule for the privilege against self-incrimination, when other constitutional safeguards must be knowingly waived, relegates the Fifth Amendment's privilege to a second-rate position. Moreover, today's holding creates this dilemma for witnesses: On the one hand, they risk imprisonment for contempt by asserting the privilege prematurely; on the other, they might lose the privilege if they answer a single question. The Court's view makes the protection depend on timing so refined that lawyers, let alone laymen, will have difficulty in knowing when to claim it." 340 U. S. at 377-8.

In *Brunner v. U. S.*, 190 F. 2d 167 (C. A. 9, 1951) the Court of Appeals upheld the District Court in refusing to allow a witness to invoke the privilege against self-incrimination as to questions concerning his membership in the Communist Party in 1937 and 1938, before passage of the Smith Act in 1940. The Supreme Court reversed per curiam, citing the first *Blau* case. 343 U. S. 918 (1952).

In *U. S. v. Field*, 193 F. 2d 92 (C. A. 2, 1951), cert. den. 342 U. S. 894 (1951), the court refused to permit the trustees of the Civil Rights Congress Bail Fund to rely upon the privilege as grounds for withholding the names of donors to the Fund, where the names were being sought by a court inquiring into bail jumping by four defendants in the *Dennis* case, whose bail had been supplied by the Fund. The case is noted in 65 Harv. L. Rev. 691 (1952). See also *Field v. U. S.*, 193 F.2d 86 (C. A. 2, 1951).

For the basic cases involving the privilege against self-incrimination, see Chapter II, *supra*.

3. It is generally accepted that the privilege against self-incrimination may be asserted against a legislative committee. See *U. S. v. Bryan*, 339 U. S. 323, 94 L. Ed. 884, 70 S. Ct. 724 (1950), and cases cited below. Following the indictment of the Communist Party leaders under the Smith Act in July 1948, the privilege has been frequently claimed by witnesses summoned before the Committee on Un-American Activities. For some period of time the Committee continued to cite such recalcitrant witnesses for contempt. In 1950 the House ordered the prosecution of some 56 witnesses. 96 Cong. Rec. 12234-83. But the prosecutions, which continued even after the *Blau* decision, failed in all but isolated instances where the courts have held that the privilege was improperly invoked or was waived. See *e. g.*, *U. S. v. Fitzpatrick*, 96 F. Supp. 491 (D. C. D. C., 1951); *U. S. v. Raley*, 96 F. Supp. 495 (D. C. D. C., 1951); *U. S. v. Jaffe*, 98 F. Supp. 191 (D. C. D. C., 1951); *U. S. v. Nelson*, 103 F. Supp. 215 (D. C. D. C., 1952) (admission of membership in Communist Party held not to waive privilege to refuse to answer further questions concerning Communist activities). *Cf. U. S. v. Emspak*, 95 F. Supp. 1010, 1012 (D. C. D. C., 1951).

4. The rule of the *Rogers* case has also proved an important factor in limiting testimony before the Committee on Un-American Activities. Thus Miss Lillian Hellman, called to testify, wrote the Committee as follows:

". . . I am ready and willing to testify before the representatives of our Government as to my own opinions and my own actions, regardless of any risks or consequences to myself.

"But I am advised by counsel that if I answer the committee's questions about myself, I must also answer questions about other people, and that if I refuse to do so, I can be cited for contempt. My counsel tells me that if I answer questions about myself, I will have waived my rights under the Fifth Amendment and could be forced legally to answer questions about others.

"This is very difficult for a layman to understand. But there is one principle that I do understand: I am not willing, now or in the future, to bring bad trouble to people who, in my past association with them, were completely innocent of any talk or any action that was disloyal or subversive.

"I do not like subversion or disloyalty in any form, and if I had ever seen any I would have considered it my duty to have reported it to the proper authorities. But to hurt innocent people whom I knew many years ago in order to save myself is, to me, inhuman and indecent and dishonorable.

"I cannot and will not cut my conscience to fit this year's fashions, even though I long ago came to the conclusion that I was not a political person and could have no comfortable place in any political group.
. . .

"I am prepared to waive the privilege against self-incrimination and to tell you anything you wish to know about my views or actions, if your committee will agree to refrain from asking me to name other people. If the committee is unwilling to give me this assurance, I will be forced to plead the privilege of the Fifth Amendment at the hearing."

Committee Chairman Wood refused the offer, saying that the Committee could not permit a witness to set forth terms for testifying or be "placed in the position of trading with a witness." N. Y. Times, May 22, 1952.

5. Proposals have been made for legislation authorizing Congressional Committees to grant witnesses immunity from Federal prosecution, thereby forcing them to testify on pain of contempt. See S. 1570 and 1747, 82d Cong., 1st Sess. (1951). A prior Federal statute did authorize such granting of immunity, 11 Stat. 155 (1857), but was later modified so as to curtail immunity in such a way as apparently not to meet constitutional requirements. 12 Stat. 333 (1862). See 18 U. S. C. § 3486 (1951); *U. S. v. Bryan, supra.* Whether for fear of permitting committees to grant immunity in cases not justified, or for other reasons, no action has been taken on the new legislative proposals. See Carr, *The Un-American Activities Committee and the Courts,* 11 La. L. Rev. 282, 290–5 (1951).

6. For discussion of the use of privilege against self-incrimination

before legislative committees, see Carr, *supra*, at 290–5; Morgan, *The Privilege Against Self-Incrimination*, 34 Minn. L. Rev. 1, 30–4 (1949); Notes, 49 Col. L. Rev. 87 (1949); 51 Col. L. Rev. 206 (1951); 61 Yale L. J. 105 (1952); 18 Brook. L. Rev. 287 (1952).

## Procedural and Other Protections to Persons Attacked by or before Legislative Committees

Some of the most severe criticism of legislative investigating committees has been directed toward the absence of adequate procedural safeguards or effective remedy against damaging but unwarranted charges. Eric Johnston, head of the Motion Picture Association, expressed forcefully the dilemma facing persons attacked before a legislative committee:

"With no vested right to be heard and no vested right to challenge accusations against him, the innocent citizen is helpless. He can be indicted and convicted in the public mind on the unchallenged say-so of a witness who may be completely sincere, but can be either misinformed or riddled with prejudice. Without fear of reprisal, a prejudiced witness can exercise venom as well as veracity."[1]

The courts have never undertaken to supervise the procedures of legislative committees. In *Christoffel v. United States*, 338 U. S. 84, 93 L. Ed. 1826, 69 S. Ct. 1447 (1949), the Supreme Court did hold that a witness before a legislative committee can be found guilty of perjury only where a quorum of the committee is present at the time the perjury is committed; and that in a prosecution for perjury it is not enough to prove that a quorum was present when the hearing began but it must be shown affirmatively that a quorum existed at the time of the offense. Chief Justice Vinson and Justices Jackson, Reed and Burton dissented. But this decision was qualified in *United States v. Bryan*, 339 U. S. 323, 94 L. Ed. 884, 70 S. Ct. 724 (1950). Here it was held that a witness subpoenaed to produce records and failing to produce them at a committee hearing could not raise the issue of a lack of quorum, particularly where it had not been raised at the hearing. Justices Black and Frankfurter dissented on grounds not involving the quorum point.[2] Aside from the quor-

---

[1] Motion Picture Association Press Release for Oct. 26, 1947, quoted in Glassie and Cooley, *Congressional Investigations—Salvation in Self Regulation*, 38 Geo. L. J. 343, 356 (1950). See also Lattimore, *Ordeal by Slander* (1950).

[2] See also *Meyers v. U. S.*, 181 F. 2d 802 (C. A. D. C., 1950), refusing to vacate the judgment in the case of Gen. Bennett Meyers for perjury in testimony concerning fraud in government contracts. See Note, 11 Law. Guild Rev. 36 (1951).

um issue, however, the courts have shown no signs of interfering with committee procedure.

Nor does any judicial remedy exist through a private suit against committee members or witnesses for defamatory statements made in committee proceedings. Members of Congress are immune to suit under Article I, Section 6, of the Constitution which provides that "for any Speech or Debate in either House, they shall not be questioned in any other Place." Witnesses compelled to testify and fair and accurate press reports of Congressional proceedings are privileged by common law decision. See Chapter V, *infra*.

A number of proposals for affording greater protection to persons attacked by or before legislative committees have been put forward. One suggestion has been that all "investigations" as distinct from "legislative" hearings be conducted by impartial commissions on the order of the British Royal Commissions. Senator Hunt has proposed that the immunity provisions of Article I, Section 6, be repealed. S. J. R. 203, 81st Cong., 2d Sess. (1950). Another suggestion has been that suit for libel or slander be allowed against the government. See the Hunt Bill, S. 4113, 81st Cong., 2d Sess. (1950).

Many proposals have been advanced for legislation or committee rules to afford greater procedural protections. Lindsay Rogers has proposed that the provisions of the Administrative Procedure Act be made applicable to legislative committee proceedings. See Rogers, *Congressional Investigations: The Problem and its Solution*, 18 U. of Chi. L. Rev. 464 (1951). Other proposals, embodied in various bills, include affording persons attacked the right to be advised in advance, to present evidence, to appear with counsel and cross-examine (usually to a limited extent) adverse witnesses, to file statements, to subpoena favorable witnesses, and the like. Additional proposals would require that committee reports be approved by a majority of the whole committee before issuance, that minority reports be issued simultaneously with the majority report, and that members of committees be prohibited from lecturing or writing about investigations for compensation. See, *e g.*, H. Con. Res. 4, 81st Cong., 1st Sess. (1949) (embodying the proposals of the American Civil Liberties Union) ; S. Con. Res. 44, 82d Cong., 1st Sess. (1951).

None of these bills or proposals has thus far been adopted. But several of the Congressional Committees have on their own initiative accepted some of the more limited proposals. See N. Y. Times, April 6, 1950.

## Note

1. On the proposal for impartial commissions see the article by Senator Ives, *In Place of Congressional "Circuses"*, N. Y. Times Magazine, Aug. 27, 1950, p. 20. The suggestions for ending Congressional immunity are discussed by Senator Hunt in *Dangers in Congressional Immunity*, N. Y. Times Magazine, June 24, 1951, p. 14. The remedy by way of a damage suit against the government is considered in Paul and Mandel, *A Remedy for Smear-by-Congress*, The New Republic, Feb. 27, 1950; Note, 3 Stan. L. Rev. 486 (1951). See also Cutler and Packer, *Make Them Tell Congress the Truth*, Harper's Magazine, Mar. 1952, p. 82, advocating that a person injured by false testimony be allowed to bring a suit for damages against the witness. On proposals for procedural changes, see Carr, *How to Improve Congressional Inquiries*, N. Y. Times Magazine, Aug. 29, 1948, p. 5; Lucas (then Senator from Illinois), *Congressional Hearings: A Plea for Reform*, N. Y. Times Magazine, Mar. 19, 1950, p. 13; Wyzanski, *Standards for Congressional Investigations*, Record of the Bar Ass'n of the City of New York (Mar. 1948), reprinted in 94 Cong. Rec. A 1547 (1948); Meader, *Limitations on Congressional Investigation*, 47 Mich. L. Rev. 775 (1949); Glassie and Cooley, *supra*, 38 Geo. L. J. 343 (1950) (including a draft of proposed committee rules); Report of Subcommittee of Senate Committee on Labor and Public Welfare, *Ethical Standards in Government*, 82d Cong., 1st Sess., pp. 55–7 (1951); Galloway, *Congressional Investigations: Proposed Reforms*, 18 U. of Chi. L. Rev. 478 (1951) (discussing the proposed bills).

2. The televising of the Kefauver Crime Committee proceedings aroused considerable controversy over the wisdom of television and radio coverage of committee proceedings. See Taylor, *The Issue Is Not TV, but Fair Play*, N. Y. Times Magazine, April 15, 1951, p. 12. On February 25, 1952, Speaker Sam Rayburn barred the use of radio and television in all House committee hearings. N. Y. Times, Feb. 26, 1952.

## 2. Anti-Sedition Legislation

The period since the Second World War has witnessed a significant revival of prosecutions under anti-sedition legislation. Federal anti-sedition legislation, known as the Smith Act, was adopted by Congress in 1940. Invoked only twice in the following eight years, in 1948 the Smith Act became the basis of a series of prosecutions against leaders of the Communist Party. Some states, which did not have anti-sedition laws, adopted them in the post-war period, and the number of state prosecutions increased.

The Smith Act and similar legislation must be viewed in the context of the whole body of law available to the government for protection against violence, attempted violence or other anti-democratic action.

## EMERSON AND HELFELD—LOYALTY AMONG GOVERNMENT EMPLOYEES

### 58 Yale L. J. 1, 27–8 (1948)

Sabotage in the form of willful injury or destruction of any national defense material, or the defective making of any national defense material, is punishable as a criminal offense.[120] Likewise, theft of, injury to or depredation against any property of the United States is punishable.[121]

The espionage statutes provide penalties not only for the intentional communication to a foreign power of information relating to national defense, to the injury of the United States or advantage of a foreign power, but also for willful communication of such information to any person not entitled to receive it and for gross negligence in allowing such information to be delivered to anyone in violation of trust or to be lost, stolen, abstracted or destroyed.[122] The Atomic Energy Act of 1946 includes a series of carefully prepared provisions designed to control the dissemination of data relating to atomic energy where disclosure would adversely affect the common defense and security.[123]

Treason consists of levying war against the United States or giving aid and comfort to its enemies; concealment of treason is also subject to punishment.[124] In addition, correspondence or intercourse with a foreign government, or counseling, advising or assisting in such correspondence, with the intent to influence the conduct of such foreign government in relation to any dispute with the United States or to defeat the measures of the United States Government, would subject an employee to criminal penalties.[125] . . .

[The insurrection statute, cited at this point, is set forth in full below.]

A conspiracy to engage in any of the foregoing acts is punishable under the general conspiracy statute and, in some cases, under specific conspiracy provisions.[127]

---

[120] 54 Stat. 1220–1 (1940), 50 U. S. C. §§ 104–6 (1946). Other provisions of the same character apply to war materials in time of war, 40 Stat. 534 (1918), as amended, 50 U. S. C. §§ 101–3 (1946), and also to trespass upon, injury or destruction of fortifications or harbor-defense systems, 30 Stat. 717 (1898), as amended, 18 U. S. C. § 96 (1946).

[121] 35 Stat. 1095 (1909), as amended, 18 U. S. C. § 82 (1946).

[122] 40 Stat. 217–8 (1917), 50 U. S. C. §§ 31–2 (1946). See also 40 Stat. 219 (1917), 50 U. S. C. § 33 (1946); 40 Stat 226, 230 (1917), 18 U. S. C. § 98 (1946).

[123] 60 Stat. 766 (1946), 40 U. S. C. A. 1810 (Supp. 1947).

[124] 35 Stat. 1088 (1909), 18 U. S. C. §§ 1–3 (1946).

[125] 35 Stat. 1088 (1909), 18 U. S. C. § 5 (1946).

[127] 35 Stat. 1096 (1909), 18 U. S. C. § 88 (1946); 54 Stat. 671 (1940), 18 U. S. C. § 11 (1946); 40 Stat. 219 (1917), 50 U. S. C. § 34 (1946).

Under the McCormack Act any individual acting as agent for a foreign principal must register with the Attorney General.[128] This would include any person who collects information for, or reports it to, a foreign principal. The Voorhis Act requires every organization, including an organization subject to foreign control, which aims wholly or in part to control by force or overthrow the government, to file a registration statement with the Attorney General including, among other data, the name and address of every officer and contributor.[129]

## REBELLION OR INSURRECTION
### 18 U. S. C. § 2383 (1948)

Whoever incites, sets on foot, assists, or engages in any rebellion or insurrection against the authority of the United States or the laws thereof, or gives aid or comfort thereto, shall be fined not more than $10,000 or imprisoned not more than ten years, or both; and shall be incapable of holding any office under the United States.

## SEDITIOUS CONSPIRACY
### 18 U. S. C. § 2384 (1948)

If two or more persons in any State or Territory, or in any place subject to the jurisdiction of the United States, conspire to overthrow, put down, or to destroy by force the Government of the United States, or to levy war against them, or to oppose by force the authority thereof, or by force to prevent, hinder, or delay the execution of any law of the United States, or by force to seize, take, or possess any property of the United States contrary to the authority thereof, they shall each be fined not more than $5,000 or imprisoned not more than six years, or both.

### Note

1. Recent prosecutions for treason include *Cramer v. U. S.*, 325 U. S. 1, 89 L. Ed. 1441, 65 S. Ct. 918 (1945); *Haupt v. U. S.*, 330 U. S. 631, 91 L. Ed. 1145, 67 S. Ct. 874 (1947); *Best v. U. S.*, 184 F. 2d 131 (C. A. 1, 1950), cert. den. 340 U. S. 939 (1951); *D'Aquino v. U. S.*, 192 F. 2d 338 (C. A. 9, 1951), cert. den. 343 U. S. 935 (1952) (Tokyo Rose); *Kawakita v. U. S.*, 343 U. S. —, 96 L. Ed. —, 72 S. Ct 950 (1952) See, generally, on treason Hurst, *Treason in the United States*, 58 Harv.

[128] 40 Stat. 226 (1917), 22 U. S. C. § 601 (1946), and 56 Stat. 248–58 (1942), 22 U. S. C. §§ 611–21 (1946).
[129] 54 Stat. 670–1 (1940), 18 U. S. C. §§ 9–11 (1946).

L. Rev. 226, 395, 806 (1945); Weyl, *Treason* (1950). See also Rebecca West, *The Meaning of Treason* (1947).

2. Prosecutions for espionage include *U. S. v. Coplon,* 185 F. 2d 629 (C. A. 2, 1950), and *Coplon v. U. S.,* 191 F. 2d 749 (C. A. D. C., 1951) (both cases reversing convictions; see Chapter II, *supra*), cert. den. 342 U. S. 920, 926 (1952); *U. S. v. Rosenberg,* 195 F. 2d 583 (C. A. 2, 1952). Recent amendments to the espionage laws are now included in 18 U. S. C. §§ 791–7 (1951).

3. Prosecutions under the provisions of the original Espionage Act of 1917 during World War II were few. Only one case was decided by the Supreme Court. *Hartzel v. U. S.,* 322 U. S. 680, 88 L. Ed. 1534, 64 S. Ct. 1233 (1944). See also *U. S. v. Pelley,* 132 F. 2d 170 (C. A. 7, 1942), cert. den. 318 U. S. 764 (1943).

4. Prosecutions for perjury growing out of alleged subversive activities include *U. S. v. Remington,* 191 F. 2d 246 (C. A. 2, 1951) (reversing conviction), cert. den. 343 U. S. 907 (1952); *U. S. v. Hiss,* 185 F. 2d 822 (C. A. 2, 1950), cert. den. 340 U. S. 948 (1951).

5. As of the end of 1950 all states and territories except New Mexico had laws against treason, 25 had laws against rebellion and insurrection, 31 had laws against sabotage. These statutes are collected in Gellhorn, *The States and Subversion,* Appen. A and B (1952). See also Groner, *State Control of Subversive Activities in the United States,* 9 Fed. B. J. 61, 71–93 (1947). Of course, all states have general legislation directed against the use of force and violence, which is also applicable to violence in connection with political activity.

## ALIEN REGISTRATION ACT (SMITH ACT)
54 Stat. 670–1 (1940), now
incorporated in 18 U. S. C. §§ 2385 and 2387 (1948)

### TITLE I

Section 1. (a) It shall be unlawful for any person, with intent to interfere with, impair, or influence the loyalty, morale, or discipline of the military or naval forces of the United States—

(1) to advise, counsel, urge, or in any manner cause insubordination, disloyalty, mutiny, or refusal of duty by any member of the military or naval forces of the United States; or

(2) to distribute any written or printed matter which advises, counsels, or urges insubordination, disloyalty, mutiny, or refusal of duty by any member of the military or naval forces of the United States. . . .

Sec. 2. (a) It shall be unlawful for any person—

(1) to knowingly or willfully advocate, abet, advise, or teach the duty, necessity, desirability, or propriety of overthrowing or destroying any government in the United States

461

by force or violence, or by the assassination of any officer of any such government;

(2) with the intent to cause the overthrow or destruction of any government in the United States, to print, publish, edit, issue, circulate, sell, distribute, or publicly display any written or printed matter advocating, advising, or teaching the duty, necessity, desirability, or propriety of overthrowing or destroying any government in the United States by force or violence;

(3) to organize or help to organize any society, group, or assembly of persons who teach, advocate, or encourage the overthrow or destruction of any government in the United States by force or violence; or to be or become a member of, or affiliate with, any such society, group, or assembly of persons, knowing the purposes thereof. . . .

Sec. 3. It shall be unlawful for any person to attempt to commit, or to conspire to commit, any of the acts prohibited by the provisions of this title. . . .

Sec. 5. (a) Any person who violates any of the provisions of this title shall, upon conviction thereof, be fined not more than $10,000 or imprisoned for not more than ten years, or both.

## Note

1. The Smith Act was modeled on the New York Criminal Anarchy Act of 1902. See Section C, *supra*. For references to the legislative history of the Smith Act see Chafee, *Free Speech in the United States*, pp. 440–1 (1941). With the adoption of the new Title 18, Crimes and Criminal Procedure, in 1948 the conspiracy provisions of Section 3 were incorporated into the general conspiracy statute, 18 U. S. C. § 371, with the effect of reducing the penalty for conspiracy from ten to five years.

2. For discussion of the background of the Smith Act see Chafee, *Free Speech in the United States*, pp. 439–90 (1941); Note, *Recent Federal Legislation Against Subversive Influences*, 41 Col. L. Rev. 159 (1941); Note, *Recent Legislative Attempts to Curb Subversive Activities in the United States*, 10 Geo. Wash. L. Rev. 104 (1941).

3. Prior to the *Dennis* case, *infra*, the Smith Act had been invoked only twice. In 1941, 18 members of the Socialist Workers Party were convicted of conspiracy to violate Sections 1 and 2 of the Act. The convictions were sustained by the Court of Appeals, relying upon the *Gitlow* case, and the Supreme Court denied certiorari. *Dunne v. U. S.*, 138 F. 2d 137 (C. A. 8, 1943), cert. den. 320 U. S. 790 (1943). In 1942, 28 alleged pro-Nazis were indicted for conspiracy to violate Section 1 of the Smith Act. The trial went on for seven and a half months in 1944 before Judge Eicher in the District of Columbia. Judge Eicher died before completion of the trial and no retrial was had. The in-

dictment was later dismissed for failure to prosecute. *U. S. v. Mc-Williams,* 163 F. 2d 695 (C. A. D. C., 1947).

4. As of the end of 1950, 31 states and territories had anti-sedition laws similar to the Smith Act, 20 had criminal syndicalism laws, 16 had criminal anarchy laws. Altogether 39 jurisdictions had one or more of these laws on the books. In addition 34 had red flag laws. These statutes are collected in Gellhorn, *The States and Subversion,* Appen. A and B (1952). See also Prendergast, *State Legislatures and Communism: The Current Scene,* 44 Am. Pol. Sci. Rev. 556 (1950); Note, *Conduct Proscribed as Promoting Violent Overthrow of the Government,* 61 Harv. L. Rev. 1215 (1948); and materials cited *infra.* For state laws which go beyond outlawing advocacy of force and violence for political objectives see the Note following the Internal Security Act, *infra.*

5. A number of municipalities have also adopted anti-sedition ordinances. One of the more extreme is that of Lafayette, Indiana (Ordinance No. 1015, adopted 1950):

"Whereas the City of Lafayette, Indiana is chargeable with the responsibility of preserving the individual rights guaranteed by the Constitution of the State of Indiana, the Constitution of the United States of America and our Declaration of Independence, now therefore

"BE IT ORDAINED BY THE COMMON COUNCIL OF THE CITY OF LAFAYETTE, INDIANA, AS FOLLOWS:

"SECTION 1. Hereafter it shall be unlawful for any person, group of persons or corporation, either singly or collectively to promote, advocate, support, encourage, advertise, disseminate or otherwise advance either by words, signs, gestures, writings, pictures or other form of communication the ideology known as Communism as herein defined.

"SECTION 2. Any person guilty of violation of any provision of this ordinance shall be punished by a fine of not more than $500.00 or by imprisonment for not more than 180 days or by both such fine and imprisonment."

## DENNIS ET AL. v. UNITED STATES

Supreme Court of the United States, 1951
341 U. S. 494, 95 L. Ed. 1137, 71 S. Ct. 857

MR. CHIEF JUSTICE VINSON announced the judgment of the Court and an opinion in which MR. JUSTICE REED, MR. JUSTICE BURTON and MR. JUSTICE MINTON join.

Petitioners were indicted in July, 1948, for violation of the conspiracy provisions of the Smith Act, 54 Stat. 671, 18 U. S. C. (1946 ed.) § 11, during the period of April, 1945, to July, 1948. The pre-trial motion to quash the indictment on the grounds, *inter alia,* that the statute was unconstitutional was denied, *United States v. Foster,* 80 F. Supp. 479, and the case was set for trial on January 17, 1949. A verdict of guilty as to all the petitioners was returned by the jury on October 14, 1949. The Court of Appeals affirmed the convictions. 183 F. 2d 201. We granted certiorari, 340 U. S. 863, limited to the following two questions: (1) Whether either § 2 or § 3 of the Smith Act, inherently or as construed and applied in the instant case, violates the First Amendment and other provisions of the Bill of Rights; (2) whether either § 2 or § 3 of the Act, inherently or as construed and applied in the instant case, violates the First and Fifth Amendments because of indefiniteness. . . .

The indictment charged the petitioners with wilfully and knowingly conspiring (1) to organize as the Communist Party of the United States of America a society, group and assembly of persons who teach and advocate the overthrow and destruction of the Government of the United States by force and violence, and (2) knowingly and wilfully to advocate and teach the duty and necessity of overthrowing and destroying the Government of the United States by force and violence. The indictment further alleged that § 2 of the Smith Act proscribes these acts and that any conspiracy to take such action is a violation of § 3 of the Act.

The trial of the case extended over nine months, six of which were devoted to the taking of evidence, resulting in a record of 16,000 pages. Our limited grant of the writ of certiorari has removed from our consideration any question as to the sufficiency of the evidence to support the jury's determination that petitioners are guilty of the offense charged. Whether on this record petitioners did in fact advocate the overthrow of the Government by force and violence is not before us, and we must base any discussion of this point upon the conclusions stated in the opinion of the Court of Appeals, which treated the issue in great detail. That court held that the record in this case amply supports the necessary finding of the jury that petitioners, the leaders of the Communist Party in this country, were unwilling to work within our framework of democracy, but intended to initiate a violent revolution whenever the propitious occasion appeared. Petitioners dispute the meaning to be drawn from the evidence, contending that the Marxist-Leninist doctrine they advocated taught that force and violence to achieve a Communist form of government in an existing democratic state would be necessary only because the ruling classes of that state would never permit the transformation to be accomplished peacefully, but would use force and violence to defeat any peaceful political and economic gain the Communists could achieve. But the Court of Appeals held that the record supports the following broad conclusions: By virtue of their control over the political apparatus of the

464

Communist Political Association,[1] petitioners were able to transform that organization into the Communist Party; that the policies of the Association were changed from peaceful cooperation with the United States and its economic and political structure to a policy which had existed before the United States and the Soviet Union were fighting a common enemy, namely, a policy which worked for the overthrow of the Government by force and violence; that the Communist Party is a highly disciplined organization, adept at infiltration into strategic positions, use of aliases, and double-meaning language; that the Party is rigidly controlled; that Communists, unlike other political parties, tolerate no dissension from the policy laid down by the guiding forces, but that the approved program is slavishly followed by the members of the Party; that the literature of the Party and the statements and activities of its leaders, petitioners here, advocate, and the general goal of the Party was, during the period in question, to achieve a successful overthrow of the existing order by force and violence.

## I.

It will be helpful in clarifying the issues to treat next the contention that the trial judge improperly interpreted the statute by charging that the statute required an unlawful intent before the jury could convict. More specifically, he charged that the jury could not find the petitioners guilty under the indictment unless they found that petitioners had the intent "to overthrow . . . the Government of the United States by force and violence as speedily as circumstances would permit." . . .

[The Chief Justice held that "the structure and purpose of the statute demand the inclusion of intent as an element of the crime."]

## II.

The obvious purpose of the statute is to protect existing Government, not from change by peaceable, lawful and constitutional means, but from change by violence, revolution and terrorism. That it is within the *power* of the Congress to protect the Government of the United States from armed rebellion is a proposition which requires little discussion. Whatever theoretical merit there may be to the argument that there is a "right" to rebellion

---

[1] Following the dissolution of the Communist International in 1943, the Communist Party of the United States dissolved and was reconstituted as the Communist Political Association. The program of this Association was one of cooperation between labor and management, and, in general, one designed to achieve national unity and peace and prosperity in the post-war period.

[Emerson]—30

against dictatorial governments is without force where the existing structure of the government provides for peaceful and orderly change. We reject any principle of governmental helplessness in the face of preparation for revolution, which principle, carried to its logical conclusion, must lead to anarchy. No one could conceive that it is not within the power of Congress to prohibit acts intended to overthrow the Government by force and violence. The question with which we are concerned here is not whether Congress has such *power*, but whether the *means* which it has employed conflict with the First and Fifth Amendments to the Constitution.

One of the bases for the contention that the means which Congress has employed are invalid takes the form of an attack on the face of the statute on the grounds that by its terms it prohibits academic discussion of the merits of Marxism-Leninism, that it stifles ideas and is contrary to all concepts of a free speech and a free press. Although we do not agree that the language itself has that significance, we must bear in mind that it is the duty of the federal courts to interpret federal legislation in a manner not inconsistent with the demands of the Constitution. *American Communications Assn.* v. *Douds,* 339 U. S. 382, 407 (1950). . . .

The very language of the Smith Act negates the interpretation which petitioners would have us impose on that Act. It is directed at advocacy, not discussion. Thus, the trial judge properly charged the jury that they could not convict if they found that petitioners did "no more than pursue peaceful studies and discussions or teachings and advocacy in the realm of ideas." He further charged that it was not unlawful "to conduct in an American college and university a course explaining the philosophical theories set forth in the books which have been placed in evidence." Such a charge is in strict accord with the statutory language, and illustrates the meaning to be placed on those words. Congress did not intend to eradicate the free discussion of political theories, to destroy the traditional rights of Americans to discuss and evaluate ideas without fear of governmental sanction. Rather Congress was concerned with the very kind of activity in which the evidence showed these petitioners engaged.

### III.

But although the statute is not directed at the hypothetical cases which petitioners have conjured, its application in this case has resulted in convictions for the teaching and advocacy of the overthrow of the Government by force and violence, which, even though coupled with the intent to accomplish that overthrow, contains an element of speech. For this reason, we must pay

[Emerson]

special heed to the demands of the First Amendment marking out the boundaries of speech.

We pointed out in *Douds, supra,* that the basis of the First Amendment is the hypothesis that speech can rebut speech, propaganda will answer propaganda, free debate of ideas will result in the wisest governmental policies. It is for this reason that this Court has recognized the inherent value of free discourse. An analysis of the leading cases in this Court which have involved direct limitations on speech, however, will demonstrate that both the majority of the Court and the dissenters in particular cases have recognized that this is not an unlimited, unqualified right, but that the societal value of speech must, on occasion, be subordinated to other values and considerations. . . .

[The Chief Justice here discusses the Supreme Court decisions in the Espionage Act cases of World War I, noted in Section C, *supra.*]

The rule we deduce from these cases is that where an offense is specified by a statute in nonspeech or nonpress terms, a conviction relying upon speech or press as evidence of violation may be sustained only when the speech or publication created a "clear and present danger" of attempting or accomplishing the prohibited crime, *e.g.,* interference with enlistment. The dissents, we repeat, in emphasizing the value of speech, were addressed to the argument of the sufficiency of the evidence.

The next important case before the Court in which free speech was the crux of the conflict was *Gitlow* v. *New York,* 268 U. S. 652 (1925). There New York had made it a crime to advocate "the necessity or propriety of overthrowing . . . organized government by force. . . ." The evidence of violation of the statute was that the defendant had published a Manifesto attacking the Government and capitalism. The convictions were sustained, Justices Holmes and Brandeis dissenting. The majority refused to apply the "clear and present danger" test to the specific utterance. Its reasoning was as follows: The "clear and present danger" test was applied to the utterance itself in *Schenck* because the question was merely one of sufficiency of evidence under an admittedly constitutional statute. *Gitlow,* however, presented a different question. There a legislature had found that a certain kind of speech was, itself, harmful and unlawful. The constitutionality of such a state statute had to be adjudged by this Court just as it determined the constitutionality of any state statute, namely, whether the statute was "reasonable." Since it was entirely reasonable for a state to attempt to protect itself from violent overthrow, the statute was perforce reasonable. The only question remaining in the case became whether there was evidence to support the conviction, a question which gave the majority no difficulty. Justices Holmes and Brandeis refused to accept this approach, but insisted that wherever speech was the evidence of the violation, it was necessary to show that the speech created the "clear and present danger" of the substantive evil which the legislature had the right to prevent. Justices Holmes and Brandeis, then, made no distinction between a federal statute which made certain acts unlawful, the evidence to support the conviction being speech, and a statute which made speech itself the crime. This approach was emphasized in *Whitney* v. *California,* 274 U. S. 357 (1927), where the Court was confronted with a conviction under the California Criminal Syndicalist statute. The Court sustained the conviction, Justices Brandeis and Holmes concurring in the result. In their concurrence they repeated that even though the legislature had designated certain speech as criminal, this could not prevent the defendant from showing that there was no danger that the substantive evil would be brought about.

Although no case subsequent to *Whitney* and *Gitlow* has expressly overruled the majority opinions in those cases, there is little doubt that subsequent opinions have inclined toward the Holmes-Brandeis rationale.[5] And in *American Communications Assn.* v. *Douds, supra,* we were called upon to decide the validity of § 9 (h) of the Labor-Management Relations Act of 1947. That section required officials of unions which desired to avail themselves of the facilities of the National Labor Relations Board to take oaths that they did not belong to the Communist Party and that they did not believe in the overthrow of the Government by force and violence. We pointed out that Congress did not intend to punish belief, but rather intended to regulate the conduct of union affairs. We therefore held that any indirect sanction on speech which might arise from the oath requirement did not present a proper case for the "clear and present danger" test, for the regulation was aimed at conduct rather than speech. In discussing the proper measure of evaluation of this kind of legislation, we suggested that the Holmes-Brandeis philosophy insisted that where there was a direct restriction upon speech, a

---

[5] *Contempt of Court: Craig v. Harney,* 331 U. S. 367, 373 (1947); *Pennekamp v. Florida,* 328 U. S. 331, 333–336 (1946); *Bridges v. California,* 314 U. S. 252, 260–263 (1941).

*Validity of state statute: Thomas v. Collins,* 323 U. S. 516, 530 (1945); *Taylor v. Mississippi,* 319 U. S. 583, 589–590 (1943); *Thornhill v. Alabama,* 310 U. S. 88, 104–106 (1940).

*Validity of local ordinance or regulation: West Virginia Board of Education v. Barnette,* 319 U. S. 624, 639 (1943); *Carlson v. California,* 310 U. S. 106, 113 (1940).

*Common law offense: Cantwell v. Connecticut,* 310 U. S. 296, 308, 311 (1940).

"clear and present danger" that the substantive evil would be caused was necessary before the statute in question could be constitutionally applied. And we stated, "[The First] Amendment requires that one be permitted to believe what he will. It requires that one be permitted to advocate what he will unless there is a clear and present danger that a substantial public evil will result therefrom." 339 U. S. at 412. But we further suggested that neither Justice Holmes nor Justice Brandeis ever envisioned that a shorthand phrase should be crystallized into a rigid rule to be applied inflexibly without regard to the circumstances of each case. Speech is not an absolute, above and beyond control by the legislature when its judgment, subject to review here, is that certain kinds of speech are so undesirable as to warrant criminal sanction. Nothing is more certain in modern society than the principle that there are no absolutes, that a name, a phrase, a standard has meaning only when associated with the considerations which gave birth to the nomenclature. See *American Communications Assn.* v. *Douds,* 339 U. S. at 397. To those who would paralyze our Government in the face of impending threat by encasing it in a semantic straitjacket we must reply that all concepts are relative.

In this case we are squarely presented with the application of the "clear and present danger" test, and must decide what that phrase imports. We first note that many of the cases in which this Court has reversed convictions by use of this or similar tests have been based on the fact that the interest which the State was attempting to protect was itself too insubstantial to warrant restriction of speech. In this category we may put such cases as *Schneider* v. *State,* 308 U. S. 147 (1939); *Cantwell* v. *Connecticut,* 310 U. S. 296 (1940); *Martin* v. *Struthers,* 319 U. S. 141 (1943); *West Virginia State Board of Education* v. *Barnette,* 319 U. S. 624 (1943); *Thomas* v. *Collins,* 323 U. S. 516 (1945); *Marsh* v. *Alabama,* 326 U. S. 501 (1946); but cf. *Prince* v. *Massachusetts,* 321 U. S. 158 (1944); *Cox* v. *New Hampshire,* 312 U. S. 569 (1941). Overthrow of the Government by force and violence is certainly a substantial enough interest for the Government to limit speech. Indeed, this is the ultimate value of any society, for if a society cannot protect its very structure, from armed internal attack, it must follow that no subordinate value can be protected. If, then, this interest may be protected, the literal problem which is presented is what has been meant by the use of the phrase "clear and present danger" of the utterances bringing about the evil within the power of Congress to punish.

Obviously, the words cannot mean that before the Government may act, it must wait until the *putsch* is about to be executed, the plans have been laid and the signal is awaited. If Government is aware that a group aiming at its overthrow is attempting to indoctrinate its members and to commit them to a course whereby they will strike when the leaders feel the circumstances permit, action by the Government is required. The argument that there is no need for Government to concern itself, for Government is strong, it possesses ample powers to put down a rebellion, it may defeat the revolution with ease needs no answer. For that is not the question. Certainly an attempt to overthrow the Government by force, even though doomed from the outset because of inadequate numbers or power of the revolutionists, is a sufficient evil for Congress to prevent. The damage which such attempts create both physically and politically to a nation makes it impossible to measure the validity in terms of the probability of success, or the immediacy of a successful attempt. In the instant case the trial judge charged the jury that they could not convict unless they found the petitioners intended to overthrow the Government "as speedily as circumstances would permit." This does not mean, and could not properly mean, that they would not strike until there was certainty of success. What was meant was that the revolutionists would strike when they thought the time was ripe. We must therefore reject the contention that success or probability of success is the criterion.

The situation with which Justices Holmes and Brandeis were concerned in *Gitlow* was a comparatively isolated event, bearing little relation in their minds to any substantial threat to the safety of the community. Such also is true of cases like *Fiske* v. *Kansas*, 274 U. S. 380 (1927), and *DeJonge* v. *Oregon*, 299 U. S. 353 (1937) ; but cf. *Lazar* v. *Pennsylvania*, 286 U. S. 532 (1932). They were not confronted with any situation comparable to the instant one—the development of an apparatus designed and dedicated to the overthrow of the Government, in the context of world crisis after crisis.

Chief Judge Learned Hand, writing for the majority below, interpreted the phrase as follows: "In each case [courts] must ask whether the gravity of the 'evil,' discounted by its improbability, justifies such invasion of free speech as is necessary to avoid the danger." 183 F. 2d at 212. We adopt this statement of the rule. As articulated by Chief Judge Hand, it is as succinct and inclusive as any other we might devise at this time. It takes into consideration those factors which we deem relevant, and relates their significances. More we cannot expect from words.

Likewise, we are in accord with the court below, which affirmed the trial court's finding that the requisite danger existed. The mere fact that from the period 1945 to 1948 petitioners' activities did not result in an attempt to overthrow the Government by force and violence is of course no answer to the fact that there was a group that was ready to make the attempt. The formation by petitioners of such a highly organized conspiracy, with rigidly disciplined members subject to call when the leaders, these petitioners, felt that the time had come for action, coupled with the inflammable nature of world conditions, similar uprisings in other countries, and the touch-and-go nature of our relations with countries with whom petitioners were in the very least ideologically attuned, convince us that their convictions were justified on this score. And this analysis disposes of the contention that a conspiracy to advocate, as distinguished from the advocacy itself, cannot be constitutionally restrained, because it comprises only the preparation. It is the existence of the conspiracy which creates the danger. Cf. *Pinkerton* v. *United States,* 328 U. S. 640 (1946); *Goldman* v. *United States,* 245 U. S. 474 (1918); *United States* v. *Rabinowich,* 238 U. S. 78 (1915). If the ingredients of the reaction are present, we cannot bind the Government to wait until the catalyst is added.

IV.

Although we have concluded that the finding that there was a sufficient danger to warrant the application of the statute was justified on the merits, there remains the problem of whether the trial judge's treatment of the issue was correct. He charged the jury, in relevant part, as follows:

"In further construction and interpretation of the statute I charge you that it is not the abstract doctrine of overthrowing or destroying organized government by unlawful means which is denounced by this law, but the teaching and advocacy of action for the accomplishment of that purpose, by language reasonably and ordinarily calculated to incite persons to such action. Accordingly, you cannot find the defendants or any of them guilty of the crime charged unless you are satisfied beyond a reasonable doubt that they conspired to organize a society, group and assembly of persons who teach and advocate the overthrow or destruction of the Government of the United States by force and violence and to advocate and teach the duty and necessity of overthrowing or destroying the Government of the United States by force and violence, with the intent that such teaching and advocacy be of a rule or principle of action and by language reasonably and ordinarily calculated to incite persons to such action, all with the intent to cause the overthrow or destruction of the Government of the United States by force and violence as speedily as circumstances would permit. . . .

"If you are satisfied that the evidence establishes beyond a reasonable doubt that the defendants, or any of them, are guilty of a violation of the statute, as I have interpreted it to you, I find as a matter of law that there is sufficient danger of a substantive evil that the Congress has a right to prevent to justify the application of the statute under the First Amendment of the Constitution.

"This is matter of law about which you have no concern. It is a finding on a matter of law which I deem essential to support my ruling that the case should be submitted to you to pass upon the guilt or innocence of the defendants. . . ."

It is thus clear that he reserved the question of the existence of the danger for his own determination, and the question becomes whether the issue is of such a nature that it should have been submitted to the jury.

The first paragraph of the quoted instructions calls for the jury to find the facts essential to establish the substantive crime, violation of §§ 2 (a) (1) and 2 (a) (3) of the Smith Act, involved in the conspiracy charge. There can be no doubt that if the jury found those facts against the petitioners violation of the Act would be established. The argument that the action of the trial court is erroneous, in declaring as a matter of law that such violation shows sufficient danger to justify the punishment despite the First Amendment, rests on the theory that a jury must decide a question of the application of the First Amendment. We do not agree.

When facts are found that establish the violation of a statute the protection against conviction afforded by the First Amendment is a matter of law. The doctrine that there must be a clear and present danger of a substantive evil that Congress has a right to prevent is a judicial rule to be applied as a matter of law by the courts. The guilt is established by proof of facts. Whether the First Amendment protects the activity which constitutes the violation of the statute must depend upon a judicial determination of the scope of the First Amendment applied to the circumstances of the case. . . .

## V.

There remains to be discussed the question of vagueness—whether the statute as we have interpreted it is too vague, not sufficiently advising those who would speak of the limitations upon their activity. It is urged that such vagueness contravenes the First and Fifth Amendments. This argument is particularly

472

nonpersuasive when presented by petitioners, who, the jury found, intended to overthrow the Government as speedily as circumstances would permit. See *Abrams* v. *United States,* 250 U. S. 616, 627–629 (1919) (dissenting opinion) ; *Whitney* v. *California,* 274 U. S. 357, 373 (1927) (concurring opinion) ; *Taylor* v. *Mississippi,* 319 U. S. 583, 589 (1943). A claim of guilelessness ill becomes those with evil intent. *Williams* v. *United States,* 341 U. S. 97, 101–102 (1951) ; *Jordan* v. *De George,* 341 U. S. 223, 230–232 (1951) ; *American Communications Assn.* v. *Douds,* 339 U. S. at 413; *Screws* v. *United States,* 325 U. S. 91, 101 (1945).

We agree that the standard as defined is not a neat, mathematical formulary. Like all verbalizations it is subject to criticism on the score of indefiniteness. But petitioners themselves contend that the verbalization "clear and present danger" is the proper standard. We see no difference from the standpoint of vagueness, whether the standard of "clear and present danger" is one contained *in haec verba* within the statute, or whether it is the judicial measure of constitutional applicability. We have shown the indeterminate standard the phrase necessarily connotes. We do not think we have rendered that standard any more indefinite by our attempt to sum up the factors which are included within its scope. We think it well serves to indicate to those who would advocate constitutionally prohibited conduct that there is a line beyond which they may not go—a line which they, in full knowledge of what they intend and the circumstances in which their activity takes place, will well appreciate and understand. *Williams, supra,* at 101–102; *Jordan, supra,* at 230–232; *United States* v. *Petrillo,* 332 U. S. 1, 7 (1948) ; *United States* v. *Wurzback,* 280 U. S. 396, 399 (1930) ; *Nash* v. *United States,* 229 U. S. 373, 376–377 (1913). Where there is doubt as to the intent of the defendants, the nature of their activities, or their power to bring about the evil, this Court will review the convictions with the scrupulous care demanded by our Constitution. But we are not convinced that because there may be borderline cases at some time in the future, these convictions should be reversed because of the argument that these petitioners could not know that their activities were constitutionally proscribed by the statute.

We have not discussed many of the questions which could be extracted from the record, although they were treated in detail by the court below. Our limited grant of the writ of certiorari has withdrawn from our consideration at this date those questions, which include, *inter alia,* sufficiency of the evidence, composition of jury, and conduct of the trial.

We hold that §§ 2 (a) (1), 2 (a) (3) and 3 of the Smith Act do not inherently, or as construed or applied in the instant case, violate the First Amendment and other provisions of the Bill of Rights, or the First and Fifth Amendments because of indefiniteness. Petitioners intended to overthrow the Government of the United States as speedily as the circumstances would permit. Their conspiracy to organize the Communist Party and to teach and advocate the overthrow of the Government of the United States by force and violence created a "clear and present danger" of an attempt to overthrow the Government by force and violence. They were properly and constitutionally convicted for violation of the Smith Act. The judgments of conviction are

*Affirmed.*

MR. JUSTICE CLARK took no part in the consideration or decision of this case.

MR. JUSTICE FRANKFURTER, concurring in affirmance of the judgment. . . .

Few questions of comparable import have come before this Court in recent years. The appellants maintain that they have a right to advocate a political theory, so long, at least, as their advocacy does not create an immediate danger of obvious magnitude to the very existence of our present scheme of society. On the other hand, the Government asserts the right to safeguard the security of the Nation by such a measure as the Smith Act. Our judgment is thus solicited on a conflict of interests of the utmost concern to the well-being of the country. This conflict of interests cannot be resolved by a dogmatic preference for one or the other, nor by a sonorous formula which is in fact only a euphemistic disguise for an unresolved conflict. If adjudication is to be a rational process we cannot escape a candid examination of the conflicting claims with full recognition that both are supported by weighty title-deeds. . . .

In all fairness, the argument cannot be met by reinterpreting the Court's frequent use of "clear" and "present" to mean an entertainable "probability." In giving this meaning to the phrase "clear and present danger," the Court of Appeals was fastidiously confining the rhetoric of opinions to the exact scope of what was decided by them. We have greater responsibility for having given constitutional support, over repeated protests, to uncritical libertarian generalities. . . .

[Mr. Justice Frankfurter then reviewed six types of cases in which the Court has "recognized and resolved conflicts between speech and competing interests."]

I must leave to others the ungrateful task of trying to reconcile all these decisions. . . . Viewed as a whole, however, the decisions express an attitude toward the judicial function and a standard of values which for me are decisive of the case before us.

*First.*—Free-speech cases are not an exception to the principle that we are not legislators, that direct policy-making is not our province. How best to reconcile competing interests is the business of legislatures, and the balance they strike is a judgment not to be displaced by ours, but to be respected unless outside the pale of fair judgment. . . .

*Second.*—A survey of the relevant decisions indicates that the results which we have reached are on the whole those that would ensue from careful weighing of conflicting interests. The complex issues presented by regulation of speech in public places, by picketing, and by legislation prohibiting advocacy of crime have been resolved by scrutiny of many factors besides the imminence and gravity of the evil threatened. The matter has been well summarized by a reflective student of the Court's work. "The truth is that the clear-and-present danger test is an oversimplified judgment unless it takes account also of a number of other factors: the relative seriousness of the danger in comparison with the value of the occasion for speech or political activity; the availability of more moderate controls than those which the state has imposed; and perhaps the specific intent with which the speech or activity is launched. No matter how rapidly we utter the phrase 'clear and present danger,' or how closely we hyphenate the words, they are not a substitute for the weighing of values. They tend to convey a delusion of certitude when what is most certain is the complexity of the strands in the web of freedoms which the judge must disentangle." Freund, On Understanding the Supreme Court, 27–28. . . .

*Third.*—Not every type of speech occupies the same position on the scale of values. There is no substantial public interest in permitting certain kinds of utterances: "the lewd and obscene, the profane, the libelous, and the insulting or 'fighting' words—those which by their very utterance inflict injury or tend to incite an immediate breach of the peace." *Chaplinsky* v. *New Hampshire*, 315 U. S. 568, 572. We have frequently indicated that interest in protecting speech depends on the circumstances of the occasion. See *Niemotko* v. *Maryland,* 340 U. S. at 275–283. It is pertinent to the decision before us to consider where on the scale of values we have in the past placed the type of speech now claiming constitutional immunity.

The defendants have been convicted of conspiring to organize a party of persons who advocate the overthrow of the Government by force and violence. The jury has found that the object of the conspiracy is advocacy as "a rule or principle of action," "by language reasonably and ordinarily calculated to incite persons to such action," and with the intent to cause the overthrow "as speedily as circumstances would permit."

On any scale of values which we have hitherto recognized, speech of this sort ranks low. . . .

These general considerations underlie decision of the case before us.

On the one hand is the interest in security. The Communist Party was not designed by these defendants as an ordinary political party. For the circumstances of its organization, its aims and methods, and the relation of the defendants to its organization and aims we are concluded by the jury's verdict. The jury found that the Party rejects the basic premise of our political system—that change is to be brought about by nonviolent constitutional process. The jury found that the Party advocates the theory that there is a duty and necessity to overthrow the Government by force and violence. It found that the Party entertains and promotes this view, not as a prophetic insight or as a bit of unworldly speculation, but as a program for winning adherents and as a policy to be translated into action.

In finding that the defendants violated the statute, we may not treat as established fact that the Communist Party in this country is of significant size, well-organized, well-disciplined, conditioned to embark on unlawful activity when given the command. But in determining whether application of the statute to the defendants is within the constitutional powers of Congress, we are not limited to the facts found by the jury. We must view such a question in the light of whatever is relevant to a legislative judgment. We may take judicial notice that the Communist doctrines which these defendants have conspired to advocate are in the ascendency in powerful nations who cannot be acquitted of unfriendliness to the institutions of this country. We may take account of evidence brought forward at this trial and elsewhere, much of which has long been common knowledge. In sum, it would amply justify a legislature in concluding that recruitment of additional members for the Party would create a substantial danger to national security.

case that the membership was organized in small units, linked by an intricate chain of command, and protected by elaborate precautions designed to prevent disclosure of individual identity. There are no reliable data tracing acts of sabotage or espionage

In 1947, it has been reliably reported, at least 60,000 members were enrolled in the Party.[11] Evidence was introduced in this

---

[11] See the testimony of the Director of the Federal Bureau of Investigation. Hearings before the House Committee on Un-American Activities, on H. R. 1884 and H. R. 2122, 80th Cong., 1st Sess., Part 2, p. 37.

directly to these defendants. But a Canadian Royal Commission appointed in 1946 to investigate espionage reported that it was "overwhelmingly established" that "the Communist movement was the principal base within which the espionage network was recruited."[12] The most notorious spy in recent history was led into the service of the Soviet Union through Communist indoctrination.[13] Evidence supports the conclusion that members of the Party seek and occupy positions of importance in political and labor organizations.[14] Congress was not barred by the Constitution from believing that indifference to such experience would be an exercise not of freedom but of irresponsibility.

On the other hand is the interest in free speech. The right to exert all governmental powers in aid of maintaining our institutions and resisting their physical overthrow does not include intolerance of opinions and speech that cannot do harm although opposed and perhaps alien to dominant, traditional opinion. The treatment of its minorities, especially their legal position, is among the most searching tests of the level of civilization attained by a society. It is better for those who have almost unlimited power of government in their hands to err on the side of freedom. We have enjoyed so much freedom for so long that we are perhaps in danger of forgetting how much blood it cost to establish the Bill of Rights.

Of course no government can recognize a "right" of revolution, or a "right" to incite revolution if the incitement has no other purpose or effect. But speech is seldom restricted to a single purpose, and its effects may be manifold. A public interest is

[12] Report of the Royal Commission to Investigate Communication of Secret and Confidential Information to Agents of a Foreign Power, June 27, 1946, p. 44. There appears to be little reliable evidence demonstrating directly that the Communist Party in this country has recruited persons willing to engage in espionage or other unlawful activity on behalf of the Soviet Union. The defection of a Soviet diplomatic employee, however, led to a careful investigation of an espionage network in Canada, and has disclosed the effectiveness of the Canadian Communist Party in conditioning its members to disclose to Soviet agents vital information of a secret character. According to the Report of the Royal Commission investigating the network, conspiratorial characteristics of the Party similar to those shown in the evidence now before us were instrumental in developing the necessary motivation to cooperate in the espionage. See pp. 43–83 of the Report.

[13] The Communist background of Dr. Klaus Fuchs was brought out in the proceedings against him. See The [London] Times, Mar. 2, 1950, p. 2, col. 6.

[14] See American Communications Assn. v. Douds, 339 U. S. 382. Former Senator Robert M. La Follette, Jr., has reported his experience with infiltration of Communist sympathizers into congressional committee staffs. Collier's, Feb. 8, 1947, p. 22.

not wanting in granting freedom to speak their minds even to those who advocate the overthrow of the Government by force. For, as the evidence in this case abundantly illustrates, coupled with such advocacy is criticism of defects in our society. Criticism is the spur to reform; and Burke's admonition that a healthy society must reform in order to conserve has not lost its force. Astute observers have remarked that one of the characteristics of the American Republic is indifference to fundamental criticism. Bryce, The American Commonwealth, c. 84. It is a commonplace that there may be a grain of truth in the most uncouth doctrine, however false and repellent the balance may be. Suppressing advocates of overthrow inevitably will also silence critics who do not advocate overthrow but fear that their criticism may be so construed. No matter how clear we may be that the defendants now before us are preparing to overthrow the Government at the propitious moment, it is self-delusion to think that we can punish them for their advocacy without adding to the risks run by loyal citizens who honestly believe in some of the reforms these defendants advance. It is a sobering fact that in sustaining the conviction before us we can hardly escape restriction on the interchange of ideas.

We must not overlook the value of that interchange. Freedom of expression is the well-spring of our civilization—the civilization we seek to maintain and further by recognizing the right of Congress to put some limitation upon expression. Such are the paradoxes of life. For social development of trial and error, the fullest possible opportunity for the free play of the human mind is an indispensable prerequisite. The history of civilization is in considerable measure the displacement of error which once held sway as official truth by beliefs which in turn have yielded to other truths. Therefore the liberty of man to search for truth ought not to be fettered, no matter what orthodoxies he may challenge. Liberty of thought soon shrivels without freedom of expression. Nor can truth be pursued in an atmosphere hostile to the endeavor or under dangers which are hazarded only by heroes. . . .

It is not for us to decide how we would adjust the clash of interests which this case presents were the primary responsibility for reconciling it ours. Congress has determined that the danger created by advocacy of overthrow justifies the ensuing restriction on freedom of speech. The determination was made after due deliberation, and the seriousness of the congressional purpose is attested by the volume of legislation passed to effectuate the same ends.

Can we then say that the judgment Congress exercised was

denied it by the Constitution? Can we establish a constitutional doctrine which forbids the elected representatives of the people to make this choice? Can we hold that the First Amendment deprives Congress of what it deemed necessary for the Government's protection?

To make validity of legislation depend on judicial reading of events still in the womb of time—a forecast, that is, of the outcome of forces at best appreciated only with knowledge of the topmost secrets of nations—is to charge the judiciary with duties beyond its equipment. We do not expect courts to pronounce historic verdicts on bygone events. Even historians have conflicting views to this day on the origin and conduct of the French Revolution. . . . It is as absurd to be confident that we can measure the present clash of forces and their outcome as to ask us to read history still enveloped in clouds of controversy. . . .

The wisdom of the assumptions underlying the legislation and prosecution is another matter. In finding that Congress has acted within its power, a judge does not remotely imply that he favors the implications that lie beneath the legal issues. Considerations there enter which go beyond the criteria that are binding upon judges within the narrow confines of their legitimate authority. The legislation we are here considering is but a truncated aspect of a deeper issue. . . .

In the context of this deeper struggle, another voice has indicated the limitations of what we decide today. No one is better equipped than George F. Kennan to speak on the meaning of the menace of Communism and the spirit in which we should meet it.

"If our handling of the problem of Communist influence in our midst is not carefully moderated—if we permit it, that is, to become an emotional preoccupation and to blind us to the more important positive tasks before us—we can do a damage to our national purpose beyond comparison greater than anything that threatens us today from the Communist side. The American Communist party is today, by and large, an external danger. It represents a tiny minority in our country; it has no real contact with the feelings of the mass of our people; and its position as the agency of a hostile foreign power is clearly recognized by the overwhelming mass of our citizens.

"But the subjective emotional stresses and temptations to which we are exposed in our attempt to deal with this domestic problem are not an external danger: they represent a danger within ourselves—a danger that something may occur in our own minds and souls which will make us no longer like the persons by whose efforts this republic was

founded and held together, but rather like the representatives of that very power we are trying to combat: intolerant, secretive, suspicious, cruel and terrified of internal dissension because we have lost our own belief in ourselves and in the power of our ideals. The worst thing that our Communists could do to us, and the thing we have most to fear from their activities, is that we should become like them."
. . . George F. Kennan, Where Do You Stand on Communism? New York Times Magazine, May 27, 1951, pp. 7, 53, 55.

Civil liberties draw at best only limited strength from legal guaranties. Preoccupation by our people with the constitutionality, instead of with the wisdom of legislation or of executive action, is preoccupation with a false value. Even those who would most freely use the judicial brake on the democratic process by invalidating legislation that goes deeply against their grain, acknowledge, at least by paying lip service, that constitutionality does not exact a sense of proportion or the sanity of humor or an absence of fear. Focusing attention on constitutionality tends to make constitutionality synonymous with wisdom. When legislation touches freedom of thought and freedom of speech, such a tendency is a formidable enemy of the free spirit. Much that should be rejected as illiberal, because repressive and envenoming, may well be not unconstitutional. The ultimate reliance for the deepest needs of civilization must be found outside their vindication in court of law; apart from all else, judges, howsoever they may seek to discipline themselves against it, unconsciously are too apt to be moved by the deep undercurrents of public feeling. A persistent, positive translation of the liberating faith into the feelings and thoughts and actions of men and women is the real protection against attempts to strait-jacket the human mind. Such temptations will have their way, if fear and hatred are not exorcised. The mark of a truly civilized man is confidence in the strength and security derived from the inquiring mind. We may be grateful for such honest comforts as it supports, but we must be unafraid of its uncertitudes. Without open minds there can be no open society. And if society be not open the spirit of man is mutilated and becomes enslaved.

[The Appendix to Mr. Justice Frankfurter's opinion, analyzing the cases requiring an imminent danger, is omitted.]

MR. JUSTICE JACKSON, concurring. . . .
The "clear and present danger" test was an innovation by Mr. Justice Holmes in the *Schenck* case, reiterated and refined by him and Mr. Justice Brandeis in later cases, all arising before

the era of World War II revealed the subtlety and efficacy of modernized revolutionary techniques used by totalitarian parties. In these cases, they were faced with convictions under so-called criminal syndicalism statutes aimed at anarchists but which, loosely construed, had been applied to punish socialism, pacifism, and left-wing ideologies, the charges often resting on far-fetched inferences which, if true, would establish only technical or trivial violations. They proposed "clear and present danger" as a test for the sufficiency of evidence in particular cases.

I would save it, unmodified, for application as a "rule of reason" in the kind of case for which it was devised. When the issue is criminality of a hot-headed speech on a street corner, or circulation of a few incendiary pamphlets, or parading by some zealots behind a red flag, or refusal by a handful of school children to salute our flag, it is not beyond the capacity of judicial process to gather, comprehend, and weigh the necessary materials for decision whether it is a clear and present danger of substantive evil or a harmless letting off of steam. It is not a prophecy, for the danger in such cases has matured by the time of trial or it was never present. . . .

I think reason is lacking for applying that test to this case.

If we must decide that this Act and its application are constitutional only if we are convinced that petitioner's conduct creates a "clear and present danger" of violent overthrow, we must appraise imponderables, including international and national phenomena which baffle the best informed foreign offices and our most experienced politicians. We would have to foresee and predict the effectiveness of Communist propaganda, opportunities for infiltration, whether, and when, a time will come that they consider propitious for action, and whether and how fast our existing government will deteriorate. And we would have to speculate as to whether an approaching Communist *coup* would not be anticipated by a nationalistic fascist movement. No doctrine can be sound whose application requires us to make a prophecy of that sort in the guise of a legal decision. The judicial process simply is not adequate to a trial of such far-flung issues. The answers given would reflect our own political predilections and nothing more. . . .

What really is under review here is a conviction of conspiracy, after a trial for conspiracy, on an indictment charging conspiracy, brought under a statute outlawing conspiracy. . . .

The Constitution does not make conspiracy a civil right. The Court has never before done so, and I think it should not do so now. Conspiracies of labor unions, trade associations, and news agencies have been condemned, although accomplished, evidenced

[Emerson]—31

and carried out, like the conspiracy here, chiefly by letter-writing, meetings, speeches and organization. Indeed, this Court seems. particularly in cases where the conspiracy has economic ends, to be applying its doctrines with increasing severity. While I consider criminal conspiracy a dragnet device capable of perversion into an instrument of injustice in the hands of a partisan or complacent judiciary, it has an established place in our system of law, and no reason appears for applying it only to concerted action claimed to disturb interstate commerce and withholding it from those claimed to undermine our whole Government.[13] . . .

I do not suggest that Congress could punish conspiracy to advocate something, the doing of which it may not punish. Advocacy or exposition of the doctrine of communal property ownership, or any political philosophy unassociated with advocacy of its imposition by force or seizure of government by unlawful means could not be reached through conspiracy prosecution. But it is not forbidden to put down force or violence, it is not forbidden to punish its teaching or advocacy, and the end being punishable, there is no doubt of the power to punish conspiracy for the purpose. . . .

When our constitutional provisions were written, the chief forces recognized as antagonists in the struggle between authority and liberty were the Government on the one hand and the individual citizen on the other. It was thought that if the state could be kept in its place the individual could take care of himself.

In more recent times these problems have been complicated by the intervention between the state and the citizen of permanently organized, well-financed, semisecret and highly disciplined political organizations. Totalitarian groups here and abroad perfected the technique of creating private paramilitary organizations to coerce both the public government and its citizens. These organizations assert as against our Government all of the constitutional rights and immunities of individuals and at the same time exercise over their followers much of the authority which they deny to the Government. The Communist Party realistically is a state within a state, an authoritarian dictatorship within a republic. It demands these freedoms, not for its members, but for the organized party. It denies to its own members at the same time the freedom to dissent, to debate, to deviate from the party line, and enforces its authoritarian rule by crude purges, if nothing more violent.

The law of conspiracy has been the chief means at the Gov-

---

[13] These dangers were more fully set out in *Krulewitch v. United States*, 336 U. S. 440, 445.

[Emerson]

ernment's disposal to deal with the growing problems created by such organizations. I happen to think it is an awkward and inept remedy, but I find no constitutional authority for taking this weapon from the Government. There is no constitutional right to "gang up" on the Government.

While I think there was power in Congress to enact this statute and that, as applied in this case, it cannot be held unconstitutional, I add that I have little faith in the long-range effectiveness of this conviction to stop the rise of the Communist movement. Communism will not go to jail with these Communists. No decision by this Court can forestall revolution whenever the existing government fails to command the respect and loyalty of the people and sufficient distress and discontent is allowed to grow up among the masses. Many failures by fallen governments attest that no government can long prevent revolution by outlawry. Corruption, ineptitude, inflation, oppressive taxation, militarization, injustice, and loss of leadership capable of intellectual initiative in domestic or foreign affairs are allies on which the Communists count to bring opportunity knocking to their door. Sometimes I think they may be mistaken. But the Communists are not building just for today—the rest of us might profit by their example.

MR. JUSTICE BLACK, dissenting.

Here again, as in *Breard* v. *Alexandria* [341 U. S. 622], decided this day, my basic disagreement with the Court is not as to how we should explain or reconcile what was said in prior decisions but springs from a fundamental difference in constitutional approach. Consequently, it would serve no useful purpose to state my position at length.

At the outset I want to emphasize what the crime involved in this case is, and what it is not. These petitioners were not charged with an attempt to overthrow the Government. They were not charged with overt acts of any kind designed to overthrow the Government. They were not even charged with saying anything or with writing anything designed to overthrow the Government. The charge was that they agreed to assemble and to talk and to publish certain ideas at a later date: The indictment is that they conspired to organize the Communist Party and to use speech or newspapers and other publications in the future to teach and advocate the forcible overthrow of the Government. No matter how it is worded, this is a virulent form of prior censorship of speech and press, which I believe the First Amendment forbids. I would hold § 3 of the Smith Act authorizing this prior restraint unconstitutional on its face and as applied.

But let us assume, contrary to all constitutional ideas of fair criminal procedure, that petitioners although not indicted for the crime of actual advocacy, may be punished for it. Even on this radical assumption, the other opinions in this case show that the only way to affirm these convictions is to repudiate directly or indirectly the established "clear and present danger" rule. This the Court does in a way which greatly restricts the protections afforded by the First Amendment. The opinions for affirmance indicate that the chief reason for jettisoning the rule is the expressed fear that advocacy of Communist doctrine endangers the safety of the Republic. Undoubtedly, a governmental policy of unfettered communication of ideas does entail dangers. To the Founders of this Nation, however, the benefits derived from free expression were worth the risk. They embodied this philosophy in the First Amendment's command that "Congress shall make no law abridging . . . the freedom of speech, or of the press. . . ." I have always believed that the First Amendment is the keystone of our Government, that the freedoms it guarantees provide the best insurance against destruction of all freedom. At least as to speech in the realm of public matters, I believe that the "clear and present danger" test does not "mark the furthermost constitutional boundaries of protected expression" but does "no more than recognize a minimum compulsion of the Bill of Rights." *Bridges v. California*, 314 U. S. 252, 263.

So long as this Court exercises the power of judicial review of legislation, I cannot agree that the First Amendment permits us to sustain laws suppressing freedom of speech and press on the basis of Congress' or our own notions of mere "reasonableness." Such a doctrine waters down the First Amendment so that it amounts to little more than an admonition to Congress. The Amendment as so construed is not likely to protect any but those "safe" or orthodox views which rarely need its protection. I must also express my objection to the holding because, as MR. JUSTICE DOUGLAS' dissent shows, it sanctions the determination of a crucial issue of fact by the judge rather than by the jury. . . .

Public opinion being what it now is, few will protest the conviction of these Communist petitioners. There is hope, however, that in calmer times, when present pressures, passions and fears subside, this or some later Court will restore the First Amendment liberties to the high preferred place where they belong in a free society.

MR. JUSTICE DOUGLAS, dissenting.

If this were a case where those who claimed protection under the First Amendment were teaching the techniques of sabotage, the assassination of the President, the filching of documents from public files, the planting of bombs, the art of street warfare, and the like, I would have no doubts. The freedom to speak is not absolute; the teaching of methods of terror and other seditious conduct should be beyond the pale along with obscenity and immorality. This case was argued as if those were the facts. The argument imported much seditious conduct into the record. That is easy and it has popular appeal, for the activities of Communists in plotting and scheming against the free world are common knowledge. But the fact is that no such evidence was introduced at the trial. There is a statute which makes a seditious conspiracy unlawful. Petitioners, however, were not charged with a "conspiracy to overthrow" the Government. They were charged with a conspiracy to form a party and groups and assemblies of people who teach and advocate the overthrow of our Government by force or violence and with a conspiracy to advocate and teach its overthrow by force and violence. It may well be that indoctrination in the techniques of terror to destroy the Government would be indictable under either statute. But the teaching which is condemned here is of a different character.

So far as the present record is concerned, what petitioners did was to organize people to teach and themselves teach the Marxist-Leninist doctrine contained chiefly in four books:[3]  Stalin, Foundations of Leninism (1924); Marx and Engels, Manifesto of the Communist Party (1848); Lenin, The State and Revolution (1917); History of the Communist Party of the Soviet Union (B.) (1939).

Those books are to Soviet Communism what Mein Kampf was to Nazism. If they are understood, the ugliness of Communism is revealed, its deceit and cunning are exposed, the nature of its activities becomes apparent, and the chances of its success less likely. That is not, of course, the reason why petitioners chose these books for their classrooms. They are fervent Communists to whom these volumes are gospel. They preached the creed with the hope that some day it would be acted upon.

The opinion of the Court does not outlaw these texts nor condemn them to the fire, as the Communists do literature offensive to their creed. But if the books themselves are not outlawed, if they can lawfully remain on library shelves, by what reasoning does their use in a classroom become a crime? It would not be a crime under the Act to introduce these books to a class, though that would be teaching what the creed of violent overthrow of

---

[3] Other books taught were Stalin, Problems of Leninism; Strategy and Tactics of World Communism (H. R. Doc. No. 619, 80th Cong., 2d Sess.), and Program of the Communist International.

the government is. The Act, as construed, requires the element of intent—that those who teach the creed believe in it. The crime then depends not on what is taught but on who the teacher is. That is to make freedom of speech turn not on *what is said,* but on the *intent* with which it is said. Once we start down that road we enter territory dangerous to the liberties of every citizen.

There was a time in England when the concept of constructive treason flourished. Men were punished not for raising a hand against the king but for thinking murderous thoughts about him. The Framers of the Constitution were alive to that abuse and took steps to see that the practice would not flourish here. Treason was defined to require overt acts—the evolution of a plot against the country into an actual project. The present case is not one of treason. But the analogy is close when the illegality is made to turn on intent, not on the nature of the act. We then start probing men's minds for motive and purpose; they become entangled in the law not for what they did but *for what they thought;* they get convicted not for what they said but for the purpose with which they said it.

Intent, of course, often makes the difference in law. An act otherwise excusable or carrying minor penalties may grow to an abhorrent thing if the evil intent is present. We deal here, however, not with ordinary acts but with speech, to which the Constitution has given a special sanction.

The vice of treating speech as the equivalent of overt acts of a treasonable or seditious character is emphasized by a concurring opinion, which by invoking the law of conspiracy makes speech do service for deeds which are dangerous to society. The doctrine of conspiracy has served divers and oppressive purposes and in its broad reach can be made to do great evil. But never until today has anyone seriously thought that the ancient law of conspiracy could constitutionally be used to turn speech into seditious conduct. Yet that is precisely what is suggested. I repeat that we deal here with speech alone, not with speech *plus* acts of sabotage or unlawful conduct. Not a single seditious act is charged in the indictment. To make a lawful speech unlawful because two men conceive it is to raise the law of conspiracy to appalling proportions. That course is to make a radical break with the past and to violate one of the cardinal principles of our constitutional scheme.

Free speech has occupied an exalted position because of the high service it has given our society. Its protection is essential to the very existence of a democracy. The airing of ideas releases pressures which otherwise might become destructive. When ideas compete in the market for acceptance, full and free

486

discussion exposes the false and they gain few adherents. Full and free discussion even of ideas we hate encourages the testing of our own prejudices and preconceptions. Full and free discussion keeps a society from becoming stagnant and unprepared for the stresses and strains that work to tear all civilizations apart.

Full and free discussion has indeed been the first article of our faith. We have founded our political system on it. It has been the safeguard of every religious, political, philosophical, economic, and racial group amongst us. We have counted on it to keep us from embracing what is cheap and false; we have trusted the common sense of our people to choose the doctrine true to our genius and to reject the rest. This has been the one single outstanding tenet that has made our institutions the symbol of freedom and equality. We have deemed it more costly to liberty to suppress a despised minority than to let them vent their spleen. We have above all else feared the political censor. We have wanted a land where our people can be exposed to all the diverse creeds and cultures of the world.

There comes a time when even speech loses its constitutional immunity. Speech innocuous one year may at another time fan such destructive flames that it must be halted in the interests of the safety of the Republic. That is the meaning of the clear and present danger test. When conditions are so critical that there will be no time to avoid the evil that the speech threatens, it is time to call a halt. Otherwise, free speech which is the strength of the Nation will be the cause of its destruction.

Yet free speech is the rule, not the exception. The restraint to be constitutional must be based on more than fear, on more than passionate opposition against the speech, on more than a revolted dislike for its contents. There must be some immediate injury to society that is likely if speech is allowed. The classic statement of these conditions was made by Mr. Justice Brandeis in his concurring opinion in *Whitney* v. *California*, 274 U. S. 357, 376–377, . . .

I had assumed that the question of the clear and present danger, being so critical an issue in the case, would be a matter for submission to the jury. It was squarely held in *Pierce* v. *United States*, 252 U. S. 239, 244, to be a jury question. Mr. Justice Pitney, speaking for the Court, said, "Whether the statement contained in the pamphlet had a natural tendency to produce the forbidden consequences, as alleged, was a question to be determined not upon demurrer but by the jury at the trial." That is the only time the Court has passed on the issue. None of our other decisions is contrary. Nothing said in any of the nonjury cases has detracted from that ruling. The statement in *Pierce* v. *United States, supra,* states the law as it has been and as it should be. The Court, I think, errs when it treats the question as one of law.

Yet whether the question is one for the Court or the jury, there should be evidence of record on the issue. This record, however, contains no evidence whatsoever showing that the acts charged, *viz.,* the teaching of the Soviet theory of revolution with the hope that it will be realized, have created any clear and present danger to the Nation. The Court, however, rules to the contrary. It says, "The formation by petitioners of such a highly organized conspiracy, with rigidly disciplined members subject to call when the leaders, these petitioners, felt that the time had come for action, coupled with the inflammable nature of world conditions, similar uprisings in other countries, and the touch-and-go nature of our relations with countries with whom petitioners were in the very least ideologically attuned, convince us that their convictions were justified on this score."

That ruling in my view is not responsive to the issue in the case. We might as well say that the speech of petitioners is outlawed because Soviet Russia and her Red Army are a threat to world peace.

The nature of Communism as a force on the world scene would, of course, be relevant to the issue of clear and present danger of petitioners' advocacy within the United States. But the primary consideration is the strength and tactical position of petitioners and their converts in this country. On that there is no evidence in the record. If we are to take judicial notice of the threat of Communists within the nation, it should not be difficult to conclude that *as a political party* they are of little consequence. Communists in this country have never made a respectable or serious showing in any election. I would doubt that there is a village, let alone a city or county or state which the Communists could carry. Communism in the world scene is no bogeyman; but Communism as a political faction or party in this country plainly is. Communism has been so thoroughly exposed in this country that it has been crippled as a political force. Free speech has destroyed it as an effective political party. It is inconceivable that those who went up and down this country preaching the doctrine of revolution which petitioners espouse would have any success. In days of trouble and confusion when bread lines were long, when the unemployed walked the streets, when people were starving, the advocates of a short-cut by revolution might have a chance to gain adherents. But today there are no such conditions. The country is not in despair; the people know Soviet

Communism; the doctrine of Soviet revolution is exposed in all of its ugliness and the American people want none of it.

How it can be said that there is a clear and present danger that this advocacy will succeed is, therefore, a mystery. Some nations less resilient than the United States, where illiteracy is high and where democratic traditions are only budding, might have to take drastic steps and jail these men for merely speaking their creed. But in America they are miserable merchants of unwanted ideas; their wares remain unsold. The fact that their ideas are abhorrent does not make them powerful.

The political impotence of the Communists in this country does not, of course, dispose of the problem. Their numbers; their positions in industry and government; the extent to which they have in fact infiltrated the police, the armed services, transportation, stevedoring, power plants, munitions works, and other critical places—these facts all bear on the likelihood that their advocacy of the Soviet theory of revolution will endanger the Republic. But the record is silent on these facts. If we are to proceed on the basis of judicial notice, it is impossible for me to say that the Communists in this country are so potent or so strategically deployed that they must be suppressed for their speech. I could not so hold unless I were willing to conclude that the activities in recent years of committees of Congress, of the Attorney General, of labor unions, of state legislatures, and of Loyalty Boards were so futile as to leave the country on the edge of grave peril. To believe that petitioners and their following are placed in such critical positions as to endanger the Nation is to believe the incredible. It is safe to say that the followers of the creed of Soviet Communism are known to the F. B. I.; that in case of war with Russia they will be picked up overnight as were all prospective saboteurs at the commencement of World War II; that the invisible army of petitioners is the best known, the most beset, and the least thriving of any fifth column in history. Only those held by fear and panic could think otherwise.

This is my view if we are to act on the basis of judicial notice. But the mere statement of the opposing views indicates how important it is that we know the facts before we act. Neither prejudices nor hate nor senseless fear should be the basis of this solemn act. Free speech—the glory of our system of government—should not be sacrificed on anything less than plain and objective proof of danger that the evil advocated is imminent. On this record no one can say that petitioners and their converts are in such a strategic position as to have even the slightest chance of achieving their aims.

The First Amendment provides that "Congress shall make no

law . . . abridging the freedom of speech." The Constitution provides no exception. This does not mean, however, that the Nation need hold its hand until it is in such weakened condition that there is no time to protect itself from incitement to revolution. Seditious conduct can always be punished. But the command of the First Amendment is so clear that we should not allow Congress to call a halt to free speech except in the extreme case of peril from the speech itself. The First Amendment makes confidence in the common sense of our people and in their maturity of judgment the great postulate of our democracy. Its philosophy is that violence is rarely, if ever, stopped by denying civil liberties to those advocating resort to force. The First Amendment reflects the philosophy of Jefferson "that it is time enough for the rightful purposes of civil government for its officers to interfere when principles break out into overt acts against peace and good order." The political censor has no place in our public debates. Unless and until extreme and necessitous circumstances are shown, our aim should be to keep speech unfettered and to allow the processes of law to be invoked only when the provocateurs among us move from speech to action.

Vishinsky wrote in 1948 in The Law of the Soviet State, "In our state, naturally, there can be no place for freedom of speech, press, and so on for the foes of socialism."

Our concern should be that we accept no such standard for the United States. Our faith should be that our people will never give support to these advocates of revolution, so long as we remain loyal to the purposes for which our Nation was founded.

[The Appendix to Mr. Justice Douglas' opinion, analyzing the cases on whether the existence of clear and present danger is a question for the court or jury, is omitted.]

## Note

1. For discussion of the issues raised by the *Dennis* case, see Boudin, *"Seditious Doctrines"* and the *"Clear and Present Danger"* Rule, 38 Va. L. Rev. 143, 315 (1952); Richardson, *Freedom of Expression and the Function of Courts*, 65 Harv. L. Rev. 1 (1951); Garfinkel and Mack, *Dennis v. United States and the Clear and Present Danger Rule*, 39 Calif. L. Rev. 475 (1951); Nathanson, *The Communist Trial and the Clear-and-Present Danger Test*, 63 Harv. L. Rev. 1167 (1950). See also Antieau, *Dennis v. United States—Precedent, Principle or Perversion*, 5 Vand. L. Rev. 141 (1952); Note, *Clear and Present Danger Re-Examined*, 51 Col. L. Rev. 98 (1951); Wiener, *"Freedom for the Thought That We Hate": Is it a Principle of the Constitution*, 37 A. B. A. J. 177 (1951), answered by Katz in 37 A. B. A. J. 901 (1951); Notes, 50 Mich. L. Rev. 451 (1952); 5 Rutgers L. Rev. 413 (1951).

On the issues arising out of use of the conspiracy provisions in Smith

Act prosecutions, see Note, *The Conspiracy Dilemma: Prosecution of Group Crime or Protection of Individual Defendants*, 62 Harv. L. Rev. 276 (1948). See also Arens, *Nuremberg and Group Prosecution*, 1951 Wash. U. L. Q. 329 (1951).

2. In testimony before the House Appropriations Committee in January 1950 an official of the Department of Justice stated: ". . . there is a program of extensive suits to prosecute members of the Communist Party who can be shown to be sympathetic and appreciative of its views. We prosecute them as individuals under the Smith Act. . . . If the Government is sustained in the Supreme Court of the United States [in the *Dennis* case], it will be about the fiscal year 1951 when that program will come up. That is the work load which we must look forward to as possible, and indeed very probable." He estimated the work load of cases as "roughly, 12000." Hearings on the Department of Justice Appropriations before the Subcommittee of the Committee on Appropriations, 81st Cong., 2d Sess., pp. 85–6 (1950). Later the Department of Justice denied that it presently contemplated bringing prosecutions against 12,000 Communist Party members. American Civil Liberties Weekly Bulletin, July 3, 1950. The extent of future prosecutions thus remains uncertain.

Several weeks after the Supreme Court's decision in the *Dennis* case the Department of Justice did institute prosecutions against some of the secondary Communist Party leadership. Indictments were obtained against more than 50 persons in New York, California, Pennsylvania, Michigan, Maryland, the District of Columbia and Hawaii. N. Y. Times, June 21, July 27, Aug. 1, 8, 18, 29, 1951. Motions to dismiss the indictments were denied. See, e. g., *U. S. v. Flynn*, unreported (S. D. N. Y., Dec. 21, 1951); *U. S. v. Frankfeld*, 101 F. Supp. 449 (D. Md., 1951). As of the middle of 1952 the trial of the Baltimore and Washington cases had resulted in convictions of six defendants in the District Court of Maryland. N. Y. Times, April 2, 1952. Lengthy trials were in progress in New York and Los Angeles.

3. Among the prosecutions instituted under state anti-sedition laws following the *Dennis* case were the indictment of Prof. Dirk J. Struik of M. I. T. and another under the Massachusetts statute, N. Y. Times, Sept. 13, 1951, and the conviction of Steve Nelson, Communist Party leader in Pennsylvania, and two others under the Pennsylvania statute. N. Y. Times, Feb. 1, 1952.

4. In *Gara v. U. S.*, 178 F. 2d 38 (C. A. 6, 1949), the defendant, dean of men at Bluffton College, Ohio, was convicted for counseling one of the students to refuse to register under the Selective Service Act. The Supreme Court affirmed by an equally divided vote. 340 U. S. 857, 95 L. Ed. 628, 71 S. Ct. 87 (1950).

## 3. Denial of Privileges or Positions of Influence to Persons Declared Subversive

In the period since the Second World War there has emerged a growing body of legislative and administrative measures designed to deny certain privileges, or eliminate from certain positions of influence, persons found to be subversive. These measures do not involve, at least in the first instance, the use of criminal sanctions and hence their administration and application are not restricted by the traditional safeguards embodied in the criminal law. For this reason, and because of the increasing use of such sanctions, the problems have assumed special significance in recent years.

The most important of these non-criminal measures are probably the loyalty programs,—Federal, state and private. This phase of the problem is considered subsequently. At this point we are concerned with other measures, including the Taft-Hartley non-Communist affidavit, the denial of a place on the ballot, limitations on freedom of movement, restrictions upon aliens, and the like. The leading Supreme Court decision is the *Douds* case.

## AMERICAN COMMUNICATIONS ASSOCIATION v. DOUDS

Supreme Court of the United States, 1950
339 U. S. 382, 94 L. Ed. 925, 70 S. Ct. 674

MR. CHIEF JUSTICE VINSON delivered the opinion of the Court.
These cases present for decision the constitutionality of § 9 (h) of the National Labor Relations Act, as amended by the Labor Management Relations Act, 1947.[1] This section, commonly referred to as the non-Communist affidavit provision, reads as follows: "No investigation shall be made by the [National Labor Relations] Board of any question affecting commerce concerning the representation of employees, raised by a labor organization under subsection (c) of this section, no petition under section 9 (e) (1) shall be entertained, and no complaint shall be issued pursuant to a charge made by a labor organization under subsection (b) of section 10, unless there is on file with the Board an affidavit executed contemporaneously or within the preceding twelve-month period by each officer of such labor organization and the officers of any national or international labor organization of which it is an affiliate or constituent unit that he is not a member of the Communist Party or affiliated with such party, and that he does not believe in, and is not a member of or supports any organization that believes in or teaches, the overthrow of the United States Government by force or by any illegal or

---

[1] 61 Stat. 136, 146, 29 U. S. C. (Supp. III) §§ 141, 159 (h), amending the National Labor Relations Act of 1935, 49 Stat. 449, 29 U. S. C. § 151 *et seq.*

unconstitutional methods. The provisions of section 35A of the Criminal Code shall be applicable in respect to such affidavits."
. . .

## I.

The constitutional justification for the National Labor Relations Act was the power of Congress to protect interstate commerce by removing obstructions to the free flow of commerce. *National Labor Relations Board v. Jones & Laughlin Steel Corp.,* 301 U. S. 1 (1937). That Act was designed to remove obstructions caused by strikes and other forms of industrial unrest, which Congress found were attributable to the inequality of bargaining power between unorganized employees and their employers. It did so by strengthening employee groups, by restraining certain employer practices, and by encouraging the processes of collective bargaining.

When the Labor Management Relations Act was passed twelve years later, it was the view of Congress that additional impediments to the free flow of commerce made amendment of the original Act desirable. . . .

One such obstruction, which it was the purpose of § 9 (h) of the Act to remove, was the so-called "political strike." Substantial amounts of evidence were presented to various committees of Congress, including the committees immediately concerned with labor legislation, that Communist leaders of labor unions had in the past and would continue in the future to subordinate legitimate trade union objectives to obstructive strikes when dictated by Party leaders, often in support of the policies of a foreign government. And other evidence supports the view that some union leaders who hold to a belief in violent overthrow of the Government for reasons other than loyalty to the Communist Party likewise regard strikes and other forms of direct action designed to serve ultimate revolutionary goals as the primary objectives of labor unions which they control.[3] At the committee hearings, the incident most fully developed was a strike at the Milwaukee plant of the Allis-Chalmers Manufacturing Company in 1941, when that plant was producing vital materials for the national defense program. A full hearing was given not only to company officials, but also to leaders of the international and local unions involved. Congress heard testimony that the strike

---

[3] A detailed description of the aims and tactics of the Socialist Workers Party, for example, may be found in the transcript of record in *Dunne v. United States,* 320 U. S. 790 (1943), certiorari denied. We cite the record as evidence only and express no opinion whatever on the merits of the case. See record, pp. 267–271, 273–274, 330–332, 439, 475, 491–492, 495–496, 535, 606, 683–688, 693, 737, 804–805.

had been called solely in obedience to Party orders for the purpose of starting the "snowballing of strikes" in defense plants.[4]

No useful purpose would be served by setting out at length the evidence before Congress relating to the problem of political strikes, nor can we attempt to assess the validity of each item of evidence. It is sufficient to say that Congress had a great mass of material before it which tended to show that Communists and others proscribed by the statute had infiltrated union organizations not to support and further trade union objectives, including the advocacy of change by democratic methods, but to make them a device by which commerce and industry might be disrupted when the dictates of political policy required such action.

## II.

. . . It cannot be denied that the practical effect of denial of access to the Board and the denial of a place on the ballot in representation proceedings is not merely to withhold benefits granted by the Government but to impose upon noncomplying unions a number of restrictions which would not exist if the Board had not been established.[6] The statute does not, however, specifically forbid persons who do not sign the affidavit from holding positions of union leadership nor require their discharge from office. The fact is that § 9 (h) may well make it difficult for unions to remain effective if their officers do not sign the affidavits. How difficult depends upon the circumstances of the industry, the strength of the union and its organizational discipline. We are, therefore, neither free to treat § 9 (h) as if it merely withdraws a privilege gratuitously granted by the Government, nor able to consider it a licensing statute prohibiting those persons who do not sign the affidavit from holding union office. The practicalities of the situation place the proscriptions of § 9 (h) somewhere between those two extremes. The difficult question that emerges is whether, consistently with the First Amendment, Congress, by statute, may exert these pressures

---

[4] See Hearings before House Committee on Education and Labor on Bills to Amend and Repeal the National Labor Relations Act, 80th Cong., 1st Sess. 3611–3615.

[6] For example, a union whose officers do not file an affidavit in compliance with § 9 (h) may not enter into a union shop contract with an employer, as it was free to do before passage of the National Labor Relations Act. A noncomplying union is excluded from the ballot in representation proceedings. If another union is certified, the noncomplying union incurs the disabilities of §§ 8 (b) 4 (C), and 303 (a) (3), as it would not have done prior to 1935. Similarly, certain strikes and boycotts are prohibited to noncomplying unions by §§ 8 (b) (4) (B), 8 (b) (4) (C), 8 (b) (4) (D) of the Act.

upon labor unions to deny positions of leadership to certain persons who are identified by particular beliefs and political affiliations.

## III.

There can be no doubt that Congress may, under its constitutional power to regulate commerce among the several States, attempt to prevent political strikes and other kinds of direct action designed to burden and interrupt the free flow of commerce. We think it is clear, in addition, that the remedy provided by § 9 (h) bears reasonable relation to the evil which the statute was designed to reach. Congress could rationally find that the Communist Party is not like other political parties in its utilization of positions of union leadership as means by which to bring about strikes and other obstructions of commerce for purposes of political advantage, and that many persons who believe in overthrow of the Government by force and violence are also likely to resort to such tactics when, as officers, they formulate union policy.

The fact that the statute identifies persons by their political affiliations and beliefs, which are circumstances ordinarily irrelevant to permissible subjects of government action, does not lead to the conclusion that such circumstances are never relevant. *In re Summers*, 325 U. S. 561 (1945); *Hamilton v. Regents*, 293 U. S. 245 (1934). We have held that aliens may be barred from certain occupations because of a reasonable relation between that classification and the apprehended evil, *Clarke v. Deckebach*, 274 U. S. 392 (1927); *Pearl Assurance Co. v. Harrington*, 313 U. S. 549 (1941), even though the Constitution forbids arbitrary banning of aliens from the pursuit of lawful occupations. *Truax v. Raich*, 239 U. S. 33 (1915); *Takahashi v. Fish and Game Commission*, 334 U. S. 410 (1948). Even distinctions based solely on ancestry, which we declared "are by their very nature odious to a free people," have been upheld under the unusual circumstances of wartime. *Hirabayashi v. United States*, 320 U. S. 81 (1943). If accidents of birth and ancestry under some circumstances justify an inference concerning future conduct, it can hardly be doubted that voluntary affiliations and beliefs justify a similar inference when drawn by the legislature on the basis of its investigations.

This principle may be illustrated by reference to statutes denying positions of public importance to groups of persons identified by their business affiliations. One federal statute,[8] for ex-

---

[8] Sections 30 and 32 of the Banking Act of 1933, 48 Stat. 162, 193, 194, as amended, 49 Stat. 684, 709, 12 U. S. C. §§ 77, 78 [upheld in *Board of Governors v. Agnew*, 329 U. S. 441.]

**495**

ample, provides that no partner or employee of a firm primarily engaged in underwriting securities may be a director of a national bank. . . . In this respect, § 9 (h) is not unlike a host of other statutes which prohibit specified groups of persons from holding positions of power and public interest because, in the legislative judgment, they threaten to abuse the trust that is a necessary concomitant of the power of office.

If no more were involved than possible loss of position, the foregoing would dispose of the case. But the more difficult problem here arises because, in drawing lines on the basis of beliefs and political affiliations, though it may be granted that the proscriptions of the statute bear a reasonable relation to the apprehended evil, Congress has undeniably discouraged the lawful exercise of political freedoms as well. Stated otherwise, the problem is this: Communists, we may assume, carry on legitimate political activities. Beliefs are inviolate. *Cantwell v. Connecticut*, 310 U. S. 296, 303 (1940). Congress might reasonably find, however, that Communists, unlike members of other political parties, and persons who believe in overthrow of the Government by force, unlike persons of other beliefs, represent a continuing danger of disruptive political strikes when they hold positions of union leadership. By exerting pressures on unions to deny office to Communists and others identified therein, § 9 (h) undoubtedly lessens the threat to interstate commerce, but it has the further necessary effect of discouraging the exercise of political rights protected by the First Amendment. Men who hold union offices often have little choice but to renounce Communism or give up their offices. Unions which wish to do so are discouraged from electing Communists to office. To the grave and difficult problem thus presented we must now turn our attention.

## IV.

The unions contend that once it is determined that this is a free speech case, the "clear and present danger" test must apply. See *Schenck v. United States*, 249 U. S. 47 (1919). But they disagree as to how it should be applied. Appellant in No. 10 would require that joining the Communist Party or the expression of belief in overthrow of the Government by force be shown to be a clear and present danger of some substantive evil, since those are the doctrines affected by the statute. Petitioner in No. 13, on the other hand, would require a showing that political strikes, the substantive evil involved, are a clear and present danger to the security of the Nation or threaten widespread industrial unrest.

This confusion suggests that the attempt to apply the term,

**496**

"clear and present danger," as a mechanical test in every case touching First Amendment freedoms, without regard to the context of its application, mistakes the form in which an idea was cast for the substance of the idea. . . .

[The] question with which we are here faced is not the same one that Justices Holmes and Brandeis found convenient to consider in terms of clear and present danger. Government's interest here is not in preventing the dissemination of Communist doctrine or the holding of particular beliefs because it is feared that unlawful action will result therefrom if free speech is practiced. Its interest is in protecting the free flow of commerce from what Congress considers to be substantial evils of conduct that are not the products of speech at all. Section 9 (h), in other words, does not interfere with speech because Congress fears the consequences of speech; it regulates harmful conduct which Congress has determined is carried on by persons who may be identified by their political affiliations and beliefs. The Board does not contend that political strikes, the substantive evil at which § 9 (h) is aimed, are the present or impending products of advocacy of the doctrines of Communism or the expression of belief in overthrow of the Government by force. On the contrary, it points out that such strikes are called by persons who, so Congress has found, have the will and power to do so *without* advocacy or persuasion that seeks acceptance in the competition of the market. Speech may be fought with speech. Falsehoods and fallacies must be exposed, not suppressed, unless there is not sufficient time to avert the evil consequences of noxious doctrine by argument and education. That is the command of the First Amendment. But force may and must be met with force. Section 9 (h) is designed to protect the public not against what Communists and others identified therein advocate or believe, but against what Congress has concluded they have done and are likely to do again.

The contention of petitioner in No. 13 that this Court must find that political strikes create a clear and present danger to the security of the Nation or of widespread industrial strife in order to sustain § 9 (h) similarly misconceives the purpose that phrase was intended to serve. In that view, not the relative certainty that evil conduct will result from speech in the immediate future, but the extent and gravity of the substantive evil must be measured by the "test" laid down in the *Schenck* case. But there the Court said that: "The question in every case is whether the *words* used are used in such circumstances and are of such a nature as to create a clear and present danger that they will bring about the substantive evils that Congress has a right to prevent." *Schenck v. United States, supra* at 52. (Emphasis supplied.)

So far as the *Schenck* case itself is concerned, imminent danger of any substantive evil that Congress may prevent justifies the restriction of speech. Since that time this Court has decided that however great the likelihood that a substantive evil will result, restrictions on speech and press cannot be sustained unless the evil itself is "substantial" and "relatively serious," Brandeis, J., concurring in *Whitney v. California* [274 U. S. at 374, 377], or sometimes "extremely serious," *Bridges v. California,* 314 U. S. 252, 263 (1941). And it follows therefrom that even harmful conduct cannot justify restrictions upon speech unless substantial interests of society are at stake. But in suggesting that the substantive evil must be serious and substantial, it was never the intention of this Court to lay down an absolutist test measured in terms of danger to the Nation. When the effect of a statute or ordinance upon the exercise of First Amendment freedoms is relatively small and the public interest to be protected is substantial, it is obvious that a rigid test requiring a showing of imminent danger to the security of the Nation is an absurdity. We recently dismissed for want of substantiality an appeal in which a church group contended that its First Amendment rights were violated by a municipal zoning ordinance preventing the building of churches in certain residential areas. *Corporation of the Presiding Bishop of the Church of Jesus Christ of Latter-Day Saints v. Porterville,* 338 U. S. 805 (1949). And recent cases in this Court involving contempt by publication likewise have no meaning if imminent danger of national peril is the criterion.[12]

. . .

When particular conduct is regulated in the interest of public order, and the regulation results in an indirect, conditional, partial abridgment of speech, the duty of the courts is to determine which of these two conflicting interests demands the greater protection under the particular circumstances presented. The high place in which the right to speak, think, and assemble as you will was held by the Framers of the Bill of Rights and is held today by those who value liberty both as a means and an end indicates the solicitude with which we must view any assertion of personal freedoms. We must recognize, moreover, that regulation of "conduct" has all too frequently been employed by public authority as a cloak to hide censorship of unpopular ideas. We have been reminded that "It is not often in this country that we now meet with direct and candid efforts to stop speaking or publication as such. Modern inroads on these rights come from associ-

---

12 *Bridges v. California,* 314 U. S. 252 (1941); *Pennekamp v. Florida,* 328 U. S. 331 (1946); *Craig v. Harney,* 331 U. S. 367 (1947).

[Emerson]

ating the speaking with some other factor which the state may regulate so as to bring the whole within official control." [13]

On the other hand, legitimate attempts to protect the public, not from the remote possible effects of noxious ideologies, but from present excesses of direct, active conduct, are not presumptively bad because they interfere with and, in some of its manifestations, restrain the exercise of First Amendment rights. *Reynolds v. United States* [98 U. S. 145]; *Prince v. Massachusetts* [321 U. S. 158]; *Cox v. New Hampshire* [312 U. S. 569]; *Giboney v. Empire Storage Co.* [336 U. S. 490]. In essence the problem is one of weighing the probable effects of the statute upon the free exercise of the right of speech and assembly against the congressional determination that political strikes are evils of conduct which cause substantial harm to interstate commerce and that Communists and others identified by § 9 (h) pose continuing threats to that public interest when in positions of union leadership. We must, therefore, undertake the "delicate and difficult task . . . to weigh the circumstances and to appraise the substantiality of the reasons advanced in support of the regulation of the free enjoyment of the rights." *Schneider v. State*, 308 U. S. 147, 161 (1939).

## V.

The "reasons advanced in support of the regulation" are of considerable weight, as even the opponents of § 9 (h) agreed. They are far from being "[m]ere legislative preferences or beliefs respecting matters of public convenience [which] may well support regulation directed at other personal activities, but be insufficient to justify such as diminishes the exercise of rights so vital to the maintenance of democratic institutions." [14] It should be emphasized that Congress, not the courts, is primarily charged with determination of the need for regulation of activities affecting interstate commerce. This Court must, if such regulation unduly infringes personal freedoms, declare the statute invalid under the First Amendment's command that the opportunities for free public discussion be maintained. But insofar as the problem is one of drawing inferences concerning the need for regulation of particular forms of conduct from conflicting evidence, this Court is in no position to substitute its judgment as to the necessity or desirability of the statute for that of Congress. . . .

When compared with ordinances and regulations dealing with

---

[13] MR. JUSTICE JACKSON, concurring in *Thomas v. Collins*, 323 U. S. 516, 547 (1945).

[14] *Schneider v. State*, 308 U. S. 147, 161 (1939).

littering of the streets or disturbance of householders by itinerant preachers, the relative significance and complexity of the problem of political strikes and how to deal with their leaders becomes at once apparent. It must be remembered that § 9 (h) is not an isolated statute dealing with a subject divorced from the problems of labor peace generally. It is a part of some very complex machinery set up by the Federal Government for the purpose of encouraging the peaceful settlement of labor disputes. Under the statutory scheme, unions which become collective bargaining representatives for groups of employees often represent not only members of the union but nonunion workers or members of other unions as well. Because of the necessity to have strong unions to bargain on equal terms with strong employers, individual employees are required by law to sacrifice rights which, in some cases, are valuable to them. See *J. I. Case Co. v. Labor Board,* 321 U. S. 332 (1944). The loss of individual rights for the greater benefit of the group results in a tremendous increase in the power of the representative of the group—the union. But power is never without responsibility. And when authority derives in part from Government's thumb on the scales, the exercise of that power by private persons becomes closely akin, in some respects, to its exercise by Government itself. See *Graham v. Brotherhood of Locomotive Firemen,* 338 U. S. 232 (1949) ; *Steele v. Louisville & N. R. Co.,* 323 U. S. 192 (1944) ; *Tunstall v. Brotherhood of Locomotive Firemen,* 323 U. S. 210 (1944) ; *Railway Mail Association v. Corsi,* 326 U. S 88, 94 (1945).

We do not suggest that labor unions which utilize the facilities of the National Labor Relations Board become Government agencies or may be regulated as such. But it is plain that when Congress clothes the bargaining representative "with powers comparable to those possessed by a legislative body both to create and restrict the rights of those whom it represents," [15] the public interest in the good faith exercise of that power is very great.

What of the effects of § 9 (h) upon the rights of speech and assembly of those proscribed by its terms? The statute does not prevent or punish by criminal sanctions the making of a speech, the affiliation with any organization, or the holding of any belief. But as we have noted, the fact that no direct restraint or punishment is imposed upon speech or assembly does not determine the free speech question. Under some circumstances, indirect "discouragements" undoubtedly have the same coercive effect upon the exercise of First Amendment rights as imprisonment, fines, injunctions or taxes. A requirement that adherents

---

[15] *Steele v. Louisville & N. R. Co.,* 323 U. S. 192, 202 (1944).

of particular religious faiths or political parties wear identifying arm-bands, for example, is obviously of this nature.

But we have here no statute which is either frankly aimed at the suppression of dangerous ideas nor one which, although ostensibly aimed at the regulation of conduct, may actually "be made the instrument of arbitrary suppression of free expression of views." *Hague v. Committee for Industrial Organization,* 307 U. S. 496, 516 (1939). There are here involved none of the elements of censorship or prohibition of the dissemination of information that were present in the cases mainly relied upon by those attacking the statute. The "discouragements" of § 9 (h) proceed, not against the groups or beliefs identified therein, but only against the combination of those affiliations or beliefs with occupancy of a position of great power over the economy of the country. Congress has concluded that substantial harm, in the form of direct, positive action, may be expected from that combination. In this legislation, Congress did not restrain the activities of the Communist Party as a political organization; nor did it attempt to stifle beliefs. Compare *West Virginia State Board of Education v. Barnette,* 319 U. S. 624 (1943). Section 9 (h) touches only a relative handful of persons, leaving the great majority of persons of the identified affiliations and beliefs completely free from restraint. And it leaves those few who are affected free to maintain their affiliations and beliefs subject only to possible loss of positions which Congress has concluded are being abused to the injury of the public by members of the described groups. • • •

It is contended that the principle that statutes touching First Amendment freedoms must be narrowly drawn dictates that a statute aimed at political strikes should make the calling of such strikes unlawful but should not attempt to bring about the removal of union officers, with its attendant effect upon First Amendment rights. We think, however, that the legislative judgment that interstate commerce must be protected from a continuing threat of such strikes is a permissible one in this case. The fact that the injury to interstate commerce would be an accomplished fact before any sanctions could be applied, the possibility that a large number of such strikes might be called at a time of external or internal crisis, and the practical difficulties which would be encountered in detecting illegal activities of this kind are factors which are persuasive that Congress should not be powerless to remove the threat, not limited to punishing the act. • • •

## VI.

Previous discussion has considered the constitutional questions raised by § 9 (h) as they apply alike to members of the Communist Party and affiliated organizations and to persons who believe in overthrow of the Government by force. The breadth of the provision concerning belief in overthrow of the Government by force would raise additional questions, however, if it were read very literally to include all persons who might, under any conceivable circumstances, subscribe to that belief.

But we see no reason to construe the statute so broadly. . . . Its manifest purpose was to bring within the terms of the statute only those persons whose beliefs strongly indicate a will to engage in political strikes and other forms of direct action when, as officers, they direct union activities. The congressional purpose is therefore served if we construe the clause, "that he does not believe in, and is not a member of or supports any organization that believes in or teaches, the overthrow of the United States Government by force or by any illegal or unconstitutional methods," to apply to persons and organizations who believe in violent overthrow of the Government as it presently exists under the Constitution as an objective, not merely a prophecy. . . .

As thus construed, we think that the "belief" provision of the oath presents no different problem from that present in that part of the section having to do with membership in the Communist Party. Of course we agree that one may not be imprisoned or executed because he holds particular beliefs. But to attack the straw man of "thought control" is to ignore the fact that the sole effect of the statute upon one who believes in overthrow of the Government by force and violence—and does not deny his belief —is that he may be forced to relinquish his position as a union leader. That fact was crucial in our discussion of the statute as it relates to membership in the Communist Party. . . .

If the principle that one may under no circumstances be required to state his beliefs on any subject nor suffer the loss of any right or privilege because of his beliefs be a valid one, its application in other possible situations becomes relevant. Suppose, for example, that a federal statute provides that no person may become a member of the Secret Service force assigned to protect the President unless he swears that he does not believe in assassination of the President. Is this beyond the power of Congress, whatever the need revealed by its investigations? An affirmative answer hardly commends itself to reason unless, indeed, the Bill of Rights has been converted into a "suicide pact." *Terminiello v. Chicago*, 337 U. S. 1, 37 (1949) (dissenting opinion). Yet the example chosen is far-fetched only because of the manifest absurdity of reliance upon an oath in such a situation. One can have no doubt that the screening process in the selection of persons to occupy such positions probes far deeper than mere oath-taking can possibly do. . . .

Insofar as a distinction between beliefs and political affiliations is based upon absence of any "overt act" in the former case, it is relevant, if at all, in connection with problems of proof. In proving that one swore falsely that he is not a Communist, the act of joining the Party is crucial. Proof that one lied in swearing that he does not believe in overthrow of the Government by force, on the other hand, must consist in proof of his mental state. . . .

Considering the circumstances surrounding the problem—the deference due the congressional judgment concerning the need for regulation of conduct affecting interstate commerce and the effect of the statute upon rights of speech, assembly and belief— we conclude that § 9 (h) of the National Labor Relations Act, as amended by the Labor Management Relations Act, 1947, does not unduly infringe freedoms protected by the First Amendment. Those who, so Congress has found, would subvert the public interest cannot escape all regulation because, at the same time, they carry on legitimate political activities. Cf. *Valentine* v. *Chrestensen*, 316 U. S. 52 (1942). To encourage unions to displace them from positions of great power over the national economy, while at the same time leaving free the outlets by which they may pursue legitimate political activities of persuasion and advocacy, does not seem to us to contravene the purposes of the First Amendment. That Amendment requires that one be permitted to believe what he will. It requires that one be permitted to advocate what he will unless there is a clear and present danger that a substantial public evil will result therefrom. It does not require that he be permitted to be the keeper of the arsenal.

## VII.

There remain two contentions which merit discussion. One is that § 9 (h) is unconstitutionally vague. The other is that it violates the mandate of Art. I, § 9 of the Constitution that "No Bill of Attainder or ex post facto Law shall be passed."

The argument as to vagueness stresses the breadth of such terms as "affiliated," "supports" and "illegal or unconstitutional methods." There is little doubt that imagination can conjure up hypothetical cases in which the meaning of these terms will be in nice question. The applicable standard, however, is not one of wholly consistent academic definition of abstract terms. It is, rather, the practical criterion of fair notice to those to whom the statute is directed. The particular context is all important.

**503**

The only criminal punishment specified is the application of § 35 (A) of the Criminal Code, 18 U. S. C. § 1001, which covers only those false statements made "knowingly and willfully." The question in any criminal prosecution involving a non-Communist affidavit must therefore be whether the affiant acted in good faith or knowingly lied concerning his affiliations, beliefs, support of organizations, etc. And since the constitutional vice in a vague or indefinite statute is the injustice to the accused in placing him on trial for an offense, the nature of which he is given no fair warning, the fact that punishment is restricted to acts done with knowledge that they contravene the statute makes this objection untenable. As this Court pointed out in *United States v. Ragen,* 314 U. S. 513, 524 (1942), "A mind intent upon willful evasion is inconsistent with surprised innocence." Cf. *Omaechevarria v. Idaho,* 246 U. S. 343 (1918) ; *Hygrade Provision Co. v. Sherman,* 266 U. S. 497 (1925) ; *Screws v. United States,* 325 U. S. 91 (1945). Without considering, therefore, whether in other circumstances the words used in § 9 (h) would render a statute unconstitutionally vague and indefinite, we think that the fact that under § 35 (A) of the Criminal Code no honest, untainted interpretation of those words is punishable removes the possibility of constitutional infirmity.

The unions' argument as to bill of attainder cites the familiar cases, *United States v. Lovett,* 328 U. S. 303 (1946) ; *Ex parte Garland,* 4 Wall. 333 (1867) ; *Cummings v. Missouri,* 4 Wall. 277 (1867). Those cases and this also, according to the argument, involve the proscription of certain occupations to a group classified according to belief and loyalty. But there is a decisive distinction: in the previous decisions the individuals involved were in fact being punished for *past* actions; whereas in this case they are subject to possible loss of position only because there is substantial ground for the congressional judgment that their beliefs and loyalties will be transformed into *future* conduct. Of course, the history of the past conduct is the foundation for the judgment as to what the future conduct is likely to be; but that does not alter the conclusion that § 9 (h) is intended to prevent future action rather than to punish past action.

This distinction is emphasized by the fact that members of those groups identified in § 9 (h) are free to serve as union officers if at any time they renounce the allegiances which constituted a bar to signing the affidavit in the past. Past conduct, actual or threatened by their previous adherence to affiliations and beliefs mentioned in § 9 (h), is not a bar to resumption of the position. In the cases relied upon by the unions on the other hand, this Court has emphasized that, since the basis of disqualification

**504**

was past action or loyalty, nothing that those persons proscribed by its terms could ever do would change the result. . . .

In their argument on this point, the unions seek some advantage from references to English history pertinent to a religious test oath. That experience is written into our Constitution in the following provision of Article VI: "The Senators and Representatives before mentioned, and the Members of the several State Legislatures, and all executive and judicial Officers, both of the United States and of the several States, shall be bound by Oath or Affirmation, to support this Constitution; but no religious Test shall ever be required as a Qualification to any Office or public Trust under the United States." It is obvious that not all oaths were abolished; the mere fact that § 9 (h) is in oath form hardly rises to the stature of a constitutional objection. All that was forbidden was a "religious Test." We do not think that the oath here involved can rightly be taken as falling within that category.

Clearly the Constitution permits the requirement of oaths by officeholders to uphold the Constitution itself. The obvious implication is that those unwilling to take such an oath are to be barred from public office. For the President, a specific oath was set forth in the Constitution itself. Art. II, § 1. And Congress has detailed an oath for other Federal officers.[22] Obviously, the Framers of the Constitution thought that the exaction of an affirmation of minimal loyalty to the Government was worth the price of whatever deprivation of individual freedom of conscience was involved. All that we need hold here is that the casting of § 9 (h) into the mold of an oath does not invalidate it, if it is otherwise constitutional.

We conclude that § 9 (h) of the National Labor Relations Act, as amended by the Labor Management Relations Act, 1947, as herein construed, is compatible with the Federal Constitution and may stand. The judgments of the courts below are therefore

*Affirmed.*

MR. JUSTICE DOUGLAS, MR. JUSTICE CLARK and MR. JUSTICE MINTON took no part in the consideration or decision of these cases.

MR. JUSTICE FRANKFURTER concurring in the Court's opinion except as to Part VII. . . .

In my view Congress has cast its net too indiscriminately in some of the provisions of § 9 (h). To ask avowal that one "does not believe in, and is not a member of or supports any organization that believes in . . . the overthrow of the United States

---

[22] 23 Stat. 22, 5 U. S. C. § 16.

Government . . . by any illegal or unconstitutional methods" is to ask assurances from men regarding matters that open the door too wide to mere speculation or uncertainty. It is asking more than rightfully may be asked of ordinary men to take oath that a method is not "unconstitutional" or "illegal" when constitutionality or legality is frequently determined by this Court by the chance of a single vote. It does not meet the difficulty to suggest that the hazard of a prosecution for perjury is not great since the convictions for perjury must be founded on willful falsity. To suggest that a judge might not be justified in allowing a case to go to a jury, or that a jury would not be justified in convicting, or that, on the possible happening of these events, an appellate court would be compelled to reverse, or, finally, that resort could be had to this Court for review on a petition for certiorari, affords safeguards too tenuous to neutralize the danger. See *Musser v. Utah*, 333 U. S. 95. The hazards that were found to be fatal to the legislation under review in *Winters v. New York*, 333 U. S. 507, appear trivial by comparison with what is here involved. . . .

I cannot deem it within the rightful authority of Congress to probe into opinions that involve only an argumentative demonstration of some coincidental parallelism of belief with some of the beliefs of those who direct the policy of the Communist Party, though without any allegiance to it. To require oaths as to matters that open up such possibilities invades the inner life of men whose compassionate thought or doctrinaire hopes may be as far removed from any dangerous kinship with the Communist creed as were those of the founders of the present orthodox political parties in this country.

The offensive provisions of § 9 (h) leave unaffected, however, the valid portions of the section. In § 16, Congress has made express provision for such severance. Since the judgments below were based in part on what I deem unconstitutional requirements, I cannot affirm but would remand to give opportunity to obey merely the valid portions of § 9 (h).

MR. JUSTICE JACKSON, concurring and dissenting, each in part.

If the statute before us required labor union officers to forswear membership in the Republican Party, the Democratic Party or the Socialist Party, I suppose all agree that it would be unconstitutional. But why, if it is valid as to the Communist Party?

The answer, for me, is in the decisive differences between the Communist Party and every other party of any importance in the long experience of the United States with party government. In order that today's decision may not be useful as a precedent

506

for suppression of any political opposition compatible with our free institutions, I limit concurrence to grounds and distinctions explicitly set forth herein, without which I should regard this Act as unconstitutional. . . .

## I.

From information before its several Committees and from facts of general knowledge, Congress could rationally conclude that, behind its political party façade, the Communist Party is a conspiratorial and revolutionary junta, organized to reach ends and to use methods which are incompatible with our constitutional system. A rough and compressed grouping of this data would permit Congress to draw these important conclusions as to its distinguishing characteristics.*

1. *The goal of the Communist Party is to seize powers of government by and for a minority rather than to acquire power through the vote of a free electorate.* It seeks not merely a change of administration, or of Congress, or reform legislation within the constitutional framework. Its program is not merely to socialize property more rapidly and extensively than the other parties are doing. While the difference between other parties in these matters is largely as to pace, the Communist Party's difference is one of direction. . . .

2. *The Communist Party alone among American parties past or present is dominated and controlled by a foreign government.* It is a satrap party which, to the threat of civil disorder, adds the threat of betrayal into alien hands. . . .

3. *Violent and undemocratic means are the calculated and indispensable methods to attain the Communist Party's goal.* It would be incredible naïveté to expect the American branch of this movement to forego the only methods by which a Communist Party has anywhere come into power. In not one of the countries it now dominates was the Communist Party chosen by a free or contestible election; in not one can it be evicted by any election. The international police state has crept over Eastern Europe by deception, coercion, *coup d'etat*, terrorism and assassination. Not only has it overpowered its critics and opponents; it has usually liquidated them. The American Communist Party has copied the organizational structure and its leaders have been schooled in the same technique and by the same tutors.

4. *The Communist Party has sought to gain this leverage and hold on the American population by acquiring control of the*

---

* [Mr. Justice Jackson's footnotes, citing the material upon which his conclusions are based, are omitted.]

**507**

*labor movement*. All political parties have wooed labor and its leaders. But what other parties seek is principally the vote of labor. The Communist Party, on the other hand, is not primarily interested in labor's vote, for it does not expect to win by votes. It strives for control of labor's coercive power—the sit-down, the slow-down, sabotage, or other means of producing industrial paralysis. . . .

5. *Every member of the Communist Party is an agent to execute the Communist program.* What constitutes a party? Major political parties in the United States have never been closely knit or secret organizations. Anyone who usually votes the party ticket is reckoned a member, although he has not applied for or been admitted to membership, pays no dues, has taken no pledge, and is free to vote, speak and act as he wills. . . .

Membership in the Communist Party is totally different. The Party is a secret conclave. Members are admitted only upon acceptance as reliable and after indoctrination in its policies, to which the member is fully committed. They are provided with cards or credentials, usually issued under false names so that the identification can only be made by officers of the Party who hold the code. Moreover, each pledges unconditional obedience to party authority. Adherents are known by secret or code names. They constitute "cells" in the factory, the office, the political society, or the labor union. For any deviation from the party line they are purged and excluded.

Inferences from membership in such an organization are justifiably different from those to be drawn from membership in the usual type of political party. Individuals who assume such obligations are chargeable, on ordinary conspiracy principles, with responsibility for and participation in all that makes up the Party's program. The conspiracy principle has traditionally been employed to protect society against all "ganging up" or concerted action in violation of its laws. No term passes that this Court does not sustain convictions based on that doctrine for violations of the antitrust laws or other statutes. However, there has recently entered the dialectic of politics a cliché used to condemn application of the conspiracy principle to Communists. "Guilt by association" is an epithet frequently used and little explained, except that it is generally accompanied by another slogan, "guilt is personal." Of course it is; but personal guilt may be incurred by joining a conspiracy. That act of association makes one responsible for the acts of others committed in pursuance of the association. It is wholly a question of the sufficiency of evidence of association to imply conspiracy. There is certainly sufficient evidence that all members owe allegiance to every de-

508

tail of the Communist Party program and have assumed a duty actively to help execute it, so that Congress could, on familiar conspiracy principles, charge each member with responsibility for the goals and means of the Party.

Such then is the background which Congress could reasonably find as a basis for exerting its constitutional powers, and which the judiciary cannot disregard in testing them. On this hypothesis we may revert to consideration of the contention of unconstitutionality of this oath insofar as it requires disclosure of Communist Party membership or affiliation.

## II.

I cannot believe that Congress has less power to protect a labor union from Communist Party domination than it has from employer domination. This Court has uncompromisingly upheld power of Congress to disestablish labor unions where they are company-dominated and to eradicate employer influence, even when exerted only through spoken or written words which any person not the employer would be free to utter.

Congress has conferred upon labor unions important rights and powers in matters that affect industry, transport, communications, and commerce. And Congress has not now denied any union full self-government nor prohibited any union from choosing Communist officers. It seeks to protect the union from doing so unknowingly. And if members deliberately choose to put the union in the hands of Communist officers, Congress withdraws the privileges it has conferred on the assumption that they will be devoted to the welfare of their members. It would be strange indeed if it were constitutionally powerless to protect these delegated functions from abuse and misappropriation to the service of the Communist Party and the Soviet Union. Our Constitution is not a covenant of nonresistance toward organized efforts at disruption and betrayal, either of labor or of the country. . . .

I conclude that we cannot deny Congress power to take these measures under the Commerce Clause to require labor union officers to disclose their membership in or affiliation with the Communist Party.

## III.

Congress has, however, required an additional disclaimer, which in my view does encounter serious constitutional objections. A union officer must also swear that "he does not believe in . . . the overthrow of the United States Government by force or by any illegal or unconstitutional methods."

If Congress has power to condition any right or privilege of

**509**

an American citizen upon disclosure and disavowal of belief on any subject, it is obviously this one. But the serious issue is whether Congress has power to proscribe any opinion or belief which has not manifested itself in any overt act. While the forepart of the oath requires disclosure and disavowal of relationships which depend on overt acts of membership or affiliation, the afterpart demands revelation and denial of mere beliefs or opinions, even though they may never have matured into any act whatever or even been given utterance. In fact, the oath requires one to form and express a conviction on an abstract proposition which many good citizens, if they have thought of it at all, have considered too academic and remote to bother about.

That this difference is decisive on the question of power becomes unmistakable when we consider measures of enforcement. The only sanction prescribed, and probably the only one possible in dealing with a false affidavit, is punishment for perjury. If one is accused of falsely stating that he was not a member of, or affiliated with, the Communist Party, his conviction would depend upon proof of visible and knowable overt acts or courses of conduct sufficient to establish that relationship. But if one is accused of falsely swearing that he did not believe something that he really did believe, the trial must revolve around the conjecture as to whether he candidly exposed his state of mind.

The law sometimes does inquire as to mental state, but only so far as I recall when it is incidental to, and determines the quality of, some overt act in question. From its circumstances, courts sometimes must decide whether an act was committed intentionally or whether its results were intended, or whether the action taken was in malice, or after deliberation, or with knowledge of certain facts. But in such cases the law pries into the mind only to determine the nature and culpability of an act, as a mitigating or aggravating circumstance, and I know of no situation in which a citizen may incur civil or criminal liability or disability because a court infers an evil mental state where no act at all has occurred. Our trial processes are clumsy and unsatisfying for inferring cogitations which are incidental to actions, but they do not even pretend to ascertain the thought that has had no outward manifestation. Attempts of the courts to fathom modern political meditations of an accused would be as futile and mischievous as the efforts in the infamous heresy trials of old to fathom religious beliefs. . . .

I conclude that today's task can only be discharged by holding that all parts of this oath which require disclosure of overt acts of affiliation or membership in the Communist Party are within the competence of Congress to enact and that any parts of it that call for a disclosure of belief unconnected with any overt act are beyond its power.

MR. JUSTICE BLACK, dissenting.

We have said that "Freedom to think is absolute of its own nature; the most tyrannical government is powerless to control the inward workings of the mind."[1] But people can be, and in less democratic countries have been, made to suffer for their admitted or conjectured thoughts. Blackstone recalls that Dionysius is "recorded to have executed a subject, barely for dreaming that he had killed him; which was held for a sufficient proof, that he had thought thereof in his waking hours."[2] Such a result, while too barbaric to be tolerated in our nation, is not illogical if a government can tamper in the realm of thought and penalize "belief" on the ground that it might lead to illegal conduct. Individual freedom and governmental thought-probing cannot live together. As the Court admits even today, under the First Amendment "Beliefs are inviolate."

Today's decision rejects that fundamental principle. The Court admits, as it must, that the "proscriptions" of § 9 (h) of the National Labor Relations Act, as amended by the Taft-Hartley Act rest on "beliefs and political affiliations," and that "Congress has undeniably discouraged the lawful exercise of political freedoms" which are "protected by the First Amendment." These inescapable facts should compel a holding that § 9 (h) conflicts with the First Amendment.

Crucial to the Court's contrary holding is the premise that congressional power to regulate trade and traffic includes power to proscribe "beliefs and political affiliations." No case cited by the Court provides the least vestige of support for thus holding that the Commerce Clause restricts the right to think. On the contrary, the First Amendment was added after adoption of the Constitution for the express purpose of barring Congress from using previously granted powers to abridge belief or its expression. Freedom to think is inevitably abridged when beliefs are penalized by imposition of civil disabilities.

Since § 9 (h) was passed to exclude certain beliefs from one arena of the national economy, it was quite natural to utilize the test oath as a weapon. History attests the efficacy of that instrument for inflicting penalties and disabilities on obnoxious minorities. It was one of the major devices used against the Huguenots in France, and against "heretics" during the Spanish Inquisition.

---

[1] Dissenting opinion in *Jones v. Opelika*, 316 U. S. 584, 618, adopted as the Court's opinion in 319 U. S. 103. See also *Cantwell v. Connecticut*, 310 U. S. 296, 303.

[2] 4 Blackstone, Commentaries 79 (6th ed. Dublin 1775).

It helped English rulers identify and outlaw Catholics, Quakers, Baptists, and Congregationalists—groups considered dangerous for political as well as religious reasons. And wherever the test oath was in vogue, spies and informers found rewards far more tempting than truth. Painful awareness of the evils of thought espionage made such oaths "an abomination to the founders of this nation," *In re Summers*, 325 U. S. 561, 576, dissenting opinion. Whether religious, political, or both, test oaths are implacable foes of free thought. By approving their imposition, this Court has injected compromise into a field where the First Amendment forbids compromise.

The Court assures us that today's encroachment on liberty is just a small one, that this particular statutory provision "touches only a relative handful of persons, leaving the great majority of persons of the identified affiliations and beliefs completely free from restraint." But not the least of the virtues of the First Amendment is its protection of each member of the smallest and most unorthodox minority. Centuries of experience testify that laws aimed at one political or religious group, however rational these laws may be in their beginnings, generate hatreds and prejudices which rapidly spread beyond control. Too often it is fear which inspires such passions, and nothing is more reckless or contagious. In the resulting hysteria, popular indignation tars with the same brush all those who have ever been associated with any member of the group under attack or who hold a view which, though supported by revered Americans as essential to democracy, has been adopted by that group for its own purposes.

Under such circumstances, restrictions imposed on proscribed groups are seldom static, even though the rate of expansion may not move in geometric progression from discrimination to armband to ghetto and worse. Thus I cannot regard the Court's holding as one which merely bars Communists from holding union office and nothing more. For its reasoning would apply just as forcibly to statutes barring Communists and their suspected sympathizers from election to political office, mere membership in unions, and in fact from getting or holding any jobs whereby they could earn a living. . . .

Today the "political affiliation" happens to be the Communist Party: testimony of an ex-Communist that some Communist union officers had called "political strikes" is held sufficient to uphold a law coercing union members not to elect any Communist as an officer. Under this reasoning, affiliations with other political parties could be proscribed just as validly. Of course there is no practical possibility that either major political party would turn this weapon on the other, even though members of one party were accused of "political lockouts" a few years ago and members of the other are now charged with fostering a "welfare state" alien to our system. But with minor parties the possibility is not wholly fanciful. One, for instance, advocates socialism; another allegedly follows the Communist "line"; still another is repeatedly charged with a desire and purpose to deprive Negroes of equal job opportunities. Under today's opinion Congress could validly bar all members of these parties from officership in unions or industrial corporations; the only showing required would be testimony that some members in such positions had, by attempts to further their party's purposes, unjustifiably fostered industrial strife which hampered interstate commerce.

It is indicated, although the opinion is not thus limited and is based on threats to commerce rather than to national security, that members of the Communist Party or its "affiliates" can be individually attainted without danger to others because there is some evidence that as a group they act in obedience to the commands of a foreign power. This was the precise reason given in Sixteenth-Century England for attainting all Catholics unless they subscribed to test oaths wholly incompatible with their religion. Yet in the hour of crisis, an overwhelming majority of the English Catholics thus persecuted rallied loyally to defend their homeland against Spain and its Catholic troops. And in our own country Jefferson and his followers were earnestly accused of subversive allegiance to France. At the time, imposition of civil disability on all members of his political party must have seemed at least as desirable as does § 9 (h) today. For at stake, so many believed, was the survival of a newly-founded nation, not merely a few potential interruptions of commerce by strikes "political" rather than economic in origin.

These experiences underline the wisdom of the basic constitutional precept that penalties should be imposed only for a person's own conduct, not for his beliefs or for the conduct of others with whom he may associate. Guilt should not be imputed solely from association or affiliation with political parties or any other organization, however much we abhor the ideas which they advocate. *Schneiderman v. United States*, 320 U. S. 118, 136–139. Like anyone else, individual Communists who commit overt acts in violation of valid laws can and should be punished. But the postulate of the First Amendment is that our free institutions can be maintained without proscribing or penalizing political belief, speech, press, assembly, or party affiliation. This is a far bolder philosophy than despotic rulers can afford to follow. It is the heart of the system on which our freedom depends.

Fears of alien ideologies have frequently agitated the nation and inspired legislation aimed at suppressing advocacy of those ideologies. At such times the fog of public excitement obscures the ancient landmarks set up in our Bill of Rights. Yet then, of all times, should this Court adhere most closely to the course they mark. . . .

## Note

1. The same issues were raised in *Osman v. Douds*, 339 U. S. 846, 94 L. Ed. 1328, 70 S. Ct. 901 (1950), decided per curiam a month later. Justices Douglas and Minton, who had not participated in the first case, voted in the *Osman* case. Mr. Justice Minton agreed with Chief Justice Vinson. Mr. Justice Douglas joined Justices Black, Frankfurter and Jackson in holding the belief portion of the provision invalid, but found it unnecessary to pass on the remaining provisions. Mr. Justice Clark did not participate. The result was that the Court was equally divided on the belief portion of the affidavit and 6 to 1 in favor of the validity of the other provisions.

2. Discussion of the legal issues involving Section 9(h), written before the *Doud's* decision, appears in Leonard Boudin, *Supersedure and the Purgatory Oath Under the Taft-Hartley Law*, 23 N. Y. U. L. Q. Rev. 72 (1948); Barnett, *The Constitutionality of the Expurgatory Oath Requirement of the Labor Management Relations Act of 1947*, 27 Ore. L. Rev. 85 (1948); Notes, 48 Col. L. Rev. 253 (1948); 42 Ill. L. Rev. 487 (1947). For discussion after the *Douds* case, see Meiklejohn, *The First Amendment and Evils That Congress Has a Right to Prevent*, 26 Ind. L. J. 477 (1951); Louis Boudin, *"Seditious Doctrines" and the "Clear and Present Danger" Rule*, 38 Va. L. Rev. 143, 315, at pp. 315–24 (1952); Greenwald, *Non-Communist Affidavits: Taft-Hartley Sound and Fury*, 12 La. L. Rev. 407 (1952); Notes 51 Col. L. Rev. 130 (1951); 24 So. Calif. L. Rev. 197 (1951); 99 U. of Pa. L. Rev. 409 (1950). Compare Mr. Justice Jackson's analysis of the strategy and tactics of the Communist Party with that of Louis Boudin, *supra*, at pp. 181–6, 340–8.

In connection with Mr. Justice Black's discussion of the historical function of loyalty oaths, see Koenigsberg and Stavis, *Test Oaths: Henry VIII to the American Bar Association*, 11 Law. Guild Rev. 111 (1951); Dunham, *Doctrines of Allegiance in Late Medieval English Law*, 26 N. Y. U. L. Rev. 41 (1951). See also H. M. Jones, *Do You Know the Nature of an Oath?*, 37 Am. Assn. U. Prof. Bull. 442 (1951).

3. In *N.L.R.B. v. Highland Park Mfg. Co.*, 341 U. S. 322, 95 L. Ed. 969, 71 S. Ct. 758 (1951), the Court held that Section 9(h) required that the officers of parent organizations, such as the American Federation of Labor and the Congress of Industrial Organizations, must file affidavits before affiliated unions could obtain the benefits of the Act. Other cases dealing with the administration of Section 9(h) are collected in 95 L. Ed. at 979–93. For discussion see Daykin, *The Operation of the Taft-Hartley Act's Non-Communist Provisions*, 36 Iowa L. Rev. 607 (1951); Note, 18 U. of Chi. L. Rev. 783 (1951).

4. The National Labor Relations Act does not protect an employee

[Emerson]

from discharge by his employer for Communist or other political beliefs or activities. See Statement of N.L.R.B. General Counsel, N. Y. Times, Mar 30, 1951. Under the Taft-Hartley amendments, where the union has a union shop it is an unfair labor practice for the union to cause the employer to discharge an employee for reasons "other than his failure to tender the periodic dues." 29 U. S. C. § 158 (b) (2) (1951). But the General Counsel of the Board has refused to issue a complaint where the union procured the dismissal of an employee who had signed the Communist-sponsored Stockholm Peace Pledge. N. Y. Times, Mar. 30, 1951. See also *In the Matter of Gamble-Skogmo, Inc.*, 75 N.L.R.B. Dec. 1068 (1948); *Lockheed Aircraft Corp. v. Superior Court*, 28 Cal. 2d 481, 171 Pac. 2d 21 (1946) (statute prohibiting discharge for political activity does not prevent discharge of employee who advocates overthrow of government by force and violence or whose loyalty has not been established). But cf. *In re Kingston Cake Co.*, 29 LRRM 1239 (1952).

5. The constitutions of many unions exclude Communists from membership. See Summers, *The Right to Join a Union*, 47 Col. L. Rev. 33, 35 (1947); Summers, *Admission Policies of Labor Unions*, 61 Q. J. of Ec. 66, 75–6 (1946) (pointing out that these provisions are not always rigorously administered). And the courts have declined to interfere where, in the absence of express constitutional provision, unions have expelled members for Communist activity. See *Shein v. Rose*, 12 N. Y. Supp. 2d 87 (Sup. Ct., N. Y. Co., 1939); *Weinstock v. Ladisky*, 197 Misc. 859, 98 N. Y. Supp. 2d 85 (Sup. Ct., N. Y. Co., 1950); *Ames v. Dubinsky*, 70 N. Y. Supp. 2d 706 (1947); and note *Harmon v. United Mine Workers*, 166 Ark. 255, 266 S. W. 84 (1924) (expulsion for membership in Ku Klux Klan upheld). See also Note, 96 U. of Pa. L. Rev. 381, 398–400 (1948).

6. In 1948 the Atomic Energy Commission instructed the General Electric Company to withdraw recognition from the United Electrical and Radio Workers Union (then C. I. O.) at the Knolls Atomic Power Laboratory because of "alleged Communist affiliation or association of various officers of UE taken together with the failure of UE officers to file non-Communist affidavits under the Labor Management Relations Act." N. Y. Times, Oct. 9, 1948. A suit by the UE to prevent this action ended in failure. *United Electrical Workers v. Lilienthal*, 84 F. Supp. 640 (D. C. D. C., 1949).

7. In 1949 and 1950 the C.I.O. expelled ten unions on grounds they were dominated by Communists and consistently followed the Communist Party line. N. Y. Times, Nov. 3, 1949, Feb. 16, June 16, Aug. 30, 1950; see Fitch, *The C.I.O. and Its Communists*, The Survey, Dec. 1949, p. 642. Efforts to block the expulsion by legal proceedings proved futile. See *Tisa v. Potofsky*, 90 F. Supp. 175 (S. D. N. Y., 1950) and *Chase v. Rieve*, 90 F. Supp. 184 (S. D. N. Y., 1950) (motion to dismiss denied but motion for temporary injunction also denied); *Durkin v. Murray*, 90 F. Supp. 367 (D. C. D. C., 1950) (suit dismissed for failure to exhaust administrative remedies). Other purges of left wing elements in the labor unions have also taken place in the last few years. See David Beck, *Communism and American Labor Unions*,

Vital Speeches, Dec. 1, 1950; Eggleston, *Labor and Civil Liberties*, The Nation, June 28, 1952, p. 647.

8. For material on the influence of Communist and left wing groups in the labor movement, see Hearings before Subcommittee of House Committee on Education and Labor, 80th Cong., 2d Sess. (1948) (hearings on New York distributive trades and fur industry); *Communist Infiltration of Labor Unions*, Hearings before the Committee on Un-American Activities, 81st Cong., 1st Sess. (1949), 81st Cong., 2d Sess. (1950); Report of Subcommittee of Senate Committee on Labor and Public Welfare, Sen. Doc. 89, 82d Cong., 1st Sess. (1951); Murray, *American Labor and the Threat of Communism*, 274 Annals of the Am. Acad. of Pol. and Soc. Sci. 125 (1951); Conn, *Communist-Led Unions and U. S. Security*, New Republic, Feb. 18, 1952.

## Restrictions on Access to the Election Process

Restrictions on access to the election process have taken two principal forms: (1) the exclusion of a party from the ballot; (2) the requirement that candidates for election to public office meet certain qualifications or take some form of oath.

Some 15 states and territories have statutes falling within the first category.[1] The leading case on the constitutionality of this form of legislation is *Communist Party v. Peek*, 20 Calif. 2d 536, 127 Pac. 2d 889 (1942). Various provisions of the California election law were involved. One provided that no party "shall be recognized or qualified to participate in any primary election which uses or adopts as any part of its party designation the word 'communist' or any derivative of the word 'communist.'" This provision the California Supreme Court held invalid as having no reasonable relation to the objective of eliminating subversive parties from the election process. Another portion of the law imposed the same limitation upon any party "which is directly or indirectly affiliated, by any means whatsoever, with the Communist Party of the United States, the Third Communist International, or any other foreign agency, political party, organization or government." This provision was also held invalid, the specific designation of the Communist Party being outlawed by the provision of the California Constitution prohibiting special legislation and the remainder being too broad in its sweep. A third prohibition against any party "which either directly or indirectly carries on, advocates, teaches, justifies, aids, or abets a program of sabotage, force and violence, sedition or treason against, the Government of the United States or this State" was held constitutional under the doctrine of *Whitney v. California*.

---

[1] These statutes, as of January 1, 1951, are collected in Gellhorn, *The States and Subversion*, Appen. A (1952).

But this third provision could be applied to any particular party only after opportunity for notice, hearing and judicial review.

An Arkansas statute, similar to the third provision of the California law, was held valid in *Field v. Hall*, 201 Ark. 77, 143 S. W. 2d 567 (1940). The Arkansas Court differed with the California Court, however, in holding that the Communist Party could be excluded from the ballot under the statute without notice or hearing by the secretary of state, the trial in a mandamus proceeding affording sufficient due process. A similar provision, with the additional exclusion of a party "which has in any manner any connection with any foreign government or power," was upheld against attack by the Prohibition Party in *State ex rel. Berry v. Hummel*, 42 Ohio Law Abs. 40, 59 N. E. 2d 238 (1944).[2]

In practice the flexibilities of administration by election officials, as well as the difficulties and delays of judicial review, sometimes make it difficult for radical parties to secure their full privileges. See Ward, *The Communist Party and the Ballot*, 1 Bill of Rights Rev. 286 (1941); Note, 96 U. of Pa. L. Rev. 381, 388–91 (1948).

The other form of restriction upon use of the elective process by radical parties is found in the laws of ten states. See Gellhorn, *supra*. Recent legislation has tended to take this pattern, as in the New Jersey statute passed in 1949 and the Maryland Subversive Activities Act, known as the Ober law, passed in the same year. The New Jersey legislation required every candidate for public office to take an oath that he does not "believe in, advocate or advise the use of force, or violence, or other unlawful or unconstitutional means, to overthrow or make any change in the Government established in the United States or in this State," or belong to or is affiliated with any organization that does so. This provision was declared invalid on the ground that the oath to support the constitution required in the New Jersey constitution

---

[2] In *Feinglass v. Reinecke*, 48 F. Supp. 438 (N. D. Ill., 1942), a Federal Court held invalid, as being too vague and uncertain, an Illinois statute excluding from the ballot any organization which was "associated, directly or indirectly, with Communist, Fascist, Nazi or other un-American principles and engages in activities or propaganda designed to teach subservience to the political principles and ideals of foreign nations or the overthrow by violence of the established constitutional form of government of the United States and the State of Illinois." Since the ballots had already been printed, however, the court refused to grant an injunction to Communist Party candidates restraining election officials from excluding them from the ballot. In *Washington ex rel. Huff v. Reeves*, 5 Wash. 2d 637, 106 Pac. 2d 729 (1940), an attempt by election officials to bar the Communist Party from the ballot, in the absence of any statutory provision, was disallowed.

was exclusive. *Imbrie v. Marsh,* 3 N. J. 578, 71 Atl. 2d 352 (1950).

The Ober law required that no person could become a candidate for public office unless he filed an affidavit that he is not a "subversive person." "Subversive person" is defined as "any person who commits, attempts to commit, or aids in the commission, or advocates, abets, advises or teaches by any means any person to commit, attempt to commit, or aid in the commission of any act intended to overthrow, destroy or alter . . . the constitutional form of the Government . . . by revolution, force, or violence;" or who is a member of an organization engaged in such conduct. The Maryland Court sustained the provision as to candidates for state office but rejected it as to candidates for Federal office. *Shub v. Simpson,* 76 Atl. 2d 332 (1950). The provision came before the Supreme Court of the United States in the *Gerende* case.

## GERENDE v. BOARD OF SUPERVISORS OF ELECTIONS OF BALTIMORE

Supreme Court of the United States, 1951
341 U. S. 56, 95 L. Ed. 745, 71 S. Ct. 565

PER CURIAM.

This is an appeal from a decision of the Court of Appeals of the State of Maryland the effect of which is to deny the appellant a place on the ballot for a municipal election in the City of Baltimore on the ground that she has refused to file an affidavit required by state law. Md. Laws 1949, c. 86, § 15. — Md. —, 78 A. 2d 660. The scope of the state law was passed on in *Shub v. Simpson,* — Md —, 76 A. 2d 332. We read this decision to hold that to obtain a place on a Maryland ballot a candidate need only make oath that he is not a person who is engaged "in one way or another in the attempt to overthrow the government *by force or violence,*" and that he is not knowingly a member of an organization engaged in such an attempt. — Md. at —, 76 A. 2d at 338. At the bar of this Court the Attorney General of the State of Maryland declared that he would advise the proper authorities to accept an affidavit in these terms as satisfying in full the statutory requirement. Under these circumstances and with this understanding, the judgment of the Maryland Court of Appeals is

*Affirmed.*

MR. JUSTICE REED concurs in the result.

## Note

1. In an advisory opinion the Alabama Supreme Court held that a

proposed constitutional amendment providing a loyalty oath as a qualification for voting would not violate the Fourteenth Amendment. *Opinion of the Justices,* 252 Ala. 351, 40 So. 2d 849 (1949).

2. See, generally, on the right of alleged subversive groups to access to the electoral process, Notes, 54 Harv. L. Rev. 155 (1940); 1 Stan. L. Rev. 85, 90–1 (1948); 34 Va. L. Rev. 450 (1948); 25 Notre Dame Law. 319 (1950); 3 Vand. L. Rev. 811 (1950). See also *Wilson v. Council of Highland Park,* 284 Mich. 96, 278 S. W. 778 (1938) (court refused to remove city councilman for membership in Black Legion).

## Restrictions on Movement

The chief restrictions imposed for political reasons on freedom of movement have been in connection with the denial of passports to citizens wishing to travel abroad and the denial of visas to persons desiring to visit the United States.

Under present Federal legislation it is a criminal offense for United States citizens to travel outside the Americas without a passport during the existence of a national emergency. 22 U. S. C. §§ 223–6 (1946). Such an emergency has been in effect since 1941. The legislation authorizing issuance of passports provides only that the Secretary of State "may" issue them to citizens under regulations set forth by the President. 22 U. S. C. §§ 211a, 212 (1946). Presidential regulations empower the Secretary to issue, deny or invalidate passports "in his discretion." Ex. Order No. 7856, 22 Code Fed. Regs. § 51.75 (1949). With increasing frequency in recent years the Secretary of State denied or invalidated passports giving as the only reason that "travel abroad at this time would be contrary to the best interests of the United States." See Note, 61 Yale L. J. 171, 173 (1952). It was clear that the denial in many instances was based upon the political activities or associations of the applicant. *Ibid.*

Passport denials that were reported in the press included refusals to Prof. Corliss Lamont of Columbia University (N. Y. Times, Oct. 15 and 16, 1951), Dr. Linus Pauling of the California Institute of Technology (N. Y. Times, May 12, 1952),[1] Rev. Henry J. Carpenter of Brooklyn (N. Y. Times, May 19, 1952), and from 20 to 25 "United States citizens assigned by the United Nations to go to Paris for the General Assembly meetings" (N. Y. Times, Nov. 1, 1951). Passports already issued were revoked in the cases of Paul Robeson (N. Y. Times, Aug. 4, 1950) and Dr. Ralph Spitzer (N. Y. Times, Sept. 19, 1950).[2] In May 1952

[1] Subsequently Dr. Pauling, on filing an affidavit that he had never been a member of the Communist Party, was given a "limited passport" to visit France and England. New Haven Register, July 17, 1952.

[2] The N. Y. Times identifies Dr. Spitzer as a former associate professor

the State Department reported that about 300 Americans had been barred from traveling abroad in the previous 12 months. N. Y. Times, May 25, 1952.

Issues were raised also with respect to the procedures employed by the State Department in making decisions on issuance of passports. No formal hearing on the question is held; the reasons for refusal are not stated beyond that it is "contrary to the best interests of the United States"; the applicant does not know the evidence upon which the decision is based, and has no opportunity to rebut it or cross-examine adverse witnesses. The applicant's only recourse is to ask for reconsideration and submit such evidence in writing as he may feel is relevant. Informal conferences with State Department officials may also take place. The State Department's position is that the matter rests entirely within its discretion and is not subject to court review.

In the spring of 1952 both the standards and procedures of the State Department in issuing passports were severely criticized by the American Civil Liberties Union and others. *Report by the American Civil Liberties Union on the Issuance of Passports* (Feb. 18, 1952); Note, *Passport Refusals for Political Reasons: Constitutional Issues and Judicial Review*, 61 Yale L. J. 171 1952); Rev. John Paul Jones, N. Y. Times, May 19, 1952. Shortly afterwards the Secretary of State issued a formal statement of the Department's position:

"It was decided that, in view of the findings by the court [in the *Dennis* case] and the Congress [in the Internal Security Act of 1950], it would be inappropriate and inconsistent for the Department to issue a passport to a person if information in its files *gave reason to believe* that he is knowingly a member of a Communist organization or that his conduct abroad is likely to be contrary to the best interests of the United States. This policy has been followed since February 1951, and, in view of the national emergency proclaimed by President Truman and the conditions existing in various areas of the world, it is believed that it should be closely adhered to.

"A passport certifies to foreign governments not only the citizenship and identity of the bearer, but requests them to permit him safely and freely to pass and, in case of need, to give all lawful aid and protection. Possession of the passport indicates the right of the bearer to receive the protection and good offices of

---

of chemistry at Oregon State University, "dismissed by the University in February, 1949, for supporting the genetic theories of the Russian biologist, Trofim D. Lysenko."

In September, 1951 the Army denied Prof. John K. Fairbank of Harvard a permit to visit Japan. N. Y. Times, Sept. 5, 1951.

American diplomatic and consular officers abroad. The right to receive the protection of this Government is correlative with the obligation to give undivided allegiance to the United States. A person whose activities, either at home or abroad, promote the interests of a foreign country or a political faction therein to the detriment of the United States or of friendly foreign countries should not be the bearer of an American passport.

"Passports are refused only on the basis of very clear and definite reports from the investigative and security offices of this Department and of other Government departments and agencies and from foreign governments containing well-authenticated information concerning past and present activities and associations of the applicant. . . .

"Any applicant who has been refused a passport has every right and is given every opportunity to request further consideration of his case and may present any evidence or information which he may wish to have considered. The particularity with which he may be informed of the contents of the reports in the Department's file depends, of course, upon the source and classification of such reports, but it is usually possible to inform him in a general way of the nature of the evidence and the information upon which he has been refused a passport. Any new evidence or information which the applicant may submit is referred to the officers who first examined the case for evaluation and expression of opinion as to whether a passport may be issued. The Department cannot violate the confidential character of passport files by making public any information contained therein."[3]

The State Department has also refused visas to persons desiring to visit the United States on grounds that they were Communists or Communist adherents. Thus in March 1950 it denied entry to twelve members of the World Congress of Partisans of Peace, including Pablo Picasso, the French artist, and Rev. Hewlett Johnson, Dean of Canterbury, for the reason that they were "known Communists and fellow-travelers." N. Y. Times, March 4, 1950.

The Internal Security Act of 1950, passed in September, tightened substantially the restrictions on foreign visitors. It makes mandatory the exclusion of numerous classes of aliens, including all who "at any time" have been members of "the Communist or other totalitarian party" of any country. 8 U. S. C. § 137 (1950) ; see *infra*. Under these provisions a number of well known foreign visitors have been barred from entry. Thus

---

[3] Department of State Press Release, May 24, 1952, reprinted in The Department of State Bulletin, June 9, 1952, pp. 919–20.

in September 1951 "a dozen of the world's leading chemists, some of them official delgates to the International Congress of Pure and Applied Chemistry," were denied visas. N. Y. Times, Sept. 7, 1951. The Federation of American Scientists, at its annual meeting in 1952, reported that "United States visa restrictions had prevented or 'indefinitely delayed' the visits of more than 200 foreign scientists in the last year and one-half." N. Y. Times, Apr. 30, 1952.

Numerous protests, from scientists and others, have been made against this visa policy. Typical is the statement of four members of the University of Chicago to Secretary of State Acheson: "It has become very difficult for a reputable university in the United States to invite foreign scholars to participate even temporarily in the intellectual life of the institution and this at a time at which a feeling of communion among the universities of the free world is greatly to be desired." N. Y. Times, Jan. 31, 1952.

### Note

1. For a detailed account of the State Department's policy on passports and a discussion of the legal issues, see Note, *supra*, 61 Yale L. J. 171 (1952). See also Note, *"Passport Denied": State Department Practice and Due Process*, 3 Stan. L. Rev. 312 (1951). For material supporting the argument for stringent regulation of travel by members of left wing groups, see Cohen and Fuchs, *Communism's Challenge and the Constitution*, 34 Corn. L. Q. 182, 187–90 (1948).

2. Two suits in the District of Columbia—one by Paul Robeson and the other by the American Civil Liberties Union in the case of Anne Bauer—were brought to test the State Department's policy and procedure on passports. On July 9, 1952, a three-judge court ruled in the *Bauer* case that the State Department must grant a hearing before revoking or refusing to renew a passport. *Bauer v. Acheson*, — F. Supp. — (1952).

3. For other aspects of freedom of movement see *Edwards v. California*, 314 U. S. 160, 86 L. Ed. 119, 62 S. Ct. 164 (1941); *Hague v. C. I. O.*, 307 U. S. 496, 83 L. Ed. 1423, 59 S. Ct. 954 (1939); Meyers, *Federal Privileges and Immunities: Application to Ingress and Egress*, 29 Corn. L. Q. 489 (1944).

### Restrictions on Aliens

Congress was early held to have unlimited power of exclusion of aliens from the United States,[1] and, flowing from this, plenary

---

[1] *Head Money Cases*, 112 U. S. 580, 28 L. Ed. 798, 5 S. Ct. 247, (1884), *Ekiu v. U. S.*, 142 U. S. 651, 35 L. Ed. 1146, 12 S. Ct. 336 (1892).

power to deport aliens.[2]  Under this deportation power various restrictions have been placed upon political activities of aliens.

The governing statute in this field is the Nationalities Act of 1940.[3]  It provides for deportation of aliens who are anarchists, opposers of organized government, advocates or members of organizations advocating violent overthrow of the government, publishers of such doctrines, or affiliates or contributors to organizations who are publishers of such doctrines.[4]  Under the original Act the Supreme Court had held that, in order to warrant deportation, the proscribed statutory beliefs or actions must exist at the time of the proceedings.[5]  Thereafter the law was amended to include past beliefs or activity, even if discontinued, as grounds for deportation.[6]  These 1940 provisions were declared constitutional in the *Harisiades* case.[7]

In *Bridges v. Wixon* in 1945 the Supreme Court set a high standard of proof for a showing of "affiliation" with a proscribed organization (in this case the Communist Party) as grounds for deportation.[8]  No decision as to the subversive character of the Communist Party was made.  Since the *Dennis* case, however, it is established that membership in the Communist Party constitutes sufficient grounds for deportation.[9]

The Internal Security Act of 1950 expanded the grounds for deportation for political activity.  It makes statutory the finding that the Communist Party and its affiliates advocate the

---

[2] *Fong Yue Ting v. U. S.*, 149 U. S. 698, 37 L. Ed. 905, 13 S. Ct. 1016 (1893).

The power over aliens is subject to certain requirements of due process. *Japanese Immigrant Case*, 189 U. S. 86, 47 L. Ed. 721, 23 S. Ct. 611 (1903). See *Bilokumsky v. Tod*, 263 U. S. 149, 68 L. Ed. 221, 44 S. Ct. 54 (1923). From time to time vigorous dissents have called for the application of greater due process protections.  See, *e. g.*, Justices Field and Brewer dissenting in *Fong Yue Ting v. U. S., supra;* Justice Murphy concurring in *Bridges v. Wixon*, 326 U. S. 135, 89 L. Ed. 2103, 65 S. Ct. 1443 (1945); Justice Douglas dissenting in *Harisiades v. Shaughnessy*, 342 U. S. 580, 96 L. Ed. —, 72 S. Ct. 512 (1952).  For recent cases involving procedural requirements see *U. S. ex rel. Knauff v. Shaughnessy*, 338 U. S. 537, 94 L. Ed. 317, 70 S. Ct. 309 (1950); *Ludecke v. Watkins*, 335 U. S. 160, 92 L. Ed. 1881, 68 S. Ct. 1429 (1948).

[3] 54 Stat. 673, 8 U. S. C. 137 (1940), amended 64 Stat. 1006 (1950).

[4] 8 U. S. C. 137 (a)–(f).

[5] *Kessler v. Strecker*, 307 U. S. 22, 83 L. Ed. 1082, 59 S. Ct. 694 (1939).

[6] See 54 Stat. 673 (1940).

[7] *Supra*, note 2.  The original statute of 1906 was declared constitutional in a case holding that philosophical belief in anarchism was sufficient to constitute an alien an "anarchist" and justify deportation.  *U. S. ex rel. Turner v. Williams*, 194 U. S. 279, 48 L. Ed. 979, 24 S. Ct. 719 (1904).

[8] 326 U. S. 135, 89 L. Ed. 2103, 65 S. Ct. 1443 (1945).

[9] *U. S. ex rel. Kaloudis v. Shaughnessy*, 180 F. 2d 489 (C. A. 2, 1950); *Vergas v. Shaughnessy*, 97 F. Supp. 335 (S. D. N. Y., 1951); *Harisiades v. Shaughnessy, supra.*

overthrow of the government by force, and explicitly orders deportation of aliens who at any time advocated, or wrote or circulated written matter advocating the overthrow of the government or "the economic, international, and governmental doctrines of world communism," or belonged to any organization that did any of these things.[10] Under this Act aliens whose political activities or beliefs fall within the proscribed limits are not only subject to deportation but are also subject to detention in jail without bail pending hearing, at the Attorney-General's discretion.[11] The statute also makes it a felony not to begin in good faith to take steps to leave the country within six months of a deportation order.[12]

The power over naturalization is specifically granted to Congress in the Constitution[13] and, despite rare dissents,[14] the power to denaturalize has been held to be granted thereby also.[15] The Nationalities Act of 1906[16] with amendments added in 1940 not important here,[17] governed naturalization proceedings until 1950. Under it an alien could not be naturalized if he had advocated, circulated literature advocating, or belonged to any organization advocating, overthrow of the government by force, at any time within ten years of his petition for naturalization;[18] and the alien must during all of the five years preceding the petition be attached to the principles of the Constitution.[19] If the alien had already been naturalized his naturalization could be revoked as illegally procured for non-compliance with these provisions, or as fraudulently procured for having falsely stated his attachment or falsely sworn on oath as to his loyalty.[20] The Supreme Court, however, has imposed strict requirements of proof on denaturalization actions for fraudulent procurement, holding that membership in a "subversive" organization, or one with ties to a foreign government in the case of the German-American Bund, by itself is not enough evidence to prove lack of attach-

---

[10] 8 U. S. C. § 137 (1951).
[11] *Carlson v. Landon*, 342 U. S. 524, 96 L. Ed. —, 72 S. Ct. 525 (1952).
[12] 8 U. S. C. § 156 (1951). See *U. S. v. Spector*, 343 U. S. 169, 96 L. Ed. —, 72 S. Ct. 591 (1952).
[13] Art. I, Sec. 8.
[14] Mr. Justice Rutledge dissenting in *Knauer v. U. S.*, 328 U. S. 654, 678, 90 L. Ed. 1500, 66 S. Ct. 1304 (1946).
[15] *Johannessen v. U. S.*, 225 U. S. 227, 56 L. Ed. 1066, 32 S. Ct. 613 (1912); *Luria v. U. S.*, 231 U. S. 9, 58 L. Ed. 101, 34 S. Ct. 10 (1913).
[16] 34 Stat. 596 (1906).
[17] 54 Stat. 1137 (1941).
[18] 8 U. S. C. § 705 (1950).
[19] 8 U. S. C. § 707 (1950).
[20] 8 U. S. C. § 738 (1950). See *Baumgartner v. U. S.*, 322 U. S. 665, 88 L. Ed. 1525, 64 S. Ct. 1240 (1944); *U. S. ex rel. Eichenlaub v. Shaughnessy*, 338 U. S. 521, 94 L. Ed. 307, 70 S. Ct. 329 (1950); *Knauer v. U. S., supra.*

ment, but that a showing of personal disloyalty to the United States is required.[21] Strict limitations were also placed on the wide latitude which had formerly been allowed[22] for introducing evidence of activities or beliefs subsequent to naturalization as retroactively showing lack of attachment.[23]

The Internal Security Act of 1950 imposes greater restrictions on the permissible political activities of aliens desiring naturalization. The question of the subversiveness of the Communist Party and Communist-front organizations is decided by statute. Any person is ineligible for naturalization, or subject to denaturalization, who within ten years prior to his petition for naturalization advocated, or circulated any material advocating, or belonged to any organization advocating, the overthrow of the government by force, or advocated the ideas of world communism; and membership in a Communist-front organization within ten years prior to naturalization raises a presumption of lack of attachment. The Act also contains a provision that membership in any of the above organizations or advocacy of any of the above ideas within five years *after* the petition for naturalization is filed shall be prima facie evidence of lack of attachment at the time of naturalization, and sufficient evidence to support a denaturalization order. Activities even prior to the ten-year period established in the statute may prevent naturalization if a deportation proceeding, for which there is no period of limitation, has been instituted.[24]

## Note

Generally on political restrictions on aliens, see Konvitz, *The Alien and the Asiatic in American Law*, ch. 1–4 (1946); Preuss, *Denaturalization on the Ground of Disloyalty*, 36 Am. Pol. Sci. Rev. 701 (1942); Balch, *Denaturalization Based on Disloyalty*, 29 Minn. L. Rev. 405 (1945); Louis Boudin, *The Settler Within Our Gates*, 26 N. Y. U. L. Rev. 266, 451 (1951); Notes, 52 Yale L. J. 108 (1942); 44 Col. L. Rev. 736 (1944); 96 U. of Pa. L. Rev. 381, 385–7 (1948); 1 Stan. L. Rev. 85, 86–8 (1948); 34 Va. L. Rev. 439, 442–3 (1948). On the effect of the Internal Security Act see King and Ginger, *The McCarran Act and the Immigration Laws*, 11 Law. Guild Rev. 128 (1951); Notes, 51 Col. L. Rev. 606, 629–46 (1951); 60 Yale L. J. 152 (1951); 24 Temple L. Q. 302 (1951).

---

[21] *Schneiderman v. U. S.*, 320 U. S. 118, 87 L. Ed. 1796, 63 S. Ct. 1333 (1943); *Baumgartner v. U. S.*, *supra*; *Knauer v. U. S.*, *supra*.

[22] See *U. S. v. Wursterbarth*, 249 Fed. 908 (D. N. J., 1918); *U. S. v. Swelgin*, 254 Fed. 884 (D. Ore., 1918); *cf.* Notes, 18 A. L. R. 1185 (1922), 44 Col. L. Rev. 736 (1944).

[23] *Schneiderman v. U.S.*, *supra*.

[24] Section 25 of the Internal Security Act, amending Section 305 of the Nationality Act of 1940.

Since the *Dennis* case and the passage of the Internal Security Act the Government has substantially intensified its efforts to deport alleged subversive aliens. See, *e. g.,* N. Y. Times, Oct. 24, 1950.

[After the above material was in proof Congress passed, over President Truman's veto, the Immigration and Nationality Act, codifying and revising all laws relating to immigration, naturalization and nationality. June 27, 1952. The new law incorporates and strengthens all the above restrictions relating to the political activities of aliens.]

## Restrictions on Lawyers

In 1950 the American Bar Association adopted a resolution that "the legislature, the court or other appropriate authority of each state or territory . . . be requested to require each member of its Bar, within a reasonable time and periodically thereafter, to file an affidavit stating whether he is or ever has been a member of the Communist Party or affiliated therewith, and stating also whether he is or ever has been a member or supporter of any organization that espouses the overthrow by force or by any illegal or unconstitutional means" of the government; and in the event such affidavit reveals such membership, "that the appropriate authority promptly and thoroughly investigate the activities and conduct of said member of the Bar to determine his fitness for continuance as an attorney." 36 A.B.A.J. 972 (1950). This proposal was criticized by a number of individuals and organizations, including a group of 26 prominent members of the Association headed by former Supreme Court Justice Roberts. 37 A.B.A.J. 123 (1951). For the National Lawyers Guild opposition see 11 Law. Guild Rev. 42 (1951). See also the articles by Professor Chafee in Harvard Law School Record, Nov. 1 and 8, 1950. In support see 37 A.B.A.J. 128 (1951).

After further consideration the American Bar Association in 1952 adopted new resolutions, the major features of which were: (1) that the Association "expel from its membership any and every individual who is a member of the Communist Party of the United States, or who advocates Marxism-Leninism"; (2) that State and Local Bar Associations be urged to do the same; and (3) that "State and Local Bar Associations or appropriate authorities immediately commence disciplinary actions of disbarment" against all such lawyers. 37 A.B.A.J. 312–3 (1951).

Some State and Local Bar Associations have accepted the A.B.A. proposals. Thus the Michigan State Bar Association voted to request the Michigan Supreme Court to amend the Canons of Professional Ethics to allow disbarment proceedings for "acts of disloyalty"; and to ask the legislature for a statute permitting confidential information gathered by the State police to be used in disbarment proceedings. N. Y. Times, Sept. 28, 1951. The Boston Bar Association voted to ask the Massachusetts Supreme Court to disbar Communists and also voted to require a loyalty oath for new members. American Civil Liberties Union Weekly Bulletin, Nov. 26, 1951. And the New Jersey State Bar Association voted to expel members of the Communist Party or persons advocating overthrow of the government by force or violence. N. Y. Times, May 24, 1952.

The New Jersey loyalty oath considered in *Imbrie v. Marsh, supra,* is also applicable to lawyers.

## Note

In support of the A. B. A.'s proposals see American Bar Association, *Brief on Communism: Marxism-Leninism* (Sept. 17, 1951); in opposition see Koenigsberg and Stavis, *Test Oaths: Henry VIII to the American Bar Association,* 11 Law. Guild Rev. 111 (1951); resolution of National Lawyers Guild, 11 Law. Guild Rev. 95 (1951). With respect to the legal issues see *Ex parte Garland,* 4 Wall. 333, 18 L. Ed. 366 (1867); *In re Summers,* 325 U. S. 561, 89 L. Ed. 1795, 65 S. Ct. 1307 (1945); *Application of Cassidy,* 51 N. Y. Supp. 2d 202, 268 App. Div. 282, aff'd 296 N. Y. 926, 73 N. E. 2d 41 (1947); Note, 18 A. L. R. 2d 268, 283–91, 335–6.

For a survey of political restrictions in the professions see Countryman, *The Bigots and the Professionals,* The Nation, June 28, 1952, p. 641.

### Note on Other Deprivations of Privileges and Positions

Among other situations in which persons charged with subversive activities or associations have been deprived of privileges or positions of influence, the following may be noted:

*Public relief.* The Emergency Relief Act of 1941 prohibited relief employment to any "communist" or "member of any Nazi Bund organization." 54 Stat. 611, 620 (1941). This provision was held invalid by a Federal District Court in *U. S. v. Schneider,* 45 F. Supp. 848 (E. D. Wis., 1942), on the ground that there was no reasonable connection between political beliefs and financial distress. But the court did sustain that part of the indictment which charged falsification of facts in concealing Communist membership. See also *U. S. v. Hautau,* 43 F. Supp. 507 (D. N. J., 1942).

A Pennsylvania law makes individuals engaged in subversive activities ineligible for public assistance, unless blind. Pa. Stat. Ann., tit. 62, § 2509 (Supp. 1949).

*Unemployment compensation.* The Ohio Unemployment Compensation Law was amended in 1949 to provide that no person is eligible for benefits who the administrator finds "advocates, or is a member of a party which advocates, the overthrow of our government by force";

**527**

and that every claimant for benefits must file an affidavit stating whether or not he advocates, or is a member of a party that advocates, overthrow of the government by force. Ohio G. C. § 1345–6, par. c (4). The provision was upheld in *Dworken v. Collopy*, 91 N. E. 2d 564 (Ct. Com. Pleas Ohio, 1950). See Note, 29 Chi.-Kent L. Rev. 255 (1951).

*Right to conduct a benefit society.* In *In re International Workers Order*, 106 N. Y. Supp. 2d 953 (Sup. Ct., N. Y. Co., 1951), the Court granted the application of the Superintendent of Insurance for an order directing him to take possession of and liquidate the International Workers Order, Inc., a fraternal benefit society, found to be dominated by the Communist Party. The liquidation was ordered under a provision of the New York Insurance Law authorizing liquidation of an insurance company found to be "in such condition that its further transaction of business will be hazardous to its policyholders, or to its creditors, or to the public"; and further on the ground that the society had, through its association with the Communist Party, exceeded its corporate powers and practiced a fraud on the state.

*Position in judicial proceedings.* In *Fawick Airflex Co. v. United Electrical Workers*, 92 N. E. 2d 431 (C. A. Ohio, 1950), app. dis. 93 N. E. 2d 480 (Ohio, 1950), a union official was charged with violation of a restraining order issued in a labor dispute. The union official took the stand in his own defense and, on cross-examination, was asked questions concerning membership in the Communist Party. He refused to answer and was adjudged guilty of contempt. On appeal the court sustained the contempt citation, holding that the questions were relevant and material. The witness was charged with acts of violence in a situation which "had all of the aspects of a dangerous and subversive revolt"; and further "it is well known that the sanctity of the truth and an oath may be, and is, pushed aside [by Communist Party members] with impunity if warranted by the occasion." 92 N. E. 2d at 433, 434. See Notes, 26 Notre Dame Law. 130 (1950); 4 Vand. L. Rev. 916 (1951).

In *State of N. Y. ex rel. Choolokian v. Mission of the Immaculate Virgin*, 192 Misc. 454, 76 N. Y. Supp. 2d 509 (1947), aff'd 274 App. Div. 1049 (1949), aff'd 300 N. Y. 43, 88 N. E. 2d 362 (1949), cert. den. 339 U. S. 912 (1950), the court refused to grant a father custody of three of his children, previously placed by him in welfare institutions, on the ground that the parent intended to emigrate to Soviet Armenia and take the children there.

For a collection of cases see Note, 18 A. L. R. 2d 268. On the use of public buildings, see Chapter VI, *infra*. On problems of academic freedom, see Chapter VII, *infra*. See also the material relating to the Internal Security Act, *infra*.

## 4. Loyalty Qualifications for Employment

One of the most significant developments in freedom of political expression in the period following the Second World War has been the establishment of loyalty qualifications for employment. Major emphasis on loyalty requirements has been in government employment—Federal, state and local—but programs have been established and proposed in a wide area of private employment as well.

Loyalty qualifications in employment have assumed two major forms. One is the requirement of taking a loyalty oath as a condition of employment. By constitution and statute public officials and employees have customarily been required to take oaths to support the constitution and laws. See *American Communications Ass'n v. Douds* and *Marsh v. Imbrie, supra.* The issue arises as to oaths which carry beyond the traditional scope. The other major form of loyalty qualification has been the requirement that persons meet certain standards of loyalty as a condition of obtaining or retaining employment.

An additional characteristic of current loyalty programs has been the provision made for comprehensive investigation of loyalty among the employees involved and the maintenance of elaborate machinery for administration of the program.

The initial and major emphasis on employee loyalty came from the Federal government in the period following the establishment of the Committee on Un-American Activities in 1938. Prior to that time no loyalty program had existed in the Federal Government. In fact Civil Service Rule I, issued in 1884, required that no inquiry could be made of "the political or religious opinions or affiliations of any applicant."[1] In 1939 Congress passed the Hatch Act, which made it unlawful for any person employed by the Federal Government "to have membership in any political party or organization which advocates the overthrow of our constitutional form of government in the United States." 53 Stat. 1147, 1148 (1939), 5 U. S. C. § 118j (1939). And beginning in 1941 Congress incorporated in all appropriation acts a provision that none of the funds could be used to pay the salary or wages of "any person who advocates, or who is a member of an organization that advocates, the overthrow of the Government of the United States by force or violence." 55 Stat. 5, 6 (1941).

Throughout the war years administration of these provisions was largely uncoordinated and somewhat haphazard. In March 1947, however, President Truman promulgated Executive Order 9835, which has served as the principal basis of the Federal loyalty program since that time.

---

[1] Presidential promulgation, issued under authority of 22 Stat. 403 (1883), 5 U. S. C. 633 (1946).

## EXECUTIVE ORDER 9835

PRESCRIBING PROCEDURES FOR THE ADMINISTRA-
TION OF AN EMPLOYEES LOYALTY PROGRAM IN
THE EXECUTIVE BRANCH OF THE GOVERNMENT

Mar. 21, 1947, 12 Fed. Reg. 1935

WHEREAS each employee of the Government of the United States is endowed with a measure of trusteeship over the democratic processes which are the heart and sinew of the United States; and

WHEREAS it is of vital importance that persons employed in the Federal service be of complete and unswerving loyalty to the United States; and

WHEREAS, although the loyalty of by far the overwhelming majority of all Government employees is beyond question, the presence within the Government service of any disloyal or subversive person constitutes a threat to our democratic processes; and

WHEREAS maximum protection must be afforded the United States against infiltration of disloyal persons into the ranks of its employees, and equal protection from unfounded accusations of disloyalty must be afforded the loyal employees of the Government;

NOW, THEREFORE, by virtue of the authority vested in me by the Constitution and statutes of the United States, including the Civil Service Act of 1883 (22 Stat. 403), as amended, and section 9A of the act approved August 2, 1939 (18 U.S.C. 61i), and as President and Chief Executive of the United States, it is hereby, in the interest of the internal management of the Government, ordered as follows:

### PART I—INVESTIGATION OF APPLICANTS

1. There shall be a loyalty investigation of every person entering the civilian employment of any department or agency of the executive branch of the Federal Government. . . .

3. An investigation shall be made of all applicants at all available pertinent sources of information and shall include reference to:

    a. Federal Bureau of Investigation files.

    b. Civil Service Commission files.

    c. Military and naval intelligence files.

    d. The files of any other appropriate government investigative or intelligence agency.

    e. House Committee on un-American Activities files.

[Emerson]

f. Local law-enforcement files at the place of residence and employment of the applicant, including municipal, county, and State law-enforcement files.

g. Schools and colleges attended by applicant.

h. Former employers of applicant.

i. References given by applicant.

j. Any other appropriate source.

4. Whenever derogatory information with respect to loyalty of an applicant is revealed a full field investigation shall be conducted. A full field investigation shall also be conducted of those applicants, or of applicants for particular positions, as may be designated by the head of the employing department or agency, such designations to be based on the determination by any such head of the best interests of national security.

## PART II—INVESTIGATION OF EMPLOYEES

1. The head of each department and agency in the executive branch of the Government shall be personally responsible for an effective program to assure that disloyal civilian officers or employees are not retained in employment in his department or agency. . . .

2. The head of each department and agency shall appoint one or more loyalty boards, each composed of not less than three representatives of the department or agency concerned, for the purpose of hearing loyalty cases arising within such department or agency and making recommendations with respect to the removal of any officer or employee of such department or agency on grounds relating to loyalty, and he shall prescribe regulations for the conduct of the proceedings before such boards.

a. An officer or employee who is charged with being disloyal shall have a right to an administrative hearing before a loyalty board in the employing department or agency. He may appear before such board personally, accompanied by counsel or representative of his own choosing, and present evidence on his own behalf, through witnesses or by affidavit.

b. The officer or employee shall be served with a written notice of such hearing in sufficient time, and shall be informed therein of the nature of the charges against him in sufficient detail, so that he will be enabled to prepare his defense. The charges shall be stated as specifically and completely as, in the discretion of the employing department or agency, security considerations permit, and the officer or employee shall be informed in the notice (1) of his right to reply to such charges in writing within a specified reasonable period of time, (2) of his right to an administrative hearing on such charges before a loyalty board, and (3) of his right to appear before such board personally, to be accompanied by counsel or representative of his own choosing, and to present evidence on his behalf, through witness or by affidavit.

3. A recommendation of removal by a loyalty board shall be subject to appeal by the officer or employee affected, prior to his removal, to the head of the employing department or agency or to such person or persons as may be designated by such head, under such regulations as may be prescribed by him, and the decision of the department or agency concerned shall be subject to appeal to the Civil Service Commission's Loyalty Review Board, hereinafter provided for, for an advisory recommendation. . . .

[Section 4 authorizes suspension of an employee pending a determination of loyalty.]

## PART III—RESPONSIBILITIES OF CIVIL SERVICE COMMISSION

1. There shall be established in the Civil Service Commission a Loyalty Review Board of not less than three impartial persons, the members of which shall be officers or employees of the Commission.

a. The Board shall have authority to review cases involving persons recommended for dismissal on grounds relating to loyalty by the loyalty board of any department or agency and to make advisory recommendations thereon to the head of the employing department or agency. Such cases may be referred to the Board either by the employing department or agency, or by the officer or employee concerned.

b. The Board shall make rules and regulations, not inconsistent with the provisions of this order, deemed necessary to implement statutes and Executive orders relating to employee loyalty. . . .

3. The Loyalty Review Board shall currently be furnished by the Department of Justice the name of each foreign or domestic organization, association, movement, group or combination of persons which the Attorney General, after appropriate investigation and determination, designates as totalitarian, fascist, communist or subversive, or as having adopted a policy of advocating or approving the commission of acts of force or violence to deny others their rights under the Constitution of the United States, or as seeking to alter the form of government of the United States by unconstitutional means.

a. The Loyalty Review Board shall disseminate such information to all departments and agencies.

## PART IV—SECURITY MEASURES IN INVESTIGATIONS

1. At the request of the head of any department or agency of the executive branch an investigative agency shall make available to such head, personally, all investigative material and information collected by the investigative agency concerning any employee or prospective employee of the requesting department or agency, or shall make such material and information available to any officer or officers designated by such head and approved by the investigative agency.

2. Notwithstanding the foregoing requirement, however, the investigative agency may refuse to disclose the names of confidential informants, provided it furnishes sufficient information about such informants on the basis of which the requesting department or agency can make an adequate evaluation of the information furnished by them, and provided it advises the requesting department or agency in writing that it is essential to the protection of the informants or to the investigation of other cases that the identity of the informants not be revealed. Investigative agencies shall not use this discretion to decline to reveal sources of information where such action is not essential.

3. Each department and agency of the executive branch should develop and maintain, for the collection and analysis of information relating to the loyalty of its employees and prospective employees, a staff specially trained in security techniques, and an effective security control system for protecting such information generally and for protecting confidential sources of such information particularly.

## PART V—STANDARDS

1. The standard for the refusal of employment or the removal from employment in an executive department or agency on grounds relating to loyalty shall be that, on all the evidence, reasonable grounds exist for belief that the person involved is disloyal to the Government of the United States.[1]

2. Activities and associations of an applicant or employee which may be considered in connection with the determination of disloyalty may include one or more of the following:

"a. Sabotage, espionage, or attempts or preparations therefor, or knowingly associating with spies or saboteurs;

"b. Treason or sedition or advocacy thereof;

---

[1] By Executive Order 10241, issued April 28, 1951, this section was amended to make the last portion read: ". . . on all the evidence, there is a reasonable doubt as to the loyalty of the person involved to the Government of the United States." 16 Fed. Reg. 3690.

"c. Advocacy of revolution or force or violence to alter the constitutional form of government of the United States;

"d. Intentional, unauthorized disclosure to any person, under circumstances which may indicate disloyalty to the United States, of documents or information of a confidential or non-public character obtained by the person making the disclosure as a result of his employment by the Government of the United States:

"e. Performing or attempting to perform his duties, or otherwise acting, so as to serve the interests of another government in preference to the interests of the United States.

"f. Membership in, affiliation with or sympathetic association with any foreign or domestic organization, association, movement, group or combination of persons, designated by the Attorney General as totalitarian, fascist, communist, or subversive, or as having adopted a policy of advocating or approving the commission of acts of force or violence to deny other persons their rights under the Constitution of the United States, or as seeking to alter the form of government of the United States by unconstitutional means." . . .

## Note

1. In addition to the Loyalty Program established by Executive Order 9835, the complete loyalty and security program of the Federal Government comprises the following:

a. *Security risk program for sensitive agencies:* By a series of statutes beginning in 1942 the heads of certain "sensitive" agencies were empowered to remove summarily any employee whose dismissal, in their judgment, was "warranted by the demands of national security." See, *e. g.*, 56 Stat. 1053 (1942). These powers were embodied in permanent legislation in 1950. This statute provides that the head of the Department of State, Commerce, Justice and Defense (including Army, Navy and Air Force), the Coast Guard, the Atomic Energy Commission, the National Security Resources Board, or the National Advisory Commission for Aeronautics, "may in his absolute discretion and when deemed necessary in the interest of national security, suspend, without pay, any civilian officer or employee" in these agencies; that "to the extent that such agency head determines that the interests of the national security permit, the employee concerned shall be notified of the reasons for his suspension and within thirty days after such notification any such person shall have an opportunity to submit any statements or affidavits . . . to show why he should be reinstated;" that "the agency head concerned may, following such investigation and review as he deems necessary, terminate the employment of such suspended civilian officer or employee whenever he shall determine such termination necessary or advisable in the interest

534

RIGHT OF POLITICAL EXPRESSION

of the national security of the United States, and such determination
by the agency head concerned shall be conclusive and final." A permanent employee is entitled, before final dismissal, to a hearing, a review by the agency head or official designated by the agency head, and
"a written statement of the decision of the agency head." Dismissal
under the statute "shall not affect the right of such officer or employee
to seek or accept employment in any other department or agency of
the Government," provided the Civil Service Commission is consulted
and, upon request, approves. The President is authorized to apply the
provisions of the act to other departments or agencies. 5 U. S. C. § 22
(1950).

The statute is intended to authorize dismissal as a "security risk"
on a broader basis than on grounds of "loyalty". The machinery for
administering the two programs is completely integrated in those
agencies which operate under both programs.

For description and discussion of the security risk program, see
Gellhorn, *Security, Loyalty and Science,* ch. IV (1950); Barth, *The
Loyalty of Free Men,* ch. VI (1951).

b. *Security clearance for access to classified information:* Acting
under various statutory provisions the Federal agencies, particularly
the Department of Defense and the State Department, classify certain matter, including documents, physical goods and oral information, as "security information", and no person may have access to such
information unless he has received security clearance. Provision for
obtaining such clearance is embodied in all government contracts involving security information. The Defense Department program is
administered by the Army-Navy-Air Force Personnel Security Board,
with appeal to the Industrial Employment Review Board. The principal statutory provisions upon which the program is based are 18
U. S. C. §§ 793, 794, 795, 797, 2151-6 (1948); 50 U. S. C. App. §§ 781-3
(1947); P. L. 831, 81st Cong. (1950) (the Internal Security Act);
P. L. 518, 81st Cong. (1950); Exec. Order 10104, 15 Fed. Reg. 597
(1950), and 10290, 16 Fed. Reg. 9795 (1951).

The Atomic Energy Act contains express provisions for clearance
of all persons having access to "restricted data". 42 U. S. C. § 1810
(b) (5) (B) (1946).

The impact of these provisions falls primarily upon persons not
employed by the Government but working for private concerns or institutions having Government contracts or for subcontractors. That
there is some tendency for the program to spread to employees not
having access to classified information see American Civil Liberties
Weekly Bulletin, Jan. 23, 1950 and Mar. 6, 1950.

See Department of Defense Munitions Board, *Industrial Security
Manual For Safeguarding Classified Security Information* (Dec. 31,
1951); Gellhorn, *supra,* ch. IV.

c. *Maritime workers security program:* Under the Magnuson Act
and Presidential regulations issued pursuant thereto, workers on vessels and on the waterfront must obtain a "Coast Guard Port Security
Card". Such cards may not be issued by the local Coast Guard Commandant "if the Commandant is satisfied that the character and habits

of life of the applicant therefor are such as to authorize the belief that the presence of such individual on board a vessel or within a waterfront facility would be inimical to the security of the United States." 50 U. S. C. §§ 191, 192, 194 (1950); Exec. Order 10173, 15 Fed. Reg. 7005 (1950). A preliminary injunction to restrain enforcement of the program was denied in *Parker v. Lester*, 98 F. Supp. 300 (N. D. Cal., 1951), app. dis. 191 F. 2d 1020 (C. A. 9, 1951).

d. *Miscellaneous.* A number of other Federal statutes impose special loyalty requirements or require specific F. B. I. clearance of particular classes of Federal employees or recipients of Federal benefits. Typical of these laws are the statute requiring special loyalty oaths from holders of National Science Foundation scholarships and fellowships, 42 U. S. C. § 1874d (1950), and special investigation of persons holding positions "of critical importance" in the civilian defense program. 50 U. S. C. App. § 2255 (1950).

See also Section 5(a) of the Internal Security Act, the state and local loyalty programs, and private loyalty programs, *infra.*

No estimate of the total number of persons covered by loyalty programs has been published.

2. For material on the background of the Federal loyalty program, see Emerson and Helfeld, *Loyalty Among Government Employees,* 58 Yale L. J. 1, 8–26 (1948); Biddle, *Fear of Freedom,* pp. 197–211 (1951). For comment on the loyalty program generally, see, in addition to the materials collected in Emerson and Helfeld, *supra,* Hoover, *A Comment on the Article "Loyalty Among Government Employees,"* 58 Yale L. J. 401 (1949); Donovan and Jones, *Program For a Democratic Counter Attack to Communist Penetration of Government Service,* 58 Yale L. J. 1211 (1949); Arnold, *The Case Against the Federal Loyalty Program,* and Sutherland, *Additional Thoughts on the Federal Loyalty Program,* both in *The Strengthening of American Political Institutions,* pp. 53, 74 (Cornell U. Press, 1949); Gellhorn, *supra;* Richardson (first Chairman of the Loyalty Review Board), *The Federal Employee Loyalty Program,* 51 Col. L. Rev. 546 (1951); Barth, *supra,* ch. V, VI, VII and VIII; Bontecou, *Does the Loyalty Program Threaten Civil Rights?,* 275 Annals of the Am. Acad. of Pol. and Soc. Sci. 117 (1951). A comprehensive study by Miss Eleanor Bontecou is to be published shortly as part of the Cornell Studies in Civil Liberty.

On the broader question of loyalty in a democratic society, see Commager, *Who is Loyal to America?,* Harper's Magazine, Sept. 1947, p. 193; Schlesinger, *What is Loyalty? A Difficult Question,* N. Y. Times Magazine, Nov. 2, 1947, p. 7; Weyl, *The Battle Against Disloyalty* (1951); Public Affairs Pamphlet No. 179, *Loyalty in a Democracy* (1952).

3. The first case to raise some of the legal issues involved in a loyalty program was *Friedman v. Schwellenbach*, 159 F. 2d 22 (C. A. D. C., 1946), cert. den. 330 U. S. 838 (1947). An employee was refused permanent civil service status, and thereby dismissed from his government position, on charges of disloyalty. The proceedings took place under Civil Service Commission Regulations, prior to the issuance of Executive Order 9835. In a suit for injunction and reinstatement

the court held the regulations valid and refused to consider the merits of the discharge.

The major legal challenge to Executive Order 9835 came in *Bailey v. Richardson.*

## BAILEY v. RICHARDSON

United States Court of Appeals, District of Columbia Circuit, 1950
182 F. 2d 46

PRETTYMAN, Circuit Judge.

This is a civil action brought in the United States District Court for the District of Columbia for a declaratory judgment and for an order directing plaintiff-appellant's reinstatement in Government employ. The defendants-appellees are the Administrator of the Federal Security Agency, the members of the Civil Service Commission, members of its Loyalty Review Board, and members of its Loyalty Board of the Fourth Civil Service Region. Answer to the complaint was made by the defendants-appellees, and affidavits were filed. Both plaintiff and defendants made motions for summary judgment. The District Court granted the motion of the defendants. This appeal followed. . . .

*The Facts.*

Appellant Bailey was employed in the classified civil service of the United States Government from August 19, 1939, to June 28, 1947. Upon the latter date she was separated from the service due to reduction in force. On March 25, 1948, she was given a temporary appointment, and on May 28, 1948, she was reinstated [subject to loyalty clearance].

[On July 31, 1948, Miss Bailey was served with interrogatories requesting answers concerning the following matters:]

"The Commission has received information to the effect that you are or have been a member of the Communist Party or the Communist Political Association; that you have attended meetings of the Communist Party, and have associated on numerous occasions with known Communist Party members.

. . . . . . . . .

"The Commission has received information to the effect that you are or have been a member of the American League for Peace and Democracy, an organization which has been declared by the Attorney General to come within the purview of Executive Order 9835.

. . . . . . . . .

"The Commission has received information to the effect

**537**

that you are or have been a member of the Washington Committee for Democratic Action, an organization which has been declared by the Attorney General to come within the purview of Executive Order 9835.

. . . . . . . . . .

"Are you now, or have ever been, a member of, or in any manner affiliated with, the Nazi or Fascist movements or with any organization or political party whose objective is now, or has ever been, the overthrow of the Constitutional Government of the United States?"

Miss Bailey answered the interrogatories directly and specifically, denying each item of information recited therein as having been received by the Commission, except that she admitted past membership for a short time in the American League for Peace and Democracy. She vigorously asserted her loyalty to the United States. She requested an administrative hearing. A hearing was held before the Regional Board. She appeared and testified and presented other witnesses and numerous affidavits. No person other than those presented by her testified.

On November 1, 1948, the Regional Board advised the Federal Security Agency, in which Miss Bailey was employed, that:

"As a result of such investigation and after a hearing before this Board, it was found that, on all the evidence, reasonable grounds exist for belief that Miss Bailey is disloyal to the Government of the United States.

"Therefore, she has been rated ineligible for Federal employment; she has been barred from competing in civil service examinations for a period of three years, and your office is instructed to separate her from the service." . . .

Miss Bailey appealed to the Loyalty Review Board and requested a hearing. Hearing was held before a panel of that Board. Miss Bailey appeared, testified, and presented affidavits. No person other than Miss Bailey testified, and no affidavits other than hers were presented on the record.

On February 9, 1949, the Chairman of the Loyalty Review Board advised the Federal Security Agency that the finding of the Regional Board was sustained, and he requested that the Agency remove Miss Bailey's name from the rolls. Notice to that effect was sent to counsel for Miss Bailey on the same day. The full Board subsequently declined to review the conclusions of its panel.

Miss Bailey's position from May 29, 1948, to November 3, 1948, was that of a training officer (general fields) CAF–13.

*The Question.*

The rights claimed by and for appellant must be discovered accurately and defined precisely. The events with which we are concerned were not accidental, thoughtless or mere petty tyrannies of subordinate officials. They were the deliberate design of the executive branch of the Government, knowingly supported by the Congress.

The case presented for Miss Bailey is undoubtedly appealing. She was denied reinstatement in her former employment because Government officials found reasonable ground to believe her disloyal. She was not given a trial in any sense of the word, and she does not know who informed upon her. Thus viewed, her situation appeals powerfully to our sense of the fair and the just. But the case must be placed in context and in perspective.

The Constitution placed upon the President and the Congress, and upon them alone, responsibility for the welfare of this country in the arena of world affairs. It so happens that we are presently in an adversary position to a government whose most successful recent method of contest is the infiltration of a government service by its sympathizers. This is the context of Miss Bailey's question.

The essence of her complaint is not that she was denied reinstatement; the complaint is that she was denied reinstatement without revelation by the Government of the names of those who informed against her and of the method by which her alleged activities were detected. So the question actually posed by the case is whether the President is faced with an inescapable dilemma, either to continue in Government employment a person whose loyalty he reasonably suspects or else to reveal publicly the methods by which he detects disloyalty and the names of any persons who may venture to assist him. . . .

The presentation of appellant's contentions is impressive. Each detail of the trial which she unquestionably did not get is depicted separately, in a mounting cumulation into analogies to the *Dreyfus* case and the Nazi judicial process. Thus, a picture of a simple black-and-white fact—that appellant did not get a trial in the judicial sense—is drawn in bold and appealing colors. But the question is not whether she had a trial. The question is whether she should have had one. . . .

[The Court first held that the procedure followed in Miss Bailey's case complied with the requirements of Executive Order 9835, and that the Lloyd-La Follette Act, 37 Stat. 555 (1912), 5 U. S. C. § 652, was inapplicable.]

## III.

### Validity of the Bar to Employment

Appellant next says that the order of the Board which barred her from the federal service for three years, was constitutionally invalid under the decision of the Supreme Court in the *Lovett* case.[27] We agree with that contention. The Court in that case clearly held that permanent proscription from Government service is "punishment" and that punishment can be inflicted only upon compliance with the Sixth Amendment. The difference between permanent and limited proscription is merely one of degree and not one of principle. So far as this record shows, this proscription of employment was not pursuant to a general regulation. It was not required by a general classification by Congress or by general regulation of the Civil Service Commission or of the Loyalty Board. No reference to proscription appears in the Executive Order, the Attorney General's orders, or the statements of the Loyalty Board. A general order that no person who is denied permanent employment after a conditional appointment be reemployed for three years might well be valid. The bar in the present proceeding appears on the record to be one imposed by the Board upon this particular individual in this particular case as a matter of individual adjudication. We hold that the portions of the orders and directions of the defendants-appellees which purported to bar Miss Bailey from federal employ for three years, are invalid.

## IV.

### Constitutionality of the Dismissal

We did not understand appellant to urge the unconstitutionality of her dismissal, apart from the three-year bar. But there is a difference of opinion among us in that respect, and we, therefore, state our views upon the point. First we consider the contentions respecting the constitutionality of the procedure pursued, and then we consider the constitutionality of the condition imposed upon the reinstatement. For the first purpose, we must assume that Miss Bailey was in the classified service without condition at the time of her removal from the rolls and that she was, therefore, dismissed from employment and not merely denied appointment; although, as we have indicated, we do not agree with that view of her status. If her status was merely that of an applicant for appointment, as we think it was, her non-appointment in-

---

[27] *United States v. Lovett*, 1946, 328 U. S. 303, 66 S. Ct. 1073, 90 L. Ed. 1252.

volved no procedural constitutional rights. Obviously, an applicant for office has no constitutional right to a hearing or a specification of the reasons why he is not appointed. We, therefore, consider the constitutionality of the procedure followed in this case upon the assumption that a Government employee in the classified service is being dismissed because her superiors have grounds, which to them are reasonable, to believe that she is disloyal.

### Sixth Amendment.

. . . We are of opinion that compliance with the Sixth Amendment is not a prerequisite to the dismissal of an employee from the Federal Government classified civil service. It is apparently admitted on behalf of appellant that this conclusion is true generally speaking, but it is said that dismissal for suspicion of disloyalty is an exception and that an employee cannot be dismissed for that one particular reason without a jury trial, confrontation by witnesses, etc., in a judicial proceeding. We shall discuss that claim of exception in a moment.

### Fifth Amendment.

It is next said on behalf of appellant that the due process clause of the Fifth Amendment requires that she be afforded a hearing of the quasi-judicial type before being dismissed. The due process clause provides: "No person shall . . . be deprived of life, liberty, or property, without due process of law; . . . ." It has been held repeatedly and consistently that Government employ is not "property"[36] and that in this particular it is not a contract.[37] We are unable to perceive how it could be held to be "liberty". Certainly it is not "life". So much that is clear would seem to dispose of the point. In terms the due process clause does not apply to the holding of a Government office.

Other considerations lead to the same conclusion. Never in our history has a Government administrative employee been entitled to a hearing of the quasi-judicial type upon his dismissal from Government service. That record of a hundred and sixty years of Government administration is the sort of history which speaks with great force. It is pertinent to repeat in this connection that the Lloyd-Lafollette Act, sponsored and enacted by advocates of a merit classified government service, expressly denies the

---

[36] *Taylor v. Beckham*, 1900, 178 U. S. 548, 20 S. Ct. 890, 1009, 44 L. Ed. 1187, and cases there cited; *Ex parte Sawyer*, 1888, 124 U. S. 200, 8 S. Ct. 482, 31 L. Ed. 402; 2 Cooley, Constitutional Limitations 746, n. 1 (8th ed. 1927), and cases there cited.

[37] *Butler v. Commonwealth of Pennsylvania*, 1850, 10 How. 402, 13 L. Ed. 472; *Crenshaw v. United States*, 1890, 134 U. S. 99, 10 S. Ct. 431, 33 L. Ed. 825.

right to such a hearing. Moreover, in the acute and sometimes bitter historic hundred-year contest over the wholesale summary dismissal of Government employees, there seems never to have been a claim that, absent congressional limitation, the President was without constitutional power to dismiss without notice, hearing or evidence; except for the question as to officials appointed with the advice and consent of the Senate. . . .

The Constitution makes the President responsible for the execution of the laws and makes the Congress responsible for the vesting of appointments in the executive branch. Those two authorities are, therefore, responsible for the ability, the integrity, and the loyalty of the personnel of the executive branch. That responsibility necessarily includes the power to choose employees for executive duty, and the power to remove those deemed not qualified is a correlative power. No function is more completely internal to a branch of government than the selection and retention or dismissal of its employees. So it has been held many times that the power of removal is an incident of the power of appointment.

In the absence of statute or ancient custom to the contrary, executive offices are held at the will of the appointing authority, not for life or for fixed terms. If removal be at will, of what purpose would due process be? To hold office at the will of a superior and to be removable therefrom only by constitutional due process of law are opposite and inherently conflicting ideas. Due process of law is not applicable unless one is being deprived of something to which he has a right.

Constitutionally, the criterion for retention or removal of subordinate employees is the confidence of superior executive officials. Confidence is not controllable by process. What may be required by acts of the Congress is another matter, but there is no requirement in the Constitution that the executive branch rely upon the services of persons in whom it lacks confidence. The opinions in the *Myers* case [272 U. S. 52] make this proposition amply clear, and those in *United Public Workers* v. *Mitchell* [330 U. S. 75] amply confirm it . . . .

We do not reach the question whether, if the due process of law clause does apply, it requires more than this appellant was given. Miss Bailey was not summarily cut off the rolls. She was advised in writing that information concerning her qualifications for Government employ had been received; she was asked specific questions; and she was told that those questions reflected the information received. The questions revealed the nature of the alleged activities giving rise to the inquiry and the names of the organizations in which she was alleged to have been active.

**542**

Everything that she wished to present was received; all affidavits offered by her were accepted, and all witnesses presented by her testified. She was twice heard orally. She was represented at all stages by competent counsel. Her case was considered by two separate groups of executive officials. On the other hand, she was not told the names of the informants against her. She was not permitted to face or to cross-examine those informants. She was not given the dates or places at which she was alleged to have been active in the named alleged subversive organizations. So the claim in her behalf necessarily goes farther than an abstract claim for due process of law. The claim must be that the due process clause requires, in dismissals of subordinate Government employees, specificity in charges equivalent to that of valid criminal charges, confrontation by witnesses, cross examination of them, and hearing upon evidence openly submitted. Even if the due process clause applies, we would think it does not require so much.

Here again it is apparently conceded on behalf of appellant that our conclusions in respect to the Fifth Amendment are sound generally speaking, but an exception is claimed in the cases of those dismissed for suspicion of disloyalty. As we have said, we shall discuss that claimed exception in a moment.

*First Amendment.*

It is next said that appellant's dismissal impinged upon the rights of free speech and assembly protected by the First Amendment, since the dismissal was premised upon alleged political activity. This suggestion goes not to the procedure but to the ultimate validity of the dismissal itself. But the plain hard fact is that so far as the Constitution is concerned there is no prohibition against the dismissal of Government employees because of their political beliefs, activities or affiliations. That document, standing alone, does not prevent Republican Presidents from dismissing Democrats or Democratic Presidents from dismissing Republicans. From the beginning, such has been the practice, with variations in scope. The reason that it has not continued to so great an extent is because the people became convinced that it was not good government and the Congress and the President wrote that view into statutes and regulations. They, not the Constitution, give Government employees such protection as they have against dismissal for political reasons. . . .

[*United Public Workers v. Mitchell*] sets at rest the broad contention that Congress and the President may not, in the interest of efficiency, impinge upon otherwise inviolate rights of Government employees to free participation in political speech and assembly.

**543**

The situation of the Government employee is not different in this respect from that of private employees. A newspaper editor has a constitutional right to speak and write as he pleases. But the Constitution does not guarantee him a place in the columns of a publisher with whose political views he does not agree. . . .

*Discrimination.*

It is said that the loyalty program as applied in this particular case went beyond the power of the Congress and of the President to regulate the conduct of Government employees.

We must at this point be careful to note the precise ground upon which appellant was dismissed. It was that in the judgment of authorized executive officials "reasonable grounds exist for belief that Miss Bailey is disloyal to the Government of the United States." So far as we have been able to ascertain, it is nowhere disputed that employees in fact disloyal to the Government may and should be removed. A classification of loyal and disloyal is undoubtedly a proper one descriptive of qualification and disqualification for public office. Appellant says: "We are of course not suggesting that a government employee who is reinstated in his job is immune from inquiry into his loyalty." So the points made in behalf of appellant must be these: (1) That mere belief on the part of executive officials of disloyalty, even though supported by grounds reasonable to them, is not a sufficient basis for valid removal. (2) That if the power to remove be limited, some authority other than executive or legislative must be able to determine whether the limitation be transgressed, and so the grounds for executive belief must be fully revealed. (3) That the information concerning appellant, as reflected in the interrogatory sent to her, does not, even if true, constitute reasonable ground for belief in her disloyalty.

The first proposition is in effect that reasonable ground for belief of disloyalty is not sufficient prerequisite to dismissal. But we can perceive no basis for holding that the executive departments must retain in the service those whose loyalty is reasonably doubtful. Reasonably grounded suspicion of disloyalty indicates a risk, and no concept of the Constitution requires the executive to endure recognizable and preventable risks in the administration of the law. He may decide to do so, but we see no basis for saying that he must. The Constitution does not require the President to continue to use in the training of Government personnel, the work performed by this appellant, a person whose loyalty to the Government he suspects. There is no reason in the Constitution why the President should not limit the training staff to persons whose loyalty is beyond the faintest shadow of suspicion.

**544**

The clear and present danger rule does not help us in this matter, because Government employ, with which we are here dealing, is not a right. The argument that the rule does apply confuses the subject matter of the controversy. No one denies Miss Bailey the right to any political activity or affiliation she may choose. What is denied her is Government employ. The argument upon the clear and present danger rule, therefore, must be that Miss Bailey has a right to Government employ unless her presence there would constitute a clear and present danger. There simply is no such right. To state the proposition is to demonstrate its untenability. The President certainly does not have to appoint any and all qualified persons to public office. And the Constitution does not require him to keep in office everyone who is qualified. Even if appellant had been qualified beyond shadow of suspicion, she could have been released from the service, so far as the Constitution is concerned. The clear and present danger rule is entirely foreign to the whole matter.

The second proposition concerns the mode of determining the sufficiency of a doubt of loyalty. If reasonable grounds for belief of disloyalty suffice for dismissal, in whose mind must such reasonable grounds be established?

Much argument at this point is premised upon the possibility of abuse of the removal power. It is said that if executive officers have power to remove without compliance with restrictive measures they may by terror destroy free thought and action in the Government service and so establish a tyranny. This fear is not new. It was held by some members of the First Congress and urged by them in the debate upon the removal power. But under our system of government the courts cannot assume a possible abuse of constitutional power as a reason for denying that power. Almost every power, constitutional, statutory, regulatory, contractual or whatnot, is susceptible of abuse. . . . Abuse of power is, of course, forbidden, but the mere potentiality of abuse does not constitute invalidity of power. We cannot declare an act unconstitutional merely because under it there is a possibility of abuse. . . .

This brings us to the third proposition upon this subject, which is that the revealed information in this particular case is insufficient ground for suspicion of disloyalty. It is said that the interrogatory showed that the basis for Miss Bailey's dismissal was an alleged membership in the Communist Party and other allegedly "subversive" organizations, and that this is an invalid discrimination.

It is perfectly true, as the Supreme Court said in the *United Public Workers* case, that Congress could not legislate that "no

Republican, Jew or Negro shall be appointed to federal office" [330 U. S. at 100]. But if a Democratic President were to appoint few, if any, Republicans to office, or vice versa, he would not be violating any provision of the Constitution. Vigorous as the condemnation of the practice has been, even in recent years, nowhere, so far as we are aware, has it been responsibly asserted that such selection is invalid. In blunt terms, the President can discriminate for political reasons. We do not think the Supreme Court meant, by the quoted sentence, that if the President or his authorized aides exercised the prerogative of selecting employees by selecting no Republicans, the choices would be constitutionally void. Some astonishing results would ensue from any such holding. The Court was referring to permanent, blanket proscription by the Congress. Of more importance, the classifications named in the quoted suggestion have no discernible bearing upon qualification for office. Such a statute would be purely arbitrary and capricious in the most obnoxious meaning of those words. . . .

*An Exception is Claimed.*

Thus the controversy develops, step by step, to its ultimate crisis. It is urged upon us that dismissal from Government employ for suspicion of disloyalty is an exception to the established doctrines and rules generally applicable to Government employees and their dismissal from service.

It is said on behalf of appellant that disloyalty is akin to treason and that dismissal is akin to conviction. Forthwith it is asserted that Miss Bailey has been convicted of disloyalty. As we have seen, nothing resembling a conviction from the legal standpoint has been visited upon her. She was merely refused Government employment for reasons satisfactory to the appointing authorities.

But it is said that the public does not distinguish, that she has been stigmatized and her chance of making a living seriously impaired. The position implicit in that assertion dissolves into two contentions. One is that even if executive authorities had power to dismiss Miss Bailey without a judicial hearing, they had no power to hurt her while doing so; that is, they had no power to call her disloyal even if they had power to dismiss her for that reason. But it has long been established that if the Government, in the exercise of a governmental power, injures an individual, that individual has no redress. Official action beyond the scope of official authority can be prevented or nullified by the courts, and so official action which violates a constitutional right of an individual can be rectified. But if no constitutional right of the individual is being impinged and officials are acting

[Emerson]

within the scope of official authority, the fact that the individual concerned is injured in the process neither invalidates the official act nor gives the individual a right to redress. So, in the present case, if Miss Bailey had no constitutional right to her office and the executive officers had power to dismiss her, the fact that she was injured in the process of dismissal neither invalidates her dismissal nor gives her right to redress; this under a rule of law established long ago. . . .

The line of cases in which this court has said that courts will not review the action of executive officials in dismissing executive employees, except to insure compliance with statutory requirements, is unvaried. As early as 1904, this court said that the rule had been announced so many times as not to require citation of authority.[70] In *Levy* v. *Woods*[71] we said, quoting the Court of Claims, "The allegations that the plaintiff was innocent of the charges preferred against him . . . and that the investigation which resulted in his removal was biased, prejudiced, and unfair, are immaterial."

The rule is applied even when the charges involve offenses of serious moral turpitude. . . .

It should be remarked parenthetically that, in so far as the case before us is concerned, any publicity which it received was not pursuant to but in flat contradiction of the Executive Order, the Attorney General's instructions, and the Loyalty Board's rules, all of which forbid publicity. Moreover, Miss Bailey accepted voluntarily the conditional reappointment which was premised upon her successful passage of the loyalty test laid down in the Executive Order.

The other contention implicit in the assertion that Miss Bailey has been stigmatized and injured, is that disloyalty is a thing apart, suspicion of which gives rise to constitutional rights not applicable to suspicion of criminal offenses. It seems to us that in so far as suspicion of disloyalty has peculiarities which distinguish it from suspicions of bribery, seduction and other offenses, they are adverse to appellant's conclusions. We must look not only at appellant's but also at the public side of this controversy. From that point of view, the retention in the Government service of one suspected of theft or a similar offense would not be of great importance, and the revelation of the method of detection and the names of informants would probably not affect the public interest. But disloyalty in the Government service under present circumstances is a matter of great public concern, and revelation

[70] *United States ex rel. Taylor v. Taft* [24 App. D. C. 95, dismissed 203 U. S. 461].

[71] 1948, 84 U. S. App. D. C. 138, 171 F. 2d 145, 146.

of the methods of detecting it and of the names of witnesses involve public considerations of compelling importance.

We cannot ignore the world situation in which not merely two
ideologies but two potentially adverse forces presently exist, and
certainly we cannot require that the President and the Congress
ignore it. Infiltration of government service is now a recognized
technique for the overthrow of government. We do not think
that the individual rights guaranteed by the Constitution necessarily mean that a government dedicated to those rights cannot
preserve itself in the world as it is. This case presents a small
segment of that momentous question. In the light of all that
is well known, much of which is recited in opinions of the Supreme Court, we cannot say that a policy of caution in respect
to members of the Communist Party in the Government service
under current circumstances is forbidden by any restriction in
the Constitution. The risks are for the President to estimate,
and the assumption of risk is for him to decide. If he thinks
that under present circumstances only those whose loyalty is
beyond suspicion should be employed by this Government, the
policy is his to make. The responsibility in this field is his, and
the power to meet it must also be his. The judiciary cannot
dictate that he must either retain in Government service those
whom he reasonably suspects or else reveal publicly the means
and methods by which he detects disloyalty. . . .

Reversed in part, affirmed in part, and remanded with instructions.

EDGERTON, Circuit Judge (dissenting).

Without trial by jury, without evidence, and without even
being allowed to confront her accusers or to know their identity,
a citizen of the United States has been found disloyal to the government of the United States.

For her supposed disloyal thoughts she has been punished by
dismissal from a wholly nonsensitive position in which her efficiency rating was high. The case received nation-wide publicity.
Ostracism inevitably followed. A finding of disloyalty is closely
akin to a finding of treason. The public hardly distinguishes
between the two.

No charges were served on appellant. The chairman of the
Regional Board said "Nobody has presented any charges." The
Board told appellant it was inquiring whether there were reasonable grounds for believing she was disloyal to the government
of the United States. The Federal Bureau of Investigation had
reported that informants believed to be reliable had made general statements purporting to connect her with the Communist
Party. These reports were not disclosed to the appellant and have

not been disclosed in court. The informants were not identified to the appellant or even to the Board. Their statements were admittedly not made under oath. The appellant denied under oath any membership in and any relationship or sympathy with the Communist Party, any activities connected with it or with communism, and any affiliation with any organization that advocated overthrow of the government of the United States. She asserted her loyalty to the government of the United States. She admitted attending one Communist meeting in 1932 in connection with a seminar study of the platforms of the various parties while she was a student at Bryn Mawr.

Appellant had no power to subpoena witnesses. Though it takes courage to appear as a voluntary defense witness in a loyalty case, four appeared. One was the pastor of the Methodist church of which appellant is an active member. He testified: "When this charge or information came to me I was not only surprised, I was dumbfounded. . . . People in our community and in our church think of her and her family in the highest terms." Three officials of appellant's government agency, the United States Employment Service, who had known appellant professionally and socially for years, testified respectively that they were "extremely shocked" by the suggestion of her being disloyal, that it was "inconceivable" and "out of reason". Persons prominent in business, government and education who knew appellant but could not be present submitted affidavits.

No witness offered evidence, even hearsay evidence, against appellant. No affidavits were introduced against her. The record consists entirely of evidence in her favor. Yet the Board purported to find "on all the evidence" that there were reasonable grounds for believing she was disloyal to the government of the United States. Appellees admit the Board made this finding "after considering all the evidence, including the confidential reports of the Federal Bureau of Investigation." . . .

Appellant appeared and testified before a panel of the Loyalty Review Board. She submitted her own affidavit and the affidavits of some 70 persons who knew her, including bankers, corporate officials, federal and state officials, union members, and others. Again no one testified against her. She proved she had publicly and to the knowledge of a number of the affiants taken positions inconsistent with Communist sympathies. She showed not only by her own testimony but by that of other persons that she favored the Marshall Plan, which the Communist Party notoriously opposed, and that in 1940, during the Nazi-Soviet Pact, she favored Lend-Lease and was very critical of the Soviet position. In her union she urged its officers to execute non-communist affidavits, opposed a foreign policy resolution widely publicized as pro-Russian, and favored what was then the official CIO resolution on foreign policy.

Against all this, there were only the unsworn reports in the secret files to the effect that unsworn statements of a general sort, purporting to connect appellant with Communism, had been made by unnamed persons. Some if not all of these statements did not purport to be based on knowledge, but only on belief. Appellant sought to learn the names of the informants or, if their names were confidential, then at least whether they had been active in appellant's union, in which there were factional quarrels. The Board did not furnish or even have this information. Chairman Richardson said: "I haven't the slightest knowledge as to who they were or how active they have been in anything." All that the Board knew or we know about the informants is that unidentified members of the Federal Bureau of Investigation, who did not appear before the Board, believed them to be reliable. To quote again from the record: "Chairman Richardson: I can only say to you that five or six of the reports come from informants certified to us by the Federal Bureau of Investigation as experienced and entirely reliable." "Mr. Seasongood: Here is a statement that it was ascertained you were a member of the Communist Party in the District of Columbia as early as 1935, and that in the early days of her Party membership she attended Communist Party meetings. . . . Here is another that says you were a member of the Communist Party, and he bases his statement on his knowledge of your association with known Communists for the past seven or eight years. That is part of the evidence that was submitted to us." "Mr. Porter: Is it under oath? Chairman Richardson: I don't think so. Mr. Seasongood: It is a person of known responsibility who had proffered information concerning Communist activity in the District of Columbia. . . . Here is another one: 'considers appointee a member of the Communist Party, and if not an actual member, one who is entirely controlled by the wishes of the Communist Leaders in the District of Columbia.'"

On such material, the Review Board sustained the action of the Regional Board and directed the Federal Security Agency to dismiss the appellant. However respectable her anonymous accusers may have been, if her dismissal is sustained the livelihood and reputation of any civil servant today and perhaps of any American tomorrow are at the mercy not only of an innocently mistaken informer but also of a malicious or demented one unless his defect is apparent to the agent who interviews him.

Appellant's dismissal violates both the Constitution and the Executive Order. . . .

II. *Dismissal for disloyalty is punishment and requires all the safeguards of a judicial trial.* Most dismissals, including among others dismissals for colorless or undisclosed reasons and dismissals for incompetence, are plainly not punitive. They do not require a judicial trial or even a full administrative hearing. They are within the authority of the executive. Likewise most tax laws are within the authority of the legislature. It does not follow that all legislative taxation is constitutional or that all executive dismissals are constitutional.

Punishment is infliction of harm, usually for wrong conduct but in appellant's case for wrong views. Dismissals to provide jobs for persons of certain affiliations, whatever else may be said of such dismissals, are not punitive. But dismissals for disloyal views are punitive. This is what the Supreme Court squarely held in the *Lovett* case.[15] It overruled no cases in so holding. The earlier decisions of the Supreme Court on which this court relies are irrelevant because they involved dismissals for undisclosed reasons, not for disloyal views.

The question whether the rule of the *Lovett* case extends to dismissals of "disloyal" persons from sensitive positions in which their presence might threaten substantial harm to the government does not arise in the present case and I express no opinion on it. Appellant was dismissed from a nonsensitive position. She was a staff training officer in the United States Employment Service. . . .

Since dismissal from government service for disloyalty is punishment, due process of law requires that the accused employee be given all the safeguards of a judicial trial before it is imposed. The Supreme Court in the *Lovett* case did not stop with holding that *Congress* could not dismiss employees for disloyalty. It went on to say, with particular reference to this punishment: "Those who wrote our Constitution . . . intended to safeguard the people of this country from punishment without trial by duly constituted courts. . . . And even the courts to which this important function was entrusted were commanded to stay their hands until and unless certain tested safeguards were observed. An accused in court must be tried by an impartial jury, . . . he must be clearly informed of the charge against him, the law which he is charged with violating must have been passed before he committed the act charged, he must be confronted by the witnesses against him . . . and even after conviction no cruel and unusual punishment can be inflicted upon him."[19]

---

[15] *United States v. Lovett,* 328 U. S. 303, 66 S. Ct. 1073, 90 L. Ed. 1252.
[19] 328 U. S. at 317–318.

Not only the basic right to judicial trial but every one of these basic safguards, unless it be the last, was violated here.
. . .

III. *Appellant's dismissal abridges freedom of speech and assembly.* Mr. Justice Holmes' famous statement, made in 1892 when he was a member of the Supreme Judicial Court of Massachusetts, that "the petitioner may have a constitutional right to talk politics, but he has no constitutional right to be a policeman"[24] is greatly oversimplified. "As pointed out in *Frost v. Railroad Comm.*, 271 U. S. 583, 594, 46 S. Ct. 605, 607, 70 L. Ed. 1101, even in the granting of a privilege, the state 'may not impose conditions which require the relinquishment of constitutional rights . . .' "[25] including the rights of free speech, press, and assembly. In the *Esquire* case the Supreme Court said: "We may assume that Congress . . . need not open second-class mail to publications of all types. . . . But grave constitutional questions are immediately raised once it is said that the use of the mails is a privilege which may be extended or withheld on any grounds whatsoever. See the dissents of Mr. Justice Brandeis and Mr. Justice Holmes in *Milwaukee Publishing Co. v. Burleson*, 255 U. S. 407, 421–423, 430–432, 437–438. Under that view the second-class rate could be granted on condition that certain economic or political ideas not be disseminated."[26] Similarly, the premise that government employment is a privilege does not support the conclusion that it may be granted on condition that certain economic or political ideas not be entertained. Though members of minority parties have often been dismissed, in the past, to make room for members of a party in power, any comprehensive practice of that sort would today be unthinkable as well as illegal, and the Supreme Court has plainly indicated it would also be unconstitutional. The Court pointed out in the *Mitchell* case that Congress could not " 'enact a regulation providing that no Republican, Jew or Negro shall be appointed to federal office, or that no federal employee shall attend Mass or take active part in missionary work.' "[27]

The dismissal which the court upheld in the *Mitchell* case was not based on views but on conduct. The Hatch Act sought to restrain civil servants, regardless of their views, from devoting more than a limited amount of energy to politics. The Court held that "For regulation of employees it is not necessary that the act regulated be anything more than an act reasonably deemed

---

[24] *McAuliffe v. Mayor of New Bedford*, 155 Mass. 216, 220, 29 N. E. 517.
[25] *Alston v. School Board of City of Norfolk*, 112 F. 2d 992, 997 (C. A. 4th). . . .
[26] *Hannegan v. Esquire, Inc.*, 327 U. S. 146, 155, 156.
[27] *United Public Workers v. Mitchell*, 330 U. S. 75, 100.

by Congress to interfere with the efficiency of the public service."[28] Since the present appellant was not a policy-making officer, had no access to state secrets, and was not even in a sensitive agency, it is doubtful whether any political opinions of hers, however obnoxious, could reasonably be deemed to interfere with the efficiency of the service. But the question is, I think, immaterial here, for the "vague and indeterminate . . . boundaries"[29] of the term "disloyal" have made the Executive Order as construed and applied a restraint on many opinions that certainly cannot be deemed to interfere with the efficiency of the service.

"In loyalty hearings the following questions have been asked of employees against whom charges have been brought. . . . 'Do you read a good many books?' 'What books do you read?' 'What magazines do you read?' 'What newspapers do you buy or subscribe to?' 'Do you think that Russian Communism is likely to succeed?' 'How do you explain the fact that you have an album of Paul Robeson records in your home?' . . . 'Is it not true . . . that you lived next door to and therefore were closely associated with a member of the I.W.W.?' "[30] "Too often the line of questioning has revolved around conformity with prevailing mores in personal habits and personal opinion. . . . A woman employee was accused of disloyalty because, at the time of the siege of Stalingrad, she collected money for Russian war relief (she also collected money for British and French relief)."[31] A record filed in this court shows that an accused employee was taken to task for membership in Consumers Union and for favoring legislation against racial discrimination. The record in the present case contains the following colloquy between a member of the Regional Board and the present appellant: "Mr. Blair: Did you ever write a letter to the Red Cross about the segregation of blood? Miss Bailey: I do not recall. Mr. Blair: What was your personal position about that? Miss Bailey: Well, the medical —. Mr. Blair: I am asking yours."[32]

No doubt some boards are quite aware that unconventional views and conduct have no tendency to indicate disloyalty. But the fact remains that some boards imagine the contrary. This fact is only too well known. It puts government employees under economic and social pressure to protect their jobs and reputations

[28] *Id.* at 101.
[29] *Herndon v. Lowry*, 301 U. S. 242, 264.
[30] Freedom vs. Security, by Robert E. Cushman, Goldwin Smith Professor of Government at Cornell University; in Physics Today, March 1949, pp. 14, 18.
[31] Editorial in The Washington Post, Feb. 6, 1949.
[32] Miss Bailey replied "I have no personal opinion."

by expressing in words and conduct only the most orthodox opinions on political, economic, and social questions.

A regulation that restrains constitutionally protected speech along with other speech cannot be enforced against either. Legislation is unconstitutional as a whole if it "does not aim specifically at evils within the allowable area of state control but . . . sweeps within its ambit other activities that in ordinary circumstances constitute an exercise of freedom of speech or of the press. The existence of such a statute . . . results in a continuous and pervasive restraint on all freedom of discussion that might reasonably be regarded as within its purview . . ."[33] . . .

Appellant's dismissal abridges not only freedom of speech but freedom of thought. Whatever loyalty means in the present connection, it is not speech but a state of mind. The appellant was dismissed for thinking prohibited thoughts. A constitution which forbids speech control does not permit thought control.

Appellant's dismissal attributes guilt by association, and thereby denies both the freedom of assembly guaranteed by the First Amendment and the due process of law guaranteed by the Fifth. The appellant was dismissed as disloyal because she was believed to be a member or associate of the Communist Party. Undoubtedly many such persons are disloyal in every sense to the government of the United States. But the Supreme Court has held that a particular member of the Communist Party may be "attached to the principles of the Constitution" within the meaning of those words in a naturalization act. . . .[38]

The court thinks Miss Bailey's interest and the public interest conflict. I think they coincide. Since Miss Bailey's dismissal from a nonsensitive job has nothing to do with protecting the security of the United States, the government's right to preserve itself in the world as it is has nothing to do with this case. The ominous theory that the right of fair trial ends where defense of security begins is irrelevant.

On this record we have no sufficient reason to doubt Miss Bailey's patriotism, or that her ability and experience were valuable to the government. We have no reason to suppose that an unpatriotic person in her job could do substantial harm of any kind. Whatever her actual thoughts may have been, to oust her as disloyal without trial is to pay too much for protection against any harm that could possibly be done in such a job. The cost is too great in morale and efficiency of government workers, in appeal of government employment to independent and inquiring minds, and in public confidence in democracy. But even if such

---

[33] *Thornhill v. Alabama,* 310 U. S. 88, 97–98.
[38] *Schneiderman v. United States,* 320 U. S. 118, 138, 136.

dismissals strengthened the government instead of weakening it, they would still cost too much in constitutional rights. We cannot preserve our liberties by sacrificing them.

## Note

1. The *Bailey* case was affirmed, without opinion, by an equally divided Supreme Court, Mr. Justice Clark not participating. *Bailey v. Richardson*, 341 U. S. 918, 95 L. Ed. 1352, 71 S. Ct. 669 (1951). In *Washington v. McGrath*, 182 F. 2d 375 (C. A. D. C., 1950), a group of 26 employees of the Post Office Department who had received notice of proposed dismissal under the Loyalty Order filed a suit for injunction and declaratory judgment. The issues were the same as in the *Bailey* case except that the plaintiffs here alleged that a majority of those removed were Jewish or Negro and averred unconstitutional discrimination. The government filed affidavits denying that race or religion entered into the proceedings. The Court of Appeals, holding that as to discrimination there was "no genuine issue of fact," upheld the District Court's dismissal. The Supreme Court, again equally divided, affirmed without opinion. 341 U. S. 923, 95 L. Ed. 1356, 71 S. Ct. 795 (1951).

2. In November 1947 the Attorney General furnished the Loyalty Review Board with a list of more than 80 organizations which he designated as subversive under Part III, Section 3 of Executive Order 9835. The Board made this list public shortly afterwards. 13 Fed. Reg. 1473 (1948). From time to time the Attorney General has added additional names. The most recent list, totaling 261 organizations, is printed in 15 Federal Register 8145–7 (Nov. 29, 1950). No notice or hearing was afforded by the Attorney General to these organizations prior to including them on the list; nor was any subsequent hearing provided.

Shortly after promulgation of the initial list three organizations brought suit against the Attorney General and members of the Loyalty Review Board for declaratory and injunctive relief. The Joint Anti-Fascist Refugee Committee, one of the three, alleged that it was a charitable organization engaged in raising and disbursing funds for the benefit of anti-Fascist refugees; that inclusion of its name on the Attorney General's list had seriously and irreparably impaired its reputation and the moral support and good will of the American people, and had caused many contributors to reduce or discontinue contributions; that members and participants in its activities had been "vilified and subjected to public shame, disgrace, ridicule and obliquy"; that it had been hampered in securing meeting places; and that many people had refused to take part in its fund-raising activities. The other organizations made similar allegations, together with an express denial that they came within any of the classifications of Part III, Section 3 of the Loyalty Order. The government moved to dismiss the complaints for failure to state a claim upon which relief could be granted. The District Court granted the motion and the Court of Appeals affirmed. 177 F. 2d 79 (C. A. D. C., 1949).

The Supreme Court reversed, holding that the complaints stated a valid cause of action. *Joint Anti-Fascist Refugee Committee v. McGrath*, 341 U. S. 123, 95 L. Ed. 817, 71 S. Ct. 624 (1951). All the justices (except Mr. Justice Clark, who did not participate) agreed that the organizations had standing to bring a suit challenging the Attorney General's action. Five justices agreed on reversal and three dissented. But there was considerable difference among the majority justices, each writing his own opinion, as to the grounds for reversal. The material below summarizes the various viewpoints and quotes short extracts from the opinions.

Mr. Justice Burton voted for reversal on narrow procedural grounds. Taking the allegations of the complaints as admitted by the motion to dismiss he held that the complaints in effect alleged that the Attorney General had included the organizations on the list without factual basis for finding them subversive. He therefore concluded that, on this state of the pleadings, the Attorney General had acted beyond the scope of his authority.

Mr. Justice Black agreed with the Burton position on the procedural issue, and agreed with Mr. Justice Frankfurter that there had been a denial of procedural due process, but went on to hold that no constitutional power existed for the Attorney General to list organizations as subversive:

"In the present climate of public opinion it appears certain that the Attorney General's much publicized findings, regardless of their truth or falsity, are the practical equivalents of confiscation and death sentences for any blacklisted organization not possessing extraordinary financial, political or religious prestige and influence. . . .

"[In] my judgment the executive has no constitutional authority, with or without a hearing, officially to prepare and publish the lists challenged by petitioners. In the first place, the system adopted effectively punishes many organizations and their members merely because of their political beliefs and utterances, and to this extent smacks of a most evil type of censorship. This cannot be reconciled with the First Amendment as I interpret it. See my dissent in *American Communications Assn.* v. *Douds*, 339 U. S. 382, 445. Moreover, officially prepared and proclaimed governmental blacklists possess almost every quality of bills of attainder, the use of which was from the beginning forbidden to both national and state governments. U. S. Const., Art. I, §§ 9, 10. It is true that the classic bill of attainder was a condemnation by the legislature following investigation by that body, see *United States* v. *Lovett*, 328 U. S. 303, while in the present case the Attorney General performed the official tasks. But I cannot believe that the authors of the Constitution, who outlawed the bill of attainder, inadvertently endowed the executive with power to engage in the same tyrannical practices that had made the bill such an odious institution.

"There is argument that executive power to issue these pseudo-bills of attainder can be implied from the undoubted power of the Government to hire and discharge employees and to protect itself against treasonable individuals or organizations. Our basic law, however,

556

wisely withheld authority for resort to executive investigations, condemnations and blacklists as a substitute for imposition of legal types of penalties by courts following trial and conviction in accordance with procedural safeguards of the Bill of Rights. . . ."

Mr. Justice Frankfurter thought that the issue could not be disposed of by Mr. Justice Burton's interpretation of the pleadings and concluded that the procedure employed by the Attorney General violated due process:

"It would be blindness . . . not to recognize that in the conditions of our time such designation drastically restricts the organizations, if it does not proscribe them. Potential members, contributors or beneficiaries of listed organizations may well be influenced by use of the designation, for instance, as ground for rejection of applications for commissions in the armed forces or for permits for meetings in the auditoriums of public housing projects. Compare Act of April 3, 1948, § 110 (c), 62 Stat. 143, 22 U. S. C. (Supp. III) § 1508 (c). Yet, designation has been made without notice, without disclosure of any reasons justifying it, without opportunity to meet the undisclosed evidence or suspicion on which designation may have been based, and without opportunity to establish affirmatively that the aims and acts of the organization are innocent. It is claimed that thus to maim or decapitate, on the mere say-so of the Attorney General, an organization to all outward-seeming engaged in lawful objectives is so devoid of fundamental fairness as to offend the Due Process Clause of the Fifth Amendment. . . .

"That a hearing has been thought indispensable in so many other situations, leaving the cases of denial exceptional, does not of itself prove that it must be found essential here. But it does place upon the Attorney General the burden of showing weighty reason for departing in this instance from a rule so deeply imbedded in history and in the demands of justice. Nothing in the Loyalty Order requires him to deny organizations opportunity to present their case. The Executive Order, defining his powers, directs only that designation shall be made 'after appropriate investigation and determination.' This surely does not preclude an administrative procedure, however informal, which would incorporate the essentials of due process. Nothing has been presented to the Court to indicate that it will be impractical or prejudicial to a concrete public interest to disclose to organizations the nature of the case against them and to permit them to meet it if they can. Indeed, such a contention could hardly be made inasmuch as the Loyalty Order itself requires partial disclosure and hearing in proceedings against a Government employee who is a member of a proscribed organization. Whether such procedure sufficiently protects the rights of the employee is a different story. Such as it is, it affords evidence that the wholly summary process for the organizations is inadequate. And we have controlling proof that Congress did not think that the Attorney General's procedure was indispensable for the protection of the public interest. The McCarran Act, passed under circumstances certainly not more serene than when the Loyalty Order was issued, grants organizations a full administrative hearing, subject to judicial review, before they are required to register as 'Communist-action' or 'Communist-front.'

"We are not here dealing with the grant of Government largess. We have not before us the measured action of Congress, with the pause that is properly engendered when the validity of legislation is assailed. The Attorney General is certainly not immune from the historic requirements of fairness merely because he acts, however conscientiously, in the name of security. Nor does he obtain immunity on the ground that designation is not an 'adjudication' or a 'regulation' in the conventional use of those terms. Due process is not confined in its scope to the particular forms in which rights have heretofore been found to have been curtailed for want of procedural fairness. Due process is perhaps the most majestic concept in our whole constitutional system. While it contains the garnered wisdom of the past in assuring fundamental justice, it is also a living principle not confined to past instances."

Mr. Justice Douglas, concurring with Mr. Justice Burton, wrote a separate opinion finding the Loyalty Order as a whole unconstitutional:

"The resolution of the constitutional question presents one of the gravest issues of this generation. There is no doubt in my mind of the need for the Chief Executive and the Congress to take strong measures against any Fifth Column worming its way into government—a Fifth Column that has access to vital information and the purpose to paralyze and confuse. The problems of security are real. So are the problems of freedom. The paramount issue of the age is to reconcile the two.

"In days of great tension when feelings run high, it is a temptation to take short-cuts by borrowing from the totalitarian techniques of our opponents. But when we do, we set in motion a subversive influence of our own design that destroys us from within. The present cases, together with No. 49, *Bailey* v. *Richardson* . . . affirmed today by an equally divided Court, are simple illustrations of that trend. . . .

"No one can tell from the Executive Order what meaning is intended. No one can tell from the records of the cases which one the Attorney General applied. The charge is flexible; it will mean one thing to one officer, another to someone else. It will be given meaning according to the predilections of the prosecutor: 'subversive' to some will be synonymous with 'radical'; 'subversive' to others will be synonymous with 'communist.' It can be expanded to include those who depart from the orthodox party line—to those whose words and actions (though completely loyal) do not conform to the orthodox view on foreign or domestic policy. These flexible standards, which vary with the mood and political philosophy of the prosecutor, are weapons which can be made as sharp or as blunt as the occasion requires. Since they are subject to grave abuse, they have no place in our system of law. When we employ them, we plant within our body politic the virus of the totalitarian ideology which we oppose. • • •

**558**

"The system used to condemn these organizations is bad enough. The evil is only compounded when a government employee is charged with being disloyal. Association with or membership in an organization found to be 'subversive' weighs heavily against the accused. He is not allowed to prove that the charge against the organization is false. That case is closed; that line of defense is taken away. The technique is one of guilt by association—one of the most odious institutions of history. The fact that the technique of guilt by association was used in the prosecutions at Nuremberg does not make it congenial to our constitutional scheme. Guilt under our system of government is personal. When we make guilt vicarious we borrow from systems alien to ours and ape our enemies. . . .

"The Loyalty Board convicts on evidence which it cannot even appraise. The critical evidence may be the word of an unknown witness who is 'a paragon of veracity, a knave, or the village idiot.' His name, his reputation, his prejudices, his animosities, his trustworthiness are unknown both to the judge and to the accused. The accused has no opportunity to show that the witness lied or was prejudiced or venal. Without knowing who her accusers are she has no way of defending. She has nothing to offer except her own word and the character testimony of her friends.

"Dorothy Bailey was not, to be sure, faced with a criminal charge and hence not technically entitled under the Sixth Amendment to be confronted with the witnesses against her. But she was on trial for her reputation, her job, her professional standing. A disloyalty trial is the most crucial event in the life of a public servant. If condemned, he is branded for life as a person unworthy of trust or confidence. To make that condemnation without meticulous regard for the decencies of a fair trial is abhorrent to fundamental justice.

"I do not mean to imply that but for these irregularities the system of loyalty trials is constitutional. I do not see how the constitutionality of this dragnet system of loyalty trials which has been entrusted to the administrative agencies of government can be sustained. Every government employee must take an oath of loyalty. If he swears falsely, he commits perjury and can be tried in court. In such a trial he gets the full protection of the Bill of Rights, including trial by jury and the presumption of innocence. I am inclined to the view that when a disloyalty charge is substituted for perjury and an administrative board substituted for the court 'the spirit and the letter of the Bill of Rights' are offended. . . .

"The British have avoided those difficulties by applying the loyalty procedure only in sensitive areas and in using it to test the qualifications of an employee for a particular post, not to condemn him for all public employment.[8] When we go beyond that procedure and adopt

---

[8] 448 H. C. Deb. 1703 *et seq.*, 3418 *et seq.* (5th Ser. 1947–1948). The meticulous care with which this small select group is handled is reflected in the letter of the Prime Minister, dated Dec. 1, 1948, reporting on the purge of communists and fascists from the civil service. 459 H. C. Deb. 830 (5th Ser. 1948–1949).

the dragnet system now in force, we trench upon the civil rights of our people. We condemn by administrative edict, rather than by jury trial. Of course, no one has a constitutional right to a government job. But every citizen has a right to a fair trial when his government seeks to deprive him of the privileges of first-class citizenship."

Mr. Justice Jackson took the view that a finding of disloyalty against an employee on the basis of membership in or affiliation with an organization, without a hearing on the nature of the organization, constituted a denial of due process, and that the organization could bring an action to vindicate its members' rights.

Mr. Justice Reed, in an opinion in which Chief Justice Vinson and Mr. Justice Minton concurred, dissented on the ground that the Loyalty Order was valid:

"No objection is or could reasonably be made in the records or briefs to an examination by the Government into the loyalty of its employees. Although the Founders of this Republic rebelled against their established government of England and won our freedom, the creation of our own constitutional government endowed that new government, the United States of America, with the right and duty to protect its existence against any force that seeks its overthrow or changes in its structure by other than constitutional means. Tolerant as we are of all political efforts by argument or persuasion to change the basis of our social, economic or political life, the line is drawn sharply and clearly at any act or incitement to act in violation of our constitutional processes. Surely the Government need not await an employee's conviction of a crime involving disloyalty before separating him from public service. Governments cannot be indifferent to manifestations of subversion. As soon as these are significant enough reasonably to cause concern as to the likelihood of action, the duty to protect the state compels the exertion of governmental power. Not to move would brand a government with a dangerous weakness of will. The determination of the time for action rests with the executive and legislative arms. An objection to consideration of an employee's sympathetic association with an admitted totalitarian, fascist, communist or subversive group, as bearing upon the propriety of his retention or employment as a government employee would have no better standing. . . .

"Procedure under the Executive Order does not require 'proof' in

---

The number of cases considered by the end of April, 1950, was 86, classified as follows:

| | |
|---|---:|
| Transferred to nonsecret departments | 32 |
| Resigned | 5 |
| Exonerated and reinstated | 19 |
| Dismissed (including one Fascist) | 7 |
| Retired for health reasons before completion of investigations | 1 |
| On special leave, either *sub judice* or confirmed Communists awaiting transfer or dismissal | 22 |
| | 86 |

See British Information Services, Reference Division, April, 1950.

the sense of a court proceeding that these communist organizations teach or incite to force and violence to obtain their objectives. What is required by the Order is an examination and determination by the Attorney General that these organizations are 'communist.' The description 'communist' is adequate for the purposes of inquiry and listing. No such precision of definition is necessary as a criminal prosecution might require. Cf. *United States* v. *Chemical Foundation,* 272 U. S. 1, 14. Communism is well understood to mean a group seeking to overthrow by force and violence governments such as ours and to establish a new government based on public ownership and direction of productive property. Undoubtedly, there are reasonable grounds to conclude that accepted history teaches that revolution by force and violence to accomplish this end is a tenet of communists. No more is necessary to justify an organization's designation as communist. . . .

"Recognizing that the designation, rightly or wrongly, of petitioner organizations as communist impairs their ability to carry forward successfully whatever legitimate objects they seek to accomplish, we do not accept their argument that such interference is an abridgment of First Amendment guarantees. They are in the position of every proponent of unpopular views. Heresy induces strong expressions of opposition. So long as petitioners are permitted to voice their political ideas, free from suggestions for the opportune use of force to accomplish their social and economic aims, it is hard to understand how any advocate of freedom of expression can assert that their right has been unconstitutionally abridged. As nothing in the orders or regulations concerning this list limits the teachings or support of these organizations, we do not believe that any right of theirs under the First Amendment is abridged by publication of the list. . . .

"These petitioners are not ordered to do anything and are not punished for anything. Their position may be analogized to that of persons under grand jury investigation. Such persons have no right to notice by and hearing before a grand jury; only a right to defend the charge at trial. Property may be taken for government use without notice or hearing by a mere declaration of taking by the authorized official. No court has doubted the constitutionality of such summary action under the due process clause when just compensation must be paid ultimately. Persons may be barred from certain positions merely because of their associations.

"To allow petitioners entry into the investigation would amount to interference with the Executive's discretion, contrary to the ordinary operations of Government. . . .

"Listing of these organizations does not conclude the members' rights to hold government employment. It is only one piece of evidence for consideration. That mere membership in listed organizations does not normally bring about findings of disloyalty is graphically shown by a report of proceedings under the loyalty program. The procedure for removal of employees suspected of disloyalty follows the routine prescribed for the removal of employees on other grounds for dismissal. Employees under investigation have never had the

[Emerson]—36

right to confrontation, cross-examination and quasi-judicial hearing. 37 Stat. 555, as amended, 5 U. S. C. § 652. Normal removal procedure functions for permanent employees about in this way. The employing agency may remove for the efficiency of the service, including grounds for disqualification of an applicant. 5 CFR, 1947 Supp., § 9.-101. Removal requires notice and charges. Before the loyalty review boards similar procedure is followed. Where initial consideration indicates a removal of an incumbent for disloyalty may be warranted, notice is provided for. Thus, there is scrupulous care taken to see that an employee who has fallen under suspicion has notice of the charges and an opportunity to explain his actions. The employee has no opportunity to disprove the characterization placed upon the listed organization by the Attorney General for the practical reasons stated . . . *supra.* The employee does have every opportunity to explain his association with that organization. The Constitution requires for the employee no more than this fair opportunity to explain his questioned activities. Such procedure is quite similar to that followed in Great Britain in the removal or transfer of civil servants from positions 'vital to the security of the State.' The Prime Minister assumed the authority to designate membership in the Communist Party or 'other forms of continuing association' therewith as sufficient to bar employment in sensitive areas."

3. In *Deak v. Pace,* 185 F. 2d 997 (C. A. D. C., 1950), the Secretary of War had dismissed two employees under his summary removal power. The charges incorporated in the notices of removal simply said that the employees had attended Communist meetings or been active in Communist organizations, without specifying times, places and names. The court held that the charges did not satisfy the statutory requirement that the employees be "fully informed of the reasons for such removal" and reversed the lower court which had dismissed a suit for mandatory injunction. Judge Prettyman dissented. On elaboration of the charges the employees were able to clear themselves, they were reinstated, and Secretary of the Army Pace apologized to them. American Civil Liberties Weekly Bulletin, Jan. 28, 1952.

4. In *U. S. v. Remington,* 191 F. 2d 246 (C. A. 2, 1951), cert. den. 342 U. S. 895 (1951) the Court reversed the conviction of Remington for alleged perjury in testifying that he had never been a member of the Communist Party. In the course of its opinion the Court said:

"Over defense objections the prosecutor was permitted to make numerous references to the Attorney General's list of subversive organizations during the defendant's cross-examination. This was error, for the list is a purely hearsay declaration by the Attorney General, and could have no probative value in the trial of this defendant [citing the *Joint Anti-Fascist* case]. It has no competency to prove the subversive character of the listed associations and, failing that, it could have no conceivable tendency to prove the defendant's alleged perjury even if it were shown that he belonged to some or all of the organizations listed." 191 F. 2d at 252.

5. A further issue under the Loyalty Order arose in *U. S. v. Kutcher* (D. C. D. C., July 2, 1951, unreported). Kutcher, a veteran who had

[Emerson]

lost both legs in the Second World War, was discharged from his position as clerk in the Newark Office of the Veterans Administration. Kutcher was an acknowledged member of the Socialist Workers Party, an organization listed by the Attorney General as one which "seeks to alter the form of government of the United States by unconstitutional means." Under the regulations of the Loyalty Review Board membership in organizations listed in this category makes dismissal mandatory under the Hatch Act. Kutcher denied that he or the Socialist Workers Party advocated or sought the overthrow of the government by unconstitutional means. The Administrator of Veterans Affairs dismissed Kutcher without considering the issue of his personal loyalty or disloyalty, and without receiving evidence concerning the organization involved. A suit by Kutcher was dismissed and the matter was appealed to the Court of Appeals.

6. Discussion of the legal issues raised by the *Bailey* and *Joint Anti-Fascist* cases may be found in McCarran, *The Supreme Court and the Loyalty Program: The Effect of Refugee Committee v. McGrath*, 37 A. B. A. J. 434 (1951); Fraenkel, *Law and Loyalty*, 37 Iowa L. Rev. 153 (1952); Note, *The "Right" to a Government Job*, 6 Rutgers L. Rev. 451 (1952); Notes, 100 U. of Pa. L. Rev. 274 (1951); 20 Geo. Wash. L. Rev. 294 (1952). For discussion published prior to the decisions see Emerson and Helfeld, *Loyalty Among Government Employees*, 58 Yale L. J. 1, 79–120 (1948) (collecting materials up to end of 1948); Notes, 36 Calif. L. Rev. 596 (1948); 48 Col. L. Rev. 1050 (1948).

## Administration of the Loyalty Program

From the start of the Loyalty Program up to January 1952 nearly 4,000,000 persons in or seeking Federal employment were checked for loyalty. Out of this number the initial check disclosed "derogatory information" in 17,343 cases and full investigations were made by the F.B.I. Some 1,935 persons left the service of the government during the course of the investigation. The lower Loyalty Boards received 15,408 cases for adjudication. An additional 1,848 persons left government service during this stage. As a result of decisions by the Loyalty Boards 570 individuals were rated as ineligible. Most of these cases were appealed to the Loyalty Review Board, which sustained the lower boards in 315 cases and reversed them in 214 cases, with 27 cases still pending. In 324 cases decisions of the lower boards favorable to the employee were reviewed by the Loyalty Review Board and remanded to the lower boards for further consideration. Thus about 350 individuals were denied employment under the program. Interview with Hiram Bingham, Chairman of the Loyalty Review Board, released Jan. 20, 1952.

Little material is available on the nature of the investigations conducted by the F.B.I. For evidence that the F.B.I. probes deeply into political beliefs, reading habits, associations and the like, see Emerson and Helfeld, *Loyalty Among Government Employees*, 58 Yale L. J. 1, 70-2 (1948). For defense of F.B.I. procedures and practices, see Hoover, *A Comment on the Article "Loyalty Among Government Employees*," 58 Yale L. J. 401 (1949); Hoover, *Civil Liberties and Law Enforcement: The Role of the FBI*, 37 Iowa L. Rev. 175 (1952).[1]

The proceedings under the loyalty programs are not made public. Under regulations of the Loyalty Review Board no formal decisions with findings of fact and reasons are prepared. Hence there is only limited and scattered data available, such as may be obtained from persons involved in loyalty cases, showing the nature of the charges, the character of the hearings, the kind of evidence relied upon, or the criteria of disloyalty.

The charges served in the *Bailey* case have been set forth, *supra*. A more recent example of charges made against an employee, with names, dates, and places changed to avoid the possibility of identification, is as follows:

"As a result of a recent investigation made of you as an employee of this Agency, under the provisions of the above-mentioned Executive Order . . . evidence has been submitted which indicates that you have been or that you are a member of or otherwise affiliated or sympathetic with one or more organizations, associations, movements, or groups, designated by the Attorney General as subversive. On the basis of this evidence reasonable doubt as to your loyalty to the Government of the United States exists. This evidence, so far as security considerations permit its disclosure, is as follows:

"1. That, since about July 1947, you have been a close associate of Mary Jane Brown, also known as Martha J. Brown, a member of the Communist Political Association, and known as such by you.

"2. That, since about July 1947, when in New York City, you resided with Mary Jane Brown, also known as Martha J. Brown, a member of the Communist Political Association, and known as such by you, at her residence 1754 Moon Street, Brooklyn, New York.

"3. That, since about July 1947, you have been a close

---

[1] For further discussion of the role of the F. B. I. in loyalty matters, see Rauh, *Informers, G-Men, and Free Men*, The Progressive, May 1950, p. 9; J. Edgar Hoover, *Hoover Answers Ten Questions on the F. B. I.*, N. Y. Times Magazine, April 16, 1950, p. 9; *Report on Certain Alleged Practices of the FBI*, 10 Law. Guild Rev. 185 (1950); Barth, *The Loyalty of Free Men*, ch. VII (1951). See also Lowenthal, *The Federal Bureau of Investigation* (1950). On some of the legal issues see Donnelly, *Judicial Control of Informants, Spies, Stool Pigeons and Agents Provocateurs*, 60 Yale L. J. 1091 (1951).

associate of Elizabeth Henson, Clara Debaitas and Ruth Williams all members of the Communist Party; and Jane Lovell and Ann James, Communist sympathizers and all of same known as such by you.

"4. That, in about 1948 or 1949, you attended the Adams School of Social Science in New York City, a Communist front organization and known as such by you."

In another case a set of interrogatories addressed to an employee of a non-sensitive agency included the following (names and places in the first interrogatory changed to avoid identification) :

"1. While a student at X University [one of the country's best known universities] did you associate with and do research work for Professor Y?

"a. If your answer is affirmative give full details on the extent of your association with this man in both a social as well as on a student-faculty relationship.

"b. Also, give the extent of your knowledge of the Communist sympathies of this man as evidenced by his membership in either the Communist Party or Communist Front organizations or otherwise.

"c. Further, give in detail the subject matter of the research work you performed, the purpose as understood by you of the work, and in what manner you were recruited and/or chosen to perform this work."

"2. Did you support the candidacy for the office of President of the United States of Henry A. Wallace on the Progressive Party platform in 1948?

"a. If so, give your reasons for this support and state the extent of your knowledge that his candidacy was supported by the Communist Party."

For accounts of the hearings before loyalty boards, in addition to the material cited in Judge Edgerton's opinion in the *Bailey* case, see Barth, *The Loyalty of Free Men*, pp. 111–24, 136–40 (1951); Biddle, *The Fear of Freedom*, pp. 219–35 (1951); Arnold, *The Case Against the Federal Loyalty Program*, in *The Strengthening of American Political Institutions* (Cornell U. Press, 1949), pp. 66–70; Durr, *How to Measure Loyalty*, The Nation, Apr. 23, 1949, pp. 470–3; Emerson and Helfeld, *Loyalty Among Government Employees*, 58 Yale L. J. 1, 72–5 (1948).

The only published decision under the program is the decision of the State Department Loyalty-Security Board, exonerating John Service, and the decision of the Loyalty Review Board reversing the State Department and finding him a security risk. N. Y. Times, Dec. 14, 1951.

As to the attitude of Chairman Bingham of the Loyalty Review Board toward the State Department's administration of the loyalty program, see the transcript of his remarks at a meeting of the Board in 1951, reported in *State Department Lax on Loyalty Cases?*, U. S. News & World Report, Feb. 8, 1952, pp. 18, 20:[2]

" 'I think it is fair to say,' Chairman Bingham observed, 'that the State Department, as you know, has the worst record of any department in the action of its Loyalty Board. . . . The Loyalty Board, in all the cases that have been considered in the State Department, has not found anyone—shall I say, 'guilty' under our rules. It is the only Board which has acted that way.' " . . .

"Chairman Bingham: 'Your present chairman thought about that for a couple of weeks and took counsel of two persons in whom he had confidence, and then asked for an appointment with the Secretary of State. The Secretary of State, who is a very busy man, very graciously gave me an appointment last Friday afternoon . . . I called his attention to the fact that his Board was out of step with all other agency boards. In the Post Office Department, 10 per cent of all persons examined were found to be worthy of separation from the Government. In the Commerce Department, 6½ per cent. The average was about 6 per cent. The State Department, zero.

" 'The Secretary of State was very impressed by what I said. He received my remarks very kindly. . . .' "

For one comment on the political pressures that affect the administration of the Loyalty Program, see the address of President Truman to the National Civil Service League, N. Y. Times, May 3, 1952:

"The loyalty program was designed to protect innocent employes as well as the Government. When I set it up, I intended it to expose the guilty and at the same time to safeguard the rights and the reputations of those who were innocent. But I have become increasingly concerned in recent months by attempts to use the loyalty program as a club with which to beat Government employes over the head.

"Political gangsters are attempting to pervert the program into an instrument of intimidation and blackmail, to coerce or destroy any who dare oppose them. These men and those who abet them have besmirched the reputations of decent, loyal public servants. They have not hesitated to lie, under cover of Congressional immunity, of course, and to repeat the lies again and again.

---

[2] The transcript was originally released by Senator McCarthy. Most of it is printed in the Congressional Record for Jan. 15, 1952, pp. 192–4.

"This is a matter for great concern. These tactics contain the seeds of tyranny. Can we be sure that people who employ such tactics are really loyal to our form of Government, with its Bill of Rights and its tradition of individual liberty? The fact is that they are breaking these things down. They are undermining the foundation stones of our Constitution. I believe such men betray our country and all it stands for. I believe they are as grave a menace as the Communists."

Charges have frequently been made that the Loyalty Program operates to impair the morale of government workers, to discourage initiative and to prevent talented persons from entering government service. See, *e.g.,* Barth, *supra,* pp. 124–30; Biddle, *supra,* pp. 217–8; Gellhorn, *Security, Loyalty, and Science,* ch. IX (1950) ; Emerson and Helfeld, *supra,* 76–9 ; Mather, *Scientists in the Doghouse,* The Nation, June 28, 1952, p. 638 ; Brown, *6,000,000 Second-Class Citizens,* The Nation, June 28, 1952, p 644. On the other hand the program has been approved by the National Federation of Government Employees, see Richardson, *The Federal Employee Loyalty Program,* 51 Col. L. Rev. 546, 554 (1951), and staunchly defended by its supporters. See, in addition to the Richardson article, *Interview with Hiram Bingham: Catching the Disloyal,* U.S. News & World Report, Nov. 23, 1951, p. 22. For criticism that the program has not been administered with sufficient vigor, see *Investigation of Federal Employees Loyalty Program,* Interim Report of the Investigations Subcommittee of the Senate Committee on Expenditures in the Executive Departments, Sen. Rept. No. 1775, 80th Cong., 2d Sess. (1948).

The only scientific study of the impact of the Loyalty Program is the exploratory survey of Jahoda and Cook, *Security Measures and Freedom of Thought: An Exploratory Study of the Impact of Loyalty and Security Programs,* 61 Yale L. J. 295 (1952).

On the rights of individuals to sue for defamatory statements made to government investigators, in those cases where the statements are discovered, see *Moore-McCormack Lines v. Foltz,* 189 F. 2d 537 (C. A. 2, 1951), cert. den. 342 U. S. 871 (1951) ; Note, 51 Col. L. Rev. 244 (1951).

## State and Local Loyalty Programs

### GARNER v. BOARD OF PUBLIC WORKS
### OF LOS ANGELES

Supreme Court of the United States, 1951
341 U. S. 716, 95 L. Ed. 1317, 71 S. Ct. 909

MR. JUSTICE CLARK delivered the opinion of the Court.

In 1941 the California Legislature amended the Charter of the City of Los Angeles to provide in part as follows:

". . . no person shall hold or retain or be eligible for any public office or employment in the service of the City of Los Angeles, in any office or department thereof, either elective or appointive, who has within five (5) years prior to the effective date of this section advised, advocated or taught, or who may, after this section becomes effective [April 28, 1941], advise, advocate or teach, or who is now or has been within five (5) years prior to the effective date of this section, or who may, after this section becomes effective, become a member of or affiliated with any group, society, association, organization or party which advises, advocates or teaches, or has, within said period of five (5) years, advised, advocated or taught the overthrow by force or violence of the government of the United States of America or of the State of California.

"In so far as this section may be held by any court of competent jurisdiction not to be self-executing, the City Council is hereby given power and authority to adopt appropriate legislation for the purpose of effectuating the objects hereof." Calif. Stat. 1941, c. 67.

Pursuant to the authority thus conferred the City of Los Angeles in 1948 passed ordinance No. 94,004 requiring every person who held an office or position in the service of the city to take an oath prior to January 6, 1949. In relevant part the oath was as follows: "I further swear (or affirm) that I do not advise, advocate or teach, and have not within the period beginning five (5) years prior to the effective date of the ordinance requiring the making of this oath or affirmation, advised, advocated or taught, the overthrow by force, violence or other unlawful means, of the Government of the United States of America or of the State of California and that I am not now and have not, within said period, been or become a member of or affiliated with any group, society, association, organization or party which advises, advocates or teaches, or has, within said period, advised, advocated or taught, the overthrow by force, violence or other unlawful means of the Government of the United States, or of the State of California. I further swear (or affirm) that I will not, while I am in the service of the City of Los Angeles, advise, advocate or teach, or be or become a member of or affiliated with any group, association, society, organization or party which advises, advocates or teaches, or has within said period, advised, advocated or taught, the overthrow by force, violence or other unlawful means, of the Government of the United States of America or of the State of California . . ."

The ordinance also required every employee to execute an affidavit "stating whether or not he is or ever was a member of the Communist Party of the United States of America or of the Communist Political Association, and if he is or was such a member, stating the dates when he became, and the periods during which he was, such a member . . . ."

On the final date for filing of the oath and affidavit petitioners were civil service employees of the City of Los Angeles. Petitioners Pacifico and Schwartz took the oath but refused to execute the affidavit. The remaining fifteen petitioners refused to do either. All were discharged for such cause, after administrative hearing, as of January 6, 1949. In this action they sue for reinstatement and unpaid salaries. The District Court of Appeal denied relief. 98 Cal. App. 2d 493, 220 P. 2d 958 (1950). We granted certiorari, 340 U. S. 941 (1951).

Petitioners attack the ordinance as violative of the provision of Art. I, § 10 of the Federal Constitution that "No State shall . . . pass any Bill of Attainder [or] ex post facto Law . . . ." They also contend that the ordinance deprives them of freedom of speech and assembly and of the right to petition for redress of grievances.

Petitioners have assumed that the oath and affidavit provisions of the ordinance present similar constitutional considerations and stand or fall together. We think, however, that separate disposition is indicated.

1. The affidavit raises the issue whether the City of Los Angeles is constitutionally forbidden to require that its employees disclose their past or present membership in the Communist Party or the Communist Political Association. Not before us is the question whether the city may determine that an employee's disclosure of such political affiliation justifies his discharge.

We think that a municipal employer is not disabled because it is an agency of the State from inquiring of its employees as to matters that may prove relevant to their fitness and suitability for the public service. Past conduct may well relate to present fitness; past loyalty may have a reasonable relationship to present and future trust. Both are commonly inquired into in determining fitness for both high and low positions in private industry and are not less relevant in public employment. The affidavit requirement is valid.

2. In our view the validity of the oath turns upon the nature of the Charter amendment (1941) and the relation of the ordinance (1948) to this amendment. Immaterial here is any opinion we might have as to the Charter provision insofar as it purported to apply retrospectively for a five-year period prior to its effective date. We assume that under the Federal Constitution the Charter amendment is valid to the extent that it bars from the city's public service persons who, subsequent to its adoption in 1941, advise, advocate, or teach the violent overthrow of the Government or who are or become affiliated with any group doing so. The provisions operating thus prospectively were a reasonable regulation to protect the municipal service by establishing an employment qualification of loyalty to the State and the United States. Cf. *Gerende v. Board of Supervisors of Elections*, 341 U. S. 56 (1951). Likewise, as a regulation of political activity of municipal employees, the amendment was reasonably designed to protect the integrity and competency of the service. This Court has held that Congress may reasonably restrict the political activity of federal civil service employees for such a purpose, *United Public Workers v. Mitchell*, 330 U. S. 75, 102–103 (1947), and a State is not without power to do as much.

The Charter amendment defined standards of eligibility for employees and specifically denied city employment to those persons who thereafter should not comply with these standards. While the amendment deprived no one of employment with or without trial, yet from its effective date it terminated any privilege to work for the city in the case of persons who thereafter engaged in the activity proscribed.

The ordinance provided for administrative implementation of the provisions of the Charter amendment. The oath imposed by the ordinance proscribed to employees activity which had been denied them in identical terms and with identical sanctions in the Charter provision effective in 1941. The five-year period provided by the oath extended back only to 1943.

The ordinance would be *ex post facto* if it imposed punishment for past conduct lawful at the time it was engaged in. Passing for the moment the question whether separation of petitioners from their employment must be considered as punishment, the ordinance clearly is not *ex post facto*. The activity covered by the oath had been proscribed by the Charter in the same terms, for the same purpose, and to the same effect over seven years before, and two years prior to the period embraced in the oath. Not the law but the fact was posterior.

Bills of attainder are "legislative acts . . . that apply either to named individuals or to easily ascertainable members of a group in such a way as to inflict punishment on them without a judicial trial . . . ." *United States v. Lovett*, 328 U. S. 303, 315 (1946). Punishment is a prerequisite. See concurring opinion in *Lovett, supra*, at 318, 324. Whether legislative action curtailing a privilege previously enjoyed amounts to punishment depends upon "the circumstances attending and the causes of the deprivation." *Cummings v. Missouri*, 4 Wall. 277, 320 (1867). We are unable to conclude that punishment is imposed by a general regulation which merely provides standards of qualification and eligibility for employment.

*Cummings v. Missouri*, 4 Wall. 277 (1867), and *Ex parte Garland*, 4 Wall. 333 (1867), the leading cases in this Court applying the federal constitutional prohibitions against bills of attainder, recognized that the guarantees against such legislation have never been intended to preclude legislative definition of standards of qualification for public or professional employment. Carefully distinguishing an instance of legislative "infliction of punishment" from the exercise of "the power of Congress to prescribe qualifications," the Court said in *Garland's* case: "The legislature may undoubtedly prescribe qualifications for the office, to which he must conform, as it may, where it has exclusive jurisdiction, prescribe qualifications for the pursuit of any of the ordinary avocations of life." 4 Wall. at pages 379–380. See also, *Cummings v. Missouri, supra*, at 318–319. This doctrine was reaffirmed in *Dent v. West Virginia*, 129 U. S. 114 (1889), in which Mr. Justice Field, who had written the *Cummings* and *Garland* opinions, wrote for a unanimous Court upholding a statute elevating standards of qualification to practice medicine. And in *Hawker v. New York*, 170 U. S. 189 (1898), the Court upheld a statute forbidding the practice of medicine by any person who had been convicted of a felony. Both *Dent* and *Hawker* distinguished the *Cummings* and *Garland* cases as inapplicable when the legislature establishes reasonable qualifications for a vocational pursuit with the necessary effect of disqualifying some persons presently engaged in it.

Petitioners rely heavily upon *United States v. Lovett*, 328 U. S. 303 (1946), in which a legislative act effectively separating certain public servants from their positions was held to be a bill of attainder. Unlike the provisions of the Charter and ordinance under which petitioners were removed, the statute in the *Lovett* case did not declare general and prospectively operative standards of qualification and eligibility for public employment. Rather, by its terms it prohibited any further payment of compensation to named individual employees. Under these circumstances, viewed against the legislative background, the statute was held to have imposed penalties without judicial trial.

Nor are we impressed by the contention that the oath denies due process because its negation is not limited to affiliations with organizations known to the employee to be in the proscribed class. We have no reason to suppose that the oath is or will be construed by the City of Los Angeles or by California courts as affecting adversely those persons who during their affiliation with a proscribed organization were innocent of its purpose, or those who severed their relations with any such organization when its character became apparent, or those who were affiliated with organizations which at one time or another during the period covered by the ordinance were engaged in proscribed activity but not at the time of affiant's affiliation. We assume that scienter is implicit in each clause of the oath. As the city has done nothing to negative this interpretation, we take for granted that the ordinance will be so read to avoid raising difficult constitutional problems which any other application would present. *Fox v. Washington*, 236 U. S. 273, 277 (1915). It appears from correspondence of record between the city and petitioners that although the city welcomed inquiry as to its construction of the oath, the interpretation upon which we have proceeded may not have been explicitly called to the attention of petitioners before their refusal. We assume that if our interpretation of the oath is correct, the City of Los Angeles will give those petitioners who heretofore refused to take the oath an opportunity to take it as interpreted and resume their employment.

The judgment as to Pacifico and Schwartz is affirmed. The judgment as to the remaining petitioners is affirmed on the basis of the interpretation of the ordinance which we have felt justified in assuming.

*Affirmed.*

MR. JUSTICE FRANKFURTER, concurring in part and dissenting in part. . . .

A municipality like Los Angeles ought to be allowed adequate scope in seeking to elicit information about its employees and from them. It would give to the Due Process Clause an unwarranted power of intrusion into local affairs to hold that a city may not require its employees to disclose whether they have been members of the Communist Party or the Communist Political Association. In the context of our time, such membership is sufficiently relevant to effective and dependable government, and to the confidence of the electorate in its government. I think the precise Madison would have been surprised even to hear it suggested that the requirement of this affidavit was an "Attainder" under Art. I, § 10, of the Constitution. For reasons outlined in the concurring opinion in *United States v. Lovett*, 328 U. S. 303, 318, I cannot so regard it. This kind of inquiry into political affiliation may in the long run do more harm than good. But the two employees who were dismissed solely because they refused to file an affidavit stating whether or when they had been members of the Communist Party or the Communist Political Association cannot successfully appeal to the Constitution of the United States.

A very different issue is presented by the fifteen employees who were discharged because they refused to take [that part of the oath relating to membership in or affiliation with organizations].

The validity of an oath must be judged on the assumption that it will be taken conscientiously. This ordinance does not ask the employee to swear that he "knowingly" or "to the best of his knowledge" had no proscribed affiliation. Certainty is implied in the disavowal exacted. The oath thus excludes from city employment all persons who are not certain that every organization to which they belonged or with which they were affiliated (with all the uncertainties of the meaning of "affiliated") at any time since 1943 has not since that date advocated the overthrow by "unlawful means" of the Government of the United States or of the State of California. . . .

If this ordinance is sustained, sanction is given to like oaths for every governmental unit in the United States. Not only does the oath make an irrational demand. It is bound to operate as a real deterrent to people contemplating even innocent associations. How can anyone be sure that an organization with which he affiliates will not at some time in the future be found by a State or National official to advocate overthrow of government by "unlawful means"? All but the hardiest may well hesitate to join organizations if they know that by such a proscription they will be permanently disqualified from public employment. These are considerations that cut deep into the traditions of our people. Gregariousness and friendliness are among the most characteristic of American attitudes. Throughout our history they have been manifested in "joining." See Arthur M. Schlesinger, Sr., Biography of a Nation of Joiners, published in 50 American Historical Review 1, reprinted in Schlesinger, Paths to the Present 23.

Giving full scope to the selective processes open to our municipalities and States in securing competent and reliable functionaries free from allegiance to any alien political authority, I do

**573**

not think that it is consonant with the Due Process Clause for men to be asked, on pain of giving up public employment, to swear to something they cannot be expected to know. Such a demand is at war with individual integrity; it can no more be justified than the inquiry into belief which MR. JUSTICE BLACK, MR. JUSTICE JACKSON, and I deemed invalid in *American Communications Ass'n v. Douds,* 339 U. S. 382.

The needs of security do not require such curbs on what may well be innocuous feelings and associations. Such curbs are indeed self-defeating. They are not merely unjustifiable restraints on individuals. They are not merely productive of an atmosphere of repression uncongenial to the spiritual vitality of a democratic society. The inhibitions which they engender are hostile to the best conditions for securing a high-minded and high-spirited public service. . . .

[Mr. Justice Burton took the view that the oath was retrospective and hence invalid under the *Lovett, Garland* and *Cummings* cases, but that the affidavit requirement was valid.]

MR. JUSTICE DOUGLAS, with whom MR. JUSTICE BLACK joins, dissenting. . . .

The case is governed by *Cummings v. Missouri,* 4 Wall. 277, and *Ex parte Garland,* 4 Wall. 333, which struck down test oaths adopted at the close of the Civil War. The *Cummings* case involved provisions of the Missouri constitution requiring public officials and certain classes of professional people, including clergymen, to take an oath that, *inter alia,* they had never been "in armed hostility" to the United States; that they had never "by act or word" manifested their "adherence to the cause" of enemies of the country or their "desire" for the triumph of its enemies; that they had never "knowingly and willingly harbored, aided, or countenanced" an enemy; that they had never been a "member of, or connected with, any order, society, or organization inimical to the government of the United States" or engaged "in guerilla warfare" against its inhabitants; that they had never left Missouri "for the purpose of avoiding enrolment for or draft into the military service of the United States" or become enrolled as a southern sympathizer.

The *Garland* case involved certain Acts of Congress requiring public officials and attorneys practicing before the federal courts to take an oath that they had "voluntarily given no aid, countenance, counsel, or encouragement to persons engaged in armed hostility" against the United States and that they had "neither sought nor accepted, nor attempted to exercise the functions of any office whatever, under any authority or pretended authority

**574**

in hostility to the United States." The Court amended its rules of admission to require this oath.

Cummings, a Catholic priest, was indicted and convicted for teaching and preaching without having first taken the oath.

Garland, a member of the Bar of the Court, had served in the Confederate Government, for which he had received a pardon from the President conditioned on his taking the customary oath of loyalty. He applied for permission to practice before the Court without taking the new oath.

Article I, § 10 of the Constitution forbids any state to "pass any Bill of Attainder" or any "ex post facto Law". Article I, § 9 curtails the power of Congress by providing that "No Bill of Attainder or ex post facto Law shall be passed." The Court ruled that the test oaths in the *Cummings* and *Garland* cases were bills of attainder and *ex post facto* laws within the meaning of the Constitution. "A bill of attainder," wrote Mr. Justice Field for the Court, "is a legislative act which inflicts punishment without a judicial trial." *Cummings v. Missouri, supra,* p. 323, and see *United States v. Lovett,* 328 U. S. 303, 317, 318. The Court held that deprivation of the right to follow one's profession is punishment. A bill of attainder, though generally directed against named individuals, may be directed against a whole class. Bills of attainder usually declared the guilt; here they assumed the guilt and adjudged the punishment conditionally, *i.e.,* they deprived the parties of their right to preach and to practice law unless the presumption were removed by the expurgatory oath. That was held to be as much a bill of attainder as if the guilt had been irrevocably pronounced. The laws were also held to be *ex post facto* since they imposed a penalty for an act not so punishable at the time it was committed.

There are, of course, differences between the present case and the *Cummings* and *Garland* cases. Those condemned by the Los Angeles ordinance are municipal employees; those condemned in the others were professional people. Here the past conduct for which punishment is exacted is single—advocacy within the past five years of the overthrow of the Government by force and violence. In the other cases the acts for which Cummings and Garland stood condemned covered a wider range and involved some conduct which might be vague and uncertain. But those differences, seized on here in hostility to the constitutional provisions, are wholly irrelevant. Deprivation of a man's means of livelihood by reason of past conduct, not subject to this penalty when committed, is punishment whether he is a professional man, a day laborer who works for private industry, or a government employee. The deprivation is nonetheless unconstitutional whether it be for one single past act or a series of past acts. The degree of particularity with which the past act is defined is not the criterion. We are not dealing here with the problem of vagueness in criminal statutes. No amount of certainty would have cured the laws in the *Cummings* and *Garland* cases. They were stricken down because of the mode in which punishment was inflicted.

Petitioners were disqualified from office not for what they are today, not because of any program they currently espouse (cf. *Gerende v. Board of Supervisors*, 341 U. S. 56), not because of standards related to fitness for the office, cf. *Dent v. West Virginia*, 129 U. S. 114; *Hawker v. New York*, 170 U. S. 189, but for what they once advocated. They are deprived of their livelihood by legislative act, not by judicial processes. We put the case in the aspect most invidious to petitioners. Whether they actually advocated the violent overthrow of Government does not appear. But here, as in the *Cummings* case, the vice is in the presumption of guilt which can only be removed by the expurgatory oath. That punishment, albeit conditional, violates here as it did in the *Cummings* case the constitutional prohibition against bills of attainder. Whether the ordinance also amounts to an *ex post facto* law is a question we do not reach.

[Mr. Justice Black's separate opinion is omitted].

## Note

1. For prior litigation over the Los Angeles County loyalty program see *Steiner v. Darby*, 88 Cal. App. 2d 481, 199 Pac. 2d 429 (1948), dismissed as not ripe for review, *sub nom. Parker v. Los Angeles*, 338 U. S. 327, 94 L. Ed. 144, 70 S. Ct. 161 (1949). The *Garner* case is noted in 50 Mich. L. Rev. 467 (1952); 20 U. of Cin. L. Rev. 514 (1951). See also Note, 18 Geo. Wash. L. Rev. 541 (1950).

2. Prior to the Second World War state legislation imposing loyalty qualifications as a condition of state employment took the form mainly of teachers' oath laws. See Chapter VII, *infra*. Since the War, however, there has been a rapid development in state laws requiring loyalty oaths or tests for all state employees. Professor Walter Gellhorn lists 18 states and territories which, as of January 1, 1951, imposed loyalty qualifications for state employment. These are Alaska, Arkansas, California, Florida, Georgia, Hawaii, Illinois, Kansas, Maryland, Massachusetts, New Jersey, New Mexico, New York, North Carolina, Oregon, Pennsylvania, Utah and Washington. Gellhorn, *The States and Subversion*, Appen. A, pp. 407–9, Appen. B (1952).[1] Since the Gellhorn compilation was made additional legislation of this sort has

---

[1] Gellhorn also lists nine of the above states, plus Oklahoma, as imposing loyalty qualifications upon persons appointed to public "office." *Ibid*, pp. 406–7.

been enacted, including laws in New Hampshire (New Hampshire Acts, 1951, ch. 193); New York (New York Acts, 1951, ch. 233); Pennsylvania (the Pechan Act, 1951, 65 P. S. §§ 211–225); Oklahoma (51 Okla. Stat. (1951, Supp) §§ 37.1–37.8); and Texas (Texas Special and General Laws, 1951, ch. 499, art. VI). See also Laws of Miss., 1950, ch. 451.

Most of this legislation imposes standards of loyalty similar to that involved in the *Garner* case, but usually without the retrospective feature. Some of the more recent statutes, influenced by the legislation which ultimately became the McCarran Act, go beyond this. Thus the Massachusetts statute expressly disqualifies any person "who is a member of the communist party." Mass. Acts, 1949, ch. 619. Florida requires an oath that "I am not a member of the Communist Party; that I have not and will not lend my aid, support, advice, counsel or influence to the Communist Party; that I do not believe in the overthrow of the Government of the United States or of the State of Florida by force or violence" or am a member of an organization that does. Fla. Gen. Acts, 1949, ch. 25046. The Georgia oath includes the statement, "that I am not a member of the Communist Party and that I have no sympathy for the doctrines of Communism and will not lend my aid, my support, my advice, my counsel nor my influence to the Communist Party or to the teachings of Communism." Geo. Acts, 1949, No. 224. The New Jersey law includes in its oath, "I am not bound by any allegiance to any foreign prince, potentate, state or sovereignty whatever". N. J. Session Laws, 1949, ch. 22. The requirements of the Maryland Ober Law have already been noted, *supra*.

One of the most elaborate loyalty statutes is the Oklahoma law, which requires an oath that the employee has no affiliation "with any foreign political agency, party, organization or Government, or with any agency, party, organization, association, or group whatever which has been officially determined by the United States Attorney General or other authorized agency of the United States to be a communist front or subversive organization"; that the employee "will take up arms in the defense of the United States in time of War, or National Emergency, if necessary;" that "within the five (5) years immediately preceding the taking" of the oath he has "not been a member of the Communist party" or other organizations referred to above. 51 Okla. Stat., *supra*.

The sanctions provided by these statutes, in addition to ineligibility for government employment, include perjury and sometimes additional criminal penalties. Some statutes, such as Florida's, also provide criminal penalties for any state official who allows a subordinate to retain a position in violation of law. Most of the state laws are formulated in terms of requiring an oath or affidavit, but some are framed like the Federal Loyalty Order and contemplate investigation of whether the employee conforms to the standards (*e. g.* the Ober Law). No such elaborate machinery for administration as the Federal Government has established, however, exists in any state.

For analysis of some of the recent statutes see Prendergast, *State Legislatures and Communism: The Current Scene*, 44 Am. Pol. Sci. Rev. 556 (1950). Discussion of loyalty legislation in Maryland, Mich-

[Emerson]—37

577

igan and New York may be found in Gellhorn, *The States and Subversion,* ch. III, IV and V (1952).

The Maryland Ober Law was challenged in two suits and held unconstitutional by a lower Maryland court. On appeal the Court of Appeals of Maryland dismissed the suits on jurisdictional grounds. *Hammond v. Lancaster,* 71 Atl. 2d 474 (1950); *Hammond v. Frankfeld,* 71 Atl. 2d 482 (1950). The provisions relating to candidates for office were attacked in later cases. The United States Supreme Court, construing the Act narrowly, upheld these provisions in the *Gerende* case, *supra.* The New Jersey law was upheld in a suit by a teacher who refused to take the oath in *Thorp v. Board of Trustees,* 6 N. J. 498, 79 Atl. 2d 462 (1951), dismissed by the Supreme Court as moot, 342 U. S. 803 (1951). The Oklahoma law was upheld in a suit involving university employees in *Board of Regents v. Updegraff,* — Okla. —, 237 Pac. 2d 131 (1951), probable jurisdiction noted by Supreme Court, Mar. 10, 1952. See also *Pawell v. Unemployment Compensation Board,* 146 Pa. Super 147, 22 Atl. 2d 43 (1941). See Chapter VII, *infra.*

3. Loyalty programs for municipal or county employees exist in a number of areas, including, in addition to Los Angeles County, Columbus, Detroit, Topeka, Kansas City and Dade County, Florida. For an account of one of the most elaborate—the Detroit program—see Movitz, *Michigan: State and Local Attack on Subversion* in Gellhorn, *supra,* ch. IV. In some cities employees have been asked to sign loyalty oaths voluntarily, there being no legal requirement to do so. See, *e. g.,* as to Chicago, N. Y. Times, Aug. 4, 1950.

4. As to how other countries handle problems of loyalty among government employees, see Bontecou, *The English Policy as to Communists and Fascists in the Civil Service,* 51 Col. L. Rev. 564 (1951); Biddle, *The Fear of Freedom,* pp. 235–8 (1951); Emerson and Helfeld, *Loyalty Among Government Employees,* 58 Yale L. J. 1, 120–33 (1948).

## Non-Governmental Loyalty Programs

Loyalty programs sponsored by private business or other private groups have been instituted in a number of areas. The best known of these are in the motion picture industry and the radio and television industries.

Following the hearings conducted by the Committee on Un-American Activities into subversion in Hollywood the motion picture producers, acting through their trade associations, announced that, "We will not knowingly employ a Communist or a member of any party or group which advocates overthrow of the Government of the United States by force or by any illegal or unconstitutional methods." N. Y. Times, Nov. 26, 1947. See also Barth, *The Loyalty of Free Men,* pp. 62–7 (1951). Administration of such a policy is, of course, by informal methods and no data is available as to the precise extent or operation of the program. In May, 1952, the American Legion presented the motion picture producers with a list of 200 persons "suspected of Communist associations or activities." The industry undertook a further investigation. N. Y. Times, May 23, 27 and June 1, 1952.

In the radio and television industry action was precipitated by the publication in June 1950 of a book called *Red Channels,* issued by three former F. B. I. agents who are editors of *Counterattack. Red Channels* listed the names of 151 persons active in the industry, together with the alleged Communist-dominated organizations each person was "reported as" being a member of, or once having been a member of. One of those listed, Jean Muir, was dropped from the television show sponsored by General Foods Corporation in August 1950. N. Y. Times, Aug. 29, 1950. Others on the list were directly or indirectly refused employment. In December Columbia Broadcasting System announced it was asking all its employees to sign the same type of loyalty questionnaire as was required of Federal employees. N. Y. Times, Dec. 21, 1950. For a full account of the operation of loyalty requirements in the industry see the report prepared by Merle Miller under the sponsorship of the American Civil Liberties Union, published under the title, *The Judges and the Judged* (1952). See also the series of articles published by Sponsor, Oct. 8, 1951; and the articles published in the Nation, June 28, 1952. For a severe criticism of the Miller report see the book review by Pitzele in The New Leader, May 12, 1952, p. 21; see also The New Leader, June 16, 1952, p. 12 (reply by Miller) and p. 15 (rejoinder by Pitzele).

Other loyalty qualifications include the requirement of the Medical Society of the State of New York that all members take a loyalty oath to the United States as a condition of membership. N. Y. Times, May 15, 1952. It has also been reported that under the will of Sam Wood, film producer, beneficiaries of the estate were required to file an oath in court declaring that they were not members of a Communist organization or any group declared by the government to be subversive. Mr. Wood's wife was exempted from taking the oath. New Haven Register, Sept. 28, 1949.

## 5. The Internal Security Act and Related State Legislation

The development of governmental measures to combat subversion culminated in the Internal Security Act of 1950, known as the McCarran Act, passed shortly after the outbreak of hostilities in Korea. The principle features of this legislation, apart from provisions relating to aliens, are (1) the legislative findings as to the nature of the Communist movement; (2) the provisions of Section 4(a) extending anti-sedition legislation; (3) the registration provisions, and (4) the detention provisions. These are set forth below.

## INTERNAL SECURITY ACT OF 1950

Public Law 831, 81st Cong., 2d Sess., effective Sept. 23, 1950

### TITLE I—SUBVERSIVE ACTIVITIES CONTROL

Section 1. (a) This title may be cited as the "Subversive Activities Control Act of 1950".

(b) Nothing in this Act shall be construed to authorize, require, or establish military or civilian censorship or in any way to limit or infringe upon freedom of the press or of speech as guaranteed by the Constitution of the United States and no regulation shall be promulgated hereunder having that effect.

#### NECESSITY FOR LEGISLATION

Sec. 2. As a result of evidence adduced before various committees of the Senate and House of Representatives, the Congress hereby finds that—

(1) There exists a world Communist movement which, in its origins, its development, and its present practice, is a world-wide revolutionary movement whose purpose it is, by treachery, deceit, infiltration into other groups (governmental and otherwise), espionage, sabotage, terrorism, and any other means deemed necessary, to establish a Communist totalitarian dictatorship in the countries throughout the world through the medium of a world-wide Communist organization.

(2) The establishment of a totalitarian dictatorship in any country results in the suppression of all opposition to the party in power, the subordination of the rights of individuals to the state, the denial of fundamental rights and liberties which are characteristic of a representative form of government, such as freedom of speech, of the press, of assembly, and of religious worship, and results in the maintenance of control over the people through fear, terrorism, and brutality.

(3) The system of government known as a totalitarian dictatorship is characterized by the existence of a single political party, organized on a dictatorial basis, and by substantial identity between such party and its policies and the government and governmental policies of the country in which it exists.

(4) The direction and control of the world Communist movement is vested in and exercised by the Communist dictatorship of a foreign country.

(5) The Communist dictatorship of such foreign country, in exercising such direction and control and in furthering the purposes of the world Communist movement, establishes or causes the establishment of, and utilizes, in various countries, action organizations which are not free and independent organizations, but are sections of a world-wide Communist organization and are controlled, directed, and subject to the discipline of the Communist dictatorship of such foreign country.

(6) The Communist action organizations so established and utilized in various countries, acting under such control, direction, and discipline, endeavor to carry out the objectives of the world Communist movement by bringing about the overthrow of existing governments by any available means, including force if necessary, and setting up Communist totalitarian dictatorships which will be subservient to the most powerful existing Communist totalitarian dictatorship. Although such organizations usually designate themselves as political parties, they are in fact constituent elements of the world-wide Communist movement and promote the objectives of such movement by conspiratorial and coercive tactics, instead of through the democratic processes of a free elective system or through the freedom-preserving means employed by a political party which operates as an agency by which people govern themselves.

(7) In carrying on the activities referred to in paragraph (6), such Communist organizations in various countries are organized on a secret, conspiratorial basis and operate to a substantial extent through organizations, commonly known as "Communist fronts", which in most instances are created and maintained, or used, in such manner as to conceal the facts as to their true character and purposes and their membership. One result of this method of operation is that such affiliated organizations are able to obtain financial and other support from persons who would not extend such support if they knew the true purposes of, and the actual nature of the control and influence exerted upon, such "Communist fronts".

(8) Due to the nature and scope of the world Communist movement, with the existence of affiliated constituent elements working toward common objectives in various countries of the world, travel of Communist members, represent-

atives, and agents from country to country facilitates communication and is a prerequisite for the carrying on of activities to further the purposes of the Communist movement.

(9) In the United States those individuals who knowingly and willfully participate in the world Communist movement, when they so participate, in effect repudiate their allegiance to the United States, and in effect transfer their allegiance to the foreign country in which is vested the direction and control of the world Communist movement.

(10) In pursuance of communism's stated objectives, the most powerful existing Communist dictatorship has, by the methods referred to above, already caused the establishment in numerous foreign countries of Communist totalitarian dictatorships, and threatens to establish similar dictatorships in still other countries.

(11) The agents of communism have devised clever and ruthless espionage and sabotage tactics which are carried out in many instances in form or manner successfully evasive of existing law.

(12) The Communist network in the United States is inspired and controlled in large part by foreign agents who are sent into the United States ostensibly as attachés of foreign legations, affiliates of international organizations, members of trading commissions, and in similar capacities, but who use their diplomatic or semi-diplomatic status as a shield behind which to engage in activities prejudicial to the public security.

(13) There are, under our present immigration laws, numerous aliens who have been found to be deportable, many of whom are in the subversive, criminal, or immoral classes who are free to roam the country at will without supervision or control.

(14) One device for infiltration by Communists is by procuring naturalization for disloyal aliens who use their citizenship as a badge for admission into the fabric of our society.

(15) The Communist movement in the United States is an organization numbering thousands of adherents, rigidly and ruthlessly disciplined. Awaiting and seeking to advance a moment when the United States may be so far extended by foreign engagements, so far divided in counsel, or so far in industrial or financial straits, that overthrow of the Government of the United States by force and violence may seem possible of achievement, it seeks converts far and wide by

an extensive system of schooling and indoctrination. Such preparations by Communist organizations in other countries have aided in supplanting existing governments. The Communist organization in the United States, pursuing its stated objectives, the recent successes of Communist methods in other countries, and the nature and control of the world Communist movement itself, present a clear and present danger to the security of the United States and to the existence of free American institutions, and make it necessary that Congress, in order to provide for the common defense, to preserve the sovereignty of the United States as an independent nation, and to guarantee to each State a republican form of government, enact appropriate legislation recognizing the existence of such world-wide conspiracy and designed to prevent it from accomplishing its purpose in the United States.

## DEFINITIONS

Sec. 3.  For the purposes of this title  . . .

(3) The term "Communist-action organization" means—

(a) any organization in the United States (other than a diplomatic representative or mission of a foreign government accredited as such by the Department of State) which (i) is substantially directed, dominated, or controlled by the foreign government or foreign organization controlling the world Communist movement referred to in section 2 of this title, and (ii) operates primarily to advance the objectives of such world Communist movement as referred to in section 2 of this title; and

(b) any section, branch, fraction, or cell of any organization defined in subparagraph (a) of this paragraph which has not complied with the registration requirements of this title.

(4) The term "Communist front organization" means any organization in the United States (other than a Communist-action organization as defined in paragraph (3) of this section) which (A) is substantially directed, dominated, or controlled by a Communist-action organization, and (B) is primarily operated for the purpose of giving aid and support to a Communist-action organization, a Communist foreign government, or the world Communist movement referred to in section 2 of this title.

(5) The term "Communist organization" means a Communist-action organization or a Communist-front organization. . . .

(14) The term "world communism" means a revolutionary movement, the purpose of which is to establish eventually a

Communist totalitarian dictatorship in any or all of the countries of the world through the medium of an internationally coordinated Communist movement.

(15) The term "totalitarian dictatorship" and "totalitarianism" mean and refer to systems of government not representative in fact, characterized by (A) the existence of a single political party, organized on a dictatorial basis, with so close an identity between such a party and its policies and the governmental policies of the country in which it exists, that the party and the government constitute an indistinguishable unit, and (B) the forcible suppression of opposition to such party. . . .

### CERTAIN PROHIBITED ACTS

Sec. 4 (a) It shall be unlawful for any person knowingly to combine, conspire, or agree with any other person to perform any act which would substantially contribute to the establishment within the United States of a totalitarian dictatorship, as defined in paragraph (15) of section 3 of this title, the direction and control of which is to be vested in, or exercised by or under the domination or control of, any foreign government, foreign organization, or foreign individual: *Provided, however,* That this subsection shall not apply to the proposal of a constitutional amendment. . . .

(d) Any person who violates any provision of this section shall, upon conviction thereof, be punished by a fine of not more than $10,000 or imprisonment for not more than ten years, or by both such fine and such imprisonment, and shall, moreover, be thereafter ineligible to hold any office, or place of honor, profit, or trust created by the Constitution or laws of the United States. . . .

(f) Neither the holding of office nor membership in any Communist organization by any person shall constitute per se a violation of subsection (a) or subsection (c) of this section or of any other criminal statute. The fact of the registration of any person under section 7 or section 8 of this title as an officer or member of any Communist organization shall not be received in evidence against such person in any prosecution for any alleged violation of subsection (a) or subsection (c) of this section or for any alleged violation of any other criminal statute.

[Section 5 provides that no member of a registered Communist organization may be employed in the Federal Government and no member of a Communist action organization may be employed in any defense facility. Section 6 provides that no member of a registered Communist organization may apply for or use a passport].

**584**

## REGISTRATION AND ANNUAL REPORTS OF
## COMMUNIST ORGANIZATIONS

Sec. 7. [Subsections (a) to (c) provide that a Communist organization shall register with the Attorney General within 30 days after (1) enactment of the Act, (2) the date it becomes a Communist organization, or (3) the date a Board order requiring registration becomes final].

(d) The registration made under subsection (a) or (b) shall be accompanied by a registration statement, to be prepared and filed in such manner and form as the Attorney General shall by regulations prescribe, containing the following information:

(1) The name of the organization and the address of its principal office.

(2) The name and last-known address of each individual who is at the time of filing such registration statement, and of each individual who was at any time during the period of twelve full calendar months next preceding the filing of such statement, an officer of the organization, with the designation or title of the office so held, and with a brief statement of the duties and functions of such individual as such officer.

(3) An accounting, in such form and detail as the Attorney General shall by regulations prescribe, of all moneys received and expended (including the sources from which received and the purposes for which expended) by the organization during the period of twelve full calendar months next preceding the filing of such statement.

(4) In the case of a Communist-action organization, the name and last-known address of each individual who was a member of the organization at any time during the period of twelve full calendar months preceding the filing of such statement.

(5) In the case of any officer or member whose name is required to be shown in such statement, and who uses or has used or who is or has been known by more than one name, each name which such officer or member uses or has used or by which he is known or has been known.

(e) It shall be the duty of each organization registered under this section to file with the Attorney General on or before February 1 of the year following the year in which it registers, and on or before February 1 of each succeeding year, an annual report, prepared and filed in such manner and form as the Attorney General shall by regulations prescribe, containing the same information which by subsection (d) is required to be included in a registration statement, except that the information required with respect to the twelve-month period referred to in paragraph (2), (3), or (4) of such subsection shall, in such annual report, be given with respect to the calendar year preceding the February 1 on or before which such annual report must be filed.

(f) (1) It shall be the duty of each organization registered under this section to keep, in such manner and form as the Attorney General shall by regulations prescribe, accurate records and accounts of moneys received and expended (including the sources from which received and purposes for which expended) by such organization.

(2) It shall be the duty of each Communist-action organization registered under this section to keep, in such manner and form as the Attorney General shall by regulations prescribe, accurate records of the names and addresses of the members of such organization and of persons who actively participate in the activities of such organization.

(g) It shall be the duty of the Attorney General to send to each individual listed in any registration statement or annual report, filed under this section, as an officer or member of the organization in respect of which such registration statement or annual report was filed, a notification in writing that such individual is so listed; and such notification shall be sent at the earliest practicable time after the filing of such registration statement or annual report. Upon written request of any individual so notified who denies that he holds any office or membership (as the case may be) in such organization, the Attorney General shall forthwith initiate and conclude at the earliest practicable time an appropriate investigation to determine the truth or falsity of such denial, and, if the Attorney General shall be satisfied that such denial is correct, he shall thereupon strike from such registration statement or annual report the name of such individual. If the Attorney General shall decline or fail to strike the name of such individual from such registration statement or annual report within five months after receipt of such written request, such individual may file with the Board a petition for relief pursuant to section 13 (b) of this title.

(h) In the case of failure on the part of any organization to register or to file any registration statement or annual report as required by this section, it shall be the duty of the executive officer (or individual performing the ordinary and usual duties of an executive officer) and of the secretary (or individual performing the ordinary and usual duties of a secretary) of such organization, and of such officer or officers of such organization as the Attorney General shall by regulations prescribe, to register for such organization, to file such registration statement, or to file such annual report, as the case may be.

## REGISTRATION OF MEMBERS OF COMMUNIST-ACTION ORGANIZATIONS

Sec. 8 (a)  Any individual who is or becomes a member of any organization concerning which (1) there is in effect a final order of the Board requiring such organization to register under section 7 (a) of this title as a Communist-action organization, (2) more than thirty days have elapsed since such order has become final, and (3) such organization is not registered under section 7 of this title as a Communist-action organization, shall within sixty days after said order has become final or within thirty days after becoming a member of such organization, whichever is later, register with the Attorney General as a member of such organization.

(b)  Each individual who is or becomes a member of any organization which he knows to be registered as a Communist-action organization under section 7 (a) of this title, but to have failed to include his name upon the list of members thereof filed with the Attorney General, pursuant to the provisions of subsections (d) and (e) of section 7 of this title, shall, within sixty days after he shall have obtained such knowledge, register with the Attorney General as a member of such organization. . . .

[Section 9 provides that the Attorney General shall make the data filed with him open for public inspection and shall submit annual reports on such data to the President and to the Congress].

## USE OF THE MAILS AND INSTRUMENTALITIES OF INTERSTATE OR FOREIGN COMMERCE

Sec. 10.  It shall be unlawful for any organization which is registered under section 7, or for any organization with respect to which there is in effect a final order of the Board requiring it to register under section 7, or for any person acting for or on behalf of any such organization—

(1) to transmit or cause to be transmitted, through the United States mails or by any means or instrumentality of interstate or foreign commerce, any publication which is intended to be, or which it is reasonable to believe is intended to be, circulated or disseminated among two or more persons, unless such publication, and any envelope, wrapper, or other container in which it is mailed or otherwise circulated or transmitted, bears the following, printed in such manner as may be provided in regulations prescribed by the Attorney General, with the name of the organization

**587**

appearing in lieu of the blank: "Disseminated by ———,
a Communist organization"; or

(2) to broadcast or cause to be broadcast any matter over
any radio or television station in the United States, unless
such matter is preceded by the following statement, with the
name of the organization being stated in place of the blank:
"The following program is sponsored by ———, a Communist organization."

[Section 11 provides that no tax deduction shall be allowed
for contributions to any registered organization and no such
organization shall be entitled to tax exemption.

Section 12 establishes a Subversive Activities Control Board
of five members with power to determine, upon application by
the Attorney General or any organization, whether an organization is a "Communist-action" or a "Communist-front" organization; and, upon application by the Attorney General or any individual to determine whether an individual is a member of a registered organization.

Section 13 sets up an administrative procedure under which the
Board is to make its determinations and issue its orders. It goes
on to provide:]

(e) In determining whether any organization is a "Communist-
action organization", the Board shall take into consideration—

(1) the extent to which its policies are formulated and
carried out and its activities performed, pursuant to directives or to effectuate the policies of the foreign government
or foreign organization in which is vested, or under the
domination or control of which is exercised, the direction
and control of the world Communist movement referred to
in section 2 of this title; and

(2) the extent to which its views and policies do not
deviate from those of such foreign government or foreign
organization; and

(3) the extent to which it receives financial or other aid,
directly or indirectly, from or at the direction of such foreign
government or foreign organization; and

(4) the extent to which it sends members or representatives to any foreign country for instruction or training in the
principles, policies, strategy, or tactics of such world Communist movement; and

(5) the extent to which it reports to such foreign government or foreign organization or to its representatives; and

(6) the extent to which its principal leaders or a substantial number of its members are subject to or recognize

the disciplinary power of such foreign government or foreign organization or its representatives; and

(7) the extent to which, for the purpose of concealing foreign direction, domination, or control, or of expediting or promoting its objectives, (i) it fails to disclose, or resists efforts to obtain information as to, its membership (by keeping membership lists in code, by instructing members to refuse to acknowledge membership, or by any other method); (ii) its members refuse to acknowledge membership therein; (iii) it fails to disclose, or resists efforts to obtain information as to, records other than membership lists; (iv) its meetings are secret; and (v) it otherwise operates on a secret basis; and

(8) the extent to which its principal leaders or a substantial number of its members consider the allegiance they owe to the United States as subordinate to their obligations to such foreign government or foreign organization.

(f) In determining whether any organization is a "Communist-front organization", the Board shall take into consideration—

(1) the extent to which persons who are active in its management, direction, or supervision, whether or not holding office therein, are active in the management, direction, or supervision of, or as representatives of, any Communist-action organization, Communist foreign government, or the world Communist movement referred to in section 2; and

(2) the extent to which its support, financial or otherwise, is derived from any Communist-action organization, Communist foreign government, or the World Communist movement referred to in section 2; and

(3) the extent to which its funds, resources, or personnel are used to further or promote the objectives of any Communist-action organization, Communist foreign government, or the world Communist movement referred to in section 2; and

(4) the extent to which the positions taken or advanced by it from time to time on matters of policy do not deviate from those of any Communist-action organization, Communist foreign government, or the world Communist movement referred to in section 2. . . .

[Section 14 provides that any party aggrieved by an order of the Board may appeal to the Court of Appeals of the District of Columbia and, by certiorari, to the Supreme Court].

## PENALTIES

Sec. 15.  (a) If there is in effect with respect to any organization or individual a final order of the Board requiring registration under section 7 or section 8 of this title—

(1) such organization shall, upon conviction of failure to register, to file any registration statement or annual report, or to keep records as required by section 7, be punished for each such offense by a fine of not more than $10,000, and

(2) each individual having a duty under subsection (h) of section 7 to register or to file any registration statement or annual report on behalf of such organization, and each individual having a duty to register under section 8, shall, upon conviction of failure to so register or to file any such registration statement or annual report, be punished for each such offense by a fine of not more than $10,000, or imprisonment for not more than five years, or by both such fine and imprisonment.

For the purposes of this subsection, each day of failure to register, whether on the part of the organization or any individual, shall constitute a separate offense.

(b) Any individual who, in a registration statement or annual report filed under section 7 or section 8, willfully makes any false statement or willfully omits to state any fact which is required to be stated, or which is necessary to make the statements made or information given not misleading, shall upon conviction thereof be punished for each such offense by a fine of not more than $10,000, or by imprisonment for not more than five years, or by both such fine and imprisonment.  For the purposes of this subsection—

(1) each false statement willfully made, and each willful omission to state any fact which is required to be stated, or which is necessary to make the statements made or information given not misleading, shall constitute a separate offense; and

(2) each listing of the name or address of any one individual shall be deemed to be a separate statement.

(c) Any organization which violates any provision of section 10 of this title shall, upon conviction thereof, be punished for each such violation by a fine of not more than $10,000.  Any individual who violates any provision of sections 5, 6, or 10 of this title shall, upon conviction thereof, be punished for each such violation by a fine of not more than $10,000 or by imprisonment for not more than five years, or by both such fine and imprisonment.

## TITLE II—EMERGENCY DETENTION
### SHORT TITLE

Sec. 100. This title may be cited as the "Emergency Detention Act of 1950".

### FINDINGS OF FACTS AND DECLARATION OF PURPOSE

Sec. 101. As a result of evidence adduced before various committees of the Senate and the House of Representatives, the Congress hereby finds that—

[Subsections (1) through (9) of Section 101 are substantially the same as subsections (1) through (6) and (9) through (11) of Section 2 of Title I, *supra*.]

(10) The experience of many countries in World War II and thereafter with so-called "fifth columns" which employed espionage and sabotage to weaken the internal security and defense of nations resisting totalitarian dictatorships demonstrated the grave dangers and fatal effectiveness of such internal espionage and sabotage.

(11) The security and safety of the territory and Constitution of the United States, and the successful prosecution of the common defense, especially in time of invasion, war, or insurrection in aid of a foreign enemy, require every reasonable and lawful protection against espionage, and against sabotage to national-defense material, premises, forces and utilities, including related facilities for mining, manufacturing, transportation, research, training, military and civilian supply, and other activities essential to national defense.

(12) Due to the wide distribution and complex interrelation of facilities which are essential to national defense and due to the increased effectiveness and technical development in espionage and sabotage activities, the free and unrestrained movement in such emergencies of members or agents of such organizations and of others associated in their espionage and sabotage operations would make adequate surveillance to prevent espionage and sabotage impossible and would therefore constitute a clear and present danger to the public peace and the safety of the United States.

(13) The recent successes of Communist methods in other countries and the nature and control of the world Communist movement itself present a clear and present danger to the security of the United States and to the existence of free American institutions, and make it necessary that Congress, in order to provide for the common defense, to preserve the sovereignty of the United States as an independent nation,

and to guarantee to each State a republican form of government, enact appropriate legislation recognizing the existence of such world-wide conspiracy and designed to prevent it from accomplishing its purpose in the United States.

(14) The detention of persons who there is reasonable ground to believe probably will commit or conspire with others to commit espionage or sabotage is, in a time of internal security emergency, essential to the common defense and to the safety and security of the territory, the people and the Constitution of the United States.

(15) It is also essential that such detention in an emergency involving the internal security of the Nation shall be so authorized, executed, restricted and reviewed as to prevent any interference with the constitutional rights and privileges of any persons, and at the same time shall be sufficiently effective to permit the performance by the Congress and the President of their constitutional duties to provide for the common defense, to wage war, and to preserve, protect and defend the Constitution, the Government and the people of the United States.

## DECLARATION OF "INTERNAL SECURITY EMERGENCY"

Sec. 102. (a) In the event of any one of the following:
(1) Invasion of the territory of the United States or its possessions,
(2) Declaration of war by Congress, or
(3) Insurrection within the United States in aid of a foreign enemy,

and if, upon the occurrence of one or more of the above, the President shall find that the proclamation of an emergency pursuant to this section is essential to the preservation, protection and defense of the Constitution, and to the common defense and safety of the territory and people of the United States, the President is authorized to make public proclamation of the existence of an "Internal Security Emergency".

(b) A state of "Internal Security Emergency" (hereinafter referred to as the "emergency") so declared shall continue in existence until terminated by proclamation of the President or by concurrent resolution of the Congress.

## DETENTION DURING EMERGENCY

Sec. 103. (a) Whenever there shall be in existence such an emergency, the President, acting through the Attorney General, is hereby authorized to apprehend and by order detain, pursuant to the provisions of this title, each person as to whom there is reasonable ground to believe that such person probably will engage in, or probably will conspire with others to engage in, acts of espionage or of sabotage.

(b) Any person detained hereunder (hereinafter referred to as "the detainee") shall be released from such emergency detention upon—

(1) the termination of such emergency by proclamation of the President or by concurrent resolution of the Congress;

(2) an order of release by the Attorney General;

(3) a final order of release after hearing by the Board of Detention Review, hereinafter established;

(4) a final order of release by a United States court, after review of the action of the Board of Detention Review, or upon a writ of habeas corpus.

[Sections 104 to 111 provide the procedure for apprehension and detention. Any person apprehended has a right to a preliminary hearing before a hearing officer appointed by the President. "Such person may introduce evidence in his own behalf, and may cross-examine witnesses against him, except that the Attorney General or his representative shall not be required to furnish information the revelation of which would disclose the identity or evidence of Government agents or officers which he believes it would be dangerous to national safety and security to divulge. . . . If from the evidence it appears to the preliminary hearing officer that there is probable cause for the detention of such person pursuant to this title, such hearing officer shall forthwith issue an order for the detention of such person. . . ."

Thereafter the person detained may appeal to the Board of Detention Review, consisting of nine members appointed by the President, which shall determine "whether there is reasonable ground to believe that such detainee probably will engage in, or conspire with others to engage in, espionage or sabotage." The Board "shall require the Attorney General to inform such detainee of grounds on which his detention was instituted, and to furnish to him as full particulars of the evidence as possible, including the identity of informants, subject to the limitation that the Attorney General may not be required to furnish information the revelation of which would disclose the identity or evidence of Government agents or officers which he believes it would be dangerous to national safety and security to divulge." The Board and its hearing examiners "are authorized to consider under regulations designed to protect the national security any evidence of Government agencies and officers the full text or content of which cannot be publicly revealed for reasons of national security, but which the Attorney General in his discretion offers to present."

[Emerson]—38

From the decision of the Board of Detention Review an appeal lies to the appropriate Federal Court of Appeals. "The findings of the Board as to the facts, if supported by reliable, substantial, and probative evidence, shall be conclusive." Commencement of proceedings for judicial review, if made by the Attorney General, shall at his request operate as a stay of the Board's order. Application for certiorari may be made to the Supreme Court. "In case of Board or court review of any detention order, the Attorney General, or such review officers as he may designate, shall present to the Board, the court, and the detainee to the fullest extent possible consistent with national security, the evidence supporting a finding of reasonable ground for detention in respect to the detainee, but he shall not be required to offer or present evidence of any agents or officers of the Government the revelation of which in his judgment would be dangerous to the security and safety of the United States."]

## CRIMINAL PROVISIONS

Sec. 112.  Whoever, being named in a warrant for apprehension or order of detention as one as to whom there is reasonable ground to believe that he probably will engage in, or conspire with others to engage in, espionage or sabotage, or being under confinement or detention pursuant to this title, shall resist or knowingly disregard or evade apprehension pursuant to this title or shall escape, attempt to escape or conspire with others to escape from confinement or detention ordered and instituted pursuant to this title, shall be fined not more than $10,000 or imprisoned not more than ten years, or both.

Sec. 113.  Whoever knowingly—

(a) advises, aids, assists, or procures the resistance, disregard, or evasion of apprehension pursuant to this title by any person named in a warrant or order of detention as one as to whom there is reasonable ground to believe that such person probably will engage in, or conspire with others to engage in, espionage or sabotage; or

(b) advises, aids, assists, or procures the escape from confinement or detention pursuant to this title of any person so named; or

(c) aids, relieves, transports, harbors, conceals, shelters, protects, or otherwise assists any person so named for the purpose of the evasion of such apprehension by such person or the escape of such person from confinement or detention; or

(d) attempts to commit or conspires with any other person to commit any acts punishable under subsection (a),

•

(b) , or (c) of this section,
shall be fined not more than $10,000, or imprisoned not more than ten years, or both.

## Note

1. The legislative history of the Internal Security Act, in summary form, is as follows:
Numerous hearings into subversive activities in the United States were conducted by the Committee on Un-American Activities and other committees in the late 1940's. See Note, 51 Col. L. Rev. 606, 608–9 (1951). In February 1948 the Subcommittee on Legislation of the Un-American Activities Committee held hearings on two bills. Hearings on Proposed Legislation to Curb or Control the Communist Party of the United States, H. R. 4422 and H. R. 4581, 80th Cong., 2d Sess. (1948). In April the Committee reported the Mundt-Nixon bill (H. R. 5852), containing anti-sedition and registration provisions. H. Rept. 1844, 80th Cong., 2d Sess. This bill passed the House on May 19, 1948, by a vote of 319 to 58. 94 Cong. Rec. 5838–6150. The Senate Committee on the Judiciary held hearings in May. Control of Subversive Activities, Hearings before the Committee on the Judiciary, on H. R. 5852, 80th Cong., 2d Sess. The Committee did not report the bill and it died with the close of the Eightieth Congress.

In April, 1949, Senate committee hearings reopened on a modified Mundt-Nixon bill. Control of Subversive Activities, Hearings before a Subcommittee of the Committee on the Judiciary, on S. 1194 and 1196, 81st Cong., 1st Sess. Similar bills were considered in House committee hearings in March 1950. Hearings on Legislation to Outlaw Certain Un-American and Subversive Activities, Hearings before the Committee on Un-American Activities on H. R. 3903 and H. R. 7595, 81st Cong., 2d Sess.

After the outbreak of Korean hostilities, at the end of June 1950, interest in the bills revived. The Senate Judiciary Committee reported the McCarran bill on August 17. S. 4037; S. Rept. 2369, 80th Cong., 2d Sess. The House Un-American Activities Committee reported the Wood bill on August 22. H. R. 9490; H. Rept. 2980, 80th Cong., 2d Sess. The House passed the Wood bill on August 29 by a vote of 354 to 20. 96 Cong. Rec. 13721–70. During Senate debate on the McCarran bill a group of liberal Senators introduced the Kilgore bill (S. 4130) as a substitute measure. 96 Cong. Rec. 14229. Their substitution move failed (96 Cong. Rec. 14599–606) and part of the Kilgore bill was instead incorporated into the McCarran bill as Title II. 96 Cong. Rec. 14623. After five days debate (96 Cong. Rec. 14170–14628) the Senate substituted the amended McCarran text, which included the Mundt-Nixon and other bills as well as the Kilgore emergency detention provisions, for that of the House bill (H. R. 9490). The Senate adopted H. R. 9490 by a vote of 70 to 7 on September 12. 96 Cong. Rec. 14628. The Senate-House conference report on the new version of H. R. 9490 (H. Rept. 3112) was adopted by both houses on September 20. The vote was 51 to 7 in the Senate and 313 to 20 in the House.

96 Cong. Rec. 15185–260, 15265–298. On September 22, President Truman vetoed the bill. 96 Cong. Rec. 15629–32. The House immediately overrode the veto, 286 to 48. 96 Cong. Rec. 15632–3. The Senate, after debating all night, likewise overrode the veto, by a vote of 57 to 10. 96 Cong. Rec. 15520–726.

2. On October 20, 1950, the Attorney General issued regulations prescribing in detail the data to be filed by Communist organizations and members of such organizations. 15 Fed. Reg. 7011 (1950). No organization or individual registered. On November 22 the Attorney General filed a petition with the Subversive Activities Control Board for an order to compel the Communist Party to register as a Communist-action organization. N. Y. Times, Nov. 23, 1950 (carrying the text of the petition). A motion to dismiss the petition was denied, the Board stating it was not empowered to consider the constitutionality of the statute which created it. Thereupon the Communist Party filed suit to enjoin the Board from proceeding. The injunction was denied by a three-judge court on the ground that administrative remedies had not been exhausted, and the Supreme Court refused a stay. *Communist Party v. McGrath,* 96 F. Supp. 47 (D. C., 1951), petition for stay denied 340 U. S. 950 (1951). After further motions the Communist Party filed an answer and hearings commenced before a panel of the Board on April 23, 1951.

Meanwhile the Senate, after some delay, confirmed the appointments of three Board members but refused to confirm Chairman Seth Richardson and Charles M. LaFollette. Richardson then resigned. A second suit to halt proceedings against the Communist Party on these grounds was dismissed. N. Y. Times, Feb. 6, 1952 (unreported, D. C. D. C.).

On April 23, 1952, the government finished the presentation of its case. The Communist Party's defense commenced on June 9, 1952. N. Y. Times, June 10, 1952.

For an account of these proceedings see the 1st and 2nd Annual Reports of the Subversive Activities Control Board (1951, 1952).

3. No prosecutions have been instituted under Section 4(a). Nor have the detention provisions gone into effect. With funds provided in its appropriations for 1951–52, however, the Department of Justice has undertaken to rehabilitate six World War II installations to serve as detention camps in the event Title II comes into operation. N. Y. Times, Jan. 1, 1952; American Civil Liberties Union Weekly Bulletin, Jan. 28, 1952.

4. For an exhaustive analysis of the Internal Security Act see Note, *The Internal Security Act of 1950,* 51 Col. L. Rev. 606 (1951). For other discussions see Sutherland, *Freedom and Internal Security,* 64 Harv. L. Rev. 383 (1951); McCarran, *The Internal Security Act of 1950,* 12 U. Pitts. L. Rev. 481 (1951); Notes, 39 Geo. L. J. 440 (1951); 46 Ill. L. Rev. 274 (1951); 25 St. John's L. Rev. 397 (1951); 24 Temple L. Q. 462 (1951). Discussion of the Mundt-Nixon bill may be found in Chafee, *The Registration of "Communist-Front" Organizations in the Mundt-Nixon Bill,* 63 Harv. L. Rev. 1382 (1950); Cohen and Fuchs, *Communism's Challenge and the Constitution,* 34 Corn. L. Q. 182, 352

(1948, 1949); Notes, 49 Col. L. Rev. 363 (1949); 23 Notre Dame Law. 577 (1948). On the self-incrimination issue raised by the registration provisions see Notes, 1951 Wis. L. Rev. 704; 51 Col. L. Rev. 206, 216-7 (1951). With respect to the detention camp provisions see Dunbar, *Beyond Korematsu: The Emergency Detention Act of 1950*, 13 U. Pitts. L. Rev. 221 (1952). See also Brecht, *The Concentration Camp*, 50 Col. L. Rev. 761 (1950). For a discussion of British legislation interning enemy aliens during World War II (which served in part as a model for Title II of the Internal Security Act) see Cohn, *Legal Aspects of Internment*, 4 Modern L. Rev. 200 (1941).

As to the impact of the Act upon freedom of association see *If in Doubt, Don't Join!*, U. S. News & World Report, Sept. 22, 1950, p. 20.

5. Other Federal registration laws include the Foreign Agents Registration Act, 22 U. S. C. §§ 611 et seq., and the Voorhis Act, 18 U. S. C. § 2386 (formerly 18 U. S. C. §§ 9-11). See summary, *supra*. In 1951 the Peace Information Center, engaged in soliciting signatures for the so-called Stockholm Peace Pledge, and its officers were indicted for failure to register under the Foreign Agents Registration Act. A motion to dismiss the indictment was denied in *U. S. v. Peace Information Center*, 97 F. Supp. 255 (D. C. D. C., 1951), but the defendants were acquitted. N. Y. Times, Nov. 21, 1951. See also *Viereck v. U. S.*, 318 U. S. 236, 87 L. Ed. 734, 63 S. Ct. 561 (1943).

6. Early in World War II Japanese living on the West Coast were removed from that area and confined in detention camps. The program was upheld by the Supreme Court as justified by military requirements. *Hirabayashi v. U. S.*, 320 U. S. 81, 87 L. Ed. 1774, 63 S. Ct. 1375 (1943); *Korematsu v. U. S.*, 323 U. S. 214, 89 L. Ed. 194, 65 S. Ct. 193 (1944); *cf. Ex parte Endo*, 323 U. S. 283, 89 L. Ed. 243, 65 S. Ct. 208 (1944). For discussion see Rostow, *The Japanese American Cases—A Disaster*, 54 Yale L. J. 489 (1945); Konvitz, *The Alien and the Asiatic in American Law*, ch. 11 (1946). But martial law in Hawaii was held invalid under the Hawaiian Organic Act in *Duncan v. Kahanamoku*, 327 U. S. 304, 90 L. Ed. 688, 66 S. Ct. 606 (1946). See Frank, *Ex Parte Milligan v. The Five Companies: Martial Law in Hawaii*, 44 Col. L. Rev. 639 (1944); Fairman, *The Supreme Court on Military Jurisdiction: Martial Rule in Hawaii and the Yamashita Case*, 59 Harv. L. Rev. 833 (1946). Generally on martial law see Rankin, *When Civil Law Fails* (1939) (bibliography on p. 206); Fairman, *The Law of Martial Rule* (2d ed. 1943).

6. An increasing number of states have enacted laws going beyond the sedition statutes of the Smith Act type or requiring registration of certain groups. Prior to the drafting of the Mundt-Nixon bill California and Michigan had registration statutes. The California law requires any group to register which advocates overthrow of the government or which is subject to foreign control. Persons attending a meeting of such an organization, knowing it has failed to register, are guilty of a misdemeanor. Cal. Corp. Code, §§ 35000-35302 (1948). In *People v. Noble*, 68 Cal. App. 2d 853, 158 Pac. 2d 225 (1945), a conviction under this law was reversed for lack of evidence and the court indicated doubts as to its constitutionality. The Michigan statute—

known as the Callahan Act—was ratified by referendum in 1948. It requires registration of foreign agents, defined as any individual or group "subsidized by a foreign government or serving directly or indirectly the purposes, aims, or objects of a foreign power." Mich. Stat. Ann. § 18.58. No organization has thus far registered. Several Michigan attorney generals have expressed doubts as to the law's validity. See Morvitz, *Michigan: State and Local Attack on Subversion*, in Gellhorn, *The States and Subversion*, pp. 191–6 (1952). On the question of exclusive Federal power over foreign agents see *Hines v. Davidowitz*, 312 U. S. 52, 85 L. Ed. 581, 61 S. Ct. 399 (1941).

See also the New York statute requiring registration of oath bound societies, N. Y. Civil Rights Law §§ 53–7, upheld as to the Ku Klux Klan in *Bryant v. Zimmerman*, 278 U. S. 63, 73 L. Ed. 184, 49 S. Ct. 61 (1928).

Following the drafting of the Mundt-Nixon bill several states passed somewhat similar legislation. Thus the Maryland Ober Law makes it a felony for any person to "assist in the formation or participate in the management or to contribute to the support of any . . . foreign subversive organization", or to remain a member, knowing the said organization to be such. A "foreign subversive organization" is defined as "any organization directed, dominated or controlled directly or indirectly by a foreign government which engages in or advocates, abets, advises or teaches . . . activities intended to overthrow, destroy or alter . . . the constitutional form of government" of the United States or Maryland, "and to establish in place thereof any form of government the direction and control of which is to be vested in, or exercised by or under, the domination or control of any foreign government, organization, or individual." Such an organization may also be dissolved by the state and its property forfeited. Laws of Md., 1949, ch. 86.

Late in 1951 Massachusetts passed a statute (Ann. L. of Mass., 1951 Supp., ch. 264, §§ 16 et seq.), described by the American Civil Liberties Union as follows (Weekly Bulletin, Dec. 3, 1951):

"In the first state action of its kind, the Massachusetts Legislature declared the Communist Party a subversive organization and unlawful. Any person who remains a member of it knowing it to be subversive may be punished by a fine and imprisonment up to $1,000 and three years in jail.

"Massachusetts thus became the first state to outlaw the Communist Party by name. The bill also makes any other organization of three or more persons associated for the common purpose of advocating the violent or unlawful overthrow of the state or federal governments a subversive organization, and requires the state Attorney General to bring an action in court against any group he has reasonable cause to believe is subversive. If the court finds the group subversive, it may order it dissolved and all its assets are turned over to the state. Continued membership in a group known to be subversive is punishable in the same way as is membership in the Party. Any person convicted of a violation of the act cannot hold public office or be a teacher, although after five years a person's disability can be removed if a court adjudges him to be loyal. The law also makes it a criminal offense to knowingly permit a meeting place to be used by the Communist Party or by a group ruled subversive. Contribution of money or other property to a group known to be subversive is also punishable. The Communist Party and other groups ruled as subversive are barred from the ballot. Candidates nominated by such groups may run for office, although they may not use the name of the Communist Party or other political organizations in their political designation."

Legislation of a similar character—known as the Trucks Act—was enacted in Michigan in 1952. Mich. Stat. Ann., 1952, § 28.243(11) et seq. See also Laws of Miss., 1950, ch. 451.

See Prendergast, *State Legislatures and Communism: The Current Scene*, 44 Am. Pol. Sci. Rev. 556 (1950); Gellhorn, *The States and Subversion*, Appen. A and B (1952). For Gov. Stevenson's veto of similar legislation in Illinois (the Broyles bill), see Busch, *Adlai E. Stevenson of Illinois*, pp. 136–44 (1952).

7. In 1950 and 1951 a large number of municipalities passed local anti-subversive ordinances. These were of two major types. In one form, as in New Rochelle, N. Y., the ordinance required registration with the police of any member of a "communist organization" who "resides in, is employed in, has a regular place of business in, or who regularly enters or travels through any part of the City of New Rochelle." A "communist organization" is defined as one "organized, or which operates, primarily for the purposes of advancing the objectives of the world communist movement."

A second form, less common, is typified by the Birmingham, Ala., ordinance which provided a $100 fine and a maximum of 180 days in jail for each day that a known Communist remained in the City. The ordinance further provided that membership in the Communist Party would be presumed if a person "shall be found in any secret or non-public place in voluntary association or communication with any person or persons established to be or to have been members of the Communist Party." N. Y. Times, July 19, 1950.

The number of these ordinances passed has not been officially calculated, but it probably is in the neighborhood of 100. See Marquis Child's estimate of 150, New Haven Journal Courier, Feb. 16, 1951. Some of them have been declared unconstitutional by state and Federal lower courts, including those in Birmingham, Jacksonville, Miami, Los Angeles, Erie and McKeesport.

8. For discussion of anti-subversive legislation in other countries see Loewenstein, *Militant Democracy and Fundamental Rights*, 31 Am. Pol. Sci. Rev. 417, 638 (1937) (anti-fascist legislation); Loewenstein, *Legislative Control of Political Extremism in European Democracies*, 38 Col. L. Rev. 591, 725 (1938); Loewenstein, *Legislation Against Subversive Activities in Argentina*, 56 Harv. L. Rev. 1261 (1943); Antieau, *"The Limitation of Liberty"—A Comparative Survey*, 24 So. Calif. L. Rev. 238 (1951). Legislation outlawing the Communist Party in Australia was declared unconstitutional by the Australian Supreme Court as not within the powers granted to the Federal Government by the Australian Constitution. *Australian Communist Party v. Com-*

_..nwealth_ [1951] Argus L. R. 129. For discussion see Beasley, _Australia's Communist Party Dissolution Act_, 29 Can. B. Rev. 490 (1951). Legislation in non-Communist countries to outlaw or restrict the Communist Party has been steadily increasing. See N. Y. Times, May 16, 1950, June 11, 1950, for surveys of the extent of such legislation. Communist countries outlaw all parties except the Communist Party.

## E. RIGHT OF COMMENT ON JUDICIAL PROCEEDINGS

The right to comment on judicial proceedings involves two issues. One concerns the right of the individual litigant to a fair trial, uninfluenced by public pressures. See Chapter II, _supra_. The other involves the extent to which individuals may criticize judges and judicial proceedings. In both cases the courts have attempted to protect judicial processes through use of the contempt power.

As to the Federal courts the statute conferring the contempt power, 18 U. S. C. § 401 (1951 Supp.), has been strictly construed to authorize contempts only where interference takes place in the immediate physical presence of the court. _Nye v. United States_, 313 U. S. 33, 85 L. Ed. 1172, 61 S. Ct. 810 (1941). The federal courts thus seem to have very limited contempt power against publications. But _cf. Smotherman v. U. S._, 186 F. 2d 676 (C. A. 10, 1950) (reversed contempt for publication on free speech grounds but seemed to find no lack of power under the statute).

The Internal Security Act of 1950 prohibits "pickets or parades in or near a building housing a court of the United States", or a building or residence used by a judge, juror, witness or court officer, or "any other demonstration in or near any such building or residence", with intent to interfere with the administration of justice or influence any judge, juror, witness, or court officer. 18 U. S. C. § 1507 (1951 Supp.).

As to the states, the Supreme Court has ruled that punishment by contempt violates the free speech guarantees of the First and Fourteenth Amendments unless the publication constitutes a clear and present danger to a fair adjudication of pending cases. _Craig v. Harney_, 331 U. S. 367, 91 L. Ed. 1546, 67 S. Ct. 1249 (1947) (criticism of judge during frequent refusals to accept jury verdict) ; _Pennekamp v. Florida_, 328 U. S. 331, 90 L. Ed. 1295, 66 S. Ct. 1029 (1946) (criticism for dismissing indictments) ; _Bridges v. California_, 314 U. S. 252, 86 L. Ed. 192, 62 S. Ct. 190 (1941) (publication of telegram and editorials to influence judge in fixing a sentence). In all of these cases the Supreme Court reversed state court convictions. The Court's approach seems to be that the honor, fortitude and similar qualifications of the judge make it improbable that he would be influenced; and that if the pressure proves sufficient to affect his judgment it is probably due to surrounding circumstances which are not likely to be altered by being stated in a publication. None of the cases involved jury determinations. Mr. Justice Frankfurter, dissenter in the *Bridges* and *Craig* cases, indicated in a Court opinion in a later case that the Court might find juries more susceptible to influence than judges. *Shepherd v. Florida,* 341 U. S. 50, 52, 95 L. Ed. 740, 71 S. Ct. 549, 550 (1951). But *cf. Baltimore Radio Show v. Maryland,* 67 Atl. 2d 497 (Md. 1949), cert. den. 338 U. S. 912 (1950).

## Note

For discussion see Nelles and King, *Contempt by Publication in the United States,* 28 Col. L. Rev. 525 (1928); Radin, *Freedom of Speech and Contempt of Court,* 36 Ill. L. Rev. 599 (1942); Note, *Contempt by Publication,* 59 Yale L. J. 534 (1950); Notes, 17 U. of Chi. L. Rev. 540 (1950); 1948 Wis. L. Rev. 125; 23 Ind. L. J. 192 (1948); 63 Harv. L. Rev. 840 (1950); 4 Stan. L. Rev. 101 (1951); 3 Syracuse L. Rev. 150 (1951); 37 Iowa L. Rev. 249 (1952).

# CHAPTER V

# FREEDOM OF SPEECH: UNTRUTHFUL AND HARMFUL COMMUNICATION

## A. OBSCENITY AND RELATED MATTERS

### COMMONWEALTH v. ISENSTADT

Supreme Judicial Court of Massachusetts, 1945
318 Mass. 543, 62 N.E.2d 840

QUA, J. The defendant has been found guilty by a judge of the Superior Court sitting without jury upon two complaints charging him respectively with selling and with having in his possession for the purpose of sale, exhibition, loan, or circulation a book published under the title "Strange Fruit," which is "obscene, indecent or impure, or manifestly tends to corrupt the morals of youth." G. L. (Ter. Ed.) c. 272, § 28, as amended by St. 1934, c. 231, and St. 1943, c. 239. The section (except the part describing the penalty) is reproduced in the footnote.[1] . . .

We do not pretend ignorance of the controversy which has been carried on in this Commonwealth, sometimes with vehemence, over so called "literary censorship."[2] With this background in mind it may not be out of place to recall that it is not our function to assume a "liberal" attitude or a "conservative" attitude. As in other cases of statutory construction and application, it is our plain but not necessarily easy duty to read the words of the statute in the sense in which they were intended, to accept and enforce the public policy of the Commonwealth as disclosed by its policy-making body, whatever our own personal opinions

---

[1] "Whoever imports, prints, publishes, sells or distributes a book, pamphlet, ballad, printed paper, phonographic record or other thing which is obscene, indecent or impure, or manifestly tends to corrupt the morals of youth, or an obscene, indecent or impure print, picture, figure, image or description, manifestly tending to corrupt the morals of youth, or introduces into a family, school or place of education, or buys, procures, receives or has in his possession any such book, pamphlet, ballad, printed paper, phonographic record, obscene, indecent or impure print, picture, figure, image or other thing either for the purpose of sale, exhibition, loan or circulation or with intent to introduce the same into a family, school or place of education, shall . . . be punished . . . ." . . .

[2] See "Massachusetts and Censorship," by S. S. Grant and S. E. Angoff, 10 Boston Univ. L. Rev. 147; "Judicial Censorship of Obscene Literature," by L. M. Alpert, 52 Harv. L. Rev. 40.

may be, and to avoid judicial legislation in the guise of new constructions to meet real or supposed new popular viewpoints, preserving always to the Legislature alone its proper prerogative of adjusting the statutes to changed conditions.

We are fully aware of the uselessness of all interpretations of the crucial words of this statute which merely define each of those words by means of the others or of still other words of practically the same signification. We do not now attempt by any single formula to furnish a test for all types of publications, including scientific and medical treatises, religious and educational works, newspapers and periodicals, and classical and recent literature, as well as phonograph records, prints, pictures, paintings, images, statuary and sculpture, artistic or otherwise, all of which are within the literal words of the statute and might conceivably fall within its prohibitions. In this case we are dealing with a recent work of fiction—a novel. We shall, in general, confine our observations to the case in hand, without necessarily binding ourselves to apply all that is here said to entirely different forms of writing or to representations by picture or image.

We deal first with a number of pertinent propositions advanced in the able briefs filed in behalf of the defendant. We agree with some of them.

(1) We agree that since the amendment of the section as it appeared in the General Laws by St. 1930, c. 162, the book is to be treated as a whole in determining whether it violates the statute.[3] It is not to be condemned merely because it may contain somewhere between its covers some expressions which, taken by themselves alone, might be obnoxious to the statute. *Halsey* v. *New York Society for the Suppression of Vice*, 234 N. Y. 1, 4. *United States* v. *One Book Entitled Ulysses*, 72 Fed. (2d) 705, 707. *United States* v. *Levine*, 83 Fed. (2d) 156. But this does not mean that every page of the book must be of the character described in the statute before the statute can apply to the book. It could never have been intended that obscene matter should escape proscription simply by joining to itself some innocent matter. A reasonable construction can be attained only by saying that the book is within the statute if it contains prohibited matter in such quantity or of such nature as to flavor the whole and impart to the whole any of the qualities mentioned in the

---

[3] Before this amendment the section read, "Whoever . . . sells . . . a book . . . *containing obscene, indecent or impure language,* or manifestly tending to corrupt the morals of youth . . . ." After the amendment it read, "Whoever . . . sells . . . a book . . . *which is obscene, indecent or impure,* or manifestly tends to corrupt the morals of youth . . . ." (Emphasis ours) See *Commonwealth v. Friede*, 271 Mass. 318, 321–322.

statute, so that the book as a whole can fairly be described by any of the adjectives or descriptive expressions contained in the statute. The problem is to be solved, not by counting pages, but rather by considering the impressions likely to be created. For example, a book might be found to come within the prohibition of the statute although only a comparatively few passages contained matter objectionable according to the principles herein explained if that matter were such as to offer a strong salacious appeal and to cause the book to be bought and read on account of it.

(2) We agree with the weight of authority that under each of the prohibitions contained in the statute the test of unlawfulness is to be found in the effect of the book upon its probable readers and not in any classification of its subject matter or of its words as being in themselves innocent or obscene.[4] A book is "obscene, indecent or impure" within the statutory prohibition if it has a substantial tendency to deprave or corrupt its readers by inciting lascivious thoughts or arousing lustful desire. It also violates the statute if it "manifestly tends to corrupt the morals of youth." The latter prohibition is expressly limited to the kind of effect specified—the corruption of morals. Under this branch of the statute it is not enough that a book may tend to coarsen or vulgarize youth if it does not manifestly tend to corrupt the morals of youth. *People* v. *Wendling*, 258 N. Y. 451, 453.

Although in their broadest meaning the statutory words "obscene, indecent or impure" might signify offensive to refinement, propriety and good taste, we are convinced that the Legislature did not intend by those words to set up any standard merely of taste, even if under the Constitution it could do so. Taste depends upon convention, and sometimes upon irrational taboo. It varies "with the period, the place, and training, environment and characteristics of persons." *Reddington* v. *Reddington,* 317 Mass. 760, 765. A penal statute requiring conformity to some current standard of propriety defined only by the statutory words quoted above would make the standard an uncertain one, shifting with every new judge or jury. It would be like a statute penalizing a citizen

---

[4] *The Queen v. Hicklin*, L. R. 3 Q. B. 360, 371. *Commonwealth v. Allison,* 227 Mass. 57, 61. *Commonwealth v. Friede,* 271 Mass. 318, 321. *Rosen v. United States*, 161 U. S. 29, 43. *Dunlop v. United States*, 165 U. S. 486, 500. *Dysart v. United States,* 272 U.S. 655. *United States v. Bennett,* 16 Blatchf. C. C. 338, 365–366. *United States v. Males,* 51 Fed. 41. *Knowles v. United States,* 170 Fed. 409, 412. *United States v. Kennerley,* 209 Fed. 119. *Griffin v. United States,* 248 Fed. 6, 8–9. *Krause v. United States,* 29 Fed. (2d) 248, 250. *United States v. Dennett,* 39 Fed. (2d) 564, 568. *Duncan v. United States,* 48 Fed. (2d) 128, 132. *People v. Brainard,* 192 App. Div. (N. Y.) 816, 820–821. See also *People v. Wendling,* 258 N. Y. 451, 81 Am. L. R. 799.

for failing to act in every situation in a gentlemanly manner. Such a statute would be unworkable if not unconstitutional, for in effect it would "license . . . the jury to create its own standard in each case," ex post facto. *Herndon* v. *Lowry*, 301 U. S. 242, 263. Such a test must be rejected. The prohibitions of the statute are concerned with sex and sexual desire. The statute does not forbid realistically coarse scenes or vulgar words merely because they are coarse or vulgar, although such scenes or words may be considered so far as they bear upon the test already stated of the effect of the book upon its readers.

(3) Since effect is the test, it follows that a book is to be judged in the light of the customs and habits of thought of the time and place of the alleged offense. Although the fundamentals of human nature change but slowly, if indeed they change at all, customs and habits of thought do vary with time and place. That which may give rise to impure thought and action in a highly conventional society may pass almost unnoticed in a society habituated to greater freedom. *United States* v. *Kennerley*, 209 Fed. 119, 121. *Parmelee* v. *United States*, 113 Fed. (2d) 729, 731–732. To recognize this is not to change the law. It is merely to acknowledge the facts upon which the application of the law has always depended. And of the operation of this principle it would seem that a jury of the time and place, representing a cross section of the people, both old and young, should commonly be a suitable arbiter. *United States* v. *Clarke*, 38 Fed. 500. *United States* v. *Kennerley*, 209 Fed. 119, 121.

(4) So, too, we think it proper to take into account what we may call the probable "audience" of the book, just as the effect of a lecture might depend in large degree upon the character of those to whom it is addressed. At one extreme may be placed a highly technical medical work, sold at a great price and advertised only among physicians. At the other extreme may be placed a rather well known type of the grossest pornography obviously prepared for persons of low standards and generally intended for juvenile consumption and distributed where it is most likely to reach juvenile eyes. Most questioned books will fall between these extremes. Moreover, the statute was designed for the protection of the public as a whole. Putting aside for the moment the reference in the statute itself to that which manifestly tends to corrupt the morals of youth, a book placed in general circulation is not to be condemned merely because it might have an unfortunate effect upon some few members of the community who might be peculiarly susceptible. The statute is to be construed reasonably. The fundamental right of the public to read is not to be trimmed down to the point where a few prurient

persons can find nothing upon which their hypersensitive imaginations may dwell. *United States* v. *Kennerley,* 209 Fed. 119, 120. The thing to be considered is whether the book will be appreciably injurious to society in the respects previously stated because of its effect upon those who read it, without segregating either the most susceptible or the least susceptible, remembering that many persons who form part of the reading public and who cannot be called abnormal are highly susceptible to influences of the kind in question and that most persons are susceptible to some degree, and without forgetting youth as an important part of the mass, if the book is likely to be read by youth. *United States* v. *Harmon,* 45 Fed. 414, 417. *United States* v. *Levine,* 83 Fed. (2d) 156. *Parmelee* v. *United States,* 113 Fed. (2d) 729, 731. The jury must ask themselves whether the book will in some appreciable measure do the harm the Legislature intended to prevent. This is not a matter of mathematics. The answer cannot be found by saying, for example, that only about one third of probable readers would be adversely affected and then classifying that one third as "abnormal" and concluding that as the book does not adversely affect "normal" persons it is not within the statute. A book that adversely affects a substantial proportion of its readers may well be found to lower appreciably the average moral tone of the mass in the respects hereinbefore described and to fall within the intended prohibition.[5] It seems to us that the statute cannot be construed as meaning less than this without impairing its capacity to give the protection to society which the Legislature intended it should give.

(5) We cannot accept the proposition which seems to have been accorded hospitality in a few of the more recent cases in another jurisdiction and which perhaps has been suggested rather than argued in the present case, to wit, that even a work of fiction, taken as a whole, cannot be obscene, indecent or impure if it is written with a sincere and lawful purpose and possesses artistic merit, and if sincerity and artistry are more prominent features of the book than obscenity.[6] In dealing with such a

---

[5] It is for this reason, if not for others, that we think it was not error to deny the defendant's fifteenth request for ruling, which reads, "As a matter of law the defendant cannot be found to be guilty of violating the provisions of General Laws (Ter. Ed.) Chap. 272, sec. 28 as amended, unless it is found that the manifest tendency of the book is to corrupt the morals of the normal youth or adult as compared to the abnormal." This request seeks to classify rigidly all persons with respect to susceptibility as "normal" or "abnormal" and overlooks the possible harmful effect upon a substantial proportion of readers who may be less than a majority and therefore overlooks the possible harm to the mass.

[6] See *United States v. One Book Entitled Ulysses,* 72 Fed. (2d) 705, 707–

practical matter as the enforcement of the statute here involved there is no room for the pleasing fancy that sincerity and art necessarily dispel obscenity. The purpose of the statute is to protect the public from that which is harmful. The public must be taken as it is. The mass of the public may have no very serious interest in that which has motivated the author, and it can seldom be said that the great majority of the people will be so rapt in admiration of the artistry of a work as to overlook its salacious appeal. Sincerity and literary art are not the antitheses of obscenity, indecency, and impurity in such manner that one set of qualities can be set off against the other and judgment rendered according to an imaginary balance supposed to be left over on one side or the other. The same book may be characterized by all of these qualities. Indeed, obscenity may sometimes be made even more alluring and suggestive by the zeal which comes from sincerity and by the added force of artistic presentation. We are not sure that it would be impossible to produce even a serious treatise on gynecology in such a manner as to make it obscene. Certainly a novel can be so written, even though the thoughtful reader can also find in it a serious message. Sincerity and art can flourish without pornography, and seldom, if ever, will obscenity be needed to carry the lesson. See *United States* v. *Kennerley*, 209 Fed. 119, 120–121; *United States* v. *Dennett*, 39 Fed. (2d) 564, 569. The statute contains no exception of works of sincerity and art, or of works in which those elements predominate, if the proscribed elements are also present in such manner and degree as to remain characteristic of the book as a whole. If it is thought that modern conditions require that such an exception be made, the Legislature and not this court should make it. This subject was the principal point of the decision in *Commonwealth* v. *Buckley*, 200 Mass. 346, where apt illustration is used. We adhere to the reasoning of that case. See further, *Commonwealth* v. *Friede*, 271 Mass. 318, 322–323; *Halsey* v. *New York Society for the Suppression of Vice*, 234 N. Y. 1, 6; and *People* v. *Pesky*, 230 App. Div. (N. Y.) 200 (citing *Commonwealth v. Buckley, supra*).

In taking this position, to which we believe ourselves compelled by the words of the statute, the necessity of enforcing it to accomplish its purposes, and our own previous construction of it, we do not go so far as to say that sincerity of purpose and literary merit are to be entirely ignored. These elements may be considered in so far as they bear upon the question whether the book, considered as a whole is or is not obscene,

---

708; *United States* v. *Levine*, 83 Fed. (2d) 156, 158; *Parmelee* v. *United States*, 113 Fed. (2d) 729, 736.

indecent, or impure. It is possible that, even in the mind of the general reader, overpowering sincerity and beauty may sometimes entirely obscure or efface the evil effect of occasional questionable passages, especially with respect to the classics of literature that have gained recognized place as part of the great heritage of humanity. The question will commonly be one of fact in each case, and if, looking at the book as a whole, the bad is found to persist in substantial degree alongside the good, as the law now stands, the book will fall within the statute.

A brief description of the book "Strange Fruit" now seems necessary. The scene is laid in a small town in Georgia. A white boy, Tracy Deen, who lacks the forcefulness to get ahead in the world, and an educated but compliant colored girl, Nonnie Anderson, fall genuinely in love, but because of race inhibitions and pressures they cannot marry. Nonnie supplies to Tracy the sympathy and the nourishment of his self-esteem which his other associations deny him. Illicit intercourse occurs, resulting in pregnancy. Tragedy follows in the form of the murder of Tracy committed by Nonnie's outraged brother and the lynching of an innocent colored man for that crime. Distributed through this book (consisting of two hundred fifty pages in the edition submitted with the record) are four scenes of sexual intercourse, including one supposed to have been imagined. The immediate approaches to these acts and the descriptions of the acts themselves vary in length from a few lines to several pages. They differ in the degree of their suggestiveness. Two of them might be thought highly emotional, with strongly erotic connotations. In addition to these there is a fifth scene in an old abandoned cabin in which there are amatory attitudes, kissing, a loosened blouse, exposed breasts, and circumstances suggesting but perhaps not necessarily requiring an act of intercourse. In still another scene Tracy in a confused drunken frenzy "saw somebody" (himself) tear off Nonnie's clothes "until there was nothing between his hands and her body," "press her down against the floor," "press her body hard—saw him try and fail, try and fail, try and fail", but he "couldn't." In addition to the scenes just mentioned there are distributed fairly evenly throughout the book approximately fifty instances where the author introduces into the story such episodes as indecent assaults upon little girls, an instance of, and a soliloquy upon, masturbation by boys, and references to acts of excretion, to "bobbing" or "pointed" breasts, to "nice little rumps, hard . . . light, bouncy . . . ," to a group of little girls "giggling mightily" upon discovering a boy behind a bush and looking at his "bared genitals." We need not recite more of these. The instances mentioned will indicate the general character of the others. Some of these minor incidents might be dismissed as of little or no consequence if there were fewer of them, but when they occur on an average on every fifth page from beginning to end of the book it would seem that a jury or a judge performing the function of a jury might find that they had a strong tendency to maintain a salacious interest in the reader's mind and to whet his appetite for the next major episode.

The principal question in the case is whether, consistently with the principles hereinbefore stated, we can say as matter of law that an honest jury, or an honest trial judge taking the place of a jury with the consent of the defendant, as in this case, would not be acting as reasonable men in concluding beyond a reasonable doubt that this book, taken as a whole, possesses the qualities of obscenity, indecency, or impurity. The test is not what we ourselves think of the book, but what in our best judgment a trier of the facts might think of it without going beyond the bounds of honesty and reason. This distinction, difficult for laymen to grasp, is familiar enough to all lawyers. It is constantly applied by appellate courts and must be preserved if jury trial is to be preserved.

It is urged that this book was written with a serious purpose; that its theme is a legitimate one; that it possesses great literary merit; and that it has met with a generally favorable reception by reviewers and the reading public. We agree that it is a serious work. It brings out in bold relief the depth and the complexity of the race problem in the South, although, so far as we can see, it offers no remedy. We agree that the theme of a love which because of social conditions and conventions cannot be sanctioned by marriage and which leads to illicit relations is a permissible theme. That such a theme can be handled with power and realism without obscenity seems sufficiently demonstrated in George Eliot's "Adam Bede," which we believe is universally recognized as an English classic. We assume that the book before us is a work of literary merit. We are also prepared to assume for the purposes of this opinion that it has been favorably received by reviewers generally and widely sold to the public, although we do not find it necessary to decide whether the opinions of reviewers and the extent of sale are such well known facts that we ought to take judicial notice of them, if the result of the case depended upon our doing so. We hold, however, that the matters mentioned in this paragraph are not decisive of the issue before us.

Regarding the book as a whole, it is our opinion that a jury of honest and reasonable men could find beyond a reasonable doubt that it contains much that, even in this post-Victorian era, would tend to promote lascivious thoughts and to arouse lustful desire in the minds of substantial numbers of that public into whose hands this book, obviously intended for general sale, is likely to fall; that the matter which could be found objectionable is not necessary to convey any sincere message the book may contain and is of such character and so pervades the work as to give to the whole a sensual and licentious quality calculated to produce the harm which the statute was intended to prevent; and that that quality could be found to persist notwithstanding any literary or artistic merit. We are therefore of opinion that the book could be found to be obscene, indecent, and impure within the meaning of the statute. We think that not only the legislators of 1835 who inserted the substance of the present wording in the statute but also the legislators of later years down to 1943 who amended the statute without greatly altering its substance would be surprised to learn that this court had held that a jury or a judge trying the facts could not even consider whether a book which answers the description already given of "Strange Fruit" falls within the statute.

For the same reasons we are of opinion that an honest and reasonable judge or jury could find beyond a reasonable doubt that this book "manifestly tends to corrupt the morals of youth." The statute does not make fitness for juvenile reading the test for all literature regardless of its object and of the manner of its distribution. Yet it cannot be supposed that the Legislature intended to give youth less protection than that given to the community as a whole by the general proscription of that which is "obscene, indecent or impure." Rather it would seem that something in the nature of additional protection of youth was intended by proscribing anything that manifestly tends to corrupt the morals of youth, even though it may not be obscene, indecent, or impure in the more general sense. At any rate, we think that almost any novel that is obscene, indecent or impure in the general sense also "manifestly tends to corrupt the morals of youth," if it is likely to fall into the hands of youth. The judge could find that the book in question would be read by many youths. Many adolescents are avid readers of novels.

It is contended that the conviction of the defendant violates the Fourteenth Amendment to the Constitution of the United States. See *Near* v. *Minnesota*, 283 U. S. 697, 707; *De Jonge* v. *Oregon*, 299 U. S. 353, 364. If, however, we are right in holding that an honest and reasonable jury could have found the defendant guilty, it seems to us that no substantial constitutional question remains. The State must have power to protect its citizens,

[Emerson]

and especially its youth, against obscenity in its various forms, including that which is written or printed. Statutes to this end have long existed. The distribution of obscene printed matter was a crime at common law. *Commonwealth* v. *Holmes,* 17 Mass. 336. Our own statute was held constitutional in *Commonwealth* v. *Allison,* 227 Mass. 57, 62, where this court said, "The subject matter is well within one of the most obvious and necessary branches of the police power of the State." *State* v. *McKee,* 73 Conn. 18. In *Near* v. *Minnesota,* 283 U. S. 697, at page 716, Chief Justice Hughes, after asserting the right of government in time of war to prevent the publication of the sailing dates of transports or of the number and location of troops, added this, "On similar grounds, the primary requirements of decency may be enforced against obscene publications." See *Gitlow* v. *New York,* 268 U. S. 652, 667; *Fox* v. *Washington,* 236 U. S. 273. And in *Chaplinsky* v. *New Hampshire,* 315 U. S. 568, at pages 571, 572, the court said that the use of certain well defined and narrowly limited classes of speech, including "the lewd and obscene" may be prevented and punished. If the so-called "clear and present danger" doctrine enunciated in such cases as *Schenck* v. *United States,* 249 U. S. 47, 52, *Herndon* v. *Lowry,* 301 U. S. 242, *Bridges* v. *California,* 314 U. S. 252, and *Thomas* v. *Collins,* 323 U. S. 516, applies to cases like the present, it would seem that danger of corruption of the public mind is a sufficient danger, and that actual publication and sale render that danger sufficiently imminent to satisfy the doctrine.

The defendant complains of the exclusion of testimony offered by him through three witnesses—a writer and teacher of literature, a child psychiatrist, and a professor of theology who was the editor of "Zion's Herald" and who had also been pastor of a church, had taught in a junior college and had been director of a boys' camp—tending to show as matter of expert opinion that the book was sincerely written; that it would elevate rather than corrupt morals; that it would not create lustful or lecherous desires in any one; that it is "perfectly consistent with the regular flow of literature now publicly sold in the Commonwealth . . . "; and that books containing material more likely to corrupt the morals of youth are sold daily without prosecution.

We cannot regard this exclusion as error. The principal matter about which expert opinion was sought was nothing more than the reaction of normal human beings to a kind of stimulation which is well within the experience of all mankind. Since the inquiry relates to the probable effect upon the general public who may read the book, there is reason to believe that a jury, being composed of men drawn from the various segments of that public, would be as good a judge of the effects as experts in literature or psychiatry whose points of view and mental reactions in such matters are likely to be entirely different from those of the general public. If expert testimony is to be admitted in this instance it is difficult to see why it would not likewise be competent in a vast number of civil and criminal cases where issues of fact depend upon the emotions and reactions of normal persons in the conditions to which they are exposed. If such evidence becomes competent it will follow that an immense number of cases now submitted without hesitation to the good sense of juries and of trial judges performing the functions of juries cannot be adequately tried without an expensive array of experts on both sides. Experience in those fields in which expert testimony is now admittedly necessary does not lead us to look with favor upon such a sweeping extension. Without prejudging the indefinite future, we are not convinced that the time has come for it. In this we agree with *People* v. *Muller,* 96 N. Y. 408, and *St. Hubert Guild* v. *Quinn,* 64 Misc. (N. Y.) 336, 341–342. See *Commonwealth* v. *Buckley,* 200 Mass. 346, 352; *United States* v. *Harmon,* 45 Fed. 414, 418. Compare *Parmelee* v. *United States,* 113 Fed. (2d) 729, 732. In so far as the excluded evidence was expected to show that other books of the same kind, or worse, were being sold without prosecution it was obviously incompetent. *Commonwealth* v. *Buckley,* 200 Mass. 346, 349, 350–351, 354 (request 26). See *Commonwealth* v. *Friede,* 271 Mass. 318, 322.

What has already been said covers all of the defendant's requests for rulings that were refused, excepting numbers fourteen and sixteen. Request fourteen was rightly refused on the ground stated by the judge that it makes the effect upon youth the sole test of applicability of the statute. Request sixteen asked the judge "as a matter of law" to "take into consideration the attitude of the community in accepting or rejecting the book. . . ." Since there was no evidence bearing upon the "attitude of the community," this seems to be a request that the judge take judicial notice of that "attitude." We do not feel called upon to prolong this opinion by entering upon a discussion as to whether "attitude of the community" in any of its possible aspects might have any bearing upon any of the issues before the judge. Some courts seem to have favored the taking of judicial notice of literary reviews and criticisms. *Halsey* v. *New York Society for the Suppression of Vice,* 234 N. Y. 1. *United States* v. *One Book Entitled Ulysses,* 72 Fed. (2d) 705, 708. In one case it was said that published reviews of qualified critics might reasonably be allowed "in evidence," which was said to be "quite another thing

. . . from expert witnesses at the trial." *United States* v. *Levine,* 83 Fed. (2d) 156, 158. Whether these decisions are consistent with our own rules, we need not determine. Neither need we determine whether the views of literary critics show the "attitude of the community" or merely that of a very specialized part of the community, or whether they bear upon anything more than the literary value of the work. For purposes of the present case we are satisfied that the defendant could not compel the judge to commit himself to a ruling upon such vague and sweeping generalities as "attitude of the community" and "accepting or rejecting the book." These seem to us to be composite conclusions which, if they could have been determined at all, could have been determined only by weighing subsidiary facts, some of which might perhaps be susceptible of judicial notice and others of which might well require proof by competent evidence. We cannot say that at the time of the trial the generalization, "attitude of the community in accepting or rejecting" this new book, had become in any aspect an established fact so notorious and indisputable that the judge could be compelled against his own judgment to ascertain it without evidence. Wigmore on Evidence (3d ed.) §§ 2568, 2568a. . . .

*Exceptions overruled.*

LUMMUS, J. The opinion seems to me to construe the statute rightly. My dissent is only from the conclusion that the evidence warranted a finding of guilty.

It must be conceded that the book in question is blemished by coarse words and scenes, some of which appear irrelevant to the plot. Yet in them I can discover no erotic allurement such as the opinion makes necessary for a conviction. On the contrary, their coarseness is repellent.

The book is a serious study of the relations of different races in a small southern town. It is a grim tragedy, not relieved even by humor. Virtue is not derided, neither is vice made attractive. In the book, the wages of sin is literally death. The reader is left depressed, unable to solve a tragic problem.

The opinion rests its support of the conviction upon the statutory words "manifestly tends to corrupt the morals of youth," as well as upon the other prohibition of the statute. It asserts that "Many adolescents are avid readers of novels." The record contains no evidence to warrant that assertion, or to show that any adolescent ever read the book or would read it under normal conditions. Neither is there, in my judgment, any common knowledge upon which in the absence of evidence a court might conclude that under normal conditions the book would be read by any substantial number of adolescents. Of course, conditions that exist after prosecution for obscenity has been brought or publicly threatened, are abnormal and furnish no test of what the opinion calls the "probable audience" of the book. The market for any novel can be artificially stimulated and widened through curiosity aroused by actual or threatened prosecution in this Commonwealth, frequently to the satisfaction and profit of the publisher elsewhere.

Such knowledge as I have leads me to believe that without such artificial stimulation novels of the class into which the book in question falls are read by few girls and by practically no boys. The great mass of readers are mature women. Plainly the book was not written for juveniles. They would find it dull reading. Under normal conditions I think the book could do no substantial harm to the morals of youth, for few juveniles would ever see it, must less read it. And if by chance some should wade through it, I think it could not reasonably be found to have any erotic allurement, even for youth.*

## Note

1. Recent cases in which defendants sought to introduce other publications for purposes of establishing the community standard are *State v. Weitershausen*, 11 N. J. Super. 487, 78 Atl. 2d 595 (1951); *Commonwealth v. Donaducy*, 167 Pa. Super. 611, 76 Atl. 2d 440 (1950) (held irrelevant); *Gore v. State*, 79 Ga. App. 696, 54 S. E. 2d 669 (1949) (involved motion pictures; held inadmissible). Judge Frank's concurrence in *Roth v. Goldman*, 172 F. 2d 788 (C. A. 2, 1949), cert. den. 337 U. S. 938 (1949), concludes that a study of off-color content in circulation in the community is the most readily available index of community mores in relation to literature and community shock-threshold. See also *People v. London*, 63 N. Y. Supp. 2d 227 (N. Y. City Mag. Ct., 1946) (fact that the book has been sold in reputable book shops irrelevant). At least one judge has made a valiant attempt to free the standard of its ambiguity by requiring a showing "beyond a reasonable doubt" and without opinion evidence that "there is a reasonable and demonstrable cause to believe that a crime or misdemeanor has been committed or is about to be committed as the perceptible result of the publication and distribution of the writing in question." *Commonwealth v. Gordon*, 66 D. & C. 101, 156 (Ct. of Quarter Sessions, Phila., 1949). See De Voto, *The Easy Chair*, 199 Harper's 62 (July 1949).

Prof. Chafee has suggested that in obscenity cases a clear and probable danger test be substituted for the clear and present danger test: "There we could argue to a censor who wanted to ban a really good novel . . . 'Very likely, as you say, it would be very damaging to society if these passages were translated into illegal acts by many persons, but is it really likely that this will happen? Isn't the risk

* The *Isenstadt* case is noted in 40 Ill. L. Rev. 417 (1946).

small enough to be worth running for the sake of giving the public the benefit of all the good material that the author has put into his work?'" *Government and Mass Communications*, pp. 59–60 (1947). Compare the statement in *State v. Lerner*, 81 N. E. 2d 282, 289 (Ct. Com. Pleas, Ohio, 1948): "The community concept of what is 'obscene' literature is approximately ascertainable. It goes without saying that public opinion, community concepts condemn sexually nasty, perversive publications, prints, pictures, drawings or photographs as 'obscene', not because they might excite sexually impure ideas in minds susceptible . . . because that is a mere matter of conjecture, but because they offend the moral concepts of people as a whole, and the people have the right to establish codes of right conduct for literature as well as for other forms of community conduct."

Some judges seem to be somewhat reluctant to discuss a standard. They feel that little can be accomplished by further intellectual hairsplitting and seem to rely on their own intuitive impression or that of administrative officials. This appears to have been the view of at least two judges in *Roth v. Goldman, supra*. One might thus also explain the reluctance of three courts in New York to write an opinion in finding the publisher of *Memoirs of Hecate County* guilty of violating the obscenity law. See 272 App. Div. 799, 71 N. Y. Supp. 2d 736 (1947); 297 N. Y. 687, 77 N. E. 2d 6 (1947). The United States Supreme Court affirmed the case by an equally divided Court. *Doubleday and Co. v. New York*, 335 U. S. 848, 93 L. Ed. 398, 69 S. Ct. 79 (1948). See Notes, 34 Corn. L. Q. 442 (1949); 47 Col. L. Rev. 686 (1947).

2. The Massachusetts law was subsequently amended to permit the introduction of evidence relating to the "literary, cultural or educational character" of the book. Mass. Gen. Laws c. 272, § 28 F. The Massachusetts courts, however, still do not pay much attention to such evidence. See *Attorney General v. "God's Little Acre,"* 326 Mass. 281, 93 N. E. 2d 819 (1950); *Attorney General v. "Forever Amber,"* 323 Mass. 302, 81 N. E. 2d 663 (1948).

In *United States v. Two Obscene Books*, 92 F. Supp. 934, 99 F. Supp. 760 (N. D. Calif., 1950, 1951) the court felt that opinions of so-called experts and critics were immaterial but nevertheless gave consideration to book reviews and statements of critics expressing the opinion that Henry Miller's *Tropic of Cancer* and *Tropic of Capricorn* are works of art. The court in holding the books obscene adopted the stricter test of "whose minds are open to such influences" and commented: "The Claimant here, as well as some of the critics and reviewers who speak in his behalf, have presented a species of 'confession and avoidance' defense of Henry Miller. The many long filthy descriptions of sexual experiences, practices and organs are of themselves admitted to be lewd. They are sought to be justified by the claim that the books as a whole have an artistic pattern, into which the obscene and scatological portions fit as part of a whole literary mosaic. But I must conclude that this is mere sophistry. The filthy scatological portions are written in a bluntly different and distinct style from the pretentious metaphysical reflective manner of writing

**615**

otherwise. Thus the conclusion is justified that either the alleged literary ability of the author deserted him or that he had his eye upon 'the box office.'" 99 F. Supp. at 762.

For an enlightening discussion of the art exception see Jenkins, *The Laissez-Faire Theory of Artistic Censorship*, 9 Journal of the History of Ideas 71 (July 1944); Jenkins, *Legal Basis of Literary Censorship*, 31 Va. L. Rev. 83 (1944). A recent case is *People v. Vanguard Press*, 192 Misc. 127, 89 N. Y. Supp. 2d 427 (N. Y. City Mag. Ct., 1947) (sincerity of purpose and literary worth are relevant factors). For more elaborate treatment of freedom of art and the proper role of control with special emphasis on the movies, see Adler, *Art and Prudence* (1937), which also contains an analysis showing the many possible meanings of the word obscenity (ch. 6). Cases dealing with the charge of obscenity in connection with scientific publications are collected in 76 A. L. R. 1099 (1932). Where a book is of value to scientists or other special users, the book is sometimes allowed to circulate only among those specialists. See *People v. Sanger*, 222 N. Y. 192, 188 N. E. 637 (1918) (involving information about contraception). See also materials on the customs laws, *infra*.

A serious film about birth called *Birth of a Baby* was banned by New York State censors. A later publication by Life Magazine of still shots from the film was suppressed in several cities. However, the Magazine was acquitted in a criminal trial. See *People v. Larsen*, 5 N. Y. Supp. 2d 55 (Ct. Spec. Sess., 1938).

Courts at times indicate that they give newspapers a greater latitude in the publication of straight news accounts of trials containing material that ordinarily might be considered obscene. See *U. S. v. Journal Co.*, 197 F. 415 (D. Va., 1912); *Commonwealth v. Herald Publishing Co.*, 121 Ky. 424, 108 S. W. 892 (1908). Under the British Judicial Proceedings Act of 1926, 16 & 17 Geo. 5, c. 61, publication of indecent material in connection with the reporting of trials and other judicial proceedings is prohibited. Even in the United States newspapers or periodicals primarily or exclusively devoted to publishing spicy judicial news have been successfully prosecuted. See, *e. g.*, *In re Banks*, 56 Kan. 242, 42 Pac. 693 (1895); *Strohm v. People*, 160 Ill. 582, 43 N. E. 622 (1896) (statute prohibiting circulation to minors); *State v. Van Wye*, 136 Mo. 227, 37 S. W. 938 (1896). *Cf. Near v. Minnesota*, Chapter IV, *supra*, and *Winters v. New York*, *infra*.

Compare the distinction between art and science and other communication with judicial attempts to differentiate "entertainment" from communication protected by the First Amendment in connection with plays and motion picture censorship, *infra*.

3. There seems to be little conclusive scientific evidence of the effect of crime and sex literature upon youth. See materials collected in Clinard, *Secondary Community Influences and Juvenile Delinquency*, 261 Annals of the Am. Acad. of Pol. and Soc. Sci., 42, 46–9 (1949). The following statement, however, is attributed to J. Edgar Hoover, Chief of the Federal Bureau of Investigation: "The increase in the number of sex crimes is due precisely to sex literature madly presented in certain magazines. Filthy literature is the great moral wrecker. It is creat-

ing criminals faster than jails can be built." Noll, *Manual of the National Organization for Decent Literature,* p. 122, quoted in 34 Marq. L. Rev. at 302 (1951). For the effect of motion pictures see *infra.* For other studies of the effect, and studies on the function and operation of the communication process and related subjects, see bibliography at end of this Section, *infra.*

## The Problem of Vagueness

Obscenity statutes have generally not been declared unconstitutional because of their vague standard so long as the language has remained within traditional confines. In *Winters* v. *New York,* 333 U. S. 507, 92 L. Ed. 840, 68 S. Ct. 665 (1948), the Court stated that statutes using typical terms like "obscene," "lewd," "lascivious," "filthy," "indecent" and "disgusting" have that "permissible uncertainty . . . caused by describing crimes by words well understood through long use in the criminal law." 333 U. S. at 518. In that case the defendant attacked the constitutionality of a section of the New York Penal Code which made it a misdemeanor to publish or distribute in any way any publication "devoted to . . . and principally made up of criminal news, police reports, or accounts of criminal deeds, or pictures, or stories of deeds of bloodshed, lust or crime. . . ." The New York Court of Appeals had by construction limited the meaning of the Section so as "not to outlaw all commentaries on crime from detective tales to scientific treatises." It held that so far as applicable in the *Winters* case the statute merely extended the meaning of "indecent or obscene" which in New York previously had been construed to refer only to matters of sexual impurity. The extended notion of obscenity and indecency was designed to include only criminal deeds of bloodshed and lust "so massed as to become vehicles for inciting violent and depraved crimes against a person." 294 N. Y. 545, 63 N. E. 2d 98, 294 N. Y. 979, 63 N. E. 2d 713 (1945). In holding the statute unconstitutional the Supreme Court stated:

"Even though all detective tales and treatises on criminology are not forbidden, and though publications made up of criminal deeds not characterized by bloodshed or lust are omitted from the interpretation of the Court of Appeals, we think fair use of collections of pictures and stories would be interdicted because of the utter impossibility of the actor or the trier to know where this new standard of guilt would draw the line between the allowable and the forbidden publications. No intent or purpose is required —no indecency or obscenity in any sense heretofore known to the law. 'So massed as to incite to crime' can become meaningful only by concrete instances. This one example is not enough. The

**617**

clause proposes to punish the printing and circulation of publications that courts or juries may think influence generally persons to commit crimes of violence against the person. No conspiracy to commit a crime is required. . . . It is not an effective notice of new crime. The clause has no technical or common law meaning. Nor can light as to the meaning be gained from the section as a whole or the Article of the Penal Law under which it appears." 333 U. S. at 519.

Mr. Justice Frankfurter took sharp issue with the majority's view:

"In these matters legislatures are confronted with a dilemma. If a law is framed with narrow particularity, too easy opportunities are afforded to nullify the purposes of the legislation. If the legislation is drafted in terms so vague that no ascertainable line is drawn in advance between innocent and condemned conduct, the purpose of the legislation cannot be enforced because no purpose is defined. . . . The reconciliation of these two contradictories is necessarily an empiric enterprise largely depending on the nature of the particular legislative problem.

"What risks do the innocent run of being caught in a net not designed for them? How important is the policy of the legislation, so that those who really like to pursue innocent conduct are not likely to be caught unaware? How easy is it to be explicitly particular? How necessary is it to leave a somewhat penumbral margin but sufficiently revealed by what is condemned to those who do not want to sail close to the shore of questionable conduct? These and like questions confront legislative draftsmen. Answers to these questions are not to be found in any legislative manual nor in the work of great legislative draftsmen. They are not to be found in the opinions of this Court. These are questions of judgment, peculiarly within the responsibility and the competence of legislatures. The discharge of that responsibility should not be set at naught by abstract notions about 'indefiniteness.'

". . . I assume, that New York may punish crimes of lust and violence. Presumably also, it may take appropriate measures to lower the crime rate. But he must be a bold man indeed who is confident that he knows what causes crime. Those whose lives are devoted to an understanding of the problem are certain only that they are uncertain regarding the role of the various alleged 'causes' of crime. Bibliographies of criminology reveal a depressing volume of writings on theories of causation. See, *e.g.*, Kuhlman, A Guide to Material on Crime and Criminal Justice (1929) Item Nos. 292 to 1211; Culver; Bibliography of Crime and Criminal Justice (1927–1931) Item Nos. 877–1475, and (1932–1937) Item Nos. 799–1560. Is it to be seriously questioned, however, that the State of New York, or the Congress of the United States, may make incitement to crime itself an offense? He too would indeed be a bold man who denied that incitement may be caused by the written word no less than by the spoken. If 'the Fourteenth Amendment does not enact Mr. Herbert Spencer's Social Statics,' (Holmes, J., dissenting in *Lochner* v. *New York,* 198 U. S. 45, 75), neither does it enact the psychological dogmas of the Spencerian era. The painful experience which resulted from confusing economic dogmas with constitutional edicts ought not to be repeated by finding constitutional barriers to a State's policy regarding crime, because it may run counter to our inexpert psychological assumptions or offend our presuppositions regarding incitement to crime in relation to the curtailment of utterance. This Court is not ready, I assume, to pronounce on causative factors of mental disturbance and their relation to crime. Without formally professing to do so, it may actually do so by invalidating legislation dealing with these problems as too 'indefinite.'

"Not to make the magazines with which this case is concerned part of the Court's opinion is to play 'Hamlet' without Hamlet. But the Court sufficiently summarizes one aspect of what the State of New York here condemned when it says 'we can see nothing of any possible value to society in these magazines.' From which it jumps to the conclusion that, nevertheless, 'they are as much entitled to the protection of free speech as the best of literature.' Wholly neutral futilities, of course, come under the protection of free speech as fully as do Keats' poems or Donne's sermons. But to say that these magazines have 'nothing of any possible value to society' is only half the truth. This merely denies them goodness. It disregards their mischief. As a result of appropriate judicial determination, these magazines were found to come within the prohibition of the law against inciting 'violent and depraved crimes against the person,' and the defendant was convicted because he exposed for sale such materials. The essence of the Court's decision is that it gives publications which have 'nothing of any possible value to society' constitutional protection but denies to the States the power to prevent the grave evils to which, in their rational judgment, such publications give rise. The legislatures of New York and the other States were concerned with these evils and not with neutral abstractions of harmlessness. Nor was the New York Court of Appeals merely resting, as it might have done, on a deep-seated conviction as to the existence of an evil and as to the appropriate means for checking it. That court drew on its experience, as revealed by 'many recent records' of criminal convictions before it, for its understanding of the practical concrete reasons that led the legislatures of a score of States to pass the enactments now here struck down."

## Note

After the *Winters* case the New York legislature attempted to ban comic books which contained *"fictional* deeds of crime, bloodshed, lust or heinous acts, which tend to incite minors to violent or depraved or immoral acts." Governor Dewey vetoed the bill remarking: "The minor changes in language do not cure the deficiency of the earlier law." N. Y. Times, Mar. 13, 1952.

For ordinances designed to overcome the objections advanced in the *Winters* case see Rhyne, *Comic Books: Municipal Control of Sale and Distribution—A Preliminary Study,* National Institute of Municipal Law Officers, Rept. No. 124 (1948).

## Methods of Control

1. *Criminal Prosecutions.* The special problems of criminal prosecutions are (1) the risk the bookseller undertakes in selling a book for which he might be prosecuted and (2) the opportunity this gives to chiefs of police, aided by local watchdog societies, to exercise informal censorship by suggesting that the sale of certain books constitutes a possible violation. In Massachusetts a statute, which became effective after the decision in the *Isenstadt* case, attempts to alleviate these problems. It authorizes prosecutors to start an equity proceeding against the book. The judge examines it summarily and notifies all persons interested to come and defend the book, if he finds there is reasonable cause to believe it obscene. Any interested party may ask for a jury trial. If the judge or jury finds the book obscene, the result is a declaratory judgment which conclusively establishes knowledge on the part of the bookseller in a later prosecution for selling the book to a person "knowing it to be obscene." Mass. Gen. Laws c. 272, § 28c (Supp. 1950). See Note, 59 Harv. L. Rev. 813 (1946). Recent cases under this statute are *Attorney General* v. *Book Named "Serenade,"* 326 Mass. 324, 94 N. E. 2d 259 (1950); *Attorney General* v. *"Forever Amber," supra; Attorney General* v. *"God's Little Acre," supra.*

Another difficulty that sometimes proves important is that the burden of defense is placed on the bookseller who cannot afford it. See Chafee, *Free Speech in the United States,* pp. 536–7, 538 (1941). Entrapment also seems to be a problem. See 18 A. L. R. 171 (1922); 86 A. L. R. 269 (1933).

In *People* v. *Wepplo,* 78 Cal. App. 2d Supp. 959, 178 Pac. 2d 853 (1947), the statute provided that any person who "wilfully and lewdly" sells an obscene book is guilty of a misdemeanor. The court held that the provision required proof of specific intent. The requirement was not satisfied where the evidence showed merely sale of the book and there was nothing in the title or otherwise on the cover to apprise the defendant of the content.

2. *Customs.* The applicable statute provides for seizure by the Collector of (1) any obscene book "or any cast, instrument or other article which is obscene or immoral;" (2) books which contain matter "advocating or urging treason or insurrection" or "forcible resistance to any law" or "containing any threat to take the life of or inflict bodily harm upon any person;" and (3) any advertisement of any lottery. 19 U. S. C. § 1305 (1946) ; see also 18 U. S. C. § 1462 (Supp. 1951) for criminal penalties. Once the articles are seized the district attorney proceeds against them in the district court. Any party of interest may demand a jury trial and has the right of review. If the articles are found to come within the prohibition they are ordered destroyed. The statute also contains the following provision: "That the Secretary of the Treasury may, in his discretion, admit the so-called classics or books of recognized and established literary or scientific merit, but may, in his discretion, admit such classics or books only when imported for noncommercial purposes."

A special Undersecretary of the Treasury, with the aid of experts, attempts to make careful discriminations between art or science and obscenity. See, Chafee, *Government and Mass Communications,* pp. 242–275 (1947). For views of the Undersecretary on where the line should be drawn, see Cairns, *Freedom of Expression in Literature,* 200 Annals of the Am. Acad. of Pol. and Soc. Sci. 76 (1938).

3. *Post Office.* The postmaster has power to exclude from the mails: (1) seditious matter, 18 U. S. C. § 1717 (Supp. 1951) ; (2) obscene matter, 18 U. S. C. §§ 1461, 1463 (Supp. 1951) ; (3) information concerning birth control, *ibid;* (4) matter tending to incite to arson, murder or assassination, 18 U. S. C. § 1461 (Supp. 1951) ; (5) fraudulent matter, 18 U. S. C. § 1341 (Supp. 1951) ; and (6) libelous matter on envelopes, 18 U. S. C. § 1718 (Supp. 1951). See also the Internal Security Act, Chapter IV, *supra.*

In *Roth* v. *Goldman,* 172 F. 2d 788 (C. A. 2, 1949), an injunction was sought against the exclusion of three books. Two were excluded for violating the fraudulent mail provisions in claiming in their advertisements that they were salacious while in reality they were not, and one was excluded for being obscene. The court affirmed the denial of the injunction. With respect to the fraud provisions it had little difficulty "because the standards of fraud are at least somewhat clearer than those of obscenity." As to the difficulty with the latter concept the court simply shrugged its shoulders: "It is urged that such material is not of the sort to stimulate lust. Waiving the question how a court may test such a claim, we may suggest the curious dilemma involved in the view that the duller a book, the more its lewdness is to be excused or at least accepted. . . . But in any event, a decision under the law here applicable is committed in the first instance to an administrative official; and under normal rules, therefore, judicial review channelled within the confines of a plea for an injunction should not be overextensive. Certainly material such as this does not afford much stimulus or basis for a finding of abuse of administrative discretion or power." 175 F. 2d at 789. Judge Frank wrote an interesting and entertaining concurrence.

The Postmaster also grants second class mail privileges to printed publications issued at stated intervals. One of the statutory prerequisites for receiving these privileges is that the publication must be for "the dissemination of information of a public character or devoted to literature, the sciences, arts or some special industry." In *United States ex rel. Milwaukee Social Democratic Publishing Co.* v. *Burleson*, 255 U. S. 407, 65 L. Ed. 704, 41 S. Ct. 352 (1921), the Supreme Court, without referring to any specific condition in the second class mail statute, upheld a determination by the postmaster that where past issues were non-mailable because of seditious matter second class mailing privileges may be withdrawn from future issues. The postmaster sought more extensive powers in *Hannegan* v. *Esquire*, 327 U. S. 146, 90 L. Ed. 586, 66 S. Ct. 456 (1946). There he had denied second class mailing privileges to *Esquire* because it had not met the statutory requirement quoted above. On the basis of general language in the *Milwaukee* case, he had construed the requirement to mean at least that the magazine must contribute to the public good and the public welfare, which, in his opinion, *Esquire* failed to do. The Supreme Court held that the postmaster's power does not extend that far:

"But grave constitutional questions are immediately raised once it is said that the use of the mails is a privilege which may be extended or withheld on any grounds whatsoever. See the dissents of Mr. Justice Brandeis and Mr. Justice Holmes in *Milwaukee Publishing Co.* v. *Burleson*, 255 U. S. 407, 421–423, 430–432, 437–438. Under that view the second class rate could be granted on condition that certain economic and political ideas not be disseminated. The provisions of the Fourth condition would have to be far more explicit for us to assume that Congress made such a radical departure from our traditions and undertook to clothe the Postmaster-General with the power to supervise the tastes of the reading public of the country.

"It is plain, as we have said, that the favorable second class rates were granted periodicals meeting the requirements of the Fourth condition, so that the public good might be served through a dissemination of the class of periodicals described. But that is a far cry from assuming that Congress had any idea that each applicant for the second class rate must convince the Postmaster-General that his publication positively contributes to the public good or public welfare." 327 U. S. at 156–8.

On post office censorship see generally: Chafee, *Government and Mass Communications*, pp. 276–366 (1947) ; Kadin, *Administrative Censorship: A Study of the Mails, Motion Pictures and Radio Broadcasting*, 19 B. U. L. Rev. 533 (1939). The *Esquire* case is discussed in Note, 53 Yale L. J. 733 (1944), an excellent treatment written prior to the Supreme Court decision.

4. *Censorship and Licensing*. Previous restraint of the press was firmly prohibited in *Near* v. *Minnesota*, 283 U. S. 697, 75 L. Ed. 1357, 51 S. Ct. 625 (1931). See Chapter IV, *supra*. Except to the extent employed by the Post Office and Customs Bureau, it is generally not in use as a technique for controlling printed publication or miscellaneous utterances. See Note, 49 Col. L. Rev. 1001 (1949). Compare the Massachusetts declaratory judgment technique, *supra*. Censorship is used extensively in connection with the movies. See *infra*. Licensing is used most frequently in connection with any forum involving the problem of limited facilities, such as parks, streets or wave lengths. See Chapter VI, *infra*. As to censorship of plays, see *People* v. *Wendling*, 258 N. Y. 451, 180 N. E. 169 (1932) ; *Opinion of the Justices*, 247 Mass. 589, 143 N. E. 808 (1924) ; Chafee, *Free Speech in the United States*, pp. 529–36 (1941). Of course the possibility of withdrawing licenses from theatres and exhibition halls, which is one of the techniques of movie censorship, is also used to control the content of plays. See Chapter VI, *infra*. On the notion, now rejected by the Supreme Court, that motion pictures are mere entertainment and therefore the type of communication to which the principle of freedom from prior restraint does not apply, see Chapter VI, *infra*. For the origins of American attitudes toward the theater, see Knowles, *The Censor, The Drama and the Film* (1934) ; 2 DeTocqueville, *Democracy in America*, pp. 75–6 (Reeve ed. 1889).

## Note

1. The sanctions imposed for the use of obscene and abusive language in our society take on various forms in addition to the ones mentioned above and sometimes reach out to the most intimate corners of private life. See, *e. g.*, 19 A. L. R. 2d 1428 (1951) (abusive and obscene language as constructive desertion in divorce proceedings); 20 A. L. R. 2d 567 (1951) (as ground for expulsion from private association); 12 A. L. R. 2d 971 (1950) (indecent proposal to woman as assault).

2. Blasphemy and other communication offensive to religion is another type of communication generally punishable in the United States. See *People v. Burstyn,* set forth *infra.*

3. Exhibitionism also can be regarded as a form of prohibited communication. The cases should be compared with those involving obscene literature, especially with regard to the relative lack of difficulty in discovering a standard. For collection of cases, see 110 A. L. R. 1233 (1937); 93 A. L. R. 996 (1934). Compare materials dealing with difficulties in fixing a standard in defamation cases, Section B, *infra.*

4. On the subject matter of this Section, see generally, Chafee, *Government and Mass Communications,* pp. 200–234 (1947), in addition to the articles by Alvart and Grant and Angoff cited in the *Isenstadt* case. See also Ernst and Seagle, *To the Pure* (1928); Ernst and Lindey, *The Censor Marches On* (1940). For a recent collection of statutes see Note, 28 Ky. L. Rev. 163, 169 (1949); for a collection of cases see 81 A. L. R. 801 (1932). The English cases are treated in Scott, *Into Whose Hands* (1945); Craig, *Above All Liberties* (1942); *The Banned Books of England* (1937). See further Note, 34 Corn. L. Q. 442 (1949); Schroeder, *May It Please The Court,* 48 Medico-Legal Journal 22, 60, 89 (1931); Hallis, *The Law of Obscenity* (1932). For a history of sex censorship through the ages see May, *Social Control of Sex Expression* (1931). An interesting attempt to explain the role of censorship in our society is found in Waldo Frank, *Sex Censorship and Democracy,* in Calverton and Schnallhausen, *Sex in Civilization,* pp. 168–179 (1929). For strong opposition to the legal restrictions by two prominent victims see D. H. Lawrence, *Pornography and Obscenity* (1930); Ellis, *The Revaluation of Obscenity* (1931).

Among the most famous users of obscene language are the American soldiers. Scientific study, however, shows that in the mouths of soldiers obscene language is more often devoid of sexual connotations than otherwise. See Elkin, *The Soldier's Language,* 51 Am. J. of Sociology 414 (1946); *cf.* Waterman, *Role of Obscenity in the Folk Tales of the Intellectual Stratum of Our Society,* 62 J. Am. Folklore 162 (1949).

**624**

## B. GROUP LIBEL, FALSEHOODS AND OTHER COMMUNICATION HARMFUL TO THE REPUTATION OR PRIVACY OF GROUPS AND INDIVIDUALS

### BEAUHARNAIS v. ILLINOIS

Supreme Court of the United States, 1952
343 U. S. 250, 96 L. Ed. —, 72 S. Ct. 725

MR. JUSTICE FRANKFURTER delivered the opinion of the Court.
The petitioner was convicted upon information in the Municipal Court of Chicago of violating § 224a of Division 1 of the Illinois Penal Code, Ill. Rev. Stat. 1949, c. 38, § 471. He was fined $200. The section provides:

"It shall be unlawful for any person, firm or corporation to manufacture, sell, or offer for sale, advertise or publish, present or exhibit in any public place in this state any lithograph, moving picture, play, drama or sketch, which publication or exhibition portrays depravity, criminality, unchastity, or lack of virtue of a class of citizens, of any race, color, creed or religion which said publication or exhibition exposes the citizens of any race, color, creed or religion to contempt, derision, or obloquy or which is productive of breach of the peace or riots. . . ."

Beauharnais challenged the statute as violating the liberty of speech and of the press guaranteed as against the States by the Due Process Clause of the Fourteenth Amendment, and as too vague, under the restrictions implicit in the same Clause, to support conviction for crime. The Illinois courts rejected these contentions and sustained defendant's conviction. 408 Ill. 512. We granted certiorari in view of the serious questions raised concerning the limitations imposed by the Fourteenth Amendment on the power of a State to punish utterances promoting friction among racial and religious groups. 342 U. S. 809.

The information, cast generally in the terms of the statute, charged that Beauharnais "did unlawfully . . . exhibit in public places lithographs, which publications portray depravity, criminality, unchastity or lack of virtue of citizens of Negro race and color and which exposes [sic] citizens of Illinois of the Negro race and color to contempt, derision, or obloquy. . . ." The lithograph complained of was a leaflet setting forth a petition calling on the Mayor and City Council of Chicago "to halt the further encroachment, harassment and invasion of white people, their property, neighborhoods and persons, by the Negro . . . ." Below was a call for "One million self respecting white people in Chicago to unite . . ." with the statement added that

"If persuasion and the need to prevent the white race from becoming mongrelized by the negro will not unite us, then the aggressions . . . rapes, robberies, knives, guns and marijuana of the negro, surely will." This, with more language, similar if not so violent, concluded with an attached application for membership in the White Circle League of America, Inc.

The testimony at the trial was substantially undisputed. From it the jury could find that Beauharnais was president of the White Circle League; that, at a meeting on January 6, 1950, he passed out bundles of the lithographs in question, together with other literature, to volunteers for distribution on downtown Chicago street corners the following day; that he carefully organized that distribution, giving detailed instructions for it; and that the leaflets were in fact distributed on January 7 in accordance with his plan and instructions. The court, together with other charges on burden of proof and the like, told the jury "if you find . . . that the defendant, Joseph Beauharnais, did . . . manufacture, sell, or offer for sale, advertise or publish, present or exhibit in any public place the lithograph . . . then you are to find the defendant guilty . . . ." He refused to charge the jury, as requested by the defendant, that in order to convict they must find "that the article complained of was likely to produce a clear and present danger of a serious substantive evil that rises far above public inconvenience, annoyance or unrest." Upon this evidence and these instructions, the jury brought in the conviction here for review.

The statute before us is not a catchall enactment left at large by the State court which applied it. Cf. *Thornhill* v. *Alabama*, 310 U. S. 88; *Cantwell* v. *Connecticut*, 310 U. S. 296, 307. It is a law specifically directed at a defined evil, its language drawing from history and practice in Illinois and in more than a score of other jurisdictions a meaning confirmed by the Supreme Court of that State in upholding this conviction. We do not, therefore, parse the statute as grammarians or treat it as an abstract exercise in lexicography. We read it in the animating context of well-defined usage, *Nash* v. *United States*, 229 U. S. 373, and State court construction which determines its meaning for us. *Cox* v. *New Hampshire*, 312 U. S. 569; *Chaplinsky* v. *New Hampshire*, 315 U. S. 568.

The Illinois Supreme Court tells us that § 224a "is a form of criminal libel law." 408 Ill. 512, 517. The defendant, the trial court and the Supreme Court consistently treated it as such. The defendant offered evidence tending to prove the truth of parts of the utterance, and the courts below considered and disposed

[Emerson]

of this offer in terms of ordinary criminal libel precedents.[1] Section 224a does not deal with the defense of truth, but by the Illinois Constitution, Art. II, § 4, "in all trials for libel, both civil and criminal, the truth, when published with good motives and for justifiable ends, shall be a sufficient defense." See also Ill. Rev. Stat., 1949, c. 38, § 404. Similarly, the action of the trial court in deciding as a matter of law the libelous character of the utterance, leaving to the jury only the question of publication, follows the settled rule in prosecutions for libel in Illinois and other States.[2] Moreover, the Supreme Court's characterization of the words prohibited by the statute as those "liable to cause violence and disorder" paraphrases the traditional justification for punishing libels criminally, namely their "tendency to cause breach of the peace."[3]

Libel of an individual was a common-law crime, and thus criminal in the colonies. Indeed, at common law, truth or good motives was no defense. In the first decades after the adoption of the Constitution, this was changed by judicial decision, statute or constitution in most States, but nowhere was there any suggestion that the crime of libel be abolished.[4] Today, every American jurisdiction—the forty-eight States, the District of Columbia, Alaska, Hawaii and Puerto Rico—punish libels directed at individuals.[5] "There are certain well-defined and narrowly limited

---

[1] 400 Ill. 512, 518. Illinois law requires that for the defense to prevail, the truth of all facts in the utterance must be shown together with good motive for publication. *People v. Strauch*, 247 Ill. 220; *People v. Fuller*, 238 Ill. 116; cf. *Ogren v. Rockford Star Printing Co.*, 288 Ill. 405.

[2] See, *e. g.*, *State v. Sterman*, 199 Iowa 569; *State v. Howard*, 169 N. C. 312, 313; cf. *Ogren v. Rockford Star Printing Co.*, *supra*.

[3] See, *e. g.*, *People v. Spielman*, 318 Ill. 482, 489; Odgers, Libel and Slander (6th ed.), 368; 19 A. L. R. 1470. Some States hold, however, that injury to reputation, as in civil libel, and not tendency to breach of the peace, is the gravamen of the offense. See Tanenhaus, Group Libel, 35 Cornell L. Q. 261, 273 and n. 67.

[4] For a brief account of this development see Warren, History of the American Bar, 236–239. See also correspondence between Chief Justice Cushing of Massachusetts and John Adams, published in 27 Mass. L. Q. 11–16 (Oct. 1942). Jefferson explained in a letter to Abigail Adams, dated September 11, 1804, that to strike down the Alien and Sedition Act would not "remove all restraint from the overwhelming torrent of slander which is confounding all vice and virtue, all truth and falsehood in the US. The power to do that is fully possessed by the several state legislatures." See *Dennis v. United States*, 341 U. S. 494, 522, n. 4. See Miller, Crisis in Freedom, 168–169, 231–232. See also provisions as to criminal libel in Edward Livingston's famous draft System of Penal Law for Louisiana, 2 Works of Edward Livingston 100–108.

[5] In eight States the offense is punished as at common law, without legislative enactment. *State v. Roberts*, 2 Marv. 450, 43 A. 252 (Del.); *Cole v. Commonwealth*, 222 Ky. 350, 300 S. W. 907; *Robinson v. State*, 108 Md. 644, 71 A. 433; *Commonwealth v. Canter*, 269 Mass. 359, 168 N. E. 790;

classes of speech, the prevention and punishment of which have never been thought to raise any constitutional problem. These

*State v. Burnham*, 9 N. H. 34; *State v. Spear*, 13 R. I. 324; *State v. Sutton*, 74 Vt. 12, 52 A. 116; *State v. Payne*, 87 W. Va. 102, 104 S. E. 288. Twelve other jurisdictions make "libel" a crime by statute, without defining the term. Ala. Code, 1940, Tit. 14, § 347; Alaska Comp. Laws Ann., 1949, § 65–4–28; D. C. Code, 1940, § 22–2301; Fla. Stat. Ann., 1943, § 836.01; Burns Ind. Stat., 1933, § 10–3201; Miss. Code, 1942, § 2268; Neb. Rev. Stat., 1943, § 28–440; N. J. Stat. Ann., 1939, § 2:146–1; N. C. Gen. Stat., 1943, § 14–47; Page's Ohio Gen. Code, 1939, § 13383; Wis. Stat., 1949, § 348.41; Wyo. Comp. Stat., 1945, § 9–1601. Thus, twenty American jurisdictions punish "libel" as defined by the case-by-case common-law development.

The remaining jurisdictions have sought to cast the common-law definition in a statutory form of words. Two formulas have been popular. Eleven jurisdictions, Illinois among them, have accepted with minor variations the following:

"A libel is a malicious defamation, expressed either by printing, or by signs or pictures, or the like, tending to blacken the memory of one who is dead, or to impeach the honesty, integrity, virtue or reputation or publish the natural defects of one who is alive, and thereby to expose him to public hatred, contempt, ridicule, or financial injury." Ariz. Code Ann., 1939, § 43.3501; Ark. Stat., 1947, § 41–2401; Deering's Cal. Penal Code, 1949, § 248; Colo. Stat. Ann., 1935, c. 48, § 199; Ga. Code Ann., 1936, § 26–2101; Idaho Code, 1947, § 18–4801; Smith-Hurd's Ill. Ann. Stat., 1936, c. 38, § 402; Mont. Rev. Codes, 1947, § 94–2801; Nev. Comp. Laws, 1929, § 10110; P. R. Codiga Penal, 1937, § 243; Utah Code Ann., 1943, § 103–38–1; cf. Virgin Islands Code, 1921, Tit. IV, c. 5, § 36.

The other version, again with minor variations, has found favor in twelve jurisdictions.

"A libel is a malicious defamation of a person, made public by any printing, writing, sign, picture, representation or effigy, tending to provoke him to wrath or expose him to public hatred, contempt or ridicule, or to deprive him of the benefits of public confidence and social intercourse; or any malicious defamation, made public as aforesaid, designed to blacken and vilify the memory of one who is dead, and tending to scandalize or provoke his surviving relatives or friends."

Iowa Code Ann., 1949, § 737.1; Kan. Gen. Stat., 1935, § 21–2401; Dart's La. Crim. Code, 1943, Art. 740–47; Me. Rev. Stat., 1944, c. 117, § 30; Minn. Stat., 1949, § 619.51; Mo. Rev. Stat., 1949, § 559.410; McKinney's N. Y. Laws, Penal Code, § 1340; N. D. Rev. Code, 1943, § 12–2801; Okla. Stat. Ann., 1936, Tit. 21, § 771; Purdon's Pa. Stat. Ann., 1945, Tit. 18, § 4412; William's Tenn. Code, 1934, §§ 11021, 11022; Remington's Wash. Rev. Stat., 1932, § 2424.

The remaining nine jurisdictions have definitions of criminal libel which fall into no common pattern. See Conn. Gen. Stat., 1949, § 8518; Hawaii Rev. Laws, 1945, § 11450; Mich. Comp. Laws, 1948, § 750–370; N. M. Stat., 1941, §§ 41–2701, 41–2708; Ore. Comp. Laws, 1940, § 23–437; S. C. Code, 1942, § 1395; S. D. Code, 1939, § 13–3401; Vernon's Tex. Stat. 1948, Art. 1269, 1275; Va. Code, 1950, § 18–133.

Our examination of the homogeneity of these statutory definitions of criminal libel might well begin and end with the words "virtue" and "ridicule." Of thirty-two jurisdictions, twelve outlaw statements impeaching the "virtue" of another; eleven of these, and fifteen more—twenty-six in all—prohibit utterances tending to bring another into "public ridicule."

include the lewd and obscene, the profane, the libelous, and the insulting or 'fighting' words—those which by their very utterance inflict injury or tend to incite to an immediate breach of the peace. It has been well observed that such utterances are no essential part of any exposition of ideas, and are of such slight social value as a step to truth that any benefit that may be derived from them is clearly outweighed by the social interest in order and morality. 'Resort to epithets or personal abuse is not in any proper sense communication of information or opinion safeguarded by the Constitution, and its punishment as a criminal act would raise no question under that instrument.' *Cantwell v. Connecticut*, 310 U. S. 296, 309–310." Such were the views of a unanimous Court in *Chaplinsky* v. *New Hampshire, supra,* at 571–572.[6]

No one will gainsay that it is libelous falsely to charge another with being a rapist, robber, carrier of knives and guns, user of marijuana. The precise question before us, then, is whether the protection of "liberty" in the Due Process Clause of the Fourteenth Amendment prevents a State from punishing such libels— as criminal libel has been defined, limited and constitutionally recognized time out of mind—directed at designated collectivities and flagrantly disseminated. There is even authority, however dubious, that such utterances were also crimes at common law.[7] It is certainly clear that some American jurisdictions have sanc-

---

For the common-law definition, applicable in the twenty jurisdictions first noted above, see L. Hand, J., in *Grant v. Reader's Digest Assn.*, 151 F. 2d 733, 735, where he speaks of defining libel "in accordance with the usual rubric, as consisting of utterances which arouse 'hatred, contempt, scorn, obloquy or shame,' and the like." Cf. Restatement, Torts, § 559, *comment* (b) ; Odgers, Libel and Slander (6th ed.), 16–17; Newell, Slander and Libel (4th ed.), 1–2.

Even a cursory examination of these enactments and common-law pronouncements demonstrates that Illinois, in § 224a, was using a form of words which invoked the familiar common law of libel to define the prohibited utterances. The defendant and the Illinois courts, as we have seen, understood this and acted upon it.

[6] In all but five States, the constitutional guarantee of free speech to every person is explicitly qualified by holding him "responsible for the abuse of that right." See *Pennekamp v. Florida*, 328 U. S. 331, 356, n. 5. See Jefferson in Kentucky Resolutions of 1798 and 1799, 4 Elliott's Debates 540–541, and in an undated draft prepared, but not used, for his December 8, 1801, Message to Congress, Library of Congress Jefferson Papers, Vol. 119, Leaf 20569. In *Carlson v. California*, 310 U. S. 106, 112, we noted that the statute there invalidated made "no exceptions with respect to the truthfulness and restraint of the information conveyed . . . ."

[7] Compare reports of *King v. Osborne* in 2 Barn. K. B. 138, 166, 94 Eng. Rep. 406, 425; 2 Swans. 503, n. (c), 36 Eng. Rep. 705, 717; W. Kel. 230, 25 Eng. Rep. 584 (1732). The present Attorney General of England asserted that this case obviated the need of special group libel legislation

tioned their punishment under ordinary criminal libel statutes.[8] We cannot say, however, that the question is concluded by history and practice. But if an utterance directed at an individual may be the object of criminal sanctions, we cannot deny to a State power to punish the same utterance directed at a defined group, unless we can say that this is a wilful and purposeless restriction unrelated to the peace and well-being of the State.

Illinois did not have to look beyond her own borders or await the tragic experience of the last three decades[9] to conclude that wilful purveyors of falsehood concerning racial and religious groups promote strife and tend powerfully to obstruct the manifold adjustments required for free, ordered life in a metropolitan, polyglot community. From the murder of the abolitionist Lovejoy in 1837 to the Cicero riots of 1951, Illinois has been the scene of exacerbated tension between races, often flaring into violence and destruction.[10] In many of these outbreaks, utterances of the character here in question, so the Illinois legislature could conclude, played a significant part.[11] The law was passed on June 29, 1917, at a time when the State was struggling to assimilate vast numbers of new inhabitants, as yet concentrated in discrete racial or national or religious groups—foreign-born brought to it by the crest of the great wave of immigration, and Negroes attracted by jobs in war plants and the allurements

---

for Great Britain. See The [London] Times, March 26, 1952, p. 2, col. 4. See also Odgers, Libel and Slander (6th ed.), 369; Tanenhaus, Group Libel, 35 Cornell L. Q. 261, 267–269.

[8] One of the leading cases arose in Illinois. *People v. Speilman*, 318 Ill. 482 (1925) sustaining a conviction for libel on the members of the American Legion. The authorities are collected and discussed in Tanenhaus, Group Libel, 35 Cornell L. Q. 261, 269–276.

[9] See, *e. g.*, Loewenstein, Legislative Control of Political Extremism in European Democracies, 38 Col. L. Rev. 591 and 725; Riesman, Democracy and Defamation, 42 Col. L. Rev. 727, 1085 and 1282; Public Order Act, 1936, 1 Edw. VIII and 1 Geo. VI, c. 6, and 317 H. C. Deb. 1350–1474 (5th ser. 1936); 318 H. C. Deb. 50–194, 582–710, 1659–1786, 2782–2784 (5th ser. 1936); 103 H. L. Deb. 742–774, 962–971 (5th ser. 1936).

[10] See generally The Chicago Commission on Race Relations, The Negro in Chicago, 1–78, and *passim* (University of Chicago Press, 1922); Research Memorandum No. 5, First Annual Rep. Ill. Inter-Racial Comm'n (1944).

[11] The May 28, 1917, riot in East St. Louis, Illinois, was preceded by a violently inflammatory speech to unemployed workmen by a prominent lawyer of the town. Report of the Special Committee Authorized by Congress to Investigate the East St. Louis Riots, H. R. Doc. No. 1231, 65th Cong., 2d Sess. 11; Chicago Commission on Race Relations, The Negro in Chicago, 75. And see *id.*, at 118–122 for literature circulated by real estate associations and other groups during the series of bombings leading up to the Chicago riots of 1919. For the Commission's comments on the role of propaganda in promoting race frictions, see *id.*, at 589, 638–639.

of Northern claims.[12] Nine years earlier, in the very city where the legislature sat, what is said to be the first northern race riot had cost the lives of six people, left hundreds of Negroes homeless and shocked citizens into action far beyond the borders of the State.[13] Less than a month before the bill was enacted, East St. Louis had seen a day's rioting, prelude to an outbreak, only four days after the bill became law, so bloody that it led to Congressional investigation.[14] A series of bombings had begun which was to culminate two years later in the awful race riot which held Chicago in its grip for seven days in the summer of 1919.[15] Nor has tension and violence between the groups defined in the statute been limited in Illinois to clashes between whites and Negroes.

In the face of this history and its frequent obligato of extreme racial and religious propaganda, we would deny experience to say that the Illinois legislature was without reason in seeking ways to curb false or malicious defamation of racial and religious groups, made in public places and by means calculated to have a powerful emotional impact on those to whom it was presented. "There are limits to the exercise of these liberties [of speech and of the press]. The danger in these times from the coercive activi-

---

[12] Tables in Drake and Cayton, Black Metropolis, 8, show that between 1900 and 1920 the number of foreign born in Chicago increased by over ⅓ and the Negro population trebled. United States census figures show the following population growth for the State as a whole and selected counties:

|  | Illinois | | Cook-County (Chicago) | | St. Clair County (East St. Louis) | |
|---|---|---|---|---|---|---|
|  | Total | Negro | Total | Negro | Total | Negro |
| 1900 | 4,821,550 | 85,078 | 1,838,735 | 31,838 | 86,685 | 3,987 |
| 1910 | 5,638,591 | 109,049 | 2,405,233 | 46,627 | 119,870 | 8,110 |
| 1920 | 6,485,280 | 182,274 | 3,053,017 | 115,238 | 136,520 | 10,136 |
| 1930 | 7,330,654 | 328,972 | 3,982,123 | 246,992 | 157,775 | 15,550 |
| 1940 | 7,897,241 | 387,446 | 4,063,342 | 249,157 | 166,899 | 21,567 |
| 1950 | 8,712,176 | 645,989 | 4,508,792 | 521,007 | 205,995 | 34,566 |

For an account of these vast population movements entailing great social maladjustments, see Drake and Cayton, Black Metropolis, 8–18, 31–65; Chicago Commission on Race Relations, The Negro in Chicago, 79–105; Carl Sandburg, The Chicago Race Riots, 9–30.

[13] See Walling, Race War in the North, 65 The Independent 529 (1908). This article apparently led to the founding of the National Association for Advancement of Colored People. Ovington, How the National Association for the Advancement of Colored People Began, 8 Crisis 184 (1914). See also Chicago Commission on Race Relations, The Negro in Chicago 67–71.

[14] Report of the Special Committee Authorized by Congress to Investigate the East St. Louis Riots, H. R. Doc. No. 1231, 65th Cong., 2d Sess. See also The Massacre of East St. Louis, 14 Crisis 219 (1917).

[15] Chicago Commission on Race Relations, The Negro in Chicago 122–133.

ties of those who in the delusion of racial or religious conceit would incite violence and breaches of the peace in order to deprive others of their equal right to the exercise of their liberties, is emphasized by events familiar to all. These and other transgressions of those limits the States appropriately may punish."[16] This was the conclusion, again of a unanimous Court, in 1940. *Cantwell* v. *Connecticut, supra,* at 310.

It may be argued, and weightily, that this legislation will not help matters; that tension and on occasion violence between racial and religious groups must be traced to causes more deeply embedded in our society than the rantings of modern Knownothings.[17] Only those lacking responsible humility will have a confident solution for problems as intractable as the frictions attributable to differences of race, color or religion. This being so, it would be out of bounds for the judiciary to deny the legislature a choice of policy, provided it is not unrelated to the problem and not forbidden by some explicit limitation on the State's power. That the legislative remedy might not in practice mitigate the evil, or might itself raise new problems, would only manifest once more the paradox of reform. It is the price to be paid for the trial-and-error inherent in legislative efforts to deal with obstinate social issues. "The science of government is the most abstruse of all sciences; if, indeed, that can be called a science which has but few fixed principles, and practically consists in little more than the exercise of a sound discretion, applied to the exigencies of the state as they arise. It is the science of experiment." *Anderson* v. *Dunn,* 6 Wheat. 204, 226. Certainly the Due Process Clause does not require the legislature to be in the vanguard of science—especially sciences as young as human ecology and cultural anthropology. See *Tigner* v. *Texas,* 310 U. S. 141, 148.

Long ago this Court recognized that the economic rights of an individual may depend for the effectiveness of their enforcement

---

[16] The utterances here in question "are not," as a detached student of the problem has noted, "the daily grist of vituperative political debate. Nor do they represent the frothy imaginings of lunatics, or the 'idle' gossip of a country town. Rather, they indicate the systematic avalanche of falsehoods which are circulated concerning the various groups, classes and races which make up the countries of the western world." Riesman, Democracy and Defamation; Control of Group Libel, 42 Col. L. Rev. at 727. Professor Riesman continues: "Such purposeful attacks are nothing new, of course. . . . What is new, however, is the existence of a mobile public opinion as the controlling force in politics, and the systematic manipulation of that opinion by the use of calculated falsehood and vilification." *Id.,* at 728.

[17] See, *e. g.,* L. Hand, J., in a symposium in The Saturday Review of Literature, Mar. 15, 1947, pp. 23–24; Report of the Committee on the Law of Defamation, Cmd. 7536, 11 (1948).

on rights in the group, even though not formally corporate, to which he belongs. *American Foundries* v. *Tri-City Council*, 257 U. S. 189. Such group-protection on behalf of the individual may, for all we know, be a need not confined to the part that a trade union plays in effectuating rights abstractly recognized as belonging to its members. It is not within our competence to confirm or deny claims of social scientists as to the dependence of the individual on the position of his racial or religious group in the community. It would, however, be arrant dogmatism, quite outside the scope of our authority in passing on the powers of a State, for us to deny that the Illinois Legislature may warrantably believe that a man's job and his educational opportunities and the dignity accorded him may depend as much on the reputation of the racial and religious group to which he willynilly belongs, as it does on his own merits. This being so, we are precluded from saying that speech concededly punishable when immediately directed at individuals cannot be outlawed if directed at groups with whose position and esteem in society the affiliated individual may be inextricably involved.

We are warned that the choice we permit the Illinois legislature here may be abused, that the law may be discriminatorily enforced; prohibiting libel of a creed or of a racial group, we are told, is but a step from prohibiting libel of a political party.[18] Every power may be abused, but the possibility of abuse is a poor reason for denying Illinois the power to adopt measures against criminal libels sanctioned by centuries of Anglo-American law. "While this Court sits" it retains and exercises authority to nullify action which encroaches on freedom of utterance under the guise of punishing libel. Of course discussion cannot be denied and the right, as well as the duty, of criticism must not be stifled.

The scope of the statute before us, as construed by the Illinois court, disposes of the contention that the conduct prohibited by the law is so ill-defined that judges and juries in applying the statute and men in acting cannot draw from it adequate standards to guide them. The clarifying construction and fixed usage which govern the meaning of the enactment before us were not

---

[18] It deserves emphasis that there is no such attempt in this statute. The rubric "race, color, creed or religion" which describes the type of group libel which is punishable, has attained too fixed a meaning to permit political groups to be brought within it. If a statute sought to outlaw libels of political parties, quite different problems not now before us would be raised. For one thing, the whole doctrine of fair comment as indispensable to the democratic political process would come into play. See *People v. Fuller, supra,* at 125; *Commonwealth v. Pratt,* 208 Mass. 553, 559. Political parties, like public men, are, as it were, public property.

present, so the Court found, in the New York law held invalid in *Winters* v. *New York*, 333 U. S. 507. Nor, thus construed and limited, is the act so broad that the general verdict of guilty on an indictment drawn in the statutory language might have been predicated on constitutionally protected conduct. On this score, the conviction here reviewed differs from those upset in *Stromberg* v. *California*, 283 U. S. 359, *Thornhill* v. *Alabama*, *supra*, and *Terminiello* v. *Chicago*, 337 U. S. 1. Even the latter case did not hold that the unconstitutionality of a statute is established *because* the speech prohibited by it raises a ruckus.

[Here Mr. Justice Frankfurter takes up the further contention that the statute violates Due Process by not permitting the "(1) defense of truth; (2) justification of the utterance as "fair comment"; and (3) its privilege as a means for redressing grievances." He disposes of privilege and "fair comment" on the basis that these were not raised by "proffer of evidence, requests for instructions, motion before or after verdict" or as a ground for reversal urged to the Supreme Court. As to the defense of truth, Illinois requires, in common with many other States, "not only that the utterance state the facts, but also that the publication be made 'with good motives and for justifiable ends.'" Defendant offered to show that in Negro districts there were more crimes than in those where whites predominated, "three crimes specifically committed by Negroes, and . . . that property values declined when Negroes moved into the neighborhood." Even if one assumes that this offer was adequate as to the defense of truth it did not meet the additional requirement of "good motives for justifiable ends."]

Libellous utterances, not being within the area of constitutionally protected speech, it is unnecessary, either for us or for the State courts, to consider the issue behind the phrase "clear and present danger." Certainly no one would contend that obscene speech, for example, may be punished only upon a showing of such circumstances. Libel, as we have seen, is in the same class.

We find no warrant in the Constitution for denying to Illinois the power to pass the law here under attack.[23] But it bears repeating—although it should not—that our finding that the law is not constitutionally objectionable carries no implication of approval of the wisdom of the legislation or of its efficacy. These questions may raise doubts in our minds as well as in others.

---

[23] The law struck down by the New Jersey court in *Klapprott* v. *New Jersey*, 127 N. J. L. 395, was quite different than the one before us and was not limited, as is the Illinois statute, by construction or usage. Indeed, in that case the court emphasized that "It is not a case of libel," and contrasted the history at common law of criminal prosecutions for written and spoken defamation.

It is not for us, however, to make the legislative judgment. We are not at liberty to erect those doubts into fundamental law.

*Affirmed.*

[Mr. Justice Reed's dissenting opinion in which Mr. Justice Douglas joined, after reiterating that the Fourteenth Amendment makes the First applicable to the states, concluded that the statutory language was so broad as to include "punishment of incidents fairly within the protection of the guarantee of free speech." The language of the statute did not limit the meaning of words like "virtue," "derision" or "obloquy." The fact that the statute is described as a criminal libel law, or that the word "virtue" is found in an individual libel statute does not clarify the meaning of these words. No cases are cited to support the majority's notion of an existing "clarifying construction" and "fixed usage."

Mr. Justice Douglas' separate dissenting opinion deplored what he felt was the Court's recent tendency to engraft "the rights of regulation onto the First Amendment by placing in the hands of the legislative branch the right to regulate 'within reasonable limits' the right of free speech." The law that today convicts a white man for "protesting in unseemly language against our decisions invalidating restrictive covenants" may tomorrow convict a Negro for denouncing "lynch law in heated terms." Shouting and raving, intemperate speech, "exaggerating weakness, magnifying error, viewing with alarm" were well known to the framers of the Constitution who, though they lived in dangerous days, chose liberty against restrictions which might result in the abuse of liberty. The Court's opinion "is notice to the legislatures that they have the power to control unpopular blocs" and "a warning to every minority that when the Constitution guarantees free speech it does not mean what it says."

Mr. Justice Jackson's dissenting opinion primarily expounds a new thesis "that the Fourteenth Amendment did not 'incorporate' the First," and that the restrictions on the states are not of the same dimensions as those imposed on Congress. While the Court has never sustained a federal criminal libel law and the validity of such a law would be "extremely doubtful" the validity of ordinary state criminal libel statutes is well established. Indeed, they were tolerated by "the very authors and partisans of the Fourteenth Amendment." The power of the states is limited by the "concept of ordered liberty." This includes restrictions on libel prosecutions generally accepted by states, such as defenses of truth and good motives, fair comment and privilege. And where expression "is punished, although it has not actually caused injuries or disorders but is thought to

**635**

have a tendency to do so" the Supreme Court has imposed the "clear and present danger test" in addition to the above safeguards which the states have "voluntarily taken upon themselves." Here the traditional defenses were not entertained by the courts below. Moreover "no actual violence and no specific injury was charged or proved. . . . The conviction rests on judicial attribution of a likelihood of evil results." Yet the "trial court . . . refused to charge the jury that it must find some clear and present danger. . . ."]

MR. JUSTICE BLACK, with whom MR. JUSTICE DOUGLAS concurs, dissenting . . .

Today's case degrades First Amendment freedoms to the "rational basis" level. It is now a certainty that the new "due process" coverall offers far less protection to liberty than would adherence to our former cases compelling states to abide by the unequivocal First Amendment command that its defined freedoms shall not be abridged.

The Court's holding here and the constitutional doctrine behind it leave the rights of assembly, petition, speech and press almost completely at the mercy of state legislative, executive, and judicial agencies. I say "almost" because state curtailment of these freedoms may still be invalidated if a majority of this Court conclude that a particular infringement is "without reason," or is "a wilful and purposeless restriction unrelated to the peace and well being of the State." But lest this encouragement should give too much hope as to how and when this Court might protect these basic freedoms from state invasion, we are cautioned that state legislatures must be left free to "experiment" and to make "legislative" judgments. We are told that mistakes may be made during the legislative process of curbing public opinion. In such event the Court fortunately does not leave those mistakenly curbed, or any of us for that matter, unadvised. Consolation can be sought and must be found in the philosophical reflection that state legislative error in stifling speech and press "is the price to be paid for the trial-and-error inherent in legislative efforts to deal with obstinate social issues." My own belief is that no legislature is charged with the duty or vested with the power to decide what public issues Americans can discuss. In a free country that is the individual's choice, not the state's. State experimentation in curbing freedom of expression is startling and frightening doctrine in a country dedicated to self-government by its people. I reject the holding that either state or nation can punish people for having their say in matters of public concern. . . .

**636**

This statute imposes state censorship over the theater, moving pictures, radio, television, leaflets, magazines, books and newspapers. No doubt the statute is broad enough to make criminal the "publication, sale, presentation or exhibition" of many of the world's great classics, both secular and religious.

The Court condones this expansive state censorship by painstakingly analogizing it to the law of criminal libel. As a result of this refined analysis, the Illinois statute emerges labeled a "group libel law." This label may make the Court's holding more palatable for those who sustain it, but the sugar-coating does not make the censorship less deadly. However tagged, the Illinois law is not that criminal libel which has been "defined, limited and constitutionally recognized time out of mind."[4] For as "constitutionally recognized" that crime has provided for punishment of false, malicious, scurrilous charges against individuals, not against huge groups. This limited scope of the law of criminal libel is of no small importance. It has confined state punishment of speech and expression to the narrowest of areas involving nothing more than purely private feuds. Every expansion of the law of criminal libel so as to punish discussions of matters of public concern means a corresponding invasion of the area dedicated to free expression by the First Amendment.

Prior efforts to expand the scope of criminal libel beyond its traditional boundaries have not usually met with widespread popular acclaim. "Seditious libel" was such an expansion and it did have its day, particularly in the English Court of Star Chamber. But the First Amendment repudiated seditious libel for this country. And one need only glance through the parliamentary discussion of Fox's Libel Law passed in England in 1792, to sense the bad odor of criminal libel in that country even when confined to charges against individuals only.

---

[4] The Court's finding of a close kinship between "criminal libel" and "group-libel" because both contain the word "libel" and have some factors in common is reminescent of what Earl Stanhope said in 1792 in discussing Mr. Fox's Libel Bill. He was arguing that a jury of laymen might more likely protect liberty than judges, because judges were prone to rely too heavily on word books. "He put the case, that an action for a libel was brought for using a modern word, not to be found in any grammar or glossary, viz. for saying that a man was 'a great bore;' a jury would laugh at such a ground of prosecution, but the judges would turn to their grammars and glossaries, and not being able to meet with it, would say they could not find such a phrase as 'a great bore,' but they had found a wild boar, which no doubt it meant; and yet it could not be, as a wild boar had four legs, and a man was a two legged animal; then it must mean, that the plaintiff was like a wild boar in disposition, which was a wicked libel, and therefore let the defendant be hanged." 29 Hansard, Parliamentary History of England, p. 1411.

The Court's reliance on *Chaplinsky* v. *New Hampshire,* 315 U. S. 568, is also misplaced. New Hampshire had a state law making it an offense to direct insulting words at an *individual* on a public street. Chaplinsky had violated that law by calling a man vile names "face-to-face." We pointed out in that context that the use of such "fighting words" was not an essential part of exposition of ideas. Whether the words used in their context here are "fighting words" in the same sense is doubtful, but whether so or not they are not addressed to or about *individuals*. Moreover, the leaflet used here was also the means adopted by an assembled group to enlist interest in their efforts to have legislation enacted. And the "fighting" words were but a part of arguments on questions of wide public interest and importance. Freedom of petition, assembly, speech and press could be greatly abridged by a practice of meticulously scrutinizing every editorial, speech, sermon or other printed matter to extract two or three naughty words on which to hang charges of "group libel." The *Chaplinsky* case makes no such broad inroads on First Amendment freedoms. Nothing Mr. Justice Murphy wrote for the Court in that case or in any other case justifies any such inference.

Unless I misread history the majority is giving libel a more expansive scope and more respectable status than it was ever accorded even in the Star Chamber. For here it is held to be punishable to give publicity to any picture, moving picture, play, drama or sketch, or any printed matter which a judge may find unduly offensive to any race, color, creed or religion. In other words, in arguing for or against the enactment of laws that may differently affect huge groups, it is now very dangerous indeed to say something critical of one of the groups. And any "person, firm or corporation" can be tried for this crime. "Person, firm or corporation" certainly includes a book publisher, newspaper, radio or television station, candidate or even a preacher.

It is easy enough to say that none of this latter group have been proceeded against under the Illinois Act. And they have not —yet. But emotions bubble and tempers flare in racial and religious controversies, the kind here involved. It would not be easy for any court, in good conscience, to narrow this Act so as to exclude from it any of those I have mentioned. Furthermore, persons tried under the Act could not even get a jury trial except as to the bare fact of publication. Here, the court simply charged the jury that Beauharnais was guilty if he had caused distribution of the leaflet. Such trial by judge rather than by jury was outlawed in England in 1792 by Fox's Libel Law. . . .

We are told that freedom of petition and discussion are in no danger "while this Court sits." This case raises considerable doubt. Since those who peacefully petition for changes in the law are not to be protected "while this Court sits," who is? I do not agree that the Constitution leaves freedom of petition assembly, speech, press or worship at the mercy of a case-by-case, day-by-day majority of this Court. I had supposed that our people could rely for their freedom on the Constitution's commands, rather than on the grace of this Court on an individual case basis. To say that a legislative body can, with this Court's approval, make it a crime to petition for and publicly discuss proposed legislation seems as farfetched to me as it would be to say that a valid law could be enacted to punish a candidate for President for telling the people his views. I think the First Amendment, with the Fourteenth, "absolutely" forbids such laws without any "ifs" or "buts" or "whereases." Whatever the danger, if any, in such public discussions, it is a danger the Founders deemed outweighed by the danger incident to the stifling of thought and speech. The Court does not act on this view of the Founders. It calculates what it deems to be the danger of public discussion, holds the scales are tipped on the side of state suppression, and upholds state censorship. This method of decision offers little protection to First Amendment liberties "while this Court sits."

If there be minority groups who hail this holding as their victory, they might consider the possible relevancy of this ancient remark:

"Another such victory and I am undone."

[The appendix containing a copy of the brochure involved is omitted.]

## Note

1. In the *Klapprott case*, 127 N. J. L. 395, 22 Atl. 2d 877 (1941), distinguished in the *Beauharnais* opinion, the New Jersey statute provided:

"Any person who shall, in the presence of two or more persons, in any language, make or utter any speech, statement or declaration, which in any way incites, counsels, promotes, or advocates hatred, abuse, violence or hostility against any group or groups of persons residing or being in this state by reason of race, color, religion or manner of worship, shall be guilty of a misdemeanor."

The Court's opinion, holding the statute unconstitutional, reads in part as follows:

"It is our view that the statute, *supra*, by punitive sanction, tends to restrict what one may say lest by one's utterances there be incited or advocated hatred, hostility or violence against a group 'by reason of race, color, religion or manner of worship.' But additionally and looking now to strict statutory construction, is the statute definite, clear and precise so as to be free from the constitutional infirmity of the vague and indefinite? That the terms 'hatred,' 'abuse,' 'hostility,' are abstract and indefinite admits of no contradiction. When do they arise? Is it to be left to a jury to conclude beyond reasonable doubt when the emotion of hatred or hostility is aroused in the mind of the listener as a result of what a speaker has said? Nothing in our criminal law can be invoked to justify so wide a discretion. The criminal code must be definite and informative so that there may be no doubt in the mind of the citizenry that the interdicted act or conduct is illicit. The element of 'violence,' mentioned in the statute, is universally understood to connote the unlawful exercise of force, *i. e.*, a breach of the peace, but in the indictments before us neither breach of the peace nor resulting violence are alleged. Unbridled license in the matter of speech has no absolute immunity either in the federal courts or the courts of the states generally (*cf. Gitlow v. New York* [268 U. S. 652]); but in the matter of free speech the utterances subject to punishment must be of the class that bring injury to society as such or are intended so to do. The cases cited above make this abundantly clear." 127 N. J. L. at 401.

The Supreme Court quoted this opinion with approval in *Winters v. New York, supra.*

Other group libel statutes are Ind. Stat. §§ 10–904 to 10–914 (Burns) (contains also a provision for a civil suit for an injunction); Conn. Rev. Stat. c. 417, § 8376 (1949) (limited to advertisements); West Va. Code § 6109 (1949) (limited to picture and theatre performances); Mass. Laws c. 272 § 98 c (Supp. 1951) (provides that any person who publishes ". . . any false, written or printed material with the intent to maliciously promote hatred of any group of persons in the commonwealth because of race, color or religion shall be guilty of libel . . ."). See discussion in Note, 28 Mass. L. Q. 104 (Dec. 1943); Perlman and Ploscowe, *False, Defamatory, Anti-racial and Anti-religious Propoganda and the Use of the Mails,* 4 Law. Guild Rev. 13 (1944). For a collection of local group libel ordinances, see Tanenhaus, *Group Libel,* 35 Corn. L. Q. 261, 283–5 (1950).

## AN ACT TO MAKE UNLAWFUL THE DEFAMATION OF RACIAL, RELIGIOUS OR NATIONAL GROUPS

Proposed model statute suggested in Note, 47 Col. L. Rev. 595, 609–12 (1947)

*Section I. Findings.*
The State has a special interest in the preservation of harmonious relations among its people. In order that the people be permitted to reach decisions on matters of public concern on the basis of free choice among conflicting doctrines, freedom of speech must be guarded jealously, not only from governmental interference but from private restraint and obstruction as well. Where such doctrines involve discussion of racial, religious and

national groups, special problems arise. False representations of fact about these groups made in support of a course of action impede the free interchange and wise choice of ideas because the enormity and repetition of such falsehoods have been shown to increase their acceptance. Free interchange and wise choice are also impeded when resort is had to violence, or when threats or insults are uttered for the purpose of intimidation. Experience has shown that substitution of such conduct for free and frank discussion endangers the peace of the community by engendering unrest, anger, violent resentment and a clear and present danger of grave evil in the community.

*Section II. Definitions.* As used in this Act:

A. *Public place* means any publicly owned place, any public conveyance, any place where at the time of the offense the public is present by invitation or sufferance with or without the payment of a fee, or any place where 20 or more persons are present;

B. *Utter* means to communicate, cause to be communicated, or assist in communicating, by the spoken or written word or by any sign, picture, or symbol including, but not limited to, communication by any electrical or mechanical means;

C. *Person* means any individual, partnership, corporation, unincorporated association, or organization;

D. *Defamatory statement* means any utterance which, directly or by innuendo, holds up the group, person or persons concerning whom it is uttered, to public contempt, hatred, shame, disgrace, or obloquy, or causes him or them to be shunned, avoided or injured in his or their business, profession, or occupation;

E. *Racial, religious or national group* means any racial, religious or national group, a portion thereof, or a person because of his belonging to such group or portion thereof;

F. *Authorized corporation* means a non-profit corporation, chartered by the United States or any state thereof, authorized to do business in this State and which has as its purpose, or among its purposes, the protection of the civil or political liberties or other rights of the aggrieved group.

[G. *Breach of the peace* means an utterance which, when judged by the probable reactions of a person of normal self-control, tends to provoke violence, or incites to violence, or which tends to stir anger, unrest or violent resentment on the part of those abused or on the part of others against those abused, or tends to create a disturbance.]*

---

* The criminal provisions of the proposed statute are bracketed; removal of the bracketed portions would leave a complete civil statute.

[Emerson]—41                                                     

*Section III. Group libel and slander prohibited.*

A. No person shall utter in a public place any false and defamatory statement of fact concerning a racial, religious or national group.

B. An action authorized by this section may be commenced by:

    (1) a representative number of individuals who are members of an aggrieved racial, religious or national group,

    (2) an authorized corporation,

    (3) the Attorney General, or

    (4) the district attorney of any county.

C. Any person who has violated subsection A of this section shall be ordered to retract, in a manner deemed appropriate by the court, the false and defamatory statement which he uttered, and may be ordered (1) to refrain from repeating the false and defamatory statement which he uttered or its substantial equivalent, and (2) to post a bond in a reasonable amount and for a reasonable period of time conditioned upon his not violating this section; *provided* that after a person has had three judgments rendered against him under this section, an order to post such a bond shall be mandatory. No money damages shall be awarded to a plaintiff in an action brought under this section.

D. An action commenced under this section may be discontinued only with the court's permission.

E. If an action under this section is commenced by a plaintiff or plaintiffs authorized by paragraph (1), subsection B of this section, the defendant may move to dismiss the action on the ground that the plaintiff or plaintiffs are not representative of the defamed group, but such motion may be made only before answering. If the court finds for the defendant on the motion, the court, before dismissing such action, shall afford the plaintiff or plaintiffs a reasonable period in which to join as parties plaintiff additional members of the group. A dismissal of an action upon such a motion shall not be deemed or stated by the defendant to have been upon the merits. Such a statement is a defamatory statement.

F. Actions brought under this section must be commenced within one year after the occurrence of the defamatory conduct complained of.

G. An action under this section may be brought in any court of general jurisdiction in this State.

H. Upon motion of the defendant in an action commenced by a plaintiff or plaintiffs authorized under paragraphs (1) or (2) of subsection B of this section, an undertaking shall be provided by such plaintiff or plaintiffs in the amount of $300 conditioned upon the action's being carried forward and upon the payment of costs should the action be unsuccessful.

I. Any judgment on the merits rendered in an action authorized by this section shall constitute a defense in any subsequent suit brought under this section based on the same utterance.

[*Section IV. Breach of peace prohibited.*

A. It shall be unlawful for any person to utter, in a public place, concerning a racial, religious or national group under circumstances tending to a breach of the peace:

(1) any threat of violence,

(2) any offensive, abusive, insulting or derogatory words except when used in the course of and as part of an exposition primarily directed to the advocacy of ideas on matters of public concern, or

(3) any false and defamatory statement of fact.

B. Any person violating this section shall, upon the first conviction thereof, be fined not less than $25 nor more than $250, or imprisoned for not more than 3 months, or both and upon the second or subsequent conviction, be fined not less than $50 nor more than $1000 or imprisoned for not more than 6 months, or both. In addition to such punishment the Court may order the defendant to post a bond in a reasonable amount and for a reasonable period of time conditioned upon his not violating this section. An order to post such a bond shall be mandatory upon the third conviction for violating this section.]

*Section V. Burden of proof.*

Whenever in an action under section 3 [or in a prosecution under paragraph (3), subsection A of section 4] the plaintiff [or prosecution] has shown that the utterance is defamatory, the burden shall be upon the defendant to come forward with evidence of its truth until, but only until, a prima facie case of its truth has been established.

*Section VI. Separability of provisions.*

If any provision of this Act, or the application thereof to any person or circumstances, is held invalid, the remainder of this Act and the application of such provisions to other persons or circumstances shall not be affected thereby.

### Note

1. For Federal group libel bills which would make it unlawful to bring defamatory literature into the country or ship it across state lines, see Baum, *Good and Bad Libel Bills*, Congress Weekly, Sept.

19, 1949, pp. 9–12; National Community Relations Advisory Council Bulletin No. 11, *Federal Group Libel Legislation* (1949).

2. In some situations actions against group libel have been attempted under the general libel laws:

(a) In some states the criminal libel laws seem broad enough to cover aspects of group defamation. See Nev. Laws § 10110 (Hillyer 1929); N. Mex. Stat. §§ 41–2725 to 41–2727 (1941); Cal. Pen. Code, c. 11 § 258 (Deering 1949) (defines "slander"). See also California Educational Code, §§ 8271–2 (Deering 1943), which forbids teachers and textbooks to cast aspersion upon the race and color of citizens. In some cases, as in the *Spielman* case cited by Mr. Justice Frankfurter, prosecutions against defamers of groups have been upheld even though there is no showing that particular individuals have been affected. See, *e. g., People v. Turner*, 28 Cal. App. 766, 154 Pac. 34 (1915); *Crane v. State*, 14 Okla. Crim. 30, 166 Pac. 1110 (1917); *People v. Gordon*, 63 Cal. App. 627, 219 Pac. 486 (1923); *Alumbaugh v. State*, 39 Ga. App. 559, 147 S. E. 714 (1929) (defamatory remarks about Knights of Columbus). For cases holding that harm to individuals must be shown, see *Drozda v. State*, 86 Tex. Crim. 614, 218 S. W. 765 (1920); *People v. Edmondson*, 168 Misc. 142, 4 N. Y. Supp. 2d 257 (1938). Despite the possibility of prosecution in many jurisdictions, action against group defamers is rarely taken under criminal libel statutes. See Tanenhaus, *Group Libel*, 35 Corn. L. Q. 261, 263–76 (1950); Note, 61 Yale L. J. 252 (1952).

(b) A civil action can generally not be brought for defamation of a large group (sometimes designated a "class") unless the individual can show that the communication applies to him in a special way. In case of a small group, individuals may sue if the definition clearly applies to every single member or if the group is so small that there can be no doubt that it covers all belonging to it. Groups also have been allowed to sue. Partnerships and corporations, though not in a position to claim mental anguish, can show pecuniary harm because of disparagement of business reputation or credit standing. Unincorporated groups face considerable procedural obstacles. For a successful suit brought by a union, see *Kirkwood v. Westchester Newspapers*, 287 N. Y. 373, 39 N. E. 2d 919 (1942) (under N. Y. Gen. Assoc. Law § 12 (1942), permitting suit by president or treasurer). For a more typical case, however, see *Fowler v. Curtis Publishing Co.*, 182 F. 2d 377 (C. A. D. C., 1950). Here the Court described an article in a popular magazine as a "caustic, merciless diatribe depicting taxicab drivers in the Nation's capital as ill-mannered, brazen, and contemptuous of their patrons . . . cheating their customers when opportunity arose." The article was illustrated by a picture which showed one of the cabs of the company for which the plaintiff driver was working in such a way that the name could be clearly identified by the reader. The Court nevertheless affirmed the lower court's dismissal of the complaint of one of the drivers, for failure to state a cause of action.

**644**

According to Tanenhaus, *supra,* pp. 263–5:

"Courts have held that actions could not be maintained by individuals when the 'Stivers clan,' 'wine-joint' owners, insurance agents, correspondence schools, trading-stamp concerns, the officials of a labor union, and antique dealers were libeled. Plaintiffs were permitted to sustain actions when the 'Fenstermaker family,' the members of a partnership, a staff of young doctors at a particular hospital, a court-martial, the occupants of a house, a jury, a county commission, a board of town trustees, an election board, the administrative board of a university, a group of coroner's physicians, and a group of harness-makers in a fire department were defamed. Actions by individuals were unsuccessful against publications alleging that most of the persons at a donation party were there for the liquor, part of a named association consisted of a gang of blackmailers, some members of a particular hose company had committed a theft, one of a man's sons was a thief, and that several of a group of six witnesses would be indicted for perjury. The courts did, on the other hand, find that 'subordinate engineers of a construction company or some of them,' and 'all radio editors save one' were sufficiently narrow categories to permit suits."

3. In addition to ethnic and religious minorities, political groups and parties are of course frequent objects of vilification. The question has been raised whether libel actions should be available to these groups. For the view that all such groups, except official parties, should be protected, provided the justification of "fair comment" is retained and the range of actionable words is limited, see Note, 98 U. of Pa. L. Rev. 865 (1950).

4. The effectiveness of group libel laws has been seriously questioned. Some of the objections are: (a) Prosecuting attorneys would be reluctant to prosecute and juries would rarely represent the point of view of minority groups. (b) Because of their necessarily vague language group libel laws might be used to suppress legitimate controversial opinions, contrary to their original purpose. (c) Such laws might make the courtroom a sounding-board for professional propagandists who would attempt to benefit from the prosecution by representing themselves as martyrs. (d) In the case of statutes permitting civil suits one libel might destroy a publisher who was sued separately by every member of a group. (e) Such a situation might also result in the clogging of court calendars. (f) Damages would be difficult to assess. (g) One member of an injured group might jeopardize its reputation by submitting what might be delicate and controversial issues to the official judgment of the jury. See 1 Chafee, *Government and Mass Communications,* pp. 122–130 (1947); Note, 61 Yale L. J. 252, 259–261; Tanenhaus, *supra,* pp. 297–302.

5. Generally on the subject of group libel laws, see Chafee, *Free Speech in the United States,* p. 174 (1941); 1 Chafee, *Government and Mass Communications,* pp. 116–130 (1947); Fraenkel, *Our Civil Liberties,* pp. 18–20, 73, 87–88 (1944); American Civil Liberties Union, *The Case Against Legal Restraints on Racial Libels and Anonymous Publications* (1946); Fineberg, *Can Anti-Semitism Be Outlawed?,* 6 Con-

temporary Jewish Record 619 (1943); Vishniak, *An International Convention Against Anti-Semitism* (1946); Pekelis, *Law and Social Action*, pp. 187–203 (1950). For descriptions and analysis of literature and other propaganda fomenting hatred of minority groups, see *e. g.*, Anti-Defamation League, *Anti-Semitism in the United States in 1947* (1948); Forster, *A Measure of Freedom*, pp. 36–79 (1950); Forster and Epstein, *The Troublemakers* (1952); Myrdal, *An American Dilemma*, pp. 455–62 (1944); Weintraub, *How Secure These Rights?*, pp. 92–5 (1949); Curtiss, *An Appraisal of the Protocols of Zion* (1942); Strong, *Organized Anti-Semitism in the United States* (1941); Adorno, *Anti-Semitism and Fascist Propaganda*, in Simmel, *Anti-Semitism: A Social Disease* (1946); Kris and Speier, *German Radio Propaganda* (1944); Kracauer, *From Caligari to Hitler, A Psychological History of the German Film* (1947); see also Noble, *The Negro in Films* (1948); Kracauer, *National Types as Hollywood Presents Them*, 13 Pub. Op. Q. 53 (1949). As to defamation of political groups see Bone, *"Smear" Politics—An Analysis of 1940 Campaign Literature*, American Council on Public Affairs (1941); Britt and Menefee, *Did the Publicity of the Dies Committee Influence Public Opinion?*, 3 Pub. Op. Q. 449 (1939). For a brief summary of the psychology of prejudice against minority groups, see Doob, *Social Psychology* (1952). See also materials cited in Chapter VI, *infra*.

## Alternative Proposals for Combatting Hate Propaganda

Alternative proposals that have been suggested for combatting hate propaganda include:

(1) "Compulsory reply" statutes requiring publishers to print a rebuttal. Under one such proposal an Advisory Committee composed of members of minority groups is to decide whether to reply and to designate a writer. See Rothenberg, *The Right of Reply to Libels in the Press*, 23 J. Comp. Legis. & Int. L. 38 (1941).

(2) "Disclosure" measures which forbid anonymously published defamation and compel groups that "attempt to influence public opinion" to register. See, Report of the President's Committee on Civil Rights, *To Secure These Rights*, pp. 164–5 (1947); Institute of Living Law, *Combatting Totalitarian Propaganda: The Method of Exposure*, 10 U. of Chi. L. Rev. 107 (1943); Smith, *Democratic Control of Propaganda Through Registration and Disclosure I*, 6 Pub Op. Q. 27 (1942). Florida has a statute requiring disclosure with respect to libels of religious groups. Fla. Stat. Ann. § 836.11 (Supp. 1950). Federal legislation has been proposed which would deny use of the mails to anonymous hate propaganda. S. 990, 77th Cong., 1st Sess. (1941).

## Note

For the belief that it is impossible to seriously affect prejudice by legal means, see Lippit and Radke, *New Trends in the Investigation of Prejudice*, 244 Annals of the Am. Acad. of Pol. and Soc. Sci. 167 (1946). For the suggestion that counterpropaganda programs be instituted by the government, see Institute of Living Law, *Combatting Totalitarian Propaganda: The Method of Enlightenment*, 27 Minn. L. Rev. 545 (1943); Riesman, *Government Education for Democracy*, 5 Pub. Op. Q. 199 (1941); Riesman, *Democracy and Defamation: Fair Game and Fair Comment II*, 42 Col. L. Rev. 1282, 1318 (1942). For studies of specific attempts at counterpropaganda, see, e. g., Rosen, *Effect of Motion Picture Gentleman's Agreement on Attitude Toward Jews*, 26 J. Psych. 525 (1948); *Two Social Scientists View No Way Out*, 10 Commentary 388 (1950); *Analysis of the Film Don't Be A Sucker: A Study in Communication*, 15 Pub. Op. Q. 243 (1951); Wiese and Cole, *A Study of Children's Attitudes and the Influence of a Commercial Picture*, 21 J. Psych. 151 (1946) (effect of film Tomorrow the World, which is story of American college professor who adopts 12 year old boy, on attitude of youth toward Nazi and American way of life); Cooper and Jahoda, *The Essence of Propaganda: How Prejudiced People Respond to Anti-Prejudice Propaganda*, 32 J. of Psych. 15 (1947); Kendall and Wolf, *The Analysis of Deviant Cases*, in Lazarsfeld (ed.), *Communications Research 1948–1949*, p. 132 (1949) (study of process through which readers misunderstood message of anti-prejudice cartoon); Wilmer, *Attitude as a Determinant of Perception in the Mass Media of Communication: Reaction to the Motion Picture Home of the Brave* (unpub. dissertation, Univ. of Cal., 1951) cited in 6 Quarterly of Film, Radio and Television 291 (1952); Raths and Trager, *Public Opinion and "Crossfire,"* 21 J. of Ed. Sociology 345 (1948); Sherif and Sargent, *Ego-Involvement and the Mass Media*, 3 J. of Social Issues 8 (No. 3, 1947). See also, Flowerman, *Mass Propaganda and the War Against Bigotry*, 42 J. of Abnormal and Social Psych. 429 (1947); Parsons, *Propaganda and Social Control*, 5 Psychiatry 551 (1942); Rose, *Studies in Reduction of Prejudice* (1947); Bierstedt, *Information and Attitudes*, Appen. 5 in MacIver, *The More Perfect Union* (1948); Williams, *The Reduction of Intergroup Tensions*, Soc. Sci. Res. Bull. No. 57 (1947); Watson, *Action for Unity* (1947). For suggested additional research see Citron, *Anti-Minority Remarks; A Problem for Action Research*, 45 J. Abnormal and Social Psych. 99 (1950); Van Til and Denemark, *Intercultural Education*, Rev. of Ed. Research, p. 274 (Oct. 1950), reprinted in part in Chapter IX, *infra*. See also other materials discussed in Chapter IX.

## Note on the General Law of Libel and Slander of Individuals

This entire branch of the common law, which grants money damages in civil suits to those whose reputations have been harmed by disparaging and defamatory statements, fits directly within the general scope of this chapter. The subject is too vast for treatment here, however, and is generally covered in a course on Torts. A brief mention of matters of special interest and reference to some of the general literature is all that space permits.

(1) *Privilege and Immunity:* A problem of special current interest is that of legislators and witnesses who harm the reputation of individuals and groups on the floor of the legislature or at committee hearings. Statements made under such circumstances are generally held privileged. Moreover, so-called fair and accurate newspaper accounts without malice are likewise privileged. Thus persons who are falsely accused in legislative proceedings are left virtually defenseless against possible harm done to their reputations, and the ensuing social and economic consequences. See, generally, Note, *Defamation Immunity,* 18 U. of Chi. L. Rev. 591 (1951); Yankwich, *The Immunity of Congressional Speech—Its Origin, Meaning and Scope,* 99 U. of Pa. L. Rev. 960 (1951); Notes, 36 Va. L. Rev. 767 (1950); 16 U. of Chi. L. Rev. 544 (1949); Barnett, *The Privilege of Defamation by Private Report of Public Official Proceedings,* 31 Ore. L. Rev. 185 (1952). On the immunity of executive officers, see 132 A. L. R. 1340 (1941). Cf. *Joint Anti-Fascist Refugee Committee v. McGrath,* set forth in Chapter IV, *supra.* As to privilege of witnesses informing the FBI about government employees, see also Chapter IV, *supra.*

In addition to fair and accurate news reports, newspapers are generally permitted to make fair comment on matters of public concern. This includes matters of government, problems involving religious, educational and charitable institutions and their officers and employees, the administration of justice, and plays, books and motion pictures. All persons in public life, such as candidates for office, actors, ministers, educators, players in sports, and public contractors are also included. The legal doctrine has it that fair comment must be based on facts truly stated. It must not contain imputations as to corrupt motives not justified by the facts. The comment should express the writer's honest opinion. All attacks on motives or character or a person's private life or accusations of crime or in terms of degrading or insulting epithets must be related to the subject of criticism. The application of these standards is of course not always simple. For a brief discussion see Yankwich, *The Protection of Newspaper Comment on Public Men and Public Matters,* 11 La. L. Rev. 327 (1951). An extensive discussion is in Riesman, *Democracy and Defamation: Fair Game and Fair Comment II,* 42 Col. L. Rev. 1282 (1942). See also Noel, *Defamation of Public Officers and Candidates,* 49 Col. L. Rev. 875 (1949); Note, 62 Harv. L. Rev. 1207 (1949). For a recent unsuccessful attempt to prosecute five newspaper men under criminal libel statutes for criticizing public officials in Louisiana, see New York Times, April 19, 1952.

(2) *The Standard.* Some of the difficulties in formulating a standard with respect to group libel that concerned the dissenters in the *Beauharnais* case apply to all types of defamation actions. An interesting problem, focusing attention on the difficulties of regulating com-

**648**

munication according to majority rule, arises in certain cases where the courts attempt to decide what constitutes defamation *per se*. In the case of utterances that some segments of the community would consider laudatory and other segments would think defamatory, which segment of the community should set the standard for the case? Suppose what is involved is a false accusation that the plaintiff obeyed a certain law and suppose that segment of the community to which the plaintiff belongs considers such obedience of the law disreputable? Would granting relief to one falsely accused of obeying the law mean that the courts encourage illegality by (a) not discouraging law breakers in denying recovery and (b) lending their prestige to values of a minority strongly opposed to the law? See *Connelly v. McKay,* 176 Misc. 685, 28 N. Y. Supp. 2d 327 (1941) ; Note, 58 Yale L. J. 1387 (1949). A somewhat similar problem arises where a person is falsely accused of being a member of an unpopular political minority. Compare *Garriga v. Richfield,* 174 Misc. 315, 20 N. Y. Supp. 2d 544 (1940) (as long as party is legal, accusation of membership not defamatory *per se;* case brought prior to Russo-German non-aggression pact), with *Levy v. Gelber,* 175 Misc. 746, 25 N. Y. Supp. 2d 148 (1941) and *Spanel v. Pegler,* 160 F. 2d 619 (C. A. 7, 1947) (libel *per se*). See also, Donnelly, *The Right of Reply: An Alternative to an Action for Libel,* 34 Va. L. Rev. 867, 870–71 (1948) ; Notes, 14 U. of Chi. L. Rev. 697 (1947) ; 22 N. Y. U. L. Q. Rev. 513 (1947).

(3) *Additional Difficulties with Common Law Remedies for Defamation.* Some of the additional problems involved in common law remedies for defamation are:

(a) Great risks in bringing suit because of: (1) Vagueness of the standard alluded to above (i.e., has the plaintiff been held up to contempt and ridicule) varies from time to time, area to area and group to group. (2) It is a defense that the accusation is substantially true. In mitigation of damages the defendant can prove that plaintiff's reputation is already tarnished. The result of the suit may be a greater injury to the plaintiff's reputation than existed before. (3) Damages are highly uncertain. A small award may mean to the public that plaintiff's reputation is not worth much. (4) Victory in court may not be sufficiently publicized to overcome the effect of defamatory publication. On the contrary the type of publicity given the case may further impair the plaintiff's reputation.

(b) Great risk in publishing because of: (1) Newspaper's strict liability for libelous material it publishes unless it is privileged. (2) The common law considered each copy sold a new libel. Newspapers could thus be subjected to chain libel suits for a single libelous statement in a single issue. (Recent decisions do not generally follow the common law on this point).[1] (3) Time and expense of libel suit to

---

[1] An example of a chain libel suit is that of Annie Oakley who in 48 proceedings recovered against 50 newspapers. Awards varied from $500 to as much as $2500. See Ernst and Lindey, *Hold Your Tongue,* p. 190 (rev. ed. 1950). See also suits brought by Congressman Sweeny because of an article charging him with opposing the appointment of a federal

publisher is very great.  (4) Pre-publication censorship by publisher's own lawyers does not on the whole prevent suits.  These arise largely because of errors in fact that could not be discovered by censors.  Moreover censorship tends to interfere with the smooth workings of a newspaper.  Other techniques for controlling some of the risks of publishing are a contract with the syndicate supplying a story  to save the newspaper or radio station harmless, and libel insurance.  These, of course, still increase the over-all cost of publishing.

(c) At times, when fear of libel prosecutions results in weakening the vigor of debate on controversial issues, they may be said to interfere with the proper function of the free interchange of ideas in a democratic society.

(4) *Suggested Reforms.*  Reforms that have been suggested include:

(a) Optional retraction:  Under the common law a retraction does not excuse a publisher from liability but may go to show no malice and thus eliminate or reduce punitive damages.  Statutes to the same effect exist in several states.  In some others, where they have been broader in scope, such statutes have been declared unconstitutional. Minnesota and California are exceptions.  California, which has a very liberal statute, provides for the elimination of all but special damages if a retraction is published without regard to whether the original item was published with malice.  In Minnesota the retraction has this effect only where the original publication was inadvertently libelous.

(b) Compulsory retraction:  The judgment requires the defendant to print a revised version of the facts.

(c)  The right of reply.  This would provide that newspapers or other media must give space for a reply within a short time to an adversely affected group or individual.  If they fail to do so, a speedy judgment compelling publication of the reply may be obtained.

For an elaboration of these points see:  Donnelly, *The Right of Reply: An Alternative to an Action for Libel,* 34 Va. L. Rev. 867 (1948) ; 1 Chafee, *Government and Mass Communications,* ch. 4 (1947).  For a blackletter summary of the law see, 3 *Restatement of Torts,* §§ 558–623 (1938).  For a historical discussion, see Veeder, *The History and Theory of the Law of Defamation,* 3 Col. L. Rev. 546 (1903), 4 Col. L. Rev. 33 (1904).  For a broadly oriented discussion see Riesman, *Democracy and Defamation,* 42 Col. L. Rev. 727, 1282 (1942).  See also Ernst and Lindey, *Hold Your Tongue* (rev. ed. 1950) ; Courtney, *Absurdities of the Law of Slander and Libel,* 36 Am. L. Rev. 552 (1902).

On the risk because of the uncertainty of outcome and the particular role of the jury see, further, Green, *Relational Interest,* 30 Ill. L. Rev. 314 (1935) ; Wellman, *Luck and Opportunity* (1938).  Consider the possibilities of content analysis for the development of a more scientific approach.  See *infra.*

---

judge because he was a Jew.  Plaintiff brought 68 suits seeking a total of $7,500,000 in damages.  See Donnelly, *The Law of Defamation: Proposals for Reform,* 33 Minn. L. Rev. 609, 627 (1949).  For a ruling that would not permit such suits see *Hartmann v. Time, Inc.,* 166 F. 2d 127 (C. A. 3, 1948), cert. den. 334 U. S. 838 (1948).

On retraction statutes see Notes, 38 Calif. L. Rev. 951 (1950); 64 Harv. L. Rev. 678 (1951); and the cases upholding the Minnesota and California Laws, *Allen v. Pioneer Press Co.*, 40 Minn. 117, 41 N. W. 936 (1889); *Werner v. Southern California Associated Newspapers*, 206 Pac. 2d 952 (Cal. App., 1949), aff'd (5–2) 35 Cal. 2d 121, 216 Pac. 2d 825, 13 A. L. R. 2d 252 (1950), appeal dismissed 340 U. S. 910 (1951).

## Right of Privacy

The individual's right to privacy is another restriction on communication recognized by the weight of authority in those jurisdictions where the matter has been considered. This right is invaded by the use in publication or broadcasting of a person's name or likeness without permission. Intrusion into personal affairs such as eavesdropping, examination of probate records or publication of private letters, also violates the right. The police power and the interest of the public to be informed are of course limitations on its scope. See Warren and Brandeis, *The Right to Privacy*, 4 Harv. L. Rev. 193 (1890) (the classic article that virtually shaped the law). For contemporary discussion and collection of cases see 14 A.L.R.2d 750 (1950); 168 A.L.R. 446 (1947); Ludwig, *"Peace of Mind" in 48 Pieces vs. Uniform Right of Privacy*, 32 Minn. L. Rev. 734 (1948). See also 13 A.L.R.2d 1213 (1950) and *State v. Evjue*, 253 Wis. 146, 33 N. W. 2d 305, 13 A.L.R.2d 1201 (1948), on the constitutionality of a statute prohibiting the publication of the identity of a female who might have been raped. For analysis of broader issues involved in the right to privacy, see Lasswell, *The Threat to Privacy*, ch. XI in MacIver (ed.), *Conflict of Loyalties* (1952).

# CHAPTER VI

# FREEDOM OF SPEECH: CONTROL OVER THE SPECIFIC MEDIA OF COMMUNICATION

## A. STREETS, PARKS AND HALLS: THE RIGHT OF ASSEMBLY, CANVASSING AND PICKETING

### KUNZ v. NEW YORK

Supreme Court of the United States, 1951

340 U. S. 290, 95 L. Ed. 280, 71 S. Ct. 312

MR. CHIEF JUSTICE VINSON delivered the opinion of the Court.
New York City has adopted an ordinance which makes it unlawful to hold public worship meetings on the streets without first obtaining a permit from the city police commissioner.[1] Ap-

---

[1] Section 435–7.0 of chapter 18 of the Administrative Code of the City of New York reads as follows:

"a. Public worship.—It shall be unlawful for any person to be concerned or instrumental in collecting or promoting any assemblage of persons for public worship or exhortation, or to ridicule or denounce any form of religious belief, service or reverence, or to preach or expound atheism or agnosticism, or under any pretense therefor, in any street. A clergyman or minister of any denomination, however, or any person responsible to or regularly associated with any church or incorporated missionary society, or any lay-preacher, or lay-reader may conduct religious services, or any authorized representative of a duly incorporated organization devoted to the advancement of the principles of atheism or agnosticism may preach or expound such cause, in any public place or places specified in a permit therefor which may be granted and issued by the police commissioner. This section shall not be construed to prevent any congregation of the Baptist denomination from assembling in a proper place for the purpose of performing the rites of baptism, according to the ceremonies of that church.

"b. Interference with street services.—It shall be unlawful for any person to disturb, molest or interrupt any clergyman, minister, missionary, lay-preacher or lay-reader, who shall be conducting religious services by authority of a permit, issued hereunder, or any minister or people who shall be performing the rite of baptism as permitted herein, nor shall any person commit any riot or disorder in any such assembly.

"c. Violations.—Any person who shall violate any provision of this section, upon conviction thereof, shall be punished by a fine of not more than twenty-five dollars, or imprisonment for thirty days, or both."

This ordinance was previously challenged in *People v. Smith*, 263 N. Y. 255, 188 N. E. 745, appeal dismissed for want of a substantial federal question, *Smith v. New York*, 292 U. S. 606 (1934). Smith, who had not applied for a permit under the ordinance, argued that the regulation of religious speakers alone constituted an unreasonable classification. None

**652**

pellant, Carl Jacob Kunz, was convicted and fined $10 for violating this ordinance by holding a religious meeting without a permit. The conviction was affirmed by the Appellate Part of the Court of Special Sessions, and by the New York Court of Appeals, three judges dissenting, 300 N. Y. 273, 90 N. E. 2d 455 (1950). The case is here on appeal, it having been urged that the ordinance is invalid under the Fourteenth Amendment.

Appellant is an ordained Baptist minister who speaks under the auspices of the "Outdoor Gospel Work," of which he is the director. He has been preaching for about six years, and states that it is his conviction and duty to "go out on the highways and byways and preach the word of God." In 1946, he applied for and received a permit under the ordinance in question, there being no question that appellant comes within the classes of persons entitled to receive permits under the ordinance.[2] This permit, like all others, was good only for the calendar year in which issued. In November, 1946, his permit was revoked after a hearing by the police commissioner. The revocation was based on evidence that he had ridiculed and denounced other religious beliefs in his meetings.

Although the penalties of the ordinance apply to anyone who "ridicules and denounces other religious beliefs," the ordinance does not specify this as a ground for permit revocation. Indeed, there is no mention in the ordinance of any power of revocation. However, appellant did not seek judicial or administrative review of the revocation proceedings, and any question as to the propriety of the revocation is not before us in this case. In any event, the revocation affected appellant's rights to speak in 1946 only. Appellant applied for another permit in 1947, and again in 1948, but was notified each time that his application was "disapproved," with no reason for the disapproval being given. On September 11, 1948, appellant was arrested for speaking at Columbus Circle in New York City without a permit. It is from the conviction which resulted that this appeal has been taken.

Appellant's conviction was thus based upon his failure to possess a permit for 1948. We are here concerned only with the propriety of the action of the police commissioner in refusing to issue that permit. Disapproval of the 1948 permit application by the police commissioner was justified by the New York courts on the ground that a permit had previously been revoked "for

of the questions involved in the instant appeal were presented in the previous case.

[2] The New York Court of Appeals has construed the ordinance to require that all initial requests for permits by eligible applicants must be granted. 300 N. Y. at 276, 90 N. E. 2d at 456.

good reasons."[3] It is noteworthy that there is no mention in the ordinance of reasons for which such a permit application can be refused. This interpretation allows the police commissioner, an administrative official, to exercise discretion in denying subsequent permit applications on the basis of his interpretation, at that time, of what is deemed to be conduct condemned by the ordinance. We have here, then, an ordinance which gives an administrative official discretionary power to control in advance the right of citizens to speak on religious matters on the streets of New York. As such, the ordinance is clearly invalid as a prior restraint on the exercise of First Amendment rights.

In considering the right of a municipality to control the use of public streets for the expression of religious views, we start with the words of Mr. Justice Roberts that "Wherever the title of streets and parks may rest, they have immemorially been held in trust for the use of the public and, time out of mind, have been used for purposes of assembly, communicating thoughts between citizens, and discussing public questions." *Hague* v. *C. I. O.*, 307 U. S. 496, 515 (1939). Although this Court has recognized that a statute may be enacted which prevents serious interference with normal usage of streets and parks, *Cox* v. *New Hampshire*, 312 U. S. 569 (1941), we have consistently condemned licensing systems which vest in an administrative official discretion to grant or withhold a permit upon broad criteria unrelated to proper regulation of public places. In *Cantwell* v. *Connecticut*, 310 U. S. 296 (1940), this Court held invalid an ordinance which required a license for soliciting money for religious causes. Speaking for a unanimous Court, Mr. Justice Roberts said: "But to condition the solicitation of aid for the perpetuation of religious views or systems upon a license, the grant of which rests in the exercise of a determination by state authority as to what is a religious cause, is to lay a forbidden burden upon the exercise of liberty protected by the Constitution." 310 U. S. at 307. To the same effect are *Lovell* v. *Griffin*, 303 U. S. 444 (1938); *Hague* v. *C. I. O.*, 307 U. S. 496 (1939); *Largent* v. *Texas*, 318 U. S. 418 (1943). In *Saia* v. *New York*, 334 U. S. 558 (1948), we reaffirmed the invalidity of such prior restraints upon the right to speak: "We hold that § 3 of this ordinance is unconstitutional on its face, for it establishes a previous restraint on the right of free speech in violation of the First Amendment which is protected by the Fourteenth Amendment against State

---

[3] The New York Court of Appeals said: "The commissioner had no reason to assume, and no promise was made, that defendant wanted a new permit for any uses different from the disorderly ones he had been guilty of before." 300 N. Y. at 278, 90 N. E. 2d at 457.

action. To use a loudspeaker or amplifier one has to get a permit from the Chief of Police. There are no standards prescribed for the exercise of his discretion." 334 U. S. at 559–560.

The court below has mistakenly derived support for its conclusion from the evidence produced at the trial that appellant's religious meetings had, in the past, caused some disorder. There are appropriate public remedies to protect the peace and order of the community if appellant's speeches should result in disorder or violence. "In the present case, we have no occasion to inquire as to the permissible scope of subsequent punishment." *Near* v. *Minnesota*, 283 U. S. 697, 715 (1931). We do not express any opinion on the propriety of punitive remedies which the New York authorities may utilize. We are here concerned with suppression—not punishment. It is sufficient to say that New York cannot vest restraining control over the right to speak on religious subjects in an administrative official where there are no appropriate standards to guide his action.

*Reversed.*

MR. JUSTICE BLACK concurs in the result.

[Mr. Justice Frankfurter concurred in this case, the *Fiener* case, and the *Niemotko* case, both *infra,* in a single opinion, reprinted in part *infra* in connection with the *Niemotko* case.]

MR. JUSTICE JACKSON, dissenting.
Essential freedoms are today threatened from without and within. It may become difficult to preserve here what a large part of the world has lost—the right to speak, even temperately, on matters vital to spirit and body. In such a setting, to blanket hateful and hate-stirring attacks on races and faiths under the protections for freedom of speech may be a noble innovation. On the other hand, it may be a quixotic tilt at windmills which belittles great principles of liberty. Only time can tell. But I incline to the latter view and cannot assent to the decision.

## I.

. . . At these meetings, Kunz preached, among many other things of like tenor, that "The Catholic Church makes merchandise out of souls," that Catholicism is "a religion of the devil," and that the Pope is "the anti-Christ." The Jews he denounced as "Christ-killers," and he said of them, "All the garbage that didn't believe in Christ should have been burnt in the incinerators. It's a shame they all weren't."

These utterances, as one might expect, stirred strife and threatened violence. Testifying in his own behalf, Kunz stated that he "became acquainted with" one of the complaining wit-

655

nesses, whom he thought to be a Jew, "when he happened to sock one of my Christian boys in the puss." Kunz himself complained to the authorities, charging a woman interrupter with disorderly conduct. He also testified that when an officer is not present at his meetings "I have trouble then," but "with an officer, no trouble."

The contention which Kunz brings here and which this Court sustains is that such speeches on the streets are within his constitutional freedom and therefore New York City has no power to require a permit. He does not deny that this has been and will continue to be his line of talk. He does not claim that he should have been granted a permit; he attacks the whole system of control of street meetings and says the Constitution gives him permission to speak and he needs none from the City.

## II.

The speeches which Kunz has made and which he asserts he has a *right* to make in the future were properly held by the courts below to be out of bounds for a street meeting and not constitutionally protected. This Court, without discussion, makes a contrary assumption which is basic to its whole opinion. It says New York has given "an administrative official discretionary power to control in advance *the right* of citizens to speak on religious matters on the streets." Again, it says that "prior restraint on the exercise of First Amendment *rights*" invalidates the ordinance. (Emphasis supplied.) This seems to take the last step first, assuming as a premise what is in question. Of course, if Kunz is only exercising his constitutional *rights,* then New York can neither restrain nor punish him. But I doubt that the Court's assumption will survive analysis.

This Court today initiates the doctrine that language such as this, in the environment of the street meeting, is immune from prior municipal control. We would have a very different question if New York had presumed to say that Kunz could not speak his piece in his own pulpit or hall. But it has undertaken to restrain him only if he chooses to speak at street meetings. There is a world of difference. The street preacher takes advantage of people's presence on the streets to impose his message upon what, in a sense, is a captive audience. A meeting on private property is made up of an audience that has volunteered to listen. The question, therefore, is not whether New York could, if it tried, silence Kunz, but whether it must place its streets at his service to hurl insults at the passer-by.

What Mr. Justice Holmes said for a unanimous Court in *Schenck* v. *United States,* 249 U. S. 47, 52, has become an axiom:

"The most stringent protection of free speech would not protect a man in falsely shouting fire in a theatre and causing a panic." This concept was applied in one of its few unanimous decisions in recent years, when, through Mr. Justice Murphy, the Court said: "There are certain well-defined and narrowly limited classes of speech, *the prevention and punishment* of which *have never been thought to raise any Constitutional problem*. These include the lewd and obscene, the profane, the libelous, and *the insulting or 'fighting' words*—those which by their very utterance inflict injury or *tend to incite* an immediate breach of the peace. . . ." (Emphasis supplied.) *Chaplinsky* v. *New Hampshire*, 315 U. S. 568, 571–572.

There held to be "insulting or 'fighting' words" were calling one a "God damned racketeer" and a "damned Fascist." Equally inciting and more clearly "fighting words," when thrown at Catholics and Jews who are rightfully on the streets of New York, are statements that "The Pope is the anti-Christ" and the Jews are "Christ-killers." These terse epithets come down to our generation weighted with hatreds accumulated through centuries of bloodshed. They are recognized words of art in the profession of defamation. They are not the kind of insult that men bandy and laugh off when the spirits are high and the flagons are low. They are not in that class of epithets whose literal sting will be drawn if the speaker smiles when he uses them. They are always, and in every context, insults which do not spring from reason and can be answered by none. Their historical associations with violence are well understood, both by those who hurl and those who are struck by these missiles. Jews, many of whose families perished in extermination furnaces of Dachau and Auschwitz, are more than tolerant if they pass off lightly the suggestion that unbelievers in Christ should all have been burned. Of course, people might pass this speaker by as a mental case, and so they might file out of a theatre in good order at the cry of "fire." But in both cases there is genuine likelihood that someone will get hurt.

This Court's prior decisions, as well as its decisions today, will be searched in vain for clear standards by which it does, or lower courts should, distinguish legitimate speaking from that acknowledged to be outside of constitutional protection. One reason for this absence is that this Court has had little experience in deciding controversies over city control of street meetings.
• • •
What evidences that a street speech is so provocative, insulting or inciting as to be outside of constitutional immunity from community interference? Is it determined by the actual reaction

of the hearers? Or is it a judicial appraisal of the inherent quality of the language used? Or both? . . .

It is peculiar that today's opinion makes no reference to the "clear and present danger" test which for years has played some part in free-speech cases. . . .

A hostile reception of his subject certainly does not alone destroy one's right to speak. A temperate and reasoned criticism of Roman Catholicism or Judaism might, and probably would, cause some resentment and protest. But in a free society all sects and factions, as the price of their own freedom to preach their views, must suffer that freedom in others. Tolerance of unwelcome, unorthodox ideas or information is a constitutionally protected policy not to be defeated by persons who would break up meetings they do not relish.

But emergencies may arise on streets which would become catastrophes if there was not immediate police action. The crowd which should be tolerant may be prejudiced and angry or malicious. If the situation threatens to get out of hand for the force present, I think the police may require the speaker, even if within his rights, to yield his right temporarily to the greater interest of peace. Of course, the threat must be judged in good faith to be real, immediate and serious. But silencing a speaker by authorities as a measure of mob control is like dynamiting a house to stop the spread of a conflagration. It may be justified by the overwhelming community interest that flames not be fed as compared with the little interest to be served by continuing to feed them. But this kind of disorder does not abridge the right to speak except for the emergency and, since the speaker was within his constitutional right to speak, it could not be grounds for revoking or refusing him a permit or convicting him of any offense because of his utterance. If he resisted an officer's reasonable demand to cease, he might incur penalties.

And so the matter eventually comes down to the question whether the "words used are used in such circumstances and are of such a nature" that we can say a reasonable man would anticipate the evil result. In this case the Court does not justify, excuse, or deny the inciting and provocative character of the language, and it does not, and on this record could not, deny that when Kunz speaks he poses a "clear and present" danger to peace and order. Why, then, does New York have to put up with it? . . .

### III.

It is worthwhile to note that the judicial technique by which this Court strikes down the ordinance is very different from that

[Emerson]

employed by the New York Court of Appeals, which sustained it. The contrary results appear to be largely due to this dissimilarity.

The Court of Appeals did not treat the ordinance as existing in a vacuum but considered all the facts of the controversy. While it construed the ordinance "as *requiring* the commissioner to give an annual permit for street preaching, *to anyone* who, like defendant, is a minister of religion," 300 N. Y. 273, 276, 90 N. E. 2d 455, 456 (emphasis supplied), it held on the facts that when, as here, the applicant "claims a constitutional right to incite riots, and a constitutional right to the services of policemen to quell those riots," then a permit need not be issued. *Id.* at 278, 90 N. E. 2d at 457.

This Court, however, refuses to take into consideration Kunz's "past" conduct or that his meetings have "caused some disorder." Nor does it deny that disorders will probably occur again. It comes close to rendering an advisory opinion when it strikes down this ordinance without evaluating the factual situation which has caused it to come under judicial scrutiny. If it were not for these characteristics of the speeches by Kunz, this ordinance would not be before us, yet it is said that we can hold it invalid without taking into consideration either what he has done or what he asserts a right to do.

It may happen that a statute will disclose by its very language that it is impossible of construction in a manner consistent with First Amendment rights. Such is the case where it aims to control matters patently not a proper subject of the police power. *Lovell* v. *Griffin,* 303 U. S. 444, 451. Cf. *Hague* v. *C. I. O.,* 307 U. S. 496; *Thornhill* v. *Alabama,* 310 U. S. 88; *Saia* v. *New York,* 334 U. S. 558. Usually, however, the only proper approach takes into consideration both the facts of the case and the construction which the State has placed on the challenged law. *Near* v. *Minnesota,* 283 U. S. 697, 708; *Cantwell* v. *Connecticut, supra,* at 303; *Kovacs* v. *Cooper,* 336 U. S. 77; *Terminiello* v. *Chicago,* 337 U. S. 1. And in the absence of facts in the light of which the statute may be construed, we have said the proper procedure is not to pass on whether it conflicts with First Amendment rights. *United States* v. *Petrillo,* 332 U. S. 1. That the approach will determine the result is indicated by comparison of the *Saia* case, in which an ordinance was held void on its face, with the *Kovacs* case, in which a similar ordinance, when tested as construed and applied, was held valid. The vital difference, as this case demonstrates, is that it is very easy to read a statute to permit some hypothetical violation of civil rights but difficult to draft one which will not be subject to the same infirmity.

**659**

This Court has not applied, and, I venture to predict, will not apply, to federal statutes the standard that they are unconstitutional if it is possible that they may be unconstitutionally applied. We should begin consideration of this case by deciding whether the opportunity to repeat his vituperative street speeches is within Kunz's constitutional rights, and here he must win on the strength of his own right.

## IV.

The question remains whether the Constitution prohibits a city from control of its streets by a permit system which takes into account dangers to public peace and order. I am persuaded that it does not do so, provided, of course, that the city does not so discriminate as to deny equal protection of the law or undertake a censorship of utterances that are not so defamatory, insulting, inciting, or provocative as to be reasonably likely to cause disorder and violence.

The Court does not hold that New York has abused the permit system by discrimination or actual censorship, nor does it deny the abuses on Kunz's part. But neither, says the Court, matters, holding that any prior restraint is bad, regardless of how fairly administered or what abuses it seeks to prevent.

It strikes rather blindly at permit systems which indirectly may affect First Amendment freedoms. Cities throughout the country have adopted permit requirements to control private activities on public streets and for other purposes.[5] The universality of this type of regulation demonstrates a need and indicates widespread opinion in the profession that it is not necessarily incompatible with our constitutional freedoms. Is everybody out of step but this Court? . . .

In the *Chaplinsky* case, *prevention* as well as *punishment* of "limited classes of speech . . . have never been thought to raise *any* Constitutional problem." (Emphasis supplied.) Mr. Justice Holmes pointed out in the *Schenck* case that the Constitution would not protect one from an injunction against uttering words that lead to riot. . In *Cox* v. *New Hampshire*, 312 U. S. 569, 577–578, Chief Justice Hughes, for a unanimous Court, dis-

---

[5] New York, for example, has found a permit system the practical means of controlling meetings in its parks. This Court, as presently constituted, only last Term dismissed an attack on the park permit system "for want of a substantial federal question," JUSTICES BLACK and DOUGLAS dissenting. *Hass v. New York*, 338 U. S. 803. New York also has used the requirement of a permit for assemblages which mask their faces to suppress the Ku Klux Klan, without stopping harmless masquerade balls and the like. Penal Law § 710. The permit system is used in many other situations where conceivable civil liberties are involved.

tinguished the requirement of a license for a parade or procession from other cases now relied on by this Court. He found requirement of a permit there constitutional and observed that such authority "has never been regarded as inconsistent with civil liberties but rather as one of the means of safeguarding the good order upon which they ultimately depend." *Id.*, at 574. The concept of civil liberty without order is the contribution of later-day jurists.

The Court, as authority for stripping New York City of control of street meetings, resurrects *Saia* v. *New York, supra,* which I, like some who now rely on it, had supposed was given decent burial by *Kovacs* v. *Cooper, supra.* Must New York, if it is to avoid chaos in its streets, resort to the sweeping prohibitions sanctioned in *Kovacs,* instead of the milder restraints of this permit system? Compelling a choice between allowing all meetings or no meetings is a dubious service to civil liberties.

Of course, as to the press, there are the best of reasons against any licensing or prior restraint. Decisions such as *Near* v. *Minnesota, supra,* hold any licensing or prior restraint of the press unconstitutional, and I heartily agree. But precedents from that field cannot reasonably be transposed to the street-meeting field. The impact of publishing on public order has no similarity with that of a street meeting. Publishing does not make private use of public property. It reaches only those who choose to read, and, in that way, is analogous to a meeting held in a hall where those who come do so by choice. Written words are less apt to incite or provoke to mass action than spoken words, speech being the primitive and direct communication with the emotions. Few are the riots caused by publication alone, few are the mobs that have not had their immediate origin in harangue. The vulnerability of various forms of communication to community control must be proportioned to their impact upon other community interests.

It is suggested that a permit for a street meeting could be required if the ordinance would prescribe precise standards for its grant or denial. . . .

Of course, standards for administrative action are always desirable, and the more exact the better. But I do not see how this Court can condemn municipal ordinances for not setting forth comprehensive First Amendment standards. This Court never has announced what those standards must be, it does not now say what they are, and it is not clear that any majority could agree on them. In no field are there more numerous individual opinions among the Justices. The Court as an institution not infrequently disagrees with its former self or relies on distinctions that are not very substantial. . . . It seems hypercritical to strike down local laws on their faces for want of standards when we have no standard. And I do not find it required by existing authority. I think that where speech is outside of constitutional immunity the local community or the State is left a large measure of discretion as to the means for dealing with it.

## V.

If the Court is deciding that the permit system for street meetings is so unreasonable as to deny due process of law, it would seem appropriate to point out respects in which it is unreasonable. This I am unable to learn, from this or any former decision. The Court holds, however, that Kunz must not be required to get permission, the City must sit by until some incident, perhaps a sanguinary one, occurs and then there are unspecified "appropriate public remedies." We may assume reference is to the procedure of the *Feiner* case which, with one-third of the Court dissenting, is upheld.[9] This invites comparison of the merits of the two methods both as to impact on civil liberties and as to achieving the ends of public order. . . .

Turning then to the permit system as applied by the Court of Appeals, whose construction binds us, we find that issuance the first time is required. Denial is warranted only in such unusual cases as where an applicant has had a permit which has been revoked for cause and he asserts the right to continue the conduct which was cause for revocation. If anything less than a reasonable certainty of disorder was shown, denial of a permit would

---

[9] I join in *Feiner v. New York*. When in a colored neighborhood Feiner urged the colored people to rise up in arms and fight, he was using words which may have been "rhetorical," but it was the rhetoric of violence. Of course, we cannot tell, from a cold record, whether the action taken was the wisest way of dealing with the situation. But some latitude for honest judgment must be left to the locality. It is a startling proposition to me that serious public utterance which advises, encourages, or incites to a crime may not be made a crime because within constitutional protection. . . .

However, the case of *Niemotko v. Maryland* illustrates the danger of abuse of the permit system which the Court should be alert to prevent. There is no evidence that those applicants were, ever had been, or threatened to be, disorderly or abusive in speech or manner, or that their speaking would be likely to incite or provoke any disorder. The denial of permission for the meeting was charged and appears to have been due to applicants' religious belief that they should not salute any flag, which they may not be compelled to do, and their conscientious objections to bearing arms in war, which Congress has accepted as a valid excuse from combat duty. In the courts of Maryland, this denial, so based, was conclusive against the right to speak. This was use of the permit system for censorship, and the convictions cannot stand.

**662**

be improper. The procedure by which that decision is reached commends itself to the orderly mind—complaints are filed, witnesses are heard, opportunity to cross-examine is given, and decision is reached by what we must assume to be an impartial and reasonable administrative officer, and, if he denies the permit, the applicant may carry his cause to the courts. He may thus have a civil test of his rights without the personal humiliation of being arrested as presenting a menace to public order. It seems to me that this procedure better protects freedom of speech than to let everyone speak without leave, but subject to surveillance and to being ordered to stop in the discretion of the police.

It is obvious that a permit is a source of security and protection for the civil liberties of the great number who are entitled to receive them. It informs the police of the time and place one intends to speak, which allows necessary steps to insure him a place to speak where overzealous police officers will not order everyone who stops to listen to move on, and to have officers present to insure an orderly meeting. Moreover, disorder is less likely, for the speaker knows that if he provokes disorder his permit may be revoked, and the objector may be told that he has a remedy by filing a complaint and does not need to take the law in his own hands. Kunz was not arrested in 1946, when his speeches caused serious objections, nor was he set upon by the crowd. Instead, they did the orderly thing and made complaints which resulted in the revocation of his permit. This is the method that the Court frustrates today.

Of course, emergencies may arise either with or without the permit system. A speaker with a permit may go beyond bounds and incite violence, or a mob may undertake to break up an authorized and properly conducted meeting. In either case, the policeman on the spot must make the judgment as to what measures will most likely avoid violent disorders. But these emergencies seem less likely to occur with the permit system than if every man and his adversary take the law in their own hands.

The law of New York does not segregate, according to their diverse nationalities, races, religions, or political associations, the vast hordes of people living in its narrow confines. Every individual in this frightening aggregation is legally free to live, to labor, to travel, when and where he chooses. In streets and public places, all races and nationalities and all sorts and conditions of men walk, linger and mingle. Is it not reasonable that the City protect the dignity of these persons against fanatics who take possession of its streets to hurl into its crowds defamatory epithets that hurt like rocks?

**663**

If any two subjects are intrinsically incendiary and divisive, they are race and religion. Racial fears and hatreds have been at the root of the most terrible riots that have disgraced American civilization. They are ugly possibilities that overhang every great American city. The "consecrated hatreds of sect" account for more than a few of the world's bloody disorders. These are the explosives which the Court says Kunz may play with in the public streets, and the community must not only tolerate but aid him. I find no such doctrine in the Constitution.

In this case there is no evidence of a purpose to suppress speech, except to keep it in bounds that will not upset good order. If there are abuses of censorship or discrimination in administering the ordinance, as well there may be, they are not proved in this case. This Court should be particularly sure of its ground before it strikes down, in a time like this, the going, practical system by which New York has sought to control its street-meeting problem.

Addressing himself to the subject, "Authority and the Individual," one of the keenest philosophers of our time observes: "The problem, like all those with which we are concerned, is one of balance; too little liberty brings stagnation, and too much brings chaos."[11] Perhaps it is the fever of our times that inclines the Court today to favor chaos. My hope is that few will take advantage of the license granted by today's decision. But life teaches one to distinguish between hope and faith.

## FEINER v. NEW YORK

Supreme Court of the United States, 1951
340 U. S. 315, 95 L. Ed. 295, 71 S. Ct. 303

MR. CHIEF JUSTICE VINSON delivered the opinion of the Court.

Petitioner was convicted of the offense of disorderly conduct, a misdemeanor under the New York penal laws, in the Court of Special Sessions of the City of Syracuse and was sentenced to thirty days in the county penitentiary. The conviction was affirmed by the Onondaga County Court and the New York Court of Appeals, 300 N. Y. 391, 91 N. E. 2d 316 (1950). The case is here on certiorari, 339 U. S. 962 (1950), petitioner having claimed that the conviction is in violation of his right of free speech under the Fourteenth Amendment.

In the review of state decisions where First Amendment rights are drawn in question, we of course make an examination of the evidence to ascertain independently whether the right has been

---

[11] Russell, Authority and the Individual, 25.

violated. Here, the trial judge, who heard the case without jury, rendered an oral decision at the end of the trial, setting forth his determination of the facts upon which he found the petitioner guilty. His decision indicated generally that he believed the state's witnesses, and his summation of the testimony was used by the two New York courts on review in stating the facts. Our appraisal of the facts is, therefore, based upon the uncontroverted facts and, where controversy exists, upon that testimony which the trial judge did reasonably conclude to be true.

On the evening of March 8, 1949, petitioner Irving Feiner was addressing an open-air meeting at the corner of South McBride and Harrison Streets in the City of Syracuse. At approximately 6:30 p. m., the police received a telephone complaint concerning the meeting, and two officers were detailed to investigate. One of these officers went to the scene immediately, the other arriving some twelve minutes later. They found a crowd of about seventy-five or eighty people, both Negro and white, filling the sidewalk and spreading out into the street. Petitioner, standing on a large wooden box on the sidewalk, was addressing the crowd through a loud-speaker system attached to an automobile. Although the purpose of his speech was to urge his listeners to attend a meeting to be held that night in the Syracuse Hotel, in its course he was making derogatory remarks concerning President Truman, the American Legion, the Mayor of Syracuse, and other local political officials.

The police officers made no effort to interfere with petitioner's speech, but were first concerned with the effect of the crowd on both pedestrian and vehicular traffic. They observed the situation from the opposite side of the street, noting that some pedestrains were forced to walk in the street to avoid the crowd. Since traffic was passing at the time, the officers attempted to get the people listening to petitioner back on the sidewalk. The crowd was restless and there was some pushing, shoving and milling around. One of the officers telephoned the police station from a nearby store, and then both policemen crossed the street and mingled with the crowd without any intention of arresting the speaker.

At this time, petitioner was speaking in a "loud, high-pitched voice." He gave the impression that he was endeavoring to arouse the Negro people against the whites, urging that they rise up in arms and fight for equal rights. The statements before such a mixed audience "stirred up a little excitement." Some of the onlookers made remarks to the police about their inability to handle the crowd and at least one threatened violence

**665**

if the police did not act. There were others who appeared to be favoring petitioner's arguments. Because of the feeling that existed in the crowd both for and against the speaker, the officers finally "stepped in to prevent it from resulting in a fight." One of the officers approached the petitioner, not for the purpose of arresting him, but to get him to break up the crowd. He asked petitioner to get down off the box, but the latter refused to accede to his request and continued talking. The officer waited for a minute and then demanded that he cease talking. Although the officer had thus twice requested petitioner to stop over the course of several minutes, petitioner not only ignored him but continued talking. During all this time, the crowd was pressing closer around petitioner and the officer. Finally, the officer told petitioner he was under arrest and ordered him to get down from the box, reaching up to grab him. Petitioner stepped down, announcing over the microphone that "the law has arrived, and I suppose they will take over now." In all, the officer had asked petitioner to get down off the box three times over a space of four or five minutes. Petitioner had been speaking for over a half hour.

On these facts, petitioner was specifically charged with violation of § 722 of the Penal Law of New York, the pertinent part of which is set out in the margin.[1] The bill of particulars, demanded by petitioner and furnished by the state, gave in detail the facts upon which the prosecution relied to support the charge of disorderly conduct. Paragraph C is particularly pertinent here: "By ignoring and refusing to heed and obey reasonable police orders issued at the time and place mentioned in the Information to regulate and control said crowd and to prevent a breach or breaches of the peace and to prevent injury to pedestrians attempting to use said walk, and being forced into the highway adjacent to the place in question, and prevent injury to the public generally."

We are not faced here with blind condonation by a state court of arbitrary police action. Petitioner was accorded a full, fair trial. The trial judge heard testimony supporting and contradicting the judgment of the police officers that a clear danger of dis-

---

[1] Section 722. "Any person who with intent to provoke a breach of the peace, or whereby a breach of the peace may be occasioned, commits any of the following acts shall be deemed to have committed the offense of disorderly conduct:

"1. Uses offensive, disorderly, threatening, abusive or insulting language, conduct or behavior;

"2. Acts in such a manner as to annoy, disturb, interfere with, obstruct, or be offensive to others;

"3. Congregates with others on a public street and refuses to move on when ordered by the police; . . . ."

order was threatened. After weighing this contradictory evidence, the trial judge reached the conclusion that the police officers were justified in taking action to prevent a breach of the peace. The exercise of the police officers' proper discretionary power to prevent a breach of the peace was thus approved by the trial court and later by two courts on review.[2] The courts below recognized petitioner's right to hold a street meeting at this locality, to make use of loud-speaking equipment in giving his speech, and to make derogatory remarks concerning public officials and the American Legion. They found that the officers in making the arrest were motivated solely by a proper concern for the preservation of order and protection of the general welfare, and that there was no evidence which could lend color to a claim that the acts of the police were a cover for suppression of petitioner's views and opinions. Petitioner was thus neither arrested nor convicted for the making or the content of his speech. Rather, it was the reaction which it actually engendered.

The language of *Cantwell* v. *Connecticut*, 310 U. S. 296 (1940), is appropriate here. "The offense known as breach of the peace embraces a great variety of conduct destroying or menacing public order and tranquility. It includes not only violent acts but acts and words likely to produce violence in others. No one would have the hardihood to suggest that the principle of freedom of speech sanctions incitement to riot or that religious liberty connotes the privilege to exhort others to physical attack upon those belonging to another sect. When clear and present danger of riot, disorder, interference with traffic upon the public streets, or other immediate threat to public safety, peace, or order, appears, the power of the state to prevent or punish is obvious." 310 U. S. at 308. The findings of the New York courts as to the condition of the crowd and the refusal of petitioner to obey the police requests, supported as they are by the record of this case, are persuasive that the conviction of petitioner for violation of public peace, order and authority does not exceed the bounds of proper state police action. This Court respects, as it must, the

---

[2] The New York Court of Appeals said: "An imminent danger of a breach of the peace, of a disturbance of public order, perhaps even of riot, was threatened. . . . the defendant, as indicated above, disrupted pedestrian and vehicular traffic on the sidewalk and street, and, with intent to provoke a breach of the peace and with knowledge of the consequences, so inflamed and agitated a mixed audience of sympathizers and opponents that, in the judgment of the police officers present, a clear danger of disorder and violence was threatened. Defendant then deliberately refused to accede to the reasonable request of the officer, made within the lawful scope of his authority, that the defendant desist in the interest of public welfare and safety." 300 N. Y. 391, 400, 402, 91 N. E. 2d 316, 319, 321.

interest of the community in maintaining peace and order on its streets. *Schneider* v. *State,* 308 U. S. 147, 160 (1939) ; *Kovacs* v. *Cooper,* 336 U. S. 77, 82 (1949). We cannot say that the preservation of that interest here encroaches on the constitutional rights of this petitioner.

We are well aware that the ordinary murmurings and objections of a hostile audience cannot be allowed to silence a speaker, and are also mindful of the possible danger of giving overzealous police officials complete discretion to break up otherwise lawful public meetings. "A State may not unduly suppress free communication of views, religious or other, under the guise of conserving desirable conditions." *Cantwell* v. *Connecticut, supra,* at 308. But we are not faced here with such a situation. It is one thing to say that the police cannot be used as an instrument for the oppression of unpopular views, and another to say that, when as here the speaker passes the bounds of argument or persuasion and undertakes incitement to riot, they are powerless to prevent a breach of the peace. Nor in this case can we condemn the considered judgment of three New York courts approving the means which the police, faced with a crisis, used in the exercise of their power and duty to preserve peace and order. The findings of the state courts as to the existing situation and the imminence of greater disorder coupled with petitioner's deliberate defiance of the police officers convince us that we should not reverse this conviction in the name of free speech.

*Affirmed.*

MR. JUSTICE BLACK, dissenting.

The record before us convinces me that petitioner, a young college student, has been sentenced to the penitentiary for the unpopular views he expressed[1] on matters of public interest while lawfully making a street-corner speech in Syracuse, New York.[2]

---

[1] The trial judge framed the question for decision as follows: "The question here, is what was said and what was done? And it doesn't make any difference whether whatever was said, was said with a loud speaker or not. There are acts and conduct an individual can engage in when you don't even have to have a crowd gathered around which would justify a charge of disorderly conduct. The question is, what did this defendant say and do at that particular time and the Court must determine whether those facts, concerning what the defendant did or said, are sufficient to support the charge." There is no suggestion in the record that petitioner "did" anything other than (1) speak and (2) continue for a short time to invite people to a public meeting after a policeman had requested him to stop speaking.

[2] There was no charge that any city or state law prohibited such a meeting at the place or time it was held. Evidence showed that it was customary to hold public gatherings on that same corner every Friday night, and the trial judge who convicted petitioner admitted that he under-

Today's decision, however, indicates that we must blind ourselves to this fact because the trial judge fully accepted the testimony of the prosecution witnesses on all important points.[3] Many times in the past this Court has said that despite findings below, we will examine the evidence for ourselves to ascertain whether federally protected rights have been denied; otherwise review here would fail of its purpose in safeguarding constitutional guarantees. Even a partial abandonment of this rule marks a dark day for civil liberties in our Nation.

But still more has been lost today. Even accepting every "finding of fact" below, I think this conviction makes a mockery of the free speech guarantees of the First and Fourteenth Amendments. The end result of the affirmance here is to approve a simple and readily available technique by which cities and states can with impunity subject all speeches, political or otherwise, on streets or elsewhere, to the supervision and censorship of the local police. I will have no part or parcel in this holding which I view as a long step toward totalitarian authority.

Considering only the evidence which the state courts appear to have accepted, the pertinent "facts" are: Syracuse city authorities granted a permit for O. John Rogge, a former Assistant Attorney General, to speak in a public school building on March 8, 1948 on the subject of racial discrimination and civil liberties. On March 8th, however, the authorities cancelled the permit. The Young Progressives under whose auspices the meeting was scheduled then arranged for Mr. Rogge to speak at the Hotel Syracuse. The gathering on the street where petitioner spoke was held to protest the cancellation and to publicize the meeting at the hotel. In this connection, petitioner used derogatory but not profane language with reference to the city authorities, President Truman and the American Legion. After hearing some of these remarks, a policeman, who had been sent to the meeting by his superiors, reported to Police Headquarters by telephone. To whom he reported or what was said does not appear in the record, but after returning from the call, he and another policeman started through the crowd toward petitioner. Both officers swore they did not intend to make an arrest when they started, and the trial court accepted their statements. They

---

stood the meeting was a lawful one. Nor did the judge treat the lawful meeting as unlawful because a crowd congregated on the sidewalk. Consequently, any discussion of disrupted pedestrian and vehicular traffic, while suggestive coloration, is immaterial under the charge and conviction here. . . .

[3] The trial court made no findings of fact as such. A decision was rendered from the bench in which, among other things, the trial judge expressed some views on the evidence. See note 11, *infra*.

also said, and the court believed, that they heard and saw "angry mutterings," "pushing," "shoving and milling around" and "restlessness." Petitioner spoke in a "loud, high pitched voice." He said that "colored people don't have equal rights and they should rise up *in arms* and fight for them." One man who heard this told the officers that if they did not take that "S ... O ... B ..." off the box, he would. The officers then approached petitioner for the first time. One of them first "asked" petitioner to get off the box, but petitioner continued urging his audience to attend Rogge's speech. The officer next "told" petitioner to get down, but he did not. The officer finally "demanded" that petitioner get down, telling him he was under arrest. Petitioner then told the crowd that "the law would take over" and asked why he was arrested. The officer first replied that the charge was "unlawful assembly" but later changed the ground to "disorderly conduct."[6]

The Court's opinion apparently rests on this reasoning: The policeman, under the circumstances detailed, could reasonably conclude that serious fighting or even riot was imminent; therefore he could stop petitioner's speech to prevent a breach of peace; accordingly, it was "disorderly conduct" for petitioner to continue speaking in disobedience of the officer's request. As to the existence of a dangerous situation on the street corner, it seems far-fetched to suggest that the "facts" show any imminent threat of riot or uncontrollable disorder.[7] It is neither unusual

---

[6] "A charge of using language likely to cause a breach of the peace is a convenient catchall to hold unpopular soapbox orators." Chafee, Free Speech in the United States, 524. The related charge of conducting a "disorderly house" has also been used to suppress and punish minority views. For example, an English statute of 1799 classified as disorderly houses certain unlicensed places ("House, Room, Field, or other Place") in which "any Lecture or Discourse shall be publickly delivered, or any publick Debate shall be had on any Subject . . ." or which was used "for the Purpose of reading Books, Pamphlets, Newspapers or other Publications . . . ." 39 Geo. III, c. 79, § 15.

[7] The belief of the New York Court of Appeals that the situation on the street corner was critical is not supported by the record and accordingly should not be given much weight here. Two illustrations will suffice: The Court of Appeals relied upon a specific statement of one policeman that he interfered with Feiner at a time when the crowd was "getting to the point where they would be unruly." But this testimony was so patently inadmissible that it was excluded by the trial judge in one of the rare instances where the defendant received a favorable ruling. Secondly, the Court of Appeals stated that after Feiner had been warned by the police, he continued to "blare out his provocative utterances over loud speakers to a milling, restless throng . . . ." I am unable to find anything in the record to support this statement unless the unsworn arguments of the assistant district attorney are accepted as evidence. The principal prosecution witness testified that after he asked Feiner to get down from the box, Feiner merely "kept telling [the audience] to go to the Syracuse Hotel and hear

**670**

nor unexpected that some people at public street meetings mutter, mill about, push, shove, or disagree, even violently, with the speaker. Indeed, it is rare where controversial topics are discussed that an outdoor crowd does not do some or all of these things. Nor does one isolated threat to assault the speaker forbode disorder. Especially should the danger be discounted where, as here, the person threatening was a man whose wife and two small children accompanied him and who, so far as the record shows, was never close enough to petitioner to carry out the threat.

Moreover, assuming that the "facts" did indicate a critical situation, I reject the implication of the Court's opinion that the police had no obligation to protect petitioner's constitutional right to talk. The police of course have power to prevent breaches of the peace. But if, in the name of preserving order, they ever can interfere with a lawful public speaker, they first must make all reasonable efforts to protect him.[8] Here the policemen did not even pretend to try to protect petitioner. According to the officers' testimony, the crowd was restless but there is no showing of any attempt to quiet it; pedestrians were forced to walk into the street, but there was no effort to clear a path on the sidewalk; one person threatened to assault petitioner but the officers did nothing to discourage this when even a word might have sufficed. Their duty was to protect petitioner's right to talk, even to the extent of arresting the man who threatened to interfere.[9] Instead, they shirked that duty and acted only to suppress the right to speak.

John Rogge." And this same witness even answered "No" to the highly suggestive question which immediately followed, "Did he say anything more about arming and fighting at that time?"

[8] Cf. *Hague v. C. I. O.*, 307 U. S. 496; *Terminiello v. Chicago*, 337 U. S. 1; *Sellers v. Johnson*, 163 F. 2d 877; see also, summary of Brief for Committee on the Bill of Rights of the American Bar Association as *amicus curiae*, *Hague v. C. I. O.*, *supra*, reprinted at 307 U. S. 678–682.

[9] In *Schneider v. State*, 308 U. S. 147, we held that a purpose to prevent littering of the streets was insufficient to justify an ordinance which prohibited a person lawfully on the street from handing literature to one willing to receive it. We said at page 162, "There are obvious methods of preventing littering. Amongst these is the punishment of those who actually throw papers on the streets." In the present case as well, the threat of one person to assault a speaker does not justify suppression of the speech. There are obvious available alternative methods of preserving public order. One of these is to arrest the person who threatens an assault. Cf. *Dean Milk Co. v. Madison*, 340 U. S. 349, decided today, in which the Court invalidates a municipal health ordinance under the Commerce Clause because of a belief that the city could have accomplished its purposes by reasonably adequate alternatives. The Court certainly should not be less alert to protect freedom of speech than it is to protect freedom of trade.

Finally, I cannot agree with the Court's statement that petitioner's disregard of the policeman's unexplained request amounted to such "deliberate defiance" as would justify an arrest or conviction for disorderly conduct. On the contrary, I think that the policeman's action was a "deliberate defiance" of ordinary official duty as well as of the constitutional right of free speech. For at least where time allows, courtesy and explanation of commands are basic elements of good official conduct in a democratic society. Here petitioner was "asked" then "told" then "commanded" to stop speaking, but a man making a lawful address is certainly not required to be silent merely because an officer directs it. Petitioner was entitled to know why he should cease doing a lawful act. Not once was he told. I understand that people in authoritarian countries must obey arbitrary orders. I had hoped that there was no such duty in the United States.

In my judgment, today's holding means that as a practical matter, minority speakers can be silenced in any city. Hereafter, despite the First and Fourteenth Amendments, the policeman's club can take heavy toll of a current administration's public critics.[10] Criticism of public officials will be too dangerous for all but the most courageous.[11] This is true regardless of the fact that in two other cases decided this day, *Kunz* v. *New York*, 340 U. S. 290; *Niemotko* v. *Maryland*, 340 U. S. 268, a majority, in obedience to past decisions of this Court, provides a theoretical

---

[10] Today the Court characterizes petitioner's speech as one designed to incite riot and approves suppression of his views. There is an alarming similarity between the power thus possessed by the Syracuse (or any other) police and that possessed by English officials under an act passed by Parliament in 1795. In that year Justices of the Peace were authorized to arrest persons who spoke in a manner which could be characterized as "inciting and stirring up the People to Hatred or Contempt . . ." of the King or the Government. 36 Geo. III, c. 8, § 7. This statute "was manifestly intended to put an end for ever to all popular discussion either on political or religious matters." 1 Buckle, History of Civilization in England (2d London ed.) 350.

[11] That petitioner and the philosophy he espoused were objects of local antagonism appears clearly from the printed record in this case. Even the trial judge in his decision made no attempt to conceal his contempt for petitioner's views. He seemed outraged by petitioner's criticism of public officials and the American Legion. Moreover, the judge gratuitously expressed disapproval of O. John Rogge by quoting derogatory statements concerning Mr. Rogge which had appeared in the Syracuse press. The court approved the view that freedom of speech should be denied those who pit "class against class . . . and religion against religion." And after announcing its decision, the court persistently refused to grant bail pending sentence.

Although it is unnecessary for me to reach the question of whether the trial below met procedural due process standards, I cannot agree with the opinion of the Court that "Petitioner was accorded a full, fair trial."

safeguard for freedom of speech. For whatever is thought to be guaranteed in *Kunz* and *Niemotko* is taken away by what is done here. The three cases read together mean that while previous restraints probably cannot be imposed on an unpopular speaker, the police have discretion to silence him as soon as the customary hostility to his views develops.

In this case I would reverse the conviction, thereby adhering to the great principles of the First and Fourteenth Amendments . . .

MR. JUSTICE DOUGLAS, with whom MR. JUSTICE MINTON concurs, dissenting.

Feiner, a university student, made a speech on a street corner in Syracuse, New York, on March 8, 1949. The purpose of the speech was to publicize a meeting of the Young Progressives of America to be held that evening. A permit authorizing the meeting to be held in a public school auditorium had been revoked and the meeting shifted to a local hotel.

Feiner delivered his speech in a small shopping area in a predominantly colored residential section of Syracuse. He stood on a large box and spoke over loudspeakers mounted on a car. His audience was composed of about 75 people, colored and white. A few minutes after he started two police officers arrived.

The speech was mainly devoted to publicizing the evening's meeting and protesting the revocation of the permit. It also touched on various public issues. The following are the only excerpts revealed by the record:

"Mayor Costello (of Syracuse) is a champagne-sipping bum; he does not speak for the negro people."

"The 15th Ward is run by corrupt politicans, and there are horse rooms operating there."

"President Truman is a bum."

"Mayor O'Dwyer is a bum."

"The American Legion is a Nazi Gestapo."

"The negroes don't have equal rights; they should rise up in arms and fight for their rights."

There was some pushing and shoving in the crowd and some angry muttering. That is the testimony of the police. But there were no fights and no "disorder" even by the standards of the police. There was not even any heckling of the speaker.

But after Feiner had been speaking about 20 minutes a man said to the police officers, "If you don't get that son of a bitch off, I will go over and get him off there myself." It was then that the police ordered Feiner to stop speaking; when he refused, they arrested him.

Public assemblies and public speech occupy an important role in American life. One high function of the police is to protect these lawful gatherings so that the speakers may exercise their constitutional rights. When unpopular causes are sponsored from the public platform there will commonly be mutterings and unrest and heckling from the crowd. When a speaker mounts a platform it is not unusual to find him resorting to exaggeration, to vilification of ideas and men, to the making of false charges. But those extravagances, as we emphasized in *Cantwell* v. *Connecticut*, 310 U. S. 296, do not justify penalizing the speaker by depriving him of the platform or by punishing him for his conduct.

A speaker may not, of course, incite a riot any more than he may invite a breach of the peace by the use of "fighting words". See *Chaplinsky* v. *New Hampshire*, 315 U. S. 568. But this record shows no such extremes. It shows an unsympathetic audience and the threat of one man to haul the speaker from the stage. It is against that kind of threat that speakers need police protection. If they do not receive it and instead the police throw their weight on the side of those who would break up the meetings, the police become the new censors of speech. Police censorship has all the vices of the censorship from city halls which we have repeatedly struck down. See *Lovell* v. *City of Griffin*, 303 U. S. 444; *Hague* v. *C. I. O.*, 307 U. S. 496; *Cantwell* v. *Connecticut*, *supra; Murdock* v. *Pennsylvania*, 319 U. S. 105; *Saia* v. *New York*, 334 U. S. 558.

## NIEMOTKO v. MARYLAND

Supreme Court of the United States, 1951
340 U. S. 268, 95 L. Ed. 267, 71 S. Ct. 325

MR. JUSTICE FRANKFURTER, concurring in the result.*

The issues in these cases concern living law in some of its most delicate aspects. To smother differences of emphasis and nuance will not help its wise development. When the way a result is reached may be important to results hereafter to be reached, law is best respected by individual expression of opinion.

These cases present three variations upon a theme of great importance. Legislatures, local authorities, and the courts have for years grappled with claims of the right to disseminate ideas in public places as against claims of an effective power in govern-

---

*[In this case, *Kunz* v. *New York*, and *Feiner* v. *New York*, *supra*. The majority opinion, written by Chief Justice Vinson, is omitted. Mr. Justice Black concurred without opinion.]

[Emerson]

ment to keep the peace and to protect other interests of a civilized community.  These cases are of special interest because they show the attempts of three communities to meet the problem in three different ways.  It will, I believe, further analysis to use the three situations as cross-lights on one another.

### I.

.  .  .  Havre de Grace, Maryland, sought to solve this tangled problem by permitting its park commissioner and city council to act as censors.  The city allowed use of its park for public meetings, including those of religious groups, but by custom a permit was required.  In this case, the city council questioned the representatives of Jehovah's Witnesses, who had requested a license, about their views on saluting the flag, the Catholic Church, service in the armed forces, and other matters in no way related to public order or public convenience in use of the park. The Mayor testified that he supposed the permit was denied "because of matters that were brought out at [the] meeting."  When Niemotko and Kelley, Jehovah's Witnesses, attempted to speak, they were arrested for disturbing the peace.  There was no disturbance of the peace and it is clear that they were arrested only for want of a permit.  .  .  .

[The statement of facts in the *Kunz* and *Feiner* cases is omitted.]

### II.

Adjustment of the inevitable conflict between free speech and other interests is a problem as persistent as it is perplexing. It is important to bear in mind that this Court can only hope to set limits and point the way.  It falls to the lot of legislative bodies and administrative officials to find practical solutions within the frame of our decisions.  There are now so many of these decisions, arrived at by the *ad hoc* process of adjudication, that it is desirable to make a cruise of the timber.

In treating the precise problem presented by the three situations before us—how to reconcile the interest in allowing free expression of ideas in public places with the protection of the public peace and of the primary uses of streets and parks—we should first set to one side decisions which are apt to mislead rather than assist.  Contempt cases and convictions under State and Federal statutes aimed at placing a general limitation upon what may be said or written, bring additional factors into the equation.  Cases like *Near* v. *Minnesota*, 283 U. S. 697, and *Grosjean* v. *American Press Co.*, 297 U. S. 233, are rooted in historic experience regarding prior restraints on publication.

**675**

They give recognition to the role of the press in a democracy, a consideration not immediately pertinent. The picketing cases are logically relevant since they usually involve, in part, dissemination of information in public places. But here also enter economic and social interests outside the situations before us. See *Hughes v. Superior Court*, 339 U. S. 460, 464–465.

The cases more exclusively concerned with restrictions upon expression in its divers forms in public places have answered problems varying greatly in content and difficulty.

1. The easiest cases have been those in which the only interest opposing free communication was that of keeping the streets of the community clean. This could scarcely justify prohibiting the dissemination of information by handbills or censoring their contents. In *Lovell* v. *Griffin,* 303 U. S. 444, an ordinance requiring a permit to distribute pamphlets was held invalid where the licensing standard was "not limited to ways which might be regarded as inconsistent with the maintenance of public order or as involving disorderly conduct, the molestation of the inhabitants, or the misuse or littering of the streets." *Id.,* at 451. In *Hague* v. *C. I. O.,* 307 U. S. 496, a portion of the ordinance declared invalid prohibited the distribution of pamphlets. In *Schneider* v. *State,* 308 U. S. 147, three of the four ordinances declared invalid by the Court prohibited the distribution of pamphlets. In *Jamison* v. *Texas,* 318 U. S. 413, the Court again declared invalid a municipal ordinance prohibiting the distribution of all handbills.

2. In a group of related cases, regulation of solicitation has been the issue. Here the opposing interest is more substantial— protection of the public from fraud and from criminals who use solicitation as a device to enter homes. The fourth ordinance considered in *Schneider* v. *State, supra,* allowed the chief of police to refuse a permit if he found, in his discretion, that the canvasser was not of good character or was canvassing for a project not free from fraud. The ordinance was found invalid because the officer who could, in his discretion, make the determinations concerning "good character" and "project not free from fraud" in effect held the power of censorship. In *Cantwell* v. *Connecticut,* 310 U. S. 296, conviction was, in part, under a State statute requiring a permit for religious solicitation. The statute was declared invalid because the licensing official could determine what causes were religious, allowing a "censorship of religion." *Id.,* at 305. Again, in *Largent* v. *Texas,* 318 U. S. 418, an ordinance requiring a permit from the mayor, who was to issue the permit only if he deemed it "proper or advisable," was declared invalid as creating an administrative censorship.

**676**

The Court has also denied the right of those in control of a company town or Government housing project to prohibit solicitation by Jehovah's Witnesses. *Marsh* v. *Alabama*, 326 U. S. 501; *Tucker* v. *Texas*, 326 U. S. 517. In *Thomas* v. *Collins*, 323 U. S. 516, the solicitation was in the interest of labor rather than religion. There a State statute requiring registration of labor organizers was found unconstitutional when invoked to enjoin a speech in a public hall. The interest of the State in protecting its citizens through the regulation of vocations was deemed insufficient to support the statute.

3. Whether the sale of religious literature by Jehovah's Witnesses can be subjected to nondiscriminatory taxes on solicitation has introduced another opposing interest—the right of the community to raise funds for the support of the government. In *Jones* v. *Opelika*, 319 U. S. 103, vacating 316 U. S. 584, and in *Murdock* v. *Pennsylvania*, 319 U. S. 105, the Court held that imposition of the tax upon itinerants was improper. In *Follett* v. *McCormick*, 321 U. S. 573, the Court went further to hold unconstitutional the imposition of a flat tax on book agents upon a resident who made his living selling religious books.

4. *Martin* v. *Struthers*, 319 U. S. 141, represents another situation. An ordinance of the City of Struthers, Ohio, forbade knocking on the door or ringing the doorbell of a residence in order to deliver a handbill. Prevention of crime and assuring privacy in an industrial community where many worked on night shifts, and had to obtain their sleep during the day, were held insufficient to justify the ordinance in the case of handbills distributed on behalf of Jehovah's Witnesses.

5. In contrast to these decisions, the Court held in *Prince* v. *Massachusetts*, 321 U. S. 158, that the application to Jehovah's Witnesses of a State statute providing that no boy under 12 or girl under 18 should sell periodicals on the street was constitutional. Claims of immunity from regulation of religious activities were subordinated to the interest of the State in protecting its children.

6. Control of speeches made in streets and parks draws on still different considerations—protection of the public peace and of the primary uses of travel and recreation for which streets and parks exist.

(a) The pioneer case concerning speaking in parks and streets is *Davis* v. *Massachusetts*, 167 U. S. 43, in which this Court adopted the reasoning of the opinion below written by Mr. Justice Holmes, while on the Massachusetts Supreme Judicial Court. *Commonwealth* v. *Davis*, 162 Mass. 510, 39 N. E. 113. The Boston ordinance which was upheld required a permit from the mayor for any person to "make any public address, discharge any cannon or firearm, expose for sale any goods, . . ." on public grounds. This Court respected the finding that the ordinance was not directed against free speech but was intended as "a proper regulation of the use of public grounds." 162 Mass. at 512, 39 N. E. at 113.

An attempt to derive from *dicta* in the *Davis* case the right of a city to exercise any power over its parks, however arbitrary or discriminatory, was rejected in *Hague* v. *C. I. O., supra.* The ordinance presented in the *Hague* case required a permit for meetings on public ground, the permit to be refused by the licensing official only "for the purpose of preventing riots, disturbances or disorderly assemblage." *Id.*, at 502. The facts of the case, however, left no doubt that the licensing power had been made an "instrument of arbitrary suppression of free expression of views on national affairs." *Id.*, at 516. And the construction given the ordinance in the State courts gave the licensing officials wide discretion. See *Thomas* v. *Casey,* 121 N. J. L. 185, 1 A. 2d 866. The holding of the *Hague* case was not that a city could not subject the use of its streets and parks to reasonable regulation. The holding was that the licensing officials could not be given power arbitrarily to suppress free expression, no matter under what cover of law they purported to act.

*Cox* v. *New Hampshire,* 312 U. S. 569, made it clear that the United States Constitution does not deny localities the power to devise a licensing system if the exercise of discretion by the licensing officials is appropriately confined. A statute requiring a permit and license fee for parades had been narrowly construed by the State courts. The license could be refused only for "considerations of time, place and manner so as to conserve the public convenience," and the license fee was "to meet the expense incident to the administration of the Act and to the maintenance of public order in the matter licensed." *Id.*, at 575–576, 577. The licensing system was sustained even though the tax, ranging from a nominal amount to $300, was determined by the licensing officials on the facts of each case.

(b) Two cases have involved the additional considerations incident to the use of sound trucks. In *Saia* v. *New York,* 334 U. S. 558, the ordinance required a license from the chief of police for use of sound amplification devices in public places. The ordinance was construed not to prescribe standards to be applied in passing upon a license application. In the particular case, a license to use a sound truck in a small city park had been denied because of complaints about the noise which resulted when sound amplifiers had previously been used in the park. There was no indication that the license had been refused because of the content of the speeches. Nevertheless, the Court held the ordinance unconstitutional. In *Kovacs* v. *Cooper*, 336 U. S. 77, part of the Court construed the ordinance as allowing conviction for operation of any sound truck emitting "loud and raucous" noises, and part construed the ordinance to ban all sound trucks. The limits of the decision of the Court upholding the ordinance are therefore not clear, but the result in any event does not leave the *Saia* decision intact.

(c) On a few occasions the Court has had to pass on a limitation upon speech by a sanction imposed after the event rather than by a licensing statute. In *Cantwell* v. *Connecticut, supra,* one of the convictions was for common-law breach of the peace. The problem was resolved in favor of the defendant by reference to *Schenck* v. *United States*, 249 U. S. 47, 52, in view of the inquiry whether, on the facts of the case, there was "such clear and present menace to public peace and order as to render him liable to conviction of the common law offense in question." 310 U. S. at 311.

In *Chaplinsky* v. *New Hampshire,* 315 U. S. 568, a State statute had enacted the common-law doctrine of "fighting words": "No person shall address any offensive, derisive or annoying word to any other person who is lawfully in any street or other public place, nor call him by any offensive or derisive name . . . ." The State courts had previously held the statute applicable only to the use in a public place of words directly tending to cause a breach of the peace by the persons to whom the remark was addressed. The conviction of a street speaker who called a policeman a "damned racketeer" and "damned Fascist" was upheld.

7. One other case should be noted, although it involved a conviction for breach of peace in a private building rather than in a public place. In *Terminiello* v. *Chicago*, 337 U. S. 1, the holding of the Court was on an abstract proposition of law, unrelated to the facts in the case. A conviction was overturned because the judge had instructed the jury that "breach of the peace" included speech which "stirs the public to anger, invites dispute, brings about a condition of unrest, or creates a disturbance . . . ." The holding apparently was that breach of the peace may not be defined in such broad terms, certainly as to speech in a private hall.

The results in these multifarious cases have been expressed in language looking in two directions. While the Court has emphasized the importance of "free speech," it has recognized that "free speech" is not in itself a touchstone. The Constitution is not unmindful of other important interests, such as public order, if interference with free expression of ideas is not found to be the overbalancing consideration. More important than the phrasing of the opinions are the questions on which the decisions appear to have turned.

(1) What is the interest deemed to require the regulation of speech? The State cannot of course forbid public proselyting or religious argument merely because public officials disapprove the speaker's views. It must act in patent good faith to maintain the public peace, to assure the availability of the streets for their primary purposes of passenger and vehicular traffic, or for equally indispensable ends of modern community life.

(2) What is the method used to achieve such ends as a consequence of which public speech is constrained or barred? A licensing standard which gives an official authority to censor the content of a speech differs *toto cœlo* from one limited by its terms, or by nondiscriminatory practice, to considerations of public safety and the like. Again, a sanction applied after the event assures consideration of the particular circumstances of a situation. The net of control must not be cast too broadly.

(3) What mode of speech is regulated? A sound truck may be found to affect the public peace as normal speech does not. A man who is calling names or using the kind of language which would reasonably stir another to violence does not have the same claim to protection as one whose speech is an appeal to reason.

(4) Where does the speaking which is regulated take place? Not only the general classifications—streets, parks, private buildings—are relevant. The location and size of a park; its customary use for the recreational, esthetic and contemplative needs of a community; the facilities, other than a park or street corner, readily available in a community for airing views, are all pertinent considerations in assessing the limitations the Fourteenth Amendment puts on State power in a particular situation.

## III.

Due regard for the interests that were adjusted in the decisions just canvassed affords guidance for deciding the cases before us.

1. In the *Niemotko* case, neither danger to the public peace, nor consideration of time and convenience to the public, appears to have entered into denial of the permit. Rumors that there would be violence by those opposed to the meeting appeared only after the Council made its decision, and in fact never materialized. The city allowed other religious groups to use the park. To allow expression of religious views by some and deny the same privilege to others merely because they or their views are un-

popular, even deeply so, is a denial of equal protection of the law forbidden by the Fourteenth Amendment.

2. The *Kunz* case presents a very different situation. We must be mindful of the enormous difficulties confronting those charged with the task of enabling the polyglot millions in the City of New York to live in peace and tolerance. Street-preaching in Columbus Circle is done in a milieu quite different from preaching on a New England village green. Again, religious polemic does not touch the merely ratiocinative nature of man, and the ugly facts disclosed by the record of this case show that Kunz was not reluctant to offend the deepest religious feelings of frequenters of Columbus Circle. Especially in such situations, this Court should not substitute its abstract views for the informed judgment of local authorities confirmed by local courts.

I cannot make too explicit my conviction that the City of New York is not restrained by anything in the Constitution of the United States from protecting completely the community's interests in relation to its streets. But if a municipality conditions holding street meetings on the granting of a permit by the police, the basis which guides licensing officials in granting or denying a permit must not give them a free hand, or a hand effectively free when the actualities of police administration are taken into account. It is not for this Court to formulate with particularity the terms of a permit system which would satisfy the Fourteenth Amendment. No doubt, finding a want of such standards presupposes some conception of what is necessary to meet the constitutional requirement we draw from the Fourteenth Amendment. But many a decision of this Court rests on some inarticulate major premise and is none the worse for it. A standard may be found inadequate without the necessity of explicit delineation of the standards that would be adequate, just as doggerel may be felt not to be poetry without the need of writing an essay on what poetry is.

Administrative control over the right to speak must be based on appropriate standards, whether the speaking be done indoors or out-of-doors. The vice to be guarded against is arbitrary action by officials. The fact that in a particular instance an action appears not arbitrary does not save the validity of the authority under which the action was taken.

In the present case, Kunz was not arrested for what he said on the night of arrest, nor because at that time he was disturbing the peace or interfering with traffic. He was arrested because he spoke without a license, and the license was refused because the police commissioner thought it likely on the basis of past performance that Kunz would outrage the religious sensibilities of others. If such had been the supportable finding on the basis of fair standards in safeguarding peace in one of the most populous centers of New York City, this Court would not be justified in upsetting it. It would not be censorship in advance. But here the standards are defined neither by language nor by settled construction to preclude discriminatory or arbitrary action by officials. The ordinance, as judicially construed, provides that anyone who, in the judgment of the licensing officials, would "ridicule" or "denounce" religion creates such a danger of public disturbance that he cannot speak in any park or street in the City of New York. Such a standard, considering the informal procedure under which it is applied, too readily permits censorship of religion by the licensing authorities. *Cantwell* v. *Connecticut*, 310 U. S. 296. The situation here disclosed is not, to reiterate, beyond control on the basis of regulation appropriately directed to the evil.[2]

3. . . . Feiner forced pedestrians to walk in the street by collecting a crowd on the public sidewalk, he attracted additional attention by using sound amplifiers, he indulged in name-calling, he told part of his audience that it should rise up in arms. In the crowd of 75 to 80 persons, there was angry muttering and pushing. Under these circumstances, and in order to prevent a disturbance of the peace, an officer asked Feiner to stop speaking. When he had twice ignored the request, Feiner was arrested. The trial judge concluded that "the officers were fully justified in feeling that a situation was developing which could very, very easily result in a serious disorder." His view was sustained by an intermediate appellate court and by a unanimous decision of the New York Court of Appeals. 300 N. Y. 391, 91 N. E. 2d 316. The estimate of a particular local situation thus comes here with the momentum of the weightiest judicial authority of New York.

This Court has often emphasized that in the exercise of our authority over state court decisions the Due Process Clause must not be construed in an abstract and doctrinaire way by disregarding local conditions. In considering the degree of respect to be given findings by the highest court of a State in cases

2. . . . So far as the special circumstances relating to the City of New York are concerned, it is pertinent to note that all three dissenting judges below are residents of New York City, whereas not one of the four constituting the majority is a denizen of that City. The three New York City dissenting judges are presumably as alive to the need for securing peace among the various racial and religious groups in New York, and to the opportunity of achieving it within the constitutional limits, as one who has only a visitor's acquaintance with the tolerant and genial communal life of New York City.

involving the Due Process Clause, the course of decisions by that court should be taken into account. Particularly within the area of due process colloquially called "civil liberties," it is important whether such a course of decisions reflects a cavalier attitude toward civil liberties or real regard for them. Only unfamiliarity with its decisions and the outlook of its judges could generate a notion that the Court of Appeals of New York is inhospitable to claims of civil liberties or is wanting in respect for this Court's decisions in support of them. It is pertinent, therefore, to note that all members of the New York Court accepted the finding that Feiner was stopped not because the listeners or police officers disagreed with his views but because these officers were honestly concerned with preventing a breach of the peace. This unanimity is all the more persuasive since three members of the Court had dissented, only three months earlier, in favor of Kunz, a man whose vituperative utterances must have been highly offensive to them.

As was said in *Hague* v. *C. I. O., supra,* uncontrolled official suppression of the speaker "cannot be made a substitute for the duty to maintain order." 307 U. S. at 516. Where conduct is within the allowable limits of free speech, the police are peace officers for the speaker as well as for his hearers. But the power effectively to preserve order cannot be displaced by giving a speaker complete immunity. Here, there were two police officers present for 20 minutes. They interfered only when they apprehended imminence of violence. It is not a constitutional principle that, in acting to preserve order, the police must proceed against the crowd, whatever its size and temper, and not against the speaker.

It is true that breach-of-peace statutes, like most tools of government, may be misused. Enforcement of these statutes calls for public tolerance and intelligent police administration. These, in the long run, must give substance to whatever this Court may say about free speech. But the possibility of misuse is not alone a sufficient reason to deny New York the power here asserted or so limit it by constitutional construction as to deny its practical exercise.

## Note

1. For discussion see Notes, 19 Geo. Wash. L. Rev. 637 (1951) ; 26 N. Y. U. L. Rev. 489 (1951) ; 49 Mich. L. Rev. 1185 (1951) : Richardson, *Freedom of Expression and the Function of Courts,* 65 Harv. L. Rev. 1 (1951). See also Dembitz, *Free Speech vs. Free-for-All,* The Nation, July 14, 1951, p. 29; Countryman, *Freedom For Insulting Speech—A Reply,* The Nation, July 21, 1951, p. 50.

2. Other situations where speech was sought to be prohibited because allegedly dangerous when uttered in the particular locale under the particular circumstances include the following:

In *Sellers v. Johnson*, 163 F. 2d 877 (C. A. 8, 1947), cert. den. 332 U. S. 851 (1948), a prior attempt by Jehovah's Witnesses to speak in the park had resulted in their being attacked by a crowd. When the Witnesses planned to meet again the police blockaded the town and turned away all strangers including the Witnesses. The Witnesses then applied for a permit which was denied. The Court in granting the Witnesses equitable relief, stated:

"While we do not question the good faith of the Mayor or the Sheriff in concluding that the best and easiest way to maintain peace and order in Lacona on September 15 was to blockade the roads leading into the Town, we are convinced that evidence of unconfirmed rumors, talk, and fears cannot form the basis of a finding of the existence of such a clear and present danger to the State as to justify a deprivation of fundamental and essential constitutional rights. We think that is particularly true in a situation where no effort whatever was made to protect those who were attempting lawfully to exercise those rights. There is no evidence that it was beyond the competency of the Sheriff and the Mayor to secure enough peace officers to police the park on September 15. The fact that the Sheriff was able to deputize approximately 100 persons to assist him in blockading the highways leading into Lacona militates against any inference that he would have been unable to preserve law and order in Lacona on September 15. The record shows that the Mayor did not exercise the authority given him by the Town Council to deputize peace officers." 163 F. 2d at 883.

Compare *Beatty v. Gillbanks,* 9 Q. B. D. 308 (1882), for a similar liberal view in Great Britain. But see Note, 47 Yale L. J. 404 (1938), for a collection of more typical British cases.

In *Miller v. Oklahoma*, 75 Okla. Cr. 428, 133 Pac. 2d 223 (1943), a Jehovah's Witness stated in answer to questions that he did not believe in man-made law, that he would obey only Jehovah's laws, and that he would not salute the flag. Bystanders became angry. The Court in holding that the defendant should be acquitted of breach of the peace stated that this was not abusive and insulting language and that there was no clear and present danger of a riot.

In a recent case brought by the American Civil Liberties Union two ordinances passed by the Town of Cortlandt, New York, after the Peekskill riots (see Chapter I, *supra*) were declared invalid by a New York Supreme Court. The first, requiring a permit from the Town Council, was declared invalid for giving unlimited discretionary power to that agency. The second was a breach-of-the-peace ordinance which contained the following provisions:

"Any person who with intent to provoke a breach of the peace . . . commits any of the following acts shall be guilty of a misdemeanor . . . . 5. Knowingly assembles with others at a meeting, assembly or demonstration held for the purpose of breaking down law enforcement, or disturbing the public peace, and carried out in a manner tending to the breaking down of law enforcement or the disturbance of the public peace; 6. Knowingly arranges for or joins or enters into a scheme or plan with others to arrange for a meeting, assembly or demonstration held for the purpose of breaking down law enforcement or disturbing the public peace and carried out in a manner tending to the breakdown of law enforcement or the disturbance of the public peace."

The Court held that the phrase "breaking down law enforcement" was too vague.

The Court's discussion was in part as follows:

"The enforcement of what law, or laws, must the assembly seek to 'break down' ? Could it be a tax law, or, perhaps, a zoning ordinance? . . . The portion of the ordinance that states it shall not be construed as to prevent lawful freedom of speech or lawful assembly does not save its constitutionality. Even a plan or scheme by two or more persons formulated in the sanctuary of a home to hold a public meeting against some innocuous ordinance might well come within the dragnet of these subdivisions. It is almost impossible to envisage where the heritage of protest ends and the violation of this ordinance begins. . . . Such dragnets must be declared void." *American Civil Liberties Union v. Town of Cortlandt*, 109 N. Y. Supp. 2d 165 (Sup. Ct. 1951).

In *New Orleans v. Hood*, 212 La. 485, 32 So. 2d 899 (1947), the Court held that an ordinance forbidding distribution on city streets of "dodgers or hand advertisements whether of theatrical nature or otherwise" could not be constitutionally applied to political circulars favoring "the communist element of the National Maritime Union." The Court stated, ". . . it matters not that the doctrines circulated are adverse to democratic principles of free speech and a free press and that their purveyor is, paradoxically, relying upon those constitutional guarantees to shield him from prosecution and punishment."

For a discussion of the *Terminiello* case, referred to in the principal opinions, see Notes, 61 Harv. L. Rev. 537 (1948) ; 49 Col. L. Rev. 1118 (1949) ; Rosenwein, *The Supreme Court and Freedom of Speech— Terminiello v. City of Chicago*, 9 Law. Guild Rev. 70 (1949) ; 23 Temple L. Q. 393 (1950) ; 24 N. Y. U. L. Q. Rev. 885 (1949). In the *Terminiello* case the Court made an exceptional departure from two of its self imposed limitations: (1) to review only issues raised in the Court below, and (2) to review issues only when properly presented in the petition for certiorari. The conviction was reversed on the ground that the trial court in charging the jury had construed the statute so broadly as to make it unconstitutional. Petitioner had not excepted to this aspect of the charge, nor was the issue raised in the state courts or mentioned in the petition for certiorari. This aspect of the case is discussed in Note, 59 Yale L. J. 971 (1950).

3. See also cases dealing with the red flag laws which forbid the display of a red flag on the theory that the person so doing will be mobbed. *People v. Altman*, 241 App. Div. 858 (1st Dept. 1934) (unconstitutional) ; *People v. Immonen*, 271 Mich. 384, 261 N. W. 59 (1935) (statute upheld) ; *cf. Stromberg v. California*, 283 U. S. 359, 75 L. Ed. 1117, 51 S. Ct. 532 (1931), *supra* Chapter IV. Massachusetts once had a statute prohibiting a red or black flag. It was repealed because it would have made the Harvard crimson illegal. Said Professor

Chafee, he hoped "other portions of the land of the brave will also be willing to face valiantly a piece of cloth." Chafee, *Free Speech in the United States*, p. 162 (1941). For legislation prohibiting public wearing of foreign uniforms, see Note, 53 Harv. L. Rev. 150 (1939). See also statutes designed to curb activities of the Ku Klux Klan by prohibiting the wearing of hoods and masks, Chapter I, *supra*.

On the use of anti-riot and unlawful assembly statutes against mass-picketing, see *infra*.

## The Use of Public Auditoriums

In *Danskin v. San Diego Unified School District*, 28 Cal. 2d 536, 171 Pac. 2d 885 (1946), the Court held invalid a regulation denying use of a school auditorium to a "subversive element" and requiring prospective users to file affidavits stating facts to show whether or not they were subversive. The term "subversive element" was defined as a group "which advocates or has for its object . . . the overthrow of the present government . . . by force or violence or other unlawful means." Holding that such activity could not be made unlawful in the absence of a clear and present danger, the Court reasoned: "The state is under no duty to make school buildings available for public meetings. See *Merryman* v. *School Dist.*, 43 Wyo. 376, 5 P. 2d 267, 86 A. L. R. 1195, 47 Am. Jur. 344. If it elects to do so, however, it cannot arbitrarily prevent any members of the public from holding such meetings. *State of Missouri ex rel. Gaines* v. *Canada*, 305 U. S. 337, 349, 59 S. Ct. 232, 83 L. Ed. 208, see *Marsh* v. *Alabama* [326 U. S. 501] . . . Nor can it make the privilege of holding them dependent on conditions that would deprive any members of the public of their constitutional rights. A state is without power to impose an unconstitutional requirement as a condition for granting a privilege even though the privilege is the use of state property. . . ."

In *Stanton* v. *Board of Education of City of New York*, 190 Misc. 1012, 76 N. Y. Supp. 2d 559 (1948), the problem under consideration in the *Danskin* case was litigated in somewhat different form. Plaintiff in that case, a taxpayer, was asking for judicial review of the action of the Board of Education of the City of New York in voting down a resolution to deny the use of school buildings to organizations which the Superintendent of Schools had reason to believe to be Communist, Nazi, or Fascist. In deciding the case in favor of the defendant, Justice Froessel, then sitting on the New York Supreme Court, did not in any way intimate that the resolution if adopted, would have been violative of the United States Constitution. Instead, he stressed the fact that the rights of free speech and assembly are subject to limitations in the interest of the preservation of the public welfare and of organized constitutional government, citing the majority decision in the *Gitlow* case with approval. In the case before him, however, he felt it was within the area of discretion reserved to the Board to reject the resolution, its action being neither arbitrary nor in violation of any statute.

In 1951 the Board of Education, reversing itself, voted to authorize the Superintendent to bar the use of school buildings to groups he believed to be totalitarian, Fascist, Communist or subversive. American Civil Liberties Union Bulletin, Sept. 3, 1951.

See also *Greisinger* v. *Grand Rapids Board of Education*, 88 Ohio App. 364, 100 N. E. 2d 294 (1949), where out-of-town Jehovah's Witnesses sought to compel the Board of Education to permit the use of a school auditorium. The Court held that the statute gave the Board broad discretionary power, that the Board exercised this reasonably, and that the denial did not constitute an unreasonable infringement on freedom of speech, assembly and worship. In the course of its opinion the Court gave the following as evidence for the reasonableness of the Board's action: "It is averred in the answer of respondents that a vast majority of the citizens, residents and taxpayers of the school district, and also many civic organizations, have requested the board not to permit the use of the school auditorium by appellants. These averments are not denied. Over the objection of appellants, evidence was introduced by way of written petitions addressed to the board and resolutions adopted by various civic organizations in the village of Grand Rapids. In the performance of their duties, the members of the board had a right to be informed and to inform themselves of the attitude of the residents and taxpayers of the school district. Having this right, the board of education could properly take cognizance of such petitions and resolutions and was required to do so, having regard for the 'welfare of the community' in relation to the use of school property.

"No bad faith on the part of the board having been shown in the method employed to ascertain the attitude of the citizens of the school district, it was within the discretion of the trial court to receive this evidence and appellants were not prejudiced by its admission."

### Restrictions in Connection with Space Allocation

In certain cases restriction is justified on grounds involving common police regulations to (1) assure that streets and playgrounds will be available for various purposes, such as transportation and recreation as well as speech, and (2) assure that competing communicators do not drown each other out or seek to use the same space at the same time. These problems are very real and must of course be dealt with. Such regulations, however, raise important issues with respect to freedom of communication: Are they designed to preserve the maximum amount and variety of communication possible while at the same time meeting the problem the regulation is designed to control? Are they so drawn as to permit easy abuse by using them as tools for suppressing unpopular speech? Are they being abused in the particular case?

### Streets

In *Ex parte Bodkin,* 86 Cal. App. 2d 208, 194 Pac. 2d 588 (1948), an ordinance provided: "Wherever the free passage of any street or sidewalk in the town . . . shall be obstructed by a crowd, the persons composing such crowd shall disperse or move on when directed to do so by a police officer. It shall be unlawful for any person to refuse. . . ." The Court in upholding the ordinance stated that the street need not be busy. It held that it was a reasonable exercise of the police power for a city to require the dispersal of a crowd even if only one pedestrian is obstructed thereby. The clear and present danger test was held to be inapplicable since the ordinance "is solely a regulation of the use of the public streets, preserving them for the benefit of the public against obstructions and not a restriction on what may be uttered or published. . . ."

Compare *Commonwealth* v. *Carpenter,* 325 Mass. 519, 91 N. E. 2d 666 (1950), where the Court held that an ordinance prohibiting wilful and unreasonable sauntering for more than seven minutes after being ordered by a policeman to move on violates the due process clause of the Fourteenth Amendment. The Court objected to the lack of standard and added that the ordinance's broad sweep "is unnecessary to the suppression of disorder or even of congestion in the streets."

### Parks

In *People* v. *Naham,* 298 N. Y. 95, 81 N. E. 2d 36 (1948), the challenged New York City Park Department regulation read: "No person shall erect any structures, stand or platform, hold any meeting, perform any ceremony, make a speech, address or harangue; exhibit or distribute any sign, placard, notice, declaration or appeal of any kind or description; exhibit any dramatic performance, or the performance in whole or in part of any interlude, tragedy, comedy, opera, ballet, play, farce, minstrelsy, dancing, entertainment, motion picture, public fair, circus, juggling, rope-walking or any other acrobatics, or show of any kind or nature; or run or race any horse, or other animal, or, being in or on a vehicle, race with another vehicle or horse, whether such race be founded on any stake, bet or otherwise; in any park or upon any park street except by permit. No parade, drill or manoeuver of any kind shall be conducted, nor shall any procession form for parade or proceed in any park or park street without a permit." Rules and Regulations of New York City Agencies, Dept. of Parks, § 21. The Court held that the Commission's discretion was limited by section 532 of the New York City charter which provided: "The commissioner shall have the power and it shall be his duty: . . . 3. To maintain the beauty and utility of all parks, squares, public places and playgrounds and other recreational properties, except those within the jurisdiction of the department of education, and to institute and execute all measures for the improvement thereof for ornamental purposes and for the beneficial uses of the people of the city." The Court concluded that the regulation thus limited is a valid exercise of the police power: "As is well known there are areas of the park system of the city of New York—e. g., children's playgrounds and horticultural gardens—that cannot be used for meetings, parades and like affairs. More than that, such affairs, when held in other areas of the system, must be so placed that ornamental improvements—e.g., lawns and shrubbery—will not be damaged, and also, must be so scheduled in point of time and separateness as not unduly to interfere with the beneficial uses of the system by the people of the city. For the public parks of that vast and congested community are the only places where a great part of its population can have any real opportunity for recreation in the open air and the only places where large numbers of its children can safely play." To the same effect see *People* v. *Hass*, 299 N. Y. 190, 86 N. E. 2d 169 (1949), app. dis. 338 U. S. 803 (1949). *Cf. Commonwealth* v. *Gilfedder*, 321 Mass. 335, 73 N. E. 2d 241 (1947).

In *Commonwealth* v. *Dubin*, 327 Mass. —, 100 N. E. 2d 843 (1951), the rule governing reservations under control of the metropolitan district provided that no one should post or print any sign, placard or any "other advertising device." The defendant had posted signs on streets at a public beach reading "We Want Peace" and so on. The Court refused to give the rule a narrow construction to the effect that it covered commercial advertising only. In the light of this interpretation it held the rule invalid: "It is not aptly and narrowly phrased to protect the public from annoyance or danger or to protect public property. It does not merely regulate the size or position of signs.

It seeks to prohibit altogether in a public place one of the common and normally harmless means of communicating ideas. . . . This decision is confined to the precise issue here discussed. It is not necessary to consider what position we should take if, for example, instead of simply displaying signs, the defendants had painted a sign upon some permanent structure or had violated any other of the several prohibitions which are joined in Rule 3."

## Note

See, generally, Notes, 65 Harv. L. Rev. 690 (1952); 32 B. U. L. Rev. 101 (1952).

On the soundtruck cases see Notes, 58 Yale L. J. 335 (1949); 34 A. B. A. J. 589, 591 (1948). A model ordinance, drafted prior to the *Kovacs* case, is found in National Institute of Municipal Law Officers, Report No. 123 (1948). For studies of the effect of noise in general see Bartlett, *The Problem of Noise* (1934); McLachlan, *Noise* (1935).

A somewhat similar problem is that of the captive audience on public transportation systems. In Washington, D. C. the Capital Transit Company had installed FM receivers in buses and streetcars to play music and make commercial announcements. The Public Utility Commission held a hearing at which passengers intervened to object to the programs. In *P. U. C. v. Pollak,* 343 U. S. 451, 96 L. Ed. —, 72 S. Ct. 813 (1952), the Supreme Court held there was no infringement of the First and Fifth Amendments. The First Amendment was not violated because there was no showing that ordinary conversations could not take place due to the broadcasts, and the broadcasts did not involve objectionable propaganda. The Fifth Amendment does not guarantee a right to privacy on buses. For discussion of the transit radio problem see Note, 100 U. of Pa. L. Rev. 271 (1951); Shipley, *Some Constitutional Aspects of Transit Radio,* 11 Fed. Com. B. J. 150 (1950).

On the distinction between commercial and political and religious communication see *infra*.

## Activities on Privately Owned Property

In contrast with the *Struthers* case, discussed in the principal opinions above, note the more recent case of *Breard* v. *Alexandria,* 341 U. S. 622, 95 L. Ed. 1233, 71 S. Ct. 920 (1951). Here the Court upheld an ordinance declaring all uninvited soliciting to be a nuisance punishable as a misdemeanor. The defendant, a magazine subscription solicitor, objected on the grounds that he was arbitrarily deprived of his occupation, that the ordinance was an unreasonable burden on interstate commerce, and that it violated guarantees of freedom of speech. Mr. Justice Reed, who had dissented in the *Struthers* case, wrote the majority opinion in the *Breard* case, commenting on *Struthers* as follows: "There was dissent even to this carefully phrased application of the principles of the First Amendment. As no element of the commercial entered into this free solicitation and the opinion was narrowly limited to the precise fact of the free distribution of an invitation to religious services, we feel that it is not necessarily inconsistent with the conclusion reached in this case." Mr. Justice Reed distinguished the *Marsh* and *Tucker* cases (see Mr. Justice Frankfurter's opinion in the *Niemotko* case, *supra*) as follows: "In *Marsh* v. *Alabama*, 326 U. S. 501, and *Tucker* v. *Texas*, 326 U. S. 517, a state was held by this Court unable to punish for trespass, after notice under a state criminal statute, certain distributors of printed matter, more religious than commercial. The statute was held invalid under the principles of the First Amendment. In the *Marsh* case it was a private corporation, in the *Tucker* case the United States, that owned the property used as permissive passways in company and government-owned towns. In neither case was there dedication to public use but it seems fair to say that the permissive use of the ways was considered equal to such dedication. Such protection was not extended to colporteurs offending against similar state trespass laws by distributing, after notice to desist, like publications to the tenants in a private apartment house. *Hall* v. *Commonwealth*, 188 Va. 72, 49 S. E. 2d 369, appeal, after conviction, on the ground of denial of First Amendment rights, dismissed on motion of appellee to dismiss because of lack of substance in the question, 335 U. S. 875, 912. . . .

"Since it is not private individuals but the local and federal governments that are prohibited by the First and Fourteenth Amendments from abridging free speech or press, *Hall* v. *Virginia* does not rule a conviction for trespass after notice by ordinance. However, if as we have shown above, p. 640, a city council may speak for the citizens on matters subject to the police power, we would have in the present prosecution the time-honored offense of trespass on private grounds after notice. Thus the *Marsh* and *Tucker* cases are not applicable here." 341 U. S. at 643–4.

Mr. Justice Black's dissent in which Mr. Justice Douglas joined bluntly stated that the old cases were in effect overruled: "Since this decision cannot be reconciled with the *Jones, Murdock* and *Martin v. Struthers* cases, it seems to me that good judicial practice calls for their forthright overruling." 341 U. S. at 649. See also *Slater v. Salt Lake City*, 115 Utah 476, 206 Pac. 2d 153 (1949); *Ex parte Mares*, 75 Cal. App. 2d 798, 171 Pac. 2d 762 (1946) (city may prohibit sale of magazine subscriptions in congested business district); 127 A.L.R. 962 (1940); 9 A.L.R.

2d 728 (1950) ; 88 A.L.R. 183 (1934) ; 116 A.L.R. 1189 (1938) ; Note, 37 Iowa L. Rev. 261 (1952).

In *Watchtower Bible and Trust Soc. v. Metropolitan Life Ins. Co.*, 297 N. Y. 339, 79 N. E. 2d 433 (1948), cert. den. 335 U. S. 886 (1948), the regulation of a privately owned housing development prohibited canvassing and similar actions except with the consent of the manager or upon written consent or invitation of one of the tenants. The Court held that the exception was reasonable since it did not keep plaintiffs, the Jehovah's Witnesses, off streets and sidewalks and permitted them to enter the buildings upon invitation of the tenants. The Court felt, therefore, that it did not need to reach the larger constitutional question of whether the Constitution of the United States and of New York "have anything to do with rules made by any dwelling proprietors governing conduct inside other edifices." Cf. *Commonwealth v. Richardson*, 313 Mass. 632, 48 N. E. 2d 678 (1943), in which the Court held that tenants have an easement over the common passageways of the apartment house which extends to all other guests and invitees including Jehovah's Witnesses who had persuaded tenants to release the lock on the inner vestibule door. Once tenants extended their permission the landlord could not keep the Witnesses out. Their entering after his warning in these circumstances did not violate a "trespass after warning" law. See also *State v. Korich*, 219 Minn. 268, 17 N. W. 2d 497 (1945) (Jehovah's Witness' quiet and orderly solicitation in apartment house, though annoying, does not violate Minneapolis "disorderly conduct" ordinance). For comment on the *Watchtower Bible* case see Note, 48 Col. L. Rev. 1105 (1948).

## Note

1. The distinction between literature primarily for commercial rather than religious purposes was made by the Supreme Court in an earlier case not quite analogous to the *Breard* case. *Valentine v. Chrestensen*, 316 U. S. 52, 86 L. Ed. 1262, 62 S. Ct. 920 (1942) (state may prohibit use of street for commercial leaflet distribution even though these contain a religious message). See also *Slater v. Salt Lake City* and *Ex Parte Mares, supra*. As to the city's power to regulate outdoor advertising, see 72 A. L. R. 465 (1931) ; 156 A. L. R. 581 (1945) ; 79 A. L. R. 551 (1932) ; 121 A. L. R. 977 (1939) (by soundtrucks and other vehicles in the streets).

2. With respect to union activity on company property, see the following: (a) *Distribution of literature—Republic Aviation Corp. v. N. L. R. B.*, 324 U. S. 793, 89 L. Ed. 1372, 65 S. Ct. 982 (1945) (where plant surrounded by many acres of company property the company must make some provision for allowing distribution of literature near the plant) ; *Maryland Drydock Co. v. N. L. R. B.*, 183 F. 2d 538 (C. A.

4, 1950) (company may prohibit passing out of literature that insults and libels management and supervisory personnel). (b) *Posting notices—N. L. R. B. v. Thompson Products*, 162 F. 2d 287, 300 (C. A. 6, 1947) (reversing N. L. R. B. ruling that company could not make a contract with one of two rival unions in such a way as to give one union, which was exclusive bargaining representative, a monopoly on posting notices). (c) *Assembly and miscellaneous activity—N. L. R. B. v. Lake Superior Lumber Corp.*, 167 F. 2d 147 (C. A. 6, 1948) (union officials allowed to come to camp where workers lived only one evening a week on a particular day). See also *People v. Barisi*, 193 Misc. 934, 86 N. Y. Supp. 2d 277 (Mg. Ct. 1948).

3. On indirect controls that can be exercised by the police through licensing of public halls or by withdrawing licenses from those who rent such halls to dangerous groups, see Note, 47 Yale L. J. 404, 421 (1938); Jarnett and Mund, *The Right of Assembly*, 9 N. Y. U. L. Q. Rev. 1, 29 (1931). In *Local 309, U. F. W. v. Gates*, 75 F. Supp. 620 (N. D. Ind., 1948), the Indiana state police attended membership meetings of the Union and took notes. Evidence showed that this activity had the same effect on freedom of discussion as more direct interference. The Court granted an injunction upon the request of a number of individual members.

4. In *City of Richmond Heights v. Richmond Heights Memorial Post Benevolent Ass'n*, 358 Mo. 70, 213 S. W. 2d 479 (1948), plaintiff city sued to enjoin defendant American Legion post from maintaining a meeting place and recreation building in an area zoned as "Single Family Dwelling District." The court ruled for the plaintiff. It rejected the allegation that the zoning ordinance as applied here was unconstitutional, declaring that "the right to peaceably assemble [is] subject to the legitimate exercise of the police power of the state . . . The facts . . . of this case do not demonstrate that the power was so arbitrarily or unreasonably used as to violate due process."

## Picketing

### PICKETING AND FREE SPEECH—THE GAZZAM, HANKE AND HUGHES CASES

26 N. Y. U. L. Rev. 183 (1951)

Since picketing was first identified with free speech in *Thornhill v. Alabama*,[1] the extent of constitutional protection afforded to picketing under the Fourteenth Amendment has been a subject of extensive controversy in the courts and legal journals. From its inception, the doctrine that picketing is in fact another form of traditional "free speech" has been criticized[2] by those who have urged that it is essentially a form of economic coercion

---

[1] 310 U. S. 88 (1940).

[2] See Teller, *Picketing and Free Speech*, 56 HARV. L. REV. 180 (1942); Gregory, *Peaceful Picketing and Free Speech*, 26 A. B. A. J. 709 (1940); Petro, *Picketing and Freedom of Speech*, 1 LABOR L. J. 675 (1950).

entitled to no constitutional protection. The critics of the doctrine have argued that picketing, even when peaceful, relies on sympathy, habit, embarrassment, and obedience to union regulation, rather than an appeal to the reason of those towards whom it is directed. In rebuttal,[3] it may be contended that picketing should be entitled to free speech protection, as are other forms of communication (advertising for instance) which appeal to the eye rather than to reason. The Supreme Court, in a wavering retreat from *Thornhill,* appears to have attempted to steer a course somewhere between the above contentions. The Court's three recent picketing decisions in the *Gazzam, Hanke* and *Hughes* cases invite a renewed discussion of the problem in order to determine what survives of the picketing-free-speech doctrine.

In *Building Service Employees Union v. Gazzam,*[4] the union, having failed in its efforts to enlist the membership of Gazzam's employees, demanded that he sign an agreement which would have the ultimate effect of compelling his employees to join the union. Upon his refusal to accede to this demand, peaceful picketing of Gazzam's hotel was commenced. Compliance with the union's demand would have violated a Washington statute[5] providing that workers shall be free from employer coercion in the selection of their collective bargaining representatives. An injunction against picketing for the unlawful objective[6] was affirmed by the highest state court[7] and the Supreme Court. In *International Brotherhood v. Hanke,*[8] another case arising in Washington, a teamsters union picketed an automobile dealer in order to force him and his co-partners to become union members. The real objective was to compel the dealer's adherence to the union rule against week-end and evening work. Although this time the granting of the union's demand would have violated no statutory proscription, the Supreme Court found the state court's injunction to be constitutional. In *Hughes v. Superior Court,*[9] the Court upheld a California injunction against picketing by the Progressive Citizens of America to induce a retail chain store

[3] See Dodd, *Picketing and Free Speech: A Dissent,* 56 HARV. L. REV. 513 (1943); Armstrong, *Where Are We Going With Picketing,* 36 CALIF. L. REV. 1; Note, 34 CORNELL L. Q. 81 (1948).

[4] 339 U. S. 532 (1950).

[5] WASHINGTON LABOR DISPUTES ACT, WASH. REV. STAT. ANN. § 7612 (Supp. 1940).

[6] The Court stressed the fact that the court injunction was directed specifically at picketing for the unlawful objective, not at picketing generally, 339 U. S. 532, 533 (1950).

[7] *Building Service Employees Union v. Gazzam,* 207 P. 2d 699, 34 Wash. 2d 38 (1949).

[8] 399 U. S. 470 (1950).

[9] 339 U. S. 460 (1950).

**694**

to institute hiring practices whereby the proportion of Negro to white employees would approximate the proportion of Negro to white customers. California did not have a fair employment practices statute. On grounds similar to those underlying the *Hanke* decision, the Court held that California might constitutionally implement its public policy against selective hiring based on race by prohibiting picketing for such a purpose.

The limitations on picketing approved in the above cases raise the question whether the constitutional law on picketing has returned to the pre-Thornhill position.

## II.

At common law, picketing was considered to be prima facie tortious as constituting an intentional interference with property, and therefore subject to injunction. Picketing was privileged as an activity in promotion of labor's legitimate interests only when its conduct and objectives were considered to be "lawful" by the courts.[10] Prior to *Thornhill*, therefore, picketing enjoyed no federal constitutional protection, except that states had to satisfy the due process requirement inherent in all economic regulation, *i.e.*, the exercise of the state police power had to have a rational basis.[11]

Although language analogizing picketing to speech may be found in several earlier state court decisions,[12] the activity was for the first time linked with free speech by the Supreme Court in a dictum voiced by Mr. Justice Brandeis in *Senn v. Tile Layers Protective Union*[13] in 1937. The Senn dictum was elevated to

---

[10] See, *e. g.*, *Robison v. Hotel and Restaurant Employees*, 35 Idaho 418, 207 Pac. 132 (1922); *Lindsay and Co. v. Montana Federation of Labor*, 37 Mont. 264, 96 Pac. 127 (1908); RESTATEMENT, TORTS § 775 (1934); TELLER, LABOR DISPUTES AND COLLECTIVE BARGAINING §§ 45, 112–117 (1940); FRANKFURTER AND GREENE, THE LABOR INJUNCTION (1930).

[11] *Cf. Malinski v. New York*, 324 U. S. 401 (1944); *Drochy v. Kansas*, 272 U. S. 306 (1926); *Hickman Coal & Coke Co. v. Mitchell*, 245 U. S. 229 (1917); *Truax v. Raich*, 239 U. S. 33 (1915).

[12] *E. g.*, *Kirmse v. Adler*, 311 Pa. 78, 166 Atl. 566 (1933); *Truax v. Bisbee*, 19 Ariz. 379, 171 Pac. 121 (1918); *Empire Theater v. Cloke*, 53 Mont. 183, 163 Pac. 107 (1917); *Ex parte Lyons*, 27 Cal. App. 2d 293, 81 P. 2d 190 (1938); *Wood Mowing and Reaping Machine Co. v. Toohey*, 114 Misc. 185, 186 N. Y. Supp. 95 (Sup. Ct. 1921).

[13] 301 U. S. 468, 478 (1937). The Court held that state legislation legalizing peaceful picketing by a labor union of a self-employed person did not deprive the employer of due process of law or equal protection of the laws. In the opinion, Justice Brandeis pronounced this memorable dictum: "Members of a union might, without special statutory authorization by a State, make known the facts of a labor dispute, for freedom of speech is guaranteed by the Federal Constitution." It has been forcefully argued that Justice Brandeis was not referring to picketing, but to other means

**695**

holding in *Thornhill v. Alabama*[14] which involved a blanket statutory proscription of picketing. Speaking for the Court, Justice Murphy applied Holmes' clear and present danger rule in testing the validity of the legislation.[15] The statute was held to be unconstitutional on its face as violative of the due process clause of the Fourteenth Amendment which protects freedom of speech from state abridgment.

In *American Federation of Labor v. Swing*[16] the Supreme Court applied its new doctrine to a case involving stranger picketing. The Court dissolved a state injunction restraining picketing of a beauty parlor by an outside union which was attempting to unionize the shop, none of whose employees desired to join the union. Stating that state policy, whether declared by statute or by the common law, was subject to the limitations of the Fourteenth Amendment, the Court held that "a state cannot exclude workingmen from peacefully exercising the right of free communication by drawing the circle of economic competition between employers and workers so small as to contain only an employer and those directly employed by him."[17] The Thornhill doctrine reached its broadest development in *Cafeteria Employees Union v. Angelos*[18] wherein the Court dissolved a New York injunction which restrained a union from picketing two restaurants which were operated by their owners without any employees.

The first seed of doubt as to continued strict adherence to the

---

of publicizing facts when he made the above statement. See GREGORY, LABOR AND THE LAW 340 (1946). In any event, the dictum has been heavily relied upon in establishing constitutional law on picketing.

[14] 310 U. S. 88 (1940). See also *Carson v. California*, 310 U. S. 106 (1940), which invalidated a municipal ordinance prohibiting all forms of employee picketing.

[15] "In the circumstances of our times the dissemination of information concerning the facts of a labor dispute must be regarded as within that area of free discussion that is guaranteed by the Constitution. . . . Abridgement of the liberty of such discussion can be justified only where the clear danger of substantive evils arises under circumstances affording no opportunity to test the merits of ideas by competition for acceptance in the market place of public opinion. We hold that the danger of injury to an industrial concern is neither so serious nor so imminent as to justify the sweeping proscription of freedom of discussion embodied in [the statute]." *Thornhill v. Alabama*, 310 U. S. 88, 102, 104–5.

[16] 312 U. S. 321 (1941), *rehearing denied*, 312 U. S. 715 (1941).

[17] *Id.* at 326.

[18] 320 U. S. 293 (1943). The contention that the picketing involved was enjoinable because it was untruthful in that the picket signs tended to give the impression that the pickets had been previously employed by the restaurant, and that by patronizing it customers "were aiding the cause of Fascism" was met by the Court's finding that the use of such language was "part of the conventional give-and-take of our economic and political controversies" and did not falsify the facts. *Id.* at 295.

**696**

doctrine was planted in *Bakery Drivers Local v. Wohl*,[19] a case decided a year prior to *Angelos*. Therein a truck drivers union was held entitled to picket bakers which were supplying nonunion peddlers with bakery products. The Court indicated, however, that picketing may be subject to greater state control than other forms of communication.[20] In a concurring opinion, Mr. Justice Douglas was more explicit. He stated:

> Picketing by an organized group is more than free speech, since it involves patrol of a particular locality and since the very presence of a picket line may induce action of one kind or another, quite irrespective of the ideas disseminated.[21]

This statement foreshadowed much of the Supreme Court thinking which was to follow. In *Carpenters Union v. Ritter's Cafe*,[22] a sharply divided court held that Texas could, on the basis of its anti-trust statute, restrain picketing of a cafe, whose owner had awarded a building contract to a firm employing nonunion labor. It is significant to note that the clear and present danger approach was not applied, this time, in testing the validity of the injunction. The holding was premised, instead, on the narrow ground that a state had the power to confine picketing to the area of industry in which the labor dispute arose.

## III.

Except for *Angelos,* no further word on picketing was forthcoming from the Court until *Giboney v. Empire Storage Co.*[23] was decided in 1949. During this period of Supreme Court silence[24] state courts put varying interpretations on the cases heretofore discussed.[25] Although a few accepted the picketing-

---

[19] 315 U. S. 769 (1942).

[20] "A state is not required to tolerate in all places and in all circumstances even peaceful picketing by an individual." *Bakery Drivers Union v. Wohl, supra* note 22, at 775. That picketing "in the context of violence" is entitled to no constitutional protection had been previously made clear in *Milk Wagon Drivers Union of Chicago v. Meadowmoor Dairies*, 312 U. S. 287 (1941).

[21] 315 U. S. 769, 776 (1942).

[22] 315 U. S. 722 (1942).

[23] 336 U. S. 490 (1949).

[24] See *Wolferman, Inc. v. Root*, 356 Mo. 976, 204 S. W. 2d 733 (1947), *cert. denied*, 333 U. S. 837 (1948); *Hotel & Restaurant Employees International Alliance v. Greenwood*, 249 Ala. 265, 30 So. 2d 696 (1947), *cert. denied*, 332 U. S. 847 (1948); *Wisconsin Employment Relations Board v. Milk & Ice Cream Drivers Union*, 238 Wis. 379, 299 N. W. 31 (1941), *cert. denied*, 316 U. S. 668 (1942). See also *Denver Milk Producers Inc. v. International Brotherhood*, 116 Colo. 389, 183 P. 2d 529 (1947), *aff'd mem.*, 344 U. S. 809 (1948).

[25] For a detailed discussion of state court decisions on picketing, see

free-speech concept,[26] the majority continued to enjoin picketing when it was in furtherance of an objective which was considered unlawful under local legislation[27] or ran counter to state public policy as defined by its judiciary.[28] Citing *Ritter,* these courts reasoned that inasmuch as no unequivocal Supreme Court pronouncement had invalidated the "unlawful objective" doctrine, they were not constrained to change their approach to the picketing problem.[29] A novel approach seems to have been taken in several cases wherein the court attempted to separate picketing for an "unlawful" purpose which was predominantly coercive (non-speech) from picketing for the same purpose in which the aspects of communication predominated. While enjoining the former, the effectiveness of which depended on union discipline, and which prevented deliveries by union drivers, the courts permitted continuation of the latter, which was directed at the general public.[30] . . .

---

Franz, *Picketing for an Unlawful Objective,* 28 N. L. C. REV. (1950); Note, 98 U. OF PA. L. REV. 545 (1950).

[26] *State ex rel. Culinary Workers Union v. Eighth Judicial District,* 207 P. 2d 990 (Nev. 1949) (injunction against picketing for a closed shop dissolved, although picketing was conducted by outside union which did not represent employer's workers); *American Federation of Labor v. Bain,* 165 Ore. 183, 106 P. 2d 544 (1940) (clear and present danger test applies to picketing as it does to other forms of speech).

[27] *E. g., Wilbank v. Chester and Delaware Bartenders Union,* 360 Pa. 48, 60 A. 2d 21 (1948), *cert. denied,* 336 U. S. 945 (1949) (objective sought an unfair labor practice under state law); *Swenson v. Seattle Central Labor Council,* 27 Wash. 2d 192, 177 P. 2d 873 (1947); *Harper v. Brennan,* 311 Mich. 489, 18 N. W. 2d 905 (1945) (objective sought violative of state anti-trust statute).

[28] *Colonial Press v. Ellis,* 321 Mass. 495, 74 N. E. 2d 1 (1947) (picketing for a closed shop); *James v. Marinship Corp.,* 25 Cal. 2d 721, 155 P. 2d 329 (closed union may not picket for a closed shop); *Mayer Bros. Poultry Farms v. Meltzer,* 274 App. Div. 169, 80 N. Y. S. 2d 874 (1st Dep't 1948) (objective sought held to be an embargo against importation of food into New York City).

[29] See *Colonial Press v. Ellis,* 321 Mass. 495, 501, 74 N. E. 2d 1, 4 (1947) ("Until there is an unequivocal pronouncement to that effect [that picketing for an unlawful objective may not be enjoined] we adhere to the view of the law laid down in our own decisions."). But see Armstrong, *Where Are We Going With Picketing,* 36 CALIF. L. REV. 1, 36 (1948) for the view that the application of the unlawful objective doctrine is unconstitutional "[u]nless the achievement of the objective would be productive of 'extremely serious' social evil."

[30] *Wolferman, Inc. v. Root,* 356 Mo. 976, 204 S. W. 2d 733 (1947), *cert. denied,* 333 U. S. 839 (1948); *accord, Lubbers v. Hurst,* 78 N. E. 2d 580 (Ohio C. P. 1946) (union restrained from attempting to prevent deliveries to employer, but employer not entitled to injunction against picketing generally).

## IV.

In *Giboney v. Empire Storage Co.*[41] a truck drivers union picketed a wholesale ice dealer in an effort to obtain an agreement whereby the dealer would supply ice to union drivers only. The Missouri Supreme Court approved an injunction of all picketing on the ground that the proposed agreement was violative of a state anti-trust statute,[42] and the Supreme Court affirmed unanimously. Although the *Giboney* decision gave strong support to the "unlawful objective" approach,[43] the Court took pains to observe that "there was clear danger, imminent and immediate, that unless restrained, appellants would succeed in making that [the state's] policy a dead letter insofar as purchases by nonunion men were concerned."[44] Moreover, the picketing involved, which was directed at drivers who were subject to union penalties if they crossed the picket lines, was essentially coercive rather than speech.[45] Another question which remained open was whether picketing was enjoinable when its purpose ran counter to a state's common law rather than its legislation.

These caveats were largely resolved by the three subsequent Supreme Court cases. The *Gazzam* case, which involved picketing for a union shop, was very similar on its facts to the *Swing* case. The cases were distinguished, however, on the ground that in the latter the state's injunction had been based "solely on the absence of an employer-employee relationship,"[46] whereas in *Gazzam* an adequate basis for the injunction was found in "the unlawful objective of the picketing, namely, coercion of the employer of the employees' selection of a bargaining representative."[47]

[41] 336 U. S. 490 (1949).

[42] 357 Mo. 671, 210 S. W. 2d 55 (1948).

[43] "Nor can we say that the publication here should not have been restrained because of the possibility of separating the picketing conduct into illegal and legal parts. . . . For the placards were to effectuate the purposes of an unlawful combination, and their sole, unlawful immediate objective was to induce Empire to violate the Missouri law. . . ." *Giboney v. Empire Storage Co.*, 336 U. S. 490, 502 (1949).

[44] *Id.* at 503.

[45] "These Union truck drivers refused to deliver goods to or from Empire's place of business. Had any one of them crossed the picket line he would have been subject to a fine or suspension by the union of which he was a member." *Id.* at 493.

[46] *Building Service Employees Union v. Gazzam*, 339 U. S. 532, 539 (1950).

[47] *Ibid.* The objective ran counter to Washington's public policy as declared by statute. Whereas in *Giboney* the state law which made the objective unlawful had criminal sanctions, this was not the case in *Gazzam*. The Court refused to distinguish the two cases on this narrow ground. *Id.* at 540.

In *Hanke,* a case whose facts closely resemble those in *Angelos,* the Court in a five to three decision retreated considerably further from the Thornhill doctrine. This time Washington's public policy was declared by the state supreme court and not by the legislature. The union objective (to have self-employed persons become union members) violated no state law, and could have been legally accomplished had Hanke agreed to the union's demand. Nevertheless the picketing injunction was affirmed, the Court concluding that it was immaterial whether a state's policy was made by statute or by the judiciary.

Even more significant than the Court's actual holding appears to be Justice Frankfurter's approach to the picketing problem, which was accepted by the three justices who concurred in his opinion.[48] Justice Frankfurter observed at the outset that picketing cannot be equated with speech,[49] and limited previous cases narrowly to their facts.[50] He proceeded to state that it was up to the states, in the regulation of their economic affairs, to strike a balance between the unions' interests on the one hand, and the employers' on the other. The state, having in *Hanke* decided in favor of the self-employer, it remained for the Supreme Court only to determine whether the state "has struck a balance so inconsistent with rooted traditions of a free people that it must be found an unconstitutional choice."[51] This approach would seem to indicate that picketing is to be afforded no substantially greater protection than other non-speech activities whose regulation must have a rational basis in order to meet the due process requirement.[52] Should this be the case, the fact that picketing has some speech aspects may, however, remain a weighty factor in the application of a "rational basis test."[53]

---

[48] The opinion was written by Justice Frankfurter. Justice Clark concurred in the result. Justices Black, Minton, and Reed dissented. Justice Douglas took no part in the consideration of the case.

[49] "[W]hile picketing has an ingredient of communication it cannot dogmatically be equated with the constitutionally protected freedom of speech." *International Brotherhood of Teamsters v. Hanke,* 339 U. S. 470, 474 (1950).

[50] It is "the Court's duty to restrict general expressions of opinion in earlier cases to their specific context. . . ." *Id.* at 480, n. 6. "In those cases we held only that a state could not proscribe picketing merely by setting artificial bounds, unreal in the light of modern circumstances, to what constitutes an industrial relationship or a labor dispute." *Id.* at 479–80.

[51] *Id.* at 479. "A state's judgment in striking such a balance is of course subject to the limitation of the Fourteenth Amendment." *Id.* at 474–75.

[52] See cases cited note 13 *supra.*

[53] Justice Minton, dissenting, urged that the picketing involved in the *Hanke* case was constitutionally protected. He stated: "It seems to me too late now to deny that those [prior] cases were rooted in the free speech

The *Hughes* decision,[54] also written by Justice Frankfurter, was arrived at by means of the same reasoning as was applied in the *Hanke* case.[55] Again the state's public policy was made by the state supreme court. A distinguishing factor, however, was the fact that the picketing involved was not conducted by a labor union, but by the Progressive Citizens of America, in an effort to induce a store to hire more Negroes. Thus coercive elements were at a minimum. The picket's appeal was to the customers and not to a group which was subject to union discipline. No heed was paid to this distinction, however, and the injunction was sustained.[56]

In view of the above decisions, very little appears to be left of the Thornhill doctrine. Although Justice Frankfurter's language indicating a "rational basis" approach is not explicit in withdrawing all free speech protection from picketing, the activity would seem to be entitled to no speech protection if his approach is followed in future decisions. Moreover, all the Justices seem to have accepted the "unlawful objective" approach set forth in *Giboney* and *Gazzam*.

---

doctrine. I think we should not decide the instant cases in a manner so alien to the basis of prior decisions." 339 U. S. 470, 483 (1950).

[54] For a discussion of the propriety of the injunction in the *Hughes* case, apart from the constitutional question, see Note, 22 So. CALIF. L. REV. 442, 450 (1949). The note discusses the state supreme court case: *Hughes v. Superior Court*, 32 Cal. 2d 850, 198 P. 2d 885 (1948).

[55] The three Justices who had dissented in *Hanke* concurred in the result in *Hughes* without adopting the Court's language. Justices Black and Minton stated that the case was controlled by the principles announced in *Giboney*. Justice Reed concurred separately on the ground that the picketing had been for an unlawful objective under California Law. Justice Douglas was absent during the consideration of the case.

[56] Relying on the *Hanke, Hughes* and *Gazzam* decisions, picketing was restrained in two recent instances by New York courts on the ground that the picketing was for an unlawful objective. *Haber and Fink, Inc. v. Jones*, 277 App. Div. 176, 98 N. Y. S. 2d 393 (1st Dep't 1950) (picketing to coerce an employer to bargain with a labor union which had been defeated in an election under the State Labor Relations Act); *Wilson v. Hacker*, 19 U. S. L. Week 2217 (Sup. Ct. Nov. 13, 1950) (picketing for a union shop by a union which excluded women from membership).

That broad prohibitions of picketing may still be considered unconstitutional is indicated in *Edwards v. Virginia*, 191 Va. 272, 60 S. E. 2d 916 (1950). Therein a state statute forbidding picketing by nonemployees was invalidated. The court concluded that "[t]he pattern which emerges [from the recent Supreme Court decisions] to shape the boundaries of state action seems to be that picketing is subject to regulation by the State, either by legislation or by court action. But such regulation must have a reasonable basis in prevention of disorder, restraint of coercion, protection of life and property, or promotion of the general welfare." 60 S. E. 2d 916, 922. Distinguishing *Hanke, Hughes*, and *Gazzam*, the court determined that the statutory prohibition involved had overstepped the boundaries of permissible state action.

The *Hanke* and *Hughes* cases have made it clear that a state's public policy concerning the lawfulness of picketing objectives may be determined by the courts as well as by the legislature. While jurisprudential consistency may demand this result, it is now more uncertain than ever whether a given trial court's injunction is constitutional. Whereas under *Giboney* the picketing objective could be tested against a statute, it now must also be tested against the policy of the judiciary. The resulting uncertainty is unfortunate, as in labor disputes a speedy and predictable settlement of the legality of the picketing involved is vital.

### Note

1. In addition to the articles and books cited in the above, see Gordon, *Giboney v. Empire Storage & Ice Co.: A Footnote to Free Speech,* 36 Va. L. Rev. 25 (1950); Cox, *Strikes, Picketing and the Constitution,* 4 Vand. L. Rev. 574 (1951); 174 A. L. R. 593 (1947); Rehmus, *Picketing and Freedom of Speech,* 30 Ore. L. Rev. 115 (1950); Note, 19 Geo. Wash. L. Rev. 287 (1950).

2. Supreme Court decisions upholding restrictions upon picketing imposed by Section 8(b) of the Taft-Hartley Act include: *N. L. R. B. v. Denver Building Council,* 341 U. S. 675, 95 L. Ed. 1284, 71 S. Ct. 943 (1951); *Electrical Workers v. N. L. R. B.,* 341 U. S. 694, 95 L. Ed. 1299, 71 S. Ct. 954 (1951); *Carpenters Union v. N. L. R. B.,* 341 U. S. 707, 95 L. Ed. 1309, 71 S. Ct. 966 (1951). See also *N. L. R. B. v. Rice Milling Co.,* 341 U. S. 665, 95 L. Ed. 1277, 71 S. Ct. 961 (1951).

On the issue of the employer's right of free speech in his relations with labor, see Daykin, *The Employers' Right of Free Speech Under the Taft-Hartley Act,* 37 Iowa L. Rev. 212 (1952).

On picketing of courts, see 18 U. S. C. § 1507 (Supp. III, 1950).

## B. UNTRUTHFUL AND HARMFUL COMMUNICATIONS IN THE NEWER MASS MEDIA

### 1. Motion Pictures

### BURSTYN v. WILSON

Supreme Court of the United States, 1952
343 U. S. 495, 96 L. Ed. —, 72 S. Ct. 777

[That portion of Mr. Justice Frankfurter's opinion which summarizes the background of the case is printed before the prevailing opinion of the Court.]

MR. JUSTICE FRANKFURTER, concurring.

A practised hand has thus summarized the story of "The Miracle":

"A poor, simple-minded girl is tending a herd of goats on a mountainside one day, when a bearded stranger passes. Suddenly it strikes her fancy that he is St. Joseph, her favorite saint, and that he has come to take her to heaven, where she will be happy and free. While she pleads with him to transport her, the stranger gently plies the girl with wine, and when she is in a state of tumult, he apparently ravishes her. (This incident in the story is only briefly and discreetly implied.)

"The girl awakens later, finds the stranger gone, and climbs down the mountain not knowing whether he was real or a dream. She meets an old priest who tells her that it is quite possible that she did see a saint, but a younger priest scoffs at the notion. 'Materialist!' the old priest says.

"There follows now a brief sequence—intended to be symbolic, obviously—in which the girl is reverently sitting with other villagers in church. Moved by a whim of appetite, she snitches an apple from the basket of a woman next to her. When she leaves the church, a cackling beggar tries to make her share the apple with him, but she chases him away as by habit and munches the fruit contentedly.

"Then, one day, while tending the village youngsters as their mothers work at the vines, the girl faints and the women discover that she is going to have a child. Frightened and bewildered, she suddenly murmurs, 'It is the grace of God!' and she runs to the church in great excitement, looks for the statue of St. Joseph, and then prostrates herself on the floor.

"Thereafter she meekly refuses to do any menial work and the housewives humor her gently but the young people are not so kind. In a scene of brutal torment, they first flatter and laughingly mock her, then they cruelly shove and hit her and clamp a basin as a halo on her head. Even abused by the beggars, the poor girl gathers together her pitiful rags and sadly departs from the village to live alone in a cave.

"When she feels her time coming upon her, she starts towards the village. But then she sees the crowds in the streets; dark memories haunt her; so she turns towards a church on a high hill and instinctively struggles towards it, crying desperately to God. A goat is her sole companion. She drinks water dripping from a rock. And when she comes to the church and finds the door locked, the goat attracts her to a small side door. Inside the church, the poor girl braces herself for her labor pains. There is a dissolve, and when we next see her sad face, in close-up, it is full of a tender light. There is the cry of an unseen baby. The girl reaches towards it and murmurs, 'My son! My love! My flesh!' "

"The Miracle"—a film lasting forty minutes—was produced in Italy by Roberto Rosselini. Anna Magnani played the lead as the demented goat-tender. It was first shown at the Venice Film Festival in August, 1948, combined with another moving picture, "L'Umano Voce," into a diptych called "Amore." According to an affidavit from the Director of that Festival, if the motion picture had been "blasphemous" it would have been barred by the Festival Committee. In a review of the film in L'Osservatore Romano, the organ of the Vatican, its film critic, Piero Regnoli, wrote: "Opinions may vary and questions may arise—even serious ones—of a religious nature (not to be diminished by the fact that the woman portrayed is mad [because] the author who attributed madness to her is not mad) . . . ." While acknowledging that there were "passages of undoubted cinematic distinction," Regnoli criticized the film as being "on such a pretentiously cerebral plane that it reminds one of the early d'Annunzio." The Vatican newspaper's critic concluded: "we continue to believe in Rosselini's art and we look forward to his next achievement." In October, 1948, a month after the Rome premiere of "The Miracle," the Vatican's censorship agency, the Catholic Cinematographic Centre, declared that the picture "constitutes in effect an abominable profanation from religious and moral viewpoints." By the Lateran agreements and the Italian Constitution the Italian Government is bound to bar whatever may offend the Catholic religion. However, the Catholic Cinematographic Centre did not invoke any governmental sanction thereby afforded. The Italian Government's censorship agency gave "The Miracle" the regular *nulla osta* clearance. The film was freely shown throughout Italy, but was not a great success. Italian movie critics divided in opinion. The critic for Il Popolo, speaking for the Christian Democratic Party, the Catholic party, profusely praised the picture as "a beautiful thing, humanly felt, alive, true and without religious profanation as someone has said, because in our opinion the meaning of the characters is clear and there is no possibility of misunderstanding." Regnoli again reviewed "The Miracle" for L'Osservatore Romano. After criticising the film for technical faults, he found "the most courageous and interesting passage of Rosselini's work" in contrasting portrayals in the film; he added: "Unfortunately, concerning morals, it is necessary to note some slight defects." He objected to its "carnality" and to the representation of illegitimate motherhood. But he did not suggest that the picture was "sacrilegious." The tone of Regnoli's critique was one of respect for Rosselini, "the illustrious Italian producer."

**704**

On March 2, 1949, "The Miracle" was licensed in New York State for showing without English titles. However, it was never exhibited until after a second license was issued on November 30, 1950, for the trilogy, "Ways of Love," combining "The Miracle" with two French films, Jean Renoir's "A Day in the Country" and Marcel Pagnol's "Jofroi." All had English subtitles. Both licenses were issued in the usual course after viewings of the picture by the Motion Picture Division of the New York State Education Department. The Division is directed by statute to "issue a license" "unless [the] film or part thereof is obscene, indecent, immoral, inhuman, sacrilegious, or is of such a character that its exhibition would tend to corrupt morals or incite to crime." N. Y. Education Law, § 122. The trilogy opened on December 12, 1950, at the Paris Theatre on 58th Street in Manhattan. It was promptly attacked as "a sacrilegious and blasphemous mockery of Christian religious truth" by the National Legion of Decency, a private Catholic organization for film censorship, whose objectives have intermittently been approved by various non-Catholic church and social groups since its formation in 1933. However, the National Board of Review (a non-industry lay organization devoted to raising the level of motion pictures by mobilizing public opinion, under the slogan "Selection Not Censorship") recommended the picture as "especially worth seeing." New York critics on the whole praised "The Miracle"; those who dispraised did not suggest sacrilege. On December 27 the critics selected the "Ways of Love" as the best foreign language film in 1950. Meanwhile, on December 23, Edward T. McCaffrey, Commissioner of Licenses for New York City, declared the film "officially and personally blasphemous" and ordered it withdrawn at the risk of suspension of the license to operate the Paris Theatre. A week later the program was restored at the theatre upon the decision by the New York Supreme Court that the City License Commissioner had exceeded his authority in that he was without powers of movie censorship.

Upon the failure of the License Commissioner's effort to cut off showings of "The Miracle," the controversy took a new turn. On Sunday, January 7, 1951, a statement of His Eminence, Francis Cardinal Spellman, condemning the picture and calling on "all right thinking citizens" to unite to tighten censorship laws, was read at all masses in St. Patrick's Cathedral.

The views of Cardinal Spellman aroused dissent among other devout Christians. Protestant clergymen, representing various denominations, after seeing the picture, found in it nothing "sacrilegious or immoral to the views held by Christian men and women," and with a few exceptions agreed that the film was "unquestionably one of unusual artistic merit."

In this estimate some Catholic laymen concurred. Their opinion is represented by the comment by Otto L. Spaeth, Director of the American Federation of Arts and prominent in Catholic lay activities:

"At the outbreak of the controversy, I immediately arranged for a private showing of the film. I invited a group of Catholics, competent and respected for their writings on both religious and cultural subjects. The essential approval of the film was unanimous.

"There was indeed 'blasphemy' in the picture—but it was the blasphemy of the villagers, who stopped at nothing, not even the mock singing of a hymn to the Virgin, in their brutal badgering of the tragic woman. The scathing indictment of their evil behaviour, implicit in the film, was seemingly overlooked by its critics."

William C. Clancy, a teacher at the University of Notre Dame, wrote in The Commonweal, the well-known Catholic weekly, that "the film is not *obviously* blasphemous or obscene, either in its intention or execution." The Commonweal itself questioned the wisdom of transforming Church dogma which Catholics may obey as "a free act" into state-enforced censorship for all. Allen Tate, the well-known Catholic poet and critic, wrote: "The picture seems to me to be superior in acting and photography but inferior dramatically. . . . In the long run what Cardinal Spellman will have succeeded in doing is insulting the intelligence and faith of American Catholics with the assumption that a second-rate motion picture could in any way undermine their morals or shake their faith."

At the time "The Miracle" was filmed, all the persons having significant positions in the production—producer, director, and cast—were Catholics. Roberto Rosselini, who had Vatican approval in 1949 for filming a life of St. Francis, using in the cast members of the Franciscan Order, cabled Cardinal Spellman protesting against boycott of "The Miracle":

"In 'The Miracle' men are still without pity because they still have not come back to God, but God is already in the faith, however confused, of that poor, persecuted woman; and since God is wherever a human being suffers and is misunderstood, 'The Miracle' occurs when at the birth of the child the poor, demented woman regains sanity in her eternal love."

[Emerson]

In view of the controversy thus aroused by the picture, the Chairman of the Board of Regents appointed a committee of three Board members to review the action of the Motion Picture Division in granting the two licenses. After viewing the picture on Jan. 15, 1951, the committee declared it "sacrilegious." The Board four days later issued an order to the licensees to show cause why the licenses should not be cancelled in that the picture was "sacrilegious." The Board of Regents rescinded the licenses on Feb. 16, 1951, saying that the "mockery or profaning of these beliefs that are sacred to any portion of our citizenship is abhorrent to the laws of this great State." On review the Appellate Division upheld the Board of Regents, holding that the banning of any motion picture "that may fairly be deemed sacrilegious to the adherents of any religious group . . . is directly related to public peace and order" and is not a denial of religious freedom, and that there was "substantial evidence upon which the Regents could act." 278 App. Div. 253, 257, 258, 260.

The New York Court of Appeals, with one judge concurring in a separate opinion and two others dissenting, affirmed the order of the Appellate Division. 303 N. Y. 242. . . . Both State courts, as did this Court, viewed "The Miracle."

MR. JUSTICE CLARK delivered the opinion of the Court. . . .

Appellant brought the present action in the New York courts to review the determination of the Regents. Among the claims advanced by appellant were (1) that the statute violates the Fourteenth Amendment as a prior restraint upon freedom of speech and of the press; (2) that it is invalid under the same Amendment as a violation of the guaranty of separate church and state and as a prohibition of the free exercise of religion; and, (3) that the term "sacrilegious" is so vague and indefinite as to offend due process. . . .

As we view the case, we need consider only appellant's contention that the New York statute is an unconstitutional abridgment of free speech and a free press. In *Mutual Film Corp.* v. *Industrial Comm'n*, 236 U. S. 230 (1915), a distributor of motion pictures sought to enjoin the enforcement of an Ohio statute which required the prior approval of a board of censors before any motion picture could be publicly exhibited in the state, and which directed the board to approve only such films as it adjudged to be "of a moral, educational or amusing and harmless character." The statute was assailed in part as an unconstitutional abridgment of the freedom of the press guaranteed by the First and Fourteenth Amendments. The District Court rejected this contention, stating that the first eight Amendments were not a restriction on state action. 215 F. 138, 141 (D. C. N. D. Ohio 1914). On appeal to this Court, plaintiff in its brief abandoned this claim and contended merely that the statute in question violated the freedom of speech and publication guaranteed by the Constitution of Ohio. In affirming the decree of the District Court denying injunctive relief, this Court stated:

> "It cannot be put out of view that the exhibition of moving pictures is a business pure and simple, originated and conducted for profit, like other spectacles, not to be regarded, nor intended to be regarded by the Ohio constitution, we think, as part of the press of the country or as organs of public opinion."

In a series of decisions beginning with *Gitlow* v. *New York*, 268 U. S. 652 (1925), this Court held that the liberty of speech and of the press which the First Amendment guarantees against abridgment by the federal government is within the liberty safeguarded by the Due Process Clause of the Fourteenth Amendment from invasion by state action. That principle has been followed and reaffirmed to the present day. Since this series of decisions came after the *Mutual* decision, the present case is the first to present squarely to us the question whether motion pictures are within the ambit of protection which the First Amendment, through the Fourteenth, secures to any form of "speech" or "the press."

It cannot be doubted that motion pictures are a significant medium for the communication of ideas. They may affect public attitudes and behavior in a variety of ways, ranging from direct espousal of a political or social doctrine to the subtle shaping of thought which characterizes all artistic expression.[10] The importance of motion pictures as an organ of public opinion is not lessened by the fact that they are designed to entertain as well as to inform. As was said in *Winters* v. *New York*, 333 U. S. 507, 510 (1948):

> "The line between the informing and the entertaining is too elusive for the protection of that basic right [a free press]. Everyone is familiar with instances of propaganda through fiction. What is one man's amusement, teaches another's doctrine."

It is urged that motion pictures do not fall within the First Amendment's aegis because their production, distribution, and exhibition is a large-scale business conducted for private profit.

---

[10] See Inglis, Freedom of the Movies (1947), 20–24; Klapper, The Effects of Mass Media (1950), *passim;* Note, Motion Pictures and the First Amendment, 60 Yale L. J. 696, 704–708 (1951), and sources cited therein.

We cannot agree. That books, newspapers, and magazines are published and sold for profit does not prevent them from being a form of expression whose liberty is safeguarded by the First Amendment.[11] We fail to see why operation for profit should have any different effect in the case of motion pictures.

It is further urged that motion pictures possess a greater capacity for evil, particularly among the youth of a community, than other modes of expression. Even if one were to accept this hypothesis, it does not follow that motion pictures should be disqualified from First Amendment protection. If there be capacity for evil it may be relevant in determining the permissible scope of community control, but it does not authorize substantially unbridled censorship such as we have here.

For the foregoing reasons, we conclude that expression by means of motion pictures is included within the free speech and free press guaranty of the First and Fourteenth Amendments. To the extent that language in the opinion in *Mutual Film Corp.* v. *Industrial Comm'n, supra,* is out of harmony with the views here set forth, we no longer adhere to it.[12]

To hold that liberty of expression by means of motion pictures is guaranteed by the First and Fourteenth Amendments, however, is not the end of our problem. It does not follow that the Constitution requires absolute freedom to exhibit every motion picture of every kind at all times and all places. That much is evident from the series of decisions of this Court with respect to other media of communication of ideas. Nor does it follow that motion pictures are necessarily subject to the precise rules governing any other particular method of expression. Each method tends to present its own peculiar problems. But the basic principles of freedom of speech and the press, like the First Amendment's command, do not vary. Those principles, as they have frequently been enunciated by this Court, make freedom of expression the rule. There is no justification in this case for making an exception to that rule.

The statute involved here does not seek to punish, as a past offense, speech or writing falling within the permissible scope of subsequent punishment. On the contrary, New York requires that permission to communicate ideas be obtained in advance

---

[11] See *Grosjean v. American Press Co.*, 297 U. S. 233 (1936); *Thomas v. Collins*, 323 U. S. 516, 531 (1945).

[12] See *United States v. Paramount Pictures, Inc.*, 334 U. S. 131, 166 (1948): "We have no doubt that moving pictures, like newspapers and radio, are included in the press whose freedom is guaranteed by the First Amendment." It is not without significance that talking pictures were first produced in 1926, eleven years after the *Mutual* decision. Encyclopedia Britannica (1951), "Motion Pictures."

from state officials who judge the content of the words and pictures sought to be communicated. This Court recognized many years ago that such a previous restraint is a form of infringement upon freedom of expression to be especially condemned. *Near* v. *Minnesota ex rel. Olson*, 283 U. S. 697 (1931). The Court there recounted the history which indicates that a major purpose of the First Amendment guaranty of a free press was to prevent prior restraints upon publication, although it was carefully pointed out that the liberty of the press is not limited to that protection. It was further stated that "the protection even as to previous restraint is not absolutely unlimited. But the limitation has been recognized only in exceptional cases." *Id.*, at 716. In the light of the First Amendment's history and of the *Near* decision, the State has a heavy burden to demonstrate that the limitation challenged here presents such an exceptional case.

New York's highest court says there is "nothing mysterious" about the statutory provision applied in this case: "It is simply this: that no religion, as that word is understood by the ordinary, reasonable person, shall be treated with contempt, mockery, scorn and ridicule . . . ."[15] This is far from the kind of narrow exception to freedom of expression which a state may carve out to satisfy the adverse demands of other interests of society. In seeking to apply the broad and all-inclusive definition of "sacrilegious" given by the New York courts, the censor is set adrift upon a boundless sea amid a myriad of conflicting currents of religious views, with no charts but those provided by the most vocal and powerful orthodoxies. New York cannot vest such unlimited restraining control over motion pictures in a censor. Cf. *Kunz* v. *New York*, 340 U. S. 290 (1951). Under

---

[15] 303 N. Y. 242, 258, 101 N. E. 2d 665, 672. At another point the Court of Appeals gave "sacrilegious" the following definition: "the act of violating or profaning anything sacred." *Id.*, at 255, 101 N. E. 2d at 670. The Court of Appeals also approved the Appellate Division's interpretation: "As the court below said of the statute in question, 'All it purports to do is to bar a visual caricature of religious beliefs held sacred by one sect or another . . . .'" *Id.*, at 258, 101 N. E. 2d at 672. Judge Fuld, dissenting, concluded from all the statements in the majority opinion that "the basic criterion appears to be whether the film treats a religious theme in such a manner as to offend the religious beliefs of any group of persons. If the film does have that effect, and it is 'offered as a form of entertainment,' it apparently falls within the statutory ban regardless of the sincerity and good faith of the producer of the film, no matter how temperate the treatment of the theme, and no matter how unlikely a public disturbance or breach of the peace. The drastic nature of such a ban is highlighted by the fact that the film in question makes no direct attack on, or criticism of, any religious dogma or principle, and it is not claimed to be obscene, scurrilous, intemperate or abusive." *Id.*, at 271–272, 101 N. E. 2d at 680.

such a standard the most careful and tolerant censor would find it virtually impossible to avoid favoring one religion over another, and he would be subject to an inevitable tendency to ban the expression of unpopular sentiments sacred to a religious minority. Application of the "sacrilegious" test, in these or other respects, might raise substantial questions under the First Amendment's guaranty of separate church and state with freedom of worship for all. However, from the standpoint of freedom of speech and the press, it is enough to point out that the state has no legitimate interest in protecting any or all religions from views distasteful to them which is sufficient to justify prior restraints upon the expression of those views. It is not the business of government in our nation to suppress real or imagined attacks upon a particular religious doctrine, whether they appear in publications, speeches, or motion pictures.

Since the term "sacrilegious" is the sole standard under attack here, it is not necessary for us to decide, for example, whether a state may censor motion pictures under a clearly-drawn statute designed and applied to prevent the showing of obscene films. That is a very different question from the one now before us. We hold only that under the First and Fourteenth Amendments a state may not ban a film on the basis of a censor's conclusion that it is "sacrilegious."

*Reversed.*

[Mr. Justice Frankfurter's concurring opinion does not reach the free speech issue. In his view "sacrilegious" lacks "the necessary precision of meaning which the Due Process clause enjoins for statutes regulating men's activities." After a thorough history of the origin and various meanings of the word "sacrilege" he concludes that it has no single meaning and that none of its various meanings include the one attributed to it by the New York Court. The opinion continues:]

History teaches us the indefiniteness of the concept "sacrilegious" in another respect. In the case of most countries and times where the concept of sacrilege has been of importance there has existed an established church or a state religion. That which was "sacred," and so was protected against "profaning," was designated in each case by ecclesiastical authority. What might have been definite when a controlling church imposed a detailed scheme of observances, becomes impossibly confused and uncertain when hundreds of sects, with widely disparate and often directly conflicting ideas of sacredness, enjoy, without discrimination and in equal measure, constitutionally guaranteed religious freedom. In the Rome of the late emperors, the England of James I, or the Geneva of Calvin, and today in Roman Catholic

**711**

Spain, Mohammedan Saudi Arabia, or any other country with a monolithic religion, the category of things sacred might have clearly definable limits. But in America the multiplicity of the ideas of "sacredness" held with equal but conflicting fervor by the great number of religious groups makes the term "sacrilegious" too indefinite to satisfy constitutional demands based on reason and fairness.

If "sacrilegious" bans more than the physical abuse of sacred persons, places, or things, if it permits censorshp of religious opinions, which is the effect of the holding below, the term will include what may be found to be "blasphemous." England's experience with that treacherous word should give us pause, apart from our requirements for the separation of Church and State. The crime of blasphemy in Seventeenth Century England was the crime of dissenting from whatever was the current religious dogma.[51] King James I's "Book of Sports" was first required reading in the churches; later all copies were consigned to the flames. To attack the mass was once blasphemous; to perform it became so. At different times during that century, with the shifts in the attitude of government towards particular religious views, persons who doubted the doctrine of the Trinity (e. g., Unitarians, Universalists, etc.) or the divinity of Christ, observed the Sabbath on Saturday, denied the possibility of witchcraft, repudiated child baptism or urged methods of baptism other than sprinkling, were charged as blasphemers, or their books were burned or banned as blasphemous. Blasphemy was the chameleon phrase which meant the criticism of whatever the ruling authority of the moment established as orthodox religious doctrine. While it is true that blasphemy prosecutions have continued in England—although in lessening numbers—into the present century,[53] the existence there of an established church gives more definite contours to the crime in England than the term "sacrilegious" can possibly have in this country. Moreover, the scope of the English common-law crime of blasphemy has been considerably limited by the declaration that "if the decencies of controversy are observed, even the fundamentals of religion may be attacked,"[54] a limitation which the New York

---

[51] Schroeder, Constitutional Free Speech (1919), 178–373, makes a lengthy review of "Prosecutions for Crimes Against Religion." The examples in the text are from Schroeder. See also Encyclopaedia of the Social Sciences, "Blasphemy"; Encyclopaedia of Religion and Ethics, "Blasphemy"; Nokes, A History of the Crime of Blasphemy (1928).

[53] See, e. g., Rex v. Bouller, 72 J. P. 188 (1908); Bowman v. Secular Society, Ltd., [1917] A. C. 406.

[54] Rex v. Ramsey, 15 Cox's C. C. 231, 238 (1883) (Lord Coleridge's charge to the jury); Bowman v. Secular Society Ltd., [1917] A. C. 406.

court has not put upon the Board of Regents' power to declare a motion picture "sacrilegious." . . .

It is this impossibility of knowing how far the form of words by which the New York Court of Appeals explained "sacrilegious" carries the proscription of religious subjects that makes the term unconstitutionally vague.[56] To stop short of proscribing all subjects that might conceivably be interpreted to be religious, inevitably creates a situation whereby the censor bans only that against which there is a substantial outcry from a religious group. And that is the fair inference to be drawn, as a matter of experience, from what has been happening under the New York censorship. Consequently the film industry, normally not guided by creative artists, and cautious in putting large capital to the hazards of courage, would be governed by its notions of the feelings likely to be aroused by diverse religious sects, certainly the powerful ones. The effect of such demands upon art and upon those whose function is to enhance the culture of a society need not be labored.

To paraphrase Doctor Johnson, if nothing may be shown but what licensors may have previously approved, power, the yea or nay saying by officials, becomes the standard of the permissible. Prohibition through words that fail to convey what is permitted and what is prohibited for want of appropriate objective standards, offends Due Process in two ways. First, it does not sufficiently apprise those bent on obedience of law of what may reasonably be foreseen to be found illicit by the law-enforcing authority, whether court or jury or administrative agency. Secondly, where licensing is rested, in the first instance, in an administrative agency, the available judicial review is in effect rendered inoperative. On the basis of such a portmanteau word as "sacrilegious," the judiciary has no standards with which to judge the validity of administrative action which necessarily involves, at least in large measure, subjective determinations. Thus, the administrative first step becomes the last step. . . .

---

[56] It is not mere fantasy to suggest that the effect of a ban of the "sacrilegious" may be to ban all motion pictures dealing with any subject that might be deemed religious by any sect. The industry's self-censorship has already had a distorting influence on the portrayal of historical figures. "Pressure forced deletion of the clerical background of Cardinal Richelieu from *The Three Musketeers*. The [Motion Picture Production] Code provision appealed to was the section providing that ministers should not be portrayed as villains." Note, "Motion Pictures and the First Amendment," 60 Yale L. J. 696, 716, n. 42.

The press recently reported that plans are being made to film a "Life of Martin Luther." N. Y. Times, April 27, 1952, § 2, p. 5, col. 7. Could Luther be sympathetically portrayed and not appear "sacrilegious" to some; or unsympathetically, and not to others?

## Note

1. See also *Texas v. Gelling*, 247 S. W. 2d 95 (Tex. Crim. App. 1952) rev'd on the basis of the *Burstyn* case, 343 U. S. 960, 96 L. Ed. —, 72 S. Ct. 1002 (1952). The state court had upheld censorship of the motion picture *Pinky*, under a municipal ordinance providing no standards for the censor, on the ground that motion pictures are not protected by the First Amendment. In two other recent cases the Supreme Court denied certiorari. *RD–DR Corp. and Film Classics, Inc. v. Smith*, 183 F. 2d 562 (C. A. 5, 1950) cert. den. 340 U. S. 853 (1950) (*Lost Boundaries* banned in Atlanta because it would "adversely affect peace, morals, and good order;" affirmed on grounds that motion pictures are not covered by the First Amendment) ; *United Artists Corp. v. Board of Censors of Memphis*, 189 Tenn. 397, 225 S. W. 2d 550 (1949), cert. den. 339 U. S. 952 (1950) (motion picture *Curley* banned on ground that "south does not permit negroes in white schools nor recognize social equality between races even in children;" Tennessee Supreme Court's decision turned on distributor's standing to sue).

2. For material on the effectiveness of motion pictures as a medium for communicating serious ideas see, in addition to the Note in 60 Yale L. J. 696, cited in the principal opinion, the bibliography at the end of this chapter and the materials cited *supra*.

3. The methods used by states and cities to censor motion pictures vary considerably. A number of states have permanent boards that ban or delete portions of the film prior to exhibition. See, in addition to the New York law discussed in the *Burstyn* case, Kan. Gen. Stat. Ann. c. 51, c. 74, art. 22 (1949) ; Md. Ann. Code Gen. Laws Art. 66A (Flock 1939) ; Ohio Gen. Code Ann. § 154–47 (Page Supp. 1950) ; Pa. Stat. Ann. tit. 4, §§ 42–4 (Purdon Supp. 1950) ; Va. Code Ann. §§ 2–98— 2–116 (1950). Some municipalities have censorship boards or an individual censor. See Note, 60 Yale L. J. 696, 697 fn. 2. In others a censoring agency such as the police or a license commissioner takes action against an objectionable film either upon complaint or upon its own initiative. Where specific authorization is lacking informal pressure is used in the form of a suggestion that the theatre license might be withdrawn. Criminal prosecution under obscenity or breach of the peace laws is another technique used. At least in one city this has been employed in such a way as to require those who wish to show questionable educational films to consult with the head of the morals division. He might permit that such films be shown under certain restrictions such as segregated audiences. See Note, 60 Yale L. J. 696, 697 fn. 3 and 4.

State censorship statutes provide for administrative appeal and appeal to the courts. While some municipalities fail to make provision for judicial review, others expressly allow limited review. See Memphis Digest § 1139 (1931) (board's findings of fact and conclusions of law final). Where the law contains no review provisions mandamus or injunction may be available. *Schuman v. Pickert*, 277 Mich. 225, 269 N. W. 152 (1936) ; *United Artists Corp. v. Thompson*, 339 Ill. 595, 171 N. E. 742 (1930). Where available, review is generally limited to whether the Board exceeded its statutory authority. See, *e.g.*, *Hygienic Productions v. Keenan,* 1 N. J. Super. 461, 62 A. 2d 150 (Cha. Div. 1948); *Distinguished Films v. Stoddard,* 271 App. Div. 715, 68 N. Y. Supp. 2d 737 (3d Dept., 1947) and other cases described in Note, 60 Yale L. J. 696, 698–9 fn. 6.

The Federal government has confined its prohibitions to interstate transportation and customs, 18 U. S. C. § 1462 (1951); 19 U. S. C. 1305 (1951). The interstate transportation provision does not seem to be enforced. See 60 Yale L. J. 696 fn. 1, which also contains references to proposed federal censorship legislation.

4. For general discussion of motion picture censorship see also Chafee, *Free Speech in the United States,* pp. 540–48 (1941); Ernst, *The First Freedom,* pp. 181–244 (1946); Harley, *World Wide Influences of the Cinema* (1940); Inglis, *Freedom of the Movies* (1947); Kupferman and O'Brien, *Motion Picture Censorship—The Memphis Blues,* 36 Corn. L. Q. 273 (1951); Notes, 49 Yale L. J. 87 (1939); 39 Col. L. R. 1383 (1939).

5. For a collection of state blasphemy cases see Torpey, *Judicial Doctrines of Religious Rights in America,* p. 58 (1948).

# THE MOTION PICTURE PRODUCERS AND DISTRIBUTORS OF AMERICA, INC.—THE PRODUCTION CODE

1949–50 International Motion Picture Almanac, p. 647 (1949)

GENERAL PRINCIPLES

1. No picture shall be produced which will lower the moral standards of those who see it. Hence the sympathy of the audience shall never be thrown to the side of crime, wrong-doing, evil or sin.

2. Correct standards of life, subject only to the requirements of drama and entertainment, shall be presented.

3. Law, natural or human, shall not be ridiculed, nor shall sympathy be created for its violation.

I. CRIMES AGAINST THE LAW

These shall never be presented in such a way as to throw sympathy with the crime as against law and justice or to inspire others with a desire for imitation.

1. *Murder*
   a. The technique of murder must be presented in a way that will not inspire imitation.
   b. Brutal killings are not to be presented in detail.
   c. Revenge in modern times shall not be justified.
2. *Methods of crime* should not be explicitly presented.
   a. Theft, robbery, safe-cracking, and dynamiting of trains, mines, buildings, etc., should not be detailed in method.

**715**

b. Arson must be subject to the same safeguards.

c. The use of firearms should be restricted to essentials.

d. Methods of smuggling should not be presented.

3. *The illegal drug traffic* must not be portrayed in such a way as to stimulate curiosity concerning the use of, or traffic in, such drugs; nor shall scenes be approved which show the use of illegal drugs, or their effects, in detail (as amended September 11, 1946).

4. *The use of liquor* in American life, when not required by the plot or for proper characterization, will not be shown.

## II. Sex

The sanctity of the institution of marriage and the home shall be upheld. Pictures shall not infer that low forms of sex relationship are the accepted or common thing.

1. *Adultery and illicit Sex,* sometimes necessary plot material, must not be explicitly treated or justified, or presented attractively.

2. *Scenes of passion*

a. These should not be introduced except where they are definitely essential to the plot.

b. Excessive and lustful kissing, lustful embraces, suggestive postures and gestures are not to be shown.

c. In general, passion should be treated in such manner as not to stimulate the lower and baser emotions.

3. *Seduction or Rape*

a. These should never be more than suggested, and then only when essential for the plot. They must never be shown by explicit method.

b. They are never the proper subject for comedy.

4. *Sex perversion* or any inference of it is forbidden.

5. *White slavery* shall not be treated.

6. *Miscegenation* (sex relationship between the white and black races) is forbidden.

7. *Sex hygiene* and venereal diseases are not proper subjects for theatrical motion pictures.

8. Scenes of *actual childbirth,* in fact or in silhouette, are never to be presented.

9. *Children's sex organs* are never to be exposed.

## III. Vulgarity

The treatment of low, disgusting, unpleasant, though not necessarily evil, subjects should be guided always by the dictates of good taste and a proper regard for the sensibilities of the audience.

**716**

## IV. OBSCENITY

Obscenity in word, gesture, reference, song, joke, or by suggestion (even when likely to be understood only by part of the audience) is forbidden.

## V. PROFANITY

Pointed profanity and every other profane or vulgar expression, however used, is forbidden.

No approval by the Production Code Administration shall be given to the use of words and phrases in motion pictures including, but not limited to, the following:

*Alley-cat* (applied to a woman); *bat* (applied to a woman); *broad* (applied to a woman); *"Bronx Cheer"* (the sound); *chippie; cocotte; God, Lord, Jesus, Christ* (unless used reverently); *cripes; fanny; fairy* (in a vulgar sense); *finger* (the); *fire*—cries of; *Gawd; goose* (in a vulgar sense); *"hold your hat"* or *"hats"; hot* (applied to a woman); *"in your hat"; louse; lousy; Madam* (relating to prostitution); *nance; nerts; nuts* (except when meaning crazy); *pansy; razzberry* (the sound); *slut* (applied to a woman); *S.O.B.; son-of-a; tart; toilet gags; tom-cat* (applied to a man); *Traveling salesman and Farmer's daughter jokes; whore; damn, hell* (excepting when the use of said last two words shall be essential and required for portrayal, in proper historical context, of any scene or dialogue based upon historical fact or folklore, or for the presentation in proper literary context of a Biblical, or other religious quotation, or a quotation from a literary work provided that no such use shall be permitted which is intrinsically objectionable or offends good taste).

In the administration of Section V of the Production Code, the Production Code Administration may take cognizance of the fact that the following words and phrases are obviously offensive to the patrons of motion pictures in the United States and more particularly to the patrons of motion pictures in foreign countries:

Chink, Dago, Frog, Greaser, Hunkie, Kike, Nigger, Spig, Wop, Yid.

## VI. COSTUME

1. *Complete nudity* is never permitted. This includes nudity in fact or in silhouette, or any licentious notice thereof by other characters in the pictures.
2. *Undressing scenes* should be avoided, and never used save where essential to the plot.
3. *Indecent or undue exposure* is forbidden.

**717**

4. *Dancing costumes* intended to permit undue exposure or indecent movements in the dance are forbidden.

## VII. DANCES
1. Dances suggesting or representing sexual actions or indecent passion are forbidden.
2. Dances which emphasize indecent movements are to be regarded as obscene.

## VIII. RELIGION
1. No film or episode may throw *ridicule* on any religious faith.
2. *Ministers of religion* in their character as ministers of religion should not be used as comic characters or as villains.
3. *Ceremonies* of any definite religion should be carefully and respectfully handled.

## IX. LOCATIONS
The treatment of bedrooms must be governed by good taste and delicacy.

## X. NATIONAL FEELINGS
1. *The use of the flag* shall be consistently respectful.
2. *The history,* institutions, prominent people and citizenry of all nations shall be represented fairly.

## XI. TITLES
The following shall not be used: titles which are salacious, indecent, obscene, profane or vulgar; titles which suggest or are currently associated in the public mind with material, characters, or occupations unsuitable for the screen; titles which are otherwise objectionable.

## XII. REPELLENT SUBJECTS
The following subjects must be treated within the careful limits of good taste:
1. *Actual hangings* or electrocutions as legal punishments for crime.
2. *Third-degree* methods.
3. *Brutality* and possible gruesomeness.
4. *Branding* of people or animals.
5. *Apparent cruelty* to children or animals.
6. *The sale of women,* or a woman selling her virtue.
7. *Surgical operations.*

## Note

"About 95% of all pictures released in the United States receive the approval of the Production Code Authority before release.[43] Member producers are required to submit all scripts and finished pictures for approval. Defenders of the Code point to it as the best alternative to legal censorship and contend that producers are free to bring any social problem to the screen provided it is presented in a morally acceptable manner.[44] Critics claim that the Code is limited in its effectiveness and that it makes realistic portrayal of some problems difficult if not impossible.[45] Some modification of the Code may be required if the removal of legal censorship is to promote honest treatment of contemporary problems and avoid a succession of stereotyped films." [46] Note, 60 Yale L. J. 696, 715–7 (1951).

[43] The Code comes into operation even before the purchase of a book, play or story for a movie. Producers seek an opinion as to acceptability under the code of material they wish to purchase. The next stage is the submission of the shooting script. If this basic story outline is acceptable an opinion will be sent to the producer, indicating what parts must be eliminated to make all details conform to the Code. If the basic story is unacceptable, producers and Code officials confer to arrive at revisions which will bring the script within Code requirements. These close working arrangements continue throughout production. When the film is completed, the Authority reviews it again and if it is satisfied issues a certificate of approval. See DOOB, PUBLIC OPINION AND PROPAGANDA, 507–510 (1948); Shurlock, *The Motion Picture Production Code*, 254 ANNALS OF THE AMERICAN ACADEMY 140 (1947).

[44] See Shurlock, *supra*, note 43, at 145; Schary, *Censorship and Stereotypes*, Saturday Review of Literature, April 30, 1949, p. 9. For a defense of the code as self-protection for movie makers see Hodgins, *A Roundtable on the Movies*, Life, June 27, 1949, p. 90.

[45] In certain respects the code defeats its own purposes. By close attention to detail the technical appearance of virtue is maintained, while movies are full of sex, crime and violence. On the effectiveness of the code see SELDES, THE GREAT AUDIENCE 64–88 (1950); POWDERMAKER, HOLLYWOOD: THE DREAM FACTORY 73–78, 80–81 (1950). . . .

[46] The code as now formulated and administered reflects the existing requirements of the many state and local censor boards. Abolition of censorship should bring some relaxation in the code. However, the primary reason for its existence is a public relations function. Formulated at a time when the public standing of the movie industry was low, the code has been developed on the thesis that the way to keep the public favorably disposed toward the industry is to eliminate material objectionable to important segments of public opinion. For the history of the formation and development of the Code see INGLIS, FREEDOM OF THE MOVIES 116 (1947). This pressure may continue to be influential even if movies are accorded First Amendment protection. Since the application of obscenity statutes and clear and present danger test might be influenced by popular attitudes toward the movies, the industry may want to continue its present policy of minimizing offense whenever possible.

## NOTE—MOTION PICTURES AND THE FIRST AMENDMENT

60 Yale L. J. 696, 713–5 (1951)

Organized interest groups, possessing potential power of boycott, can cause a producer to abandon certain stories or make changes in screen plays.[39] Religious, social, professional, racial, national, and business groups actively apply such pressures.[40]

[39] Actual boycott is the ultimate sanction at the disposal of interest groups and the threat of this economic weapon makes such groups influential at all stages of movie production. Boycott can take the form of suggestions to membership that they not attend a certain picture, picketing before a theatre showing an objectionable film, and public appeals to avoid the picture. Still more persuasive is the threat that members will boycott any picture shown at the offending theatre or any film produced by an offending studio. Another threat which Hollywood feels from these groups is their political power to get restrictive legislation passed.

For examples of boycotts see the threat by Cardinal Dougherty in Philadelphia to boycott the showing *Forever Amber* as well as any other theatre presenting films made by the same studio, POWDERMAKER, HOLLYWOOD: THE DREAM FACTORY 69 (1950); recent picketing in New York over the showing of *The Miracle*, Crowther, *Strange Case of the Miracle*, Atlantic, April, 1951, pp. 35–39; negro protests against *Song of the South*, NOBLE, THE NEGRO IN FILMS 218–219 (1948); and agitation against the showing of *Oliver Twist* by the Anti-Defamation League of B'nai B'rith, 159 PUBLISHER'S WEEKLY 254 (1951). The Sons of Liberty also protested against *Oliver Twist* by boycotting all productions of the British producer and then extending the boycott to pictures made by other British firms. SELDES, THE GREAT AUDIENCE 100 (1950).

The theatre showing *The Iron Curtain* in 1948 was picketed by left wing groups and counter picketed by Catholic War Veterans. The theatre also received a threat that it would be bombed if it did not withdraw the controversial film. See New York Times May 14, 1948, p. 28 col. 6. A bombing threat was made during the *Miracle* controversy. See Crowther *supra*.

[40] Many organizations maintain committees which preview films for one or more of the following reasons: (1) to inform their membership generally about recent films; (2) to supervise moral content; (3) to further specific aims of the organization. National reviewing committees are maintained by the following organizations: The American Library Association, American Legion Auxiliary, General Federation of Women's Clubs, National Council of Jewish Women, National Federation of Music Clubs, National Legion of Decency, National Society, Daughters of the American Revolution, and National Protestant Motion Picture Council. In addition, state or regional committees are maintained by such groups as the American Association of University Women, California Congress of Parents and Teachers, California Federation of Business and Professional Womens Clubs and Southern California Council of Church Women. Other organizations which preview films are the Associated Women of the American Farm Bureau Federation and Girl Scouts of the United States. Opinions of the previewers are publicized through the publications of the organizations and movie trade publications such as the *Joint Estimate of Current Motion Pictures* published weekly by the Motion Picture Association of

Producers use information gained from these sources in determining profit potentialities of pictures. Industry organizations

America. The National Legion of Decency puts out a weekly "moral estimate" of current motion pictures. Films are listed in four general categories: Morally Unobjectionable for General Patronage; Morally Unobjectionable for Adults; Morally Objectionable in part for all; Condemned. In the issue of December 7, 1950, 70 films were listed as unobjectionable for all, 75 for adults only; 115 were objectionable in part and 71 were condemned.

An industry-supported agency which previews pictures is the National Board of Review. The Board, whose activities are financed by fees charged producers for review of their films, classifies pictures, disseminates information about them, and organizes audience support for films it considers worthy. The agency has also worked closely with organizations seeking to improve motion picture content but opposing legal censorship. For description of the history and functioning of the National Board of Review see INGLIS, FREEDOM OF THE MOVIES 74–82 (1947).

Operations of the General Federation of Women's Clubs were described in communication to YALE LAW JOURNAL from Mrs. Joseph R. Chesser, Adviser, Division of Motion Pictures, dated December 7, 1950, in Yale Law Library. The organization maintains a preview committee in New York which sees films before they are released for public exhibition. During the period June, 1947–Feb. 1950 647 films were previewed. 42% were found suitable for young people; 23.2% were classified for adult consumption only and 34.8% were recommended for children. Only about 1% were not recommended for public exhibition. This group has protested vigorously against use of source material based on the life of notorious criminals. The clubwomen protested against the production of a film based on the life of Al Capone.

Two groups making concerted efforts with respect to treatment of negroes in films are the National Association for the Advancement of Colored People and the International Film and Radio Guild. These groups led a campaign against the filming of *Uncle Tom's Cabin* in 1946 and were successful in having the producer abandon the project. NOBLE, NEGRO IN FILMS 218 (1948).

Reactions of other nations to the way in which their nationals and history are presented are quite influential because a substantial portion of film rentals comes from abroad. Kracauer, *National Types as Portrayed by Hollywood*, PUB. OP. Q., Fall, 1947, p. 346.

A scene in one film was reshot at the request of the State Department which objected to showing a group of Mexican school children without shoes. To assist in the Good Neighbor program the producers took the scene with shoes on. POWDERMAKER, HOLLYWOOD: DREAM FACTORY 120 (1950).

Some control over movie content is exercised by the armed forces. As a result of the help which producers obtain from the Army and Navy there has developed a practice of cooperation between the armed forces and the motion picture industry. In return for assistance in production the armed forces received the right to censor films produced with their aid. See Litzky, *Censorship of Motion Pictures in the United States* (Thesis submitted for Degree of Doctor of Philosophy in the School of Education of New York University 1947).

For a detailed study of all films in which judges, lawyers, courtrooms and the law were involved, see *Factual Study of Judges, Lawyers in Motion*

work with committees of these groups to reduce objectionable features in films previewed by the committees and to get the views of these groups on future productions.[41]

## PRESSURE PROBLEM
### DIRECTOR DISCUSSES CUTS COMPELLED IN "A STREETCAR NAMED DESIRE"
### BY ELIA KAZAN
New York Times, October 21, 1951

This newspaper has asked me for a statement about a reported dispute between Warner Brothers and myself with regard to cuts which the studio made in "A Streetcar Named Desire," directed by me.

The cuts, it must be said at once, are minor although, to me, painful. They do not hurt the total impact of the picture.

Even if it were otherwise, I can think of nothing of less general interest than a conflict between a director and a picture studio. However, I met a situation here which extended beyond the studio. The producers have implored me to keep silent about it, for they regard it as a passing headache with a happy ending

_Pictures_, 33 A. B. A. J. 650 (1947). The survey concluded, after analysis of 104 pictures in which lawyers appeared, that the legal profession was being treated fairly. Sixty-five pictures were sympathetic, 21 indifferent and 18 unsympathetic. Before filming _Mad With Much Heart_ which concerns a policeman who turns sadist under the pressure of his job the producers sought and obtained the approval of police departments in Los Angeles and Boston. New York Times, April 23, 1950, sect. II, p. 5 col. 1.

Recent activity by pressure groups includes the attack on _Born Yesterday_ in some Catholic papers as a "marxist satire," New York Times, Dec. 1, 1950, p. 31 col. 1, and the cancellation of the showing of _Bicycle Thief_ in Queens because of protests from local Knights of Columbus that the movie "glorifies a thief." New York Times, Feb. 16, 1951, p. 27, col. 7.

The American Humane Association enforces a general rule against the killing or wounding of an animal on the screen. Hence adjustments were necessary in the filming of _The Brave Bulls_. Cutting techniques and special camera angles had to be used to convey the three climaxes in the bullfight. New York Times, April 16, 1950, sec. II, p. 6, col. 5.

[41] For a description of the close working arrangements between producers and interest groups see SELDES, THE GREAT AUDIENCE, 89–104 (1950).

It seems doubtful that any serious production of art which probes at all deeply into the vast range of human experience can avoid treading on the sensibilities of some racial, religious, economic, political, or other interest group. If approval of all the groups involved must always be had the results will tend to be unreal and insipid. On the subject of movie pressure groups generally see Brown, _Wishful Banning_, Saturday Review of Literature, March 12, 1949, p. 24; Holmes, _Sensitivity as Censor_, Saturday Review of Literature, Feb. 26, 1949, p. 9: and sources cited note 40 _supra_.

[Emerson]

at the box office. On sober thought, I cannot see it that way. I feel the public should hear this kind of story and make its own conclusions. I want to tell it, although, ironically, I was in the position of an outsider as it occurred.

Warner Brothers and Charles K. Feldman, who jointly produced "Streetcar," had shown courage in purchasing a fine and unusual play. They had been extremely cooperative and exceptionally generous throughout the making of the picture. They had provided me with the best possible scenic designer, cameraman, cutter, composer—and cast. What differences we had had were normal differences of taste and opinion, and were resolved as such.

*Background.*

By last summer the picture was finished. We had received the seal of approval of the Breen Office, certifying that it conformed to the requirement of the picture industry's moral code. Prevues were behind us. The last cuts had been agreed upon. "Streetcar" was booked into Radio City Music Hall, and I was in Hollywood once more, at work on another picture for another studio.

Then I heard that Warners had canceled the booking.

Then one day, quite by accident, I learned that the cutter who had worked with me on "Streetcar" had been sent to New York. I began to ask questions. After delays and evasions, which are significant only for the nervousness they betrayed, I received reluctant answers. An executive of Warners was kind enough to explain to me, at least in part, what was going on:

Warners had learned that the Legion of Decency was about to give the picture a "C" or "Condemned" rating. This would mean that people of the Roman Catholic faith would be instructed not to see it.

The studio's reaction was one of panic. They had a sizable investment in the picture, and they at once assumed that no Catholic would buy a ticket. They feared further that theatres showing the picture would be picketed, might be threatened with boycotts of as long as a year's duration if they dared to show it, that priests would be stationed in the lobbies to take down the names of parishioners who attended. I was told that all these things had happened in Philadelphia when a picture with a "C" rating was shown there, and, further, that the rating was an invitation for every local censor board in the country to snipe at a picture, to require cuts or to ban it altogether.

**723**

*Legion's Position.*

The explanation continued: the Legion of Decency did not want to appear as censors. They simply view finished work and pronounce their verdict. As nearly as I could gather, Warners were begging to be told what changes might be made in order to avoid the dreaded rating, while the Legion repeated that it was not theirs to censor, but only to say if the picture was decent for Catholic eyes and ears. But of course if a new version were submitted, they could not refuse to rule upon it.

The next thing I knew was that the cutter, David Weisbart, was back in Hollywood with a cut print which either subsequently received, or already had, the desired "B" rating.

I was then allowed to see it.

I decided to get to New York as fast as I could. Here I was introduced to a prominent Catholic layman, who informed me that he himself, giving time and thought and great care to the matter, had suggested the cuts in my picture. His presence was at the invitation of Warner Brothers, and he had striven to bridge between the picture's artistic achievement—which he praised highly—and "the primacy of the moral order" as interpreted by himself, in conformity with the Legion's standards. There had been no overt involvement of the Legion, which had then passed the cut version.

I could not help wondering where this process left the moral responsibility of the makers of the picture, including the author and myself, or how the end result differed from direct censorship by the Legion.

However that may be, I—and for that matter the public—was presented with a finished fact. My picture had been cut to fit the specifications of a code which is not my code, is not the recognized code of the picture industry, and is not the code of the great majority of the audience.

And that was that. There was no recourse, as I discovered when I tried to reopen the matter.

As to the cuts themselves, I believe that if the audience—any audience—could see projected on the screen the footage which was cut out of "A Streetcar Named Desire" in order to protect the morals of that portion of them who are Roman Catholics, they would be overwhelmed by a bewilderment which would leave them, ever after, suspicious of censorship. For when something is cut out of a picture on such grounds, it is only natural to assume that it is something of special and daring character, somehow very different from what is permitted to remain. If you could see the banned footage, you would find it just about indistinguishable from the body of the picture, which you are

**724**

allowed to see. You might even echo the producers' anxious and repeated and almost reasonable question: What difference does it make?

### Director's View.

As the director of the picture I see the deleted film somewhat differently. It does make a difference. I see it as small but necessary bits that built mood or motivation as I needed them, and whose rough excision leaves small holes or unprepared climaxes that make my work appear cruder than it was. I see it as lost fragments of a subtly told story, whose omission leaves the characters less fully explained than the author intended and than the actors, before, conveyed.

There were twelve cuts altogether, which remove some three or four minutes from the film. They range from a trivial cut of three words, "—on the mouth" (following the words, "I would like to kiss you softly and sweetly—"), to a recutting of the wordless scene in which Stella, played by Kim Hunter, comes down the stairway to Stanley after a quarrel.

This scene was carefully worked out in an alternation of close and medium shots, to show Stella's conflicting revulsion and attraction to her husband, and Miss Hunter played it beautifully. The censored version protects the audience from the close shots and substitutes a long shot of her descent. It also, by explicit instruction, omits a wonderful piece of music. It was explained to me that both the close shots and the music made the girl's relation to her husband "too carnal."

Another cut comes directly before Stanley attacks Blanche. It takes out his line, "You know, you might not be bad to interfere with." Apart from forcing a rather jerky transition, this removes the clear implication that only here, for the first time, does Stanley have any idea of harming the girl. This obviously changes the interpretation of the character, but how it serves the cause of morality is obscure to me, though I have given it much thought.

### Other Deletions.

The other cuts are of like nature. Certain of them were interpreted to me as stemming from the thought that if one character—Stella was the candidate—could be shown as "good," the film would be redeemed. Such a thought, of course, is directly opposed to Tennessee Williams' thought. All his characters are a mixture of the qualities we label "good" and "bad," and that is their humanity.

**725**

A final incident: I asked Warner Brothers if we could not send the original version of "Streetcar" to the Venice Film Festival where, in international competition, American films are often at a disadvantage because of their removal from life as Europeans (and the rest of us) know it. The producers reported back to me that if the uncut version were shown, even once, in Venice, the Legion would be compelled to give the (cut) picture a "C" rating in this country.

Now Warner Brothers, as the owners of the film, had the right to make these—or any other—cuts. From a business standpoint, it is easy to understand why they acceded to them. The Legion's point of view is also clear: they believe that certain things should be seen and others should not be seen by those who follow their dictates. If a picture, especially an important picture, can be brought into line with their code, they are naturally pleased.

That leaves the public, the author and myself to be considered. Meanwhile the box office is breaking records.

## Note

In May, 1952, all of Gide's and Moravia's works were put on the index of forbidden books by the Vatican's Sacred Congregation of the Holy Office. The Vatican paper L'Osservatore Romano commented: "The church could not keep silent any longer. . . . The work of this author is to be condemned both for what it affirms and for what it denies. Let it therefore be explicitly condemned. The gifts he possessed, both of interior intelligence and of rich poetry, render the condemnation all the more painful, but also all the more necessary. The church, as his dearest friends, waited to the very end for the prodigal son to return. He did not return. Let at least his place in the Catholic line-up be marked among the enemies and corruptors— among the followers of the adversary." The New York Times story on the subject reports: "L'Osservatore said the condemnation of M. Gide after his death was unexpected and even heartrending. It added, however, that he had lived all his life 'as a non-Christian, or rather as a deliberate anti-Christian.' His 'taste for profanation' was 'carried as far as blasphemy,' the newspaper declared, saying that the last pages he had written before his death were 'filled with bitter negations of Christ as well as with vice and ugly references to Catholics.' M. Gide's idea of 'sincerity,' L'Osservatore said, was to 'roll over deeper in filth and to defile what is purest in the life of men, namely, the figure of Christ and the love of men for Christ.' " N. Y. Times, June 1, 1952, p. 7. For discussion of the system of censorship in the Catholic Church, see Pernicone, *The Ecclesiastical Prohibition of Books* (Catholic University Studies in Canon Law, No. 72, 1932); Blanchard, *American Freedom and Catholic Power,* ch. 9 (1949).

## 2. Radio

### Defamation

The states are divided on the question of whether a radio station is absolutely liable for defamation by a speaker, or whether a station is liable only where it is itself at fault. The majority of states follow the latter rule. Compare *Sorenson v. Wood,* 123 Neb. 348, 243 N. W. 82 (1932), app. dis. *sub. nom. KFAB Broadcasting Co. v. Sorenson,* 290 U. S. 599 (1933), holding there is absolute liability, with *Summit Hotel Co. v. National Broadcasting Co.,* 336 Pa. 182, 8 Atl. 2d 302 (1939). For a collection of cases and statutes see Note, 61 Yale L. J. 87, 90, 91 fn. 13 and 14 (1951). For a full discussion of defamation by radio see Remmers, *Recent Legislative Trends in Defamation by Radio,* 64 Harv. L. Rev. 727 (1951); Note, 46 Ill. L. Rev. 634 (1951); NAB General Counsel's Memorandum, *Liability of Broadcasters for Defamation* (1949); Donnelly, *Defamation by Radio: A Reconsideration,* 34 Iowa L. Rev. 12 (1948).

A special problem arises because Section 315 of the Federal Communications Act requires that broadcasting stations give equal opportunity to political candidates and at the same time prohibits censorship of scripts. 47 U. S. C. § 315 (1948). Does this section force upon radio stations a liability against which they cannot protect themselves, at least in those areas where an absolute liability rule prevails? In *Port Huron Broadcasting Co.,* 4 R.R. 1 (1948), the licensee had made a contract for broadcast time with three speakers. The station in reviewing the scripts prior to the broadcast found one of them defamatory and cancelled all three speeches. The Commission held that once the licensee had entered the field of political broadcasts withdrawal of facilities constituted censorship. By way of dictum the opinion added that the Federal Act immunized licensees from liability for defamation in political broadcasts over which the station had no control as a result of the Federal law.[1]

The *Port Huron* case was considered at length in a Congressional investigation. See H. Rep. No. 2461, 80th Cong. 2d Sess. (1948); Final Report of the Select Committee to Investigate the Federal Communications Commission, H. Rep. No. 2479, 80th Cong. 2d Sess. (1949). In the course of the investigation the Chairman of the Commission gave assurance that pending Congressional action a licensee seeking to protect himself in good

---

[1] In an early court decision it was held that the *Port Huron* statement was not an "order" entitling the plaintiff to judicial review. *Houston Post Co. v. U. S.,* 79 F. Supp. 199 (S. D. Tex., 1948).

faith without political bias would not be in jeopardy. The Committee proposed no legislation and none was enacted.

In a later opinion the Commission reviewed its absolute no-censorship rule. *WDSU Broadcasting Corp.*, 7 R.R. 769 (1952). The following part of the opinion refers to possible liability under State law: "We have stated what we believe to be the proper interpretation of § 315 in the Port Huron decision. No statute supplanting the existing law and our interpretation . . . has been enacted . . . [H]ereafter we will not accept the plea of doubt and uncertainty in the state of the law as a reason for not administering the law as we read it. Nor will we accept the argument that state statutes or common law on the subject of libel in some way supplant or modify the unqualified pronouncement of Congress on the use of the interstate facilities of radio by candidates in making political broadcasts."

In *Yates v. Associated Broadcasts*, 7 R.R. 2088 (N. D. Cal., 1951), the Court granted a mandatory injunction to force a radio station to permit a dramatization in behalf of a Communist political candidate facing charges under the Smith Act. The judge's oral remarks were in part as follows: ". . . there is no responsibility on the part of the station for what is said there. The station cannot be sued for libel and it has a right to make a disclaimer . . . What is in the script is the Committee's responsibility and not the station's and if it happens to be communist propaganda that has the name of a candidate . . . on it, that's not the fault of the station." This does not necessarily support the Commission's view since California does not impose liability for radio defamation where the station cannot censor. Calif. Civ. Code Ann. § 48.5 (Deering 1949). States following strict liability have thus far held that Section 315 is no defense. The leading case is *Sorensen v. Wood, supra.*

## Note

Examples of legislation similar to that of California are Mich. Stat. Ann. § 27.1406 (Supp. Ann. 1951); Colo. Stat. Ann. c. 138 B § 1 (Repl. 1949). For a collection of other statutes dealing specifically with the problem of political candidates, see Note, 61 Yale L. J. 87, 91 fn. 14; for a model law see NAB General Counsel's Memorandum, *supra*, at p. 8. The view that the Federal Act supersedes state law is strengthened by *DuMont Laboratories v. Carroll*, 184 F. 2d 153 (C. A. 3, 1950), cert. den. 340 U. S. 929 (1951), where a Pennsylvania statute providing for censorship of movies used on television was declared unconstitutional on the ground that Congress had preempted the entire television field.

In *Felix v. Westinghouse Radio Stations*, 186 F. 2d 1 (C. A. 3, 1950), cert. den. 341 U. S. 909 (1951), the court held that Section 315 does not apply to supporters of political candidates. The radio station may therefore censor such speeches and is not entitled to use Section 315 as a defense. The Commission has held that Section 315 does not apply to a candidate who does not qualify to be put on a ballot in a state where there are no write-in votes. See 7 R. R. 766 (1952). For proposed rules see 1 R. R. 53:445 (1950). For a recent bill extending the coverage of Section 315 to political supporters authorized by the candidate, see S. 1379, 82d Cong., 1st Sess. (1951).

## *Lotteries*

Section 316 of the Federal Communications Act prohibited the broadcasting with knowledge of "any advertisement of or information concerning any lottery, gift enterprise or similar scheme offering prizes dependent in whole or in part upon lot or chance." It also forbade the broadcasting of any list of such prizes. As part of the revision of the Criminal Code in 1948 this provision was deleted from the Communications Act and incorporated in the Criminal Code. 18 U. S. C. § 1304 (1951). Although the statutory provision is confined to criminal sanctions the Commission has used it as a proper standard of what constitutes public interest in licensing proceedings. Moreover, the Commission decided to promulgate general rules concerning lottery broadcasts, instead of relying simply on case to case determination. These rules repeat the statutory language and interpret it to cover typical radio give away programs (§ 3.192, 1 R. R. 53 : 295–6) :

". . . the Commission will in any event consider that a program comes within the provisions of subsection (a) if in connection with such program a prize consisting of money or thing of value is awarded to any person whose selection is dependent in whole or in part upon lot or chance, if as a condition of winning or competing for such prize:

(1) such winner or winners are required to furnish any money or thing of value or are required to have in their possession any product sold, manufactured, furnished or distributed by a sponsor of a program broadcast on the station in question; or

(2) such winner or winners are required to be listening to or viewing the program in question on a radio or television receiver; or

(3) such winner or winners are required to answer correctly a question, the answer to which is given on a program broadcast over the station in question or where aid to answering the question correctly is given on a program broadcast over the station in question. For the purpose of this provision the broadcasting of the question to be answered over the radio station on a previous

**729**

program will be considered as an aid in answering the question correctly; or

(4) such winner or winners are required to answer the phone in a prescribed manner or with a prescribed phrase, or are required to write a letter in a prescribed manner or containing a prescribed phrase, if the prescribed manner of answering the phone or writing the letter or the prescribed phrase to be used over the phone or in the letter (or an aid in ascertaining the prescribed phrase or the prescribed manner of answering the phone or writing the letter) is, or has been, broadcast over the station in question."

The regulations are suspended pending court review. Objections to the Commission's power to promulgate the rules are made primarily on the following grounds: First, the Commission has no power to promulgate rules setting forth types of programs that fall within the scope of a criminal statute, especially where such rules go beyond existing judicial interpretations of the criminal provisions. For arguments pro and con, see *Promulgation of Rules Governing Broadcast of Lottery Information,* 1 R. R. 91:22 (1949). Second, the rules do not set forth substantive violations of the criminal statute. On this issue, it is generally agreed that there must be three elements present to constitute a lottery: a prize, chance, and consideration. The most dubious element under the Commission's rules is whether consideration exists. With respect to this issue see *Promulgation of Rules Governing Broadcast of Lottery Information,* 1 R. R. 91:22 (1949). In that report the Commission argued: "Where such a scheme is designed to induce members of the public to listen to the program and be at home available for selection as a winner or possible winner, there results detriment to those who are so induced to listen when they are under no duty to do so. And this detriment to the members of the public results in a benefit to the licensee who sells the radio time and 'circulation' to the sponsor, and to the sponsor as well, who presents his advertising to the audience secured by means of the scheme."

## Note

Compare *Affiliated Enterprises, Inc. v. Gruber,* 86 F. 2d 958 (C. A. 1, 1936). Where the answering of questions is a prerequisite to winning it might be argued that the program gives prizes for skill not chance. See *Peek v. United States,* 61 F. 2d 973 (C. A. 5, 1932), and *Northern Virginia Broadcasters, Inc. (WARL)* 4 R. R. 660 (1949). See also Note 60 Yale L. J. 1396, 1406–7 (1951). In a recent case the Commission denied renewal of a license because excessive time was devoted to the broadcast of horse-racing information. *Port Frere Broadcasting Co., Inc. (WTUX),* 5 R. R. 1137 (1950).

## Obscenity

Formerly Section 326 of the Act, which prohibits all censorship by the Commission, contained a second sentence prohibiting the broadcast of "obscene," "indecent" or "profane" language. This sentence was deleted and incorporated in the Criminal Code. 18 U. S. C. § 1464 (1948). The question as to the Commission's power under this provision is similar to that raised with respect to former Section 316, *supra*. Moreover, other objections might be urged since, in view of the deletion, the anti-censorship provision is left without specific qualifications. On the other hand, Section 303 (m) of the Act, 47 U. S. C. § 303 (m) (1) (D), authorizing the Commission to suspend licenses for obscene broadcasts, has remained intact. For cases on these issues see *Re Shaeffer (KVEP)*, F. R. C. Docket No. 5228, June 24, 1930 ("the question in every case is whether the words were used under such circumstances and are of such a nature to create the impression that they are what Congress intended to prevent;" this case involved a broadcast by a third party); In *Re Application of Norman Baker*, F. R. C. Docket No. 967, June 5, 1931; *Trinity Methodist Church, South v. Federal Radio Com.*, 62 F. 2d 850 (C. A. D. C., 1932), cert. den. 288 U. S. 599 (1933); *KFKB Broadcasting Association, Inc. v. Federal Radio Commission*, 47 F. 2d 670 (C. A. D. C., 1931); *Scroggin & Company Bank*, 1 F. C. C. 194 (1935); *Brooklyn Cases*, 2 F. C. C. 208 (1935) (scandalous language in astrologer programs); *Knickerbocker Broadcasting Co. Inc.*, 2 F. C. C. 76 (1935) (advertising contraceptives). See also the investigation by the F. C. C. of the Columbia Broadcasting System and the Blue Network, and the investigation by Congress of the FCC, for broadcasting suggestive Spanish songs. Warner, *Radio and Television Law*, p. 337 (1949). For censure by the Commission of the National Broadcasting Company for broadcasting certain Mae West programs, and its citing of stations for obscenity for broadcasting Eugene O'Neill's *Beyond the Horizon* because it contained "damn", "hell" and "for God's sake," see Warner, *supra*, pp. 338–9. In the case of O'Neill's play, public indignation forced the Commission to reconsider. *Ibid.* Both the Standards of Practice of the National Association of Broadcasters (1946) and NBC Program Policies and Working Manual (1944) prohibit "obscene," "vulgar," "profane," "blasphemous," and "sacrilegious" language. See Warner, *supra*, p. 339, fn. 16 and 17 and p. 389, fn. 4 and 5.

### Note

1. For problems concerning the relative amount of time alloted to advertising see *infra*. For early experiences see Friedrich and Sayre,

*The Development of the Control of Advertising on the Air* (Studies in the Control of Radio No. 1), p. 9 (1940). The Commission generally now seems to be content to leave it to the industry to control annoying and distasteful aspects of the specific content of advertising. Content control is exercised by the Federal Trade Commission and the Food and Drug Administration. See Gatling, *Radio Advertising and the Federal Trade Commission,* 9 Fed. Com. B. J. 74 (1948) ; Warner, *supra,* pp. 417–419. Warner also describes the work of state agencies in attempts of the industry at self regulation of advertising content. *Id.* pp. 419–23. On liquor advertising see Warner, p. 411, fn. 11 and 12. The Commission has stated that in communities where such advertising raises serious social, economic and political issues the station must make time available to groups or individuals advocating temperance or abstinence. See *Broadcast of Programs Advertising Alcoholic Beverages,* 5 R. R. 595 (1949).

2. When radio broadcasting began there were a great number of fortune telling and astrology programs on the air. The predecessor to the Federal Communications Commission, the Federal Radio Commission, acted against a number of stations. On the whole these programs now seem to have disappeared. See Haley, *The Law on Radio Programs* (1938) reprinted with additions from 5 Geo. Wash. L. Rev. 157 (1937) ; Warner, *supra,* p. 390.

3. In *WNAX Broadcasting Company,* 6 F. C. C. 397, 399 (1938), the advertiser solicited farmers to let him handle tax-refund claims to which they would be entitled if certain legislation pending in Congress had been enacted. There was to be an original service charge and a further charge of five per cent for every refund obtained. The station's fee for radio time was contingent on the amount of money thus collected. The Commission held that this was solicitation of funds to influence Congress and that such use of the radio was against the "public interest."

4. On state censorship of televised films, see *DuMont Laboratories v. Carroll,* 184 F. 2d 153 (C. A. 3, 1950), cert. den. 340 U. S. 929 (1951), discussed *supra;* Note, 25 St. John's L. Rev. 244, 263 (1951).

## C. OPENING THE CHANNELS OF MASS COMMUNICATION TO A GREATER VARIETY AND QUANTITY OF COMMUNICATION

### 1. The Problem

### THE COMMISSION ON FREEDOM OF THE PRESS— A FREE AND RESPONSIBLE PRESS

The University of Chicago Press, pp. 37–51 (1947)

#### NEWSPAPER CONCENTRATION

For a considerable period (since 1909) the number of daily English-language newspapers has fallen at a fairly constant rate. At the same time there has been a growth in literacy, in total population, and in total circulation. The peak of 2,600 dailies reached in 1909 has been steadily reduced to the present 1,750. Dr. R. B. Nixon, who has done the most recent research on this subject, reported in the *Journalism Quarterly* for June, 1945, that only 117 (approximately one out of twelve) of the cities in which daily newspapers are published now have competing dailies. He also found that in ten states of the Union no cities have competing dailies; in twenty-two states no cities have competing Sunday newspapers. Altogether 40 per cent of the estimated total daily newspaper circulation of forty-eight millon is noncompetitive. Rival newspapers exist only in the larger cities.

Twenty-five hundred of the 16,000 and more weekly newspapers of the nation disappeared between 1910 and 1920, another 1,300 between 1920 and 1930, and 1,750 more in the next decade. Fewer than 10,000 now survive.[1]

#### MAGAZINE AND BOOK CONCENTRATION

A few big houses own the magazines of largest circulation.[2] The eight leading publishers include the so-called "Big Five": Curtis, with the *Ladies' Home Journal, Saturday Evening Post, Country Gentleman,* and the new *Holiday;* Time-Life, Inc., with *Life, Time, Fortune,* and *Architectural Forum;* Crowell-Collier's, with *Colliers, American,* and *Woman's Home Companion;* Hearst, with *Good Housekeeping, Harper's Bazaar, House Beautiful,* and

---

[1] The approximately 100 foreign-language dailies and 150 Negro dailies and weeklies have shown neither marked increase nor decline.

[2] There is a top group of magazines, a dozen to fifteen, each of which has a circulation of 2,000,000 or more, and a second group of seventy to eighty with circulations over 100,000.

the new *Junior Bazaar;* and McCall's, with *McCall's Magazine* and *Red Book.* To these should be added the *Reader's Digest,* which had at the end of the war an estimated domestic circulation of 8,500,000, plus Spanish, Portuguese, Swedish, Arabic, Danish, and Finnish editions totaling another 1,500,000; all but the last of these had the largest circulations in their languages. Among the giants must be included also the Capper group of farm periodicals and the separately owned *Farm Journal,* which together have a circulation over six million. Very recently the Coronet-Esquire group, with a reported circulation of four million for *Coronet,* has jumped into the higher brackets.

Thirty years ago there were nearly two dozen major women's magazines and a group of six large magazines which was just emerging. Now the six largest in a reduced field have nearly nine-tenths of the total circulation.

Though there is still a lively interest in new ventures in magazines and the attempt to launch one is frequently made, the advantages in promotion possessed by the big groups give their publications a head start in the race for readers.

In book publishing the competitive area is comparatively broad. New book houses appear frequently, and some rapidly achieve financial success. Approximately two hundred houses provide 90 per cent of the books published in the United States each year. More than a quarter of the annual titles are produced by the ten largest publishers.

There is a Big Five in trade or general publishing. They are headed by Doubleday-Doran, which printed forty million volumes in 1945, with gross receipts somewhere near thirty million dollars. The next four, Macmillan, Pocket Books, William Wise, and Harper's, do not approach this size. (The Book-of-the-Month Club could be included in this group.) In the textbook and subscription book field a small number of still other publishers do a large percentage of the total business which equals or exceeds the trade publication total.

In the field of technical books McGraw-Hill deserves special mention. It accounts for approximately 25 per cent of such books and, in addition, dominates the field of business and industrial magazines. The importance of these magazines, and hence of concentration in this area, should not be underestimated.

## RADIO COMPETITION AND THE NETWORKS

The situation in radio is distinguished by the fact that the number of stations which can broadcast without interference is limited by nature and the further fact that the maintenance of competition among these stations is enjoined by law. The result is that the number of stations at present is just over a thousand, of which only twenty-five are Class IA clear channel stations, and that single ownership of more than one in any locality or more than eight in all is effectively prevented by the Federal Communications Commission. In spite of these facts, however, the prevalent trend in the communications industry has dominated radio. The broadcasting networks which provide programs to the stations are outside the regulative power of the F. C. C., except as they own stations subject to regulation, or except as regards their contracts with affiliated stations. Over the last twenty years, four great networks have emerged—the National Broadcasting Company, the Columbia Broadcasting System, the American Broadcasting Company, and the Mutual Broadcasting System. The natural tendency of national advertisers to gravitate toward the networks has induced nearly eight hundred of the thousand stations to become affiliated with the chains.

## MOTION PICTURE CONCENTRATION

The eight major motion picture companies are Loew's (M-G-M), RKO, Warner Brothers, Paramount, and Twentieth Century-Fox, which five produce, distribute, and exhibit pictures; Columbia and Universal, which produce and distribute alone; and United Artists, which distributes for a group of independent producing companies and exhibits in England. Approximately a fifth of the theater capacity of this country has been affiliated with the five producing companies among the eight majors. The theaters in the best city locations with the largest audiences, the highest admissions, and the longest runs have been controlled by the eight major companies.[3]

## CHAINS

Large individual units in a single medium are not the only types of Big Press that have grown up. Another kind of development, especially in the newspaper field and in motion pictures, is the ownership of more than one newspaper or other mass medium in one or several cities by a single person or corporation. These are technically called chain ownerships.

The number of papers controlled by national chains has actually declined in recent years, the papers included in the Hearst chain having dropped from twenty-six to seventeen in the ten depres-

---

[3] Other large and well-established companies dealing in production and distribution are Monogram, Republic, and PRC. There are a number of other "satellite" producing companies which distribute their pictures through one or the other of the majors.

sion years, and those in the Scripps-Howard chain from twenty-three to eighteen. At present only a dozen chains among newspapers extend beyond seven dailies, and all but three or four are limited to a single region.

The number of regional chains or, more properly, single ownership of papers in two to a dozen different communities has, however, increased. In 1935 there were 63 such combined ownerships, and in 1945, 76. Fourteen were cases of single ownership of 8 or more papers. The 76 chains—national, regional, and local—own 375 dailies altogether, or 25 per cent of all English-language dailies. In addition, there are 174 localities in which there are partial combinations of separately published newspapers through joint use of the single printing establishment, so that a Republican and a Democratic newspaper run peacefully through the same press but at different times of day.

Whatever the tendency is, the fact remains that the local and regional chains, together with the Hearst, Scripps-Howard, and McCormick-Patterson ownership groups, control more than half (53.8 per cent) of the total newspaper circulation of the nation. Fourteen newspaper owners control 25 per cent of the daily circulation, with less than fifty owners controlling nearly half the total Sunday circulation.

## LOCAL NEWS MONOPOLIES

Monopoly, in the strict sense of single control of all current information coming into an area, does not exist in the communications industry. The nearest thing to it—and it is too near for comfort—is unitary ownership in a single locality. This does exist. Ninety-two per cent of the communities in this country, all but the bigger cities, have only one local newspaper. In a hundred small communities the only newspaper owner also owns the only radio station. This creates a *local* monopoly of local news.[4] Joint newspaper-radio ownership is increasing. About a third of the radio stations in the United States are controlled by newspapers, and the applications for FM licenses so far received exceed this ratio.

## THE COMMUNICATIONS EMPIRES

The Commission doubts that any regional or national monopoly of communications by a single owner is possible. Mr. Hearst

---

[4] There are cases of significant concentration of newspaper and radio ownership in some *regions*, such as that of Frank E. Gannett, whose chain of papers does not extend outside upstate New York. His hegemony, powerful as it is, falls far short of giving him an actual monopoly in that region.

at the top of his fortunes, not many years ago, had accumulated twenty-six newspapers, thirteen magazines (mainly with large circulation), eight radio stations, a newsreel company, a substantial interest in a motion picture feature producing company, a leading feature syndicate, and one of the three press associations, for a total of an estimated thirty million readers and a huge motion picture and radio audience. But at this peak Hearst's organization was in brisk competition with rivals in each medium. It was a communications empire of great size and influence; but it was no monopoly. And it has visibly decreased in size in recent years.

The Luce interests, the Cowles interests, and the Marshall Field interests are powerful combinations in the various media. The Radio Corporation of America, if not an empire in the Hearst sense, was at its moment of greatest extent a mass communications principality of extraordinary scope.

The Luce interests have owned, at one time or another, a weekly news magazine (*Time*), a weekly picture magazine (*Life*), two monthly magazines (*Fortune* and *Architectural Forum*), a documentary motion picture producing company and a radio program ("March of Time"), and interest in a metropolitan radio station (WQXR) and a radio network (A.B.C.)—the two latter now sold. The Cowles brothers own four midwest newspapers, four radio stations, and a weekly picture magazine. The Radio Corporation of America, which is a leading manufacturer of radio and sound and color equipment, owns the National Broadcasting Company, had a substantial interest in RKO-Radio Pictures, Inc., and is one of the two leading American companies handling the international radio telegraph business to and from the United States.

Big money made in other fields is now going into communications. The Atlas Corporation has recently bought *Liberty Magazine*, with a circulation of a million and a half, and has a substantial interest in RKO-Radio Pictures, Inc., and Walt Disney Productions, as well as three movie-fan magazines. Marshall Field owns two metropolitan dailies, four radio stations, a farm journal, and a Sunday newspaper magazine supplement used by more than forty papers. He also has a controlling interest in a large book publishing house and its related reprint house. Edward Noble used money from the sale of Lifesavers to buy the Blue network. The Pew interests (Sun Oil) control one of the biggest farm journals, a group of trade papers including *Iron Age*, and *Pathfinder* magazine with a large circulation in small town and rural areas.

## NEWS AGENCIES, FEATURES, AND SYNDICATES

The press associations and some one hundred and seventy-five companies offer feature services with nation-wide coverage, so that, as compared with fifty years ago, an increasing sameness appears in news stories, photographs, cartoons, and columns. Even editorials are mass-produced for certain categories of papers. Almost all of the ten thousand weekly newspapers still surviving, for example, have for a long time used the services of the Western Newspaper Union, a manufacturer of editorials, features, and columns, owned by John H. Perry, the so-called "Boiler Plate King." Nearly three thousand of them use an eight-page paper provided by Western Newspaper Union, four of the pages of which are pre-written, pre-edited, and pre-printed by syndicate. Perry is also developing a chain of small papers including seven dailies, fourteen weeklies, and four radio stations. He owns the principal trade magazine for the weekly press and has an interest in plants producing printing machinery which he sells to his clients.

Of the 1,750 remaining general English daily newspapers in the United States, 95 per cent, serving all but one-fifth of 1 per cent of the total daily circulation, take the services of one or more of the three major press associations—the Associated Press, United Press, and International News Service. This standardization is made more uniform still by the fact that International News Service is owned by interests identified with Hearst, United Press by interests identified with Scripps-Howard, and the Associated Press by a limited, and until recently self-limiting group of newspaper publishers. (Radio stations and news magazines are now admitted to associate membership without a vote.)

The same interrelationship within an interrelationship appears in the syndicate news and photo feature business which sells photographs, comic strips, feature columns, and the like, thus providing a central control of content far more extensive than any control through ownership. Perry's Western Newspaper Union is itself one of the country's biggest newspaper syndicates in terms of papers served. Of the five or six biggest syndicates, among the hundred-and-seventy-odd now operating, King Features is connected with the Hearst interests; United Features and Newspaper Enterprise Association, with the Scripps-Howard interests. Associated Press operates one of the largest and most complete feature services. Large syndicates are owned or controlled by metropolitan newspapers: the *Chicago Tribune* and the *New York Daily News* (jointly), one of the largest of all the syndicates, the *New York Herald Tribune*, the *Des Moines*

*Register and Tribune,* the *Chicago Sun, PM,* the *New York Evening Post,* and the *Chicago Times.*

## Monopolistic Practices

The main causes of the trend toward concentration in the communication industries have been the advantages inherent in operating on a large scale using the new technology. High labor costs have also contributed to the elimination of the smaller, marginal owner.

Other forces are at work as well. They are *personal* forces; they have nothing to do with technological change. They exist, and always have existed, in all branches of the economy, and the communications industries are no exception. These forces are those exaggerated drives for power and profit which have tended to restrict competition and to promote monopoly throughout the private enterprise system. As in other industries, the means employed in specific instances have varied all the way from complicated economic pressures down to the simple instruments of physical violence.

Hearst and McCormick fought an epic newsstand war in Chicago early in the present century, which involved not only the destruction of papers but also the shooting of employees. These battles, and the private armies which fought on either side, were a factor in promoting the gang warfare which has distressed the city since. Violence as a curb on competition has not, however, been confined to Chicago. The New York papers, including the *Times* and the *Herald Tribune,* had newsstand fights in the thirties; and *PM* faced serious difficulties in finding a place on the newsstands.

Potential competitors have divided territory as Hearst, Gannett, and Block did in upstate New York and as motion picture theaters have done elsewhere. Small publishers are now complaining that giant concerns, such as Time-Life and Curtis, have pre-empted paper stocks and printing facilities under long-term contracts. In recent litigation the Associated Press was compelled to give up a practice which the Supreme Court found monopolistic, since it permitted one publisher to deny the Association's service to a competitor. Antitrust actions, now on appeal, against the eight great motion picture companies are designed to separate the control of production from exhibition, a combination which is claimed to amount to monopoly. These companies have produced 80 per cent of American feature films and distributed 95 per cent of the films reaching the public.

**739**

## THE COST OF NEW VENTURES

Monopolistic practices, together with the cost of machinery and the momentum of big, going concerns, have made it hard for new ventures to enter the field of mass communications.[5]

Although there is no such thing as a going price for a great city newspaper, it is safe to assume that it would cost somewhere between five and ten million dollars to build a new metropolitan daily to success. The investment required for a newspaper in a medium-sized city is estimated at three-quarters of a million to several million; for a small-town paper, $25,000–$100,000. Radio stations have been sold at figures well over a million dollars, though such prices must include, in the words of Commissioner Durr, "something [the sellers] do not own and have no right to sell; namely, the use of a radio channel." The equity needed for a new feature motion picture producing company would probably be at least $100,000, but this is merely a shoestring; one cannot sensibly initiate a producing unit without a contract with one of the major distributors. A publisher should not start a magazine aimed at the mass market unless he is prepared to lose two or three million dollars at the outset. On the other hand, a book publishing house might be established for as little as $100,000.

Our survey of the instruments and the organization of the communications industry leaves us with certain questions. To what extent has the reduction in the number of units of the press reduced variety? Has the reduction in the number of units cut down the opportunity to reach an audience on the part of those who have something to say? Has the struggle for power and profit been carried to such a point in this field that the public interest has suffered? Have the units of the press, by becoming big business, lost their representative character and developed a common bias—the bias of the large investor and employer? Can the press in the present crisis rise to its responsibility as an essential instrument for carrying on the political and social life of a nation and a world of nations seeking understanding? If not, will its irresponsibility deprive it of its freedom?

### Note

The Commission on Freedom of the Press considered, in addition to the monopolistic structure of the communications industry, the following effects on the press of the "economic logic of private enterprise": (1) the tendency to maximize circulation by disseminating

---

[5] This is especially true in the newspaper, magazine, and radio network fields; not so much so in book publishing and radio station ownership.

a wide variety of information, such as advertising, specialized knowledge, and entertainment, and reducing the volume and quality of information and discussion regarding public affairs; (2) the "distortion" of information and discussion of public affairs, through emphasis on the novel and sensational; (3) the imposition of pressures by private groups, advertisers, and the personal interests of owners; (4) the reluctance of the press to correct its own errors through mutual public self-criticism; and (5) the inadequate distribution of all types of publication to each segment of the population. Commission on Freedom of the Press, *supra*, pp. 52–68. See also bibliography at end of this Chapter.

## 2. Technique of Limiting Concentration of Communication Enterprise

### a. Motion Pictures

### UNITED STATES v. PARAMOUNT PICTURES

Supreme Court of the United States, 1948
334 U. S. 131, 92 L. Ed. 1161, 68 S. Ct. 915

MR. JUSTICE DOUGLAS delivered the opinion of the Court.

These cases are here on appeal from a judgment of a three-judge District Court holding that the defendants had violated § 1 and § 2 of the Sherman Act, 26 Stat. 209, as amended, 50 Stat. 693, 15 U. S. C. §§ 1, 2, and granting an injunction and other relief. 66 F. Supp. 323; 70 F. Supp. 53.

The suit was instituted by the United States under § 4 of the Sherman Act to prevent and restrain violations of it. The defendants fall into three groups: (1) Paramount Pictures, Inc., Loew's, Incorporated, Radio-Keith-Orpheum Corporation, Warner Bros. Pictures, Inc., Twentieth Century-Fox Film Corporation, which produce motion pictures, and their respective subsidiaries or affiliates which distribute and exhibit films. These are known as the five major defendants or exhibitor-defendants. (2) Columbia Pictures Corporation and Universal Corporation, which produce motion pictures, and their subsidiaries which distribute films. (3) United Artists Corporation, which is engaged only in the distribution of motion pictures. The five majors, through their subsidiaries or affiliates, own or control theatres; the other defendants do not.

The complaint charges that the producer defendants had attempted to monopolize and had monopolized the production of motion pictures. The District Court found to the contrary and that finding is not challenged here. The complaint charged that all of the defendants, as distributors, had conspired to restrain

**741**

and monopolize and had restrained and monopolized interstate trade in the distribution and exhibition of films by specific practices which we will shortly relate. It also charged that the five major defendants had engaged in a conspiracy to restrain and monopolize, and had restrained and monopolized, interstate trade in the exhibition of motion pictures in most of the larger cities of the country. It charged that the vertical combination of producing, distributing, and exhibiting motion pictures by each of the five major defendants violated § 1 and § 2 of the Act. It charged that each distributor-defendant had entered into various contracts with exhibitors which unreasonably restrained trade. Issue was joined; and a trial was had.[3]

*First. Restraint of Trade—(1) Price fixing.*
No film is sold to an exhibitor in the distribution of motion pictures. The right to exhibit under copyright is licensed. The District Court found that the defendants in the licenses they issued fixed minimum admission prices which the exhibitors agreed to charge, whether the rental of the film was a flat amount or a percentage of the receipts. It found that substantially uniform minimum prices had been established in the licenses of all defendants. Minimum prices were established in master agreements or franchises which were made between various defendants as distributors and various defendants as exhibitors and in joint operating agreements made by the five majors with each other and with independent theatre owners covering the operation of certain theatres.[4] By these later contracts minimum admission prices were often fixed for dozens of theatres owned by a particular defendant in a given area of the United States. Minimum prices were fixed in licenses of each of the five major

---

[3] Before trial, negotiations for a settlement were undertaken. As a result, a consent decree against the five major defendants was entered November 20, 1940. The consent decree contained no admission of violation of law and adjudicated no issue of fact or law, except that the complaint stated a cause of action. The decree reserved to the United States the right at the end of a three-year trial period to seek the relief prayed for in the amended complaint. After the end of the three-year period the United States moved for trial against all the defendants.

[4] A master agreement is a licensing agreement or "blanket deal" covering the exhibition of features in a number of theatres, usually comprising a circuit.

A franchise is a licensing agreement, or series of licensing agreements, entered into as part of the same transaction, in effect for more than one motion picture season and covering the exhibition of features released by one distributor during the entire period of the agreement.

An independent as used in these cases means a producer, distributor, or exhibitor, as the context requires, which is not a defendant in the action, or a subsidiary or affiliate of a defendant.

defendants. The other three defendants made the same requirement in licenses granted to the exhibitor-defendants. We do not stop to elaborate on these findings. They are adequately detailed by the District Court in its opinion. See 66 F. Supp. 334–339.

The District Court found that two price-fixing conspiracies existed—a horizontal one between all the defendants; a vertical one between each distributor-defendant and its licensees. The latter was based on express agreements and was plainly established. The former was inferred from the pattern of price-fixing disclosed in the record. We think there was adequate foundation for it too. It is not necessary to find an express agreement in order to find a conspiracy. It is enough that a concert of action is contemplated and that the defendants conformed to the arrangement. *Interstate Circuit* v. *United States,* 306 U. S. 208, 226–227; *United States* v. *Masonite Corp.,* 316 U. S. 265, 275. That was shown here.

On this phase of the case the main attack is on the decree which enjoins the defendants and their affiliates from granting any license, except to their own theatres, in which minimum prices for admission to a theatre are fixed in any manner or by any means. The argument runs as follows: *United States* v. *General Electric Co.,* 272 U. S. 476, held that an owner of a patent could, without violating the Sherman Act, grant a license to manufacture and vend, and could fix the price at which the licensee could sell the patented article. . . .

We start, of course, from the premise that so far as the Sherman Act is concerned, a price-fixing combination is illegal *per se. United States* v. *Socony-Vacuum Oil Co.,* 310 U. S. 150; *United States* v. *Masonite Corporation, supra.* We recently held in *United States* v. *Gypsum Co.,* 333 U. S. 364, 400, that even patentees could not regiment an entire industry by licenses containing price-fixing agreements. . . . The case where a distributor fixes admission prices to be charged by a single independent exhibitor, no other licensees or exhibitors being in contemplation, seems to be wholly academic, as the District Court pointed out. It is, therefore, plain that *United States* v. *General Electric Co., supra,* as applied in the patent cases, affords no haven to the defendants in this case. For a copyright may no more be used than a patent to deter competition between rivals in the exploitation of their licenses. See *Interstate Circuit* v. *United States, supra,* p. 230.

## (2) *Clearances and Runs.*

Clearances are designed to protect a particular run of a film against a subsequent run.[6] The District Court found that all of the distributor-defendants used clearance provisions and that they were stated in several different ways or in combinations: in terms of a given period between designated runs; in terms of admission prices charged by competing theatres; in terms of a given period of clearance over specifically named theatres; in terms of so many days' clearance over specified areas or towns; or in terms of clearance as fixed by other distributors.

The Department of Justice maintained below that clearances are unlawful *per se* under the Sherman Act. But that is a question we need not consider, for the District Court ruled otherwise and that conclusion is not challenged here. In its view their justification was found in the assurance they give the exhibitor that the distributor will not license a competitor to show the film either at the same time or so soon thereafter that the exhibitor's expected income from the run will be greatly diminished. A clearance when used to protect that interest of the exhibitor was reasonable, in the view of the court, when not unduly extended as to area or duration. Thus the court concluded that although clearances might indirectly affect admission prices, they do not fix them and that they may be reasonable restraints of trade under the Sherman Act. . . .

The District Court enjoined defendants and their affiliates from agreeing with each other or with any exhibitors or distributors to maintain a system of clearances, or from granting any clearance between theatres not in substantial competition, or from granting or enforcing any clearance against theatres in substantial competition with the theatre receiving the license for exhibition in excess of what is reasonably necessary to protect the licensee in the run granted. In view of the findings this relief was plainly warranted.

Some of the defendants ask that this provision be construed (or, if necessary, modified) to allow licensors in granting clearances to take into consideration what is reasonably necessary for a fair return to the licensor. We reject that suggestion. If that were allowed, then the exhibitor-defendants would have an

---

[6] A clearance is the period of time, usually stipulated in license contracts, which must elapse between runs of the same feature within a particular area or in specified theatres.

Runs are successive exhibitions of a feature in a given area, first-run being the first exhibition in that area, second-run being the next subsequent, and so on, and include successive exhibitions in different theatres, even though such theatres may be under a common ownership or management.

easy method of keeping alive at least some of the consequences of the effective conspiracy which they launched. For they could then justify clearances granted by other distributors in favor of their theatres in terms of the competitive requirements of those theatres, and at the same time justify the restrictions they impose upon independents in terms of the necessity of protecting their film rental as licensor. . . .

(3) *Pooling Agreements; Joint Ownership.*

The District Court found the exhibitor-defendants had agreements with each other and their affiliates by which theatres of two or more of them, normally competitive, were operated as a unit, or managed by a joint committee or by one of the exhibitors, the profits being shared according to prearranged percentages. Some of these agreements provided that the parties might not acquire other competitive theatres without first offering them for inclusion in the pool. The court concluded that the result of these agreements was to eliminate competition *pro tanto* both in exhibition and in distribution of features,[8] since the parties would naturally direct the films to the theatres in whose earnings they were interested.

The District Court also found that the exhibitor-defendants had like agreements with certain independent exhibitors. Those alliances had, in its view, the effect of nullifying competition between the allied theatres and of making more effective the competition of the group against theatres not members of the pool. The court found that in some cases the operating agreements were achieved through leases of theatres, the rentals being measured by a percentage of profits earned by the theatres in the pool. The District Court required the dissolution of existing pooling agreements and enjoined any future arrangement of that character.

These provisions of the decree will stand. The practices were bald efforts to substitute monopoly for competition and to strengthen the hold of the exhibitor-defendants on the industry by alignment of competitors on their side. Clearer restraints of trade are difficult to imagine.

There was another type of business arrangement that the District Court found to have the same effect as the pooling agreements just mentioned. Many theatres are owned jointly by two or more exhibitor-defendants or by an exhibitor-defendant and an independent. The result is, according to the District Court, that the theatres are operated "collectively, rather than com-

---

[8] A feature is any motion picture, regardless of topic, the length of film of which is in excess of 4,000 feet.

petitively." And where the joint owners are an exhibitor-defendant and an independent the effect is, according to the District
Court, the elimination by the exhibitor-defendant of "putative
competition between itself and the other joint owner, who otherwise would be in a position to operate theatres independently."
The District Court found these joint ownerships of theatres to be
unreasonable restraints of trade within the meaning of the
Sherman Act.

The District Court ordered the exhibitor-defendants to dis-
affiliate by terminating their joint ownership of theatres; and it
enjoined future acquisitions of such interests. One is authorized
to buy out the other if it shows to the satisfaction of the District
Court and that court first finds that such acquisition "will not
unduly restrain competition in the exhibition of feature motion
pictures." This dissolution and prohibition of joint ownership
as between exhibitor-defendants was plainly warranted. To the
extent that they have joint interests in the outlets for their films
each in practical effect grants the other a priority for the exhibition of its films. . . .

The District Court also ordered disaffiliation in those instances
where theatres were jointly owned by an exhibitor-defendant and
an independent, and where the interest of the exhibitor-defendant was "greater than five per cent unless such interest shall be
ninety-five per cent or more," an independent being defined for
this part of the decree as "any former, present or putative motion
picture theatre operator which is not owned or controlled by the
defendant holding the interest in question." The exhibitor-defendants are authorized to acquire existing interests of the independents in these theatres if they establish, and if the District
Court first finds, that the acquisition "will not unduly restrain
competition in the exhibition of feature motion pictures." All
other acquisitions of such joint interests were enjoined.

This phase of the decree is strenuously attacked. We are asked
to eliminate it for lack of findings to support it. . . .

It is conceded that the District Court made no inquiry into the
circumstances under which a particular interest had been acquired. It treated all relationships alike, insofar as the disaffiliation provision of the decree is concerned. In this we think
it erred.

We have gone into the record far enough to be confident that
at least some of these acquisitions by the exhibitor-defendants
were the products of the unlawful practices which the defendants
have inflicted on the industry. To the extent that these acquisitions were the fruits of monopolistic practices or restraints of
trade, they should be divested. And no permission to buy out the

other owner should be given a defendant. *United States* v. *Crescent Amusement Co.* [323 U. S. 173, 189]; *Schine Chain Theatres, Inc.* v. *United States* [334 U. S. 110]. Moreover, even if lawfully acquired, they may have been utilized as part of the conspiracy to eliminate or suppress competition in furtherance of the ends of the conspiracy. In that event divestiture would likewise be justified. *United States* v. *Crescent Amusement Co., supra,* pp. 189–190. In that situation permission to acquire the interest of the independent would have the unlawful effect of permitting the defendants to complete their plan to eliminate him.

Furthermore, if the joint ownership is an alliance with one who is or would be an operator but for the joint ownership, divorce should be decreed even though the affiliation was innocently acquired. For that joint ownership would afford opportunity to perpetuate the effects of the restraints of trade which the exhibitor-defendants have inflicted on the industry.

It seems, however, that some of the cases of joint ownership do not fall into any of the categories we have listed. Some apparently involve no more than innocent investments by whose who are not actual or potential operators. If in such cases the acquisition was not improperly used in furtherance of the conspiracy, its retention by defendants would be justified absent a finding that no monopoly resulted. And in those instances permission might be given the defendants to acquire the interests of the independents on a showing by them and a finding by the court that neither monopoly nor unreasonable restraint of trade in the exhibition of films would result. In short, we see no reason to place a ban on this type of ownership, at least so long as theatre ownership by the five majors is not prohibited. The results of inquiry along the lines we have indicated must await further findings of the District Court on remand of the cause.

(4) *Formula Deals, Master Agreements, and Franchises.*

A formula deal is a licensing agreement with a circuit of theatres in which the license fee of a given feature is measured, for the theatres covered by the agreement, by a specified percentage of the feature's national gross. The District Court found that Paramount and RKO had made formula deals with independent and affiliated circuits. The circuit was allowed to allocate playing time and film rentals among the various theatres as it saw fit. The inclusion of theatres of a circuit into a single agreement gives no opportunity for other theatre owners to bid for the feature in their respective areas and, in the view of the District Court, is therefore an unreasonable restraint of trade. The Dis-

**747**

trict Court found some master agreements[10] open to the same objection. Those are the master agreements that cover exhibition in two or more theatres in a particular circuit and allow the exhibitor to allocate the film rental paid among the theatres as it sees fit and to exhibit the features upon such playing time as it deems best, and leaves other terms to the discretion of the circuit. The District Court enjoined the making or further performance of any formula deal of the type described above. It also enjoined the making or further performance of any master agreement covering the exhibition of features in a number of theatres.

The findings of the District Court in these respects are supported by facts.

[The Court here states that former deeds and master agreements are restraints of trade: (1) they eliminate the possibility of theatre by theatre bidding to the disadvantage of the small competitor. (2) ". . . the pooling of the purchasing power of an entire circuit in bidding for films is a misuse of monopoly power insofar as it combines the theatres in closed towns with competitive situations."]

The District Court also enjoined the making or further performance of any franchise. A franchise is a contract with an exhibitor which extends over a period of more than a motion picture season and covers the exhibition of features released by the distributor during the period of the agreement. The District Court held that a franchise constituted a restraint of trade because a period of more than one season was too long and the inclusion of all features was disadvantageous to competitors. At least that is the way we read its findings. . . .

[We] cannot say on this record that franchises are illegal *per se* when extended to any theatre or circuit no matter how small. The findings do not deal with the issue doubtlessly due to the fact that any system of franchises would necessarily conflict with the system of competitive bidding adopted by the District Court. Hence we set aside the findings on franchises so that the court may examine the problem in the light of the elimination from the decree of competitive bidding. . . .

### (5) *Block-Booking.*

Block-booking is the practice of licensing, or offering for license, one feature or group of features on condition that the exhibitor will also license another feature or group of features released by the distributors during a given period. The films are licensed in blocks before they are actually produced. All the defendants, except United Artists, have engaged in the practice.

---

[10] See note 4, *supra.*

Block-booking prevents competitors from bidding for single features on their individual merits. The District Court held it illegal for that reason and for the reason that it "adds to the monopoly of a single copyrighted picture that of another copyrighted picture which must be taken and exhibited in order to secure the first." That enlargement of the monopoly of the copyright was condemned below in reliance on the principle which forbids the owner of a patent to condition its use on the purchase or use of patented or unpatented materials. See *Ethyl Gasoline Corporation* v. *United States,* 309 U. S. 436, 459; *Morton Salt Co.* v. *Suppiger Co.,* 314 U. S. 488, 491; *Mercoid Corp.* v. *Mid-Continent Investment Co.,* 320 U. S. 661, 665. The court enjoined defendants from performing or entering into any license in which the right to exhibit one feature is conditioned upon the licensee's taking one or more other features.

We approve that restriction. The copyright law, like the patent statutes, makes reward to the owner a secondary consideration. . . .

We do not suggest that films may not be sold in blocks or groups, when there is no requirement, express or implied, for the purchase of more than one film. All we hold to be illegal is a refusal to license one or more copyrights unless another copyright is accepted.

## (6) *Discrimination.*

The District Court found that defendants had discriminated against small independent exhibitors and in favor of large affiliated and unaffiliated circuits through various kinds of contract provisions. These included suspension of the terms of a contract if a circuit theatre remained closed for more than eight weeks with reinstatement without liability on reopening; allowing large privileges in the selection and elimination of films; allowing deductions in film rentals if double bills are played; granting moveovers[13] and extended runs; granting road show privileges;[14] allowing overage and underage;[15] granting unlimited playing time; excluding foreign pictures and those of independent producers; and granting rights to question the classification of features for rental purposes. The District Court found that the

---

[13] A moveover is the privilege given a licensee to move a picture from one theatre to another as a continuation of the run at the licensee's first theatre.

[14] A road show is a public exhibition of a feature in a limited number of theatres, in advance of its general release, at admission prices higher than those customarily charged in first-run theatres in those areas.

[15] Underage and overage refer to the practice of using excess film rental earned in one circuit theatre to fulfill a rental commitment defaulted by another.

competitive advantages of these provisions were so great that their inclusion in contracts with the larger circuits and their exclusion from contracts with the small independents constituted an unreasonable discrimination against the latter. Each discriminatory contract constituted a conspiracy between licensor and licensee. Hence the District Court deemed it unnecessary to decide whether the defendants had conspired among themselves to make these discriminations. No provision of the decree specifically enjoins these discriminatory practices because they were thought to be impossible under the system of competitive bidding adopted by the District Court.

These findings are amply supported by the evidence. . . .

There is some suggestion on this as well as on other phases of the cases that large exhibitors with whom defendants dealt fathered the illegal practices and forced them onto the defendants. But as the District Court observed, that circumstance if true does not help the defendants. For acquiescence in an illegal scheme is as much a violation of the Sherman Act as the creation and promotion of one.

*Second—Competitive Bidding.*

The District Court concluded that the only way competition could be introduced into the existing system of fixed prices, clearances and runs was to require that films be licensed on a competitive bidding basis. Films are to be offered to all exhibitors in each competitive area.[16] The license for the desired run is to be granted to the highest responsible bidder, unless the distributor rejects all offers. The licenses are to be offered and taken theatre by theatre and picture by picture. Licenses to show films in theatres in which the licensor owns directly or indirectly an interest of ninety-five per cent or more are excluded from the requirement for competitive bidding. . . .

At first blush there is much to commend the system of competitive bidding. . . . [A]fter reflection we have concluded that competitive bidding involves the judiciary so deeply in the daily operation of this nation-wide business and promises such dubious benefits that it should not be undertaken.

Each film is to be licensed on a particular run to "the highest responsible bidder, having a theatre of a size, location and equipment adequate to yield a reasonable return to the licensor."

---

[16] Competitive bidding is required only in a "competitive area" where it is "desired by the exhibitors." As the District Court said, "the decree provides an opportunity to bid for any exhibitor in a competitive area who may desire to do so."

The details of the competitive bidding system will be found in 70 F. Supp. pp. 73–74.

The bid "shall state what run such exhibitor desires and what he is willing to pay for such feature, which statement may specify a flat rental, or a percentage of gross receipts, or both, or any other form of rental, and shall also specify what clearance such exhibitor is willing to accept, the time and days when such exhibitor desires to exhibit it, and any other offers which such exhibitor may care to make." We do not doubt that if a competitive bidding system is adopted all these provisions are necessary. For the licensing of films at auction is quite obviously a more complicated matter than the like sales for cash of tobacco, wheat, or other produce. [The Court here discusses some of the difficult problems that would arise in connection with judicial administration of a competitive bidding system.]

We mention these matters merely to indicate the character of the job of supervising such a competitive bidding system. It would involve the judiciary in the administration of intricate and detailed rules . . . The judiciary is unsuited to affairs of business . . . Yet delegation of the management of the system to the discretion of those who had the genius to conceive the present conspiracy and to execute it with the subtlety which this record reveals, could be done only with the greatest reluctance. . . .

If each feature must go to the highest responsible bidder, those with the greatest purchasing power would seem to be in a favored position. . . . In this connection it should be noted that, even though the independents in a given competitive area do not want competitive bidding, the exhibitor-defendants can invoke the system.

Our doubts concerning the competitive bidding system are increased by the fact that defendants who own theatres are allowed to pre-empt their own features. They thus start with an inventory which all other exhibitors lack. The latter have no prospect of assured runs except what they get by competitive bidding. The proposed system does not offset in any way the advantages which the exhibitor-defendants have by way of theatre ownership. It would seem in fact to increase them. For the independents are deprived of the stability which flows from established business relationships. Under the proposed system they can get features only if they are the highest responsible bidders. They can no longer depend on their private sources of supply which their ingenuity has created. Those sources, built perhaps on private relationships and representing important items of good will, are banned, even though they are free of any taint of illegality. . . .

The competitive bidding system was perhaps the central arch of the decree designed by the District Court. Its elimination may affect the cases in ways other than those which we expressly mention. Hence on remand of the cases the freedom of the District Court to reconsider the adequacy of decree is not limited to those parts we have specifically indicated.

*Third.  Monopoly, Expansion of Theatre Holdings, Divestiture.*
There is a suggestion that the hold the defendants have on the industry is so great that a problem under the First Amendment is raised. Cf. *Associated Press* v. *United States,* 326 U. S. 1. We have no doubt that moving pictures, like newspapers and radio, are included in the press whose freedom is guaranteed by the First Amendment. That issue would be focused here if we had any question concerning monopoly in the production of moving pictures. But monopoly in production was eliminated as an issue in these cases, as we have noted. The chief argument at the bar is phrased in terms of monopoly of exhibition, restraints on exhibition, and the like. Actually, the issue is even narrower than that. The main contest is over the cream of the exhibition business—that of the first-run theatres. By defining the issue so narrowly we do not intend to belittle its importance. It shows, however, that the question here is not *what* the public will see or *if* the public will be permitted to see certain features. It is clear that under the existing system the public will be denied access to none. If the public cannot see the features on the first-run, it may do so on the second, third, fourth, or later run. The central problem presented by these cases is which exhibitors get the highly profitable first-run business. That problem has important aspects under the Sherman Act. But it bears only remotely, if at all, on any question of freedom of the press, save only as timeliness of release may be a factor of importance in specific situations.

The controversy over monopoly relates to monopoly in exhibition and more particularly monopoly in the first-run phase of the exhibition business.

The five majors in 1945 had interests in somewhat over 17 per cent of the theatres in the United States—3,137 out of 18,076. Those theatres paid 45 per cent of the total domestic film rental received by all eight defendants.

In the 92 cities of the country with populations over 100,000 at least 70 per cent of all the first-run theatres are affiliated with one or more of the five majors. In 4 of those cities the five majors have no theatres. In 38 of those cities there are no independent first-run theatres. In none of the remaining 50 cities did less than three of the distributor-defendants license their product on first run to theatres of the five majors. In 19 of the 50 cities less than three of the distributor-defendants licensed their product on first run to independent theatres. In a majority of the 50 cities the greater share of all of the features of defendants were licensed for first-run exhibition in the theatres of the five majors.

In about 60 per cent of the 92 cities having populations of over 100,000, independent theatres compete with those of the five majors in first-run exhibition. In about 91 per cent of the 92 cities there is competition between independent theatres and the theatres of the five majors or between theaters of the five majors themselves for first-run exhibition. In all of the 92 cities there is always competition in some run even where there is no competition in first runs.

In cities between 25,000 and 100,000 populations the five majors have interests in 577 of a total of 978 first-run theatres or about 60 per cent. In about 300 additional towns, mostly under 25,000 an operator affiliated with one of the five majors has all of the theatres in the town. . . .

The District Court did, however, enjoin the five majors from expanding their present theatre holdings in any manner. It refused to grant the request of the Department of Justice for total divestiture by the five majors of their theatre holdings. . . .

It is clear, so far as the five majors are concerned, that the aim of the conspiracy was exclusionary, *i.e.* it was designed to strengthen their hold on the exhibition field. In other words, the conspiracy had monopoly in exhibition for one of its goals, as the District Court held. . . .

It is, therefore, not enough in determining the need for divestiture to conclude with the District Court that none of the defendants was organized or has been maintained for the purpose of achieving a "national monopoly," nor that the five majors through their present theatre holdings "alone" do not and cannot collectively or individually have a monopoly of exhibition. For when the starting point is a conspiracy to effect a monopoly through restraints of trade, it is relevant to determine what the results of the conspiracy were even if they fell short of monopoly. . . .

[T]he findings of the District Court do not cover this point beyond stating that monopoly was an objective of the several restraints of trade that stand condemned.

Moreover, the problem under the Sherman Act is not solved merely by measuring monopoly in terms of size or extent of holdings or by concluding that single ownerships were not obtained.

"for the purpose of achieving a national monopoly." It is the relationship of the unreasonable restraints of trade to the position of the defendants in the exhibition field (and more particularly in the first-run phase of that business) that is of first importance on the divestiture phase of these cases. . . .

[T]here is no finding as to the presence or absence of monopoly on the part of the five majors in the *first-run* field for the entire country, in the *first-run* field in the 92 largest cities of the country, or in the *first-run* field in separate localities. Yet the *first-run* field, which constitutes the cream of the exhibition business, is the core of the present cases. Section 1 of the Sherman Act outlaws unreasonable restraints irrespective of the amount of trade or commerce involved (*United States* v. *Socony-Vacuum Oil Co.*, 310 U. S. 150, 224, 225, n. 59), and § 2 condemns monopoly of "any part" of trade or commerce. "Any part" is construed to mean an appreciable part of interstate or foreign trade or commerce. *United States* v. *Yellow Cab Co.*, 332 U. S. 218, 225. Second, we pointed out in *United States* v. *Griffith* [334 U. S. 100], that "specific intent" is not necessary to establish a "purpose or intent" to create a monopoly but that the requisite "purpose or intent" is present if monopoly results as a necessary consequence of what was done. The findings of the District Court on this phase of the cases are not clear, though we take them to mean by the absence of "purpose" the absence of a specific intent. So construed they are inconclusive. In any event they are ambiguous and must be recast on remand of the cases. Third, monopoly power, whether lawfully or unlawfully acquired, may violate § 2 of the Sherman Act though it remains unexercised (*United States* v. *Griffith, ante,* p. 100), for as we stated in *American Tobacco Co.* v. *United States*, 328 U. S. 781, 809, 811, the existence of power "to exclude competition when it is desired to do so" is itself a violation of § 2, provided it is coupled with the purpose or intent to exercise that power. The District Court, being primarily concerned with the number and extent of the theatre holdings of defendants, did not address itself to this phase of the monopoly problem. Here, also, parity of treatment as between independents and the five majors as theatre owners, who were tied into the same general conspiracy, necessitates consideration of this question.

Exploration of these phases of the cases would not be necessary if, as the Department of Justice argues, vertical integration of producing, distributing and exhibiting motion pictures is illegal *per se.* But the majority of the Court does not take that view. In the opinion of the majority the legality of vertical integration under the Sherman Act turns on (1) the purpose or intent with which it was conceived, or (2) the power it creates and the attendant purpose or intent. First, it runs afoul of the Sherman Act if it was a calculated scheme to gain control over an appreciable segment of the market and to restrain or suppress competition, rather than an expansion to meet legitimate business needs. *United States* v. *Reading Co.*, 253 U. S. 26, 57; *United States* v. *Lehigh Valley R. Co.*, 254 U. S. 255, 269–270. Second, a vertically integrated enterprise, like other aggregations of business units (*United States* v. *Aluminum Co. of America*, 148 F. 2d 416), will constitute monopoly which, though unexercised, violates the Sherman Act provided a power to exclude competition is coupled with a purpose or intent to do so. As we pointed out in *United States v. Griffith, ante,* pp 100, 107, n. 10, size is itself an earmark of monopoly power. For size carries with it an opportunity for abuse. And the fact that the power created by size was utilized in the past to crush or prevent competition is potent evidence that the requisite purpose or intent attends the presence of monopoly power. See *United States* v. *Swift & Co.* 286 U. S. 106, 116; *United States* v. *Aluminum Co. of America, supra,* p. 430. Likewise bearing on the question whether monopoly power is created by the vertical integration, is the nature of the market to be served (*United States* v. *Aluminum Co. of America, supra,* p. 430), and the leverage on the market which the particular vertical integration creates or makes possible.

These matters were not considered by the District Court. For that reason, as well as the others we have mentioned, the findings on monopoly and divestiture which we have discussed in this part of the opinion will be set aside. There is an independent reason for doing that. As we have seen, the District Court considered competitive bidding as an alternative to divestiture in the sense that it concluded that further consideration of divestiture should not be had until competitive bidding had been tried and found wanting. Since we eliminate from the decree the provisions for competitive bidding, it is necessary to set aside the findings on divestiture so that a new start on this phase of the cases may be made on their remand.

It follows that the provision of the decree barring the five majors from further theatre expansion should likewise be eliminated. For it too is related to the monopoly question; and the District Court should be allowed to make an entirely fresh start on the whole of the problem. We in no way intimate, however, that the District Court erred in prohibiting further theatre expansion by the five majors.

The Department of Justice maintains that if total divestiture is denied, licensing of films among the five majors should be barred. As a permanent requirement it would seem to be only an indirect way of forcing divestiture. For the findings reveal that the five majors could not operate their theatres full time on their own films. Whether that step would, in absence of competitive bidding, serve as a short-range remedy in certain situations to dissipate the effects of the conspiracy (*United States* v. *Univis Lens Co.*, 316 U. S. 241, 254; *United States* v. *Bausch & Lomb Co.* [321 U. S. 707, 724] ; *United States* v. *Crescent Amusement Co., supra*, p. 188) is a question for the District Court.

*Fourth.*

[The portions of the opinion which follow the above are omitted. They deal with the power of the District Court to continue an arbitration system for clearances and runs established under the 1940 consent decree and the right of certain independent exhibitors to intervene especially to protest against the competitive bidding system.]

The judgment in these cases is affirmed in part and reversed in part, and the cases are remanded to the District Court for proceedings in conformity with this opinion.

[MR. JUSTICE FRANKFURTER, dissenting in part, would give greater weight to the discretion of the District Court in fashioning the decree. His opinion is omitted.]

## Note

1. On remand the District Court held that the vertical integrations were a means of carrying out a conspiracy to fix prices, runs and clearances and therefore illegal restriction of trade. The Court found that the theatre holdings were so distributed as to result in a practical absence of competition among the defendants. It further found monopoly power in the power to exclude and in the actual exclusion of competitors effected in part through the vertical integration. A decree was issued prescribing among other things divorcement of the distributor-producer and exhibitor businesses. *U. S. v. Paramount Pictures*, 85 F. Supp. 881 (S. D. N. Y., 1949).

Prior to this decision, consent decrees were entered against R. K. O. and Paramount. The R. K. O. decree gave the principal stockholder the option to sell his stock in either the producing or exhibiting company or until such sale to deposit his stock with the trustee. The later decree removed the second alternative. The Supreme Court reversed on this point. *Hughes* v. *U. S.*, 342 U. S. 353, 96 L. Ed. 281, 72 S. Ct. 306 (1952). For a discussion and criticism of the consent decrees and the opinion in the Supreme Court, see McDonough and Linslow, *The Motion Picture Industry: United States v. Oligopoly*, 1 Stan. L. Rev. 385 (1949). See also Marcus, *Anti-Trust Laws and the Right to Know*, 24 Ind. L. J. 513 (1949). A consent decree not discussed in these articles was later entered against Loew's, Inc.

2. For other recent government civil actions brought against independent theatre circuits as exhibitors and the Big Eight as distributors charging monopolistic practices and restrictions of trade preventing effective competition by non-circuit exhibitors, see *Interstate Circuit v. U. S.*, 306 U. S. 208, 83 L. Ed. 610, 59 S. Ct. 467 (1939); *U. S. v. Crescent Amusement Co.*, 323 U. S. 173, 89 L. Ed. 160, 65 S. Ct. 254 (1944); *Schine Chain Theatres v. U. S.*, 334 U. S. 110, 92 L. Ed. 1245, 68 S. Ct. 947 (1948); *U. S. v. Griffith*, 334 U. S. 100, 92 L. Ed. 1236, 68 S. Ct. 941 (1948).

The eight major companies also feel the effect of anti-trust laws in private suits of which there are about forty each year. See, *e.g.,* *Ball v. Paramount Pictures*, 169 F. 2d 317 (C. A. 3, 1948); *William Goldman Theatres v. Loew's, Inc.*, 150 F. 2d 738 (C. A. 3, 1945); *Milgram v. Loew's, Inc.*, 94 F. Supp. 416 (E. D. Pa., 1950); *Bigelow v. R. K. O. Radio Pictures, Inc.*, 327 U. S. 251, 90 L. Ed. 652, 66 S. Ct. 574 (1946) (finding violation); *Dipson Theatres, Inc. v. Buffalo Theatres, Inc.*, 190 F. 2d 951 (C. A. 2, 1951); *Fanchon & Marco v. Paramount Pictures*, 100 F. Supp. 84 (S. D. Calif., 1951) (finding no violation).

The legality of franchises and other agreements is frequently challenged on anti-trust grounds in collateral proceedings. See *e.g.,* *Paramount Pictures v. Partmar*, 97 F. Supp. 552 (S. D. Calif., 1951); *Warner Bros. Theatres v. Cooper Foundation*, 189 F. 2d 825 (C. A. 10, 1951); *Solomont & Sons Trust v. New England Theatres*, 326 Mass. 99, 93 N. E. 2d 241 (1950).

## NOTE—MOTION PICTURES AND THE FIRST AMENDMENT

### 60 Yale L. J. 696, 717–9 (1951)

A third non-legal restraint on motion picture expression is the organization of the industry and the nature of its audience. The major theatre circuits, closely allied with the large producing studios, have had a powerful voice in determining the type of films produced.[47] Exhibitors generally are more interested in

---

[47] The motion picture industry is divided into three mutually dependent parts: production, distribution, and exhibition. The great bulk of American movies are produced by eight major companies. These same companies control the major centers of distribution. Prior to recent anti-trust actions the five largest producers also owned theatres. In determining the type of pictures to be produced the large theatre circuits affiliated with the major producing studios have been most influential. The five major producing studios have in the past made substantial portions of their profits from theatre operation as against production. Income statistics for 1939 showed that film rentals accounted for an average of only 36.4% of the volume of business. HUETTIG, ECONOMIC CONTROL OF THE MOTION PICTURE INDUSTRY 70, Table VI (1944). The effect of the anti-trust action is shown by figures of net income for Paramount. In the first quarter of 1949 when Paramount owned its large theatre chain

assuring steady attendance by the same people than in attracting new customers. Hence there is pressure by exhibitors for formula movies designed for instant acceptance by the regular audiences.[48] As a result of this pressure, producers may try to aim their films at a mass audience representing many diverse cultural groups. Moreover, the high cost of making a feature film,[49] added to the influence of financing banks,[50] encourages concentration on production of pictures assured of immediate appeal. However, there are indications that this fear of arousing controversy may be diminishing. With revenues declining,[51]

it netted $5,675,000. In the first quarter of 1950 after it had lost its theatres the figure was $1,441,000. Business Week, June 24, 1950, p. 26. When confronted with the choice of producing films or staying in the theatre management business all producers decided to continue to make pictures. Reasons for this decision are falling theatre revenues and the advent of television which may cut more deeply into the theatre business, than into the demand for movie production. Divorcement of producers from their theatres may reduce the power of the distribution and former theatre management departments of the major studios. But the influence on production of the circuits created by this divorcement is difficult to determine. The divorcement of producers from their theatres may make it more difficult for studios to undertake experimentation. Darryl F. Zanuck, production head of Twentieth Century Fox, has said it would have been difficult to produce *Wilson* had it not been for the possibility of exploiting the film in the studio's own theatres. *Hollywood's Magic Mountain*, Fortune, Feb. 1945, p. 208. For discussion of the economic structure of the movie industry see HUETTIG, *op. cit. supra*, at 54–95, 113–142; INGLIS, FREEDOM OF THE MOVIES 36–54 (1947); MOTION PICTURE INDUSTRY—A PATTERN OF CONTROL, TNEC MONOGRAPH No. 43, 76th Cong., 2d Sess. (1941).

[48] It has been estimated that 13–15 million individuals see the average Hollywood class "A" production. Since the size of the audience is thus limited, repetitive attendance is of great concern to theatre owners. A public opinion survey shows that 52% of the public goes to movies more than once a month. CANTRIL, PUBLIC OPINION, 1935–1946 (1951). To develop movie going as a habit it has been thought necessary to concentrate on themes with tested box office success. Another factor making for sameness of product is the fact that exhibitors are greatly influenced by attendance on the first day of a picture's run in a metropolitan theatre. It is important to get a large audience on the first day in order to ensure subsequent bookings. To guarantee this type of response it is necessary to have films to which the regular audience will go almost automatically. See SELDES, THE GREAT AUDIENCE 13, 38–39 (1950).

[49] If a movie costs less than $1,000,000 it is tagged as a Class B film. The major features cost about $3,000,000. The most expensive film of all time is now in production. *Quo Vadis* will cost about $10,000,000. See Schulberg, *Movies in America: After 50 Years*, Atlantic, Nov. 1947, p. 115; *Hollywood's Magic Mountain*, Fortune, Feb. 1945, p. 153.

[50] Film production is financed largely through banks which demand regular fixed charges. Bank financing tends to restrict variety and experimentation. POWDERMAKER, HOLLYWOOD: THE DREAM FACTORY 51–52 (1950).

[51] Surveys of postwar trends in movie revenues have indicated a steady decline. The contribution to national income of motion pictures dropped

some critics are calling for films that will satisfy more kinds of interest in order to attract a larger proportion of the population to the movie theatres.[52]  Such a movement would increase the number of films dealing with issues of significance to political and social discussion.

## Note

For a detailed account of how the anticipation of audience reaction and box office returns, and the actual reaction of the audience, including "kids in blue jeans" at sneak previews, influence "art" in Hollywood, see Ross, *Onward and Upward with the Arts*, The New Yorker, May 24 through June 21, 1952 (describing the production of *Red Badge of Courage*).

•

### b. Radio

## NOTE—THE IMPACT OF THE FCC'S CHAIN BROADCASTING RULES

### 60 Yale L. J. 78, 80–111 (1951)

Prior to the issuance of the Network Rules, the affiliation contracts contained highly restrictive provisions.  The heart of the

---

from a high of $1,116,000,000 in 1946 to $871,000,000 in 1949.  Motion Picture Division, Office of Industry and Commerce, U. S. Dept. of Commerce. In September, 1950 Audience Research reported that the average person is buying 7% fewer movie tickets than in 1940.  During the first six months of 1950 attendance was off 9% from that of 1949.  Monday Morning Post, Sept. 25, 1950.  A survey of profits on 146 pictures during 1950 showed that only 12 brought back more in the domestic market than the amount spent on production and distribution.  Brady, *Hollywood Takes Stock*, New York Times, March 12, 1950, sec. II, p. 5, col. 7.

[52] The suggestion has been made that the industry develop additional first-run circuits of medium-sized theatres.  Producers could then make medium-budget films which would not have to possess record-breaking mass appeal in order to make money.  See Walter Wanger quoted in SELDES, THE GREAT AUDIENCE 39 (1950).  A call for abandonment of the old aspiration of making movies with universal appeal in favor of films made for a particular audience is given in Variety, quoted in Crowther, *Is There An Audience?*, New York Times, Oct. 11, 1950 sec. II., p. 1, col., 8. See also Hodgins, *A Roundtable on the Movies*, Life, June 27, 1949, p. 90.

Research in radio casts doubt on the idea that the only way for a mass medium to make money is to produce the same type of product continually. Demand for any commodity, particularly movies, is not fixed but is susceptible of influence from changes in the product itself.  Since the supply of a mass medium tends itself to create demand, if more movies on serious themes were produced more people might develop a greater interest in them.  Movies with serious theme have been successful at the box office in recent years. See note 21 *supra*.  These theories on the importance of availability of the communication in determining the size of its audience are discussed in Lazarsfeld, *Audience Research* in READER IN PUBLIC

contract was an exclusive option clause. Under this provision the most desirable portions of the broadcasting day were designated "option time." The net work could require its affiliates, on 28 days' notice, to "clear" option time of any local programs previously scheduled and to substitute the network's commercial program. The station owner theoretically retained the power to reject any network program not in the public interest. But NBC required that he affirmatively justify his rejection, and CBS insisted that he give the network notice of rejection three weeks before the scheduled date of the program. An "affiliation exclusivity" clause prevented member stations from carrying programs of competing networks even during unoptioned time. In return, the network granted "territorial exclusivity," promising not to supply programs to any rival station within an affiliate's primary service area—even programs rejected by the affiliate. The chains generally controlled station rates for sale of time to network advertisers, and NBC further retained the power to penalize an affiliate whenever its independent national advertising rates varied from those established for network sales. The affiliation contracts were usually binding for five years on member stations, but could be terminated by the networks on one or two years' notice.

The effect of these provisions was to restrict competition between stations and between networks and to make the individual station owner a less responsible operator in the public interest. The territorial exclusivity clause foreclosed independent stations from a large part of the national advertising market and denied them access to popular network programs. The network option clause restricted affiliates' ability to enter into binding commitments with advertisers for sponsorship of local programs and national non-network, or "spot," programs. In the case of NBC stations, the threat of being penalized for any variance between network and non-network rates further discouraged affiliates from independent solicitation of national advertising. The contracts were equally effective in hindering the growth of new chains. The affiliation exclusivity clause barred new networks from purchasing time during popular broadcasting hours on stations affiliated with National and Columbia, and the five-year contract term made it well nigh impossible to wean stations away from these established networks. Mutual, for example, had great difficulty attracting advertisers because of its inability to place its programs on the powerful outlets. And when a fifth

OPINION AND COMMUNICATION 345–346 (Berelson & Janowitz ed. 1950); WAPLES & TYLER, WHAT THE PEOPLE WANT TO READ ABOUT: A STUDY OF GROUP INTERESTS and a SURVEY OF PROBLEMS IN ADULT READING (1938).

network threatened to enter the field in 1939, Mutual in turn adopted the same restrictive provisions. The affiliation contracts further hampered a station licensee in building up a balanced program schedule and in developing local live programs. The option clause forced him to abdicate control over much of the broadcasting day to the network or to its advertisers. And in practice his technical right to reject undesirable programs was often limited by inability to ascertain in advance the precise content of programs offered by the network.

## ENTER THE NETWORK RULES

After three years of exhaustive investigation, the FCC in 1941 issued its Network Rules to deal with these abuses. The Communications Act gives the Commission no direct authority over the networks. But under that statute the FCC does have the power to grant, modify, or renew the licenses of individual stations if it finds that such action would be in the "public convenience, interest, or necessity." Therefore the Rules took the form of statements of policy by the Commission that it would not grant a license to any station owner who entered into a proscribed arrangement with a network.

Through the abolition of restrictive practices embodied in affiliation contracts, the Commission first of all sought to promote competition between stations. Territorial exclusivity was prohibited in order to give independent stations a chance at rejected network programs.[35] To enable affiliates to bargain more freely for non-network advertising, the broadcasting day was divided into four segments and option time was limited to three hours in each segment. The notice required before a network could demand clearance for its own programs during option time was increased from 28 to 56 days.[36] Outside of option time, stations

---

[35] "No license shall be granted to a standard broadcasting station having any contract, arrangement, or understanding, express or implied, with a network organization which prevents or hinders another station serving substantially the same area from broadcasting the network's programs not taken by the former station, or which prevents or hinders another station serving a substantially different area from broadcasting any program of the network organization. This section shall not be construed to prohibit any contract, arrangement, or understanding between a station and a network organization pursuant to which the station is granted the first call in its primary service area upon the programs of the net-work organization." 47 CODE FED. REGS. § 3.102 (1949). . . .

[36] "No license shall be granted to a standard broadcasting station which options for network programs any time subject to call on less than 56 days' notice, or more time than a total of three hours within each of four segments of the broadcast day as herein described. The broadcast day is divided into four segments as follows: 8 a.m. to 1 p.m.; 1 p.m.

were to be left free to make long-range commitments. Network control over the rates of time which it did not actually purchase was outlawed.[37]

Even more extensive efforts were made to foster network competition for stations and advertising. NBC was forced to divest itself of one of its networks.[38] Ownership by any network of two stations in one market or of one station in a market not otherwise adequately served was proscribed.[39] Under the Rules a network could not contractually bind a station to exclusive affiliation,[40] or require clearance of time sold to competing networks even during option hours.[41] Affiliation contracts themselves were limited to two years.[42]

---

to 6 p.m.; 6 p.m. to 11 p.m.; 11 p.m. to 8 a.m. Such options may not be exclusive as against other net work organizations and may not prevent or hinder the station from optioning or selling any or all of the time covered by the option, or other time, to other network organizations." 47 CODE FED. REGS. § 3.104 (1949).

This regulation was the most significant concession to the networks embodied in the Commission's amendments of October, 1941. The original Rules permitted no option power whatsoever. CHAIN BROADCASTING REPORT 92.

[37] "No license shall be granted to a standard broadcasting station having any contract, arrangement, or understanding, express or implied, with a network organization under which the station is prevented or hindered from, or penalized for, fixing or altering its rates for the sale of broadcast time for other than the network's programs." 47 CODE FED. REGS. § 3.108 (1949).

[38] "No license shall be issued to a standard broadcast station affiliated with a network organization which maintains more than one network: Provided, that this section shall not be applicable if such networks are not operated simultaneously, or if there is no substantial overlap in the territory served by the group of stations comprising each such network." 47 CODE FED REGS. § 3.107 (1949). . . .

[39] "No license will be granted to a network organization, or to any person directly or indirectly controlled by or under common control with a network organization, for more than one standard broadcast station where one of the stations covers substantially the service area of the other station, or for any standard broadcast station in any locality where the existing standard broadcast stations are so few or of such unequal desirability (in terms of coverage, power, frequency, or other related matters) that competition would be substantially restrained by such licensing." 47 CODE FED. REGS. § 3.106 (1949).

[40] "No license shall be granted to a standard broadcast station having any contract, arrangement, or understanding, express or implied, with a network organization under which the station is prevented or hindered from, or penalized for, broadcasting the programs of any other network organization." 47 CODE FED. REGS. § 3.101 (1949).

[41] See § 3.104, note 36 *supra*.

[42] "No license shall be granted to a standard broadcast station having any contract, arrangement, or understanding, express or implied, with a network organization which provides, by original term, provisions for renewal, or otherwise for the affiliation of the station for a period longer

Finally the regulations were designed to restore to the individual licensee a greater measure of control over programming. No longer could he option away his entire broadcasting day or bind himself to exclusive affiliation.[43] The requirement of increased notice for clearance orders assured greater continuity for local and spot programs. The Rules insisted that the licensee have full discretion to reject unsatisfactory or unsuitable network commercial offers and to substitute local interest programs.[44] The licensee was to be free to build up a balanced program structure from a diversity of sources—network, spot, and local—in order to fulfill his statutory responsibility of operating his station in the public interest.

### PRESENT STATUS OF BROADCASTING UNDER THE RULES

While the FCC hailed the Rules as the magna charta of radio, network spokesmen prophesied the doom of chain broadcasting. The networks warned that radio advertising revenues would dwindle; that small stations in particular would suffer because businessmen would advertise, if at all, only through powerful outlets in rich markets; that public service programs would be sharply curtailed; and that the rules were in reality a prelude to government operation of radio in America. Instead, under the Rules network revenues have soared, broadcasters have more than trebled in number, any diminution in sustaining programs can more accurately be attributed to increased expenditure for advertising, and government operation of radio is no closer today than ever. But despite the disappearance of all prohibited clauses from affiliation contracts, the hopes of the FCC for a new era in the radio industry have proven largely illusory.

*Competition on the station level*

Competition between stations continues on extremely unequal terms. Since affiliation guarantees both a minimum of profitable

---

than 2 years: Provided, that a contract, arrangement, or understanding for a period up to 2 years may be entered into within six months prior to the commencement of such period." 47 CODE FED. REGS. § 3.103 (1949).

[43] See § 3.101 note 40 *supra*; § 3.104 note 36 *supra*.

[44] "No license shall be granted to a standard broadcast station having any contract, arrangement, or understanding, express or implied, with a network organization which (a) with respect to programs offered pursuant to an affiliation contract, prevents or hinders the station from rejecting or refusing network programs which the station reasonably believes to be unsatisfactory or unsuitable; or which (b) with respect to network programs so offered or already contracted for, prevents the station from rejecting or refusing any program which in its opinion, is contrary to public interest, or from substituting a program of outstanding local or national importance." 47 CODE FED. REGS. § 3.105 (1949).

network programs and a competitive advantage in bargaining for other advertising—national and local—the goal of most stations is still to join a network. Occasionally an independent station can prosper by catering to minority tastes or foreign language groups or by specializing in local events. But in general unaffiliated stations must be content with advertising left-overs. Although the tremendous expansion in the number of stations since the war has brought competition to areas where previously one or two broadcasters had a monopoly, it has also made it increasingly difficult for independent stations to obtain network programs. In the pre-war period many markets were not served by a sufficient number of full-time outlets to permit all national networks to secure exclusive affiliates; hence unaffiliated stations in those areas could successfully bargain for network programs. Now there are stations eager for affiliation wherever coverage is sought. The result is that any local station which is unwilling or unable to sign an affiliation contract must operate without network programs. . . .

Any expectation that the rule against territorial exclusivity would alleviate the competitive disadvantage of unaffiliated stations was short-lived. In the first place, networks are under no affirmative obligation to offer rejected programs to independents. Secondly, popular commercial programs are rarely rejected by affiliates, and independents can seldom afford the expense of sustainers. Finally, even if an independent station owner obtains a network program, his tenure is insecure, so that he may lose the program as soon as local popularity is achieved. An affiliate can reclaim the program at the end of the independent's contract term, which is usually limited to a period of a few months.

Competition among stations for national advertising is further threatened by the networks' practice of representing certain key affiliates in the sale of non-network time to national sponsors in the spot market. Ordinarily a station, affiliated or unaffiliated, deals with spot market advertisers through independent station representation agencies who are in direct competition with the networks for advertising money. Within this framework all stations should have reasonable access to spot advertising. When a network represents its affiliates in the spot market, however, it is in a position to exercise powerful bargaining leverage on a national advertiser who is seeking choice hours for programs which he sponsors over the network. As yet the networks' invasion of the spot field has been limited. Indeed, the initial influence of their competitive challenge has forced independent representation agencies to improve their service. But there are dangers inherent in the possible expansion of network representa-

**764**

tion of key stations. If ABC, CBS, and NBC were to represent only twelve to fifteen more of their affiliates, together they could control 50% of the spot market. Furthermore, when a network represents an affiliate in the sale of spot advertising, it controls the great bulk of the affiliate's revenues and is in the anomalous position of competing with itself for the sale of station time. The Rules do not touch this problem.

*Competition at the network level*

The separation of the Blue Network from NBC and its transformation into the American Broadcasting Company represents the one solid achievement of the Rules. No doubt the listening public has benefitted from the added diversity of program fare. But American and Mutual are still far from being the competitive equals of National and Columbia. Their limited financial success in recent years reflects the prosperity of the times and radio's overall increased share of the advertising dollar, rather than competitive inroads on their older rivals.

The newer networks are at a disadvantage in competing for advertising because NBC and CBS still control most of the nation's powerful stations. Sponsors prefer to reach a particular market through one dominant outlet; the newer networks, however, have been able to serve many areas only by combining a number of small stations. Conversely, the most powerful outlets cannot be induced to switch allegiance to American and Mutual because these networks do not have the high-paying advertisers and the most popular programs. The two year limitation on network-station contracts has in no way affected this basic dilemma, and the prohibition of exclusivity has not resulted in extensive dual affiliation.

Since the four networks were not competitive equals at the time the Rules went into effect, the Rules, to the extent that they have made clearance less automatic, have actually hindered the development of the younger chains. By 1943 both National and Columbia were already distributing a full schedule of popular programs, but American and Mutual were still very much in the building process. Inasmuch as affiliates are more likely to object to network requests for additional hours than to mere maintenance of the status quo, American at least has lost substantial advertising revenue because of failure or delay in securing the necessary number of outlets.

*Station responsibility*

The Network Rules have not materially increased local station responsibility. Affiliation contracts have been revised so that they comply scrupulously with the FCC mandate. But despite the fact that the Rules cover informal as well as contractual arrangements, networks can subtly bring pressure to bear on affiliates in ways that are very difficult to uncover. The pressure is effective because the networks still have a superior bargaining position. The manager of an affiliated station realizes that networks naturally prefer to deal with outlets that will accept without protest all commercial programs which are offered, whether inside or outside option time. He knows that if he protests too much he may fall into disfavor and ultimately be disaffiliated. As a result, any station associated with a network is strongly tempted to forget about local obligations and become a mere conduit for network programs. Moreover, chain representation of affiliates in the spot market involves yet another threat to independent operation. When a network assumes this dual function of selling network and spot time, it is in a position to influence non-network rates and to exert control over theoretically independent station time.

An illustration of extreme network dominance of station operation was presented by the recent FCC hearings on renewal of licenses of stations belonging to Don Lee Broadcasting System, West Coast associate of Mutual.[85] Don Lee's affiliation contracts were in strict conformity with the Network Rules. But by the exertion of constant pressure and thinly veiled threats of disaffiliation, the network was able to vitiate the protection which the Rules were designed to afford member stations. Don Lee informed its member stations that they must choose between independent operation and affiliation, and that the contractual rights guaranteed affiliates by the FCC Rules were inimical to efficient operation and expansion of the network. Affiliates were discouraged from carrying programs of other networks. Demands for clearance on as little as two weeks' notice frustrated development of local programs. Don Lee assured its members of only three and a half hours a day for non-network operations, insisting that almost all the popular listening hours be reserved for network programs. No disruption of network schedules was tolerated even to permit coverage of such events as state election returns and political conventions, local news, and local athletic contests and religious services. The network repeatedly tried to substitute its standards of taste and public interest for those of its affiliates. In one instance Don Lee even tried to purge a local station of an executive who had in the past demonstrated his independence. Although the FCC has made no full-scale investigation of any other network, at least one Commissioner felt that parallel activities were indicated in other chains. . . .

---

[85] [5 Pike & Fischer Radio Regulations 1179 (1949).]

[The Note here discusses FM and TV and also deplores the general lack of enforcement of the chain broadcasting rules. The editors feel that because of the uniform limited service area of FM stations an integrated AM-FM system would alleviate the shortage of broadcasting frequencies and competitive inequalities among stations and among networks without sacrifice of local programming control.]

Many of the problems of competitive inequality at both network and station levels could be solved by a change in the Commission's station allocation policies. The most effective, but at the same time most drastic, step would be to set a deadline before which all AM stations except clear channel stations serving primarily rural areas must convert to FM. Obviously such a change-over would entail great expense not only to station owners but also to listeners who would be forced to purchase FM receivers. Much of this waste could have been avoided by a foresighted FCC in 1945 when there were far fewer AM stations and many prewar receiving sets were in need of replacement. Perhaps 1950 is a bad time to force such a change in view of the uncertainty as to the full economic effects of television. But if the Commission waits another 10 years until adjustments have been made to reflect the influence of TV, this will probably mean the sacrifice of the 700 odd FM stations which are now struggling for existence. In any event, since the possibility of a dominant FM system declines with the construction of each new AM station and the purchase of each new AM receiver, the time for Commission action, if action is ever to be taken, is now.

Short of ordering a shift to FM, the Commission could replace those high-powered clear channel stations which are located in densely populated areas, and hence are neither designed nor needed to serve rural listeners, with 5,000-watt regional stations. In the essentially metropolitan northeastern section of the country there are 12 Class I-A and 13 Class I-B clear channel stations, most of them affiliated with NBC and CBS. If these clear channel frequencies were redesignated as regional channels, at least 200 new regional outlets could be licensed in addition to those needed to replace the deleted stations. This action would lessen the competitive advantage of NBC and CBS in the profitable northeastern market and would put all the stations in that area on a far more equal footing.

But if the Commission is unwilling to take either of these steps, there are several less ambitious measures which it should take in an effort to breathe new life into the Chain Rules.

In order to reduce the inequality of competition at the station level, the FCC should:

**767**

a) require the networks to provide a uniform and convenient mechanism by which independent stations can obtain, with assurance of reasonable tenure, network programs rejected by an affiliate;

b) restrict network representation of stations in the spot market to stations actually owned and operated by the network.

As long as networks exist, affiliates will probably have a competitive advantage over independents. But adoption of these proposals would temper the competitive disparity, without unduly hindering efficient network operations.

To promote competition among networks, the FCC should:

a) favor American and Mutual affiliates whenever applications for increased power are made; and

b) adopt, as quickly as possible, its proposed rule to limit the number of hours which TV stations may take from any single network until a community is served by at least four stations.

The task of safeguarding licensee independence is largely one of enforcement. In order to strengthen the Commission's enforcement policy, Congress should:

a) arm the FCC with intermediate sanctions; and

b) give the Commission jurisdiction over the networks to enable it to take direct action against any network which violates the Rules.

Finally, the most effective step that could be taken to revitalize the Rules would be a change of attitude on the part of the FCC. Until the Commission demonstrates that it will punish networks which unduly coerce their affiliates, and licensees who disregard their public service responsibilities, the Network Rules will never cut their baby teeth, much less their six-year molars.

## Note

1. For further discussion of the connection between the chain broadcasting regulations and freedom of speech, see Hearings Before Committee on Interstate Commerce on S. Res. 113, 77th Cong., 1st Sess. 151 (1941). See further F. C. C., *Report on Chain Broadcasting* (1941); F. C. C., *Supplementary Report on Chain Broadcasting* (1941) F. C. C., *An Economic Study of Standard Broadcasting* (1947); Robinson, *Radio Networks and the Federal Government* (1943); Columbia Broadcasting System, *What the New Radio Rules Mean* (1941); Trammel (National Broadcasting Company President), *Statement Before Senate Committee on Interstate Commerce* (1941); Note, 51 Yale L. J. 448 (1941).

2. When the chain broadcasting rules were issued the National Broadcasting Company and the Columbia Broadcasting System brought suits to enjoin their enforcement. In upholding the rules the Supreme Court stated that Congress in providing that licenses be granted on

the basis of the "public interest, convenience, and necessity gave the Commission broad powers to regulate." The nature of radio, permitting only a limited number of stations, meant that such regulations must go beyond mere technical and emergency matters. The public interest standard is not too vague and indefinite. Nor does the fact that Section 311 specifically provides for the withholding of licenses from those convicted of violating the anti-trust laws preclude the Commission from considering the effect of monopolistic practices on the "public interest, convenience and necessity" where there have been no convictions. The Court also rejected contentions that the regulations were arbitrary and violated the First Amendment. On this latter point the Court stated:

"We come, finally to an appeal to the First Amendment. The Regulations, even if valid in all other respects, must fall because they abridge, say the appellants, their right of free speech. If that be so, it would follow that every person whose application for a license to operate a station is denied by the Commission is thereby denied his constitutional right of free speech. Freedom of utterance is abridged to many who wish to use the limited facilities of radio. Unlike other modes of expression, radio inherently is not available to all. That is its unique characteristic, and that is why, unlike other modes of expression, it is subject to governmental regulation. Because it cannot be used by all, some who wish to use it must be denied. But Congress did not authorize the Commission to choose among applicants upon the basis of their political, economic, or social views, or upon any other capricious basis. If it did, or if the Commission by these Regulations proposed a choice among applicants upon some such basis, the issue before us would be wholly different. The question here is simply whether the Commission, by announcing that it will refuse licenses to persons who engage in specified network practices (a basis for choice which we hold is comprehended within the statutory criterion of 'public interest'), is thereby denying such persons the constitutional right of free speech. The right of free speech does not include, however, the right to use the facilities of radio without a license. The licensing system established by Congress in the Communications Act of 1934 was a proper exercise of its power over commerce. The standard it provided for the licensing of stations was the 'public interest, convenience, or necessity'. Denial of a station license on that ground, if valid under the Act, is not a denial of free speech." *National Broadcasting Co. v. U. S.*, 319 U. S. 190, 226–7, 87 L. Ed. 1344, 63 S. Ct. 997 (1943).

## NOTE—FCC COMPARATIVE HEARINGS
### 64 Harv. L. Rev. 947, 948–54 (1951)

Section 307(b) of the Communications Act directs that the Commission "shall make such distribution of licenses, frequencies, hours of operation, and of power among the several States and communities as to provide a fair, efficient, and equitable distribution of radio service to each of the same."[11]  This criterion of "equitable distribution" is unique, in that here a comparison of the needs of different communities is in issue rather than a comparison of the relative abilities of different applicants.

The Commission has interpreted Section 307(b) as indicating a desire to have every locality supplied with a "primary service"[12] and will, therefore, prefer an applicant who shows that his proposed signal will cover an area, commonly called a "white area," not theretofore served.[13]  This is the strongest case that an applicant can make, for even though the "white area" covered by the proposed signal is small and includes but few persons, the applicant will be favored.[14]  If both applicants propose to render a first primary service, the Commission will favor the one reaching the largest number of persons.[15]

The general mandate of Section 307(b), however, includes much more than merely cases involving a first primary service.  It has been invoked to favor an applicant who would render service to a community with fewer local stations than the community proposed to be served by his opponent.[16]  It has also been held applicable to regional stations, thus favoring a community having no regional stations.[17]  Its mandate has been translated into a policy favoring a grant which will provide the first local station in a community already receiving primary services from stations elsewhere, thereby fostering a medium of expression to satisfy purely local needs.[18]  . . .

The Commission has a clearly enunciated policy that a station seeking to improve its facilities will be favored over a new ap-

[11] 48 STAT. 1083 (1934), as amended, 49 STAT. 1475 (1936), 47 U. S. C. § 307(b) (1946).

[12] See Scripps-Howard Radio, Inc. (WCPO), 3 R. R. 1796, 1802 (1948). A "primary service" means a broadcast service to an area in which the ground wave is not subject to objectionable interference or fading.  FCC Rules, 47 CODE FED. REGS. § 3.11 (1949).

[13] E.g., East Texas Broadcasting Co., 5 R. R. 413 (1949).

[14] E.g., Scripps-Howard Radio, Inc. (WCPO), 5 R. R. 810 (1950); William M. Drace, 4 R. R. 741 (1948) (losing applicant would have provided daytime service to 5 times as many persons and nighttime service to about 2½ times as many but no first primary service).

[15] E.g., Manistee Radio Corp., 5 R. R. 302 (1950).

[16] E.g., Newark Broadcasting Corp., 3 R. R. 839 (1947); cf. WJIM, Inc., 3 R. R. 1692 (1947), aff'd sub nom. Radio Cincinnati, Inc. v. FCC, 177 F. 2d 92 (D. C. Cir. 1949) (although opponent would serve around 800,000 persons, as opposed to 225,000 persons served by the preferred applicant, the latter would furnish a first primary service, daytime only, to 5000 persons).

[17] Booth Radio Stations, Inc., 4 R. R. 616 (1949).

[18] Enid Broadcasting Co., 5 R. R. 1232 (1950); Seaside Broadcasting Co., 5 R. R. 930c (1949).

[Emerson]

plicant, if all other factors are equal and the existing station has a satisfactory past record.[20]   One case emphasized that the existing station's "record of past achievement furnishes assurance that its proposal will actually be placed into effect."[21]   Another justification frequently given for this policy, though of dubious validity, is that an existing station seeking to improve would always be barred by a new qualified applicant if the result were otherwise.[22]   But more fundamentally, the policy is a reflection of an understandable tendency to favor one seeking to improve his position and his service to the public.

While this test appears to be clear and simple in application, it conflicts with another strong Commission policy to the effect that the establishment of an additional and competitive service is desired to prevent the monopolization of the media of communication and to promote competition.[23]   As might be expected, the Commission has relied on each, ignoring[24] or dismissing the other as not controlling.[25]   And since the qualification to the policy that all other factors be equal is seldom met, the policy favoring the existing station is of illusory force.[26]   Thus, the Court of Appeals for the District of Columbia has recently upheld the FCC in its refusal to favor the existing station where the proposed programming of the new applicant was found by the Commission to be superior to that of the old station.[27]   Similarly, a new station has been favored where it proposed to bring into the locality the programs of a large network, not theretofore received in the area.[28]   . . .

In accord with the strong policy of the Commission favoring competition and disapproving the monopolization of communications media, there is an FCC policy disfavoring an applicant who controls or has an interest in a newspaper.[29]   While the Commis-

[20] *E.g.*, Valdosta Broadcasting Co., 11 F. C. C. 769 (1946).   An even stronger Commission policy, but closely related to this one, is that disfavoring the deletion of an existing station by the grant of a mutually exclusive license to a new applicant.   . . .

[21] Lansing Broadcasting Co., 5 R. R. 48, 67 (1949).

[22] Valdosta Broadcasting Co., 11 F. C. C. 769 (1946).

[23] *E.g.*, KVOX Broadcasting Co., 3 R. R. 972 (1947).

[24] Lansing Broadcasting Co., 5 R. R. 48 (1949).

[25] James A. Noe, 3 R. R. 1821 (1949).

[26] If an examiner's report rests upon this policy, attack by the losing party usually rests upon the grounds that all other factors are not equal. *See* James A. Noe, 3 R. R. 1821, 1826e (1949) (Chairman Coy, dissenting).

[27] Kentucky Broadcasting Corp. v. FCC, 174 F. 2d 38 (D. C. Cir. 1949). For subsequent history, see Mid-America Broadcasting Corp., 6 R. R. 269 (1950).

[28] Fetzer Broadcasting Co., 11 F. C. C. 515 (1946).

[29] *E.g.*, Port Huron Broadcasting Co., 5 F. C. C. 177 (1938).   In Scripps-

sion has not seen fit to incorporate this into a Rule, due to a desire not to discourage qualified applicants from applying for licenses, the policy has been publicly announced in the Federal Register.[30]

Insofar as the applicant controls the only local newspaper and there is inadequate competition by newspapers published in other cities, there is perhaps some vigor to this policy.[31] However, where the degree of competition is greater, the policy's true impact is largely a matter of conjecture, for it seems to have been more honored in the breach than in the observance.[32] For example, in one significant case, *Midland Broadcasting Co.*,[33] the local newspaper owner was preferred for two reasons. First, the majority of the officers and directors of the competing applicant were so closely affiliated with the local industrial corporation which dominated the city that the Commission feared a grant to them would only increase this domination. Hence, there were two conflicting monopoly aspects, each of which seemed to the Commission to balance the other. Second, the newspaper applicant showed a greater degree of local ownership and of integration between ownership and management. Seemingly also of some influence were the excellent public service record of the newspaper and the substantial amount of newspaper competition from nearby cities.

Perhaps contributing to the sporadic application of the policy against newspaper ownership of radio stations is the Commission's realization that newspapers—already experts in the field of news dissemination and keenly aware of the needs of the community—will naturally gravitate towards the radio business and will probably provide excellent service to the public.[34] Therefore, it is not surprising that other policy considerations are

Howard Radio, Inc., 4 R. R. 525 (1949), this was listed as a factor favoring the nonnewspaper applicant, even though there were two other papers and five AM stations in the city not connected with either applicant. However, the weight of this factor in the case is conjectural.

[30] Public Notice, 9 FED. REG. 702 (1944).

[31] Norman Broadcasting Co., 5 R. R. 120 (1949). It also has considerable validity when combined with another policy, for example, that of favoring expansion of existing stations. Kokomo Pioneer Broadcasters, 6 R. R. 285 (1950).

[32] *E.g.*, Orlando Daily Newspapers, Inc., 11 F. C. C. 760 (1946). If applicable, § 307(b) would clearly be controlling. Hanford Publishing Co., 3 R. R. 1281 (1947).

[33] 3 R. R. 1961 (1948).

[34] But see Mansfield Journal Co. v. F. C. C., 180 F. 2d 28 (D. C. Cir. 1950), 59 YALE L. J. 1342.

normally more controlling than the fact of newspaper owner-ship.[35] . . .

Motivated by the same general policy which led to a disapproval of licensing newspaper owners, the Commission will consider and under certain circumstances disfavor one person's owner-ship interest in more than a single station.[36] But unlike the newspaper case, multiple ownership disapprobation has resulted in a Commission Rule, Section 3.35,[37] which forbids multiple ownership if the proposed station would render a primary service to a substantial portion of the primary-service area of another station owned by the same parties. The principle of this Rule has been frequently invoked to deny licenses in comparative hearings.[38] But an exception embodied in the Rule does allow multiple ownership "upon a showing that public interest, con-venience and necessity will be served" thereby. That this pro-viso has been used to allow a grant to a multiple owner[39] stands as cogent evidence that even the Commission's Rules may be so phrased as to furnish little assurance of standardized treatment.

However, the policy against multiple ownership has extended beyond the confines of Section 3.35. For multiple ownership, even where no overlap of primary services would result, has been the basis for preferring another applicant.[40] Further, where both applicants are already or would be multiple owners, the Commission has favored the applicant who would have relatively fewer stations.[41]

One outstanding example of the length to which the Commis-sion must go at times to find a basis for preference is illustrated

---

[35] One case has indicated that a deviation from the policy against news-paper applicants is not an abuse of discretion. *See* Tri-State Broadcast-ing Co. v. F. C. C., 96 F. 2d 564, 566 (D. C. Cir. 1938).

[36] *E.g.*, Lubbock County Broadcasting Co., 4 R. R. 493 (1948). Al-though this case was reversed on appeal, Plains Radio Broadcasting Co. v. F. C. C., 175 F. 2d 359 (D. C. Cir. 1949), the court approved the Com-mission's action on this point. *Id.* at 363.

[37] F. C. C. Rules, 47 CODE FED. REGS. § 3.35 (1949).

[38] *E.g.*, The Yankee Network, Inc., 3 R. R. 1766, 1782 (1947) (as be-tween five mutually exclusive applicants for three FM channels, two dis-favored by invocation of policy against monopoly, although grant to oth-er three would result in a duplication of network programs already heard in the area) ; *cf.* Wichita Broadcasting Co., 3 R. R. 865 (1947).

[39] Norfolk Broadcasting Co., 3 R. R. 1699 (1947).

[40] *E.g.*, The Finger Lakes Broadcasting System, 11 F. C. C. 528, 546 (1946) ; Associated Broadcasters, Inc., 3 R. R. 1826f (1948).

[41] Granite City Broadcasting Co., 4 R. R. 1322i (1949). The FCC has put a ceiling on the number of FM and TV stations which one person may own, control or operate. 47 CODE FED. REGS. § 3.240 (1949) (six FM stations) ; *id.* § 3.640 (five TV stations).

by *Cedar Rapids Broadcasting Corp.*[42] Applicants *A* and *B* were both corporations, and shareholders of each had interests in other radio stations. Since all other factors were equal, the Commission was forced to rely upon the policy favoring diversification of control as the determinative factor. Two shareholders of corporation *A* owned 50 per cent of *A*'s stock; they also owned 57 per cent of another station—Carpenter, one of the two shareholders, owning only 7 per cent of the other station. Similarly, two shareholders of corporation *B* owned 40.6 per cent of *B*'s stock; and also they controlled another station—Sexton, one of the two shareholders, owning less than 1 per cent of the other station. Solely on the basis of these facts the Commission granted the application of *B,* finding that a greater diversification of control would result. The difference between the two applicants was that the two shareholders of *B* owned 9.4 per cent less stock than did the shareholders of *A* in their respective applicant corporations, and Sexton owned slightly over 6 per cent less stock than did Carpenter in their respective outside radio interests. . . .

Other miscellaneous factors of judgment may be grouped together because they are similar in impact and are the somewhat pragmatic by-products of selecting the best qualified. The Commission has favored the policies of: (1) local residency of the owners, who are expected to be thoroughly conversant with local needs,[60] (2) integration of ownership and management, whereby the owners will take an active part in the day-to-day operation of the station,[61] (3) active participation by applicants in civic affairs,[62] (4) broad diversification of background and interests,[63] and (5) past broadcast experience.[64]

## Note

1. The Commission also considers such additional factors as the applicant's character, including integrity, temperament, altruism and the like, see *Mester v. United States,* 70 F. Supp. 118 (E. D. N. Y., 1947) aff'd 332 U. S. 749 (1947); *Calumet Broadcasting Co. v. F. C. C.,* 160 F. 2d 285 (C. A. D. C., 1947), and his personal ability, *Kansas City*

---

[42] 3 R. R. 1853 (1948).

[60] *E.g.,* Norman Broadcasting Co., 5 R. R. 120 (1949); Midland Broadcasting Co., 3 R. R. 1961 (1948).

[61] *E.g.,* Southern Broadcasting Co., 3 R. R. 1711 (1947); Frank M. Helm, 4 R. R. 1297, *modified on other grounds,* 4 R. R. 1312 (1949); *cf.* Bay State Beacon, Inc. v. F. C. C., 171 F. 2d 826 (D. C. Cir. 1948).

[62] *E.g.,* Norfolk Broadcasting Corp., 3 R. R. 1699 (1947).

[63] *E.g.,* Jackson Broadcasting Co., 4 R. R. 690 (1948).

[64] *E.g.,* Pocahontas Broadcasting Corp. 3 R. R. 1744 (1947); *cf.* Scripps-Howard Radio, Inc., 4 R. R. 525 (1949).

*Broadcasting Co.,* 6 R. R. 607 (1950). For brief discussion, see Note, 25 St. John's L. Rev. 245, 259–260 (1951).

2. Suggested devices for improving the pattern of the television industry with a view toward better program service include: (a) Allocation of channels to educational institutions. See Hearings before a Subcommittee of the Committee on Interstate and Foreign Commerce on Sen. Res. 127, 82d Cong., 1st Sess. (1951); Siepmann, *Radio, Television and Society,* pp. 272–9 (1950); White, *The American Radio,* pp. 101–111 (1947). (b) Theatre-TV—the broadcast of programs to theatres on closed circuits or over cables, with admission charged to patrons. (c) Subscription—TV: (1) Phonevision—scrambled image sent over TV with impulse sent over telephone wire needed to unscramble it, the use of the wire being paid for, when used, as part of regular telephone bill. (2) Subscribe-vision—punched plastic card unscrambles image. (3) Telemeter—coin slot attached to set. See Note, 19 U. of Chi. L. Rev. 556, 569 *et seq.* (1952). For FCC view on subscription programs in connection with FM stations broadcasting music see *Further Letter to FM Stations Engaged in "Functional Music" or "Planned Music" Operations,* Public Notice 62825 (Apr. 12, 1951); *Policy Statements Concerning "Functional Music" Operations,* Public Notice F. C. C. 51445, 62347 (May 4, 1951) (holding "planned music" contrary to Federal Communications Act).

For recent indications of FCC policy in the FM and television fields, see *FM Service for Tax Exempt Non-Profit Organizations,* 1 R. R. 91: 571 (1951); *Sixth Report on Television Allocations,* 1 R. R. 91:599 (1952), esp. pars. 33–62 dealing with the policy of reserving certain channels for education.

## c. Press

## UNITED STATES v. ASSOCIATED PRESS

Supreme Court of the United States, 1945
326 U. S. 1, 89 L. Ed. 2013, 65 S. Ct. 1416

[The Associated Press, a cooperative membership association consisting of some 1200 newspapers located throughout the nation, operated in the following manner. The members contributed news gathered in their respective localities exclusively to the A.P. The A.P. staff covered the rest of the world. The news thus gathered was edited and redistributed among all the members. Expenses were defrayed by assessments. Service thus provided was universally regarded in the industry as highly efficient and most complete. At the time of the suit, 81 per cent of the morning papers with 96 per cent of the circulation and 59 per cent of the evening papers with 77 per cent of the circulation were members of the A.P. Out of the papers having a circulation of over 50,000, all but one, the Chicago Sun, were members. There existed only two other news services of similar scope, United Press and International News Service. They operated on a profit basis and generally did not have access to the local news gathered by A.P. members for A.P.'s exclusive use. The Anti-Trust Division of the Department of Justice attacked two A.P. by-law provisions as violating the Sherman Act. The first was the exclusive local news provision already mentioned. The second provision, until amended in 1942, granted any member with which a new applicant might compete a "right to protest" the newcomer's admission. The application would then be voted on by the entire membership and four-fifths' approval was required. If the protesting member put up any fight at all, the other papers, expecting similar favors in return, were very unlikely to vote for admission. On the other hand, non-competing applicants who were new sources of local news were welcome and simply had to be voted on by the Board of Directors. After complaints by the Washington Times-Herald and Chicago Sun to the Department of Justice, the above provision was changed in 1942 to omit reference to a "right to protest" and reduced the vote necessary for the admission of competing members from four-fifths to a majority. However, other restrictions were imposed. If elected, the applicant could join only if he relinquished to A.P. members any exclusive news source he had available and an amount of money equal to 10 per cent of the total amount of regular assessments received by A.P. from members in the field (morning, evening, or Sunday) in the applicant's city since October 1, 1900. In the case of the Chicago Sun, this would have amounted to $400,000. A morning newspaper in New York would have had to pay $1,500,000. This money was to be distributed among the competing members in the city.

The defendant admitted that membership in the A.P. generally gave a newspaper a competitive advantage over non-members. The District Court held that the exclusionary provisions violated the Sherman Act, and enjoined the A.P. from observing them. At the same time it permitted the fashioning of new by-laws. The requirement that members must furnish local news exclusively to A.P. was held not to be a violation standing alone.

The Supreme Court upheld this decision. The opinion stated that trade in news carried on among several states is interstate commerce. It dismissed arguments that the by-laws imposed reasonable restrictions, viz., that they should be treated like a reporter's contract, or that they are reasonable because an owner of property should have a right to choose his associates. Mr. Justice Black stated that while such agreements without more might be reasonable, "They assume quite a different aspect if utilized as essential features of a program to hamper or destroy competition." The fact that there were other news services in the field did not alter the fact that A.P. membership nevertheless amounted to a competitive advantage. The Court continued:]

Nevertheless, we are asked to reverse these judgments on the ground that the evidence failed to show that AP reports, which might be attributable to their own "enterprise and sagacity," are clothed "in the robes of indispensability." The absence of "indispensability" is said to have been established under the following chain of reasoning: AP has made its news generally available to the people by supplying it to a limited and select group of publishers in the various cities; therefore, it is said, AP and its member publishers have not deprived the reading public of AP news; all local readers have an "adequate access" to AP news, since all they need do in any city to get it is to buy, on whatever terms they can in a protected market, the particular newspaper selected for the public by AP and its members. We reject these contentions. The proposed "indispensability" test would fly in the face of the language of the Sherman Act and all of our previous interpretations of it. Moreover, it would make that law a dead letter in all fields of business, a law which Congress has consistently maintained to be an essential safeguard to the kind of private competitive business economy this country has sought to maintain.

The restraints on trade in news here were no less than those held to fall within the ban of the Sherman Act with reference to combinations to restrain trade outlets in the sale of tiles, *Montague & Co.* v. *Lowry*, 193 U. S. 38; or enameled ironware, *Standard Sanitary Mfg. Co.* v. *United States*, 226 U. S. 20, 48–49; or lumber, *Eastern States Lumber Dealers' Assn.* v. *United States*, 234 U. S. 600, 611; or women's clothes, *Fashion Originators' Guild* v. *Federal Trade Commission*, [312 U. S. 457]; or motion pictures, *United States* v. *Crescent Amusement Co.*, 323 U. S. 173. Here as in the *Fashion Originators' Guild* case, *supra*, 465, "the combination is in reality an extra-governmental agency, which prescribes rules for the regulation and restraint of interstate commerce, and provides extra-judicial tribunals for determination and punishment of violations, and thus 'trenches upon the power of the national legislature and violates the statute.' *Addyston Pipe & Steel Co.* v. *United States*, 175 U. S. 211, 242." By the restrictive By-Laws each of the publishers in the combination has, in effect, "surrendered himself completely to the control of the association," *Anderson* v. *Shipowners Assn.*, 272 U.S. 359, 362, in respect to the disposition of news in interstate commerce. Therefore this contractual restraint of interstate trade, "designed in the interest of preventing competition," cannot be one of the "normal and usual agreements in aid of trade and commerce which may be found not to be within the [Sherman] Act . . ." *Eastern States Lumber Dealers' Assn.* v. *United States, supra*, 612, 613. It is further said that we reach our conclusion by application of the "public utility" concept to the newspaper business. This is not correct. We merely hold that arrangements or combinations designed to stifle competition cannot be immunized by adopting a membership device accomplishing that purpose.

Finally, the argument is made that to apply the Sherman Act to this association of publishers constitutes an abridgment of the freedom of the press guaranteed by the First Amendment. Perhaps it would be a sufficient answer to this contention to refer to the decisions of this Court in *Associated Press* v. *Labor Board* [301 U. S. 103], and *Indiana Farmer's Guide Co.* v. *Prairie Farmer Co.*, 293 U. S. 268. It would be strange indeed, however, if the grave concern for freedom of the press which prompted adoption of the First Amendment should be read as a command that the government was without power to protect that freedom. The First Amendment, far from providing an argument against application of the Sherman Act, here provides powerful reasons to the contrary. That Amendment rests on the assumption that the widest possible dissemination of information from diverse and antagonistic sources is essential to the welfare of the public, that a free press is a condition of a free society. Surely a command that the government itself shall not impede the free flow of ideas does not afford non-governmental combinations a refuge if they impose restraints upon that constitutionally guaranteed freedom. Freedom to publish means freedom for all and not for some. Freedom to publish is guaranteed by the Constitution, but freedom to combine to keep others from publishing is not. Freedom of the press from governmental interference under the First Amendment does not sanction repression of that freedom by private interests.[18] The First Amendment affords not the slightest support for the contention that a combination to restrain trade in news and views has any constitutional immunity.

---

[18] It is argued that the decree interferes with freedom "to print as and how one's reason or one's interest dictates." The decree does not compel AP or its members to permit publication of anything which their "reason" tells them should not be published. It only provides that after their "reason" has permitted publication of news, they shall not, for their own financial advantage, unlawfully combine to limit its publication. The only compulsion to print which appears in the record is found in the By-Laws, previously set out, which compel members of the Association to print some AP news or subject themselves to fine or expulsion from membership in the Association.

[The Court then took up various objections to the way in which the decree was formulated including the objection by the government that the by-law requiring members to furnish local news exclusively to A.P. should also be held invalid. The Court concluded that the findings justified the decree and that it was within the limits of the discretion of the District Court.

Mr. Justice Douglas' and Mr. Justice Frankfurter's concurring opinions are omitted.

Mr. Justice Roberts' and Mr. Justice Murphy's dissenting opinions are omitted.]

### Note

1. Subsequent requirements for admission to the press associations and their application in practice are set forth in Note, 61 Yale L. J. 948, 968 (1952):

"Under the terms of its present by-laws . . . AP may not refuse membership to applicants on grounds of their potential competition with present members.[116] In recent years, however, AP has denied membership to some dailies who "could not meet the required standards of qualification." [117] And AP assessments, which have risen in the postwar period,[118] are set at the absolute discretion of the Board of Directors.[119] Moreover, the guiding principle for assessment determination is population size of the daily's locale,[120] a criterion which ignores page-size or circulation differences among AP members in the same town. But because of the extensive news coverage which AP's co-oper-

---

[116] Under the new by-law, Art II (7), passed in 1945, "no member or director shall take into consideration in passing upon such applicant the effect of his or its admission upon the ability of such applicant to compete with members in the same city and field." Ed. & Pub., Dec. 1, 1945, p. 66. Yet under a literal reading, the members *can* take into account an applicant's competitive status if he is in the same city but not in the same "field" (morning, evening, or Sunday). The limited wording resulted from the fact that outlawed, old by-laws imposed special restrictions only on applicants in the same city and "field" as an existing member. See District Court decree, ¶ 1, United States v. Associated Press, Civil No. 19–163, S.D.N.Y. Jan. 13, 1944.

[117] Communication, *supra* note 111. It is not precisely clear what such standards are, since they are not specified in the by-laws. Some of the standards considered, however, are existence of a paid subscription list; ability to supply AP with local news; and size of staff and plant. Communication, *supra* note 114. The Board of Directors can elect to Associate Membership, while the annual membership meeting elects to Regular Membership. Communication, *supra* note 111.

[118] Communication, *supra* note 114.

[119] By-laws, Art VI (3), VII (1), VIII (1) (1945). Moreover, "[t]he nature and extent of the news service to be furnished to a member shall be determined by the Board of Directors, upon the member's admission. . . ." By-laws, Art. VII (1), reprinted in Ed. & Pub., Dec. 1, 1945, p. 67.

[120] Communication, *supra* note 111.

ative structure provides, few publishers willingly go without AP service, whatever the cost.[121]

"UP and INS subscriptions are often sold with special bonus guarantees for early buyers. Both services grant many subscribers 'asset value' contracts. These guarantee the publisher a special payment which a subsequent competing subscriber must pay in addition to standard service charges.[122] Such extra fees for new applicants a few years ago averaged approximately $25,000 for UP and $30,000 for INS.[123] Although in most of the very largest cities dailies do not hold 'asset value' contracts,[124] elsewhere 'asset value' contracts with both UP and INS ensure the sole publisher, frequently a member of AP, a cost advantage over potential competitors.[125]"

2. For discussion of the *Associated Press* case, see Lewin, *The Associated Press Decision—An Extension of the Sherman Act?*, 13 U. of Chi. L. Rev. 247 (1946); 2 Chafee, *Government and Mass Communications*, 542 et seq. (1947); see especially 588 and 666 et seq. for critical appraisal of the effectiveness of anti-trust laws in the communication field and pp. 618 and 678 et seq. for discussion of alternative remedies such as (a) treating the press as a public utility and making its experiences and services available to all or (b) aiding and facilitating the entrance of new enterprise through subsidies. For an able reply see Brown, book review, 57 Yale L. J. 894 (1948).

3. The F. T. C. has unsuccessfully sought to prosecute magazine publishers for entering into contracts with distributors whereby the latter agreed not to sell certain competing publications and to maintain prices established by the publisher. *F. T. C. v. Curtis Publishing Co.*, 260 U. S. 568, 67 L. Ed. 408, 43 S. Ct. 210 (1923). See also *U. S. v. Times Picayune Publishing Co.*, — F. Supp. — (E. D. La., 1952) (prac-

---

[121] See note 114 *supra*.

[122] Associated Press v. United States, 326 U. S. 1, 13 n. 11 (1945); *Hearings before Subcommittee No. 2 of the Committee on the Judiciary on H. R. 110*, 30th Cong., 1st Sess., 18–9, 40–1, 55 (1947). In 1944, UP had "asset value" contracts with 215 subscribers in 144 cities, and INS had such contracts with 64 subscribers in 62 cities, Government's Proposed Findings of Fact, Comparison of Proposed Findings of Fact and Conclusions of Law Submitted by the Government and Those Submitted by the Defendants, p. 66, United States v. Associated Press, Civil No. 19–163 (S. D. N. Y. 1944). In addition, 13 INS subscribers held territorially exclusive contracts. *Id.* at p. 68. Smaller new services often sell their reports on a territorially exclusive basis. See *Hearings on H. R. 110, supra*, at 5, 44; United States v. Associated Press, 52 F. Supp. 362, 367 (S. D. N. Y. 1944).

[123] Averages compiled from figures, *ibid.* For description of how asset values are computed, see *Hearings on H. R. 110, supra* note 122, at 18.

[124] In 1944, no morning or evening daily in New York, Washington, Philadelphia, Detroit, Baltimore, Cleveland, St. Louis, or Boston held such contracts with UP; no morning paper in Los Angeles or Chicago; and no evening paper in Pittsburgh. Defendants' Proposed Findings, Comparison of Finding, *supra* note 122, at p. 68.

[125] In 1944, the only publisher in 26 monopoly newspaper cities had UP and INS asset value contracts plus AP membership. In 18 other cities, the only morning or evening paper had the same status. *Ibid.*

tice of forcing advertisers to buy space in a morning-evening package held violation of Sections 1 and 2 of the Sherman Act). For additional F. T. C. and state cases see Note, 61 Yale L. J. 948 (1952).

4. In *Lorain Journal Co. v. U. S.*, 342 U. S. 143, 96 L. Ed. —, 72 S. Ct. 181 (1951), a newspaper which already enjoyed a substantial monopoly in the locality had refused to accept local advertising from those using a local radio station. The Court upheld an injunction on the theory that the defendant was attempting to monopolize interstate commerce. See also *Mansfield Journal Co. v. F. C. C.*, 180 F. 2d 28 (C. A. D. C., 1950) where the Commission, in passing on the Journal's application for a license, considered not only the monopolistic effect of ownership of a station by the newspaper but also the newspaper's past efforts to monopolize by driving out a competing radio station. This case is discussed in Note, 59 Yale L. J. 1342 (1950).

It has been said that many small communities probably have insufficient means to support competing information outlets. In these areas blind adherence to anti-trust policies would probably not achieve the desired diversity of communication. See Report of the United States Senate Special Committee To Study Problems of American Small Business, *Survival of a Free, Competitive Press, The Small Newspaper*, 80th Cong., 1st Sess. (1947). On opposition to the anti-trust approach in general as a means for achieving diversity and high quality in communication, see materials cited *infra*.

5. On monopoly in the newspaper field, see also Ernst, *The First Freedom*, pp. 68–71 (1946); Bird, *Newspaper Monopoly and Political Independence*, 17 Journalism Qu. 207 (1940); Villard, *The Disappearing Daily* (1944); Nixon, *Concentration and Absenteeism in Daily Newspaper Ownership*, 22 Journalism Qu. 97 (1945). On the economics of the newspaper business, its big business character, the role of profits and the difficulty of launching a new enterprise, see Johnson, *Great Newspapers, If Any*, Harper's Magazine, June, 1948, p. 540; Poynter, *The Economic Problems of the Press and the Changing Newspaper*, 219 Annals of the Am. Acad. of Pol. and Soc. Sci. 82 (1942); Mott, *American Journalism* (1941). On the entire subject see the excellent summary in Note, 61 Yale L. J. 948 (1952). See also materials in bibliography at end of this Chapter.

6. Government regulation of business and economic aspects of the communication industry is of course quite extensive. Space permits only a brief mention of some of the controls which have been thought relevant to the problem of freedom. *Subsidies:* (a) second-class mail privileges have been mentioned in connection with post office control of harmful literature, *supra*. (b) Copyright in one sense favors freedom by encouraging new creation; in another sense it is an obstacle to free circulation as was seen in the Paramount case. For further discussion see 2 Chafee, *Government and Mass Communications*, p. 486 (1947); Chafee, *Reflections on the Law of Copyright*, 45 Col. L. Rev. 503, 719 (1945). In addition there are specific provisions in the Federal Communications Act against rebroadcasting programs without permit from the originating station. 47 U. S. C. § 325 (1946). *Compulsory Disclosure.* This has already been mentioned as a pos-

sible alternative to group libel laws, and in connection with the Internal Security Act, *supra*. Periodicals that want second-class mail rates also must disclose ownership and financial organization and so must broadcasting stations. See 2 Chafee, *Government and Mass Communications*, pp. 489–94 (1947); White, *The American Radio*, pp. 178–82 (1947). *Others:* In addition communication industries are subject to taxation, rationing of paper, laws against unfair competition, and labor laws, all of which can become restrictions on freedom to communicate. See 2 Chafee, *supra*, ch. 21 and 22. On taxation see *Grosjean v. American Press Co.*, 297 U. S. 233, 80 L. Ed. 660, 56 S. Ct. 444 (1936) (invalidating license tax imposed by Huey Long regime of two per cent on gross receipt of newspapers with circulation over 20,000 because it was not a general tax but a device in the "guise of a tax to limit the circulation of information to which the public is entitled in virtue of the constitutional guarantees"). On labor laws see *Oklahoma Press Publishing Co. v. Walling*, 327 U. S. 186, 90 L. Ed. 614, 66 S. Ct. 494 (1946); *Associated Press v. N. L. R. B.*, 301 U. S. 103, 81 L. Ed. 953, 57 S. Ct. 650 (1937).

### 3. Direct Positive Control of Content—Radio as an Example of Partial Control

The Federal Communications Commission has for many years attempted to induce its licensees to improve the diversity and quality of radio programs. Though there are no specific provisions in the Federal Communications Act authorizing the Commission to generally survey, evaluate and rule on program content, the Commission has claimed this power on the basis of Sections 307 and 309(a) which provide that a license shall be granted or renewed only if "public convenience, interest, or necessity will be served thereby." The industry has largely disagreed with this construction. The contentions are first, that the Commission in its licensing function may consider only financial and technical matters and, second, that overall program control constitutes a violation of the First Amendment and of Section 326 of the Act which prohibits censorship by the Commission. The Courts, however, have sustained the Commission whenever it was challenged.[1]

The Commission has acted with respect to overall program planning in two ways: (1) It has made proposed program schedules an important factor in granting new licenses. It also has

---

[1] *Johnston Broadcasting Co. v. F. C. C.*, 175 F. 2d 351 (C. A. D. C., 1949); *Kentucky Broadcasting Co. v. F. C. C.*, 174 F. 2d 38 (C. A. D. C. 1949); *Simmons v. F. C. C.*, 169 F. 2d 670 (C. A. D. C., 1948), cert. den. 335 U. S. 846 (1948); *KFKB Broadcasting Ass'n. v. F. R. C.*, 47 F. 2d 670, 672 (C. A. D. C., 1931); *Trinity Methodist Church, South v. F. R. C.*, 62 F. 2d 850, 853 (C. A. D. C., 1932).

purported to make much of past program records in considering applications for renewal; but in this area, perhaps because of the severity of the penality of not renewing a license, action thus far has largely been limited to warnings and admonitions. (2) These warnings and admonitions sometimes are issued in the form of more formal integrated reports. The most famous of these was the so-called Blue Book, which contained a study of bad program habits of the industry and promulgated some general standards. The following is an excerpt from the conclusions of that report. The notes following indicate the range of applications and some of the problems that arise.

## FEDERAL COMMUNICATIONS COMMISSION— PUBLIC SERVICE RESPONSIBILITY OF BROADCAST LICENSEES

### pp. 55–6, Mar. 7, 1946

While much of the responsibility for improved program service lies with the broadcasting industry and with the public, the Commission has a statutory responsibility for the public interest, of which it cannot divest itself. The Commission's experience with the detailed review of broadcast renewal applications since April 1945, together with the facts set forth in this report, indicate some current trends in broadcasting which, with reference to licensing procedure, require its particular attention. . . .

(1) *Sustaining programs.* The carrying of sustaining programs has always been deemed one aspect of broadcast operation in the public interest. Sustaining programs . . . perform a five-fold function in (a) maintaining an overall program balance, (b) providing time for programs inappropriate for sponsorship, (c) providing time for programs serving particular minority tastes and interests, (d) providing time for non-profit organizations—religious, civic, agricultural, labor, educational, etc., and (e) providing time for experiment and for unfettered artistic self-expression.

Accordingly, the Commission concludes that one standard of operation in the public interest is a reasonable proportion of time devoted to sustaining programs.

Moreover, if sustaining programs are to perform their traditional functions in the American system of broadcasting, they must be broadcast at hours when the public is awake and listening. The time devoted to sustaining programs, accordingly, should be reasonably distributed among the various segments of the broadcast day. . . .

[The] Commission, in considering overall program balance, will also take note of network sustaining programs available to but not carried by a station, and of the programs which the station substitutes therefor.

(2) *Local live programs.* The Commission has always placed a marked emphasis, and in some cases perhaps an undue emphasis, on the carrying of local live programs as a standard of public interest. The development of network, transcription, and wire news services is such that no sound public interest appears to be served by continuing to stress local live programs exclusively at the expense of these other categories. Nevertheless, reasonable provision for local self-expression will remain an essential function of a station's operation . . . and will continue to be so regarded by the Commission. In particular, public interest requires that such programs should not be crowded out of the best listening hours.

(3) *Programs devoted to the discussion of public issues.* The crucial need for discussion programs, at the local, national, and international levels alike is universally realized . . . Accordingly, the carrying of such programs in reasonable sufficiency, and during good listening hours, is a factor to be considered in any finding of public interest.

(4) *Advertising excesses.* The evidence set forth above . . . warrants the conclusion that some stations during some or many portions of the broadcast day have engaged in advertising excesses which are incompatible with their public responsibilities, and which threaten the good name of broadcasting itself.

As the broadcasting industry itself has insisted, the public interest clearly requires that the amount of time devoted to advertising matter shall bear a reasonable relationship to the amount of time devoted to programs. Accordingly, in its application forms the Commission will request the applicant to state how much time he proposes to devote to advertising matter in any one hour.

This by itself will not, of course, result in the elimination of some of the particular excesses. . . . This is a matter in which self-regulation by the industry may properly be sought and indeed expected. The Commission has no desire to concern itself with the particular length, content, or irritating qualities of particular commercial plugs.

### Note

1. *Sustaining Programs:* Recent cases involving this aspect of the Blue Book are: *Bay State Beacon Inc.,* 3 R. R. 1455 (1947) ; aff'd 171 F. 2d 826 (C. A. D. C., 1948) (applicant who limited commercial pro-

grams to 60% of total broadcast time preferred to applicant who proposed to limit such programs to 80% of broadcast time and to limit "institutional" sponsorship to 15%); *Eugene J. Roth*, 3 R. R. 1377 (1947), discussed *infra*.

The Commission has also on occasion applied its underlying general standard of program balance so as to require program schedules to reflect the interest of different segments of the community. One of these cases is *Port Frere Broadcasting Co. Inc.*, 5 R. R. 1137 (1949) (use of the entire afternoon five days a week for the broadcast of sports programs does not properly serve the interests of the community). Some earlier cases are: *Citizens Broadcasting Corp., et al.*, 6 F. C. C. 669 (1938); *Voice of Detroit, Inc.*, 6 F. C. C. 363 (1938). Compare *Norfolk Broadcasting Corp.*, 3 R. R. 1699 (1947); *Hazard Broadcasting System*, 11 F. C. C. 1211 (1947).

2. *Local Live Programs:* Prior to the Blue Book several cases stressed this standard. See *Hannibal Broadcasting Co.*, 4 F. C. C. 505 (1937); *Courier Post Publishing Co. v. F. C. C.*, 104 F. 2d 213 (C. A. D. C., 1939). Since publication of the Blue Book the Commission has held that an applicant who proposes to set aside a considerable portion of the broadcast day to network programs abdicates his program responsibility. *Simmons v. F. C. C.*, 169 F. 2d 670 (C. A. D. C., 1948), cert. den. 335 U. S. 846 (1948). See also *Rossmoyne Corp.*, 7 R. R. 117 (1952). The Commission has also favored applicants who carefully survey local needs by discussion with civic, religious, charitable, and educational groups and who implement the survey with local sustaining programs. See *Norfolk Broadcasting Corp.* and *Hazard Broadcasting System, supra*.

Special consideration is given the tastes and needs of rural populations in the licensing of Clear Channel Stations. See Bureau of Agricultural Economics, *Attitudes of Rural People Toward Radio Service* (U. S. Dept. of Agric. 1946), cited in the Blue Book, p. 17 fn. 10.

3. *Discussion of Public Issues:* In a more recent report which followed hearings conducted on its own motion the Commission somewhat clarified its view with regard to this standard and especially with regard to editorializing by radio stations, an area in which the Commission's earlier pronouncement had caused some confusion: "The Commission believes that under the American system of broadcasting the individual licensees of radio stations have the responsibility for determining the specific program material to be broadcast over their stations. This choice, however, must be exercised in a manner consistent with the basic policy of the Congress that radio be maintained as a medium of free speech for the general public as a whole rather than as an outlet for the purely personal or private interests of the licensee. This requires that licensees devote a reasonable percentage of their broadcasting time to the discussion of public issues of interest in the community served by their stations and that such programs be designed so that the public has a reasonable opportunity to hear different opposing positions on the public issues of interest and importance in the community. The particular format best suited for the presentation of such programs in a manner consistent with the public

interest must be determined by the licensee in the light of the facts of each individual situation. Such presentation may include the identified expression of the licensee's personal viewpoint as part of the more general presentation of views or comments on the various issues, but the opportunity of licensees to present such views as they may have on matters of controversy may not be utilized to achieve a partisan or one-sided presentation of issues. Licensee editorialization is but one aspect of freedom of expression by means of radio. Only insofar as it is exercised in conformity with the paramount right of the public to hear a reasonably balanced presentation of all responsible viewpoints on particular issues can such editorialization be considered to be consistent with the licensee's duty to operate in the public interest. For the licensee is a trustee impressed with the duty of preserving for the public generally radio as a medium of free expression and fair presentation." *Editorializing by Broadcast Licensees*, 1 R. R. 91:201, 91:211–212 (1949).

The Commission labeled as "extreme" two opposite standards of fairness proposed at the hearings. The first would impose an affirmative obligation on a station to assure fair presentation of all sides before any time could be allocated to the discussion of controversial issues. The Commission thought that such a requirement would give a veto power on whether the subject should be discussed at all to any one party to a controversy and would create difficulty in connection with subjects that at first seem non-controversial but later cause substantial opposition. On the other hand, the Commission regarded as insufficient the second proposed standard which simply called for tolerance of opposing views and required no more than that a station make time available when requested. The Commission felt that licensees "have an affirmative duty generally to encourage and implement the broadcast of all sides of controversial public issues over their facilities. . . ." *Id.* at 91:206.

Prior to the 1949 Report the Commission was thought to be opposed to all editorializing. The basis of this view was its opinion in *Mayflower Broadcasting Corp.*, 8 F. C. C. 333 (1940). The Commission in renewing the license of the Yankee Network rebuked it for broadcasting editorials in support of candidates for public office: "The public interest can never be served by a dedication of any broadcast facility to the support of [the licensee's] partisan ends. Radio can serve as an instrument of democracy only when devoted to the communication of information and the exchange of ideas fairly and objectively presented. A truly free radio cannot be used to advocate the cause of the licensee. It cannot be used to support the candidacies of his friends. It cannot be devoted to the support of principles he happens to regard most favorably. In brief, the broadcaster cannot be an advocate.

"Freedom of speech on the radio must be broad enough to provide full and equal opportunity for the presentation to the public of all sides of public issues. Indeed, as one licensed to operate in a public domain the licensee has assumed the obligation of presenting all sides of important public questions, fairly, objectively and without bias.

[Emerson]

The public interest—not the private—is paramount. These requirements are inherent in the conception of public interest set up by the Communications Act as the criterion of regulation." 8 F. C. C. at 340.

The considerations involved in the Commission's rejection of the stricter policy were: Labelling an opinion as that of the station would not lend it so much additional weight as to render the practice unfair per se. Nor would it necessarily tend to reduce the chance that the station would afford fair opportunity to the opposition. Open advocacy helps enforcement of the fairness standard because unfairness becomes more readily detectable. Elimination of open advocacy would fail to reduce and probably increase the more frequent and probably more effective indirect means by which stations make their views felt and would tend in a general way to discourage radio stations from allowing open airing of public issues. *Editorializing by Broadcast Licensees, supra,* pp 91:207–208. See also discussion in Note, 59 Yale L. J. 759, 766–9 (1950). The Note adds the contention that in case of a ban "the FCC might well place unjustified reliance on this supposedly automatic device, diluting the force behind the general formula and deflecting attention from more important sources of abuse." 59 Yale L. J. *supra,* p. 768.

However, even without the ban serious questions have been raised about the extent of enforcement of the fairness standard: "In the past the FCC has appraised the manner in which broadcasters have presented public issues only when some question has been raised in a license proceeding by a competing applicant or by a person who has been refused broadcasting time by a station. Furthermore, the Commission has done virtually nothing to identify the apparently large volume of partisan propaganda which now escapes scrutiny under the 'fairness' formula because it has not been labelled at the source as 'opinion.'

"A more effective plan of enforcement might embody the following suggestions. First, the FCC could require all applicants for license renewal to make and substantiate an affirmative claim that they have allotted a reasonable amount of time to discussion of controversial issues, and that such discussion has, in the overall, been presented in a fair and representative manner. Second, in line with this suggestion, the Commission could specifically require all such applicants to enumerate and summarize all partisan expressions emanating from their stations, whether formally tagged 'opinion' or not.[41] Finally, if more direct measures prove necessary, the Commission might establish a permanent impartial body to analyze the contents of broadcast programs on a random sampling basis. The purpose would not be to evaluate the ideas expressed, but rather to earmark partisan expressions and make an initial determination as to whether the require-

---

[41] A comprehensive audit of the "controversial" content of broadcast programs is essential to consistent enforcement of the "fairness" formula. The difficulty of this task is far outweighed by the importance of securing fair treatment of public issues over radio. It would not seem unreasonable to impose the task of making an initial "tabulation" on the broadcasters.

ments of representative presentation are being met." Note, 59 Yale
L. J., *supra*, pp. 769–770.

Compare with these suggestions the Commission's defense against
the charge that enforcement of the fairness standard would necessarily
force the Commission to take a stand on the merits of particular issues.
*Editorializing by Broadcast Licensees, supra,* pp. 91:209–210. Compare
also *WBNX Broadcasting Co.,* 4 R. R. 242 (1948).

Before the *Mayflower* case, the policy of fairness came up in cases
where religious, labor or other special interest groups sought to use
stations for presentation of their views. See, *e. g., Great Lakes Broadcasting Co. v. F. R. C.* (F. R. C., Dec. 17, 1928) rev'd on other grounds,
37 F. 2d 993 (C. A. D. C., 1930), cert. dis. 281 U. S. 706 (1929); *Chicago Federation of Labor v. F. R. C.* (F. R. C. May 20, 1929) aff'd 41
F. 2d 422 (C. A. D. C., 1930); *KFKB Broadcasting Ass'n v. F. R. C.,*
47 F. 2d 670 (C. A. D. C., 1931); *Trinity Methodist Church, South v.
F. R. C.,* 62 F. 2d 850 (C. A. D. C., 1932); *Young People's Association
for the Propagation of the Gospel,* 6 F C. C. 178 (1938).

Since the *Mayflower* case the issue of fairness has been raised and
discussed in several license proceedings. In *United Broadcasting
Corp.,* 10 F. C. C. 515 (1945), the F. C. C. condemned the station's policy
of not selling time to labor unions and censoring their scripts when
sustaining time was allotted, while commentators critical of labor were
permitted complete freedom. In *Homer P. Rainey,* 3 R. R. 737 (1947),
the Commission stated that a station must make available a reasonable
amount of time for broadcasts connected with an important election
campaign. In *Robert Harold Scott,* 3 R. R. 259 (1946), the Commission ruled that where atheism was attacked reasonable time must be
made available for reply though atheists represent only a very small
segment of the community. The *Scott* case brought about a Congressional investigation. See Final Report of the Select Committee to Investigate the Federal Communications Commission, H. Rept. No. 2479,
80th Cong., 2d Sess. (1949), and hearings before the same Committee
pursuant to H. R. 691, 80th Cong., 2d Sess. (1948). See also Harness,
*The FCC Still Needs Investigation,* 42 Public Utility Fortnightly 835
(1948).

In *WBNX Broadcasting Co.,* the American Jewish Congress offered
in evidence qualitative and quantitative content analyses intended to
show bias and hostility against Jews and Negroes on the part of the
New York Daily News which was applying for an FM channel. On a
motion to strike the evidence the Commission issued two memorandum
opinions. In the first it indicated that the qualitative content analysis
had no probative value and that the quantitative analysis had no evidentiary significance. In the second memorandum the Commission
ruled that while the particular evidence was insufficient a body of experts need not insulate itself from this type of evidence. 3 R. R. 948
(1947), 4 R. R. 205, 242, 653 (1948). For a discussion of the use of
content analysis as evidence in administrative and judicial proceedings, see Note, 15 U. of Chi. L. Rev. 910 (1948).

Some of the recent cases have dealt with somewhat more detailed
problems of administration. See *e. g., Fostoria Broadcasting Co.,* 3 R.

R. 2014a (1948) (the applicant was permitted to charge for political broadcasts more than the regular commercial rate where the time requested diminished the station's income by necessitating the removal of an existing commercial program); *The Evening News Assn.*, 6 R. R. 283 (1950) (station cannot, as a prerequisite for granting time for the discussion of public issues, demand that the opposing parties make joint requests and joint use of the station's facilities); *New Broadcasting Co.*, 6 R. R. 258 (1950) (a station which broadcasts editorials must take affirmative steps to find and present opposing view points); *G. A. Richards*, 5 R. R. 1292 (1950) (the Commission will look into charges that the station instructed its employes to slant the news and took disciplinary action for disobedience). For material dealing with application of Section 315, which requires the allotment of equal time to political candidates see *supra*.

4. *Advertising Excesses:* In accordance with the policy enunciated in the Blue Book the Commission has generally not looked at the content of advertising, but has concerned itself largely with the relative time allotted to advertising. See *supra*. Illustrative cases are: *The Walmac Co.*, 3 R. R. 1371 (1947) (applicant promised to limit spot announcements to station breaks and to limit such announcements in participating programs to three in any fourteen and one half minute period); *Eugene J. Roth*, 3 R. R. 1377 (1947) (applicant promised to limit announcements to three in every fifteen minutes, with the total time not to exceed two minutes, and to limit commercial programs to a maximum of 65% of the broadcast day as against 95% under past practice). See also *Community Broadcasting Co.*, 3 R. R. 1360 (1947).

5. For discussion see Notes, 47 Col L. Rev. 1041 (1947); 57 Yale L. J. 275 (1947); 36 Va. L. Rev. 232 (1950) (on the whole opposed to program control); 18 U. of Chi. L. Rev. 78 (1950); 19 Geo. Wash. L. Rev. 312 (1951); 19 U. of Chi. L. Rev. 556 (1952). These comments collect the general literature in the field.

6. For a proposed Commission to prepare annual reports on television programs with suggestions for their improvement, see the bill introduced by Senator Benton, S. 1579, 82d Cong., 1st Sess. (1951).

7. In addition to restricting and facilitating communication government also participates as a communicator. Space does not permit extensive presentation of materials, but see Merritt, *The United States Government as Publisher* (1943); McCamy, *Government Publicity: Its Practice in Federal Administration* (1939); McCamy, *Government Publications For The Citizen* (1949); Pollard, *The Presidents and the Press* (1947); Catlin, *Propaganda as a Function of Democratic Government* in Childs, *Propaganda and Dictatorship* (1936); Hemming, *Public Administration and the Public Interest*, pp. 362 et seq. (1935); Coatman, *The B. B. C., Government and Politics*, 15 Pub. Op. Q. 287 (1951); Couse, *British Broadcasting: A Study in Monopoly* (1950). Recently the British Government published a White Paper proposing measures which would limit the B. B. C. monopoly and open the way to the establishment of some private broadcasting stations, N. Y. Times, May 16, 1952.

## General Bibliography

The following is a representative selection of the more important literature in the field. Some of the material cited previously in specific context is repeated here for the reader's convenience.

1. *General:* Commission on the Freedom of the Press, *A Free and Responsible Press* (1947); Chafee, *Government and Mass Communications* (1947); Hocking, *Freedom of the Press* (1947); Inglis, *Freedom of the Movies* (1947); White, *The American Radio* (1947); Ernst, *The First Freedom* (1946); Hughes, *Prejudice and the Press* (1950) (a reply to Mr. Ernst and the Commission); *Communication and Social Action,* 250 Annals of the Acad. of Pol. and Soc. Sci. (1947); Berelson and Janowitz, *Reader in Public Opinion and Communication* (1950); Bird and Merwin, *The Press and Society* (1951); Brucker, *Freedom of Information* (1949); Bryson, *The Communication of Ideas* (1948); Cantril, *Public Opinion, 1935–1946* (1951); Doob, *Public Opinion and Propaganda* (1948); Irion, *Public Opinion and Propaganda* (1950); Schramm, *Mass Communications* (1949); Schramm, *Communications in Modern Society* (1948); Seldes, *The Great Audience* (1950); Smith, Lasswell and Casey, *Propaganda, Communication and Public Opinion* (1946) (best general bibliography).

Many important references contained in these books are not repeated here. The reader should consult them to get a more complete picture. For complete bibliographies including graduate student theses in the field of mass communications see The Journalism Quarterly. For good selected bibliographies containing some references that are not cited here see 6 Quarterly of Film, Radio and Television 283 (1952); Berelson and Janowitz, *supra,* pp. 497–505. See also Bureau of Applied Social Research, *List of Publications, 1935–1952* (Columbia University, mimeo., 1952).

2. *Studies Concerned with the Total Process and Function of Human Communication:* Blumer, *Social Attitudes and Non Symbolic Interaction,* 9 Journal of Educational Sociology, 515–523 (1936); Burke, K., *A Rhetoric of Motives* (1950); De Grazia, *Shostakovich's Seventh Symphony,* 6 Psychiatry 117 (1943); Dewey and Bentley, *Knowing and the Known* (1949); Efron, *Gesture and Environment* (1941); Hayakawa, *Language in Action* (1941) (semantics); Heise and Miller, *Problem Solving by Small Groups Using Various Communication Nets,* 46 J. Abnormal Soc. Psych. 327 (1951); Hull, *Principles of Behavior* (1943); Johnson, *People in Quandaries: The Semantics of Personal Adjustment* (1946); Korzybski, *Science and Sanity* (1941) (semantics); Lasswell, Leites et al., *Language of Politics, Studies in Quantitative Semantics* (1949); Lee, *The Language of Wisdom and Folly* (1949) (semantics); Lewin, *Principles of Topological Psychology* (1936); Lowenthal, *Historical Perspectives of Popular Culture,* 55 American J. of Sociology 323 (1950) (historical and philosophical frame of reference for communication research); Merton, *Social Theory and Social Structure* 199–216 (1949); Miller, *Language and Communication* (1951); McGeoch, *The Psychology of Human Learning* (1942); Morris, *Signs, Language and Behavior* (1946) (integration of semantics and

psychological approaches); Pronko, *Language and Psycholinguistics: A Review,* 43 Psych. Bull. 189 (1946); Riley and Riley, *A Sociological Approach to Communications Research,* 15 Pub. Op. Q. 445 (1951); Ruesch and Bateson, *Communication, The Social Matrix of Psychiatry* (1951) (attempt to integrate psychiatric and sociological approaches); Sapir, *Language, An Introduction to the Study of Speech* (1921) (anthropological approach); Sharron and Weaver, *The Mathematical Theory of Communication* (1949); Shils, *The Study of the Primary Group,* in Lasswell and Lerner, *The Policy Sciences* (1951); Smith, *The Communicative Act,* 31 J. Soc. Psych. 271 (1950); Thorndike, *The Psychology of Wants, Interests and Attitudes* (1935); Whorf, *Science and Linguistics,* 42 Technology Rev. 229 (1940); Wiener, *The Human Use of Human Beings—Cybernetics and Society* (1950) (an attempt to treat social problems of communication in the light of earlier scientific findings summarized in Wiener, *Cybernetics or Control and Communication in the Animal and the Machine* (1948)).

3. *Studies of Public Opinion:* (a) General Theory: Allport, *Toward a Science of Public Opinion,* 1 Pub. Op. Q. 7 (1937); Bauer, *Public Opinion,* 12 Encyclopedia Soc. Sciences 669 (1934); Mannheim, *Ideology and Utopia: An Introduction to the Sociology of Knowledge* (1936); Riezler, *What is Public Opinion,* 11 Social Res. 397 (1944); Speier, *Historical Development of Publc Opinion,* 55 Am. J. Sociology 376 (1950); (b) Formation: Bogardus, *The Making of Public Opinion* (1951); Goldhamer, *Public Opinion and Personality,* 55 Am. J. of Sociology 346 (1950); Kornhauser, *Public Opinion and Social Class,* 55 Am. J. of Sociology 333 (1950); Lazarsfeld, Berelson and Gaudet, *The People's Choice: How the Voter Makes Up His Mind in a Presidential Campaign* (1944); Stouffer et al., *The American Soldier* in Studies in Social Psychology in World War II (1949–50); (c) Impact of Public Opinion: Bean, *How to Predict Elections* (1948); Bruner, *Mandate from the People* (1944); Leiserson, *Opinion Research and the Political Process,* 13 Pub. Op. Q. 31 (1949); Markel (ed.), *Public Opinion and Foreign Policy* (1949); Rogers, *The Pollsters* (1949); (d) Measurement: Cantril, *Gauging Public Opinion* (1944); Lazarsfeld, *The Obligations of the 1950 Pollster to the 1984 Historian,* 14 Pub. Op. Q. 617 (1950); Meier and Saunders, *The Polls and Public Opinion* (1949); Mosteller and others, *The Pre-Election Polls of 1948* (1949); Stouffer et al., *Measurement and Prediction* (1950).

4. *General Studies of Mass Media Communication:* (a) General: Adorno, *On Popular Music,* 9 Studies in Philosophy and Social Science, p. 17 (1941); Borden, *The Economic Effects of Advertising* (1942); Farrell, *The Fate of Writing in America* (1946); Fearing (ed.), *Mass Media: Content, Function and Measurement,* 3 Journal of Social Issues, No. 3 (1947); Herme, Brooks and Ersted, *Youth, Communication and Libraries* (1949); Lazarsfeld and Stanton, *Communications Research 1948–1949* (1949); see also Lerner (ed.), *Propaganda in War and Crisis: Materials for American Policy* (1951); MacDougald, *The Popular Music Industry* (1941); Merton, *Mass Persuasion: The Social Psychology of a War Bond Drive* (1946); Mott, *Golden Multitudes:*

**791**

*The Story of Best Sellers in the United States* (1947); Rose, *Communication and Participation in a Small City as Viewed by Its Leaders,* 5 International Journal of Opinion and Attitude Research 367 (Fall, 1951); Waples, *Print, Radio and Film in a Democracy* (1942), *People and Print* (1938), *What Reading Does to People* (1940) (with Berelson and Bradshaw); Whyte, *Is Anybody Listening* (1952); (b) Newspapers: Note, 61 Yale L. J. 948 (1952) (economic study of newspaper concentration); Bent, *Newspaper Crusaders* (1939); Bigman, *Rivals in Conformity: A Study of Two Competing Dailies,* 25 Jour. Q. 127 (1948); Bird, *This Fascinating Advertising Business* (1947); Casey, *Pressure Groups and the Press,* in Meier and Saunders, *The Polls and Public Opinion* (1949); Clark, *The Rural Press and the New South* (1948); Ickes, *Freedom of the Press Today,* 181, 183 (1941); Kingsbury, Hart and others, *Newspapers and the News: An Objective Measurement of Ethical and Unethical Behavior by Representative Newspapers* (1937); Liebling, *The Wayward Pressman* (1947); Lyons (ed.), *The Nieman Fellows Report* (1948); MacDougall, *Newsroom Problems and Policies* (1941); Neurath, *One-Publisher Communities: Factors Influencing Trend,* 21 Jour. Q. 230 (1944); Nixon, *Concentration and Absenteeism in Daily Newspaper Ownership,* 22 Journ. Q. 97 (1945); Oak, *The Negro Newspaper* (1948); Ray, *Economic Forces as Factors in Daily Newspaper Concentration,* 29 Journ. Q. 31 (1952); Seldes, *1000 Americans* (1948); Seldes, *Lords of the Press* (1938); Rept. of the U. S. Senate Special Committee to Study Problems of American Small Business, *Survival of a Free, Competitive Press, The Small Newspaper,* 80th Cong. 1st Sess. (1947); Waugh, *The Comics* (1947); Winship and Allport, *Do Rosy Headlines Sell Newspapers?* 7 Pub. Op. Q. 205 (1943); (c) Film: Huettig, *Economic Control of the Motion Picture Industry* (1944); Bertrand, Evers, and Blanchard, *The Motion Picture Industry: A Pattern of Control* (TNEC Monograph 43, 1941); Fiske and Handel, *Motion Picture Research: Content and Audience Analysis,* 11 Journal of Marketing 129 (1946); Handel, *Hollywood Looks at Its Audience* (1950); Hodgins, *A Round Table on the Movies,* Life Magazine, June 27, 1949, p. 90; Mayer, *Sociology of Film* (1946); Powdermaker, *Hollywood: The Dream Factory* (1950); Schmidt, Schmalenbach and Bächlin, *The Film, Its Economic, Social and Artistic Problems* (1948); (d) Radio and Television: Cantril and Allport, *The Psychology of Radio* (1935); Lazarsfeld and Kendall, *Radio Listening in America* (1948); Lazarsfeld and Stanton, *Radio Research 1941* (1941); *Radio Research 1942–43* (1944); Lazarsfeld and Field, *The People Look at Radio* (1946); Lazarsfeld, *Radio and the Printed Page* (1940); Shayon, *Television and Our Children* (1951) (in favor of TV); Siepmann, *Radio's Second Chance* (1947); Siepmann, *Radio, Television and Society* (1950).

5. *Content in General and of Printed Matter:* Berelson and Salter, *Majority and Minority Americans: An Analysis of Magazine Fiction,* 10 Pub. Op. Q. 168 (1946); Bureau of Applied Social Research, Columbia University, *Front-Page Bias in Newspapers* (1944); Harris, *Presentation of Crime in Newspapers* (1932); Johns-Heine, Patrike, and Gerth, *Values in Mass Periodical Fiction, 1921–40,* 13 Pub. Op. Q.

105 (1949); Leigh, *The Public Library in the U. S.* (1950); Miller, *The Book Industry* (1949); Lowenthal, *Historical Perspectives of Popular Culture,* 55 Am. J. Sociology 323 (1950); Orwell, *Dickens, Dali and Others* (1946); Rosenberg and Bellin, *Value Patterns in the Trade Union Press,* 3 International J. of Op. and Att. Research 555 (1949); Spiegelman, Terwilliger and Fearing, *The Content of Comic Strips: A Study of A Mass Medium of Communication,* 35 J. Soc. Psych. 37 (1952).

6. *Content of Radio and Television Programs:* Baker, *An Analysis of Radio's Programming* in *Communications Research 1948-49,* p. 51 (1949); Smythe, *An Analysis of Television Programs,* 184 Scientific Amer., 15 (1951). See Klots, *Trial by Television,* Harper's Magazine, Oct. 1951, p. 90.

7. *Content of Motion Pictures:* Dale, *The Content of Motion Pictures* (1935); Jones, *Quantitative Analysis of Motion Picture Content,* 14 Pub. Op. Q. 554 (1950) (1200 films over 30-year period); Wolfenstein and Leites, *Movies: A Psychological Study* (1950).

8. *Effect and Audience Studies in General and with Respect to Printed Matter:* Berelson, *What Missing the Newspaper Means* in *Communications Research 1948-49* (1949); Berelson and Asheim, *The Library's Public* (1949); Wolf and Fiske, *The Children Talk About Comics,* in *Communications Research 1948-49,* p. 3 (1949); Hovland, *Changes in Attitude Through Communication,* 46 J. Abnorm. Soc. Psych. 424 (1951); Janis, Lumsdaine and Gladstone, *Effects of Preparatory Communications on Reactions to a Subsequent News Event,* 15 Pub. Op. Q. 487 (1951); Klapper and Glock, *Trial by Newspaper,* 180 Scientific Amer. p. 16 (1949); Lasswell, *Radio as an Instrument of Reducing Personal Insecurity,* 9 Studies in Philosophy and Social Sciences 49 (1941); Leavitt, *Some Effects of Certain Communication Patterns on Group Performance,* 46 J. Abnorm. Soc. Psych. 38 (1951) (effects of imposing restrictions among members of a small group); Lyness, *The Place of the Mass Media in the Lives of Boys and Girls,* 29 Journ. Q. 43 (1952); Schramm, *The Effects of Mass Communications: A Review,* 26 Journ. Q. 397 (1949); Waples, Berelson and Bradshaw, *What Reading Does to People* (1940).

9. *Effect and Audience Studies of Radio and Television Programs:* Beville, *The ABCD's of Radio Audiences,* 4 Pub. Op. Q. 195 (1940); Berelson and Asheim, *The Library's Public* (1949); Cantril, Gaudet and Hertzog, *Invasion from Mars* (1940); Coffin, *Television's Effects on Leisure-Time Activities,* 32 J. Applied Psych. 550 (1948); Geiger, Theodore, *A Radio Test of Musical Taste,* 14 Pub. Op. Q. 453 (1950); Lazarsfeld and Kendall, *Radio Listening in America* (1949); Maccoby, *Television: Its Impact on School Children,* 15 Pub. Op. Q. 421 (1951); McDonagh, *Television and the Family,* 35 Sociol. and Soc. Research 113 (1950); Peterson and Thurstone, *Motion Pictures and the Social Attitudes of Children* (1933); Ricciuti, *Children and Radio: A Study of Listeners and Nonlisteners to Various Types of Radio Programs in Terms of Selected Ability, Attitude and Behavior Measures,* 44 Genetic Psychology Monographs 69 (1951); Riley, Cantwell and Ruttiger, *Some Observations on the Social Effects of Television,* 13 Pub. Op. Q. 223

(1949); Robinson, *Radio Audience Measurement and Its Limitations*, 3 J. of Social Issues 42 (1947); Seagoe, *Children's Television Habits and Preferences*, 6 Quarterly of Film, Radio and Television 143 (1951).

10. *Effect and Audience Studies in Motion Picture:* Fearing, *Influence of the Movies on Attitudes and Behavior*, 254 Annals of the Am. Acad. of Pol. and Soc. Sci. 70 (1947); Fiske and Handel, *New Techniques for Studying the Effectiveness of Films*, 11 J. of Marketing 390 (1947); Fiske and Handel, *Motion Picture Research: Response Analysis*, 11 J. of Marketing 273 (1947); Hovland, Lumsdaine and Sheffield, *Experiments on Mass Communication* (1949) (effects of Army films).

# CHAPTER VII

# ACADEMIC FREEDOM

## A. THE PRINCIPLES OF ACADEMIC FREEDOM

### THEODORE M. GREENE—THE FUNCTION OF THE SCHOOL IN A MODERN DEMOCRATIC SOCIETY [1]

## I

The "school," as one of our major institutions has a unique and all-important function to perform in a modern democratic society. To understand this function we must understand the relation of the school to other basic institutions in our society, the relation of a democratic society to the individuals who compose it, and the vital role of the prevailing ethos of a society.

Whatever may be the case, in claim and in actuality, in non-democratic societies, a democratic society is committed to the ultimate value of the individual person. The one and only proper function of its institutions is therefore to safeguard the rights and to promote the welfare of its citizens. It is essential that the people reserve ultimate political power to themselves, for only thus can they determine, in the long run, what institutions shall serve them and in what manner.

This control is important because the institutions of every society affect so profoundly the life of the individual citizen. Their multiple impact upon the individual is continuous, powerful and inescapable, for better or for worse. Native endowment and individual temperament are also, of course, important determinants of character and behavior; but the language we speak, the values we cherish, our motivations and attitudes, and our patterns of conduct are all profoundly influenced by our social institutions.

No less influential, though more intangible, is the prevailing ethos of a society. This ethos is hard to define generically and hard to describe in specific societies. It might be defined, but only roughly and inadequately, as the prevailing spirit or dominant temper of a society, reflecting its hierarchy of accepted values and the characteristic attitudes and motivations of most

---

[1] Theodore M. Greene is Professor of Philosophy, Yale University. This essay has been written specially for this volume, but the author hopes to publish an expanded version of this material in book form in the not too distant future.

of its members. More concretely, the ethos of ancient Sparta is usually described as more warlike, more prone to regimentation, and less speculative and artistically creative, than that of Athens. A similar attempt could be made to distinguish the ethos of a totalitarian from that of a democratic society, or the ethos of England from that of the United States, or the ethos of New England from the somewhat different ethos of the deep South, the Middle West, or the Western States. However intangible and indefinable, this social ethos is a third factor (over and above the individual and the institution) whose importance we dare not minimize. It seems to be both cause and effect—the conjoint product of the members of a society and its institutions and, simultaneously, a powerful influence upon these institutions and upon the lives of individual citizens.

## II

For the purpose of this analysis we can usefully distinguish five basic institutions in our modern democratic society—government and the family, the school and the church, and, finally, that rather amorphous aggregate of corporate activities entitled business and industry. Each of these has a distinctive character of its own and each has a unique and irreplacable function in our society. Government and the family, moreover, constitute a complementary pair, and the school and the church, a second complementary pair; business and industry are dependent upon these four, and serve all of them, in a very distinctive way. These large generalizations call for some explanation and justification.

Government, or the state in its political and legal aspects, is all-inclusive in its jurisdiction over its citizens and its responsibility to them. Its chief functions are to provide security for the body politic, to define and administer justice with impartiality, and to promote the welfare of all within its domain by appropriate legislation and administration. The family unit is, in contrast, the most exclusive, the smallest, and the most intimate and personal institution in our society. Its function, too, is multiple—to assure its members shelter and sustenance, to provide for procreation and the nurture of the young, and, above all, to promote within the family circle the companionship and love of husband and wife, parents and children, brother and sister.

These two institutions complement each other as do impersonality and intimacy, force and persuasion, justice and love. Each institution, it is true, must exhibit in appropriate ways the characteristics of the other. Thus, the state can and should, in its administration of justice, deal with persons humanely, with an eye to their special aptitudes and needs; political democracy should rely on persuasion rather than force in the selection of its representatives and in the enactment and even the enforcement of legislation. Yet the state must finally be able to resort to force to prevent or quell civil disobedience and disorder and to defend its people against external threats to their corporate safety; and however humanely it functions, its highest and ultimate virtue is impartial justice rather than charity. Similarly, the family must occasionally resort to force in its attempt to protect the young and the senile from harm; persuasion is practicable only in proportion to the maturity and reasonableness of its members; companionship depends on fair play, and love which if not rooted in justice quickly degenerates into sentimentality. Yet, despite such overlappings and borrowings, these two basic institutions differ so profoundly in structure and purpose that neither could possibly perform the proper function of the other.

The school and the church complement one another in a totally different way. The school, i.e., the institution which is specifically charged with responsibility for formal education at all levels, has as its primary object the conservation, dissemination and extension of human knowledge. Its chief concern is truth and the psychological prerequisite for the attainment of truth—an honest, critical, inquiring mind. In contrast, the church, i.e., the institution dedicated to the corporate worship and service of the Diety, is basically credal rather than critical, receptive rather than exploratory, rooted in faith rather than in man-initiated human inquiry.

School and church resemble one another in proportion as both are socially oriented and liberal rather than exclusive and authoritarian. The church has too often been indifferent to social welfare; the school has too frequently exhibited an aristocratic indifference to the common man; and both institutions have been, and still are, guilty of illiberal dogmatism. Yet both institutions at their liberal best have defended man's honest search for truth, and both, in the degree that each realizes its peculiar genius, are vitally concerned with the good life of the individual and mankind. Both realize, moreover, that the good can be achieved only through wisdom, discipline and unselfish devotion. Both, therefore, seek to conserve man's intellectual and spiritual heritage and both try, in their respective ways, to use the fresh resources of the present to promote man's moral and spiritual well-being.

No less important, however, are the major differences of orientation and emphasis between school and church. The school is, by its very nature, rooted in human initiative and dedicated to intellectual inquiry, whereas the church in all its traditional forms, both authoritarian and liberal, is man's corporate response to what is judged to be the Divine Initiative. This response, in turn, involves an ultimate act of acceptance and of faith. In this sense the church is as basically credal as the school is basically critical; its ultimate anchorage is faith in a self-revealing Deity, whereas the school's ultimate reliance is on human reason and human initiative. Hence the inevitable prior emphasis of the church on commitment and orthodoxy, in contrast to the prior emphasis of the school on critical reflection and on originality and heterodoxy.

The fifth great institution in our society is business and industry. Its social function is to produce and sell all the goods which we need to support life, to provide us with our comforts, and to implement our multifarious social programs and individual projects. The social function of business and industry is distinctively utilitarian in that its primary task is to provide the physical means requisite for humane and spiritual ends. Thus, justice and love, truth and holiness, can be regarded as ends in themselves, or as ends which possess intrinsic value for man, whereas economic goods are valuable only in proportion as they contribute to the attainment of non-economic values. The prime virtues of business and industry are, therefore, ingenuity, efficiency and moral integrity; a commercial enterprise which exhibits these virtues will make its contribution to the common good. This obligation to be of public service need not conflict with the motive of private gain which plays so important a role in our system of competitive enterprise, since private gain can, at least in principle, be made compatible with usefulness to the public.

### III

When we survey the distinguishing characteristics of each of these five major institutions with an eye to their several special contributions to our modern democratic society, four conclusions seem inescapable.

1. Each of these institutions has a unique function which no other can properly perform. Every society must have a government of some sort or lapse into anarchy. Every utopian attempt of the state to assume some of the normal functions of the family has been unsuccessful and has presently been abandoned; witness the most recent abortive experiment along these lines in Communist Russia. The social results of over-reliance in China on the family for social solidarity, rather than on a local and national government, illustrate the opposite danger. History, East and West, has given us many demonstrations of the disastrous effect of ecclesiastical control of political power, and we have just wit-

798

nessed in Germany, Italy and Russia the incomparable harm to free intellectual inquiry and to enlightened corporate worship that results from rigid governmental controls over school and church. Less immediately evident, but no less real, is the loss in business and industrial efficiency when the state substitutes state ownership and absolute economic controls for a just control of economic exploitation and judicious governmental aid where such aid is needed. Reversely, a wholly laissez-faire economy without proper governmental supervision results inevitably in unjust riches and power for the privileged few and cruel poverty for the unprivileged many. Finally, a society which fails to provide its citizens, under the guidance of a righteous and enlightened church, with the opportunity for the worship of the Deity seems condemned to some form of secular idolatry—a dictator, or the nation, or wealth, or power, or social prestige becomes the false god who is idolatrously worshipped. The health and vitality of our own society, in short, seems to depend upon the health and vitality of all these five basic institutions, each performing its unique function at least reasonably well.

2. It is also evident that, of the five institutions under review, only two, the church and the school, possess within themselves, as institutions, the intellectual and spiritual resources for new discovery, self-criticism and self-reform. The school possesses these resources in its scholarship—its dedication to ceaseless intellectual inquiry on every front. The comparable resources of the church (if the claims of a mature and enlightened religious faith are to be credited) are God's revelations of Himself to mankind, today as well as yesterday. A church which has lost its faith in a continuing vital revelation and which tries to live exclusively off its ancient dogmas has ceased to be a vital religious institution, however well entrenched it may be in its society, just as a school which has abandoned the quest for new knowledge is no longer a vital academic institution but merely an organ of propaganda. The capacity for new insights and self-criticism is the surest criterion of vitality in both school and church.

This might appear to be equally applicable to government, the family, and business and industry, and in a sense it is. All these institutions do indeed become rigidified in the absence of fresh thought and lively criticism. But at this point we must ask, What are the primary institutional sources of inquiry, discovery and criticism? Does government by its very nature welcome criticism from without or from within? Does the family, as an institution? Does business and industry? The multiplicity and persistence of autocratic governments, the prevalence in all cultures of autocratic matriarchal and patriarchal family systems, and the notable lack of significant innovation in man's economic activities in most cultures and historical epochs preclude an affirmative answer to these questions. Historically, the well-springs of criticism and self-criticism have been primarily academic and religiously prophetic; every society which has lacked a vital scholarly or a vital religious tradition or both has sooner or later become static and autocratic. How long would criticism be welcomed, or even tolerated, in our own society—in politics and law, in the family, and in business and industry—if our schools and churches were to close their doors and cease to function? Our other three basic institutions are today as amenable as they are to criticism, and therefore as capable of improvement, because of the open-minded and critically-minded men and women in them; and these men and women exhibit these traits because, ultimately, the church and the school, separately or conjointly, have inspired them with these ideals and taught them the techniques and attitudes of critical inquiry and new discovery.

In short, it is the peculiar task of church and school to generate in men a respect for their fellowmen, a respect for integrity and truth, and a faith in a Deity worthy of their reverence. This task is not an easy one, since both are subject to all the temptations and social pressures of their society. If they become too ineffective in the body politic, an ungodly and ignorant government will eventually persecute and suppress them. If they abandon their proper calling and become the tools of a competitive economy, the very economy which they seek to serve will retrogress and they will wither on the vine. If they fail to educate young men and women for enlightened parenthood and companionship, the families of the next generation will revert to a more primitive autocratic level. If church and school do not educate people in righteousness, justice, and truth, their society will relapse more or less rapidly into barbarism, and this reversion will eventually destroy both the church and the school which have failed to perform their proper functions.

3. In the foregoing account of the church I have assumed the validity of its basic claims and, consequently, its unique and irreplaceable institutional function. This is an assumption which many thoughtful and less thoughtful people in our society today are unable or unwilling to make; all our churches in combination fail to reach at least half of our total population. This puts an enormous extra cultural responsibility upon the school which it must do its best to meet despite the attendant danger—the danger of assuming, as a secular institution, the priestly and prophetic role of a church. All the more urgent is it that, in our semi-secular society, the school set its spiritual sights as high as

**800**

possible, and that it do its utmost to conserve and revitalize our rich spiritual heritage whose origin is partly Hebraic-Christian and partly Greek and Roman. To do so, the school must be on its guard, on the one hand, against the temptation of intellectualism in modern dress, i.e., a spiritually impoverished scientism which eulogizes scientific procedure and logical clarity at the expense of responsible moral and spiritual evaluation, and, on the other hand, against the even subtler temptation of a short-range pragmatic relativism which undermines man's deepest moral and spiritual convictions. The school today has indeed a tremendous and terrifying task—the task of educating a largely secular society not only vocationally, in the skills of a technological culture, and intellectually, for joyful critical inquiry, but also socially, for responsible citizenship and leadership, and, above all, morally and spiritually, for the preservation and strengthening of our humane God-fearing heritage.

Since, moreover, the church in our society wields a notable and perhaps growing influence, the school has another very important responsibility, namely, to the church itself—a responsibility complementary to that of the church to the school. It is the church's responsibility to try to save the school from secular idolatry—from the worship of false gods, and from secular self-righteousness. It is the school's responsibility to save the church from blind dogmatism and bigotry. Whenever the church is not subjected to criticism and when it loses its respect for honest doubt and fearless inquiry it lapses inevitably into an arrogant authoritarianism. Then the rituals of its cult become magical, the articles of its creed become frozen dogmas, its social policies become reactionary, and its faith becomes superstitious and blind. Only under the continuing and lively impact of the spirit of criticism which it is the special responsibility of the school to engender can the church hope to achieve and maintain the intellectual integrity, the humility and the openness of heart and mind which characterize "high" religion at its best. Witness the fate of churches in autocratic societies which do not respect intellectual inquiry and the freedoms of thought and expression, and which do not have strong schools as champions of the honest and untrammelled mind.

4. This brings us to the school's most general responsibility in a modern democratic society which is dedicated to the intrinsic dignity of man, to the basic freedoms, to the importance of democratic self-government, and to justice for all. This high objective calls for appropriate social organization and legislation and for a continual battle against injustice, political corruption, and every threat to human dignity and freedom. But if we are to advance

towards our goal we must, as a society, have a pervasive and dynamic democratic ethos. The animating spirit of our society, if it is to be truly democratic, must be the spirit of passionate devotion to liberty, of high respect for intellectual and moral integrity, of righteous zeal for justice, of spiritual humility and assurance. Only if this ethos, this social temper, is strong and vital, will our society find the wise leaders and the enlightened citizenry requisite for democratic strength.

Of all the basic institutions in our society, the school can do the most to foster this democratic ethos. The other major institutions must, of course, make their several contributions—the state, by legislation, legal process and public example; the family, in the nurture of the young and in the companionship of man and wife; business and industry, in all the dealings of management and labor with one another and with the public; the church, as the prophetic voice of righteousness and love. All these institutions, along with other influential agencies such as the press, the radio and television, can and should share in the total educational task in their several ways. But their educational function is subsidiary to a more basic function in each case, whereas education is the primary function of the school. It, uniquely among all our institutions, must teach men how and why to be free. It must lead the way to ever greater freedom by example and precept. Only thus can our citizenry hope to select its leaders wisely and to follow their lead with cautious confidence. Only thus can we hope to lessen corruption in government and exploitation in our economy. Only thus will our democratic ethos be strong and vital enough to impel men and women of unusual ability in every walk of life to assume the responsibilities of mature leadership. Only thus can our democratic society maintain its health and develop the strength to defend itself against foreign aggression.

## IV

Why is it that the school has this special responsibility? The answer is not far to seek. Our society is genuinely democratic, and the school is true to its peculiar genius, only in proportion as each is genuinely liberal. Our society is democratic only to the extent to which it cherishes the freedoms which are most precious to man as a reflective and believing being. Freedom from want and freedom from fear are important because starvation and cruelty are inhumane, even for animals, but more particularly because economic and political security are prerequisite to the higher freedoms, i.e., the freedom to think and speak and the freedom to believe and act as one's own conscience dictates. The school is, par excellence, the well-spring of these higher freedoms

[Emerson]

since its special task is to make available man's wisest thoughts and beliefs, to extend his knowledge and deepen his spiritual insights, and, above all, to promote in all men an understanding of these highest freedoms and a passionate devotion to them. The school is thus the nurse and tutor, as government is the champion, of man's most precious rights—the rights without which man loses his human stature and becomes an animal, however well fed, well organized, and well protected he may be.

That the school is, by its very nature, liberal is evident in its ultimate faith and in its characteristic activities. Its faith is in the power of truth and in man's ability to discover truth more and more adequately by means of rational reflection upon his total response to his total environment—natural, human and Divine. Its characteristic activities are partly scholarly, partly pedagogical, and both are, in their essence, liberal and liberating.

Scholarship in all fields of inquiry is directed to the discovery of new facts and to the formulation of ever more illuminating interpretations of these facts. Such scholarship is the product of individual research and reflection but, no less, of collaboration among scholars. Such collaboration, in turn, would be impossible without mutual respect and an open-minded eagerness to learn from others and to share with others what one knows. And scholarship is morally responsible only if it is oriented ultimately to man's most significant needs and aspirations.

The teacher shares the ultimate faith of the scholar. It is his task not only to disseminate available knowledge but also to teach the methods and criteria of objective inquiry and responsible evaluation and, above all, to instill a profound respect for fact and value, intellectual and spiritual integrity. Teaching, so conceived, not only enriches and gives meaning to the life of the individual; it is the only effective training for responsible citizenship and leadership in a free democratic society.

The ethos of the healthy school is thus the prototype of the ethos of a healthy democracy, and academic freedom is the quintessence of man's most cherished freedoms. Academic freedom requires the school to see to it that all responsible opinions on controversial issues are voiced and argued—and so do the freedoms of speech and assembly in a democracy. The four cardinal virtues requisite to academic freedom are intellectual competence, sincerity, a deep concern for human welfare, and tolerance rooted in humility. These constitute the only valid basis for hiring teachers and scholars, and their opposites— intellectual incompetence, insincerity, cynical sophistication, and intolerant dogmatism—are the only proper grounds for firing them. Hence the iniquity of all attempts of business, church, or state to make political, social, or religious orthodoxy a criterion of scholarly or pedagogical competence, or to ascribe guilt "by association," or to compel loyalty by special oaths. But these are precisely the virtues which are needed, and the vices to be combatted, by a democracy dedicated to enlightened leadership, popular suffrage, private and public integrity, and the basic freedoms guaranteed by our Constitution and our Bill of Rights. The more scrupulously and staunchly the school exemplifies academic freedom in its own institutional life, the more will it vitalize the cause of freedom beyond its academic walls.

The school's responsibility to society and to mankind cannot be fully discharged, however, unless it also concerns itself explicitly with the healthy functioning of our other major institutions. Any ivory tower retreat from the affairs of men will quickly destroy its own inner integrity and social usefulness. The school must teach its society the nature and value of responsible fearless criticism of all our major institutions—church and state, family and business. It must also demonstrate its own high regard for criticism by welcoming all responsible criticisms of itself. For in a democracy no institution can be allowed to flaunt a socially irresponsible autonomy. Each is responsible to all the others and, above all, to the society which all should serve. Finally, the school cannot be true to its own principles if it defends nationalistic isolationism or imperialistic exploitation of other peoples. For if its own principles are valid, they are the basic principles of humanity and therefore equally applicable to all mankind. The freedoms which the school must finally espouse are the freedoms of man as man, the freedoms that transcend all the barriers—national and racial, social and religious—which still keep peoples apart and foster tyranny and exploitation. If our democratic cause of freedom is the righteous cause of all men, as we believe it is, the school must here too lead the way by showing what it means to be intelligently and passionately concerned with the freedom of all men everywhere.

To measure up to its high calling the school must therefore be wise and fearless. It must find, train, and hold able and devoted teachers at all levels of instruction. It must discover and develop scholars of first rate intellectual ability, high moral integrity, and genuine spiritual humility. It must have administrators who understand their responsibilities and who discharge them with justice and courage. It must provide all its students, the ablest as well as the less able, with the instruction and the inspiration they most need. It must win the confidence, respect, and support of the public. This total task is, indeed, too great to permit of complete success at any time, but the school can and, I believe, will rise to the challenge of our times with ever growing enthusiasm and vigor.

## POPE LEO XIII—LIBERTAS PRAESTANTISSIMUM[1]
### June 20, 1888

Human liberty necessarily stands in need of light and strength to direct its actions to good and to restrain them from evil. Without this, the freedom of our will would be our ruin. First of all there must be law; that is, a fixed rule of teaching what is to be done and what is to be left undone. . . . Nothing more foolish can be uttered or conceived than the notion that because man is free by nature, he is therefore exempt from law. Were this the case, it would follow that to become free we must be deprived of reason; whereas the truth is that we are bound to submit to law precisely because we are free by our very nature. For law is the guide of man's actions; it turns him towards good by its rewards, and deters him from evil by its punishments.

Foremost in this office comes the natural law, which is written and engraved in the mind of every man; and this is nothing but our reason, commanding us to do right and forbidding sin. Nevertheless all prescriptions of human reason can have force of law only in as much as they are the voice and the interpreters of some higher power on which our reason and liberty necessarily depend. For, since the force of law consists in the imposing of obligations and the granting of rights, authority is the one and only foundation of all law—the power, that is, of fixing duties and defining rights, as also of assigning the necessary sanctions of reward and chastisement to each and all of its commands. But all this, clearly, cannot be found in man, if, as his own supreme legislator, he is to be the rule of his own actions. It follows therefore that the law of nature is the same thing as the eternal law, implanted in rational creatures, and inclining them to their right action and end; and can be nothing else but the eternal reason of God, the Creator and Ruler of all the world. . . .

From this it is manifest that the eternal law of God is the sole standard and rule of human liberty, not only in each individual man, but also in the community and civil society which men constitute when united. Therefore, the true liberty of human society does not consist in every man doing what he pleases, for this would simply end in turmoil and confusion, and

---

[1] The extracts are taken from the Encyclical Letter as printed in Ryan and Boland, *Catholic Principles of Politics*, pp. 169–78 (1947).

bring on the overthrow of the State; but rather in this, that through the injunctions of the civil law all may more easily conform to the prescriptions of the eternal law. Likewise, the liberty of those who are in authority does not consist in the power to lay unreasonable and capricious commands upon their subjects, which would equally be criminal and would lead to the ruin of the commonwealth; but the binding force of human laws is in this, that they are to be regarded as applications of the eternal law, and incapable of sanctioning anything which is not contained in the eternal law, as in the principle of all law. Thus St. Augustine most wisely says: "I think that you can see, at the same time, that there is nothing just and lawful in that temporal law, unless what men have gathered from this eternal law."[1] If, then, by any one in authority, something be sanctioned out of conformity with the principles of right reason, and consequently hurtful to the commonwealth, such an enactment can have no binding force of law, as being no rule of justice, but certain to lead men away from that good which is the very end of civil society. . . .

We must now consider briefly liberty of speech, and liberty of the Press. It is hardly necessary to say that there can be no such right as this, if it be not used in moderation, and if it pass beyond the bounds and end of all true liberty. For right is a moral power which—as We have before said and must again and again repeat—it is absurd to suppose that nature has accorded indifferently to truth and falsehood, to justice and injustice. Men have a right freely and prudently to propagate throughout the State what things soever are true and honorable, so that as many as possible may possess them; but lying opinions, than which no mental plague is greater, and vices which corrupt the heart and moral life, should be diligently repressed by public authority, lest they insidiously work the ruin of the State. . . . In regard, however, to all matters of opinion which God leaves to man's free discussion, full liberty of thought and of speech is naturally within the right of every one; for such liberty never leads men to suppress the truth, but often to discover it and make it known.

A like judgment must be passed upon what is called liberty of teaching. There can be no doubt that truth alone should imbue the minds of men; for in it are found the well-being, the end, and the perfection of every intelligent nature; and therefore nothing but truth should be taught both to the ignorant and to the educated, so as to bring knowledge to those who have it not, and to preserve it in those who possess it. For this reason it is

---

[1] *De Libero Arbitrio,* lib. i, cap. 6, n. 15.

plainly the duty of all who teach to banish error from the mind, and by sure safeguards to close the entry to all false convictions. From this it follows, as is evident, that the liberty of which We have been speaking, is greatly opposed to reason, and tends absolutely to pervert men's minds, in as much as it claims for itself the right of teaching whatever it pleases—a liberty which the State cannot grant without failing in its duty. And the more so, because the authority of teachers has great weight with their hearers, who can rarely decide for themselves as to the truth or falsehood of the instruction given to them.

Wherefore, this liberty also, in order that it may deserve the name, must be kept within certain limits, lest the office of teaching be turned with impunity into an instrument of corruption. Now truth, which should be the only subject-matter of those who teach, is of two kinds, natural and supernatural. Of natural truths, such as the principles of nature and whatever is derived from them immediately by our reason, there is a kind of common patrimony in the human race. On this, as on a firm basis, morality, justice, religion, and the very bonds of human society rest; and to allow people to go unharmed who violate or destroy it would be most impious, most foolish, and most inhuman. But with no less religious care must we preserve that great and sacred treasure of the truths which God Himself has taught us. . . . Thus it is manifest that man's best and surest teacher is God, the source and principle of all truth; and the only-begotten Son, who is in the bosom of the Father, the Way, the Truth, and the Life, the true Light which enlightens every man and to whose teaching all must submit: *And they shall all be taught of God.* In faith and in teaching of morality, God Himself made the Church a partaker of His divine authority, and through His heavenly gift she cannot be deceived. She is therefore the greatest and most reliable teacher of mankind, and in her dwells an inviolable right to teach them. . . . Now, reason itself clearly teaches that the truths of divine revelation and those of nature cannot really be opposed to one another, and that whatever is at variance with them must necessarily be false. Therefore the divine teaching of the Church, so far from being an obstacle to the pursuit of learning and the progress of science, or in any way retarding the advance of civilization, in reality brings to them the sure guidance of shining light. And for the same reason it is of no small advantage for the perfecting of human liberty, since our Saviour Jesus Christ has said that by truth is man made free: *You shall know the truth, and the truth shall make you free.* Therefore there is no reason why genuine liberty should grow indignant,

**807**

or true science feel aggrieved, at having to bear the just and
necessary restraint of laws by which, in the judgment of the
Church and of Reason itself, human teaching has to be controlled. . . . Lastly, we must not forget that a vast field
lies freely open to man's industry and genius, containing all
those things which have no necessary connection with Christian
faith and morals, or as to which the Church, exercising no
authority, leaves the judgment of the learned free and uncon-
strained. . . .

## MAX WEBER—THE MEANING OF "ETHICAL NEUTRALITY" IN SOCIOLOGY AND ECONOMICS (1917)

From Weber, The Methodology of the Social Sciences, translated
and edited by Edward A. Shils and Henry A. Finch,
copyright 1949 by The Free Press of Glencoe, Illinois,
pp. 1–10

By "value-judgments" are to be understood, where nothing
else is implied or expressly stated, practical evaluations of the
unsatisfactory or satisfactory character of phenomena subject
to our influence. The problem involved in the "freedom" of a
given science from value-judgments of this kind, i.e., the validity and the meaning of this logical principle, is by no means
identical with the question which is to be discussed shortly,
namely, whether in teaching one should or should not declare
one's acceptance of practical value-judgments, deduced from
ethical principles, cultural ideals or a philosophical outlook.
This question cannot be discussed scientifically. It is itself
entirely a question of practical valuation, and cannot therefore
be definitively settled. With reference to this issue, a wide variety
of views is held, of which we shall only mention the two extremes. At one pole we find (a) the standpoint that the distinction between purely logically deducible and empirical factual assertions on the one hand, and practical, ethical or philosophical value-judgments on the other, is correct, but that,
nevertheless (or perhaps, precisely because of this), both
classes of problems properly belong within the area of instruction. At the other pole we encounter (b) the proposition that
even when the distinction cannot be made in a logically complete manner, it is nevertheless desirable that the assertion of
value-judgments should be held to a minimum.

The latter point of view seems to me to be untenable. Especially untenable is the distinction which is rather often made
in our field between value-judgments of a partisan character

and those which are non-partisan. This distinction only obscures the practical implications of the preferences which are suggested to the audience. Once the assertion of value-judgments from the academic platform is admitted, the contention that the university teacher should be entirely devoid of "passion" and that he should avoid all subjects which threaten to arouse over-heated controversies constitutes a narrow-minded, bureaucratic opinion which every independent teacher must reject. Of the scholars who believed that they should not renounce the assertion of practical value-judgments in empirical discussions, it was the most passionate of them—such as Treitschke—and in his own way, Mommsen, who were the most tolerable. As a result of their intensely emotional tone, their audiences were enabled to discount the influence of their evaluations in whatever distortion was introduced into their factual assertions. Thereby the audiences did for themselves what the lecturers were temperamentally prevented from doing. The effect on the minds of the students was thus guaranteed the same depth of moral feeling which, in my opinion, the proponents of the assertion of practical value-judgments in teaching want to protect, without the audience's being confused as to the logical disjunction between the different spheres. This confusion must of necessity occur whenever the exposition of empirical facts and the exhortation to take an evaluative position on important issues are both done with the same cool dispassionateness.

The first point of view (a) is acceptable and, can indeed be acceptable from the standpoint of its own proponents, only when the teacher sets as his unconditional duty, in every single case, even to the point where it involves the danger of making his lecture less lively or attractive, to make relentlessly clear to his audience, and especially to himself, which of his statements are statements of logically deduced or empirically observed facts and which are statements of practical evaluations. Once one has acknowledged the logical disjunction between the two spheres, it seems to me that the assumption of this attitude is an imperative requirement of intellectual honesty; in this case it is the absolutely minimal requirement.

On the other hand, the question whether one should in general assert practical value-judgments in teaching (even with this reservation) is one of practical university policy. On that account, it must in the last analysis, be decided only with reference to those tasks which the individual, according to his own value-system, assigns to the universities. Those who on the basis of their qualifications as teachers assign to the universities and thereby to themselves the universal role of moulding human beings, of inculcating political, ethical, aesthetic, cultural or other attitudes, will take a different position than those who believe it necessary to affirm the fact (and its consequences) that the academic lecture-hall achieves a really valuable influence only through specialized training by specially qualified persons. For the latter, therefore, "intellectual integrity" is the only specific virtue which it should seek to inculcate. The first point of view can be defended from as many different ultimate value-positions as the second. The second (which I personally accept) can be derived from a most enthusiastic as well as from a thoroughly modest estimate of the significance of specialized training (*Fachbildung*). In order to defend this view, one need not be of the opinion that everyone should become as specialized as possible. One may, on the contrary, hold the view in question because one does not wish to see the ultimate and highest personal decisions which a person must make regarding his life, confounded with specialized training— however highly one may estimate the significance of specialized training not only for general intellectual training but indirectly also for the self-discipline and ethical attitude of the young person. One may hold the latter view because one does not wish to see the student so influenced by the teacher's suggestions that he is prevented from solving his problems on the basis of his own conscience.

Professor Schmoller's favorable disposition towards the teacher's assertion of his own value-judgments in the classroom is thoroughly intelligible to me personally as the echo of a great epoch which he and his friends helped to create. But even he cannot deny the fact that for the younger generation the objective situation has changed considerably in one important respect. Forty years ago there existed among the scholars working in our discipline, the widespread belief that of the various possible points of view in the domain of practical-political preferences, ultimately only one was the correct one. (Schmoller himself to be sure took this position only to a limited extent). Today this is no longer the case among the proponents of the assertion of professorial evaluations—as may easily be demonstrated. The legitimacy of the assertion of professorial evaluations is no longer defended in the name of an ethical imperative whose comparatively simple postulate of justice, both in its ultimate foundations as well as in its consequences, partly was, and partly seemed to be, relatively unambiguous and above all relatively impersonal (due to its specifically suprapersonal character). Rather, as the result of an inevitable development, it is now done in the name of a patch-work of cultural values, i.e., actually subjective demands on culture, or quite openly, in the name of the alleged "rights of the teacher's personality." One may well wax indignant over this, but one cannot—because it is a value-judgment—refute this point of view. Of all the types of prophecy, this "person-ally" tinted professorial type of prophecy is the only one which is altogether repugnant. An unprecedented situation exists when a large number of officially accredited prophets do not do their preaching on the streets, or in churches or other public places or in sectarian conventicles, but rather feel themselves competent to enunciate their evaluations on ultimate questions "in the name of science" in governmentally privileged lecture halls in which they are neither controlled, checked by discus-sion, nor subject to contradiction. It is an axiom of long stand-ing, which Schmoller on one occasion vigorously espoused that what took place in the lecture hall should be held separate from the arena of public discussion. Although it is possible to con-tend that even scientifically this may have its disadvantages, I take the view that a "lecture" should be different from a "speech." The calm rigor, matter-of-factness and sobriety of the lecture declines with definite pedagogical losses, when the substance and manner of public discussion are introduced, in the style of the press. This privilege of freedom from outside control seems in any case to be appropriate only to the sphere of the specialized qualifications of the professor. There is, however, no specialized qualification for personal prophecy, and for this reason it is not entitled to that privilege of freedom from external control. Furthermore, there should be no ex-ploitation of the fact that the student, in order to make his way, must attend certain educational institutions and take courses with certain teachers, with the result that in addition to what is required, i.e., the stimulation and cultivation of his capacity for observation and reasoning, and a certain body of factual information, the teacher slips in his own uncontradictable eval-uations, which though sometimes of considerable interest, are often quite trivial.

Like everyone else, the professor has other facilities for the diffusion of his ideals. When these facilities are lacking, he can easily create them in an appropriate form, as experience has shown in the case of every honest attempt. But the pro-fessor should not demand the right as a professor to carry the marshal's baton of the statesman or reformer in his knapsack. This is just what he does when he uses the unassailability of the academic chair for the expression of political (or cultural-political) evaluations. In the press, in public meetings, in associations, in essays, in every avenue which is open to every other citizen, he can and should do what his God or daemon demands. Today the student should obtain, from his teacher in the lecture hall, the capacity: (1) to fulfill a given task in a workmanlike fashion; (2) definitely to recognize facts, even those which may be personally uncomfortable, and to distinguish them from his own evaluations; (3) to subordinate himself to his task and to repress the impulse to exhibit his personal tastes or other sentiments unnecessarily. This is vastly more important today than it was forty years ago when the problem did not even exist in this form. It is not true—as many people have insisted—that the "personality" is and should be a "whole" in the sense that it is injured when it is not exhibited on every possible occasion.

Every professional task has its own "inherent norms" and should be fulfilled accordingly. In the execution of his professional responsibility, a man should confine himself to it alone and should exclude whatever is not strictly *proper to it*—particularly his own loves and hates. The powerful personality does not manifest itself by trying to give everything a "personal touch" at every possible opportunity. The generation which is now growing up should, above all, again become used to the thought that "being a personality" is something that cannot be deliberately striven for and that there is only one way by which it can (perhaps!) be achieved: namely, the whole-hearted devotion to a "task" whatever it (and its derivative "demands of the hour") may be. It is poor taste to mix personal questions with specialized factual analyses. We deprive the word "vocation" of the only meaning which still retains ethical significance if we fail to carry out that specific kind of self-restraint which it requires. But whether the fashionable "cult of the personality" seeks to dominate the throne, public office or the professorial chair—its impressiveness is superficial. Intrinsically, it is very petty and it always has prejudicial consequences. Now I hope that it is not necessary for me to emphasize that the proponents of the views against which the present essay is directed can accomplish very little by this sort of cult of the "personality" for the very reason that it is "personal." In part they see the responsibilities of the professorial chair in another light, in part they have other educational ideals which I respect but do not share. For this reason we must seriously consider not only what they strive to achieve but also how the views which they legitimate by their authority influence a generation with an already extremely pronounced predisposition to overestimate its own importance.

Finally, it scarcely needs to be pointed out that many ostensible opponents of the assertion of political value-judgments from the academic chair are by no means justified when, in seeking to discredit cultural and social-political discussions which take place in public, they invoke the postulate of "ethical neutrality" which they often misunderstand so gravely. The indubitable existence of this spuriously "ethically neutral" tendentiousness, which (in our discipline) is manifested in the obstinate and deliberate partisanship of powerful interest groups, explains why a significant number of intellectually honest scholars still continue to assert their personal evaluations from their chair. They are too proud to identify themselves with this psuedo-ethical neutrality. Personally I believe that, in spite of this, what is right (in my opinion) should be done and that the influence of the value-judgments of a scholar who confines himself to championing them at appropriate occasions outside the classroom, will increase when it becomes known that he does only his "task" inside the classroom. But these statements are in their turn, all matters of evaluation, and hence scientifically undemonstrable.

In any case the fundamental principle which justifies the practice of asserting value-judgments in teaching can be consistently held only when its proponents demand that the spokesman for all party-preferences be granted the opportunity of demonstrating their validity on the academic platform. But in Germany, insistence on the right of professors to state their evaluations has been associated with the opposite of the demand for the equal representation of all (even the most "extreme") tendencies. Schmoller thought that he was being entirely consistent from his own premises when he declared that "Marxists and Manchesterites" were disqualified from holding academic positions although he was never so unjust as to ignore their scientific accomplishments. It is exactly on these points that I could never agree with our honored master. One obviously ought not justify the expression of evaluations in teaching—and then when the conclusions are drawn therefrom, point out that the university is a state institution for the training of "loyal" administrators. Such a procedure makes the university, not into a specialized technical school (which appears to be so degrading to many teachers) but rather into a theological seminary—except that it does not have the latter's religious dignity.

Attempts have been made to set up certain purely "logical" limits to the range of value-judgments which should be allowed from the academic chair. One of our foremost jurists once explained, in discussing his opposition to the exclusion of socialists from university posts, that he too would not be willing to accept an "anarchist" as a teacher of law since anarchists deny the validity of law in general—and he regarded his argument as conclusive. My own opinion is exactly the opposite. An anarchist can surely be a good legal scholar. And if he is such, then indeed the Archimedean point of his convictions, which is outside the conventions and presuppositions which are so self-evident to us, can equip him to perceive problems in the fundamental postulates of legal theory which escape those who take them for granted. Fundamental doubt is the father of knowledge. The jurist is no more responsible for "proving" the value of those cultural objects which are relevant to "law" than the physician is responsible for demonstrating that the prolongation of life is desirable under all conditions. Neither of them is in a position to do this with the means at their disposal. If, however, one wishes to turn the university into a forum for the discussion of values, then it obviously becomes a duty to permit the most unrestrained freedom of discussion of fundamental questions from all value-positions. Is this possible? Today the most decisive and important questions of practical and political values are *excluded* from German universities by the very nature of the present political situation. . . . Everyone knows, however, that these vital questions of our national life cannot be discussed with full freedom in German universities.[2] In view of the fact that certain value-questions which are of decisive political significance are permanently banned from university discussion, it seems to me to be only in accord with the dignity of a representative of science *to be silent* as well about such value-problems as he is allowed to treat.

But in no case, however, should the unresolvable question—unresolvable because it is ultimately a question of evaluation—as to whether one may, must, or should champion certain practical values in teaching, be confused with the purely logical discussion of the relationship of value-judgments to empirical disciplines such as sociology and economics. Any confusion on this point will impede the thoroughness of the discussion of the actual logical problem. Its solution will, however, not give any directives for answering the other question beyond two purely logical requirements, namely: clarity and an explicit separation of the different types of problems.

Nor need I discuss further whether the distinction between empirical statements of fact and value-judgments is "difficult" to make. It is. All of us, those of us who take this position as well as others, encounter the subject time and again. But the

---

[2] This is by no means peculiar to Germany. In almost every country there exist, openly or hidden, actual restraints. The only differences are in the character of the particular value-questions which are thus excluded.

exponents of the so-called "ethical economics" particularly should be aware that even though the moral law is perfectly unfulfillable, it is nonetheless "imposed" as a duty. The examination of one's conscience would perhaps show that the fulfillment of our postulate is especially difficult, just because we reluctantly refuse to enter the very alluring area of values without a titillating "personal touch." Every teacher has observed that the faces of his students light up and they become more attentive when he begins to set forth his personal evaluations, and that the attendance at his lectures is greatly increased by the expectation that he will do so. Everyone knows furthermore that in the competition for students, universities in making recommendations for advancement, will often give a prophet, however minor, who can fill the lecture halls, the upper hand over a much superior scholar who does not present his own preferences. Of course, it is understood in those cases that the prophecy should leave sufficiently untouched the political or conventional preferences which are generally accepted at the time. The pseudo-"ethically-neutral" prophet who speaks for the dominant interests has, of course, better opportunities for ascent due to the influence which these have on the political powers-that-be. I regard all this as very undesirable, and I will also therefore not go into the proposition that the demand for the exclusion of value-judgments is "petty" and that it makes the lectures "boring." I will not touch upon the question as to whether lecturers on specialized empirical problems must seek above all to be "interesting." For my own part, in any case, I fear that a lecturer who makes his lectures stimulating by the insertion of personal evaluations will, in the long run, weaken the students' taste for sober empirical analysis.

I will acknowledge without further discussion that it is possible, under the semblance of eradicating all practical value-judgments, to suggest such preferences with especial force by simply "letting the facts speak for themselves." The better kind of our parliamentary and electoral speeches operate in this way— and quite legitimately, given their purposes. No words should be wasted in declaring that all such procedures on the university lecture platform, particularly from the standpoint of the demand for the separation of judgments of fact from judgments of value, are, of all abuses, the most abhorrent. The fact, however, that a dishonestly created illusion of the fulfillment of an ethical imperative can be passed off as the reality, constitutes no criticism of the imperative itself. At any rate, even if the teacher does not believe that he should deny himself the right of asserting value-judgments, he should make them absolutely *explicit* to the students and to himself.

Finally, we must oppose to the utmost the widespread view that scientific "objectivity" is achieved by weighing the various evaluations against one another and making a "statesman-like" compromise among them. Not only is the "middle way" just as undemonstrable scientifically (with the means of the empirical sciences) as the "most extreme" evaluations; rather, in the sphere of evaluations, it is the least unequivocal. It does not belong in the university—but rather in political programs and in parliament. The sciences, both normative and empirical, are capable of rendering an inestimable service to persons engaged in political activity by telling them that (1) these and these "ultimate" positions are conceivable with reference to this practical problem; (2) such and such are the facts which you must take into account in making your choice between these positions. And with this we come to the real problem.

## EDUCATIONAL POLICIES COMMISSION—AMERICAN EDUCATION AND INTERNATIONAL TENSIONS[1]
### pp. 35–6 (1949)

How will continuing international tensions, involving both ideological conflict now and the threat of armed conflict in the future, affect American schools?

If the schools develop programs that contribute to the nation's needs in this time of crisis, and if they can convince the public that these contributions are useful, then education can command the support it will deserve as an instrument of national policy. The national interest requires that educators take a candid view of the world about them and shape school programs to help discharge the obligations which that disordered world presents.

This does not mean that the schools must abandon their traditional purposes. The schools' responsibilities for transmitting the social heritage, for building in children and youth the skills, attitudes, and appreciative capacities requisite for effective and satisfying living, will continue. But other responsibilities, deriving from the hard fact that continuing international tensions and the threat of war place all our traditional values in jeopardy, must also be assumed.

It is fortunate, however, that so many of the special tasks that schools must undertake to meet present needs will also con-

---

[1] The Educational Policies Commission is a joint commission of the National Education Association and the American Association of School Administrators and consists of twenty leading American educators headed by John K. Norton and including Dwight D. Eisenhower and James B. Conant. It is concerned with all major problems of educational policy.

tribute to the long-range purposes of education. Thus, the challenge of anti-democratic ideologies reinforces the schools' basic obligation to teach democracy, just as the need for healthy young people to wear uniforms and man machines tells the schools to intensify and improve their programs of health and vocational education.

The schools of the United States will certainly be expected and required to continue their work in developing strong national loyalties. Their task, however, may reach beyond present typical practice to include a more penetrating understanding of the elements in our national tradition that merit the greatest devotion, of the qualities of our national greatness that are most worthy to be admired and fostered, and of the historical background and reasonable national aspirations of other peoples.

## AMERICAN ASSOCIATION OF UNIVERSITY PROFESSORS—STATEMENT OF PRINCIPLES OF ACADEMIC FREEDOM AND TENURE*

### 1940

The purpose of this statement is to promote public understanding and support of academic freedom and tenure and agreement upon procedures to assure them in colleges and universities. Institutions of higher education are conducted for the common good and not to further the interest of either the individual teacher[1] or the institution as a whole. The common good depends upon the free search for truth and its free exposition.

Academic freedom is essential to these purposes and applies to both teaching and research. Freedom in research is fundamental to the advancement of truth. Academic freedom in its teaching aspect is fundamental for the protection of the rights of the teacher in teaching and of the student to freedom in learning. It carries with it duties correlative with rights.

Tenure is a means to certain ends; specifically: (1) Freedom of teaching and research and of extramural activities, and (2) A sufficient degree of economic security to make the profession attractive to men and women of ability. Freedom and economic security, hence tenure, are indispensable to the

---

* Published annually in the Spring issue of the Bulletin of The American Association of University Professors.

[1] The word "teacher" as used in this document is understood to include the investigator who is attached to an academic institution without teaching duties.

success of an institution in fulfilling its obligations to its students and to society.

## Academic Freedom

(a) The teacher is entitled to full freedom in research and in the publication of the results, subject to the adequate performance of his other academic duties; but research for pecuniary return should be based upon an understanding with the authorities of the institution.

(b) The teacher is entitled to freedom in the classroom in discussing his subject, but he should be careful not to introduce into his teaching controversial matter which has no relation to his subject. Limitations of academic freedom because of religious or other aims of the institution should be clearly stated in writing at the time of the appointment.

(c) The college or university teacher is a citizen, a member of a learned profession, and an officer of an educational institution. When he speaks or writes as a citizen, he should be free from institutional censorship or discipline, but his special position in the community imposes special obligations. As a man of learning and an educational officer, he should remember that the public may judge his profession and his institution by his utterances. Hence he should at all times be accurate, should exercise appropriate restraint, should show respect for the opinions of others, and should make every effort to indicate that he is not an institutional spokesman.

## Academic Tenure

(a) After the expiration of a probationary period teachers or investigators should have permanent or continuous tenure, and their services should be terminated only for adequate cause, except in the case of retirement for age, or under extraordinary circumstances because of financial exigencies.

In the interpretation of this principle it is understood that the following represents acceptable academic practice:

(1) The precise terms and conditions of every appointment should be stated in writing and be in the possession of both institution and teacher before the appointment is consummated.

(2) Beginning with appointment to the rank of full-time instructor or a higher rank, the probationary period should not exceed seven years, including within this period full-time service in all institutions of higher education; but subject to the proviso that when, after a term of probationary service of more than three years in one or more institutions, a teacher is called to another institution it may be agreed in writing that his new

**818**                                            [Emerson]

appointment is for a probationary period of not more than four years, even though thereby the person's total probationary period in the academic profession is extended beyond the normal maximum of seven years. Notice should be given at least one year prior to the expiration of the probationary period if the teacher is not to be continued in service after the expiration of that period.

(3) During the probationary period a teacher should have the academic freedom that all other members of the faculty have.

(4) Termination for cause of a continuous appointment, or the dismissal for cause of a teacher previous to the expiration of a term appointment, should, if possible, be considered by both a faculty committee and the governing board of the institution. In all cases where the facts are in dispute, the accused teacher should be informed before the hearing in writing of the charges against him and should have the opportunity to be heard in his own defense by all bodies that pass judgment upon his case. He should be permitted to have with him an adviser of his own choosing who may act as counsel. There should be a full stenographic record of the hearing available to the parties concerned. In the hearing of charges of incompetence the testimony should include that of teachers and other scholars, either from his own or from other institutions. Teachers on continuous appointment who are dismissed for reasons not involving moral turpitude should receive their salaries for at least a year from the date of notification of dismissal whether or not they are continued in their duties at the institution.

(5) Termination of a continuous appointment because of financial exigency should be demonstrably bona fide.

## Note

1. Some leading discussions of the role of academic institutions and education in modern society are: American Historical Association, Report of the Commission on the Social Studies, *Conclusions and Recommendations* (1934); Bode, *Democracy as a Way of Life* (1921); Brameld, *Patterns of Educational Philosophy—A Democratic Interpretation* (1950); Childs, *Education and Morals* (1950); Coe, *Educating for Citizenship*, ch. IV (1932); Counts, *Dare the School Build a New Social Order?* (1932); Dewey, *Democracy and Education* (1916); Dewey, *Problems of Men* (1946); Esipov and Goncharov, *I Want to be Like Stalin* (1947); Finney, *Sociological Philosophy of Education* (1928); Gentile, *The Reform of Education* (1922); Guinan, *Freedom and Authority in Education* (1936); Hook, *Education for Modern Man* (1946); Horne, *The Democratic Philosophy of Education* (1935); Kallen, *The Education of Free Men* (1949); Kandel, *Comparative Education*, ch. 3 (1933); Kilpatrick, *Education and the Social Crisis*

(1932); Kneller, *The Educational Philosophy of National Socialism* (1941); Lasswell and McDougal, *Legal Education and Public Policy: Professional Training in the Public Interest*, 52 Yale L. J. 203 (1943); McCallister, *The Growth of Freedom in Education* (1931) (an historical treatment of the concept of freedom in educational theory and practice); Meiklejohn, *Education Between Two Worlds* (1942); National Education Association, *The Unique Function of Education in American Democracy* (1937) (a statement by the Educational Policies Commission); Pinkevitch, *The New Education in the Soviet Republic* (1929); Pittenger, *Indoctrination for American Democracy*, ch. 3 (1941); Redden and Ryan, *A Catholic Philosophy of Education* (1942); Russell, *Principles of Social Reconstruction*, ch. 5 (1917); Slesinger, Z., *Education and the Class Struggle* (1937); Symposium, *Freedom and the University* (Cornell U. Press, 1950). See also the material in Section A of Chapter VIII, *infra*.

For more complete and classified material and bibliographies see Brubacher, J. S., *Modern Philosophies of Education* (1950); and Brubacher, J. S., *Eclectic Philosophy of Education* (1951).

2. For discussion of the principles of academic freedom, see Alberty and Bode (eds.), *Educational Freedom and Democracy* (1938); Bagley, *Teachers Rights, Academic Freedom, and the Teaching of Controversial Issues*, 40 Teachers College Record 99 (1938); Brubacher, *Loyalty to Freedom*, 70 School and Society 369 (1949); Capen, *Academic Freedom*, 68 School and Society 70 (1948); Childs, *Academic Freedom in a Period of Transition*, in National Education Ass'n, *Addresses and Proceedings*, pp. 233–237 (1935); Childs, *Education and Morals*, pp. 199–207 (1950); Conant, *Education in a Divided World*, pp. 172–180 (1949); Dewey, *Academic Freedom*, 2 Cyclopedia of Ed. 700 (1911); Dewey, *The Social Significance of Academic Freedom*, 2 Social Frontier 165 (1936); Eklund, *Academic Freedom*, 33 Am. Teacher 5 (1948); Gideonse, *Changing Issues in Academic Freedom in the United States Today*, 94 Proceedings of Amer. Phil. Society 91 (1950); Gosling, *Academic Freedom*, 40 School and Society 79 (1934); Guthrie, *The Sacred Fetish of Academic Freedom*, 16 Vital Speeches 632 (1950); Johnson, *Academic Freedom*, in Anshen (ed.), *Freedom: Its Meaning* (1940); Karelsen, *A Layman Looks at Academic Freedom*, 69 School and Society 241 (1949); Lowell, *At War With Academic Traditions in America*, pp. 269–72 (1934); Lovejoy, *Academic Freedom*, 1 Encl. of Soc. Sci. 384 (1930); Meiklejohn, *Freedom and the College* (1923); National Education Association, Report of the Committee on Academic Freedom, *The Limits of Academic Freedom* (1939) (case studies, and an analysis of lay and professional opinion); Stevenson et al., *Academic Freedom—Its Meaning, Scope and Limitations*, 2 Social Frontier 169 (1936); Weschler, *Freedom to Learn*, 2 Social Frontier 176 (1936); Wright, *The Citizens' Stake in Academic Freedom*, 20 J. Higher Ed. 339 (1949).

For other expressions of the Catholic point of view, see Pius XI, *Christian Education of Youth*, 28 Cath. Ed. Rev. 129 (1930); Ryan *Truth and Freedom*, 20 J. Higher Ed. 349 (1949); Jordan, *The Bogey of Indoctrination,* 37 Cath. Ed. Rev. 20 (1939); Redden and Ryan, *Freedom Through Education,* p. 23 (1944).

For discussions of the propriety of limitations upon the freedom of the teacher employed in sectarian institutions, see Soper, *Academic Freedom in a Christian College,* 30 School and Society 521 (1929); Coe, *Academic Liberty in Denominational Colleges,* 30 School and Society 678 (1929) (an answer to President Soper); Mallon, *Faculty Ranks, Tenure and Academic Freedom,* 39 Nat'l. Cath. Ed. Ass'n Bulletin 177, 190–4 (1942).

3. Studies of the social, economic and political context in which educational theories and practices have developed include Beale, *A History of Freedom of Teaching in American Schools* (1941); Counts, *The Social Foundations of Education* (1934); Curti, *The Social Ideas of American Educators* (1935).

4. For an historical account of problems of academic freedom see Beale, *A History of Freedom of Teaching in American Schools* (1941); Tyler and Cheyney, *Academic Freedom,* 200 Annals of the Amer. Acad. of Pol. & Soc. Science 102 (1938); Ludlum, *Academic Freedom and Tenure: A History,* 10 Antioch Rev. 3 (1950); Brubacher, *A History of the Problems of Education* (1947). These matters are raised inferentially in McCallister, *The Growth of Freedom in Education* (1931).

5. Statements of the concrete application of the principles of academic freedom, in addition to that of the A. A. U. P. set forth *supra,* may be found in American Civil Liberties Union, *Civil Liberties of Teachers and Students—Academic Freedom* (1949 and supplements, Nov. 1949, May 1952); National Education Association Platform, printed in Proceedings of the Eighty-ninth Annual Meeting, 1951, pp. 117 et seq.; Progressive Education Association, *Educational Freedom: A Study Guide for Use by Professional Groups and Educational Organizations* (1937).

6. Problems of academic freedom at elementary and secondary educational levels would appear to differ at some points from the issues raised at the level of higher education. Thus the lack of maturity of the students may be thought to require different teaching methods as well as different controls over the teaching staff. Hence issues of academic freedom at the lower school levels may be framed more in terms of democratic as opposed to authoritarian methods of education. For a discussion of these differences see Alberty and Bode, *supra,* ch. IV–VII.

7. For discussion of some of the current issues of academic freedom in other countries, see *Academic Freedom and the State,* 166 Nature 449 (1950) (Great Britain); Munger, *Academic Freedom under Peron,* 7 Antioch Rev. 275 (1947); *McGill Drops Behind,* 27 Can. Forum 268 (1948); see also Esipov and Goncharov, *I Want to be Like Stalin* (1947); Counts, *American Education through the Soviet Looking Glass* (1951).

## B. SOME CURRENT ISSUES OF ACADEMIC FREEDOM

Issues which have aroused controversy and have provoked isolated or concerted struggles over the principles of academic freedom vary with the times and with the specific social, economic and political conflicts of the period. Whenever the unorthodox intellectual challenges the values or practices of a society, whether by proposing radical innovations or merely by casting doubt upon the merits of the existing system, he is likely to be countered by pressures from interests representing the more conservative elements in the society. Notable instances of such controversies have marked the intellectual progress of every civilization. See, Bury, *A History of Freedom of Thought* (1913).

In the course of modern industrial development in the United States many struggles over academic freedom have taken place. Thus in the decades before the Civil War tense and heated conflict over the issue of abolition of slavery brought about the dismissal of several professors. Shortly after the Civil War, and even into the twentieth century, teaching the theory of evolution resulted in the discharge of many faculty members, particularly in sectarian schools. At the turn of the century, the most serious economic and political issue was that of bimetallism. The dismissal of Professor Edward A. Ross from Leland Stanford Jr. University in 1900 for having advocated free silver, almost alone among economists, aroused open and, for the first time, organized protest on the part of teachers and scholars. During the early years of the century concern with the activities of anarchists and other radicals was reflected in pressures upon educational institutions. Later, the First World War and the Bolshevik Revolution greatly accentuated the tensions and resulted in a series of dismissals, attacks upon textbooks and curriculum, legislative investigations, and legislation establishing loyalty oaths and loyalty tests for teachers. In the decade and a half before the Second World War, as the temper of the country calmed, controversy became less frequent and less bitter. Yet even through this period important problems of academic freedom were raised and debated.

Some of the issues involving academic freedom have been peculiar to a given locality, or to particular sub-strata of society. For example, resistance may be found to the discussion of racial problems in the south and southwest; or labor problems in urban industrial sections of the north; or religious questions in rural, fundamentalist areas all over the country. These and other issues have frequently tested the principle that a teacher should be permitted to explore matters which in his community are of consequence.

For a discussion of some of the major controversies in past eras see the material cited in the Note at the end of Section A, *supra*.  See also Chapter IV, Section B, *supra*.

In the period following the Second World War there has been a sharp revival of controversy over the principles and practices of academic freedom.  Concern has been expressed by many that infringements upon academic freedom have become so widespread as to endanger the entire tradition.  Thus in a report to the ninetieth annual convention of the National Education Association on July 1, 1952, Dr. Martin Essex, Chairman of the Association's Committee on Tenure and Academic Freedom, was reported as asserting that "the academic freedom of the American public school teacher is threatened to a greater extent than at any time in the last 100 years."  N. Y. Times, July 2, 1952. For other comments see *infra*.

The following material sets forth briefly some of the important controversies that have taken place in recent years.  The incidents have been selected as illustrative of various kinds of issues that pose problems in academic freedom today.

### 1. Issues Involving Teachers and Others Representing the Academic Profession

#### a. Olivet College

In 1948 Dr. T. Barton Akeley and his wife, the college librarian, were discharged from Olivet College in Michigan, for their "ultra-liberal" views.  Their dismissal was followed by that of five others, one of whom, Tucker P. Smith, was Socialist candidate for Vice President.  "Subsequently ten more faculty members resigned, making a total of seventeen who were dismissed or left voluntarily.  This was more than half of the original number of thirty."  N. Y. Times, May 29, 1949.  See also American Civil Liberties Union, *In the Shadow of Fear*, 20th Annual Rep't., 1949, pp. 25–6.

#### b. The Parker Case

Professor George F. Parker, assistant professor of religion and philosophy at Evansville College, Evansville, Indiana, was dismissed in 1948 for serving as chairman of the Vanderburgh County Citizens for Wallace Committee and presiding at a Wallace-for-President meeting held in Evansville.  The College announced that "his activities both on and off the campus . . . put an end to his usefulness to the institution."  N. Y. Times,

**823**

May 29, 1949. The dismissal was subsequently investigated by the American Association of University Professors and Evansville College was placed on its list of "censored administrations." See 35 A.A.U.P. Bull. 74 (1949). For further discussion of the case see Biddle, *The Fear of Freedom*, pp. 172–4 (1951), and Barth, *The Loyalty of Free Men*, p. 223 (1951).[1]

### c. The Spitzer Case

At Oregon State University, Dr. Ralph Spitzer, associate professor of chemistry, was discharged for "supporting the genetics teachings of Lysenko, the Russian Communist, who advocates the theory that acquired characteristics can be inherited." N. Y. Times, Feb. 24, 1949. Dr. A. L. Strand, President of the University and an entomologist, was quoted as saying, "Any scientist who has such poor power of discrimination so as to choose to support Lysenko's genetics against all the weight of evidence against it is not much of a scientist or has lost the freedom that an instructor or investigator should possess." *Ibid.*[2]

### d. The May Quinn Case

May Quinn, a teacher in a New York elementary school, was charged with making anti-Negro statements in her classroom. On the particular occasion in question a student had brought in a newspaper clipping describing a suit brought by a Negro in the South to obtain admission to a university. Miss Quinn was alleged to have said, "I would not go where I was not wanted;" "the Negroes were happy before they knew about racial discrimination. Now that they know about it, are they any happier?;" and "if people wouldn't talk so much about racial discrimination, there would be less of it." Several years before Miss Quinn had been suspended and fined for making anti-Semitic statements in her classroom. Various individuals and organizations demanded that she be permanently dropped as a teacher. The Superintendent of Schools reprimanded Miss Quinn but refused to discharge her, saying she had made a "positive effort, both before and after the incident, to foster proper interracial attitudes among her pupils." See N. Y. Times, Dec. 17, 19, 20, 22, 23, 1949.

---

[1] A number of other complaints were made to the American Association of University Professors concerning discharge for activity or affiliation with the Progressive Party. See A. A. U. P. Bull., *supra;* N. Y. Times, May 29, 1949. No action on these cases seems to have been taken.

[2] The American Civil Liberties Union reported that Spitzer was dismissed "for writing that the biological theories of a Russian Communist scientist should be studied." *In the Shadow of Fear*, 20th Annual Rep't, 1949, p. 25.

**824**

## e. University of California
## Loyalty Oath

Investigations, accusations and legislative proposals of the California Tenney Committee led the Board of Regents of the University of California to adopt, in March of 1949, a resolution requiring faculty members to sign an oath as a condition of receiving their salary.[3] This oath, to be added to the traditional oath to support the Constitution required of all "public officials" of the state by the California Constitution, was as follows:

"I do not believe in and am not a member of nor do I support any party or organization that believes in, advocates or teaches the overthrow of the United States government by force or violence."

The faculty, while substantially agreeing with the University policy which barred Communists from employment, objected to taking this special oath. Following conferences between the faculty Senate Advisory Committee and President Sproul, a "compromise" oath was adopted by resolution of the Board of Regents on June 24, 1949, which read:

"I am not a member of the Communist Party, or under any oath, or a party to any agreement, or under any commitment that is in conflict with my obligations under this oath."

The Board of Regents justified the oath as necessary to implement its policy, adopted in 1940, that "membership in the Communist Party is incompatible with membership in the faculty of a state university."

Substantial numbers of faculty members continued to oppose the oath. Their reasons were summarized by George R. Stewart, one of their number, as follows:

"In the first place . . . it must be emphasized that no professor, so far as is known, refused to sign for the obvious reason; that is, that he actually was a Communist. . . .

"As to why the professors actually did not sign, some of the reasons may seem to be of small moment in themselves, but these seemingly innocent details represented to the faculty the beginnings of dangerous tendencies—to be combated immediately before they became serious. As one professor put it: 'The way to prevent a flood is to keep the first crack from opening in the dam.' . . .

"1. *Ambiguity*. In the first arguments, which involved the as-yet-unrevised oath, the charge of ambiguity ranked high. It was pointed out that anyone swearing to such a text would

---

[3] For an account of the activities of the Tenney Committee at the University, see Barrett, *The Tenney Committee*, pp. 121–58 (1951).

not be certain as to what he was committing himself. After the revision of the text in June, this argument disappeared. It left, however, a heritage of distrust. . . .

"2. *Political Test.* Since the Communist Party is a legal party in California, many professors believed that the oath constituted a political test for membership in the faculty and was therefore contrary, certainly to the spirit, and probably to the letter, of the articles in the state Constitution under which the University operates. They believed also that the establishment of any kind of political test was extremely dangerous. Having been admitted for the Communist Party, it might easily at some later time be extended to include any other party, or any unpopular group. The whole procedure was thus, they believed, contrary to basic American practices and should not be condoned.

"3. *Guilt by Association.* Many professors believed that the blanket condemnation of all members of the Communist Party constituted a recognition of 'guilt by association.' In other words, people were to be convicted and punished merely because they kept disreputable company, not because they themselves had actually committed any offense or had even been shown likely to commit an offense. . . .

"4. *Personal.* In the last analysis the very strongest argument with many individuals has been a complex of ideas which may all be placed under the general term 'personal.' Men and women of spirit objected to having the knife put at their throats; that is, at being forced to swear under penalty of losing their means of livelihood. Moreover, the mere fact of being thus required to swear that you are not a Communist implies that you are under suspicion of being a Communist and is therefore insulting and to be resisted. . . .

"Another strong personal argument was that of discrimination. Why should a particular group of citizens—that is, the professors—be required to swear an oath that is not required of other citizens, not even of state officials? This reduces the professor to a second-class citizen, a person under suspicion. It is comparable to a Jim Crow law. . . .

"5. *Not a Good Communist Preventive.* Another argument against the oath was that, since Communists would presumably swear to it readily, its imposition was not a practical means of freeing the University from alleged Communist influence. . . .

"6. *University Welfare.* By February most members of the faculty had become convinced that the oath was not of preeminent importance in itself but that certain of the regents

**826**

were trying by means of it to force their arbitrary will upon the faculty, destroy any effective faculty autonomy, and thus gain direct control of the University in a way not warranted by the spirit of the Constitutional Act or by tradition. . . .

"7. *Academic Tenure*. From the very beginning the faculty had recognized that the imposition of the oath was obviously overthrowing the principle of Academic Tenure. . . .

"8. *Academic Freedom*. Since Tenure and Academic Freedom are inseparably bound, the argument against the oath on the basis of Academic Freedom had, from the beginning, run parallel with that on the basis of Tenure. The imposition of the oath, moreover, struck directly at Freedom by setting up a field within which thought was no longer free. Having signed the oath, a professor might still think about Communism, but he necessarily had always to come out with the answer that Communism was bad. . . ."[4]

Some faculty members met and agreed not to sign the oath. It became apparent that refusal to sign was equivalent to resigning. The faculty Senate than took a firm stand, requesting that the Board of Regents delete, rather than revise, the oath. The Board agreed to continue negotiations but refused to rescind its resolution. Many faculty members then agreed to sign. The non-signers were given until April 30 to sign or consider themselves dismissed. After further negotiations the Board of Regents on April 21, 1950, voted to rescind the requirement of the oath; but it adopted a new resolution stipulating that, as a condition precedent to employment, each member of the faculty would be required to execute the Constitutional oath and to accept appointment by a letter containing the following provisions:

"Having taken the constitutional oath of office required of public officials of the State of California, I hereby formally acknowledge my acceptance of the position and salary named, and also state that I am not a member of the Communist Party or any other organization which advocates the overthrow of the government by force or violence, and that I have no commitments in conflict with my responsibilities with respect to impartial scholarship and free pursuit of truth. I understand that the foregoing statement is a condition of my employment and a consideration of payment of my salary."

The resolution further provided:

"In the event that a member of the faculty fails to comply with any foregoing requirement applicable to him he shall have the right to petition the President of the University for

---

[4] Stewart, *The Year of the Oath*, pp. 21–6 (1950).

a review of his case by the Committee on Privilege and Tenure of the Academic Senate, including an investigation of and full hearing on the reasons for his failure so to do. Final action shall not be taken by the Board of Regents until the Committee on Privilege and Tenure, after such investigation and hearing, shall have had an opportunity to submit to the Board, through the President of the University, its findings and recommendations. It is recognized that final determination in each case is the prerogative of the Regents."[5]

Thirty-nine faculty members who had refused to sign the oath appeared before the Faculty Committee. Six others refused to do either. The hearing resulted in favorable recommendations to the Board of Regents as to each of those who appeared. On July 21, 1950, the Board of Regents voted to dismiss the six who had refused to sign or appear before the Committee and to appoint the 39 others for the coming year. But at the next meeting the latter decision was reconsidered and reversed, and a motion unanimously carried to give the faculty members 10 days in which to sign the statement prescribed in the resolution of April 21, 1950.

Twenty-six faculty members, none of whom was charged with being either a member of the Communist Party or in any way "subversive," refused to comply with this order and 18 of these non-signers brought proceedings for a writ of mandamus to compel the Regents to reappoint them. On April 6, 1951, the court ordered their reinstatement, and in October the Board of Regents rescinded the requirement of its resolution of April 21.[6]

Meanwhile in October 1950 the California Legislature had passed the Levering Act which required all state employees, including members of the University faculty, to take a loyalty oath. This requirement is now applicable.[7]

A report issued by the Committee on Academic Freedom to

---

[5] For an account of the controversy up to this point, see Stewart, *supra*.

[6] The court's decision, discussed in Section D, *infra*, went on the ground that the Constitutional oath was exclusive. *Tolman v. Underhill*, — Cal. App. —, 229 Pac. 2d 447 (1951).

[7] The Levering Act oath requires an employee to swear that "I do not advocate, nor am I a member of any party or organization . . . that now advocates the overthrow of the Government of the United States or of the State of California by force or violence or other unlawful means; that within the five years immediately preceding the taking of this oath . . . I have not been a member of [any such organization] except as follows ——————— . . . and that during such time as I am [an employee] I will not advocate nor become a member of [any organization] that advocates the overthrow of the Government . . . by force or violence or other unlawful means." Stat. of Cal., 3d Sess. 1950, ch. 7.

the Academic Senate of the Northern Section of the University in February, 1951, summarized the effect of the loyalty oath controversy in the following terms:

(1) Twenty-six members of the faculty were dismissed, including such well-known scholars as the historian E. H. Kantorowicz, who accepted a position with the Institute for Advanced Study at Princeton; Professor Harold Winkler, appointed visiting lecturer in Government by Harvard University as "the best available man"; and Professor G. C. Wick, appointed as "a first rate scientist" to a new professorship at Carnegie Institute of Technology. Others on the list included "figures of international reputation in psychology, history, mathematics, philosophy, physics and classics."

(2) Thirty-seven other faculty members resigned in protest, many of them also well-known scholars.

(3) Forty-seven persons who were offered positions at the University refused to accept them because of the loyalty requirements.

(4) Fifty-five courses were dropped from the curriculum as a result of the dismissals and resignations, and the inability to obtain replacements.

(5) Numerous professional associations had protested the action of the Board of Regents, many of which urged their members not to accept positions at the University of California.

(6) Great difficulty had been encountered by many departments of the University in attracting qualified men to fill vacancies.[8]

## 2. Issues Involving Curriculum, Textbooks and Other Teaching Material

### a. The Nation

On June 24, 1948, the Board of Education of the City of New York suspended *The Nation* from the public schools indefinitely for having carried a series of articles by Paul Blanshard highly critical of the Catholic church. *The Nation* (and the magazine *Soviet Russia Today*) had been banned several months earlier from the Newark, New Jersey schools. In both cases, the magazines were removed as a result of protests from Catholic parents. The superintendent of Schools in Newark stated that "Publications that are patently anti-Catholic, anti-

---

[8] The report is summarized in N. Y. Times, Mar. 11, 1951. For further discussion of the controversy see American Civil Liberties Union of Northern California, *Crisis at the University of California* (Nov. 1949 and Dec. 1950); Barth, *The Loyalty of Free Men*, pp. 213–8 (1951). For additional material on loyalty oaths and tests for teachers see Sections D and E, *infra*.

Protestant, anti-Semitic, anti-Negro, or anti-American have no place as teaching or reference materials in a public school." The Board of Education in New York justified its exclusion of *The Nation* on the ground that "American public school tradition was opposed to bringing religious controversies into the classroom." See Note, *School Boards, Schoolbooks, and the Freedom to Learn,* 59 Yale L. J. 928, 935 (1950).

### b. *Magruder's American Government*

In October 1949 the Houston Independent District School Board voted to discontinue the use of Dr. Frank Magruder's *American Government* in the Houston high schools. Objection was taken to a passage which read:

"The United States is called a capitalistic country, but it does not have pure capitalism. It has capitalism subject to increasing government control as our manner of living becomes more complex. The country is capitalistic with strong socialistic and even communistic trends. The postal system, power projects and progressive taxes are bits of socialism; and public free education and old age assistance are examples of communism * * * to each according to his need."

Publishers of the book stated that the text had been used in the majority of United States senior high school civic classes and in Army and Navy schools during the war. They also said that the passage in question was from an earlier edition and had been "removed from subsequent editions." N. Y. Times, Oct. 26, 1949.[9]

### c. *Oliver Twist and The Merchant of Venice*

In 1949 several Jewish organizations in New York City strongly protested to the Board of Education the use of Dickens' *Oliver Twist* and Shakespeare's *The Merchant of Venice* as approved reading and study material in the public and secondary schools. It was alleged that the books were objectionable as engendering hatred of the Jew as a person and as a race. The Board of Education refused to withdraw the books. A suit to compel removal of the books from classrooms and school libraries was dismissed. *Rosenberg v. Board of Education,* 196 Misc. 542, 92 N. Y. Supp. 2d 344 (1949). See *infra.*

### d. *The Sapulpa Incident*

In Sapulpa, Oklahoma, books of the school library, after hav-

---

[9] The earlier edition of the Magruder book was also dropped as a text in Little Rock (although retained as a reference) and in Georgia. N. Y. Times, May 25, 1952.

ing been "criticized by a women's civic group for their attitude toward socialism and sex," were burned. The vice president of the High School Board was quoted as saying that "only five or six" books were destroyed, that they "were volumes of no consequence," and that he could not remember their authors or titles. N. Y. Times, February 12, 1952.

### e. Other Cases

Benjamin Fine, educational editor of the New York Times, in a nation-wide survey published in the Times on May 25, 1952, reported:

"Widespread attacks have been made in recent months on schoolbooks and other reading materials. The attacks have been based on the grounds that the texts contain subversive passages or have been written by authors suspected of un-American views. . . .

"A summary of *The Times* findings, based on the nation-wide reports, follows:

"1. A concerted campaign is under way over the country to censor school and college textbooks, reading materials and other visual aids.

"2. Voluntary groups are being formed in nearly every state to screen books for 'subversive' or un-American statements. These organizations, not accountable to any legal body, are sometimes doing great harm in their communities.

"3. Librarians are intimidated by outside pressures in their choice of books and other materials. Unwilling to risk a public controversy, they meekly accept the requests of the self-appointed censorship groups.

"4. Several textbooks and other materials have already been removed from school or college libraries and are effectively on 'the blacklist.'

"5. The attacks on the 'subversive' school texts appear to be part of a general campaign against public schools and other educational institutions."[10]

---

[10] The Fine survey was attacked by Henry Hazlitt as "one-sided" and "loaded," and as not considering the "possibility" that "the real menace to our educational system may come from some of those within it, or from the doctrines endorsed by some of the textbooks criticized." Hazlitt, *Educators vs. Free Inquiry*, The Freeman, June 30, 1952, p. 663.

For a summary of many of the controversies over textbooks and a discussion of the problem, see Saveth, *What To Do About "Dangerous" Textbooks*, Commentary, Feb. 1952, p. 99. See also Josephson, *The Battle of the Books*, The Nation, June 28, 1952, p. 619.

## 3. Issues Relating to Campus Activities

### a. Speakers at Ohio State

In July 1951 Dr. Harold C. Rugg, professor emeritus at
Columbia University and author of several social science textbooks which have been criticized as being "socialistic," was
invited to speak on the Ohio State campus. His appearance
resulted in protests by the American Legion, two Columbus
newspapers, and others. As a result of this incident the Board
of Trustees in September adopted a resolution barring "disloyal" public speakers from the campus and requiring that all
campus speakers be cleared with the president's office. The
Board defended its action in a statement issued in October in
which it said:

"As trustees of the Ohio State University, we encourage the
fullest academic freedom consistent with national security. The
facilities of the university will not be made available to known
Communists or members of other groups who seek to undermine basic liberties of America. We recognize no inalienable
right to any freedom which has for its purpose the destruction of our government." N. Y. Times, Oct. 16, 1951.

Under the clearance procedure President Howard L. Bevis
refused to approve Dr. Cecil E. Hinshaw, a Quaker pacifist, as
a speaker. Strong objections to the procedure and policy were
voiced by faculty members, the local chapter of the American
Association of University Professors, and other groups and
individuals. Doubts were expressed as to whether various professional meetings would be held at Ohio State. Dr. Bevis defended the action of the Board of Trustees, saying that "he
believed that both the trustees and the faculty were honestly
seeking the same goal: How to prevent the facilities of the University from being used and exploited by subversive groups and
people." N. Y. Times, Oct. 29, 1951. Later Dr. Bevis relaxed
the rule in a series of interpretations which provided that no
prior clearance was necessary for (1) speakers invited by a
faculty member to participate in his class, (2) heads of the
religious foundations recognized by the University, and (3)
speakers at meetings of professional, scientific or religious
groups recognized by the university. N. Y. Times, Nov. 8, 1951.

Objections were still raised, however, and two speakers who
had been cleared by the screening process declined invitations
to speak. Finally, in December, the Board of Trustees issued
a "further interpretation" which permitted faculty members
to be responsible for speakers brought to the campus but provided:

"In case of doubt, the faculty member concerned shall consult with his colleagues and cause the matter to be referred to his appropriate department chairman and dean to the president's office for advice and action." N. Y. Times, Dec. 14, 1951.

For accounts of the controversy see N. Y. Times Oct. 16, 26, 28, 29, 30, Nov. 8, 11, and Dec. 14, 1951; American Civil Liberties Weekly Bulletin, Nov. 12, 1951; Ohio State University Monthly, Nov. 15, 1951.

### b. Howard Fast

New York University refused to allow Howard Fast to speak after he had been convicted of contempt of the Committee on Un-American Activities and while awaiting sentence. Subsequently, after his release from prison, Fast was refused permission to speak at Columbia. American Civil Liberties Union Weekly Bull., Apr. 9, 1951. Later he was permitted to speak at Columbia and at Yale. See The Harvard Crimson, *Academic Freedom Survey*, June 17, 1952, p. M–4.

### c. The Zarichny Case

In 1947 the President of Michigan State College, approving a recommendation of the Faculty Committee on Student Organizations, placed on "disciplinary probation" all members of the campus chapter of the American Youth for Democracy, an organization that had been refused recognition by the Student Council. The terms of the probation were that the students in question could not "participate in any extra-curricular activities" or "in the affairs of any student organization" during the period of the probation. Subsequently, in December 1948 the College refused to permit James Zarichny, one of the students involved, to re-enroll for the next term, on the grounds he had violated his probation. The basis for the expulsion was that Zarichny had arranged a meeting in a building across the street from the campus at which Carl Winters, one of the defendants convicted in the first Smith Act prosecution of the Communist Party leaders, was the principal speaker. Zarichny contended the meeting was not sponsored by any student organization but by the county Civil Rights Committee.

Zarichny's suit for mandamus to compel his reinstatement was dismissed and the United States Supreme Court denied certiorari. *Zarichny v. State Board of Agriculture*, 338 U. S. 816 (1949).[11]

---

[11] For an account of the case, otherwise unreported, see 18 U. S. Law Week 3014. The facts recited above are taken in part from the report in U. S. Law Week and in part from a leaflet reproducing the letters from

### d. Other Student Activities

At the University of Chicago, Alan Kimmel, graduate student in geography, was removed by University officials as editor of the weekly university newspaper, *The Maroon*, "because he had been a sponsor and participant in the Communist World Youth Festival in East Berlin." N. Y. Times, October 5, 1951. Another student received permission to register at Cornell after the faculty committee determined that reports of his allegedly un-American remarks at the conference of International Union of Students at Prague (accusing the United States of being the aggressor in Korea) were erroneous. N. Y. Times, Sept. 17, 1950.

After having refused a charter to a chapter of the Labor Youth League (designated by the Attorney General as "subversive"), Columbia University issued a policy statement granting "recognized" student organizations the privilege of inviting guest speakers of their own choosing. At the same time it reserved for a faculty-student-administration committee the right to deny recognition to any campus group whose conduct is "irresponsible." The term "irresponsible" was defined to include "illegal or immoral actions, actions contrary to the organizations' stated objectives and action taken without fair regard for the interests and good name of the university." N. Y. Times, Oct. 25, 1951.

## 4. Issues Involving the General Operation of Particular Educational Institutions

### a. Sarah Lawrence College

A glimpse of the controversy over Sarah Lawrence College may be obtained from the following news items in the New York Times:

"Denying that any Communist could get or keep a job on its faculty, Sarah Lawrence College disclosed tonight the torments that veiled communism were causing there.

"Under a barrage of sudden criticism from certain writers and American Legion leaders, the college is even asked to justify its real estate tax exemption. Officials said that Dr. Harold Taylor, president, now spends two-thirds of his time fighting 'completely unfounded' charges. . . .

"The issue was discussed by Dr. Taylor and Harrison Tweed, board chairman of the college and senior partner in the New

the College to Zarichny issued by the Provisional Committee for Students and Faculty Rights.

[Emerson]

York law firm of Milbank, Tweed, Hope & Hadley, in a public statement.

" 'Until recently,' they said, 'Sarah Lawrence College has been spared the kind of attacks on freedom in education which have occurred at many other institutions. No one inside the college has ever suggested that we should have less freedom than we do, nor have we had any threats or accusations from outside the college.

" 'However, during the past two months we have had such attacks. One was a newspaper article in the Hearst press, another came from Counter Attack, whose publisher also issues Red Channels. To add to the variety, on the same day as the Counter Attack issue, the Communist Party Daily Worker denounced us for alleged discrimination against Negro students on a college-sponsored trip to the T.V.A.

" 'Another attack appeared in a circular issued by Allen Zoll, listing faculty members with "subversive connections" teaching in women's colleges, including Wellesley, Smith, Mount Holyoke and Sarah Lawrence. Another appeared in an article by Louis Budenz in the November issue of the American Legion Magazine which attempted to throw suspicion of "harboring subversives" on fifteen colleges and universities, among them Harvard, Cornell, Amherst, Columbia, Pittsburgh, New York University, California, Chicago and Sarah Lawrence.

" 'Early in November the Americanism committee of the Westchester County Legion, no doubt stimulated by Mr. Budenz' article, asked to talk to the president, and members of the committee came to the college for an interview. The names of three faculty members, one of whom has been at the college since it opened in 1928 and another with ten years of service, out of seventy-one members of the teaching staff, were brought into the discussion by the visitors. They were informed that the persons mentioned were good and honest teachers who enjoyed the confidence and respect of their students, their colleagues, the president and the board of trustees.

" 'The commander of the Bronxville Post of the American Legion then entered the situation and wrote a letter which demanded, under threat of the "fullest publicity," that the president give an "official" answer to questions relating to possible Communist party membership or sympathy on the part of Sarah Lawrence faculty members.' " N. Y. Times, Jan. 23, 1952.

"At a meeting here tonight the American Legion returned to its attack on Sarah Lawrence College of Bronxville, accusing it of ignoring charges that one of its faculty members is a Communist.

"The accused man is Joseph Barnes, former foreign editor of The New York Herald-Tribune, and now an editor for Simon [and] Schuster, publishers, who denied the charges when they were made by witnesses before the Senate subcommittee on internal security. Dr. Harold Taylor, president of the college, has denounced the Legion's attacks, of which tonight's is the third, as an infringement upon academic security. . . .

"After detailing these and other charges, Mr. Saunders asserted that the most restrained description his committee could formulate for Mr. Barnes was that he was 'an academic security risk.' He charged the college with 'academic betrayal' in entrusting to him the teaching of young women in a course on 'contemporary issues.' Quoting the college catalogue to the effect that the purpose of this course was to teach students how to 'recognize distortion' and 'become familiar with the influence on news of pressure groups and propagandists,' he said that this statement 'deserves some sort of award for unconscious humor.'

"Mr. Saunders also criticized Dr. Taylor for having described Mr. Barnes, after the charges against him had been disclosed, as 'a valuable addition to our faculty.' When Mr. Barnes offered to resign from the faculty, according to Mr. Saunders, Mr. Taylor rejected the resignation. . . .

"Mr. Saunders continued, the Legion is entitled to specific replies, not generalities. He charged the newspapers with hanging up a 'paper curtain concealing the facts of our dispute with Sarah Lawrence College.' " N. Y. Times, Apr. 10, 1952.

### b. Controversies over School Systems

For a dramatic account of a successful challenge to the "progressive" educational policies of Willard Goslin, Superintendent of Schools in Pasadena, see Hulburd, *This Happened in Pasadena* (1951). Similar controversies have taken place in Scarsdale, N. Y., Englewood, N. J., and other places. See N. Y. Times, April 4 and 8, 1952 (Scarsdale); McWilliams, *Our Town in Turmoil*, The Nation, June 16, 1951, p. 558 (Englewood).

### 5. The General Picture

In 1951 the New York Times made a survey of the status of academic freedom at 72 major colleges in the United States. Reporting numerous infringements of the principles of academic freedom, it drew the following conclusions:

"A subtle, creeping paralysis of freedom of thought and speech is attacking college campuses in many parts of the country, limiting both students and faculty in the area traditionally reserved for the free exploration of knowledge and truth.

"These limitations on free inquiry take a variety of forms, but their net effect is a widening tendency toward passive acceptance of the status quo, conformity, and a narrowing of the area of tolerance in which students, faculty and administrators feel free to speak, act and think independently. . . .

"Discussions with student leaders, teachers and administrators—in most instances names were withheld for fear of reprisal or criticism—disclosed that this censorship, wariness, caution and inhibition largely took these forms:

"1. A reluctance to speak out on controversial issues in and out of class.

"2. A reluctance to handle currently unpopular concepts even in classroom work where they may be part of the study program.

"3. An unwillingness to join student political clubs.

"4. Neglect of humitarian causes because they may be suspect in the minds of politically unsophisticated officials.

"5. An emphasis on lack of affiliations.

"6. An unusual amount of serio-comic joking about this or that official investigating committee 'getting you.'

"7. A shying away, both physically and intellectually, from any association with the words, 'liberal,' 'peace,' 'freedom,' and from classmates of a liberal stripe.

"8. A sharp turning inward to local college problems, to the exclusion of broader current questions." N. Y. Times, May 10, 1951.[12]

In a study of conditions in the lower schools the New York Times reached similar conclusions regarding the effect of pressures in restraining freedom of thought and discussion among

---

[12] The Times report summarized other factors in the picture as follows:

"Among college administrators, faculties and students there is a small but alert and growing army of defenders of free inquiry and speech, pressing with increasing vigor against repression. . . .

"Broadly speaking, the study showed that caution, wariness and inhibition, induced by current pressures, live side by side with free scholarship and independent inquiry.

"Some institutions reported no basic change in their academic freedom, no inhibitions among students or faculties.

"Others reported that restrictions in and out of the classroom have themselves stimulated a growing concern for the need for preserving independent thinking and speech." New York Times, May 11, 1951.

**837**

teachers, students and administrators. N. Y. Times, Jan. 18, 1952.[13]

A statement of the point of view which underlies and supports the challenge to some of the current trends in educational theory and practice appears in Kuhn, *Your Child is Their Target,* American Legion Magazine, June 1952, p. 18:

"There has been a subtle, dangerous movement inside our educational system, slow and tentative at first, picking up speed as it accumulated strength and power, especially in the past fifteen years. The movement has been more than an adaptation to changing times of teaching trends and methods, as its proponents have openly asserted. It has been a deliberate, calculated action by a small but powerful group of educators not only to change the character of American education radically, but to capture the 'whole child,' usurp parental authority and so nullify moral and spiritual influences. . . .

"Generally speaking, then, the course of the radical educators toward their aims and objectives was smooth enough after their first serious set-back—the discontinuance by many schools of the use of Dr. Rugg's books 'The Rugg Social Science Series.' It might almost be said that the victory won by their perceptive early critics had put these self-styled 'frontier thinkers' on guard; and while sporadic and isolated criticisms continued to be made against them; they were usually able to fend their critics off and continue the subtle change-over from traditional, disciplined education to the socialistic type known variously as 'progressive education,' 'common learnings,' and 'activity program,' this last a name Dr. Dewey favored in his efforts to substitute 'experience curricula' for well-thought-out courses of study. . . .

"The battle is joined now and the controversy is raging between the groups of aroused parents and patriotic citizens and the professional opposition. The parents are as yet largely unorganized, but their strength lies in their hardy individualism. . . . The professional opposition is far from solid among the country's teachers. Most of them are where

---

[13] For a detailed account of 53 incidents involving issues of academic freedom, occurring at colleges and universities during the academic year 1951–52, see The Harvard Crimson, *Academic Freedom Survey,* June 17, 1952 (the fourth annual survey conducted by the Crimson). For other surveys and expressions of concern see Watson, *Teachers and the "Thing",* The Nation, Nov. 3, 1951, p. 371; Barth, *The Loyalty of Free Men,* ch. IX (1951); Biddle, *The Fear of Freedom,* pp. 155–81 (1951); Watson, *The Public Schools Retreat from Freedom,* The Nation, June 28, 1952, p. 653; Wilson, *Academic Freedom and American Society,* The Nation, June 28, 1952, p. 658.

they've always been—on the side of sound American teaching, adjusted to meet changing conditions and times, but not dedicated to deliberate excesses and continuous experimentation. The organized minority entrenched in power and well financed, is supported by the alien ideological groups within the country as well as the cynical native architects of revolutionary change. . . .

"Let us not forget, too, that jobs are involved. Many of the professional educators and lobbyists involved in the agitation are actually rightists, even extreme conservatives, but as administrators or highly paid educational executives connected with high power, high pressure educational lobbies they are more concerned with the perpetuation of the 'educational trust' than they are with pedagogical methods or left-wing education. These people protect the pinkoes, collectivists, Marxists and commies because they are part of their gang and the gang must stand together. However, even though these people are not ideologically sympathetic with the commies, they can be almost as dangerous.

"The controversy will rage and flare even higher, because emotions as well as jobs are involved. Charges and counter-charges will be hurled. The smear will spread and deepen as the fight goes on to *recapture* the lost values of traditional American education and return the schools to teachers who want to use them as schools to educate students, not as experimental stations where the children are guinea pigs for the development of new social and political attitudes to help mould the welfare-socialist state. . . .

". . . the socialist character of education . . . is extremely strong; and educators today who believe in and disseminate socialist doctrines as part of school curricula are numerous indeed. In fact, these 'frontier thinkers' were few in number but they were able to go a long way and acquire a big following before any real barriers were thrown up against them."[14]

For the point of view which supports "progressive" trends in education but believes the Communist influence in academic institutions has been underestimated, see Hook, *Academic Integrity and Academic Freedom*, Commentary, October 1949, p. 329; Kristol, *"Civil Liberties," 1952—A Study in Confusion*, Commentary, March 1952, p. 228.

---

[14] Don Wilson, National Commander of the American Legion, was reported as saying that the Kuhn article accurately represented the Legion point of view. N. Y. Times, July 3, 1952.

## C. THE PATTERN OF CONTROL

The extent to which the principles of academic freedom are or may be realized in practice depends, in the first instance, upon the pattern of control over academic institutions. This section attempts to survey briefly the basic structure of power in which the educational system operates.

The institutions exercising legal and actual control over education—state legislatures and local boards of education elected by majority vote, state boards appointed by the executive, school administrations, faculties, and private groups—left to themselves might not in practice produce a result always consistent with principles of academic freedom. It is necessary to examine, therefore, what legal or institutional devices are available to limit or temper the basic powers in order to approach academic freedom in reality. Section D considers possible constitutional and judicial protections, Section E deals with statutory and contractual protections, and Section F takes up protections based upon voluntary association and self-organization.

### 1. State Legislatures

Ultimate legal power over academic institutions rests primarily in the state legislature. The state constitution usually provides that the state shall establish and maintain a "free and uniform" system of education. Over this public school system the legislature exercises a direct and plenary control, subject to constitutional restrictions to be discussed later. Thus the legislature is empowered to create, alter and classify school districts; to levy taxes and make appropriations in furtherance of educational purposes; to build and maintain buildings, equipment and other school facilities and to deny or extend use of these facilities to private citizens and organizations. It may authorize the purchase and distribution of textbooks, and control the curriculum by compelling or prohibiting the teaching of certain subjects. As proprietor of the public school system, the legislature may specify the qualifications, such as the achievement of minimum educational standards, for employment of teachers and other personnel; determine wages, hours of work, vacation periods and other conditions of employment; create, alter or abolish teaching and administrative positions; provide for the hiring, promotion, discipline and discharge of personnel; and otherwise control the efficiency of the school system.

The legislature ordinarily delegates much of its authority to subordinate agencies such as state and local school boards.

It may at any time amend its action, however, and hence change or divest subordinate agencies of powers delegated to them. Moreover, through use of the appropriating and investigating powers it may keep constant surveillance over the activities of these administrative bodies.

As a proper exercise of its power to regulate "in the interest of public health, safety and morals," the State may compel all children to attend public school or otherwise to satisfy the educational requirements specified by law. In this, the natural right of the parent to the control of his child is subservient to the interest of the State in guaranteeing an intelligent and informed citizenry.

For discussions of the extent of legislative control over the school system see Edwards, *The Courts and the Public Schools*, pp. 1–25 (1933); Garber, *Yearbook of School Law*, pp. 1–8 (1950); Elliott and Chambers, *The Colleges and the Courts*, pp. 146–54 (1936); Chambers, *The Colleges and the Courts* (1941, 1946 and 1952); Hill, *Control of Tax Supported Higher Education in the United States* (1934) (studies of the development and control of tax supported institutions in each of the states). See, generally, Council of State Governments, *The Forty-Eight State School Systems* (1949).

On the extent and exercise of legislative control over the curriculum see also Flanders, *Legislative Control of the Elementary Curriculum* (1925); Turck, *State Control of Public School Curriculum*, 15 Ky. L. J. 277 (1927); Brudney, *Legislative Regulation of Social Studies in Secondary Schools*, 9 Yearbook of School Law 140 (1941); Keesecker, *Education for Freedom as Provided by State Laws* (United States Office of Education, Bulletin 11, 1948); Kelly and McNeely, *The State and Higher Education*, Part I (1933); Note, *Academic Freedom and the Law*, 46 Yale L. J. 670 (1937).

Beyond the area of the public school system, however, the power of the state becomes more limited. Thus it is well established that state power over education does not extend so far as to deny parents the right to provide their children the education required by law in other than the public schools. Hence parents may educate their children at home, provided the minimum educational standards are met.

More important, the Supreme Court has ruled that a state may not prohibit the establishment of private schools. *Pierce v. Society of Sisters*, 268 U. S. 510, 69 L. Ed. 1070, 45 S. Ct. 571 (1925). In that case an Oregon statute sought to eliminate the private and parochial school systems by compelling all children between the ages of eight and sixteen to attend the public

**841**

school. The Supreme Court held the Act invalid as a violation of the due process clause of the Fourteenth Amendment:

". . . we think it entirely plain that the Act of 1922 unreasonably interferes with the liberty of parents and guardians to direct the upbringing and education of children under their control. As often heretofore pointed out, rights guaranteed by the Constitution may not be abridged by legislation which has no reasonable relation to some purpose within the competency of the State. The fundamental theory of liberty upon which all governments in this Union repose excludes any general power of the State to standardize its children by forcing them to accept instruction from public teachers only. The child is not the mere creature of the State; those who nurture him and direct his destiny have the right, coupled with the high duty, to recognize and prepare him for additional obligations." 268 U. S. at 534–5.[1]

The state may, of course, exercise its general police power to regulate or even prohibit private schools to the extent necessary in the interests of public health, safety or morals. Thus it may require private schools to obtain a license to operate, prescribe minimum standards of operation, provide for regular inspection to ensure that the standards are being maintained, control the right to confer degrees, and require licenses of the schools' graduates, as in medicine and law.[2]

At one time Article I, Section 10 of the Federal Constitution, prohibiting the States from impairing the obligation of contracts, threatened to become a serious limitation upon state power over private educational institutions functioning under state charter. Thus in the famous *Dartmouth College Case* the Supreme Court held unconstitutional an act of the New Hampshire legislature changing the powers and composition of the Board of Trustees of Dartmouth College without its consent, on the ground that the charter constituted a contract obligation which could not be impaired by the State. *Dartmouth*

---

[1] In accord is *Columbia Trust Co. v. Lincoln Institute of Kentucky*, 138 Ky. 804, 129 S. W. 113 (1910), in which an act prohibiting the establishment of a private school without the consent of the majority of voters in the precinct where the proposed school was to be erected and maintained was held unconstitutional. The court said that the legislature could not prohibit the establishment of a private school unless it could be shown that it was "in some way inimical to the public safety, the public health, or the public morals."

[2] Such licensing and other regulations may not be couched in such general terms as to violate constitutional requirements concerning delegation of legislative power. See *Packer Collegiate Institute v. University of the State of New York*, 298 N. Y. 184, 81 N. E. 2d 80 (1948), noted in 49 Col. L. Rev. 573 (1949).

*College v. Woodward,* 4 Wheat. 518, 4 L. Ed. 629 (1819).
Since that decision, however, most charters granted by the
states to educational institutions expressly reserve the right
to amend, alter or repeal. This has been effective in avoiding
the limitations of the contract clause. Thus Kentucky granted
to Berea College a charter defining its business as "the education of all persons who may attend its institution of learning. . . ." But the charter reserved to the state the right
to alter or repeal. Subsequently Kentucky passed a law prohibiting the maintenance of any school where white and Negro
students were received together as pupils for instruction, unless they were taught in separate branches at a distance of at
least twenty-five miles from each other. Berea College contended that the statute so changed its charter as to violate the
contract clause. But the Supreme Court upheld the statute,
saying that the state had reserved the power to alter or repeal
and the law did not "defeat or substantially impair the object
of the grant." *Berea College v. Kentucky,* 211 U. S. 45, 53
Ed. 81, 29 S. Ct. 33 (1908).[3]

The states have long encouraged the establishment of privately owned and controlled schools by allowing them exemption
from taxation. Some states have supplied textbooks, transportation and other services to children attending private as well
as public schools. See *Cochran v. Board of Education,* 281
U. S. 370, 74 L. Ed. 913, 50 S. Ct. 335 (1930) ; on the church-
state issue involved here, see Chapter VIII, *infra.* Presumably
a direct grant of funds to private schools would be invalid as
not constituting an expenditure for a public purpose. But the
states may enter into contracts with private institutions, and
in this manner supply them with public funds in return for
services performed. All these forms of assistance give the
state an indirect control of substantial importance over private
institutions.

See, generally, Bartlett, *State Control of Private Incorporated Institutions of Higher Education* (1926) ; Chambers,
*supra,* pp. 44–69 (1946), pp. 77–81 (1952) ; Elliott and Chambers, *supra,* pp. 179–199 ; Elliott and Chambers, *Charters and
Basic Laws of Selected American Universities and Colleges*
(1934) ; Graves, *The Administration of American Education*
(1932) ; McLaughlin, *A History of State Legislation Affecting Private Elementary and Secondary Schools in the United
States, 1870–1945* (1946) ; Note, *supra,* 46 Yale L. J. 670
(1937).

---

[3] For material dealing with other constitutional limitations, see Section
D, *infra.*

## 2. Federal Government

While the principal control over academic institutions is exercised at the state and local level, the influence of the Federal Government is not without significance. Under its taxing and spending powers the Federal Government provides various forms of tax exemption of benefit to educational institutions; has made various grants of funds to land-grant colleges and for school buildings, hot lunches, vocational educational programs, scholarships, and the like; and has established the Office of Education to administer Federal grants, conduct research programs, and advise and consult with State and local, public and private, educational institutions. These powers carry with them the authority to make the receipt of government benefits conditional upon compliance with Federally imposed requirements that are reasonably related to the use of the original power. See *Steward Machine Co. v. Davis*, 301 U. S. 548, 81 L. Ed. 1279, 57 S. Ct. 883 (1937); *Helvering v. Davis*, 301 U. S. 619, 81 L. Ed. 1307, 57 S. Ct. 904 (1937). Bills establishing a system of direct grants in aid to the states for educational purposes have thus far failed to pass because of disagreement over such conditions. See Chapter VIII, *infra*.

In addition, the Federal Government, particularly through the Defense Department and the Atomic Energy Commission, has been awarding educational institutions large sums under contract arrangements. It is not unusual to find certain departments of universities largely dependent upon such contracts. The arrangement gives the Federal Government potentially great influence over personnel and methods of operation of educational institutions.

The Federal legislature also possesses a significant control over academic institutions through the use of the investigatory power. Congressional investigating committees have frequently probed into alleged subversive activities on the part of persons affiliated with educational institutions, and the power to investigate the textbooks, curriculum and other aspects of academic operation would appear to exist and has been exercised. See Chapter IV, *supra*.

Finally, the Federal Government exercises the same powers as a State over education in the District of Columbia. The example it sets in this regard can have an important influence upon the States and localities.

For discussion see *A Symposium in Federal Legislation Relating to Education*, 30 Iowa L. Rev. 155 (1945); Note, 23 Temple L. Q. 227 (1950); Mitchell, *Religion and Federal Aid to Education,* 14 Law and Contemp. Prob. 113 (1949); Russell, *Federal Activities in Higher Education After the Second World War* (1951) (containing bibliography); House Committee on Education and Labor, *Federal Educational Activities and Educational Issues before Congress,* 82d Cong., 1st Sess., vol. 1, pts. 1–2 (1951).

## 3. State and Local School Boards

Control over actual operation of public educational institutions is customarily delegated to a state board of education and to local boards of education. The state board is normally appointed by the governor, often subject to legislative confirmation, but the local boards are more frequently elected. Governing boards of state colleges and universities are usually also appointed by the governor, subject to confirmation. The relationship between state and local boards varies in the different states but the normal pattern is for the local boards to exercise extensive direct control, subject to state legislation and general regulations of the state boards.

Subject to controlling regulations the appropriate school boards usually possess broad authority to employ, promote, discipline and discharge teachers and other personnel; to determine their compensation; to prescribe the curriculum, textbooks and teaching methods; to control the use of school property; to provide transportation and supplies; and generally to carry on the operation of the public school system.

These powers of the school boards are often exercised in detailed and far-reaching ways. Thus it has not been infrequent for the boards to impose extensive restrictions upon the social and intellectual activities of teachers, including rules concerning their right to join organizations, the extent of their participation in community life, and their personal conduct, such as smoking, getting married, or even "falling in love." In general the courts have shown extreme reluctance to interfere with the decisions of school boards except where it clearly appears that the board is acting in disregard of statutory requirements or in a malicious, arbitrary or unreasonable fashion. See Section E, *infra.*

For general accounts of the powers and practices of school boards see Beale, *Are American Teachers Free?* (1936); *The Status and Practices of Boards of Education,* 24 Nat'l Ed. Ass'n Research Bull., No. 2 (1946); Hill, *supra;* Messick, *The Discretionary Powers of School Boards* (1949) and cases there cited; *Yearbook of School Law* (1950, 1951, 1952); Note, *supra,* 46 Yale L. J. 670.

A number of studies have been made of the economic and social status of school board members and their basic social outlook. In general these surveys have shown that members of school boards are drawn almost entirely from the upper-economic business and professional classes. Rarely are members of minority groups, or lower income groups, chosen to serve on the school board. Furthermore, elections are usually on a political basis, as is the case with other municipal offices, and rarely is educational policy determined independently of political considerations. See 24 Nat'l Ed. Ass'n Research Bull. *supra;* McKendree, *Composition of State Boards of Education in the United States* (1941); Counts, *Social Composition of Boards of Education* (1927); Arnett, *Social Beliefs and Attitudes of American School Board Members* (1932); Beck, *Men Who Control Our Universities* (1947); Tenth Yearbook of the John Dewey Society (Benjamin, ed.), *Democracy in the Administration of Higher Education,* ch. IX (1950). See also Curti, *Social Ideas of American Educators,* esp. ch. VI, *The School and the Triumph of Business Enterprise* (1935); Veblen, *The Higher Learning in America* (1918).

## 4. Administration of Private Educational Institutions

Administrative control of private educational institutions is usually vested in a board of trustees or comparable body, the administrative head, and the faculty. The relationship between these groups varies considerably. In most institutions of higher learning the faculty exercises considerable autonomy over the curriculum, methods of instruction, research, and the hiring, promotion and discharge of faculty members. The same tends to be true of state supported universities and colleges. This tradition of faculty autonomy is one of the most significant factors in maintaining academic freedom in higher education.[4]

---

[4] For one statement of the tradition see Hutchins (then Chancellor of the University of Chicago), *The Freedom of the University,* 37 Am. Ass'n of U. Prof. Bull. 238, 248–9 (1951): "Obviously a high degree of responsibility, forbearance, and understanding is required of trustees under the American system if they are to allow it to become a center of independent thought and are not to follow the natural lines suggested by the fact that a large university looks like any other large corporation. The complete legal control of the board of regents or trustees is undoubted. But as the minister of education in a European country is required to restrain the impulse to use his legal powers because of the traditional rights of faculties, and the faculties of Oxford and Cambridge are not irresponsible, though they might be if they wished, so the American board of trustees, in spite of its legal control of the university, might limit itself to criticism of the educational and scientific program of the university, to the conservation and development of its funds, and to the interpretation of the

On the other hand faculty control in itself creates important problems of academic freedom; for a faculty or department can and often does exert substantial pressure toward academic conformity, particularly on younger faculty members or students and graduates seeking teaching positions.

In general see John Dewey Society, *Democracy in the Administration of Higher Education* (1950); Flexner, *Universities: American, English, German* (1930).

## 5. The Influence of Private Groups

Private individuals and pressure groups exercise considerable influence over policy formulated by boards of education, trustees, and other controlling bodies. Among those which have been most successful in their educational campaigns are various military groups such as the American Legion and the Veterans of Foreign Wars, the Freemasons, the Knights of Columbus, religious groups, the Chambers of Commerce, public utilities, the Woman's Christian Temperance Union and the Anti-Saloon League. Occasionally trade-unions have successfully exerted influence, particularly with regard to anti-labor bias in school texts. See Lynd and Lynd, *Middletown in Transition*, pp. 233–40 (1937); Beale, *Are American Teachers Free?* (1936); Pierce, *Citizens' Organizations and the Civic Training of Youth* (1933); Jorgensen, *The Betrayal of Our Public Schools* (1930); Blanshard, *American Freedom and Catholic Power*, ch. IV

---

university to the public. Those who have the legal control should be wise enough to refrain from exercising it. In this view the trustees become not the managers of the university but its best friends and severest critics, laymen who are interested in the university, who believe in it, and who wish to assist it. I do not subscribe to the notion that the board should operate the university as the representative of the community. Nor do I subscribe to the notion that the board is a kind of supreme court that should decide educational issues brought before it. This would mean that the board would be determining the educational policy of the institution, something that even the best boards are not qualified to do.

"An extreme statement of this position would be that the faculties could ask the trustees or regents to take an oath supporting the aims of the faculties, since the principal duty of trustees and regents is to further those aims, but that the trustees and regents could not exact such expressions from faculties in regard to the aims of trustees and regents. To put the extreme position another way: a trustee, or a board of trustees, who did not like what the faculty or a faculty member was doing should resign. It should never occur to trustees that faculty members should resign because they do not share the opinions of trustees. The most important right that the trustees have is the right of criticism. I think that two propositions are true: first, a university is a center of independent thought and, second, uncriticized groups inevitably deteriorate. The solution of the problem lies, then, not in regulation or in control but in criticism."

(1949) ; Gellermann, *The American Legion as Educator* (1938) ; Raup, *Education and Organized Interests in America* (1936) ; Duffield, *King Legion* (1931) ; Hapgood, *Professional Patriots* (1927) ; Pierce, *Public Opinion and the Teaching of History* (1926) ; Sinclair, *The Goslings* (1924) ; Waller, *Outside Demands and Pressures on the Public Schools* (1932) ; Note, *School Boards, Schoolbooks, and the Freedom to Learn,* 59 Yale L. J. 928 (1950). For an account of the activities of the public utilities in the educational field, see Note, 56 Yale L. J. 304, 311–3 (1947). See also Section B, *supra.*

Insofar as private institutions are supported financially to a considerable extent by alumni contributions, the alumni may exercise great influence over the educational policies of the administration. See Hutchins, *The Freedom of the University,* 37 A. A. U. P. Bull. 238, 249 (1951) ; Buckley, *God and Man at Yale* (1951) (urging alumni to demand adherence to their policies as a condition of making contributions) ; *cf.* the Ober-Conant-Clark correspondence, Harvard Alumni Bulletin, June 25, 1949, p. 730 (President Conant and Trustee Clark rejecting proposals of Alumnus Ober to restrain Harvard faculty members in outside political activities).

## D. CONSTITUTIONAL PROTECTION OF ACADEMIC FREEDOM

### SCOPES v. STATE
Supreme Court of Tennessee, 1927
154 Tenn. 105, 289 S. W. 363

CHIEF JUSTICE GREEN delivered majority opinion; JUDGE CHAMBLISS concurring opinion, and JUSTICE COOK concurred; JUDGE COLIN P. MCKINNEY, opinion dissenting, and JUDGE SWIGGART did not participate.

Scopes was convicted of a violation of chapter 27 of the Acts of 1925 for that he did teach in the public schools of Rhea county a certain theory that denied the story of the divine creation of man, as taught in the Bible, and did teach instead thereof that man had descended from a lower order of animals. After a verdict of guilty by the jury, the trial judge imposed a fine of $100, and Scopes brought the case to this court by an appeal in the nature of a writ of error. . . .

Chapter 27 of the Acts of 1925, known as the Tennessee Anti-evolution Act is set out in the margin.[1] . . .

---

[1] An Act prohibiting the teaching of the Evolution Theory in all the Universities, Normals and all other public schools of Tennessee, which are

[The] Act's title clearly indicates the purpose of the Statute to be the prohibition of teaching in the Schools of the State that man has developed or descended from some lower type or order of animals. . . .

It thus seems plain that the Legislature in this enactment only intended to forbid teaching that man descended from a lower order of animals. The denunciation of any theory denying the Bible story of creation is restricted by the caption and by the final clause of section 1.

So interpreted the Statute does not seem to be uncertain in its meaning nor incapable of enforcement for such a reason, notwithstanding the great argument to the contrary. The indictment herein follows the language of the Statute. . . . The assignments of error which challenge the sufficiency of the indictment and the certainty of the Act are accordingly overruled.

It is contended that the Statute violates section 8 of article 1 of the Tennessee Constitution, and section 1 of the Fourteenth Amendment to the Constitution of the United States—the Law of the Land clause of the State Constitution, and the Due Process of Law clause of the Federal Constitution, which are practically equivalent in meaning.

We think there is little merit in this contention. The plaintiff in error was a teacher in the public schools of Rhea county. He was an employee of the State of Tennessee or of a municipal agency of the State. He was under contract with the State to work in an institution of the State. He had no right or privilege to serve the State except upon such terms as the State prescribed. His liberty, his privilege, his immunity to teach and proclaim the theory of evolution, elsewhere than in the service of the State, was in no wise touched by this law.

The Statute before us is not an exercise of the police power of the State undertaking to regulate the conduct and contracts of individuals in their dealings with each other. On the other hand it is an Act of the State as a corporation, a proprietor, an employer. It is a declaration of a master as to the character of work the master's servant shall, or rather shall not, perform. In dealing with its own employees engaged upon its

---

supported in whole, or in part, by the public school funds of the State, and to provide penalties for the violation, thereof.

Section 1. Be it enacted by the General Assembly of the State of Tennessee, That it shall be unlawful for any teacher in any of the Universities, Normals, and all other public schools of the State, which are supported in whole or in part by the public school funds of the State, to teach any theory that denies the story of the Divine Creation of man, as taught in the Bible, and to teach instead, that man has descended from a lower order of animals. . . .

own work, the State is not hampered by the limitations of section 8 of article 1 of the Tennessee Constitution, nor of the Fourteenth Amendment to the Constitution of the United States. . . .

Since the State may prescribe the character and the hours of labor of the employees on its works, just as freely may it say what kind of work shall be performed in its service—what shall be taught in its schools, so far at least as section 8 of article 1 of the Tennessee Constitution, and the Fourteenth Amendment to the Constitution of the United States are concerned.

But it is urged that chapter 27 of the Acts of 1925 conflicts with section 12 of article 11, the Education clause, and section 3 of article 1, the Religious Preference clause of the Tennessee Constitution. It is to be doubted if the plaintiff in error, before us only as the State's employee, is sufficiently protected by these constitutional provisions to justify him in raising such questions. Nevertheless as the State appears to concede that these objections are properly here made, the court will consider them.

The relevant portion of section 12 of article 11 of the Constitution is in these words:

". . . It shall be the duty of the General Assembly in all future periods of this government to cherish Literature and Science."

The argument is that the theory of the descent of man from a lower order of animals is now established by the preponderance of scientific thought and that the prohibition of the teaching of such theory is a violation of the legislative duty to cherish Science.

While this clause of the Constitution has been mentioned in several of our cases, these references have been casual, and no Act of the Legislature has ever been held inoperative by reason of such provision. In one of the opinions in *Green* v. *Allen*, 24 Tenn. (5 Humph.), 170, the provision was said to be directory. Although this court is loath to say that any language of the Constitution is merely directory, *State* v. *Burrow*, 119 Tenn., 376; *Webb* v. *Carter*, 129 Tenn., 182, we are driven to the conclusion that this particular admonition must be so treated. It is too vague to be enforced by any court. To cherish Science means to nourish, to encourage, to foster Science.

In no case can the court directly compel the Legislature to perform its duty. In a plain case the court can prevent the Legislature from transgressing its duty under the Constitution

[Emerson]

by declaring ineffective such a legislative Act. The case, however, must be plain and the legislative Act is always given the benefit of any doubt. . . .

If the Legislature thinks that by reason of popular prejudice, the cause of education and the study of Science generally will be promoted for forbidding the teaching of evolution in the schools of the State, we can conceive of no ground to justify the courts' interference. The courts cannot sit in judgment on such Acts of the Legislature or its agents and determine whether, or not, the omission or addition of a particular course of study tends "to cherish Science."

The last serious criticism made of the Act is that it contravenes the provision of section 3 of article 1 of the Constitution, "that no preference shall ever be given by law to any religious establishment or mode of worship." . . .

We are not able to see how the prohibition of teaching the theory that man has descended from a lower order of animals gives preference to any religious establishment or mode of worship. So far as we know there is no religious establishment or organized body that has [in] its creed or confession of faith any article denying or affirming such a theory. So far as we know the denial or affirmation of such a theory does not enter into any recognized mode of worship. Since this cause has been pending in this court, we have been favored, in addition to briefs of counsel and various *amici curiae*, with a multitude of resolutions, addresses and communications from scientific bodies, religious factions, and individuals giving us the benefit of their views upon the theory of evolution. Examination of these contributions indicates that Protestants, Catholics, and Jews are divided among themselves in their beliefs, and that there is no unanimity among the members of any religious establishment as to this subject. Belief or unbelief in the theory of evolution is no more a characteristic of any religious establishment or mode of worship than is belief or unbelief in the wisdom of the prohibition laws. It would appear that members of the same churches quite generally disagree as to these things.

Furthermore, chapter 27 of the Acts of 1925 *requires* the teaching of nothing. It only forbids the teaching of the evolution of man from a lower order of animals. Chapter 102 of the Acts of 1915 requires that ten verses from the Bible be read each day at the opening of every public school, without comment and provided the teacher does not read the same verses more than twice during any session. It is also provided in this Act that pupils may be excused from the Bible readings upon the written request of their parents.

As the law thus stands, while the theory of evolution of man may not be taught in the schools of the State, nothing contrary to that theory is required to be taught. It could scarcely be said that the statutory scriptural reading just mentioned would amount to the teaching of a contrary theory.

Our school authorities are, therefore, quite free to determine how they shall act in this state of the law. Those in charge of the educational affairs of the State are men and women of discernment and culture. If they believe that the teaching of the Science of Biology has been so hampered by chapter 27 of the Acts of 1925 as to render such an effort no longer desirable, this course of study may be entirely omitted from the curriculum of our schools. If this be regarded as a misfortune, it must be charged to the Legislature. It should be repeated that the Act of 1925 deals with nothing but the evolution of man from a lower order of animals. . . .

Much has been said in argument about the motives of the Legislature in passing this Act. But the validity of a Statute must be determined by its natural and legal effect, rather than proclaimed motives. *Lochner v. New York*, 198 U. S. 45; *Grainger v. Douglas Park Jockey Club*, 148 Fed. 513; 6 R. C. L. 111, 81. . . .

This record discloses that the jury found the defendant below guilty but did not assess the fine. The trial judge himself undertook to impose the minimum fine of $100 authorized by the Statute. This was error. Under section 14 of article 6 of the Constitution of Tennessee, a fine in excess of $50 must be assessed by a jury. The Statute before us does not permit the imposition of a smaller fine than $100.

Since a jury alone can impose the penalty this Act requires and as a matter of course no different penalty can be inflicted, the trial judge exceeded his jurisdiction in levying this fine and we are without power to correct his error. The judgment must accordingly be reversed. *Upchurch v. The State*, 153 Tenn., 198.

The court is informed that the plaintiff in error is no longer in the service of the State. We see nothing to be gained by prolonging the life of this bizarre case. On the contrary we think the peace and dignity of the State, which all criminal prosecutions are brought to redress, will be the better conserved by the entry of a *nolle prosequi* herein. Such a course is suggested to the Attorney-General.

[The concurring opinion of Judge Chambliss is omitted.

**852**

Judge McKinney dissented on the ground that the statute was invalid for uncertainty.]

## Note

1. The *Scopes* case attracted world-wide attention and has been widely commented upon in leading texts and journals. See Waller, *The Constitutionality of the Tennessee Anti-Evolution Act*, 35 Yale L. J. 191 (1925); Keebler, *Limitations Upon the State's Control of Public Education: A Critical Analysis of State of Tennessee v. Scopes*, 6 Tenn. L. Rev. 153 (1928); Lippmann, *American Inquisitors* (1928); Shipley, *The War on Modern Science* (1927). See also Chapter VIII *infra*. The transcript of the Scopes trial has been published under the title, *The World's Most Famous Court Trial* (1925). For a description of the trial, by one of Scopes' counsel, see Hays, *Let Freedom Ring*, pp. 26–89 (rev. ed., 1937).

2. In 1940, when Bertrand Russell was appointed as Professor of Philosophy in the City College of New York, the appointment was challenged by a taxpayer's suit. *Kay v. Board of Higher Education,* 173 Misc. 943, 18 N. Y. Supp. 2d 821 (1940), aff'd without opinion 259 App. Div. 879, 20 N. Y. Supp. 2d 1016 (1940). The court, after finding that Bertrand Russell was neither a citizen nor competent under the standards of fitness required by state law, and hence on both grounds disqualified to teach, turned to the question whether the appointment was against public policy:

"In this consideration I am completely dismissing any question of Mr. Russell's attacks upon religion, but there are certain basic principles upon which this government is founded. If a teacher, who is a person not of good moral character, is appointed by any authority the appointment violates these essential prerequisites. One of the prerequisites of a teacher is good moral character. In fact, this is a prerequisite for appointment in civil service in the city and state, or political subdivisions, or in the United States. It needs no argument here to defend this statement. It need not be found in the Education Law. It is found in the nature of the teaching profession. Teachers are supposed not only to impart instruction in the classroom but by their example to teach the students. The taxpayers of the City of New York spend millions to maintain the colleges of the City of New York. They are not spending that money nor was the money appropriated for the purpose of employing teachers who are not of good moral character. However, there is ample authority in the Education Law to support this contention."

The court then considers various views of Bertrand Russell, particularly on sex and marriage, as expressed in his writings. It concludes:

"Considering Dr. Russell's principles, with reference to the Penal Law of the State of New York, it appears that not only would the morals of the students be undermined, but his doctrines would tend to bring them, and in some cases their parents and guardians, in conflict with the Penal Law, and accordingly this court intervenes.

"The appointment of Dr. Russell is an insult to the people of the

**853**

City of New York and to the thousands of teachers who were obligated upon their appointment to establish good moral character and to maintain it in order to keep their positions. Considering the instances in which immorality alone has been held to be sufficient basis for removal of a teacher and mindful of the aphorism 'As a man thinketh in his heart, so he is,' the court holds that the acts of the Board of Higher Education of the City of New York in appointing Dr. Russell to the Department of Philosophy of the City College of the City of New York, to be paid by public funds, is in effect establishing a chair of indecency and in doing so has acted arbitrarily, capriciously and in direct violation of the public health, safety and morals of the people and of the petitioner's rights herein, and the petitioner is entitled to an order revoking the appointment of the said Bertrand Russell and discharging him from his said position, and denying to him the rights and privileges and the powers appertaining to his appointment."

For comment on the case see Hamilton, *Trial by Ordeal, New Style*, 50 Yale L. J. 778 (1941); Kennedy, *Portrait of a Realist, New Style*, 10 Ford. L. Rev. 196 (1941); White, *Professor Hamilton's Law*, 10 Ford. L. Rev. 205 (1941); Notes, 53 Harv. L. Rev. 1192 (1940); 8 U. of Chi. L. Rev. 316 (1941). See also Dewey and Kallen, *The Bertrand Russell Case* (1941); American Civil Liberties Union, *The Story of the Bertrand Russell Case* (1941); Cohen, *Faith of a Liberal*, ch. 21 (1946).

A similar effort to prevent Bertrand Russell from teaching at the University of California failed, the court holding plaintiff had not exhausted administrative remedies. *Wall v. Board of Regents*, 38 Cal. App. 2d 698, 102 Pac. 2d 533 (1940).

## MEYER v. NEBRASKA

Supreme Court of the United States, 1923
262 U. S. 390, 67 L. Ed. 1042, 43 S. Ct. 625

MR. JUSTICE MCREYNOLDS delivered the opinion of the Court.

Plaintiff in error was tried and convicted in the District Court for Hamilton County, Nebraska, under an information which charged that on May 25, 1920, while an instructor in Zion Parochial School, he unlawfully taught the subject of reading in the German language to Raymond Parpart, a child of ten years, who had not attained and successfully passed the eighth grade. The information is based upon "An act relating to the teaching of foreign languages in the State of Nebraska," approved April 9, 1919, which follows [Laws 1919, c. 249.]:

"Section 1. No person, individually or as a teacher, shall, in any private, denominational, parochial or public school, teach any subject to any person in any language other than the English language.

"Sec. 2. Languages, other than the English language, may

be taught as languages only after a pupil shall have attained and successfully passed the eighth grade as evidenced by a certificate of graduation issued by the county superintendent of the county in which the child resides. . . ."

The problem for our determination is whether the statute as construed and applied unreasonably infringes the liberty guaranteed to the plaintiff in error by the Fourteenth Amendment. "No State shall . . . deprive any person of life, liberty, or property, without due process of law."

While this Court has not attempted to define with exactness the liberty thus guaranteed, the term has received much consideration and some of the included things have been definitely stated. Without doubt, it denotes not merely freedom from bodily restraint but also the right of the individual to contract, to engage in any of the common occupations of life, to acquire useful knowledge, to marry, establish a home and bring up children, to worship God according to the dictates of his own conscience, and generally to enjoy those privileges long recognized at common law as essential to the orderly pursuit of happiness by free men. . . . The established doctrine is that this liberty may not be interfered with, under the guise of protecting the public interest, by legislative action which is arbitrary or without reasonable relation to some purpose within the competency of the State to effect. Determination by the legislature of what constitutes proper exercise of police power is not final or conclusive but is subject to supervision by the courts. *Lawton v. Steele,* 152 U. S. 133, 137.

The American people have always regarded education and acquisition of knowledge as matters of supreme importance which should be diligently promoted. The Ordinance of 1787 declares, "Religion, morality, and knowledge being necessary to good government and the happiness of mankind, schools and the means of education shall forever be encouraged." Corresponding to the right of control, it is the natural duty of the parent to give his children education suitable to their station in life; and nearly all the States, including Nebraska, enforce this obligation by compulsory laws.

Practically, education of the young is only possible in schools conducted by especially qualified persons who devote themselves thereto. The calling always has been regarded as useful and honorable, essential, indeed, to the public welfare. Mere knowledge of the German language cannot reasonably be regarded as harmful. Heretofore it has been commonly looked upon as helpful and desirable. Plaintiff in error taught this language in school as part of his occupation. His right thus to teach and the right of parents to engage him so to instruct their children, we think, are within the liberty of the Amendment.

The challenged statute forbids the teaching in school of any subject except in English; also the teaching of any other language until the pupil has attained and successfully passed the eighth grade, which is not usually accomplished before the age of twelve. The Supreme Court of the State has held that "the so-called ancient or dead languages" are not "within the spirit or the purpose of the act." *Nebraska District of Evangelical Lutheran Synod v. McKelvie,* 187 N. W. 927. Latin, Greek, Hebrew are not proscribed; but German, French, Spanish, Italian, and every other alien speech are within the ban. Evidently the legislature has attempted materially to interfere with the calling of modern language teachers, with the opportunities of pupils to acquire knowledge, and with the power of parents to control the education of their own.

It is said the purpose of the legislation was to promote civic development by inhibiting training and education of the immature in foreign tongues and ideals before they could learn English and acquire American ideals; and "that the English language should be and become the mother tongue of all children reared in this State." It is also affirmed that the foreign born population is very large, that certain communities commonly use foreign words, follow foreign leaders, move in a foreign atmosphere, and that the children are thereby hindered from becoming citizens of the most useful type and the public safety is imperiled.

That the State may do much, go very far, indeed, in order to improve the quality of its citizens, physically, mentally and morally, is clear; but the individual has certain fundamental rights which must be respected. The protection of the Constitution extends to all, to those who speak other languages as well as to those born with English on the tongue. Perhaps it would be highly advantageous if all had ready understanding of our ordinary speech, but this cannot be coerced by methods which conflict with the Constitution—a desirable end cannot be promoted by prohibited means. . . .

The desire of the legislature to foster a homogeneous people with American ideals prepared readily to understand current discussions of civic matters is easy to appreciate. Unfortunate experiences during the late war and aversion toward every characteristic of truculent adversaries were certainly enough to quicken that aspiration. But the means adopted, we think, exceed the limitations upon the power of the State and conflict with rights assured to plaintiff in error. The interference is plain enough and no adequate reason therefor in time of peace and domestic tranquility has been shown.

The power of the State to compel attendance at some school and to make reasonable regulations for all schools, including a requirement that they shall give instructions in English, is not questioned. Nor has challenge been made of the State's power to prescribe a curriculum for institutions which it supports. Those matters are not within the present controversy. Our concern is with the prohibition approved by the Supreme Court. *Adams v. Tanner* [244 U. S. 590, 594], pointed out that mere abuse incident to an occupation ordinarily useful is not enough to justify its abolition, although regulation may be entirely proper. No emergency has arisen which renders knowledge by a child of some language other than English so clearly harmful as to justify its inhibition with the consequent infringement of rights long freely enjoyed. We are constrained to conclude that the statute as applied is arbitrary and without reasonable relation to any end within the competency of the State.

As the statute undertakes to interfere only with teaching which involves a modern language, leaving complete freedom as to other matters, there seems no adequate foundation for the suggestion that the purpose was to protect the child's health by limiting his mental activities. It is well known that proficiency in a foreign language seldom comes to one not instructed at an early age, and experience shows that this is not injurious to the health, morals or understanding of the ordinary child.

The judgment of the court below must be reversed and the cause remanded for further proceedings not inconsistent with this opinion.

*Reversed.*

[Mr. Justice Holmes, with whom Mr. Justice Sutherland concurred, dissented. His opinion which appears in a companion case, *Bartels v. Iowa*, 262 U. S. 407, 67 L. Ed. 1947, 43 S. Ct. 628 (1923), is as follows:]

We all agree, I take it, that it is desirable that all the citizens of the United States should speak a common tongue, and therefore that the end aimed at by the statute is a lawful and proper one. The only question is whether the means adopted deprive teachers of the liberty secured to them by the Fourteenth Amendment. It is with hesitation and unwillingness that I differ from my brethren with regard to a law like this but I cannot bring my mind to believe that in some circumstances, and circumstances existing it is said in Nebraska, the statute might not be regarded as a reasonable or even necessary method of reaching the desired result. The part of the act with which we are concerned deals with the teaching of young children. Youth is the time when familiarity with a language is established and if there are sections in the State where a child would hear only Polish or French or German spoken at home I am not prepared to say that it is unreasonable to provide that in his early years he shall hear and speak only English at school. But if it is reasonable it is not an undue restriction of the liberty either of teacher or scholar. No one would doubt that a teacher might be forbidden to teach many things, and the only criterion of his liberty under the Constitution that I can think of is "whether, considering the end in view, the statute passes the bounds of reason and assumes the character of a merely arbitrary fiat." *Purity Extract & Tonic Co. v. Lynch*, 226 U. S. 192, 204. *Hebe Co. v. Shaw*, 248 U. S. 297, 303. *Jacob Ruppert v. Caffey*, 251 U.S. 264. I think I appreciate the objection to the law but it appears to me to present a question upon which men reasonably might differ and therefore I am unable to say that the Constitution of the United States prevents the experiment being tried.

I agree with the Court as to the special proviso against the German language contained in the statute dealt with in *Bohning v. Ohio.*

## Note

1. The language of teaching in the public schools had long been the subject of state regulation. Early laws required that English be taught, as a subject, in schools conducted in a foreign language. During the period of the first World War, English was made mandatory as the basic language of the public schools in many states; by 1923 thirty-four states had statutes of this kind. At the same time attempts were made to eliminate all foreign languages from the lower grades. This legislation, passed in 11 states, was directed primarily against the German language. See Beale, *Are American Teachers Free?*, pp. 332–5 (1936). Comment on the *Meyer* decision may be found in Notes, 12 Calif. L. Rev. 136 (1924); 10 Marq. L. Rev. 94 (1926); 22 Mich. L. Rev. 248 (1924); 4 Tex. L. Rev. 93 (1925); 72 U. Pa. L. Rev. 46 (1923).

In accord with the *Meyer* case are *Farrington v. Tokushige*, 273 U. S. 284, 71 L. Ed. 646, 47 S. Ct. 406 (1927) (holding unconstitutional the Foreign Language School Act of Hawaii, which the Court found imposed unreasonable language and other requirements upon schools taught in a foreign language); *Mo Hock Ke Lok Po v. Stainback*, 74 F. Supp. 852 (D. Haw., 1947) (holding unconstitutional later legislation prohibiting the teaching of a foreign language to children below a specified age or grade), reversed on other grounds, 336 U. S. 368, 93 L. Ed. 741, 69 S. Ct. 606 (1949).

2. The courts have passed upon issues of academic freedom involving the school curriculum without reference to constitutional provisions. Thus in *Rosenberg v. Board of Education*, 196 Misc. 542, 92 N. Y. Supp. 2d 344 (1949), discussed in Section B, *supra*, suit was

brought to compel the Board of Education to remove *Oliver Twist* and *The Merchant of Venice* from school classrooms and libraries. The court, in dismissing the suit, said:

"Except where a book has been maliciously written for the apparent purpose of promoting and fomenting a bigoted and intolerant hatred against a particular racial or religious group, public interest in a free and democratic society does not warrant or encourage the suppression of any book at the whim of any unduly sensitive person or group of persons, merely because a character described in such book as belonging to a particular race or religion is portrayed in a derogatory or offensive manner. The necessity for the suppression of such a book must clearly depend upon the intent and motive which has actuated the author in making such a portrayal. . . .

"Educational institutions are concerned with the development of free inquiry and learning. The administrative officers must be free to guide teachers and pupils toward that goal. Their discretion must not be interfered with in the absence of proof of actual malevolent intent. Interference by the court will result in suppression of the intended purpose of aiding those seeking education."

3. In general with respect to constitutional issues concerning curriculum, textbooks and the like, see Note, *School Boards, Schoolbooks, and the Freedom to Learn,* 59 Yale L. J. 928 (1950). On the specific problem of standing to raise these issues, see 59 Yale L. J. at 945–9.


## ADLER v. BOARD OF EDUCATION

Supreme Court of the United States, 1952
342 U. S. 485, 96 L. Ed. —, 72 S. Ct. 380

MR. JUSTICE MINTON delivered the opinion of the Court.

Appellants brought a declaratory judgment action in the Supreme Court of New York, Kings County, praying that § 12-a of the Civil Service Law,[1] as implemented by the so-called Feinberg Law,[2] be declared unconstitutional, and that action by the Board of Education of the City of New York thereunder be enjoined. On motion for judgment on the pleadings, the court held that subdivision (c) of § 12-a, the Feinberg Law, and the Rules of the State Board of Regents promulgated thereunder violated the Due Process Clause of the Fourteenth Amendment, and issued an injunction. 196 Misc. 873, 95 N.Y.S.2d 114. The Appellate Division of the Supreme Court reversed, 276 App.Div. 527, 96 N.Y.S.2d 466, and the Court of Appeals affirmed the judgment of the Appellate Division, 301 N.Y. 476, 95 N.E.2d 806. The appellants come here by appeal under 28 U.S.C. § 1257.

Section 12-a of the Civil Service Law, hereafter referred to

---

[1] N. Y. Laws 1939, c. 547, as amended N. Y. Laws 1940, c. 564.
[2] N. Y. Laws 1949, c. 360.

as § 12-a, is set forth in the margin.[3] To implement this law, the Feinberg Law was passed, adding a new section, § 3022, to the Education Law of the State of New York, which section so far as here pertinent is set forth in the margin.[4] The Fein-

[3] "§ 12-a. *Ineligibility*

"No person shall be appointed to any office or position in the service of the state or of any civil division or city thereof, nor shall any person presently employed in any such office or position be continued in such employment, nor shall any person be employed in the public service as superintendents, principals or teachers in a public school or academy or in a state normal school or college, or any other state educational institution who: (a) By word of mouth or writing wilfully and deliberately advocates, advises or teaches the doctrine that the government of the United States or of any state or of any political subdivision thereof should be overthrown or overturned by force, violence or any unlawful means; or,

"(b) Prints, publishes, edits, issues or sells, any book, paper, document or written or printed matter in any form containing or advocating, advising or teaching the doctrine that the government of the United States or of any state or of any political subdivision thereof should be overthrown by force, violence or any unlawful means, and who advocates, advises, teaches, or embraces the duty, necessity or propriety of adopting the doctrine contained therein;

"(c) Organizes or helps to organize or becomes a member of any society or group of persons which teaches or advocates that the government of the United States or of any state or of any political subdivision thereof shall be overthrown by force or violence, or by any unlawful means;

"(d) A person dismissed or declared ineligible may within four months of such dismissal or declaration of ineligibility be entitled to petition for an order to show cause signed by a justice of the supreme court, why a hearing on such charges should not be had. Until the final judgment on said hearing is entered, the order to show cause shall stay the effect of any order of dismissal or ineligibility based on the provisions of this section. The hearing shall consist of the taking of testimony in open court with opportunity for cross-examination. The burden of sustaining the validity of the order of dismissal or ineligibility by a fair preponderance of the credible evidence shall be upon the person making such dismissal or order of ineligibility."

[4] "§ 3022. *Elimination of subversive persons from the public school system*

"1. The board of regents shall adopt, promulgate, and enforce rules and regulations for the disqualification or removal of superintendents of schools, teachers or employees in the public schools in any city or school district of the state who violate the provisions of section three thousand twenty-one of this article or who are ineligible for appointment to or retention in any office or position in such public schools on any of the grounds set forth in section twelve-a of the civil service law and shall provide therein appropriate methods and procedure for the enforcement of such sections of this article and the civil service law.

"2. The board of regents shall, after inquiry, and after such notice and hearing as may be appropriate, make a listing of organizations which it finds to be subversive in that they advocate, advise, teach or embrace the doctrine that the government of the United States or of any state or of any political subdivision thereof shall be overthrown or overturned by force, violence or any unlawful means, or that they advocate, advise, teach or

berg Law was also to implement § 3021 of the Education Law of New York.[5] The constitutionality of this section was not attacked in the proceedings below.

The preamble of the Feinberg Law, § 1, makes elaborate findings that members of subversive groups, particularly of the Communist Party and its affiliated organizations, have been infiltrating into public employment in the public schools of the State; that this has occurred and continues notwithstanding the existence of protective statutes designed to prevent the appointment to or retention in employment in public office, and particularly in the public schools, of members of any organizations which teach or advocate that the government of the United States or of any state or political subdivision thereof shall be overthrown by force or violence or by any other unlawful means. As a result, propaganda can be disseminated among the children by those who teach them and to whom they look for guidance, authority, and leadership. The Legislature further found that the members of such groups use their positions to advocate and teach their doctrines, and are frequently bound by oath, agreement, pledge, or understanding to follow, advocate and teach a prescribed party line or group dogma or doctrine without regard to truth or free inquiry. This propaganda, the Legislature declared, is sufficiently subtle to escape detection in the classroom; thus, the menace of such infiltration into the classroom is difficult to measure. Finally, to protect the children from such influence, it was thought essential that the laws prohibiting members of such groups, such as the Communist Party or its affiliated organizations, from obtaining or retaining employment in the public schools be rig-

---

embrace the duty, necessity or propriety of adopting any such doctrine, as set forth in section twelve-a of the civil service law. Such listings may be amended and revised from time to time. The board, in making such inquiry, may utilize any similar listings or designations promulgated by any federal agency or authority authorized by federal law, regulation or executive order, and for the purposes of such inquiry, the board may request and receive from such federal agencies or authorities any supporting material or evidence that may be made available to it. The board of regents shall provide in the rules and regulations required by subdivision one hereof that membership in any such organization included in such listing made by it shall constitute prima facie evidence of disqualification for appointment to or retention in any office or position in the public schools of the state."

[5] "§ 3021. *Removal of superintendents, teachers and employees for treasonable or seditious acts or utterances*

"A person employed as superintendent of schools, teacher or employee in the public schools, in any city or school district of the state, shall be removed from such position for the utterance of any treasonable or seditious word or words or the doing of any treasonable or seditious act or acts while holding such position."

orously enforced. It is the purpose of the Feinberg Law to provide for the disqualification and removal of superintendents of schools, teachers, and employees in the public schools in any city or school district of the State who advocate the overthrow of the Government by unlawful means or who are members of organizations which have a like purpose.

Section 3022 of the Education Law, added by the Feinberg Law, provides that the Board of Regents, which has charge of the public school system in the State of New York, shall, after full notice and hearing, make a listing of organizations which it finds advocate, advise, teach, or embrace the doctrine that the government should be overthrown by force or violence or any other unlawful means, and that such listing may be amended and revised from time to time.

It will be observed that the listings are made only after full notice and hearing. In addition, the Court of Appeals construed the statute in conjunction with Article 78 of the New York Civil Practice Act, Gilbert-Bliss' N. Y. Civ. Prac., Vol. 6B, so as to provide listed organizations a right of review.

The Board of Regents is further authorized to provide in rules and regulations, and has so provided, that membership in any listed organization, after notice and hearing, "shall constitute prima facie evidence for disqualification for appointment to or retention in any office or position in the school system";[6] but before one who is an employee or seeks employment is severed from or denied employment, he likewise must be given a full hearing with the privilege of being represented by counsel and the right to judicial review. It is § 12-a of the

---

[6] "§ 254. *Disqualification or removal of superintendents, teachers and other employees.*

· · · · · · · · · · · ·

"2. *List of subversive organizations to be issued.* Pursuant to chapter 360 of the Laws of 1949, the Board of Regents will issue a list, which may be amended and revised from time to time, of organizations which the Board finds to be subversive in that they advocate, advise, teach or embrace the doctrine that the Government of the United States, or of any state or of any political subdivision thereof, shall be overthrown or overturned by force, violence or any unlawful means, or that they advocate, advise, teach or embrace the duty, necessity or propriety of adopting any such doctrine, as set forth in section 12-a of the Civil Service Law. Evidence of membership in any organization so listed on or after the tenth day subsequent to the date of official promulgation of such list shall constitute *prima facie* evidence of disqualification for appointment to or retention of any office or position in the school system. Evidence of membership in such an organization prior to said day shall be presumptive evidence that membership has continued, in the absence of a showing that such membership has been terminated in good faith." Official Compilation of Codes, Rules and Regulations of the State of New York (Fifth Supp.), Vol. 1, pp. 205–206.

Civil Service Law, as implemented by the Feinberg Law as above indicated, that is under attack here.

It is first argued that the Feinberg Law and the rules promulgated thereunder constitute an abridgment of the freedom of speech and assembly of persons employed or seeking employment in the public schools of the State of New York.

It is clear that such persons have the right under our law to assemble, speak, think and believe as they will. *Communications Ass'n v. Douds,* 339 U. S. 382. It is equally clear that they have no right to work for the State in the school system on their own terms. *United Public Workers v. Mitchell,* 330 U. S. 75. They may work for the school system upon the reasonable terms laid down by the proper authorities of New York. If they do not choose to work on such terms, they are at liberty to retain their beliefs and associations and go elsewhere. Has the State thus deprived them of any right to free speech or assembly? We think not. Such persons are or may be denied, under the statutes in question, the privilege of working for the school system of the State of New York because, first, of their advocacy of the overthrow of the government by force or violence, or, secondly, by unexplained membership in an organization found by the school authorities, after notice and hearing, to teach and advocate the overthrow of the government by force or violence, and known by such persons to have such purpose.

The constitutionality of the first proposition is not questioned here. *Gitlow v. New York,* 268 U. S. 652, 667–672, construing § 161 of the New York Penal Law.

As to the second, it is rather subtly suggested that we should not follow our recent decision in *Garner v. Los Angeles Board,* 341 U. S. 716. We there said:

> "We think that a municipal employer is not disabled because it is an agency of the State from inquiring of its employees as to matters that may prove relevant to their fitness and suitability for the public service. Past conduct may well relate to present fitness; past loyalty may have a reasonable relationship to present and future trust. Both are commonly inquired into in determining fitness for both high and low positions in private industry and are not less relevant in public employment." 341 U.S., at p. 720.

We adhere to that case. A teacher works in a sensitive area in a schoolroom. There he shapes the attitude of young minds towards the society in which they live. In this, the state has a vital concern. It must preserve the integrity of the schools.

That the school authorities have the right and the duty to screen the officials, teachers, and employees as to their fitness to maintain the integrity of the schools as a part of ordered society, cannot be doubted. One's associates, past and present, as well as one's conduct, may properly be considered in determining fitness and loyalty. From time immemorial, one's reputation has been determined in part by the company he keeps. In the employment of officials and teachers of the school system, the state may very properly inquire into the company they keep, and we know of no rule, constitutional or otherwise, that prevents the state, when determining the fitness and loyalty of such persons, from considering the organizations and persons with whom they associate.

If, under the procedure set up in the New York law, a person is found to be unfit and is disqualified from employment in the public school system because of membership in a listed organization, he is not thereby denied the right of free speech and assembly. His freedom of choice between membership in the organization and employment in the school system might be limited, but not his freedom of speech or assembly, except in the remote sense that limitation is inherent in every choice. Certainly such limitation is not one the state may not make in the exercise of its police power to protect the schools from pollution and thereby to defend its own existence.

It is next argued by appellants that the provision in § 3022 directing the Board of Regents to provide in rules and regulations that membership in any organization listed by the Board after notice and hearing, with provision for review in accordance with the statute, shall constitute prima facie evidence of disqualification, denies due process, because the fact found bears no relation to the fact presumed. In other words, from the fact found that the organization was one that advocated the overthrow of government by unlawful means and that the person employed or to be employed was a member of the organization and knew of its purpose,[8] to presume that such member is disqualified for employment is so unreasonable as to be a denial of due process of law. We do not agree.

"The law of evidence is full of presumptions either of fact or law. The former are, of course, disputable, and the strength of any inference of one fact from proof of another depends upon the generality of the experience upon which it is founded. . . .

---

[8] In the proceedings below, both the Appellate Division of the Supreme Court and the Court of Appeals construed the statute to require such knowledge. 276 App. Div. 527, 530, 96 N. Y. S. 2d 466, 470–471; 301 N. Y. 476, 494, 95 N. E. 2d 806, 814–815.

"Legislation providing that proof of one fact shall constitute *prima facie* evidence of the main fact in issue is but to enact a rule of evidence, and quite within the general power of government. Statutes, National and state, dealing with such methods of proof in both civil and criminal cases abound, and the decisions upholding them are numerous." *Mobile, J. & K. C. R. Co. v. Turnipseed,* 219 U. S. 35, at p. 42.

Membership in a listed organization found to be within the statute and known by the member to be within the statute is a legislative finding that the member by his membership supports the thing the organization stands for, namely, the overthrow of government by unlawful means. We cannot say that such a finding is contrary to fact or that "generality of experience" points to a different conclusion. Disqualification follows therefore as a reasonable presumption from such membership and support. Nor is there here a problem of procedural due process. The presumption is not conclusive but arises only in a hearing where the person against whom it may arise has full opportunity to rebut it. The holding of the Court of Appeals below is significant in this regard:

"The statute also makes it clear that . . . proof of such membership 'shall constitute prima facie evidence of disqualification' for such employment. But, as was said in *Potts v. Pardee* (220 N. Y. 431, 433): 'The presumption growing out of a *prima facie* case . . . remains only so long as there is no substantial evidence to the contrary. When that is offered the presumption disappears, and unless met by further proof there is nothing to justify a finding based solely upon it.' Thus the phrase '*prima facie* evidence of disqualification' as used in the statute, imports a hearing at which one who seeks appointment to or retention in a public school position shall be afforded an opportunity to present substantial evidence contrary to the presumption sanctioned by the *prima facie* evidence for which subdivision 2 of section 3022 makes provision. Once such contrary evidence has been received, however, the official who made the order of ineligibility has thereafter the burden of sustaining the validity of that order by a fair preponderance of the evidence. (Civil Service Law, § 12-a, subd. [d].) Should an order of ineligibility then issue, the party aggrieved thereby may avail himself of the provisions for review prescribed by the section of the statute last cited above. In that view

there here arises no question of procedural due process."
301 N. Y. 476, at p. 494, 95 N. E. 2d 806, at 814–815.

Where, as here, the relation between the fact found and the
presumption is clear and direct and is not conclusive, the requirements of due process are satisfied.

Without raising in the complaint or in the proceedings in
the lower courts the question of the constitutionality of § 3021
of the Education Law of New York, appellants urge here for
the first time that this section is unconstitutionally vague.
The question is not before us. We will not pass upon the constitutionality of a state statute before the state courts have
had an opportunity to do so. *Asbury Hospital v. Cass County,*
326 U. S. 207, 213–216; *Alabama State Federation of Labor v.
McAdory,* 325 U. S. 450, 460–462; *Plymouth Coal Co. v. Pennsylvania,* 232 U. S. 531, 546.

It is also suggested that the use of the word "subversive" is
vague and indefinite. But the word is first used in § 1 of the
Feinberg Law, which is the preamble to the Act, and not in a
definitive part thereof. When used in subdivision 2 of § 3022,
the word has a very definite meaning, namely, an organization
that teaches and advocates the overthrow of government by
force or violence.

We find no constitutional infirmity in § 12-a of the Civil
Service Law of New York or in the Feinberg Law which implemented it, and the judgment is

*Affirmed.*

MR. JUSTICE BLACK, dissenting.

While I fully agree with the dissent of MR. JUSTICE DOUGLAS,
the importance of this holding prompts me to add these thoughts.

This is another of those rapidly multiplying legislative enactments which make it dangerous—this time for school teachers—
to think or say anything except what a transient majority happen to approve at the moment. Basically these laws rest on
the belief that government should supervise and limit the flow
of ideas into the minds of men. The tendency of such governmental policy is to mould people into a common intellectual
pattern. Quite a different governmental policy rests on the
belief that government should leave the mind and spirit of
man absolutely free. Such a governmental policy encourages
varied intellectual outlooks in the belief that the best views will
prevail. This policy of freedom is in my judgment embodied
in the First Amendment and made applicable to the states by
the Fourteenth. Because of this policy public officials cannot
be constitutionally vested with powers to select the ideas people

[Emerson]

can think about, censor the public views they can express, or choose the persons or groups people can associate with. Public officials with such powers are not public servants; they are public masters.

I dissent from the Court's judgment sustaining this law which effectively penalizes school teachers for their thoughts and their associates.

[Mr. Justice Frankfurter dissented on the ground that the issues were not ripe for constitutional review and that the plaintiffs lacked standing to sue.]

MR. JUSTICE DOUGLAS, with whom MR. JUSTICE BLACK concurs, dissenting.

I have not been able to accept the recent doctrine that a citizen who enters the public service can be forced to sacrifice his civil rights.* I cannot for example find in our constitutional scheme the power of a state to place its employees in the category of second-class citizens by denying them freedom of thought and expression. The Constitution guarantees freedom of thought and expression to everyone in our society. All are entitled to it; and none needs it more than the teacher.

The public school is in most respects the cradle of our democracy. The increasing role of the public school is seized upon by proponents of the type of legislation represented by New York's Feinberg law as proof of the importance and need for keeping the school free of "subversive influences." But that is to misconceive the effect of this type of legislation. Indeed the impact of this kind of censorship on the public school system illustrates the high purpose of the First Amendment in freeing speech and thought from censorship.

The present law proceeds on a principle repugnant to our society—guilt by association. A teacher is disqualified because of her membership in an organization found to be "subversive." The finding as to the "subversive" character of the organization is made in a proceeding to which the teacher is not a party and in which it is not clear that she may even be heard. To be sure, she may have a hearing when charges of disloyalty are leveled against her. But in that hearing the finding as to the "subversive" character of the organization apparently may not be reopened in order to allow her to show the truth of the matter. The irrebuttable charge that the organization is "subversive" therefore hangs as an ominous cloud over her own hearing. The mere fact of membership in the organization

* *United Public Workers* v. *Mitchell*, 330 U. S. 75; *Garner* v. *Board of Public Works of Los Angeles*, 341 U. S. 716.

**867**

raises a prima facie case of her own guilt. She may, it is said, show her innocence. But innocence in this case turns on knowledge; and when the witch hunt is on, one who must rely on ignorance leans on a feeble reed.

The very threat of such a procedure is certain to raise havoc with academic freedom. Youthful indiscretions, mistaken causes, misguided enthusiasms—all long forgotten—become the ghosts of a harrowing present. Any organization committed to a liberal cause, any group organized to revolt against an hysterical trend, any committee launched to sponsor an unpopular program becomes suspect. These are the organizations into which Communists often infiltrate. Their presence infects the whole, even though the project was not conceived in sin. A teacher caught in that mesh is almost certain to stand condemned. Fearing condemnation, she will tend to shrink from any association that stirs controversy. In that manner freedom of expression will be stifled.

But that is only part of it. Once a teacher's connection with a listed organization is shown, her views become subject to scrutiny to determine whether her membership in the organization is innocent or, if she was formerly a member, whether she has *bona fide* abandoned her membership.

The law inevitably turns the school system into a spying project. Regular loyalty reports on the teachers must be made out. The principals become detectives; the students, the parents, the community become informers. Ears are cocked for tell-tale signs of disloyalty. The prejudices of the community come into play in searching out the disloyal. This is not the usual type of supervision which checks a teacher's competency; it is a system which searches for hidden meanings in a teacher's utterances.

What was the significance of the reference of the art teacher to socialism? Why was the history teacher so openly hostile to Franco Spain? Who heard overtones of revolution in the English teacher's discussion of the Grapes of Wrath? What was behind the praise of Soviet progress in metallurgy in the chemistry class? Was it not "subversive" for the teacher to cast doubt on the wisdom of the venture in Korea?

What happens under this law is typical of what happens in a police state. Teachers are under constant surveillance; their pasts are combed for signs of disloyalty; their utterances are watched for clues to dangerous thoughts. A pall is cast over the classrooms. There can be no real academic freedom in that environment. Where suspicion fills the air and holds scholars in line for fear of their jobs, there can be no exercise

**868**

of the free intellect. Supineness and dogmatism take the place of inquiry. A "party line"—as dangerous as the "party line" of the communists—lays hold. It is the "party line" of the orthodox view, of the conventional thought, of the accepted approach. A problem can no longer be pursued with impunity to its edges. Fear stalks the classroom. The teacher is no longer a stimulant to adventurous thinking; she becomes instead a pipe line for safe and sound information. A deadening dogma takes the place of free inquiry. Instruction tends to become sterile; pursuit of knowledge is discouraged; discussion often leaves off where it should begin.

This, I think, is what happens when a censor looks over a teacher's shoulder. This system of spying and surveillance with its accompanying reports and trials cannot go hand in hand with academic freedom. It produces standardized thought, not the pursuit of truth. Yet it was the pursuit of truth which the First Amendment was designed to protect. A system which directly or inevitably has that effect is alien to our system and should be struck down. Its survival is a real threat to our way of life. We need be bold and adventuresome in our thinking to survive. A school system producing students trained as robots threatens to rob a generation of the versatility that has been perhaps our greatest distinction. The Framers knew the danger of dogmatism; they also knew the strength that comes when the mind is free, when ideas may be pursued wherever they lead. We forget these teachings of the First Amendment when we sustain this law.

Of course the school systems of the country need not become cells for Communist activities; and the classrooms need not become forums for propagandizing the Marxist creed. But the guilt of the teacher should turn on overt acts. So long as she is a law-abiding citizen, so long as her performance within the public school system meets professional standards, her private life, her political philosophy, her social creed should not be the cause of reprisals against her.

## Note

1. The Rules issued by the Board of Regents on July 15, 1949, to implement the Feinberg Law included, in addition to the extract quoted in the majority opinion, the following provisions (Official Compilation of Codes, Rules and Regulations of the State of New York (5th Supp; 1950), vol. I, § 254, pp. 205–6):

"b. *Reports on teachers or other employes.* The school authorities shall require one or more of the officials in their employ, whom they shall designate for such purpose, to submit to them in writing not later than October 31, 1949, and not later than September 30th of each school year thereafter, a report on each teacher or other employe. Such report shall either (1) state that there is no evidence indicating that such teacher or other employe has violated the statutory provisions herein referred to, including the provisions with respect to membership in organizations listed by the Regents as subversive in accordance with paragraph 2 hereof; or (2) where there is evidence indicating a violation of said statutory provisions, including membership in such a subversive organization, recommend that action be taken to dismiss such teacher or other employe, on the ground of a specified violation or violations of the law.

"c. *Reports on superintendents of schools and other officials.* The school authorities shall themselves prepare such reports on the superintendent of schools and such other officials as may be directly responsible to them, including the officials designated by them in accordance with subdivision b. of this paragraph. . . .

"3. *Report of school authorities to Commissioner of Education.* On or before the first day of December of each year, the school authorities of each school district shall render to the Commissioner of Education a full report, officially adopted by the school authorities and signed by their presiding officer, of the measures taken by them for the enforcement of these regulations during the calendar year ending on the 31st day of October preceding. . . ."

In September 1949 the Superintendent of Schools of the City of New York issued a circular to implement the Rules of the Board of Regents, which included the following provisions with respect to the filing of annual reports (N. Y. Times, Sept. 15, 1949):

"Every principal and other reporting officer shown below will file a report, containing two parts.

"Section 1. A certification as to the persons against whom there is no evidence of any violation of the law. . . .

"Section 2. Number of employes not included in above list, about whom special reports have been filed—give number.

"If there is evidence against any employe, a report containing the evidence should be prepared without aid of stenographic or other clerical help and mailed separately to the Superintendent of Schools. Every effort should be made to protect an employe against whom there may be evidence from any publicity until there has been an opportunity to consider the evidence and to decide whether there is any basis for charges. . . .

"Reports are to be made as follows [in each classification the group is listed and then the reporting officer]:

"Teachers, et al, assigned to a school—principal.

"Principals of elementary, junior high and vocational high schools and staff assigned to office of assistant superintendents—assistant superintendents assigned to districts.

"Principals of academic high schools—associate superintendent in charge.

"Special teachers—directors.

"Custodians, civil service personnel—heads of bureaus.

"Community centers staffs, evening elementary schools, after school playground teachers, if any, who are not employed in day schools—Director of Community Education.

"Evening high schools—principals of said schools.

"Principals of evening high and vocational high schools—associate superintendents in charge.

"Vacation playgrounds—Director of Community Education.

"Summer day schools—associate superintendent in charge.

"All staff members of Bureau of Child Guidance—acting director of bureau.

"Staff of Attendance Bureau—acting director of bureau.

"Staff of Bureau of C. R. M. D. except teachers assigned to schools—director of C. R. M. D.

"Teachers of homebound—acting assistant director of physically handicapped children.

"Lunch room staff (No report need be made on cafeteria workers in senior high schools where these persons are not our employes)—director of school lunches or manager of school lunches (J. H. S.)

"Associate superintendents, assistant superintendents, directors, heads of bureaus—Superintendent of Schools.

"Superintendent of Schools—Board of Education. . . ."

The comment of the *New Yorker* was:

"Now if we can just get Feinberg to O.K. the Supervisor, and get the Attorney General to O.K. Feinberg, we're all set. That is, we're all set provided we can get somebody to O.K. the Attorney General."

2. Legislation requiring loyalty oaths from public school teachers was first passed during the Civil War period. Seven states enacted such laws at that time. But the practice did not become widespread until the First World War, when a number of states passed laws requiring oaths or establishing loyalty qualifications for teachers. For the history of teachers' loyalty legislation see Reutter, *The School Administrator and Subversive Activities*, ch. 2 (1951); Linville, *Oaths of Loyalty for Teachers* (1935); National Education Association, *Teachers Oaths* (1936) and *Revised Report* (1937); Beale, *Are American Teachers Free?*, ch. V (1936).

The most famous of the World War I statutes were the Lusk Laws of New York, enacted in 1921. One law required of teachers a certificate of loyalty:

"Such certificate shall state that the teacher holding the same is a person of good moral character and that he has shown satisfactorily that he is loyal and obedient to the government of this state and of the United States; no such certificate shall be issued to any person who, while a citizen of the United States, has advocated, either by word of mouth or in writing, a form of government other than the government of the United States or of this state, or who advocates or has advocated, either by word of mouth or in writing, a change in the form of government of the United States or of this state by force, violence or any unlawful means." New York Session Laws, 1921, ch. 666.

Another provided that no school should operate in the state without a license, and that:

"No license shall be granted for the conduct of any such school, institute, class or course . . . where it shall appear that the instruction proposed to be given includes the teaching of the doctrine that organized governments shall be overthrown by force, violence or unlawful means, or where it shall appear that such school, institute, class or course is to be conducted in a fraudulent manner." N. Y. Session Laws, 1921, ch. 667.

The passage of these laws led to a widespread investigation of teachers. In New York City a committee was set up to hear charges and pass upon suspected cases of disloyalty. Principals of schools were required to report on the loyalty of each teacher. Proceedings were commenced to force the Rand School of Social Science to cease operation. See *People of New York v. American Socialist Society*, 202 App. Div. 640, 195 N. Y. Supp. 801 (1922).

The Lusk Laws were repealed in 1923. For an account of their operation see Beale, *supra*, pp. 59–73; Sinclair, *The Goslings*, pp. 81–87 (1924); Chafee, *Free Speech in the United States*, ch. 8 (1941). See also, on the events of this period, Pierce, *Public Opinion and the Teaching of History* (1926).

Legislation pertaining to teacher loyalty increased during the early and middle thirties. By 1940 twenty states had either oath requirements or other legal provisions by means of which the "disloyal" teacher could be excluded from the public schools.

Some state laws give state officials express authority to ban subversive texts or other materials from the schools. Thus the New York Education Law directs the Commissioner of Education, on his own motion, or on complaint of any person, to forbid the use of textbooks containing "any matter or statements of any kind which are seditious in character, disloyal to the United States or favorable to the cause of any foreign country with which the United States may be at war." N. Y. Ed. Law § 704.

See Reutter and other references, *supra*.

3. In the period following the Second World War a number of additional states passed teachers' loyalty legislation and some states strengthened existing laws. By 1951 loyalty legislation for teachers existed in 33 states. In 11 states this legislation took the form of an oath; in seven it imposed loyalty qualifications; and in 15 it included both an oath and loyalty qualifications.

The form of oath required by the 26 states varies. In many it is in the form of the traditional pledge to support the constitution. In 10 it contains prohibitions against belonging to "subversive" groups, teaching or advocating "subversive" doctrines, or both. Most of these latter are framed in terms of not advocating overthrow of the government by force or violence or belonging to organizations that do. But several of the more recent statutes go further. See, *e. g.*, the Georgia, Florida, New Jersey and Oklahoma oaths (applicable to all state employees, including teachers) set forth in Chapter IV, *supra*, pp. 517, 577.

In the 22 states having loyalty qualifications, the requirements also vary. Most provide for dismissal of teachers who advocate overthrow of the government by force or violence or belong to an organization

**872**

that so advocates. Again the most recent statutes frequently go beyond this. See, *e. g.*, the Maryland Ober Law (likewise applicable to teachers as well as other state employees) set forth in Chapter IV, *supra*, p. 518.

In most states teachers' loyalty legislation applies only to the personnel of the public schools. But some statutes apply to private educational institutions as well.

For a full analysis of state legislation through 1950, see Reutter, *supra*, ch. 3. See also Gellhorn, *The States and Subversion* (1952) (legislation collected in Appen. A and B). On local legislation, see Reutter, *supra*, ch. 4. For legislation passed since the Reutter and Gellhorn compilations, see Chapter IV, *supra*.

4. For the Supreme Court's position on teachers' loyalty legislation, in addition to the *Adler* case, see *Gerende v. Board of Supervisors*, 341 U. S. 56, 95 L. Ed. 745, 71 S. Ct. 565 (1951) and *Garner v. Board of Public Works*, 341 U. S. 716, 95 L. Ed. 1317, 71 S. Ct. 909 (1951), both printed in Chapter IV, *supra*. Compare with these decisions *West Virginia State Board of Education v. Barnette*, 319 U. S. 624, 87 L. Ed. 1628, 63 S. Ct. 1178 (1943) (printed in part in Chapter VIII, *infra*), in which the Court held invalid the requirement that school children must pledge allegiance to the flag.

5. State courts, except in the *Tolman* case, *infra*, have consistently upheld teachers' loyalty legislation. The earlier cases are *People v. American Socialist Society*, *supra* (upholding licensing provisions of the Lusk Laws); *Sauder v. District Board*, 271 Mich. 413, 261 N. W. 66 (1935) (teacher's contract not including required oath to support the constitution held void); *Scalf v. L'Anse Tp. Single School*, 276 Mich. 662, 268 N. W. 773 (1936) (same); *Board of Education v. Jewett*, 21 Cal. App. 2d 64, 68 Pac. 2d 404 (1937) (statements of teacher held to violate oath and constitute grounds for dismissal; see *infra*); cf. *Epstein v. Board of Examiners*, 162 Misc. 718, 295 N. Y. Supp. 796 (1936).

The more recent cases have reached the same result. In *Thorp v. Board of Trustees*, 6 N. J. 498, 79 Atl. 2d 462 (1951), the New Jersey loyalty oath was upheld. (For the wording of the oath see Chapter IV, *supra*, pp. 517, 577). The court distinguished the *Imbrie* case, which had invalidated the oath as applied to candidates for public office (see Chapter IV, *supra*), on the ground that teachers were not "public officers" and hence the oath required by the Constitution for public officers did not exclude additional oaths for teachers. On the freedom of speech and due process issues the court, citing the *Douds* case, said: "It is of the very nature of the social compact that the individual freedoms at issue here are subject to reasonable restraint in the service of an interest deemed essential to the life of the community." It then found the requirement of an oath reasonably related to "the essential common security":

"The maintenance of the purity of the educational process against corruption by subversive influences is of the highest concern to society. It is in no real sense a denial of academic freedom to require of a teacher, as a condition to employment, a sworn disavowal of allegiance to the doctrine of force or violence as a mode of overthrowing government. That would seem to be axiomatic. Loyalty to government and its free democratic institutions is a first requisite for the exercise of the teaching function. Freedom from belief in force or violence as a justifiable weapon for the destruction of government is of the very essence of a teacher's qualifications. The apprehended danger is real and abiding. We have long had evidences of the pressure here of a godless ideology ruthlessly fostered by a foreign power which has for its aim the violent overthrow of government and free society. And one of its weapons is the debasement of teaching as a softening measure in the consummation of the subversive process. The school system affords the opportunity and means for subtle infiltration. There is no intrusion upon personal freedoms when government intervenes, as it has here, to avert this peril to its very existence. A teacher who is bereft of the essential quality of loyalty and devotion to his government and the fundamentals of our democratic society is lacking in a basic qualification for teaching. The teacher is not obliged to take the oath; but if he refuses to do so he is not entitled to teach. In the current struggle for men's minds, the State is well within its province in ensuring the integrity of the educational process against those who would pervert it to subversive ends." 6 N. J. at 511–4, 79 Atl. 2d at 468–70.

The Oklahoma oath (set forth in Chapter IV, *supra*, p. 577), was upheld in *Board of Regents v. Updegraff*, — Okla. —, 237 Pac. 2d 131 (1951). The court held the oath to be not unreasonable, arbitrary or capricious and hence a valid exercise of the police power. It rejected arguments based upon constitutional prohibitions against impairment of contract, bills of attainder, ex post facto laws and abridgment of freedom of religion. On the due process issue the Court said:

"The statute and the required loyalty oath do not deprive public officials and employees of property or liberty without due process of law. The intervenors are employees of the state as teachers in a public institution. They have no constitutional right to be so employed. They have no right to so serve the state except upon such terms as the state prescribes. The act does not purport to take away their right to teach. Public institutions do not have to hire nor retain employees except on terms suitable to them. . . ." — Okla. at —, 237 Pac. 2d at 137.

See also *Dworken v. Cleveland Board of Education*, 94 N. E. 2d 18 (Ct. Com. Pleas, Ohio, 1950) (upholding the loyalty oath required by the Cleveland Board of Education).

6. The loyalty oath required by the Board of Regents of the University of California (see Section B, *supra*) was held invalid in *Tolman v. Underhill*, — Cal. App. 2d —, 229 Pac. 2d 447 (1951). The decision was based upon the ground that the California Constitution prescribed the form of oath for all officers, and provided that "no other oath, declaration, or test, shall be required as a qualification for any office or public trust." The court held that the faculty members involved were included within the term "office or public trust" and hence the Constitutional oath was exclusive:

". . . [We] conclude that the people of California intended, at least, that no one could be subjected, as a condition to holding office, to any test of political or religious belief other than his pledge to support the Constitutions of this state and of the United States; that that pledge is the highest loyalty that can be demonstrated by any citizen, and that the exacting of any other test of loyalty would be antithetical to our fundamental concept of freedom. Any other conclusion would be to approve that which from the beginning of our government has been denounced as the most effective means by which one special brand of political or economic philosophy can entrench and perpetuate itself to the eventual exclusion of all others; the imposition of any more inclusive test would be the forerunner of tyranny and oppression."

Pointing to Article IX, Section 9 of the Constitution, which provided that the University "shall be entirely independent of all political or sectarian influence," the court said:

"Hence, if the faculty of the University can be subjected to any more narrow test of loyalty than the constitutional oath, the constitutional mandate in Section 9 of Article IX would be effectively frustrated, and our great institution now dedicated to learning and the search for truth reduced to an organ for the propagation of the ephemeral political, religious, social and economic philosophies, whatever they may be, of the majority of the Board of Regents of that moment." 229 Pac. 2d at 452.

The Levering Act (see Section B, *supra*) has not yet been tested.

7. For discussion of the legal problems involved in teachers' loyalty legislation, see Gardner and Post, *The Constitutional Questions Raised by the Flag Salute and Teachers' Oath Acts in Massachusetts*, 16 Bos. U. L. Rev. 803 (1936); Twohy, *The Feinberg Law*, 24 St. John's L. Rev. 197 (1950); Note, *The 'Little Red Schoolhouse' and the Communist: New York State Struggles with the Problem of Educating for a Free Society*, 35 Corn. L. Q. 824 (1950); Note, *Legislative Control of Loyalty in the School System*, 29 Neb. L. Rev. 485 (1950); Note, *The New York and California Experiments with Academic Control*, 18 U. of Chi. L. Rev. 293 (1951); Marshall, *The Defense of Public Education From Subversion*, 51 Col. L. Rev. 587 (1951); Reutter, *supra*, ch. 5; see also Notes, 45 Ill. L. Rev. 274 (1950); 25 St. John's L. Rev. 345 (1951); 25 Temp. L. Q. 207 (1951); 49 Mich. L. Rev. 1219 (1951).

8. In *Samson v. Trustees of Columbia University*, 101 Misc. 146, 167 N. Y. Supp. 202 (1917), the court upheld the dismissal of a student for making a speech attacking the Government, the draft and the war: ". . . it was one of the implied terms of the agreement [implied from the student's admission] that the plaintiff would comport himself in such manner as not to destroy or interfere with the discipline, good order and fair name of the University." No constitutional issues were considered. See also *Zarichny v. State Board of Agriculture*, discussed in Section B, *supra*. On the rights of students generally see Note, *supra*, 29 Neb. L. Rev. at 499–501 (1950).

9. For situations in which loyalty oaths or tests have been applied to teachers in the absence of legislative provision, and hence raise questions of tenure or contract (as in the University of Washington cases), see Section E, *infra*. With respect to constitutional limitations

in matters involving racial discrimination in education, see Chapter IX, *infra*. On the Church-State issue, see Chapter VIII, *infra*.

## E. PROTECTION OF ACADEMIC FREEDOM THROUGH TENURE AND CONTRACT RIGHTS

### 1. History of Tenure Legislation

### McSHERRY v. CITY OF ST. PAUL

Supreme Court of Minnesota, 1938
202 Minn. 102, 277 N. W. 541

[Plaintiff, a substitute teacher, had been summarily discharged. She sued to recover the balance of her salary, claiming that she had tenure rights and had been discharged in violation of the Minnesota tenure law. The tenure statute provided that, after completion of a probationary period of three years, teachers "shall continue in service and hold their respective position during good behavior and efficient and competent service and shall not be discharged or demoted except for one or more of the causes as specified . . . and after a hearing as specified. . . ." The statute went on to enumerate specific causes justifying discharge or demotion. The Court took occasion to summarize the history of tenure legislation.]

JULIUS J. OLSON, Justice. . . .

Teachers' tenure, like civil service and other similar movements, dates back now over a period of many years. The abuses existing by reason of the "spoils system" which came into prominence during Jackson's administration, later followed by national and other administrations, led to much-deserved criticism. That is why on January 16, 1883 ("An act to regulate and improve the civil service of the United States," 22 Stat. 403), the first civil service act was passed. In 1885, the National Education Association brought forth the question of tenure of school officials. A committee of that association studied the matter and later submitted a report. Generally speaking, the tenure so sought was interpreted to mean, in substance, the application of the principles of civil service to the teaching profession. It was thought that for the good of the schools and the general public the profession should be made independent of personal or political influence, and made free from the malignant power of spoils and patronage. In 1886 the state of Massachusetts enacted a law "relating to the tenure of office of teachers." St. Mass. 1886, c. 313. Thereunder school districts were permitted to enter into contracts with teachers for a longer period than one year. In 1889 the committee on rules of the Boston School Committee suggested a tenure law providing for a probationary period of one year, four years of annual elections, and thereafter permanent tenure subject to removal for cause after proper hearing. The bases for recommendations were that better talent would be attracted to the teaching profession; that annual contracts theretofore in vogue had not resulted in the elimination of poor, incompetent, and inefficient teachers; that the principle of annual election or appointment was not generally applied to policemen, firemen, or judicial officers, and in the very nature of things should not apply to teachers; that not infrequently the best teachers were discharged for inadequate reasons. (See report of Committee on Tenure of National Education Association for the year 1921.) Foreign countries have long recognized the principle of teachers' tenure. (See report of Committee on Tenure of National Education Association for the year 1936.) Since 1900 the principle of teachers' tenure in this country has developed more rapidly. In a general way it has followed the civil service plan. The objectives sought have been to protect the teachers against unjust removal after having undergone an adequate probationary period; that the movement itself has for its basis public interest, in that most advantages go to the youth of the land and to the schools themselves, rather than the interest of the teachers as such. (See report of Committee on Civil Service for Teachers of National Education Association for July, 1934.)

Many states have adopted teachers' tenure acts. We shall not stop to enumerate them. The general purposes and advantages of these acts and the reasons therefor are interestingly set forth in "Bulletin of National Education Association on Teachers' Tenure for 1937." . . .

Plainly, the legislative purposes sought were stability, certainty, and permanency of employment on the part of those who had shown by educational attainment and by probationary trial their fitness for the teaching profession. By statutory direction and limitation there is provided means of prevention of *arbitrary* demotions or discharges by school authorities. The history behind the act justifies the view that the vicissitudes to which teachers had in the past been subjected were to be done away with or at least minimized. It was enacted for the *benefit and advantage of the school system* by providing such machinery as would tend to minimize the part that malice, political or partisan trends, or caprice might play. It established

**877**

*merit* as the essential basis for the *right* of permanent employment. On the other hand, it is equally clear that the act does not impair *discretionary* power of school authorities to make the best selections consonant with the public good; but their conduct in this behalf is strictly circumscribed and must be kept within the boundaries of the act. The provision for a probationary period is intended for that very purpose. The right to demote or discharge provides remedies for safeguarding the future against incompetence, insubordination, and other grounds stated in the act. The act itself bespeaks the intent. Provisions for notice and hearing, the requirements of specified causes for discharge or demotion, are indicative of the general purpose. With these considerations in mind, it is our duty so to construe such parts of the act which on their face do not clearly delineate the legislative intent as will bring about a result in harmony with the expressed legislative policy. . . .

[The Court held that plaintiff had tenure rights and should recover.]

## 2. The Scope of Tenure Legislation

State tenure laws covering public schools usually provide that after a teacher has served a specified probationary period he cannot be dismissed or otherwise disciplined except for "cause." Some laws provide protection for all teachers employed by the state; others cover only teachers in cities of a certain size; and others leave the adoption of tenure regulations optional with those communities not specifically covered by statute. Frequently there is no provision for tenure in rural areas.

Laws not providing for permanent tenure may contain no provision at all regarding length of employment, may specify that teachers be annually appointed, may permit contracts for more than one year, or may be of the "continuing contract" type which provide that a teacher is automatically reappointed each year unless notified of dismissal before a certain date. Where statutes are silent with regard to the length of employment, there may exist other legislation which affects the employment of teachers. For example, there may be statutes governing cause for discharge, demotion, transferral, or disciplinary action; providing for notice and hearing before discharge during the term of the contract; and so on. Teachers may also be included within the scope of state or municipal civil service acts.

Tenure acts may be of the type creating a private contractual

878

relationship or of the policy-stating type which creates "legislative status" for the teacher. In *Phelps v. Board of Education,* 300 U.S. 319, 81 L.Ed. 674, 57 S.Ct. 483 (1937), the Court held that the New Jersey Tenure Act was intended merely to regulate the conduct of boards of education and did not create a contractual right. Hence the legislature could, without violating the contract clause of the Constitution, reduce the salaries of public school teachers protected by the Act from dismissal or reduction in salary except for "inefficiency, incapacity, conduct unbecoming a teacher, or other just cause." A similar decision was reached in *Dodge v. Board of Education,* 302 U.S. 74, 82 L.Ed. 57, 58 S.Ct. 98 (1937), where an Illinois statute reducing retirement annuities payable to teachers who had been retired under an earlier act, was held not to impair the obligations of a contract or deprive the teachers of a vested right without due process of law.

But in *Indiana ex rel. Anderson v. Brand,* 303 U.S. 95, 82 L.Ed. 685, 58 S.Ct. 443 (1938), the Court held that an Indiana statute amending the Teachers Tenure Act of 1927 so as to exclude township schools and teachers from its provisions constituted an unconstitutional abrogation of a vested contractual right. The Court distinguished the *Phelps* and *Dodge* cases by the language used in the several statutes, finding that the Indiana act expressly intended to create a contractual status.

Where the teachers' tenure act is construed as merely an expression of public policy, the teacher is afforded less protection than under the contract-type legislation. If he is considered an "officer" rather than an "employee", with "status" rather than "contract," he is not secure from the periodic interference of the legislature itself, which may provide for dismissal or reduce salary and retirement benefits, without "cause," or may, as the Court pointed out in *Malone v. Hayden,* 329 Pa. 213, 197 Atl. 344 (1938), abolish the law altogether.[1]

Some statutes protect all certificated employees of the school system; some include only teachers, principals and at times superintendents.

The causes for dismissal or disciplinary action are frequently stated in general terms in tenure laws. Some simply provide

---

[1] As in the case of any civil service system there are various administrative devices which under certain circumstances can be used to circumvent the tenure laws. Thus it is possible to reorganize the school system, abolish jobs, transfer teachers to inconvenient posts, and the like. Where the teacher can prove that the purpose of such a move was to avoid the tenure laws he has been given judicial relief. *Gassen v. St. Charles Parish School Board,* 199 La. 954, 7 So. 2d 217 (1942); *State ex rel. Karnes v. Board of Regents,* 222 Wis. 542, 269 N. W. 284 (1936).

that a teacher may not be dismissed except for "cause," or for "reasonable and just cause." Most list specific grounds, such as "incompetency," "inefficiency," "evident unfitness for service," "conduct unbecoming a teacher," "cruelty," "immorality," "intemperance," "insubordination," "dishonesty," "conviction for felony or crime involving moral turpitude," "committing or advocating criminal syndicalism," "violation of school laws and regulations," and "physical or mental disability." Many laws which state specific grounds such as these reaffirm the wide discretionary authority entrusted to the school board by concluding the list with "or for other good and just cause." Some laws specifically state that a teacher may not be dismissed for "political or personal reasons," or for "marriage."

For a collection and analysis of the type and coverage of state tenure laws see National Education Association, Committee on Tenure, *Teacher Tenure: Its Status Critically Appraised* (1942) and *Critical Analysis of Teacher Tenure Legislation* (1939). See also, National Education Association, Committee on Tenure, *Opinions on Tenure: School Board Members and Superintendents* (1939); National Education Association, *The Legal Status of the Public School Teacher*, 25 Res. Bull. 42–50 (1947); Notes, 21 Notre Dame Law. 25 (1945); 25 B. U. Law Rev. 292 (1945); 8 U. of Pitt. L. Rev. 144 (1942).

The faculties of state-controlled colleges and universities do not qualify for protection under these tenure laws. Some states have passed special tenure laws comparable to those applicable to secondary school teachers. Normally, however, the matter rests in the hands of the Board of Regents or other governing board. The governing boards of many of the state colleges and universities have adopted regulations providing for tenure, causes for discharge or other disciplinary action, and procedures to be followed in verifying charges.

Private educational institutions are not subject to tenure legislation. Again, many of the governing boards of such institutions have adopted rules covering tenure matters. The American Association of University Professors has been active in securing the adoption of such regulations. In some institutions, particularly those of long standing, an unwritten agreement regarding tenure has become traditional.[2]

---

[2] There is no current compilation of tenure rules and practices presently in force in American colleges and universities. Columbia University is engaged in a study of "the contemporary situation [with regard to academic freedom], including a study of the respective roles of governing boards, administrative officers, faculties, and students," which will provide a comprehensive survey of existing tenure regulations. Publication is planned for the fall of 1953.

## 3. Provisions for Hearing, Appeal and Review

Tenure laws governing the public schools usually provide that the teacher shall be given notice of the school board's decision to discharge or take other disciplinary action, together with a copy of the charges on which the decision is based. In some states a hearing, either private or public, is required by law; in others a hearing is held only if requested by the teacher. The teacher may usually decide whether he wishes the hearing to be private or public, and may be represented by counsel of his choice.

In many states an appeal from the decision of a school board may be taken to higher school authorities, for example, to the county or state superintendent of schools or to a specially appointed tenure commission. In some states there is no provision for appeal to school authorities but the courts are given express jurisdiction to review. Where the statutes are silent on the question of appeal or review the courts will normally take jurisdiction.

The scope of court review is limited. The courts will consider jurisdictional and procedural matters. But, unless it is clearly shown that an action of the school authorities is arbitrary, fraudulent, discriminatory or malicious, or exceeds the statutory limitations upon their power, the courts will not interfere with decisions affecting educational policy, or disturb the administrative tribunal's findings of fact.

There are two forms of relief normally available for the wrongfully discharged teacher: a mandamus proceeding to compel reinstatement, and an action for damages for breach of contract. The former is available only to teachers whose tenure position is not based solely on contract but is secured by law.

See, National Education Association, Committee on Tenure, *To Whom May Aggrieved Teachers Appeal?* (1941) (contains a state-by-state digest of statutes and judicial decisions); National Education Association, Committee on Tenure, *Teacher Tenure: Its Status Critically Appraised*, pp. 27–32 (1942); National Education Association, *The Legal Status of the Public School Teacher*, 25 Res. Bull. 37–40 (1947); Chambers, *The Colleges and the Courts*, 1936–40, ch. V and VI (1941); Note, *Tenure for Teachers—A Continuing Struggle*, 23 Tex. L. Rev. 265 (1945); Note, 37 Mich. L. Rev. 430 (1939); Note, *Academic Freedom and the Law*, 46 Yale L. J. 670 (1937); Notes, 45 Ill. L. Rev. 274 (1950); 127 A. L. R. 1298.

## 4. Causes for Dismissal Under Tenure Laws— Elementary and Secondary Schools

Innumerable decisions by school boards, appeal boards and the courts deal with the question of allowable grounds for discharge or discipline under the tenure laws. This whole body of decision is, in one sense, relevant to considerations of academic freedom. The extent to which a teacher is protected against dismissal, for any cause, affects his freedom as a teacher and as an individual. But we are more directly concerned with dismissals or disciplinary action related to such issues as the right of the teacher to discuss controversial matters in the class room, to express political views, to engage in outside political activities, and the like. The material in this section is therefore confined to problems of this nature.

The cases summarized below include the major decisions that illustrate the manner in which the courts and administrative bodies have dealt with these problems. It should be remembered that, as is true of any system of statutory administration, the great bulk of the cases arising under the tenure laws never reach the courts.

### The Teacher as Citizen

(1) On the right of the teacher to run for political office:

*School City of East Chicago v. Sigler,* 219 Ind. 9, 36 N.E.2d 760, 136 A.L.R. 1149 (1941). The teacher brought an action to recover salary withheld during his temporary suspension while campaigning for election to Congress. After the teacher had notified the School Board of his intention to run, the Board adopted a resolution requiring candidates for political office to take a leave of absence without pay. The court denied recovery on the ground that this rule was a reasonable exercise of the school board's discretion, but added that a teacher "has the same privilege as any other citizen to become a candidate for public office. Such candidacy should not be and is not ground for cancellation of his contract as a permanent teacher."

*Watkins v. Special School District of Lepanto,* 194 S. W. 32 (Ark., 1917). In an action by a teacher for breach of contract, the court held that the school board was without authority to discharge him on the basis of a rumor that he intended to run for the office of county superintendent.

(2) On the right of the teacher to hold political views and join political associations:

*McDowell v. Board of Education,* 104 Misc. 564, 172 N. Y. Supp. 590 (1918). This was one of the most famous First World War cases. Petitioner, a Quakeress, was an assistant

[Emerson]

teacher of Latin in high school. She was dismissed for "conduct unbecoming a teacher," under a statute which provided that a teacher should hold her position "during good behavior and efficient and competent service, and shall not be removable except for cause after a hearing. . . ." Interrogated by the board of superintendents, she stated her unwillingness to uphold the country in resisting invasion or in carrying out the war; to urge her pupils to support the war or to perform Red Cross services or to buy thrift stamps; and she further believed a teacher was under no obligation to train her pupils to support the war policies of the government. The Court held that her dismissal was for an offense within the meaning of the statute: "the grounds of removal contemplated by the statute may in a given instance be wholly unrelated to the discharge of the scholastic duties, and a teacher may be both incompetent and inefficient, even though her class shows most gratifying results in the ordinary subjects of the curriculum. It is of the utmost importance to the state that the association of teacher and pupil should tend to inculcate in the latter principles of justice and patriotism and a respect for our laws. This end cannot be accomplished, if the pupil finds his teacher unwilling to submit to constituted authority." Her application for writ of mandamus to compel her reinstatement was denied.

*Matter of Pratt*, 25 N. Y. State Dept. Repts. 65 (Ed. Dep't., 1921). Where a statute permitted discharge of a teacher for "lack of good behavior" or "lack of efficient and competent service," a teacher who became a member of the Communist Party, engaged actively in its work, and resigned only out of fear of losing her position, was properly discharged for "misbehavior." Her appeal asking for reinstatement was dismissed. *Cf. Epstein v. Board of Examiners*, 162 Misc. 718, 295 N. Y. Supp. 796 (1936).

*Board of School Directors of Wilmerding v. Gillies*, 343 Pa. 382, 23 Atl.2d 447 (1942), noted in 8 U. of Pitts. L. Rev. 144 (1942). A high school teacher of English and History appealed from an order directing his discharge on grounds of "immorality" and "incompetency." The principal evidence on which the charges were based was that he had signed nomination papers of the Communist Party candidate for Congress, but it was not shown that he himself was a member of the Communist Party. The court held that the evidence did not support the charges, and that his dismissal was unlawful.

*State ex rel. Schweitzer v. Turner*, 19 So.(2d) 832 (Fla., 1944), noted in 25 B. U. L. R. 292 (1945). Mandamus proceedings were brought to compel the reinstatement of a teacher discharged for "incompetency." A statute required the teaching of "morals . . . truth, honesty and patriotism . . . and every Christian virtue." The teacher was a conscientious objector and announced his refusal to participate in the war, either in a combatant or noncombatant capacity. This refusal the court held was sufficient to justify his dismissal on grounds of "incompetency," although it was "admitted that, professionally, [the teacher] is well qualified, conscientious, and experienced and is highly esteemed in Dade County." Nonetheless, his conduct and attitude were "inimical to the responsibilities of good citizenship," and "his manifested ideals were detrimental to the minds of the students and welfare of the public school system."

*Matter of Koral v. Board of Education,* 197 Misc. 221, 94 N. Y. Supp. 2d 378 (1950). Petitioner, a permanent employee of the Board of Education, sought reinstatement to his position as assistant mechanical engineer. He was dismissed, without the hearing guaranteed all regular employees of the Board by the Education Law, for asserting his privilege against self-incrimination and for refusing to answer questions regarding his membership in the Communist Party and espionage activities put to him by the House Committee on Un-American Activities. A section of the New York City Charter authorized dismissal of any public employee for refusal to answer, on grounds of self-incrimination, questions relating to the "property, government, or affairs of the city." The court held that this Charter provision "supersedes and overrides the provisions of the Education Law requiring a hearing on the charges," and that Koral was lawfully dismissed.

See also *Reinecke v. Loper,* 77 F. Supp. 333 (D. Haw., 1948); *Albert v. School District of Pittsburgh,* 181 F. 2d 690 (C.A. 3, 1950.)

(3) On the right of the teacher to participate in the determination of school policy:

*Gardner v. North Little Rock Special School District,* 161 Ark. 466, 257 S.W. 73 (1923). School superintendent brought an action to recover the amount of his salary due under two-year contract after wrongful discharge for "insubordination." He had actively led one of two bitterly opposed factions in an effort to improve school facilities and raise teachers' salaries, on which issues the school board was sharply divided. It was not contended that his political activity was injurious to the school's interests. The court held that the superintendent was wrongfully discharged, as his "impropriety" did not constitute insubordination or misconduct, and that he was entitled to recover damages.

*Harrison v. State Board of Education,* 134 N.J.L. 502, 48 Atl. 2d 579 (1946). A school principal with tenure was dismissed on charges of "conduct unbecoming a principal," "insubordination," "conduct in excess of authority," and for "making unwarranted attacks upon her superiors and their professional qualifications and administrative efficiency." The court upheld the dismissal: "It is not a question merely of bona fide criticism of and disagreement with the policies and acts of her superiors, but rather of disobedience and refusal to observe the orders and directions of duly constituted authority."

## Note

Other cases involving activities outside the classroom include:
*Hopkins v. Inhabitants of Bucksport,* 119 Me. 437, 111 Atl. 734 (1920). Teacher with 17 years experience, dismissed without knowing in advance what the charges against her were, brought an action to recover under her contract. A statute authorized dismissal on two grounds: "unfitness to teach" and "failure of practical success in the work of the school, rendering the teacher's services unprofitable." She was dismissed for having associated with a German enemy alien, from whom she took driving lessons. The court held this discharge unlawful, as the committee acted not on evidence of actual unfitness but in anticipation of future results.

*Reed v. Orleans Parish School Board,* 21 So. 2d 895 (La. App., 1945). In this case a teacher with permanent status was suspended without pay for "wilful neglect of duty" in that she refused to fill out a questionnaire regarding the nature and amount of war work she was doing. She sought an annullment of the suspension order and an order compelling the Board to pay her salary withheld during the period of suspension, on the grounds that the Board was without authority to demand information regarding her activities after school. The court held that inasmuch as the purpose of the questionnaire was to determine the possibilities of expanding the school curriculum, in compliance with a recommendation of the U. S. Office of Education, the request of the Board was a reasonable one and the discharge of the teacher for a wilful neglect of duty was lawful.

*Horosko v. School District of Mt. Pleasant Township,* 335 Pa. 369, 6 Atl. 2d 866 (1939). A teacher who, after school hours and during summer vacation, acted as waitress and bartender, and drank beer, shook dice, played pinball machine with customers in presence of pupils, was held to have been justifiably dismissed on grounds of "incompetency."

On dismissal of women teachers for marriage see *State ex rel. Wood v. Board of Education of St. Louis,* 357 Mo. 147, 206 S. W. 2d 566 (1947).

In 1950 the Superintendent of Schools in New York City called in a number of teachers and questioned them concerning present and past membership in and association with the Communist Party. Eight teachers refused to answer the questions. They were suspended without pay and charges were brought against them of "insubordination and conduct unbecoming a teacher." N. Y. Times, May 4, 1950. Hearings were held before a trial examiner, who recommended dismissal. N. Y. Times, Dec. 13, 1950. The Board of Education, approving the trial examiner's report, dismissed them. N. Y. Times, Feb. 9, 1951. Although the Feinberg Law was in effect at the time it was not invoked in the proceeding. The eight teachers filed suit to review the Board of Education's ruling. N. Y. Times, April 12, 1951. Subsequently the Superintendent questioned additional teachers along the same lines. As a result four teachers resigned and eight more were suspended. N. Y. Times, Oct. 16, 1951, Feb. 1, 1952. In December, 1951, the Board of Education adopted a resolution ordering the dismissal of any "teacher or other school employee who is a member of the Communist Party or of a group advocating overthrow of the government by force and violence," directing the Superintendent to inquire into such activity, and declaring it the duty of all teachers to answer questions on the subject. N. Y. Times, Dec. 7, 1951.

For further discussion of the question whether members of the Communist Party, and those "affiliated" or "associated" with it or "sympathetic" to it, should be permitted to teach, see the University of Washington Tenure Cases, *infra,* and the following Note.

## The Teacher in his Professional Capacity

In considering the cases involving the dismissal of a teacher for inadequate performance of teaching obligations in his classroom, it is important to note that much, and in some cases all, of the evidence in support of charges against him are based upon the testimony of his students. The problems this raises are obvious.

*Foreman v. School District No. 25 of Columbia County,* 81 Ore. 587, 159 Pac. 1155 (1916). A high school teacher under contract was discharged for teaching her pupils "principles of anarchy and disloyalty to their government, among other things, that the government under which she and they live is 'rotten to the core' "; and "that there is no God, and that Jesus Christ is not the Son of God." She sought damages for breach of contract. A rule of the State Board of Education required that teachers inculcate in their pupils "correct principles of morality, and a proper regard for the laws of society, and for the government under which they live." The court held that her conduct violating this rule constituted a breach of her teaching contract, for which she could be discharged without notice or hearing, under a statute permitting dismissal only for "good cause shown."

*Matter of Mufson,* 18 N. Y. State Dep't. Reports 393 (Ed.

Dep't., 1918). The tenure law permitted discharge for cause. Three high school teachers of English were dismissed for "conduct unbecoming a teacher." The charges against Mufson were that he "fails to live up to his duty as teacher, inasmuch as he conceives it proper to maintain before his classes an attitude of strict neutrality in class discussions dealing with . . . the duty of every one to support the Government of the United States in all measures taken by the Federal Government to insure the proper conduct of the present war." At a hearing before the Board of Education Mufson declined to answer questions concerning his "obligation to inculcate respect for the President of the United States in the minds of your pupils" and his "sympathy with the United States in this war against the German Government." Schneer was charged with circulating a bibliography among the students "which contained references to works which should not have been called to the attention of the students of that school." The chief charge against Schmalhausen was that he "considered it not to be his duty to develop in the students under his control instinctive respect for the President of the United States as such, . . . and other federal, state and municipal officers as such." The principal evidence was that Schmalhausen had required his students to write a "frank letter" to the President on the conduct of the war and, when critical letters were written, "had failed to make such criticisms . . . as would lead the pupil to perceive the gross disloyalty involved in his point of view." All the dismissals were upheld by the Commissioner of Education.

*Matter of Glassberg,* 33 N. Y. State Dep't. Reports 261 (Ed. Dep't, 1925). Glassberg, a high school teacher of history, was dismissed for "conduct unbecoming a teacher." The evidence on which the charges were based, produced by the conflicting testimony of students, was that on one occasion he had made remarks to his class such as "being a public school teacher he was not allowed to tell the truth to his pupils;" "that the Government of the United States of America was and still is systematically suppressing true reports with regard to the Russian Bolsheviki;" that if the truth were "permitted to be made public . . . it would be found that the said Bolsheviki are not so bad as most people think;" and that, when asked if it "was ever right to put the red flag above the American flag," he had replied, "Yes, in a sense." The Commissioner of Education sustained the dismissal.

*Board of Education of Eureka v. Jewett,* 21 Cal. App. 2d 64, 68 Pac. 2d 404 (1937). A permanent teacher of social studies in a junior high school was dismissed on grounds of "unprofessional conduct." He had made statements to his pupils that it was "silly and foolish to salute the American flag"; that "Russia had the best government in the world, and that we had one of the worst"; that "Russia always pays its debts, it is this country that doesn't pay its debts"; that the United States was "the aggressor in every war we have been in." He had also made other statements of the same nature and, when accused by one of his pupils of being a communist, he had not denied it. In order to obtain his teaching credentials, the teacher had subscribed to an oath to "support the Constitution and laws of the United States and of the State of California, and by precept and example to promote respect for the flag, and undivided allegiance to the government of the United States." It was held that his classroom behavior violated this oath and justified revocation of his credentials and his dismissal.

*Joyce v. Board of Education of Chicago*, 325 Ill. App. 543, 60 N.E.(2d) 431 (1945.) The school board discharged a high school history teacher for "conduct unbecoming a school teacher in the Chicago public schools." Two months after Pearl Harbor the teacher had written a letter, which was publicized, congratulating a former student on the "courageous and idealistic stand" he had taken in refusing to register for the draft as required by the Selective Service Act. In discussing current affairs with her class the day following the attack on Pearl Harbor, she made statements "derogatory to the United States government" and favorable to Germany and Japan. The court found that the letter alone constituted adequate cause for discharge, and did not consider the evidence regarding her classroom remarks, about which the testimony of her students was conflicting.

## Note

1. Other cases involving conduct in the classroom include:

*Goldsmith v. Board of Education of Sacramento*, 66 Cal. App. 157, 225 Pac. 783 (1924). A teacher who had been suspended without pay for ten weeks for "unprofessional conduct" brought mandamus to compel his reinstatement. The teacher had expressed in class his support of a particular candidate for election to superintendency of schools, and urged students to tell their parents to vote for him. The court held that such advocacy was "foreign to the purposes and objects" of the school and affirmed the suspension order.

*Bump v. Union High School District*, 144 Ore. 390, 24 Pac. 2d 330 (1933). A high school teacher was discharged for "failure to maintain order in classroom, to follow directions of the school board with regard to course of study, and failure to conduct himself so as to command the respect of his pupils," in that he performed acts of contortion by scratching the back of his head with his foot, flirted with girl pupils, used vulgar language, told risqué stories, discussed sex problems, advocated nudism, inculcated disrespect for the Bible as a religious authority and disrespect for the United States Government. A State Board of Education rule, which the court held to be part of the contract, required teachers to teach "correct moral principles and regard for law." Bump was dismissed "for good cause shown." The court held that the Board could determine whether he had breached the terms of his contract without notifying him of its intention to do so, and that only if he were discharged for an act not amounting to a breach of his contract of teaching was he entitled to notice and hearing.

2. The National Education Association's Committee on Tenure and Academic Freedom publishes an annual report, *Court Decisions on Teacher Tenure*, which digests all cases of dismissal or other disciplinary action against teachers under tenure. See also Garber, *Yearbook of School Law* (published annually); Notes, 46 Yale L. J. 670 (1937); 16 Tenn. L. Rev. 1002 (1941); 21 Notre Dame Law. 25 (1945); 29 Neb. L. Rev. 485, 495–9 (1950); 127 A.L.R. 1298. For a discussion of the innumerable restrictions upon the activities of teachers see Beale, *Are American Teachers Free?* (1936).

## 5. Tenure and Contract Protection in Higher Education

Only isolated cases involving teachers in institutions of higher learning have reached the courts. Rights in the nature of tenure rights, accruing through university rules or contract arrangements, have been recognized. In *State ex rel. Keeney v. Ayers,* 108 Mont. 547, 92 Pac.2d 306 (1939), the plaintiff was a librarian with professorial rank at the University of Montana. He had, for a period of six consecutive years, signed an annual contract, subject to tenure regulations printed on its reverse side. These regulations stipulated that after three years of continuous service reappointment would be considered permanent. This provision was stricken from the last contract, but the plaintiff had accepted this contract under protest. His employment was subsequently terminated, without the hearing and investigation guaranteed permanent faculty members by the regulations. He sought mandamus to compel reinstatement. The Court granted the petition, holding that the tenure rules were not merely for the guidance of the governing board, but became part of the contract entitling the professor to permanent status and the right of hearing and investigation prior to his dismissal. In a dictum, relying on the United States Supreme Court's decision in *Anderson v. Brand, supra,* the Court indicated that the regulations governing tenure could not be repealed or so altered by the Board as to impair its contract with the employee.

See also *Ironside v. Tead,* 13 N. Y. Supp. 2d 17 (1939) (instructor, given written notice of his acquisition of tenure at time when no specific rules had been formally adopted by governing board, and discharged without notice or hearing immediately prior to the board's formal adoption of specific tenure regulations eight years later, held entitled to reinstatement). And note the court's reference to the fact that the University of California faculty members possessed tenure right in *Tolman v. Underhill,* — Cal. App. —, 229 Pac.2d 447, 448 (1951). But *cf. Cobb v. Howard University,* 106 F.2d 860 (C.A.D.C., 1939) (no tenure rights accrued where enabling statute specifically provided for removal in the judgment of the trustees).

The courts do not appear to have passed upon causes of dismissal raising direct questions of academic freedom at the university level. *Cf. State ex rel. Bourgeois v. Board of Supervisors of Louisiana State University,* 205 La. 177, 17 So. 2d 25 (1944); *Fuller v. DePaul University,* 293 Ill. App. 261, 12 N. E. 2d 213 (1938). But such questions are more frequently considered in administrative proceedings within the university. Among the best known cases of this kind are the University of Washington Tenure Cases.

## THE TENURE CASES AT THE UNIVERSITY OF WASHINGTON

Extracts from *Communism and Academic Freedom,*
University of Washington Press (1949)

### I

INTRODUCTION—A REVIEW OF THE CASES AND A STATEMENT OF POLICY BY PRESIDENT RAYMOND B. ALLEN

. . . The tenure cases emerged from this special background. For many years the University had been charged with being a hotbed of Communism and the harbor of what was called "a nest of Communist professors." The many years of charges concerning Communist activity at the University and elsewhere in the state of Washington culminated in 1947 in the establishment by the state legislature of a Joint Legislative Fact-Finding Committee on Un-American Activities (popularly known as the Canwell Committee). . . . The Committee was charged with inquiring into alleged subversive activities and objectives of individuals and organizations in the state of Washington, and was asked to report its findings to the next session of the legislature. The Committee was instructed by the legislature to give special attention to Communist Party activities that might affect "the functioning of any state agency, unemployment relief, and other forms of public assistance, educational institutions of this state supported in whole or in part by state funds." The second investigation undertaken by the legislative Committee had as its subject alleged Communist activities on the University of Washington campus.

After some weeks of preliminary investigation, the Committee held an open public hearing in Seattle starting on July 19, 1948, and lasting for one week. Throughout its investigation and hearings the University attempted to cooperate with this committee. . . .

It should be said also that in the open Committee hearings no effort was made by Committee members to elicit testimony on the political or social views of faculty members other than those who, for some concrete reason, were believed to be, or to have been, members of the Communist Party. It is to the credit of the Committee that it limited its inquiry to those situations where there was an actual question of Communist Party membership.

In the hearings of the legislative Committee ten members of the University faculty, all enjoying tenure under University rules, were named as being or having been members of the Communist Party. Two of the ten flatly denied any association with the Party. Five admitted past membership but denied present membership. The three others refused to testify as to past or present membership in the Communist Party.*

Following the open hearings of the legislative Committee, and after the information elicited by the Committee had been studied carefully by the University Administration, complaints were filed with the University faculty Committee on Tenure and Academic Freedom against six members of the faculty by Dean Edward H. Lauer of the College of Arts and Sciences. The six respondents included the three faculty members who had refused to testify as to past or present membership in the Communist Party and three of those who had admitted past membership but denied present membership. Following the filing of complaints by Dean Lauer on September 8, 1948, and subsequent to formal replies by the six respondents, the faculty Committee on Tenure and Academic Freedom began its closed hearings in the cases on October 27, 1948. The hearings, lasting through thirty-three sessions, were closed December 15, 1948. Testimony was taken from seventy-three witnesses. The expenses and

---

* There were approximately 700 full-time members of the University faculty and about the same number of part-time and subfaculty members.

witness fees for both Administration and respondents' witnesses were paid by the University.

The faculty Committee on Tenure and Academic Freedom is established by the University's Administrative Code, which in Chapter IV specifies University regulations on tenure and the preservation of academic freedom. The Committee is composed of eleven members of the University faculty, and it is appointed by the University Senate and not by the President, who has absolutely no voice in its selection. The President, however, is an ex officio member of all University committees, and therefore he sat with the Committee during its hearings although he (by regulation in the Administrative Code) was specifically excluded from its deliberations in executive session. According to the Code, the Committee is charged with making effective the following statement of principles:

> 1. *Principles.* It is desirable that regular action by both a faculty committee and the administration of the University should precede the dismissal for cause of a faculty member. The accused teacher should always have the opportunity to face his accusers and to be heard in his own defense by all bodies that pass judgment on his case. In the trial of charges of professional incompetence, the testimony of scholars in the same field, either from his own or from other institutions, should always be taken. . . .

## II

### REPORT OF THE COMMITTEE ON TENURE AND ACADEMIC FREEDOM

#### General Nature of Tenure Code

Inasmuch as the determination of each of the six cases rests in large part on the interpretation to be given to those parts of the Tenure Code dealing with grounds for dismissal, it is deemed desirable to discuss this subject before taking up any individual case.

The relevant provisions read as follows:

> Univ. Admin. Code, Ch. IV, Part I, Sec. I: Definitions. "Tenure" means the right of a person to hold his position during good behavior and efficient and competent service, and not to be removed therefrom except for cause in the manner hereinafter provided.
> *Ibid.,* Sec. IV. Removal for Cause.
> Persons having tenure under the provisions of this act

may be removed from the faculty of the University for one or more of the following reasons:

(a) Incompetency
(b) Neglect of duty
(c) Physical or mental incapacity
(d) Dishonesty or immorality
(e) Conviction of a felony involving moral turpitude

Proceedings for the removal of such a person shall be conducted in accordance with the rules of procedure hereinafter described (see Chapter IV, Part II).

Complainant contends that the listing of causes for removal in Section I is merely illustrative, and not definitive. . . . In particular, it is urged that any conduct bringing the University into disrepute should be deemed an absence of good behavior and hence ground for recommendation of dismissal.

Naturally, respondents contend that the causes listed in Sec. IV are definitive.

In the opinion of the Committee the latter is the correct interpretation of the Code in this respect. . . .

### Cases of Lauer vs. Butterworth and Lauer vs. Phillips

*Statement of Professors Densmore, Gose, Hatch, Rowntree, and Thompson*

Joseph Butterworth is an Associate in English, which position he has held since he joined the faculty in 1929. Herbert J. Phillips has been a member of the University faculty since 1920 and holds the position of Assistant Professor of Philosophy, which rank he attained in 1934. . . .

Both Butterworth and Phillips admitted at the outset of the hearing that they are presently members of the Communist Party, U. S. A., and have been such since the year 1935. There is, therefore, no issue of fact as to their status as party members. . . .

Before proceeding to consider our immediate problem, it must be said, in fairness to respondents Butterworth and Phillips, that not all rank-and-file Communists privately subscribe unqualifiedly to all Communist doctrine or interpret it in the same way. However, any publicly expressed difference by any Party member on any important point settled by the Party is ground for expulsion from the Party.

We are not at all sure that a member of the Communist Party, in stating his understanding of party policy or doctrine, uses

**893**

language in quite the same sense as we do. Respondent Phillips has, for example, testified that he does not believe in the violent overthrow of the government and that the Communist Party does not stand for such a program in this country. We believe that he is sincere in making this statement. However, we suspect that, on a given set of facts, we might assert that the Communist Party was attempting to overthrow the government by force, and he might assert that it was merely defending itself against the unwarranted attacks of a reactionary minority bent on suppressing the will of the majority. Precisely that view was taken by every pro-Communist witness in this hearing concerning the rise to power of Communist governments in foreign countries, which we, as non-Communists, believe was accomplished by force. The Communist point of view is so different from our own that any apparent agreement in principle is often entirely unreal in actual practice. Nevertheless, we give to respondent Phillips the benefit of the doubt and assume that he would not condone seizure of power by violent methods. The respondent Butterworth did not indicate his views on this subject with the same clarity, but we shall proceed on the assumption that his views as to the impropriety of seizing power by violent means are the same.

Nevertheless, the fact remains that both of these respondents adhere to the fundamentals of Marxism. To their credit it should be said that they have frankly admitted their membership in the Communist Party and make no apologies for their beliefs. The very core of Marxist doctrine, to which they subscribe, calls for a complete change of the structure of the state so as to substitute for the present system a government entirely dominated by one class and party, with complete and permanent suppression of all opposition. It is merely a figure of speech to say that this would be nothing more than an orderly amendment of the present system by constitutional means. The program calls for far more than amendment, as that term is commonly understood. It calls for revolution—with or without force—after which the present form of government would no longer exist. The republican form of government, guaranteed by the United States Constitution, or, to use the more popular modern term, democracy in the American sense, would be replaced by a philosophy and a legal system utterly alien to our institutions. Whether so sweeping a change can ever be imposed on the American people may be debatable. Nevertheless, it is the program for which every member of the Communist Party, including these respondents, must stand if there is to be no "watering down of Marxism-Leninism." (See Com-

**894**

plainant's Exhibit 2, "Theory and Practice of Communist Party.")

We have then this anomalous situation. These respondents seek and assert the right to remain in the employ of a state which they hope to destroy and, as members of a minority group, seek and assert a right to protection when their own political faith denies any such right to any other minority once Communism becomes dominant. Only the magnanimity of a most benevolent government can be invoked to honor these requests.

There are undoubtedly many people in the United States today who would at this point end all debate by discharging these respondents from their present positions without more ado. There are undoubtedly many others who would and do condone the position taken by respondents, not because they agree with them but because of deeply rooted respect for freedom of thought and conscience. . . .

It is not within our competence as members of this faculty Committee to form new policies as to tenure, much less as to status of the Communist Party and its members. . . . We cannot . . . add grounds for removal to those stated therein or ignore grounds which are so stated. Such addition or subtraction must be accomplished by some change in the Code under which we operate.

Our problem then is simply this: Taking the admitted fact that respondents Phillips and Butterworth are members of the Communist Party, U. S. A., is there a case for removal present under the Administrative Code? It must be kept in mind that nothing concerning the conduct of these respondents other than the simple fact of their Party membership, plus its necessary implications, is before us. None of their actions in the classroom or elsewhere is to be considered. All material of that character was eliminated from the case at the instance of complainant to present a "clear-cut issue." . . .

Of the foregoing [causes for dismissal set forth in the Tenure Code, *supra*], it is at once obvious that (c) physical or mental incapacity and (e) conviction of a felony involving moral turpitude are not involved as to these respondents. There then remain, as the only possible grounds, incompetency, neglect of duty, dishonesty or immorality and, conceivably, misbehavior, if that is not of necessity already included in one of the other grounds.

Incompetency, as here used, refers to the scholarship and teaching ability of a faculty member in his field of study. It has no reference to his attainments or activities in other fields.

The complainant conceded during the hearing that the general scholarship and teaching ability of respondents Phillips and Butterworth in their respective fields, were not challenged. It is impossible to conceive how the mere fact of membership in the Communist Party could, in any way, affect the competency of respondent Butterworth as a teacher of Old English literature. As to respondent Phillips, there is potentially a closer question. As a teacher of philosophy, it might be suggested that, without specific proof, his objectivity as a teacher would necessarily be impaired by his strong bias in favor of a doctrinaire political philosophy. However, the testimony of his colleagues and students is directly to the contrary. Although he does have occasion to discuss Marxian philosophy in his teaching, it appears that his practice is to warn his students of his bias and to request that they evaluate his lectures in light of that fact. Under the circumstances, we cannot find either respondent to be incompetent within the meaning of the Code.

Dishonesty is doubtless susceptible of several connotations. These would include financial dishonesty, untruthfulness, and the rather broad field of intellectual dishonesty. Of these, only the last named is a possibility. Intellectual dishonesty, however, is of necessity a subjective thing. We have no reason to believe that either of these respondents is insincere. On the contrary, we believe that both sincerely accept Communism. The fact that we believe Communist doctrines to be absurd and erroneous does not mean that those who accept them are dishonest.

Immorality is also quite possibly calculated to cover a wide range of conduct. We cannot, however, believe that it was intended to apply to a political belief. It is true that, using the term in the broadest sense, one might brand membership in the Communist Party as an immoral act, depending on how strong one's opinions on the subject might be. This, however, would give the word a much broader meaning than we suppose was intended by the framers of the Code, or would be attributed to it by any member of the faculty reading the Code to determine what conduct would be permissible.

There remain then only neglect of duty and misbehavior. In our opinion, misbehavior is not really a separate ground for dismissal but rather is simply one phase of neglect of duty. In its most restricted form, the duty of a member of the faculty is to teach, diligently and effectively, the courses assigned to him. But duty includes substantially more than this. It calls for such matters as reasonable cooperation with the Administration and the department or school with which one is connected. It includes, for example, the duty of serving on faculty committees to a reasonable extent. It includes also an obligation to conduct oneself both on and off the campus in a manner consistent with the dignity of one's professional position and to refrain from conduct which would discredit the University or bring it into disrepute.

This is not to say that there should be a puritanical censorship of the private life of a faculty member. Within reasonable limits, he is entitled to live his own life as he sees fit. There are, however, limits beyond which he cannot go without violating his duty to the University. Many examples could be given. It would, we believe, be beyond the bounds of propriety for a University teacher to undertake, in his spare time, the occupation of bartender. There is, of course, nothing illegal in such an occupation, but it cannot be denied that such work would be regarded as unacceptable conduct by a very great majority of the faculty and the general public.

We come to the vital question whether simple and unelaborated membership in the Communist Party constitutes neglect of duty on the part of a member of the University faculty. When we consider this question, we find ourselves confronted by a highly confused situation. We think that neglect of duty, as a general proposition, refers to some standard of conduct that is quite universally recognized by the faculty and public alike as being below the standard suitable for a faculty member. Our difficulty is that we find no such universality of opinion upon the subject now under discussion. . . .

It is not necessary that all of the duties of a faculty member be committed to formal statements. There are some duties that are so well understood by all as to require no formal action. The difficulty here is that we cannot be certain even of the majority opinion on the subject. We do know that there is a rather sharp difference of opinion among faculty members and college executives on this whole question. We do know that Committee A of the American Association of University Professors has taken the stand that open membership in the Communist Party should not subject a faculty member to removal. We do know that the administration of this University has, during the period of at least thirteen years in which some of its faculty members have been members of the Communist Party, taken no clear action on the subject. We do know that at least two successive departmental heads in the Department of Philosophy (of which respondent Phillips is a member) took the extreme view that they did not wish the members of their department to inform them in any way of their political affiliations. We do know that there have been debates upon the subject of outlawing the Communist Party, such as the one conducted by Mr. Dewey and Mr. Stassen in Oregon within the past year. We do know that membership in the Communist Party is not illegal in the state of Washington; that it may and does name candidates for public office; and that these candidates could, in theory and in law, be elected to the highest executive and legislative positions in the state. We do know that membership in the Communist Party on the part of a faculty member brings the University into disrepute with a large section of the public, but whether that section is a majority or not has never been authoritatively determined.

Under these ambiguous and confused conditions, it is impossible for us to say there is or has been an established standard of duty making membership in the Communist Party ground for removal of a faculty member. Persons who are members have received encouragement from various sources, many of them high in the educational world. Much of the argument pro and con on the question may be quite specious, but the fact remains that nothing has been done to determine the question one way or another. We are therefore unable to find a neglect of duty where no duty has been clearly established.

We again repeat, so that there may be no doubt, it is not within the power of this Committee to invent new duties or raise new standards. This Committee can only deal with duties as they exist. If it were within the power of this Committee to determine policy, it appears that its members would divide rather sharply on whether the simple fact of Communist Party membership should be made cause for removal of a member of the faculty. Those of us who join in this statement agree, as a matter of policy, with the views expressed in the dissenting statement of Professors Benson and Goodspeed in these cases but do not join therein because we believe that we would thereby assume a policy-making function beyond our powers. We believe that it is time that a policy be laid down by some competent authority, whether it be the faculty as a whole, the President, the Regents, or the legislature, so as to put this vexed subject upon a basis that cannot be misunderstood. . . .

We conclude that in the cases of respondents Butterworth and Phillips the fact of membership in the Communist Party alone furnishes no basis for removal under the Administrative Code, as presently constituted. If some other body having suitable powers sees fit to lay down a new policy, that is another matter. . . .

[Emerson]

## Separate Statement of Professors Robinson, Sholley, and Huber

The undersigned members of the Committee concur in the recommendations contained in the preceding majority statement, but do not agree with all of the reasoning and factual conclusions contained therein. The following statement was drafted in the hope that it would secure the adherence of a majority of those members concurring in the recommendations. Although that hope has been disappointed, time considerations have caused us to submit it in its original form rather than cause delay by preparation of a different version. . . .

Complainant introduced a large volume of literature issued or sponsored by the Communist Party, U. S. A., and the testimony of expert witnesses in an effort to prove that the Communist Party, U. S. A., is dominated by a foreign power; that it openly advocates overthrow of government by force and violence; that it enforces strict adherence to the "party line" by rigid discipline imposed upon all of its members to such an extent that they must surrender their intellectual integrity and honesty; and that it seeks to achieve its ends by secret methods, including the "infiltration" of other organizations. Since no evidence was introduced to show that either Butterworth or Phillips engaged in any illegal or improper activity, complainant's position necessarily is that *every* member of the Communist Party is unfit to remain a faculty member, regardless of his scholarship, teaching ability, or the general propriety of all of his overt conduct.

Respondents introduced expert testimony and documentary material tending to show that the Communist Party, U. S. A., is not foreign dominated, does not advocate illegal means to achieve its ultimate goal of establishing socialism, does not attempt to discipline its rank-and-file members or insist upon their unquestioning adherence to the party line, and is a lawful political party. Respondents testified that each joined the Communist Party in 1935 and has continued such membership since, that their Party activities were and are almost entirely confined to paying dues and attending discussion meetings of their unit, that they believe the Party to be a legitimate political party of the nature described by their general evidence, and that they have not surrendered their intellectual independence and freedom of belief. Testimony of colleagues and of former and present students was introduced to prove respondents' reputation and performance as sound scholars and able and unbiased teachers. Complainant made no effort to refute this last line of testimony.

The Committee conceives the issues of fact properly before it to be narrower than the scope of the evidence might suggest. The Communist Party is not on trial, nor are any of its members other than, for present purposes, respondents Butterworth and Phillips. Our authority is limited to determining whether they have by virtue of admitted membership in the Communist Party been guilty of conduct which in our judgment constitutes cause for dismissal as defined by the Code. We sit to try Butterworth and Phillips, not Foster and Dennis. We may, and must, consider the general nature of the Communist Party, U.S.A., insofar as may be necessary to assay the conduct of respondents, but to that extent only. We conceive that we have neither duty nor authority to make "findings of fact" completely unnecessary to the decision of cases submitted to us. . . . We turn to the listed causes.

(a) *Incompetency.* This term obviously refers to the knowledge, skill, and temperament requisite to the adequate performance of teaching and research duties. On these points no charge is leveled at respondents Butterworth and Phillips, and the only evidence in the record is favorable to them. However, complainant's charge presupposes that the term "incompetency" has a broader meaning.

It is urged that the rigid adherence to the party line enforced by strict discipline upon all members of the Communist Party renders any member "incompetent", because such member is not a free agent, free to follow truth wherever it may lead; his research is distorted into a search for evidence to support his beliefs; his teaching is slanted to induce his students to share these beliefs; in short, he is incapable of sound scholarship and objective teaching. We pass over the fundamental question posed by this contention—whether academic freedom extends to teachers of strong beliefs and fighting faith—because the question *is* fundamental and most difficult to answer, and because we find in the record nothing to support the allegations, other than general statements of the duty of all Party members to follow policy determinations made by the national leadership, and testimony that disobedient Party functionaries are from time to time expelled. Against this, respondents testified that they had never been subjected to discipline, that they felt free to do their own thinking and reach their own conclusions, and that they remained in the Party through personal conviction and not from fear of persecution. As to academic activities, in the case of Butterworth, whose area of specialty is Old and Middle English language and literature, it would be astonishing if the impact of Marxism could be detected, and there is direct evidence that it is, if present, imperceptible. The case of Phillips is otherwise, for he is a philosopher and a teacher of courses in which certain philosophical aspects of Marxism are directly introduced as subject matter of study and discussion. However, there is no evidence of distortion in research, and there is evidence that Dr. Phillips in his classes treats Marxism in an objective manner. Indeed, it appears that he seeks to guard against the effects of unwitting slant in his teaching by warning the class of his personal bias.

A further contention is that respondents Butterworth and Phillips are "incompetent" in the sense of lacking intellectual capacity and balance because they hold economic and political beliefs and adhere to an organization devoted to their furtherance, which beliefs are abhorred and which organization is hated and feared by the great majority of Americans. Here complainant opens a door through which we dare not pass. Surely we may not outlaw all professors who hold beliefs contrary to whatever may be the current conceptions, superstitions, and emotions of the general populace; we must not close the academic doors to a modern Galileo or Darwin. And just as surely, we may not set up our own beliefs, or those of the University faculty as a whole, as the standard of competence. Our profession is ornamented by many men who hold religious beliefs which contravene the findings of physical science. On a more mundane level, would anyone have the effrontery to declare that George Bernard Shaw is incompetent to teach drama because he holds—and proclaims most vigorously—a strong opinion that vaccination is a menace to mankind? True, these examples involve beliefs deemed relatively harmless today, but what is innocuous today was deadly yesterday, and may be again tomorrow; and, in any event, neither the truth of a belief nor the intellect of its holder is to be assayed by measuring the social disturbance which would attend the general acceptance of such belief. In short, the contention cuts too deep for us to adopt it without a much clearer mandate than that before us.

Finally, we are urged to read "incompetency" as "unfitness" and to hold these respondents unfit because their membership in the Communist Party brings discredit and disrepute upon the University in the minds of the citizenry of this state. This, in essence, is the same argument as that grounded on the phrase "good behavior" which was considered and rejected above. It is even less admissible in this context. In any event, there is nothing in the record to indicate that the University has suffered in the estimation of the public, and we would hardly be warranted in conjecturing that such has been the case.

(b) *Neglect of duty.* In its obvious connotation, this phrase comprehends inadequate performance of duties as a scholar and

as a teacher, and of those other duties, such as service on this Committee, properly imposed upon academic employees of the University. Some members of the Committee believe the phrase should be so limited in meaning; others are of the view that it may properly be given a somewhat broader scope. Since a majority concludes that complainant has failed to prove his case even under the broadest acceptable reading, the question is left open.
. . .

(c) *Dishonesty or immorality*. The interpretative problem here posed is to what extent these terms comprehend extramural conduct. We pass this question, because again we conclude that complainant's factual contention is not supported by the evidence.

Complainant strongly urges that respondents are "dishonest" in the sense of being secret enemies of our state and national governments because they are members of long standing in an organization which proclaims as its long-range objective the overthrow of these governments by force and violence, and which organization is actually controlled by a foreign power whose present international policy is inimical to the interests of this country. There is much evidence in the record bearing on the nature of the Communist Party, some of which supports this contention and some of which points the other way. But, as we pointed out above, we are not trying the Communist Party. The real issue is the honesty of respondents. If they, however foolishly, believe the Party to be an independent seeker after socialism by peaceful and constitutional means, they can not be branded as "dishonest." . . .

By way of summation, the Committee concludes that complainant has failed to sustain his charges against respondents Butterworth and Phillips, because the various supporting contentions are either unsubstantiated by the evidence or involve interpretations of the Tenure Code which we deem inadmissible. . . .


*Separate and Dissenting Statement of Professors*
*Benson and Goodspeed*

The interpretation placed on the language of the Tenure Code by the Committee majority has led it to conclusions which we must reject. To accept the causes for removal listed in Section IV as definitive, and to declare all other possible grounds for dismissal outside the Committee's jurisdiction, is to deny to members of the faculty, and the University, the full protection the Tenure Code was intended to provide. In our view the listed causes must be accepted as merely illustrative. . . .

Suppose a member of the faculty refused to support his family and neglected his children in a fashion so outrageous as to arouse the hostility of the community; that he was so irresponsible financially and so reckless in the incurring of debts, which he refused to pay, that the University Comptroller's routine was continually interrupted by garnishment actions against him. Clearly, such a person would be unfit for retention on the faculty, yet nowhere does the Tenure Code, if narrowly interpreted, provide machinery for his dismissal. . . .

That the Communist Party is not on trial before this Committee we readily agree; but we must insist that Communism, the Communist Party, and their relationship to University faculty members and to academic freedom are properly before us, both in specific pleadings and in the voluminous record of this Committee's hearings.

Academic freedom has been defined as freedom to seek the truth wherever it shall lead. It is one of the duties of this Committee to protect that freedom. The principle of democratic centralism, which is basic in Communist teachings and Communist Party practices, directly opposes this freedom we would protect. To say that we may not assess Communism in terms of its significance to academic freedom lest we trench on that freedom, is to ignore the world in which we live and to foster in the name of academic freedom that which would avowedly destroy it. To insist that we may not appraise Communism in terms of its contribution to individual dignity and liberty, again is to close our eyes—to the terrors, the purges, the physical slavery it has brought to many lands, and the enslavement it has brought to men's minds everywhere Communists have been able to enforce their "party line" in science, music, literature, the theater, and the arts. . . .

It is therefore our considered judgment that membership in the Communist Party, U. S. A., should not be regarded as similar to, or even vaguely suggestive of, membership in the traditional American political parties. It is our opinion that active present membership in the Communist Party, U. S. A., is an overt act of such reckless, uncritical, and intemperate partisanship as to be inimical to, and incompatible with, the highest traditions of academic freedom and responsible scholarship, and that such active present membership should be declared sufficient grounds for dismissal of any faculty member so committed. As a corollary, it is further recommended that present active membership in the Communist Party be deemed adequate reason for refusal to employ an applicant for a position on the faculty of the University of Washington.

The strict construction placed upon the wording of the Tenure

**903**

Code, in our view, does violence to the ordinary and generally understood meanings of the words employed. Webster defines "incompetence" as "unfitness," and we find no difficulty in applying these terms to the instant situations. To insist that the principles of academic freedom bar us from such a course, is to argue that we should shelter on our faculty men who believe the world is flat, and is to extend tolerance into the realm of nonsense. History has yet to witness the closing of academic doors to a Bacon or a Newton through a critical appraisal and rejection of dogma by his fellows. . . .

The respondents Phillips and Butterworth, by their active present membership in the Communist Party, U. S. A., have disqualified themselves for retention on the faculty of the University of Washington. The undersigned therefore recommend that these respondents be dismissed with such severance pay in lieu of notice as will be compatible with the principles of academic freedom and tenure laid down by the American Association of University Professors.

*Separate and Dissenting Statement of Professor Williams*

I join with Professors Benson and Goodspeed in recommending that respondents Joseph Butterworth and Herbert J. Phillips be dismissed as members of the faculty. My reasons are as follows:

Both are admitted members of the Communist Party, U. S. A. This fact, in my opinion, disqualifies them as faculty members and renders them subject to dismissal on the ground of "incompetency."

My opinion is based upon two fundamental considerations. In the first place, I do not accept the exclusively legalistic basis taken in the majority report. Whether the Communist Party, U. S. A., is legal or not is not the sole consideration upon which the decision should be made, in my opinion. I hold that membership in many legally constituted organizations might render one incompetent to perform the duties of a member of the faculty.

In the second place, my opinion is based upon the consideration of the nature, functions, control, and administration of American public education. Public education in the United States is in the nature of a social enterprise in which the general welfare is one of the prime considerations. Public educational institutions are instruments created by legislation at the behest of the public on the assumption that they will perform their public functions in terms of the spirit, philosophy, and under the general climate of ideas acceptable to the government of the people who create, patronize, and support them.

The people are sovereign in respect to American public education. They have the right to establish the policies governing the conduct of educational institutions. One well-established policy, generally accepted in the United States, is that one of the functions of education is that of training for citizenship. I have no doubt that it is the expectation of the parents of students at the University of Washington that their children shall not be instructed by members of the Communist Party, U. S. A. I hold that a member of the Communist Party is incompetent to teach in a publicly created institution of learning because such membership is incompatible with citizenship in a government such as ours founded upon democratic principles and unquestionably opposed to the rule of any one class as advocated by the Communist Party.

I do not question the right of an instructor to entertain a belief of his choice, but active membership in any organization incompatible with the government of the United States is disqualifying and is ground for dismissal.

[The Committee voted 7 to 4 that Prof. Gundlach, in failing to answer frankly questions relating to his Communist Party membership at a conference with President Allen prior to the Canwell hearings, had been guilty of neglect of duty and should be dismissed. The Committee voted unanimously that Profs. Eby, Ethel and Jacobs, who were no longer members of the Communist Party, should not be dismissed.]

## III

### THE PRESIDENT'S ANALYSIS

. . . While incompetency is a relative term without fixed technical meaning, it does have a common and approved usage. The following has been frequently used by the courts:

> It [incompetency] may be employed as meaning disqualification; inability; incapacity; lack of ability, legal qualification or fitness to discharge the required duty.
>
> — *Corpus Juris*

In my opinion, a teacher may be rendered incompetent, even within the restricted legal meaning of the term, by any action, condition, or attitude which interferes with the proper and adequate performance of his duties. . . .

I would point out that the teacher and the scholar have special obligations with respect to the sincerity of their convictions which involve questions of intellectual honesty and integrity. Men in academic life—teachers, scholars, and scientists—are engaged in a vocation which is concerned with the finding of truth and its dissemination, with the pursuit of truth wherever it may lead. Is it possible for an individual, however sincere, to embrace both this unhampered pursuit of truth and, at the same time, the doctrines and dogmas of a political party which admits of no criticism of its fundamental principles and programs? Put in another way, a teacher may be ever so sincere in his belief in Communism, but can he at the same time be a sincere seeker after truth, which is the first obligation and duty of the teacher? My answer to these questions is, "He cannot." Therefore, I believe these men, by reason of their admitted membership in the Communist Party described in the above findings, to be incompetent, intellectually dishonest, and derelict in their duty to find and teach the truth.

There is, in other words, a higher duty imposed upon members of the academic community than upon other men. For centuries universities have survived in the Western world, not without difficulties and serious attacks from both without and within, primarily because of their impartiality, objectivity, and determination to seek truth and not be propagandists in partisan political, economic, and other debates. The University of Washington could not exist if every member of its faculty were to engage in clandestine political activity and to take sides secretly on every partisan political and economic issue that comes before the people. Clandestine activity such as Butterworth's and Phillips' in the Communist Party means that they have forsaken their duty to protect the University's integrity and to pursue an objective quest of truth in favor of a propagandistic mission entirely unrelated to real educational and scholarly effort. In my opinion every member of the faculty must discharge this higher duty if a University is to maintain its corporate function, identity, and integrity. The integrity of an institution begins and ends with the integrity of the people that comprise it and give it meaning and life. . . .

I recommend that the Board hold with the minority that respondents Butterworth and Phillips are disqualified from membership on the faculty of the University of Washington on the ground that they are members of the Communist Party, U. S. A., and, until these proceedings, kept this fact secret, and therefore are unfit for faculty membership. In these proceedings it has been adequately proved, in my opinion, that they are incompetent, that they are intellectually dishonest, and that they have neglected their duties as members of the faculty. They should be dismissed within the generally accepted meaning of these words as they are listed as causes for dismissal in Section IV of the Administrative Code. . . .

[President Allen agreed with the Committee's recommendations as to the other four professors.]

## IV

### MINUTES OF THE BOARD OF REGENTS

The Board of Regents voted to adopt the President's recommendations for the dismissal of Messrs. Butterworth, Phillips, and Gundlach from the faculty of the University of Washington as of February 1, 1949.

The Board voted to adopt the President's recommendations against dismissal of Messrs. Jacobs, Eby, and Ethel, subject to the following conditions:

(a) That these men shall severally sign and file affidavits that they are not now members of the Communist Party, and have not been members of the Communist Party since the respective dates stated in their testimony before the faculty Tenure Committee. Failure to file such affidavits with the President of the University prior to February 1, 1949, shall result in immediate dismissal.

(b) That Messrs. Jacobs, Eby, and Ethel be further placed on probation for a period of two years.

### Note

1. For further background on the Canwell Committee and the University of Washington proceedings, see Countryman, *Un-American Activities in the State of Washington* (1951).

2. Most colleges and universities take the position that members of the Communist Party are not qualified to teach and will not be employed or retained on the faculty. See summary of views in N. Y. Times, May 30, 1949, Oct. 8, 1950. Many have formally adopted rules banning Communists and some require loyalty oaths of faculty members. See, *e. g.*, N. Y. Times, Mar. 25 and June 3, 1949, Oct. 10 and 11, 1950, June 14, 1951, Mar. 29, 1952. Others take an intermediate position that they will not knowingly employ Communists but will not institute elaborate procedures to search for them. See N. Y. Times, Feb. 18, 1952.

3. Professional organizations of educators opposed to the employment of Communists as teachers are the National Educational Association (resolution adopted at 87th Annual Meeting, 1949); The Educational Policies Commission (see *Education and International Tensions*, 1949); the American Association of School Administrators (resolution adopted at Convention, 1950). Resolutions against the employment of "subversive" teachers which have been adopted by state education associations are described in Reutter, *The School Administrator and Subversive Activities*, pp. 66–7 (1951). Organizations which oppose disciplinary action against teachers solely on the basis of mem-

bership in the Communist Party are the American Federation of Teachers (which bars Communists from membership), see 34 Amer. Teacher 5 (1949); the American Civil Liberties Union (which bars Communists from positions as officers or members of committees), see *Civil Liberties of Teachers and Students* (1949, and Supplements, Nov. 1949 and May 1952); the American Association of University Professors, see *Report of Committee for 1947,* 34 A. A. U. P. Bull. 121 (1948).

4. The classic debate upon the question of Communists as teachers in universities is Hook, *Should Communists be Permitted to Teach?,* N. Y. Times Mag. Feb. 27, 1949, p. 7 (no) versus Meiklejohn, *Should Communists be Allowed to Teach?,* N. Y. Times Mag. Mar. 27, 1949, p. 10 (A. A. U. P. position). See also Havighurst and Peck, *Communism and American Education,* 57 School Rev. 453 (1949) (a summary of opinions regarding Communists as teachers, with bibliography); Gallup, *Barring of Communist Teachers is Favored by Big Vote in Survey,* Public Opinion News Service (Sept. 21, 1949); Allen, *Communists Should Not Teach in American Colleges,* 13 Ed. Forum 433 (1949); Axtelle, *Should Communists Teach in American Universities?,* 13 Ed. Forum 425 (1949); Childs, *Communists and the Right to Teach,* The Nation, Feb. 26, 1949, p. 230; Commager, *Red Baiting in the Colleges,* The New Republic, July 25, 1949, p. 10; Fuchs and Hunter, *Communists in the Colleges: Two Views,* 9 Antioch Rev. 199 (1949); Hook, *Academic Integrity and Academic Freedom,* Commentary 329 (Oct. 1949); Kandel, *The Teaching Profession and Communists,* 70 Sch. and Soc. 73 (1949); Lerner, *The Mandarins and the Pariahs,* 18 Am. Scholar 337 (1949); Lovejoy, *Communism versus Academic Freedom,* 18 Am. Scholar 332 (1949); Morse, *Academic Freedom versus Communistic Indoctrination,* 15 Vital Speeches 400 (1949); Norton, *Communists as Teachers,* 119 Am. School Board J. 49 (1949); Norton, *Keeping American Education Free,* 14 Ed. Forum 277 (1950); Schlesinger, *The Right to Loathsome Ideas,* Sat. Rev. Lit., May 14, 1949; Smith, *Academic Expediency as Democratic Justice in re Communists,* 18 Am. Scholar 342 (1949); Stoke, *Freedom is Not Academic,* 20 J. Higher Ed. 346 (1949); Thayer, *Should Communists and Fascists Teach in the Schools?,* 12 Harv. Ed. Rev. 7 (1942); Wecter, *Commissars of Loyalty,* Sat. Rev. Lit., May 13, 1950.

## F. PROTECTION OF ACADEMIC FREEDOM THROUGH SELF-ORGANIZATION

Realization of the principles of academic freedom, in practice, will of course depend upon the effort and activity of those persons who have an interest in furthering its doctrines. See Caughey, *Trustees of Academic Freedom,* 37 A. A. U. P. Bull. 427 (1951). Under modern conditions an interest of this nature is usually expressed most effectively through an organization. Professional educational associations, teachers' unions, groups

**908**

such as the American Civil Liberties Union, and other organizations play a part in this process.

## 1. Professional Organizations

The American Association of University Professors, a professional organization comparable to the American Medical and Bar Associations, was first organized in 1915. Its primary purposes are to raise professional standards and defend academic freedom. Anyone who has had three years' teaching experience in a college or university is eligible for membership. The Association reported in 1949 a membership of 33,638 teachers in 792 institutions—roughly one quarter of the total number of faculty members in institutions of higher education in 1944. See 35 A. A. U. P. Bull. 176 (1949); President's Commission on Higher Education, *Higher Education for American Democracy: Resource Data*, Vol. 6, p. 36 (1948). Through its Committee on Academic Freedom and Tenure (Committee A), the Association investigates alleged violations of academic freedom, attempts negotiation and mediation with the college administration and, where these efforts fail to secure the reinstatement of a wrongfully discharged teacher, imposes its final sanction by placing the institution on its list of "Censored Administrations." As of 1950, eight administrations were so censored. A considerable number of controversies are brought to the attention of the Committee each year, but only those few which offer the greatest chances of success, in that they involve clear violations of academic freedom or tenure principles, are pursued with vigor and determination. The effectiveness of the Association is due largely to its publicity measures. The nature of Committee A's operation is described in its Report for 1947, 34 A. A. U. P. Bull. 110–133; its history, with a brief reference to and commentary on cases investigated by it, is discussed by Ludlum, *Academic Freedom and Tenure: A History*, 10 Antioch Rev. 3 (1950); its activities are summarized in its annual reports, published in the A. A. U. P. Bulletin.

Learned societies organized prior to the American Association of University Professors relegated their interest in matters pertaining to academic freedom to that organization upon its inception in 1915. Recently, however, these societies have taken a renewed interest. For example, as a result of the action of the Board of Regents of the University of California in dismissing professors who refused to sign the "loyalty oath" (see *supra*) the American Psychological Association, and its 17 divisions, which include the nation's social psychologists, anthropologists, educators, economists and specialists in industrial and group relations, urged its members not to accept positions at the University of California "until such time as tenure conditions meet acceptable standards." N. Y. Times, Sept. 7, 1950. For other expressions of learned society protest over the loyalty oath situation at California, see the Interim Report of the Committee on Academic Freedom, *The Consequences of the Abrogation of Tenure* (1951).

The National Education Association, an organization of teachers and other professional educators operating largely in the area of lower education, was first organized in 1857. It has changed considerably both in organization and purposes during its history, but has always remained under the control of administrators and supervisors. It has a large membership and its spokesmen are leading American educators. One of its primary functions is to report annually to the public its views on general educational problems, such as Federal aid to education, the shortage of teachers, buildings and equipment, and so forth. Its interests extend to issues of academic freedom but its activity in this area is of a general nature and does not include machinery for investigation of particular cases. The NEA Committee on Academic Freedom and Tenure publishes annual reports of *Court Decisions on Teacher Tenure,* and occasional surveys of opinion on problems involving academic freedom. For a discussion of the NEA's activities during the 1920's and 1930's see Beale, *Are American Teachers Free?,* pp. 692–701 (1936); Sinclair, *The Goslings,* pp. 234–275 (1924); for a less derogatory and more disinterested study see, Selle, *The Organization and Activities of the National Education Association* (1932); the NEA's own history is Fenner, *NEA History* (1945).[1]

## 2. Teachers' Unions

The right of teachers to join labor organizations has been severely restricted in the past. Thus in *People ex rel. Fursman v. Chicago,* 278 Ill. 318, 116 N. E. 158 (1917), the court upheld a regulation of the Board of Education forbidding teachers to become members of a union. The court said:

"No person has a right to demand that he or she shall be employed as a teacher. The board has the absolute right to decline to employ or to re-employ any applicant for any reason whatever or for no reason at all. The board is responsible for its action only to the people of the city, from whom, through the mayor, the members have received their appointments. It is no infringe-

---

[1] For a case in which a voluntary association of colleges removed from its accredited list an institution which dismissed seven faculty members in violation of tenure standards, see *North Dakota v. North Central Ass'n,* 99 F. 2d 697 (C. A. 7, 1938).

ment upon the constitutional rights of anyone for the board to decline to employ him as a teacher in the schools, and it is immaterial whether the reason for the refusal to employ him is because the applicant is married or unmarried, is of fair complexion or dark, is or is not a member of a trades union, or whether no reason is given for such refusal. The board is not bound to give any reason for its action. It is free to contract with whomsoever it chooses. Neither the Constitution nor the statute places any restriction upon this right of the board to contract, and no one has any grievance which the courts will recognize simply because the board of education refuses to contract with him or her. Questions of policy are solely for determination of the board, and when they have once been determined by it the courts will not inquire into their propriety." 278 Ill. at 325–6.

In accord, *Frederich v. Owens,* 25 Ohio Cir. Ct. R. 581 (1915) ; *Seattle High School Ch. No. 200 v. Sharples,* 159 Wash. 424, 293 Pac. 994 (1930) ; *Chapin v. Board of Education of Peoria* (Cir. Ct. Ill., Dec. 9, 1939) text quoted in Rhyne, *Labor Unions and Municipal Employee Law,* p. 157 (1946).

Opposition to the teacher's right to organize and bargain collectively is based upon two grounds: (1) the board of education has been delegated by the legislature absolute authority to engage whom it will, and this authority cannot be diminished by any agreement with a private organization such as a union; (2) collective bargaining implies the right to strike, and this right has uniformly been denied employees of the government.

A position more favorable toward organization by teachers was taken in the recent case of *Norwalk Teachers' Assn. v. Board of Education,* 138 Conn. 269, 83 Atl. (2d) 482 (1951). Here a declaratory judgment was requested defining rights to organize, bargain collectively, demand recognition, and strike. The court declared that, in absence of any statute expressly prohibiting collective bargaining on the part of public employees, teachers might so organize, but that strikes, work stoppages or collective refusal to enter upon duties was forbidden: "The strike is not a permissible method of enforcing the plaintiff's demands. . . . There is no objection to the organization of the plaintiff as a labor union but if its organization is for the purpose of 'demanding' recognition and collective bargaining the demands must be kept within legal bounds. What we have said does not mean that the plaintiff has the right to organize for all of the purposes for which employees in private enterprise may unite . . . Nor does it mean that, having organized, it is necessarily protected against unfair labor practices . . . or that it shall be the exclusive bargaining agent for all employees of the unit.

**911**

. . . It means nothing more than that the plaintiff may organize and bargain collectively for the pay and working conditions which it may be in the power of the board of education to grant." 138 Conn. at 277.

The case is noted in 26 Conn. B. J. 116 (1952). See also *Fowler v. Town of Enfield*, 138 Conn. 521, 86 Atl. 2d 662 (1952). In general see Spero, *Government as Employer* (1948).

Despite legal and other obstacles there has been an increase in the membership and activities of teachers' unions. Notable among them are the American Federation of Teachers, an affiliate of the American Federation of Labor, which publishes a monthly bulletin, *The American Teacher;* the Chicago Teachers Federation; and the Teachers Union of New York, Local 555.[2] These and other organizations have taken an active interest in issues of academic freedom.

The faculties of 29 universities are organized into trade unions. See Derbigny, *Labor Unionism in American Colleges*, 69 School and Society 172 (1949); Eggerston, *Some Practices in Faculty Organization*, in Benjamin et al, *Democracy in the Administration of Higher Education*, pp. 105–116 (1950).

For an account of the activities of the American Civil Liberties Union in the field of academic freedom, see Bunting, *Liberty and Learning* (1942).

---

[2] In June 1950 the New York City Board of Education barred the Teachers Union from all official dealings with the public school system, pointing out that the parent union of the Teachers Union (the United Public Workers of America) had recently been expelled from the Congress of Industrial Organizations as Communist dominated. N. Y. Times, June 2, 1950.

# CHAPTER VIII

# FREEDOM OF RELIGION

## A. HERITAGE — AND NOW

### MR. JUSTICE RUTLEDGE—DISSENTING OPINION IN EVERSON v. BOARD OF EDUCATION

330 U. S. 1, 33–43, 91 L. Ed. 711, 732–7, 67 S. Ct. 504, 520–4 (1947)

No provision of the Constitution is more closely tied to or given content by its generating history than the religious clause of the First Amendment. It is at once the refined product and the terse summation of that history. The history includes not only Madison's authorship and the proceedings before the First Congress, but also the long and intensive struggle for religious freedom in America, more especially in Virginia,[11] of which the Amendment was the direct culmination.[12] In the documents of the times, particularly of Madison, who was leader in the Virginia struggle before he became the Amendment's sponsor, but also in the writings of Jefferson and others and in the issues which engendered them is to be found irrefutable confirmation of the Amendment's sweeping content.

For Madison, as also for Jefferson, religious freedom was the crux of the struggle for freedom in general. Remonstrance, Par. 15, Appendix hereto. Madison was coauthor with George

---

[11] Conflicts in other states, and earlier in the colonies, contributed much to generation of the Amendment, but none so directly as that in Virginia or with such formative influence on the Amendment's content and wording. See Cobb, Rise of Religious Liberty in America (1902); Sweet, The Story of Religion in America (1939). The Charter of Rhode Island of 1663, II Poore, Constitutions (1878) 1595, was the first colonial charter to provide for religious freedom.

The climactic period of the Virginia struggle covers the decade 1776–1786, from adoption of the Declaration of Rights to enactment of the Statute for Religious Freedom. For short accounts see Padover, Jefferson (1942) c. V; Brant, James Madison, The Virginia Revolutionist (1941) cc. XII, XV; James, The Struggle for Religious Liberty in Virginia (1900) cc. X, XI; Eckenrode, Separation of Church and State in Virginia (1910). These works and Randall [The Life of Thomas Jefferson (1858)] will be cited in this opinion by the names of their authors. Citations to "Jefferson" refer to The Works of Thomas Jefferson (ed. by Ford, 1904–1905); to "Madison," to The Writings of James Madison (ed. by Hunt, 1901–1910).

[12] Brant, cc. XII, XV; James, cc. X, XI; Eckenrode.

Mason of the religious clause in Virginia's great Declaration of Rights of 1776. He is credited with changing it from a mere statement of the principle of tolerance to the first official legislative pronouncement that freedom of conscience and religion are inherent rights of the individual.[13] He sought also to have the Declaration expressly condemn the existing Virginia establishment.[14] But the forces supporting it were then too strong.

Accordingly Madison yielded on this phase but not for long. At once he resumed the fight, continuing it before succeeding legislative sessions. As a member of the General Assembly in 1779 he threw his full weight behind Jefferson's historic Bill for Establishing Religious Freedom. That bill was a prime phase of Jefferson's broad program of democratic reform undertaken on his return from the Continental Congress in 1776 and submitted for the General Assembly's consideration in 1779 as his proposed revised Virginia code.[15] With Jefferson's departure for Europe in 1784, Madison became the Bill's prime sponsor.[16] Enactment failed in successive legislatures from its introduction in June, 1779, until its adoption in January, 1786. But during all this time the fight for religious freedom moved forward in Virginia on various fronts with growing intensity. Madison

---

[13] See Brant, c. XII, particularly at 243. Cf. Madison's Remonstrance, Appendix to this opinion. Jefferson of course held the same view. See note 15. . . .

[14] See Brant, 245–246. Madison quoted liberally from the Declaration in his Remonstrance and the use made of the quotations indicates that he considered the Declaration to have outlawed the prevailing establishment in principle, if not technically.

[15] Jefferson was chairman of the revising committee and chief draftsman. Corevisers were Wythe, Pendleton, Mason and Lee. The first enacted portion of the revision, which became known as Jefferson's Code, was the statute barring entailments. Primogeniture soon followed. Much longer the author was to wait for enactment of the Bill for Religious Freedom; and not until after his death was the corollary bill to be accepted in principle which he considered most important of all, namely, to provide for common education at public expense. See V Jefferson, 153. However, he linked this with disestablishment as corollary prime parts in a system of basic freedoms. I Jefferson, 78.

Jefferson, and Madison by his sponsorship, sought to give the Bill for Establishing Religious Freedom as nearly constitutional status as they could at the time. Acknowledging that one legislature could not "restrain the acts of succeeding Assemblies . . . and that therefore to declare this act irrevocable would be of no effect in law," the Bill's concluding provision as enacted nevertheless asserted: "Yet we are free to declare, and do declare, that the rights hereby asserted are of the natural rights of mankind, and that if any act shall be hereafter passed to repeal the present or to narrow its operation, such act will be an infringement of natural right." 1 Randall, 220.

[16] See I Jefferson, 70–71; XII Jefferson, 447; Padover, 80.

[Emerson]

led throughout, against Patrick Henry's powerful opposing leadership until Henry was elected governor in November, 1784.

The climax came in the legislative struggle of 1784–1785 over the Assessment Bill. . . . This was nothing more nor less than a taxing measure for the support of religion, designed to revive the payment of tithes suspended since 1777. So long as it singled out a particular sect for preference it incurred the active and general hostility of dissentient groups. It was broadened to include them, with the result that some subsided temporarily in their opposition.[17] As altered, the bill gave to each taxpayer the privilege of designating which church should receive his share of the tax. In default of designation the legislature applied it to pious uses.[18] But what is of the utmost significance here, "in its final form the bill left the taxpayer the option of giving his tax to education."[19]

Madison was unyielding at all times, opposing with all his vigor the general and nondiscriminatory as he had the earlier particular and discriminatory assessments proposed. The modified Assessment Bill passed second reading in December, 1784, and was all but enacted. Madison and his followers, however, maneuvered deferment of final consideration until November, 1785. And before the Assembly reconvened in the fall he issued his historic Memorial and Remonstrance.[20]

This is Madison's complete, though not his only, interpretation of religious liberty.[21] It is a broadside attack upon all forms of "establishment" of religion, both general and particular, nondiscriminatory or selective. Reflecting not only the many legislative conflicts over the Assessment Bill and the Bill for Establishing Religious Freedom but also, for example, the struggles for religious incorporations and the continued maintenance of the glebes, the Remonstrance is at once the most concise and the most accurate statement of the views of the First Amendment's author concerning what is "an establishment of religion." . . .

The Remonstrance, stirring up a storm of popular protest,

[17] Madison regarded this action as desertion. See his letter to Monroe of April 12, 1785; II Madison, 129, 131–132; James, cc. X, XI. But see Eckenrode, 91, suggesting it was surrender to the inevitable. . . .

[18] Eckenrode, 99, 100.

[19] *Id.*, 100; II Madison, 113. . . .

[20] See generally Eckenrode, c. V; Brant, James, and other authorities cited in note 11 above.

[21] II Madison, 183; and the Appendix to this opinion. Eckenrode, 100 ff. See also Fleet, Madison's "Detached Memoranda" (1946) III William & Mary Q. (3d Series) 534, 554–562.

killed the Assessment Bill.[22]  It collapsed in committee shortly before Christmas, 1785.  With this, the way was cleared at last for enactment of Jefferson's Bill for Establishing Religious Freedom.  Madison promptly drove it through in January of 1786, seven years from the time it was first introduced.  This dual victory substantially ended the fight over establishments, settling the issue against them.  See note 33.

The next year Madison became a member of the Constitutional Convention.  Its work done, he fought valiantly to secure the ratification of its great product in Virginia as elsewhere, and nowhere else more effectively.[23]  Madison was certain in his own mind that under the Constitution "there is not a shadow of right in the general government to intermeddle with religion"[24] and that "this subject is, for the honor of America, perfectly free and unshackled.  The government has no jurisdiction over it . . . ."[25]  Nevertheless he pledged that he would work for a Bill of Rights, including a specific guaranty of religious freedom, and Virginia, with other states, ratified the Constitution on this assurance.[26]

Ratification thus accomplished, Madison was sent to the first Congress.  There he went at once about performing his pledge to establish freedom for the nation as he had done in Virginia.  Within a little more than three years from his legislative victory at home he had proposed and secured the submission and ratification of the First Amendment as the first article of our Bill of Rights.[27]

All the great instruments of the Virginia struggle for religious liberty thus became warp and woof of our constitutional

---

[22] The major causes assigned for its defeat include the elevation of Patrick Henry to the governorship in November of 1784; the blunder of the proponents in allowing the Bill for Incorporations to come to the floor and incur defeat before the Assessment Bill was acted on; Madison's astute leadership, taking advantage of every "break" to convert his initial minority into a majority, including the deferment of action on the third reading to the fall; the Remonstrance, bringing a flood of protesting petitions; and the general poverty of the time.  See Eckenrode, c. V, for an excellent short, detailed account.

[23] See James, Brant, *op. cit. supra* note 11.

[24] V Madison, 176.  Cf. notes 33, 37.

[25] V Madison, 132.

[26] Brant, 250. . . .

[27] The amendment with respect to religious liberties read, as Madison introduced it: "The civil rights of none shall be abridged on account of religious belief or worship, nor shall any national religion be established, nor shall the full and equal rights of conscience be in any manner, or on any pretext, infringed." 1 Annals of Congress 434.  In the process of debate this was modified to its present form.  See especially 1 Annals of Congress 729–731, 765; also note 34.

tradition, not simply by the course of history, but by the common unifying force of Madison's life, thought and sponsorship. He epitomized the whole of that tradition in the Amendment's compact, but nonetheless comprehensive, phrasing.

As the Remonstrance discloses throughout, Madison opposed every form and degree of official relation between religion and civil authority. For him religion was a wholly private matter beyond the scope of civil power either to restrain or to support.[28] Denial or abridgment of religious freedom was a violation of rights both of conscience and of natural equality. State aid was no less obnoxious or destructive to freedom and to religion itself than other forms of state interference. "Establishment" and "free exercise" were correlative and coextensive ideas, representing only different facets of the single great and fundamental freedom. The Remonstrance, following the Virginia statute's example, referred to the history of religious conflicts and the effects of all sorts of establishments, current and historical, to suppress religion's free exercise. With Jefferson, Madison believed that to tolerate any fragment of establishment would be by so much to perpetuate restraint upon that freedom. Hence he sought to tear out the institution not partially but root and branch, and to bar its return forever.

In no phase was he more unrelentingly absolute than in opposing state support or aid by taxation. Not even "three pence" contribution was thus to be exacted from any citizen for such a purpose. Remonstrance, Par. 3.[29] Tithes had been the lifeblood of establishment before and after other compulsions dis-

---

[28] See text of the Remonstrance, Appendix; also notes 13, 15, 24, 25 *supra* and text.

Madison's one exception concerning restraint was for "preserving public order." Thus he declared in a private letter, IX Madison, 484, 487, written after the First Amendment was adopted: "The tendency to a usurpation on one side or the other, or to a corrupting coalition or alliance between them, will be best guarded agst. by an entire abstinance of the Govt. from interference in any way whatever, beyond the necessity of preserving public order, & protecting each sect agst. trespasses on its legal rights by others." . . .

[29] The third ground of remonstrance . . . bears repetition for emphasis here: "Because, it is proper to take alarm at the first experiment on our liberties . . . The freemen of America did not wait till usurped power had strengthened itself by exercise, and entangled the question in precedents. They saw all the consequences in the principle, and they avoided the consequences by denying the principle. We revere this lesson too much, soon to forget it. Who does not see that . . . the same authority which can force a citizen to *contribute three pence* only of his property for the support of any one establishment, may force him to conform to any other establishment in all cases whatsoever?" (Emphasis added.) II Madison 183, 185–186.

appeared. Madison and his coworkers made no exceptions or abridgments to the complete separation they created. Their objection was not to small tithes. It was to any tithes whatsoever. "If it were lawful to impose a small tax for religion, the admission would pave the way for oppressive levies."[30] Not the amount but "the principle of assessment was wrong." And the principle was as much to prevent "the interference of law in religion" as to restrain religious intervention in political matters.[31] In this field the authors of our freedom would not tolerate "the first experiment on our liberties" or "wait till usurped power had strengthened itself by exercise, and entangled the question in precedents." Remonstrance, Par. 3. Nor should we.

In view of this history no further proof is needed that the Amendment forbids any appropriation, large or small, from public funds to aid or support any and all religious exercises. But if more were called for, the debates in the First Congress and this Court's consistent expressions, whenever it has touched on the matter directly, supply it.

By contrast with the Virginia history, the congressional debates on consideration of the Amendment reveal only sparse discussion, reflecting the fact that the essential issues had been settled.[33]

---

[30] Eckenrode, 105, in summary of the Remonstrance.

[31] "Because the bill implies either that the Civil Magistrate is a competent Judge of Religious truth; or that he may employ Religion as an engine of Civil policy. The first is an arrogant pretention falsified by the contradictory opinions of Rulers in all ages, and throughout the world: The second an unhallowed perversion of the means of salvation." Remonstrance, Appendix, Par. 5; II Madison 183, 187.

[33] See text *supra* at notes 24, 25. Madison, of course, was but one of many holding such views, but nevertheless agreeing to the common understanding for adoption of a Bill of Rights in order to remove all doubt engendered by the absence of explicit guaranties in the original Constitution.

By 1791 the great fight over establishments had ended, although some vestiges remained then and later, even in Virginia. The glebes, for example, were not sold there until 1802. Cf. Eckenrode, 147. Fixing an exact date for "disestablishment" is almost impossible, since the process was piecemeal. Although Madison failed in having the Virginia Bill of Rights declare explicitly against establishment in 1776, cf. note 14 and text *supra*, in 1777 the levy for support of the Anglican clergy was suspended. It was never resumed. Eckenrode states: "This act, in effect, destroyed the establishment. Many dates have been given for its end, but it really came on January 1, 1777, when the act suspending the payment of tithes became effective. This was not seen at the time. . . . But in freeing almost half of the taxpayers from the burden of the state religion, the state religion was at an end. Nobody could be forced to support it, and an attempt to levy tithes upon Anglicans alone would be to recruit the ranks of dissent." P. 53. See also pp. 61, 64. The question of assessment however was revived "with far more strength than ever, in the summer of 1784." *Id.*, 64. It would seem more factual therefore to fix the time of disestablishment as of December, 1785–January, 1786, when the issue in large was finally settled.

Indeed the matter had become so well understood as to have been taken for granted in all but formal phrasing. Hence, the only enlightening reference shows concern, not to preserve any power to use public funds in aid of religion, but to prevent the Amendment from outlawing private gifts inadvertently by virtue of the breadth of its wording.[34] . . .

## Note

1. For another discussion throwing a different light on the views of Jefferson and Madison see the dissenting opinion of Mr. Justice Reed in the *McCollum* case, printed *infra*.

2. On the movement toward separation and religious freedom in Virginia and other colonies see discussions and materials in 1 Stokes, *Church and State in the United States* (1950); Howe, *Cases on Church and State in the United States*, ch. 1 (1952); Blau, *Cornerstones of Religious Freedom in America* (1949); Greene, *Religion and the State, The Making and Testing of an American Tradition* (1941); Konvitz, *Separation of Church and State: The First Freedom*, 14 Law and Contemp. Prob. 44 (1949). See also Eliot, in *Pioneers of Religious Liberty in America* (1903); Meyer, *The Blaine Amendment and the Bill of Rights*, 64 Harv. L. Rev. 939 (1951); Ernst, *The Political Thought of Roger Williams* (1929) and *Roger Williams, New England Firebrand* (1932); Greene, *The Development of Religious Liberty in Connecticut* (1905); Purcell, *Connecticut in Transition 1775–1818* (1918); Meyer, *Church and State in Massachusetts from 1740 to 1833* (1930); Sweet, *The Story of Religion in America* (1950), *Religion in Colonial America* (1942), and *The American Churches, An Interpretation* (1947 and 1948); Weigle, *American Idealism*, ch. IV, V and VI

---

[34] At one point the wording was proposed: "No religion shall be established by law, nor shall the equal rights of conscience be infringed." 1 Annals of Congress 729. Cf. note 27. Representative Huntington of Connecticut feared this might be construed to prevent judicial enforcement of private pledges. He stated "that he feared . . . that the words might be taken in such latitude as to be extremely hurtful to the cause of religion. He understood the amendment to mean what had been expressed by the gentleman from Virginia; but others might find it convenient to put another construction upon it. The ministers of their congregations to the Eastward were maintained by the contributions of those who belonged to their society; the expense of building meeting-houses was contributed in the same manner. These things were regulated by by-laws. If an action was brought before a Federal Court on any of these cases, the person who had neglected to perform his engagements could not be compelled to do it; for a support of ministers or building of places of worship might be construed into a religious establishment." 1 Annals of Congress 730.

To avoid any such possibility, Madison suggested inserting the word "national" before "religion," thereby not only again disclaiming intent to bring about the result Huntington feared but also showing unmistakably that "establishment" meant public "support" of religion in the financial sense. 1 Annals of Congress 731. See also IX Madison, 484–487.

(1928) (title pages, documents, pictures, contemporary with the establishment of religious freedom in the United States); Bryce, *The American Commonwealth*, ch. III and IV (1888); Campbell, *The Puritan in Holland, England and America* (1893); Eaton, *Freedom of Thought in the Old South* (1940) (decline of liberalism in the Old South).

For history of the struggle for religious liberty throughout the ages, see Bainton, *The Struggle for Religious Liberty* (1941); Bury, *A History of Freedom of Thought*, ch. V and VIII (1913); Geffcken, *Church and State, Their Relations Historically Developed* (1877); Garrison, *Intolerance* (1934); Jordan, *The Development of Religious Toleration in England* (1940); Lecky, *Democracy and Liberty*, ch. VI and VII (1899); Ruffini, *Religious Liberty* (1912).

## MURRAY—LAW OR PREPOSSESSIONS?

14 Law and Contemp. Prob. 23, 30–4, 36–7, 39 (1949); published by
Duke University School of Law, Durham, N. C.
Copyright, 1949, by Duke University.

. . . We have got here a paradox that would be laughable were it not so serious in its consequences: in the effort to prove that "no establishment of religion" means "no aid to religion" the Supreme Court proceeds to establish a religion—James Madison's. In order to make separation of church and state absolute, it unites the state to a "religion without a church"—a deistic version of fundamentalist Protestantism. In the name of freedom of religion it decrees that the relations of government to religion are to be controlled by the fundamental tenet of secularism—the social irrelevance of religion, its exclusion from the secular affairs of the City and its educational system, its relegation to the private forum of conscience or at best to the hushed confines of the sacristy. . . . [The] philosophizing of the whole Court . . . reminds one of Byron's Julia, who, in momentary disregard of her original lines and the exigencies of metre, "screaming, 'I will ne'er consent to an establishment of religion,' imposed one on the American people."

The issue here is serious. And, I repeat, it concerns the reasoning of the Court, as it shapes itself into a philosophy of separation. If there is to be a sort of official American philosophy in the matter, promulgated by the Supreme Court, it must be constructed in the absence of all appeal to sectarian dogmas—Madison's as well as anybody else's. I do not deny that the dogma in question is widely held—by educationists like Kilpatrick, Thayer, Hook *et al.*; by jurists in the tradition of Holmes and by jurisprudents of the positivistic schools . . . If today the Court were to take as a premise of argument Madison's particular theory

**920**

of "natural rights" as deriving from a pre-social "state of nature" (a theory borrowed from Locke), there would be legal howlings. It is not more legitimate to adopt Madison's particular theory of religion in its relation to organized society. . . .

Be it noticed that in all this I am arguing only against Madison's (and the Court's) absolutism, on the ground that it can rest only on a religious absolute, a theological premise. Take away this premise, and you can combine Madison's other arguments into a satisfactory theory of separation of church and state—a satisfactory theory because it will not make separation an absolute, and its reasons will be such as to command consensus. The distinction of the ecclesiastical and civil jurisdictions, the immunity of conscience from coercion by civil authority in the free exercise of religion, the principle of political equality, the legitimate demands of political unity in a religiously divided society, the general requirements of the common good (which include the need of society to be a "good" society)—these are proper and adequate materials from which to fashion an acceptable American philosophy of separation of church and state. They were in fact the original materials from which that philosophy was fashioned and made the premise of the First Amendment. Madison's added element, the absolutizing element, was not included.

There were two merits to this original philosophy, both of which perish in the new philosophy of the Court. The first is that separation of church and state, thus put on its proper grounds, appears in its true relation to the free exercise of religion. It appears as instrumental to freedom, therefore as a relative, not an absolute in its own right. As a Congregationalist writer recently put it: "Separation of church and state, then, is simply a means, a technique, a policy to implement the principle of religious freedom. It assumes organic separation but dynamic interaction between church and state; it functions through cooperation without favoritism. As a method, separation of church and state can never be an absolute."[38a] . . .

The second great merit of the original American philosophy (pragmatic as it was in the best sense, as a political philosophy, based on sound concepts of freedom, equality, and the common good) is that it would permit an equitable, socially healthy solution to a new American problem for which there is no solution in the new ideological and doctrinaire philosophy of the First Amendment. I mean the educational problem—the relation of

[38a] Keehn, *Church-State Relations*, Social Action, Nov. 15, 1948, p. 31.

religion to public education, and of government to the religious school. . . .

The essential question concerns the juridical status, within the American system of education, of the non-profit school with religious affiliations, that serves a public purpose by educating for the public life of citizenship, without being a "public" school in the narrow sense, because it is only under partial, not total, governmental supervision and control. This problem of juridical status is fundamental, antecedent to all questions of financial support of any kind—questions which cannot in fact be solved except by prior solution of the fundamental problem.

Moreover, this problem is posited today concretely, in a set of particular circumstances. A determinant circumstance is the existence of a powerful and articulate philosophy of "American" education in whose explicit tendency is the denial or diminishing of the juridical status of these schools. The major premise of this philosophy is a concept of the "historic unity" of the American people and a rather mystical concept of "democracy." The minor premise is the "divisiveness" of "segregation" in education on religious grounds; it is a manifestation of "isolationist religious practices," that are "disruptive" of the "democratic community." The conclusion of the philosophy was put, for example, in a resolution of the American Federation of Teachers, which asserts "the basic principle that the interests of the democratic community are best served where children of all component groups of American society are enrolled in a common public school." This is the "rightful" position; any other is to be given only toleration, more or less provisional. The conclusion is further supported by some theorists on grounds that only in the public schools can children be nourished with a robust, quasi-religious faith in the "unifying secularism" of American democracy. And a final rib in the theory is the principle that, although (at least for the moment) the child may not be the creature of the state, the school definitely is. Government is the primary educator; its interests are paramount; in particular, it makes its own interests (democratic unity and "faith" in democracy) the controlling norm of parental interests, by right of superior situation in the hierarchy of social values. . . .

[The] parental right in education is the very pivotal point of a democratic system. It is, to change the metaphor again, the touchstone of difference between democratic education and the monolithic systems of cultural totalitarianism, whether on the Soviet or even on the Third Republic style. When the modern

**922**

state with its immense power embarks (as indeed it must) on
the spiritual mission of educating its children, its whole native
tendency (as recent developments in United States educational
theory and practice abundantly show) is toward state monopoly.
And it is only held back on its plunging course toward the extreme
of *l'école unique,* symbol of the *Kulturstaat,* by the frail barrier
of the parental right to control and direct the education of their
children. . . .

The public school is not a temple in which our children are
to be baptized into the unity of the secular democratic faith,
while those who stand without are somehow faintly heretical.
Viewed realistically and with all respect for its idealisms and
achievements, it is actually the symbol of our religious disunity
and the sign of an experiment in dealing in a particular way—
there are other ways—with the fact of that disunity. And it is
the symbol of our democracy only in so far as it deals with this
fact honestly and fairly, not blinking it or chipping away at it
in the name of some dubious ideal of national unity. . . .

## JACQUES MARITAIN—MAN AND THE STATE

pp. 184–6; published by The University of Chicago Press,
Chicago, Ill. Copyright, 1951, by The University of Chicago.

The Catholic Church is sometimes reproached with being an
"authoritarian Church," as if the authority—that is, the right
to be listened to—that she exercises on her faithful in seeing to
the preservation of revealed truth and Christian morality were
to result in fostering authoritarian trends in the sphere of
civil life and activities. May I be allowed to say that those who
make such reproaches lack both in theological and historical
insight.

They lack in historical insight, because they do not grasp
the significance of the diversity of historical climates which in
past times made the authority of the Church over the State—
and now make the mutual freedom of the State and the Church—
requisites of the common good of civilization.

They lack in theological insight, for they do not see that the
authority of the Church in her own spiritual sphere is nothing
else than her bondage to God and to her mission. This authority
concerns her own organization precisely as contrasted in essence
with the organization of civil society. . . .

Be it noted, furthermore, that, as a matter of fact, no government is less authoritarian than the government of the Catholic
Church. It governs without police force and physical coer-

cion the immense people for whose spiritual common good it is responsible. Here we have a society the order of which primarily depends on the non-material influence on human souls of teaching, preaching, worshipping, and the sacramental life, and only secondarily on the external power of the law. . . .

The Church in her very essence is an object of theological faith—belongs to the order of those realities hidden in divine life and made known by divine revelation which are called supernatural mysteries. As a result, between the believer, who thinks of the Church in terms of faith, and the unbeliever, who thinks of her in terms merely human, there is a kind of unavoidable mutual misapprehension. The first one knows that the life which animates her is the life of the God-given grace of Christ, which is received in deficient human beings, and from which these human beings slip away each time they do evil. He knows, therefore, that she is sinless while composed of sinful members.

## Note

1. For a more elaborate discussion by Maritain of the problem of education, see his *Education at the Crossroads* (1943).

2. For other material on the Catholic position see Ryan and Millar, *The State and the Church* (1936); Ryan and Boland, *Catholic Principles of Politics* (1947); Parsons, *The First Freedom: Considerations on Church and State in the United States* (1948); Sheppard, *Religion and the Concept of Democracy: A Thomistic Study in Social Philosophy* (1949); Dawson, *Religion and the Modern State* (1935); Garrison, *Religion and Civil Liberty in the Roman Catholic Tradition* (1947); Antieau, *The Limitation of Religious Liberty,* 18 Ford. L. Rev. 221 (1949); Marshall, *The Roman Catholic Church in the Modern State* (1931); Sturzo, *Church and State* (1939); Vermeersch, *Tolerance* (1913); Rommen, *The State in Catholic Thought* (1945). For treatment of rationalism as a type of American religious thought see Koch, *Republican Religion: The American Revolution and the Cult of Reason* (1933); see also Morais, *Deism in Eighteenth Century America* (1934).

## HORACE KALLEN—THE EDUCATION OF FREE MEN

pp. 224-9; copyright 1949 by Horace Kallen, Farrar, Straus & Young, Inc.

The goal of the free public school of democratic society has to be the support and strengthening of the common faith in the democratic way of life and thought by the development of habits of thinking and doing which, to repeat Aristotle's phrase, should contribute most to the permanence of the democratic constitution. The trend in free society is to accept the instincts and impulses with which children are born for what they are; to provide them with enchanneling action on the environment that disciplines them into habits by the methods of free inquiry rather than authoritarian rehearsal; and to open up new ways for the continual growth and reconstruction of personal traits and social relations. John Dewey says that the primary business of the school, in democratic society, is to train all the children in co-operative and mutually helpful living. . . .

The primary business of sectarian instruction is naturally enough the growth and prosperity of the sectarian organization. Each needs devout communicants who will believe beyond any question that their special sectarian discipline and doctrine and theirs alone can save the human soul. Their method requires the minimizing of observation, experiment, analysis, reflection, and of choosing between alternatives; it requires the maximizing of indoctrination, repetition, *memoriter,* and exhortation. Their goal requires that minds should be molded into automatic acquiescence in dogmas regarding all sorts of matters, from the Immaculate Conception to birth control. . . .

The springs of religion are inveterate, and the religions of the world are among the latest as well as the most ancient and the most pervasive components of the world's cultures. But their mutual exclusions and intolerances are also among the most passionate and inveterate, and their pretensions are among the most absolutist and totalitarian. Yet, given their numbers and variety, none, in its character and consequences, can be an ineffable; nor, in a democratic society which takes democracy in a truly religious spirit, may the study of any or all be ordained as a grammar of assent, or the argument of a foregone conclusion. The truth of their relations to one another, to the qualities of men, and to the peace and freedom of humankind can be studied only as each and every human enterprise is studied, not by the rehearsal of a doctrine and the indrill of a discipline, but by way of inquiry into causes and consequences, on their merits, without privilege and without favor.

## Note

1. See also, Conference on the Scientific Spirit and Democratic Faith, *The Authoritarian Attempt to Capture Education,* esp. ch. 8 (1945); Dewey, *Education Today,* ch. 6 (1940). For a contemporary attempt to describe religious propositions in a way that would allow for the integration of psychological, cultural and some philosophical approaches to religion, see Ruesch and Bateson, *Communication,* ch. 8, Conventions of Communication: Where Validity Depends upon Belief (1951).

2. In addition to the questions raised about the relation of educa-

tional techniques to religious education and the aim of training citizens for a democracy consider also the connection between religious diversification and church schools, and economic and social stratification, as well as cultural isolation of minority groups. See *e. g.*, Pope, *Religion and the Class Structure*, 256 Annals of Am. Acad. of Pol. and Soc. Sci. 84 (1948); Chapman, *Church Schools, Some Factors in the Relation Among Private, Public and Parochial Schools*, 18 J. of Ed. Sociology 340 (1945).

## KARL MANNHEIM—FREEDOM, POWER, AND DEMOCRATIC PLANNING

pp. 286–9; copyright 1950 by Oxford University Press, Inc.

The problem presents itself quite differently for the Third Way, which would seek to transform society without endangering its fundamental integration. It would have to pay equal attention to the factors conducive to dynamic and creative change on the one hand and to fundamental integration on the other. The old-fashioned *laissez-faire* thinker or the radical would disregard the significance of tradition and religion and the forces making for stability and continuity, because in his time these matters took care of themselves. In the new situation, the strategist of reform will have to maintain integration in the midst of rapid change. He will have to concentrate on stability and continuity at the same time that he seeks to change society. This is when he realizes the need for religion and quasi-religious integrating powers in society. But with him religion is not allowed to become, as in the case of the reactionary, a bulwark of vested interests, but rather a force to help to bring about change and, in the process, regenerate man and society.

In another context we have tried to show that the age of Liberalism was rather exceptional in thinking that change could be accomplished without bothering about religious and other forms of basic integration. John Stuart Mill even went so far as to say that it was to the interest of society that the fundamental issues of creed be continually revised and that, therefore, there should be no basic agreement on them. Otherwise they were bound to be a groundwork for hierarchy and arbitrary institutions so incompatible with a dynamic society. There is, no doubt, penetrating insight in Mill's statement as far as one aspect of the story is concerned. He points very clearly to the difficulty which every planned society meets when it sets out to develop a totalitarian philosophy for the whole system, whether it happens to be a racial dogma or the Marxist theory of economic determination and class struggle. Once such philosophies become the sacred source of interpretation for all events—a form of basic theology—they lead to a new sort of clericalism. . . .

A planned society should make up its mind about ultimate issues. On the other hand it is saved from becoming totalitarian, rigid, and a strait jacket to the community by making the search for basic truth a dynamic issue, honestly putting a question mark after statements that require it. But even if the question mark were often to point to infinity, to the insoluble problematic nature of human knowledge, this would not mean that in the next five or ten years that same society need live in uncertainty. After having ironed out our differences we could agree on a certain plan, even if we know that all the social and philosophical implications have not finally been settled.

Democratically decided principles will be valid for practical purposes over a limited period, and fundamental revision will only be forthcoming when a new start seems necessary. Even so, certain circles in society will continue to discuss the fundamentals of life, religion, and society. Such discussions will have their place in a democratically planned social order. There will be provision for discussion, though no license will be granted for destructive action or sabotage of co-operation whenever it pleases the objector.

Certain unchanging aspects of the human mind seem to indicate the need for a transcendental religious foundation in society; and several factors make this need even more urgent in our present situation. There exist some archaic patterns in the human mind and in the nature of human action that lead to the quest for certainty and deeper foundations. The very fact that in our practical procedures we always think in terms of means and ends and have a purpose in mind when we perform something makes it difficult for us to conceive of a universe without such an end. Although this may be a thought habit acquired through the process of living and doing things, it is so deeply rooted that a world without purpose would mean a kind of homelessness hardly tolerable to a thoughtful being. It is one of the great paradoxes of our age that the more our technical skill permeates the details of everyday life, where we seek for purposeful arrangements, the more our philosophy tends toward the idea that purpose as a concept does not apply to Nature as such: even those things that seem to be purposeful are the result of selection, the chance product of endless variety and forms of adaptation. Such an idea can be conceived, but it can hardly be lived. It is like admitting in theory that the earth moves

**927**

round the sun while still experiencing the sun as a rising disc that radiates light day by day. In the same way, calm assurance that the highest thing in life is communion with One to whom we can speak and who will respond with unfailing understanding and forgiveness is so deeply ingrained that despondency would reign if this religious belief were lost. Only through satisfaction of these deep-rooted aspirations (that there is a Purpose in what we are doing, and that there is a Personal Power to whom man can appeal) can man develop the sense of belonging in a world where he can find his place and where there is an order that supports him and dispels his anxieties.

These are some of the inalienable features in human nature that in one way or another will always make for some form of religion. They will not be satisfied with 'scientific' interpretations that fail to answer the basic needs of the inquiring mind.

---

Man's efforts lightly flag and seek too low a level,
Soon doth he pine for all untrammeled sloth—
Wherefore a mate I give him, nothing loth,
Who spurs and shapes and must create though Devil.
—Goethe

## Note

1. Compare T. S. Eliot, *The Idea of a Christian Society* (1939) and *Notes Toward the Definition of Culture* (1948).

2. The following are standard reference works on the subjects of this Chapter: Stokes, *Church and State in the United States* (1950); Johnson and Yost, *Separation of Church and State in the United States* (1948); Torpey, *Judicial Doctrines of Religious Rights in America* (1948). See also Religious Liberty Association, *American State Papers on Freedom in Religion* (1943). For further discussions both legal and non-legal see, Sutherland, *Due Process and Disestablishment*, 62 Harv. L. Rev. 1306 (1949); Symposium, *Religion and the State*, 14 Law and Contemp. Problems 1 (1949); Pear, *The U. S. Supreme Court and Religious Freedom*, 12 Mod. L. Rev. 167 (1949); Fellman, *Separation of Church and State in the United States, A Summary View*, 1950 Wis. L. Rev. 427; Pfeffer, *The Supreme Court as Protector of Civil Rights: Freedom of Religion*, 275 Annals of the Am. Acad. of Pol. and Soc. Sci. 75 (1951) and *Church and State, Something Less than Separation*, 19 U. of Chi. L. Rev. 1 (1951); Van Dusen, *Church and State in the Modern World* (1937).

3. For discussion of religions in America see *Organized Religions in the United States*, 256 Annals of the Am. Acad. of Pol. and Soc. Sci. (1948); May, *Protestant Churches and Industrial America* (1949); Maynard, *The Story of American Catholicism* (1941); Finkelstein, Ross and Brown, *The Religions of Democracy: Judaism, Catholicism,*

*Protestantism in Creed and Life* (1946); Mays and Nicholson, *Negro's Church* (1933); Clark, *The Small Sects in America* (1949); Stroup, *The Jehovah's Witnesses* (1945).

4. For critical evaluation of the connection of religious thought and institutions with the development of political and economic theory in America see Bates, *American Faith: Its Religious, Political and Economic Foundations* (1940); Gabriel, *The Course of American Democratic Thought* (1943); Curti, *Growth of American Thought* (1951); Dorfman, *The Economic Mind in American Civilization, 1606–1918* (1946–9); Schneider, *History of American Philosophy* (1946); Perry, *Puritanism and Democracy* (1944).

5. For a brief scholarly discussion of the history, development and teachings of the various major religions of the world see Bouquet, *Comparative Religion* (1941). See also Jurji (ed.), *The Great Religions of the Modern World* (1946). For a sociological study of religion, including the nature of religious experience and its expression, the impact of religion on society, the nature of religious groups and of religious authority, and the relation of religion to the state throughout the world and throughout history, see Wach, *Sociology of Religion* (1944). This study contains extensive bibliographical references. For critical philosophical treatments of religion see Hume, *Dialogues Concerning Natural Religion* (1779); Feuerbach, *Das Wesen der Religion* (1849); Santayana, *Reason in Religion* (1905); Russell, *Religion and Science* (1935); Koehler, *The Place of Value in a World of Facts* (1938). For an extensive bibliography of philosophical treatments of religion see Brightman, *A Philosophy of Religion*, pp. 490–522 (1940). See also Hocking, *Living Religions and a World Faith* (1940); Mumford, *The Conduct of Life* (1951); Whyte, *The Next Development in Man* (1948); Burtt, *Types of Religious Philosophy* (1939); Collingwood, *Religion and Philosophy* (1916); D'Arcy, *The Mind and Heart of Love, Lion and Unicorn: A Study in Eros and Agape* (1947) (theology and psychoanalysis); Dewey, *A Common Faith* (1934); Freud, *The Future of an Illusion* (1928); Fromm, *Psychoanalysis and Religion* (1950); Jung, *Psychology and Religion* (1938); Macmurray, *The Structure of Religious Experience* (1836); Brierley, *Recent Trends in Psychoanalysis*, ch. VI (1951).

•

## B. ORGANIZED RELIGION AND EDUCATION

### 1. History of Secular and Religious Education in the United States

MR. JUSTICE FRANKFURTER—CONCURRING
OPINION IN ILLINOIS EX REL. McCOLLUM
v. BOARD OF EDUCATION

333 U. S. 203, 213–225, 92 L. Ed. 649, 660–5, 68 S. Ct. 461, 466–72
(1948)

. . . Traditionally, organized education in the Western
world was Church education. It could hardly be otherwise when
the education of children was primarily study of the Word and
the ways of God. Even in the Protestant countries, where there
was a less close identification of Church and State, the basis of
education was largely the Bible, and its chief purpose inculcation
of piety. To the extent that the State intervened, it used its
authority to further aims of the Church.

The emigrants who came to these shores brought this view
of education with them. Colonial schools certainly started with
a religious orientation. When the common problems of the
early settlers of the Massachusetts Bay Colony revealed the
need for common schools, the object was the defeat of "one chief
project of that old deluder, Satan, to keep men from the knowledge of the Scriptures." The Laws and Liberties of Massachusetts, 1648 edition (Cambridge 1929) 47.[1]

The evolution of colonial education, largely in the service of
religion, into the public school system of today is the story of
changing conceptions regarding the American democratic society, of the functions of State-maintained education in such a
society, and of the role therein of the free exercise of religion
by the people. The modern public school derived from a philosophy of freedom reflected in the First Amendment. It is appropriate to recall that the Remonstrance of James Madison, an event
basic in the history of religious liberty, was called forth by a
proposal which involved support to religious education. . . .
As the momentum for popular education increased and in turn
evoked strong claims for State support of religious education,
contests not unlike that which in Virginia had produced Madi-

---

[1] For an exposition of the religious origins of American education, see
S. W. Brown, The Secularization of American Education (1912) cc. I, II;
Knight, Education in the United States (2d rev. ed. 1941) cc. III, V; Cub-
berley, Public Education in the United States (1934) cc. II, III.

[Emerson]

son's Remonstrance appeared in various forms in other States. New York and Massachusetts provide famous chapters in the history that established dissociation of religious teaching from State-maintained schools. In New York, the rise of the common schools led, despite fierce sectarian opposition, to the barring of tax funds to church schools, and later to any school in which sectarian doctrine was taught.[2] In Massachusetts, largely through the efforts of Horace Mann, all sectarian teachings were barred from the common school to save it from being rent by denominational conflict.[3] The upshot of these controversies, often long and fierce, is fairly summarized by saying that long before the Fourteenth Amendment subjected the States to new limitations, the prohibition of furtherance by the State of religious instruction became the guiding principle, in law and feeling, of the American people. In sustaining Stephen Girard's will, this Court referred to the inevitable conflicts engendered by matters "connected with religious polity" and particularly "in a country composed of such a variety of religious sects as our country." *Vidal v. Girard's Executors*, 2 How. 127, 198. That was more than one hundred years ago.

Separation in the field of education, then, was not imposed upon unwilling States by force of superior law. In this respect the Fourteenth Amendment merely reflected a principle then dominant in our national life. To the extent that the Constitution thus made it binding upon the States, the basis of the restriction is the whole experience of our people. Zealous watchfulness against fusion of secular and religious activities by Government itself, through any of its instruments but especially through its educational agencies, was the democratic response of the American community to the particular needs of a young and growing nation, unique in the composition of its people.[4] . . . The secular public school did not imply indifference to the

[2] See Boese, Public Education in the City of New York (1869) c. XIV; Hall, Religious Education in the Public Schools of the State and City of New York (1914) cc. VI, VII; Palmer, The New York Public School (1905) cc. VI, VII, X, XII. And see New York Laws 1842, c. 150, § 14, amended, New York Laws 1844, c. 320, § 12.

[3] S. M. Smith, The Relation of the State to Religious Education in Massachusetts (1926) c. VII; Culver, Horace Mann and Religion in the Massachusetts Public Schools (1929).

[4] It has been suggested that secular education in this country is the inevitable "product of 'the utter impossibility of harmonizing multiform creeds.'" T. W. M. Marshall, *Secular Education in England and the United States*, 1 American Catholic Quarterly Review 278, 308. It is precisely because of this "utter impossibility" that the fathers put into the Constitution the principle of complete "hands-off," for a people as religiously heterogeneous as ours.

basic role of religion in the life of the people, nor rejection of religious education as a means of fostering it. The claims of religion were not minimized by refusing to make the public schools agencies for their assertion. The non-sectarian or secular public school was the means of reconciling freedom in general with religious freedom. The sharp confinement of the public schools to secular education was a recognition of the need of a democratic society to educate its children, insofar as the State undertook to do so, in an atmosphere free from pressures in a realm in which pressures are most resisted and where conflicts are most easily and most bitterly engendered. . . .

This development of the public school as a symbol of our secular unity was not a sudden achievement nor attained without violent conflict.[5] While in small communities of comparatively homogeneous religious beliefs, the need for absolute separation presented no urgencies, elsewhere the growth of the secular school encountered the resistance of feeling strongly engaged against it. . . .

[By] 1875 the separation of public education from Church entanglements, of the State from the teaching of religion, was firmly established in the consciousness of the nation. In that year President Grant made his famous remarks to the Convention of the Army of the Tennessee:

> "Encourage free schools, and resolve that not one dollar appropriated for their support shall be appropriated to the support of any sectarian schools. Resolve that neither the State nor nation, nor both combined, shall support institutions of learning other than those sufficient to afford every child growing up in the land the opportunity of a good common-school education, unmixed with sectarian, pagan, or atheistical dogmas. Leave the matter of religion to the family altar, the church, and the private school, supported entirely by private contributions. Keep the church and the state forever separate." "The President's Speech at Des Moines," 22 *Catholic World* 433, 434–35 (1876).

So strong was this conviction, that rather than rest on the

---

[5] See Cubberley, Public Education in the United States (1934) pp. 230 *et seq.;* Zollmann, *The Relation of Church and State,* in Lotz and Crawford, Studies in Religious Education (1931) 403, 418 *et seq.;* Payson Smith, *The Public Schools and Religious Education,* in Religion and Education (Sperry, Editor, 1945) pp. 32 *et seq.;* also Mahoney, The Relation of the State to Religious Education in Early New York 1633–1825 (1941) c. VI; McLaughlin, A History of State Legislation Affecting Private Elementary and Secondary Schools in the United States, 1870–1945 (1946) c. I; and see note 10, *infra.*

comprehensive prohibitions of the First and Fourteenth Amendments, President Grant urged that there be written into the United States Constitution particular elaborations, including a specific prohibition against the use of public funds for sectarian education,[6] such as had been written into many State constitutions.[7] By 1894, in urging the adoption of such a provision in the New York Constitution, Elihu Root was able to summarize a century of the nation's history: "It is not a question of religion, or of creed, or of party; it is a question of declaring and maintaining the great American principle of eternal separation between Church and State." Root, Addresses on Government and Citizenship, 137, 140. The extent to which this principle was deemed a presupposition of our Constitutional system is strikingly illustrated by the fact that every State admitted into the Union since 1876 was compelled by Congress to write into its constitution a requirement that it maintain a school system "free from sectarian control."

Prohibition of the commingling of sectarian and secular instruction in the public school is of course only half the story.

---

[6] President Grant's Annual Message to Congress, December 7, 1875, 4 Cong. Rec. 175 *et seq.;* Ames, The Proposed Amendments to the Constitution of the United States During the First Century of its History, H. R. Doc. No. 353, Pt. 2, 54th Cong., 2d Sess., pp. 277–78. In addition to the first proposal, "The Blaine Amendment," five others to similar effect are cited by Ames. The reason for the failure of these attempts seems to have been in part that the "provisions of the State constitutions are in almost all instances adequate on this subject, and no amendment is likely to be secured." *Id.*

In the form in which it passed the House of Representatives, the Blaine Amendment read as follows: "No State shall make any law respecting an establishment of religion, or prohibiting the free exercise thereof; and no religious test shall ever be required as a qualification to any office or public trust under any State. No public property, and no public revenue of, nor any loan of credit by or under the authority of, the United States, or any State, Territory, District, or municipal corporation, shall be appropriated to, or made or used for, the support of any school, educational or other institution, under the control of any religious or anti-religious sect, organization, or denomination, or wherein the particular creed or tenets of any religious or anti-religious sect, organization, or denomination shall be taught. And no such particular creed or tenets shall be read or taught in any school or institution supported in whole or in part by such revenue or loan of credit; and no such appropriation or loan of credit shall be made to any religious or anti-religious sect, organization, or denomination, or to promote its interests or tenets. This article shall not be construed to prohibit the reading of the Bible in any school or institution; and it shall not have the effect to impair rights of property already vested. . . ." H. Res. 1, 44th Cong., 1st Sess. (1876).

[7] See *Constitutions of the States and United States,* III Report of the New York State Constitutional Convention Committee (1938) Index, pp. 1766–67.

**933**

A religious people was naturally concerned about the part of the child's education entrusted "to the family altar, the church, and the private school." The promotion of religious education took many forms. Laboring under financial difficulties and exercising only persuasive authority, various denominations felt handicapped in their task of religious education. Abortive attempts were therefore frequently made to obtain public funds for religious schools.[10] But the major efforts of religious inculcation were a recognition of the principle of Separation by the establishment of church schools privately supported. Parochial schools were maintained by various denominations. These, however, were often beset by serious handicaps, financial and otherwise, so that the religious aims which they represented found other directions. There were experiments with vacation schools, with Saturday as well as Sunday schools.[11] They all fell short of their purpose. It was urged that by appearing to make religion a one-day-a-week matter, the Sunday school, which acquired national acceptance, tended to relegate the child's religious education, and thereby his religion, to a minor role not unlike the enforced piano lesson.

Out of these inadequate efforts evolved the week-day church school, held on one or more afternoons a week after the close of the public school. But children continued to be children;

---

[10] See, e. g., the New York experience, including, *inter alia*, the famous Hughes controversy of 1840–42, the conflict culminating in the Constitutional Convention of 1894, and the attempts to restore aid to parochial schools by revision of the New York City Charter, in 1901, and at the State Constitutional Convention of 1938. See McLaughlin, A History of State Legislation Affecting Private Elementary and Secondary Schools in the United States, 1870–1945 (1946) pp. 119–25; Mahoney, The Relation of the State to Religious Education in Early New York 1633–1825 (1941) c. VI; Hall, Religious Education in the Public Schools of the State and the City of New York (1914) pp. 46–47; Boese, Public Education in the City of New York (1869) c. XIV; compare New York Laws 1901, vol. 3 § 1152, p. 492, with amendment, *id.*, p. 668; see Nicholas Murray Butler, *Religion and Education* (Editorial) in 22 Educational Review 101, June, 1901; New York Times, April 8, 1901, p. 1, col. 1; April 9, 1901, p. 2, col. 5; April 19, 1901, p. 2, col. 2; April 21, 1901, p. 1, col. 3; Editorial, April 22, 1901, p. 6, col. 1.

Compare S. 2499, 79th Cong., 2d Sess., providing for Federal aid to education, and the controversy engendered over the inclusion in the aid program of sectarian schools, fully discussed in, *e. g.*, "The Nation's Schools," January through June, 1947.

[11] For surveys of the development of private religious education, see, *e. g.*, A. A. Brown, A History of Religious Education in Recent Times (1923); Athearn, Religious Education and American Democracy (1917); Burns and Kohlbrenner, A History of Catholic Education in the United States (1937); Lotz and Crawford, Studies in Religious Education (1931) Parts I and IV.

**934**

they wanted to play when school was out, particularly when other children were free to do so. Church leaders decided that if the week-day church school was to succeed, a way had to be found to give the child his religious education during what the child conceived to be his "business hours."

The initiation of the movement[12] may fairly be attributed to Dr. George U. Wenner. The underlying assumption of his proposal, made at the Interfaith Conference on Federation held in New York City in 1905, was that the public school unduly monopolized the child's time and that the churches were entitled to their share of it.[13] This, the schools should "release." Accordingly, the Federation, citing the example of the Third Republic of France,[14] urged that upon the request of their parents children be excused from public school on Wednesday afternoon, so that the churches could provide "Sunday school on Wednesday." This was to be carried out on church premises under church au-

[12] Reference should be made to Jacob Gould Schurman, who in 1903 proposed a plan bearing close resemblance to that of Champaign. See Symposium, 75 The Outlook 635, 636, November 14, 1903; Crooker, Religious Freedom in American Education (1903) pp. 39 *et seq.*

[13] For the text of the resolution, a brief in its support, as well as an exposition of some of the opposition it inspired, see Wenner's book, Religious Education and the Public School (rev. ed. 1913).

[14] The French example is cited not only by Wenner but also by Nicholas Murray Butler, who thought released time was "restoring the American system in the state of New York." *The Place of Religious Instruction in Our Educational System,* 7 Vital Speeches 167, 168 (Nov. 28, 1940); see also Report of the President of Columbia University, 1934, pp. 22–24. It is important to note, however, that the French practice must be viewed as the result of the struggle to emancipate the French schools from control by the Church. The leaders of this revolution, men like Paul Bert, Ferdinand Buisson, and Jules Ferry, agreed to this measure as one part of a great step towards, rather than a retreat from, the principle of Separation. The history of these events is described in Muzzey, *State, Church, and School in France,* The School Review, March through June, 1911.

In effect, moreover, the French practice differs in crucial respects from both the Wenner proposal and the Champaign system. The law of 1882 provided that "Public elementary schools will be closed one day a week in addition to Sunday in order to permit parents, if they so desire, to have their children given religious instruction outside of school buildings." Law No. 11,696, March 28, 1882, Bulletin des Lois, No. 690. This then approximates that aspect of released time generally known as "dismissed time." No children went to school on that day, and the public school was therefore not an alternative used to impel the children towards the religious school. The religious education was given "outside of school buildings."

The Vichy Government attempted to introduce a program of religious instruction within the public school system remarkably similar to that in effect in Champaign. The proposal was defeated by intense opposition which included the protest of the French clergy, who apparently feared State control of the Church. See Schwartz, *Religious Instruction under Pétain,* 58 Christian Century 1170, (Sept. 24, 1941).

**935**

thority. Those not desiring to attend church school would continue their normal classes. Lest these public school classes unfairly compete with the church education, it was requested that the school authorities refrain from scheduling courses or activities of compelling interest or importance.

The proposal aroused considerable opposition and it took another decade for a "released time" scheme to become part of a public school system. Gary, Indiana, inaugurated the movement. At a time when industrial expansion strained the communal facilities of the city, Superintendent of Schools Wirt suggested a fuller use of the school buildings. Building on theories which had become more or less current, he also urged that education was more than instruction in a classroom. The school was only one of several educational agencies. The library, the playground, the home, the church, all have their function in the child's proper unfolding. Accordingly, Wirt's plan sought to rotate the schedules of the children during the school-day so that some were in class, others were in the library, still others in the playground. And some, he suggested to the leading ministers of the City, might be released to attend religious classes if the churches of the City cooperated and provided them. They did, in 1914, and thus was "released time" begun. The religious teaching was held on church premises and the public schools had no hand in the conduct of these church schools. They did not supervise the choice of instructors or the subject matter taught. Nor did they assume responsibility for the attendance, conduct or achievement of the child in a church school; and he received no credit for it. The period of attendance in the religious schools would otherwise have been a play period for the child, with the result that the arrangement did not cut into public school instruction or truly affect the activities or feelings of the children who did not attend the church schools.[15]

From such a beginning "released time" has attained substantial proportions. In 1914–15, under the Gary program, 619 pupils left the public schools for the church schools during one period a week. According to responsible figures almost 2,000,-000 in some 2,200 communities participated in "released time" programs during 1947.[16]

[15] Of the many expositions of the Gary plan, see, e. g., A. A. Brown, *The Week-Day Church Schools of Gary, Indiana,* 11 Religious Education 5 (1916) ; Wirt, *The Gary Public Schools and the Churches, id.* at 221 (1916).

[16] See the 1947 Yearbook, International Council of Religious Education, p. 76; also New York Times, September 21, 1947, p. 22, col. 1.

## Note

1. See Butts, *American Tradition in Religion and Education* (1950);
Moehlman, *School and Church: The American Way* (1944); Sweets,
*Church and Education* (1939); Pfeffer, *Religion, Education and the
Constitution*, 8 Law. Guild Rev. 387 (1948); Stewart, *A History of
Religious Education in Connecticut to the Middle of the Nineteenth
Century* (1924).

2. On religion and education in general see: National Education
Association, *The Status of Religious Education in the Public Schools*
(1949) (contains extensive bibliography); American Council on Edu-
cation, *The Relation of Religion to Public Education* (1947); Chave,
*A Functional Approach to Religious Education* (1947); Mattox, *The
Teaching of Religion in the Public Schools* (1948); Moehlman, *The
Church As Educator* (1947); Lotz (ed.), *Orientation in Religious Edu-
cation* (1950); O'Neill, *Religion and Education Under the Constitution*
(1949); Williams, *The New Education and Religion, A Challenge to
Secularism in Education* (1945); Kilpatrick, *Religion in Education:
The Issues*, Prog. Ed. 98 (1949); Thayer, *Religion in Public Education*
(1947); Weary, *Democracy's Case Against Religious Education on
School Time* (1947); Synagogue Council of America, *Conference on Religious Education and the Public Schools* (1941); Brubacher (ed.), *The
Public Schools and Spiritual Values* (1944); Meiklejohn, *Educational
Cooperation Between Church and State*, 14 Law and Contemp. Prob. 61
(1949); American Jewish Committee, *Church, State and Education*
(1951); Cushman, *Public Support of Religious Education in American
Constitutional Law*, 45 Ill. L. Rev. 333 (1950); Cosway and Toepfer, *Religion and the Schools*, 17 U. Cin. L. Rev. 117 (1948); Burke, *Busses, Released Time and the Political Process*, 32 Marq. L. Rev. 311 (1948);
Note, *Catholic Schools and Public Money*, 50 Yale L. J. 917 (1941)
(containing a thorough discussion of aid to religion).

## 2. Aid to Education

### EVERSON v. BOARD OF EDUCATION

Supreme Court of the United States, 1947
330 U. S. 1, 91 L. Ed. 711, 67 S. Ct. 504

MR. JUSTICE BLACK delivered the opinion of the Court.

A New Jersey statute authorizes its local school districts to
make rules and contracts for the transportation of children to
and from schools.[1] The appellee, a township board of educa-

---

[1] "Whenever in any district there are children living remote from any
schoolhouse, the board of education of the district may make rules and
contracts for the transportation of such children to and from school, including the transportation of school children to and from school other than
a public school, except such school as is operated for profit in whole or in
part.

tion, acting pursuant to this statute, authorized reimbursement to parents of money expended by them for the bus transportation of their children on regular busses operated by the public transportation system. Part of this money was for the payment of transportation of some children in the community to Catholic parochial schools. These church schools give their students, in addition to secular education, regular religious instruction conforming to the religious tenets and modes of worship of the Catholic Faith. The superintendent of these schools is a Catholic priest.

The appellant, in his capacity as a district taxpayer, filed suit in a state court challenging the right of the Board to reimburse parents of parochial school students. He contended that the statute and the resolution passed pursuant to it violated both the State and the Federal Constitutions. That court held that the legislature was without power to authorize such payment under the state constitution. 132 N. J. L. 98, 39 A. 2d 75. The New Jersey Court of Errors and Appeals reversed, holding that neither the statute nor the resolution passed pursuant to it was in conflict with the State constitution or the provisions of the Federal Constitution in issue. 133 N. J. L. 350, 44 A. 2d 333. The case is here on appeal under 28 U. S. C. § 344(a).

Since there has been no attack on the statute on the ground that a part of its language excludes children attending private schools operated for profit from enjoying State payment for their transportation, we need not consider this exclusionary language; it has no relevancy to any constitutional question here presented.[2] Furthermore, if the exclusion clause had been prop-

---

"When any school district provides any transportation for public school children to and from school, transportation from any point in such established school route to any other point in such established school route shall be supplied to school children residing in such school district in going to and from school other than a public school, except such school as is operated for profit in whole or in part." New Jersey Laws, 1941, c. 191, p. 581; N. J. R. S. Cum. Supp., tit. 18, c. 14, § 8.

[2] Appellant does not challenge the New Jersey statute or the resolution on the ground that either violates the equal protection clause of the Fourteenth Amendment by excluding payment for the transportation of any pupil who attends a "private school run for profit." Although the township resolution authorized reimbursement only for parents of public and Catholic school pupils, appellant does not allege, nor is there anything in the record which would offer the slightest support to an allegation, that there were any children in the township who attended or would have attended, but for want of transportation, any but public and Catholic schools. It will be appropriate to consider the exclusion of students of private schools operated for profit when and if it is proved to have occurred, is made the basis of a suit by one in a position to challenge it, and New Jersey's highest court has ruled adversely to the challenger. Striking down a state law

**938**

erly challenged, we do not know whether New Jersey's highest court would construe its statutes as precluding payment of the school transportation of any group of pupils, even those of a private school run for profit. Consequently, we put to one side the question as to the validity of the statute against the claim that it does not authorize payment for the transportation generally of school children in New Jersey.

The only contention here is that the state statute and the resolution, insofar as they authorized reimbursement to parents of children attending parochial schools, violate the Federal Constitution in these two respects, which to some extent overlap. *First.* They authorize the State to take by taxation the private property of some and bestow it upon others, to be used for their own private purposes. This, it is alleged, violates the due process clause of the Fourteenth Amendment. *Second.* The statute and the resolution forced inhabitants to pay taxes to help support and maintain schools which are dedicated to, and which regularly teach, the Catholic Faith. This is alleged to be a use of state power to support church schools contrary to the prohibition of the First Amendment which the Fourteenth Amendment made applicable to the states.

*First.* The due process argument that the state law taxes some people to help others carry out their private purposes is framed in two phases. The first phase is that a state cannot tax A to reimburse B for the cost of transporting his children to church schools. This is said to violate the due process clause because the children are sent to these church schools to satisfy the personal desires of their parents, rather than the public's interest in the general education of all children. This argument, if valid, would apply equally to prohibit state payment for the transportation of children to any non-public school, whether operated by a church or any other non-government individual or group. But, the New Jersey legislature has decided that a public purpose will be served by using tax-raised funds to pay the bus fares of all school children, including those who attend parochial schools. The New Jersey Court of Errors and Appeals has reached the same conclusion. The fact that a state law, passed to satisfy a public need, coincides with the personal desires of the individuals most directly affected is certainly an inadequate reason for us to say that a legislature has erroneously appraised the public need

• • • •

---

is not a matter of such light moment that it should be done by a federal court *ex mero motu* on a postulate neither charged nor proved, but which rests on nothing but a possibility. *Cf. Liverpool, N. Y. & P. S. S. Co. v. Comm'rs of Emigration,* 113 U. S. 33, 39.

**939**

It is much too late to argue that legislation intended to facilitate the opportunity of children to get a secular education serves no public purpose. *Cochran v. Louisiana State Board of Education*, 281 U. S. 370; Holmes, J., in *Interstate Ry. v. Massachusetts*, 207 U. S. 79, 87. See opinion of Cooley, J., in *Stuart v. School District No. 1 of Kalamazoo*, 30 Mich. 69 (1874). The same thing is no less true of legislation to reimburse needy parents, or all parents, for payment of the fares of their children so that they can ride in public busses to and from schools rather than run the risk of traffic and other hazards incident to walking or "hitchhiking." See *Barbier v. Connolly* [113 U. S. 27, 31]. See also cases collected 63 A. L. R. 413; 118 A. L. R. 806. Nor does it follow that a law has a private rather than a public purpose because it provides that tax-raised funds will be paid to reimburse individuals on account of money spent by them in a way which furthers a public program. See *Carmichael v. Southern Coal & Coke Co.*, 301 U. S. 495, 518. Subsidies and loans to individuals such as farmers and home-owners, and to privately owned transportation systems, as well as many other kinds of businesses, have been commonplace practices in our state and national history. . . .

*Second.* The New Jersey statute is challenged as a "law respecting an establishment of religion." The First Amendment, as made applicable to the states by the Fourteenth, *Murdock v. Pennsylvania*, 319 U. S. 105, commands that a state "shall make no law respecting an establishment of religion, or prohibiting the free exercise thereof . . . ." These words of the First Amendment reflected in the minds of early Americans a vivid mental picture of conditions and practices which they fervently wished to stamp out in order to preserve liberty for themselves and for their posterity. Doubtless their goal has not been entirely reached; but so far has the Nation moved toward it that the expression "law respecting an establishment of religion," probably does not so vividly remind present-day Americans of the evils, fears, and political problems that caused that expression to be written into our Bill of Rights. Whether this New Jersey law is one respecting an "establishment of religion" requires an understanding of the meaning of that language, particularly with respect to the imposition of taxes. Once again, therefore, it is not inappropriate briefly to review the background and environment of the period in which that constitutional language was fashioned and adopted. . . .

[The opinion here reviews the history of the First Amendment.]

**940**

The meaning and scope of the First Amendment, preventing establishment of religion or prohibiting the free exercise thereof, in the light of its history and the evils it was designed forever to suppress, have been several times elaborated by the decisions of this Court prior to the application of the First Amendment to the states by the Fourteenth.[21]  The broad meaning given the Amendment by these earlier cases has been accepted by this Court in its decisions concerning an individual's religious freedom rendered since the Fourteenth Amendment was interpreted to make the prohibitions of the First applicable to state action abridging religious freedom.  There is every reason to give the same application and broad interpretation to the "establishment of religion" clause.  The interrelation of these complementary clauses was well summarized in a statement of the Court of Appeals of South Carolina,[23] quoted with approval by this Court in *Watson v. Jones*, 13 Wall. 679, 730:  "The structure of our government has, for the preservation of civil liberty, rescued the temporal institutions from religious interference. On the other hand, it has secured religious liberty from the invasion of the civil authority."

The "establishment of religion" clause of the First Amendment means at least this:  Neither a state nor the Federal Government can set up a church.  Neither can pass laws which aid one religion, aid all religions, or prefer one religion over another. Neither can force nor influence a person to go to or to remain away from church against his will or force him to profess a belief or disbelief in any religion.  No person can be punished for entertaining or professing religious beliefs or disbeliefs, for church attendance or non-attendance.  No tax in any amount, large or small, can be levied to support any religious activities or institutions, whatever they may be called, or whatever form they may adopt to teach or practice religion.  Neither a state nor the Federal Government can, openly or secretly, participate in the affairs of any religious organizations or groups and *vice versa*.  In the words of Jefferson, the clause against establishment of religion by law was intended to erect "a wall of separation between church and State."  *Reynolds v. United States, supra* at 164.

We must consider the New Jersey statute in accordance with the foregoing limitations imposed by the First Amendment. But we must not strike that state statute down if it is within

---

[21] *Terrett v. Taylor*, 9 Cranch 43; *Watson v. Jones*, 13 Wall. 679; *Davis v. Beason*, 133 U. S. 333; *Cf. Reynolds v. United States* [98 U. S. 145, 162]; *Reuben Quick Bear v. Leupp*, 210 U. S. 50.

[23] *Harmon v. Dreher*, Speer's Equity Reports (S. C., 1843), 87, 120.

the State's constitutional power even though it approaches the verge of that power. See *Interstate Ry. v. Massachusetts,* Holmes, J., *supra* at 85, 88. New Jersey cannot consistently with the "establishment of religion" clause of the First Amendment contribute tax-raised funds to the support of an institution which teaches the tenets and faith of any church. On the other hand, other language of the amendment commands that New Jersey cannot hamper its citizens in the free exercise of their own religion. Consequently, it cannot exclude individual Catholics, Lutherans, Mohammedans, Baptists, Jews, Methodists, Non-believers, Presbyterians, or the members of any other faith, *because of their faith, or lack of it,* from receiving the benefits of public welfare legislation. While we do not mean to intimate that a state could not provide transportation only to children attending public schools, we must be careful, in protecting the citizens of New Jersey against state-established churches, to be sure that we do not inadvertently prohibit New Jersey from extending its general state law benefits to all its citizens without regard to their religious belief.

Measured by these standards, we cannot say that the First Amendment prohibits New Jersey from spending tax-raised funds to pay the bus fares of parochial school pupils as a part of a general program under which it pays the fares of pupils attending public and other schools. It is undoubtedly true that children are helped to get to church schools. There is even a possibility that some of the children might not be sent to the church schools if the parents were compelled to pay their children's bus fares out of their own pockets when transportation to a public school would have been paid for by the State. The same possibility exists where the state requires a local transit company to provide reduced fares to school children including those attending parochial schools, or where a municipally owned transportation system undertakes to carry all school children free of charge. Moreover, state-paid policemen, detailed to protect children going to and from church schools from the very real hazards of traffic, would serve much the same purpose and accomplish much the same result as state provisions intended to guarantee free transportation of a kind which the state deems to be best for the school children's welfare. And parents might refuse to risk their children to the serious danger of traffic accidents going to and from parochial schools, the approaches to which were not protected by policemen. Similarly, parents might be reluctant to permit their children to attend schools which the state had cut off from such general government services as ordinary police and fire protection, connections for sewage disposal, public highways and sidewalks. Of course, cutting off church schools from these services, so separate and so indisputably marked off from the religious function, would make it far more difficult for the schools to operate. But such is obviously not the purpose of the First Amendment. That Amendment requires the state to be a neutral in its relations with groups of religious believers and non-believers; it does not require the state to be their adversary. State power is no more to be used so as to handicap religions than it is to favor them.

This Court has said that parents may, in the discharge of their duty under state compulsory education laws, send their children to a religious rather than a public school if the school meets the secular educational requirements which the state has power to impose. See *Pierce v. Society of Sisters,* 268 U. S. 510. It appears that these parochial schools meet New Jersey's requirements. The State contributes no money to the schools. It does not support them. Its legislation, as applied, does no more than provide a general program to help parents get their children, regardless of their religion, safely and expeditiously to and from accredited schools.

The First Amendment has erected a wall between church and state. That wall must be kept high and impregnable. We could not approve the slightest breach. New Jersey has not breached it here.

*Affirmed.*

MR. JUSTICE JACKSON, dissenting. . . .
Whether the taxpayer constitutionally can be made to contribute aid to parents of students because of their attendance at parochial schools depends upon the nature of those schools and their relation to the Church. The Constitution says nothing of education. It lays no obligation on the states to provide schools and does not undertake to regulate state systems of education if they see fit to maintain them. But they cannot, through school policy any more than through other means, invade rights secured to citizens by the Constitution of the United States. *West Virginia State Board of Education v. Barnette,* 319 U. S. 624. One of our basic rights is to be free of taxation to support a transgression of the constitutional command that the authorities "shall make no law respecting an establishment of religion, or prohibiting the free exercise thereof . . . ." U. S. Const., Amend. I; *Cantwell v. Connecticut,* 310 U. S. 296.

The function of the Church school is a subject on which this record is meager. It shows only that the schools are under super-

**943**

intendence of a priest and that "religion is taught as part of the curriculum." But we know that such schools are parochial only in name—they, in fact, represent a world-wide and age-old policy of the Roman Catholic Church. Under the rubric "Catholic Schools," the Canon Law of the Church, by which all Catholics are bound, provides:

"1215. Catholic children are to be educated in schools where not only nothing contrary to Catholic faith and morals is taught, but rather in schools where religious and moral training occupy the first place. . . . (Canon 1372.)"

"1216. In every elementary school the children must, according to their age, be instructed in Christian doctrine.

"The young people who attend the higher schools are to receive a deeper religious knowledge, and the bishops shall appoint priests qualified for such work by their learning and piety. (Canon 1373.)"

"1217. Catholic children shall not attend non-Catholic, indifferent, schools that are mixed, that is to say, schools open to Catholics and non-Catholics alike. The bishop of the diocese only has the right, in harmony with the instructions of the Holy See, to decide under what circumstances, and with what safeguards to prevent loss of faith, it may be tolerated that Catholic children go to such schools. (Canon 1374.)"

"1224. The religious teaching of youth in any schools is subject to the authority and inspection of the Church.

"The local Ordinaries have the right and duty to watch that nothing is taught contrary to faith or good morals, in any of the schools of their territory.

"They, moreover, have the right to approve the books of Christian doctrine and the teachers of religion, and to demand, for the sake of safeguarding religion and morals, the removal of teachers and books. (Canon 1381.)" (Woywod, Rev. Stanislaus, The New Canon Law, under imprimatur of Most Rev. Francis J. Spellman, Archbishop of New York and others, 1940.)

It is no exaggeration to say that the whole historic conflict in temporal policy between the Catholic Church and non-Catholics comes to a focus in their respective school policies. The Roman Catholic Church, counseled by experience in many ages and many lands and with all sorts and conditions of men, takes what, from the viewpoint of its own progress and the success of its mission, is a wise estimate of the importance of education to religion. It does not leave the individual to pick up religion by chance. It relies on early and indelible indoctrination in the faith and order of the Church by the word and example of persons consecrated to the task.

Our public school, if not a product of Protestantism, at least is more consistent with it than with the Catholic culture and scheme of values. It is a relatively recent development dating from about 1840.[1] It is organized on the premise that secular education can be isolated from all religious teaching so that the school can inculcate all needed temporal knowledge and also maintain a strict and lofty neutrality as to religion. The assumption is that after the individual has been instructed in worldly wisdom he will be better fitted to choose his religion. Whether such a disjunction is possible, and if possible whether it is wise, are questions I need not try to answer.

I should be surprised if any Catholic would deny that the parochial school is a vital, if not the most vital, part of the Roman Catholic Church. If put to the choice, that venerable institution, I should expect, would forego its whole service for mature persons before it would give up education of the young, and it would be a wise choice. Its growth and cohesion, discipline and loyalty, spring from its schools. Catholic education is the rock on which the whole structure rests, and to render tax aid to its Church school is indistinguishable to me from rendering the same aid to the Church itself. . . .

It is of no importance in this situation whether the beneficiary of this expenditure of tax-raised funds is primarily the parochial school and incidentally the pupil, or whether the aid is directly bestowed on the pupil with indirect benefits to the school. The state cannot maintain a Church and it can no more tax its citizens to furnish free carriage to those who attend a Church. The prohibition against establishment of religion cannot be circumvented by a subsidy, bonus or reimbursement of expense to individuals for receiving religious instruction and indoctrination.

The Court, however, compares this to other subsidies and loans to individuals and says, "Nor does it follow that a law has a private rather than a public purpose because it provides that tax-raised funds will be paid to reimburse individuals on account of money spent by them in a way which furthers a public program. See *Carmichael v. Southern Coal & Coke Co.,* 301 U. S. 495, 518." Of course, the state may pay out tax-raised funds to

---

[1] See Cubberley, Public Education in the United States (1934) ch. VI; Knight, Education in the United States (1941) ch. VIII.

relieve pauperism, but it may not under our Constitution do so to induce or reward piety. It may spend funds to secure old age against want, but it may not spend funds to secure religion against skepticism. It may compensate individuals for loss of employment, but it cannot compensate them for adherence to a creed.

It seems to me that the basic fallacy in the Court's reasoning, which accounts for its failure to apply the principles it avows, is in ignoring the essentially religious test by which beneficiaries of this expenditure are selected. A policeman protects a Catholic of course—but not because he is a Catholic; it is because he is a man and a member of our society. The fireman protects the Church school—but not because it is a Church school; it is because it is property, part of the assets of our society. Neither the fireman nor the policeman has to ask before he renders aid "Is this man or building identified with the Catholic Church—" But before these school authorities draw a check to reimburse for a student's fare they must ask just that question, and if the school is a Catholic one they may render aid because it is such, while if it is of any other faith or is run for profit, the help must be withheld. To consider the converse of the Court's reasoning will best disclose its fallacy. That there is no parallel between police and fire protection and this plan of reimbursement is apparent from the incongruity of the limitation of this Act if applied to police and fire service. Could we sustain an Act that said the police shall protect pupils on the way to or from public schools and Catholic schools but not while going to and coming from other schools, and firemen shall extinguish a blaze in public or Catholic school buildings but shall not put out a blaze in in Protestant Church schools or private schools operated for profit? That is the true analogy to the case we have before us and I should think it pretty plain that such a scheme would not be valid. . . .

MR. JUSTICE FRANKFURTER joins in this opinion.

MR. JUSTICE RUTLEDGE, with whom MR. JUSTICE FRANKFURTER, MR. JUSTICE JACKSON and MR. JUSTICE BURTON agree, dissenting. . . .

[The first part of Mr. Justice Rutledge's opinion has been printed *supra*.]

It is not because religious teaching does not promote the public or the individual's welfare, but because neither is furthered when the state promotes religious education, that the Constitution forbids it to do so. Both legislatures and courts are bound by that

[Emerson]

distinction. In failure to observe it lies the fallacy of the "public function"—"social legislation" argument, a fallacy facilitated by easy transference of the argument's basing from due process unrelated to any religious aspect to the First Amendment.

By no declaration that a gift of public money to religious uses will promote the general or individual welfare, or the cause of education generally, can legislative bodies overcome the Amendment's bar. Nor may the courts sustain their attempts to do so by finding such consequences for appropriations which in fact give aid to or promote religious uses. Cf. *Norris v. Alabama,* 294 U. S. 587, 590; *Hooven & Allison Co. v. Evatt,* 324 U. S. 652, 659; *Akins v. Texas,* 325 U. S. 398, 402. Legislatures are free to make, and courts to sustain, appropriations only when it can be found that in fact they do not aid, promote, encourage or sustain religious teaching or observances, be the amount large or small. No such finding has been or could be made in this case. The Amendment has removed this form of promoting the public welfare from legislative and judicial competence to make a public function. It is exclusively a private affair.

The reasons underlying the Amendment's policy have not vanished with time or diminished in force. Now as when it was adopted the price of religious freedom is double. It is that the church and religion shall live both within and upon that freedom. There cannot be freedom of religion, safeguarded by the state, and intervention by the church or its agencies in the state's domain or dependency on its largesse. Madison's Remonstrance, Par. 6, 8.[44] The great condition of religious liberty is that it be maintained free from sustenance, as also from other interferences, by the state. For when it comes to rest upon that secular foundation it vanishes with the resting. *Id.,* Par.7, 8.[45] Public money devoted to payment of religious costs, educational or other, brings the quest for more. It brings too the struggle of sect against sect for the larger share or for any. Here one by numbers alone will benefit most, there another. That is precisely the history of societies which have had an established

---

[44] "Because the establishment proposed by the Bill is not requisite for the support of the Christian Religion. To say that it is, is a contradiction to the Christian Religion itself; for every page of it disavows a dependence on the powers of this world. . . . Because the establishment in question is not necessary for the support of Civil Government. . . . What influence in fact have ecclesiastical establishments had on Civil Society? . . . in no instance have they been seen the guardians of the liberties of the people." II Madison 183, 187, 188.

[45] "Because experience witnesseth that eccleciastical establishments, instead of maintaining the purity and efficacy of Religion, have had a contrary operation." II Madison 183, 187.

religion and dissident groups. *Id.,* Par. 8, 11. It is the very thing Jefferson and Madison experienced and sought to guard against, whether in its blunt or in its more screened forms. *Ibid.* The end of such strife cannot be other than to destroy the cherished liberty. The dominating group will achieve the dominant benefit; or all will embroil the state in their dissensions. *Id.,* Par. 11.[46]

Exactly such conflicts have centered of late around providing transportation to religious schools from public funds.[47] The issue and the dissension work typically, in Madison's phrase, to "destroy that moderation and harmony which the forbearance of our laws to intermeddle with Religion, has produced amongst its several sects." *Id.,* Par. 11. This occurs, as he well knew, over measures at the very threshold of departure from the principle. *Id.,* Par 3, 9, 11.

In these conflicts wherever success has been obtained it has been upon the contention that by providing the transportation the general cause of education, the general welfare, and the welfare of the individual will be forwarded; hence that the matter lies within the realm of public function, for legislative determination. State courts have divided upon the issue, some taking the view that only the individual, others that the institution receives the benefit. A few have recognized that this dichotomy is false, that both in fact are aided.

The majority here does not accept in terms any of those views. But neither does it deny that the individual or the school or indeed both, are benefited directly and substantially. . . .

Notwithstanding the recognition that this two-way aid is given and the absence of any denial that religious teaching is thus furthered, the Court concludes that the aid so given is not "support" of religion. . . .

---

[46] "At least let warning be taken at the first fruits of the threatened innovation. The very appearance of the Bill has transformed that 'Christian forbearance, love and charity,' which of late mutually prevailed, into animosities and jealousies, which may not soon be appeased." II Madison 183, 189.

[47] In this case briefs *amici curiae* have been filed on behalf of various organizations representing three religious sects, one labor union, the American Civil Liberties Union, and the states of Illinois, Indiana, Louisiana, Massachusetts, Michigan and New York. All these states have laws similar to New Jersey's and all of them, with one religious sect, support the constitutionality of New Jersey's action. The others oppose it. Maryland and Mississippi have sustained similar legislation. . . . No state without legislation of this sort has filed an opposing brief. But at least six states have held such action invalid, namely, Delaware, Oklahoma, New York, South Dakota, Washington and Wisconsin. . . . The New York

[This] approach, if valid, supplies a ready method for nullifying the Amendment's guaranty, not only for this case and others involving small grants in aid for religious education, but equally for larger ones. The only thing needed will be for the Court again to transplant the "public welfare—public function" view from its proper nonreligious due process bearing to First Amendment application, holding that religious education is not "supported" though it may be aided by the appropriation, and that the cause of education generally is furthered by helping the pupil to secure that type of training. . . .

[Mr. Justice Rutledge goes on to say that no discrimination against those attending religious schools is involved, for they can always choose to attend public schools. The hardship entailed by those attending religious schools is a necessary consequence of the principle of separation. He states further that even if it were shown that all religions received aid under the statute, it could not stand.]

For then the adherent of one creed still would pay for the support of another, the childless taxpayer with others more fortunate. Then too there would seem to be no bar to making appropriations for transportation and other expenses of children attending public or other secular schools, after hours in separate places and classes for their exclusively religious instruction. The person who embraces no creed also would be forced to pay for teaching what he does not believe. Again, it was the furnishing of "contributions of money for the propagation of opinions which he disbelieves" that the fathers outlawed. That consequence and effect are not removed by multiplying to all-inclusiveness the sects for which support is exacted. The Constitution requires, not comprehensive identification of state with religion, but complete separation. . . .

I have chosen to place my dissent upon the broad ground I think decisive, though strictly speaking the case might be decided on narrower issues. The New Jersey statute might be held invalid on its face for the exclusion of children who attend private, profit-making schools.[58] I cannot assume, as does the majority, that the New Jersey courts would write off this explicit limitation from the statute. Moreover, the resolution by which the statute was applied expressly limits its benefits to students

---

ruling was overturned by amendment to the state constitution in 1938. Constitution of New York, Art. XI, 4. . . .

[58] It would seem at least a doubtfully sufficient basis for reasonable classification that some children should be excluded simply because the only school feasible for them to attend, in view of geographic or other situation, might be one conducted in whole *or in part* for profit. . . .

of public and Catholic schools.[59] There is no showing that there are no other private or religious schools in this populous district.[60] I do not think it can be assumed there were none. But in the view I have taken, it is unnecessary to limit grounding to these matters. . . .

### Note

1. Several jurisdictions have held that the furnishing of free transportation to pupils of non-public schools is prohibited: *Gurney v. Ferguson*, 190 Okla. 254, 122 Pac. 2d 1002 (1941); *Mitchell v. Consolidated School Dist.*, 17 Wash. 2d 61, 135 Pac. 2d 79 (1943); *Sherrard v. Jefferson County Bd. of Education*, 294 Ky. 469, 171 S. W. 2d 963 (1942) (not for "public purpose"); *State ex rel. Van Straten v. Milquet*, 180 Wis. 109, 192 N. W. 392 (1928); *State ex rel. Traub v. Brown*, 36 Del. 181, 172 Atl. 835 (1934), writ of error dismissed, 39 Del. 187, 197 Atl. 478 (1938); *Judd v. Board of Education*, 278 N. Y. 200, 15 N. E. 2d 576 (1938). To the same effect as the *Everson* case, see *Bowler v. Baker*, 73 Cal. App. 653, 167 Pac. 2d 256 (1946); *Adams v. St. Mary's County*, 180 Md. 550, 26 Atl. 2d 377 (1942); *Zellers v. Huff*, 55 N. M. 501, 236 Pac. 2d 949 (1951).

2. The *Everson* case is discussed in Cosgrove and Flattery, *Transportation of Parochial School Pupils*, 22 Notre Dame Law. 192 (1947); Cahill, *Constitutionality of Indirect State Aid to Sectarian Schools*, 3 Intramural L. Rev. 147 (1948); Hopkins, *State Transportation of Students to Parochial Schools*, 36 Ky. L. J. 328 (1948).

### Total and Partial Integration of Religious and Public School Systems

In *Zellers v. Huff*, 55 N. M. 501, 236 Pac. 2d 949 (1951), the Supreme Court of New Mexico enjoined the State Board of Education from continuing its support of parochial schools and schools substantially managed by the Roman Catholic Church. The schools were part of the public school system, the state had to maintain two sets of textbooks, and in some communities they were the only schools even for non-Catholics. Religious

---

[59] . . . The resolution was as follows, according to the school board's minutes read in proof: "The transportation committee recommended the transportation of pupils of Ewing to the Trenton and Pennington High Schools *and Catholic Schools* by way of public carrier as in recent years. On Motion of Mr. Ralph Ryan and Mr. M. French the same was adopted." (Emphasis added.) The New Jersey court's holding that the resolution was within the authority conferred by the state statute is binding on us. *Reinman v. Little Rock*, 237 U. S. 171, 176; *Hadacheck v. Sebastian*, 239 U. S. 394, 414.

[60] The population of Ewing Township, located near the City of Trenton, was 10,146 according to the census of 1940. Sixteenth Census of the United States, Population, Vol. 1, 674.

instruction and religious exercises were part of the program and religious comic books, prayer books and other equipment were used. The court held that the following violated the religious provisions of Federal and state constitutions: (1) the wearing of religious garbs by teachers in public schools; (2) the teaching of sectarian religion and the dissemination of religious literature; (3) the supervision of school teachers and public school system by a church. The court authorized, in accordance with provisions of a state statute, the discharge of teachers who knowingly taught sectarian doctrine. But it held that the payment by teachers of their salaries to religious orders did not render state payment of those salaries state aid to religion.

For an account of the background of this case see 2 Stokes, *Church and State in the United States*, pp. 662–71 (1950). See also *Knowlton v. Baumhover*, 182 Ia. 691, 166 N. W. 202 (1918) (appropriating rent for schoolroom with relics and teaching by sister with garb, as alternative to requiring public school room, held invalid); *State ex rel. Public School District v. Taylor*, 122 Neb. 454, 240 N. W. 573 (1932); *Harfst v. Hoegen*, 349 Mo. 808, 163 S. W. 2d 609 (1942) (Roman Catholic school made part of public school system—state textbooks and course of instruction adopted, name of building, graven images, holy water fonts, garbed teachers and religious instruction persisted—held invalid); *Wright v. School District*, 151 Kan. 485, 99 Pac. 2d 737 (1940); *Williams v. Stanton School Dist.*, 173 Ky. 708, 191 S. W. 507 (1917); *Richter v. Cordes*, 100 Mich. 278, 58 N. W. 1110 (1894).

For cases upholding the use and renting of religious property for public schools, see *Millard v. Board of Education*, 121 Ill. 297, 10 N. E. 669 (1887) (emergency measure—there were religious exercises but no compulsion against wishes of parents); *Scripture v. Burns*, 59 Ia. 70, 12 N. W. 760 (1882) (public funds available only for a six-month school; justification was that by using sectarian school building and contributions by the church, school could be taught for ten months); *New Haven v. Torrington*, 132 Conn. 194, 43 Atl. 2d 455 (1945) (Board of Education ran school in Catholic orphanage taught in part by garbed nuns who conducted religious exercises but not immediately prior to classes; the school was open to all children in the neighborhood but attended only by Catholics; held that a city whose residents were taught in it must reimburse the city which ran the school; the school met the two prerequisites of (1) exclusive control by Board of Education and (2) no sectarian instruction); *State ex rel. Johnson v. Boyd*, 217 Ind. 348, 28 N. E. 2d 256

(1940); *Crain v. Walker,* 222 Ky. 828, 2 S. W. 2d 654 (1928); *Matter of Roche,* 26 N. Y. St. Dep't. Rep. 217 (1921). See also *Quick Bear v. Leupp,* 210 U. S. 50, 52 L. Ed. 954, 28 S. Ct. 690 (1908) (payment of Indian claims by federal government intended to be used in support of Catholic parochial system, did not constitute violation of separation of church and state).

## Other Aids to Religious Schools

*Tuition.* The following cases hold use of state funds to pay parochial school tuition invalid: *Otken v. Lamkin,* 56 Miss. 758 (1879) (holding unconstitutional a statute permitting child attending private school to receive from the school fund share he would have been entitled to were he attending public school); *Synod of Dakota v. State,* 2 S. D. 366, 50 N. W. 632 (1891) (tuition of students being trained as public school teachers in sectarian college could not be paid out of state funds); *Williams v. Stanton School Dist.,* 173 Ky. 708, 191 S. W. 507 (1917) (payment of tuition fees of public school students taught in rooms, and in part by teachers, of a sectarian college unlawful).

*Free textbooks to parochial school students.* In addition to the *Cochran* case discussed in the *Everson* case see *Chance v. Mississippi State Textbook Rating and Purchasing Board,* 190 Miss. 453, 200 So. 706 (1941) (valid); *Smith v. Donahue,* 202 App. Div. 656, 195 N. Y. Supp. 715 (1922) (invalid); *Donahoe v. Richards,* 38 Me. 376 (1854) (invalid).

*Exemption from state taxes of parents sending children to private schools. Underwood v. Wood,* 93 Ky. 177, 19 S. W. 405 (1892) (invalid).

*Use of school property.* Primarily in connection with the Sunday School movement a number of cases have dealt with the question of the use of public school property for religious purposes. Cases authorizing use are: *Nichols v. School Directors,* 93 Ill. 61 (1879) (statute explicitly authorizing use of public school building for religious meetings, and Sunday School sessions not interfering with regular school work, held not to violate constitutional provision that no person should be required to support a place of worship against his consent, nor any preference given to any denomination; the "incidental benefit" received by the religious organizations did not constitute state aid to religion); to the same effect see, *State ex rel. Gilbert v. Dilley,* 95 Neb. 527, 145 N. W. 999 (1914) (the occasional use of school for Sunday Schools did not convert it into a place of worship—mandamus not available to taxpayer who cannot show extent of his contribution to cost of Sunday meetings): *Davis v. Boget,* 50 Ia. 11 (1878) (relies on earlier case, *Townsend v. Hagen,* 35 Ia. 194 (1872), for holding that statute broadly authorizing disposition by electors of school building for religious purposes is constitutional). See also *Bull v. Stichman,* 298 N. Y. 516, 80 N. E. 2d 661 (1948) (appropriation by Emergency Joint Housing Board to remodel building of a Jesuit college; held taxpayer and citizen without any special or personal interest has no standing to sue). Cases prohibiting use are: *Spencer v. School District,* 15 Kan. 259 (1875) (religious and other private uses violate prohibition of expending funds for "private purpose") ; *Hysong v. Gallitzin School Dist.,* 164 Pa. 629, 30 Atl. 482 (1894) (violates financial aid to religion provisions) ; *Bender v. Streabich,* 17 Pa. Co. Ct. 609 (1896) (violates financial aid to religion provisions). See also *Scofield v. Eighth School District,* 27 Conn. 499 (1858) ; *George v. Second School District,* 6 Met. (Mass.) 497 (1843).

## Note

1. The church-state controversy has played an important part in Federal Aid to Education bills introduced in Congress. See, *e.g.,* the exchange between Mrs. Roosevelt and Cardinal Spellman, N. Y. Times, July 23 and 30, 1949. The proposals vary in their treatment of private schools, from complete exclusion, to leaving it up to the states, to complete inclusion. See Note, 23 Temple L. Q. 227 (1950) ; and see Chapter VII, *supra.* Among the forms of Federal aid to religious education now in operation are (1) Veteran's contributions for training for the ministry at denominational schools, 38 U. S. C. § 693 (1948) ; (2) Religious activities at United States Naval and Military Academies. See U. S. Naval Acad. Reg. Art. 4301 (b) (prescribing attendance at services on Sunday) ; Reg. for the U. S. Corps of Cadets (1947) 47 (attendance at church and religious training in either Protestant, Catholic or Jewish faith).

2. While aid in connection with education has been the major subject of current litigation, other government aids to religion have also been challenged on constitutional grounds:

(a) *Tax exemption of church property:* Religious organizations are generally exempt from federal income taxation and contributions to them are deductible up to 15% of adjusted gross income. Gifts and bequests to religious organizations are also deductible for purposes of federal gift and estates tax. States grant tax exemptions to religious organizations either under State statutes or under constitutional provisions. For state cases upholding the exemptions see *Garrett Biblical Inst. v. Elmhurst State Bank,* 331 Ill. 308, 163 N. E. 1 (1928) (upheld on grounds (1) that Christian nation should encourage religious establishment, and (2) that exemption to all religious denominations without discrimination does not violate the Constitution); *Trustees of Griswold College v. Iowa,* 46 Iowa 275, (1877) (upheld without specific grounds). *Cf.* also, *Chicago Theological Seminary v.*

*Illinois,* 188 U. S. 662, 47 L. Ed. 641, 23 S. Ct. 386 (1903) (exemption from taxation by statute must be plainly granted and does not exist by implication). The statutes limit tax exemptions either in terms of the area of the church holdings or in terms of their total value, or in terms of their use. Use exemptions give birth to a great deal of litigation. For a collection of cases see Torpey, *Judicial Doctrines of Religious Rights in America,* pp. 171–197 (1948). For a general discussion of the constitutional question see, Paulsen, *Preferment of Religious Institutions in Tax and Labor Legislation,* 14 Law and Contemp. Prob. 144 (1949).

(b) *Appropriations for institutions other than schools:* Cases holding these invalid under specific constitutional prohibitions are: *State ex rel. Nevada Orphan Asylum v. Hallock,* 16 Nev. 373 (1882) (sectarian asylum); *Cook County v. Chicago Industrial School for Girls,* 125 Ill. 540, 18 N. E. 183 (1888) (tuition, board, clothing and medical care furnished delinquent girls committed to Catholic institutions); *Bennett v. City of La Grange,* 153 Ga. 428, 112 S. E. 482 (1922) (Salvation Army aided by contract with city whereby the former assumed care of the poor of the city at actual cost). Direct financial aid to sectarian institutions is sometimes permitted because they are explicitly exempt from the state constitutional prohibition, or because they allegedly service the general community: *Sargent v. Board of Education,* 177 N. Y. 317, 69 N. E. 722 (1904) (explicit exemption); *cf. People ex rel. Orphan Asylum v. Board of Education,* 13 Barb. 400 (N. Y. Sup. Ct., 1851); *Craig v. Mercy Hospital–Street Memorial,* 209 Miss. 427, 47 So. 2d 867 (1950); *Kentucky Building Commission v. Effron,* 310 Ky. 355, 220 S. W. 2d 836 (1949) (state funds allocated for hospitals which serviced patients regardless of creed and conducted no religious ceremonies). See also *Bradfield v. Roberts,* 175 U. S. 291, 44 L. Ed. 168, 20 S. Ct. 121 (1899) (appropriation for building in connection with congressionally chartered hospital run by a monastic order upheld as long as hospital carried out purposes of charter). See, Johnson and Yost, *Separation of Church and State in the United States,* pp. 100–114 (1948); Stokes, *Church and State in the United States* (1950).

## Parental Control of Religious Education

*In relation to the public school system.* As indicated in the *Everson* case, the *Pierce* case held that parents cannot be forced to send their children to public schools. However, the State may compel parents to educate their children in accordance with minimum standards set by compulsory education laws. See Chapter VII, *supra.* Where the required private education is not furnished and parents refuse to send children to public school, the courts have held that prosecutions under the compulsory education laws do not violate religious freedom, because such laws do not interfere with religious belief but with practices detrimental to the public interest which the state may

**954**

properly regulate. Cases holding that the private instruction furnished was adequate are: *Wright v. State,* 21 Okla Crim. 430, 209 Pac. 179 (1922) ; *People v. Levisen,* 404 Ill. 574, 90 N. E. 2d 213 (1950), noted in 36 Va. L. Rev. 682 (1950) ; *State v. Peterman,* 32 Ind. App. 665, 70 N. E. 550 (1904). For cases holding the private instruction inadequate, see *Rice v. Commonwealth,* 188 Va. 224, 49 S. E. 2d 342 (1948) ; *Shapiro v. Dorin,* 99 N. Y. Supp. 2d 830 (Dom. Rel. Court, 1950) ; *People v. Donner,* 302 N. Y. 857, 100 N. E. 2d 57 (1951), cert. den. 342 U. S. 884 (1951). See also *State v. Counort,* 69 Wash. 361, 124 Pac. 910 (1912) ; *State v. Hoyt,* 84 N. H. 38, 146 Atl. 170 (1929) (stressing difficulty of inspection) ; *State v. Will,* 99 Kan. 167, 160 Pac. 1025 (1916). For a case where the children were removed from public school and received no instruction at all, see *Commonwealth v. Beiler,* 168 Pa. Super. 462, 79 Atl. 2d 134 (1951). For annotations see 3 A. L. R. 2d 1392; 14 A. L. R. 2d 1369; see also 113 A. L. R. 697 (on what constitutes a public school).

*Disputes among parents and guardians.* In *Matter of Santos,* 278 App. Div. 373, 105 N. Y. Supp. 2d 716 (1951), a divorced mother had placed two children with a Jewish refugee for board. The mother disappeared and the court remanded them to the custody of the refugee. They received continuous Jewish training for three years through the auspices of Jewish agencies and foster parents. The mother reappeared and demanded custody. The Appellate Division held that since the children's mother was Catholic and they were baptized accordingly they should be placed in a Catholic institution. See N. Y. Domestic Relations Court Act §§ 86(3) and 88(1) (5). The former section states that an earlier commitment based on mistaken adjudication of religion may be vacated; the latter provides that the original assignment must be to an institution of the same religion as the child's if available. Compare *Matter of Krenkel,* 278 App. Div. 573, 102 N. Y. Supp. 2d 456 (1951), motion to appeal to Court of Appeals den., 278 App. Div. 664, 103 N. Y. Supp. 2d 295 (1951) (Catholic mother after placing child in Jewish family and consenting to adoption married the father, also a Catholic, and sought to withdraw earlier consent; court held welfare of child best served by refusing to allow withdrawal of consent; facts taken from record on appeal). See Note, 65 Harv. L. Rev. 694 (1952).

See also *State v. Hand,* 1 Ohio Dec. 238 (1848) (father who wanted to take child to Shaker Colony was denied custody on ground that in communistic settlement the ordinary parent-child feelings would not be fostered). Compare *People v. Labrenz,* 411 Ill. 618, 104 N. E. 2d 769 (1952) (parents temporarily deprived of the custody of their child where they refused on religious grounds to permit a blood transfusion without which the child would probably have died; court held that the statute governing its decision does not violate religious freedom). See also cases cited *infra*.

Generally both parents or the survivor are held to have control over the religious education of the children. Where the parents agree or there is only a mild dispute that does not seriously threaten to affect the interest and welfare of the child, courts tend to adopt a hands-off policy unless religious practices violate the laws. Where one or both parents have lost custody or where the disagreement between parents about religious upbringing seems to interfere seriously with the health and welfare of the child, courts take into consideration such factors as baptism or induction into a religion with the consent of one or both parents, ante-nuptial agreements, the religious beliefs of the parents, the past religious upbringing of the children and whether the children have reached the age of discretion. See Torpey, *Judicial Doctrines of Religious Rights in America,* ch. 8 (1948); Friedman, *The Parental Right to Control the Religious Education of a Child,* 29 Harv. L. Rev. 485 (1916); Note, 11 St. Johns L. Rev. 126 (1936); Allred, *The Legal Status of the Ante-Nuptial Promise Before Mixed Marriage,* 12 Jurist 1 (1952); Note, 50 Yale L. J. 1286 (1941) (ante-nuptial contracts).

### 3. Released Time

## ILLINOIS EX REL. McCOLLUM v. BOARD OF EDUCATION

Supreme Court of the United States, 1948
333 U. S. 203, 92 L. Ed. 649, 68 S. Ct. 461

MR. JUSTICE BLACK delivered the opinion of the Court.

This case relates to the power of a state to utilize its tax-supported public school system in aid of religious instruction insofar as that power may be restricted by the First and Fourteenth Amendments to the Federal Constitution.

The appellant, Vashti McCollum, began this action for mandamus against the Champaign Board of Education in the Circuit Court of Champaign County, Illinois. Her asserted interest was that of a resident and taxpayer of Champaign and of a parent whose child was then enrolled in the Champaign public schools. Illinois has a compulsory education law which, with exceptions, requires parents to send their children, aged seven

956

to sixteen, to its tax-supported public schools where the children are to remain in attendance during the hours when the schools are regularly in session. Parents who violate this law commit a misdemeanor punishable by fine unless the children attend private or parochial schools which meet educational standards fixed by the State. District boards of education are given general supervisory powers over the use of the public school buildings within the school districts. Ill. Rev. Stat. ch. 122, §§ 123, 301 (1943).

Appellant's petition for mandamus alleged that religious teachers, employed by private religious groups, were permitted to come weekly into the school buildings during the regular hours set apart for secular teaching, and then and there for a period of thirty minutes substitute their religious teaching for the secular education provided under the compulsory education law. The petitioner charged that this joint public-school religious-group program violated the First and Fourteenth Amendments to the United States Constitution. The prayer of her petition was that the Board of Education be ordered to "adopt and enforce rules and regulations prohibiting all instruction in and teaching of religious education in all public schools in Champaign School District Number 71, . . . and in all public school houses and buildings in said district when occupied by public schools." . . .

[The Court holds that the appellant has standing to maintain the action.]

Although there are disputes between the parties as to various inferences that may or may not properly be drawn from the evidence concerning the religious program, the following facts are shown by the record without dispute.[1] In 1940 interested members of the Jewish, Roman Catholic, and a few of the Protestant faiths formed a voluntary association called the Champaign Council on Religious Education. They obtained permission

---

[1] Appellant, taking issue with the facts found by the Illinois courts, argues that the religious education program in question is invalid under the Federal Constitution for any one of the following reasons: (1) In actual practice certain Protestant groups have obtained an overshadowing advantage in the propagation of their faiths over other Protestant sects; (2) the religious education program was voluntary in name only because in fact subtle pressures were brought to bear on the students to force them to participate in it; and (3) the power given the school superintendent to reject teachers selected by religious groups and the power given the local Council on Religious Education to determine which religious faiths should participate in the program was a prior censorship of religion.

In view of our decision we find it unnecessary to consider these arguments or the disputed facts upon which they depend.

from the Board of Education to offer classes in religious instruction to public school pupils in grades four to nine inclusive. Classes were made up of pupils whose parents signed printed cards requesting that their children be permitted to attend;[2] they were held weekly, thirty minutes for the lower grades, forty-five minutes for the higher. The council employed the religious teachers at no expense to the school authorities, but the instructors were subject to the approval and supervision of the superintendent of schools.[3] The classes were taught in three separate religious groups by Protestant teachers,[4] Catholic priests, and a Jewish rabbi, although for the past several years there have ap-

[2] The Supreme Court described the request card system as follows: ". . . Admission to the classes was to be allowed only upon the express written request of parents, and then only to classes designated by the parents. . . . Cards were distributed to the parents of elementary students by the public-school teachers requesting them to indicate whether they desired their children to receive religious education. After being filled out, the cards were returned to the teachers of religious education classes either by the public-school teachers or the children. . . ." On this subject the trial court found that ". . . those students who have obtained the written consent of their parents therefor are released by the school authorities from their secular work, and in the grade schools for a period of thirty minutes' instruction in each week during said school hours, and forty-five minutes during each week in the junior high school, receive training in religious education. . . . Certain cards are used for obtaining permission of parents for their children to take said religious instruction courses, and they are made available through the offices of the superintendent of schools and through the hands of principals and teachers to the pupils of the school district. Said cards are prepared at the cost of the council of religious education. The handling and distribution of said cards does not interfere with the duties or suspend the regular secular work of the employees of the defendant. . . ."

[3] The State Supreme Court said: "The record further discloses that the teachers conducting the religious classes were not teachers in the public schools but were subject to the approval and supervision of the superintendent. . . ." The trial court found: "Before any faith or other group may obtain permission from the defendant for the similar, free and equal use of rooms in the public school buildings said faith or group must make application to the superintendent of schools of said School District Number 71, who in turn will determine whether or not it is practical for said group to teach in said school system." The president of the local school board testified: ". . . The Protestants would have one group and the Catholics, and would be given a room where they would have the class and we would go along with the plan of the religious people. They were all to be treated alike, with the understanding that the teachers they would bring into the school were approved by the superintendent. . . . The superintendent was the last word so far as the individual was concerned. . . ."

[4] There were two teachers of the Protestant faith. One was a Presbyterian and had been a foreign missionary for that church. The second testified as follows: "I am affiliated with the Christian church. I also work in the Methodist Church and I taught at the Presbyterian. I am married to a Lutheran."

parently been no classes instructed in the Jewish religion. Classes were conducted in the regular classrooms of the school building. Students who did not choose to take the religious instruction were not released from public school duties; they were required to leave their classrooms and go to some other place in the school building for pursuit of their secular studies. On the other hand, students who were released from secular study for the religious instructions were required to be present at the religious classes. Reports of their presence or absence were to be made to their secular teachers.[5]

The foregoing facts, without reference to others that appear in the record, show the use of tax-supported property for religious instruction and the close cooperation between the school authorities and the religious council in promoting religious education. The operation of the State's compulsory education system thus assists and is integrated with the program of religious instruction carried on by separate religious sects. Pupils compelled by law to go to school for secular education are released in part from their legal duty upon the condition that they attend the religious classes. This is beyond all question a utilization of the tax-established and tax-supported public school system to aid religious groups to spread their faith. And it falls squarely under the ban of the First Amendment (made applicable to the States by the Fourteenth Amendment) as we interpreted it in *Everson v. Board of Education*, 330 U. S. 1. . . . The majority in the *Everson* case, and the minority . . . , agreed that the First Amendment's language, properly interpreted, had erected a wall of separation between Church and State. They disagreed as to the facts shown by the record and as to the proper application of the First Amendment's language to those facts.

Recognizing that the Illinois program is barred by the First and Fourteenth Amendments if we adhere to the views expressed both by the majority and the minority in the *Everson* case, counsel for the respondents challenge those views as dicta and urge that we reconsider and repudiate them. They argue that historically the First Amendment was intended to forbid only government preference of one religion over another, not an impartial governmental assistance of all religions. In addition

---

[5] The director of the Champaign Council on Religious Education testified: ". . . If any pupil is absent we turn in a slip just like any teacher would to the superintendent's office. The slip is a piece of paper with a number of hours in the school day and a square, and the teacher of the particular room for the particular hour records the absentees. It has their names and the grade and the section to which they belong. It is the same sheet that the geography and history teachers and all the other teachers use, and is furnished by the school. . . ."

they ask that we distinguish or overrule our holding in the *Everson* case that the Fourteenth Amendment made the "establishment of religion" clause of the First Amendment applicable as a prohibition against the States. After giving full consideration to the arguments presented we are unable to accept either of these contentions.

To hold that a state cannot consistently with the First and Fourteenth Amendments utilize its public school system to aid any or all religious faiths or sects in the dissemination of their doctrines and ideals does not, as counsel urge, manifest a governmental hostility to religion or religious teachings. A manifestation of such hostility would be at war with our national tradition as embodied in the First Amendment's guaranty of the free exercise of religion. For the First Amendment rests upon the premise that both religion and government can best work to achieve their lofty aims if each is left free from the other within its respective sphere. Or, as we said in the *Everson* case, the First Amendment has erected a wall between Church and State which must be kept high and impregnable.

Here not only are the State's tax-supported public school buildings used for the dissemination of religious doctrines. The State also affords sectarian groups an invaluable aid in that it helps to provide pupils for their religious classes through use of the State's compulsory public school machinery. This is not separation of Church and State.

The cause is reversed and remanded to the State Supreme Court for proceedings not inconsistent with this opinion.

*Reversed and remanded.*

[Mr. Justice Frankfurter delivered a concurring opinion in which Justices Jackson, Rutledge and Burton joined. Part of this opinion has been reprinted *supra*. The remainder of the opinion makes the following points: The Champaign plan works "an obvious pressure upon children to attend" and "sharpens the consciousness of religious differences at least among some of the children." These "are precisely the consequences against which the Constitution was directed." The problem is not simply one of the short period of time allocated to religious education. "If that were all, Champaign might have drawn upon the French system, known in its American manifestation as 'dismissed time,' whereby one school day is shortened to allow all children to go where they please, leaving those who so desire to go to a religious school. The momentum of the whole school atmosphere and school planning is presumably put behind religious instruction, as given in Champaign, precisely in order to secure for the re-

**960**

ligious instruction such momentum and planning." "Separation means separation, not something less." "The public school is at once the symbol of our democracy and the most pervasive means for promoting our common destiny."

Mr. Justice Jackson's concurring opinion in part warns that the Court went too far in granting without qualification Mrs. McCollum's sweeping request that it not only end released time but "ban every form of teaching which suggests or recognizes that there is a God. . . . The fact is that, for good or ill, nearly everything in our culture worth transmitting, everything which gives meaning to life, is saturated with religious influences, derived from paganism, Judaism, Christianity—both Catholic and Protestant—and other faiths accepted by a large part of the world's peoples. One can hardly respect a system of education that would leave the student wholly ignorant of the currents of religious thought that move the world society for a part in which he is being prepared." Mr. Justice Jackson adds: "The opinions in this case show that public educational authorities have evolved a considerable variety of practices in dealing with the religious problem. . . . [It] must be expected that, no matter what practice prevails, there will be many discontented and possibly belligerent minorities. We must leave some flexibility to meet local conditions, some chance to progress by trial and error. . . . To lay down a sweeping constitutional doctrine as demanded by complainant . . . is to decree a uniform, rigid and . . . unchanging standard for countless school boards. . . . It seems to me that to do so is to allow zeal for our own ideas of what is good in public instruction to induce us to accept the rule of a super board of education for every school district in the nation." Neither the Constitution nor any other "legal source" are a guide to where the "secular ends and the sectarian begins."]

MR. JUSTICE REED, dissenting. . . .
The phrase "an establishment of religion" may have been intended by Congress to be aimed only at a state church. When the First Amendment was pending in Congress in substantially its present form, "Mr. Madison said, he apprehended the meaning of the words to be, that Congress should not establish a religion, and enforce the legal observation of it by law, nor compel men to worship God in any manner contrary to their conscience."[7] Passing years, however, have brought about acceptance of a broader meaning, although never until today, I believe,

---

[7] 1 Annals of Congress 730.

has this Court widened its interpretation to any such degree as holding that recognition of the interest of our nation in religion, through the granting, to qualified representatives of the principal faiths, of opportunity to present religion as an optional, extracurricular subject during released school time in public school buildings, was equivalent to an establishment of religion. A reading of the general statements of eminent statesmen of former days, referred to in the opinions in this case and in *Everson v. Board of Education, supra,* will show that circumstances such as those in this case were far from the minds of the authors. The words and spirit of those statements may be wholeheartedly accepted without in the least impugning of the judgment of the State of Illinois.[8]

Mr. Jefferson, as one of the founders of the University of Virginia, a school which from its establishment in 1819 has been wholly governed, managed and controlled by the State of Virginia, was faced with the same problem that is before this Court today: the question of the constitutional limitation upon religious education in public schools. In his annual report as Rector, to the President and Directors of the Literary Fund, dated October 7, 1822, approved by the Visitors of the University of whom Mr. Madison was one,[10] Mr. Jefferson set forth his views at some length.[11] These suggestions of Mr. Jefferson were

---

[8] For example, Mr. Jefferson's striking phrase as to the "wall of separation between church and State" appears in a letter acknowledging "The affectionate sentiments of esteem and approbation" included in a testimonial to himself. In its context it reads as follows:

"Believing with you that religion is a matter which lies solely between man and his God, that he owes account to none other for his faith or his worship, that the legislative powers of Government reach actions only, and not opinions, I contemplate with sovereign reverence that act of the whole American people which declared that their legislature should 'make no law respecting an establishment of religion, or prohibiting the free exercise thereof,' thus building a wall of separation between church and State." 8 The Writings of Thomas Jefferson (Washington ed., 1861) 113.

[10] 19 The Writings of Thomas Jefferson (Memorial edition, 1904) 408, 409.

[11] *Id.,* pp. 414–17:

"It was not, however, to be understood that instruction in religious opinion and duties was meant to be precluded by the public authorities, as indifferent to the interests of society. On the contrary, the relations which exist between man and his Maker, and the duties resulting from those relations, are the most interesting and important to every human being, and the most incumbent on his study and investigation. The want of instruction in the various creeds of religious faith existing among our citizens presents, therefore, a chasm in a general institution of the useful sciences. . . . A remedy, however, has been suggested of promising aspect, which, while it excludes the public authorities from the domain of religious freedom, will give to the sectarian schools of divinity the full

[Emerson]

adopted[12] and ch. II, § 1, of the Regulations of the University of October 4, 1824, provided that:

"Should the religious sects of this State, or any of them, according to the invitation held out to them, establish within, or adjacent to, the precincts of the University, schools for instruction in the religion of their sect, the students of the University will be free, and expected to attend religious worship at the establishment of their respective sects, in the morning, and in time to meet their school in the University at its stated hour."[13]

Thus, the "wall of separation between church and State" that Mr. Jefferson built at the University which he founded did not exclude religious education from that school. The difference between the generality of his statements on the separation of church and state and the specificity of his conclusions on education are considerable. A rule of law should not be drawn from a figure of speech.

Mr. Madison's *Memorial and Remonstrance against Religious*

benefit the public provisions made for instruction in the other branches of science. . . . It has, therefore, been in contemplation, and suggested by some pious individuals, who perceive the advantages of associating other studies with those of religion, to establish their religious schools on the confines of the University, so as to give to their students ready and convenient access and attendance on the scientific lectures of the University; and to maintain, by that means, those destined for the religious professions on as high a standing of science, and of personal weight and respectability, as may be obtained by others from the benefits of the University. Such establishments would offer the further and greater advantage of enabling the students of the University to attend religious exercises with the professor of their particular sect, either in the rooms of the building still to be erected, and destined to that purpose under impartial regulations, as proposed in the same report of the commissioners, or in the lecturing room of such professor. . . . Such an arrangement would complete the circle of the useful sciences embraced by this institution, and would fill the chasm now existing, on principles which would leave inviolate the constitutional freedom of religion, the most inalienable and sacred of all human rights, over which the people and authorities of this state, individually and publicly, have ever manifested the most watchful jealousy; and could this jealousy be now alarmed, in the opinion of the legislature, by what is here suggested, the idea will be relinquished on any surmise of disapprobation which they might think proper to express."
Mr. Jefferson commented upon the report on November 2, 1822, in a letter to Dr. Thomas Cooper, as follows: "And by bringing the sects together, and mixing them with the mass of other students, we shall soften their asperities, liberalize and neutralize their prejudices, and make the general religion a religion of peace, reason, and morality." 12 Ford, *The Works of Thomas Jefferson*, (Fed. ed., 1905), 272.

[12] 3 Randall, Life of Thomas Jefferson (1858) 471.

[13] 19 The Writings of Thomas Jefferson (Memorial edition, 1904) 449.

*Assessments*,[14] relied upon by the dissenting Justices in *Everson*, is not applicable here. Mr. Madison was one of the principal opponents in the Virginia General Assembly of *A Bill Establishing a Provision for Teachers of the Christian Religion*. The monies raised by the taxing section of that bill were to be appropriated "by the Vestries, Elders, or Directors of each religious society, . . . to a provision for a Minister or Teacher of the Gospel of their denomination, or the providing places of divine worship, and to none other use whatsoever . . . " The conclusive legislative struggle over this act took place in the fall of 1785, before the adoption of the Bill of Rights. The *Remonstrance* had been issued before the General Assembly convened and was instrumental in the final defeat of the act, which died in committee. Throughout the *Remonstrance*, Mr. Madison speaks of the "establishment" sought to be effected by the act. It is clear from its historical setting and its language that the *Remonstrance* was a protest against an effort by Virginia to support Christian sects by taxation. Issues similar to those raised by the instant case were not discussed. Thus, Mr. Madison's approval of Mr. Jefferson's report as Rector gives, in my opinion, a clearer indication of his views on the constitutionality of religious education in public schools than his general statements on a different subject.

This Court summarized the amendment's accepted reach into the religious field, as I understand its scope, in *Everson v. Board of Education, supra*. The Court's opinion quotes the gist of the Court's reasoning in *Everson*. I agree, as there stated, that none of our governmental entities can "set up a church." I agree that they cannot "aid" all or any religions or prefer one "over another." But "aid" must be understood as a purposeful assistance directly to the church itself or to some religious group or organization doing religious work of such a character that it may fairly be said to be performing ecclesiastical functions. "Prefer" must give an advantage to one "over another." I agree that pupils cannot "be released in part from their legal duty" of school attendance upon condition that they attend religious classes. But as Illinois has held that it is within the discretion of the School Board to permit absence from school for religious instruction no legal duty of school attendance is violated. 396 Ill. 14, 71 N. E. 2d 161. If the sentence in the Court's opinion, concerning the pupils' release from legal duty,

14 The texts of the *Memorial and Remonstrance* and the bill against which it was aimed, to wit, *A Bill Establishing a Provision for Teachers of the Christian Religion* are set forth in *Everson v. Board of Education*, 330 U. S. 1, 28, 63–74.

is intended to mean that the Constitution forbids a school to excuse a pupil from secular control during school hours to attend voluntarily a class in religious education, whether in or out of school buildings, I disagree. Of course, no tax can be levied to support organizations intended "to teach or practice religion." I agree too that the state cannot influence one toward religion against his will or punish him for his beliefs. Champaign's religious education course does none of these things. . . .

## Note

1. In *Zorach v. Clauson,* 343 U. S. 306, 96 L. Ed. —, 72 S. Ct. 679 (1952), the Supreme Court upheld the New York City released time system. The New York system provides for the release of the students on written request of parents, for purposes of attending religious instruction and devotional exercises in religious centers outside of school. Students not released under the system stay in classrooms. The churches send weekly reports to the schools on attendance of the released pupils. Mr. Justice Douglas, writing for the Court, distinguished the *McCollum* case as follows:

"In the *McCollum* case the classrooms were used for religious instruction and the force of the public school was used to promote that instruction. Here, as we have said, the public schools do no more than accommodate their schedules to a program of outside religious instruction. We follow the *McCollum* case. But we cannot expand it to cover the present released time program unless separation of Church and State means that public institutions can make no adjustments of their schedules to accommodate the religious needs of the people. We cannot read into the Bill of Rights such a philosophy of hostility to religion."

Concerning the principle of separation the Court said:

"The First Amendment within the scope of its coverage permits no exception; the prohibition is absolute. The First Amendment, however, does not say that in every and all respects there shall be a separation of Church and State. Rather, it studiously defines the manner, the specific ways, in which there shall be no concert or union or dependency one on the other. That is the common sense of the matter. Otherwise the state and religion would be aliens to each other—hostile, suspicious, and even unfriendly. Churches could not be required to pay even property taxes. Municipalities would not be permitted to render police or fire protection to religious groups. Policemen who helped parishioners into their places of worship would violate the Constitution. Prayers in our legislative halls; the appeals to the Almighty in the messages of the Chief Executive; the proclamations making Thanksgiving Day a holiday; "so help me God" in our courtroom oaths—these and all other references to the Almighty that run through our laws, our public rituals, our ceremonies would be flouting the First Amendment. A fastidious atheist or agnostic could

**965**

even object to the supplication with which the Court opens each session: 'God save the United States and this Honorable Court.' "

Mr. Justice Douglas added:

"Government may not finance religious groups nor undertake religious instruction nor blend secular and sectarian education nor use secular institutions to force one or some religion on any person. But we find no constitutional requirement which makes it necessary for government to be hostile to religion and to throw its weight against efforts to widen the effective scope of religious influence. The government must be neutral when it comes to competition between sects. It may not thrust any sect on any person. It may not make a religious observance compulsory. It may not coerce anyone to attend church, to observe a religious holiday, or to take religious instruction. But it can close its doors or suspend its operations as to those who want to repair to their religious sanctuary for worship or instruction. No more than that is undertaken here."

Justices Black, Frankfurter and Jackson dissented. They felt that the state was involved in the administration of the system and both explicitly and implicitly used its coercive power to implement the program.

2. In the courts below the plaintiffs had sought to introduce evidence that the system on the administrative level actually worked coercively. See paragraph 3 of this Note, *infra*. This evidence was not admitted. One of Mr. Justice Douglas' grounds for upholding the system was that the record showed no actual coercion. Mr. Justice Frankfurter's dissent levels special criticism at this aspect of the opinion.

For an earlier New York case upholding the New York released time system see *Lewis v. Spaulding*, 193 Misc. 66, 85 N. Y. Supp. 2d 682 (1948).

3. The following extract from Note, *Released Time Reconsidered: The New York Plan is Tested*, 61 Yale L. J. 405, 411–5 (1952), describes released time systems in operation, based primarily upon the New York experience. The Note was written prior to the Supreme Court's opinion in the *Zorach* case:

"Continuance of released time would sanction infringement of the 'separation doctrine' by state aid existing in three aspects of the program's operation. One element of aid is the New York Education Law. It requires through its truancy provisions that those students who are released actually attend their religious classes. A released child who fails to attend religious classes has no excused absence from public school and is thus a truant. In enforcing the truancy law upon released time truants some school districts interview the child to find out why he did not attend the religious instruction. Other districts, if the child is frequently truant, refuse him permission to be released for religious instruction. Still others use these techniques jointly. In addition to the actual enforcement sanctions, the very existence of the law may influence the released child to attend his religious classes. Use of the compulsory education law in a released time program was expressly condemned in the *McCollum* decision.

**966**

"The machinery of the public school also makes a substantial contribution to the operation and success of released time. Time and labor of teachers and school officials is required to administer the program. They must obtain and file cards of excused children; prepare, distribute, and keep current lists for classroom teachers of released time students; supervise an additional classroom dismissal; and secure and check absence reports of religious centers. Some teachers, despite the Board of Education's prohibition of comment on the attendance or non-attendance of pupils at religious classes, encourage children to attend religious classes or actually recruit them for such instruction.[37] The persistence of this practice over the years, despite its prohibition, suggests that this is an abuse inherent in the program.[39] The teacher exerts considerable influence on the children,[40] and her contribution to the religious education program can be important.[41]

---

[37] Examples of this type of coercion are: "Miss Jeffries (a teacher) distributed blank consent cards to the children in her class and asked the children publicly for a show of hands of those who were going to participate in the released time program . . . Miss Jeffries scolded those students who had participated in the released time program the term before but who did not raise their hands to show that they were continuing." Affidavit of Wendy Gluck, Affidavits, Kings County Clerk's Number 10327/1948, Supreme Court of the State of New York, County of Kings. "A student in her class became ill and vomited in the classroom. Miss Jeffries said to the sick student that she did not object at looking at the vomit as much as she objected to looking at the student's face because he did not participate in the released time program." Affidavit of Esta Gluck, *ibid.* See also affidavit of Anne Stewart. . . .

[39] It is important to study the actual practice since there are indications that the rules are not always literally followed. Rule 4 of the New York City Board of Education's Regulations before September 24, 1941 read, "Pupils of any grade will be dismissed from school for the last hour of each week, except that in classes on a departmental schedule release will be limited to the last period of the program." Mr. William Hendrie, who was then a principal in a school employing the departmental schedule, released his children at 2:30 as instructed by the regulation. Mr. Jansen, then Associate Superintendent of Schools and now Superintendent of Schools called and told Mr. Hendrie not to interpret the rules literally and to dismiss the students in the departmentally scheduled classes promptly at 2:00 p. m. Affidavit of Mr. William Hendrie, Kings County Clerk's Number 10327/1948, Supreme Court of the State of New York, County of Kings.

[40] See National Education Association, Department of School Principals, *Personality Adjustment of the Elementary School Child* 385 (1936); Carrington, *Teacher Personality as a Factor in Child Adjustment*, National Education Association of the United States, Department of Elementary School Principals 15th Yearbook 586–94 (1936).

[41] Another, though more infrequent, practice used by teachers to induce attendance at the released time program is the giving of onerous work to the children who remain in the public school. A student reports, "My sixth grade teacher, Miss Croft, urged the children in the class to participate in the released time program and she stated that those students who did not participate would be required to do long division arithmetic problems during every released time hour, whereas those children who did participate were to be excused from this exercise. While I was in Miss Croft's class,

Moreover, high schools aid the released time program by allowing scholastic credit for religious instruction.[42]

"Further state aid for religion exists in the substantial contribution made by the school milieu to the recruitment of children for religious classes. The public school environment is a significant factor in motivating behavior,[43] and it must be considered in evaluating the total contribution of the school, as an institution, to religious education. Holding religious classes during school hours aids religious instruction since it can more easily compete with classroom time than with recreational time. Such encouragement may be lessened in some schools because the released time period activities may be enjoyable, or may include important school work which the children may not want to miss. In addition, group interactions are an effective assistance to recruitment of children for religious classes and this has been regarded as 'state action' in aid of religion. Children belong to social groups not ordinarily based on religion or released time attendance.[51] Studies have shown that a group influences children so strongly that they frequently accept its judgment even when they know that judgment is wrong,[52] and in matters of opinion, children follow their friends almost completely.[53] Thus, when a child in the public school

---

the students who remained in the public school after 2 o'clock on Thursdays were given long division arithmetic problems beyond the level of the normal expectation of sixth grade." Affidavit of Anne Stewart, Affidavits, King County Clerk's Number 10327/1948, Supreme Court of the State of New York, County of Kings. Also Affidavit of Mrs. Gussie Finer, *ibid*.

. . .

[42] . . . A study of released time programs in high school indicates that one of the principal motivations for students to take released time courses in high school was to obtain credit toward graduation. McClure, *Weekday Religious Education at the High School Level*, 46 Religious Education 345, 352 (1951).

[43] For a description of the school environment and its impact on the individual see: Bossard, The Sociology of Child Development 459–92 (1948); Lee & Lee, The Child and His Curriculum 74, 95–103 (2d ed. 1950); Waller, The Sociology of Teaching c. 2 (1932).

[51] Group unity forms among children in the early primary school. Hurlock, Child Development 236 (1942); Thorpe, Child Psychology and Development 558 (1946). The primary bases for friendship formation of primary school children are: propinquity of the children, same mental and physical age. Hurlock, *op. cit. supra* at 247; Murphy, Murphy, & Newcomb, Experimental Social Psychology 513 (1931); Thorpe, *op. cit. supra* at 595.

[52] . . . Berenda, Influence of the Group on the Judgment of Children 14–32 (1950). On the strong control of the peer group see, Brown, Sociology of Childhood 164, 169–70 (1939); Bossard, *op. cit. supra* note 43, at 504, 507; Hurlock, *op. cit. supra* note 51 at 218, 233, 236–7; Lee & Lee, *op. cit. supra* note 43, at 74.

[53] In a test of food preferences there was virtually complete identification of choices between close friends. Duncker, *Experimental Modification of Children's Food Preference Through Social Suggestion*, 33 Jour. of Abnormal and Social Psychology 489 (1938). *Cf.* Riesman, The Lonely Crowd (1950).

sees his friends leave to attend religious classes, the social interactions of the school, as an institution, impel him toward religious instruction.  When parents refuse to allow children to attend religious classes with their friends, the children may become emotionally disturbed.[54]  This reaction indicates the coercion on the children to attend religious classes.  Such coercion, even though not completely successful in forcing conformity in all situations, was regarded in the *McCollum* case as one of the abridgments of the separation doctrine."

4. See also on the New York released time system, Public Education Association, *Released Time For Religious Education in New York City Schools* (1949).  For a full discussion of the variety of released time systems in the United States and an extensive bibliography see Mr. Justice Frankfurter's opinion in the *McCollum* case, 233 U. S. at 222–31.

5. For discussion of the legal issues see Lassiter, *The McCollum Decision and the Public School*, 37 Ky. L. J. 402 (1949); Manion, *The Church, The State and Mrs. McCollum*, 23 Notre Dame Law. 456 (1948); Owen, *The McCollum Case*, 22 Temp. L. Q. 159 (1948); Michenfelder, *The McCollum Decision: A Criticism*, 1 Intramural L. Rev. 26 (St. Louis Univ., 1949); Notes, 49 Col. L. Rev. 836 (1949); 61 Harv. L. Rev. 1248 (1948).

## 4. Bible Reading

In a number of states Bible reading in the public schools seems to be clearly prohibited:  *Illinois:  People ex rel. Ring v. Board of Education*, 245 Ill. 334, 92 N. E. 251 (1910).  The King James

---

[54] A former non-released student describes her experiences as follows: "When the released time children departed at 2:00 p.m. on Wednesdays, I felt left behind.  The released children made remarks about my being Jewish and I was made very much aware of the fact that I did not participate with them in the released time program.  I endured a great deal of anguish as a result of this and decided that I would like to go along with the other children to the church center rather than continue to expose myself to such embarrassment.  I asked my mother for permission to participate in the released time program to accompany my Catholic classmates to their religious center, but she forbade it.  The divisiveness created by the released time program among the public school children became a part of our after school play.  Following the introduction of released time at P. S. 163, Brooklyn, I began to notice I was ostracized by other children in after school activities.  I was not permitted to share in their play, and they made unflattering remarks about my not going to the church center because I was Jewish.  As a result of arguments about my nonparticipation in released time, my classmates called me such names as 'Christ killer' and 'dirty Jew.'  I still live in the same neighborhood and to this day I do not talk to many of the girls with whom I went to school because of the arguments and fights which developed among us as a result of our differences which developed from the released time program."  Statement of Leah Cunn, Affidavits, Kings County Clerk's Number 10327/1948, New York Supreme Court, County of Kings.  See also affidavits by Gussie Finer and Charles Stewart, *ibid.*

version was read and teachers made comments. Pupils were supposed to stand, assume a devotional attitude and answer questions about the reading. They also had to sing hymns and say the Lord's Prayer. The court held that this violated both freedom of worship as well as a provision of the Illinois Constitution against the use of public funds in aid of "church or sectarian" purposes. It stated further that it made no difference which version of the Bible was used. The Bible itself is a sectarian book to any non-Christian. Moreover, the compulsion to join in any form of worship violated the Illinois Constitution. *Louisiana: Herold v. Parish Board of School Directors*, 136 La. 1034, 68 So. 116 (1915). The Board resolution required reading of the Bible without comment and recital of the Lord's Prayer if the teacher wished it. The court held that reading of the "Christian Bible" in any version was an invasion of freedom of conscience of the Jews and violated constitutional prohibitions against the expenditure of public funds "in aid of any church, sect, or denomination of religion." Excusing minority pupils would subject them to stigma and therefore fail to remedy the situation. *Nebraska: State ex rel. Freeman v. Scheve*, 65 Nebr. 853, 91 N. W. 846 (1902). Although Bible reading in itself may not be unconstitutional it becomes so when accompanied by singing of hymns and the saying of sectarian prayers. *South Dakota: State ex rel. Finger v. Weedman et al. School District Board*, 55 S. D. 343, 226 N. W. 348 (1929). The court ordered the school board to reinstate pupils dismissed for refusing to attend religious exercises, which consisted of reading from the King James version of the Bible and recitation of the Lord's Prayer. The question of the right to read from the Bible in the public schools was not determined, but the court strongly suggested that it was violative of the guarantee of religious freedom. *Washington: State ex rel. Clithero v. Showalter*, 159 Wash. 519, 293 Pac. 1000 (1930) app. dis. 284 U. S. 573 (1931). Daily Bible reading and compulsory instruction in the Bible twice a week held unconstitutional. See also *State ex rel. Dearle v. Frazier*, 102 Wash. 369, 173 Pac. 35 (1918). *Wisconsin: State ex rel. Weiss v. Dist. Bd.* 76 Wis. 177, 44 N. W. 967 (1890). The case involved reading of the King James Bible without comments or accompanying hymns or prayers. Those who did not wish to participate were excused. The court held the practice violated a state statute prohibiting the use of textbooks "which would have a tendency to inculcate sectarian ideas." It further held that the reading interfered with freedom of worship and was contrary to constitutional prohibitions against "sectarian instruction" and ex-

**970**

penditure of public funds for religious schools. *Cf. State ex rel. Conway v. Dist. Bd.*, 162 Wis. 482, 156 N. W. 477 (1916) (the saying of nonsectarian prayer by priest or minister at graduation held not to constitute sectarian instruction).

The following states have upheld Bible reading: *Colorado: People ex rel. Vollmar v. Stanley*, 81 Col. 276, 255 Pac. 610 (1927). Reading of King James Bible without comment does not violate freedom of religion, nor prohibitions against sectarian instruction, compulsory religious service, and expenditure of public funds for church or sectarian schools, provided attendance is made optional. The court's reply to the argument that absence from religious instruction would put a stigma on the absentees was as follows: "The shoe is on the other foot. We have known many boys to be ridiculed for complying with religious regulations, but never one for neglecting them or absenting himself from them." The court left open the possibility that the reading of certain portions of the King James Bible might be "sectarian instruction" and indicated that when the specific question was presented it would consider it. *Georgia: Wilkerson v. City of Rome*, 152 Ga. 762, 110 S. E. 895 (1922). Reading of the King James Bible without comment accompanied by offering of a prayer was upheld. The court said that mere listening to the reading of a portion of the King James Bible and to the saying of a prayer does not amount to interference with free worship of Catholics and Jews, and since only "an insignificant fraction of time would be consumed in the reading" it was not violative of prohibitions against the expenditure of public funds for sectarian purposes. *Iowa: Moore v. Monroe*, 64 Ia. 367, 20 N. W. 475 (1884). Religious exercises, from which children might be excused, consisted of Bible reading, singing of hymns, and prayer, unaccompanied by comments from the teacher. The court held that the religious liberty clause of the Iowa constitution did not prevent the casual use of a public building for religious worship, but was designed to prevent the enactment of a law compelling any person to pay taxes for a building used distinctively as a place of worship. The objection that religious exercises, made part of the educational system, into which the child must either be drawn or made conspicuous and inconvenienced by being excused, was not regarded "as one of great weight," so long as the child was not required to attend the exercises. *Kansas: Billard v. Board of Education of Topeka*, 69 Kan. 53, 76 Pac. 422 (1904). Recitation of Lord's Prayer and Twenty-third Psalm, without comment or remark, as a morning exercise designed to quiet the children but from which they might be excused, did not constitute religious worship or teaching of sectarian doctrine, within the meaning of the Constitution. The Court contended that Bible reading encouraged intellectual and moral improvement, and provided the "noblest ideals of moral character" which it is the duty of the public schools to promote.

*Kentucky: Hackett v. Brooksville Graded School District,* 120 Ky. 608, 87 S. W. 792 (1905). The court held that neither the Constitution nor the statutes prohibiting interference with religious freedom were violated by services, from which children might be excused, which consisted of prayers, denominational hymn-singing and reading, without comment, from the King James version of the Bible. The court did not regard the King James Bible as a sectarian book, when read without comment, because it did not teach the dogmas of a sect as such, although it might be accepted and used by certain sects. *Maine: Donahoe v. Richards,* 38 Me. 376 (1854). The court held that the regulation adopting the King James version of the Bible as a textbook, binding upon all pupils even though of different religious faiths, was constitutional and did not infringe upon the rights of conscience or of freedom of worship. The power of the "committee" to select texts was held to be "general and unlimited", and "it was neither expected nor intended that there should be entire uniformity in the course of instruction or in the books to be used in the several towns of the state." *Massachusetts: Spiller v. Inhabitants of Woburn,* 94 Mass. 127 (1866). The court held lawful an order of the town committee requiring schools to be opened with prayer and Bible reading, during which each pupil should bow his head, unless his parents requested that he be excused. The bowing of the head did not constitute a religious rite, or compel participation in services which might be in conflict with the pupil's religious belief or conscientious scruples, as prohibited by the religious liberty clause of the Massachusetts Constitution. *Michigan: Pfeiffer v. Board of Education of Detroit,* 118 Mich. 560, 77 N. W. 250 (1898). Reading from a book composed almost entirely of Bible extracts emphasizing the moral precepts of the Ten Commandments, where the teacher made no comment and was required to excuse any pupil if requested to do so by his parents or guardian was held by the court not to have violated any constitutional rights of the complainants. But the court left the problem of Bible reading, not here involved, to the discretion of the State Board of Education.

*Minnesota: Kaplan v. Independent School District of Virginia,* 171 Minn. 142, 214 N. W. 18 (1927). The reading of the

King James version of the Bible, exclusively from the old Testament and without commentary, did not constitute the teaching of religious doctrine in violation of the constitutional guarantees protecting religious liberty. Pupils might be excused if they or their parents so desired, and hence were not compelled to worship according to the tenets of any creed or to learn any sectarian creed. The question of the propriety of Bible reading was left to the discretion of local school authorities. *New York: Lewis v. Board of Education,* 157 Misc. 520, 285 N. Y. Supp. 164 (1935). A charter provision of the City of New York prohibiting the Board of Education from excluding the Holy Scripture from any of the local schools was held constitutional, and the practice of reading from the Bible not destructive of the proper division between church and state. *Ohio: Board of Education of Cincinnati v. Minor,* 23 Oh. St. 211 (1872). The court left to the discretion of the school officials the question of Bible reading, but upheld a resolution passed by the Board of Education prohibiting religious instruction and the reading of religious books in the public schools. *Texas: Church v. Bullock,* 104 Tex. 1, 109 S. W. 115 (1908). A resolution of the school board requiring the presence but not the participation of pupils in morning religious exercises which consisted of reading, without comment, from the King James version of the Bible, recitation of the Lord's Prayer and the singing of hymns, did not convert the school into a sectarian or religious society within the meaning of the Constitution.

## Note

1. For the history of the requirement of Bible reading in public schools and its connection with anti-Catholic sentiment in nineteenth century America, see Billington, *The Protestant Crusade,* 1800–1860 (1938). For instances of severe punishment of Catholic and Jewish children who refused to participate in the reading of Protestant versions of the Bible, see Synagogue Council of America, *Report of Conference on Religious Education and the Public Schools,* p. 26 (1944); Beale, *A History of Freedom of Teaching in American Schools,* p. 211 (1941); Whipple, *The Story of Civil Liberty in the United States,* pp. 63–4 (1927).

2. In *Evans v. Selma Union High School Dist.,* 193 Cal. 54, 222 Pac. 801, 31 A. L. R. 1121 (1924), objections were raised to a purchase for the High School's library of Bibles in the King James version. The statute provided that "No publication of a sectarian, partisan. or denominational character must be used or distributed in any school or be made part of any school library; nor must any sectarian or denominational doctrine be taught therein." The court, holding that the King James version of the Bible is not a sectarian book, said

that neither the authorship of a book, nor its predominant use by particular sects, nor the fact that it states the doctrine of a particular sect necessarily makes it sectarian.

3. Religion also appears in the public schools in the form of Christmas and Easter parties and other celebrations of religious holidays. For a brief outline of the extent and variety of practices and some suggestions as to community attitudes and effects see Synagogue Council of America and National Community Relations Advisory Council, *Joint Conference on Religious Holiday Observances in the Public Schools, Fact Sheet* (1949). For an approach to the problem in terms of joint celebrations of the holidays of various groups, see Edman and Collins, *Promising Practices in Intergroup Education* (1947).

4. For examples of tensions arising from religious observances in public schools, see N. Y. Times, June 15, 16, 18, 20, 21, 1950 (Catholic-Protestant tensions arising out of Protestant baccalaureate services).

5. In *Doremus v. Board of Education*, 342 U. S. 429, 96 L. Ed. —, 72 S. Ct. 394 (1952), the plaintiffs sought a declaratory judgment to declare unconstitutional as in violation of the First Amendment a state statute which provided for reading without comment five verses of the Old Testament at the opening of each public-school day. No issue was raised under the state Constitution. The Supreme Court held that it lacked jurisdiction because of the plaintiff's lack of standing and was not bound by the state court's willingness to consider the case on the merits. One plaintiff was the father of a child in school, but the child had graduated before the appeal reached the Supreme Court. Mr. Justice Jackson gave as further reasons for lack of standing: "There is no assertion that she was injured or even offended . . . or that she was compelled to accept, approve or confess agreement with any dogma or creed or even to listen when the Scriptures were read. . . . [There] was a . . . stipulation that any student, at his own or his parents' request, could be excused. . . . [No] such excuse was asked." As to the plaintiffs' standing as taxpayers he stated in part: "There is no allegation that this activity is supported by any separate tax or paid for from any particular appropriation or that it adds any sum whatever to the cost of conducting the school. No information is given as to what kind of taxes are paid by appellants and there is no averment that the Bible reading increases any tax they do pay or that as taxpayers they are, will, or possibly can be out of pocket because of it." The Court, relying on *Massachusetts v. Mellon*, 262 U. S. 447, 67 L. Ed. 1078, 43 S. Ct. 597 (1923) held that there is no "case or controversy" where the taxpayer cannot show any immediate special pecuniary injury. The *Everson* case was distinguished on the ground that "Everson showed a measurable appropriation or disbursement of school-district funds occasioned solely by the activities complained of." Justices Douglas, Reed and Burton dissented. They contended that *Massachusetts v. Mellon* does not limit the jurisdiction of the Court in cases involving state statutes where the state was willing to take the case on the merits.

**974**

For a discussion of the procedural difficulties in bringing various church-state issues to the courts see Sutherland, *Due Process and Disestablishment,* 62 Harv. L. Rev. 1306 (1949).

## 5. Flag Salute and Other Compulsory Practices Offensive to Certain Religions

In *Minersville School District v. Gobitis,* 310 U. S. 586, 84 L. Ed. 1375, 60 S. Ct. 1010 (1940), the Supreme Court upheld the expulsion of Jehovah's Witnesses' children for refusing to salute the flag, as they were required to do by state law, on the ground that the salute was contrary to their religious belief. The opinion, written by Mr. Justice Frankfurter, and a dissent written by Mr. Justice Stone were the subject of a great deal of public debate. In *West Virginia State Board of Education v. Barnette,* 319 U. S. 624, 87 L. Ed. 1628, 63 S. Ct. 1178 (1943), the issue came up a second time. Mr. Justice Jackson's opinion, overruling the Court's *Gobitis* decision, formulated the principal issue as whether the state has power to compel affirmance of a belief and reasoned that the clear and present danger test is just as applicable where the government compels affirmance of a belief as where it seeks to suppress one. The opinion rejected the view of the *Gobitis* case that the matter was one within the special province of local school boards and legislatures and one in which the Court had little competence, and asserted that in matters of fundamental constitutional rights the Court acted by virtue of its commission and not its competence. Mr. Justice Jackson concluded:

"Lastly, and this is the very heart of the *Gobitis* opinion, it reasons that 'National unity is the basis of national security', that the authorities have 'the right to select appropriate means for its attainment', and hence reaches the conclusion that such compulsory measures toward 'national unity' are constitutional. *Id.* at 595. Upon the verity of this assumption depends our answer in this case.

"National unity as an end which officials may foster by persuasion and example is not in question. The problem is whether under our Constitution compulsion as here employed is a permissible means for its achievement.

"Struggles to coerce uniformity of sentiment in support of some end thought essential to their time and country have been waged by many good as well as by evil men. Nationalism is a relatively recent phenomenon but at other times and places the ends have been racial or territorial security, support of a dynasty or regime, and particular plans for saving souls. As first and moderate methods to attain unity have failed, those bent on its accomplishment must resort to an ever-increasing severity. As governmental pressure toward unity becomes greater, so strife becomes more bitter as to whose unity it shall be. Probably no deeper division of our people could proceed from any provocation than from finding it necessary to choose what doctrine and whose program public educational officials shall compel youth to unite in embracing. Ultimate futility of such attempts to compel coherence is the lesson of every such effort from the Roman drive to stamp out Christianity as a disturber of its pagan unity, the Inquisition, as a means to religious and dynastic unity, the Siberian exiles as a means to Russian unity, down to the fast failing efforts of our present totalitarian enemies. Those who begin coercive elimination of dissent soon find themselves exterminating dissenters. Compulsory unification of opinion achieves only the unanimity of the graveyard.

"It seems trite but necessary to say that the First Amendment to our Constitution was designed to avoid these ends by avoiding these beginnings. There is no mysticism in the American concept of the State or of the nature or origin of its authority. We set up government by the consent of the governed, and the Bill of Rights denies those in power any legal opportunity to coerce that consent. Authority here is to be controlled by public opinion, not public opinion by authority.

"The case is made difficult not because the principles of its decision are obscure but because the flag involved is our own. Nevertheless, we apply the limitations of the Constitution with no fear that freedom to be intellectually and spiritually diverse or even contrary will disintegrate the social organization. To believe that patriotism will not flourish if patriotic ceremonies are voluntary and spontaneous instead of a compulsory routine is to make an unflattering estimate of the appeal of our institutions to free minds. We can have intellectual individualism and the rich cultural diversities that we owe to exceptional minds only at the price of occasional eccentricity and abnormal attitudes. When they are so harmless to others or to the State as those we deal with here, the price is not too great. But freedom to differ is not limited to things that do not matter much. That would be a mere shadow of freedom. The test of its substance is the right to differ as to things that touch the heart of the existing order.

"If there is any fixed star in our constitutional constellation, it is that no official, high or petty, can prescribe what shall be

**976**

orthodox in politics, nationalism, religion, or other matters of opinion or force citizens to confess by word or act their faith therein. If there are any circumstances which permit an exception, they do not now occur to us.[19]

"We think the action of the local authorities in compelling the flag salute and pledge transcends constitutional limitations on their power and invades the sphere of intellect and spirit which it is the purpose of the First Amendment to our Constitution to reserve from all official control." 319 U. S. at 640–2.

Mr. Justice Frankfurter, dissenting, said in part:
"We are told that a flag salute is a doubtful substitute for adequate understanding of our institutions. The states that require such a school exercise do not have to justify it as the only means for promoting good citizenship in children, but merely as one of diverse means for accomplishing a worthy end. We may deem it a foolish measure, but the point is that this Court is not the organ of government to resolve doubts as to whether it will fulfill its purpose. Only if there be no doubt that any reasonable mind could entertain can we deny to the states the right to resolve doubts their way and not ours.

"That which to the majority may seem essential for the welfare of the state may offend the consciences of a minority. But, so long as no inroads are made upon the actual exercise of religion by the minority, to deny the political power of the majority to enact laws concerned with civil matters, simply because they may offend the consciences of a minority, really means that the consciences of a minority are more sacred and more enshrined in the Constitution than the consciences of a majority.

"We are told that symbolism is a dramatic but primitive way of communicating ideas. Symbolism is inescapable. Even the most sophisticated live by symbols. But it is not for this Court to make psychological judgments as to the effectiveness of a particular symbol in inculcating concededly indispensable feelings, particularly if the state happens to see fit to utilize the symbol that represents our heritage and our hopes. And surely only flippancy could be responsible for the suggestion that constitutional validity of a requirement to salute our flag implies equal validity of a requirement to salute a dictator. The significance of a symbol lies in what it represents. To reject the swastika does not imply rejection of the Cross. And so it bears

---

[19] The Nation may raise armies and compel citizens to give military service. *Selective Draft Law Cases*, 245 U. S. 366. It follows, of course, that those subject to military discipline are under many duties and may not claim many freedoms that we hold inviolable as to those in civilian life.

repetition to say that it mocks reason and denies our whole history to find in the allowance of a requirement to salute our flag on fitting occasions the seeds of sanction for obeisance to a leader. To deny the power to employ educational symbols is to say that the state's educational system may not stimulate the imagination because this may lead to unwise stimulation. . . .

"To talk about 'clear and present danger' as the touchstone of allowable educational policy by the states whenever school curricula may impinge upon the boundaries of individual conscience, is to take a felicitous phrase out of the context of the particular situation where it arose and for which it was adapted. Mr. Justice Holmes used the phrase 'clear and present danger' in a case involving mere speech as a means by which alone to accomplish sedition in time of war. By that phrase he meant merely to indicate that, in view of the protection given to utterance by the First Amendment, in order that mere utterance may not be proscribed, 'the words used are used in such circumstances and are of such a nature as to create a clear and present danger that they will bring about the substantive evils that Congress has a right to prevent.' *Schenck v. United States*, 249 U. S. 47, 52. The 'substantive evils' about which he was speaking were inducement of insubordination in the military and naval forces of the United States and obstruction of enlistment while the country was at war. He was not enunciating a formal rule that there can be no restriction upon speech and, still less, no compulsion where conscience balks, unless imminent danger would thereby be wrought 'to our institutions or our government'.

"The flag salute exercise has no kinship whatever to the oath tests so odious in history. For the oath test was one of the instruments for suppressing heretical beliefs. Saluting the flag suppresses no belief nor curbs it. Children and their parents may believe what they please, avow their belief and practice it. It is not even remotely suggested that the requirement for saluting the flag involves the slightest restriction against the fullest opportunity on the part both of the children and of their parents to disavow as publicly as they choose to do so the meaning that others attach to the gesture of salute. All channels of affirmative free expression are open to both children and parents. Had we before us any act of the state putting the slightest curbs upon such free expression, I should not lag behind any member of this Court in striking down such an invasion of the right to freedom of thought and freedom of speech protected by the Constitution." 319 U. S. at 661–4.

**978**                                                         [Emerson]

## Note

Instances other than those involving compulsory flag salute where children have objected to public school requirements on religious grounds are: (1) Absence from school on religious holiday: *Commonwealth v. Bey,* 166 Pa. Super. 136, 70 Atl. 2d 693 (1950), noted in 98 U. of Pa. L. Rev. 923 (1950) (Moslem students absent on Friday; held prosecution under compulsory education law constitutional). (2) Compulsory dancing lessons: *Hardwick v. Board of School Trustees,* 54 Cal. App. 696, 205 Pac. 49 (1921) (held unreasonable). (3) Compulsory military training: *Hamilton v. Univ. of Calif.,* 293 U. S. 245, 79 L. Ed. 343, 55 S. Ct. 197 (1934) (students voluntarily attending state-maintained university cannot refuse to accept military training which offended their religious beliefs). See also *Univ. of Md. v. Coale,* 165 Md. 224, 167 Atl. 54 (1933). In *Miami Military Institute v. Leff,* 129 Misc. 481, 220 N. Y. Supp. 799 (1926), it was held that a private school may not compel Jewish students to attend Christian churches. See also the vaccination cases, *infra,* and the *Scopes* case, *supra* Chapter VII.

## C. POLICE REGULATION

### UNITED STATES v. BALLARD

Supreme Court of the United States, 1944

322 U. S. 78, 88 L. Ed. 1148, 64 S. Ct. 882

[Guy, Edna and Donald Ballard were indicted for conspiracy and mail fraud in connection with organizing a religious sect known as the I Am movement. The indictment charged that the defendants falsely represented with the intent to defraud certain religious doctrines and beliefs, well knowing the falsity thereof, in order to convert money and valuable property obtained from their followers for their own benefit. Some of the beliefs were as follows: (1) That Guy Ballard, alias Saint Germain, and the other Ballards, had been selected as divine messengers to transmit the words of the alleged divine entity Saint Germain to mankind under teachings commonly known as the I Am movement; (2) that by reasons of their supernatural attainments they could cure persons of diseases either curable or incurable and had in fact cured hundreds of persons. With the acquiescense of both sides the charge to the jury eliminated the question of truth and falsity of the religious belief. The District Court presented the issue as follows: "Did these defendants honestly and in good faith believe these things? If they did they should be acquitted." Defendants were convicted. The Court of Appeals reversed on the ground that the allegations

**979**

in the indictment required a finding by the jury that at least some of the representations were false. Defendants attacked the constitutionality of the indictment as violative of the guarantees of free exercise of religion extended by the First and Fourteenth Amendments. They also attacked the charge to the jury as error on the theory that it amounted to an amendment of the indictment.]

MR. JUSTICE DOUGLAS delivered the opinion of the Court. . . . [We] do not agree that the truth or verity of respondents' religious doctrines or beliefs should have been submitted to the jury. Whatever this particular indictment might require, the First Amendment precludes such a course, as the United States seems to concede. "The law knows no heresy, and is committed to the support of no dogma, the establishment of no sect." *Watson v. Jones*, 13 Wall. 679, 728. The First Amendment has a dual aspect. It not only "forestalls compulsion by law of the acceptance of any creed or the practice of any form of worship" but also "safeguards the free exercise of the chosen form of religion." *Cantwell v. Connecticut*, 310 U. S. 296, 303. "Thus the Amendment embraces two concepts,—freedom to believe and freedom to act. The first is absolute but, in the nature of things, the second cannot be." *Id.*, pp. 303–304. Freedom of thought, which includes freedom of religious belief, is basic in a society of free men. *Board of Education v. Barnette*, 319 U. S. 624. It embraces the right to maintain theories of life and of death and of the hereafter which are rank heresy to followers of the orthodox faiths. Heresy trials are foreign to our Constitution. Men may believe what they cannot prove. They may not be put to the proof of their religious doctrines or beliefs. Religious experiences which are as real as life to some may be incomprehensible to others. Yet the fact that they may be beyond the ken of mortals does not mean that they can be made suspect before the law. Many take their gospel from the New Testament. But it would hardly be supposed that they could be tried before a jury charged with the duty of determining whether those teachings contained false representations. The miracles of the New Testament, the Divinity of Christ, life after death, the power of prayer are deep in the religious convictions of many. If one could be sent to jail because a jury in a hostile environment found those teachings false, little indeed would be left of religious freedom. The Fathers of the Constitution were not unaware of the varied and extreme views of religious sects, of the violence of disagreement among them, and of the lack of any one religious creed on which all men would agree.

They fashioned a charter of government which envisaged the widest possible toleration of conflicting views. Man's relation to his God was made no concern of the state. He was granted the right to worship as he pleased and to answer to no man for the verity of his religious views. The religious views espoused by respondents might seem incredible, if not preposterous, to most people. But if those doctrines are subject to trial before a jury charged with finding their truth or falsity, then the same can be done with the religious beliefs of any sect. When the triers of fact undertake that task, they enter a forbidden domain. The First Amendment does not select any one group or any one type of religion for preferred treatment. It puts them all in that position. *Murdock v. Pennsylvania,* 319 U. S. 105. As stated in *Davis v. Beason,* 133 U. S. 333, 342, "With man's relations to his Maker and the obligations he may think they impose, and the manner in which an expression shall be made by him of his belief on those subjects, no interference can be permitted, provided always the laws of society, designed to secure its peace and prosperity, and the morals of its people, are not interfered with." See *Prince v. Massachusetts,* 321 U. S. 158. So we conclude that the District Court ruled properly when it withheld from the jury all questions concerning the truth or falsity of the religious beliefs or doctrines of respondents. . . .

[The case was reversed and remanded to the Court of Appeals to consider other grounds urged by the defendants which that Court had not reached.]

MR. CHIEF JUSTICE STONE, dissenting:

I am not prepared to say that the constitutional guaranty of freedom of religion affords immunity from criminal prosecution for the fraudulent procurement of money by false statements as to one's religious experiences, more than it renders polygamy or libel immune from criminal prosecution. *Davis v. Beason,* 133 U. S. 333; see *Chaplinsky v. New Hampshire,* 315 U. S. 568, 572; cf. *Patterson v. Colorado,* 205 U. S. 454, 462; *Near v. Minnesota,* 283 U. S. 697, 715. I cannot say that freedom of thought and worship includes freedom to procure money by making knowingly false statements about one's religious experiences. To go no further, if it were shown that a defendant in this case had asserted as a part of the alleged fraudulent scheme, that he had physically shaken hands with St. Germain in San Francisco on a day named, or that, as the indictment here alleges, by the exertion of his spiritual power he "had in fact cured . . . hundreds of persons afflicted with diseases and ailments," I should not doubt that it would be open to the Gov-

**981**

ernment to submit to the jury proof that he had never been in San Francisco and that no such cures had ever been effected. In any event I see no occasion for making any pronouncement on this subject in the present case. . . .

With the assent of the prosecution and the defense the trial judge withdrew from the consideration of the jury the question whether the alleged religious experiences had in fact occurred, but submitted to the jury the single issue whether petitioners honestly believed that they had occurred, with the instruction that if the jury did not so find, then it should return a verdict of guilty. . . . The state of one's mind is a fact as capable of fraudulent misrepresentation as is one's physical condition or the state of his bodily health. See *Seven Cases v. United States*, 239 U. S. 510, 517; cf. *Durland v. United States*, 161 U. S. 306, 313. . . . Since the indictment and the evidence support the conviction, it is irrelevant whether the religious experiences alleged did or did not in fact occur or whether that issue could or could not, for constitutional reasons, have been rightly submitted to the jury. Certainly none of respondents' constitutional rights are violated if they are prosecuted for the fraudulent procurement of money by false representations as to their beliefs, religious or otherwise. . . .

[Justices Roberts and Frankfurter joined in the Stone opinion. Mr. Justice Jackson dissented in a separate opinion.]

## Note

1. When the case reached the Supreme Court for a second time, the indictment was ordered dismissed on the ground that women were intentionally and systematically excluded from the federal grand jury panel. The Court again refused to pass on the central issue of whether the mail may be used to obtain money by fraud when the fraud is a false claim of belief concerning religion. *Ballard v. U. S.*, 329 U. S. 187, 91 L. Ed. 181, 67 S. Ct. 261 (1946).

2. Compare *Brown v. Father Divine*, 163 Misc. 796, 298 N. Y. Supp. 642 (1937), in which a follower of Father Divine sought appointment of a receiver for the rents and profits of the property of the Peace Mission on the ground that the money contributed had not been deposited in the Heavenly Treasure. The plaintiff was successful.

3. Among state police regulations that have been challenged on religious grounds are: (1) *Statutes forbidding fortune-telling and spiritualism or vagrancy laws construed to cover these practices. State v. De Laney*, 122 Atl. 890 (N. J. 1923) (charter of church permitted teaching of spiritualism; freedom of religion defense upheld); *People v. Miller*, 46 N. Y. Supp. 2d 206 (1943) (statute specifically exempted spiritualists acting in good faith and without personal fee; client made contribution; defense upheld); for an earlier case prior to the statute

in which a spiritualist was convicted, see *People v. Ashley,* 184 App. Div. 520, 172 N. Y. Supp. 282 (1918). To the same effect see *People v. Neitzel,* 69 Wash. 567, 125 Pac. 939 (1912); *City of St. Louis v. Hellscher,* 295 Mo. 293, 242 S. W. 652 (1922); *McMasters v. State,* 21 Okla. Cr. 318, 207 Pac. 566 (1922). For full description and historical background see Rubenstein, *A Treatise on Contemporary Religious Jurisprudence* (1948). (2) *Liquor prohibition.* The granting of an exemption for sacramental wine has been upheld against challenges that it is discriminatory or an aid to religion. See *People v. Marquis,* 291 Ill. 121, 125 N. E. 757 (1919); *cf. State v. Kramer,* 49 S. D. 56, 206 N. W. 468 (1925) (refusal by a state to exempt an unlimited quantity for sacramental purposes has been held not to violate freedom of religion).

3. Many health regulations have also been challenged on constitutional grounds. The following are examples:

(1) *Prohibition of spiritual healing.* For an account of the controversy subsequent to the founding of the Christian Science movement and the eventual recognition of Christian Science healing in most states, see 2 Stokes, *Church and State in the United States,* pp. 322–5 (1950). For report on recent legal and professional status of Christian Science heading, see N. Y. Times, June 3, 1952. The religious right to heal by prayer does not extend so far as to compel a state to permit the practice of medicine for a fee to an unqualified and unlicensed physician. *Fealy v. City of Birmingham,* 15 Ala. App. 367, 73 So. 296 (1916); *Smith v. People,* 51 Colo. 270, 117 Pac. 612 (1911); *State v. Verbon,* 167 Wash. 140, 8 Pac. 2d 1083 (1932); *State v. Miller,* 59 N. D. 286, 229 N. W. 569 (1930); *People v. Vogelgesang,* 221 N. Y. 290, 116 N. E. 977 (1917); *State v. Buswell,* 40 Neb. 158, 58 N. W. 728 (1894); *People v. Cole,* 219 N. Y. 98, 113 N. E. 790 (1916); *State v. Marble,* 72 Oh. St. 21, 73 N. E. 1063 (1905). The problem also arises in prosecution of parents for breach of duty imposed by statute to furnish recognized medical care to a child. The defense that medical care contradicts the defendant's religious beliefs, such as Divine Healing through prayer, is not accepted on ground that the law is directed at acts which the state could regulate under the police power, not beliefs. *People v. Pierson,* 176 N. Y. 201, 68 N. E. 243 (1903); *State v. Chenoweth,* 163 Ind. 94, 71 N. E. 197 (1904); *Owens v. State,* 6 Okla. Cr. 110, 116 Pac. 345, 36 L.R.A. N.S. 633 (1911); *Beck v. State,* 29 Okla. Cr. 240, 233 Pac. 495 (1925); see also *Mitchell v. Davis,* 205 S. W. 2d 812 (Tex. Civ. App. 1947) (mother loses custody of dying child); Note, 12 A.L.R. 2d 1042. For other custody cases involving the elements of religious upbringing and health and well-being of child, see *infra.*

(2) *Vaccination and physical examination.* The well-established power of a state to require vaccination, *Jacobson v. Massachusetts,* 197 U. S. 11, 49 L. Ed. 643, 25 S. Ct. 358 (1905); *Zucht v. King,* 260 U. S. 174, 67 L. Ed. 194, 43 S. Ct. 24 (1922), has been challenged specifically on the ground that it interferes with religious freedom. The cases on the whole involve prosecution of parents under the compulsory education laws, for failing to vaccinate children as a condition

for admission to the public school: *Seubold v. Fort Smith Special School District*, 218 Ark. 560, 237 S. W. 2d 884 (1951); *Anderson v. State*, 84 Ga. App. 259, 65 S. E. 2d 848 (1951); *Vonnegut v. Baun*, 206 Ind. 172, 188 N. E. 677 (1934); *Mosier v. Barren County Board of Health*, 308 Ky. 829, 215 S. W. 2d 967 (1948); *Commonwealth v. Green*, 268 Mass. 585, 168 N. E. 101 (1929); *State v. Drew*, 89 N. H. 54, 192 Atl. 629 (1937); *Sadlock v. Board of Education*, 137 N. J. 85, 58 Atl. 2d 218 (1948); *In re Whitmore*, 47 N. Y. Supp. 2d 143 (1944); *Viemeister v. White*, 179 N. Y. 235, 72 N. E. 97 (1904); *City of New Braunfels v. Waldschmidt*, 109 Tex. 302, 207 S. W. 303 (1918); see also, *Walker v. Dallas Independent School District*, 75 F. Supp. 552 (N. D. Tex., 1948). For a case in which the court upheld a requirement of physical examination and report by a physician as prerequisite of admission to public school against religious freedom objections, see *Streich v. Board of Education*, 34 S. D. 169, 147 N. W. 779 (1914). In *Peterson v. Widule*, 157 Wis. 641, 147 N. W. 966 (1914), the court held that it was not a violation of freedom of religion for a state to require examination for venereal disease prior to obtaining a marriage license.

(3) *Snake handling*. Some religious sects make snake handling part of their religious ritual. Statutes outlawing these practices have been upheld. *Harden v. State*, 188 Tenn. 17, 216 S. W. 2d 708 (1948), noted in 2 Vand. L. Rev. 694 (1949); *State v. Massey*, 229 N. C. 734, 51 S. E. 2d 179 (1949), app. dis. *sub. nom. Bunn v. N. C.*, 336 U. S. 942 (1949); *Lawson v. Commonwealth*, 291 Ky. 437, 164 S. W. 2d 972 (1942); *cf. Kirk v. Commonwealth*, 186 Va. 839, 44 S. E. 2d 409 (1947) (defense of religious belief not available in prosecution for death due to snake handling).

## NOTE—SUNDAY LAWS—APPLICATION TO PERSONS OBSERVING A DIFFERENT SABBATH

### 25 So. Cal. L. Rev. 131, 132–4 (1951)

The tradition of "blue laws" in this country is a facet of our colonial heritage, rooted in the theocratic spirit permeating Puritan New England and Anglican Virginia, and reflected in the legislative enactments of the various colonial commonwealths.[7] The prototype of pre-Revolutionary War laws for the observance of Sunday was an English statute forbidding any person to exercise "worldly labor or business or work of their ordinary calling on the Lord's Day, works of necessity and charity excepted."[8] The explicit religious character of this law was reproduced with marked exactitude in many of the original Sunday laws of the colonial epoch and laid the foundation for subsequent Sunday

---

[7] Harris, Sunday Laws (1892), 29, § 22; 21 Encyc. Brit., Sunday (14th Ed. 1929), 565.

[8] 29 Car. II, c. 7 (1676). . . .

legislation in this country.[9]  The avowed objective of these laws was to compel church attendance and prevent the profanation of a day consecrated to the worship of God.[10]  Stringent punishment was meted out to "Sunday-breakers" who engaged in secular vocations or indulged in mundane pleasures.[11]

With various but not essential modifications, such laws remained in force when the victorious colonies changed their status to that of sovereign states in the new federal union.  They served as models for similar legislation adopted by the later-admitted states.  Today, most state jurisdictions impose restrictions upon the performance of work or the conduct of business of one's ordinary calling on Sundays, except where exemptions are specifically granted. . . .

Many early opinions upholding the comprehensive scope of various state laws proscribing Sunday labor, sports, amusements, contracts and business transactions are forthright in their pronouncements that the purpose of such enactments is to preserve the sacred character of the first day of the week because of its religious significance.[18]  Certain courts have espoused the view that the devout men who framed the Constitution could not have intended that the secular authorities should be indifferent to the furtherance of religious ideals despite the separation of Church and State.[19]  A New York case has held that Christianity was a part of the common law of the state and entitled to protection by the secular authorities.[20]  All of these decisions are predicated on a thorough study of the historical antecedents of the Sunday laws, which quite plainly indicate that their purpose was to foster the established religions of early colonial times.

Contrariwise, California once declared a Sunday law unconstitutional as an attempt to enforce a religious institution.[21]  One jurisdiction has invalidated a Sunday statute on the basis of particular phraseology, which was construed as designed to enforce

---

[9] *Rodman v. Robinson*, 134 N. C. 503, 47 S. E. 19 (1904); Johnson, Sunday Legislation, 23 Ky. L. Jour. 131, 140, 142 (1934).

[10] 2 Encyc. Soc. Sci., Blue Laws (1930), 600.

[11] 26 Encyc. Amer., Sunday (1950), 30.

[18] *O'Donnell v. Sweeney*, 5 Ala. 467 (1843); *Brimhall v. Van Campen*, 8 Minn. 13 (1862).

[19] *State v. Ambs*, 20 Mo. 214 (1854); *Lindenmuller v. People*, 33 Barb. (N. Y.) 548 (1861); *City Council v. Benjamin*, 2 Strob. (S. C.) 508, 49 Am. Dec. 608 (1846).

[20] *People v. Ruggles*, 8 Johns. (N. Y.) 290 (1811).

[21] *Ex parte Newman*, 9 Cal. 502 (1858).  This decision was overruled in *Ex parte Andrews*, 18 Cal. 678 (1861).  In 1883, the Sunday legislation in California was repealed.

Sunday observance as a religious duty.[22] An intermediate view has suggested that the laws for the cessation of work on Sunday are not the product of efforts to create state-induced adherence to a religious doctrine but the natural interweaving of Christian ideals into the civil matrix of our social order.[23]

Although the earlier cases grappled with this problem from the standpoint of the propriety of Sunday laws as a means of compelling religious observance, this approach, whether well taken or not, seems largely to have been abandoned. Sunday laws are now almost universally sustained as a valid exercise of the state's police power in safeguarding health and preserving the morals and good order of society.[24] The state's objective is to assure the physical, intellectual and moral welfare of its citizens by providing one day's rest in seven from the strain of uninterrupted labor.[25] Thus, limitations on Sunday labor are construed as civil regulations designed to achieve uniformity as to a day of rest, and its enforcement is to protect those entitled to its benefits.[26] The fact that it coincides with a day celebrated by a particular church does not detract from its character as a civil regulation under the police power.[27]

Using this rationale, many recent cases have decided that Sunday laws do not encroach upon the religious liberty either of Christians who might desire to work on Sunday or of members of religious groups which hold sacred a day other than Sunday.[28] Before a court will invalidate a statute prohibiting the doing of otherwise legal acts on Sunday as an invasion of religious liberty, the statute must show that it tends to the establishment of a religion, provides for compulsory support of religious instruction, or restricts the practice of one's religion or the expression of one's religious beliefs.[29] . . . [I]t is arguable that where a shopkeeper voluntarily suspends his business on a certain day in

---

[22] *Dist. of Columbia v. Robinson*, 30 App. D. C. 283, 12 Ann. Cas. 1094 (1908).

[23] *Church of the Holy Trinity v. United States*, 143 U. S. 457, 471, 12 Sup. Ct. 511, 517, 36 L. Ed. 226, 232 (1892); *Ex parte Burke*, 59 Cal. 6, 14 (1881).

[24] *Carr v. State*, 175 Ind. 241, 93 N. E. 1071 (1911); *People v. Havnor*, 149 N. Y. 195, 43 N. E. 541 (1896).

[25] *State v. Petit*, 24 Minn. 376, 77 N. W. 225 (1898); *State v. Powell*, 58 Ohio St. 324, 50 N. E. 900, 41 L. R. A. 854 (1898).

[26] *Ex parte Andrews*, 18 Cal. 678 (1861); *Frolickstein v. Mayor of Mobile*, 40 Ala. 725 (1867).

[27] *Ex parte Andrews*, 18 Cal. 678 (1861); *Judefind v. State*, 78 Md. 510, 28 Atl. 405, 22 L. R. A. 721 (1894).

[28] *Rogers v. State*, 60 Ga. App. 722, 4 S. E. (2d) 918 (1939); *State v. Grabinski*, 33 Wash. (2d) 603, 206 Pac. (2d) 1022 (1949).

[29] *State ex rel. Temple v. Barnes*, 22 N. D. 18, 132 N. W. 215 (1911).

keeping with his religious convictions, and is also required by law to close his shop on the following day, he is confronted with the choice of either suffering severe economic hardship or compromising his religious scruples. The freedom to practice one's religion under the competitive handicap of two days of enforced leisure each week may thus well depend on the size of the individual's purse.[31]

Ultimately, the valid exercise of the state's police power requires that there be a substantial nexus between the end to be achieved and the legislation enacted for that purpose, accomplished without interference with the fundamental rights guaranteed to the individual.[32] While it is within a state's prerogative to provide its citizenry with a day of rest from customary labor, it would seem desirable to exempt from these enactments those who, following their religious dictates, select as their day of rest one other than Sunday. A minority of courts have in fact held that such an exemption is a *sine qua non* for the validity of general Sunday laws.[33] This has the virtue not only of promoting the health of the community in conformity with the professed purpose of these laws, but eliminates any possibility of religious discrimination or of the imputation that the state is making a law "respecting an establishment of religion." Five states have moved in this direction by repealing their Sunday laws and replacing them with statutes requiring one day of rest in seven, without signifying the day.[34]

## Note

See also Lewis, *Sunday Legislation: Its History to the Present Time and its Results* (1902); Note, *Sunday Statutes in a Modern Community,* 61 Yale L. J. 427 (1952).

---

[31] "Freedom of speech, freedom of the press, freedom of religion are available to all, not merely to those who can pay their own way." *Murdock v. Pennsylvania*, 319 U. S. 105, 111, 63 Sup. Ct. 870, 874, 87 L. Ed. 1292, 1297 (1943).

[32] *Mugler v. Kansas*, 123 U. S. 623, 8 Sup. Ct. 273, 31 L. Ed. 205 (1887).

[33] *City of Canton v. Nist*, 9 Ohio St. 439 (1859). See *Johns v. State*, 78 Ind. 332, 334 (1881), where the court discusses the Indiana Sunday statute as follows: "The framers of the statute meant to leave it to the consciences and judgments of the citizens to choose between the first and the seventh day of the week. One or the other of these days they must refrain from common labor. . . . It was not the purpose . . . to compel any class of conscientious persons to abstain from labor two days in every week. . . . If the [exemption] proviso were wrenched from the statute, these classes of citizens would be compelled, in obedience to their religious convictions, to rest from labor on the seventh day, and, by the law, also compelled to refrain from common labor on the first day of the week. A leading and controlling element of our system of government is, that there shall be absolute freedom in all matters of religious belief."

[34] These states are Arizona, California, Oregon, Wisconsin and Wyoming.

## D. OTHER ASPECTS OF FREEDOM OF RELIGION

### 1. Marriage and Divorce

Laws prohibiting polygamy and bigamy have been upheld against the objection that they interfered with religious beliefs of members of the Mormon Church that permitted and required these practices. See *Reynolds v. U. S.*, 98 U. S. 145, 25 L. Ed. 244 (1878) ; *Davis v. Beason*, 133 U. S. 333, 33 L. Ed. 637, 10 S. Ct. 299 (1890) (upholding Utah territorial law requiring that every voter swear that he does not practice and advocate polygamy privately or publicly). See also *Church of Latter-Day Saints v. U. S.*, 136 U. S. 1, 34 L. Ed. 478, 10 S. Ct. 792 (1890), where the Court said: " . . . the Thugs of India imagined that their belief in the right of assassination was a religious belief; but their thinking so did not make it so . . . The offering of human sacrifices by our own ancestors in Britain was no doubt sanctioned by an equally conscientious impulse. But no one, on that account, would hesitate to brand these practices, now, as crimes against society, and obnoxious to condemnation and punishment by the civil authority." See further *State v. Barlow*, 107 Utah 292, 153 Pac. 2d 647 (1944), app. dis. 324 U. S. 829 (1945) (state bigamy law) ; *Cleveland v. U. S.*, 329 U. S. 14, 91 L. Ed. 12, 67 S. Ct. 13 (1946) (Federal anti-white slave law). For a discussion of British cases see Bartholomew, *Polygamous Marriages*, 15 Mod. L. Rev. 35 (1952).

In *People ex rel. Bernat v. Bicek*, 405 Ill. 510, 91 N.E. 2d 588 (1950), the Illinois Domestic Relations Act of 1949 authorized divorce courts to seek the assistance of representatives of religious denominations to which the parties belonged for purposes of effecting a reconciliation. The court in holding the Act invalid gave as one of its reasons that it violated the principle of separation of Church and State. It relied principally on the *McCollum* case, *supra*.

It is generally held that only the state may dissolve marriages and religious divorces are not recognized. Certain grounds for seeking a divorce also touch on the issue of separation of Church and State and religious freedom. These include religious oppression and refusal to cohabit on religious grounds. For a collection of cases see Torpey, *Judicial Doctrines of Religious Rights in America*, pp. 207 et seq. (1948). See *Hughes v. Holman*, 110 Ore. 415, 223 Pac. 730 (1924) (alienation of affection of wife by church; held that proof of intent and causal connection insufficient).

## 2. Conscientious Objectors

*History.* Madison's original draft of the Bill of Rights contained exemptions for religious objectors. Bills in some of the states proposed such exemptions but they were not enacted. During the Civil War religious objectors were gradually recognized and given the alternative of paying a fee or participating in noncombatant service. Political and ethical objectors were not recognized. In World War I again only religious objectors were recognized initially by the draft laws. At first these had to belong to pacifist churches and were required to participate in noncombatant service. Gradually the pacifist church membership requirement was partially lifted and individual conscientious scruples based on religion received some recognition. Moreover, conscientious objectors who would not participate in any activities within the armed services were furloughed to agriculture and industry. The World War II statute recognized all conscientious opposition based "on religious training and belief," and also permitted the assignment of CO's who could not work within military establishments to work of national importance under civilian control. 50 U.S.C. App. § 305 (g) (1946). The phrase "on religious training and belief" received conflicting interpretations by the Courts of Appeals. The Second Circuit believed it included ethical objectors. The Ninth Circuit believed it did not. Cf. *U.S. ex rel. Reel v. Badt,* 141 F. 2d 845 (C.A. 2, 1944) with *Berman v. United States,* 156 F.2d 377 (C.A. 9, 1946). The 1948 Act eliminated the claims of ethical objectors by making belief in a Supreme Being a prerequisite to classification as a CO. Work of national importance under civilian control was eliminated. Depending on the nature of his opposition an objector was either assigned to noncombatant service or deferred. Under the 1951 Act the draft boards may prescribe that deferred objectors "perform such civilian work contributing to the maintenance of the national health, safety or interest as the local board may deem appropriate." 50 U.S.C. App. § 456 (j) (1951). In February 1952 President Truman issued regulations implementing this provision. N. Y. Times, Feb. 21, 1952. See Russell, *Development of Conscientious Objector Recognition in the United States,* 20 Geo. Wash. L. Rev. 409 (1952).

*Litigated Issues.* It has been held that Congressional powers to raise an Army and Navy permit both war and peacetime drafts, and that such laws do not violate the Thirteenth Amendment. *Selective Draft Law Cases,* 245 U.S. 366, 62 L.Ed. 349, 38 S.Ct. 159 (1918) ; *U.S. v. Herling,* 120 F.2d 236 (C.A. 2, 1941). Exemptions of religious groups from combatant service have been held not to violate the disestablishment clause of the First Amendment. *Selective Draft Law Cases, supra.* At the same time the First Amendment does not guarantee such an exemption. It is no defense to a charge of failure to register that the Act violates one's religious belief. *U.S. v. Kime,* 188 F.2d 677 (C.A. 7, 1951); *U.S. v. Henderson,* 180 F.2d 711 (C.A. 7, 1950); *Richter v. U.S.,* 181 F.2d 591 (C.A. 9, 1950); *Cannon v. U.S.,* 181 F.2d 354 (C.A. 9, 1950); *Michener v. U.S.,* 184 F.2d 712 (C.A. 10, 1950). Nor may a registrant who has been classified as a conscientious objector refuse on religious grounds to do work of national importance under the provisions of the 1940 Act. *Roodenko v. U.S.,* 147 F.2d 752 (C.A. 10, 1944), cert. den. 324 U.S. 860 (1945). See also *Atherton v. U.S.,* 176 F.2d 835 (C.A. 9, 1949) (fact that civilian camp contained army officers did not render camp part of the army); *U.S. v. Emery,* 168 F.2d 454 (C.A. 2, 1948) (conscientious objector in "detached service" from camp was paid only $15 per month by the government out of the prevailing wage it received for his dairy herd testing; the government deposited the rest of the money in a separate fund in the Treasury; held no violation of First or Fifth Amendments).

As to the conclusiveness of the draft boards' classification see, *Cox v. United States,* 332 U.S. 442, 92 L.Ed. 59, 68 S.Ct. 115 (1947); *Estep v. U.S.,* 327 U.S. 114, 90 L.Ed. 567, 66 S.Ct. 423 (1946). As to the proper procedure for obtaining review see *Estep v. U.S., supra; Gibson v. U.S.,* 329 U.S. 338, 91 L.Ed. 331, 67 S. Ct. 301 (1946); *Sunal v. Large,* 332 U. S. 174, 91 L. Ed. 1982, 67 S. Ct. 1588 (1947).

The draft acts also exempt ministers of religion and theological students. The exemption of a "minister" has been interpreted by the courts not to exempt everyone a particular group or religion may designate as a minister but only those Congress intended. Jehovah's Witnesses, according to whose belief every member of the sect is a "minister," have been classified otherwise by the draft boards and such classifications have been upheld. *U. S. v. Mroz,* 136 F.2d 221 (C.A. 7, 1943); *Baxley v. U.S.,* 134 F.2d 998 (C.A. 4, 1943); *Rase v. U.S.,* 129 F.2d 204 (C.A. 6, 1942); *Martin v. U.S.,* 190 F.2d 775 (C.A. 4, 1951). Draft boards also have used theological panels to hold hearings and advise them on whether a particular applicant is a bona fide minister or student for the ministry. The Supreme Court has upheld this practice as authorized by the statute and not violative of due process so long as the draft board itself makes the final adjudication. *Eagles v. U.S. ex rel. Samuels,* 329 U.S. 304, 91 L.Ed. 308, 68 S.Ct. 313 (1946). The 1951 act tends to support these holdings by specifically excluding from the classification those who "irregularly" or "incidentally" preach. 50 U.S.C.App. § 456(g) (1951). It has been held, however, that the claim of a Jehovah's Witness may not be referred to a panel of Protestant members. *U.S. v. Balough*, 157 F.2d 939 (C.A. 2, 1946), vacated on other grounds, 329 U.S. 692 (1947).

See also *In re Summers*, 325 U.S. 561, 89 L.Ed. 1795, 65 S.Ct. 1307 (1945) (denial of admission to the bar for refusal to take oath which includes willingness to serve in state militia does not violate First or Fourteenth Amendments; majority relied by analogy on the *Schwimmer* and *MacIntosh* cases, *infra*).

Religious belief has been held to be no defense to a charge of violation of the Selective Service Act by knowingly counseling one who is required to register to fail and refuse to do so. *Warren v. U.S.*, 177 F.2d 596 (C.A. 10, 1949), cert. den. 338 U.S. 947 (1950); *Gara v. U.S.*, 178 F.2d 38 (C.A. 6, 1949), affirmed by equally divided Court, 340 U.S. 857, 95 L.Ed. 628, 71 S. Ct. 87 (1950).

For a general discussion of the law governing conscientious objectors and its administration see Selective Service System, *Conscientious Objection* (Special Monograph No. 11, 1950); Russell, *supra;* Cornell, *The Conscientious Objector and the Law* (1943); Cornell, *Exemption from the Draft: A Study in Civil Liberties*, 56 Yale L. J. 258 (1947); see also Elloff, *Jehovah's Witnesses and the Selective Service Act*, 31 Va. L. Rev. 811 (1945); Mittlebeeler, *Laws and the Conscientious Objector*, 20 Ore. L. Rev. 301 (1941).

## Note

1. The Supreme Court had held prior to 1946 that an alien who refuses to bear arms will not be admitted to citizenship. *U. S. v. Schwimmer*, 279 U. S. 644, 73 L. Ed. 889, 49 S. Ct. 448 (1929); *U. S. v. MacIntosh*, 283 U. S. 605, 75 L. Ed. 1302, 51 S. Ct. 570 (1931); and *U. S. v. Bland*, 283 U. S. 636, 75 L. Ed. 1319, 51 S. Ct. 569 (1931). In *Girouard v. U. S.*, 328 U. S. 61, 90 L. Ed. 1084, 66 S. Ct. 826 (1946), the Court held that an alien who is willing to serve as a non-combatant and take the oath of allegiance but does not want to bear arms because of his religious beliefs can become a citizen under the provisions of the Nationality Act. The earlier cases were overruled. See also *Cohnstaedt v. Immigration and Naturalization Service*, 339 U. S. 901, 94 L. Ed. 1331, 70 S. Ct. 516 (1950) (refusal to manufacture munitions or deliver them to combat troops on religious grounds is no bar); *cf. In re Clarke*, 301 Pa. 321, 152 Atl. 92 (1930) (citizenship refused where petitioner wanted to add to customary oath: "So far as they are in accord with the moral law of the United States").

2. Some other Church-State problems not covered in this Chapter are:

(a) *Disputes between factions within religious organizations*. These frequently involve disposition of church property. The general trend of American decisions has been to rule that the determinations of the supreme hierarchical authority are conclusive. See *Watson v. Jones,* 13 Wall. 679, 20 L. Ed. 666 (1872); *Trustees of Presbytery v. Westminster Presbyterian Church,* 222 N. Y. 305, 118 N. E. 800 (1918). But *cf. Saint Nicholas Cathedral v. Kedroff,* 302 N. Y. 1, 96 N. E. 2d 56 (1950) (legislative action taking church away from supposedly Soviet controlled hierachy upheld in part by construing it as a legislative declaration that church has become perverted to secular purposes). See Note, 64 Harv. L. Rev. 1360 (1951). For collection of materials see, Howe, *Cases on Church and State in the United States,* ch 11 (1952).

(b) *Incorporation of church property.* For full discussion see Dignan, *History of the Legal Incorporation of Catholic Church Property in the United States* (1935).

(c) *Appointment of Ambassador to the Vatican*: See Feiertag, *American Public Opinion on the Diplomatic Relations between the United States and the Papal States (1847–1867)* (1933); Stock, *United States Ministers to the Papal States* (1933); Cullinan, *The White House and the Vatican,* 38 A. B. A. J. 471, 530 (1952).

# CHAPTER IX

# DISCRIMINATION

## A. HOUSING

### 1. Introduction

## TO SECURE THESE RIGHTS—THE REPORT OF THE PRESIDENT'S COMMITTEE ON CIVIL RIGHTS

Washington: U. S. Government Printing Office,
1947, pp. 67–70

Equality of opportunity to rent or buy a home should exist for every American. Today, many of our citizens face a double barrier when they try to satisfy their housing needs. They first encounter a general housing shortage which makes it difficult for any family without a home to find one. They then encounter prejudice and discrimination based upon race, color, religion or national origin, which places them at a disadvantage in competing for the limited housing that is available. The fact that many of those who face this double barrier are war veterans only underlines the inadequacy of our housing record.

Discrimination in housing results primarily from business practices. The practices may arise from special interests of business groups, such as the profits to be derived from confining minorities to slum areas, or they may reflect community prejudice. One of the most common practices is the policy of landlords and real estate agents to prevent Negroes from renting outside of designated areas. Again, it is "good business" to develop exclusive "restricted" suburban developments which are barred to all but white gentiles. When Negro veterans seek "GI" loans in order to build homes, they are likely to find that credit from private banks, without whose services there is no possibility of taking advantage of the GI Bill of Rights, is less freely available to members of their race. Private builders show a tendency not to construct new homes except for white occupancy. These interlocking business customs and devices form the core of our discriminatory policy. But community prejudice also finds expression in open public agitation against construction of public housing projects for Negroes, and by violence against Negroes who seek to occupy public housing projects or to build in "white" sections.

*The restrictive covenant.*[1]—Under rulings of the Supreme Court, it is legally impossible to segregate housing on a racial or religious basis by zoning ordinance. Accordingly, the restrictive covenant has become the most effective modern method of accomplishing such segregation. Restrictive covenants generally take the form of agreements written into deeds of sale by which property owners mutually bind themselves not to sell or lease to an "undesirable." These agreements have thus far been enforceable by court action. Through these covenants large areas of land are barred against use by various classes of American citizens. Some are directed against only one minority group, others against a list of minorities. These have included Armenians, Jews, Negroes, Mexicans, Syrians, Japanese, Chinese, and Indians.

While we do not know how much land in the country is subject to such restrictions, we do know that many areas, particularly large cities in the North and West, such as Chicago, Cleveland, Washington, D. C., and Los Angeles, are widely affected. The amount of land covered by racial restrictions in Chicago has been estimated at 80 percent. Students of the subject state that virtually all new subdivisions are blanketed by these covenants. Land immediately surrounding ghetto areas is frequently restricted in order to prevent any expansion in the ghetto. Thus, where old ghettos are surrounded by restrictions, and new subdivisions are also encumbered by them, there is practically no place for the people against whom the restrictions are directed to go. Since minorities have been forced into crowded slum areas, and must ultimately have access to larger living areas, the restrictive covenant is providing our democratic society with one of its most challenging problems. . . .

*Public housing.*—The federal government has been closely concerned with minority housing problems in recent years through its aid to local public housing authorities, through its insurance of loans to private builders and through its war and veterans' programs. Much of the improvement in the housing conditions of minorities in recent years has resulted from public building. The Federal Public Housing Authority has tried to allocate public housing fairly, and to make certain that equal standards are maintained. Many housing projects with mixed racial occupancy have been operated with great success.

The Committee is glad to note that the Federal Housing Agency, which guarantees loans for certain types of private build-

---

[1] [Ed. note: This Report was issued prior to the Supreme Court's decision in *Shelley v. Kramer*, printed *infra*, which held restrictive covenants unenforceable.]

**994** [Emerson]

ing, has recently abandoned the policy by which it encouraged the placing of racial restrictive covenants on projects supported by government guarantees.

It must be noted, however, that even if government, local or federal, does not encourage racial restrictions, private interests may put discriminatory practices into effect if proper safeguards are not devised. The experience of Stuyvesant Town in New York City is a case in point. There the city made great financial concessions to a private corporation, the Metropolitan Life Insurance Company, to induce construction of a large housing project, which was to be subject to a variety of restrictions designed to make it serve community housing needs. But, in the absence of any direct requirement of equitable distribution of the benefits of the project the Company barred Negroes from occupancy in Stuyvesant Town. Yet New York is a city in which mixed public housing projects have been maintained for many years.

## HELFELD AND GRONER—RACE DISCRIMINATION IN HOUSING

### 57 Yale L. J. 426, 426–33 (1948)

#### NEGRO HOUSING IN AMERICA

The condition of Negro occupied residences best illustrates the problem of racial discrimination in housing. All available data demonstrate that Negro homes are substandard, overcrowded, segregated, generally inferior—in every section of the country, and on every income level.[3]

---

[3] The statistical data to be presented are corroborated by sociological descriptions of Negro housing. "Nothing is so obvious about the Negroes' level of living as the fact that most of them suffer from poor housing conditions." MYRDAL, AN AMERICAN DILEMMA 376 (1944). See also, *e.g.*, DRAKE AND CAYTON, BLACK METROPOLIS (1945); WOOFTER, NEGRO PROBLEMS IN CITIES (1928).

The intensive study of Negro youth prepared for the American Youth Commission in 1940 attested to the inferiority of Negro housing. The summary statement was: "Negro homes, all in all, are dreary dwellings, on neglected streets without pavements, littered by accumulated wastes, in the oldest sections of the city." REID, IN A MINOR KEY 25 (1940). Reports from each section of the country described poor housing. ATWOOD, WYATT, DAVIS AND WALKER, THUS BE THEIR DESTINY 2, 12–3, 43, 68–70 (1941) (Milton, Pa., Greensboro, N. C. and Galesburg, Ill.); DAVIS, GARDNER AND GARDNER, DEEP SOUTH 22, 50–4, 387–8, 468–70 (1941) (urban and rural); FRAZIER, NEGRO YOUTH AT THE CROSSWAYS, 6–18, 200, 290 (1940) (middle states); JOHNSON, GROWING UP IN THE BLACK BELT 6, 11, 18, 23, 27, 35, 55–8, 226, at 68 quoting a Negro girl in Georgia, "I'd like to have a house that don't leak, a house with no leaks in it anywhere. I wants a comfortable house,

In urban areas, for example, a few comparative percentages from an official study indicate the extent of the inferiority; in Hartford, 29.9% of the Negro families as contrasted with 2.5% of the whites lived in dwellings unfit for use or in need of major repairs; in Milwaukee, the corresponding contrast was 67.7% for Negroes to 6.5% for whites; in Detroit, 33.7% and 6.8%; and in Birmingham, 56.5% and 19.7%.[4] Other investigations into the availability of heating, kitchen and toilet facilities, reveal similar racial disparities.[5]

a house you won't freeze in in winter. I'd like to have nice things in the house, nice furniture so you could be comfortable. I'd like for it to have smooth floors, not big loose planks." (1941) (rural South); REID, op. cit. supra, at 26–7 (summary); SUTHERLAND, COLOR, CLASS AND PERSONALITY 13, 15, 17, 18, 20–1, 31, 35, 45, 69, 73, 97 (1942) (summary); WARNER, JUNKER AND ADAMS, COLOR AND HUMAN NATURE 168 (1941) (Chicago). See also REUTER, THE AMERICAN RACE PROBLEM 222–3 (Rev. ed. 1938).

[4] STERNER, THE NEGRO'S SHARE 190 (1943), summarizing unpublished tabulations of the Federal Housing Administration. The following table, reproduced from p. 191, gives the occupancy by Negroes in each community in terms of a percentage of all dwelling units, of units needing major repairs, and of those unfit for use.

| City | All Dwelling Units | Needing Major Repairs | Unfit for use |
|---|---|---|---|
| Buffalo, N. Y. | 3.0% | 10.1% | 28.1% |
| Philadelphia, Pa. | 12.7 | 46.7 | 66.8 |
| Milwaukee (greater), Wis. | 1.5 | 10.1 | 51.7 |
| Raleigh, N. C. | 30.6 | 82.1 | 82.0 |
| Charlotte, N. C. | 8.5 | 14.6 | 13.1 |
| Atlanta, Ga. | 36.3 | 57.3 | 81.4 |
| Birmingham, Ala. | 42.2 | 66.9 | 84.7 |
| New Orleans, La. | 31.9 | 57.8 | 74.1 |

In 1940, 45% of dwelling units occupied by whites throughout the country were substandard, as against 85% for non-whites. Weaver, Housing in a Democracy, 244 ANNALS 94 (1946). An FHA study found 12.2% of the homes in "white" blocks in need of major repairs, 38.6% in "mixed" blocks, and 50.9% in "non-white" blocks. FHA, THE STRUCTURE AND GROWTH OF RESIDENTIAL NEIGHBORHOODS IN AMERICAN CITIES 71 (1939). An official study in Dallas in 1924–25 concluded that "a little less than 50 per cent of the houses presently occupied by Negroes are reasonably fit for good family life, while nearly 20 per cent of the houses ought actually to be destroyed." 6 PRESIDENT'S CONFERENCE ON HOME BUILDING AND HOME OWNERSHIP (NEGRO HOUSING) 126 (1932), hereafter cited as PRESIDENT'S CONFERENCE. In Richmond, many of the new houses opened for Negroes in 1931 were "built in open violation of the building code." Id. at 73. A sample inspection of one block in Harlem by the Urban League in recent years revealed a violation of the building code in every instance. MOON, THE HIGH COST OF PREJUDICE 37 (1947). The documentation could be multiplied; see generally, STERNER, op. cit. supra, at 166–209.

[5] See U. S. Dept. of Commerce, Consumer Use of Selected Goods and Services, by Income Classes, MARKET RESEARCH SERIES 5–12, Table 5 (1935–7); STERNER, THE NEGRO'S SHARE 186–92 (1943).

Furthermore, overcrowding is characteristic of Negro housing. Before the war, 24% of Negro homes in Philadelphia housed more than one person per room, as compared to 12% of the white homes; in Detroit the percentages were 26% Negro and 12% white; in Norfolk, 27% and 11%.[6] Certain areas of the Black Belt in Chicago have a population density of 90,000 per square mile, while neighboring white apartments have a density of 20,000.[7] Baltimore Negroes, 20% of the city's population are jammed into 2% of the homes.[8]

In addition, Negro homes are cut off from the rest of the community. Official and unofficial mapping of the location of Negro residences reveals clearly defined segregated areas.[9] An FHA study concluded that the intensity of segregation increases directly with the number and proportion of the non-white population.[10] In Chicago, for example, it has been estimated that over 90% of the Negroes live in areas predominantly Negro.[11] Segregation distinguishes Negro housing from slum housing in general.

[6] *Id.* at 193. In 1940, "While less than eight per cent of the dwelling units occupied by urban whites were overcrowded, almost 25 per cent of the units occupied by urban Negroes were overcrowded. Although the nonwhite urban population between 1930 and 1940 increased 7.7 per cent, as compared to 7.2 per cent for whites, the supply of housing available for non-whites increased 12.7 per cent as compared to 16.6 per cent for whites." Weaver, *supra* note 4, at 95.

[7] DRAKE AND CAYTON, BLACK METROPOLIS 204 (1945).

[8] TENENBAUM, WHY MEN HATE 335 (1947). If the national population density were the same as that of a certain Harlem block, the entire U. S. population would require only half the area of New York City. *Ibid.* In the Los Angeles "little Tokyo" area which housed 7,500 before the war, 30,000 Negroes lived during the war. NAT. URBAN LEAGUE, RACIAL PROBLEMS IN HOUSING, BULL. No. 2 at 16 (3d ed. 1945). In Detroit, while the average unit housed 3.8, "To house all Negro families at an average of 4.0 persons per occupied dwelling unit would require 53,000 dwellings, or an increase of 19,000 over the number of dwellings occupied by Negroes in 1940. However, 8,000 homes occupied by Negroes in 1940 were physically sub-standard. Since many of the remaining homes occupied by Negroes are aged frame structures, badly overcrowded, an equal number may be expected to become obsolete over the next ten years." DETROIT CITY PLANNING COMMISSION, THE PEOPLE OF DETROIT 19 (1946). On a countrywide average, the median number of rooms per dwelling unit in 1940 was 4.9 for white and 3.5 for Negro. Robinson, *Relationship Between Conditions of Dwellings and Rentals, by Race*, 22 J. LAND & PUB. UT. ECON. 296, 300 (1946).

[9] See WOOFTER, NEGRO PROBLEMS IN CITIES 40–67 (1928); FHA, *op. cit. supra* note 4, at 45, 47, 69–70.

[10] FHA, *op. cit. supra* note 4, at 68.

[11] DRAKE AND CAYTON, BLACK METROPOLIS 174 (1945).

Since the segregation of Negroes is "indiscriminate,"[12] all social and economic segments of the race are trapped behind ghetto walls. The Negro who strives to live by the social and ethical standards of the majority must reside, nonetheless, in the neighborhood of poverty, filth and vice. As a consequence of this and other forms of enforced segregation, full assimilation of prevailing cultural values is not achieved.[13] The distortion of social values in the Negro neighborhood is manifest in higher crime rates, and in relatively greater expense to the community in required police, fire and health services.[14] In Chicago's Black Belt, for example, the rate of juvenile delinquency is eight times, and the death rate almost twice that in the rest of the city.[15]

---

[12] PRESIDENT'S CONFERENCE 26; DRAKE AND CAYTON, BLACK METROPOLIS 206 (1945).

[13] Segregation is the "pathological feature of the Negro community." It "produces an artificial situation in which inferior standards of excellence and efficiency are set up. Since the Negro is not required to compete in the larger world and to assume its responsibilities and suffer its penalties, he does not have an opportunity to mature." FRAZIER, NEGRO YOUTH AT THE CROSSWAYS 290 (1940). Consciousness of discrimination affects Negroes' attitudes towards important social issues, so that even war is looked at from a race rather than from any broader point of view. *Id.* at xxii. ". . . Many young Negroes have never experienced the American dream. They have never known a society composed of respectable, law-abiding, industrious, self-reliant families whose ambition has been rewarded by good houses, electric refrigerators, and an improved social status." SUTHERLAND, *op. cit. supra* note 3, at 15. See also Cooper, *The Frustrations of Being a Member of a Minority Group*, 29 MENTAL HYGIENE 189 (1945). Additional insight is provided by a number of novels: PETRY, THE STREET (1946); WRIGHT, BLACK BOY (1945); MOON, DARKER BROTHER (1943); WRIGHT, NATIVE SON (1940).

[14] "At least three types of social pathology have been observed to have a high and inescapable correlation with the character of Negro residence areas. These are: (1) A high rate of delinquency, (2) A high rate of mortality, and (3) A distorted standard of living." PRESIDENT'S CONFERENCE 52. Rates of "dependency, family desertion and illegitimacy . . . [are] high in those areas that were characterized by physical decay and lack of organized community life." FRAZIER, THE NEGRO FAMILY IN THE UNITED STATES 373–4 (1939). A Chicago housing conference "listed among the 'ghetto conditions' high sickness and death rates; a heavy relief load during the Depression; inadequate recreational facilities; lack of building repairs; neglect of garbage disposal and street cleaning; overcrowded schools; high rates of crime and juvenile delinquency; and rough treatment by the police." DRAKE AND CAYTON, BLACK METROPOLIS 202 (1945). Segregation can also frustrate the operation of a city plan: "Badly in need of a medical center, express highways, parks and other deferred civic improvements, Detroit must wait indefinitely for them. The land they will occupy now houses hundreds of Negro families who can't be evicted because there's no place for them to go." Velie, *Housing: Detroit's Time Bomb*, Colliers, Nov. 23, 1946, p. 15, col. 1.

[15] GERTZ, AMERICAN GHETTOS 8 (1947). Such data generally show an improvement when decent housing is provided. See GRAY, HOUSING AND

Moreover, through preoccupation with segregation, potentially creative energy is wasted by both the majority and minority races. This process of waste is most dramatically illustrated in the race riot. Inferior, segregated housing is one of the primary causes of strained race relations which periodically culminate in race warfare.[16] . . .

Attempts to justify this pervasive pattern of segregation in terms of Negro traits follow three recurring types of argument, none of which seems tenable. Thus, it is often alleged that the Negro is an irresponsible tenant, notwithstanding the excellent rent-paying[25] and maintenance[26] records of Negroes who have been given the opportunity to live in modern housing developments. Also, on the assumption that each man gets the full housing value he can pay for, it is frequently argued that

---

CITIZENSHIP 125–6 (1946); JOHNSON, INTO THE MAIN STREAM 223 (1947); MOON, THE HIGH COST OF PREJUDICE 37 (1947). In a Cincinnati housing project for Negroes, built in the twenties with private funds, the rate of arrest was 1 per 215 inhabitants annually; the rate in the city generally was 1 per 15 for whites and 1 per 7½ for Negroes. PRESIDENT'S CONFERENCE 105.

[16] LEE, RACE RIOT 60, 89, 93, 119 (1943) analyzes the Detroit riots. Even in the absence of riots, violence is part of the race housing picture. *E.g.,* "From May 1944 through July 1946—a period of twenty-seven months—59 attacks were made on Negro residences in Chicago. About half were arson-bombings. There were 22 cases of stoning, three shootings, three house-wreckings, two stench-bombings. Three persons were killed and many were injured." GERTZ, AMERICAN GHETTOS 10 (1947). See also MYRDAL, AN AMERICAN DILEMMA 624 (1944); PRESIDENT'S CONFERENCE 46; Martin, *The Truth About Sojourner Truth,* 49 CRISIS 112 (1942); BROWN, WHY RACE RIOTS (1944).

"Anyone who has investigated the problem of group tensions has always ended up with the belief that nothing radical can be achieved until the walls of segregated, hemmed-in, ghetto living have been destroyed." TENENBAUM, WHY MEN HATE 333 (1947). There appears to be unanimity among writers on race relations that housing is the crucial issue. For typical statements, see DRAKE AND CAYTON, BLACK METROPOLIS 114 (1945); MOTON, WHAT THE NEGRO THINKS 117 (1929); THE NEGRO PROBLEM: HOUSING A BASIC FACTOR (reprint by American Council on Race Relations of war time columns by Barry Bishop in the Dallas Morning News).

[25] "For 155 projects in 59 cities having two or more FPHA-aided projects, at least one of which is occupied by Negro tenants, the following results are reported: Collection losses do not exceed one percent of the total operating incomes for a total of 142 of these projects, 72 of which are occupied by Negroes and 70 by white or other tenants. Five of the 13 projects showing rental losses in excess of one per cent are tenanted by Negroes and 8 are tenanted by whites or others. The collection loss records between the two racial groups do not differ more than one per cent in 51 of the 59 cities and the records are identical in 34." Weaver, *Race Restrictive Housing Covenants,* 20 J. LAND & PUB. UT. ECON. 183, 189 (1944).

[26] For data on Negro maintenance, see PRESIDENT'S CONFERENCE 249–57; JOHNSON, TO STEM THIS TIDE 61 (1943); Weaver, *supra* note 25, at 191 n. 24.

Negroes cannot obtain better housing because of inability to pay rather than because of discrimination.  But Negro families get less for their housing dollar than white families on the same income level;[27] and, indeed, the relative inferiority actually increases as the rental value increases.[28]  Finally, it is contended that segregation is inevitable because Negroes and whites cannot live together, but this assertion is refuted by a substantial body of evidence on interracial living in federal housing projects.[29]

[27] "The rent of Negro dwellings is a plain indication of the exploitation of Negro neighborhoods.  These rents are excessive whether they are measured by the kind of house and equipment, by the relation of rents paid by Negroes and those paid by white people for similar quarters, by the steady increase in rents, by the relation of rent to the value of the property, or by the proportion which rent forms of the family budget."  WOOFTER, NEGRO PROBLEMS IN CITIES 121 (1928) with supporting data on preceding pages.  "Negro residents of the Chicago 'Black Belt' pay as much per cubic foot per room as that paid by wealthy residents for equivalent space of the Lakeside Drive."  Cayton, *Negro Housing in Action*, Social Action, April 5, 1940, p. 18.  See also FRAZIER, THE NEGRO FAMILY IN THE UNITED STATES 458 (1939); MYRDAL, AN AMERICAN DILEMMA 625 (1944); PRESIDENT'S CONFERENCE 26, 58; and note 28 *infra*.

[28] For the following data based on the 1940 Housing Census, see Robinson, *supra* note 8, at 297:

*Percentage of Sub-standard Units in Each Rental Bracket*

| Monthly Rental Value (Est.) | Total | | | 16 Northern and Western Cities | | | 26 Southern Districts | | |
|---|---|---|---|---|---|---|---|---|---|
| | White | Non-White | Ratio (Non-White to White) | White | Non-White | Ratio (Non-White to White) | White | Non-White | Ratio (Non-White to White) |
| Under $5 | 90.2 | 97.6 | 1.1 | 76.5 | 95.1 | 1.2 | 94.2 | 97.8 | 1.0 |
| $5 –$9 | 87.7 | 94.7 | 1.1 | 87.3 | 93.9 | 1.1 | 88.0 | 94.9 | 1.1 |
| $10–$14 | 69.4 | 79.4 | 1.1 | 71.7 | 81.1 | 1.1 | 66.1 | 78.5 | 1.2 |
| $15–$19 | 42.1 | 55.3 | 1.3 | 43.1 | 56.9 | 1.3 | 39.1 | 53.1 | 1.3 |
| $20–$24 | 25.0 | 43.8 | 1.8 | 24.2 | 44.2 | 1.8 | 27.2 | 42.8 | 1.6 |
| $25–$29 | 14.4 | 31.0 | 2.2 | 13.6 | 30.0 | 2.2 | 16.9 | 34.8 | 2.1 |
| $30–$39 | 7.7 | 20.9 | 2.7 | 7.1 | 20.5 | 2.9 | 10.1 | 22.8 | 2.3 |
| $40–$49 | 4.0 | 13.5 | 3.4 | 3.7 | 13.6 | 3.7 | 5.3 | 13.2 | 2.5 |
| $50–$59 | 3.2 | 10.9 | 3.4 | 3.1 | 11.5 | 3.7 | 3.7 | 9.0 | 2.4 |
| $60–$74 | 2.8 | 9.1 | 3.3 | 2.8 | 9.6 | 3.4 | 2.7 | 7.8 | 2.9 |
| $75–$99 | 2.7 | 10.7 | 3.9 | 2.9 | 11.9 | 4.1 | 2.1 | 7.2 | 3.4 |
| $100 and over | 2.8 | 13.4 | 4.8 | 3.2 | 14.9 | 4.7 | 1.8 | 7.5 | 4.2 |

Total No. of Units Reporting:

| | | | |
|---|---|---|---|
| White: | 6,365,845 | 4,772,155 | 1,593,690 |
| Non-white | 850,063 | 427,648 | 422,415 |

[29] USHA, EXPERIENCE IN PUBLIC HOUSING PROJECTS JOINTLY OCCUPIED BY NEGRO, WHITE, AND OTHER TENANTS (1944 Annual Conference of Racial Relations Advisers); ABRAMS, RACE BIAS IN HOUSING 20-5 (1947).  For a

In 325 federal projects providing for occupancy by both Negro and white tenants, the policy ranged from setting aside specific areas for a particular race, to adherence to a principle of no segregation. Harmonious race relations were most thoroughly achieved in those projects which maintained a policy of fully integrating the races, the residents accepting the new neighborhood standard of no segregation in much the same way as they had previously accepted segregation in the communities from which they came.[30] The extent of the mutual respect engendered by interracial living was demonstrated during the Detroit race riots, when Negroes and whites who had lived together in the same section of the city showed no disposition to join in the general violence.[31]

An inquiry into this pattern of discrimination should be an integral part of any thorough attack on the legal problems involved in racial segregation. Without an awareness of the implications of each decision in relation to this sociological background, analysis by the courts of the doctrinal issues would appear to be barren indeed.

## Note

1. A further argument for segregation is that the entrance of Negroes into former non-Negro neighborhoods depresses property values. See *e.g.*, May, *The Valuation of Residential Real Estate* (1942); McMichael, *Real Estate Subdivisions* (1949). Many writers feel that long run effects do not support this contention and that the depression of property values occurs largely because of fear and panic produced by what thus momentarily becomes a self-fulfilling prophecy. They believe that this could be averted if real estate interests were to take a more

report of similar experiences in employment see WEAVER, NEGRO LABOR cc. XI, XII (1946).

[30] "Where Negroes are integrated with whites into self-contained communities without segregation, reach daily contact with their co-tenants, are given the same privileges and share the same responsibilities, initial latent tensions tend to subside, distinctions become reconciled, cooperation ensues and an environment is created in which interracial harmony will be effected." ABRAMS, *op. cit supra* note 29, at 22. For a case example of how a policy of race integration succeeded see Hovde, *Negro Housing in Pittsburgh*, 16 OPPORTUNITY 356 (1938).

The meaningfulness of this body of evidence has been discounted recently in a contrasting of public and private projects: "Moreover, in the former case, the tenant, because of his economic condition, has little or no freedom of choice respecting living accommodations. In the latter case, the type of desirable tenant has great freedom of choice." Affidavit of Gove, Vice-President of Metropolitan Life Insurance Co., July 9, 1947. But see CIV. RTS. REP. 70 for a contrary view

[31] "No Negroes and whites who lived close together as neighbors showed any tendency to fight each other." LEE, RACE RIOT 17 (1943).

realistic view and plan to avoid a panic sale and exodus. See Stern, *Long Range Effect of Colored Occupancy,* The Review of the Society of Residential Appraisers 5 (1946); Weaver, *The Negro Ghetto,* ch. 15 (1948); Beehler, *Colored Occupancy Raises Values,* The Review of the Society of Residential Appraisers 3 (1945); Abrams, *The New "Gresham's Law of Neighborhood"—Fact or Fiction,* 19 Appraisal Journal 324 (1951). Abrams contends that appraisers in assigning a value to homogeneity roam beyond their field of competence and make judgments about American cultural values that require the training and experience of social scientists. See *infra* for material indicating increase of large private investment in interracial housing, and for other material showing favorable experience with heterogeneous housing and neighborhoods.

For data showing that Negroes if not stopped by discrimination would be able to afford better housing, see also Felt, *An Untapped Housing Market* (National Urban League, 1948); on the other hand for use of discriminatory rentals as one of the resistances to "invasion," see Hatt, *The Relation of Ecological Location to Status, Position, and Housing of Ethnic Minorities,* 10 Amer. Sociological Rev. 481 (1945).

2. The following material supplements some of the data and sources of the above extract:

(a) Kane, *The Nonwhite Housing Market,* 16 Insured Mortgage Portfolio, No. 2, p. 23 (FHA, 1952):

"The Census shows that in April 1950 there were 15,482,000 nonwhite persons in the United States. Of these, 14,894,000 or 96.2 percent (9.9 percent of the entire population) were Negroes.[1] Between 1940 and 1950 the nonwhite population increased 15.1 percent, while the entire population increased 14.5 percent.

"In that decade, however, a remarkable change took place in the relative proportions of the Negro population in various sections of the country. Negroes in large numbers migrated from the South to States in which war industries provided greater job opportunities, so that, while the white population increased 17 percent in the 16 States and the District of Columbia in the southern region, the nonwhite population increased only 3 percent, and in 8 of these States—Alabama, Arkansas, Georgia, Kentucky, Mississippi, Oklahoma, Texas, and West Virginia—the nonwhite population declined during the 1940's. On the other hand, the nonwhite population of eight major industrial States —California, Illinois, Michigan, Missouri, New Jersey, New York, Ohio, and Pennsylvania—increased by over a million and a half, or 55 percent, bringing their nonwhite population from 4.8 percent of their total population in 1940 to 6.4 percent in 1950.

"In California and Michigan, the proportion of nonwhites more than doubled during the 1940's. California gained 106 percent, compared with a gain of 51 percent in the white population; in Michigan

---

[1] The remaining 3.8 percent of all nonwhites were mostly American Indians, Japanese, Chinese, and Filipinos. Persons of Mexican or Puerto Rican birth or ancestry who were not of Indian, Negro, or other nonwhite race, were enumerated as white.

**1002**

the nonwhite population increased 109 percent, while the white population increased 18 percent. . . .

[The discussion of employment is reprinted in Section C, *infra*.]

"Between 1940 and 1950 the number of nonwhite households in the Nation increased by 14.4 percent. In the latter year 86 percent of all nonwhite married couples had their own households (a decrease from the 89 percent shown by the 1940 Census), compared with 94 percent of all married couples, both white and nonwhite. The relative scarcity of housing for nonwhite families was probably influential in maintaining the nonwhite population per household (3.94 persons in 1950 and 4.02 persons in 1940) well above the comparable figures for the white population (3.37 persons in 1950 and 3.64 persons in 1940).

"Although nonwhites made up over 10 percent of our population at the time of the 1950 Census, they occupied a somewhat smaller proportion—8.6 percent— of all occupied dwelling units. Of all nonwhite-occupied units, 34 percent were owner-occupied, compared with 23 percent in 1940. Owner-occupancy among Negroes increased during the decade at a higher rate than for whites—66 percent against 54 percent.

"The median number of persons in nonwhite-occupied dwellings in 1950 was 3.3, slightly more than the median of 3.1 for all occupied units. The median number of white occupants per dwelling unit declined 0.2 persons from 1940, while the median for nonwhite-occupied units remained the same as in 1940. The number of white-occupied dwellings increased 23 percent in the decade, but the nonwhite-occupied dwellings increased only 10 percent.

"Over a fifth of all nonwhite-occupied dwelling units were reported as crowded—that is, having more than 1.5 persons per room. This is a decrease from 1940, when 23.4 percent of nonwhite-occupied dwellings were crowded. Fewer dwellings occupied by nonwhite owners were crowded in 1950 than in 1940—10.7 percent as against 18 percent—but the proportion of crowded nonwhite renter-occupied units remained unchanged—25 percent.

"The condition of nonfarm dwelling units in 1950 is indicated in the following table:

| | All occupied dwelling units (percent) | Nonwhite occupied dwelling units (percent) |
|---|---|---|
| **Not dilapidated:** | | |
| With private toilet and bath and hot running water | 71.7 | 33.2 |
| With private toilet and bath and only cold water | 3.3 | 4.7 |
| With running water, lacking private toilet or bath | 11.4 | 18.1 |
| No running water | 6.5 | 17.3 |
| **Dilapidated:** | | |
| With private toilet and bath, and hot running water | 1.6 | 3.9 |
| Lacking hot water, private toilet, or private bath | 5.4 | 22.7 |

Source: Bureau of the Census, *1950 Census of Housing, Preliminary Reports,* "Housing Characteristics of the United States: April 1, 1950": Series HC–5, No. 1.

"The median contract rent paid by nonwhite occupants of nonfarm units in 1950 was $25: 2½ times the 1940 median of $10, but considerably less than the median of $35 for all renter-occupied nonfarm units. Less than 11 percent of all nonwhite renters paid $50 or more in 1950.

"The average value of nonwhite-owner-occupied nonfarm dwellings in 1950 was $5,500, having risen from $2,600 in 1940. The average value of all owner-occupied nonfarm dwellings rose from $7,200 in 1940 to $10,800 in 1950. While the over-all rate of increase was not as great as for nonwhite-owned units, the average value remained much larger. Only a little more than 7 percent of the nonwhite owners reported values of $10,000 or more, compared with 31 percent of white and nonwhite owners combined, and over a third of all nonwhite-owned homes were valued at less than $2,000.

"Altogether, 38 percent of the nonfarm dwellings occupied by nonwhite owners were mortgaged, compared with 44 percent of all owner-occupied dwellings. For nonwhite owners, this ratio of mortgaged units increased by 8 percentage points between 1940 and 1950, while the proportion of all owner-occupied dwellings with mortgages decreased 1.7 percentage points in the same period.

*"Summary*

"In summary, a number of facts are apparent from the preliminary census data on nonwhite population and housing.

"1. For the country as a whole, there has been a substantial increase of home ownership among nonwhite families since 1940.

"2. A larger proportion of mortgaged homes occupied by nonwhite owners indicates a somewhat greater availability of mortgage credit for nonwhite purchasers.

"3. There has been a notable migration of nonwhites from farms to cities, and from predominantly rural sections of the country to urban districts.

"4. The educational level of the nonwhite population is rising, and members of this group are steadily advancing to more responsible and better paid occupations and to greater security in their jobs. These conditions result in more pressing demands for better housing.

"5. The provision of housing available to nonwhite families has not kept pace with the growth of the nonwhite population. Overcrowding and dilapidation still characterize a disproportionate share of nonwhite-occupied homes.

"6. At the present time the housing demand of the nonwhite population is still for the most part a demand for low-cost and low-rent homes. Changing sociological characteristics of the group, however—among others, higher education, better employment opportunities, urbanization —affect the extent and nature of their housing demand."[2]

(b) A recent ecological study of segregation in 187 American cities indicates the following tendencies: "Cities with highest scores [greatest amount of segregation] tend to be resort cities in Florida, new industrial cities of the South, borderline cities between North and South, and industrial cities of the Great Lakes area. Low segregation scores are shown by small cities of New England, cities of the Mountain and Pacific regions and some residential suburbs. . . . Large cities reflect more segregation than small cities though the range is greater in small cities. . . . Segregation of nonwhites is least in cities with relatively few nonwhites. It increases with the proportion of nonwhite dwellings up to about 5 per cent, but decreases beyond that point." Cowgill and Cowgill, *An Index of Segregation Based on Block Statistics,* 16 Am. Soc. Rev. 825 (1951). The article criticizes earlier studies based on census tracts.

(c) Cost of Slums: Rumney, *The Social Cost of Slums,* 7 J. of Social Issues, Nos. 1 and 2, pp. 69, 78–9 (1951); National Community Relations Advisory Council, *Equality of Opportunity in Housing,* pp. 7–8 (1952); Straus, *Two-Thirds of a Nation,* pp. 42–4 (1952).

(d) Health Problems: Davie, *Negroes in American Society,* pp. 235–42 (1949); Taylor, *Health Problems and Needs of Negro Children,* 19 J. of Negro Ed. 278–283 (1950). See also Yankauer, *The Relationship of Fetal and Infant Mortality to Residential Segregation: An Inquiry into Social Epidemiology,* 15 Am. Soc. Rev. 644 (1950); Metropolitan Life Insurance Co., *Maternal and Infant Mortality by Color,* 1936–8, 1946–8 (Statistical Bulletin 1950); Tandy, *The Health Situation of Negro Mothers and Babies in the United States* (U. S. Dept. of Labor, Children's Bureau, 1940).

---

[2] [Ed. note: Part of this material is also summarized in Housing and Home Finance Agency, *The 1950 Housing Situation in Charts* (1951). The 1950 Census of Population, Advance Reports Series, PC–14, No. 1, reports that the number of nonwhites in central cities increased five times as much as that of whites. The white increase in suburban sections was greater than that for nonwhites. See also Crosby, *In These Ten Cities* (Public Affairs Committee, 1951).]

(e) Psychological effects of poor housing: Demerath, *Housing of Psyche (Social-Psychological Corollaries of Housing)*, 35 Mental Hygiene 410–17 (1951); Chapin, *Some Housing Factors Related to Mental Hygiene*, 7 J. of Social Issues, Nos. 1 and 2, p. 164 (1951) (effect of overcrowding on mental health).

(f) Crime Rates: Spero, *Negro Crime* (1940); Diggs, *Some Problems and Needs of Negro Children as Revealed by Comparative Delinquency and Crime Statistics*, 19 J. of Negro Ed. 290, 293 (1950); 1951 Statistical Abstract, pp. 140–3 (comparing numbers of white and Negro admissions to state and federal prisons and reformatories); U. S. Federal Security Agency, Children's Bureau, *Juvenile Court Statistics 1948* (1949).


# BAUER—SOCIAL QUESTIONS IN HOUSING AND COMMUNITY PLANNING

7 Jo. of Social Issues 21–3 (1951)

Race relations is a major issue in America, and the question of racial discrimination and segregation is one of the most urgent and controversial aspects of housing and planning policy. From the viewpoint of those who are concerned with the process of housing and civic development, however, this is not an isolated issue, related wholly to racial prejudice: it is part of a general tendency to separate different kinds of people and different functions, with resulting standardization of land use over wide areas.

## The Overall Trend Toward Segregation

In the more or less feudal pattern of the old South, extreme racial discrimination did not result in wholesale geographic segregation. Quite the contrary. And today there are many northern cities where "white" or "Negro" districts are relatively larger and more concentrated, than in some Southern cities. Clearly, other factors than race prejudice *per se* must have some influence.

One of these influences is undoubtedly the strong trend toward economic segregation, which has been operating in most modern cities for the past century. Zoning and building regulations, large-scale enterprise, and restrictive covenants tend to standardize dwelling types, price and rent levels, and the social-economic class of the residents, over wide areas. Within this framework, it is very easy for the private covenant to become a major instrument for racial segregation as well, and for the large developer or landlord to establish with complete efficiency any occupancy restrictions he likes. But it should be noted that the trend toward class separation on a geographic basis has

**1006**

been fairly universal, not only in America but also in England with no race problem, and even in the Scandinavian countries with much weaker class distinctions than here. It was reinforced by the upper-middle-class flight to the suburbs, which tends to result in stratification not only by districts but by whole communities and towns, and on the other hand by public housing construction in central districts, limited to "low income families." Public and private projects restricted to "veterans" are a further example.

Moreover, the geographic standardization of dwelling types also promotes the segregation of families by size, type and age-group. Families with small children gravitate toward individual homes where economically feasible, while adult households who prefer apartments must go elsewhere to developments where children are prohibited.

The functional segregation of land use that has been the primary goal of most official city plans should also be mentioned here: the trend toward vast areas that are wholly residential, wholly commercial, or wholly industrial, to the extent that "nonconforming uses" could be weeded out.

In this brief summary the picture has undoubtedly been cartooned. But the general past trend, however imperfectly realized, toward Everyone in His Place, in a standardized one-class, one-age-group, and one-color district, devoted wholly to residence, can hardly be disputed.

This was not, however, the result of any conscious overall plan or public decision to encourage maximum social segregation. It came about more or less by accident, as a side result of forces and policies employed for quite different and often distinctly progressive or idealistic ends, and because we were reluctant to assume any conscious collective responsibility whatsoever for the social pattern. In housing reform and city planning, we have been primarily concerned with plumbing and playgrounds, rent levels and rational building methods, and it was assumed that human relations would take care of themselves on the basis of personal choice. What we failed to recognize was that the powerful tools employed for civic development and home production *also* predetermine social structure to such an extent that there is little room left for free personal choice or flexible adjustment. The big social decisions are all made in advance, inherent in the planning and building process. And if these decisions are not made responsibly and democratically, then they are made irresponsibly by the accidents of technology, the myths of property interest, or the blindness and prejudice of a reactionary minority.

*The Forces Operating Against Segregation*

The fact that racial segregation is now inevitably a matter of public decision, one way or the other, is coming to be recognized. For an independent landlord or builder to say whom he will or will not accept in a building is one thing. But if he requires public finance or subsidy, and court enforcement of his racial policy on a neighborhood scale, then some responsibility also devolves upon government. Once the issue is clearly posed as a matter of conscious public policy, a policy that even has profound international implications, a great many people who took segregation for granted begin to question it. Throughout the North today, the color line is being seriously challenged, due to the new hope and political prowess of the Negroes and to the pricks of democratic conscience. The Supreme Court has outlawed the enforcement of race restrictive covenants in the courts. And even in the South, where the principle of segregation is still firmly established, in law as well as in custom, the potential effect of Supreme Court decisions and national policy is by no means disregarded.

Class segregation is somewhat less officially or dramatically questioned, but there is a growing feeling that a large area occupied wholly by people of identical social-economic status is alien both to our traditions and to our concept of social progress. The need for a greater mixture of age-groups and family types, for reasons of convenience and social health, is increasingly recognized. The zoners' ideal of a pure unsullied "residential area" is being replaced by the notion that shops and community facilities should be located for maximum convenience, and that perhaps even some non-nuisance factories might be introduced. And finally, the desire to relieve the visual as well as social monotony of over-standardized land-use is a factor of some consequence all along the line.

Once we become aware of the issues and alternatives, it is clear that our new housing and planning tools do not *inherently* produce social segregation. Indeed, they can be used to produce the opposite result quite as effectively. Even zoning laws can be drawn up and administered to encourage or insure diversity rather than uniformity. And a housing policy geared to reach all income groups is the primary requirement for the production of "balanced" communities, if that is what we want. There is no reason why public, private and cooperative projects of moderate scale and varied dwelling types cannot be combined in large development or redevelopment schemes. Also, a large project in single ownership can establish a pattern of *non*discrimination just as effectively as it can enforce a color line. A number of public housing authorities in the North have demonstrated that "mixed" living can be entirely successful, and a few private developments are now taking the same step.[1]

## ABRAMS—THE SEGREGATION THREAT IN HOUSING

Ch. XII in Straus, *Two-Thirds of a Nation,* published by Alfred A. Knopf, Inc., copyright by Nathan Straus, 1952, pp. 226–8

Public housing projects in New York City, Philadelphia, New Haven, Los Angeles, Chicago, Pittsburgh, and Seattle—to name some of the cities—have proved that whites and blacks can get along just as well as whites and whites or blacks and blacks. These mixed housing projects have had little or no attention in newspapers and magazines. For some years the local housing authorities were reluctant to publicize the success of their ventures, possibly through fear of what southern Congressmen would say about this use of a Federal subsidy. Yet such projects may mark the most important gain in the struggle for racial equality since the Civil War.

These mixed housing projects have not been uniform in pattern. Some housing authorities have deliberately and timidly assigned Negroes and whites to separate buildings in the same project. Others admitted only a few token families of Negroes. Many, however, have literally ignored the color line, with the result that Negroes comprise a substantial percentage of the tenants.

The most successful projects have been those where the Negro tenants were part of an interracial community and were sufficiently represented so they could enjoy the self-security that an ostracized race requires for its comfort in a new environment. In these projects initial tensions have disappeared, differences have been adjusted, a peaceful atmosphere has been created.

In contrast, there has been much less accomplished in projects where the minority receives only token representation or where the races have been separated by buildings or some other line of demarcation. There is no way to separate without separating. Any method used tends to emphasize the distinctions and reinforce the old prejudices. Tenants in these projects cling to the attitudes common in private developments. White and Negro children may attend the same public school, even go to the same summer camp—but when they are back on segregated ground the white children do not play with Negro youngsters.

The picture is just the opposite in projects that are completely

---

[1] [Ed. note: See also *Unsegregated Housing: A National Concern,* 5 American Council on Race Relations, Report No. 2 (1950).]

mixed. Children play together with no consciousness of color. Tenant associations hold business meetings and give parties. Neighbors visit back and forth. *If only two or three such projects had proved successful, the story would have been significant news. The fact is that every properly administered project has succeeded.*

"There has been no tendency for neighborhood people to move away because of the projects," said General Thomas F. Farrell, chairman of the New York City Housing Authority. "The projects are well built and well maintained. Business in the neighborhood improves. With rare exceptions the tenants are good neighbors."[1] The impressive number of similar experiences shows that inter-racial living is now more than an experiment. It is a signal demonstration of a workable way of life, a possible key to America's Number One problem.

The feeling of white superiority seems to subside and then disappear when people live together as neighbors and share the common responsibilities for its success. Project managers have overcome the initial objection of some of the white tenants by explaining the policies of the authority and there have been very few instances of tenants moving out even where comparable dwellings in other projects were offered them. The common use of recreational facilities has been an important factor in creating the environment for an accord. The Negroes are members of the tenant associations, participate in the cultural programs, often lead in the community activities.

There have been problems. Not all have responded as have some. But the problems have not been a fraction of what was predicted nor have they been serious. *The evils of segregation do not arise from either whites or Negroes. They come from segregation. When that barrier is removed, the whites and Negroes get along without trouble.*

## Note

1. For psychological studies in accord see Deutsch and Collins, *Interracial Housing: A Psychological Evaluation of a Social Experiment* (1951). See also Federal Public Housing Authority, *Experience in Public Housing Projects Jointly Occupied by Negroes, Whites and Other Tenants* (1949); Weaver, *Negro Ghetto*, pp. 168–9, 186–8, 189–91 (1948); National Community Relations Advisory Council, *Equality of Opportunity in Housing* (1952); Rutledge, *Integration of Racial Minor-*

---

[1] Thomas F. Farrell: "Object Lesson in Race Relations," *The New York Times Magazine*, February 12, 1950, p. 37. See also Robert P. Weaver: *The Negro Ghetto* (New York: Harcourt, Brace and Company; 1948) and Charles Abrams: *Race Bias in Housing* (New York: American Civil Liberties Union; 1946).

*ities in Public Housing Projects* (Public Housing Administration, 1951).

2. With the results of planned integration compare situations in which Negroes moving into a "restricted" neighborhood have encountered violence, riots, and bombings. Several such outbreaks occurred in Chicago in 1946 and 1947. In 1951 a mob of 5,000 persons rioted to prevent a young Negro veteran and his family from moving into a rented apartment in Cicero, a suburb of Chicago. See Chapter I, *supra*. For accounts of recent apartment-house and project bombings in Miami, Florida, see N. Y. Times Sep. 23 and December 3, 1951. For reports of a bomb-blast injuring two homes in Los Angeles see N. Y. Times, March 17, 1952. Recently Kansas City officials reported that a "home made" bomb had been placed near a Negro home in an otherwise all-white neighborhood. N. Y. Times, May 22, 1952.

Another indication of community hostility appeared when Southwood, California residents voted 174–28 to reject former Chinese Nationalist Intelligence Officer, Shing Sheng, and his family as possible neighbors. A local minister who supported the Shengs' application reported that Southwood parents withdrew their children from his Sunday School. See N. Y. Times, Feb. 17 and 25, 1952.

For further description of these and other incidents of violence see American Jewish Congress and National Association for the Advancement of Colored People, *Civil Rights in the United States in 1951*, pp. 80–3 (1952); National Community Relations Advisory Council, *supra*, pp. 13–5. See also Jones, *Invasion and Racial Attitudes, A Study of Housing in a Border City*, 27 Social Forces 285 (1949). For an analysis of interracial violence see Lee and Humphrey, *Race Riot* (1943). For a comprehensive socio-legal survey see Note, *Racial Violence and Civil Rights Law Enforcement*, 18 U. of Chi. L. Rev. 769 (1951).

3. Prognostication and evaluation of the effect of the Constitution, court decisions and legislation in the field of discrimination may be aided by an understanding of the structure, behavior and thinking patterns of minority and dominant groups, the underlying causes of discrimination and prejudice, and factors in the society favoring or opposing a change toward integration. The following text presents, in outline, a theory which seeks to synthesize Myrdal's "vicious circle" formulation, see *An American Dilemma*, Vol. 1, pp. 75–8 (1944), and other sociological, psychological and economic (largely Marxist) interpretations of dominant-minority relations in the United States. It is presented here to illustrate the range of probable relevances.

## MARDEN—MINORITIES IN AMERICAN SOCIETY

Published by American Book Company, copyright 1952, pp. 449–51

The two outstanding generalizations about dominant-minority relations in the United States have been (1) the imposition of minority status upon all the "different peoples" coming under the jurisdiction of the nation; and (2) the instability of the dominant-minority patterns thus formed, with the net trend of change in the direction of removing the disabilities of minority status from each minority. An interpretation of the first of these generalizations can be made only by considering a number of circumstances and social forces operating in conjunction. Since ethnocentrism is a universal phenomenon it engenders some degree of opposition wherever two peoples meet. The historical circumstances which brought so many other peoples in contact with "established" Americans presented the maximum of opportunity for the development of dominant-minority structures. The success of dominant Americans in imposing minority status upon all the others is in part due to their superior power. The desire to establish and maintain dominance has been powerfully motivated by the dynamics of the free enterprise system, especially in its development to the first World War. From the viewpoint of entrepreneurs, the exploitation of the possibilities for economic profit in the New World encouraged welcoming new labor willing to perform unskilled tasks. Their subsequent minority status contributed to keeping their wages lower directly by discrimination and indirectly by retarding unionization. Dominant status laborers likewise in an unstable employment economy were motivated to practice discrimination to protect their tenuous economic status. Indirectly, the individual economic insecurity of many elements in the American economy coupled with the strong urge to rise in socioeconomic status created a large volume of frustration. Discrimination against minorities served to attenuate these frustrations both by providing the ego satisfaction of having someone else to look down on and by proving an outlet for the aggressive tendencies which frustration generates by projecting it upon minorities. This diversion of frustration of the dominant status worker through discrimination also served the economic interest of the entrepreneurial elements. The dynamics of private enterprise are not in all ways and at all times in the same direction. Changing conditions create situations in which "it pays" for both employer and worker to relax their discriminatory practices. In the final analysis, the relation between capitalism and minority discrimination is not inexorable.

Once established, dominant-minority patterns tend to continue in part simply because they are traditional, supported by the mores of the dominant community. This tendency to conform is strengthened by conditioning dominant status children to accept them as "habitual," and by applying the penalties of nonconformism upon the would-be nonconformists.

Dominant-minority relations have never been completely frozen. The net trend toward the breakdown of minority status derives primarily from the dynamics of political democracy, from the beliefs in the American Creed and their expression through appropriate institutions. The institutions of democratic citizenship press persistently toward the equal participation of all and the equal protection of all. The process of democratic government likewise presses continuously for its fuller development, and in so doing affords increasing opportunity for minorities to help themselves. Democratic education tends to break down the dominant stereotype of the minority, an essential rationale for the discriminatory process. Free education for minorities destroys the illusion of their categorical inferiority. Democratic education of the dominant elements further undermines the racist ideology, as does the experience of association with minority students on a relatively equal footing. The course which dominant-minority relations has followed in the United States may be in considerable measure viewed as a conflict between the dynamics of capitalism and those of democracy. The conflict is not, however, "one to the death." However, ascendancy of the political over the economic interest is essential if the move toward "a more perfect union" between minorities and the dominants is to continue. Either the dynamics of democracy must control the exploitative tendencies of the free enterprise system or they must create conditions in which discrimination "does not pay off" in economic terms. The current trends suggest that the democratic dynamics possess this ascendancy.

## Note

For a bibliography of social science studies of the minorities problem, see Note at end of this Chapter.

## 2. Discrimination by Private Realtors and Landlords

### SHELLEY v. KRAEMER

Supreme Court of the United States, 1948
334 U. S. 1, 92 L. Ed. 1161, 68 S. Ct. 836

MR. CHIEF JUSTICE VINSON delivered the opinion of the Court. These cases present for our consideration questions relating to the validity of court enforcement of private agreements, generally described as restrictive covenants, which have as their purpose the exclusion of persons of designated race or color from the ownership or occupancy of real property. Basic constitutional issues of obvious importance have been raised.

The first of these cases comes to this Court on certiorari to the Supreme Court of Missouri. On February 16, 1911, thirty out of a total of thirty-nine owners of property fronting both sides of Labadie Avenue between Taylor Avenue and Cora Avenue in the city of St. Louis, signed an agreement, which was subsequently recorded, providing in part:

> " . . . the said property is hereby restricted to the use and occupancy for the term of Fifty (50) years from this date, so that it shall be a condition all the time and whether recited and referred to as [sic] not in subsequent conveyances and shall attach to the land as a condition precedent to the sale of the same, that hereafter no part of said property or any portion thereof shall be, for said term of Fifty-years, occupied by any person not of the Caucasian race, it being intended hereby to restrict the use of said property for said period of time against the occupancy as owners or tenants of any portion of said property for resident or other purpose by people of the Negro or Mongolian Race."

The entire district described in the agreement included fifty-seven parcels of land. The thirty owners who signed the agreement held title to forty-seven parcels, including the particular parcel involved in this case. At the time the agreement was signed, five of the parcels in the district were owned by Negroes. One of those had been occupied by Negro families since 1882, nearly thirty years before the restrictive agreement was executed. The trial court found that owners of seven out of nine homes on the south side of Labadie Avenue, within the restricted district and "in the immediate vicinity" of the premises in question, had failed to sign the restrictive agreement in 1911. At the time this action was brought, four of the premises were occupied by Negroes, and had been so occupied for periods ranging from twenty-three to sixty-three years. A fifth parcel had been occupied by Negroes until a year before this suit was instituted.

On August 11, 1945, pursuant to a contract of sale, petitioners Shelley, who are Negroes, for valuable consideration received from one Fitzgerald a warranty deed to the parcel in question. The trial court found that petitioners had no actual knowledge of the restrictive agreement at the time of purchase.

On October 9, 1945, respondents, as owners of other property subject to the terms of the restrictive covenant, brought suit in the Circuit Court of the city of St. Louis praying that petitioners Shelley be restrained from taking possession of the property and that judgment be entered divesting title out of petitioners Shelley and revesting title in the immediate grantor or in such other person as the court should direct. The trial court denied the requested relief on the ground that the restrictive agreement, upon which respondents based their action, had never become final and complete because it was the intention of the parties to that agreement that it was not to become effective until signed by all property owners in the district, and signatures of all the owners had never been obtained.

The Supreme Court of Missouri sitting *en banc* reversed and directed the trial court to grant the relief for which respondents had prayed. That court held the agreement effective and concluded that enforcement of its provisions violated no rights guaranteed to petitioners by the Federal Constitution.[2] At the time the court rendered its decision, petitioners were occupying the property in question.

The second of the cases under consideration comes to this Court from the Supreme Court of Michigan. The circumstances presented do not differ materially from the Missouri case. . . .[3]

Petitioners have placed primary reliance on their contentions, first raised in the state courts, that judicial enforcement of the restrictive agreements in these cases has violated rights guaranteed to petitioners by the Fourteenth Amendment of the Federal Constitution and Acts of Congress passed pursuant to that Amendment. Specifically, petitioners urge that they have been denied the equal protection of the laws, deprived of property without due process of law, and have been denied privileges and immunities of citizens of the United States. We pass to a consideration of those issues.

## I.

Whether the equal protection clause of the Fourteenth Amendment inhibits judicial enforcement by state courts of restrictive covenants based on race or color is a question which this Court has not heretofore been called upon to consider. Only two cases have been decided by this Court which in any way have involved the enforcement of such agreements. The first of these was the case of *Corrigan* v. *Buckley*, 271 U. S. 323 (1926). There, suit was brought in the courts of the District of Columbia to enjoin a threatened violation of certain restrictive covenants relating to lands situated in the city of Washington. Relief was

---

[2] *Kraemer v. Shelley*, 355 Mo. 814, 198 S.W.2d 679 (1946).
[3] *Sipes v. McGhee*, 316 Mich. 614, 25 N.W.2d 638 (1947).

granted, and the case was brought here on appeal. It is apparent that that case, which had originated in the federal courts and involved the enforcement of covenants on land located in the District of Columbia, could present no issues under the Fourteenth Amendment; for that Amendment by its terms applies only to the States. Nor was the question of the validity of court enforcement of the restrictive covenants under the Fifth Amendment properly before the Court, as the opinion of this Court specifically recognizes.[5] The only constitutional issue which the appellants had raised in the lower courts, and hence the only constitutional issue before this Court on appeal, was the validity of the covenant agreements as such. This Court concluded that since the inhibitions of the constitutional provisions invoked apply only to governmental action, as contrasted to action of private individuals, there was no showing that the covenants, which were simply agreements between private property owners, were invalid. Accordingly, the appeal was dismissed for want of a substantial question. Nothing in the opinion of this Court, therefore, may properly be regarded as an adjudication on the merits of the constitutional issues presented by these cases, which raise the question of the validity, not of the private agreements as such, but of the judicial enforcement of those agreements.

The second of the cases involving racial restrictive covenants was *Hansberry v. Lee*, 311 U. S. 32 (1940). In that case, petitioners, white property owners, were enjoined by the state courts from violating the terms of a restrictive agreement. The state Supreme Court had held petitioners bound by an earlier judicial determination, in litigation in which petitioners were not parties, upholding the validity of the restrictive agreement, although, in fact, the agreement had not been signed by the number of owners necessary to make it effective under state law. This Court reversed the judgment of the state Supreme Court upon the ground that petitioners had been denied due process of law in being held estopped to challenge the validity of the agreement on the theory, accepted by the state court, that the earlier litigation, in which petitioners did not participate, was in the nature of a class suit. In arriving at its result, this Court did not reach the issues presented by the cases now under consideration.

It is well, at the outset, to scrutinize the terms of the restrictive agreements involved in these cases. In the Missouri case, the covenant declares that no part of the affected property shall be "occupied by any person not of the Caucasion race, it being

---

[5] *Corrigan v. Buckley*, 271 U.S. 323, 330–331 (1926).

intended hereby to restrict the use of said property . . . against the occupancy as owners or tenants of any portion of said property for resident or other purpose by people of the Negro or Mongolian Race." Not only does the restriction seek to proscribe use and occupancy of the affected properties by members of the excluded class, but as construed by the Missouri courts, the agreement requires that title of any person who uses his property in violation of the restriction shall be divested. The restriction of the covenant in the Michigan case seeks to bar occupancy by persons of the excluded class. It provides that "This property shall not be used or occupied by any person or persons except those of the Caucasian race."

It should be observed that these covenants do not seek to proscribe any particular use of the affected properties. Use of the properties for residential occupancy, as such, is not forbidden. The restrictions of these agreements, rather, are directed toward a designated class of persons and seek to determine who may and who may not own or make use of the properties for residential purposes. The excluded class is defined wholly in terms of race or color; "simply that and nothing more."[6]

It cannot be doubted that among the civil rights intended to be protected from discriminatory state action by the Fourteenth Amendment are the rights to acquire, enjoy, own and dispose of property. Equality in the enjoyment of property rights was regarded by the framers of that Amendment as an essential pre-condition to the realization of other basic civil rights and liberties which the Amendment was intended to guarantee.[7] Thus, § 1978 of the Revised Statutes, derived from § 1 of the Civil Rights Act of 1866 which was enacted by Congress while the Fourteenth Amendment was also under consideration, provides:

> "All citizens of the United States shall have the same right, in every State and Territory, as is enjoyed by white citizens thereof to inherit, purchase, lease, sell, hold, and convey real and personal property."[9]

This Court has given specific recognition to the same principle. *Buchanan* v. *Warley*, 245 U. S. 60 (1917).

It is likewise clear that restrictions on the right of occupancy of the sort sought to be created by the private agreements in

---

[6] *Buchanan* v. *Warley*, 245 U.S. 60, 73 (1917).

[7] *Slaughter-House Cases*, 16 Wall. 36, 70, 81 (1873). See Flack, The Adoption of the Fourteenth Amendment.

[9] 14 Stat. 27, 8 U.S.C. § 42. [The provision was reenacted in § 18 of the Act of May 31, 1870, subsequent to the adoption of the Fourteenth Amendment, 16 Stat. 144.]

these cases could not be squared with the requirements of the Fourteenth Amendment if imposed by state statute or local ordinance. We do not understand respondents to urge the contrary. In the case of *Buchanan* v. *Warley, supra,* a unanimous Court declared unconstitutional the provisions of a city ordinance which denied to colored persons the right to occupy houses in blocks in which the greater number of houses were occupied by white persons, and imposed similar restrictions on white persons with respect to blocks in which the greater number of houses were occupied by colored persons. During the course of the opinion in that case, this Court stated: "The Fourteenth Amendment and these statutes enacted in furtherance of its purpose operate to qualify and entitle a colored man to acquire property without state legislation discriminating against him solely because of color."[10]

In *Harmon* v. *Tyler*, 273 U. S. 668 (1927), a unanimous court, on the authority of *Buchanan* v. *Warley, supra,* declared invalid an ordinance which forbade any Negro to establish a home on any property in a white community or any white person to establish a home in a Negro community, "except on the written consent of a majority of the persons of the opposite race inhabiting such community or portion of the City to be affected."

The precise question before this Court in both the *Buchanan* and *Harmon* cases involved the rights of white sellers to dispose of their properties free from restrictions as to potential purchasers based on considerations of race or color. But that such legislation is also offensive to the rights of those desiring to acquire and occupy property and barred on grounds of race or color is clear, not only from the language of the opinion in *Buchanan* v. *Warley, supra,* but from this Court's disposition of the case of *Richmond* v. *Deans*, 281 U. S. 704 (1930). There, a Negro, barred from the occupancy of certain property by the terms of an ordinance similar to that in the *Buchanan* case, sought injunctive relief in the federal courts to enjoin the enforcement of the ordinance on the grounds that its provisions violated the terms of the Fourteenth Amendment. Such relief was granted, and this Court affirmed, finding the citation of *Buchanan* v. *Warley, supra,* and *Harmon* v. *Tyler, supra,* sufficient to support its judgment.[11]

---

[10] *Buchanan v. Warley,* 245 U.S. 60, 79 (1917).

[11] Courts of Georgia, Maryland, North Carolina, Oklahoma, Texas, and Virginia have also declared similar statutes invalid as being in contravention of the Fourteenth Amendment. *Glover v. Atlanta*, 148 Ga. 285, 96 S.E. 562 (1918); *Jackson v. State*, 132 Md. 311, 103 A. 910 (1918); *Clinard v. Winston-Salem*, 217 N.C. 119, 6 S.E.2d 867 (1940); *Allen v. Oklahoma City*, 175 Okla 421, 52 P.2d 1054 (1936); *Liberty Annex Corp. v. Dallas*, 289 S.W. 1067

But the present cases, unlike those just discussed, do not involve action by state legislatures or city councils. Here the particular patterns of discrimination and the areas in which the restrictions are to operate, are determined, in the first instance, by the terms of agreements among private individuals. Participation of the State consists in the enforcement of the restrictions so defined. The crucial issue with which we are here confronted is whether this distinction removes these cases from the operation of the prohibitory provisions of the Fourteenth Amendment.

Since the decision of this Court in the *Civil Rights Cases*, 109 U. S. 3 (1883), the principle has become firmly embedded in our constitutional law that the action inhibited by the first section of the Fourteenth Amendment is only such action as may fairly be said to be that of the States. That Amendment erects no shield against merely private conduct, however discriminatory or wrongful.[12]

We conclude, therefore, that the restrictive agreements standing alone cannot be regarded as violative of any rights guaranteed to petitioners by the Fourteenth Amendment. So long as the purposes of those agreements are effectuated by voluntary adherence to their terms, it would appear clear that there has been no action by the State and the provisions of the Amendment have not been violated. Cf. *Corrigan* v. *Buckley, supra.*

But here there was more. These are cases in which the purposes of the agreements were secured only by judicial enforcement by state courts of the restrictive terms of the agreements. The respondents urge that judicial enforcement of private agreements does not amount to state action; or, in any event, the participation of the State is so attenuated in character as not to amount to state action within the meaning of the Fourteenth Amendment. Finally, it is suggested, even if the States in these cases may be deemed to have acted in the constitutional sense, their action did not deprive petitioners of rights guaranteed by the Fourteenth Amendment. We move to a consideration of these matters.

## II.

That the action of state courts and judicial officers in their official capacities is to be regarded as action of the State within the meaning of the Fourteenth Amendment, is a proposition

---

(Tex. Civ. App. 1927); *Irvine* v. *Clifton Forge*, 124 Va. 781, 97 S.E. 310 (1918).

[12] And see *United States* v. *Harris,* 106 U.S. 629 (1883); *United States* v. *Cruikshank,* 92 U.S. 542 (1876).

which has long been established by decisions of this Court. That principle was given expression in the earliest cases involving the construction of the terms of the Fourteenth Amendment. Thus, in *Virginia* v. *Rives,* 100 U. S. 313, 318 (1880), this Court stated: "It is doubtless true that a State may act through different agencies,—either by its legislative, its executive, or its judicial authorities; and the prohibitions of the amendment extend to all action of the State denying equal protection of the laws, whether it be action by one of these agencies or by another." In *Ex parte Virginia,* 100 U. S. 339, 347 (1880), the Court observed: "A State acts by its legislative, its executive, or its judicial authorities. It can act in no other way." In the *Civil Rights Cases,* 109 U. S. 3, 11, 17 (1883), this Court pointed out that the Amendment makes void "State action of every kind" which is inconsistent with the guaranties therein contained, and extends to manifestations of "State authority in the shape of laws, customs, or judicial or executive proceedings." Language to like effect is employed no less than eighteen times during the course of that opinion.

Similar expressions, giving specific recognition to the fact that judicial action is to be regarded as action of the State for the purposes of the Fourteenth Amendment, are to be found in numerous cases which have been more recently decided. [Here the Court quotes from *Twining* v. *New Jersey,* 211 U. S. 78 (1908) and *Brinkerhoff-Faris Trust & Savings Co.* v. *Hill,* 281 U. S. 673 (1930), and cites numerous other cases.]

One of the earliest applications of the prohibitions contained in the Fourteenth Amendment to action of state judicial officials occurred in cases in which Negroes had been excluded from jury service in criminal prosecutions by reason of their race or color. These cases demonstrate, also, the early recognition by this Court that state action in violation of the Amendment's provisions is equally repugnant to the constitutional commands whether directed by state statute or taken by a judicial official in the absence of statute. Thus, in *Strauder* v. *West Virginia,* 100 U. S. 303 (1880), this Court declared invalid a state statute restricting jury service to white persons as amounting to a denial of the equal protection of the laws to the colored defendant in that case. In the same volume of the reports, the Court in *Ex parte Virginia, supra,* held that a similar discrimination imposed by the action of a state judge denied rights protected by the Amendment, despite the fact that the language of the state statute relating to jury service contained no such restrictions.

**1020**

The action of state courts in imposing penalties or depriving parties of other substantive rights without providing adequate notice and opportunity to defend, has, of course, long been regarded as a denial of the due process of law guaranteed by the Fourteenth Amendment. *Brinkerhoff-Faris Trust & Savings Co.* v. *Hill, supra.* Cf. *Pennoyer* v. *Neff*, 95 U. S. 714 (1878).

In numerous cases, this Court has reversed criminal convictions in state courts for failure of those courts to provide the essential ingredients of a fair hearing. Thus it has been held that convictions obtained in state courts under the domination of a mob are void. *Moore* v. *Dempsey*, 261 U. S. 86 (1923). And see *Frank* v. *Mangum*, 237 U. S. 309 (1915). Convictions obtained by coerced confessions, by the use of perjured testimony known by the prosecution to be such, or without the effective assistance of counsel, have also been held to be exertions of state authority in conflict with the fundamental rights protected by the Fourteenth Amendment.

But the examples of state judicial action which have been held by this Court to violate the Amendment's commands are not restricted to situations in which the judicial proceedings were found in some manner to be procedurally unfair. It has been recognized that the action of state courts in enforcing a substantive common-law rule formulated by those courts, may result in the denial of rights guaranteed by the Fourteenth Amendment, even though the judicial proceedings in such cases may have been in complete accord with the most rigorous conceptions of procedural due process.[19] Thus, in *American Federation of Labor* v. *Swing*, 312 U. S. 321 (1941), enforcement by state courts of the common-law policy of the State, which resulted in the restraining of peaceful picketing, was held to be state action of the sort prohibited by the Amendment's guaranties of freedom of discussion. In *Cantwell* v. *Connecticut*, 310 U. S. 296 (1940), a conviction in a state court of the common-law crime of breach of the peace was, under the circumstances of the case, found to be a violation of the Amendment's commands relating to freedom of religion. In *Bridges* v. *California*, 314 U. S. 252 (1941), enforcement of the state's common-law rule relating to contempts by publication was held to be state action inconsistent with the prohibitions of the Fourteenth Amendment. And cf. *Chicago, Burlington and Quincy R. Co.* v. *Chicago*, 166 U. S. 226 (1897).

---

[19] In applying the rule of *Erie R. Co.* v. *Tompkins*, 304 U.S. 64 (1938), it is clear that the common-law rules enunciated by state courts in judicial opinions are to be regarded as a part of the law of the State.

The short of the matter is that from the time of the adoption of the Fourteenth Amendment until the present, it has been the consistent ruling of this Court that the action of the States to which the Amendment has reference includes action of state courts and state judicial officials. Although, in construing the terms of the Fourteenth Amendment, differences have from time to time been expressed as to whether particular types of state action may be said to offend the Amendment's prohibitory provisions, it has never been suggested that state court action is immunized from the operation of those provisions simply because the act is that of the judicial branch of the state government.

## III.

. . . We have no doubt that there has been state action in these cases in the full and complete sense of the phrase. The undisputed facts disclose that petitioners were willing purchasers of properties upon which they desired to establish homes. The owners of the properties were willing sellers; and contracts of sale were accordingly consummated. It is clear that but for the active intervention of the state courts, supported by the full panoply of state power, petitioners would have been free to occupy the properties in question without restraint.

These are not cases, as has been suggested, in which the States have merely abstained from action, leaving private individuals free to impose such discriminations as they see fit. Rather, these are cases in which the States have made available to such individuals the full coercive power of government to deny to petitioners, on the grounds of race or color, the enjoyment of property rights in premises which petitioners are willing and financially able to acquire and which the grantors are willing to sell. The difference between judicial enforcement and nonenforcement of the restrictive covenants is the difference to petitioners between being denied rights of property available to other members of the community and being accorded full enjoyment of those rights on an equal footing.

The enforcement of the restrictive agreements by the state courts in these cases was directed pursuant to the common-law policy of the States as formulated by those courts in earlier decisions. In the Missouri case, enforcement of the covenant was directed in the first instance by the highest court of the State after the trial court had determined the agreement to be invalid for want of the requisite number of signatures. In the Michigan case, the order of enforcement by the trial court was affirmed by the highest state court. The judicial action in each case bears the clear and unmistakable imprimatur of the State. We have noted that previous decisions of this Court have established the proposition that judicial action is not immunized from the operation of the Fourteenth Amendment simply because it is taken pursuant to the state's common-law policy. Nor is the Amendment ineffective simply because the particular pattern of discrimination, which the State has enforced, was defined initially by the terms of a private agreement. State action, as that phrase is understood for the purposes of the Fourteenth Amendment, refers to exertions of state power in all forms. And when the effect of that action is to deny rights subject to the protection of the Fourteenth Amendment, it is the obligation of this Court to enforce the constitutional commands.

We hold that in granting judicial enforcement of the restrictive agreements in these cases, the States have denied petitioners the equal protection of the laws and that, therefore, the action of the state courts cannot stand. . . .

Respondents urge, however, that since the state courts stand ready to enforce restrictive covenants excluding white persons from the ownership or occupancy of property covered by such agreements, enforcement of covenants excluding colored persons may not be deemed a denial of equal protection of the laws to the colored persons who are thereby affected.[28] This contention does not bear scrutiny. The parties have directed our attention to no case in which a court, state or federal, has been called upon to enforce a covenant excluding members of the white majority from ownership or occupancy of real property on grounds of race or color. But there are more fundamental considerations. The rights created by the first section of the Fourteenth Amendment are, by its terms, guaranteed to the individual. The rights established are personal rights.[29] It is, therefore, no answer to these petitioners to say that the courts may also be induced to deny white persons rights of ownership and occupancy on grounds of race or color. Equal protection of the laws is not achieved through indiscriminate imposition of inequalities.

Nor do we find merit in the suggestion that property owners who are parties to these agreements are denied equal protection of the laws if denied access to the courts to enforce the terms of restrictive covenants and to assert property rights which the

---

[28] It should be observed that the restrictions relating to residential occupancy contained in ordinances involved in the *Buchanan, Harmon* and *Deans* cases, cited *supra*, and declared by this Court to be inconsistent with the requirements of the Fourteenth Amendment, applied equally to white persons and Negroes.

[29] *McCabe v. Atchison, Topeka & Santa Fe R. Co.*, 235 U.S. 151, 161–162 (1914); *Missouri ex rel. Gaines v. Canada*, 305 U.S. 337 (1938); *Oyama v. California*, 332 U.S. 633 (1948).

state courts have held to be created by such agreements. The Constitution confers upon no individual the right to demand action by the State which results in the denial of equal protection of the laws to other individuals. And it would appear beyond question that the power of the State to create and enforce property interests must be exercised within the boundaries defined by the Fourteenth Amendment. Cf. *Marsh* v. *Alabama,* 326 U. S. 501 (1946).

The problem of defining the scope of the restrictions which the Federal Constitution imposes upon exertions of power by the States has given rise to many of the most persistent and fundamental issues which this Court has been called upon to consider. That problem was foremost in the minds of the framers of the Constitution, and, since that early day, has arisen in a multitude of forms. The task of determining whether the action of a State offends constitutional provisions is one which may not be undertaken lightly. Where, however, it is clear that the action of the State violates the terms of the fundamental charter, it is the obligation of this Court so to declare.

The historical context in which the Fourteenth Amendment became a part of the Constitution should not be forgotten. Whatever else the framers sought to achieve, it is clear that the matter of primary concern was the establishment of equality in the enjoyment of basic civil and political rights and the preservation of those rights from discriminatory action on the part of the States based on considerations of race or color. Seventy-five years ago this Court announced that the provisions of the Amendment are to be construed with this fundamental purpose in mind.[30] Upon full consideration, we have concluded that in these cases the States have acted to deny petitioners the equal protection of the laws guaranteed by the Fourteenth Amendment. Having so decided, we find it unnecessary to consider whether petitioners have also been deprived of property without due process of law or denied privileges and immunities of citizens of the United States.

For the reasons stated, the judgment of the Supreme Court of Missouri and the judgment of the Supreme Court of Michigan must be reversed.

*Reversed.*

MR. JUSTICE REED, MR. JUSTICE JACKSON, and MR. JUSTICE RUTLEDGE took no part in the consideration or decision of these cases.

---

[30] *Slaughter-House Cases,* 16 Wall. 36, 81 (1873); *Strauder* v. *West Virginia,* 100 U.S. 303 (1880). See Flack, The Adoption of the Fourteenth Amendment.

MR. JUSTICE FRANKFURTER, concurring.

In these cases, the plaintiffs ask equity to enjoin white property owners who are desirous of selling their houses to Negro buyers simply because the houses were subject to an original agreement not to have them pass into Negro ownership. Equity is rooted in conscience. An injunction is, as it always has been, "an extraordinary remedial process which is granted, not as a matter of right but in the exercise of a sound judicial discretion." *Morrison* v. *Work*, 266 U. S. 481, 490. In good conscience, it cannot be "the exercise of a sound judicial discretion" by a federal court to grant the relief here asked for when the authorization of such an injunction by the States of the Union violates the Constitution—and violates it, not for any narrow technical reason, but for considerations that touch rights so basic to our society that, after the Civil War, their protection against invasion by the States was safeguarded by the Constitution. This is to me a sufficient and conclusive ground for reaching the Court's result.

## Note

1. In *Hurd* v. *Hodge*, 334 U. S. 24, 92 L. Ed. 1187, 68 S. Ct. 847 (1948), a companion case to the *Shelley* case, the Supreme Court held a restrictive covenant in the District of Columbia unenforceable. The Court said it was unnecessary to reach the constitutional question and relied on 8 U.S.C. § 42, derived from § 1 of the Civil Rights Act of 1866, which provides: "All citizens of the United States shall have the same right in every state and territory as is enjoyed by white citizens thereof to inherit, purchase, lease, sell, hold and convey real and personal property." The Court stated: "White sellers, one of whom is a petitioner here, have been enjoined from selling the properties to any Negro or colored person. Under such circumstances, to suggest that Negro petitioners have been accorded the same rights as white citizens to purchase, hold, and convey real property is to reject the plain meaning of language." 334 U.S. at 34. The Court also held that the covenants violated public policy. See also Judge Edgerton's dissenting opinion in the court below, 162 F. 2d 233 (C.A.D.C., 1947).

2. The *Shelley* and *Hurd* cases are discussed in Ming, *Racial Restrictions and the Fourteenth Amendment: The Restrictive Covenant Cases*, 16 U. of Chi. L. Rev. 203 (1949); Clark and Perlman, *Prejudice and Property* (1948) (brief for U.S. *amicus curiae*), reviewed in Haber, 34 Iowa L. Rev. 388 (1949); Lowe, *Racial Restrictive Covenants*, 1 Ala. L. Rev. 15 (1948); Crooks, *The Racial Covenant Cases*, 37 Geo. L.J. 514 (1949); Notes, 61 Harv. L. Rev. 1450 (1948); 21 So. Calif. L. Rev. 358 (1948); 48 Col. L. Rev. 1241 (1948) (state action problem); Sayre, *Shelley v. Kraemer and United Nations Law*, 34 Ia. L. Rev. 1 (1948); Note, 37 Cal. L. Rev. 493 (1949).

For studies of the function and effect of restrictive covenants see Weaver, *The Negro Ghetto*, (1948); Long and Johnson, *People vs. Prop-*

*erty* (1947); Long, *Race Restrictive Housing Covenants and Social Control,* 33 Sociology and Social Research 355 (1949).

A United Press survey in 1951 reported that "thousands of Negro families have moved into white residential neighborhoods" as a result of recent Supreme Court decisions. N.Y. Times, Jan. 22, 1951. The survey revealed disagreement between white and Negro real estate brokers as to the effect of this trend on community prejudices. *Cf.* Note, *Practical effects in Tennessee of the Non-Enforceability of Restrictive Racial Covenants,* 20 Tenn. L. Rev. 679 (1949).

3. Prior to *Shelley v. Kraemer,* covenants with racial or religious restrictions had been from time to time invalidated on various grounds. See *e.g. Gandolfo v. Hartman,* 49 Fed. 181 (C.C. Cal., 1892) (violates equal protection clause and most favored nation agreement with China —the only case prior to *Shelley* decided on this ground); *Yoshida v. Gelbert Improvement Co.,* 58 Pa. D. & C. 321 (1946) (contrary to public policy); *Pickel v. McCawley,* 329 Mo. 166, 44 S.W.2d 857 (1931) (changed conditions of the neighborhood). Courts also invalidated racial and religious restrictions on the ground that they constituted illegal restraints on alienation. However, the same jurisdictions frequently upheld them if properly phrased as mere restrictions on occupancy. See Note, 3 A.L.R.2d 466, 488.

For discussion prior to the *Shelley* case of the property doctrines as well as constitutional issues see Bowman, *The Constitution and Common Law Restraints on Alienation,* 8 B.U.L. Rev. 1 (1928); Bruce, *Racial Zoning by Private Contract in the Light of the Constitutions and the Rule Against Restraints on Alienation,* 21 Ill. L. Rev. 704 (1927); McGovney, *Racial Residential Segregation by State Court Enforcement of Restrictive Agreements, Covenants or Conditions in Deeds is Unconstitutional,* 33 Calif. L. Rev. 5 (1945).

4. For full discussion of what constitutes state action within the meaning of the Fourteenth Amendment see references in Chapter I, *supra.* See also *Dorsey v. Stuyvesant Town Corp.,* reprinted *infra.*

5. Enforceability of restrictive racial covenant in action for damages: In *Weiss v. Leaon,* 359 Mo. 1054, 225 S.W.2d 127 (1949), the Supreme Court of Missouri reversed a lower court which dismissed an action for damages against a white owner who breached a covenant providing that his property may not be "devised, sold, leased or occupied by Negroes." The court stated that the *Shelley* case ruled only on the matter of injunctions and did not necessarily hold that a judgment for damages constitutes state action. For the opposite holding see *Roberts v. Curtis,* 93 F. Supp. 604 (D.D.C., 1950); *Phillips v. Naff,* 332 Mich. 389, 52 N.W.2d 158 (1952). *Cf. Old Wayne Mutual Life Assoc. v. McDonough,* 204 U.S. 8, 51 L. Ed. 345, 27 S. Ct. 236 (1907) (money judgment against defendant not within court's jurisdiction is state action violating due process). For discussion see Groves, *Judicial Interpretation of the Holdings of the United States Supreme Court in the Restrictive Covenant Cases,* 45 Ill. L. Rev. 614 (1950); Notes, 63 Harv. L. Rev. 1062 (1950) (discusses also how the concept of privity of estate may create legal difficulties for plaintiffs in damage actions that did not exist where an injunction was sought); 18 Geo. Wash. L. Rev.

[Emerson]

417 (1950) (collects cases illustrating judicial granting of variety of legal remedies that have been held to constitute state action in violation of due process) ; 98 U. of Pa. L. Rev. 588 (1950) ; 7 Wash. & Lee L. Rev. 178 (1950) ; 25 N.Y.U.L. Rev. 406 (1950).

6. In *Clifton v. Puente,* 218 S.W.2d 272 (Tex. Civ. App., 1948), a restrictive covenant contained a forfeiture clause under which the property upon breach reverted to the original grantor. Upon sale to Puente, a person of Mexican descent, the original grantor to whom the property was to return under the forfeiture clause executed a deed to another buyer who took possession. The court upheld Puente's claim for title and possession on the ground that denial of relief would amount to enforcement of the restrictive covenant. Cf. *Ralph Cohn Inc. v. Trawick,* 60 Atl.2d 926 (Mun. App. D.C., 1948) (failure to disclose existence of restrictive covenant to Negro purchaser held material misrepresentation entitling buyer to rescind—the failure to disclose occurred a year prior to the decision in *Hurd v. Hodge;* the court also emphasized that there was a duty to disclose such covenants regardless of their illegality). See also *Claremont Improvement Club v. Buckingham,* 89 Cal. App.2d 32, 200 Pac.2d 47 (1948) (refusal to grant declaratory judgment that covenant valid; it would serve no purpose since the *Shelley* case forbade any judicial process that would give judgment effect).

In *Rice v. Sioux City Memorial Park Cemetery,* 102 F. Supp. 658 (N.D. Iowa, 1952), plaintiff brought suit for breach of contract for defendant's failure to bury her non-Caucasian husband, seeking to have contract provisions restricting burial to Caucasions declared void under the State and Federal Constitutions. The case, removed to the Federal court by defendant, was remanded to the state court to decide the state questions on the ground that there was no independent claim or cause of action raising a federal question, especially since the contract was a "state created obligation."

In *Novick v. Levitt & Sons,* 200 Misc. 694, 108 N.Y. Supp.2d 615 (1951), plaintiffs sought an injunction to restrain their landlord from evicting them after the expiration of their lease. The contention was that their leases were not renewed as was customary because plaintiffs had allowed their children to play with Negro children and because they entertained Negro guests. The court dismissed the case because the complaint did not adequately support this contention and also indicated grave doubts about the adequacy of the cause of action had the pleading been properly drawn. According to the court plaintiff's premise was "that defendant may not choose to whom it shall rent its houses." The court concluded, "Plaintiffs submit no support for such a legal theory and I find the law to be to the contrary."

## NOTE—CIRCUMVENTION OF THE RULE AGAINST ENFORCEMENT OF RACIALLY RESTRICTIVE COVENANTS

37 Calif. L. Rev. 493, 494–7 (1949)

One plan is to place title to the land of a particular area in a business corporation, either at the start of a subdivision or by sale to the corporation by existing owners. The board would determine the persons to whom it would lease, being guided by the applicant's "cultural" acceptability or by some similar non-racial standard set out in the articles. This would involve, however, the practical difficulty of financing the purchase of a large tract of land and would run counter to the natural desire of persons to own their own home sites.[7]

The second plan leaves title in the individual residents but forbids the sale of the land without the permission of the board of a non-profit corporation,[8] once again acting in accord with the desired standards. The restriction on sale is contained as a covenant in each deed, as is a provision that the buyer will become a member of the corporation upon receiving title, and both are intended to run with the land.[9] This scheme would substitute individual ownership for the lease plan, but the property law of some states would declare it an unenforceable restraint upon alienation.

A third proposal provides for the formation of a non-profit corporation, title to the land once again remaining with the residents. The corporation passes upon the desirability of prospective buyers, and the use or occupancy of any property within the agreement is prohibited without a permit issued by the "permit committee" of the corporation. Any buyer accepts his deed subject to this "use and occupancy permit" covenant and automatically becomes a member of the corporation. This plan appears to be the most workable.[11] It would replace the un-

---

[7] This plan could be more easily introduced at the start of a real estate development. The experience of some leading realtors in the San Francisco area has been that in established communities the number of persons who could be persuaded to join and convey title would be well under 50 per cent.

[8] These non-profit organizations are organized with each land owner having one vote, there being no shares but certificates of membership. See CAL. CORP. CODE §§ 9601, 9607; BALLANTINE ON CORPORATIONS § 7 at 28; 1 FLETCHER, CYCLOPEDIA OF CORPORATIONS § 68. See also Green Gables Home Owners Association v. Sunlite Homes (1949) 89 A.C.A. 952, 202 P.(2d) 143.

[9] The covenants could be included in the deeds at the start of a subdivision or could be inserted subsequently by filing with the county recorder. CAL. CIV. CODE §§ 1158–1165.

[11] As a modification of the manner of giving approval in all these plans, the initial or final decision as to a prospective buyer's or lessor's desirability

popular lease scheme with individual ownership and a simpler, more easily financed plan and would place the restriction on use and occupancy rather than on alienation.[12] If a sale were made to a person who lacked an occupancy permit, a suit to enjoin occupancy, to eject him, or an action for liquidated damages against his grantor would ensue.[13]

It can be seen that each of these devices is founded on the same principle of vesting judgment in a small group subject to more or less indefinite standards. There is no absolute guarantee to any owner-member that changed conditions might not bring about the admission of a member of a minority group, such as a negro, except the express or tacit understanding between the residents and the board and between the members of the board or permit committee themselves. Although no mention is made of deliberate intention to exclude, these schemes are designed to accomplish the same end.

Suits involving the attempted enforcement of these schemes against either grantor or grantee, after a wrongful sale to a negro, fall into three groups, according to the difficulty of proving discrimination. In the simplest case, evidence of specific instances of intentional exclusion could be introduced to show that although no use is made of the words "Negro" or "Caucasian," discrimination is in fact being practiced. In the face of this evidence enforcement of the covenant would be denied.[14]

Without such evidence, proof would be more difficult. However, in those portions of a city which feel great pressure from a negro section and either surround it or impede its growth, the absence of negroes, even without any statistics showing the practice of systematic exclusion, would seem sufficient evidence of discrimination unless such absence were otherwise explained.

could be made by an appointed "block captain" or by certain of the nearest neighbors. The writer has been informed that in the Shaker Heights residential area of Cleveland, Ohio, the corporation must approve the new occupant upon his being acceptable to a majority of his nearest five neighbors.

[12] Restrictions against use and occupancy have been upheld in many more states than those against alienation. . . .

[13] As an added means of enforcement, the corporation could require a purchaser to post a bond, to be forfeited if he sold to an undesirable. This would be impractical because of the small number of persons who could buy a house and at the same time post a bond of sufficient size. Still another clause would give the corporation the right to buy before an owner sold. Both of these provisions could be found to be restraints on alienation in states which have a strict prohibition against restraints.

[14] This would follow from the rationale of Yick Wo v. Hopkins (1886) 118 U.S. 356 in which the effect of the administration of a San Francisco ordinance, rather than its wording, was held to be a violation of the equal protection clause.

In *Patton* v. *Mississippi*[15] the mere absence of negroes on juries for thirty years, without further proof of arbitrary or systematic exclusion, in itself was sufficient evidence to show discrimination. Such sufficient evidence of intentional discrimination should likewise be inferred from the pronounced absence of negro occupancy where the pressure from a negro section is strong and the problems resulting from overcrowding intense.

The most difficult situation would arise in communities where there is little pressure from negro sections. There might be a purchase by a negro only occasionally, as, for example, in a new subdivision, and proof of discrimination would be made almost impossible. If a negro were not approved, it would be hard to obtain testimony of actual discrimination in selection. The directors and members of the corporation and perhaps even the grantor could testify that the standards set out in the articles had been followed. It may be argued, however, that even under these circumstances, enforcement of the agreements would violate the Fourteenth Amendment. It has been held that a state may not place in a state officer or body the power, guided only by vague standards, to deprive a person of a fundamental right.[17] In the *Shelley* case, the judicial enforcement of the private covenants was considered to be state action[18] to the same

---

15 (1947) 332 U.S. 463. No specific evidence of exclusion was shown, but no Negro had been selected for jury duty in thirty years. The fact that there were few Negroes eligible for jury duty, the qualifications for which the Court did not examine, makes this a stronger case for the proposition that the Court will not ask for proof of acts of exclusion when its results are clearly shown. See also (1948) 33 IOWA L. REV. 728; (1948) 23 NOTRE DAME LAW. 387; and Smith v. Texas (1940) 311 U.S. 128.

17 In the Jehovah's Witnesses' cases it was held that ordinances were invalid on their face which gave to a governmental official or body the power, guided only by vague standards or standards involving a religious test, to deny licenses to itinerant evangelists to solicit funds or to pass out literature on the city streets. It was held that this would give to an official the arbitrary power to curb the freedom of religion. Cantwell v. Connecticut (1940) 310 U.S. 296; Schneider v. State (1939) 308 U.S. 147; Lovell v. Griffin (1938) 303 U.S. 444. Likewise, in the freedom of speech field, the Court, in Hague v. C.I.O. (1939) 307 U.S. 496, struck down an ordinance of Jersey City which "enabled the Director of Safety to refuse a permit on his mere opinion that such refusal will prevent 'disturbances or disorderly assemblage.' It can thus . . . be made the instrument of arbitrary suppression of views. . . ." See also Saia v. New York (1948) 334 U.S. 558.

18 Prior to the Shelley case, the concept of "state action," which had been applied originally only to the legislative, judicial and executive branches, and to political and administrative subdivisions, had been expanded to include organizations or groups of individuals which exercised normally governmental powers and became thereby instrumentalties of the states. See Comment (1948) 61 HARV. L. REV. 344. This had been the extent of the evolution of the term "state action," and enforcement of contracts violative of the Fourteenth Amendment by state courts was still considered by state courts to be

extent as if the state itself had adopted a racial zoning statute, which it is forbidden to do. Similarly, when the state enforces these housing agreements which give to the board or committee the power to deny housing guided only by standards of "cultural desirability" or "compatability," it is placing its stamp of approval on an exercise of power which would be arbitrary and unconstitutional if delegated to a public person or body. Should not judicial enforcement of these private agreements be unconstitutional?[20] This conclusion, if adopted by the Court, could charge these housing corporations with the duty to avoid any discrimination, or any system of internal organization which might bring about discrimination, in determining who shall live in a community.[21]

## Note

Other devices that have been suggested to circumvent *Shelley v. Kraemer* include: (a) the purchaser may be required to deposit with the vendor or a third party a substantial *pledge*, while undertaking not to resell to a specified class of persons under penalty of forfeiture; (b) The deed may be placed in *escrow* with a third party, who takes

---

too indirect to constitute "state action." The Shelley case took this next step, first proposed by Professor McGovney [33 Calif. L. Rev. 5, 10], by saying that court enforcement of a contract brought into play the "full panoply of state powers." See (1948) 48 Col. L. Rev. 1241.

[20] There is at present no direct authority for this position, but in other situations private bodies have been held to the same constitutional limitations as the state. In Marsh v. Alabama (1946) 326 U.S. 501, the Court held that a state could not impose criminal punishment for trespass on a member of Jehovah's Witnesses for distributing religious literature on the premises of a company-owned town contrary to the wishes of the town's management. "In our view the circumstances that the property rights to the premises where the deprivation of liberty, here involved, took place, were held by others than the public, is not sufficient to justify the State's permitting a corporation to govern a community of citizens so as to restrict their fundamental liberties and the enforcement of such restraint by the application of a state statute." 326 U.S. 501 at 509. *Cf. Tucker v. Texas* (1946) 326 U.S. 517. . . .

Although the application of the Marsh case prohibits a private body performing public functions from denying constitutional rights, it is not yet clear where the "public function" line will be drawn. In Watchtower Bible and T. Soc. v. Metropolitan Life Ins. Co. (1948) 297 N.Y. 339, 79 N.E.(2d) 433, *cert. denied* (1948) 335 U.S. 886, the New York Court of Appeals refused to apply the Marsh doctrine to a large, privately owned housing development, subsidized by the state at least to the extent of the grant of the power of eminent domain, where solicitation by Jehovah's Witnesses had been prohibited in the halls of the buildings.

[21] An objection to the logical effect of this doctrine might be its application to purely social organizations. This could be resolved by drawing a line between membership in social groups and the more fundamental right to housing.

over the function previously performed by the courts in deciding whether a restrictive covenant has been broken; (c) The deed may include a so-called *"Van Sweringen Covenant"*, preventing resale without consent of the original owner; (d) There may be a clause in the deed providing for *automatic reversion* to a prior grantor in case of attempt to resell to a member of a proscribed minority group; (e) The original grantor may reserve to himself an *option of first refusal*, by the exercise of which he can select successive owners of the same tract or building.

For further description of these devices see, National Community Relations Advisory Council, *Equality of Opportunity in Housing*, pp. 12–13 (1952); Abrams, *The Segregation Threat in Housing*, 7 Commentary 123 (Feb. 1949); Ming, *Racial Restrictions and the Fourteenth Amendment: The Restrictive Covenant Cases*, 16 U. of Chi. L. Rev. 203 (1949); Groves, *Judicial Interpretations of the Holdings of the United States Supreme Court in the Restrictive Covenant Cases*, 45 Ill. L. Rev. 614 (1950); Notes, 61 Harv. L. Rev. 1407, 1416–20 (1948); 27 N.C.L. Rev. 224, 229 *et seq.* (1949); 24 Notre Dame Law, 157 (1948).

On the possibility of the use of Anti-Trust laws in combatting some of these devices as well as agreements by middlemen see Marcus, *Civil Rights and the Anti-Trust Laws*, 18 U. of Chi. L. Rev. 171 (1951); *U.S. v. Mortgage Conf. of New York*, Civ. No. 37–247 (S.D.N.Y., 1948), 1948–49 CCH Trade Cases § 62,273 (defendants consented to a decree which among other things enjoined them from refraining to compete for mortgages or leases because of the race or nationality of the owner).

## WEAVER—THE NEGRO GHETTO

Published by Harcourt, Brace and Company, copyright by Robert C. Weaver, 1948, pp. 215–6, 222–4

In those cities where racial covenants are not widespread and in cities where they are generally used, the practices of real estate operators have been an effective deterrent to colored peoples' moving into new neighborhoods, since many realtors have entered into "gentlemen's agreements" not to sell or rent to Negroes in areas outside existing colored districts. The situation has been summarized as follows:

> Fairly effective also are the general attitudes among real-property owners and real-estate agencies, and the formal understanding which exists among them. As a result, Negroes find themselves barred from new residential developments or from purchasing properties for sale in certain areas.[6]

Often the real estate dealers operate through other agencies. They discourage financial institutions from making loans on properties bought by Negroes in white neighborhoods; they attempt,

---

[6] [Sterner, *The Negro's Share*, p. 208 (1943).]

usually successfully, to prevent financial institutions from financing new, large-scale housing developments for Negroes in white areas; or they press FHA to reject construction for Negroes in or adjacent to white neighborhoods. At the same time financial institutions act independently to perpetuate the pattern of ghetto living. . . .

In Los Angeles, the same process took place. As in Cleveland, the city real estate board disclaimed any jurisdiction over a proposed area for Negro occupancy in a white district, referring the matter to the southwest branch of the board. The latter expressed strong opposition to the project and put pressure on a large local bank to withdraw financial support. Although the bank refused to do so, the project was not built.

The basis for such action is found in the rules of real estate boards. There are irrefutable evidences of the existence of such rules. The Washington Real Estate Board, like all others, had a *Code of Ethics*. That document specifies that

> No property in a white section should ever be sold, rented, advertised, or offered to colored people. In a doubtful case advice from the Public Affairs Committee should be obtained.[7] . . .

The general lack of interest of developers and builders in housing for colored people has served to hide a much more fundamental impediment to new construction for minorities. This is the disinclination of financial institutions to take mortgages on such construction. In part, it is a purely financial consideration, since few lending institutions take kindly to investments in new housing for any but the more prosperous and secure groups in our society. The Negro, being largely in the lower income ranges, has been excluded on economic grounds. This is reflected in developments in Washington, D. C., where the sizeable Negro population has included a disproportionate number of moderate and steady income recipients. In Washington, there has been in the past decade or two a relatively small amount of new housing for colored people. Most of it, like most of the war housing for Negroes, is located in the northeast section of the city, and it has been financed without too much difficulty. FHA insurance, of course, accelerated the process. Yet a comparison of the price of all new construction in Washington with the rent-paying ability of Washingtonians in sub-standard housing in 1940 illustrates that in the period 1935–40 privately built housing was concentrated at price levels where only a small

---

[7] *Code of Ethics*, Washington Real Estate Board, section 5, par. 15. Cited in Hurd v. Hodge, p. 528.

percentage of the population most in need of shelter was distributed. . . .

Also, the general conditions of blight which developed as a result of extreme overcrowding in the Black Belts made them poor locations for new housing. This was accentuated by the high incidence of absentee ownership, the rapid amortization of much of the property in the Negro ghetto and the area's general neglect by city officials and services. On economic grounds alone, financial institutions were often justified in discouraging new, scattered building in northern Black Belts.

### Note

1. The Code of Ethics of the National Association of Real Estate Boards formerly forbade a realtor to introduce into a neighborhood members of a race whose presence would clearly be detrimental to property values. This code was binding on member boards and failure to enforce it could mean expulsion of the local board. References to race were eliminated from the code in January 1951. This change is not binding on local boards, however, and they can continue to encourage discrimination. See American Jewish Congress and National Association for the Advancement of Colored People, *Civil Rights in the United States in 1951*, p. 79 (1951).

2. Recently in various cities there has been some increase in privately financed interracial housing. These projects have proved financially and socially successful. For description see, National Community Relations Advisory Council, *Equality of Opportunity in Housing*, pp. 30–2 (1952). See also McGraw, *Financing Homes for Nonwhites: Some Views and Credit Experience*, National Savings and Loan J. 8 (Oct. 1948). For activities of the FHA see *infra*.

3. See also Isaacs, *Are Urban Neighborhoods Possible*, 5 J. of Housing 177 (1948) and *The Neighborhood Unit is an Instrument for Segregation*, 5 J. of Housing 215 (1948).

### 3. Discrimination in Public and Publicly Assisted Housing

NATIONAL COMMUNITY RELATIONS ADVISORY
COUNCIL—EQUALITY OF OPPORTUNITY
IN HOUSING

pp. 46–51 (1952)

In general, the housing programs of the Federal government fall into several broad categories. One is a low-rent public housing program administered by the Public Housing Administration, whereby Federal funds are used to assist cities in building housing for low-income groups. These projects are owned and operated by a local government agency.

A relatively new type of federal aid is provided for under Title I of the Housing Act of 1949 and administered by the Division of Slum Clearance and Urban Redevelopment. Federal loans and grants to local public agencies are authorized so that they can clear slums and blighted areas and make the land available for private *or* public development or redevelopment.

The Federal Housing Administration provides insurance against loss on several types of loans made by private lending institutions. It also insures yields on investments in rental housing for families of moderate income, where no mortgage financing is involved. The FHA does not make loans and does not build housing.

Finally, the Defense Housing and Community Facilities Act of 1951 sets up a housing program for critical defense areas.

The overall federal housing agency is the Housing and Home Finance Agency.

Through the public housing program, many low income families have been provided with their first opportunity to live in decent homes. Minority groups received a large share of benefits under this program. By 1942, one-third of all the dwelling units built with Federal aid were for Negro occupancy. Half the total low-rent units in the South and over a quarter in the North were occupied by Negro families in the fall of 1946.

The Federal government has established no standard for occupancy except that projects should conform to "community patterns and trends." Local housing authorities are given the responsibility for site selection, construction, tenant selection and operation. The racial policies followed in these projects, therefore, vary from community to community. Since most of the early low-rent projects were built in slum areas, most local authorities avoided a decision on the racial question simply by maintaining the racial composition of the neighborhood. As the program developed, however, and buildings were put up on vacant land, a policy had to be determined. . . .

Three general patterns—segregated, "checkerboard" and integrated—have evolved in public housing projects. Under a "segregated" policy separate projects are provided for Negro and white tenants. A "checkerboard" project is one where Negro and white tenants are placed in separate sections or buildings of the same project. An integrated development is one where tenants are selected and allotted vacancies on the basis of objective criteria without regard to their race or color.

**1035**

While none of the federal housing statutes specifically bars segregation, the Public Housing Administration has attempted to insure equality of treatment.

Under the most recent rules of the PHA two requirements must be met. First, the number of housing units available to Negroes must be proportionate to their need. This does not mean merely that the number must be proportionate to the Negro population in the area. Since the public housing program is designed to serve persons now in substandard dwellings, the number of units available to Negroes must be proportionate to the number of Negroes living in such sub-standard dwellings. If the PHA is not satisfied that the proposed program will meet this requirement, it may withhold approval.

Second, the facilities offered Negro and white tenants must be equal, not only in the physical aspects of the housing itself but also in such features as proximity to schools, parks, etc.

In some instances, however, PHA closes its eyes to actual violations of the federal housing laws brought about by segregation. For instance, the law sets up priorities for families eligible for federally-aided low-rent projects. But because of segregated patterns, families of one race may obtain apartments while families of another race, with higher priority, remain on the waiting list. . . .

Most plans for publicly-assisted housing in the next few years will, no doubt, take advantage of Title I of the Federal Housing Act of 1949, authorizing Federal grants to cities and states for assembling, clearance, preparation, sale or leasing of land for slum clearance and urban redevelopment. Under this legislation a local public agency may acquire slum or blighted areas, clear the land and make it available for private or public development, with the Federal Government bearing up to two-thirds of any financial losses incurred by the local government in the resale of the land.

The Housing Act of 1949 contains no provisions against discrimination or segregation. The HHFA has announced that it will not tolerate racial restrictive covenants on land sold under the Title I program—an almost meaningless ruling in the light of the United States Supreme Court decision on restrictive covenants. Beyond this, however, there has been no indication that the Federal government will make any attempt to prevent segregation under this Title.

Urban redevelopment is heralded by housing experts as the key to the future development of American cities. But it also presents a potentially grave problem for the future of intergroup relations in this country. Properly planned and administered, the urban redevelopment provisions of the Federal Housing Act of 1949 could aid materially in realizing the stated objective of the law to provide "a decent home and suitable living environment for every American family." Improperly implemented, however, these provisions can permanently impose a pattern of segregated living in the United States. . . .

The problem of relocation is basic to any large-scale building, and is intensified many-fold where Negroes are involved. In these times of general housing scarcity, it is extremely difficult for any families—and particularly those of minority racial, national or ethnic groups—to find new homes. This fact has led some housing experts to oppose any demolitions at the present time. They suggest, instead, that new projects, operated without segregation, be built on vacant land and that actual slum clearance be postponed until the total housing supply is increased.

The Housing Act of 1949 provides that families forced to move from a redevelopment site must be provided with "decent, safe and sanitary dwellings" at rentals which they can afford.

While the HHFA leaves the definition of what constitutes "decent, safe and sanitary dwellings" to local determination, it has issued some regulations to implement the law. Now before a redevelopment site will be approved, details concerning the needs of site dwellers and other housing available for them must be presented. The HHFA will study particularly the requirements of displaced minority families and the availability of other housing for them.

The Housing Act of 1949 does not contain specific relocation standards for families displaced by low-rent public housing.

In May 1950, PHA stressed the importance of using vacant sites for low-rent projects during the critical housing shortage. Despite this, however, families were being displaced from their homes, forced to fend for themselves and relocate in other slum areas. In June 1951, PHA further required local authorities to present a feasible relocation plan with detailed facts and figures which reflect recognition of the restricted housing supply for minority groups. The standard applied, however, is that the new homes be no worse than those from which the families were forced to move.

The problems inherent in slum clearance operations necessitating the rehousing of families in an extremely tight housing market were finally officially recognized by the federal housing agencies in November, 1951. At that time the HHFA in concurrence with FHA, PHA and the Division of Slum Clearance and Urban Redevelopment issued a far-reaching statement explaining the co-ordinated use of federal aids to help relocate these families. The local community is given initial responsibility for making sure that displaced families are rehoused in accordance with statutory requirements and that rehousing does not itself produce overcrowding and new areas of blight. This, the policy states, "will usually require expansion of housing facilities and living space, particularly where racial minorities are to be displaced." The policy directs both PHA and the Division of Slum Clearance and Urban Redevelopment to consider in their approval of slum clearance sites whether the locality is actually providing for expansion of housing on vacant sites. Moreover, for the first time, FHA is given the duty to "actively undertake to encourage and assist private builders in a practical program of developing both sale and rental housing suited to the needs of displaced families" with specific attention to the needs of minority families.

Implementation of this policy statement is certain to expand the housing market for minority groups. If it operates in a framework of segregation, however, it may establish new ghettoes in outlying areas of our cities.

Because of defense needs and preparations, most redevelopment programs have not progressed beyond the planning stage. But there is already some fear that slum clearance may become "Negro clearance," since areas considered for redevelopment frequently encompass the centrally-located "Black Belts." Therefore, it becomes extremely important to see that building is planned for vacant land before slums are razed, and that open occupancy patterns and strict adherence to the relocation provisions of the law are encouraged. . . .

Housing is closely related to the full utilization of labor. This was proved during World War II when qualified Negro workers could not move to labor shortage areas because of housing restrictions.

In order to provide for the housing needs of defense workers moving to new or already overcrowded industrial and military centers, Congress enacted the Defense Housing and Community Facilities Act of 1951. The law provides that, in localities declared by the President to be critical defense housing areas, credit restrictions may be suspended and housing aids provided to private builders, including a more liberal FHA mortgage insurance and advance commitment by the Federal Government to purchase mortgages. In addition the Government is authorized to provide housing and community facilities in those areas where private industry is unable to do so.

**1038**

The law itself is silent on the question of discrimination. But the Senate committee report which accompanied the measure stated: "Your committee expects that . . . there shall be equality of treatment of persons of all races, religions and national origin. . . ." There is no assurance, however, that defense housing will not be segregated.

In many areas, the expansion of industrial and military installations is resulting in the creation of entirely new cities. Thus, with all the government aids provided by the Defense Housing Act, new segregated communities may be established. On the other hand, the Federal Government has the power to insist that to qualify for assistance under this law, builders and developers must rent or sell to all eligible applicants, regardless of race, creed, or national origin. This could be done by an administrative ruling issued by the Housing and Home Finance Agency. At the planning stage, HHFA could insist that housing be programmed for the needs of *all* workers.

To date, the policy pronouncements of the Housing and Home Finance Agency with respect to private defense housing have established no such requirement. They do provide for the planning of defense housing within racial classifications and, in effect, establish quotas for minority participation. Only in the case of *federally-owned* housing is there provision that "occupancy . . . shall not be denied to any eligible defense worker on the basis of race, color, creed or national origin." It is estimated that less than 7,000 units of such housing will be available for the entire country.

## DORSEY v. STUYVESANT TOWN CORP.

New York Court of Appeals, 1949
299 N. Y. 512, 87 N.E.2d 541, cert. den. 339 U.S. 981 (1950)

BROMLEY, J. . . .
[Three Negro veterans sought an injunction against Stuyvesant Town Corporation and the Metropolitan Life Insurance Company to restrain them from refusing to rent apartments to plaintiffs and others in a like situation because of their race and color. The question on appeal was whether the exclusion of Negro tenants from Stuyvesant Town, a housing project built under the New York Redevelopment Companies Law, amounted to "state action" within the meaning of the Fourteenth Amendment.

The opinion first analyzes the provision of the New York Constitution dealing with housing, finding it "instinct with the theory, consistent with its two purposes, that low rent housing for persons of low income is to be a function of government and the rehabilitation of substandard areas is to be the function of private enterprise aided by government." The opinion continues with an analysis of the Redevelopment Law.]

Section 2 of the Redevelopment Companies Law provides as follows: " * * * It is hereby declared that in certain areas of municipalities located within this state there exist substandard conditions and insanitary housing conditions owing to obsolescence, deterioration and dilapidation of building, or excessive land coverage, lack of planning, of public facilities, of sufficient light, air and space, and improper design and arrangement of living quarters; that there is not in such areas a sufficient supply of adequate, safe and sanitary dwelling accommodations properly planned and related to public facilities; that modern standards of urban life require that housing be related to adequate and convenient public facilities; that the aforesaid substandard and insanitary conditions depress and destroy the economic value of large areas and by impairing the value of private investments threaten the sources of public revenues; that the public interest requires the clearance, replanning, reconstruction and neighborhood rehabilitation of such substandard and insanitary areas, together with adequate provision for recreational and other facilities incidental and appurtenant thereto according to the requirements of modern urban life and that such clearance, replanning, reconstruction and neighborhood rehabilitation are essential to the protection of the financial stability of such municipalities; that in order to protect the sources of public revenue it is necessary to modernize the physical plan and conditions of urban life; that these conditions cannot be remedied by the ordinary operations of private enterprise; that provision must be made to encourage the investment of funds in corporations engaged in providing redevelopment facilities to be constructed according to the requirements of city planning and in effectuation of official city plans and regulated by law as to profits, dividends and disposition of their property or franchises; that provision must be made to enable insurance companies to provide such facilities, subject to regulation by law as to the return from such facilities and the disposition of property acquired for such purpose; and that provision must also be made for the acquisition for such corporations and companies at fair prices of real property required for such purposes in substandard areas and for public assistance of such corporations and companies by the granting of partial tax exemption; that the cooperation of the state and its subdivisions is necessary to accomplish such purposes; that the clearance, replanning and reconstruction, rehabilitation and modernization of substandard and insanitary areas and the provision of adequate, safe, sanitary and properly planned housing accommodations in effectuation of official city plans by such corporations and companies in these areas are public uses and purposes for which private property may be acquired for such corporations and companies and partial tax exemption granted; that these conditions require the creation of the agencies, instrumentalities and corporations hereinafter prescribed for the purpose of attaining the ends herein recited; and the necessity in the public interest for the provisions hereinafter enacted is hereby declared as a matter of legislative determination." . . .

Sections 6 and 7 provide that the provisions of the Business Corporations Law, General Corporation Law and Stock Corporation Law shall apply to redevelopment corporations, except where such provisions are in conflict with the provisions of the Redevelopment Companies Law, and that each such corporation shall have and may exercise such of the powers conferred by the General Corporation Law as shall be necessary in conducting its business and consistent with the provisions of the Redevelopment Companies Law. Limitations are imposed upon redevelopment companies in connection with various aspects of their businesses. Section 8 provides for a limited return on investment by stipulating that there shall be paid annually out of the earnings of the redevelopment company, after providing for all expenses, taxes and assessments a sum for interest, amortization, depreciation and dividends, equal to but not exceeding 6% of the total actual final cost of the project, which obligation shall be cumulative. Any cash surplus in excess of the amount so provided shall, upon disolution of the company, be paid into the general fund of the municipality. Section 13 provides that a redevelopment company shall not have power to acquire any realty for a project unless the supervising agency and the local legislative body determine that such acquisition is necessary or convenient for the public purpose defined in the act. It also provides that no such company shall issue stock, debentures and bonds in an amount greater than the total actual final cost of the project and that no contract shall be made for the payment of salaries to officers or employees, or for the construction, substantial repair, improvement or operation of projects except subject to the approval of the supervising agency. The supervising agency referred to means only the Superintendent of Insurance where, as here, an insurance company owns the stock and debentures of a redevelopment company, and if, as here, a contract is entered into the parties to which are a municipality, a redevelopment company and an insurance company, the supervising agency shall have no continuing power of supervision once it shall have approved the contract (§§ 3, 15). This means that the general power of visitation, examination and control provided for by section 21 is inapplicable to Stuyvesant. There are other limitations upon methods of financing, mortgage, sale or disposition of property and alteration of structures (§§ 9, 10, 11, 12, 14, 16, 23).

Section 15 sets up a procedure for the submission and approval of a plan of a proposed project which requires the prior approval of the supervising agency and the local planning commission. Thereafter a contract shall be proposed which, prior to its execution, must be approved by the local legislative body. It is provided that the contract shall regulate the rents to be charged and may contain other provisions for the financing, construction, operation and supervision of the project.

The statute provides that a municipality may take property by condemnation for a redevelopment company provided the latter shall pay all sums expended in connection with such acquisition, and it authorizes the municipality to convey such land to the company (§ 20). It also authorizes any local legislative body to convey to such company land in any street which is duly closed or discontinued pursuant to the plan, upon payment therefor or upon exchange for other lands (§ 20).

Section 24 provides that after the termination of tax exemption, in any manner, a redevelopment company may dissolve and convey its property to whomsoever it desires, and all limitations of the act shall cease.

Finally, section 26 provides as follows:

"The local legislative body of any municipality in which a project of such company is or is to be located may by contract agree with any redevelopment company to exempt from local and municipal taxes, other than assessments for local improvements, all or part of the value of the property included in such project which represents an increase over the assessed valuation of the real property, both land and improvements, acquired for the project at the time of its acquisition by the redevelopment company which originally undertook the project and for such definite period of years as such contract may provide. The tax exemption shall not operate for a period of more than twenty-five years, commencing in each instance from the date on which the benefits of such exemption first become available and effective.

**1042**                                                    [Emerson]

"A redevelopment company which has been granted and has received tax exemption pursuant to this section may at any time elect to pay to the municipality the total of all accrued taxes for which exemption was granted and received, together with interest at the rate of five per centum per annum. Upon such payment the tax exemption of the project shall thereupon cease and terminate."

The Legislature deliberately and intentionally refrained from imposing any restriction upon a redevelopment company in its choice of tenants. The law contains none. Attempts, repeatedly made in the Legislature since the law was enacted, to alter the policy of the statute in this respect have failed. (See, e.g., 1948 Sess., Assem. Int. 127, Pr. No. 127; Assem. Int. 217, Pr. No. 217; Assem. Int. 1270, Pr. 1294; 1947 Sess., Assem. Int. 35, Pr. No. 35; Assem. Int. 72, Pr. No. 72.) On the other hand, the Public Housing Law (§ 223), which is applicable to State-constructed, low cost housing projects, expressly prohibits discrimination. There is no claim that the Legislature refused by amendment to make similar provision in the Redevelopment Companies Law because it thought the statute already barred discrimination, and it is undisputed, therefore, that the legislative intent is clear to leave private enterprise free to select tenants of its own choice.

The matter of the exclusion of Negroes from the development arose in connection with the approval by the Governor of the 1943 amendments to the Redevelopment Companies Law and in contract negotiations between Metropolitan and the city. Commissioner Robert Moses, active in the plan, stated publicly to the Governor and the board of estimate that if any requirement was imposed which deprived the landlord of the right to select its tenants, no private venture would go into the business. Certainly the general impression was created—which Metropolitan did nothing to dispel—that Stuyvesant Town would not rent to Negroes. For that reason and others, unsuccessful attacks were made upon the desirability of the project. In the board of estimate at least three votes were cast against approval of the contract on the ground that exclusion on racial grounds would be practiced. The contract was finally approved without any provision regarding discrimination in the selection of tenants. It may be noted in passing that thereafter the New York City Council passed legislation withholding tax exemption from any subsequent redevelopment company unless it gave assurance that no discrimination would be practiced in its rental policies. This provision, however, expressly excluded from its

**1043**

operation any project "hitherto agreed upon or contracted for" (Administrative Code of City of New York, § J41-1.2).

In 1943, respondent Stuyvesant was formed by Metropolitan pursuant to the statute. A contract with the city was approved by the board of estimate of the City of New York in June, 1943. The contract embodied a plan for the rehabilitation of a substandard area comprising eighteen city blocks in the borough of Manhattan by the erection of thirty-five apartment houses capable of accommodating about twenty-five thousand people. Under the contract the City of New York agreed to condemn and bring under one good title the entire area. Stuyvesant agreed to acquire the area, demolish the old buildings and construct new ones, all without expense to the city. Metropolitan agreed to advance the necessary funds to Stuyvesant, guaranteed performance by the latter, and, with Stuyvesant, assumed all risks of the venture. The city granted tax exemption for twenty-five years only to the extent of the enhanced value to be created by the project. Stuyvesant agreed to convey to the city bordering strips around the periphery of the project in exchange for land in streets which the city agreed to close.

The contract regulates rents at rates intended to yield the statutory limited return, prohibits mortgaging and sale of the project, gives the city certain auditing privileges, and requires payment to the city upon the dissolution of Stuyvesant of any earned cash surplus after payment of all indebtedness. Upon the termination in any way of tax exemption, Stuyvesant may dissolve and convey its property to Metropolitan, and the statute and contract become inapplicable to the project.

In formulating an answer to the questions propounded at the beginning of this opinion we first consider whether there is anything in the Constitution of the State of New York which can be said to impose any broader or different restriction than is contained in the equal protection clauses of the Fourteenth Amendment of the Federal Constitution. Our conclusion is that the problem is precisely the same under the State Constitution as it is under the Federal Constitution. . . .

Our decision then must rest on the co-ordinate commands expressed in the equal protection clauses of the Federal and State Constitutions. For many years it has been unquestioned that the great prohibitions of the Fourteenth Amendment are addressed to that action alone which "may fairly be said to be that of the States" (*Shelley* v. *Kraemer*, 334 U. S. 1, 13; *Civil Rights Cases*, 109 U. S. 3). Upon that characteristic of the constitutional inhibition these parties have joined issue. Respondents contend that they are private companies, beyond the reach of the constitutional restraint and free to select arbitrarily the tenants who will occupy Stuyvesant Town. Appellants insist that the avowed discrimination falls under the constitutional ban because they say it has been aided and made possible by the action of the State. The issue is decisive, for the policy of respondents could not be followed by a governmental body (*cf. Buchanan* v. *Warley*, 245 U. S. 60).

In an early decision of the Supreme Court under the Fourteenth Amendment we find the statement that "a State acts by its legislative, its executive, or its judicial authorities. It can act in no other way." (*Ex Parte Virginia*, 100 U. S. 339, 347.) In that case the court held the official conduct of a State judge subject to the mandate although he had acted on his own impulse and without authority from the law of the State. Subsequent cases have made it clear that the prohibited action of a State may be exerted through private individuals and corporations. Thus discrimination by private individuals offends the equal protection clause if they act under constraint of State law (*Nixon* v. *Herndon*, 273 U. S. 536; *Buchanan* v. *Warley*, 245 U. S. 60, *supra*; *Truax* v. *Raich*, 239 U. S. 33).

In a more recent series of cases the Federal courts have held private groups subject to the constitutional restraints when they perform functions of a governmental character in matters of great public interest (*Smith* v. *Allwright*, 321 U. S. 649; *Nixon* v. *Condon*, 286 U. S. 73; *Rice* v. *Elmore*, 165 F. 2d 387, certiorari denied 333 U. S. 875; *Kerr* v. *Enoch Pratt Free Lib.*, 149 F. 2d 212. But compare *Mason* v. *Hitchcock*, 108 F. 2d. 134). Speaking of the executive committee of the Democratic Party in the State of Texas, Mr. Justice CARDOZO said: "They are not acting in matters of merely private concern like the directors or agents of business corporations. They are acting in matters of high public interest, matters intimately connected with the capacity of government to exercise its functions." (*Nixon* v. *Condon, supra*, at p. 88.) The result is unchanged though the State cast off all fetters upon their discretion (*Rice* v. *Elmore, supra*). The Supreme Court of the United States has indicated that the inhibitions of the Fifth Amendment upon the action of the Federal Government would apply to a labor union whose power to act as sole collective bargaining agent for railroad employees was derived from Federal statute (see *Steele* v. *Louisville & Nashville R. R. Co.*, 323 U. S. 192, 198–199).

In a final group of cases the State has lent its power in support of the actions of private individuals or corporations, and in so doing has clothed the private act with the character of State action (*Shelley* v. *Kraemer, supra; Marsh* v. *Alabama*, 326 U. S.

501). In the latter case an Alabama conviction for trespass in disseminating religious literature on the privately owned streets of a company town offended the due process clause of the Fourteenth Amendment. The language of the court indicates that if the right had been asserted in a different context the owner's action itself would have been condemned. Thus (326 U. S., at pp. 505–506) : "We do not agree that the corporation's property interests settle the question. The State urges in effect that the corporation's right to control the inhabitants of Chickasaw is coextensive with the right of a homeowner to regulate the conduct of his guests. We cannot accept that contention. Ownership does not always mean absolute dominion. The more an owner, for his advantage, opens up his property for use by the public in general, the more do his rights become circumscribed by the statutory and constitutional rights of those who use it."

Appellants here rely upon those cases in urging that we must characterize as governmental action the rental policy of Metropolitan and Stuyvesant. They point to the acknowledged contribution made by government to the project—principally the tax exemption amounting to many millions of dollars, and aggregation of the land through use of the city's power of eminent domain and through exchange of bordering tracts for city streets which had been closed. Moreover, we are urged to consider the size of the project as in reality forming a large community within the city.

All of the previous decisions, and others cited, might be distinguished in that they disclose the exertion of governmental power directly to aid in discrimination or other deprivation of right, or the action of a private group in the exercise of a governmental function. Neither factor is present here, where the State has remained silent and has indicated that the public purpose has been fulfilled by the rehabilitation of a substandard area (*Matter of Murray* v. *La Guardia*, 291 N. Y. 320, *supra*). This conclusion is reinforced by the constitutional provision, hereinbefore referred to, which specifically negated any authorization to State or city to engage in any private business or enterprise in connection with the rehabilitation of substandard areas (art. XVIII, § 10).

However, to rest our decision solely upon conceptual distinction would be to ignore the character of the Constitution which we construe and of the decisions through which the Supreme Court of the United States has preserved its nature as a living instrument of government. The language quoted above from *Marsh* v. *Alabama* (*supra*) has a different ring from the earlier words of *Ex Parte Virginia* (*supra*). The evolution of our society has disclosed State action where doubtless it would not have been found in an earlier day. Institutions created to meet the social and industrial necessities of our times do not respond readily to the simple test enunciated in *Ex Parte Virginia* (e.g., *Marsh* v. *Alabama, supra*). Those considerations might suggest the desirability of holding that the test can be satisfied, and State action discerned, in any case where the State has tolerated discrimination respecting a matter of high public importance. Invocation of the Constitution then might depend upon a balance of the two values asserted—here the privilege of Metropolitan and Stuyvesant as against the right of appellants to equality of treatment.

Such a development in constitutional law would clash with a fundamental policy inherent in the Fourteenth Amendment and the decision of the *Civil Rights Cases* (109 U. S. 3, *supra*). Both are instinct with the idea that the rights defined in the amendment are to be protected by the States against the actions of private individuals. That high responsibility of the States, implicit in our Federal system, indicates that the political processes must furnish the appropriate means for extension of those rights in areas wherein they have not been heretofore asserted. The unquestioned value of that system suggests the limits to the expanding concept of State action, which has hitherto been found only in cases where the State has consciously exerted its power in aid of discrimination or where private individuals have acted in a governmental capacity so recognized by the State.

The State of New York has consciously and deliberately refrained from imposing any requirement of nondiscrimination upon respondents as a condition to the granting of aid in the rehabilitation of substandard areas. Furthermore, it has deliberately refrained from declaring by legislation that the opportunity to purchase and lease real property without discrimination is a civil right. To say that the aid accorded respondents is nevertheless subject to these requirements, on the ground that helpful co-operation between the State and the respondents transforms the activities of the latter into State action, comes perilously close to asserting that any State assistance to an organization which discriminates necessarily violates the Fourteenth Amendment. Tax exemption and power of eminent domain are freely given to many organizations which necessarily limit their benefits to a restricted group. It has not yet been held that the recipients are subject to the restraints of the Fourteenth Amendment.

The increasing and fruitful participation of government, both State and Federal, in the industrial and economic life of the nation—by subsidy and control analogous to that found in this case—suggests the grave and delicate problem in defining the scope of the constitutional inhibitions which would be posed if we were to characterize the rental policy of respondents as governmental action. To cite only a few examples: the merchant marine, air carriers and farmers all receive substantial economic aid from our Federal Government and are subject to varying degrees of control in the public interest. Yet it has never been suggested that those and similar groups are subject to the restraints upon governmental action embodied in the Fifth Amendment similar to the restrictions of the Fourteenth upon the States. We do not read the language in *Steele* v. *Louisville & Nashville R. R. Co.* (323 U. S. 192, *supra*) as implying such a suggestion. Such restraints as have been imposed upon their freedom of action are derived from statute or common law, and we feel that those sources of control are the most appropriate.

We are agreed that the moral end advanced by appellants cannot justify the means through which it is sought to be attained. Respondents cannot be held to answer for their policy under the equal protection clauses of either Federal or State Constitution. The aid which the State has afforded to respondents and the control to which they are subject are not sufficient to transmute their conduct into State action under the constitutional provisions here in question.

The judgment . . . should be affirmed. . . .

FULD, J. (dissenting). Undenied and undeniable is the fundamental proposition that "Distinctions between citizens solely because of their ancestry are by their very nature odious to a free people whose institutions are founded upon the doctrine of equality". (*Hirabayashi* v. *United States,* 320 U. S. 81, 100.) The average citizen, aware of that truth but unschooled in legal niceties, will, I venture, find the decision which the court now makes extremely perplexing. While the Stuyvesant Town housing project was in blueprint and under construction, the public understood, and rightly, that it was an undertaking on which the State and the City of New York had bestowed the blessings and benefits of governmental powers. Now that the development is a reality, the public is told in effect that, because the Metropolitan Life Insurance Company (hereafter referred to as Metropolitan) and Stuyvesant Town Corporation (hereafter called Stuyvestant) are private companies, they are not subject to the equal protection clause, and may, if they choose, discriminate against Negroes in selecting tenants. That conclusion strikes me as totally at odds with common understanding and not less so with the facts and circumstances disclosed by the record. . . .

**1048**

# DISCRIMINATION

The Fourteenth Amendment of the Federal Constitution, insofar as relevant, provides that "No State shall . . . deny to any person within its jurisdiction the equal protection of the laws." The Amendment, it is true, does not operate against purely private conduct (*Civil Rights Cases,* 108 U. S. 3) but it does prohibit discrimination even by private persons or agencies if such action can "fairly be said" to be that of the State. (See *Shelley* v. *Kraemer,* 334 U. S. 1, 13.) The concept of "state action" has enjoyed a career of aggressive expansion during the sixty-six years since the *Civil Rights Cases* were decided. (109 U. S. 3.). . .

As the majority opinion recognizes (p 534), the Fourteenth Amendment is no longer satisfied by a mechanical finding that the discriminatory conduct was not perpetrated by legislative, judicial or executive officials of the State. The concept of "state" action has been vitalized and expanded; the definition of "private" conduct in this context has been tightened and restricted. When private individuals or groups move beyond "matters of merely private concern" and act in "matters of high public interests", the test is not, Mr. Justice CARDOZO has written, whether they are "the representatives of the State in the strict sense in which an agent is the representative of his principal. The test is whether they are to be classified as representatives of the State to such an extent and in such a sense that the great restraints of the Constitution set limits to their action." (*Nixon* v. *Condon,* 286 U. S. 73, 88–89.)

The fact that the constitutional right is invaded in the exercise of "private" property interests is no more decisive than that the owner himself is "private". In *Marsh* v. *Alabama* (326 U. S. 501, *supra*), for instance, a Jehovah's Witness was convicted of trespass, in spite of her claim of constitutional right, for refusing to leave the streets of a company town completely owned by a private corporation. Relying upon its "private" proprietary rights, the owner urged that the Fourteenth Amendment was inapplicable to it, but the Supreme Court declared (pp. 505–506): "We do not agree that the corporation's property interests settle the question. The State urges in effect that the corporation's right to control the inhabitants of Chickasaw is coextensive with the right of a homeowner to regulate the conduct of his guests. We cannot accept that contention. Ownership does not always mean absolute dominion. The more an owner, for his advantage, opens up his property for use by the public in general, the more do his rights become circumscribed by the statutory and constitutional rights of those who use it."

**1049**

A kindred philosophy outlaws the enforcement of privately drawn restrictive covenants aimed at nonwhite ownership of property. (See *Shelley* v. *Kraemer*, 334 U. S. 1, *supra*.) It also runs through the numerous decisions which deny to the State and its subdivision, a city, the power to avoid their constitutional responsibilities by leasing or assigning to private persons important projects or functions in which discrimination is practiced. (See, e.g., *Lawrence* v. *Hancock*, 76 F. Supp. 1004; *Kern* v. *City Commissioners of City of Newton*, 151 Kan. 565; *Culver* v. *City of Warren*, 83 N. E. 2d 82 [Ohio App.].)

The teaching of this body of law is clear. On the one hand, the equal protection clause does not prohibit private persons from exercising rights of private ownership in matters merely private, however arbitrarily or capriciously they may discriminate. On the other hand, even the conduct of private individuals offends against the constitutional provision if it appears in an activity of public importance and if the State has accorded the transaction either the panoply of its authority or the weight of its power, interest and support. . . .

To intimate that this is just another instance of a government subsidy is to misconceive the case. To claim that the construction and operation of a project such as Stuyvesant is a matter of but private concern is to disregard the obvious. Unmistakable are the signs that this undertaking was a governmentally conceived, governmentally aided and governmentally regulated project in urban redevelopment. Everywhere in evidence are the voice and authority of the State and the City. Approval of the underlying constitutional housing article set in motion numerous governmental acts necessary to accomplish the "reconstruction and rehabilitation" of slum areas and to provide "incidental . . . facilities" (§ 1). Proceeding under that authority, the Legislature had in view more than merely the effacement or razing of blighted substandard buildings; their "modernization" and "reconstruction" to provide "adequate, safe, sanitary and properly planned housing accommodations in effectuation of official city plans" were declared to be "public uses and purposes" (§ 2). And it was to achieve all these ends—not merely the clearance of a slum area—that the plans for Stuyvesant Town were conceived and executed, that the City condemned property for use by defendants, closed public streets and turned over their land area—comprising 19% of the total area of the project—granted tax exemption upon improvements and insisted upon regulation of the rents, profits and financing methods of the redevelopment corporation.

**1050**

That there is "state action" here is supported and established, however, by more than the constitutional and statutory provisions which made the development possible, by more than the city and state participation and aid that brought Stuyvesant Town into being. In addition, there is the exceedingly significant fact that the City's Board of Estimate approved and authorized the contract for the construction and operation of Stuyvesant Town after having been apprised by city representatives and company officials that Negroes would be excluded from the development. Beyond that, the City Council deliberately excepted Stuyvesant from the coverage of the law, subsequently enacted, which barred discrimination in tax-exempt projects. In a most literal sense, in a most direct way, here was "action," and—if such a showing were necessary (but see, contra, *Steele v. Louisville & Nashville R. R. Co.*, 323 U. S. 192, *supra*)—action, "consciously exerted," by the State "in aid of" the discrimination being practiced (opinion, p. 535). To suggest that the Constitution's command does not apply because such action was not exerted "directly" in aid of the discrimination (opinion, p. 533), is to overlook the nature of the case. We cannot close our eyes to what led to the end result, nor properly hold that the final product of that action should be considered and appraised without regard to its roots or its background. . . .

As an enterprise in urban redevelopment, Stuyvesant Town is a far cry from a privately built and privately run apartment house. More, its peculiar features yield to those eligible as tenants tremendous advantages in modern housing and at rentals far below those charged in purely private developments. As citizens and residents of the City, Negroes as well as white people have contributed to the development. Those who have paid and will continue to pay should share in the benefits to be derived. Stuyvesant Town in its role as chosen instrument for this public purpose may not escape the obligations that accompany the privileges accorded to it.

It is impossible to balance the essence of democracy against fireproof buildings and well-kept lawns, and, fortunately, the Constitutions, Federal and State, forbid our putting the former into the judicial scales just as they forbade the city officials from putting it upon the bargaining table. The mandate that there be equal protection of the laws, designed as a basic safeguard for all, binds us and respondents as well to put an end to this discrimination.

I would reverse in the Dorsey action.

[Judges Lewis, Conway and Dye concurred with Judge Bromley; Chief Judge Loughran and Judge Desmond agreed with Judge Fuld.]

## Note

1. For an earlier attempt to raise the constitutional issue decided in the *Dorsey* case, see *Pratt v. La Guardia,* 182 Misc. 462, 47 N. Y. Supp.2d 359 (1944), aff'd without op. 268 App. Div. 973, 52 N.Y. Supp. 2d 569 (1944), app. dis. 294 N.Y. 842, 62 N.E.2d 394 (1945) (no rental policy had been adopted; the Court refused to grant equitable relief on the basis of anticipations).

2. For discussion of the principal case see Notes, 57 Yale L.J. 426 (1948) (lower court decision); 98 U. of Pa. L. Rev. 247 (1949); 35 Corn. L. Q. 399 (1950); Note, *State Action Within the Meaning of the Fourteenth Amendment of the Federal Constitution: The Stuyvesant Case,* 23 Temp. L. Q. 209 (1950); Note, 21 Miss. L. J. 407 (1950).

Subsequently the Metropolitan Life Insurance Company announced that the Stuyvesant Town Corporation "has leased some apartments to qualified Negro families." N. Y. Times, Aug. 25, 1950. In 1951 the New York City Council passed a bill to prohibit discrimination or segregation in all private housing projects enjoying total or partial exemption from city taxes or receiving direct or indirect financial aid from the city. The bill applied to existing projects and was primarily directed at Stuyvesant Town. N. Y. Times, Feb. 17 and Mar. 15, 1951.

3. Public housing and housing built with public funds: In *Seawell v. MacWithey,* 2 N. J. 563, 67 Atl.2d 309 (1949), applications for dwellings in four housing projects built with city and state funds were "screened" by the Veteran's Permanent Housing Committee of the East Orange City Council and a private group appointed by the City Council, called the Veterans Selection Committee. The Committees adopted a policy of segregation under which one of the four projects was set aside for Negroes. The lower court granted an injunction restraining the segregation based on the ground that it violated the Fourteenth Amendment, the State Constitution and a statute prohibiting racial and religious discrimination in public housing facilities. The New Jersey Supreme Court reversed on the theory that the City had taken no discriminatory action because the Committees were acting without authority by ordinance or resolution. The case is noted in 4 Rutgers L. Rev. 506 (1950).

In *Favors v. Randall,* 40 F. Supp. 743 (E.D. Pa., 1941), it was held that where the housing authority selects tenants on the basis of a quota reflecting the existing neighborhood racial pattern of occupancy there is no "discrimination." The Court relied in part on the equal but separate facilities doctrine (see *infra*): "The argument cannot be accepted that equal rights cannot be secured to the negro except by an enforced commingling of the two races. . . . In determining the question of reasonableness the Philadelphia Housing Authority was at liberty to act with reference to the established usages, customs and traditions of the people, and with a view to the preservation of public peace and good order as well as a promotion of their comfort, which was the purpose of the creation of the Authority." On the question of proof of segregation see Note, 17 U. of Chi. L. Rev. 107 (1949).

Racial segregation in public housing projects has also been upheld in *Denard v. Housing Authority of Ft. Smith*, 203 Ark. 1050, 159 S.W.2d 764 (1942); *Housing Authority v. Higginbotham*, 143 S.W.2d 95 (Tex. Civ. App., 1940) (constitutional question in these cases was raised by landowners objecting to the taking of the land by the government). The cases are collected and summarized in 14 A.L.R.2d 153.

4. Nine states have statutes dealing with discrimination in housing.

A. Basis for discrimination covered: (1) "Discrimination" based on color, race, creed or religion: Conn. Gen. Stat., 1951 Supp., § 1407b; Smith-Hurd Ill. Stats. Ann., 1951 Cum. Supp., ch. 67½, § 82; Burns Ind. Stats. Ann., 48–8503; Mass. Gen. Stats., 1951 Cum. Supp., ch. 121, § 26FF; N.J.L. 1950, ch. 105–112; N.Y. Civil Rights Law (Wicks-Austin Law), Art. 2A; Pa. Stat. (Purdon), 1951 Cum. Supp., tit. 35, § 1664; Wis. Stat. 1951, ch. 66.39(13). (2) "Discrimination" based on national origin: Indiana, Pennsylvania, Wisconsin, New Jersey and New York. (3) "Discrimination" based on ancestry: New Jersey and New York. (4) "Discrimination" based on religious, political, or other affiliations: Minn. Stats. Ann., 1951 Cum. Supp., 462.481, 462.641.

B. Type of discrimination prohibited: Most of these statutes forbid discrimination without defining more specifically the meaning of the term. The Massachusetts statute prohibits segregation as well as discrimination in the selection of tenants for public low-rent housing projects. The New York law guaranteeing equal rights to publicly-aided housing includes within the term "discriminate" the process of segregation or separation. Other specific forbidden practices under these laws include: (1) Discrimination in tenant selection: Pennsylvania, Minnesota, Wisconsin (in veteran housing only). (2) Restrictive covenants attached to conveyances by Redevelopment Commissions: Illinois. (3) Exclusion from zoned redevelopment areas: Indiana. The Pennsylvania law requires that the redevelopment contract contain a covenant that no person shall be deprived of the use or occupancy of the project and its facilities because of race, creed, color, or national origin.

C. Types of housing covered: (1) Public housing: Connecticut, Massachusetts, Minnesota, New Jersey, New York, Pennsylvania, Wisconsin. (2) Publicly-assisted housing: Connecticut, New York. (3) Urban redevelopment: Illinois, Indiana, Minnesota, New Jersey, New York, Pennsylvania, Wisconsin. (4) Veterans' housing: New Jersey, New York, Pennsylvania, Wisconsin. Most of these laws contain no enforcement procedure. The public officials are subject to suit by a party directly injured. The New York, Minnesota, and Connecticut statutes specifically provide for civil suit. The Minnesota law limits damage claims to $500. In addition, the New York law allows any taxpayer on property whose assessed value is over $1000 to seek an injunction forbidding discrimination. In Connecticut, Massachusetts, and New Jersey, commissions administering anti-discrimination laws in the area of employment and public accommodations (see *infra*) also receive complaints and hold hearings concerning alleged discrimination in public housing. These laws have already resulted in effective action on the state level. See American Jewish Congress and National Association for the Advancement of Colored People, *Civil Rights in the United States in 1951*, pp. 70–83 (1952).

5. In thirteen cities—Boston, Cleveland, Hartford, Newark, New York, Philadelphia, Pontiac (Michigan), Providence, San Francisco, Los Angeles, St. Paul, Cincinnati and Pasco (Washington) recent local ordinances and resolutions forbid discrimination (including segregation) in public and publicly-aided housing. The New York, San Francisco, Los Angeles, and Cincinnati measures cover redevelopment programs as well. Only two cities, New York and San Francisco, provide for enforcement by public authorities. In New York discrimination is a misdemeanor, subject to a $500 fine. In addition municipal tax exemption may be withdrawn upon a finding of discrimination by the State Supreme Court. The San Francisco Housing Authority is authorized to attempt conciliation and, upon its failure, to seek an injunction.

For an analysis of these municipal laws see Wisconsin Legislative Reference Library (Research Report No. 105), *A Study of State and Local Legislative and Administrative Acts Designed to Meet Problems of Human Rights*, pp. 5–8 (1952).

For model ordinances and statutes, see National Community Relations Advisory Council, *Equality of Opportunity in Housing*, pp. 56–62 (1952).

6. Zoning: In *Buchanan v. Warley*, 245 U. S. 60, 62 L. Ed. 149, 38 S. Ct. 16 (1917), discussed in the *Shelley* and *Dorsey* cases, *supra*, the Supreme Court stated:

"That there exists a serious and difficult problem arising from a feeling of race hostility which the law is powerless to control, and to which it must give a measure of consideration, may be freely admitted. But its solution cannot be promoted by depriving citizens of their constitutional rights and privileges.

"As we have seen, this court has held laws valid which separated the races on the basis of equal accommodations in public conveyances, and courts of high authority have held enactments lawful which provide for separation in the public schools of white and colored pupils where equal privileges are given. But in view of the rights secured by the Fourteenth Amendment to the Federal Constitution such legislation must have its limitations, and cannot be sustained where the exercise of authority exceeds the restraints of the Constitution. We think these limitations are exceeded in laws and ordinances of the character now before us.

"It is the purpose of such enactments, and, it is frankly avowed it will be their ultimate effect, to require by law, at least in residential districts, the compulsory separation of the races on account of color. Such action is said to be essential to the maintenance of the purity of the races, although it is to be noted in the ordinance under consideration that the employment of colored servants in white families is permitted, and nearby residences of colored persons not coming within the blocks, as defined in the ordinance, are not prohibited.

"The case presented does not deal with an attempt to prohibit the amalgamation of the races. The right which the ordinance annulled was the civil right of a white man to dispose of his property if he saw fit to do so to a person of color and of a colored person to make such disposition to a white person.

"It is urged that this proposed segregation will promote the public peace by preventing race conflicts. Desirable as this is, and important as is the preservation of the public peace, this aim cannot be accomplished by laws or ordinances which deny rights created or protected by the Federal Constitution.

"It is said that such acquisitions by colored persons depreciate property owned in the neighborhood by white persons. But property may be acquired by undesirable white neighbors or put to disagreeable though lawful uses with like results.

"We think this attempt to prevent the alienation of the property in question to a person of color was not a legitimate exercise of the police power of the State, and is in direct violation of the fundamental law enacted in the Fourteenth Amendment of the Constitution preventing state interference with property rights except by due process of law. That being the case the ordinance cannot stand." 245 U. S. at 80–2.

See also *Harmon v. Tyler*, 273 U. S. 668, 71 L. Ed. 831, 47 S. Ct. 471 (1927), and *Richmond v. Deans*, 281 U. S. 704, 74 L. Ed. 1128, 50 S. Ct. 407 (1930), also discussed in the *Shelley* and *Dorsey* cases. A recent case is *Birmingham v. Monk*, 185 F.2d 859 (C. A. 5, 1951), where the court held that evidence that an ordinance segregating white and negro residences was passed to preserve breach of the peace was irrelevant. See Notes, 37 Va. L. Rev. 612 (1951); 29 Chi-Kent L. Rev. 329 (1951). For criticism of the *Buchanan* case see Martin, *Segregation of Residences of Negroes*, 32 Mich. L. Rev. 721 (1934). Racial zoning is prohibited by statute in Colorado. Col. Stat. Ann., ch. 26, § 25 (1935). In Kansas City planning commissions may not act so as to discriminate against minorities. Kan. Gen. Stat., § 12–713 (1935). See also Note, 126 A.L.R. 638.

7. Alien land laws: Typical alien land laws are the Washington law, prohibiting landholding by non-declarant aliens, and the California law, applying the prohibition to aliens ineligible for citizenship. Wash. Stat. § 10581–92 (Supp. 1940); 1 Deering Cal. Gen. Laws, Acts 261 and 262 (1944). In *Terrace v. Thompson*, 263 U. S. 197, 68 L. Ed. 255, 44 S. Ct. 15 (1923), and *Porterfield v. Webb*, 263 U. S. 225, 68 L. Ed. 278, 44 S. Ct. 21 (1923), the Supreme Court upheld these laws. The Court reasoned that the classification was reasonable because it flowed from the naturalization law itself. Those who could not become citizens might not take sufficient interest to effectively work for the welfare of the state. This would become especially serious when one considers the possibility that all the land in the state might fall into the hands of aliens.

In *Oyama v. California*, 332 U. S. 633, 92 L. Ed. 249, 68 S. Ct. 269 (1948), the Court held that Section 9 of the California law violated the rights of citizens who are children of ineligible aliens and discriminated against them solely because of ancestry. Section 9 created a prima facie presumption of intent to evade escheat upon proof that the consideration was paid or agreed to be paid by an ineligible alien and that title was taken in the name of a citizen or eligible alien. The Court stated that it did not need to reach the question of the validity of the other provisions of the land law. Four justices favored invalidation of the entire law.

Recent state court decisions, however, have relied on the *Oyama* case, on *Takahashi v. Fish and Game Comm.*, 334 U. S. 410, 92 L. Ed. 1478, 68 S. Ct. 1138 (1948) (declaring a law denying fishing licenses to "aliens ineligible for citizenship" violative of the equal protection clause), and on *Shelley v. Kraemer, supra,* as indicating that the Court no longer regards the earlier cases as binding. These decisions have held alien land laws to violate the equal protection clause. See *Kenji Namba v. McCourt,* 185 Ore. 579, 204 Pac. 2d 569 (1949) ; *Seii Fujii v. State,* — Cal. 2d —, 242 Pac. 2d 617 (1952).

For discussion, see Note, 56 Yale L. J. 1017 (1947) ; Ferguson, *The California Alien Land Law and the Fourteenth Amendment,* 35 Calif. L. Rev. 61 (1947) ; McGovney, *The Anti-Japanese Land Laws of California and Ten Other States,* 35 Calif. L. Rev. 7 (1947).

## Lending Activities of the Federal Government

### WEAVER—THE NEGRO GHETTO

Published by Harcourt, Brace and Company, copyright by Robert C. Weaver, 1948, pp. 69–72

The depression ushered the Federal Government into the housing field. These activities of the New Deal administration were concerned with reforms in the credit system and the construction of shelter for low-income families. Of these, the latter were of more benefit to colored people.

Along with a vastly larger number of whites, colored home owners were faced with commitments to pay mortgages which were, in the early 1930's, unrealistic in light of current incomes and property values. To meet the general situation in part, the Home Owners Loan Corporation was formed in 1933, and in a period of three years it refinanced (on terms of lower mortgages and interest rates) about a million small homes. Because of several factors, many Negro home owners were not able to qualify for this aid. In the first place, the purchase price that some paid and outstanding loans were all out of proportion to the value of the properties. Then there was a paradoxical situation: because of the hesitancy of financial institutions to finance Negro homes, Negroes in general, had less of the value of their homes covered by mortgages; at the same time, Negroes who did owe a sizeable proportion of the value of their homes often had second and third mortgages at high interest rates and service charges. These secondary mortgages were less easily adjusted, and this factor combined with the location, value and smaller mortgages on Negro property to reduce the extent to which colored owners benefited from HOLC. Where they did get loans, the terms were much more favorable than they had been able to get previously. Although there are no data reflecting the extent of Negro participation in HOLC, the Housing Census for 1940 reports that at that time 24,290 non-whites had HOLC loans. The Negro mortgages were slightly less than 5 per cent of the total.

Another assistance to the credit structure came from the activities of the Federal Housing Administration. The agency had two principal programs: insured loans for home modernization, and insured loans for house construction. Between 1934–40, FHA insured mortgages for $4,400,000,000, and four out of every ten urban dwellings built in the U.S.A. during 1940 were FHA-insured. Not only were the vast majority of Negroes financially unable to participate in the FHA program, but even those who could afford to build new homes were stymied by their relegation to the Black Belt. This latter factor was most significant, since the financial institutions through which FHA operated and from which most of its key officials in Washington and the field were recruited were the very financial and real estate interests and institutions which led the campaign to spread racial covenants and residential segregation. Then, too, FHA stressed the development of suburban communities and most of its construction was concentrated in the outlying areas (in Detroit and Chicago, well over half of the FHA-insured loans in 1941 were in new subdivisions). Negroes had long been barred from most such areas. Within the Black Belt, largely because it was a congested and over-populated area and because it was usually the oldest section of the city, there were few vacant areas which could meet the neighborhood requirements of FHA. In light of these facts, it is safe to say (as observation and subsequent figures have proved) that Negroes in northern cities benefited little from the activities of the agency. . . .

FHA's chief contribution to Negroes was to complicate the ultimate solution of their housing problem. This it accomplished by devious ways. By failing to permit or promote Negro participation, while facilitating the augmentation of the total supply of new housing, it contributed greatly to widening the gap between the living conditions of whites and Negroes. FHA's emphasis on outlying projects provided whites with places to live and thus accelerated their movement away from areas where some colored people lived, increasing residential segregation in

the process.  But the most objectionable feature of FHA operations was its acceptance and championing of race restrictive
covenants.  This was probably inevitable once the government
had turned the agency's operations over to the real estate and
home finance boys.

## Note

Prior to *Shelley v. Kraemer* the FHA Underwriting Manual contained the following instructions:
"The Valuator should realize that the need for protection from adverse influences is greater in an undeveloped or partially developed
area than in any other type of neighborhood.  Generally, a high rating
should be given only where adequate and properly enforced zoning regulations exist or where effective restrictive covenants are recorded
against the entire tract, since these provide the surest protection against
undesirable encroachment and inharmonious use.  To be most effective,
deed restrictions should be imposed upon all land in the immediate environment of the subject location. . . .  Recommended restrictions
should include provision for the following . . . Prohibition of the
occupancy of properties except by the race for which they are intended."  U. S. Federal Housing Administration, *Underwriting Manual*,
§ 980 (3) (g) (1939).
The Manual also stated that for the sake of the "stability" of the
neighborhoods "properties shall continue to be occupied by the same
social and racial classes" and the agency helped frame restrictive covenants for prospective borrowers.  In 1947 a revised manual deleted all
reference to "race."  It stated: "Protective covenants are essential to
the sound development of proposed residential areas."  U. S. Federal
Housing Administration, *Underwriting Manual*, § 1354 (1947).
After *Shelley v. Kraemer* the FHA and the Veterans Administration
declared that they would not insure property with racial covenants
recorded after Feb. 15, 1950.  More recently FHA has indicated that
interracial projects will get insurance and many have.  Nevertheless,
projects like Levittown in Long Island which followed a known discriminatory policy continued to get insurance.  FHA still seems to encourage segregated Negro housing but it has been indicated that where
FHA obtains title to projects they will be non-segregated.
A full discussion may be found in Abrams, *The Segregation Threat
in Housing*, in Straus, *Two-Thirds of a Nation*, pp. 210, 219 et seq.
(1952); National Community Relations Advisory Council, *Equality of
Opportunity in Housing* (1952); National Association for the Advancement of Colored People, *Memorandum to the President of the United
States Concerning Racial Discrimination by the Federal Housing Administration* (mimeo., Feb. 7, 1949).
For examples of literature issued by federal agencies showing that
the approach was in terms of more and better housing for minority
groups by breaking the bottleneck in finance and site selection, rather
than in terms of integrated interracial housing, see *e. g.*, McGraw, *The
Neglected Tenth in Housing and Home Finance* (mimeo. 1948).  See

also Wyatt, *Better Homes for Negro Families in the South,* 28 Social Forces 297 (1950).

## B. EDUCATION, TRANSPORTATION AND PUBLIC ACCOMMODATIONS

### 1. Introduction

### TO SECURE THESE RIGHTS—THE REPORT OF THE PRESIDENT'S COMMITTEE ON CIVIL RIGHTS

Washington: U. S. Government Printing Office, 1947, pp. 62–7

The United States has made remarkable progress toward the goal of universal education for its people. The number and variety of its schools and colleges are greater than ever before. Student bodies have become increasingly representative of all the different peoples who make up our population. Yet we have not finally eliminated prejudice and discrimination from the operation of either our public or our private schools and colleges. Two inadequacies are extremely serious. We have failed to provide Negroes and, to a lesser extent, other minority group members with equality of educational opportunities in our public institutions, particularly at the elementary and secondary school levels. We have allowed discrimination in the operation of many of our private institutions of higher education, particularly in the North with respect to Jewish students.

*Discrimination in public schools.*—The failure to give Negroes equal educational opportunities is naturally most acute in the South, where approximately 10 million Negroes live. The South is one of the poorer sections of the country and has at best only limited funds to spend on its schools. With 34.5 percent of the country's population, 17 southern states and the District of Columbia have 39.4 percent of our school children. Yet the South has only one-fifth of the taxpaying wealth of the nation. Actually, on a percentage basis, the South spends a greater share of its income on education than do the wealthier states in other parts of the country. For example, Mississippi, which has the lowest expenditure per school child of any state, is ninth in percentage of income devoted to education. A recent study showed Mississippi spending 3.41 percent of its income for education as against New York's figure of only 2.61 percent. But this meant $400 per classroom unit in Mississippi, and $4,100 in New York. Negro and white school children both suffer because of the South's basic inability to match the level of educational opportunity provided in other sections of the nation.

But it is the South's segregated school system which most directly discriminates against the Negro. This segregation is found today in 17 southern states and the District of Columbia. Poverty-stricken though it was after the close of the Civil War, the South chose to maintain two sets of public schools, one for whites and one for Negroes. With respect to education, as well as to other public services, the Committee believes that the "separate but equal" rule has not been obeyed in practice. There is a marked difference in quality between the educational opportunities offered white children and Negro children in the separate schools. Whatever test is used—expenditure per pupil, teachers' salaries, the number of pupils per teacher, transportation of students, adequacy of school buildings and educational equipment, length of school term, extent of curriculum—Negro students are invariably at a disadvantage. Opportunities for Negroes in public institutions of higher education in the South—particularly at the professional graduate school level—are severely limited.

Statistics in support of these conclusions are available. Figures provided by the United States Office of Education for the school year, 1943–44, show that the average length of the school term in the areas having separate schools was 173.5 days for whites, and 164 for Negroes; the number of pupils per teacher was 28 for white and 34 for Negroes; and the average annual salary for Negro teachers was lower than that for white teachers in all but three of the 18 areas. Salary figures are as follows:

| State or District of Columbia | Average annual salary of principals, supervisors, and teachers in schools for— | |
|---|---|---|
| | Whites | Negroes |
| Alabama | $1,158 | $ 661 |
| Arkansas | 924 | 555 |
| Delaware | 1,953 | 1,814 |
| Florida | 1,530 | 970 |
| Georgia | 1,123 | 515 |
| Louisiana | 1,683 | 828 |
| Maryland | 2,085 | 2,002 |
| Mississippi | 1,107 | 342 |
| Missouri | 1,397 | [1] 1,590 |
| North Carolina | 1,380 | 1,249 |
| Oklahoma | 1,428 | 1,438 |
| South Carolina | 1,203 | 615 |
| Tennessee | 1,071 | 1,010 |
| Texas | 1,395 | 946 |
| Virginia | 1,364 | 1,129 |
| District of Columbia | 2,610 | 2,610 |

The South has made considerable progress in the last decade in narrowing the gap between educational opportunities afforded the white children and that afforded Negro children. For example, the gap between the length of the school year for whites and the shorter one for Negroes has been narrowed from 14.8 days in 1939–40 to 9.5 days in 1943–44. Similarly, the gap in student load per teacher in white and Negro schools has dropped from 8.5 students in 1939–40 to six students in 1943–44.

In spite of the improvement which is undoubtedly taking place, the Committee is convinced that the gap between white and Negro schools can never be completely eliminated by means of state funds alone. The cost of maintaining separate, but truly equal, school systems would seem to be utterly prohibitive in many of the southern states. It seems probable that the only means by which such a goal can finally be won will be through federal financial assistance. The extension of the federal grant-in-aid for educational purposes, already available to the land-grant colleges and, for vocational education, to the secondary school field, seems both imminent and desirable.

Whether the federal grant-in-aid should be used to support the maintenance of separate schools is an issue that the country must soon face.

In the North, segregation in education is not formal, and in some states is prohibited. Nevertheless, the existence of resi-

---

[1] Higher salaries due to the fact that most Negro schools are located in cities where all salaries are higher.

dential restrictions in many northern cities has had discriminatory effects on Negro education. In Chicago, for example, the schools which are most crowded and employ double shift schedules are practically all in Negro neighborhoods.

Other minorities encounter discrimination. Occasionally Indian children attending public schools in the western states are assigned to separate classrooms. Many Texas schools segregate Mexican American children in separate schools. In California segregation of Mexican American children was also practiced until recently. The combined effect of a federal court ruling, and legislative action repealing the statute under which school boards claimed authority to segregate, seems to have ended this pattern of discrimination in California schools.

*Discrimination in private schools.*—The second inadequacy in our present educational practices in America is the religious and racial discrimination that exists in the operation of some private educational institutions, both with respect to the admission of students and the treatment of them after admission.

The Committee is absolutely convinced of the importance of the private educational institution to a free society. It does not question the right of groups of private citizens to establish such institutions, determine their character and policies, and operate them. But it does believe that such schools immediately acquire a public character and importance. Invariably they enjoy government support, if only in the form of exemption from taxation and in the privilege of income-tax deduction extended to their benefactors. Inevitably, they render public service by training our young people for life in a democratic society. Consequently, they are possessed of a public responsibility from which there is no escape.

Leading educators assert that a careful selection in admissions practices may be necessary to insure a representative and diversified student body. Liberal arts colleges, in particular, have used this reasoning to limit the number of students enrolled from any one race or religion, as well as from any geographical section, preparatory school, or socio-economic background.

Nevertheless it is clear that there is much discrimination, based on prejudice, in admission of students to private colleges, vocational schools, and graduate schools. Since accurate statistical data is almost impossible to obtain this is difficult to prove. But competent observers are agreed that existence of this condition is widespread. Application blanks of many American colleges and universities include questions pertaining to the candidate's racial origin, religious preference, parents' birthplace, etc. In many of our northern educational institutions enrollment of

Jewish students seems never to exceed certain fixed points and there is never more than a token enrollment of Negroes.

The impact of discriminatory practices in private education is illustrated by the situation in New York City. The students of the city colleges of New York are predominantly Jewish, resulting in part from the discrimination practiced by some local private institutions. These colleges have high academic standards, but graduates from them with excellent records have been repeatedly denied admission to private and nonsectarian professional schools. A Special Investigating Committee of the Council of the City of New York, recently established to examine this situation, found convincing evidence of discrimination against graduates of the city colleges by the medical schools in the city in violation of the Civil Rights Act of New York. The Investigating Committee, after questioning witnesses and examining application blanks, concluded that various professional schools tried to get information about applicants which would indicate their race, religion, or national origin for "a purpose other than judging their qualifications for admission." Jews are not alone in being affected by these practices. One witness, a member of a medical school's admission committee, admitted to a prejudice against Irish Catholics which affected his judgment. The number of Negroes attending these medical schools has been extremely low; less than 50 have been graduated from them in 25 years.

Certainly the public cannot long tolerate practices by private educational institutions which are in serious conflict with patterns of democratic life, sanctioned by the overwhelming majority of our people. By the closing of the door through bigotry and prejudice to equality of educational opportunity, the public is denied the manifold social and economic benefits that the talented individual might otherwise contribute to our society.

## Note

More recent statistics on segregated schools show the following: (1) Average length of school term: white schools, 176.2, Negro, 171.0. (2) Average number of days attended by each pupil enrolled: white, 153.4, Negro, 143.1. (3) Average pupil-teacher load: white, 29, Negro, 34. (4) Current expenditure per pupil in average daily attendance (9 states): white $136.73, Negro $74.67. (5) Average salary per member of staff (19 states): white $2,271, Negro, $1,742. U. S. Federal Security Agency, Office of Education, *Statistical Summary of Education, 1947–48*, ch. 1 in *Biennial Survey of Education in the United States 1946–1948* (1951).

HIGHER EDUCATION FOR AMERICAN DEMOCRACY—
A REPORT OF THE PRESIDENT'S COMMISSION
ON HIGHER EDUCATION

Washington: U. S. Government Printing Office, 1947, vol. II, ch. III,
pp. 25–39, 43–4

## Discrimination in Higher Education

. . . Discriminatory practices deprive the Nation of a great
variety of talent, create and perpetuate serious inequalities, and
generate dangerous tensions. The impact of these social attitudes and behavior patterns adversely affects our entire society—
group relationships, the individuals who discriminate, and the
individuals who are discriminated against. This spiritual damage is not measurable; indeed it has never been recognized with
complete honesty. To the extent that intolerant attitudes against
members of minority groups are given support by our educational
institutions, the fabric of our democratic life is endangered.

A quantitative measure of discrimination at the undergraduate
level is impossible to obtain. Educational institutions are reluctant to be explicit about their selection criteria as these apply to
minority groups. Discriminatory practices are denied, ignored,
or rationalized. *But it requires no parade of statistics to know
that the situation for young people of minority groups is today
unsatisfactory, both in their opportunity to enter college and in
the happiness of their college life.* Enrollment data unmistakably
indicate the prevalence of quota systems and policies of exclusion. The nature of discrimination varies with respect to different minority groups and in different sections of the country.
But discrimination on grounds of an individual's race, creed,
color, sex, national origin, or ancestry is undoubtedly a fact in
many institutions of higher education.

The problem is not limited to the individuals who are denied
admission. Even for such of the minority group students as
are admitted, the unhappy consequences of intolerance can be
and often are profound and lifelong. The frustrations of social
discrimination—in the dormitories, in honorary societies, in
fraternities and sororities, on athletic teams, and at social functions—strike at the personal dignity of the affected students from
minority groups. There are even some college communities in
which a nonwhite student cannot get a haircut or be served in the
local restaurants. . . .

### To End Discrimination

It is often said that colleges and universities reflect rather than
shape public attitudes; that educational institutions cannot run

**1064**

counter to community sentiment, tradition, and alumni attitudes. To some extent, of course, this is true. But this factor cannot be made the excuse for inaction within the colleges.

This Commission urges educational institutions to act as pioneering agents of leadership against discrimination. Each institution should conscientiously plan and prosecute a well organized program to reduce and where possible promptly to eliminate discrimination, not only by correcting its policies and practices, but also by educating its students to seek the abolition of discriminatory practices in all their manifestations.

This Commission is fully aware of the practical difficulties confronting such a program. It is realistic about the legalities, regional attitudes, and other conditions which complicate the problem. But realism has also to admit that elimination of discrimination is the goal, and that American institutions of higher education should be committed to working progressively in specific terms to remove present inequities. . . .

Fundamentally, adherence to discriminatory procedures in privately controlled colleges has been based upon an assumption by such institutions that they had solely a private responsibility. But this view is now rapidly giving place to one of public accountability on the part of all colleges and universities. It is becoming generally acknowledged that despite a large measure of private control and private support, these institutions are vitally affected with a public interest. Not only is this reflected in the privilege of tax exemption which they are accorded, but also in the process of State accreditation in certain States, and in the recognition that they constitute part of a program of higher education dedicated to the Nation's welfare. They are thus genuinely vested with a public interest and as such are morally obligated to abandon restrictive policies. As the President's Committee on Civil Rights has stated ". . . the public cannot long tolerate practices by private educational institutions which are in serious conflict with patterns of democratic life . . . ."

In order that this mandate of public obligation shall have equal force everywhere, and not lead merely to pronouncements by individual colleges, the invoking of legislation along lines of the proposed legislation against discrimination in New York seems the logical way of advance. The Commission concludes that to assure a universal and equal regard for a policy of nondiscrimination the legal method becomes both fair and practical.

Moreover, a universal legal mandate can be a helpful defense for admission officers against undue pressure of alumni groups and of professional associations which may attempt to influence admissions policies in order to maintain the character of an institution in accord with an established tradition. There is good ground for belief that a required removal of discriminatory criteria for the selection of students would result in a more diversified distribution of students from minority groups among all institutions, with a minimum of concentration in a certain few colleges and universities. . . .

## RACIAL DISCRIMINATION[1]

*The Educational Status of the Negro* . . .

According to the U.S. Bureau of the Census, data for 1940 revealed that Negro adults 25 years and over completed on the average only 5.7 years of schooling while the average for native white adults was 8.8 years and for foreign-born white adults was 7.3 years. While 92.5 percent of the native whites and 71.0 percent of the foreign-born whites had completed at least 5 years of grade school, only 58.0 percent of the Negroes had done so. While 82.7 percent of the native whites and 56.3 percent of the foreign-born whites had completed seventh grade, only 36.1 percent of the Negroes had accomplished as much. High school data are even more significant: 7.3 percent of the Negroes completed 4 years of high school; this contrasts with 28.8 percent of the native whites and 11.6 percent of the foreign-born whites. In higher education only 1.3 percent of the Negroes in contrast to the 5.4 percent of the native whites and 2.4 percent of the foreign-born whites completed a 4-year college course. . . .

---

[1] Statement of dissent:

The undersigned wish to record their dissent from the Commission's pronouncements on "segregation," especially as these pronouncements are related to education in the South. We recognize that many conditions affect adversely the lives of our Negro citizens, and that gross inequality of opportunity, economic and educational, is a fact. We are concerned that as rapidly as possible conditions should be improved, inequalities removed, and greater opportunity provided for all our people. But we believe that efforts toward these ends must, in the South, be made within the established patterns of social relationships, which require separate educational institutions for whites and Negroes. We believe that pronouncements such as those of the Commission on the question of segregation jeopardize these efforts, impede progress, and threaten tragedy to the people of the South, both white and Negro. We recognize the high purpose and the theoretical idealism of the Commission's recommendations. But a doctrinaire position which ignores the facts of history and the realities of the present is not one that will contribute constructively to the solution of difficult problems of human relationships.

ARTHUR H. COMPTON,
DOUGLAS S. FREEMAN,
LEWIS W. JONES,
GOODRICH C. WHITE.

*The Impact of Segregation on Higher Education for Negroes* . . .

Negroes represent approximately 10 percent of the total population of the United States. Yet enrollments of Negroes in institutions of higher education during the school year 1947 accounted for only 3.1 percent of the total. An estimated 75,000 students of Negro descent were enrolled; of these, approximately 85 percent were enrolled in 105 segregated institutions.

The disparity is striking between expenditures for current education purposes by Negro and by other institutions of higher education in the District of Columbia and the 17 Southern States which require the segregation of Negroes. This is shown in an unpublished report by Mordecai W. Johnson, President of Howard University. For all types of institutions, whether publicly or privately controlled, the ratio of expenditures of institutions for whites to those of institutions for Negroes ranged from 3 to 1 in the District of Columbia to 42 to 1 in Kentucky. And nowhere in the area, except in the District of Columbia, did there appear a single institution that approximated the undergraduate, graduate, and professional offerings characteristic of a first-class State university. . . .

*Discrimination by Graduate and Professional Schools* . . .

*Table 5 well summarizes the situation in several important professional fields. But let it be noted that ratios as here cited are merely metric devices. The use of ratios is never to be construed as an endorsement of a racially determined percentage of those to be educated for either a general or a specific purpose.*

TABLE 5.—*Comparison of number of Negroes and whites in selected professions in comparison to Negro population and white population in segregated areas*[1]

| Profession | Ratio of practitioners to population | | Ratio of Negroes per Negro practitioner to Whites per White practitioner |
|---|---|---|---|
| | Negro | White | |
| Doctors ................. | 1: 4,409 | 1: 843 | 5 |
| Dentists ................. | 1: 12,101 | 1: 2,795 | 4 |
| Pharmacists .............. | 1: 22,815 | 1: 1,714 | 13 |
| Lawyers ................ | 1: 24,997 | 1:702 | 36 |
| Social Workers ........... | 1: 11,537 | 1: 2,654 | 4 |
| Engineers ................ | 1: 130,700 | 1: 1644 | 203 |

*To End Racial Discrimination*

This Commission concludes that there will be no fundamental correction of the total condition until segregation legislation is repealed.

---

[1] Source: "The Availability of Education in the Negro Separate School." *The Journal of Negro Education*, Summer, 1947, pp. 264–265.

Deep-seated, long-standing forces of opinion and sentiment are obviously involved. Segregation laws cannot be wished away or eradicated by executive order. But influences looking to their repeal are at work; time and more vigorous effort will change public sentiment. White and Negro citizens will have to continue to work together to secure the necessary legislation and then implement it adequately so that the educational opportunity for white and Negro students will become equal. Until such action is taken, the opportunities for Negroes to qualify as leaders in education, law, medicine, the church, and other areas will be limited seriously. Our national life is made poorer by the lack of such leadership. . . .

*If, as this Commission recommends, steps are taken to make Federal funds available to equalize higher educational opportunities among the States and otherwise to supplement inadequate State financial resources, all such legislation should clearly specify that there may be no discrimination in the channeling of such funds, either as regards possible individual beneficiaries under student grants-in-aid and fellowships, or as to institutions for white students as compared to institutions for Negroes only. Such provisions have not always been made in Federal legislation, the Smith-Hughes Act being a case in point. The Negro institutions should by law receive their full proportionate share of all Federal and State funds destined for the support of college instruction.*

## RELIGIOUS DISCRIMINATION

A second significant body of illustrative evidence regarding discrimination is most readily available in terms of the experience of students of Jewish heritage.

*But before advancing this second illustrative body of evidence, it is well to repeat the warning that in determining opportunities for education, it is not sound democratic doctrine to invoke the argument of maintaining the same ratios of minority group numbers enrolled in colleges to total population numbers. The only defensible basis is that total ability and interest—rather than quotas or ratios, however determined—be the criterion of admission to institutions of higher learning. . . .*

*Techniques of Discrimination . . .*

This Commission, therefore, recommends the removal from application forms of all questions pertaining to religion, color, and national or racial origin. And it points out that the proposed State legislation against discrimination above referred to would automatically lead to the elimination of all questions of this kind.

1068

# DISCRIMINATION

*Discrimination in Professional Schools* . . .

The distribution of Jewish students in medical schools requires particular consideration. The B'nai B'rith received data from the same 57 of the 79 medical schools for the falls of 1935 and 1946. Over the 11-year period there was an absolute loss of 408 Jewish students, even though the enrollment in these 57 schools rose by 557. This constitutes a relative decline in the proportion of Jewish students to total students from 16.1 percent in the fall of 1935, to 13.3 percent in the fall of 1946.

## DEMOCRACY IN HIGHER EDUCATION

If we are to realize the democratic principle of equality of opportunity in education, new ways must be found to translate this principle into practice.

Fundamental to this effort must be a greatly increased will on the part of all American citizens to see that justice is done in educational institutions. There has been too much tardiness and timidity. It now seems clear that many institutions will change their policies only under legal compulsion.

Considerable thought and study should be given to the establishment of "Fair Educational Practices" laws, paralleling the so-called fair employment practices measures enacted or considered by several states. Such laws would give those believed to be the victims of discrimination recourse to an administrative procedure which might investigate and establish the facts of each individual case. That there have been benefits from the existence of legal remedies in the realm of industrial employment is now clear. Nor have the fears of the opponents of such legislation been substantiated in practice. Laws which place equal obligation upon every institution of higher learning to admit applicants only on the basis of publicly justifiable criteria would not resolve every problem of discrimination which exists within colleges and universities. If carefully devised, however, such measures should go far to equalizing educational opportunity.

Many believe that voluntary action, if vigorously and universally pursued, would be more desirable than compulsory action. But the assumption that early and general voluntary action will be adequate to meet the need does not appear to be warranted.

When colleges admit all qualified students—when scholarship, ability, and other defensible standards are made the basis of admission rather than race, color, creed, sex, national origin or ancestry—then a democratic solution will have been reached. When our colleges and universities are being vigorously administered in ways which promote equal opportunity for all qualified students, the local communities and the community of the Nation

**1069**

cannot help but follow such leadership in other areas of our national life.

## Note

1. See also Caliver, *Certain Significant Developments in the Education of Negroes During the Past Generation*, 35 J. of Negro History 111 (1950). For a discussion of the relation of lack of educational facilities and segregation to the full realization of potential Negro leadership, see Caliver, *Education of Negro Leaders* (U. S. Federal Security Agency, Office of Education, Bull. 1948, No. 3) (1949).

2. A recent survey indicates that the personnel of southern graduate and professional schools does not agree with the sentiment on segregation generally attributed to the southern community. 70.5 per cent of the faculty members polled favored no segregation in the existing facilities. Three per cent favored segregation. Two per cent favored setting up new separate schools for Negroes. 24.5 per cent favored regional segregated graduate schools under the Southern Governors' Plan (see *infra*). See 19 J. of Negro Ed. 118 (1950). See also N. Y. Times, June 11, 1952, for ultimatum by the dean, chaplain, head of Religion Department, and five faculty members of School of Theology of the University of the South, threatening resignation if Negro students were still excluded by June 1953.

3. For more recent statistics along the lines presented under the heading "Discrimination by Graduate and Professional Schools" see Federal Security Agency, Office of Education, *Fall Enrollment in Higher Educational Institutions, 1951*, p. vi (Circ. No. 328, 1951); id., *Earned Degrees Conferred by Higher Educational Institutions 1950–51*, p. 5 (Circular No. 333a, 1951).

4. For a study of discrimination on religious grounds see Forster, *A Measure of Freedom*, ch. 7 (1950); Shosteck and Baer, *200,000 Jewish Collegians* (1948); N. Y. State Department of Education, *Decrease in College Discrimination* (1950); critically analyzed in American Jewish Congress, CLSA, *Analysis of Decrease in College Education* (Oct. 13, 1950); American Jewish Committee and Anti-Defamation League of B'nai B'rith, *Joint Memorandum on Study of Discrimination at Colleges of New York State* (Oct. 13, 1950); Brown (ed.), *Discriminations in College Admissions* (American Council on Education Studies, 1950).

## PLESSY v. FERGUSON

Supreme Court of the United States, 1896

163 U. S. 537, 41 L. Ed. 256, 16 S. Ct. 1138

[A Louisiana statute, passed in 1890, provided that "all railway companies carrying passengers in their coaches in this State, shall provide equal but separate accommodations for the white, and colored races, by providing two or more passenger coaches for each passenger train, or by dividing the passenger coaches by a partition so as to secure separate accommodations;" and that "No person or persons shall be admitted to occupy seats in coaches, other than, the ones, assigned, to them on account of the race they belong to." Criminal penalties were provided for persons or railway officials violating the foregoing provision.

Plessy, who was of seven eighths Caucasian and one eighth African blood, purchased a ticket on the East Louisiana Railway to travel from New Orleans to Covington, also in Louisiana. Plessy entered a coach reserved for whites but was ordered by the conductor to sit in the colored coach. He refused to do so, was arrested, and was charged with violation of the statute. Plessy brought a suit for writ of prohibition against the judge who was to try him. The Louisiana Supreme Court denied the writ and Plessy appealed to the United States Supreme Court.]

MR. JUSTICE BROWN, after stating the case, delivered the opinion of the court. . . .

The constitutionality of this act is attacked upon the ground that it conflicts both with the Thirteenth Amendment of the Constitution, abolishing slavery, and the Fourteenth Amendment, which prohibits certain restrictive legislation on the part of the States.

1. That it does not conflict with the Thirteenth Amendment, which abolished slavery and involuntary servitude, except as a punishment for crime, is too clear for argument. . . .

A statute which implies merely a legal distinction between the white and colored races— a distinction which is founded in the color of the two races, and which must always exist so long as white men are distinguished from the other race by color—has no tendency to destroy the legal equality of the two races, or reëstablish a state of involuntary servitude. . . .

2. . . . The object of the [Fourteenth] amendment was undoubtedly to enforce the absolute equality of the two races before the law, but in the nature of things it could not have been intended to abolish distinctions based upon color, or to enforce social, as distinguished from political equality, or a commingling of the two races upon terms unsatisfactory to either. Laws permitting, and even requiring, their separation in places where they are liable to be brought into contact do not necessarily imply the inferiority of either race to the other, and have been generally, if not universally, recognized as within the competency of the state legislatures in the exercise of their police power. The most common instance of this is connected with the establishment of separate schools for white and colored children, which has been held to be a valid exercise of the legislative power even by

courts of States where the political rights of the colored race have been longest and most earnestly enforced.

One of the earliest of these cases is that of *Roberts* v. *City of Boston,* 5 Cush. 198, in which the Supreme Judicial Court of Massachusetts held that the general school committee of Boston had power to make provision for the instruction of colored children in separate schools established exclusively for them, and to prohibit their attendance upon the other schools. "The great principle," said Chief Justice Shaw, p. 206, "advanced by the learned and eloquent advocate for the plaintiff," (Mr. Charles Sumner,) "is, that by the constitution and laws of Massachusetts, all persons without distinction of age or sex, birth or color, origin or condition, are equal before the law. . . . But, when this great principle comes to be applied to the actual and various conditions of persons in society, it will not warrant the assertion, that men and women are legally clothed with the same civil and political powers, and that children and adults are legally to have the same functions and be subject to the same treatment; but only that the rights of all, as they are settled and regulated by law, are equally entitled to the paternal consideration and protection of the law for their maintenance and security." It was held that the powers of the committee extended to the establishment of separate schools for children of different ages, sexes and colors, and that they might also establish special schools for poor and neglected children, who have become too old to attend the primary school, and yet have not acquired the rudiments of learning, to enable them to enter the ordinary schools. Similar laws have been enacted by Congress under its general power of legislation over the District of Columbia, Rev. Stat. D. C. §§ 281, 282, 283, 310, 319, as well as by the legislatures of many of the States, and have been generally, if not uniformly, sustained by the courts [citing state court decisions]. . . .

Laws forbidding the intermarriage of the two races may be said in a technical sense to interfere with the freedom of contract, and yet have been universally recognized as within the police power of the State. *State* v. *Gibson,* 36 Indiana, 389.

The distinction between laws interfering with the political equality of the negro and those requiring the separation of the two races in schools, theatres and railway carriages has been frequently drawn by this court. . . .

[The Court here discusses the cases upholding the right of Negroes to serve on juries. See Chapters I and II, *supra.* It then considers *Hall* v. *DeCuir,* 95 U. S. 485, the *Civil Rights Cases* (see Chapter I, *supra*), and *Louisville, New Orleans &c. Railway* v. *Mississippi,* 133 U. S. 587.]

**1072**

## DISCRIMINATION

It is claimed by the plaintiff in error that, in any mixed community, the reputation of belonging to the dominant race, in this instance the white race, is *property*, in the same sense that a right of action, or of inheritance, is property. Conceding this to be so, for the purposes of this case, we are unable to see how this statute deprives him of, or in any way affects his right to, such property. If he be a white man and assigned to a colored coach, he may have his action for damages against the company for being deprived of his so called property. Upon the other hand, if he be a colored man and be so assigned, he has been deprived of no property, since he is not lawfully entitled to the reputation of being a white man.

In this connection, it is also suggested by the learned counsel for the plaintiff in error that the same argument that will justify the state legislature in requiring railways to provide separate accommodations for the two races will also authorize them to require separate cars to be provided for people whose hair is of a certain color, or who are aliens, or who belong to certain nationalities, or to enact laws requiring colored people to walk upon one side of the street, and white people upon the other, or requiring white men's houses to be painted white, and colored men's black, or their vehicles or business signs to be of different colors, upon the theory that one side of the street is as good as the other, or that a house or vehicle of one color is as good as one of another color. The reply to all this is that every exercise of the police power must be reasonable, and extend only to such laws as are enacted in good faith for the promotion for the public good, and not for the annoyance or oppression of a particular class. [The Court here discusses *Yick Wo* v. *Hopkins,* 118 U. S. 356.] . . .

So far, then, as a conflict with the Fourteenth Amendment is concerned, the case reduces itself to the question whether the statute of Louisiana is a reasonable regulation, and with respect to this there must necessarily be a large discretion on the part of the legislature. In determining the question of reasonableness it is at liberty to act with reference to the established usages, customs and traditions of the people, and with a view to the promotion of their comfort, and the preservation of the public peace and good order. Gauged by this standard, we cannot say that a law which authorizes or even requires the separation of the two races in public conveyances is unreasonable, or more obnoxious to the Fourteenth Amendment than the acts of Congress requiring separate schools for colored children in the District of Columbia, the constitutionality of which does not seem to have been questioned, or the corresponding acts of state legislatures.

We consider the underlying fallacy of the plaintiff's argument to consist in the assumption that the enforced separation of the two races stamps the colored race with a badge of inferiority. If this be so, it is not by reason of anything found in the act, but solely because the colored race chooses to put that construction upon it. The argument necessarily assumes that if, as has been more than once the case, and is not unlikely to be so again, the colored race should become the dominant power in the state legislature, and should enact a law in precisely similar terms, it would thereby relegate the white race to an inferior position. We imagine that the white race, at least, would not acquiesce in this assumption. The argument also assumes that social prejudices may be overcome by legislation, and that equal rights cannot be secured to the negro except by an enforced commingling of the two races. We cannot accept this proposition. If the two races are to meet upon terms of social equality, it must be the result of natural affinities, a mutual appreciation of each other's merits and a voluntary consent of individauls. As was said by the Court of Appeals of New York in *People* v. *Gallagher*, 93 N. Y. 438, 448, "this end can neither be accomplished nor promoted by laws which conflict with the general sentiment of the community upon whom they are designed to operate. When the government, therefore, has secured to each of its citizens equal rights before the law and equal opportunities for improvement and progress, it has accomplished the end for which it was organized and performed all of the functions respecting social advantages with which it is endowed." Legislation is powerless to eradicate racial instincts or to abolish distinctions based upon physical differences, and the attempt to do so can only result in accentuating the difficulties of the present situation. If the civil and political rights of both races be equal one cannot be inferior to the other civilly or politically. If one race be inferior to the other socially, the Constitution of the United States cannot put them upon the same plane. . . .

The judgment of the court below is, therefore,

*Affirmed.*

Mr. JUSTICE HARLAN dissenting. . . .

In respect of civil rights, common to all citizens, the Constitution of the United States does not, I think, permit any public authority to know the race of those entitled to be protected in the enjoyment of such rights. Every true man has pride of race, and under appropriate circumstances when the rights of others, his equals before the law, are not to be affected, it is his privilege to express such pride and to take such action based upon it as to him seems proper. But I deny that any legislative body or judicial tribunal may have regard to the race of citizens when the civil rights of those citizens are involved. Indeed, such legislation, as that here in question, is inconsistent not only with that equality of rights which pertains to citizenship, National and State, but with the personal liberty enjoyed by every one within the United States. . . .

The white race deems itself to be the dominant race in this country. And so it is, in prestige, in achievements, in education, in wealth and in power. So, I doubt not, it will continue to be for all time, if it remains true to its great heritage and holds fast to the principles of constitutional liberty. But in view of the Constitution, in the eye of the law, there is in this country no superior, dominant, ruling class of citizens. There is no caste here. Our Constitution is color-blind, and neither knows nor tolerates classes among citizens. In respect of civil rights, all citizens are equal before the law. The humblest is the peer of the most powerful. The law regards man as man, and takes no account of his surroundings or of his color when his civil rights as guaranteed by the supreme law of the land are involved. It is, therefore, to be regretted that this high tribunal, the final expositor of the fundamental law of the land, has reached the conclusion that it is competent for a State to regulate the enjoyment by citizens of their civil rights solely upon the basis of race.

In my opinion, the judgment this day rendered will, in time, prove to be quite as pernicious as the decision made by this tribunal in the *Dred Scott case*. It was adjudged in that case that the descendants of Africans who were imported into this country and sold as slaves were not included nor intended to be included under the word "citizens" in the Constitution, and could not claim any of the rights and privileges which that instrument provided for and secured to citizens of the United States; that at the time of the adoption of the Constituion they were "considered as a subordinate and inferior class of beings, who had been subjugated by the dominant race, and, whether emancipated or not, yet remained subject to their authority, and had no rights or privileges but such as those who held the power and the government might choose to grant them." 19 How. 393, 404. The recent amendments of the Constitution, it was supposed, had eradicated these principles from our institutions. But it seems that we have yet, in some of the States, a dominant race—a superior class of citizens, which assumes to regulate the enjoyment of civil rights, common to all citizens, upon the basis of race. The present decision, it may well be apprehended, will not only

**1075**

stimulate aggressions, more or less brutal and irritating, upon the admitted rights of colored citizens, but will encourage the belief that it is possible, by means of state enactments, to defeat the beneficent purposes which the people of the United States had in view when they adopted the recent amendments of the Constitution, by one of which the blacks of this country were made citizens of the United States and of the States in which they respectively reside, and whose privileges and immunities, as citizens, the States are forbidden to abridge. Sixty millions of whites are in no danger from the presence here of eight millions of blacks. The destinies of the two races, in this country, are indissolubly linked together, and the interests of both require that the common government of all shall not permit the seeds of race hate to be planted under the sanction of law. What can more certainly arouse race hate, what more certainly create and perpetuate a feeling of distrust between these races, than state enactments, which, in fact, proceed on the ground that colored citizens are so inferior and degraded that they cannot be allowed to sit in public coaches occupied by white citizens? That, as all will admit, is the real meaning of such legislation as was enacted in Louisiana.

The sure guarantee of the peace and security of each race is the clear, distinct, unconditional recognition by our governments, National and State, of every right that inheres in civil freedom, and of the equality before the law of all citizens of the United States without regard to race. State enactments, regulating the enjoyment of civil rights, upon the basis of race, and cunningly devised to defeat legitimate results of the war, under the pretence of recognizing equality of rights, can have no other result than to render permanent peace impossible, and to keep alive a conflict of races, the continuance of which must do harm to all concerned. This question is not met by the suggestion that social equality cannot exist between the white and black races in this country. That argument, if it can be properly regarded as one, is scarcely worthy of consideration; for social equality no more exists between two races when travelling in a passenger coach or a public highway than when members of the same races sit by each other in a street car or in the jury box, or stand or sit with each other in a political assembly, or when they use in common the streets of a city or town, or when they are in the same room for the purpose of having their names placed on the registry of voters, or when they approach the ballot-box in order to exercise the high privilege of voting. . . .

The arbitrary separation of citizens, on the basis of race, while they are on a public highway, is a badge of servitude wholly inconsistent with the civil freedom and the equality before the law established by the Constitution. It cannot be justified upon any legal grounds.

If evils will result from the commingling of the two races upon public highways established for the benefit of all, they will be infinitely less than those that will surely come from state legislation regulating the enjoyment of civil rights upon the basis of race. We boast of the freedom enjoyed by our people above all other peoples. But it is difficult to reconcile that boast with a state of the law which, practically, puts the brand of servitude and degradation upon a large class of our fellow-citizens, our equals before the law. The thin disguise of "equal" accommodations for passengers in railroad coaches will not mislead any one, nor atone for the wrong this day done. . . .

## Note

1. For a historical account collecting material tending to demonstrate that "a large number" of the draftsmen of the Fourteenth Amendment thought that it forbade segregation and segregated schools, see Frank and Munro, *The Original Understanding of Equal Protection of the Laws*, 50 Col. L. Rev. 153 (1952).

2. In *Gong Lum v. Rice*, 275 U.S. 78, 72 L. Ed. 172, 48 S. Ct. 91 (1927), a child of Chinese parentage was excluded from a white school and permitted to go only to a Negro school under a segregation law. The Court stated: "The question here is whether a Chinese citizen of the United States is denied equal protection of the laws when he is classed among the colored races and furnished facilities for education equal to that offered to all, whether white, brown, yellow or black. Were this a new question, it would call for very full argument and consideration, but we think that it is the same question which has been many times decided to be within the constitutional power of the state legislature to settle without intervention of the federal courts under the Federal Constitution." 275 U.S. at 85–6. It has been contended that the case is not a square holding on whether segregation in education is illegal per se because the contention by plaintiff was that a Chinese should be classified as white. See *e.g.*, dissent by Judge Edgerton in *Carr v. Corning*, 182 F.2d 14, 32 (C.A.D.C., 1950). For other early Supreme Court cases not squarely ruling on the separate but equal doctrine, yet deciding the issues within this framework see *Cumming v. Board of Education*, 175 U.S. 528, 44 L. Ed. 262, 20 S. Ct. 197 (1899); *Berea College v. Kentucky*, 211 U.S. 45, 53 L. Ed. 81, 29 S. Ct. 33 (1908).

## 2. Education

### MISSOURI ex rel. GAINES v. CANADA

Supreme Court of the United States, 1938
305 U.S. 337, 83 L. Ed. 208, 59 S. Ct. 232

MR. CHIEF JUSTICE HUGHES delivered the opinion of the Court.

Petitioner Lloyd Gaines, a negro, was refused admission to the School of Law at the State University of Missouri. Asserting that this refusal constituted a denial by the State of the equal protection of the laws in violation of the Fourteenth Amendment of the Federal Constitution, petitioner brought this action for mandamus to compel the curators of the University to admit him. On final hearing, an alternative writ was quashed and a peremptory writ was denied by the Circuit Court. The Supreme Court of the State affirmed the judgment. 113 S.W. 2d. 783. We granted certiorari, October 10, 1938.

Petitioner is a citizen of Missouri. In August, 1935, he was graduated with the degree of Bachelor of Arts at the Lincoln University, an institution maintained by the State of Missouri for the higher education of negroes. That University has no law school. Upon the filing of his application for admission to the law school of the University of Missouri, the registrar advised him to communicate with the president of Lincoln University and the latter directed petitioner's attention to § 9622 of the Revised Statutes of Missouri (1929), providing as follows:

"Sec. 9622. *May arrange for attendance at university of any adjacent state—Tuition fees.*—Pending the full development of the Lincoln university, the board of curators shall have the authority to arrange for the attendance of negro residents of the state of Missouri at the university of any adjacent state to take any course or to study any subjects provided for at the state university of Missouri, and which are not taught at the Lincoln university and to pay the reasonable tuition fees for such attendance; *provided* that whenever the board of curators deem it advisable they shall have the power to open any necessary school or department. (Laws 1921, p. 86, § 7.)"

Petitioner was advised to apply to the State Superintendent of Schools for aid under that statute. It was admitted on the trial that petitioner's "work and credits at the Lincoln University would qualify him for admission to the School of Law of the University of Missouri if he were found otherwise eligible." He was refused admission upon the ground that it was "contrary to the constitution, laws and public policy of the State to admit a negro as a student in the University of Missouri." It appears that there are schools of law in connection with the state univer-

**1078**

sities of four adjacent States, Kansas, Nebraska, Iowa and Illinois, where nonresident negroes are admitted. . . .

In answering petitioner's contention that this discrimination constituted a denial of his constitutional right, the state court has fully recognized the obligation of the State to provide negroes with advantages for higher education substantially equal to the advantages afforded to white students. The State has sought to fulfill that obligation by furnishing equal facilities in separate schools, a method the validity of which has been sustained by our decisions. *Plessy* v. *Ferguson,* 163 U.S. 537, 544; *McCabe* v. *Atchison, T. & S. F. Ry. Co.,* 235 U.S. 151, 160; *Gong Lum* v. *Rice,* 275 U.S. 78, 85, 86. Compare *Cumming* v. *Board of Education,* 175 U.S. 528, 544, 545. Respondents' counsel have appropriately emphasized the special solicitude of the State for the higher education of negroes as shown in the establishment of Lincoln University, a state university well conducted on a plane with the University of Missouri so far as the offered courses are concerned. It is said that Missouri is a pioneer in that field and is the only State in the Union which has established a separate university for negroes on the same basis as the state university for white students. But, commendable as is that action, the fact remains that instruction in law for negroes is not now afforded by the State, either at Lincoln University or elsewhere within the State, and that the State excludes negroes from the advantages of the law school it has established at the University of Missouri.

It is manifest that this discrimination, if not relieved by the provisions we shall presently discuss, would constitute a denial of equal protection. That was the conclusion of the Court of Appeals of Maryland in circumstances substantially similar in that aspect. *University of Maryland* v. *Murray,* 169 Md. 478; 182 A. 590. It there appeared that the State of Maryland had "undertaken the function of education in the law" but had "omitted students of one race from the only adequate provision made for it, and omitted them solely because of their color"; that if those students were to be offered "equal treatment in the performance of the function, they must, at present, be admitted to the one school provided." *Id.,* p. 489. A provision for scholarships to enable negroes to attend colleges outside the State, mainly for the purpose of professional studies, was found to be inadequate (*Id.,* pp. 485, 486) and the question, "whether with aid in any amount it is sufficient to send the negroes outside the State for legal education," the Court of Appeals found it unnecessary to discuss. Accordingly, a writ of mandamus to admit the applicant was issued to the officers and regents of the

University of Maryland as the agents of the State entrusted with the conduct of that institution.

The Supreme Court of Missouri in the instant case has distinguished the decision in Maryland upon the grounds—(1) that in Missouri, but not in Maryland, there is "a legislative declaration of a purpose to establish a law school for negroes at Lincoln University whenever necessary or practical"; and (2) that "pending the establishment of such a school, adequate provision has been made for the legal education of negro students in recognized schools outside of this State." 113 S.W. 2d, p. 791.

As to the first ground, it appears that the policy of establishing a law school at Lincoln University has not yet ripened into an actual establishment, and it cannot be said that a mere declaration of purpose, still unfulfilled, is enough. The provision for legal education at Lincoln is at present entirely lacking. Respondents' counsel urge that if, on the date when petitioner applied for admission to the University of Missouri, he had instead applied to the curators of Lincoln University it would have been their duty to establish a law school; that this "agency of the State," to which he should have applied, was "specifically charged with the mandatory duty to furnish him what he seeks." . . .

The state court has not held that it would have been the duty of the curators to establish a law school at Lincoln University for the petitioner on his application. Their duty, as the court defined it, would have been either to supply a law school at Lincoln University as provided in § 9618 or to furnish him the opportunity to obtain his legal training in another State as provided in § 9622. . . . In the light of its ruling we must regard the question whether the provision for the legal education in other States of negroes resident in Missouri is sufficient to satisfy the constitutional requirement of equal protection, as the pivot upon which this case turns.

The state court stresses the advantages that are afforded by the law schools of the adjacent States,—Kansas, Nebraska, Iowa and Illinois,—which admit non-resident negroes. The court considered that these were schools of high standing where one desiring to practice law in Missouri can get "as sound, comprehensive, valuable legal education" as in the University of Missouri; that the system of education in the former is the same as that in the latter and is designed to give the students a basis for the practice of law in any State where the Anglo-American system of law obtains; that the law school of the University of Missouri does not specialize in Missouri law and that the course of study and the case books used in the five schools are substantially identical. Petitioner insists that for one intending to practice in Missouri there are special advantages in attending a law school there, both in relation to the opportunities for the particular study of Missouri law and for the observation of the local courts, and also in view of the prestige of the Missouri law school among citizens of the State, his prospective clients. Proceeding with its examination of relative advantages, the state court found that the difference in distances to be traveled afforded no substantial ground of complaint and that there was an adequate appropriation to meet the full tuition fees which petitioner would have to pay.

We think that these matters are beside the point. The basic consideration is not as to what sort of opportunities other States provide, or whether they are as good as those in Missouri, but as to what opportunities Missouri itself furnishes to white students and denies to negroes solely upon the ground of color. The admissibility of laws separating the races in the enjoyment of privileges afforded by the State rests wholly upon the equality of the privileges which the laws give to the separated groups within the State. The question here is not of a duty of the State to supply legal training, or of the quality of the training which it does supply, but of its duty when it provides such training to furnish it to the residents of the State upon the basis of an equality of right. By the operation of the laws of Missouri a privilege has been created for white law students which is denied to negroes by reason of their race. The white resident is afforded legal education within the State; the negro resident having the same qualifications is refused it there and must go outside the State to obtain it. That is a denial of the equality of legal right to the enjoyment of the privilege which the State has set up, and the provision for the payment of tuition fees in another State does not remove the discrimination.

The equal protection of the laws is "a pledge of the protection of equal laws." *Yick Wo* v. *Hopkins,* 118 U.S. 356, 369. Manifestly, the obligation of the State to give the protection of equal laws can be performed only where its laws operate, that is, within its own jurisdiction. It is there that the equality of legal right must be maintained. . . .

Nor can we regard the fact that there is but a limited demand in Missouri for the legal education of negroes as excusing the discretion in favor of whites. . . .

[Petitioner's] right was a personal one. It was as an individual that he was entitled to the equal protection of the laws, and the State was bound to furnish him within its borders facilities for legal education substantially equal to those which the

State there afforded for persons of the white race, whether or not other negroes sought the same opportunity.

It is urged, however, that the provision for tuition outside the State is a temporary one,—that it is intended to operate merely pending the establishment of a law department for negroes at Lincoln University. While in that sense the discrimination may be termed temporary, it may nevertheless continue for an indefinite period by reason of the discretion given to the curators of Lincoln University and the alternative of arranging for tuition in other States, as permitted by the state law as construed by the state court, so long as the curators find it unnecessary and impracticable to provide facilities for the legal instruction of negroes within the State. In that view, we cannot regard the discrimination as excused by what is called its temporary character. . . .

[The dissenting opinion of Mr. Justice McReynolds, with which Mr. Justice Butler concurred, is omitted.]

## Note

1. In *McCready v. Byrd*, 73 Atl.2d 8 (Md., 1950), plaintiff sought mandamus to require the University of Maryland to consider her application for admission as a first year student in the school of nursing regardless of the fact that she was a Negro. The opinion states:

"In 1948 the State of Maryland and other southern states, without the consent of Congress under section 10 of Article I of the Constitution, entered into a regional compact, which was subsequently amended and, as amended, is set out in and was ratified by Chapter 282 of the Acts of 1949, effective June 1, 1949, relating to the development and maintenance of regional educational services and schools in the southern states in the professional, technological, scientific, literary and other fields, so as to provide greater educational advantages and facilities for the citizens of the several states who reside within such region. By arrangement pursuant to the regional compact the State of Maryland has sent a number of white students to study veterinary medicine in a school in another state and has sent, or is willing to send, negro students for the same purpose to a different school in another state. No instruction in veterinary medicine is offered by the University of Maryland or any other state agency in Maryland. Pursuant to the regional compact a contract for training in nursing education, dated July 19, 1949, was made between the Board of Control for Southern Regional Education, 'a joint agency' created by the regional compact, and the State of Maryland, relating to nursing education of three first year students from the State of Maryland in Meharry Medical College, School of Nursing, at Nashville, Tennessee. Meharry Medical School and its school of nursing receive negro students only. In August, 1949 the University of Maryland offered petitioner a course in nursing at Meharry Medical College at a total over-all cost to her, including living and traveling expenses, which would not exceed the cost to her of attending the school of nursing at the University of Maryland. Petitioner declined the offer.

"From the uncontradicted testimony, in ample detail, of Doctor Pincoffs, since 1922 Professor of Medicine in the University of Maryland Medical School and chief physician at the University Hospital, and other witnesses called by respondents, it seems clear that in educational facilities and living conditions the nursing school at Meharry College is not only equal but superior to the University of Maryland nursing school. The offer to petitioner of a course in nursing at Meharry Medical College therefore included every advantage except the one she now insists upon, viz., education in a state institution within the State of Maryland. Respondents stress the regional compact and the contract for training in nursing education. The terms and details of these agreements are not now material. Neither agreement mentions race. We may assume, without deciding, that the compact is valid without the consent of Congress. Under the contract the Board are only agents —or ambassadors—to negotiate a contract for nursing education between the State of Maryland and Meharry Medical College. Obviously no compact or contract can extend the territorial boundaries or the sovereignty of the State of Maryland to Nashville. . . ."

After quoting extensively from *Missouri ex rel. Gaines v. Canada* and also referring to *Sipuel v. Oklahoma, infra,* the Court held that the mandamus should issue. Certiorari was denied. 340 U. S. 827 (1950).

2. For descriptions and favorable comments on the South's Program for Regional Education which makes graduate education available to Negroes see Gant, *The Southern Regional Education Program,* 12 Pub. Ad. Rev. 106 (1952); Nabrit, *What the Plan is and How it Works,* in *Discrimination in Higher Education,* p. 40 (So. Confer. Ed. Fund, 1950); Stoney, *In Defense of the Regional Plan,* 86 Survey 300 (June, 1950). See also statement of Colgate W. Darden, president of the University of Virginia, on non-segregation in regional graduate schools, 6 New South 3, 5–7 (1951). For more critical outlooks on the plan see Williams, *Why the Regional Plan Should be Opposed,* in *Discrimination in Higher Education, supra,* p. 46; Saveth, *Jim Crow and the Regional Plan,* 85 Survey 476 (Sept., 1949); and Myers, *The Colleges for Negroes,* 86 Survey 233 (May, 1950). See also 7 Southern Patriot No. 7 (1949) for ten arguments against the plan formulated by the Southern Conference Educational Fund, Inc.

3. In *Ex Parte Banks,* 48 So.2d 35 (Ala., 1950), Negroes accepted state aid to take law in Howard University. They were denied a license to practice that is granted graduates of University of Alabama law school. The court said: "they . . . occupy a status of voluntarily seeking legal education outside of the state, aided by the state, knowing that in doing so the law does not justify a diploma license".

## SWEATT v. PAINTER

Supreme Court of the United States, 1950

339 U.S. 629, 94 L. Ed. 1114, 70 S. Ct. 848

MR. CHIEF JUSTICE VINSON delivered the opinion of the Court.
This case and *McLaurin v. Oklahoma State Regents, post,*
p. 637, present different aspects of this general question: To
what extent does the Equal Protection Clause of the Fourteenth
Amendment limit the power of a state to distinguish between
students of different races in professional and graduate education in a state university? Broader issues have been urged for
our consideration, but we adhere to the principle of deciding
constitutional questions only in the context of the particular
case before the Court. . . .

In the instant case, petitioner filed an application for admission
to the University of Texas Law School for the February, 1946
term. His application was rejected solely because he is a Negro.[1]
Petitioner thereupon brought this suit for mandamus against the
appropriate school officials, respondents here, to compel his admission. At that time, there was no law school in Texas which
admitted Negroes.

The state trial court recognized that the action of the State in
denying petitioner the opportunity to gain a legal education while
granting it to others deprived him of the equal protection of the
laws guaranteed by the Fourteenth Amendment. The court did
not grant the relief requested, however, but continued the case
for six months to allow the State to supply substantially equal
facilities. At the expiration of the six months, in December,
1946, the court denied the writ on the showing that the authorized
university officials had adopted an order calling for the opening
of a law school for Negroes the following February. While
petitioner's appeal was pending, such a school was made available,
but petitioner refused to register therein. The Texas Court of
Civil Appeals set aside the trial court's judgment and ordered the
cause "remanded generally to the trial court for further proceedings without prejudice to the rights of any party to this
suit."

On remand, a hearing was held on the issue of the equality of
the educational facilities at the newly established school as compared with the University of Texas Law School. Finding that
the new school offered petitioner "privileges, advantages, and

---

[1] It appears that the University has been restricted to white students,
in accordance with the State law. See Tex. Const., Art. VII, §§ 7, 14; Tex.
Rev. Civ. Stat. (Vernon, 1925), Arts 2643b (Supp. 1949), 2719, 2900.

opportunities for the study of law substantially equivalent to those offered by the State to white students at the University of Texas," the trial court denied mandamus. The Court of Civil Appeals affirmed. 210 S. W. 2d. 442 (1948). Petitioner's application for a writ of error was denied by the Texas Supreme Court. We granted certiorari, 338 U.S. 865 (1949), because of the manifest importance of the constitutional issues involved.

The University of Texas Law School, from which petitioner was excluded, was staffed by a faculty of sixteen full-time and three part-time professors, some of whom are nationally recognized authorities in their field. Its student body numbered 850. The library contained over 65,000 volumes. Among the other facilities available to the students were a law review, moot court facilities, scholarship funds, and Order of the Coif affiliation. The school's alumni occupy the most distinguished positions in the private practice of the law and in the public life of the State. It may properly be considered one of the nation's ranking law schools.

The law school for Negroes which was to have opened in February, 1947, would have had no independent faculty or library. The teaching was to be carried on by four members of the University of Texas Law School faculty, who were to maintain their offices at the University of Texas while teaching at both institutions. Few of the 10,000 volumes ordered for the library had arrived;[2] nor was there ony full-time librarian. The school lacked accreditation.

Since the trial of this case, respondents report the opening of a law school at the Texas State University for Negroes. It is apparently on the road to full accreditation. It has a faculty of five full-time professors; a student body of 23; a library of some 16,500 volumes serviced by a full-time staff; a practice court and legal aid association; and one alumnus who has become a member of the Texas Bar.

Whether the University of Texas Law School is compared with the original or the new law school for Negroes, we cannot find substantial equality in the educational opportunities offered white and Negro law students by the State. In terms of number of the faculty, variety of courses and opportunity for specialization, size of the student body, scope of the library, availability of law review and similar activities, the University of Texas Law School

---

[2] Students of the interim School of Law of the Texas State University for Negroes [located in Austin, whereas the permanent School was to be located at Houston] shall have use of the State Law Library in the Capitol Building. . . ." Tex. Laws 1947, c. 29, § 11, Tex. Rev. Civ. Stat. (Vernon, 1949 Supp.), note to Art. 2643b. It is not clear that this privilege was anything more than was extended to all citizens of the State.

is superior. What is more important, the University of Texas Law School possesses to a far greater degree those qualities which are incapable of objective measurement but which make for greatness in a law school. Such qualities, to name but a few, include reputation of the faculty, experience of the administration, position and influence of the alumni, standing in the community, traditions and prestige. It is difficult to believe that one who had a free choice between these law schools would consider the question close.

Moreover, although the law is a highly learned profession, we are well aware that it is an intensely practical one. The law school, the proving ground for legal learning and practice, cannot be effective in isolation from the individuals and institutions with which the law interacts. Few students and no one who has practiced law would choose to study in an academic vacuum, removed from the interplay of ideas and the exchange of views with which the law is concerned. The law school to which Texas is willing to admit petitioner excludes from its student body members of the racial groups which number 85% of the population of the State and include most of the lawyers, witnesses, jurors, judges and other officials with whom petitioner will inevitably be dealing when he becomes a member of the Texas Bar. With such a substantial and significant segment of society excluded, we cannot conclude that the education offered petitioner is substantially equal to that which he would receive if admitted to the University of Texas Law School.

It may be argued that excluding petitioner from that school is no different from excluding white students from the new law school. This contention overlooks realities. It is unlikely that a member of a group so decisively in the majority, attending a school with rich traditions and prestige which only a history of consistently maintained excellence could command, would claim that the opportunities afforded him for legal education were unequal to those held open to petitioner. That such a claim, if made, would be dishonored by the State, is no answer. "Equal protection of the laws is not achieved through indiscriminate imposition of inequalities." *Shelley v. Kraemer*, 334 U.S. 1, 22 (1948).

It is fundamental that these cases concern rights which are personal and present. This Court has stated unanimously that "The State must provide [legal education] for [petitioner] in conformity with the equal protection clause of the Fourteenth Amendment and provide it as soon as it does for applicants of any other group." *Sipuel v. Board of Regents*, 332 U.S. 631, 633 (1948). That case "did not present the issue whether a state might not satisfy the equal protection clause of the Fourteenth Amendment by establishing a separate law school for Negroes." *Fisher v. Hurst*, 333 U.S. 147, 150 (1948). In *Missouri ex rel. Gaines v. Canada*, 305 U. S. 337, 351 (1938), the Court, speaking through Chief Justice Hughes, declared that "petitioner's right was a personal one. It was as an individual that he was entitled to the equal protection of the laws, and the State was bound to furnish him within its borders facilities for legal education substantially equal to those which the State there afforded for persons of the white race, whether or not other negroes sought the same opportunity." These are the only cases in this Court which present the issue of the constitutional validity of race distinctions in state-supported graduate and professional education.

In accordance with these cases, petitioner may claim his full constitutional right: legal education equivalent to that offered by the State to students of other races. Such education is not available to him in a separate law school as offered by the State. We cannot, therefore, agree with respondents that the doctrine of *Plessy v. Ferguson*, 163 U.S. 537 (1896), requires affirmance of the judgment below. Nor need we reach petitioner's contention that *Plessy v. Ferguson* should be reexamined in the light of contemporary knowledge respecting the purposes of the Fourteenth Amendment and the effects of racial segregation. . . .

We hold that the Equal Protection Clause of the Fourteenth Amendment requires that petitioner be admitted to the University of Texas Law School. The judgment is reversed and the cause is remanded for proceedings not inconsistent with this opinion.

*Reversed.*

## McLAURIN v. OKLAHOMA STATE REGENTS

Supreme Court of the United States, 1950
339 U. S. 637, 94 L. Ed. 1149, 70 S. Ct. 851

Mr. CHIEF JUSTICE VINSON delivered the opinion of the Court.
In this case, we are faced with the question whether a state may, after admitting a student to graduate instruction in its state university, afford him different treatment from other students solely because of his race. We decide only this issue; see *Sweatt v. Painter, ante*. . . .

Appellant is a Negro citizen of Oklahoma. Possessing a Master's Degree, he applied for admission to the University of Oklahoma in order to pursue studies and courses leading to a Doctorate in Education. At that time, his application was denied, solely because of his race. The school authorities were required to exclude him by the Oklahoma statutes, 70 Okla. Stat. (1941) §§ 455, 456, 457, which made it a misdemeanor to maintain or operate, teach or attend a school at which both whites and Negroes are enrolled or taught. Appellant filed a complaint requesting injunctive relief, alleging that the action of the school authorities and the statutes upon which their action was based were unconstitutional and deprived him of the equal protection of the laws. Citing our decisions in *Missouri ex rel. Gaines v. Canada*, 305 U.S. 337 (1938), and *Sipuel v. Board of Regents*, 332 U.S. 631 (1948), a statutory three-judge District Court held that the State had a Constitutional duty to provide him with the education he sought as soon as it provided that education for applicants of any other group. It further held that to the extent the Oklahoma statutes denied him admission they were unconstitutional and void. On the assumption, however, that the State would follow the constitutional mandate, the court refused to grant the injunction, retaining jurisdiction of the cause with full power to issue any necessary and proper orders to secure McLaurin the equal protection of the laws. 87 F. Supp. 526.

Following this decision, the Oklahoma legislature amended these statutes to permit the admission of Negroes to institutions of higher learning attended by white students, in cases where such institutions offered courses not available in the Negro schools. The amendment provided, however, that in such cases the program of instruction "shall be given at such colleges or institutions of higher education upon a segregated basis."[1] Appellant was thereupon admitted to the University of Oklahoma Graduate School. In apparent conformity with the amendment, his admission was made subject to "such rules and regulations as to segregation as the President of the University shall consider to afford to Mr. G. W. McLaurin substantially equal educational opportunities as are afforded to other persons seeking the same education in the Graduate College," a condition which does not appear to have been withdrawn. Thus he was required to sit apart at a designated desk in an anteroom adjoining the classroom; to sit at a designated desk on the mezzanine floor of the library, but not to use the desks in the regular reading room; and to sit at a designated table and to eat at a different time from the other students in the school cafeteria.

To remove these conditions, appellant filed a motion to modify the order and judgment of the District Court. That court held that such treatment did not violate the provisions of the Four-

---

[1] . . . 70 Okla. Stat. Ann. (1950) §§ 455, 456, 457. Segregated basis is defined as "classroom instruction given in separate classrooms, or at separate times." *Id.* § 455.

teenth Amendment and denied the motion. 87 F. Supp. 528. This appeal followed.

In the interval between the decision of the court below and the hearing in this Court, the treatment afforded appellant was altered. For some time, the section of the classroom in which appellant sat was surrounded by a rail on which there was a sign stating, "Reserved For Colored," but these have been removed. He is now assigned to a seat in the classroom in a row specified for colored students; he is assigned to a table in the library on the main floor; and he is permitted to eat at the same time in the cafeteria as other students, although here again he is assigned to a special table.

It is said that the separations imposed by the State in this case are in form merely nominal. McLaurin uses the same classroom, library and cafeteria as students of other races; there is no indication that the seats to which he is assigned in these rooms have any disadvantage of location. He may wait in line in the cafeteria and there stand and talk with his fellow students, but while he eats he must remain apart.

These restrictions were obviously imposed in order to comply, as nearly as could be, with the statutory requirements of Oklahoma. But they signify that the State, in administering the facilities it affords for professional and graduate study, sets McLaurin apart from the other students. The result is that appellant is handicapped in his pursuit of effective graduate instruction. Such restrictions impair and inhibit his ability to study, to engage in discussions and exchange views with other students, and, in general, to learn his profession.

Our society grows increasingly complex, and our need for trained leaders increases correspondingly. Appellant's case represents, perhaps, the epitome of that need, for he is attempting to obtain an advanced degree in education, to become, by definition, a leader and trainer of others. Those who will come under his guidance and influence must be directly affected by the education he receives. Their own education and development will necessarily suffer to the extent that his training is unequal to that of his classmates. State-imposed restrictions which produce such inequalities cannot be sustained.

It may be argued that appellant will be in no better position when these restrictions are removed, for he may still be set apart by his fellow students. This we think irrelevant. There is a vast difference—a Constitutional difference—between restrictions imposed by the state which prohibit the intellectual commingling of students, and the refusal of individuals to commingle where the state presents no such bar. *Shelley v. Kraemer,* 334 U.S. 1,

13-14 (1948). The removal of the state restrictions will not necessarily abate individual and group predilections, prejudices and choices. But at the very least, the state will not be depriving appellant of the opportunity to secure acceptance by his fellow students on his own merits.

We conclude that the conditions under which this appellant is required to receive his education deprive him of his personal and present right to the equal protection of the laws. See *Sweatt v. Painter, ante.* . . . We hold that under these circumstances the Fourteenth Amendment precludes differences in treatment by the state based upon race. Appellant, having been admitted to a state-supported graduate school, must receive the same treatment at the hands of the state as students of other races. The judgment is

*Reversed.*

## Note

1. See also *Wilson v. Board of Supervisors,* 92 F. Supp. 986 (E.D. La, 1950), motion to affirm granted 340 U.S. 909, 95 L. Ed. 657, 71 S. Ct. 294 (1951); *Parker v. University of Delaware,* 75 Atl.2d 225 (Del., 1950) (Negro admitted to white college because facilities at Negro college found inferior, but court refused to hold Negro college inferior simply because it was a segregated school).

2. The principal cases are discussed in Roche, *Education, Segregation and the Supreme Court—A Political Analysis,* 99 U. of Pa. L. Rev. 949 (1951); Taylor, *The Demise of Race Restrictions in Graduate Education,* 1 Duke B. J. 135 (1951); Note, 26 St. Johns L. Rev. 123 (1951).

3. Further examples of the application of the separate but equal doctrine to education are:

*McKissick v. Carmichael,* 187 F.2d 949 (C.A. 4, 1951), cert. den. 341 U.S. 951 (1951). The opinion, holding that the Negro law school was not equal to that provided for whites, reads in part:

"Many of defendants' experienced witnesses were of the opinion that the teaching is more effective in the colored than in the white school because of the respective size of the classes. In the University School the classes range from 80 to 116, a number entirely too large for efficient instruction, 25 was said to be the ideal number, whereas the classes in the College School are composed of 8 or 9 individuals, too small for the best results, but of such size as to permit individual instruction of each student; and it is said that this circumstance alone compensates for the deficiency in the colored school. Moreover, it is shown that colored lawyers are rarely if ever employed by white persons in North Carolina, and hence it is argued that the success of the colored graduates in active practice would be promoted far more by association and acquaintance formed with the 1300 students of the North Carolina College than by mingling with the white students at the University.

"These circumstances are worthy of consideration by any one who is responsible for the solution of a difficult racial problem; but they do

[Emerson]

not meet the complainants' case or overcome the deficiencies which it discloses. Indeed the defense seeks in part to avoid the charge of equality by the paternal suggestion that it would be beneficial to the colored race in North Carolina as a whole, and to the individual plaintiffs in particular, if they would cooperate in promoting the policy adopted by the State rather than seek the best legal education which the State provides. The duty of the federal courts, however, is clear. We must give first place to the rights of the individual citizen, and when and where he seeks only equality of treatment before the law, his suit must prevail. It is for him to decide in which direction his advantage lies." 187 F.2d at 953–4.

This case is noted in 30 N.C. L. Rev. 153 (1952); 39 Ky. L. J. 492 (1951) (lower court decision).

*Carr v. Corning,* 182 F.2d 14 (C.A.D.C., 1950). The segregated school system of the District of Columbia was challenged. The facts showed that a Junior High School for Negroes had had to operate on two shifts while that for whites was operating on one shift. When the two shifts were later eliminated in the Negro school many of the students had to be accommodated in annexes established in elementary schools. The court, holding the facilities equal, pointed out that the double shift and annexes were temporary expedients to which white students in other parts of the District were also subjected where white schools are overcrowded. The court refused to overrule the separate but equal doctrine. The plaintiffs also wanted the court to take judicial notice of the Strayer report, a Congressionally authorized survey of the District of Columbia school system, to show the relative inadequacy of school buildings, sizes of classes, and courses taught at District Negro Schools. The court declined to take judicial notice on the ground that the report contained too much opinion material. The case is noted in 18 Geo. Wash. L. Rev. 563 (1950).

*Carter v. School Bd. of Arlington,* 182 F. 2d 531 (C. A. 4, 1950). Negro students had claimed that they could not get certain courses in the Negro school that were available at the white school. The defense was in part that surveys at the beginning of each year in the Negro school showed there was little desire on the part of Negro students to take certain courses. It was also contended that discrimination might have resulted from faulty judgment by administrators, but that this was no ground for judicial interference and should be corrected by state authorities. Judge Soper's opinion read in part:

"It is established, however, that the right of the individual student to the privilege of public instruction equivalent to that given by the state to the individual student of another race, is a personal one and equivalency cannot be determined by weighing the respective advantages furnished to the two groups of which the individuals are members. In Corbin v. County School Board of Pulaski County, 4 Cir., 177 F. 2d 924, 926, we said: '* * * the question cannot be decided by averaging the facilities provided for the two classes of pupils throughout the county and comparing one with the other, since the rights created by the Fourteenth Amendment are individual and personal and the prohibitions of the Amendment are observed only when the same or equivalent treatment is accorded to persons of different races similarly situated.' . . .

"The differences between the two schools are not merely unimportant variations incident to the maintenance of separate establishments, but constitute unlawful discriminations against pupils of the colored race; and it is no defense that they flow in part from variations in the size of the respective student bodies or locations of the buildings. The burdens inherent in segregation must be met by the state which maintains the practice. Nor can it be said that a scholar who is deprived of his due must apply to the administrative authorities and not to the courts for relief. An injured person must of course show that the state has denied him advantages accorded to others in like situation, but when this is established, his right of access to the courts is absolute and complete." 182 F. 2d at 534–6.

The court, relying on its earlier decision in the *Corbin* case, also held inadequate the defense that the county had adopted a policy of sending Negro vocational pupils to a Regional School, basing its holding on "the inconvenience and loss of time imposed by transportation."

Compare *Brown v. Ramsey*, 185 F. 2d 225 (C. A. 8, 1950), where the allegations of inequality were in part that the Negro High School had no facilities for teaching metal trades, auto mechanics, photography, printing, and did not teach physics, geometry, business courses and romance languages taught in schools for white children. The court, after stating that the record contained ample evidence that the facilities were equal, stated:

". . . in the white high school with an enrollment of approximately 1,200 students the demand for some particular type of instruction may arise with a sufficient number of applicants to justify its installation, while the required number would not apply at the Lincoln High School with an enrollment of 139. A study of the cases cited in this opinion shows that this policy might result in a denial to a Negro student of the equality of treatment commanded by the 14th Amendment. That command in this case is that any individual Negro student qualified for a particular course of instruction afforded to white students is entitled of right to the same instruction, even though in the Negro school he is the sole applicant for it. The character of education made available to the Negro students can not be made to depend on the number of qualified applicants. . . .

"But we are not concerned with hypothetical issues. The question here is whether any of the appellants have been or are being denied the equality of treatment to which they are entitled. The allegations of the complaint and the evidence concerning courses of instruction are directed to an alleged custom or practice which may conceivably result in the denial of equal treatment to some Negro student at some time, rather than to an actual denial suffered by any of the appellants. Of the six appellants who are enrolled in the Lincoln High School only two appeared as witnesses. Neither testified to the denial of any course of instruction which the witness or other appellant applied for or offered to take."

**1092**

See also *State ex rel. Brewton v. Bd. of Education of St. Louis,* 361 Mo. 86, 233 S. W. 2d 697 (1950) (Negro child must be admitted to course in aerodynamics offered only at white school); *Davis v. County School Bd.,* 103 F. Supp. 337 (E. D. Va., 1952) (actual discrepancy in curriculum is not cured by tendering willingness to give any course); but *cf. Brown v. Bd. of Trustees of La Grange,* 187 F. 2d 20 (C. A. 5, 1951) (parent denied relief where daughter could not get certain course in chemistry because he had not been denied a civil right).

On the problem of inequality of distance of the schools compare *Wright v. Board of Education,* 129 Kan. 852, 284 Pac. 363 (1930), *Lehew v. Brummell,* 103 Mo. 546, 15 S. W. 765 (1891) (that Negro child is required to travel a greater distance does not matter) with *Williams v. Board of Education,* 79 Kan. 202, 99 Pac. 216 (1908) (Negro child would have to travel difficult and dangerous route—facilities held inequal).

It is generally held that the length of the academic term, the proportionate number of teachers and their qualifications must be the same. See *e. g., Lowery v. School Trustees,* 140 N. C. 33, 52 S. E. 267 (1905); *Jones v. Bd. of Education,* 90 Okla. 233, 217 Pac. 400 (1923).

For a detailed discussion of the cases applying the separate but equal facilities doctrine to education, see Note, *Equal Educational Facilities under the Equal Protection Clause of the Fourteenth Amendment,* 1950 Wash. U. L. Q. 594.

4. In *Claybrook v. Owensboro,* 16 Fed. 297 (D. Ky. 1883), it was held that an ad valorem tax for the benefit of schools could not be so used that the tax from whites paid for the white schools and the money collected from Negroes paid for the Negro schools.

5. Discrimination by semi-public schools: In *Norris v. Mayor of Baltimore,* 78 F. Supp. 451 (D. Md., 1948), a privately owned art school run without profit excluded a Negro applicant who sought an injunction against the school, the state and the city. The city rented the school, a municipal building, at a nominal rental and the school received a subsidy from the city and the State of Maryland. As a *quid pro quo* each member of the City Council and the state legislature could appoint one student free of tuition. The subsidy paid for twenty-three per cent of the school's total budget, though the students thus appointed were only five per cent of the total student body. The court held that since the management of the school was in the hands of private trustees not appointed by the government or in any sense public officials, the connection between the state and municipality and the school was not sufficient to constitute the school's action "state action." The court also held that it lacked jurisdiction to entertain the suit against the city and state because such a suit is a taxpayer's suit and, unlike one involving violation of the Civil Rights Acts, see 28 U. S. C. § 41 (14), required the jurisdictional amount of $3000 which was not shown here. See 28 U. S. C. § 41 (1) (a).

In *Kerr v. Enoch Pratt Free Library,* 149 F. 2d 212 (C. A. 4, 1942), the library was heavily supported by public funds but also managed by private trustees. The Court of Appeals reversed the same court that later decided the *Norris* case and held that a Negro applicant who had been excluded from the library's training school be granted an injunction. The court in the *Norris* case distinguished the *Kerr* case on the ground that in *Kerr* the city held title to the library's property and managed its financial affairs.

See also *Battle v. Wichita Falls Junior College Dist.*, 101 F. Supp. 82 (N. D. Tex., 1951). Negroes excluded from Junior College would have had to travel 367 miles to obtain similar education. The college was operated by a Board of Trustees and financed by taxes, tuition, endowments and gifts. The court ordered plaintiffs' admission.

## NOTE—GRADE SCHOOL SEGREGATION: THE LATEST ATTACK ON RACIAL DISCRIMINATION

### 61 Yale L. J. 730, 732–44 (1952)

The drive against segregation has now shifted to the grade schools. In *Briggs v. Elliott*[11] and *Brown v. Board of Education of Topeka*,[12] such segregation has been squarely challenged in the Supreme Court for the first time.[13]

In the *Briggs* case, Negro parents argued that the educational segregation required by South Carolina's constitution and statutes is *per se* unconstitutional.[14] They also alleged that the physical facilities afforded their children were inferior to those provided white children.[15] In the *Brown* case, a similar Kansas

---

[11] 98 F. Supp. 529 (E. D. S. C. 1951), *remanded per curiam* [342 U. S. 350 (1952)].

[12] 98 F. Supp. 797 (D. Kan. 1951), *appeal filed*, 20 U. S. L. Week 3164 (Nov. 19, 1951).

[13] The Supreme Court has repeatedly spoken of educational segregation as valid. Missouri *ex rel*. Gaines v. Canada, 305 U. S. 337; Gong Lum v. Rice, 275 U. S. 78 (1927); Cumming v. Board of Education, 175 U. S. 528 (1899). But these cases did not rule on the question of whether segregation *per se* would be unconstitutional if objective facilities were equal. See dissent of Edgerton, J., in Carr v. Corning, 182 F. 2d 14, 32 (D. C. Cir. 1950). See also Ransmeier, *The Fourteenth Amendment and the "Separate but Equal Doctrine,"* 50 Mich. L. Rev. 203, 219 (1951); Waite, *The Negro in the Supreme Court*, 30 Minn. L. Rev. 254–5 (1945); Note, 56 Yale L. J. 1059 (1947). But see Briggs v. Elliott, 98 F. Supp. 529, 533 (E. D. S. C. 1951).

[14] See S. C. Const. Art. 11, § 7: "Separate schools shall be provided for children of the white and colored races, and no child of either race shall ever be permitted to attend a school provided for children of the other race"; S. C. Code § 5377 (1942): "It shall be unlawful for pupils of one race to attend the schools provided by boards of trustees for persons of another race."

[15] Briggs v. Elliott, 98 F. Supp. 529, 530 (E. D. S. C. 1951).

law is being attacked by Negro parents.[16] In both cases special three-judge courts, relying on the "separate but equal" doctrine, sustained the constitutionality of the laws.[17] In the *Briggs* case, however, the state conceded that the Negro facilities were not equal to the white and the court ordered equalization within six months.[18] On the other hand, the *Brown* court expressly found respective Negro and white facilities substantially equal.[19] Plaintiffs in both cases took direct appeals to the Supreme Court. The Supreme Court remanded the *Briggs* case and directed the three-judge court to evaluate South Carolina's effort to equalize facilities during the six month period and to "take whatever action it may deem appropriate in light" of the present condition of the separate schools.[20] On remand, the lower court held that the state has complied with the decree.[21]

Remand of the *Briggs* case indicates that the Supreme Court is not ready to overrule the "separate but equal" doctrine and

---

[16] Kan. Stat. Ann. c. 72–1724 (1949) authorizes cities of the first class to organize and maintain separate schools for the education of white and colored children below the high school grades.

[17] Briggs v. Elliott, 98 F. Supp. 529, 536 (E. D. S. C. 1951); Brown v. Board of Education of Topeka, 98 F. Supp. 797, 800 (D. Kan. 1951).

[18] In the pleadings, the state denied that the facilities were unequal. But five months later, at the beginning of the hearing, it admitted physical inequality. The excuse advanced was that the school district was rural and lacked funds but that under the new South Carolina educational equalization bond issue, facilities would be greatly improved. Briggs v. Elliott, 98 F. Supp. 529, 531 (E. D. S. C. 1951). In deference to South Carolina's policy of segregation the court ordered prompt equalization rather than integration. *Id.* at 537–8. This order ignores the Supreme Court's decision that the right to equality is immediate under the Fourteenth Amendment. Sweatt v. Painter, 339 U. S. 629, 635 (1950); Sipuel v. Board of Regents, 332 U. S. 631, 633 (1948). In a strong dissent Judge Waring argued that the state's delayed admission of inequality was a maneuver to keep the court from reviewing the basic issue of whether segregation *per se* was unconstitutional. *Id.* at 540–41.

[19] Quality and qualification of teachers, curricula, and physical facilities were found to be comparable. The court also decided that the longer distance Negroes had to travel to school was offset by free bus service. Brown v. Board of Education of Topeka, 98 F. Supp. 797, 798 (D. Kan. 1951). This finding would seem to be an attempt to force a segregation *per se* ruling on the Supreme Court by eliminating the possibility of holding facilities unequal under the "separate but equal" doctrine. Conceivably, however, the Supreme Court will still find a way to avoid overruling *Plessy*.

[20] Briggs v. Elliott, 20 U. S. L. WEEK 4112 (Jan. 28, 1952).
A third segregation case, recently decided in Virginia, held that facilities were not substantially equal and the court ordered the county's school authorities to equalize "with all reasonable diligence and dispatch." Davis v. School Board of Prince Edward County, Civil Action No. 1188 (D. C. Va. 1952); see N. Y. Times, Mar. 8, 1952, p. 15, col. 8.

[21] [103 F. Supp. 920 (E. D. S. C., 1952)].

will require a factual showing of inequality. Proving the inequality of physical facilities is relatively simple.[22] But where segregated facilities are physically equal, it becomes necessary to prove intangible inequalities if segregation is to be successfully attacked. These are more difficult to demonstrate at the lower levels of education than in professional schools because the impact of grade school education must be measured in terms of general personality development,[23] while the impact of graduate school training can also be evaluated in terms of preparation for profes-

---

[22] Experience has shown that Negro facilities are never actually equal to the curriculum and physical plant provided for whites. This can be seen by a comparison of the statistics of teacher load, unit costs, teachers' salaries, and school term attendance. BLOSE & GUCWA, STATISTICS OF STATE SCHOOL SYSTEMS, U. S. OFFICE OF ED., BIENNIAL SURVEY OF EDUCATION IN THE UNITED STATES 1946–48, 107 (1950) (Table 45); Note, 56 Yale L. J. 1059, 1062 (1947); MYRDAL at 581. Even Washington, D. C. schools, which are probably the best Negro schools in the country, have been found inferior. STRAYER, THE REPORT OF A SURVEY OF THE PUBLIC SCHOOLS OF THE DISTRICT OF COLUMBIA 47–8, 315–21, 388 (1949). Threatened by integration, southern states are trying to improve their Negro schools. MYRDAL at 342. For increase of expenditures between 1941 and 1948, see BLOSE & GUCWA, op. cit. supra, at 28 (Table XIX). South Carolina plans to spend $75,000,000, Briggs v. Elliott, 98 F. Supp. 529, 531 (E. D. S. C. 1951), and Georgia $30,000,000 on equalization. N. Y. Times, April 22, 1951, p. 58, col. 3. See generally Fine, Negro Education in South on Rise, N. Y. Times, March 16, 1952, p. 82, col. 3. But full equalization for the whole South, kindergarten through college, would probably cost close to a billion dollars—a prohibitive price for the comparatively poorer southern states. Konvitz, The Courts Deal a Blow to Segregation, 11 COMMENTARY 158, 165–6 (1951).

Even if the separate system were equalized, segregation would still be discriminatory because intangible inequalities would remain. Beittel, Some Effects of the "Separate but Equal" Doctrine of Education, 20 J. NEGRO ED., 140, 143 (1951).

Also, equalization within the uneconomical dual system would, per dollar spent, result in a lower standard of education than could be achieved on an integrated basis. Thus, both Negroes and whites will suffer an educational loss relative to the national average if the South is forced merely to equalize. However, since segregation is only economical if the South can maintain unequal facilities for Negroes, enforced equalization will constitute an economic pressure favoring desegregation. MYRDAL at 341–2.

[23] Full group participation is crucial at the lower levels as an aid to personality development. American education seeks to help pupils develop habits of self-direction and cooperation by means of experimentation and participation in group life. Separateness, by denying full participation, necessarily compromises the goals of self-realization, human relationship, and civic responsibility. EDUCATIONAL POLICIES COMMISSION, NATIONAL EDUCATION ASSOCIATION, EDUCATION FOR ALL AMERICAN CHILDREN 112 (1948); JOHNSON, EDUCATION AND THE CULTURAL CRISIS 58–9 (1951); KILPATRICK, BODE, DEWEY, CHILDS, ROUP, HULLFISH & THAYER, THE EDUCATIONAL FRONTIER 190–191 (1933); MIDCENTURY WHITE HOUSE CONFERENCE at 175–6.

**1096**

sional work. Since personality reflects the total life experience of any given individual, it is difficult to isolate the specific psychological impact of segregation upon the individual personality. The presence of other forms of social discrimination prevents scientific measurement of educational segregation's precise effect.[24] It seems reasonable, however, to infer that the contribution of educational segregation to the total impact of discriminatory experiences affecting the Negro is substantial.[25]

In the *Briggs* case, efforts were made to demonstrate the effects of segregation by introducing into evidence the results of psychological projective tests[26] given to sixteen Negro school children

[24] Social scientists admit that we have not yet reached the point where we can measure the effects of separate factors of discrimination on the individual personality. KARDINER & OVESEY, THE MARK OF OPPRESSION xiv (1951); SUTHERLAND, COLOR, CLASS, AND PERSONALITY xxiii (1942); Long, *Some Psychogenic Hazards of Segregated Education of Negroes*, 4 J. NEGRO ED. 336 (1935).

For the latest psychodynamic material in the general field, see KARDINER & OVESEY, *op. cit. supra.* Psychological projective tests have been used with children to explore the growth of attitudes toward racial difference. See note 26 *infra.* However, empirical professional experience and observation remain the chief basis for the overwhelming social science opinion that segregation is inherently harmful. DEUTSCHER & CHEIN at 270, 271.

[25] Dr. Frederick Wertham, noted psychiatrist, testified recently that although he recognized that educational segregation is not the sole cause of emotional conflict among Negro children, it is of "paramount importance." Its force is significant to Dr. Wertham because it is a clear cut, continuous act of the state bound up with the educative process which hits the child at the moment he leaves a sheltered family life to contact society and for the first time find social groups for himself. Transcript of Record, p. 137–9, Bulah v. Gebhart, Delaware Chancery Civil Action No. 265, Oct. 25, 1951.

Recently a survey of social scientists was taken to try to focus the expert opinion of anthropologists, psychologists, and sociologists on the effects of enforced segregation, assuming facilities were equal. These experts were picked as scientists especially concerned with social adjustment of individuals from membership lists of the respective learned societies. The sociological sample was split into two groups: (a) those who listed race relations or social psychology as a dominant interest; and (b) "selected sociologists" who had published research on race relations in either the *American Journal of Sociology* or the *American Sociological Review*. A total of 849 questionnaires were sent out. 90.4% of the 517 replies stated that enforced segregation would have detrimental effects on the *segregated* group even if equal physical facilities are provided. Only 2.3% said it would not have this effect while 7.4% did not answer or had no opinion. 82.8% also felt that segregation had detrimental effects on the segregating group while 3.7% said no and 13.5% did not commit themselves. DEUTSCHER & CHEIN at 266–7.

[26] Projective tests seek to reveal conscious and unconscious attitudes or feelings by use of pictures, toys or dramatic play techniques which do not commit the subject upon issues explicitly formulated. For a full description, consult Horowitz & Murphy, *Projective Methods in the Psychological Study of Children*, 7 J. EXP. ED. 133 (1938).

involved in the controversy. The tests were similar to tests previously given to a larger sample of Negro children three to seven years old from both mixed and segregated nurseries and schools of the North and South.[27] The children in both tests were given a colored and a white doll, which were otherwise identical. They were asked to choose the "nice" doll, the "bad" looking doll, the "nice" color, and the doll they would prefer to play with. After these value judgments had been expressed, each child was asked to point out in turn the white doll, colored doll, Negro doll, and finally the doll that looked like himself.[28] Examination of total results shows a marked conflict between racial preference and racial self-identification. In the broader sample, two-thirds of the children preferred the white doll and 59 per cent expressed the more negative view that the colored doll looked "bad." At the same time two-thirds of the children identified with the colored

The doll and picture-coloring tests used here sought to establish in this order (a) racial preference (b) ability to distinguish racial differences and (c) racial self-identification. For example, each child, after being given dolls identical except for color, was asked this series of questions: "Give me the: (1) doll you like best or like to play with; (2) 'nice' doll; (3) doll that looks 'bad'; (4) doll that has the nice color; (5) doll that looks like a white child; (6) doll that looks like a colored child; (7) doll that looks like a Negro child; (8) doll that looks like you." Clark & Clark, *Racial Identification and Preference in Negro Children* in READINGS IN SOCIAL PSYCHOLOGY 169 (Newcomb & Hartley ed. 1947) (hereinafter cited as CLARK & CLARK).

[27] *Ibid.* Dr. Kenneth B. Clark, Assistant Professor of Psychology, New York City College, also tested the sixteen children in the *Briggs* case a week before trial. Transcript of Record, Vol. I, p. 89, Briggs v. Elliott, 98 F. Supp. 529 (E. D. S. C. 1951). For results of related tests, see Clark & Clark, *Emotional Factors in Racial Identification and Preference in Negro Children*, 19 J. NEGRO ED. 341 (1950); Clark & Clark, *Skin Color as a Factor in Racial Identification of Negro Preschool Children*, 11 J. Soc. PSYCH. 159 (1940); Clark & Clark, *Segregation as a Factor in the Racial Identification of Negro Preschool Children*, 11 J. Exp. Ed. 161 (1939); Clark & Clark, *The Development of Consciousness of Self and the Emergence of Racial Identification in Negro Preschool Children*, 10 J. Soc. PSYCH. 591 (1939); Horowitz, *Racial Aspects of Self Identification in Nursery School Children*, 7 J. PSYCH. 91 (1939).

A forthcoming book on the effects of discrimination, by Dr. Kenneth C. Clark, will bring together for critical analysis all of the latest psychological experiments used by the Midcentury White House Conference on Children and Youth.

[28] There was little chance of error from mistaken color selection since 94% of the children in the broader sample correctly identified the white doll as looking like a white child. CLARK & CLARK at 171. All sixteen of the children tested for the *Briggs* case correctly identified the dolls as to racial likeness. Transcript of Record, Vol. I, p. 90, Briggs v. Elliott, 98 F. Supp. 529 (E. D. S. C. 1951).

doll.[29]  The *Briggs* test produced similar results.[30]  These children would seem either to be in conflict about their status or to have resigned themselves to inferior self-images.  Those who identify themselves as white either have a confused self-image or are escaping from the reality of inferior status.[31]

The unhealthy symptoms revealed by the doll tests cannot, however, be traced with certainty to educational segregation.  A North-South breakdown of the results fails to establish any statistically significant difference in the preference for the white doll or self-identification with it.[32]  And analysis of the tests by age groups shows that Negro children are already aware of race and accompanying value judgments at the preschool age.[33]  This rules out the possibility that the schools play an initiating role in creating psychological conflicts.  The tests do indicate that the age of starting school is a crucial one in the development of the

---

[29] CLARK & CLARK at 175.  This preference is corroborated by the fact that a majority of children at every age level except seven chose white as the "nice" color.  At seven the children split evenly on which color was "nice." *Id.* at 176.

[30] Of the sixteen *Briggs* case children tested ten preferred the white doll and six the colored doll; nine considered the white doll to be the "nice" doll and seven the colored doll; and eleven said the colored doll looked "bad."  The remaining four children made no choice at all.  Transcript of Record, Vol. I, p. 90, Briggs v. Elliott, 98 F. Supp. 529 (E. D. S. C. 1951).

[31] Transcript of Record, Vol. I, pp. 90–91, Briggs v. Elliott, 98 F. Supp. 529 (E. D. S. C. 1951).  See also Clark & Clark, *Emotional Factors in Racial Identification and Preference in Negro Children*, 19 J. NEGRO ED. 341, 349–50 (1950).

[32] Clark & Clark at 174, 178, 69% of the southern children identified with the colored doll but only 61% of the northern children did so.  This can be partially accounted for by the fact that the northern sample had more light-skinned Negroes.  *Id.* at 177.

72% of the northern children preferred to play with the white doll compared with 62% of the southern children.  68% of the northern children chose the white doll as "nice" compared with 52% of the southern.  The only statistically significant differential was that 71% of the northern children chose the colored doll as "bad" compared with only 49% of the southern children.  Answering the "nice color" question, 63% of the northern and 57% of the southern children picked the white doll.  *Ibid.*

These figures at first glance would seem to indicate that the South with its segregated schools provides a healthier environment for Negro children.  Dr. Clark feels that this would be an inaccurate and superficial analysis.  He concedes that there is more overt conflict present in the northern children but stresses the fact that submission and apparent adjustment to inferior status are also unhealthy.  Communication to the YALE LAW JOURNAL from Dr. Kenneth B. Clark, dated Feb. 19, 1951, in the Yale Law Library.

It is clear, however, that these tests do not isolate school segregation as the source of emotional disturbances in Negro children.  Also, since the Negro facilities in the *Briggs* case were inferior, the tests cannot demonstrate specifically that "separate but equal" facilities harm the Negro child.

[33] Clark & Clark at 174.

child's ego structure. Because he seeks positive group identification and personal self-esteem, the tests show that the child at this time is especially sensitive to the accepted social values of his larger environment.[34] But psychologists have not yet gone far enough to produce findings that can compel direct legal consequences under the "separate but equal" doctrine.[35]

Behind the Supreme Court's insistence on a factual showing of inequality in educational segregation cases may be a reluctance to remove too abruptly the basic props of the Southern social system. In part this reluctance may stem from fear that sudden change would have harsh effects on Negro children presently in school. Forcing them into a hostile mixed school atmosphere might during the transition produce more unfortunate psychological consequences than segregation.[36] However, since this

[34] *Id.* at 177. At the ages of five and six both northern and southern Negro children showed the greatest preference for the white doll in their value judgments of "play with," "nice," and "nice color." *Id.* at 176. This corresponds roughly with the age at which most children leave the home and must adjust to groups in the wider school community. For an indication of the importance of this period in the life of the child, see testimony of Dr. Wertham, *supra* note 25.

[35] The Court could, of course, draw an inference similar to those made in the *Sweatt* and *McLaurin* cases. For instance, the court in Brown v. Board of Education of Topeka, 98 F. Supp. 797, 800 (D. Kan. 1951) found it difficult to see why segregation in separate schools was not unconstitutional if segregation within a school was held illegal in the *McLaurin* case. Nor could the district court see why commingling with the white majority group was any less educationally advantageous in the lower grades than at the graduate level. But the court felt bound by *Plessy v. Ferguson* until that case is overruled. *Id.* at 800.

In attempting to prove the psychological impact of segregation the Negro seeks to convince the Supreme Court that segregation necessarily creates inequality and hence must be held unconstitutional per se. Such a holding would put an end to lengthy litigation. But there is no way to prevent the Court from insisting that proof of a deleterious psychological impact in one case does not prove it for other cases. Thus the Court may continue to decide segregation on a case to case basis under the "separate but equal" rule. Another purpose of proving psychological or intangible inequalities is the fact that unlike physical inequalities they probably cannot be remedied by equalization.

[36] Dr. W. E. B. DuBois expressed this concern when he said that the Negro school child needed sympathy and understanding which he would be unlikely to get in a mixed school since private discrimination would continue and white teachers were unequipped to offset it. He also felt that the truth about Negro history, necessary to give the Negro child proper status, would only receive adequate attention in a Negro school. Although Dr. DuBois criticizes using the child as a "battering ram" for reform, he was mainly critical of overemphasis on desegregation to the detriment of equalization. He concedes that a mixed school offers the more natural basis of corrective education because of the wider contacts. DuBois, *Does the Negro Need Separate Schools?*, 4 J. NEGRO ED. 328 (1935).

may also occur when segregation is abolished piecemeal, some immediate harm to Negro children seems inevitable if the long-run goal of a healthy educational environment for both Negroes and whites is to be achieved.[37] A more decisive factor in the Court's "go slow" policy may be its fear of precipitating widespread social unrest and possible violence.[38] This fear could easily arise from repeated warnings of southern leaders that no interference with the established Southern racial structure will be tolerated.[39] But an examination of the available evidence makes

Dr. Henry B. Garret of Columbia University is the only recent authority to claim that given equal facilities, Negro students can get a better education in a segregated school. N.Y. Times, Mar. 1, 1952, p. 13, c. 4.

[37] There is considerable expert testimony to the effect that the self-image conflict of Negro children will never be corrected in segregated schools because the fact of segregation gives objective support to their inferior status. Testimony of Dr. David Krech, Associate Professor of Social Psychology, University of California, Transcript of Record, Vol. II, p. 159, Briggs v. Elliott, 98 F. Supp. 529 (E. D. S. C. 1951); testimony of Mrs. Helen Trager, M. A., teacher and lecturer at Vassar College, id. at Vol. II, pp. 171, 182.

Dr. Wertham, after testing and interviewing pupils of segregated schools, concluded that segregation created an insoluble emotional conflict in the mind of the Negro. He said that legislated educational segregation acted to intensify the conflict and was the most important factor impairing the mental health of Negroes. N.Y. Times, Oct. 23, 1951, p. 23, col. 5.

[38] Thus, southern briefs defend segregation as a public safety necessity. Brief of the States of Arkansas, Florida, Georgia, Kentucky, Louisiana, Mississippi, North Carolina, Oklahoma, South Carolina, Tennessee and Virginia, amici curiae in support of Respondents, p. 9, Sweatt v. Painter, 339 U. S. 629 (1950).

Technically, of course, this policy element cannot control the legal issue. But it is generally recognized that the Court avoids a per se ruling because it is reluctant to cause social revolution by judicial fiat. Berger, The Supreme Court and Group Discrimination since 1937, 49 COL. L. REV. 201, 204; Comment, 18 U. of CHI. L. REV. 769, 781, (1951); Note, 56 YALE L. J. 1059, 1067 (1947). For a full discussion of the issue's political implications, see Roche, Education, Segregation and the Supreme Court—A Political Analysis, 99 U. OF PA. L. REV. 949 (1951).

A counter policy argument is developing as a result of the growing embarrassment caused to American international prestige by domestic American racial conditions. Drake, The International Implications of Race and Race Relations, 20 J. NEGRO ED. 261 (1951); Bunche, Democracy: A World Issue, 19 J. NEGRO ED. 431, 436-7 (1950).

[39] E.g. Governor Wright of Miss. in an unprecedented state-wide radio hook-up warned Negroes that his state would not tolerate integration even if passed by Congress: "If any of you have become so deluded as to want to enter our white schools, patronize our hotels and cafes, enjoy social equality with whites, then kindness and true sympathy requires me to advise you to make your home in some other state than Mississippi." N. Y. Times, May 10, 1948, p. 5, col. 5; similarly, Governor Talmadge has predicted riots if Negroes enter white schools, id., Sept. 26, 1950, p. 22, col. 3, and says that Georgia will continue to bar Negroes so long as he is governor, id., June 6, 1950, p. 19, col. 2. Governor Byrnes in repudiating the Truman

it doubtful that major violence would accompany educational desegregation.[40]

Despite extensive educational desegregation, in only one city was there any violence during the transition.[41] As a result of recent Supreme Court cases, over a thousand Negroes have been peacefully integrated into southern graduate and professional schools.[42] Social ostracism has not been as great as was expected.[43] Furthermore, in Illinois,[44] Indiana,[45] and New Jer-

Administration's efforts to end segregation, *id.*, Jan. 17, 1951, p. 3, col. 2, has pledged continued segregation for South Carolina. *Id.*, Jan. 25, 1951, p. 19, col. 6.

[40] Although there can be no guarantee of non-violent reaction to desegregation, threats in the past have failed to materialize. See note 51 *infra*. A recent analysis of racial violence concluded that most if not all racial violence can be prevented by well-advised government action even where the enforcement of civil rights involves a direct attack on racial segregation. Comment, *Racial Violence and Civil Rights Law Enforcement*, 18 U. of CHI. L. REV. 769, 781 (1951).

[41] Protest meetings, demonstrations, and school strikes are considered here to be peaceful and lawful methods of registering protest. The only reported incidents of violence stemming from educational desegregation are the recent disorders in Cairo, Ill. See note 47 *infra*.

[42] These results are unquestionably attributable to the Supreme Court decisions in Sweatt v. Painter, 339 U.S. 629 (1950) and McLaurin v. Oklahoma State Regents, 339 U.S. 637 (1950). The New York Times surveyed one hundred institutions and found that the same officials who had predicted campus and community riots if integration occurred freely admitted that the transition had not disturbed institutional routine. N. Y. Times, Oct. 23, 1950, p. 29, col. 6; *id.*, Oct. 29, 1950, p. 9, col. 2.

[43] *Ibid.* For a review of graduate level desegregation, the reception of Negroes, and the lack of violence or injury to race relations, see AMERICAN JEWISH CONGRESS & NATIONAL ASSOCIATION FOR THE ADVANCEMENT OF COLORED PEOPLE, CIVIL RIGHTS IN THE UNITED STATES IN 1950: A BALANCE SHEET OF GROUP RELATIONS 42-6, 51-2 (hereinafter cited as 1950 BALANCE SHEET). Campus newspapers at the Universities of Alabama and Mississippi, Auburn College, and Millsaps College openly endorsed integration. Konvitz, *The Courts Deal a Blow to Segregation*, 11 COMMENTARY 158, 164 (1951).

It is not yet clear how far undergraduate schools will be affected by the *Sweatt* and *McLaurin* cases but in at least three states private colleges have voluntarily desegregated. See 1950 BALANCE SHEET at 46. Kentucky amended its laws to allow integration above the high school level, KY. REV. STAT. § 158–021 (Supp. 1950), and five institutions promptly dropped segregation. 1950 BALANCE SHEET at 46; 123 NEW REPUBLIC 9 (1950). See also Konvitz, *supra*, at 165.

[44] In 1950, East St. Louis, Ill., ended its eighty-five year old segregation of schools. Although police were alerted and some white pupils stayed home, no incidents were reported. N. Y. Times, Jan. 30, 1950, p. 22, col. 4; *id.*, Jan. 31, 1950, p. 16, col. 3. This integration was forced on East St. Louis by the Illinois legislature which voted to cut off the state subsidy to any school violating state law by separating Negro and white pupils. *Id.*, Dec. 22, 1949, p. 8, col. 3. But *cf.* the situation in Cairo, Ill., note 47 *infra*.

[45] In Indianapolis, where segregation dated from 1875, and was well en-

sey,[46] state legislatures have forced reluctant communities to eliminate segregation in their grade schools. Despite local resentment and protest, the integration of Negro and white children has generally proceeded peacefully.[47]

Other forms of desegregation have recently occurred in the South, and despite sporadic racial violence the transition has in general been peaceful. In some instances, the desegregation has occurred in activities where southern insistence on segregation has traditionally been most adamant. Thus, in St. Louis and Washington, D.C., over strong public protest, segregation in municipal swimming pools has been successfully prohibited.[48] Ex-

---

trenched because of the strong Ku Klux Klan tradition in Indiana and the proximity to the South's Jim Crow, desegregation was expected to bring trouble. For an account of these expectations and their peaceful outcome see Lewis, *The Crisis That Never Came Off*, The Reporter, Dec. 6, 1949, p. 12. Over fervent protests the Gary, Indiana school board successfully desegregated one of its main high schools without violence although at one point 1500 of its 1750 pupils were out on strike. N. Y. Times, June 7, 1947, p. 30, col. 7; *id.*, Sept. 4, 1947, p. 19, col. 5; *id.*, Sept. 5, 1947, p. 21, col. 6; *id.*, Sept. 6, 1947, p. 2, col. 1; *id.*, Sept. 7, 1947, p. 14, col. 4; *id.*, Sept. 8, 1947, p. 23, col. 6; *id.*, Sept. 9, 1947, p. 25, col. 6; *id.*, Sept. 13, 1947, p. 2, col. 3.

[46] The New Jersey Constitutional Convention adopted a ban on public school segregation in 1947. N. Y. Times, Aug. 21, 1947, p. 25, col. 5. And desegregation has been systematically enforced since 1948. *Id.* Feb. 5, 1948, p. 14, col. 3; *id.*, Feb. 20, 1948, p. 16, col. 3; *id.*, June 5, 1948, p. 18, col. 7. Although there are still some all-Negro schools due to geographical situations, forty school districts had desegregated without reported violence as of Sept. 24, 1951. NEW JERSEY DEPARTMENT OF EDUCATION, DIVISION AGAINST DISCRIMINATION, PROGRESS REPORT ON THE DESEGREGATION OF SCHOOLS (1951).

[47] The very recent limited bombing and cross-burning in Cairo, Ill., is the sole reported example of violence stemming from educational desegregation. The incidents were threats to discourage integration and proper police protection was conspicuously absent. Time, Feb. 18, 1952, p. 67; The Nation, Feb. 2, 1952, pp. 124–6. Subsequently 21 Negro children were integrated into white schools with no reported incidents. N. Y. Times, March 2, 1952, p. 71, col. 5.

Extensive integration over protests has occurred in Arizona without any violence. Communication to the YALE LAW JOURNAL from Arizona Council for Civic Unity, dated Jan. 2, 1952, on file in Yale Law Library; Time, Oct. 8, 1951, pp. 84–5.

[48] Interracial swimming carries sexual connotations and therefore is second in Myrdal's "Rank Order of Discriminations" as supported by white public opinion. MYRDAL at 61, 617. Despite a forced closing due to a riot in 1949, N. Y. Times, June 22, 1949, p. 56, col. 3, the St. Louis, Mo., municipal swimming pool was opened by court order, *id.*, July 18, 1950, p. 13, col. 2, and operated interracially without serious disturbance in 1950. Better preparation was made and after the first days extra police supervision was discontinued. 1950 BALANCE SHEET at 66. However, a near riot had to be quelled at Colonial Beach, Va., when Negroes tried to swim there. *Ibid.* In Washington, D.C., the Department of the Interior pools were interracial in 1950 with an estimated 145,000 whites and 90,000 Negroes attending without incident.

perience in the elimination of segregation in public parks, sporting events, theaters and movies has been the same.[49] And in the armed forces, where resistance to racial integration has been traditional, segregation is fast disappearing at the command of the President.[50] In allied fields of racial discrimination, such as white primaries,[51] all-white juries[52] and segregated interstate

---

*Id.* at 74. But a race riot had closed them in 1949. N. Y. Times, July 1, 1949, p. 22 Col. 3. For a detailed discussion of the swiming pool desegregation in St. Louis and Wash., D.C., see Comment, *Racial Violence and Civil Rights Enforcement*, 18 U. of CHI. L. REV. 769, 771–5 (1951).

[49] Baltimore, Md., has ended segregation on four golf courses and allows mixed tennis matches on some of its city courts. N. Y. Times, June 27, 1951, p. 22, col. 6.

The South has had several major sports events with Negro-white participation. N. Y. Times, Sept. 21, 1947, § V, p. 4, col. 5; *id.*, Oct. 13, 1947, p. 34, col. 4; *id.*, Nov. 24, 1947, p. 25, col. 2. The University of North Carolina recently stopped requiring segregation of its Negro students as spectators, *id.*, Oct. 13, 1951. p. 7, col. 8. However there has been a tendency toward voluntary self-segregation. *Id.*, Oct. 14, 1951, p. 39, col. 4.

Several theatres in Washington, D. C., 1950 BALANCE SHEET at 76; N. Y. Times, Sept. 11, 1949 § 11, p. 3, col. 8, and six motion picture houses in Wilmington, Del. have successfully dropped segregation without disturbing public order. *Id.*, March 10, 1951, p. 8, col. 1. For a survey of recent desegregation generally, see 1950 BALANCE SHEET.

[50] Exec. Order No. 9981, 13 FED. REG. 4313 (1948) called for "equality of treatment and opportunity for all persons in the armed services without regard to race, color, religion or national origin." This order resulted in an official policy and implementation of racial integration in all three services. REPORT BY THE PRESIDENT'S COMMITTEE ON EQUALITY OF TREATMENT AND OPPORTUNITY IN THE ARMED SERVICES 5–7 (1950). Integration of work, school, and living quarters, which was fastest in the Navy and Air Force, resulted in a decrease of racial friction, rather than greater tension. *Id.* at 44. Segregation policy in the Army was traditionally justified by the military opinion that it was necessary for morale and efficiency. This rationalization has been discredited and integration is the official policy and practice in the Army. *Id.* at 47–63. For the complete history of Navy integration, see NELSON, INTEGRATION OF THE NEGRO INTO THE UNITED STATES NAVY (1951). Desegregation in the armed forces would have been stopped had it impaired efficiency or morale. Exec. Order No. 9981, 13 FED. REG. 4313 (1948). And its success should establish the feasibility of integration in other areas of life, especially in schools where life contacts are far less constant and intimate.

[51] For a succinct history of the court battles to outlaw white primaries and circumvention tactics in the South, consult KEY, SOUTHERN POLITICS c. 29 (1949). On Negro suffrage in general see LOGAN, ATTITUDE OF THE SOUTHERN WHITE PRESS TOWARD NEGRO SUFFRAGE (1940); MOON, BALANCE OF POWER—THE NEGRO VOTE (1948).

Southern threats against Negro voting never materialized. Despite the exhortations of Senator Bilbo and others to use any means to bar the Negro vote, N. Y. Times, June 23, 1946, p. 30, col. 4, and his assertions to the effect that whites would continue to run the Mississippi primary, *id.*, June 25, 1946, p. 17, col. 5, only a few incidents were reported as Negroes voted for the first

travel,[53] court orders have partially overcome deeply rooted patterns of discrimination. All of this progress has been made in the face of continuous threats of violence and non-conformance by southern leaders.[54]

These instances of southern adjustment to enforced desegregation strongly suggest that the normal reaction of the South to Supreme Court decisions is not violence. Generally, the only resistance takes the form of attempted circumvention.[55] Tighter

time. *Id.*, July 3, 1946, p. 1, col. 2; *id.*, July 4, 1946, p. 1, col. 6. Despite warnings from Governor Talmadge, Negroes voted in the Georgia primaries and no incidents were reported. Undoubtedly some Negro voters stayed away from the polls but Negro participation in the primary voting was encouraging. *Id.*, Aug. 17, 1946, p. 11, col. 7. A study shows that Negro suffrage in Texas has been accepted with very little resort to extra-legal violence despite an ever-increasing Negro vote. Strong, *The Rise of Negro Voting in Texas*, 42 AM. POL. SCI. REV. 510, 512–13 (1948).

Former Federal District Judge Waring, who wrote the decision outlawing South Carolina's white primary system, Rice v. Elmore, 165 F.2d 387 (4th Cir. 1947), *cert. denied*, 333 U.S. 875 (1948) (unsuccessful attempt to avoid the rule of Smith v. Allwright, 321 U. S. 649, by repealing all the South Carolina laws relating to primaries in order to make the South Carolina Democratic party a private organization not subject to constitutional restriction) later asserted that the peaceful 1948 primaries demonstrated the emptiness of the threats of racial strife which were used to inhibit the courts. N. Y. Times, Feb. 27, 1950, p. 17, col. 1. However, later his own home was attacked. *Id.*, Oct. 10, 1950, p. 28, col., 6; *id.*, Oct. 12, 1950, p. 41, col. 1.

[52] Southern all-white juries have not been eliminated but service on mixed juries is no longer considered novel. 1950 BALANCE SHEET at 29.

[53] The reaction following the Supreme Court's requirement that interstate travel be integrated in Morgan v. Virginia, 328 U. S. 373 (1946) and Henderson v. United States, 339 U. S. 816 (1950) has not been violent. The carriers tend, however, to continue segregation informally by seating races at opposite ends of cars. 1950 BALANCE SHEET at 63. Just recently this policy received the blessing of the Interstate Commerce Commission, 20 U. S. L. WEEK 2382 (1952).

[54] The Supreme Court was directly admonished by Attorney General Daniel of Texas when he summed up his oral argument in Sweatt v. Painter, 339 U.S. 629 (1950) with the warning that segregation was necessary to avoid race conflict because "some people have feelings that make for conflict when the races associate too closely." N. Y. Times, April 5, 1950, p. 39, col. 6. But experience has shown that segregation was not necessary at the graduate level.

Liberal Virginius Dabney, who concedes that the courts have been responsible for much of the Negro's progress, cautions that these gains will be lost if pushed beyond southern public opinion. *Id.*, March 22, 1951, p. 33 col. 5. But southern public opinion has almost uniformly shifted only after judicial support of the Negro's rights. For statements of Southerners on race relations in general, see BILBO, TAKE YOUR CHOICE—SEPARATION OR MONGRELIZATION (1945); COLLINS, WHITHER SOLID SOUTH? (1947); LANDRY, THE CULT OF EQUALITY (1945).

[55] The plan in Georgia, N. Y. Times, Feb. 18, 1951, p. 48, col. 1, and in South Carolina, *id.*, March 17, 1951, p. 13, col. 4, to abandon public schools

decrees and persistent enforcement ultimately overcome even this type of resistance.[56] Thus there is little reason for the courts to allow threats of violence and civil strife to delay desegregation.[57]

and set up private schools for whites if segregation is declared unconstitutional illustrates the circumvention pattern. It resembles the election law manipulation with which the South attempted to neutralize the Court's attack on the white primary. KEY, SOUTHERN POLITICS c. 29 (1949). Recently Atlanta, Ga., cut the white-Negro vote ratio from 2-1 down to 3-1 by establishing new city boundaries which raised the white population from 67% to 72%. The Nation, Feb. 23, 1952, p. 166. The "county unit" system, used in Georgia to minimize the weight of the Negro vote, is still constitutional. South v. Peters, 339 U.S. 276 (1950). Maintenance of white political control is no less crucial to southerners than the maintenance of all white schools. And the threats of violence made when white primaries were endangered were as violent as those now voiced against educational desegregation. The informal segregated seating pattern adopted by interstate carriers is another example of passive resistance rather than violent reaction to desegregation orders. See note 53 supra.

School district gerrymander is a ready device to limit the number of Negroes actually integrated. It is still used with success in sections of the North, MYRDAL at 633, and would undoubtedly be used in the South.

[56] The history of the white primary cases is the best example of legal victories over civil intransigence. Consult KEY, SOUTHERN POLITICS c. 29 (1949).

[57] The possibility of racial violence when school segregation breaks down cannot be denied. Rose & Rose, The American Negro, 20 J. NEGRO ED. 320, 323 (1951). But actually, due to southern residential segregation patterns, it is not likely that even a general desegregation decree would in fact cause drastic and immediate integration. Thompson, Negro Teachers and the Elimination of Segregation, 20 J. NEGRO ED. 135, 138 (1951).

Even assuming a violent reaction to desegregation, this danger from the standpoint of legal theory should not control. "It is urged that this proposed segregation will promote the public peace by preventing race conflict. Desirable as this is, and important as is the preservation of the public peace, this aim cannot be accomplished by laws or ordinances which deny rights created or protected by the Federal Constitution." Buchanan v. Warley, 245 U.S. 60, 81 (1917).

Moreover, experiments in Detroit after the serious race riots of World War II demonstrate that racial conflict can be avoided if proper law enforcement precautions are taken. N. Y. Times, April 20, 1947, § VI, p. 17, col. 4. For instance, Chicago officials insisted a "mob can't run the city." And a riot protesting residential desegregation was sucessfully quelled while the city took immediate steps to improve further its riot control techniques. N. Y. Times, Dec. 11, 1946, p. 35, col. 4. The swimming pool desegregation cases also illustrate the efficacy of proper police precautions. See note 46 supra. For a complete discussion of racial disorders and the important preventive function played by the law and by enforcement agencies see Comment, Racial Violence and Civil Rights Enforcement, 18 U. OF CHI. L. REV. 769 (1951). See also LEE, RACE RIOTS AREN'T NECESSARY (Public Affairs Pamphlet 1945); MACIVER, THE MORE PERFECT UNION 178 (1948).

Finally, if the Court feels that a blanket desegregation decree would precipitate too great social resistance, it might direct that schools be integrated

[Emerson]

DISCRIMINATION

## Note

1. See also Powe, *The Constitutionality of Segregation in the Elementary Public Schools,* 11 Law. Guild Rev. 151 (1951); Notes, 4 S. C. L. Q. 177 (1951); 13 U. of Pitts. L. Rev. 157 (1951).

2. Compare with the *Briggs* and *Brown* cases, which were decided by a three judge court, *Gray v. Board of Trustees of University of Tennessee,* 100 F. Supp. 113 (E. D. Tenn., 1951). The court stated that 28 U. S. C. § 2281 requires the action of a three-judge court "only when an injunction is issued restraining the action of any officer of the State upon the ground of the unconstitutionality of" a state statute. The court held that since the state law made it mandatory for school officials to provide equal facilities the statute is not unconstitutional and what is challenged is a violation of equal protection without statutory sanctions. This should be disposed of by a one judge court. The case became moot because Negroes were admitted to the white school.

3. On the relationship of modern educational theory to the problem of school segregation, see Brief for the Committee of Law Teachers Against Segregation in Legal Education, filed in *Sweatt v. Painter, supra,* reprinted in 34 Minn. L. Rev. 289, 319–20 (1950):

"(2) Just as the principle of free public education was the first important step in realizing democratic objectives through our educational system, so completely non-segregated public education is an essential element in reaching that goal. If children have race superiority taught them as infants, we cannot expect them lightly to toss it aside in later life. The answer lies not, however, in simply indoctrinating them with the principle of racial equality. Modern educational theory, formulated in answer to the need of our society for self-reliant individuals voluntarily cooperating with others to meet the everchanging scene in our dynamic civilization,[92] postulates a more thoroughgoing solution. According to this theory, education 'is a continuous process from the be-

from kindergarten to second grade the first year and then automatically one grade higher each year. In this way integration would grow up with the children. The mixing of younger children would be less likely to excite the community and valuable administrative experience would be achieved before the upper grades were integrated. Because the decree would assure automatic progressive integration each year, this gradual solution is not subject to the usual complaint against gradualism, *i.e.,* that it is a dodge meant to give the impression of changes without any real progress. This plan would also provide time to solve the problem of surplus Negro teachers who will undoubtedly not be integrated immediately. But the overall teacher shortage should ameliorate even this difficulty. On the problem of Negro teachers, see Thompson, *supra* at 135. Such a disposition of the problem must hurdle the technical barrier of the Fourteenth Amendment's guarantee of a personal and *immediate* right to equality. See Sipuel v. Board of Regents, 332 U.S. 631, 633 (1948).

[92] See Benedict [*Transmitting our Democratic Heritage in the Schools,* 48 Am. Jo. Sociol. 722 (1943), reprinted in Lee and Lee, *Social Problems in America* 297 (1949)]; Kallen, *The Education of Free Men* cc. 10, 11, 12, 15 (1949); Kilpatrick (Ed.), *The Educational Frontier* c. 2 (1933); The President's Commission on Higher Education, 1 *Higher Education for American*

ginning to the end of life,' and it is a 'continuous reconstruction of experience.' [93] That is to say, each new thing learned is assimilated to some previous thing learned, and the new is in part conditioned by the old. 'Education in America must be education for democracy. If education is life and growth, then it must be life within a social group. . . . Schools must be democratic communities wherein children live natural, democratic lives with their companions and grow into adulthood with good citizenship a part of their experience.' [94]

"(3) This modern educational theory of learning by doing, clearly implies the necessity of non-segregated education. The principle of equality of opportunity regardless of race or creed, so much a part of our American tradition, can be fully achieved only if this element in our cultural heritage is kept alive and allowed to grow. The school, as has been shown, is the most important institution through which this heritage can be transmitted. But, as has likewise been made clear, proper teaching of the principle of equality of opportunity requires more than mere inculcation of the democratic ideal. What is essential is the opportunity, at least in the school, to practice it. This requires that the school make possible continuous actual experience of harmonious cooperation between members of various ethnic and religious groups and thus produce attitudes of tolerance and mutual sharing that will continue in later life.[95] In the segregated school, this desirable environment does not exist. The most important instrument for teaching democracy to all people is thus rendered impotent.

"Even for those who believe in the policy behind *Plessy v. Ferguson,* that it is impractical to eliminate segregation in all areas of our culture at once, education has usually been the logical step for achieving our ideal of true equality. Since segregated education cannot be effective education for equality, the principle of *Plessy v. Ferguson* should not be extended to the schools."

4. For a summary of other material from the social sciences, see Van Til and Denemark, *Intercultural Education,* in Review of Educational Research, pp. 277–86 (Oct. 1950) :[1]

*"What Schools Can Do*

"Five major approaches to developing democratic human relations have especially been studied in current research. Many of these approaches had been suggested as promising practices by educators who based them primarily on teaching experience, educational theory, and

---

Democracy 5–9, 101–2 (1947) ; 2 *id.* 3–9; Brubacher, *Modern Philosophies of Education* c. 14 (1939).

[93] Frasier and Armentrout, *An Introduction to Education* 31, 33 (3d ed. 1933).

[94] Id. at 32. See also Brubacher, *op. cit. supra* note 92 at 330–1; Dewey, *Democracy and Education* (1916) ; Mayo, *The Human Problems of an Industrial Civilization* (1933) ; Lewin, *Resolving Social Conflicts* c. 5 (1948).

[95] See Kallen, *The Education of Free Men* 182–4 *et passim* (1949) ; MacIver, *The More Perfect Union* c. 9 (1948) ; Newlon, *Education for Democracy in our Time* 92–103 (1939).

[1] The numbers in parentheses refer to materials printed in the footnote at the end of the extract.

the limited research available (41, 91, 92). It should be noted that a large number of the current research studies considered demonstrated an awareness of the necessity for developing programs which included a wide variety of approaches, even as they chose to limit their investigation to one.

"1. *The creation of a democratic atmosphere designed to reduce the personal insecurities and tensions of children.*

"Ackerman and Jahoda (1, 2) found that emotional predispositions to anti-Semitism include anxiety, confusion of the concept of self, unsatisfactory interpersonal relationships, conformity, fear of the different, poor perception of reality, an inconsistent value system, and a poorly developed conscience. Much research points to the importance of wholesome family relationships prior to and concurrent with the school experiences of children for minimizing such difficulties. There is also good reason to believe, with Kilpatrick (41), Weston (93), Taba (83), and others, that a warm, friendly, democratic atmosphere in schools may help to strengthen the healthy attitudes already present in many young people, and to some degree at least, make up for the shortcomings in home environment experienced by others. Kilpatrick and Van Til (42) indicated that perhaps the single most important factor in building good human relations thru the school is a democratic atmosphere, and defined such an atmosphere as one which involves acceptance, belongingness, and welcome as a person.

"The importance of the classroom teacher in effecting attitude changes, and the influence which teacher attitudes have upon those of the students have been pointed out by Russell and Robertson (75), Radke, H. Trager, and Davis (66), and others. Those institutions involved in the College Study in Intergroup Relations (18, 32) recognized the crucial role of the teacher and instituted surveys and reexaminations of their teacher preparation programs.

"Analyses done in the area of group dynamics (51, 62, 84) lead us to believe that a reexamination of the ways in which school groups are organized and conducted will point out possibilities for materially reducing individual tensions and insecurities. Tolman (87), in describing social learning, commented briefly on some of the possible ways of translating or dissipating aggressions against out-groups.

"2. *The encouragement of broadening intergroup contacts in situations involving cooperation.*

"The findings reported by Stouffer and others (81), drawn from data obtained by the Research Branch of the War Department, and those reported by Whittemore (94) with regard to the experiences in the 'G. I. Universities' following the war, lend strong support to the *fait accompli* as a method of intergroup education. Data from the former group, in answer to a question relating to attitudes toward serving in a company containing Negro and white platoons, disclosed that of the men not having had such experience, only 2 percent stated they would like it. Sixty-two percent indicated they would dislike it very much. A literal revolution in attitudes was apparent from the responses of men having had such experience. Thirty-two percent stated they would like it and only 7 percent indicated they would dislike it very much. As Stouffer and his associates pointed out, this technic is particularly promising when 'attention is focused on concrete tasks or goals requiring common effort rather than upon more abstract considerations of justice or of desirable policy which emphasize and arouse traditional prejudices.' A similar conclusion was reported by Wittenberg (98) with respect to neighborhood projects.

"The value of contacts in situations involving cooperation was reported by Deutsch and Collins (22) with respect to intergroup contacts in public housing projects. Findings by Phelps (64, 65) in school work camps also seem to corroborate the value of this technic. Particularly promising results are yielded by situations in which the pressures to conform to prior arrangements are lessened. The conditions of contact are important, according to B. MacKenzie (55) and as research on social distance prior to the current period of investigation has repeatedly demonstrated. One of the conclusions of the Philadelphia Early Childhood Project (66) pointed out that such contacts needed to be accompanied by other change technics to prevent some prejudiced persons from regarding the contact merely as an exception to their previously formulated generalizations.

"3. *The provision of opportunities for enhanced emotional sensitization to other intercultural groups.*

"The role of emotions in the educative process has long been underestimated in American educational thinking. The work of Prescott and his associates has been a valuable stimulus toward recognizing the emotional as well as the intellectual facets of the learning process. In human relations research the importance of building into personal frames of reference an emotional sensitivity to other persons and groups is now receiving increasing attention. Davidoff (20) found a positive correlation between empathy and attitude toward minority groups. Kramer (45), in discussing dimensions of prejudice, called attention to the emotional as well as the cognitive and action facets of such attitudes. Woodruff and DiVesta (99) observed that an important way of changing attitudes is to change the individual's concept of the object toward which the attitude is expressed, a process which must necessarily include emotional considerations.

"A significant part of the work of the staff of Intergroup Education in Cooperating Schools (85) has been devoted to developing school curriculums which emphasize human relations problems thru the medium of literature, particularly novels. Reports suggesting the potentialities of literature for both the elementary and secondary levels were made by Franc (28), Finley (25), and Rollins (71). H. Trager and Everitt (88), speaking from experiences with primary grade children in the Philadelphia public schools, doubted that books alone are sufficient, but suggested that their value lay in reinforcing, interpreting, and extending the experience of children. . . .

"4. *The promotion of situations in which individuals may be exposed to the inconsistency or invalidity of some of their existing attitudes.*

**1110**

# DISCRIMINATION

"It is notable that in contrast to the preceding half-decade, when a large number of research studies were concerned with the effectiveness of information presented in curriculum courses as a means of changing intergroup attitudes, practically no such projects were reported in the period from 1947 to 1950. Bierstedt (54), in summarizing much of this earlier research, concluded that appropriate instruction under certain conditions does have an influence on attitudes toward outgroups, but pointed to the necessity for research as to the kind of instruction and conditions which accompany it, as well as into the character of the students involved. Similar tentativeness is apparent in Rose's generalizations on the effectiveness of information (73), also based on a summary of research.

"Current researches have placed considerable emphasis upon study of persons exposed to data that contradicts their presently held attitudes. Lippitt (51), Kretch and Crutchfield (46), and others have observed that the effectiveness of facts in bringing about attitudinal changes is frequently dependent upon the extent to which those attitudes we seek to change are themselves involved in obtaining the facts. Much of the work of the Commission on Community Interrelations (13, 14, 76) has been devoted to an analysis of the role of action research in intergroup education. Chein (12), reporting upon the Montclair, Minneapolis, and Northtown community self-surveys, noted in a composite summary such concrete changes as the passage of an FEPC ordinance, the admittance of Negroes into an important local union, the construction by private builders of a 350 dwelling unit for Negro occupancy, and the first employment of Negroes as teachers, school principals, policemen, and salesclerks.

"5. *Strengthening the 'social supports' of democratic behavior.* . . . [The authors here discuss the effect of legislation and mass media propaganda.]

"It is also encouraging to note in intercultural education a heightened appreciation of interrelationships and interaction. For instance, there is a growing emphasis upon the school *in* society, both as it influences and is influenced by other social institutions and forces. There is growing recognition of the relationship between process and product, and consequent deep concern with both. The ties between emotion and intellect are emphasized. Increased cooperation is evident between psychological and social disciplines, between research workers and action agencies, and between home and school. Most of all, it is heartening to find that these emphases arising out of research concerned with improving intergroup relations closely parallel and undergird our emerging concept of what constitutes good democratic experimental education for American schools." [2]

---

[2] The references cited in the above extract are as follows:

1. Ackerman, Nathan W., and Jahoda, Marie. *Anti-Semitism and Emotional Disorder.* New York: Harper and Brothers, 1950. 130 p.

2. Ackerman, Nathan W., and Jahoda, Marie. "Toward a Dynamic Interpretation of Anti-Semitic Attitudes." *American Journal of Orthopsychiatry* 18:163–73; January 1948.

5. In *Gonzales v. Sheely,* 96 F. Supp. 1004 (D. Ariz., 1951) the court found school facilities for Mexicans inferior and granted a temporary injunction against segregation. The conclusions of law read in part as follows:

"Segregation of school children in separate school buildings because of racial or national origin, as accomplished by regulations, customs and usages of respondent, constitutes a denial of the equal protection of the laws guaranteed to petitioners as citizens of the United States

12. Chein, Isidor. "The Problems of Inconsistency: a Restatement." *Journal of Social Issues* 5:52–61; No. 3, 1949.
13. Chein, Isidor; Cook, Stuart W.; and Harding, John. "The Field of Action Research." *American Psychologist* 3:43–50; February 1948.
14. Chein, Isidor, and Others, issue editors. "Consistency and Inconsistency in Intergroup Relations." *Journal of Social Issues* 5:2–61; No. 3, 1949.
18. Cook, Lloyd Allen, editor. *College Programs in Intergroup Education.* College Study in Intergroup Relations, Vol. I. Washington, D. C.: American Council on Education, 1950. 365 p.
20. Davidoff, Melvin D. *A Study of Empathy and Correlates of Prejudice Toward a Minority Group.* Lafayette, Indiana: Division of Educational Reference, Purdue University, 1949. 61 p.
22. Deutsch, Morton, and Collins, Mary Evans. *Study of Intergroup Relations in Unsegregated and Segregated Interracial Housing Projects.* New York: Center for Human Relations Studies, New York University, 1949. 4 p.
25. Finley, Mabel S. "Book Approach: Experiment in Intergroup Education." *English Journal* 38:384–88; September 1949.
28. Franc, Lillian. "Intergroup Education Through Literature in the Fourth Grade." *Elementary English* 27:226–39; April 1950.
32. Harris, Raymond P. "Improving Intergroup Relations Through Teacher Training." *Education* 68:142–47; November 1947.
41. Kilpatrick, William H. *Modern Education and Better Human Relations.* New York: Anti-Defamation League of B'nai B'rith, 1949. 31 p.
42. Kilpatrick, William H., and Van Til, William, editors. *Intercultural Attitudes in the Making.* Ninth Yearbook, John Dewey Society. New York: Harper and Brothers, 1949. 246 p. Hymes, James L., Jr. "Parents." p. 17–47.
45. Kramer, Bernard M. "Dimensions of Prejudice." *Journal of Psychology* 27: 389–451; April 1949.
46. Kretch, David and Crutchfield, Richard S. *Theory and Problems of Social Psychology.* New York: McGraw-Hill Book Company, 1948. 621 p.
51. Lippitt, Ronald. *Training in Community Relations: A Research Exploration Toward New Group Skills.* New York: Harper and Brothers, 1949. 283 p.
54. MacIver, Robert M. *The More Perfect Union.* New York: The Macmillan Company, 1948. 302 p. Stone, L. Joseph. "Memorandum on Types of Prejudice." Appendix 4, p. 285–87. Bierstedt, Robert. "Information and Attitudes." Appendix 5, p. 288–302.
55. MacKenzie, Barbara K. "The Importance of Contact in Determining Attitudes Toward Negroes." *Journal of Abnormal and Social Psychology* 43:417–41; October 1948.
62. National Education Association and Research Center for Group Dynamics, Massachusetts Institute of Technology. *Group Growth and Educational Dynamics.* Bulletin No. 2. Washington, D. C.: National Education Association, 1948. 68 p.

by the provisions of the Fourteenth Amendment to the Constitution of the United States. Discriminations less acute than those practiced by respondents have recently been held in violation of the Equal Protection clause of the Fourteenth Amendment in McLaurin v. Oklahoma State Regents, 339 U. S. 637, 70 S. Ct. 851, 94 L. Ed. 1149, where the

64. Phelps, Seth P. "A Community Looks At a High-School Work Camp." *School Review* 51:202–209; April 1948.

65. Phelps, Seth P. "Students' Opinions of Work Camps." *School Review* 55:214–21; April 1947.

66. Radke, Marian: Trager, Helen G.; and Davis, Hadassah. "Social Perceptions and Attitudes of Children." *Genetic Psychology Monographs* 40:327–447; November 1949.

71. Rollins, Charlemae. *We Build Together.* Revised edition. Chicago: National Council of Teachers of English, 1948. 71 p.

73. Rose, Arnold M. *Studies in the Reduction of Prejudice.* Chicago: American Council on Race Relations, 1948. 112 p.

74. Rose, Arnold M. "The Use of Propaganda to Reduce Prejudice." *International Journal of Opinion and Attitude Research* 2:221–29; Summer 1948.

75. Russell, David H., and Robertson, Isabella W. "Influencing Attitudes Toward Minority Groups in a Junior High School." *School Review* 55:205–13; April 1947.

76. Selltiz, Claire, and Wormser, Margot Haas, editors. "Community Self Surveys: An Approach to Social Change." *Journal of Social Issues* 5:1–65; Spring 1949.

81. Stouffer, Samuel A., and Others. *The American Soldier: Adjustment During Army Life.* Princeton, New Jersey: Princeton University Press, 1949. 599 p.

83. Taba, Hilda. issue editor. "School Culture and Group Life." *Journal of Educational Sociology* 21:497–552; May 1948.

84. Taba, Hilda, and Others. *Curriculum in Intergroup Relations: Case Studies in Instruction for Secondary Schools.* Washington, D. C.: American Council on Education, 1949. 168 p.

85. Taba, Hilda, and Others. *Reading Ladders for Human Relations.* Revised edition. Washington, D. C.: American Council on Education, 1949. 115 p.

87. Tolman, Edward C. "The Psychology of Social Learning." *Journal of Social Issues* 5:3–18; Supplement No. 3, December 1949.

88. Trager, Helen G., and Everitt, Roberta M. "Tools for Human Relations Education." *Educational Leadership* 7:530–39; May 1950.

91. Van Til, William. "Building Intercultural Attitudes Through the School." *North Central Association Quarterly* 23:243–46; January 1949.

92. Watson, Goodwin. *Action for Unity.* New York: Harper and Brothers, 1947. 165 p.

93. Weston, Grace L., and Others. *Democratic Citizenship and the Development of Children.* Detroit, Michigan: Citizenship Education Study, 1949. 43 p.

94. Whittemore, Irving C. "An Uncontrolled Experiment in Race Relations." *Journal of Educational Sociology* 22:590–97; May 1949.

98. Wittenberg, Rudolph M. "Grass Roots and City Blocks." *Common Ground* 7:43–49; Summer 1947.

99. Woodruff, Ashel D., and DiVesta, Francis J. "The Relationship Between Values, Concepts, and Attitudes." *Educational and Psychological Measurement* 8:645–59; Winter 1948.

very act of setting plaintiff apart from other students in the same room because of the racial origin of the plaintiff was held to deny plaintiff equal protection. A paramount requisite in the American system of public education is social equality. It must be open to all children by unified school associations, regardless of lineage.

"English language deficiencies of some of the children of Mexican ancestry as such children enter elementary public school life as beginners may justify differentiation by public school authorities in the exercise of their reasonable discretion as to the pedagogical methods of instruction to be pursued with different pupils, and foreign language handicaps may exist to such a degree in the pupils in elementary schools as to require separate treatment in separate classrooms. Such separate allocations, however, can be lawfully made only after credible examination by the appropriate school authorities of each child whose capacity to learn is under consideration, and the determination of such segregation must be based wholly upon indiscriminate foreign language impediments in the individual child, regardless of his ethnic traits or ancestry. But even such situations do not justify the general and continuous segregation in separate schools of children of Mexican ancestry from the rest of the elementary school population, as has been shown to be the practice in respondent school district. Omnibus segregation of children of Mexican ancestry from the rest of the student body in the elementary grades in the schools involved in this action because of language handicaps is not warranted by the record before us." 96 F. Supp. at 1008–9.

## Fair Educational Practices Legislation

Several states have passed Fair Educational Practices Acts designed to eliminate discriminatory practices in education. Mass. Ann. Laws, ch. 151c, §§ 1–5 (1950); N. J. Stat. Ann. § 18:25 (Supp. 1949); N. Y. Ed. Law. § 313 (Supp. 1950). Though the statutes cover both private and public schools, they were enacted largely to cope with discrimination by private schools and especially by institutions of higher learning. The procedure is very similar to that of the Fair Employment laws, *infra*. Where attempts at mediation and conciliation fail, a cease and desist order enforceable by the courts may be issued after a hearing and findings of unfair educational practices. Proof of discrimination in this field presents some special difficulties because seemingly legitimate educational requirements can easily be used to cover discrimination or may produce discrimination as a secondary result. Examples are (1) qualifications of applicants, such as sociability; (2) geographical quotas; or (3) giving higher ratings to grades of better preparatory school not covered by any Fair Educational Practices law, where the preparatory school itself discriminated. For discussion see Note, 64 Harv. L. Rev. 307 (1950).

DISCRIMINATION

### Note

1. See also Notes, 24 N. Y. U. L. Q. Rev. 211 (1949); 47 Col. L. Rev. 821 (1947); 30 B. U. L. Rev. 237 (1950); Taylor, *The Demise of Race Distinctions in Graduate Education,* 1 Duke B. J. 135, 156 et seq. (1951).

2. On segregation and discrimination after admission to college which occurs as a result of practices of fraternities see Note, *Religious and Racial Barriers Breaking Down in College Fraternities,* 1 Nat'l Ass'n of Intergroup Relations Officials Reporter, No. 4, p. 3 (1951). This article also surveys a recent trend toward dropping discriminatory practices. For legal implications of fraternity discrimination at state universities see Horowitz, *Discriminatory Fraternities at State Universities—A Violation of the 14th Amendment?,* 25 S. Cal. L. Rev. 289–96 (1952).

### 3. Transportation

In *Morgan v. Virginia,* 328 U. S. 373, 90 L. Ed. 1317, 66 S. Ct. 1050 (1946), a Negro interstate passenger travelling on a bus from Virginia through the District of Columbia to Baltimore, Maryland refused to obey the request of the driver to move to a back seat partly occupied by colored passengers in order to make room for a white passenger. She was arrested and convicted of violating a Virginia segregation statute which required that she sit in designated seats. The Supreme Court held that the statute was an unconstitutional burden on interstate commerce, largely because of the inconvenience caused passengers by frequently compelling them to shift seats. The Court stressed the following facts: (1) seat designations under the statute could be changed at any time when "necessary or proper for the convenience of passengers"; (2) when the bus enters a state not requiring segregation passengers are free to sit where they wish; (3) 18 states prohibit racial segregation on motor carriers while ten require racial segregation; (4) among the latter there is no uniform standard of what constitutes a Negro. The Court's opinion concluded:

"In weighing the factors that enter into our conclusion as to whether this statute so burdens interstate commerce or so infringes the requirements of national uniformity as to be invalid, we are mindful of the fact that conditions vary between northern or western states such as Maine or Montana, with practically no colored population; industrial states such as Illinois, Ohio, New Jersey and Pennsylvania with a small, although appreciable, percentage of colored citizens; and the states of the deep south with percentages of from twenty-five to nearly fifty per cent colored, all with varying densities of the white and colored races in certain localities. Local efforts to promote amicable relations in difficult areas by legislative segregation in interstate transportation emerge from the latter racial distribution. As no state law can reach beyond its own border nor bar transportation of passengers across its boundaries, diverse seating requirements for the races in interstate journeys result. As there is no federal act dealing with the separation of races in interstate transportation, we must decide the validity of this Virginia statute on the challenge that it interferes with commerce, as a matter of balance between the exercise of the local police power and the need for national uniformity in the regulations for interstate travel. It seems clear to us that seating arrangements for the different races in interstate motor travel require a single, uniform rule to promote and protect national travel. Consequently, we hold the Virginia statute in controversy invalid." 328 U. S. at 385–6.[1]

## Note

1. In *Hall v. De Cuir*, 95 U. S. 485, 24 L. Ed. 547 (1878), Hall, an operator of a Mississippi steamboat that traveled interstate between New Orleans and Vicksburg was held liable in the state courts for damages for violating a Louisiana statute that guaranteed "equal rights and privileges in all parts of the conveyance . . . without distinction or discrimination on account of race or color." While the boat was in Louisiana the Negro plaintiff had been excluded from one of its cabins reserved for whites. The Supreme Court held that the statute was an unconstitutional burden on interstate commerce. It stated in part:

"Each State could provide for its own passengers and regulate the transportation of its own freight, regardless of the interests of others. Nay more, it could prescribe rules by which the carrier must be governed within the State in respect to passengers and property brought from without. On one side of the river or its tributaries he might be required to observe one set of rules, and on the other another. Commerce cannot flourish in the midst of such embarrassments. No carrier of passengers can conduct his business with satisfaction to himself, or comfort to those employing him, if on one side of a State line his passengers, both white and colored, must be permitted to occupy the same cabin, and on the other be kept separate. Uniformity in the regulations by which he is to be governed from one end to the other of his route is a necessity in his business, and to secure it Congress, which is untrammelled by State lines, has been invested with the exclusive legislative power of determining what such regulations shall be. If this statute can be enforced against those engaged in inter-state

---

[1] Justices Black, Frankfurter and Rutledge concurred; Mr. Justice Burton dissented; Mr. Justice Jackson did not participate.

commerce, it may be as well against those engaged in foreign; and the master of a ship clearing from New Orleans for Liverpool, having passengers on board, would be compelled to carry all, white and colored, in the same cabin during his passage down the river, or be subject to an action for damages, 'exemplary as well as actual,' by any one who felt himself aggrieved because he had been excluded on account of his color." 95 U. S. at 489.

2. In *Bob-Lo Excursion Co. v. Michigan*, 333 U. S. 28, 92 L. Ed. 455, 68 S. Ct. 358 (1948), the defendant was prosecuted for violating the Michigan Civil Rights Act by excluding a Negro because of his race from an excursion boat journey to Bois Blanc Island, known as Detroit's Coney Island, located in Canada, yet wholly owned by the defendant and practically inaccessible from the Canadian shore. Defendant challenged the Michigan statute as an undue burden on foreign commerce. The Court, upholding the statute, stressed the following points: (1) while the transportation was clearly foreign commerce, the special use and relative isolation of Bois Blanc made the foreign commerce one of highly local concern; (2) the chance that Canada or Congress would pass a law in conflict with Michigan's Civil Rights Law was remote. The Court stated that these facts distinguished the case from cases like *Hall v. De Cuir*, 95 U. S. 485, 24 L. Ed. 547 (1878): "It is difficult to imagine what national interest or policy, whether of securing uniformity in regulating commerce affecting relations with foreign nations or otherwise, could reasonably be found to be adversely affected by applying Michigan's statute to these facts or to outweigh her interest in doing so. Certainly there is no national interest which overrides the interest of Michigan to forbid the type of discrimination practiced here." 333 U. S. at 40. Mr. Justice Douglas, concurring, pointed out that the case involved more than segregation, namely total exclusion; that if another state or the Federal government should pass a law excluding Negroes altogether such laws would clearly be invalid under the equal protection clause; and that the case of a "head-on collision" with the policy of a foreign power might present a different problem, but "no such conflict is present here." Mr. Justice Jackson and Chief Justice Vinson dissented. The case is noted in 36 Calif. L. Rev. 487 (1948); 58 Yale L. J. 329 (1949).

3. The Virginia segregation statute has been upheld since the *Morgan* case in so far as it applies to intrastate transportation. See *New v. Atlantic Greyhound Corp.*, 186 Va. 726, 43 S. E. 2d 872 (1947); *Commonwealth v. Carolina Coach Co.*, 192 Va. 745, 66 S. E. 2d 572 (1951). In the latter case all the seats allocated to Negroes were occupied but seats were available next to white persons. Compare the *Henderson* case, *infra*, and the cases cited in the Note following. See also *Charles v. Norfolk and Western Ry. Co.*, 188 F. 2d 691 (C. A. 7, 1951) (suit for false arrest and assault subsequent to *Morgan* case for expulsion of plaintiff allegedly based on Virginia statute).

## HENDERSON v. UNITED STATES

Supreme Court of the United States, 1950
339 U. S. 816, 94 L. Ed. 1302, 70 S. Ct. 843

MR. JUSTICE BURTON delivered the opinion of the Court.

The question here is whether the rules and practices of the Southern Railway Company, which divide each dining car so as to allot ten tables exclusively to white passengers and one table exclusively to Negro passengers, and which call for a curtain or partition between that table and the others, violate § 3 (1) of the Interstate Commerce Act. That section makes it unlawful for a railroad in interstate commerce "to subject any particular person, . . . to any undue or unreasonable prejudice or disadvantage in any respect whatsoever: . . . ." 54 Stat. 902, 49 U. S. C. § 3 (1), 49 U. S. C. A. § 3 (1). We hold that those rules and practices do violate the Act.

This issue grows out of an incident which occurred May 17, 1942. On that date the appellant, Elmer W. Henderson, a Negro passenger, was traveling on a first-class ticket on the Southern Railway from Washington, D.C., to Atlanta, Georgia, en route to Birmingham, Alabama, in the course of his duties as an employee of the United States. The train left Washington at 2 p. m. At about 5:30 p. m., while the train was in Virginia, the first call to dinner was announced and he went promptly to the dining car. In accordance with the practice then in effect, the two end tables nearest the kitchen were conditionally reserved for Negroes. At each meal those tables were to be reserved initially for Negroes and, when occupied by Negroes, curtains were to be drawn between them and the rest of the car. If the other tables were occupied before any Negro passengers presented themselves at the diner then those two tables also were to be available for white passengers, and Negroes were not to be seated at them while in use by white passengers. When the appellant reached the diner, the end tables in question were partly occupied by white passengers but at least one seat at them was unoccupied. The dining-car steward declined to seat the appellant in the dining car but offered to serve him, without additional charge, at his Pullman seat. The appellant declined that offer and the steward agreed to send him word when space was available. No word was sent and the appellant was not served although he twice returned to the diner before it was detached at 9 p. m.

In October, 1942, the appellant filed a complaint with the Interstate Commerce Commission alleging especially that the foregoing conduct violated § 3 (1) of the Interstate Commerce Act.[3] Division 2 of the Commission found that he had been subjected to undue and unreasonable prejudice and disadvantage, but that the occurrence was a casual incident brought about by the bad judgment of an employee. The Commission declined to enter an order as to future practices. 258 I. C. C. 413. A three-judge United States District Court for the District of Maryland, however, held that the railroad's general practice, as evidenced by its instructions of August 6, 1942, was in violation of § 3 (1). Accordingly, on February 18, 1946, it remanded the case for further proceedings. 63 F. Supp. 906. Effective March 1, 1946, the company announced its modified rules which are now in effect. They provide for the reservation of ten tables, of four seats each, exclusively and unconditionally for white passengers and one table, of four seats, exclusively and unconditionally for Negro passengers. Between this table and the others a curtain is drawn during each meal.[4]

On remand, the full Commission, with two members dissenting and one not participating, found that the modified rules do not violate the Interstate Commerce Act and that no order for the future is necessary.[5] 269 I. C. C. 73. The appellant promptly in-

---

[3] "(1) *It shall be unlawful for any common carrier* subject to the provisions of this part *to make, give, or cause any undue or unreasonable preference or advantage to any particular person*, company, firm, corporation, association, locality, port, port district, gateway, transit point, region, district, territory or any particular description of traffic, *in any respect whatsoever; or to subject any particular person*, company, firm, corporation, association, locality, port, port district, gateway, transit point, region, district, territory, or any particular description of traffic *to any undue or unreasonable prejudice or disadvantage in any respect whatsover: . . . .*" (Emphasis supplied.) 54 Stat. 902, 49 U. S. C. § 3 (1).

The appellant sought an order directing the railroad not only to cease and desist from the specific violations alleged but also to establish in the future, for the complainant and other Negro interstate passengers, equal and just dining-car facilities and such other service and facilities as the Commission might consider reasonable and just, and requiring the railroad to discontinue using curtains around tables reserved for Negroes.

The appellant sought damages, but the Commission found no pecuniary damages and that issue has not been pressed further.

[4] . . . the evidence shows, and the Commission has stated, that "White and Negro soldiers are served together without distinction." 258 I. C. C. 413, 415; 63 F. Supp. 906, 910. The rules, accordingly, are treated as applicable only to civilian passengers. The company further showed that it is now substituting a five-foot high wooden partition in place of the curtain. The steward's office is being placed in the table space opposite that reserved for Negro passengers and a similar wooden partition is being erected between that office and the rest of the car.

[5] The company was permitted to introduce two tabulations, covering about ten days each, showing the comparative numbers of meals served to white and Negro passengers on trips comparable to the one which the appellant

stituted the present proceeding before the District Court, constituted of the same three members as before, seeking to have the Commission's order set aside and a cease and desist order issued. 28 U. S. C. §§ 41(28), 43–48; 49 U. S. C. § 17(9); see also, 28 U. S. C. (Supp. III) §§ 1336, 1398, 2284, 2321, 2325. With one member dissenting, the court sustained the modified rules on the ground that the accommodations are adequate to serve the average number of Negro passengers and are "proportionately fair." 80 F. Supp. 32, 39. The case is here on direct appeal. 28 U. S. C. (Supp. III) §§ 1253, 2101(b). In this Court the United States filed a brief and argued orally in support of the appellant.

It is clear that appellant has standing to bring these proceedings. He is an aggrieved party, free to travel again on the Southern Railway. Having been subjected to practices of the railroad which the Commission and the court below found to violate the Interstate Commerce Act, he may challenge the railroad's current regulations on the ground that they permit the recurrence of comparable violations. *Mitchell* v. *United States*, 313 U. S. 80, 92–93.

The material language in § 3(1) of the Interstate Commerce Act has been in that statute since its adoption in 1887. 24 Stat. 380. From the beginning, the Interstate Commerce Commission has recognized the application of that language to discriminations between white and Negro passengers. *Councill* v. *Western & Atlantic R. Co.*, 1 I. C. C. 339;[6] *Heard* v. *Georgia R. Co.*, 1 I. C. C. 428; *Heard* v. *Georgia R. Co.*, 3 I. C. C. 111; *Edwards* v. *Nashville, C. & St. L. R Co.*, 12 I. C. C. 247; *Cozart* v. *Southern R. Co.*, 16 I. C. C. 226; *Gaines* v. *Seaboard Air Line R. Co.*, 16 I. C. C. 471; *Crosby* v. *St. Louis-San Francisco R. Co.*, 112 I. C. C. 239. That section recently was so applied in *Mitchell* v. *United States, supra.*

---

had taken. These show that only about 4% of the total meals served were served to Negro passengers whereas four reserved seats exceed 9% of a total seating capacity of 44. On the other hand, the tabulations also show that at one meal 17 Negro passengers, and at each of 20 meals more than eight Negro passengers, were served. Similarly, the brief filed by the Commission states that, out of the 639 serving periods reported, on 15 occasions more than four times as many white passengers were served as there were seats reserved for them, and, on 541 occasions, there were two or more rounds of servings.

[6] "The Western and Atlantic Railroad Company will be notified to cease and desist from subjecting colored persons to undue and unreasonable prejudice and disadvantage in violation of section 3 of the Act to regulate commerce, and from furnishing to colored persons purchasing first-class tickets on its road accommodations which are not equally safe and comfortable with those furnished other first-class passengers." 1 I. C. C. at page 347.

The decision in this case is largely controlled by that in the *Mitchell* case. There a Negro passenger holding a first-class ticket was denied a Pullman seat, although such a seat was unoccupied and would have been available to him if he had been white. The railroad rules had allotted a limited amount of Pullman space, consisting of compartments and drawing rooms, to Negro passengers and, because that space was occupied, the complainant was excluded from the Pullman car and required to ride in a second-class coach. This Court held that the passenger thereby had been subjected to an unreasonable disadvantage in violation of § 3(1).[7]

The similarity between that case and this is inescapable. The appellant here was denied a seat in the dining car although at least one seat was vacant and would have been available to him, under the existing rules, if he had been white.[8] The issue before us, as in the *Mitchell* case, is whether the railroad's current rules and practices cause passengers to be subjected to undue or unreasonable prejudice or disadvantage in violation of § 3 (1). We find that they do.

The right to be free from unreasonable discriminations belongs, under § 3(1), to each particular person. Where a dining car is available to passengers holding tickets entitling them to use it, each such passenger is equally entitled to its facilities in accordance with reasonable regulations. The denial of dining service to any such passenger by the rules before us subjects him to a prohibited disadvantage. Under the rules, only four Negro passengers may be served at one time and then only at the table reserved for Negroes. Other Negroes who present themselves are compelled to await a vacancy at that table, although there may be many vacancies elsewhere in the diner. The railroad thus refuses to extend to those passengers the use of its existing and unoccupied facilities. The rules impose a like deprivation upon white passengers whenever more than 40 of them seek to be served at the same time and the table reserved for Negroes is vacant.

We need not multiply instances in which these rules sanction unreasonable discriminations. The curtains, partitions and signs emphasize the artificiality of a difference in treatment which serves only to call attention to a racial classification of passengers holding identical tickets and using the same public dining

---

[7] The rules also denied access by Negroes to the dining car and observation car. The principles there announced applied equally to those facilities.

[8] That specific denial of service was condemned by the Commission and the District Court as a violation of § 3(1). Review of that condemnation is not sought here.

facility. Cf. *McLaurin* v. *Oklahoma State Regents* [339 U. S. 637] decided today. They violate § 3 (1).

Our attention has been directed to nothing which removes these racial allocations from the statutory condemnation of "undue or unreasonable prejudice or disadvantage . . . ." It is argued that the limited demand for dining-car facilities by Negro passengers justifies the regulations. But it is no answer to the particular passenger who is denied service at an unoccupied place in the dining car that, on the average, persons like him are served. As was pointed out in *Mitchell* v. *United States*, 313 U. S. 80, 97, "The comparative volume of traffic cannot justify the denial of a fundamental right of equality of treatment, a right specifically safeguarded by the provisions of the Interstate Commerce Act." Cf. *McCabe* v. *Atchison, T. & S. F. R. Co.*, 235 U. S. 151; *Missouri ex rel. Gaines* v. *Canada*, 305 U. S. 337.

That the regulations may impose on white passengers, in proportion to their numbers, disadvantages similar to those imposed on Negro passengers is not an answer to the requirements of § 3 (1). Discriminations that operate to the disadvantage of two groups are not the less to be condemned because their impact is broader than if only one were affected. Cf. *Shelley* v. *Kraemer*, 334 U. S. 1, 22.

Since § 3 (1) of the Interstate Commerce Act invalidates the rules and practices before us, we do not reach the constitutional or other issues suggested.

The judgment of the District Court is reversed and the cause is remanded to that court with directions to set aside the order of the Interstate Commerce Commission which dismissed the original complaint and to remand the case to that Commission for further proceedings in conformity with this opinion.

It is so ordered.

## Note

1. In *Day* v. *Atlantic Greyhound Corp.*, 171 F. 2d 59 (C. A. 4, 1948), decided prior to the *Henderson* case, the plaintiff had purchased a round trip ticket from Syracuse, New York, to Florida with stop over privileges in Richmond, Va. After stopping there for three weeks she boarded the bus and when later ordered to take a rear seat, pursuant to a regulation of the carrier, refused, and was ejected and arrested. The court held that "the adoption of a reasonable regulation by an interstate carrier for the segregation of passengers does not violate the law as laid down by the Supreme Court." The court's treatment of the cases was as follows:

"The most important legal question on this appeal is raised by the contention of the plaintiff that any rule of a common carrier which imposes racial segregation upon its passengers not only contravenes the principles of the common law, but violates the Fourteenth Amendment of the Federal Constitution. This question, however, is not open to debate in this court. It is foreclosed by binding decisions of the Supreme Court which hold that an interstate carrier has a right to establish rules and regulations which require white and colored passengers to occupy separate accommodations provided there is no discrimination in the arrangement. See Hall v. DeCuir, 95 U. S. 485, 24 L. Ed. 547; Chiles v. Chesapeake & Ohio R. Co., 218 U. S. 71, 30 S. Ct. 667, 54 L. Ed. 936, 20 Ann. Cas. 980. It is true that in more recent decisions, notably Morgan v. Virginia, 328 U. S. 373, 66 S. Ct. 1050, 90 L. Ed. 1317, 165 A.L.R. 574, and Bob-Lo Excursion Co. v. Michigan, 333 U. S. 28, 68 S. Ct. 358, the right of colored passengers in public vehicles to fair and reasonable treatment has been sustained, and the limits to the power of the states to enact segregation statutes have been defined. . . . Nevertheless, in [the Morgan] case the court pointed out that it was dealing with a state statute and not with a regulation of the carrier; and the court referred specifically to its earlier decision in Chiles v. Chesapeake & Ohio R. Co., supra. . . . Since the Chiles case expressly sustained the power of an interstate carrier to issue a segregation regulation, provided that it is not discriminatory, our inquiry must be limited to the nature of the regulation enforced in the pending case, and we may not inquire whether the segregation of the races in public vehicles is in itself inherently discriminatory." 171 F. 2d at 60.

In *Whiteside v. Southern Bus Lines*, 177 F. 2d 949 (C. A. 6, 1949), which also preceded the Supreme Court's *Henderson* decision, the court felt that the distinction between a statute and a regulation was not too important in the *Morgan* case:

"It must be conceded that Kentucky has no statute compelling the segregation of races in either intrastate or interstate commerce such as the statute of Virginia held, in the Morgan case, to be inapplicable to interstate commerce. But the appellee relies upon long-settled usage and custom in Kentucky, crystallized into its unwritten law. Brumfield v. Consolidated Coach Corp., 240 Ky. 1, 40 S. W. 2d 356, 365. That case follows and cites with approval an earlier decision, Ohio Valley Ry.'s Receiver v. Lander, 104 Ky. 431, 47 S. W. 344, 882, wherein it is said, 'A common carrier of passengers for hire has the right, in the absence of a statute, to prescribe regulations for the separation of white and colored passengers, giving equal and like protection and accommodation to both.' [240 Ky. 1, 40 S. W. 2d 365.] We see no distinction in principle, when a regulation is sanctioned or required by state law, whether the law is declared by a legislature in a statute or by the highest court of the state in a decision, certainly since the Supreme Court declared in Erie R. Co. v. Tompkins, 304 U. S. 64, 78, 58 S. Ct. 817, 82 L. Ed. 1188, 114 A.L.R. 1487, that such distinction is not a matter of federal concern, and in West v. American Tel. & Tel. Co., 311 U. S. 223, 237, 61 S. Ct. 179, 85 L. Ed. 139, 132 A.L.R. 956, that it is the duty of the federal court in every case to ascertain from all the available data, what the state law is. In any event, the present appellee defends its regulation by the sanction not only of local custom, but of applicable Kentucky law. . . .

"It must also be observed that acts burdening interstate commerce are not, like those inhibited in the Fourteenth Amendment, limited to state action. Burdens may result from the activities of private persons as the great mass of federal criminal legislation validated under the authority of the Commerce Clause, discloses. But if state action is a prerequisite to the invalidity of the regulation here considered as it was applied to the appellant, state action is clearly to be perceived in the ejection of the appellant by a state police officer." 177 F. 2d at 952–3.

After the *Henderson* case Judge Soper who had written the opinion in the *Atlantic Greyhound* case, *supra,* again discussed the Supreme Court cases in *Chance v. Lambeth,* 186 F. 2d 879 (C. A. 4, 1951), but this time somewhat differently, distinguishing his own prior decision.

"These cases had to do with the effect of state segregation statutes; but as we have seen, carrier regulations or practices, as distinguished from state statutes which denied equality of treatment to the races were stricken down as violations of the Interstate Commerce Act in Mitchell v. United States and Henderson v. United States, supra. In the last mentioned cases the court did not reach certain constitutional questions suggested by the complainant, but in all the cases, whether the decision was based upon a violation of a provision of the constitution or of a statute of the United States, the problem under consideration was the standard of conduct to be observed by interstate carriers in dealing with members of the traveling public. Moreover, the ill effect upon the passengers and the disturbance of interstate traffic were much the same whether the carrier's conduct was treated technically as a denial of equal privileges to the races or as a burden upon interstate commerce. Thus, in the Mitchell case the complainant was excluded from a Pullman car and required to ride in a second class coach, and in the Henderson case the passenger was excluded from certain tables in the dining car and forced to wait until seats at other tables were vacant before he was served. The decisions which invalidated carrier regulations as contrary to the statute must therefore be considered in the instant case, although the regulation is here attacked as an undue burden upon commerce.

"We reach the conclusion that the railroad regulation now before us must be declared invalid. Not only does its enforcement interfere with the uniformity which should characterize interstate carriage from one end of the route to the other, but its irregular enforcement for the convenience of the carrier, dependent upon the number of passengers and the character of accommodations which they purchase, adds to the burden upon the traffic by increasing the confusion and discomfort of the passengers. When white and colored passengers are permitted to ride together for part of their journey through the State of Virginia, and then are compelled to separate and change cars, and when passengers in coaches are segregated on account of race while passengers in Pullman and dining cars are permitted to ride together irrespective

**1124**

of race, the burden upon interstate commerce is as clearly manifest as that imposed by the statute of Virginia which was invalidated in the Morgan case. It is true that the regulation of the carrier was not enacted by state authority, although the power of the state is customarily invoked to enforce it; but we know of no principle of law which requires the courts to strike down a state statute which interferes with interstate commerce but to uphold a railroad regulation which is infected with the same vice.

"The Railroad Company emphasizes the decisions in Chiles v. Chesapeake & O. Ry. Co., 218 U. S. 71, 30 S. Ct. 667, 54 L. Ed. 936, and our own decision in Day v. Atlantic Greyhound Corp., 171 F. 2d 59, rendered in the interval between the Morgan and Henderson decisions. In both cases the regulation of an interstate carrier segregating the passengers according to race was upheld; but they are not controlling here since in each case the passenger boarded the vehicle at a place where the rule of the carrier required segregation and he could have taken a seat and retained it to the end of his journey." 186 F. 2d at 882-3.

In *Lyons v. Illinois Greyhound Lines*, 192 F. (2d) 533 (C. A. 7, 1951), plaintiff sued for damages resulting from injuries due to segregation enforced by the bus driver. She claimed physical and mental pain as a result of being forced to stand during the entire journey. The court held that her complaint showed a violation of § 216 (d) of the Interstate Commerce Act and that under 28 U. S. C. § 1337, which gives district courts original jurisdiction of civil actions ensuing under any Congressional act regulating commerce, she could proceed directly in the District Court without prior administrative determination. See also *Solomon v. Pennsylvania R. Co.*, 96 F. Supp. 709 (S. D. N. Y., 1951); *contra: Greene v. Atlantic Coast Line*, 95 F. Supp. 761 (E. D. N. Y., 1951).

2. As to segregation in air terminals, see *Nash v. Air Terminal Service*, 85 F. Supp. 545 (E. D. Va., 1949).

3. For discussion of some of the above cases, see Notes, 13 Ga. B. J. 83 (1950); 62 Harv. L. Rev. 1389 (1949); 1 Ala. L. Rev. 263 (1949); 14 Albany L. Rev. 220 (1950); 2 Baylor L. Rev. 369 (1950); 45 Ill. L. Rev. 671 (1950); 4 Rutgers L. Rev. 719 (1950); 4 Vand. L. Rev. 689 (1951).

## 4. Public Accommodations

### NOTE—PRIVATE REMEDIES UNDER STATE EQUAL RIGHTS STATUTES

44 Ill. L. Rev. 363, 364–77 (1949)

#### History of Equal Rights Legislation

Equal rights legislation made its appearance shortly after the Civil War. Massachusetts was one of the first states to prohibit discrimination based on race or color in any public place of amusement.[4] The great impetus, however, came from the reconstructionists who had taken over the state governments of the South. By 1868 at least one southern state had an "equal rights" provision in its constitution[5] and within a few years several other southern states had enacted legislation to protect the recently emancipated negro.[6]

The initial movement for legislation of this type came to a climax with the enactment of the federal Civil Rights Bill of 1875.[7] . . .

With the demise of the federal legislation, the burden fell to the state legislatures. Many of them enacted statutes[9] closely modeled after the federal statute, but noticeably less punitive. Of those statutes, all enacted by the turn of the century, only those in eighteen states have been retained.[10]

### Equal Rights at Common Law

An understanding of the common law on this subject is essential to any treatment of the remedies afforded by the statutes for two reasons. First, the courts have declared these equal rights statutes to be in derogation of the common law, except insofar as they apply to innkeepers, common carriers, and public utilities.[11] This has resulted in a restrictive interpretation of the statutes and the application of rules of construction which have greatly narrowed their effectiveness. Second, the recognition that innkeepers and common carriers are under a common-law duty not to discriminate among members of the public seeking the enjoyment of their facilities has also generally resulted in holdings

---

[4] Mass. Laws, 1864–65, p. 650.

[5] Louisiana Constitution of 1868, Art. 13. In Joseph v. Bidwell, 28 La. Ann. 382 (1876), a colored man, denied admittance to a theater, successfully invoked this provision.

[6] For a more detailed discussion of the history of civil rights legislation in the states, see Stephenson, Race Distinctions in American Law (1909) 43 Am. L. Rev. 547.

[7] [Ed. Note: For this legislation and its invalidation by the Supreme Court in the Civil Rights Cases, see Chapter I, supra.]

[9] This second movement was limited to the western and northern states. The civil rights legislation soon disappeared from the southern scene. Stephenson, Race Distinctions in American Law (1909) 43 Am. L. Rev. 547, 559–64.

[10] [Ed. Note: These statutes are set out in the Note following this extract.]

[11] Tyson & Brother v. Banton, 273 U. S. 418 (1927). As to the common-law duty of innkeepers and common carriers: Opinion of the Justices, 247 Mass. 589, 143 N. E. 808 (1924); People v. King, 110 N. Y. 418, 18 N. E. 245 (1888). The common-law duty of public utilities rests upon the theory that their right to business is derived from a franchise granted by the state. Grannan v. Westchester Racing Ass'n, 153 N. Y. 449, 47 N. E. 896 (1897).

that a discrimination based on race, creed, or color gives rise to a cause of action coterminous with that provided for in the equal rights statutes.[12]

The common law permits the proprietor of a privately owned but public offered place of accommodation or amusement to impose such reasonable regulations as in his judgment will best serve the interests of his business.[13] *Wood* v. *Leadbitter*[14] is generally regarded as having established this doctrine of a proprietor's right to exclude. The English Court of the Exchequer ruled that tickets for admission to a race track were revocable at any time without return of the money paid and without assignment, by the owner, of any reason for the revocation.[15] This doctrine rests upon the complete freedom to refuse admission in the first instance.[16] With but few dissents the American courts have accepted this view, holding that there is no action in tort, in the absence of excessive force, for the forcible ejection of a patron by a proprietor of a public place.[17]

However, an increasing number of English and American courts, even in the absence of statute, are refusing to follow *Wood* v. *Leadbitter* and are recognizing the right to recover damages in tort for wrongful ejection.[18] The English and American cases which recognized the common law duty of innkeepers

---

[12] Odom v. East Avenue Corp., 34 N. Y. S. (2d) 312 (1942). *But see* Horn v. Ill. Cent. R. Co., 327 Ill. App. 498, 64 N. E. (2d) 574 (1946) (the court indicated that the common-law duty of common carriers would be superseded by the statutory right).

[13] Millar v. Pittsburgh Athletic Co., 91 Pa. Super. 241 (1927); De la Ysla v. Publix Theatres Corp., 82 Utah 598, 26 P. (2d) 818 (1933); Younger v. Judah, 111 Mo. 303, 19 S. W. 1109 (1892).

[14] 13 M. & W. 838, 153 Eng. Rep. 351 (1845).

[15] This conclusion was said to be inescapable since an irrevocable right to go upon the premises and remain for the duration of the races to which the plaintiff was admitted is a right in the land which can be granted only by deed.

[16] Wood v. Leadbitter, 153 Eng. Rep. 351, 354 (the court disapproved Taylor v. Waters, 129 Eng. Rep. 150 (1816), which upheld a verdict in favor of a ticket holder for wrongful denial of admission to a theater).

[17] Marrone v. Washington Jockey Club, 227 U. S. 633 (1913) (Holmes, J., referred to an argument against the doctrine "as an attempt to overthrow the rule commonly accepted in this country from the English Cases."); see Conrad, The Privilege of Forcibly Ejecting an Amusement Patron (1942) 90 U. of Pa. L. Rev. 809.

[18] Barnswell v. National Amusement Co., Ltd., 21 B. C. R. 435 (1915) (the plaintiff, a colored man, was refused admission by the doormen. The only assault was a placing of a policeman's hand on plaintiff's shoulder, who, at the manager's request told him to go away). *Accord:* Hurst v. Pictures Ltd., [1915] 1 K. B. 1; Vogel v. Saenger Theatres, 207 La. 835, 22 So. (2d) 189 (1945); *contra:* Cowell v. Rosehill Race Course Co., Ltd., 56 C. L. R. 605 (1936) (expressly disapproving the *Hurst* case).

and common carriers to accommodate all persons without discrimination proceed on the theory that the proprietors of these enterprises are engaged in businesses which are sufficiently affected with a public interest as to deprive them of some of the prerogatives of the owners of other private businesses. By holding out to the public their facilities and inviting the public to enjoy their accommodations an implied or express contract is created when the invitation is accepted. The accommodations cannot thereafter be denied on a discriminatory basis and each individual is entitled to courteous treatment and the privileges of the accommodations for the duration of the contract.[19] . . .

It seems improbable that many courts will follow the lead of these cases and extend the duty not to discriminate on the basis of race, color, or creed beyond its present limited confines. It is quite possible, however, that future decisions, reflecting a changed public sentiment, will repudiate the doctrine that equal rights statutes should be strictly construed because they are in derogation of the common law.

### Scope of the Statutes

The narrow scope of the common-law rules governing equal rights demonstrates the need for broad statutory protection. However, despite the adoption of strengthening amendments, the substantive provisions of the state equal rights statutes leave much to be desired in the breadth of their coverage. In general, all persons are guaranteed the full and equal enjoyment of the accommodations, advantages, facilities and privileges of the various enumerated businesses.[30] Discrimination based on race, color, or creed is prohibited.

There is less uniformity in the sanctions provided by the statutes. Generally, violations are termed misdemeanors and call for fines and imprisonment at the discretion of the court. Fines vary from a minimum of ten dollars to a maximum of one thousand dollars, and terms of imprisonment range from fifteen days to one year. Seven states impose only criminal sanctions.[34] In several instances, courts have decided that statutes containing only

---

[19] Innkeepers: Strauss v. County Hotel Co., 12 Q. B. D. 27 (1883); Odom v. East Avenue Corp., 34 N. Y. S. (2d) 312 (1942). Common Carriers: Gisbourn v. Hurst, 1 Salk. 249 (1710); De Wolf v. Ford, 193 N. Y. 397, 86 N. E. 527 (1908).

[30] Among the places more generally included are hotels, inns, theaters, restaurants, eating houses, soft drink parlors, common carriers, barbershops, and "other places of public accommodation and amusement."

[34] Connecticut, Iowa, Nebraska, New Jersey, Pennsylvania, Rhole Island, and Washington.

criminal sanctions may still provide the basis for a private right of action for damages.[35]

Eleven states[36] allow pecuniary as well as moral satisfaction to an aggrieved person by expressly providing for the recovery of damages in civil actions. Four states[37] provide that the institution of one action will constitute an election of remedies and thus bar the bringing of the other action. Amounts collectible in a civil suit range from twenty-five dollars to five hundred dollars. Two states provide for the recovery of actual damages, with one of them providing for the additional recovery of a fixed forfeiture of one hundred dollars.[39] One state permits the recovery of treble damages.[40]

While the statutes generally provide protection for "all persons", it is clear that their primary purpose is to protect against discrimination based on race, creed or color.[41] Persons discriminated against and excluded for other reasons have sought in vain to bring themselves within the protection of the statutes. The courts have refused to recognize a cause of action where the individual excluded was accompanied by negroes,[42] was an unescorted woman,[43] wore no tie in a restaurant,[44] wore a military uniform when civilian dress was required,[45] was a dramatic critic who displeased the proprietor by adverse criticism of his production,[46] was a gambler,[47] had purchased a ticket from a ticket broker,[48] or for any reason applicable to all alike,[49] or for no assigned reason at all.[50] . . .

---

[35] Washington. The Michigan court had so held prior to a 1937 amendment which added a civil remedy.

[36] California, Colorado, Illinois, Indiana, Kansas, Massachusetts, Michigan, Minnesota, New York, Ohio, and Wisconsin.

[37] Colorado, Indiana, Ohio, and Wisconsin.

[39] Kansas. California provides for additional recovery of $100.

[40] Michigan.

[41] *Civil Rights Cases*, 109 U. S. 3 (1883); Collister v. Hayman, 183 N. Y. 254, 76 N. E. 20 (1905).

[42] Matthews v. Hotz, 173 N. Y. S. 234 (1918) (white man accompanied by two negroes was refused service at a bar unless "extra" prices were paid for drinks).

[43] Collister v. Hayman, 183 N. Y. 254, 76 N. E. 20 (1905).

[44] Brandt v. Mink, 78 N. Y. S. 1109 (1902) (plaintiff, a white man, was refused service in a restaurant because he wore no tie).

[45] Buenzle v. Newport Amusement Ass'n., 29 R. I. 23, 68 Atl. 721 (1908) (plaintiff was offered a civilian coat and told he could go in if he put it on); Baer v. Washington Heights Cafe, 168 N. Y. S. 567 (1917).

[46] Woolcott v. Shubert, 217 N. Y. 212, 111 N. E. 829 (1916).

[47] Madden v. Queens County Jockey Club, 296 N. Y. 249, 72 N. E. (2d) 697 (1947) *cert. denied*, 332 U. S. 761 (1947) (plaintiff was barred from race track under mistaken belief that he was Frank Costello's bookmaker).

[48] Levine v. Brooklyn Nat. League Baseball Club, 36 N. Y. S. (2d) 474 (1942).

The courts have uniformly sustained[54] these acts as valid regulations of the enumerated businesses in the face of numerous attacks upon their constitutionality under both state and federal constitutions.[55]

Except for a few decisions, courts have found the statutes to be in derogation of the common law or penal in nature, thus subjecting them to a strict construction which has greatly restricted the scope of the protection afforded.[56]  Strict construction has almost uniformly lead to an application of the rule of *ejusdem generis*.  This rule has been applied to the end that saloons,[57] billiard rooms,[58] ice cream parlors,[59] soda fountains,[60] boarding houses,[61] apartment buildings,[62] restaurants,[63] and barber shops[64] among other places have been held not to be places of public accommodation, amusement, or resort.

Strict construction has also resulted in restricting the types of relief available to the remedy provided by the statute, as well as confining the recovery of damages to the statutory forfeiture.[65]

The courts which have construed the statutes strictly have

---

[49] Terrell Wells Swimming Pool v. Rodriguez, 182 S. W. (2d) 824 (Tex. Civ. App. 1944).

[50] Finnesey v. Seattle Baseball Club, 122 Wash. 276, 210 Pac. 679 (1922).

[54] Pickett v. Kuchan, 323 Ill. 138, 153 N. E. 667 (1926) People v. King, 110 N. Y. 418, 18 N. E. 245 (1888) ; Greenberg v. Western Turf Ass'n., 140 Cal. 357, 73 Pac. 1050 (1903).

[55] The attacks on the constitutionality are usually based on the contention that the entrepreneurs affected are being denied equal protection of the laws and due process of the law.  See, *e. g.*, Pickett v. Kuchan, 323 Ill. 138, 153 N. E. 667 (1926).

[56] Pickett v. Kuchan, 323 Ill. 138, 153 N. E. 667 (1926) ; Commonwealth v. Sylvester, 95 Mass. 247 (1866) ; Bowlin v. Lyon, 67 Iowa 536, 25 N. W. 766 (1885) ; Rhone v. Loomis, 74 Minn. 200, 77 N. W. 317 (1898) ; Chochos v. Burden, 74 Ind. App. 242, 128 N. E. 696 (1920) ; Cohn v. Goldgraben, 170 N. Y. S. 407 (1918) ; Brown v. Meyer Sanitary Milk Co., 150 Kan. 931, 96 P. (2d) 651 (1940) ; Darius v. Apostolos, 68 Colo. 323, 190 Pac. 510 (1920) ; Faulkner v. Solazzi, 79 Conn. 541, 65 Atl. 947 (1907) ; Bryan v. Adler, 97 Wis. 124, 72 N. W. 368 (1897) ; Messenger v. State, 25 Neb. 674, 41 N. W. 638 (1889).

[57] Rhone v. Loomis, 74 Minn. 200, 77 N. W. 31 (1898) (saloons not included in ".  .  . taverns .  .  . and other places of refreshment").

[58] Commonwealth v. Sylvester, 95 Mass. 247 (1866).

[59] Brown v. Meyer Sanitary Milk Co., 150 Kan. 931, 96 P. (2d) 651 (1940).

[60] Cecil v. Green, 161 Ill. 265, 43 N. E. 1105 (1896).

[61] Independence v. Richardson, 117 Kan. 656, 232 Pac. 1044 (1925).

[62] Alsberg v. Lucerne Hotel Co., 92 N. Y. S. 851 (1905) (a family hotel where the apartments are arranged in small suites differing in no respect from those in an ordinary apartment house, and where the apartments are rented upon annual leases and transient tenants are not solicited, is not a hotel within the meaning of the statute).

[63] State v. Brown, 112 Kan. 814, 212 Pac. 663 (1923).

[64] Faulkner v. Solazzi, 79 Conn. 541, 65 Atl. 947 (1907).

[65] Pickett v. Kuchan, 323 Ill. 138, 153 N. E. 667 (1926).

emphasized the restrictions imposed thereby upon the control and management of private property,[66] whereas the courts construing the statutes liberally stress the unequivocal right created and the importance of giving full effect to public policy and the intent of the legislature.[67]

### Recovery of Statutory Damages in Private Actions

The most important element of these equal rights statutes lies in their enforcement provisions. Recognizing the effectiveness of enforcement through private action, most statutes accord to the injured individual some positive way to assert his legal rights. Foremost among these is the provision for the recovery of damages. The majority of statutes which provide for civil actions authorize the party aggrieved to recover a forfeiture within minimum and maximum limits. . . .

In addition to the actual damages and the fixed forfeiture provided for by the California statute, the courts there have permitted the recovery of punitive damages. In *Greenberg v. Western Turf Ass'n*. [77] the fixed forfeiture was held to be a penalty for the mere violation of the statute. It is imposed apart from any consideration as to the circumstances accompanying the violation and without regard to the degree of oppressiveness or brutality involved.

### Mandamus

Aside from the recovery of damages, there remain other legal weapons which can be availed of by those deprived of their "equal rights". The method of court enforcement of the terms of the statute by private application should not be overlooked. Thus, the writ of mandamus has been held appropriate[82] for the protec-

---

[66] Delaney v. Central Valley Golf Club, Inc., 28 N. Y. S. (2d) 932 (1941), *aff'd.* 289 N. Y. 577, 43 N. E. (2d) 716 (1942) (negro denied admission to golf course which was posted "Private" but permitted the public to play frequently); *Contra: Camp-of-the-Pines v. New York Times Co.*, 53 N. Y. S. (2d) 475 (1945) (the statute . . . "strikes at the bigot and all promoters of discord and unhappiness. Every effort is made and should be made, and it is the duty of the courts to prevent as far as is humanly possible, social and economic ostracism").

[67] Orloff v. Los Angeles Turf Club, 30 Cal. (2d) 110, 180 P. (2d) 321 (1947); Randall v. Cowlitz Amusements, 194 Wash. 82, 76 P. (2d) 1017 (1938); Bolden v. Grand Rapids Operating Corp., 239 Mich. 318, 214 N. W. 241 (1927).

[77] 140 Cal. 357, 73 Pac. 1050 (1903) (punitive damages $1,000); Piluso v. Spencer, 36 Cal. App. 416, 172 Pac. 412 (1918).

[82] People *ex rel.* Peair v. Bd. of Education, 127 Ill. 613, 21 N. E. 189 (1889); Stone v. Pasadena, 47 Cal. App. (2d) 749, 118 P. (2d) 866 (1941); State *ex rel.* Pierce v. Union Dist. School Trustees, 46 N. J. L. 76 (1884); *aff'd* 47 N. J. L. 348 (1885).

tion of minorities against discrimination by public officials in connection with the operation of school and park systems.[83]

• • •

## Injunctive Relief

An obvious and perhaps more effective method of court enforcement of these rights would be through the medium of the injunction. Where injunctive relief has been sought, however, two objections have been raised. The first is the strict construction-exclusive remedy argument. The second is that equity protects only property rights and not personal rights.

The Illinois Appellate Court in *White v. Pasfield*[88] refused to enjoin the defendant from denying the complainant admission to a swimming pool in violation of the equal rights statute.[89] The court held that equity would not protect such personal rights and directed the complainant to seek redress at law in the manner prescribed by the statute. Without explanation, it was pointed out that the cases in which mandamus issued were exceptions to the rule here applied.[90]

The *Pasfield* case was rejected by the California Court in *Orloff v. Los Angeles Turf Club*.[91] The court pointed out that the opinion failed to take into consideration several factors believed to be of controlling significance. The exclusive remedy rule is inapplicable when the remedy is inadequate to compensate the party aggrieved and inadequate to fulfill the purposes of the statute. The inadequacy of damages in these cases is manifest. Not only is it difficult to apply a monetary measure of damages to injuries of this sort, but the injury is more apt to be of a continuing nature than a physical tort. Furthermore, the statute does not expressly exclude the availability of preventive relief through a specific injunction.

To apply the rule that equity protects only property rights is to place those rights in a more favorable position than personal

---

[83] Although an early case held that a permanent injunction was the proper decree to prevent segregation in the schools, Chase v. Stephenson, 71 Ill. 383 (1874), it has not been followed and the later cases have issued writs of mandamus. People v. Board of Education, 127 Ill. 613, 21 N. E. 187 (1889).

[88] 212 Ill. App. 73 (1918) (negro denied admission to swimming pool).

[89] Ill. Rev. Stat. (1947) c. 38, § 126. If, however, the legislature set limits to the recovery, to curb the jury, as the court held in Pickett v. Kuchan, 323 Ill. 138, 153 N. E. 667 (1926), it would indicate that relief other than damages is not excluded.

[90] People v. Mayor of Alton, 209 Ill. 461, 70 N. E. 640 (1904). This recognition that relief other than damages may be awarded would indicate that the personal right-equity issue was of primary importance in this decision.

[91] 30 Cal. (2d) 110, 180 P. (2d) 321 (1947) (non-racial exclusion).

rights, a proposition which the court felt to be wholly at odds with the fundamental principles of democracy. There has recently been a strong tendency to extend equitable relief to cases involving personal torts just as such relief has been extended in the property cases where the relief at law is inadequate.[92] . . .

## Conclusion

This review of the statutes and the cases arising under them indicates that the continuing disregard for the rights of minorities reflects both inadequacies in the statutes themselves and restrictive judicial interpretation resulting in a failure to invoke the full potential scope of the existing statutory provisions. Even to the casual observer it is apparent that the negro's rights under these statutes are being disregarded more frequently than the number of cases would indicate. There may be numerous reasons for the scarcity of actions which do not stem from the inadequacies of the statutes and the restrictive judicial interpretation of them. It is manifest, however, that the limited recoveries permitted in most of the states, coupled with the restrictive construction applied to the statutes by the courts is a deterrent to a party seeking to redress a discrimination. . . .

## Note

1. The pertinent state statutes are: Cal. Civ. Code (1949) § 51; Colo. Stat. Ann. (1935) 35: § 1; Conn. Gen. Laws (1949) § 8375; Ill. Ann. Stats. (Smith-Hurd) ch. 38, § 125; Ind. Stats. (Burns) §§ 10–901, 902; Iowa Code Ann. §§ 735.1, 735.2; Kan. Gen. Laws (1949) § 21–2424; Mass. Ann. Laws § 272.98; Laws of Mich. (Mason's 1933 Supp.) §§ 17115–146, 17115–148; Minn. (Mason's Stats. 1927) § 7321; Neb. Rev. Stats. (1943) § 20–101; N. J. Stats. Ann. (Supp. 1951) § 18:25–4; N. Y. Civil Rights Law, § 40; Ohio Gen. Code Ann. (Page) § 12940; Pa. Stats. Ann. (Purdon) § 18:4654; R. I. Gen. Laws (1938) § 606:28, 29; Stats. of Wash. Ann. (Remington) § 2686; Wis. Stats. (1951) § 340.75.

2. Defenses: Defenses of personal antipathy have been unsuccessful.[1] The defense of "exclusiveness" is not available where the facility is operated in effect as a public accommodation rather than a private club.[2] Problems have arisen, however where the refusal comes

---

[92] See Moscovitz, Civil Liberties and Injunctive Protection (1947) 39 Ill. L. Rev. 144; Pound, Equitable Relief Against Defamation and Injuries to Personalty (1916) 29 Harv. L. Rev. 640. *See* Kenyon v. Chicopee, 320 Mass. 528, 70 N. E. (2d) 241 (1946) (in which the court said it was by no means satisfied that personal and property rights are always as distinct and readily separable as much as the public discussion in recent years would have them).

[1] *Bailey v. Washington Theatre Co.*, 112 Ind. App. 336, 41 N. E. 2d 819 (1942).

[2] *Norman v. City Island Beach Co.*, 126 Misc. 335, 213 N. Y. Supp. 379

from a waiter or employee and the employer denies setting down a discriminatory policy. Michigan, New York, and Illinois courts have held the employee's action outside of the scope of his employment and find no ratification by the employer in continuing to hire the servant.[3] Other jurisdictions utilize agency rules to impose liability upon the more affluent employer.[4] Recently one court hurdled the problem of proving the discriminatory intent behind the immediate denial by allowing evidence of the defendant's past policy of exclusion of Negroes from his drug store lunch counter.[5]

3. Segregation in public accommodations is achieved largely through local ordinances and custom. In addition, state statutes require segregation in specific areas of public accommodations. For a summary of segregation laws see Murray, *State Laws on Race and Color* (1950). See also Konvitz, *The Constitution and Civil Rights*, ch. 8 (1947); and materials, *supra*, on segregation laws in the field of transportation.

In 1948 Senator Glenn Taylor of Idaho challenged the Birmingham, Alabama, segregation ordinance by attempting to enter a church to address a political meeting through a door marked "Negro entrance." He was prevented from entering by a police officer and, after persisting, was arrested. Senator Taylor was charged with disorderly conduct, convicted and sentenced to a fine of $50 and imprisonment for 180 days at hard labor. His efforts to raise the constitutional issues involved in the segregation ordinance were unsuccessful in the state courts, which excluded all evidence designed to show that the arrest was made for purposes of enforcing the segregation ordinance. *Taylor v. Birmingham*, 35 Ala. App. 133, 45 So. 2d 53 (1950). The Supreme Court denied certiorari. 340 U. S. 832 (1950). Senator Taylor did not return to Alabama to serve his sentence and state officials announced they would not attempt to extradite him. N. Y. Times, Oct. 11, 1950.

4. The American Bowling Congress, a private organization which conducted most of the bowling tournaments and other organized activities in bowling, had since 1916 restricted its membership to "white males." Mounting pressure to end the discrimination included suits in Illinois, Wisconsin, New York and Ohio, and threats of litigation in Michigan and Minnesota. In Illinois, where the ABC was incorpo-

---

(1926) (bathhouse with accommodations for 1500, 60 of which used by club members, held "public").

[3] *Hubert v. Jose*, 148 App. Div. 718, 132 N. Y. Supp. 811 (1912); *Goldsberry v. Kamachos*, 255 Mich. 647, 239 N. W. 513 (1931); *Wilkinson v. Hart's Drive-In, Inc.*, 338 Ill. App. 210, 86 N. E. 2d 870 (1949). But *cf. Denny v. Dorr*, 333 Ill. App. 581, 78 N. E. 2d 144 (1948), where an agency relationship was permitted.

[4] *Bryan v. Adler*, 97 Wis. 124, 72 N. W. 368 (1897); *Crosswaith v. Thomason*, 95 Colo. 309, 35 P. 2d 849 (C. A. 10, 1934). And see *Davis v. Euclid Ave. Theatre Co.*, 17 Ohio C. C. N. S. 495 (1911), where the statement appears "the principal may be civilly liable either because he has specially authorized or commanded the act complained of, or because his agent within the scope of the agency has done it even against his orders."

[5] *State v. Katz*, 241 Iowa 115, 40 N. W. 2d 41 (1949).

rated, a suit by the Attorney General under the civil rights law resulted in a fine of $2,500 and a court direction to ABC to end the discrimination or have its charter revoked.  In Wisconsin, where the ABC headquarters were located, the Attorney General brought suit to enjoin its operation as a "public nuisance."  The New York suit was brought by the Attorney General for an injunction on the ground the discrimination was contrary to public policy and that the organization had not obtained a certificate to operate in New York under the General Corporation Law.  After spending $40,000 in this litigation the ABC, at its convention in May, 1950, voted to eliminate the discriminatory bylaw.  N. Y. Times, Jan. 19 and 28, April 23 and May 13, 1950.

5. One of the most important developments in state civil rights legislation in this area has been the adoption of the techniques of the administrative process in the administration and enforcement of such legislation.  Several states have recently passed legislation establishing administrative commissions with power to enforce the civil rights laws through hearings and administrative orders.  Conn. Gen. Stats. (Supp. 1949) §§ 691a, 692a; Mass. Ann. Laws (1951 Supp.) ch. 151 B. § 5; N. J. Stats. Ann. tit. 18, § 25.8 (the Freeman Law, passed in 1949) ; N. Y. Exec. Law §§ 290ff.  (Wicks-Roman Act).  The procedures are similar to those employed in the Fair Employment Practices Acts, *infra,* and the Fair Educational Practices Acts, *supra.*  For reports on the work of state commissions in this field see *Report of the Commission on Civil Rights 1950–1951* (Conn.) p. 83, (reporting 76 complaints in the two years since passage of the statute, of which all but two were settled by conciliation); N. J. Department of Education, Division Against Discrimination, *Biennial Report* (July, 1949 to June, 1951) (reporting 113 complaints in that period, also largely settled by conciliation).

For a model municipal ordinance, providing for administration by a commission, see American Jewish Congress, Commission on Law and Social Action, Report Dec. 24, 1951 (mimeo.).

6. For discussion of state civil rights statutes dealing with public accommodations see Mangum, *The Legal Status of the Negro,* ch. III (1940); Konvitz, *The Constitution and Civil Rights,* ch 7 and 8 (1947); Konvitz, *Legislation Guaranteeing Equality of Access to Places of Public Accommodation,* 275 Annals of the Am. Acad. of Pol. and Soc. Sci. 47 (1951); Wisconsin Legislative Reference Service, *A Study of State and Local Legislative and Administrative Acts Designed to Meet Problems of Human Rights* (Res. Rept. No. 105, 1952); Note, 35 Calif. L. Rev. 571 (1947); 1 A. L. R. 2d 1165.  See also Turner and Kennedy, *Exclusion, Ejection, and Segregation of Theater Patrons,* 32 Iowa L. Rev. 625 (1947).  On the enforcement problem see Goosetrée, *The Iowa Civil Rights Statute: A Problem of Enforcement,* 37 Iowa L. Rev. 242 (1952); Note, *Equity's Role in the Protection of Civil Rights,* 37 Iowa L. Rev. 268 (1952).

7. In recent years the civil provisions of the Federal Civil Rights Acts have been invoked in a number of cases to vindicate the rights of minority groups to use places of public accommodation.  Under the

*Civil Rights Cases* Federal power to prevent discrimination in the use of such facilities exists only where the discrimination is attributable to state action. See Chapter I, *supra*. But where state action may be found the provisions of 8 U. S. C. § 43 and other provisions of the Federal Civil Rights Acts are available. Section 43 authorizes "an action at law, suit in equity, or other proper proceedings for redress" against "every person who, under color of any statute, ordinance, regulation, custom, or usage of any State . . . subjects . . . any citizen of the United States or any other person . . . to the deprivation of any rights, privileges, or immunities secured by the Constitution and laws." Two developments account, at least in part, for the increased reliance upon the Federal statutes. One is the growing activity of states and municipalities in maintaining recreational and other public facilities; the other is the tendency of the courts to expand the concept of "color of law" or "state action."

Where the state, municipality or other governmental unit owns and operates facilities such as swimming pools, golf courses, play grounds, parks and the like the courts have upheld suits by members of minority groups who have been denied access to the facilities. Thus in *Draper v. City of St. Louis*, 92 F. Supp. 546 (E. D. Mo., 1950), app. dis. 186 F. 2d 307 (C. A. 8, 1950), the court granted an injunction against the city for its refusal to allow Negroes to use a municipal swimming pool, though it declined to allow damages. In accord are *Lopez v. Seccombe*, 71 F. Supp. 769 (S. D. Cal., 1944); *Law v. Mayor and City Council of Baltimore*, 78 F. Supp. 346 (D. Md., 1948) (golf course); *Beal v. Holcombe*, 193 F. 2d 384 (C. A. 5, 1951) (golf course). The courts have reached the same result where the facilities were owned by the city and leased to private persons for operation. *Lawrence v. Hancock*, 76 F. Supp. 1004 (S. D. W. Va., 1948) (swimming pool built with municipal funds and leased to private persons could not discriminate against Negroes); see also *Culver v. City of Warren*, 83 N. E. 2d 82 (Ohio, 1948) (public pool leased to veteran's club must be open to Negroes).

In *Valle v. Stengel*, 176 F. 2d 697 (C. A. 3, 1949), the manager of a privately owned swimming pool in New Jersey, aided by the police, denied admission to the pool to Negroes who were citizens of New York. The court upheld a suit for damages and injunction on the ground that the action of the police established the necessary state action and that plaintiffs had been denied the right to enter into a contract (purchase of admission tickets), thereby being deprived of the privileges and immunities of United States citizens under Article IV, Section 2 and under the Fourteenth Amendment, and also being denied equal protection. But *cf. Watkins v. Oaklawn Jockey Club*, 183 F. 2d 440 (C. A. 8, 1950).

But where the municipality has afforded "equal facilities" to Negroes on a segregated basis relief under the Federal Civil Rights Acts has thus far been denied. In *Boyer v. Garrett*, 88 F. Supp. 353 (D. Md., 1949), aff'd 183 F. 2d 582 (C. A. 4, 1950), cert. den. 340 U. S. 912 (1951), suit was brought for injunction and damages against officials of the City of Baltimore to test municipal regulations which prohibited athletic events in which whites and Negroes participated and which set aside public athletic facilities for use by whites and Negroes at different times. Relying on *Plessy v. Ferguson* the lower Federal courts dismissed the suit. Certiorari denied for late filing. See also *Winkler v. Maryland*, 69 Atl. 2d 674 (Md., 1949) cert. den. 339 U. S. 919 (1950) (criminal prosecution arising out of same situation upheld); *Camp v. Recreation Board for District of Columbia*, 104 F. Supp. 10 (D. D. C., 952). In *Rice v. Arnold*, 45 So. 2d 195 (Fla., 1950), the court upheld regulations providing for use of municipal golf course by Negroes on Mondays only, the claim being that the allocation of time to one day was in proportion to the Negro use. The Supreme Court vacated and remanded the case for reconsideration in light of the *Sweatt* and *McLaurin* cases, 340 U. S. 848, 95 L. Ed. 621, 71 S. Ct. 77 (1950). On reconsideration the Florida Supreme Court adhered to its decision, reaffirming the "separate but equal" doctrine and saying the issue of whether the regulation in fact granted equal facilities was not properly raised. 54 So. 2d 114 (1951). The Supreme Court denied certiorari for the reason that the Florida decision was based on a nonfederal ground, Justices Black and Douglas dissenting. 342 U. S. 946 (1952). See also *Beal v. Holcombe* and *Law v. Mayor and City Council of Baltimore, supra* (facilities found unequal).

The criminal provisions of the Federal Civil Rights Acts do not appear to have been invoked in cases involving public accommodations.

For discussion see Note, *Freedom to Contract—A New Civil Right*, 59 Yale L. J. 1167 (1950); Hyman, *Segregation and the Fourteenth Amendment*, 4 Vand. L. Rev. 555 (1951).

8. For discussion of the effect of court decisions on the elimination of discrimination, and the resulting social adjustments, see Note, *Grade School Segregation: The Latest Attack on Racial Discrimination*, 61 Yale L. J. 730 (1952), printed *supra*.

9. On anti-miscegenation laws, see Note, *Constitutionality of Anti-Miscegenation Statutes*, 58 Yale L. J. 472 (1949).

## C. EMPLOYMENT

### TO SECURE THESE RIGHTS—THE REPORT OF THE PRESIDENT'S COMMITTEE ON CIVIL RIGHTS

U. S. Government Printing Office, 1947, at pp. 53–61

A man's right to an equal chance to utilize fully his skills and knowledge is essential. The meaning of a job goes far beyond the paycheck. Good workers have a pride in the organization for which they work and feel satisfaction in the jobs they are doing. A witness before a congressional committee has recently said:

Discrimination in employment damages lives, both the bodies and the minds, of those discriminated against and those who discriminate. It blights and perverts that healthy

[Emerson]—72

ambition to improve one's standard of living which we like
to say is peculiarly American. It generates insecurity, fear,
resentment, division and tension in our society.

In private business, in government, and in labor unions, the
war years saw a marked advance both in hiring policies and in
the removal of on-the-job discriminatory practices. Several factors contributed to this progress. The short labor market, the
sense of unity among the people, and the leadership provided
by the government all helped bring about a lessening of unfair
employment practices. Yet we did not eliminate discrimination
in employment. The Final Report of the federal Fair Employment Practice Committee, established in 1941 by President
Roosevelt to eliminate discrimination in both government and
private employment related to the war effort, makes this clear.
Four out of five cases which arose during the life of the Committee, concerned Negroes. However, many other minorities
have suffered from discriminatory employment practices. The
FEPC reports show that eight percent of the Committee's docket
involved complaints of discrimination because of creed, and 70
percent of these concerned Jews. It should be noted that FEPC
jurisdiction did not extend to financial institutions and the professions, where discrimination against Jews is especially prevalent.
Witnesses before this Committee, representing still other minority groups, testified as follows:
The Japanese Americans: "We know, too, what discrimination in employment is. We know what it means to be unacceptable to union membership; what it means to be the last hired
and first fired; what it means to have to work harder and longer
for less wages. We know these things because we have been
forced to experience them."
The Mexican Americans: "We opened an employment bureau
(to help Mexican Americans) in our office last year for San
Antonio. We wrote to business firms throughout the city, most
of whom didn't answer. We would call certain firms and say that
we heard they had an opening for a person in a stock room or
some other type of work; or I would go myself. But thinking I
was the same in prejudice as they, they would say, 'You know we
never hire Mexicans.' "
The American Indians: "As with the Negroes, Indians are
employed readily when there is a shortage of labor and they can't
get anyone else. When times get better, they are the first ones
to be released."
*Discriminatory hiring practices.*—Discrimination is most
acutely felt by minority group members in their inability to get
a job suited to their qualifications. Exclusions of Negroes, Jews,

**1138**                                              [Emerson]

or Mexicans in the process of hiring is effected in various ways—by newspaper advertisements requesting only whites or gentiles to apply, by registration or application blanks on which a space is reserved for "race" or "religion," by discriminatory job orders placed with employment agencies, or by the arbitrary policy of a company official in charge of hiring.

A survey conducted by the United States Employment Service and contained in the Final Report of the Fair Employment Practice Committee reveals that of the total job orders received by USES offices in 11 selected areas during the period of February 1–15, 1946, 24 percent of the orders were discriminatory. Of 38,195 orders received, 9,171 included specifications with regard to race, citizenship, religion, or some combination of these factors.

The National Community Relations Advisory Council has studied hiring practices since V-J Day. A 1946 survey of the practices of 134 private employment agencies in 10 cities (Boston, Chicago, Cincinnati, Cleveland, Detroit, Kansas City, Milwaukee, Philadelphia, St. Louis, and San Francisco) disclosed that 89 percent of these agencies included questions covering religion on their registration forms. In Chicago, a statistical count of discriminatory job orders was made by one of the largest commercial agencies in the city. This revealed that 60 per cent of the executive jobs, 50 percent of the sales executive jobs, and 41 percent of the male clerical openings, and 24 percent of the female clerical openings were closed to Jews. Fully 83 percent of all orders placed with the agency carried discriminatory specifications. A companion study of help-wanted ads conducted in eight major cities during corresponding weeks in 1945 and 1946 showed that while the total volume of help-wanted advertising had declined, there was an over-all increase of 195 percent in discriminatory ads for 1946 over 1945.

The minority job seeker often finds that there are fields of employment where application is futile no matter how able or well-trained he is. Many northern business concerns have an unwritten rule against appointing Jews to executive positions; railroad management and unions discourage the employment of Negroes as engineers or conductors.

In some of our territories which are fairly free from other discrimination, unfair employment practices occur. Some of the larger business firms in Hawaii will not hire clerical or stenographic workers of Japanese ancestry where the public can see the worker. In Puerto Rico, with its large Negro population, generally only white people or very light colored persons are employed by banks, sugar corporations, airlines, shipping companies, and large department stores in clerical and executive positions.

Discrimination in hiring has forced many minority workers into low-paying and often menial jobs such as common laborer and domestic servant. This has done much to bring about the situation reported by the Bureau of the Census in 1940—

> Striking differences between the occupations of whites and Negroes were shown in 1940 census statistics. Farmers, farm laborers, and other laborers constituted 62.2 percent of all employed Negro men and only 28.5 percent of all employed white men. Only about 5 percent of all employed Negro men, compared with approximately 30 percent of employed white men, were engaged in professional, semi-professional, proprietary, managerial, and clerical or sales occupations. Skilled craftsmen represented 15.6 percent of employed white men and only 4.4 percent of employed Negro men. More than half of the Negro craftsmen were mechanics, carpenters, painters, plasterers and cement finishers, and masons.

*On-the-job discrimination.*—If he can get himself hired, the minority worker often finds that he is being paid less than other workers. This wage discrimination is sharply evident in studies made of individual cities and is especially exaggerated in the South. A survey, conducted by the Research and Information Department of the American Federation of Labor shows that the average weekly income of white veterans ranges from 30 to 78 percent above the average income of Negro veterans in 26 communities, 25 of them in the South. In Houston, for example, 36,000 white veterans had a weekly income of $49 and 4,000 Negro veterans had average incomes of $30—a difference of 63 percent. These differences are not caused solely by the relegation of the Negroes to lower types of work, but reflect wage discriminations between white and Negroes for the same type of work. The Final Report of the FEPC states that the hourly wage rates for Negro common laborers averaged 47.4 cents in July, 1942, as compared with 65.3 cents for white laborers.

Nor can the disparity be blamed entirely on differences in education and training. The 1940 census reveals that the median annual income of Negro high school graduates was only $775 as compared with $1,454 for the white high school graduate; that the median Negro college graduate received $1,074 while his white counterpart was earning $2,046; that while 23.3 percent of white high school graduates had wage or salary incomes over $2,000, but four percent of Negro graduates achieved that level.

In presenting this evidence, the Committee is not ignoring the fact that an individual Negro worker may be less efficient than an individual white worker or vice versa. Nor does it suggest that wage differences which reflect actual differences in the competence of workers are unjustifiable. What is indefensible is a wage discrimination based, not on the worker's ability, but on his race.

While private business provided almost 70 percent of all cases docketed by the FEPC for the fiscal year 1943–44, about a fourth of the complaints were against the federal government itself. This at once calls to question the effectiveness of the Civil Service Commission rules against such discrimination, and the various departments' directives and executive orders that have restated this policy of nondiscrimination from time to time.

A case study, conducted in one government agency by the National Committee on Segregation in the Nation's Capital, demonstrates a pattern of discrimination existing in government service. Samples of Negro and white workers in this agency were matched for the variables of age, sex, marital status, educational level, length of service, division in which inducted, and job title and grade at which inducted. Out of 503 whites and 292 Negroes inducted into the agency in the fiscal year 1946, 40 pairs were perfectly matched for these variables. A few more Negroes than whites had veteran status, but the average efficiency ratings for the two groups were exactly the same.

A check on promotion and resignation for the sample was made in April, 1947. It was found that the whites had received 12 grade promotions in a total service of 22 years. This was an average of one promotion for each two man-years of service. The Negroes had received two grade promotions in a total service of 28 man-years. This was one promotion for each 14 man-years. In other words, it took the average Negro seven times as long as the average white to get a promotion, in spite of the fact that almost all of their variables which could affect promotion were exactly the same.

Finally, labor unions are guilty of discriminatory labor practices. Six percent of the complaints received by the FEPC were made against unions, and the FEPC states that when challenged, private industry eliminated discrimination much more readily than did unions. On the other hand, it should be noted that great strides have been made in the admission of minorities to unions. Both the American Federation of Labor and the Congress of Industrial Organizations have repeatedly condemned discriminatory union practices. But the national organizations have not yet fully attained their goals. Some railway unions have "Jim Crow" auxiliaries into which Negroes, Mexicans, or Orientals are shunted, with little or no voice in union affairs. Furthermore, there is a rigid upper limit on the type of job on which these members can be employed.

There is a danger that some of our wartime gains in the elimination of unfair employment practices will be lost unless prompt action is taken to preserve them. In the federal government, the employment of Negroes jumped from 40,000 before the war to 300,000 in 1944. And while only 10 percent of all Negroes employed in government held jobs other than custodial in 1938, 60 percent of the Negroes in 1944 were employed in clerical and professional categories. . . .

In private industry, minority workers were heavily concentrated in war industries, which since the end of the war have suffered drastic cutbacks. In other industries the termination of manpower controls has encouraged some employers to resume prewar policies of exclusion or discriminatory treatment of minority workers. The first sentence in the summary of the FEPC Final Report bluntly observes that "the wartime gains of Negro, Mexican American, and Jewish workers are being lost through an unchecked revival of discriminatory practices."

Such postwar economic retrenchment as has occurred has disproportionally hit the minority groups. A United States Census Bureau survey, bearing out the adage the minority workers are "the last hired, first fired," discloses that from July 1945, to April, 1946, unemployment among whites increased about one and one-half times while unemployment among nonwhites more than tripled. The situation has of course been aggravated by the accelerated migration of Negroes from the South to northern industrial areas during the war.

## Note

More recent figures on the employment of nonwhite workers are given in Kane, *The Nonwhite Housing Market,* 16 Insured Mortgage Portfolio, No. 2, pp. 23–5 (FHA, 1952):

"Important changes occurred in the employment of nonwhite workers in the 1940's. The most notable change was the decline in the proportion of these workers in agricultural occupations, from about 33 percent in 1940 to 20 percent in 1950 for the United States, and from 40 to 29 percent for the South. In the same period, the proportion of nonwhite persons employed in manufacturing rose from about 11 to 18 percent for the country as a whole and from 11 to 14 percent for the South. The relative number employed in construction and trade also increased substantially.

"The percentage of all nonwhite workers who were employed in private households fell from 21 percent in 1940 to 15 percent in 1950. Proportionately more nonwhite workers were in professional, techni-

**1142**

cal, clerical, and sales work in 1950 than in 1940. The number of non-white clerical workers tripled between 1940 and 1950, and the number of nonwhite sales workers, craftsmen, and operatives doubled. In fact, by 1950, "operatives and kindred workers" had become the most important occupational group for nonwhite workers, with one million persons included.

"A relatively large number of nonwhite women—about 37 percent of the total number 14 years and over—formed part of the civilian labor force in 1950. This was about the same proportion as in 1940. The proportion of all women, both white and nonwhite, who were in the labor force in 1950 was about 29 percent. Although private household workers still made up the largest category of nonwhite women workers—42 percent—this was substantially less than the 1940 figure of about 59 percent.

"Wage and salary workers accounted for nearly 83 percent of all employed nonwhite workers in 1950, while self-employed workers represented about 13 percent—a decline from 21 per cent in 1940, reflecting both the decline in agricultural employment and the greater opportunities now open to Negroes as wage and salary workers.

"The proportion of nonwhite persons 14 years of age and older in the labor force has been decreasing since 1920, partly as a result of an increase in school attendance. From 1940 to 1950, for example, school enrollment among nonwhites aged 14 to 24 increased about 18 percent, a rate much greater than the 2 percent increase for both whites and nonwhites. In fact, the percentage of nonwhite persons 5 to 24 years old enrolled in school is now almost equal to the percentage of all persons in those ages enrolled—59 percent compared with 61.

"The geographical shift of the nonwhite population and the substantial changes in the occupational distribution of nonwhite workers have been accompanied by a relatively large increase in the money income of this group. The median wage or salary income of nonwhite families and individuals increased from $489 in 1939 to $1,533 in 1949, an increase of 214 percent.[3] The corresponding increase for white families and individuals was only 137 percent. However, in spite of the relatively great increase in income, the level of the money income of nonwhite families of two or more persons is still low as compared with that of all families. In 1949, for the country as a whole, the median income of nonwhite families living in nonfarm areas was $1,658, as compared with $3,245 for all nonfarm families. About 81 percent of these nonwhite families had incomes under $3,000, as compared with 44 percent for white and nonwhite families taken together. About 4 percent of nonwhite families and 22 percent of all families in nonfarm areas had incomes over $5,000 in 1949."

---

[3] These data are from the Census release entitled *Current Population Reports, Consumer Income*, "Income of Families and Persons in the United States: 1949," Series P–60, No. 2, which is based on a sample survey conducted by the Bureau of the Census in March 1950 and which was not a part of the Decennial Census of 1950.

## WILLIAMS v. INTERNATIONAL BROTHERHOOD

Supreme Court of California, 1946

27 Cal.2d 586, 165 Pac.2d 903

GIBSON, C. J.

Plaintiffs, skilled Negro shipyard workers, brought this action on behalf of themselves and approximately 2,000 other Negro workers similarly situated, to restrain defendants from interfering with their employment or re-employment because they are not members of certain local labor unions, affiliated with the defendant International Brotherhood of Boilermakers, Iron Shipbuilders and Helpers of America. The trial court sustained the demurrers of all defendants, discharged an order to show cause why a preliminary injunction should not issue and dismissed the action. Plaintiffs have appealed from the order of discharge and from the judgment of dismissal.

The complaint alleges in substance as follows: Plaintiffs are employees and former employees of defendants Permanente Metals Corporation and Kaiser Company, Inc. A written contract containing a provision for a closed shop is in effect between the employers and the International Brotherhood, which dispatches workers for employment at the shipyards through the agencies of defendant local unions. Negroes are not admitted to membership in the local unions, but plaintiffs were dispatched for employment at the shipyards without permitting or requiring them to become members. Subsequently, however, the unions attempted to compel plaintiffs and other Negro workers to become members and pay dues to Negro lodges established under the authority of the International Brotherhood as auxiliaries to the local unions. These auxiliaries, it is alleged, are not bona fide labor unions but constitutes schemes and devices whereby the defendant unions segregate Negro from non-Negro workers and discriminate against Negroes, the sole reason for the segregation and discrimination being race and color. Various practices of the unions, provided for in the By-Laws Governing Auxiliary Lodges of the International Brotherhood, are set forth in the complaint and are challenged as discriminatory. Plaintiffs are willing to join the local unions upon the same terms and conditions as non-Negro workers, but they are not willing to join or pay dues to the auxiliary lodges.

The gravamen of the complaint is that the unions assert the right to obtain the discharge of the Negro workers under the closed shop contract because they are not members of the unions, although at the same time the unions will not admit Negroes to membership except under discriminatory and unequal conditions. In *James v. Marinship Corp.*, 25 Cal. 2d 721 [155 P. 2d 329], which was decided after the trial court acted in the present case, we held that an arbitrarily closed or partially closed union membership is incompatible with a closed shop; that a denial of union membership to Negroes on terms of equality with other workers is tantamount to wholly closing the union to them; and that injunctive relief will lie to prevent the maintenance of an arbitrarily closed union together with a closed shop.

Defendants point out, however, that the complaint filed herein does not allege that either the International Brotherhood or its local affiliates had attained a monoply of labor in the locality, and, therefore, they contend, the complaint does not state a cause of action under the decision in the James case. Although it is true that the court in the James case treated the existence of such a monopoly as an important reason for granting relief, the decision, contrary to defendants' contention, was not made dependent thereon. The question was expressly reserved for future determination, but we noted, however, that some states, by statute, have declared *all* labor unions to be affected with a public interest and thus subject to regulation. (25 Cal. 2d at page 734, 155 P. 2d 329.)

It is now established by a decision of the Supreme Court of the United States rendered since the James case, that a state has the power to prohibit discrimination on account of race, creed or color by any labor union with respect to membership or union services. (*Railway Mail Ass'n v. Corsi*, 326 U.S. 88 [65 S. Ct. 1483, 89 L. Ed. 2072].) The contention was there made that a New York statute which prohibits a union from denying membership or equal treatment to anyone by reason of race, color or creed was contrary to the Fourteenth Amendment in that it abridged property rights and liberty of contract. The court replied that to so hold "would be a distortion of the policy manifested in that amendment which was adopted to prevent state legislation designed to discriminate on the basis of race or color," and, particularly applicable to the present case, the court stated that there was "no constitutional basis for the contention that a state cannot protect workers from exclusion solely on the basis of race, color or creed by an *organization, functioning under the protection of the state, which holds itself out to represent the general business needs of employees.*" (Italics added.) (65 S. Ct. at page 1487.) Further, it should be noted that the New York statute was not limited in operation to unions having closed shop agreements, and no question of a labor monopoly in the locality was involved in the Corsi case. Although the relief granted in the Corsi case was derived from legislative authority, nevertheless, it is established that, where persons are subjected to certain conduct by others which is deemed unfair and contrary to public policy, the courts have full power to afford necessary protection in the absence of statute. (*James* v. *Marinship Corp.*, 25 Cal. 2d 721, 740 [155 P. 2d 329].)

The failure to allege a monopoly of labor in the entire locality is not fatal to plaintiffs' cause of action insofar as the authorities relied upon in the James case are concerned. Although it is true that certain of the cases cited emphasize the fact that such a monopoly existed (see, for example, *Wilson* v. *Newspaper & Mail Deliveries' Union* (1938), 123 N. J. Eq. 347 [197 A. 720]; *Carroll* v. *Local No. 269* (1943), 133 N. J. Eq. 144 [31 A. 2d 223]), in only one case was it stated that relief must be denied because of the failure to show that the union had obtained a monopoly over the labor market. (*Walter* v. *McCarvel* (1941), 309 Mass. 260 [34 N. E. 2d 677].) In other jurisdictions relief has been granted against the maintenance of a closed shop and an arbitrarily closed union without requiring proof of a labor monopoly in the area. *Dorrington* v. *Manning* (1939), 135 Pa. Super. 194 [4 A. 2d 886]; *Wills v. Local No. 1067*, 26 Ohio N. P. N. S. 435; *cf. Lucke* v. *Clothing Cutters' & T. Assembly No. 7507, K. of L.* (1893), 77 Md. 396 [26 A. 505, 39 Am. St. Rep. 421, 19 L. R. A. 408].)

These decisions are based upon the theory that such collective labor activity does not have a proper purpose and constitutes an unlawful interference with a worker's right to employment. The Restatement of Torts, section 810, has adopted this view, stating: "Workers who in concert procure the dismissal of an employee because he is not a member of a labor union satisfactory to the workers . . . are liable to the employee, if, but only if, he desires to be a member of the labor union but membership is not open to him on reasonable terms." This rule is not founded upon the presence of a labor monopoly in the entire locality, and the reasoning is simply that it is unfair for a labor union to interfere with a person's right to work because he does not belong to the union although he is willing to join and abide by reasonable union rules and is able to meet all reasonable conditions of membership. No purpose appropriate to the functions of a labor organization may be found in such discriminatory conduct. Here the union's efforts are directed, not toward advancing the legitimate interests of a labor union, but rather against other workers solely on the basis of race and color.

The reasons why an arbitrarily closed union should not be permitted to exist together with a closed shop are stated in 1 Teller, Labor Disputes and Collective Bargaining (1940), at page 285, as follows: "Labor unions which close their ranks to the public thereby assume a sovereignty which is not theirs to assume. . . . The closed shop as an instrumentality of a labor union, membership wherein is reasonably open to the public, establishes a desirable rule governing industrial enterprise. The closed shop at the hands of a labor union which substantially excludes the public from its benefits, on the other hand, is a means whereby an anti-social monopoly is foisted upon the industrial body politic." This reasoning is applicable whether the monopoly is limited to a single plant or covers an entire community.

The public interest is directly involved because the unions are seeking to control by arbitrary selection the fundamental right to work. While the need for protection may be greater where the union has secured closed shop contracts covering all the jobs in the locality, this is only an aggravated phase of the general problem. The individual worker denied the right to keep his job suffers a loss, and his right to protection against arbitrary and discriminatory exclusion from union membership should be recognized wherever membership is a necessary prerequisite to work. A closed shop agreement with a single employer is in itself a form of monopoly, giving a third party, the union, control over at least the plant of the signatory employer, and although such a labor monopoly is not in itself improper, it carries with it certain responsibilities, and the public clearly has an interest in preventing any abuse of it. As pointed out in the Corsi case (326 U. S. 88 [65 S. Ct. 1483, 1487, 89 L. Ed. 2072]), a labor union functioning under the protection of the state holds itself out to represent the general business needs of employees, and if, as it was there held, a state may protect workers from exclusion by *any* labor union, it is clearly warranted in doing so wherever union membership is a condition to employment although only a single employer is involved.

It is assumed in connection with another phase of the case that the shipyards are industries affecting interstate commerce and that the parties hereto are subject to the National Labor Relations Act (49 Stats. 449, 29 U. S. C. A. § 151 et seq.) The act affords a further reason for granting relief because under its provisions it is unnecessary to show that the unions have a labor monopoly in the locality. The union as the bargaining agent of the employees selected in accordance with the act has the duty to represent *all* employees, without discrimination because of race or color, and it may be compelled to do so by judicial action. (*Cf. Steele* v. *Louisville & Nashville R. R. Co.*, 323 U. S. 192 [65 S. Ct. 226, 89 L. Ed. 173]; *Tunstall* v. *Brotherhood of Locomotive Firemen & Enginemen*, 323 U. S. 210 [65 S. Ct.

235, 89 L. Ed. 187].)   The National Labor Relations Board has stated that where a union has obtained a contract requiring membership as a condition of employment, it does not have the right to compel the discharge of employees who are discriminatorily denied membership.   (See *In re Larus & Bro. Co. Inc.,* June 30, 1945, 62 N. L. R. B. No. 134; *In re Rutland Courts,* 44 N. L. R. B. 587.)

The complaint, therefore, does not fail to state a cause of action merely because it does not allege that the union defendants have attained a monopoly of the supply of labor in the locality.

The union defendants contend that their demurrers were properly sustained on the ground that the complaint did not allege unreasonable discrimination against Negro workers.   They say that the International Brotherhood is open to Negro members if they consent to segregation into separate auxiliaries and that this is not unreasonable discrimination.   In addition to segregation, however, the complaint alleges specific provisions of the by-laws of the International Brotherhood which would operate to place members of the auxiliaries in an unequal and disadvantageous position as compared with members of the local unions. Plaintiffs charge, for example, that the locals control, manage, and supervise all of the affairs and business of the auxiliaries whereas the auxiliaries have no voice or vote in the affairs of the supervising locals; that the auxiliaries are not allowed business agents or grievance committees to act for their members but must seek representation through the business agents of the local unions, "who refuse to act for the members of said auxiliaries"; and that members of the auxiliaries are dispatched to employment only through the agencies of the local unions and cannot obtain a change of classification of work from helper to journeyman without their approval.   These union rules and practices were held discriminatory in *James* v. *Marinship Corp.,* 25 Cal. 2d 721, 737–739 [155 P. 2d 329], where it was further declared that since the Negroes were denied union membership on terms of equality with other workers, the effect was the same as wholly denying them membership.

The union defendants next contend that the trial court did not have jurisdiction over the subject matter because, they assert, if an injunction were granted it would in effect destroy their closed shop contract and affect the status of the employees of the shipyards, and it would thus interfere with the rights of collective bargaining granted by the National Labor Relations Act.   This contention was determined adversely to defendants in the James case.   They now rely upon *Hill* v. *State of Florida,* 325 U. S. 538 [65 S. Ct. 1373, 89 L. Ed. 1782], which was decided after the James case. It was there held that a state has no power to impose conditions upon the rights of a union and its representatives to function as collective bargaining agents under the National Labor Relations Act.

There is nothing in the Hill case, however, that precludes a state court from enforcing against a labor union such rights of individual workers as are consistent with the provisions of the federal act. That act clearly does not give a union the authority to maintain a closed shop agreement together with an arbitrarily closed union membership. Moreover, the rights which plaintiffs seek to enforce not only are consistent with the provisions of the federal act but appear to be affirmatively granted thereby. Section 9 (a) provides that the union selected by a majority of the employees of a bargaining unit "shall be the exclusive representatives of all the employees in such unit", (49 Stats. 453, 29 U. S. C. A. § 159), and it is difficult to see how a union can fairly represent all employees of a bargaining unit if it arbitrarily excludes some from membership thereby depriving them of the opportunity to vote for union leaders and to participate in determining union policies. (See *James* v. *Marinship Corp.*, 25 Cal. 2d 721, 735 [155 P. 2d 329].)

An additional contention made by the employer in *Thompson* v. *Moore Dry Dock Co.* [27 Cal. 2d 595, 165 P. 2d 901], should be considered here, since the allegations in the complaints are substantially the same and the cases were argued together in this court. It is contended that a cause of action is not stated against the employers because it does not appear that they have committed or threatened any wrong against plaintiffs. The complaints allege that the employers have enforced, or threaten to enforce, the closed shop contracts against plaintiffs by requiring them, upon penalty of discharge, to join the auxiliary lodges, thus subjecting them to discriminatory and unequal union rules set forth in the complaint. As held in the James case, an employer may be enjoined from indirectly assisting a union in carrying out discriminatory practices against Negroes through a closed shop contract. (25 Cal. 2d 721, 742). It is argued, however, that an injunction would place the employers in a dilemma in that it would require them to judge whether, after such an order, the union had ceased its discriminatory practices, and they argue that they would thereby be subjected either to a claim by a Negro that the injunction was being violated or to a claim by the union that it no longer discriminated against Negroes. The employers, however, will not be compelled to make such a decision. They need not look behind the notice from the union that an employee is not a member in good standing. They may accept the statements of the union officials who are in charge of providing work clearances not only to the effect that a particular worker is not a member in good standing but also to the effect that the union has ceased all unequal and discriminatory treatment within the terms of the injunction. Upon receipt of such a statement the employers may refuse to hire the Negro workers, and if the union has not given truthful information and if it has continued the enjoined discriminations, it alone, and not the employers, will be subject to a charge of contempt. The primary responsibility for compliance with the order of the court is thus placed where it belongs—directly on the union. With the duties and responsibilities of the employers thus limited, there remains no force to their objection that they will be placed in an inescapable dilemma. . . .

The judgment of dismissal and the order discharging the order to show cause why a preliminary injunction should not issue are reversed.

## Note

1. In the *Steele* case, cited by the principal opinion, the Supreme Court held that enforcement of a collective agreement discriminating against Negroes as to seniority rights could be enjoined. The Court stated: "While the statute does not deny to such a bargaining labor organization the right to determine eligibility to its membership it does require the union on collective bargaining and in making contracts with the carrier to represent non-union or minority union members of the craft without hostile discrimination, fairly, impartially, and in good faith." 323 U. S. at 204. A more recent case went further. In *Brotherhood of Railroad Trainmen v. Howard*, 343 U. S. 768, 96 L. Ed. —, 72 S. Ct. 1022 (1952), Justice Black's opinion read in part as follows: "There is a difference in the circumstances of the two cases, however, which it is contended requires us to deny the judicial remedy here that was accorded in the *Steele* case. That difference is this: Steele was admittedly a locomotive fireman although not a member of the Brotherhood of Locomotive Firemen and Enginemen which under the Railway Labor Act was the exclusive bargaining representative of the entire craft of firemen. . . . In this case . . . the colored employees have for many years been treated by the carriers and the Brotherhood as a separate class for representation purposes and have in fact been represented by another union of their own choosing. Since the Brotherhood has discriminated against 'train porters' instead of minority members of its own 'craft' it is argued that the Brotherhood owed no duty at all to refrain from using its statutory bargaining power so as to abolish the jobs of the colored porters and drive them from the railroads . . . [This] argument is unsound . . . These train porters are threatened with loss of their jobs because they are not white and for no other reason. The job they did hold under its old name would be abolished by the agreement; their color alone would

disqualify them for the old job under its new name . . . The Federal Act thus prohibits bargaining agents it authorizes from using their position and power to destroy colored workers' jobs in order to bestow them on white workers. And courts can protect those threatened by such an unlawful use of power granted by a federal act." 343 U. S. at 772–4.

In *Betts v. Easley,* 161 Kan. 459, 169 Pac. 2d 831 (1946), the Brotherhood of Railway Carmen was the bargaining agent of Negroes who, though members, were forced to join a separate lodge under the jurisdiction of the nearest white local. They could not participate in the election of union officers or in determination of union policy. Negro workers sought to enjoin the union from acting as collective bargaining agent until equal privileges and full membership were bestowed on them. The court stated: "The petition alleges not only that Negro employees are denied the right to take part in such local affairs of the union as the election of officers and the fixing of dues, but are denied the right to participate in determining the position to be taken by the union, as bargaining agent for all employees, as to wages, hours, working conditions, and other such matters vitally affecting their economic welfare. Such denial is repugnant to every American concept of equality under the law. It is repugnant both to the letter and the spirit of our fundamental charter . . . The acts complained of are in violation of the fifth amendment." 161 Kan. at 469.

The National Labor Relations Board generally does not recognize bargaining units based solely on sex, race or creed. See *U. S. Bedding Co.,* 52 N. L. R. B. 382, 13 LRRM 10 (1943); but *cf. Bethlehem Alameda Shipyard, Inc.,* 53 N. L. R. B. 999, 13 LRRM 139 (1943). In *Norfolk Southern Bus Corp.,* 76 N. L. R. B. 488, 21 LRRM 1215 (1948), the bus company contended that the union ought not to represent Negro employees because they were not members of the union. The NLRB ruled against this contention since there was no evidence that the union would not represent all employees equally. The NLRB has generally followed the rule that the mere fact that Negroes are put in a separate local or simply excluded is insufficient proof, standing alone, that the members of the minority local or nonmembers are not adequately represented. See *Atlanta Oak Flooring Co.,* 62 N. L. R. B. 973, 16 LRRM 235 (1945); *Veneer Products Inc.,* 81 N. L. R. B. 492, 23 LRRM 1373 (1949); *General Motors Corp.,* 62 N. L. R. B. 427, 16 LRRM 237 (1945); *Wichita Foundry and Machine Co.,* 69 N. L. R. B. 458, 18 LRRM 1234 (1946).

See also *N. L. R. B. v. Reliable Newspaper Delivery, Inc.,* 187 F. 2d 547 (C. A. 3, 1951), 27 LRRM 2432 (court would not enforce NLRB order to give back pay to union members only where the union was a closed one admitting only sons of members).

2. *Graham v. Brotherhood of Firemen,* 338 U. S. 232, 94 L. Ed. 22, 70 S. Ct. 14 (1949), involved an agreement between the union and the company in which Negro workers were labeled as non-promotable. As a result Negro workers were displaced and demoted and gradually entirely eliminated from the jobs. They sought an injunction against the enforcement of the contract, damages, and a declaratory judgment.

The union claimed that no injunction should issue in view of the Norris-La Guardia Act. The Supreme Court held that that Act is for the protection of employees and does not bar an injunction against union-employer activities that violate employee rights under the Railway Labor Act.

In *Brotherhood of Locomotive Firemen v. Mitchell*, 190 F. 2d 308 (C. A. 5, 1951), the court held that the duty of the Firemen to represent Negroes fairly is a continuing one. The statute of limitations does not run against an injunction. It does, however, run against a claim for damages.

3. In *Williams v. Yellow Cab Co.*, 103 F. Supp. 847 (W. D. Pa., 1952), a collective bargaining contract limited Negro cab drivers to the Negro sections of the city. The drivers sought an injunction and damages because of the segregation. The court felt it lacked jurisdiction because the union was not acting under protection of Federal labor laws. It added, however, that in any event the contract was not illegal because the limitations imposed on Negroes were based on legitimate business reasons, the union members approved of the contract, and Negroes understood the arrangement when they were hired.

4. Constitutional protection: In *Truax v. Raich*, 239 U. S. 33, 60 L. Ed. 131, 36 S. Ct. 7 (1915), the plaintiff was discharged because of a state law that required employers to employ native born American citizens in the minimum amount of eighty per cent of their total working force. He sought an injunction against the employer and against the attorney general and county attorney on the ground that the act denied him equal protection of the laws. The Supreme Court in holding the act invalid stated in part:

"It is sought to justify this act as an exercise of the power of the State to make reasonable classifications in legislating to promote the health, safety, morals and welfare of those within its jurisdiction. But this admitted authority, with the broad range of legislative discretion that it implies, does not go so far as to make it possible for the State to deny to lawful inhabitants, because of their race or nationality, the ordinary means of earning a livelihood. It requires no argument to show that the right to work for a living in the common occupations of the community is of the very essence of the personal freedom and opportunity that it was the purpose of the Amendment to secure. *Butchers' Union Co. v. Crescent City Co.*, 111 U. S. 746, 762; *Barbier v. Connolly*, 113 U. S. 27, 31; *Yick Wo v. Hopkins* [118 U. S. 356]; *Allgeyer v. Louisiana*, 165 U. S. 578, 589, 590; *Coppage v. Kansas*, 236 U. S. 1, 14. If this could be refused solely upon the ground of race or nationality, the prohibition of the denial to any person of the equal protection of the laws would be a barren form of words. It is no answer to say, as it is argued, that the act proceeds upon the assumption that 'the employment of aliens unless restrained was a peril to the public welfare.' The discrimination against aliens in the wide range of employments to which the act relates is made an end in itself and thus the authority to deny to aliens, upon the mere fact of their alienage, the right to obtain support in the ordinary fields of labor is necessarily involved. It must also be said that reasonable classification implies action consistent with the legitimate interests of the State, and it will not be disputed that these cannot be so broadly conceived as to bring them into hostility to exclusive Federal power. The authority to control immigration—to admit or exclude aliens—is vested solely in the Federal Government. . . ." 239 U. S. at 41–2.

5. Picketing against discrimination: In *Hughes v. Superior Court,* 339 U. S. 460, 94 L. Ed. 985, 70 S. Ct. 718 (1950), the Progressive Citizens of America picketed a store demanding that it hire Negro clerks so that their proportion would approximate that of Negro customers. An injunction was upheld on the ground that the picketing violated the public policy of the state as expressed by the courts, opposing all discriminatory hiring, including quota systems, such as the pickets advocated. See discussion *supra.* Compare *New Negro Alliance v. Sanitary Grocery Co.,* 303 U. S. 552, 82 L. Ed. 1012, 58 S. Ct. 703 (1938), where the Alliance, an organization for the mutual improvement of its members, picketed stores urging Negroes not to buy because no Negroes were employed. The District Court enjoined the picketing. The Supreme Court reversed on the ground that this was a labor dispute within the meaning of § 113 of the Norris-La Guardia Act, 29 U. S. C. § 113.

6. See, generally, Hewitt, *Right to Membership in a Labor Union,* 99 U. of Pa. L. Rev. 919 (1951); Rosenthal, *Exclusion of Employees under Taft-Hartley Act,* 4 Ind. and Lab. Rel. Rev. 556 (1951); Forkosch, *Internal Affairs of Unions,* 18 U. of Chi. L. Rev. 729 (1951); Note, 8 Wash. & Lee L. Rev. 234 (1951); Murray, *The Right to Equal Opportunity in Employment,* 33 Calif. L. Rev. 388 (1945); Aaron and Komaroff, *Statutory Regulation of Internal Union Affairs,* 44 Ill. L. Rev. 425, 631 (1949); Harris, *Section 8(a)(3) of the Taft-Hartley Act,* 6 Nat. B. J. 242 (1948); Jenkins, *The Problem of Racial Discrimination in Union Membership,* 7 Law. Guild Rev. 37 (1947); Note, *Maritime Hiring Halls and Labor Disputes,* 1 Stan. L. Rev. 272 (1949); Reuther, *Justice on the Job Front,* Testimony before Subcommittee on Anti-Discrimination Legislation of the United States Senate Committee on Labor and Public Welfare (pub. by U.A.W.–C.I.O., 1947); Mason, *The CIO and the Negro in the South,* 14 J. Negro Ed. 552 (1945); Northrup, *Organized Labor and the Negro* (1944).

## NEW YORK LAW AGAINST DISCRIMINATION

### N. Y. Exec. Law, Art. 15, §§ 290–301[1]

**§ 290. Purposes of article.** This article shall be known as the "Law Against Discrimination." . . . [The] legislature hereby finds and declares that practices of discrimination against any of its inhabitants because of race, creed, color or national origin

---

[1] Passed as N. Y. Laws, 1945, ch. 118, Mar. 12, 1945, effective July 1, 1945; formerly N. Y. Exec. Law, Art. 12, §§ 125–36; renumbered as above by N. Y. Laws, 1951, ch. 800.

are a matter of state concern, that such discrimination threatens not only the rights and proper privileges of its inhabitants but menaces the institutions and foundation of a free democratic state. . . .

§ 291. **Opportunity for employment without discrimination a civil right.** The opportunity to obtain employment without discrimination because of race, creed, color or national origin is hereby recognized as and declared to be a civil right.

§ 292. **Definitions.** When used in this article . . .

5. The term "employer" does not include a club exclusively social, or a fraternal, charitable, educational or religious association or corporation, if such club, association or corporation is not organized for private profit, nor does it include any employer with fewer than six persons in his employ.

6. The term "employee" and this article do not include any individual employed by his parents, spouse or child, or in the domestic service of any person. . . .

§ 293. **State commission against discrimination.** There is hereby created in the executive department a state commission against discrimination. Such commission shall consist of five members, to be known as commissioners, who shall be appointed by the governor, by and with the advice and consent of the senate, and one of whom shall be designated as chairman by the governor. . . .

§ 294. **General policies of commission.** The commission shall formulate policies to effectuate the purposes of this article and may make recommendations to agencies and officers of the state or local subdivisions of government in aid of such policies and purposes.

§ 295. **General powers and duties of commission.** The commission shall have the following functions, powers and duties . . .

6. To receive, investigate and pass upon complaints alleging discrimination in employment because of race, creed, color or national origin.

7. To hold hearings, subpoena witnesses, compel their attendance, administer oaths, take the testimony of any person under oath, and in connection therewith, to require the production for examination of any books or papers relating to any matter under investigation or in question before the commission. . . .

8. To create such advisory agencies and conciliation councils, local, regional or state-wide, as in its judgment will aid in effectuating the purposes of this article and of section eleven of

article one of the constitution of this state, and the commission may empower them to study the problems of discrimination in all or specific fields of human relationships or in specific instances of discrimination because of race, creed, color or national origin, and to foster through community effort or otherwise good-will, co-operation and conciliation among the groups and elements of the population of the state, and make recommendations to the commission for the development of policies and procedures in general and in specific instances, and for programs of formal and informal education which the commission may recommend to the appropriate state agency. Such advisory agencies and conciliation councils shall be composed of representative citizens, serving without pay, but with reimbursements for actual and necessary traveling expenses. . . .

9. To issue such publications and such results of investigations and research as in its judgment will tend to promote good-will and minimize or eliminate discrimination because of race, creed, color or national origin. . . .

§ 296. **Unlawful employment practices.** It shall be an unlawful employment practice: 1. For an employer, because of the race, creed, color or national origin of any individual, to refuse to hire or employ or to bar or to discharge from employment such individual or to discriminate against such individual in compensation or in terms, conditions or privileges of employment.

2. For a labor organization, because of the race, creed, color or national origin of any individual, to exclude or to expel from its membership such individual or to discriminate in any way against any of its members or against any employer or any individual employed by an employer.

3. For any employer or employment agency to print or circulate or cause to be printed or circulated any statement, advertisement or publication, or to use any form of application for employment or to make any inquiry in connection with prospective employment, which expresses, directly or indirectly, any limitation, specification or discrimination as to race, creed, color or national origin, or any intent to make any such limitation, specification or discrimination, unless based upon a bona fide occupational qualification.

4. For any employer, labor organization or employment agency to discharge, expel or otherwise discriminate against any person because he has opposed any practices forbidden under this article or because he has filed a complaint, testified or assisted in any proceeding under this article.

5. For any person, whether an employer or an employee or not,

to aid, abet, incite, compel or coerce the doing of any of the acts forbidden under this article, or to attempt to do so.

§ 297. **Procedure.** Any person claiming to be aggrieved by an unlawful employment practice may, by himself or his attorney-at-law, make, sign and file with the commission a verified complaint in writing which shall state the name and address of the person, employer, labor organization or employment agency alleged to have committed the unlawful employment practice complained of and which shall set forth the particulars thereof and contain such other information as may be required by the commission. The industrial commissioner or attorney-general may, in like manner, make, sign and file such complaint. Any employer whose employees, or some of them, refuse or threaten to refuse to cooperate with the provisions of this article, may file with the commission a verified complaint asking for assistance by conciliation or other remedial action.

After the filing of any complaint, the chairman of the commission shall designate one of the commissioners to make, with the assistance of the commission's staff, prompt investigation in connection therewith; and if such commissioner shall determine after such investigation that probable cause exists for crediting the allegations of the complaint, he shall immediately endeavor to eliminate the unlawful employment practice complained of by conference, conciliation and persuasion. The members of the commission and its staff shall not disclose what has transpired in the course of such endeavors. In case of failure so to eliminate such practice, or in advance thereof if in his judgment circumstances so warrant, he shall cause to be issued and served in the name of the commission, a written notice, together with a copy of such complaint, as the same may have been amended, requiring the person, employer, labor organization or employment agency named in such complaint, hereinafter referred to as respondent, to answer the charges of such complaint at a hearing before three members of the commission, sitting as the commission, at a time and place to be specified in such notice. . . . The case in support of the complaint shall be presented before the commission by one of its attorneys or agents, and the commissioner who shall have previously made the investigation and caused the notice to be issued shall not participate in the hearing except as a witness, nor shall he participate in the deliberations of the commission in such case; and the aforesaid endeavors at conciliation shall not be received in evidence. The respondent may file a written verified answer to the complaint and appear at such hearing in person or otherwise, with or without counsel, and submit testimony. In the discretion of the commission, the complainant may be allowed to intervene and present testimony in person or by counsel. . . . The commission shall not be bound by the strict rules of evidence prevailing in courts of law or equity. The testimony taken at the hearing shall be under oath and be transcribed. If, upon all the evidence at the hearing the commission shall find that a respondent has engaged in any unlawful employment practice as defined in this article, the commission shall state its findings of fact and shall issue and cause to be served on such respondent an order requiring such respondent to cease and desist from such unlawful employment practice and to take such affirmative action, including (but not limited to) hiring, reinstatement or upgrading of employees, with or without back pay, or restoration to membership in any respondent labor organization, as, in the judgment of the commission, will effectuate the purposes of this article, and including a requirement for report of the manner of compliance. If, upon all the evidence, the commission shall find that a respondent has not engaged in any such unlawful employment practice, the commission shall state its findings of fact and shall issue and cause to be served on the complainant an order dismissing the said complaint as to such respondent. . . . Any complaint filed pursuant to this section must be so filed within ninety days after the alleged act of discrimination.

[Section 298 provides that any complainant, respondent or other person aggrieved by an order of the Commission may obtain judicial review, and the Commission may obtain judicial enforcement, of an order in the appropriate New York Supreme Court in accordance with usual administrative law procedures. Section 299 establishes criminal penalties for violation of an order. Section 300 declares that the act shall be liberally construed. Section 301 is a separability provision.]

## BERGER—FAIR EMPLOYMENT PRACTICES LEGISLATION

275 Annals of the Am. Acad. of Pol. and
Soc. Sci. 34, 34–9 (1951)

It is nearly six years since New York State enacted its pioneering law applying modern administrative methods to enforce the prohibition of unfair practices in private employment. . . .

### JURISDICTIONS

As the United States Congress repeatedly failed to enact a federal fair employment practices law, other states and cities followed the example of New York. New Jersey did so later in

1945, Massachusetts in 1946, and Connecticut in 1947. In 1949 Washington, Rhode Island, Oregon, and New Mexico enacted similar statutes. Meanwhile several cities outlawed discrimination in private employment: Chicago in 1945, Minneapolis in 1947, Philadelphia in 1948; and in 1950, Youngstown, Struthers, and Cleveland, Ohio, and Gary, Indiana. Still other states and cities enacted laws on the subject. Indiana and Wisconsin in 1945 authorized existing agencies to help eliminate private employment discrimination by conferring with workers and employers, but the legislatures granted no enforcement powers to these state agencies. Ordinances prohibiting discrimination in municipal employment and by firms executing city contracts were passed by Milwaukee, Wisconsin, in 1945; Phoenix, Arizona, in 1948; and Richmond, California, in 1949. In 1946 Cincinnati, Ohio, outlawed discrimination in municipal employment.

The following states and cities have fair employment practices laws which apply modern administrative techniques: New York, New Jersey, Massachusetts, Connecticut, Washington, Rhode Island, Oregon, New Mexico; and Minneapolis, Philadelphia, Youngstown, Struthers, Cleveland, and Gary. (Chicago is omitted because its law has been virtually a dead letter because of doubt as to its constitutionality and the failure to establish an agency to administer it.) This entire area includes one-quarter of the total population of the United States, about a tenth of the nation's nonwhites, and more than two-thirds of the Jews in this country. In the following discussion we shall be concerned with these eight state laws, but only with the Minnesota and Philadelphia ordinances, since the other city ordinances were enacted too recently for evaluation. Indeed, the reader should bear in mind that, while fair employment practices legislation has already proved its efficacy in general, it is a relatively new legal technique, still in its early stages of development.

## ADMINISTRATIVE TECHNIQUES

The fair employment practices laws which apply modern administrative techniques have essentially the same features. . . .[1]

## RESULTS

A study of the operation of these laws quickly reveals that they have justified the community's and the legislature's faith in their efficacy. The administrative agencies have proceeded cautiously and have made definite, if moderate, progress in carrying out

---

[1] [Ed. Note: See N. Y. Law Against Discrimination, *supra*.]

the intent of the law. The two predictions most often made about the results of fair employment practices legislation have not come true. First, there has been no deluge of complaints by "cranks" and "disgruntled failures." Second, business has not fled those states and cities which have strong fair employment practices laws.

As was to be expected, the agencies charged with the responsibility of enforcing this new and challenging kind of law have wanted to move carefully and to build up voluntary support for fair employment, rather than resort immediately to the compulsory and punitive features of the law. They have therefore stressed the educational rather than the coercive aspects of the law, and the conciliation process rather than the public hearing and cease and desist order. The agencies are proud of the fact that they have found it unnecessary (or have seldom had) to go beyond the stage of informal conciliation in achieving settlements of cases in which they discovered actual discrimination. At this writing (March 1951), only the New York and Connecticut commissions have gone so far as to hold a public hearing and to issue a cease and desist order, both in 1950.

Such a record of apparently successful conciliation is impressive; but the public is unable to form a reliable judgment as to the accomplishments of informal conciliation, because none of the enforcing agencies reveals the terms upon which its cases have been settled. Some of the agencies have provided illustrations of such settlements, but none as yet gives complete and systematic reports on the number of complainants who have actually been offered (and have accepted) employment, the number of cases in which back pay has been awarded, and so on. In other words, it is impossible for the public to judge the enforcing agencies' standards in attempting to eliminate discrimination in employment. In this connection it must be mentioned that in 1950 the Connecticut Inter-racial Commission announced that in every case of unlawful refusal to employ an applicant, the only satisfactory adjustment would be an outright offer of a job.

## PROBLEMS OF EVALUATION

There are other barriers to systematic evaluation of the fair employment practices laws. How, for example, can we separate their effects from those of the period of full employment during the last decade and the federal wartime Committee on Fair Employment Practice? The number of complaints brought to the enforcing agencies, smaller than expected, is not an adequate guide, since not all victims of discrimination know of the law or are willing to invoke it. On the other hand, one individual's complaint may lead to a fundamental change in a large firm's employment patterns and therefore affect thousands of other workers in the same firm or industry. The best criterion for the effectiveness of these new anti-discrimination laws would be, first, the number of persons who secured employment with employers or in industries from which they had been barred; and, second, the number of companies, types of employment, and industries (with the number of jobs encompassed) from which minorities had earlier been excluded but which were opened to them by the action of the enforcing agencies.

In the face of these inherent difficulties in evaluating the laws and their administration, the enforcing agencies have unfortunately not done all they might to facilitate evaluation. We have already seen that they do not reveal the terms upon which they settle cases of discrimination by informal conciliation. Nor do most of them reveal enough about their work to enable the public to learn what proportion of individual complaints is upheld. Only the New York State Commission Against Discrimination has regularly published data which enable one to compute this proportion. Thus, to the end of 1950, this commission upheld only about 28 per cent of the individual complaints filed with it (although in another 26 per cent of these complaints it found and eliminated other discriminatory practices than those which occasioned the specific complaint). It would be interesting to compare this record with that of other enforcing agencies, but no other agency presents the data to make such a comparison possible, except the Philadelphia FEPC, which presented such data for 1950.

Still another deficiency in the reporting system of the various enforcing agencies is the lack of uniformity. This problem was discussed two years ago at a conference of the New York, New Jersey, Massachusetts, and Connecticut agencies, and a committee was directed to study it. However, uniformity of complaint and disposition categories and of statistical reports has not yet been achieved.

One reason for these deficiencies of reporting, research, and self-analysis is, of course, the limitations of budget. As the accompanying table shows, New York appropriates about $350,000 annually for its enforcing agency, but each of the other states appropriates less than $65,000. The Philadelphia Fair Employment Practice Commission had a budget of about $75,000 in 1950, but it was far from able to apply much of this amount to reporting and research, when, as it reported last year:

> No privacy exists for the conduct of the Commission's
> business by the staff. Interviews with complainants and

respondents must be carried on in a public room within the hearing of stenographers and clerks and in close proximity to other members of the public awaiting interviews with the staff.

## Prejudice and Discrimination

Whatever the reason for this situation, it undoubtedly blocks adequate appreciation of the full effects of fair employment practices legislation. It is clear that the statutes we have been discussing have actually reduced discriminatory employment practices. The accompanying table shows that the agencies of seven states and two cities have handled about 5,000 cases of alleged discrimination, and that of those they have actually settled, more than half have resulted in the elimination of some form of discrimination.

It is not enough, however, to be able to compute such data. The fair employment practices laws deal ostensibly with *behavior*, but they certainly affect (as they were intended to) *attitude* and *opinions* as well. To what extent, we may ask, have the statutes thus far established the sort of social situations in which prejudical attitudes (as distinguished from discriminatory *acts*) become weaker or less prevalent? What is the reaction of employers and workers to their experience with the law and the enforcing agencies?

The answers to such questions would be not merely academically interesting, but also significant for an evaluation of the laws as written and for the state of group relations in a community. We need studies of the attitudes towards minority groups which prevail among workers before and after the liberalization of employment patterns in various kinds of work situations in offices and factories. The records of the enforcing agencies are a treasure of such vital information which their staffs, as now constituted, are not equipped to tap. In order to enable private persons or agencies to interpret the records, the enforcing agencies will have to make public much more material than they have thus far done. They can do so within the limitations imposed by the laws. . . .

SELECTED ASPECTS OF OPERATION OF SEVEN STATE AND TWO MUNICIPAL FAIR EMPLOYMENT PRACTICES STATUTES

| | N.Y. | N.J. | Mass. | Conn. | Washington State | R.I. | Oregon | Minneapolis | Phila. |
|---|---|---|---|---|---|---|---|---|---|
| Effective date[a]<br>Annual budget[c]<br>Administrative agency | July 1, 1945<br>$357,000<br>5-member State Commission Against Discrimination | Apr. 16, 1945<br>$65,000<br>Division Against Discrimination in Department of Education, and 7-member Commission on Civil Rights | Aug. 21, 1946<br>$59,000<br>3-member Commission Against Discrimination | May 14, 1947<br>$58,000<br>10-member Inter-racial Commission | June 18, 1949<br>$25,000<br>5-member State Board Against Discrimination in Employment | July 1, 1949<br>$40,000<br>5-member Commission for Fair Employment Practices | July 16, 1949<br>$15,000<br>5-member Fair Employment Practices Division, Bureau of Labor | Feb. 5, 1947<br>$8,300<br>5-member Fair Employment Practice Commission | Mar. 12, 1948<br>$75,000<br>5-member Fair Employment Practice Commission |
| Remuneration[b]<br>Full-time staff members[c]<br>Jurisdictions in addition to employment | Full<br>63<br>None | None<br>12<br>Public accommodations; Education | Partial<br>9<br>Public accommodations; Public housing | Per diem<br>14<br>Public accommodations; Public housing | Per diem<br>2<br>None | Partial<br>4<br>None | <br>2<br>None. | None<br>2<br>None | Per diem<br>12<br>None |
| Who may initiate complaints | Aggrieved person, Att'y Gen., civic organization[d] | Aggrieved person, Commissioner of Labor, Att'y Gen. | Aggrieved person, Commission, Employer, Att'y Gen. | Aggrieved person, Commission, Employer | Aggrieved person, State Board, Employer | Aggrieved person, Commission, civic organization[e] | Aggrieved person, Employer | Aggrieved person, Commission | Aggrieved person, Commission, civic organization |
| Total number of cases docketed[f] | 2,448<br>Dec. 31, 1950 | 974<br>Dec. 31, 1950 | 751<br>Nov. 30, 1950 | 177<br>Sept. 15, 1950 | 64<br>Oct. 26, 1950 | 7[k]<br>Dec. 31, 1949 | 21<br>July 1950 | 122<br>June 30, 1950 | 146<br>May 31, 1950 |
| Proportion of settled cases[g] in which<br>Discrimination was found[h]<br>Discrimination was *not found* | 54%<br>46% | 52%<br>48% | 65%<br>35% | 60%<br>40% | 25%<br>75% | [i]<br>[i] | 6[j]<br>1[j] | 55%<br>45% | 71%[i]<br>29%[i] |
| Proportion of complaints filed against<br>Employers<br>Employment agencies<br>Labor organizations<br>Others | 81%<br>8%<br>9%<br>2% | [i]<br>[i]<br>[i]<br>[i] | 64%<br>8%<br>3%<br>25%[m] | 87%<br>5%<br>8%<br>— | 53%<br>18%<br>16%<br>14%[m] | [i]<br>[i]<br>[i]<br>[i] | 16[j]<br>0[j]<br>5[j]<br>— | 78%<br>6%<br>2%<br>14%[m] | 57%[l]<br>13%[l]<br>13%[l]<br>34%[l][m] |
| Proportion of complaints based on charge of discrimination because of<br>Race or color<br>Religion<br>National origin, ancestry<br>Other reasons | 70%<br>16%<br>6%<br>8% | [i]<br>[i]<br>[i]<br>[i] | 72%<br>16%<br>12%<br>— | 96%<br>3%<br>1%<br>— | 98%[n]<br>2%[o]<br>—<br>— | [i]<br>[i]<br>[i]<br>[i] | 19[j]<br>2[j]<br>—<br>— | 75%<br>24%<br>1%[p]<br>— | 57%<br>7%<br>4%<br>32%[q] |

[a] Rounded figures, for fiscal year ending various dates in 1950.
[b] This indicates roughly the proportion of their time which members can afford to devote to this activity.
[c] 1950, including clerical workers.
[d] Includes employment agencies receiving a discriminatory order.
[e] Only under Sec. 131.3 and 131.5 of the statute.
[f] From effective date of the statute until date given below the figure for each agency.
[g] Number of cases filed which investigation showed had some basis for charge of discrimination.
[h] Omitting cases pending, withdrawn, and over which administrative agency had no jurisdiction. For New York and Washington these cases refer only to verified complaints by individuals.

[i] Includes discrimination as charged in complaint or other discriminatory acts discovered.
[j] Insufficient data made public.
[k] Absolute number, not a proportion, because of small number of cases.
[l] For period ending May 31, 1949, since no comparable data made public since then.
[m] No breakdown of this category given.
[n] Mainly state, city, and county government agencies.
[o] 50 out of 51 "formal complaints."
[p] One out of 51 "formal complaints."
[q] One out of 122 cases.
[r] All but two of these cases dealt with discriminatory application forms and advertisements.

Sources: Official reports issued by state and municipal administrative agencies, and special correspondence with them.

## Note

1. Patterns of conciliation: The General Counsel of the New York Commission in a series of articles in the New York Law Journal, April 6, 9, 10, 11 and 12, 1951, summarized the usual pattern of conciliation agreement:

"The basic or minimum terms embodied, directly or by implication, in almost all conciliation agreements, fall into four categories:

"A. An immediate elimination of all existing violations of the law disclosed by the investigation.

"B. A general commitment that the respondent will henceforth obey the letter and spirit of the law.

"C. A requirement that the respondent display the commission's poster in a conspicuous and well-lighted place where all employees and applicants for employment may see it, or where all nonmembers and applicants for union membership may see it.

"D. A requirement that the commission be permitted to make periodic reinspections of the respondent's employment pattern and practices, and that respondent's records be made available to the commission at the time of review. . . .

"In addition to the minimum bases of conciliation, there are a multiplicity of varying requirements for affirmative action which enter into the patterns of most conciliation agreements contingent upon the equities and facts in each particular case. These variants may likewise be grouped into four general categories:

"A. Provisions designed to redress the complainant directly for the wrong he has suffered and to protect him against future wrongful acts by the respondent.

"B. Provisions designed to sensitize and educate the respondent and its personnel to the problems of discrimination and the requirements of the law.

"C. Provisions designed to elicit changed policy pronouncements from the respondent and to introduce procedural changes in the respondent's personnel methods and labor relations.

"D. Provisions requiring respondent to make surveys, keep records and render reports to the commission."

The annual reports of the Commission give examples of specific settlements. See *e.g.* 1950 Rept., pp. 57–9; 1951 Rept., pp. 65–7. Some of these are: stipulations that complainant be hired "at once"; agreement that complainant will be considered for employment when new hiring begins (there being no actual vacancies on day unlawful discrimination occurred); back pay to complainant; suggestion that respondent add to pamphlet distributed to employees in the passages dealing with personnel, that selections will be made without regard to race, creed, color or national origin. In one case a psychological test sold by a testing corporation to employers to reveal the causes of maladjustment showed the religion of the employees. The commission asked the corporation to delete this aspect of the test because it was subject to abuse. The corporation felt disinclined and it was finally agreed that

**1163**

the corporation inform its clients of the existence of FEPC laws in several states and of the illegality of improper uses of the test. A theatre corporation which operated a number of theatres in the City of New York made a request for a "white cashier". As one of the terms of conciliation it agreed to show the Commission film "An Equal Chance" at each of its theatres.

2. The following summary of rulings and interpretations contained in the New York Commission's 1950 and 1951 reports throw additional light on the nature of its work. (a) *Scope of Act:* (1) Employment agency: Private business school running placement service for graduates without fee is subject to Act. *Patterson v. School of Business Practice and Speech,* 1951 Rept. p. 37; (2) Employees: For purposes of deciding whether business has sufficient employees to be covered by the Act, active corporate officers including those residing out of state who regularly come to New York on business are included. *Matter of H. H. Heinrich Inc.,* 1950 Rept., p. 26; *Garfield v. Mills Metal Partition Co.,* 1950 Rept., p. 27. Real estate salesmen working on commission are not employees of the realtor but independent contractors. *Chastang v. Herbert R. Houghton,* 1951 Rept., p. 22. (b) *General Policies:* (1) Interstate corporation: Information concerning interstate corporation engaged in discriminatory practices will be passed on to other states where corporation is active. This policy was adopted at Third Annual Conference of Eastern States Commissions Against Discrimination. 1951 Rept., p. 73. (2) "Historical and universal" exclusion of Negroes from certain branch of employment: Commission decided that this was true of beach wear models and action must therefore take the form of educational effort; conference with Knitted Outer-wear Association officials arranged. *Russel v. Annis Originals, Inc.,* 1951 Rept., p. 26. (c) *General Powers:* (1) Cooperation with other state agencies utilizing the statutory "function, power and duty of obtaining upon request and utilizing the services of all governmental departments and agencies": The Commission has concluded an agreement with the Department of Licenses of the City of New York which provides that the Commissioner of Licenses will give "great weight" to Commission findings and will inform all licensees of this policy. Any discovery of employment agency code symbols showing race, creed, or color by License Department investigators will be reported to the Commission, as will applications for new employment agencies whose proposed trade name implies racial, religious, or national discrimination. All new applications for such agency licenses will also be forwarded so that the Commission may advise the firm of its legal duty not to discriminate. See 1951 Rept., pp. 27–8. (2) Subpoenas: Where respondents have been uncooperative in appearing or producing records the Commission has achieved success through the issuance of subpoenas and subpoenas duces tecum. *Serette v. Vogt's Ice Cream, Inc., Mulzac v. Luckenbach Steamship Co. Inc.,* 1950 Rept., p. 34.

The reports discuss the following unlawful employment practices: (a) *By employers:* (1) The requirement that an employee anglicize his name, held illegal. *Riccio v. Bessie Miller and Stratford Bd. of Ed-*

**1164**

*ucation,* 1951 Rept., p. 31. (2) Defendant replacing Negro with white waiters claimed that firing was incidental to switch from "be-bop" to "girlie" show. This alleged night club custom of integrating race of waiters with type of entertainment rejected. *Thornhill and Price v. Elite Restaurant Inc.,* 1950 Rept., p. 36. (3) Negro storer complained because no action was taken on his bid for promotion to clerical position. The company maintained two seniority rosters, an A roster for clerical employees and a B roster for non-clericals. There were no Negroes on A roster. Investigating Commissioner dismissed on ground of no probable cause. *Comer v. Erie R. R. Co.,* 1950 Rept., p. 37. (4) While employer may not fire person because of religious belief he may fire Jehovah's Witness who makes religious propaganda during working hours to the annoyance of customers. *Scinto v. Bankers Trust Co.,* 1951 Rept., p. 33. (5) A number of cases challenge the job standards and salary scales claiming usually that the job standards are set suspiciously high for the salary scale of the job. The Commission consistently upholds these standards as long as they are fixed and applied without regard to race, creed or color or national origin. 1950 Rept., p. 37; 1951 Rept., p. 35–6. (6) Policy of discriminating in favor of Negroes against Puerto Ricans in predominantly Negro neighborhood not permitted. *Matter of Teddy's Shanty,* 1951 Rept., p. 33. The Commission generally has opposed any quota system of employment. In finding that such a system was contemplated in the carpenter division of the building trades industry it ordered an employer to issue a detailed memorandum to employees in charge of recruitment, hiring, promotion or discharge and to all subcontractors. The memorandum stated the requirements of the law and informed each recipient of his personal responsibility for compliance. *Saunders v. Knickerbocker Construction Corp.,* 1950 Rept., p. 37. In an earlier case, *Moe et al v. H. R. H. Construction Corp.* (stated first in 1949 report, restated in 1950 report, p. 38), the Commission rejected the contention that on a construction job in a predominantly Negro neighborhood the quota for Negroes should be in proportion to the population. (b) *By labor unions:* Union application form contained words "English-Italian". Defense was that information needed as to language of notices to be sent to members. Union agreed to delete question and substitute on reverse side of application: "Do you prefer to receive notices of meetings or other notices, written in the English or Italian language?" Union also requested photographs with application. Defense was they were needed to stop improper transfers of membership cards. Union agreed not to have photos attached to application but only to membership card after an applicant was accepted. *Ragland v. O'Dowd and Kelvin Engineering Co. and Local 731, Hodcarriers, Building & Common Laborers, AFL,* 1950 Rept., p. 39. (c) *By employment agencies:* Agencies may not make any inquiries concerning race, creed, color or national origin regardless of intent. They may not give information regarding the applicant's race to an employer over the telephone, or refuse to send employees out to advertised positions because of their creed. The argument was made by several agencies that their interviewers were independent contractors because they solicit job orders on a

commission basis and put in their own want ads under a budget which allows interviewers a percentage of their income for advertising. The Commission, however, considered it significant that agency allowed interviewer to advertise in its name, to use its name on business cards, and to use its office records and application files. 1951 Rept., p. 39.
(d) *In Help Wanted and Situation Wanted ads:* The following were considered unlawful: (i) reference to "Christian-Jewish Firm"; (ii) "Out-of-Town College Graduate," "No Met. N. Y. C. Born." 1950 Rept., pp. 39–42; 1951 Rept., pp. 40–2.

For a summary of rulings and interpretations contained in the 1948 and 1949 reports see Berger, *The New York State Law Against Discrimination: Operation and Administration,* 35 Corn. L. Q. Rev. 747–79 (1950).

3. Pre-employment inquiries: The 1951 Report, p. 43, states the following regarding the New York Commission's publicizing of its rulings on pre-employment inquiries: "In publicizing . . . the Commission is saying to those over whom it has jurisdiction that any pre-employment inquiries which it has listed as lawful may be used without question but that if use is to be made of any inquiry which it has listed as unlawful, the Commission will question such usage and request its discontinuance unless there is factual support. . . [that it does not express a qualification prohibited by the statute or] . . . that it is based on a bona fide occupational qualification." The following is a sampling of the rulings ((l) stands for lawful and (ul) for unlawful): *Place of Birth:* (ul) all inquiries. *Age:* (l) certificate of age or work permit; (ul) birth certificate or baptismal record. *Religion or Creed:* (l) Do you regularly attend house of worship; (ul) inquiry into denomination, religious affiliation, church, parish, pastor or religious holidays observed; applicant must not be told this is "Catholic organization" etc.; *Race or Color:* (l) eyes and hair; (ul) complexion, skin color. *Photograph:* (ul) any requirement or even request at option of applicant of submission of photograph prior to hiring; relaxed in case of out of town referrals by N. Y. schools. *Citizenship:* (l) Ever arrested or interned as enemy alien? Are you permanent immigrant? Are you U. S. citizen or do you intend to become one? Are parents or spouses citizens? (ul) Citizen of what country; naturalized or native born; date of becoming U. S. citizen; requirement that citizen papers be produced; naturalized or native born citizenship of parents or spouse or date of their naturalization. *National Origin:* (l) Language applicant speaks or writes fluently, or what foreign language he speaks or writes fluently; (ul) applicant's lineage, ancestry, national origin, descent, parentage, nationality, mother tongue, nationality of applicant's parent or spouse, language commonly used by applicant, how applicant comes to know a foreign language, "Is your name French?" "I've never come across a name like this, is it Czechoslovakian?" *Relatives:* (l) Name of applicant's father, mother, husband, wife or minor dependent children; address (within the United States) of these people. Applicant's relatives already employed by company? Do you live with parents? With whom do you live? (ul) Name and address of any relatives other than father, mother, husband, wife and minor de-

pendents. *Notice in case of emergency:* (1) Name and address of person to be notified in case of accident or emergency; (ul) name and address of nearest relative to be so notified. *Military Experience:* (1) Inquiry as to military service in U. S. forces; (ul) inquiry into general military experience. *Organizations:* (1) Inquiries into all affiliations, including political organizations, that specifically exclude organizations which would reveal race, religious creed, color or national origin. N. Y. SCAD, *Rulings on Pre-employment Inquiries,* Jan. 7, 1950; see also, *Rulings* (May 18, 1950) and 1950 Annual Report, p. 97 et seq.

In *Ivory v. Edwards,* 278 App. Div. 359, 105 N. Y. Supp. 2d 580 (1951), an individual agency and an association of employment agencies sought a declaratory judgment against the validity of the Commission's pre-employment inquiry rulings and against the requirement that provisions of the law be openly posted in employment offices. The court held that there was no justiciable controversy about the rules before it because no specific application of them was challenged. The court stated: "They appear to be in the nature of case rulings made on the facts of particular cases . . . published for the information of the public. While presumptively such rulings would be applied in similar cases . . . the rulings are in no way self executing or of an effect which is compelling on . . . employers or employment agencies." 278 App. Div. at 383. As to the cause of action on the posting regulation the court dismissed the complaint insofar as it was brought in behalf of the association because of lack of showing that "association" was a "real party in interest." The case was remanded for consideration on the merits on the requirement of posting insofar as it applied to the individual agency plaintiff.

4. As the Berger article points out, up to 1950 none of the state commissions had held a public hearing or issued a formal decision in any case. Since that date there have been a number of hearings, some of which have resulted in cease and desist orders and court review. The cases which reach the stage of hearing and order, however, still constitute a very small proportion of the total cases processed:

*Connecticut:* In a case involving Clark Dairy, Inc., the Commission, after hearing, found the company had refused to hire a Negro applicant because of his race and color and issued a cease and desist order, including a requirement that the company hire the applicant. The company appealed the order to the Superior Court, New Haven County, not challenging the validity of the law but arguing that the statute gave the Commission no authority to order the company to hire an applicant it had rejected. The Court held that the Commission could not affirmatively order the company to hire the applicant but that it could order the company to cease discrimination against the applicant if he presented himself for employment in the future. The Court rejected other company contentions that the complainant must be made a party and that the Commission's finding of discrimination was not supported by the evidence. *Draper v. Clark Dairy Inc.* 17 Conn. Supp. 93 (1950).

In *Commission ex rel. Young v. Travelers Insurance Co.,* Case No. 188, Aug. 30, 1951, the insurance company selected white persons for a professional job in the personnel department in preference to the Negro applicant. The Commission found that the Negro applicant was in fact "superior . . . in all respects." It also recognized that the company had "no Negroes employed either in professional or semi-professional positions." But it thought that the evidence of intent to discriminate was insufficient. The hearing examiner emphasized the courteous interview, the fact that applicant was given high ratings and that the competitor for the job had experience in writing for publication and certain intangible personal attributes which the applicant did not have. The applicant had also been offered a job at lower pay in the casualty underwriting section, which she turned down. In *Tilley v. International Brotherhood of Electrical Workers,* a union which had a long record of excluding Negroes from membership was ordered to admit the applicant. Rept. of the Commission on Civil Rights 1950–1951, p. 83.

*New York: Woorm v. Kirk Lucas Agency,* N. Y. S. C. A. D., 1950 Rept., pp. 53–6. An employment agency was ordered to discontinue inquiries about race, creed, color and national origin and to reinterview complainant for first available position. The Commission also ordered that agency's books be made available to it in the future when the Commission wanted to re-examine its practices. See also *Ivory v. Edwards, supra.*

*Massachusetts:* A cease and desist order was issued March 27, 1951, against the United Employment Bureau, an employment agency, after a public hearing. The complaint was by a Negro who alleged that the agency had refused to refer him to an available bartender's position because of his race and color. The respondent was ordered to file a monthly report for six months setting forth in detail how it was complying. The Commission refused to award $928 for alleged loss incurred. The complainant appealed. Unreported.

*Oregon:* Negroes complained because they were barred from membership in the Brotherhood of Railway Carmen by blackballs. The Commissioner found substantial prejudice in the union although the union had frequently had explanations of the law presented to them. He ordered it to cease and desist. Unreported.

*Philadelphia:* Complainant who claimed she had been discharged because she was not Jewish requested that the court order the Commission to hold a hearing on her case. The court ruled that the Commission had discretion as to whether or not a hearing should be held and could not be compelled to take action. Unreported; see Berger, *supra,* p. 39.

5. On recent inclusion of age discrimination provision in Fair Employment Practices Acts, and other methods of dealing with the problem see Note, 61 Yale L. J. 574 (1952).

6. For criticism of the New York Commission and appraisal of its activities see Berger, *The New York State Law Against Discrimination: Operation and Administration,* 35 Corn. L. Q. 747, 784–787 (1950); Berger, *Equality by Statute,* ch. IV (1952). See also Committee to Support the Ives-Quinn Law, *New York State Law Against Discrimination—An Appraisal and A Program* (1948); Mather, *Report on the Experience of the Urban League, NAACP, and American Jewish Congress with the State Commission Against Discrimination* (1948); Note, 56 Yale L. J. 837 (1947).

As Berger points out, one of the more frequent subjects of criticism, both of those favoring abolition of the Fair Employment Practice Laws and of those favoring more vigorous enforcement and procedures that are more adequately geared to the needs of individual complainants, is the relative small number of complaints. One explanation is in terms of the attitude of workers who belong to minority groups. A 1948 study has revealed that (1) these workers learn which types of jobs and firms are closed to them and avoid applying for jobs; (2) it takes time for knowledge about the law to spread among workers; (3) minority groups do not think that the law will be effective; (4) minority group members tend to rationalize their not getting hired on bases other than discrimination. Saenger and Gordon, *The Influence of Discrimination on Minority Group Members in its Relation to Attempts to Combat Discrimination* (American Jewish Congress, Commission on Community Interrelations, 1948).

7. The effectiveness of law for changing behavior without encountering too much resistance from attitudes was demonstrated by a study of reactions of department store customers to the introduction of Negro sales personnel. Saenger and Gilbert, *Customer Reactions to the Integration of Negro Sales Personnel*, 4 International Journal of Opinion and Attitude Research 57 (1950).

8. The forerunner of the State Fair Employment Practices Laws was the President's Fair Employment Practice Committee referred to *supra*. The FEPC was established by President Roosevelt in June, 1941 to counteract discrimination which seriously interfered with the quantity and morale of manpower needed for national defense. The Committee at first was part of the Office of Production Management and was later transferred to the War Man Power Commission and finally given independent status in 1943. It functioned till 1946. The Committee handled about 5000 cases involving discrimination because of race, creed and nationality by employers, unions and the government. It lacked enforcement powers and relied almost entirely on voluntary compliance. While it was authorized to recommend to the President and other Federal agencies steps to make its determinations effective, it did not achieve much in this way and its "directives," when they were resorted to, were frequently ignored without serious consequences to the violators.

For discussion see Ross, *All Manner of Men* (1948); Note, 56 Yale L. J. 837 (1947).

Federal Fair Employment Practices legislation was a major part in President Truman's Civil Rights Program. Various bills establishing Federal agencies with more or less enforcement power have been proposed in Congress. No legislation has passed Congress. For accounts of some of the political forays see Maslow, *FEPC—A Case History in Parliamentary Maneuver*, 13 U. of Chi. L. Rev. 407 (1946); Wilson, *The Proposed Legislative Death Knell of Private Discriminatory Employment Practices*, 31 Va. L. Rev. 789 (1945). See also Note, 38 Va. L. Rev. 375 (1952).

Present Federal activity in the field is limited largely to the operations of two Executive Orders. Executive Order, No. 9980, issued July

26, 1948, makes each department and agency head responsible for an "effective program to insure that fair employment policies are fully observed" in his department or agency. He may appoint a Fair Employment Officer who can appraise personnel actions to determine their conformity to fair employment policy, receive complaints from those who claim to have been discriminated against, and take corrective and disciplinary action. The Order also provides for a Fair Employment Board within the Civil Service Commission with power to review decisions of heads of departments. It also is to advise them, coordinate their programs, and disseminate information. 13 Fed. Reg. 4311 (1948).

Executive Order, No. 10308, Dec. 3, 1951, deals with enforcement of nondiscrimination clauses which must be made part of all government contracts and subcontracts. It generally authorizes heads of each government contracting agency to take all necessary steps to achieve compliance and holds them responsible. It also establishes a Committee on Contract Compliance with the following functions: (1) To examine and study rules, procedures and practice of contracting agencies in order to determine how procedures can be strengthened and approved; (2) to confer with, advise, and make recommendations to, government contracting agencies about eliminating discrimination; (3) when necessary to transmit recommendations to the Director of Defense Mobilization who, "when he deems it appropriate," shall forward the recommendations to the President accompanied by his views on their relationship to mobilization. 16 Fed. Reg. 12303 (1951).

9. On local ordinances, see Elson and Schanfield, *Local Regulation of Discriminatory Employment Practices,* 56 Yale L. J. 431 (1947).

## Bibliographical Note

Studies concerned with the theory of race and caste: Barzun, *Race: A Study in Modern Superstition* (1937); Benedict, *Race: Science and Politics* (1940); Boyd, *Genetics and the Races of Man* (1950); Boas, *Race, Language and Culture* (1940); Cox, *Caste, Class and Race: A Study in Social Dynamics* (1948); Davis and Gardner, *Deep South: A Social Anthropological Study of Caste and Class* (1941); Dollard, *Caste and Class in a Southern Town* (1949); Fairchild, *Race and Nationality* (1947); Golightly, *Race, Values, and Guilt,* 26 Social Forces 125 (1947); Krogman, *The Concept of Race* in Linton (ed.), *The Science of Man in the World Crisis* (1945); Ashley-Montagu, *Man's Most Dangerous Myth: The Fallacy of Race* (1945) and *Statement on Race* (1951); Myrdal, *An American Dilemma* (1944); Odum, *Race and Rumors of Race* (1944); Park, *Race and Culture* (1950); Powdermaker, *After Freedom: A Cultural Study in the Deep South* (1939); Radin, *The Racial Myth* (1934); Wirth, *Race and Public Policy,* 58 Scientific Monthly 302 (1944).

Studies in the history and sociology of American minority groups: Graeber and Britt, *Jews in a Gentile World* (1942); Davie, *Negroes in American Society* (1949); Du Bois, *Black Folk: Then and Now* (1939) and *Dusk of Dawn* (1940); Embree, *Brown Americans: The Story of a Tenth of the Nation* (1943); Finkelstein, *The Jews: Their History,*

[Emerson]

DISCRIMINATION

*Culture and Religion* (1949); Frazier, *Negro Family in the United States* (1939) and *The Negro in the United States* (1949); Gordon, Albert I., *Jews in Transition* (1949); Handlin, *The Uprooted* (1951); Herskovits, *The American Negro: A Study in Racial Crossing* (1928) and *The Myth of the Negro Past* (1941); Johnson, C. S., *Growing Up in the Black Belt: Negro Youth in the Rural South* (1941); Johnson, J. W., *Autobiography of an Ex-Colored Man* (1927); Kibbe, *Latin Americans in Texas* (1946); Kluckhohn and Leighton, *The Navaho* (1946); LaFarge, O. (ed.), *The Changing Indian* (1942); Lindquist, *The Indian in American Life* (1944); McKay, *Harlem: Negro Metropolis* (1940); McWilliams, *Brothers Under the Skin* (1943) and *North from Mexico: The Spanish-Speaking People of the United States* (1948); Mills, Senior and Goldsen, *The Puerto Rican Journey* (1950); Murray, *The Negro Handbook* (1949); Ottley, *Black Odyssey: The Story of the Negro in America* (1948); Redding, *On Being Negro in America* (1951) and *They Came in Chains* (1950); Schermerhorn, *These Our People: Minorities in American Culture* (1949); Smith, *Americans from Japan* (1948); Tannenbaum, *Slave and Citizen: The Negro in the Americas* (1947); Thomas, D. and Nishimoto, *The Spoilage* (1946); Thomas, W. I. and Znaniecki, *The Polish Peasant in Europe and America* (1918–20); Warner and Srole, *The Social Systems of American Ethnic Groups* (1945); Wirth, *The Ghetto* (1928).

Studies concerned with the social and psychological dynamics of prejudice: Myrdal, *An American Dilemma* (1944); Cox, *Caste, Class and Race* (1948); Dollard, *Caste and Class in a Southern Town* (1937); MacIver, *The More Perfect Union* (1948); Bettelheim and Janowitz, *Dynamics of Prejudice* (1950); Baruch, *Glass House of Prejudice* (1946); Allport and Kramer, *Some Roots of Prejudice*, 22 J. of Psychology 9 (July, 1946); Gordon, *Race Patterns and Prejudices in Puerto Rico*, 14 Am. Sociological Rev. 294 (1949); Hartley, *Problems in Prejudice* (1946); Lasker, *Race Attitudes in Children* (1929); Nettler, *The Relationship Between Attitude and Information Concerning the Japanese in America*, 11 Am. Sociological Rev. 177 (1946); Simmel, Ernst (ed.), *Anti-Semitism: A Social Disease* (1946); Zawadski, *Limitations of the Scapegoat Theory of Prejudice*, 43 J. of Abnormal and Social Psychology (1948).

Studies dealing with intergroup relations: Burma, *Race Relations and Anti-Discriminatory Legislation*, 56 Am. J. of Sociology, 416–23 (1951); Berry, *Race Relations* (1951) (contains excellent bibliographical material); Frazier, *Race Contacts and the Social Structure*, 14 Am. Sociological Rev. 1 (1949); Johnson, C. S., *Into the Main Stream: A Survey of Best Practices in Race Relations in the South* (1947) and *To Stem This Tide* (1943); La Farge, J. *The Race Question and the Negro* (1943); Lee and Humphrey, *Race Riot* (1943); Locke and Stern, *When Peoples Meet* (1946); MacIver (ed.), *Group Relations and Group Antagonisms* (1944), *Civilization and Group Relationships* (1945), *The More Perfect Union* (1948) and *Discrimination and National Welfare* (1949); Malinowski, *The Dynamics of Culture Change: An Inquiry into Race Relations in Africa* (1945); McWilliams, *A Mask for Privilege: Anti-Semitism in America* (1948) and *Prejudice; Japanese-*

*Americans: Symbol of Racial Intolerance* (1944); Myers, G., *History of Bigotry in the United States* (1943); Rose, *America Divided* (1948), *The Roots of Prejudice* (1951) and *Studies in Reduction of Prejudice* (1948); Thompson, E. (ed.), *Race Relations and the Race Problem* (1939); United Nations, Commission on Human Rights, *Race Prejudice and Discrimination* (1951); Williams, *Reduction of Intergroup Tensions* (1947); Woofter, *Races and Ethnic Groups in American Life* (1933).

Studies dealing with the personality structure of oppressed groups: Atwood, *Thus Be Their Destiny: The Personality Development of Negro Youth in Three Communities* (1941) Child, *Italian or American? The Second Generation in Conflict* (1943); Davis and Dollard, *Children of Bondage* (1940); Frazier, *Negro Youth at the Crossways: Their Personality Development in the Middle States* (1940); Goff, *Problems and Emotional Difficulties of Negro Children* (1949); Klineberg (ed.), *Characteristics of the American Negro* (1944) and *Race and Psychology* (1951); Kardiner and Ovesey, *The Mark of Oppression: A Psychosocial Study of the American Negro* (1951); Reid, *In a Minor Key: Negro Youth in Story and Fact* (1940); Rose, *The Negro's Morale: Group Identification and Protest* (1949); Sutherland, *Color, Class and Personality* (1942); Thompson, L. and Joseph, *White Pressures on Indian Personality and Culture,* 53 Am. J. of Sociology 17 (1947); Warner, Junker and Adams, *Color and Human Nature: Negro Personality Development in a Northern City* (1941).

# TABLE OF CASES

Names of those cases from which substantial extracts are reprinted appear in italics. Cases are listed only under the name of the first party, except that where the United States appears as the first party the case is listed under the name of the other party.

**1175**

# INDEX

[Emerson]—76

END OF VOLUME